BaseBall america®
2019
PROSPECT
HANDBOOK

BASEBALL AMERICA INC. DURHAM, N.C.

BaseBall america

2019
PROSPECT
HANDBOOK

Editors
J.J. COOPER, MATT EDDY AND KYLE GLASER

Assistant Editors
BEN BADLER, MICHAEL BROWN,
TEDDY CAHILL, JUSTIN COLEMAN,
CARLOS COLLAZO, JOSH NORRIS AND
KEGAN LOWE

Database and Application Development
BRENT LEWIS

Contributing Writers
MIKE BERARDINO, MIKE DIGIOVANNA,
DUSTIN DOPIRAK, TOM HAUDRICOURT, JON MEOLI,
BILL MITCHELL, NICK PIECORO,
ALEX SPEIER AND TRACY RINGOLSBY

Photo Editor
BRENDAN NOLAN

Design & Production
JAMES ALWORTH, SARA HIATT MCDANIEL
AND LINWOOD WEBB

Cover Photo
FERNANDO TATIS JR. BY JENNIFER STEWART

NO PORTION OF THIS BOOK MAY BE
REPRINTED OR REPRODUCED WITHOUT
THE WRITTEN CONSENT OF THE PUBLISHER.

FOR ADDITIONAL COPIES, VISIT OUR
WEBSITE AT BASEBALLAMERICA.COM OR
CALL 1-800-845-2726 TO ORDER.

US $34.95, PLUS SHIPPING AND HANDLING PER ORDER.
EXPEDITED SHIPPING AVAILABLE.

DISTRIBUTED BY SIMON & SCHUSTER
ISBN: 978-1-932391-82-4

STATISTICS PROVIDED BY MAJOR LEAGUE BASEBALL
ADVANCED MEDIA AND COMPILED BY
BASEBALL AMERICA.

BaseBall america

ESTABLISHED 1981 • P.O. Box 12877, Durham, NC 27709 • Phone (919) 682-9635

EDITOR AND PUBLISHER	B.J. Schecter @bjschecter
EXECUTIVE EDITORS	J.J. Cooper @jjcoop36, Matt Eddy @MattEddyBA
CHIEF REVENUE OFFICER	Don Hintze
DIRECTOR OF BUSINESS DEVELOPMENT	Ben Leigh

EDITORIAL

ASSOCIATE EDITORS	Justin Coleman
	Kegan Lowe @KeganLowe
	Josh Norris @jnorris427
SENIOR WRITER	Ben Badler @benbadler
NATIONAL WRITERS	Teddy Cahill @tedcahill
	Carlos Collazo @CarlosACollazo
	Kyle Glaser @KyleAGlaser
WEB EDITOR	Mark Chiarelli @Mark_Chiarelli
SPECIAL CONTRIBUTOR	Tim Newcomb @tdnewcomb

PRODUCTION

DESIGN & PRODUCTION DIRECTOR	Sara Hiatt McDaniel
MULTIMEDIA MANAGER	Linwood Webb
DESIGN ASSISTANT	James Alworth

BUSINESS

TECHNOLOGY MANAGER	Brent Lewis
ACCOUNT EXECUTIVE	Kellen Coleman
MARKETING AND OPERATIONS COORDINATOR	Angela Lewis
CUSTOMER SERVICE	Melissa Sunderman

STATISTICAL SERVICE
MAJOR LEAGUE BASEBALL ADVANCED MEDIA

BASEBALL AMERICA ENTERPRISES

Alliance
>>>> BASEBALL ((((

CHAIRMAN & CEO	Gary Green
PRESIDENT	Larry Botel
GENERAL COUNSEL	Matthew Pace
DIRECTOR OF MARKETING	Amy Heart
INVESTOR RELATIONS	Michele Balfour
DIRECTOR OF OPERATIONS	Joan Disalvo
PARTNERS	Jon Ashley
	Stephen Alepa
	Martie Cordaro
	Brian Rothschild
	Andrew Fox
	Maurice Haroche
	Dan Waldman
	Sonny Kalsi
	Glenn Isaacson
	Robert Hernreich
	Craig Amazeen
	Peter Ruprecht
	Beryl Snyder
	Tom Steiglehner

3STEP

MANAGING PARTNER	David Geaslen
CHIEF CONTENT OFFICER	Jonathan Segal
CHIEF FINANCIAL OFFICER	Sue Murphy
DIRECTOR OF DIGITAL CONTENT	Tom Johnson
DIRECTOR OF OPERATIONS, DATABASE/VIDEO	Brendan Nolan

INTRODUCTION

When Adrian Beltre announced his retirement, it was the end of an era. Beltre has been one of the best third basemen in baseball for nearly two decades. But it also means that we are saying goodbye to the last prospects who precede the Prospect Handbook. In Beltre's first game as a major leaguer, he played with Raul Mondesi. Cecil Fielder was part of the Angels lineup he faced. Now Mondesi's son Adalberto has graduated from the Prospect Handbook to the Royals' lineup, and Fielder's son Prince has gone from prospect to major league star to retiree himself.

Only Bartolo Colon remains active among players who were prospect eligible before the first Baseball America Prospect Handbook was published in 2001. Soon we will be saying farewell to the final remaining stars of that first Handbook—players like Albert Pujols, C.C. Sabathia and Francisco Rodriguez.

This edition of the Prospect Handbook is a hint at the to-be-told story of baseball in the 2010s, 2020s and beyond. It's possible that Wander Franco and some of the other youngest stars of this Prospect Handbook will still be playing baseball in 2040, when they likely will be facing the sons of some of the players who are currently in the Handbook.

We hope that the updates and tweaks we've made to this year's edition will make this the best Prospect Handbook you've ever purchased. Next year will surely bring some additional tweaks.

The Prospect Handbook is the biggest project the Baseball America staff undertakes each year. We're proud of that, and we want to make sure that it's well worth your purchase. We hope you enjoy it as much as we enjoyed spending the past year watching players, talking to scouts and writing up these 900 reports.

J.J. COOPER AND MATT EDDY
EXECUTIVE EDITORS, BASEBALL AMERICA

A NOTE ABOUT THIS EDITION

Baseball America introduced BA Grades in the 2012 edition of the Prospect Handbook. We also grade all tools for the 300 players who rank as Top 10 Prospects, providing an quick overview of each player's strengths and weaknesses. All grades are projected future grades.

We grade players' tools on the 20-80 scouting scale, where 50 is average. A key to the abbreviations:

Players		Pitchers*	
HIT	Ability to hit for average	**FB**	Fastball
POW	Power	**CB**	Curveball
SPD	Speed	**SL**	Slider
FLD	Fielding ability	**CHG**	Changeup
ARM	Throwing arm	**CTL**	Control

* Some pitchers receive a grade for OTH or "Other," which is typically a cutter or splitter. In the case of Rays righthander Brent Honeywell it's a screwball.

EDITOR'S NOTE: The transactions deadline for this book was Dec. 13, 2018. You can find players who changed organizations by using the handy index in the back.
>> For the purposes of this book, a prospect is any player who has not exceeded 50 innings, 30 relief appearances or 130 at-bats in the major leagues, regardless of major league service time. Finally, the grades attached to each team's draft class, as evaluated by Teddy Cahill, are based solely on the quality of the players signed, with no consideration given to any players acquired by trading those draft picks or for how many draft picks a team might have lost.

TABLE OF CONTENTS

ARIZONA DIAMONDBACKS
STARTS ON PAGE 18

No. Player, Pos.	Grade/Risk	No. Player, Pos.	Grade/Risk	No. Player, Pos.	Grade/Risk
1. Jazz Chisholm, SS	60/H	11. Taylor Clarke, RHP	45/M	21. Drew Ellis, 3B	45/H
2. Jon Duplantier, RHP	55/H	12. Andy Young, 2B	50/H	22. Luis Frias, RHP	50/X
3. Daulton Varsho, C	55/H	13. Andy Yerzy, C/1B	50/H	23. Dominic Miroglio, C	45/H
4. Carson Kelly, C	50/M	14. Matt Tabor, RHP	50/X	24. Domingo Leyba, 2B	40/M
5. Geraldo Perdomo, SS	55/X	15. Merrill Kelly, RHP	45/M	25. Emilio Vargas, RHP	45/H
6. Kristian Robinson, OF	55/X	16. Yoan Lopez, RHP	45/M	26. Matt Mercer, RHP	45/H
7. Taylor Widener, RHP	50/H	17. Pavin Smith, 1B	45/H	27. Harrison Francis, RHP	50/X
8. Alek Thomas, OF	55/X	18. Ryan Weiss, RHP	45/H	28. Jackson Goddard, RHP	45/H
9. Jake McCarthy, OF	50/H	19. Buddy Kennedy, 3B	45/H	29. Jimmie Sherfy, RHP	40/H
10. Blaze Alexander, SS	55/X	20. Marcus Wilson, OF	45/H	30. Kevin Ginkel, RHP	40/H

ATLANTA BRAVES
STARTS ON PAGE 34

No. Player, Pos.	Grade/Risk	No. Player, Pos.	Grade/Risk	No. Player, Pos.	Grade/Risk
1. Austin Riley, 3B	60/M	11. Kyle Muller, LHP	50/M	21. Tucker Davidson, LHP	45/H
2. Ian Anderson, RHP	65/H	12. Joey Wentz, LHP	50/M	22. Chad Sobotka, RHP	45/H
3. Mike Soroka, RHP	60/M	13. Patrick Weigel, RHP	55/X	23. Alex Jackson, C	45/H
4. Kyle Wright, RHP	55/M	14. Kolby Allard, LHP	45/M	24. Wes Parsons, RHP	40/M
5. Touki Toussaint, RHP	60/H	15. Greyson Jenista, OF	50/H	25. A.J. Graffanino, SS	45/H
6. Bryse Wilson, RHP	50/M	16. Freddy Tarnok, RHP	50/H	26. Jeffrey Ramos, OF	45/H
7. Drew Waters, OF	55/H	17. Tristan Beck, RHP	50/H	27. Trey Riley, RHP	50/X
8. Cristian Pache, OF	55/H	18. C.J. Alexander, 3B	50/H	28. Isranel Wilson, OF	45/X
9. William Contreras, C	55/H	19. Huascar Ynoa, RHP	50/H	29. Jasseel de la Cruz, RHP	45/X
10. Luiz Gohara, LHP	55/H	20. Jacob Webb, RHP	50/H	30. Ray-Patrick Didder, SS	40/M

BALTIMORE ORIOLES
STARTS ON PAGE 50

No. Player, Pos.	Grade/Risk	No. Player, Pos.	Grade/Risk	No. Player, Pos.	Grade/Risk
1. Yusniel Diaz, OF	55/M	11. Brenan Hanifee, RHP	50/H	21. Michael Baumann, RHP	45/H
2. DL Hall, LHP	60/H	12. Dillon Tate, RHP	50/H	22. Branden Kline, RHP	45/H
3. Ryan Mountcastle, 3B	55/H	13. Luis Ortiz, RHP	50/H	23. Rylan Bannon, 2B	45/H
4. Austin Hays, OF	55/H	14. Richie Martin, SS/2B	45/H	24. Zach Pop, RHP	45/H
5. Grayson Rodriguez, RHP	60/X	15. DJ Stewart, OF	45/M	25. Drew Rom, LHP	50/X
6. Keegan Akin, LHP	50/M	16. Zac Lowther, LHP	45/H	26. Jean Carmona, SS/2B	50/X
7. Hunter Harvey, RHP	55/X	17. Jean Carlos Encarnacion, 3B	50/X	27. Pedro Araujo, RHP	45/H
8. Ryan McKenna, OF	50/H	18. Adam Hall, SS	50/X	28. Josh Rogers, LHP	40/M
9. Dean Kremer, RHP	50/H	19. Cadyn Grenier, SS	45/H	29. Matthias Dietz, LHP	45/V
10. Blaine Knight, RHP	50/H	20. Alex Wells, LHP	40/M	30. Drew Jackson, 2B/SS	40/H

BOSTON RED SOX
STARTS ON PAGE 66

No. Player, Pos.	Grade/Risk	No. Player, Pos.	Grade/Risk	No. Player, Pos.	Grade/Risk
1. Bobby Dalbec, 3B	55/H	11. Durbin Feltman, RHP	45/H	21. Josh Ockimey, 1B	45/H
2. Michael Chavis, 3B	55/H	12. Jarren Duran, OF/2B	45/H	22. Kutter Crawford, RHP	45/H
3. Darwinzon Hernandez, LHP	50/H	13. Danny Diaz, 3B	50/X	23. Zach Schellenger, RHP	50/X
4. Jay Groome, LHP	55/X	14. Brandon Howlett, 3B	50/X	24. Chase Shugart, RHP	45/H
5. Triston Casas, 1B/3B	55/X	15. Colten Brewer, RHP	40/M	25. Eduardo Lopez, OF	50/X
6. Bryan Mata, RHP	50/H	16. Nick Decker, OF	50/X	26. Alex Scherff, RHP	50/X
7. Tanner Houck, RHP	50/H	17. Travis Lakins, RHP	40/M	27. Pedro Castellanos, 1B/OF	45/V
8. Mike Shawaryn, RHP	45/H	18. Denyi Reyes, RHP	45/H	28. Sam Travis, 1B/OF	40/H
9. Antoni Flores, SS	50/X	19. Nick Northcut, 3B	50/X	29. Brett Netzer, 2B	40/H
10. C.J. Chatham, SS	45/H	20. Gilberto Jimenez, OF	50/X	30. Yoan Aybar, LHP	45/X

CHICAGO CUBS
STARTS ON PAGE 82

No. Player, Pos.	Grade/Risk	No. Player, Pos.	Grade/Risk	No. Player, Pos.	Grade/Risk
1. Nico Hoerner, SS	55/H	11. Richard Gallardo, RHP	50/X	21. Oscar De La Cruz, RHP	45/V
2. Miguel Amaya, C	55/H	12. Luis Verdugo, SS	50/X	22. Thomas Hatch, RHP	40/H
3. Brailyn Marquez, LHP	55/V	13. Nelson Velazquez, OF	50/X	23. Reivaj Garcia, SS	45/X
4. Cole Roederer, OF	55/X	14. Alex Lange, RHP	45/H	24. Jared Young, 1B	40/H
5. Brennan Davis, OF	50/V	15. Jose Albertos, RHP	50/X	25. D.J. Wilson, OF	45/V
6. Adbert Alzolay, RHP	45/H	16. Edmond Americaan, OF	50/X	26. Jhonny Pereda, C	40/H
7. Paul Richan, RHP	45/H	17. Brendon Little, LHP	45/H	27. Jimmy Herron, OF	45/V
8. Cory Abbott, RHP	45/H	18. Dillon Maples, RHP	45/H	28. Trevor Clifton, RHP	40/H
9. Justin Steele, LHP	45/H	19. Zack Short, SS	45/H	29. Keegan Thompson, RHP	40/H
10. Aramis Ademan, SS	50/V	20. Riley Thompson, RHP	45/H	30. Erick Leal, RHP	40/H

CHICAGO WHITE SOX
STARTS ON PAGE 98

No.Player, Pos.	Grade/Risk	No.Player, Pos.	Grade/Risk	No.Player, Pos.	Grade/Risk
1. Eloy Jimenez, OF	70/M	11. Luis Basabe, OF	50/H	21. Bryce Bush, 3B	50/X
2. Michael Kopech, RHP	65/V	12. Zack Collins, C	50/H	22. Konnor Pilkington, LHP	45/H
3. Dylan Cease, RHP	60/H	13. Ian Hamilton, RHP	50/H	23. Jake Burger, 3B	50/X
4. Nick Madrigal, 2B	60/H	14. Gavin Sheets, 1B	50/H	24. Alexander Comas, OF	50/X
5. Luis Robert, OF	60/X	15. Seby Zavala, C	45/M	25. Caberea Weaver, OF	50/X
6. Micker Adolfo, OF	55/H	16. Laz Rivera, SS	50/H	26. Lincoln Henzman, RHP	45/H
7. Dane Dunning, RHP	55/H	17. Alec Hansen, RHP	50/V	27. Joel Booker, OF	45/H
8. Blake Rutherford, OF	50/H	18. Zack Burdi, RHP	50/V	28. Zach Thompson, RHP	40/M
9. Luis Gonzalez, OF	50/H	19. Jordan Stephens, RHP	45/H	29. Tyler Johnson, RHP	45/H
10. Steele Walker, OF	50/H	20. Spencer Adams, RHP	45/M	30. Kodi Medeiros, LHP	45/H

CINCINNATI REDS
STARTS ON PAGE 114

No.Player, Pos.	Grade/Risk	No.Player, Pos.	Grade/Risk	No.Player, Pos.	Grade/Risk
1. Nick Senzel, 3B	65/H	11. Jose Siri, OF	50/H	21. Aristides Aquino, OF	40/M
2. Hunter Greene, RHP	65/X	12. Stuart Fairchild, OF	45/H	22. Juan Martinez, 3B	45/X
3. Taylor Trammell, OF	60/H	13. Josiah Gray, RHP	50/H	23. Jacob Heatherly, LHP	45/X
4. Jonathan India, 3B	60/H	14. Jose Israel Garcia, SS	45/H	24. Hendrik Clementina, C	45/X
5. Tony Santillan, RHP	60/H	15. T.J. Friedl, OF	40/M	25. Alfredo Rodriguez, SS	40/H
6. Tyler Stephenson, C	50/H	16. Mariel Bautista, OF	50/X	26. Danny Lantigua, OF	45/X
7. Shed Long, 2B	50/H	17. Lyon Richardson, RHP	50/X	27. Ibandel Isabel, 1B	45/X
8. Jeter Downs, SS	50/H	18. Keury Mella, RHP	45/H	28. Scott Moss, LHP	40/H
9. Vladimir Gutierrez, RHP	50/H	19. James Marinan, RHP	50/X	29. Connor Joe, 3B/1B	40/H
10. Mike Siani, OF	50/H	20. Jimmy Herget, RHP	40/M	30. Bren Spillane, OF/1B	45/X

CLEVELAND INDIANS
STARTS ON PAGE 130

No.Player, Pos.	Grade/Risk	No.Player, Pos.	Grade/Risk	No.Player, Pos.	Grade/Risk
1. Triston McKenzie, RHP	60/M	11. Yu Chang, SS/3B	50/H	21. Will Benson, OF	50/X
2. Nolan Jones, 3B	55/H	12. Gabriel Rodriguez, SS	55/X	22. Oscar Gonzalez, OF	45/H
3. Tyler Freeman, SS	55/H	13. Carlos Vargas, RHP	55/X	23. Raynel Delgado, SS	50/X
4. Bo Naylor, C	60/X	14. Daniel Johnson, OF	50/H	24. Nick Sandlin, RHP	45/H
5. George Valera, OF	60/X	15. Aaron Civale, RHP	45/H	25. Eric Haase, C	40/M
6. Sam Hentges, LHP	55/H	16. Oscar Mercado, OF	45/H	26. Junior Sanquintin, SS	50/X
7. Bobby Bradley, 1B	50/H	17. Jean Carlos Mejia, RHP	50/X	27. Quentin Holmes, OF	50/X
8. Luis Oviedo, RHP	55/V	18. Ernie Clement, SS	45/H	28. Richie Palacios, 2B	45/H
9. Brayan Rocchio, SS	55/X	19. Aaron Bracho, SS	50/X	29. Jonathan Rodriguez, OF	50/X
10. Ethan Hankins, RHP	55/X	20. Lenny Torres, RHP	50/X	30. Kirk McCarty, LHP	45/H

COLORADO ROCKIES
STARTS ON PAGE 146

No.Player, Pos.	Grade/Risk	No.Player, Pos.	Grade/Risk	No.Player, Pos.	Grade/Risk
1. Brendan Rodgers, SS	60/M	11. Ryan Castellani, RHP	50/H	21. Daniel Montano, OF	50/X
2. Garrett Hampson, 2B/SS	50/M	12. Josh Fuentes, 3B	45/M	22. Rico Garcia, RHP	45/H
3. Peter Lambert, RHP	50/M	13. Jesus Tinoco, RHP	50/H	23. Mike Nikorak, RHP	50/X
4. Colton Welker, 3B	55/H	14. Terrin Vavra, SS	50/H	24. Vince Fernandez, OF	45/H
5. Grant Lavigne, 1B	55/V	15. Justin Lawrence, RHP	50/H	25. Brian Mundell, 1B	40/M
6. Tyler Nevin, 1B	50/H	16. Reid Humphreys, RHP	45/M	26. Breiling Eusebio, LHP	50/X
7. Ryan Rolison, LHP	50/H	17. Ben Bowden, LHP	45/H	27. Roberto Ramos, 1B	45/H
8. Riley Pint, RHP	55/X	18. Robert Tyler, RHP	45/H	28. Bret Boswell, 2B	45/H
9. Ryan Vilade, SS	50/H	19. Yonathan Daza, OF	45/H	29. Niko Decolati, OF	50/X
10. Sam Hilliard, OF	50/H	20. Ryan Feltner, RHP	45/H	30. Willie MacIver, C	45/X

DETROIT TIGERS
STARTS ON PAGE 162

No.Player, Pos.	Grade/Risk	No.Player, Pos.	Grade/Risk	No.Player, Pos.	Grade/Risk
1. Casey Mize, RHP	65/H	11. Wenceel Perez, SS	50/H	21. Spencer Turnbull, RHP	40/M
2. Matt Manning, RHP	60/H	12. Kody Clemens, 2B	45/H	22. Bryan Garcia, RHP	50/X
3. Isaac Paredes, SS/2B	55/H	13. Jake Rogers, C	45/H	23. Matt Hall, LHP	40/M
4. Franklin Perez, RHP	60/X	14. Sergio Alcantara, SS	40/M	24. Jacob Robson, OF	40/M
5. Daz Cameron, OF	50/M	15. Gregory Soto, LHP	50/X	25. Daniel Woodrow, OF	40/M
6. Beau Burrows, RHP	50/M	16. Kyle Funkhouser, RHP	45/H	26. Anthony Castro, RHP	45/V
7. Parker Meadows, OF	55/X	17. Dawel Lugo, 2B/3B	40/M	27. Sam McMillan, C	45/X
8. Christin Stewart, OF	45/M	18. Logan Shore, RHP	45/H	28. Brock Deatherage, OF	40/H
9. Willi Castro, SS	45/H	19. Sandy Baez, RHP	40/M	29. Jason Foley, RHP	45/X
10. Alex Faedo, RHP	50/H	20. Austin Sodders, LHP	45/H	30. Wilkel Hernandez, RHP	45/X

TABLE OF CONTENTS

HOUSTON ASTROS

KANSAS CITY ROYALS

LOS ANGELES ANGELS

LOS ANGELES DODGERS

MIAMI MARLINS

MILWAUKEE BREWERS
STARTS ON PAGE 258

No. Player, Pos.	Grade/Risk	No. Player, Pos.	Grade/Risk	No. Player, Pos.	Grade/Risk
1. Keston Hiura, 2B	60/M	11. Trey Supak, RHP	45/M	21. Eduarqi Fernandez, OF	50/X
2. Corbin Burnes, RHP	55/L	12. Payton Henry, C	45/H	22. Mario Feliciano, C	45/V
3. Corey Ray, OF	55/H	13. Jake Gatewood, 1B	45/H	23. Micah Bello, OF	45/X
4. Brice Turang, SS	55/X	14. Braden Webb, RHP	45/H	24. Larry Ernesto, OF	45/X
5. Zack Brown, RHP	50/H	15. Troy Stokes Jr., OF	45/H	25. Je'Von Ward, OF	45/X
6. Mauricio Dubon, 2B/SS	45/M	16. Aaron Ashby, RHP	45/H	26. Cody Ponce, RHP	40/H
7. Tristen Lutz, OF	50/H	17. Caden Lemons, RHP	50/X	27. Trent Grisham, OF	40/H
8. Lucas Erceg, 3B	50/H	18. Adrian Houser, RHP	40/M	28. Eduardo Garcia, SS	45/X
9. Joe Gray, OF	55/X	19. Carlos Rodriguez, OF	50/X	29. Carlos Herrera, RHP	40/H
10. Jacob Nottingham, C	45/M	20. Marcos Diplan, RHP	45/H	30. Chad McLanahan, 1B	45/X

MINNESOTA TWINS
STARTS ON PAGE 274

No. Player, Pos.	Grade/Risk	No. Player, Pos.	Grade/Risk	No. Player, Pos.	Grade/Risk
1. Royce Lewis, SS	65/H	11. Luis Arraez, 2B	50/H	21. LaMonte Wade, OF	50/H
2. Alex Kirilloff, OF	60/H	12. Misael Urbina, OF	55/X	22. Ben Rortvedt, C	45/H
3. Brusdar Graterol, RHP	60/H	13. Jose Miranda, 2B/3B	50/H	23. Zack Littell, RHP	40/M
4. Wander Javier, SS	60/X	14. Griffin Jax, RHP	50/H	24. Luke Raley, OF	45/H
5. Trevor Larnach, OF	55/H	15. Nick Gordon, SS/2B	45/M	25. Landon Leach, RHP	50/X
6. Brent Rooker, OF/1B	55/H	16. Jorge Alcala, RHP	50/H	26. John Curtiss, RHP	45/H
7. Jhoan Duran, RHP	55/H	17. Lewis Thorpe, LHP	50/H	27. Michael Helman, 2B	45/H
8. Blayne Enlow, RHP	50/H	18. Stephen Gonsalves, LHP	45/M	28. Aaron Whitfield, OF	45/H
9. Ryan Jeffers, C	50/H	19. Akil Baddoo, OF	50/H	29. Gabriel Maciel, OF	45/H
10. Yunior Severino, 2B	55/X	20. Jordan Balazovic, RHP	50/H	30. Gilberto Celestino, OF	45/V

NEW YORK METS
STARTS ON PAGE 290

No. Player, Pos.	Grade/Risk	No. Player, Pos.	Grade/Risk	No. Player, Pos.	Grade/Risk
1. Andres Gimenez, SS	55/M	11. Desmond Lindsay, OF	50/V	21. Adam Hill, RHP	45/H
2. Peter Alonso, 1B	55/M	12. Francisco Alvarez, C	55/X	22. Carlos Cortes, 2B	45/H
3. Ronny Mauricio, SS	60/X	13. Luis Santana, 2B	50/V	23. Ryder Ryan, RHP	45/H
4. Mark Vientos, 3B	55/V	14. Luis Guillorme, SS/2B	40/L	24. Daniel Zamora, LHP	40/M
5. Anthony Kay, LHP	50/H	15. Gavin Cecchini, 2B/SS	45/M	25. Drew Smith, RHP	40/M
6. David Peterson, LHP	50/H	16. Tomas Nido, C	40/L	26. Chris Viall, RHP	45/H
7. Shervyen Newton, SS	55/X	17. Jordan Humphreys, RHP	50/V	27. Tony Dibrell, RHP	45/H
8. Simeon Woods-Richardson, RHP	55/X	18. Ross Adolph, OF	45/H	28. Junior Santos, RHP	50/X
9. Franklyn Kilome, RHP	50/V	19. Will Toffey, 3B	45/H	29. William Lugo, 3B	50/X
10. Thomas Szapucki, LHP	55/X	20. Eric Hanhold, RHP	40/M	30. Tylor Megill, RHP	50/X

NEW YORK YANKEES
STARTS ON PAGE 306

No. Player, Pos.	Grade/Risk	No. Player, Pos.	Grade/Risk	No. Player, Pos.	Grade/Risk
1. Estevan Florial, OF	55/H	11. Luis Medina, RHP	55/X	21. Juan Then, RHP	50/X
2. Jonathan Loaisiga, RHP	55/H	12. Clarke Schmidt, RHP	50/H	22. Frank German, RHP	45/H
3. Everson Pereira, OF	60/X	13. Chance Adams, RHP	50/H	23. Domingo Acevedo, RHP	45/H
4. Anthony Seigler, C	60/X	14. Anthony Garcia, OF	55/X	24. Yoendrys Gomez, RHP	50/X
5. Michael King, RHP	50/M	15. Osiel Rodriguez, RHP	55/X	25. Luis Gil, RHP	50/X
6. Deivi Garcia, RHP	55/H	16. Oswald Peraza, SS	55/X	26. Thairo Estrada SS	45/H
7. Roansy Contreras, RHP	55/H	17. Garrett Whitlock, RHP	50/H	27. Raimfer Salinas, OF	50/X
8. Antonio Cabello, OF	55/X	18. Nick Nelson, RHP	50/H	28. Antonio Gomez, C	50/X
9. Albert Abreu, RHP	50/H	19. Trevor Stephan, RHP	45/H	29. Kevin Alcantara, OF	50/X
10. Matt Sauer, RHP	50/H	20. Jason Lopez, C	45/H	30. Josh Breaux, C	45/V

OAKLAND ATHLETICS
STARTS ON PAGE 322

No. Player, Pos.	Grade/Risk	No. Player, Pos.	Grade/Risk	No. Player, Pos.	Grade/Risk
1. Jesus Luzardo, LHP	70/H	11. Greg Deichmann, OF	50/H	21. Luis Barrera, OF	45/H
2. A.J. Puk, LHP	70/X	12. Jeremy Eierman, SS	50/H	22. Kevin Merrell, SS	45/H
3. Sean Murphy, C	55/H	13. James Kaprielian, RHP	50/V	23. Nick Allen, SS	45/H
4. Kyler Murray, OF	60/X	14. Grant Holmes, RHP	50/V	24. Tyler Ramirez, OF	45/H
5. Austin Beck, OF	50/H	15. Parker Dunshee, RHP	45/H	25. Gus Varland, RHP	45/H
6. Lazaro Armenteros, OF	50/H	16. Brian Howard, RHP	45/H	26. J.B. Wendelken, RHP	40/M
7. Jameson Hannah, OF	50/H	17. Marcos Brito, 2B	50/X	27. Brady Feigl, RHP	45/H
8. Eli White, 2B	50/H	18. Daulton Jefferies, RHP	50/X	28. Jordan Diaz, 3B	50/X
9. Jorge Mateo, SS	50/H	19. Alfonso Rivas, 1B	50/X	29. Dairon Blanco, OF	40/H
10. Sheldon Neuse, 3B	45/M	20. Skye Bolt, OF	45/H	30. Jonah Heim, C	40/H

TABLE OF CONTENTS

SEATTLE MARINERS
STARTS ON PAGE 418

No. Player, Pos.	Grade/Risk	No. Player, Pos.	Grade/Risk	No. Player, Pos.	Grade/Risk
1. Justus Sheffield, LHP	60/M	11. Erik Swanson, RHP	45/M	21. Joey Curletta, 1B	40/M
2. Jarred Kelenic, OF	60/V	12. Braden Bishop, OF	45/M	22. Joe Rizzo, 3B	40/H
3. Evan White, 1B	55/H	13. Sam Carlson, RHP	50/X	23. Nolan Hoffman, RHP	45/V
4. Julio Rodriguez, OF	60/X	14. Jake Fraley, OF	45/H	24. Joey Gerber, RHP	45/V
5. Justin Dunn, RHP	55/H	15. Matt Festa, RHP	40/M	25. Anthony Misiewicz, LHP	40/H
6. Logan Gilbert, RHP	55/H	16. Dan Vogelbach, 1B/DH	40/M	26. Donnie Walton, 2B/SS	40/H
7. Kyle Lewis, OF	55/V	17. Dom Thompson-Williams, OF	45/H	27. Art Warren, RHP	40/H
8. Noelvi Marte, SS	55/X	18. Wyatt Mills, RHP	45/H	28. Gerson Bautista, RHP	40/H
9. Josh Stowers, OF	50/H	19. Juan Querecuto, SS	50/X	29. David McKay, RHP	40/H
10. Cal Raleigh, C	50/H	20. Brayan Perez, LHP	50/X	30. Max Povse, RHP	40/H

TAMPA BAY RAYS
STARTS ON PAGE 434

No. Player, Pos.	Grade/Risk	No. Player, Pos.	Grade/Risk	No. Player, Pos.	Grade/Risk
1. Wander Franco, SS	75/V	11. Shane Baz, RHP	60/X	21. Anthony Banda, LHP	50/V
2. Brent Honeywell, RHP	65/X	12. Shane McClanahan, LHP	55/V	22. Taylor Walls, SS	45/H
3. Brendan McKay, LHP/1B	60/H	13. Nick Solak, 2B	45/M	23. Lucius Fox, SS	45/H
4. Ronaldo Hernandez, C	60/V	14. Brock Burke, LHP	50/H	24. Tyler Frank, SS	45/H
5. Matthew Liberatore, LHP	60/X	15. Nick Schnell, OF	55/X	25. Joe McCarthy, OF/1B	45/H
6. Jesus Sanchez, OF	55/H	16. Tanner Dodson, RHP/OF	50/H	26. Austin Franklin, RHP	50/X
7. Vidal Brujan, 2B	55/H	17. Josh Lowe, OF	50/H	27. David Mercado, RHP	50/X
8. Brandon Lowe, 2B/OF	50/M	18. Ian Gibaut, RHP	45/M	28. Drew Strotman, RHP	50/X
9. Nate Lowe, 1B	55/H	19. Andrew Velazquez, SS/OF	45/M	29. Jose De Leon, RHP	50/X
10. Moises Gomez, OF	55/H	20. Colin Poche, LHP	40/L	30. Matt Krook, LHP	50/X

TEXAS RANGERS
STARTS ON PAGE 450

No. Player, Pos.	Grade/Risk	No. Player, Pos.	Grade/Risk	No. Player, Pos.	Grade/Risk
1. Hans Crouse, RHP	60/V	11. Cole Ragans, LHP	55/X	21. Tyreque Reed, 1B	45/V
2. Julio Pablo Martinez, OF	55/H	12. Osleivis Basabe, SS	55/X	22. David Garcia, C	45/X
3. Leody Taveras, OF	55/V	13. C.D. Pelham, LHP	45/M	23. Jose Rodriguez, C	45/X
4. Cole Winn, RHP	60/X	14. Owen White, RHP	55/X	24. Kyle Cody, RHP	45/X
5. Anderson Tejeda, SS	55/V	15. Jonathan Ornelas, SS	50/X	25. Emmanuel Clase, RHP	45/X
6. Jonathan Hernandez, RHP	50/M	16. DeMarcus Evans, RHP	45/H	26. Scott Heineman, OF	40/M
7. Taylor Hearn, LHP	50/M	17. Chris Seise, SS	50/X	27. Diosbel Arias, SS/3B	40/V
8. Joe Palumbo, LHP	50/H	18. Tyler Phillips, RHP	45/H	28. Sam Huff, C	40/V
9. Bubba Thompson, OF	55/X	19. Randy Florentino, C	50/X	29. Keyber Rodriguez, SS	45/X
10. Mason Englert, RHP	55/X	20. A.J. Alexy, RHP	45/H	30. Alex Speas, RHP	45/X

TORONTO BLUE JAYS
STARTS ON PAGE 466

No. Player, Pos.	Grade/Risk	No. Player, Pos.	Grade/Risk	No. Player, Pos.	Grade/Risk
1. Vladimir Guerrero Jr., 3B	80/H	11. Anthony Alford, OF	45/M	21. Leonardo Jimenez, SS	45/X
2. Bo Bichette, SS	65/M	12. Adam Kloffenstein, RHP	55/X	22. Billy McKinney, OF	40/M
3. Danny Jansen, C	55/M	13. Orelvis Martinez, SS	55/X	23. David Paulino, RHP	40/H
4. Eric Pardinho, RHP	60/V	14. Ryan Noda, 1B/OF	50/V	24. T.J. Zeuch, RHP	40/H
5. Jordan Groshans, SS/3B	60/V	15. Griffin Conine, OF	50/V	25. Logan Warmoth, SS	40/H
6. Nate Pearson, RHP	60/V	16. Cal Stevenson, OF	50/X	26. Sean Wymer, RHP	40/H
7. Kevin Smith, SS/3B	55/H	17. Patrick Murphy, RHP	45/H	27. Elvis Luciano, RHP	45/X
8. Sean Reid-Foley, RHP	50/M	18. Trent Thornton, RHP	45/H	28. Reese McGuire, C	40/H
9. Cavan Biggio, 2B/3B	50/M	19. Hector Perez, RHP	45/H	29. Rowdy Tellez, 1B	40/H
10. Miguel Hiraldo, SS	55/X	20. Gabriel Moreno, C	45/V	30. Chad Spanberger, 1B	40/V

WASHINGTON NATIONALS
STARTS ON PAGE 482

No. Player, Pos.	Grade/Risk	No. Player, Pos.	Grade/Risk	No. Player, Pos.	Grade/Risk
1. Victor Robles, OF	65/M	11. Reid Schaller, RHP	45/H	21. Jackson Tetreault, RHP	45/H
2. Carter Kieboom, SS	55/H	12. Gage Canning, OF	45/H	22. Kyle Johnston, RHP	45/H
3. Luis Garcia, SS/3B	55/H	13. Raudy Read, C	45/H	23. Brigham Hill, RHP	45/H
4. Mason Denaburg, RHP	60/X	14. Telmito Agustin, OF	45/H	24. Tanner Rainey, RHP	45/X
5. Wil Crowe, RHP	50/M	15. Israel Pineda, C	50/X	25. Joan Adon, RHP	45/X
6. Tim Cate, LHP	50/H	16. Tres Barrera, C	45/H	26. Tomas Alastre, RHP	45/X
7. Seth Romero, LHP	55/X	17. Jose Sanchez, SS	50/X	27. Gabe Klobosits, RHP	45/X
8. Sterling Sharp, RHP	50/H	18. James Bourque, RHP	50/X	28. Malvin Pena, RHP	45/X
9. Yasel Antuna, SS/2B	50/X	19. Nick Raquet, LHP	45/H	29. Ronald Pena, RHP	45/X
10. Jake Irvin, RHP	45/H	20. Ben Braymer, LHP	45/H	30. Drew Ward, 3B	40/H

For the eighth year in a row, Baseball America has assigned Grades and Risk Factors for each of the 900 prospects in the Prospect Handbook. For the BA Grade, we used a 20-to-80 scale, similar to the scale scouts use, to keep it familiar. However, most major league clubs put an overall numerical grade on players, called the Overall Future Potential or OFP. Often the OFP is merely an average of the player's tools.

The BA Grade is not an OFP. It's a measure of a prospect's value, and it attempts to gauge the player's realistic ceiling. We've continued to adjust our grades to try to be more realistic, and less optimistic, and keep refining the grade vetting process. The majority of the players in this book rest in the 50 High/45 Medium range, because the vast majority of worthwhile prospects in the minors are players who either have a chance to be everyday regulars but are far from that possibility, or players who are closer to

BA GRADE

50 Risk: High

the majors but who are likely to be role players and useful contributors. Few future franchise players or perennial all-stars graduate from the minors in any given year. The goal of the Grade/Risk system is to allow readers to take a quick look at how strong their team's farm system is, and how much immediate help the big league club can expect from its prospect. Got a minor leaguer who was traded from one organization to the other after the book went to press? Use the player's Grade/Risk and see where he would rank in his new system.

It also helps with our Organization Rankings, but those will not simply flow, in formulaic fashion, from the Grade/Risk results as we incorporate a lot of factors into our talent rankings including the differences in risk between pitchers and hitters. Hitters have a lower injury risk and therefore are safer bets.

BA Grade Scale

GRADE	HITTER ROLE	PITCHER ROLE	EXAMPLES
75-80	Franchise Player	No. 1 starter	Mike Trout, Max Scherzer, Francisco Lindor
65-70	Perennial All-Star	No. 2 starter	Paul Goldschmidt, Manny Machado, Gerrit Cole
60	Occasional All-Star	No. 3 starter, Game's best reliever	George Springer, Jose Abreu, Edwin Diaz
55	First-Division Regular	No. 3/No. 4 starter, Elite closer	Eddie Rosario, Kevin Gausman, Felipe Vasquez
50	Solid-Average Regular	No. 4 starter, Elite set-up reliever	Adam Frazier, Tanner Roark, David Robertson
45	Second-Division Regular/Platoon	No. 5 starter, Lower-leverage reliever	Yolmer Sanchez, Nick Pivetta, Buck Farmer
40	Reserve	Fill-in starter, relief specialist	Craig Gentry, Dixon Machado, T.J. McFarland

RISK FACTORS

LOW: Likely to reach realistic ceiling, certain big league career barring injury.

MEDIUM: Some work left to refine their tools, but a polished player.

HIGH: Most top draft picks in their first seasons, players with plenty of projection left, players with a significant flaw left to correct or players whose injury history is worrisome.

VERY HIGH: Recent draft picks with a limited track record of success or injury issues.

EXTREME: Teenagers in Rookie ball, players with significant injury histories or players whose struggle with a key skill (especially control for pitchers or strikeout rate for hitters).

BA GRADES

Explaining The 20-80 Scouting Scale

None of the authors of this book is a scout, but we all have spoken to plenty of scouts to report on the prospects and scouting reports enclosed in the Prospect Handbook. So we use their lingo, and the 20-80 scouting scale is part of that. Many of these grades are measurable data, such as fastball velocity and speed (usually timed from home to first or in workouts over 60 yards). A fastball grade doesn't stem solely from its velocity—command and life are crucial elements as well—but throwing 100 mph will earn a player an 80 grade. Secondary pitches are graded in a similar fashion. The more swings-and-misses a pitch induces from hitters and the sharper the bite of the movement, the better the grade.

Velocity steadily has increased over the past decade. Not all that long ago an 88-91 mph fastball was considered major league average, but current data shows it is now below-average. Big league starting pitchers now sit 92-93 mph on average. You can reduce the scale by 1 mph for lefthanders as they on average throw with slightly reduced velocity. Fastballs earn their grades based on the average range of the pitch over the course of a typical outing, not touching or bumping the peak velocity on occasion.

A move to the bullpen complicates in another direction. Pitchers airing it out for one inning should throw harder than someone trying to last six or seven innings, so add 1-2 mph for relievers. Yes, nowadays an 80 fastball for a reliever needs to sit at 98-99 mph with some movement and command.

Hitting ability is as much a skill as it is a tool, but the physical elements—hand-eye coordination, swing mechanics, bat speed—are key factors in the hit tool grade. Raw power generally is measured by how far a player can hit the ball, but game power is graded by how many home runs the hitter projects to hit in the majors, preferably an average over the course of a career. We have tweaked our power grades based on the recent rise in home run rates.

Arm strength can be evaluated by observing the velocity and carry of throws, measured in workouts with radar guns or measured in games for catchers with pop times—the time it takes from the pop of the ball in the catcher's mitt to the pop of the ball in the fielder's glove at second base. Defense takes different factors into account by position but starts with proper footwork and technique, incorporates physical attributes such as hands, short-area quickness and fluid actions, then adds subtle skills such as instincts and anticipation as a last layer.

Not every team uses the wording below. Some use a 2-to-8 scale without half-grades, and others use above-average and plus synonymously. But for the Handbook, consider this BA's 20-80 scale.

20: As bad as it gets for a big leaguer. Think Billy Hamilton's power.

30: Poor, but not unplayable, such as Coco Crisp's arm or Edwin Encarnacion's speed.

40: Below-average, such as Wilmer Flores' defense, or Marco Gonzales' fastball velocity.

45: Fringe-average. Jake Odorizzi's fastball, Tanner Roark's control and Steven Vogt's defense qualify.

50: Major league average. Aaron Nola's fastball or Juan Soto's speed.

55: Above-average. Nick Castellanos' power.

60: Plus. Joe Panik's defense or Jon Lester's control.

70: Plus-Plus. Among the best tools in the game, such as Corey Seager's arm, Patrick Corbin's slider or Brandon Crawford's defense.

80: Top of the scale. Some scouts consider only one player's tool in all of the major leagues to be 80. Think of Aaron Judge's power tool, Byron Buxton's defense or Max Scherzer's fastball.

20-80 Measurables

SPEED 60-Yard Dash Times (In Seconds)	SPEED Home-First (In Secs.) RHH—LHH	POWER Grade Home Runs	FASTBALL Velocity (Starters) Grade Velocity	ARM STRENGTH Catcher: Pop Times To Second Base (In Seconds)
80 .... < 6.44	80 ....4.00—3.90	80 ....45+	80 .....97+ mph	80 .... < 1.74
70 .....6.45-6.64	70 ....4.10—4.00	70 35-44	70 96	70 ......1.75-1.84
60 .....6.65-6.84	65 ....4.15—4.05	65 30-34	65 95	60 ......1.85-1.94
50 .....6.85-6.99	60 ....4.20—4.10	60 25-29	60 94	50 ......1.95-2.04
40 .....7.00-7.24	55 ....4.25—4.15	55 21-24	55 93	40 ......2.05-2.14
30 .....7.25-7.44	50 ....4.30—4.20	50 18-20	50 91-92	30 ......2.15-2.24
20 .... > 7.45	45 ....4.35—4.25	45 15-17	45 90	20 .... > 2.25
	40 ....4.40—4.30	40 10-14	40 88-89	
	30 ....4.50—4.40	30 5-9	30 86-87	
	20 ....4.60—4.50	20 0-4	20 .....85 or less	

MINOR LEAGUE DEPTH CHART

AN OVERVIEW

Another feature of the Prospect Handbook is a depth chart of every organization's minor league talent. This shows you at a glance what kind of talent a system has and provides even more prospects beyond the Top 30.

Players are usually listed on the depth charts where we think they'll ultimately end up. To help you better understand why players are slotted at particular positions, we show you here what scouts look for in the ideal candidate at each spot, with individual tools ranked in descending order.

LF	CF	RF
Power	Fielding	Power
Hitting	Hitting	Hitting
Fielding	Speed	Arm Strength
Arm Strength	Power	Fielding
Speed	Arm Strength	Speed

3B	SS	2B	1B
Power	Fielding	Hitting	Power
Hitting	Arm Strength	Fielding	Hitting
Fielding	Hitting	Power	Fielding
Arm Strength	Power	Speed	Arm Strength
Speed	Speed	Arm Strength	Speed

C
Fielding
Hitting
Arm Strength
Power
Speed

STARTING PITCHERS

No. 1 starter	No. 2 starter	No. 3 starter	No. 4-5 starters
• Two plus pitches	• Two plus pitches	• One plus pitch	• Command of two major
• Average third pitch	• Average third pitch	• Two average pitches	league pitches
• Plus-plus command	• Average command	• Average command	• Average velocity
• Plus makeup	• Average makeup	• Average makeup	• Consistent breaking ball
			• Decent changeup

CLOSER	SETUP MAN
• One dominant pitch	• Plus fastball
• Second plus pitch	• Second above-
• Plus command	average pitch
• Plus-plus makeup	• Average command

POSITION RANKINGS

Context is crucial to prospect evaluations. So to provide yet another layer of context, we rank prospects at all all eight field positions plus righthanded and lefthanded starting pitchers. The rankings go deeper at the glamour positions, i.e. shortstop, center field and righthanded starter.

We grade players' tools on the 20-80 scouting scale, where 50 is average. The tools listed for position players are ability to hit for average (HIT), hit for power (POW), speed (SPD), fielding ability (FLD) and throwing arm (ARM). The tools listed for pitchers are fastball (FB), curveball (CB), slider (SL), changeup (CHG), other (OTH) and control (CTL). The "other" category can be a splitter, cutter or screwball.

Included as the final categories are BA Grades and Risk levels on a scale ranging from low to extreme.

CATCHER

No	Player	Org	HIT	POW	SPD	FLD	ARM	BA Grade	Risk
1.	Keibert Ruiz	Dodgers	60	45	40	55	50	60	High
2.	Francisco Mejia	Padres	60	45	40	50	80	60	High
3.	Joey Bart	Giants	50	60	40	60	60	60	High
4.	Danny Jansen	Blue Jays	60	40	30	45	45	55	Medium
5.	Ronaldo Hernandez	Rays	45	60	30	45	70	60	Very High
6.	Sean Murphy	Athletics	45	55	30	60	70	55	High
7.	Will Smith	Dodgers	45	55	55	60	55	50	Medium
8.	Miguel Amaya	Cubs	50	50	20	60	60	55	High
9.	Daulton Varsho	D-backs	55	50	55	55	45	55	High
10.	William Contreras	Braves	50	55	40	50	60	55	High

FIRST BASE

No	Player	Org	HIT	POW	SPD	FLD	ARM	BA Grade	Risk
1.	Yordan Alvarez	Astros	55	60	50	40	45	60	Medium
2.	Peter Alonso	Mets	45	70	20	40	40	55	Medium
3.	Nate Lowe	Rays	50	60	30	50	40	55	High
4.	Josh Naylor	Padres	55	55	45	40	55	50	Medium
5.	Evan White	Mariners	55	50	60	70	55	55	High
6.	Brent Rooker	Twins	45	60	40	40	40	55	High
7.	Grant Lavigne	Rockies	60	60	50	55	50	55	Very High
8.	Triston Casas	Red Sox	60	60	40	60	50	55	Extreme
9.	Nick Pratto	Royals	60	50	45	55	55	55	Very High
10.	Bobby Bradley	Indians	40	70	20	45	50	50	High

SECOND BASE

No	Player	Org	HIT	POW	SPD	FLD	ARM	BA Grade	Risk
1.	Keston Hiura	Brewers	60	55	50	50	45	60	Medium
2.	Luis Urias	Padres	70	40	45	55	55	55	Medium
3.	Nick Madrigal	White Sox	60	40	60	60	50	60	High
4.	Vidal Brujan	Rays	60	30	70	55	55	55	High
5.	Brandon Lowe	Rays	50	55	55	50	45	50	Medium
6.	Cavan Biggio	Blue Jays	45	60	50	45	50	50	Medium
7.	Kevin Kramer	Pirates	55	50	50	50	45	50	Medium
8.	Shed Long	Reds	55	50	55	45	50	50	High
9.	Jahmai Jones	Angels	50	45	60	45	50	50	High
10.	Eli White	Athletics	60	40	60	60	50	50	High

THIRD BASE

No	Player	Org	HIT	POW	SPD	FLD	ARM	BA Grade	Risk
1.	Vladimir Guerrero Jr.	Blue Jays	80	70	40	40	60	80	Medium
2.	Nick Senzel	Reds	60	60	55	60	60	65	High
3.	Austin Riley	Braves	50	70	40	60	70	60	Medium
4.	Jonathan India	Reds	55	55	50	55	55	60	High
5.	Ke'Bryan Hayes	Pirates	55	45	55	70	60	55	Medium
6.	Alec Bohm	Phillies	60	60	40	40	55	60	High
7.	Jordan Groshans	Blue Jays	60	60	50	50	60	60	Very High
8.	Nolan Gorman	Cardinals	50	70	40	50	55	60	Very High
9.	Elehuris Montero	Cardinals	60	55	45	45	60	55	High
10.	Colton Welker	Rockies	60	55	50	55	55	55	High

SHORTSTOP

No	Player	Org	HIT	POW	SPD	FLD	ARM	BA Grade	Risk
1.	Fernando Tatis Jr.	Padres	55	60	60	60	70	70	Medium
2.	Wander Franco	Rays	70	70	50	55	55	75	Very High
3.	Bo Bichette	Blue Jays	70	60	50	50	55	65	Medium
4.	Royce Lewis	Twins	70	55	60	60	55	65	High
5.	Brendan Rodgers	Rockies	60	55	50	55	60	60	Medium
6.	Andres Gimenez	Mets	50	50	50	60	60	55	Medium
7.	Jazz Chisholm	D-backs	50	60	55	55	55	60	High
8.	Luis Garcia	Phillies	60	40	55	60	60	60	Very High
9.	Carter Kieboom	Nationals	60	60	50	50	55	55	High
10.	Luis Garcia	Nationals	60	55	55	50	55	55	High
11.	Gavin Lux	Dodgers	55	50	55	55	55	55	High
12.	Oneil Cruz	Pirates	50	60	55	50	60	60	Extreme
13.	Garrett Hampson	Rockies	55	40	60	50	50	50	Medium
14.	Marco Luciano	Giants	50	60	60	50	55	60	Extreme
15.	Nico Hoerner	Cubs	60	40	55	50	50	60	High
16.	Ronny Mauricio	Mets	60	60	40	50	70	60	Extreme
17.	Kevin Smith	Blue Jays	45	60	50	50	60	55	High
18.	Wander Javier	Twins	60	50	55	55	60	60	Extreme
19.	Isaac Paredes	Tigers	60	50	40	50	55	55	High
20.	Tyler Freeman	Indians	60	45	50	50	55	55	High

CENTER FIELD

No	Player	Org	HIT	POW	SPD	FLD	ARM	BA Grade	Risk
1.	Victor Robles	Nationals	60	55	70	70	60	65	Medium
2.	Jo Adell	Angels	60	70	60	55	60	70	High
3.	Taylor Trammell	Reds	60	55	60	55	45	60	High
4.	Alex Verdugo	Dodgers	60	50	50	50	60	55	Medium
5.	Yusniel Diaz	Orioles	55	55	55	55	60	55	Medium
6.	Victor Victor Mesa	Marlins	55	45	70	60	70	60	High
7.	Jarred Kelenic	Mariners	60	55	50	50	55	60	Very High
8.	Drew Waters	Braves	55	60	60	55	60	55	High
9.	Cristian Pache	Braves	50	40	70	70	70	55	Extreme
10.	Luis Robert	White Sox	55	60	70	60	50	60	Extreme
11.	Daz Cameron	Tigers	55	50	60	55	55	50	Medium
12.	Brandon Marsh	Angels	50	50	60	60	60	55	High
13.	Julio Pablo Martinez	Rangers	55	55	60	50	50	55	High
14.	Khalil Lee	Royals	55	55	55	60	60	50	Medium
15.	Travis Swaggerty	Pirates	55	50	60	55	55	55	High
16.	Kyler Murray	Athletics	60	60	60	60	50	60	Extreme
17.	Estevan Florial	Yankees	55	55	60	60	60	60	Very High
18.	Everson Pereira	Yankees	60	60	60	55	50	60	High
19.	Austin Hays	Orioles	55	55	50	55	60	55	High
20.	Leody Taveras	Rangers	50	45	60	60	60	55	Very High

CORNER OUTFIELD

No	Player	Org	HIT	POW	SPD	FLD	ARM	BA Grade	Risk
1.	Eloy Jimenez	White Sox	60	70	40	45	40	70	Medium
2.	Kyle Tucker	Astros	60	60	40	50	50	60	Medium
3.	Alex Kirilloff	Twins	70	55	50	50	45	60	High
4.	Tyler O'Neill	Cardinals	45	70	60	60	55	55	Medium
5.	Jesus Sanchez	Rays	55	60	55	50	50	55	High
6.	Trevor Larnach	Twins	50	60	40	45	45	55	High
7.	George Valera	Indians	60	50	50	50	50	60	Extreme
8.	Moises Gomez	Rays	50	60	50	50	50	55	High
9.	Julio Rodriguez	Mariners	55	60	45	50	70	60	Extreme
10.	Micker Adolfo	White Sox	40	60	55	50	70	55	High

RIGHTHANDER

No	Pitcher	Team	FB	CB	SL	CHG	OTH	CTL	BA Grade	Risk
1.	Forrest Whitley	Astros	70	60	60	70	60†	55	70	High
2.	Sixto Sanchez	Phillies	70	—	60	60	—	70	65	High
3.	Ian Anderson	Braves	70	60	—	55	—	50	65	High
4.	Casey Mize	Tigers	70	—	55	70*	55†	60	65	High
5.	Alex Reyes	Cardinals	80	70	55	60	—	50	70	Extreme
6.	Mitch Keller	Pirates	70	60	—	50	—	60	60	Medium
7.	Michael Kopech	White Sox	80	60	60	50	—	50	65	Very High
8.	Mike Soroka	Braves	60	—	55	50	—	60	60	Medium
9.	Brent Honeywell	Rays	60	55	55	60	70^	55	65	Extreme
10.	Dylan Cease	White Sox	80	60	50	50	—	50	60	High
11.	Kyle Wright	Braves	60	60	55	—	—	55	55	Medium
12.	Touki Toussaint	Braves	60	60	—	60	—	45	60	High
13.	Hunter Greene	Reds	80	—	60	50	—	50	65	Extreme
14.	Matt Manning	Tigers	70	60	—	50	—	50	60	High
15.	Tony Santillan	Reds	70	—	55	55	—	50	60	High
16.	Triston McKenzie	Indians	60	60	—	55	—	60	60	Medium
17.	Griffin Canning	Angels	60	60	50	45	—	50	55	Medium
18.	Josh James	Astros	80	—	50	70	—	45	60	High
19.	Chris Paddack	Padres	60	40	—	70	—	70	60	High
20.	Corbin Martin	Astros	60	50	55	50	—	55	55	Medium
21.	Brusdar Graterol	Twins	70	50	60	40	—	55	60	High
22.	Eric Pardinho	Blue Jays	55	60	60	50	—	60	60	Very High
23.	Nate Pearson	Blue Jays	70	—	55	50	—	45	60	Very High
24.	Luis Patino	Padres	60	55	60	55	—	55	60	Very High
25.	Corbin Burnes	Brewers	60	50	55	50	—	60	55	Low
26.	Jonathan Loaisiga	Yankees	60	—	60	55	—	50	55	Medium
27.	Hans Crouse	Rangers	70	—	60	50	—	55	60	Very High
28.	Dakota Hudson	Cardinals	60	—	60	60	—	45	55	Medium
29.	Brady Singer	Royals	60	—	60	50	—	55	60	High
30.	Adonis Medina	Phillies	60	—	60	60	—	55	55	High
31.	Franklin Perez	Tigers	60	55	50	60	—	60	55	High
32.	J.B. Bukauskas	Astros	60	—	70	45	50†	45	55	High
33.	Bryse Wilson	Braves	70	55	—	50	—	55	50	Medium
34.	Dustin May	Dodgers	60	55	—	40	55†	60	55	High
35.	Dane Dunning	White Sox	60	60	60	55	—	55	55	High
36.	Sean Reid-Foley	Blue Jays	60	50	60	45	—	45	50	Medium
37.	Cole Winn	Rangers	60	60	50	50	—	60	60	Extreme
38.	Dennis Santana	Dodgers	60	—	55	50	—	50	50	Medium
39.	Cal Quantrill	Padres	60	—	50	60	—	50	55	High
40.	Michel Baez	Padres	60	45	50	60	—	50	55	High

LEFTHANDER

No	Pitcher	Team	FB	CB	SL	CHG	OTH	CTL	BA Grade	Risk
1.	Jesus Luzardo	Athletics	60	60	—	70	—	60	70	High
2.	A.J. Puk	Athletics	70	—	70	45	—	50	70	Extreme
3.	Justus Sheffield	Mariners	60	—	55	55	—	50	60	Medium
4.	MacKenzie Gore	Padres	60	60	55	60	—	60	65	Very High
5.	D.L. Hall	Orioles	60	60	—	60	—	55	60	High
6.	Adrian Morejon	Padres	70	60	—	55	—	50	60	High
7.	Brendan McKay	Rays	60	50	—	50	60†	60	60	High
8.	Matthew Liberatore	Rays	60	60	—	60	—	55	60	Extreme
9.	Daniel Lynch	Royals	60	50	60	60	—	60	55	Extreme
10.	Logan Allen	Padres	50	50	50	60	—	50	50	Medium
11.	Ryan Weathers	Padres	50	55	—	60	—	55	60	Extreme
12.	Jose Suarez	Angels	50	50	—	60	—	55	50	Medium
13.	Luiz Gohara	Braves	60	—	60	40	—	45	55	High
14.	Sam Hentges	Indians	60	55	—	50	50†	50	55	High
15.	Taylor Hearn	Rangers	70	—	55	50	—	50	50	Medium

* Splitter. ^ Screwball. † Cutter.

TALENT RANKINGS

Team	2018	2017	2016	2015	2014
1. San Diego Padres	3	9	25	14	6

Fernando Tatis Jr. is one of baseball's most prized prospects. Three of the Padres' top four prospects are high-end, near-ready hitters who play in the middle of the diamond, and they boast one of the game's top collections of pitchers. Throw in a wide mix of breakout candidates and you have the best farm system in baseball.

2. Tampa Bay Rays	5	11	13	17	20

Tampa Bay's system is stacked from top to bottom, with impact bats around the diamond and strong pitching, led by a potential frontline starter in Brent Honeywell. Shortstop Wander Franco is still 17 but projects as a future star who could be the No. 1 prospect in baseball next year.

3. Toronto Blue Jays	8	20	24	9	15

Vladimir Guerrero Jr. alone is carries enormous value, but the Blue Jays have serious talent at all levels of the system. Several players took significant steps forward last season, which, along with 2017 and 2018 amateur additions of players like Eric Pardinho, Nate Pearson and Jordan Groshans, adds both high-end upside and depth.

4. Atlanta Braves	1	1	3	29	26

After graduating Ronald Acuña Jr., the Braves still have high-end talent in the minor league system, led by a stellar group of starting pitchers in the upper levels, many of whom have already tasted the big leagues. From low Class A on down, though, prospects suddenly become scarce.

5. Houston Astros	11	4	2	10	5

The Astros have accomplished what every new general manager says is his goal when he takes over: Build a sustainable playoff contender while keeping the farm system fully stocked. Baseball's best pitching prospect, Forrest Whitley, should be in Houston soon, leading a core of near-ready pitching prospects.

6. Chicago White Sox	4	5	23	20	24

For a team in rebuild mode, the White Sox's depth is ordinary, but they are rich in high-ceiling prospects, led by potential cornerstone Eloy Jimenez. Nick Madrigal's advanced bat is a good balance to the higher-risk profiles of outfielder Luis Robert and Micker Adolfo, while Michael Kopech and Dylan Cease both have electric arms.

7. Cincinnati Reds	10	13	12	16	16

Picking top five overall in the draft for three straight years (and netting Nick Senzel, Hunter Greene and Jonathan India) has helped the Reds, with outfielder Taylor Trammell and righthander Tony Santillan giving Cincinnati one of the best top fives in the game. The Reds need to get more out of their Latin American program.

8. Minnesota Twins	12	22	10	2	3

With Royce Lewis and Alex Kirilloff, the Twins have two of the most exciting young hitters in the minors. None of Minnesota's top 10 prospects has played a game at Double-A, so while the system is good, most of its prospects are still at least a couple of years away from the majors.

9. Oakland Athletics	18	17	18	19	23

Most of the value in Oakland's system comes from a pair of lefties, Jesus Luzardo and A.J. Puk, both of whom have the attributes to be frontline starters, though the system's depth thins quickly. Five of the team's top 10 prospects are outfielders, led by the X-Factor in Heisman Trophy winner Kyler Murray.

10. Los Angeles Dodgers	9	2	1	3	14

The Dodgers are well stocked in catchers between Keibert Ruiz, Will Smith and Diego Cartaya, with Alex Verdugo and Gavin Lux giving them two more high-end position prospects who play up the middle. That's impressive for a team that hasn't picked higher than 20th in the draft since 2013.

11. St. Louis Cardinals	13	12	14	15	7

Alex Reyes barely hanging on to prospect eligibility props up an otherwise solid system. Their next two prospects (outfielder Tyler O'Neill and righthander Dakota Hudson) should bolster the big league club in 2019, and the Cardinals are deep in young third basemen with Nolan Gorman, Elehuris Montero and Malcom Nuñez.

12. Philadelphia Phillies	7	6	8	22	22

After graduating a wave of position prospects, the Phillies are pitching-heavy, led by Sixto Sanchez. Shortstop Luis Garcia has exciting upside, while the Phillies will look for 2018 first-round pick Alec Bohm to make up for recent disappointments at the top of their drafts.

13. Los Angeles Angels	14	30	30	27	30

Top prospect Jo Adell quickly catapulted his stock to become one of the game's elite prospects. After years of letting their farm system deteriorate, the Angels' renewed focus on that area is nearing payoff, with seven of their top 10 prospects scheduled to open 2019 at Double-A or Triple-A.

14. Detroit Tigers	20	25	26	30	28

Long accustomed to using their prospects as trade chips under former general manager Dave Dombrowski, the Tigers are now trying to build from within. Casey Mize, the No. 1 overall pick in the 2018 draft, leads the pack in a stockpile of power arms.

15. Cleveland Indians	21	18	17	23	17

Beyond Triston McKenzie, the Indians are light at the upper levels following trades and graduations. The lower levels are full of arrow-up players though, and scouts have taken notice of the team's collection of young Latin American prospects, a sign of the organization's recently revamped international program.

Team	2018	2017	2016	2015	2014
16. Washington Nationals	15	19	5	12	21

The top three prospects in the organization stack up well, led by a premium talent in center fielder Victor Robles and two more middle-of-the-diamond hitters in Carter Kieboom and Luis Garcia. Focusing on arms in the 2017 and 2018 drafts helped their pitching depth.

17. Seattle Mariners	30	21	28	24	25

The Mariners would have contended for No. 30 on this list until they decided to rebuild after the 2018 season. They added four of their top six prospects in December trades of Robinson Cano and Jean Segura, including top two prospects Justus Sheffield and Jarred Kelenic.

18. Pittsburgh Pirates	16	7	11	7	1

It's a top-heavy system, with a core group of players who could be average regulars to stars. Beyond them, the lack of depth in the organization gets revealed quickly.

19. New York Mets	27	15	15	4	10

Peter Alonso and Andres Gimenez carry the system and both should help soon in Queens. However, much of the system's position talent is several years away, with high-risk, high-reward players like Ronny Mauricio, Mark Vientos and Shervyen Newton.

20. New York Yankees	2	3	16	19	18

After graduating Aaron Judge, Gary Sanchez, Gleyber Torres and Miguel Andujar the last two years, the system has dropped without an elite, near-ready prospect, but they are deep in young pitching. The organization's Latin American pipeline under international scouting director Donny Rowland continues to flourish, with results in the big leagues (Luis Severino, Sanchez, Andujar) and the lower levels now brimming with exciting upside.

21. Arizona Diamondbacks	26	28	22	6	13

Their prospects in the upper minors are solid, though they lack upside to be elite players. The prospects in the lower levels like Jazz Chisholm, Geraldo Perdomo and Kristian Robinson have big upside but also carry big risk.

22. Baltimore Orioles	17	27	27	28	12

The Orioles are generally a disaster, with the team hiring new general manager Mike Elias and quickly gutting the organization's front office and several members of its scouting and player development staff. The farm system is better than it was a year ago after trades, including one to get No. 1 prospect Yusniel Diaz, but being a zero internationally will continue to hurt them for years.

23. Colorado Rockies	19	10	6	8	11

Proximity to the big leagues for their top three prospects (shortstops Brendan Rodgers and Garrett Hampson and righthander Peter Lambert) is a strength, because all three have Triple-A experience and should help in 2019. After that, the organization lacks high-upside, impact players.

24. Texas Rangers	22	23	7	11	9

The Rangers have a trio of promising young center fielders and a stockpile of pitching prospects at the lower levels from recent drafts, led by top prospect Hans Crouse and 2018 first-rounder Cole Winn. They don't have any of the game's elite prospects, though, and they lack pure hitters, with a position player group on the thin side with considerable risk attached to even their best ones.

25. Miami Marlins	24	29	29	25	27

For a team that traded Giancarlo Stanton, Christian Yelich, Marcell Ozuna and Dee Gordon, you would hope to have better than the game's No. 25 farm system. The Marlins got a jolt in October by signing Cuban outfielder Victor Victor Mesa, their new top prospect, but the returns on their recent first-round picks have been minimal.

26. Milwaukee Brewers	6	8	9	21	29

The Brewers had a dynamite year in the major leagues, but their farm system took one of the biggest tumbles from a year ago. Their top two prospects (second baseman Keston Hiura and righthander Corbin Burnes) could factor into their 2019 roster, but the upside dims quickly beyond their top handful of players.

27. Kansas City Royals	29	26	21	13	8

The upper levels of the system lack potential regulars, with few high-end prospects anywhere in the organization. Pitching is the focal point of the system, with the Royals bolstering their stash by drafting college pitchers with their top four picks in 2018.

28. San Francisco Giants	25	24	19	26	19

Two big amateur acquisitions in 2018—catcher Joey Bart, the No. 2 overall pick, and shortstop Marco Luciano, the No. 2 international prospect—injected the organization with two-high end talents. That's good, because it's rough beyond them, with recent draft classes that haven't netted much.

29. Chicago Cubs	28	16	20	1	4

Nico Hoerner and Miguel Amaya are both talented prospects who can play premium positions, but the cupboard is nearly bare in the upper minors. Of the Cubs' top 15 prospects, only lefthander Justin Steele has played in Double-A or higher.

30. Boston Red Sox	23	14	4	5	2

After 108 wins and another World Series trophy, the Red Sox won't be too concerned about having baseball's worst farm system. The Red Sox haven't necessarily done poorly at acquiring talent in the draft or internationally, but they've cashed in their best prospects to bolster the major league club.

Arizona Diamondbacks

BY NICK PIECORO

The second year of general manager Mike Hazen's regime saw another attempt at threading the competitive needle, with the Diamondbacks trying to win without severely sacrificing the future. They fell short on the former, but time will tell on the latter.

Arizona was on track for its second consecutive postseason appearance in 2018 before collapsing in September and finishing with an 82-80 record. To get there, the club parted ways with a whopping 15 prospects since the end of 2017 season. Eight of those 15 ranked among the system's Top 30 Prospects just a year ago.

On top of that, the D-backs were unable to sign their 2018 first-round pick. California high school shortstop Matt McLain spurned them to attend UCLA.

Yet there's a twist: It's hard to call it a lost year for player development.

The D-backs watched as incumbent prospects began to blossom, while a handful of newcomers shined in their first taste of pro ball. The system's strength remained in the lower levels, but a fascinating crop of prospects began to come together.

Outfielders Kristian Robinson and Alek Thomas and shortstops Geraldo Perdomo and Blaze Alexander have a chance to rise through the ranks together. They could be the best wave of position prospects the club has had since Justin Upton, Stephen Drew, Miguel Montero and others arrived on the scene more than a decade ago.

The D-backs have some interesting players both ahead of and behind that group. Righthanders Jon Duplantier and Taylor Widener threw well at Double-A Jackson. Shortstop Jazz Chisholm had a breakout season, reaching high Class A Visalia, where catcher Daulton Varsho also performed.

One cannot overlook the cost the D-backs paid to try to contend in 2018. They traded away rotation-caliber prospects such as lefty Anthony Banda (to the Rays) and righty Jhoan Duran (Twins).

From a major league standpoint, Arizona entered the 2018 offseason at a crossroads. Most of its current core is at or approaching free agency, thus becoming too expensive to keep together.

Still, hope remains. The D-backs will get a compensation pick for McLain in the 2019 draft, giving them two first-rounders. They'll get a pick in the supplemental second round. They will also get picks with Patrick Corbin departing in free agency and A.J. Pollock expected to follow.

And they made the painful decision to trade franchise player Paul Goldschmidt to the Cardinals after the season. In the trade, Arizona acquired three players in their early 20s—Luke Weaver,

Archie Bradley, the seventh overall pick in 2011, has matured into a high-leverage reliever.

PROJECTED 2022 LINEUP

Catcher	Daulton Varsho (25)
First Base	Jake Lamb (31)
Second Base	Ketel Marte (28)
Third Base	Eduardo Escobar (33)
Shortstop	Jazz Chisholm (24)
Left Field	David Peralta (34)
Center Field	Jake McCarthy (24)
Right Field	Marcus Wilson (25)
No. 1 Starter	Robbie Ray (30)
No. 2 Starter	Jon Duplantier (27)
No. 3 Starter	Luke Weaver (28)
No. 4 Starter	Zack Godley (32)
No. 5 Starter	Taylor Widener (27)
Closer	Archie Bradley (29)

Carson Kelly and Andy Young—as well as another draft pick in the supplemental second round.

The farm system and thus the organization's long-term outlook should benefit. Industry perception pegs the D-backs' system as middle of the road because so many players are so far way. Yet some wouldn't be surprised if the D-backs shot up the system rankings—and if their long-term future looked brighter than it may appear.

"I think the Diamondbacks have a better system than people think," a scout with an American League club said. "Most scouts don't cover short-season and Rookie ball, (but) if some of these guys continue to develop, the organization will definitely move up."

ARIZONA DIAMONDBACKS

TOP 2019 ROOKIE: Jon Duplantier, RHP. The D-backs could have rotation needs in 2019. If he stays healthy, Duplantier can help fill them.

BREAKOUT PROSPECT: Ryan Weiss, RHP. An excellent athlete, he has a plus fastball, a feel for spinning a breaking ball and the ability to pound the strike zone.

SLEEPER: Shumpei Yoshikawa, RHP. Signed out of Japan's industrial league, the 23-year-old is a polished pitch-maker with a plus changeup.

SOURCE OF TOP 30 TALENT			
Homegrown	26	Acquired	4
College	12	Trade	4
Junior college	0	Rule 5 draft	0
High school	7	Independent league	0
Nondrafted free agent	0	Free agent/waivers	0
International	7		

LF
Marcus Wilson (20)
Neyfy Castillo

CF
Alek Thomas (8)
Jake McCarthy (9)
Eduardo Diaz
Jorge Barrosa
Lioner Peguero

RF
Kristian Robinson (6)
Alvin Guzman

3B
Blaze Alexander (10)
Buddy Kennedy (19)
Drew Ellis (21)
Joey Rose

SS
Jazz Chisholm (1)
Geraldo Perdomo (5)
Brandon Leyton
Roman Ruiz
Luis Rubio

2B
Andy Young (12)
Domingo Leyba (24)
Ryan Grotjohn
Jose Caballero

1B
Andy Yerzy (13)
Pavin Smith (17)
Kevin Cron

C
Daulton Varsho (3)
Carson Kelly (4)
Dominic Miroglio (23)
Renae Martinez
Nick Dalesandro

LHP

LHSP	LHRP
Mack Lemieux	Jared Miller
Alex Young	Michel Gelabert
Cody Reed	Kenny Hernandez
Tyler Holton	

RHP

RHSP	RHRP
Jon Duplantier (2)	Yoan Lopez (16)
Taylor Widener (7)	Luis Frias (22)
Taylor Clarke (11)	Emilio Vargas (25)
Matt Tabor (14)	Jimmie Sherfy (29)
Merrill Kelly (15)	Kevin Ginkel (30)
Ryan Weiss (18)	West Tunnell
Matt Mercer (26)	Travis Moths
Harrison Francis (27)	Josh Green
Jackson Goddard (28)	
Nick Green	
Bo Takahashi	
Shumpei Yoshikawa	
Jhosmer Alvarez	
Adrian Del Moral	
Abraham Calzadilla	
Riley Smith	

DRAFT ANALYSIS

2018

BEST PURE HITTER: Arizona targeted several high-level hit tools early in the draft, but OF Alek Thomas (2) is a potential plus hitter with excellent bat speed. He has a knack for making in-game adjustments and has plenty of history squaring up some of the top pitchers in the 2018 draft class. He crushed his first stint of pro ball, hitting .333/.395/.463 in 56 games at a pair of Rookie-level stops.

BEST POWER HITTER: 1B Zack Shannon (15) led all Division II hitters in home runs as a senior at Delta State (Miss.) and continued his longball barrage with a wood bat in his pro debut, hitting 14 homers in 54 games in the Pioneer League.

FASTEST RUNNER: Thomas was one of the safer bets among the 2018 prep class to stay in center field, in large part because of his running ability. He's a plus runner who gets out of the box well and knows how to utilize his legs on the bases and in the outfield. He stole 12 bags in his debut.

BEST DEFENSIVE PLAYER: OF Jake McCarthy (1s) handled center field well in his three years at Virginia and most scouts believe he'll be a fine defender at the position. He spent most of his time there in the Northwest League but also got innings in both left and right field. McCarthy is an above-average runner and has solid defensive instincts.

BEST FASTBALL: RHP Matt Mercer (5) is a Driveline Baseball protege who built up his velocity over his career with Oregon, touching as high as 98 mph, though he more routinely sits in the low to mid-90s with a violent, high-effort delivery. He started all 13 of his games in the Arizona and Northwest leagues with a 3.10 ERA.

BEST SECONDARY PITCH: LHP Tyler Holton (9) threw just 4.2 innings this year after having Tommy John surgery. A plus changeup is his best pitch in a repertoire that also includes a well below-average fastball.

BEST PRO DEBUT: The D-backs popped SS Blaze Alexander (11), signed him for $500,000 and watched as he went out and hit .329/.417/.538 in the Arizona and Pioneer leagues. Known pri-

TOP DRAFT PICKS OF THE DECADE

Year	Player, Pos.	2018 Org
2009	Bobby Borchering, 3B	Did not play
2010	*Barret Loux, RHP	Did not play
2011	Trevor Bauer, RHP	Indians
2012	Stryker Trahan, C	Did not play
2013	Braden Shipley, RHP	D-backs
2014	Touki Toussaint, RHP	Braves
2015	Dansby Swanson, SS	Braves
2016	Anfernee Grier, OF (1st round supp)	D-backs
2017	Pavin Smith, 1B	D-backs
2018	*Matt McLain, SS	—

* Did not sign

marily for his defensive ability and 70-grade arm, Alexander has bat speed, though scouts wonder how much offensive value he would provide.

BEST ATHLETE: Thomas was a talented high school football player.

MOST INTRIGUING BACKGROUND: C Nick Dalesandro (10) is the son of Mark Dalesandro, who had a five-year major league career as a catcher and third baseman. The younger Dalesandro is an athletic backstop with a well above-average arm who has pitched some in the past as well.

CLOSEST TO THE MAJORS: McCarthy put together one of the most complete collegiate résumés in the 2018 class, hitting .337/.423/.476 in parts of three seasons in the Atlantic Coast Conference as well as a strong track record in the Cape Cod League. He is a good bet to move quickly through the system thanks to an advanced hit tool, pedigree and defensive value.

BEST LATE-ROUND PICK: Alexander could have been a Day One pick after ranking No. 85 on the BA 500 with elite defensive potential and an intriguing bat.

THE ONE WHO GOT AWAY: SS Matt McLain (1), who popped up during the spring in a down year in Southern California, impressed enough with his bat and ability to handle shortstop that the D-backs took him 25th overall. However, McLain and Arizona couldn't agree on a deal and the undersized middle infielder will head to UCLA.

—CARLOS COLLAZO

2017

1B Pavin Smith (1) has disappointed as a top-10 overall selection, but C Daulton Varsho (2s) in the early going has stood out as a solid all-around player. Prep RHPs Matt Tabor (3) and Harrison Francis (4) give the class some exciting upside.

GRADE: C

2016

RHP Jon Duplantier (3) was set back by injury but still offers solid upside, as does C Andy Yerzy (2). RHP Tommy Eveld (9) had a solid year and in July was dealt for Brad Ziegler. Top-pick OF Anfernee Grier (1s) has struggled as a pro.

GRADE: C

2015

RHP Ryan Burr (5) reached the big leagues and RHP Taylor Clarke (3) could soon join him, but this draft will likely come down to what SS Dansby Swanson (1) does in Atlanta. He was a starter on a playoff team, but the jury is still out.

GRADE: B

1 JAZZ CHISHOLM, SS

Born: Feb. 1, 1998. **B-T:** L-R. **HT:** 5-11. **WT:** 165.
Signed: Bahamas, 2015. **Signed by:** Craig Shipley.

At a showcase for Lucius Fox in the Bahamas in February 2015, D-backs scout Craig Shipley was as intrigued by Fox at short-stop as he was by Chisholm, who was playing second base. Shipley saw Chisholm again a few weeks later, this time at short, and, impressed by Chisholm's actions and athleticism, wound up signing him for $200,000 that July. He has quickly turned himself into a bargain. After an impressive debut in Rookie-level Missoula, where he hit .281 with nine homers in 249 at-bats, Chisholm played in just 29 games in 2017 before a torn meniscus ended his season. He made up for lost time in 2018, with a solid three and a half months at low Class A Kane County followed by a monster six weeks in the high Class A California League. The 25 home runs he hit in 2018 set a single-season franchise record for a shortstop. He finished with a good showing in a limited role in the Arizona Fall League.

SCOUTING REPORT: Chisholm has an exciting array of tools. He has an athletic build and strong hands, and he generates a smooth, lefthanded uppercut swing that produces loud contact with easy power. His approach is aggressive, sometimes too aggressive. Coaches say he has a tendency to try too hard to generate power to his pull side, say-ing his swing can get too steep and his approach too pull-conscious. They believe when he keeps his approach simple, the power comes naturally to all fields. He strikes out a lot—nearly 30 percent of the time—and his high swing-and-miss rate on pitches in the zone is concerning. He also struggled against lefthanded pitchers. Defensively, Chisholm has everything it takes to stick at shortstop but needs to work on his consistency. He has smooth, flashy actions but is prone to lapses in concentra-tion, making highlight-reel plays before commit-ting errors on routine ones. He's an above-average to plus runner and stole 17 bases in 21 tries. Chisholm has a bubbling, energetic personality and is brimming with confidence, and coaches and team executives say he continued to work hard despite being disappointed about starting the season in Kane County.

THE FUTURE: Chisholm is a high-risk but high-reward stock. He has some rough edges to smooth over, and if it comes together he could be a short-stop with 20-homer, 20-steal potential. Parts of his game lack maturity, which could come in time. He could open 2019 in Double-A Jackson.

GERHART

BA GRADE	SCOUTING GRADES
60 Risk: High	Hit: 50. Power: 60. Run: 55. Field: 55. Arm: 55.

Projected future grades on 20-80 scouting scale.

TOP PROSPECTS OF THE DECADE

Year	Player, Pos.	2018 Org
2009	Jarrod Parker, RHP	Did not play
2010	Jarrod Parker, RHP	Did not play
2011	Jarrod Parker, RHP	Did not play
2012	Trevor Bauer, RHP	Indians
2013	Tyler Skaggs, LHP	Angels
2014	Archie Bradley, RHP	D-backs
2015	Archie Bradley, RHP	D-backs
2016	Dansby Swanson, SS	Braves
2017	Anthony Banda, LHP	Rays
2018	Jon Duplantier, RHP	D-backs

BEST TOOLS

Best Hitter for Average	Daulton Varsho
Best Power Hitter	Kevin Cron
Best Strike-Zone Discipline	Pavin Smith
Fastest Baserunner	Tra Holmes
Best Athlete	Kristian Robinson
Best Fastball	Taylor Widener
Best Curveball	Jon Duplantier
Best Slider	Yoan Lopez
Best Changeup	Matt Tabor
Best Control	Taylor Clarke
Best Defensive Catcher	Carson Kelly
Best Defensive Infielder	Geraldo Perdomo
Best Infield Arm	Blaze Alexander
Best Defensive Outfielder	Tra Holmes
Best Outfield Arm	Alvin Guzman

Year	Club (League)	Class	AVG	G	AB	R	H	2B	3B	HR	RBI	BB	SO	SB	CS	OBP	SLG
2016	Missoula (PIO)	R	.281	62	249	42	70	12	1	9	37	19	73	13	4	.333	.446
2017	Kane County (MWL)	LoA	.248	29	109	14	27	5	2	1	12	10	39	3	0	.325	.358
2018	Kane County (MWL)	LoA	.244	76	307	52	75	17	4	15	43	30	97	8	2	.311	.472
	Visalia (CAL)	HiA	.329	36	149	27	49	6	2	10	27	9	52	9	2	.369	.597
Minor League Totals			.271	203	814	135	221	40	9	35	119	68	261	33	8	.330	.472

2 JON DUPLANTIER, RHP

Born: July 11, 1994. **B-T:** L-R. **HT:** 6-4. **WT:** 225. **Drafted:** Rice, 2016 (3rd round). **Signed by:** Rusty Pendergrass.

TRACK RECORD: Duplantier turned in one of the more dominant minor league seasons of the past 25 years in 2017, but a hamstring injury and a bout with right biceps tendinitis limited him to just 74 innings at Double-A Jackson in 2018. Given his injury history, the Diamondbacks were overly cautious with him, bringing him back slowly. Duplantier made up 21.2 innings with a strong performance in the Arizona Fall League.

SCOUTING REPORT: Duplantier still has the best stuff of any starter in the system. His legit four-pitch mix begins with a lively fastball that sits in the low-to-mid-90s. Scouts and coaches say his slider evolved into his best secondary option, with his curveball and changeup both average to plus at times. He's cerebral and inquisitive, and coaches say he understands how best to use his stuff to exploit hitters' weaknesses. He has average to above-average command and control, though his walks ticked up in 2018. For some scouts, Duplantier's recent arm issues made it harder to overlook his funky arm action.

BA GRADE

55 Risk: High

Fastball: 60.
Slider: 60. Curve: 55.
Change: 50. CTL: 60.

THE FUTURE: Scouts who like Duplantier see a mid-rotation starter and perhaps a little more, but some remain spooked by the injuries that date to his days at Rice and wonder if he's a breakdown candidate. If he keeps taking the ball he can shed that reputation, not to mention possibly reach the majors in 2019.

Year	Club (League)	Class	W	L	ERA	G	GS	CG	SV	IP	H	HR	BB	SO	K/9	WHIP	AVG
2016	Hillsboro (NWL)	SS	0	0	0.00	1	0	0	0	1	0	0	2	3	27.0	2.00	.000
2017	Kane County (MWL)	LoA	6	1	1.24	13	12	0	0	73	45	4	15	78	9.7	0.83	.180
	Visalia (CAL)	HiA	6	2	1.56	12	12	0	0	63	46	2	27	87	12.4	1.15	.204
2018	Diamondbacks (AZL)	R	0	0	1.29	2	2	0	0	7	5	0	2	9	11.6	1.00	.200
	Jackson (SL)	AA	5	1	2.69	14	14	0	0	67	52	4	28	68	9.1	1.19	.217
Minor League Totals			17	4	1.79	42	40	0	0	211	148	10	74	245	10.5	1.05	.199

3 DAULTON VARSHO, C

Born: July 2, 1996. **B-T:** L-R. **HT:** 5-10. **WT:** 190. **Drafted:** Wisconsin-Milwaukee, 2017 (2nd round supplemental). **Signed by:** Rick Short.

TRACK RECORD: After tearing up the Horizon League his junior year at Wisconsin-Milwaukee, Varsho, the son of big leaguer Gary Varsho, was taken 68th overall by the Diamondbacks in 2017. In his first full season as a pro, he jumped to a fast start for High Class A Visalia before needing surgery for a broken right hamate in June. He returned in August, and after a slow two and a half weeks, he hit like he had before the injury over his final 10 games.

SCOUTING REPORT: Varsho has a compact swing, an aggressive-yet-mature approach and a knack for finding the barrel, with scouts seeing good extension that generates loft, giving him average power with the chance for more. There are still questions about his ability to stick at catcher, but he did win over some converts in 2018. He's athletic and energetic behind the plate, and his quick transfer and throwing accuracy make up for average-at-best arm strength. Some scouts say his receiving can occasionally appear raw. He's the rare catcher who also is an above-average to plus runner.

BA GRADE

55 Risk: High

Hit: 55. Power: 50.
Run: 55. Field: 55.
Arm: 45.

THE FUTURE: Even those unsure if Varsho can catch believe he'll be a big leaguer, saying that his athleticism should allow him to handle second base or the outfield, with some saying the Diamondbacks could use him at multiple positions the way the Dodgers have with Austin Barnes.

Year	Club (League)	Class	AVG	G	AB	R	H	2B	3B	HR	RBI	BB	SO	SB	CS	OBP	SLG
2017	Hillsboro (NWL)	SS	.311	50	193	36	60	16	3	7	39	17	30	7	2	.368	.534
2018	Diamondbacks (AZL)	R	.500	3	12	4	6	2	1	1	1	0	1	0	0	.500	1.083
	Visalia (CAL)	HiA	.286	80	304	44	87	11	3	11	44	30	71	19	3	.363	.451
Minor League Totals			.301	133	509	84	153	29	7	19	84	47	102	26	5	.367	.497

4 CARSON KELLY, C

Born: July 14, 1994. **B-T:** R-R. **HT:** 6-2. **WT:** 220. **Drafted:** HS—Portland, Ore., 2012 (2nd round). **Signed by:** Matt Swanson (Cardinals).

TRACK RECORD: Drafted as a third baseman by the Cardinals, Kelly converted to catcher in 2014 and was hailed as Yadier Molina's heir apparent. But with Molina showing no signs of letting up, the Cardinals wanted Kelly playing everyday and sent him back to Triple-A Memphis in 2018 for a third straight season. In December, the Cardinals traded Kelly to the D-backs as part of the Paul Goldschmidt trade.

SCOUTING REPORT: Kelly is athletic in the box with a sound swing, a good approach and occasional power. While he hasn't had a chance to show it yet at the major league level—he has received only sporadic at-bats during his big league stints the past three years—he projects as a bottom-of-the-order hitter with on-base skills. Some evaluators believe his transition to catching meant his offensive development was put on hold, so much so that his bat could have more upside. Kelly has long been regarded as one of the best defensive catchers

BA GRADE

50 Risk: Medium

Hit: 50. Power: 40.
Run: 20. Field: 60.
Arm: 55

in the minors. He is a good receiver with a strong arm and an athletic base, and his makeup and baseball intelligence give him a chance to impact all aspects of the game.

THE FUTURE: The trade to Arizona gives Kelly a path to an everyday job. With only Alex Avila and John Ryan Murphy ahead of him, Kelly should be the Diamondbacks' starting catcher soon.

Year	Club (League)	Class	AVG	G	AB	R	H	2B	3B	HR	RBI	BB	SO	SB	CS	OBP	SLG
2016	Springfield, MO (TL)	AA	.287	64	216	29	62	7	0	6	18	14	46	0	1	.338	.403
	Memphis (PCL)	AAA	.292	32	113	14	33	10	0	0	14	11	17	0	0	.352	.381
	St. Louis (NL)	MAJ	.154	10	13	1	2	1	0	0	1	0	2	0	0	.214	.231
2017	Memphis (PCL)	AAA	.283	68	244	37	69	13	0	10	41	33	40	0	2	.375	.459
	St. Louis (NL)	MAJ	.174	34	69	5	12	3	0	0	6	5	11	0	0	.240	.217
2018	Memphis (PCL)	AAA	.269	83	294	38	79	14	1	7	41	48	48	0	0	.378	.395
	St. Louis (NL)	MAJ	.114	19	35	1	4	0	0	0	3	3	7	0	0	.205	.114
Major League Totals			.154	63	117	7	18	4	0	0	10	8	20	0	0	.227	.188
Minor League Totals			.255	622	2249	266	573	111	7	52	284	208	358	2	3	.324	.380

5 GERALDO PERDOMO, SS

Born: Oct. 22, 1999. **B-T:** B-R. **HT:** 6-2. **WT:** 184. **Signed:** Dominican Republic, 2016. **Signed by:** Junior Noboa/Elvis Cruz.

TRACK RECORD: Signed for $70,000 in 2016, Perdomo exhibited advanced plate discipline in the Dominican Summer League in his pro debut the following year. He continued to show a discerning eye in 2018, but he added some offensive impact as well, emerging as one of the Diamondbacks' most intriguing young prospects.

SCOUTING REPORT: Perdomo has an athletic frame with a high waist and an upper body that should be able to handle added bulk. He has a way of gliding on defense, and his soft hands, plus arm and instincts lead scouts to believe he'll have no trouble sticking at shortstop. A switch-hitter, he has plus bat speed, good bat-to-ball skills and pull power that could grow into more. Perdomo was overly passive in the DSL in 2017 but became more aggressive as he started facing better strike-throwers. Scouts say he's a slightly above-average runner. He impressed coaches by making big strides learning English.

BA GRADE

55 Risk: Extreme

Hit: 55. Power: 40.
Run: 50. Field: 60.
Arm: 60.

THE FUTURE: Perdomo might not have the huge ceiling of Jazz Chisholm or Kristian Robinson, but his floor could be higher, with scouts seeing a talented, instinctual, smart player in the mold of Tony Fernandez. He'll likely open 2019 in low Class A Kane County.

Year	Club (League)	Class	AVG	G	AB	R	H	2B	3B	HR	RBI	BB	SO	SB	CS	OBP	SLG
2017	D-backs (DSL)	R	.238	63	214	42	51	3	2	1	11	60	37	16	8	.410	.285
2018	Diamondbacks (AZL)	R	.314	21	86	20	27	4	2	1	8	14	17	14	1	.416	.442
	Missoula (PIO)	R	.455	6	22	3	10	0	1	0	2	7	4	1	1	.586	.545
	Hillsboro (NWL)	SS	.301	30	103	20	31	3	2	3	14	18	23	9	4	.421	.456
Minor League Totals			.280	120	425	85	119	10	7	5	35	99	81	40	14	.423	.372

6 KRISTIAN ROBINSON, OF

Born: Dec. 11, 2000. **B-T:** R-R. **HT:** 6-3. **WT:** 190. **Signed:** Bahamas, 2017.
Signed by: Cesar Geronimo/Craig Shipley.

TRACK RECORD: The Diamondbacks signed Robinson for $2.5 million in 2017 and fully expected his first season as a pro to begin in the Dominican Summer League. But he so impressed throughout the spring, with a mature approach on and off the field, that the club started him in the Rookie-level Arizona League, then pushed him to the Pioneer League to finish.

SCOUTING REPORT: Robinson has a strong, physical build and looks far more developed than his age would suggest. He has good pitch-recognition skills and some feel to hit, though some scouts see him as a power-over-hit type for now. His power could be huge, and he showed signs of tapping into it in 2018, driving balls to all fields. Given that he's a native of the Bahamas and had limited exposure to tough pitching as an amateur, he might have even more room to grow than others his age. He has the instincts, speed and athleticism to stick in center field, but his ultimate home could depend on how his body develops.

BA GRADE

55 Risk: Extreme

Hit: 50. **Power:** 60.
Run: 55. **Field:** 55.
Arm: 55.

THE FUTURE: Though he has a long way to go, the sky is the limit in terms of Robinson's upside. Some see flashes of Andruw Jones or Adam Jones if he can remain in center, while others see his physical development turning him into a Jermaine Dye or Jorge Soler type on a corner. If he doesn't open in low Class A Kane County, he'll likely get there at some point early in the 2019 season.

Year	Club (League)	Class	AVG	G	AB	R	H	2B	3B	HR	RBI	BB	SO	SB	CS	OBP	SLG
2018	Diamondbacks (AZL)	R	.272	40	162	35	44	11	0	4	31	16	46	7	5	.341	.414
	Missoula (PIO)	R	.300	17	60	13	18	1	0	3	10	11	21	5	3	.419	.467
Minor League Totals			.279	57	222	48	62	12	0	7	41	27	67	12	8	.363	.428

7 TAYLOR WIDENER, RHP

Born: Oct. 24, 1994. **B-T:** R-R. **HT:** 6-0. **WT:** 195. **Drafted:** South Carolina, 2016 (12th round). **Signed by:** Billy Godwin (Yankees).

TRACK RECORD: The Yankees traded Widener to the Diamondbacks in February 2018 as part of the three-team Steven Souza Jr. trade also involving the Rays. Widener turned in the most consistent season of any Diamondbacks starter in 2018, earning the organization's pitcher of the year honors while leading the Double-A Southern League in strikeouts and WHIP and finishing second in ERA.

SCOUTING REPORT: Widener's success is in large part built off a dominant fastball. The pitch sits around 92-93 mph and usually tops out around 95, and he generates lots of swings and misses with it, including up in the strike zone. His secondary stuff was less consistent. His changeup improved in 2018, going from a traditional offspeed/velocity-separation pitch to a power change out of the Zack Greinke mold that's more about disrupting timing and inducing ground balls. It became his best secondary offering, moving ahead of a slider that has some bite but at times can be more like a slurve.

BA GRADE

50 Risk: High

Fastball: 60.
Change: 50. **Slider:** 50.
Control: 55.

THE FUTURE: Widener is beloved for his competitiveness, but he does have some effort and aggression in his delivery and a less-than-ideal arm stroke. Combine that with the inconsistent secondary stuff and some see his ultimate home being in the bullpen. He'll get every chance to start, however, and likely will move to Triple-A Reno in 2019.

Year	Club (League)	Class	W	L	ERA	G	GS	CG	SV	IP	H	HR	BB	SO	K/9	WHIP	AVG
2016	Staten Island (NYP)	SS	2	0	0.00	6	1	0	1	15	2	0	4	25	14.7	0.39	.043
	Charleston, SC (SAL)	LoA	1	0	0.78	7	1	0	3	23	15	2	3	34	13.3	0.78	.188
2017	Tampa (FSL)	HiA	7	8	3.39	27	27	0	0	119	87	5	50	129	9.7	1.15	.206
2018	Jackson (SL)	AA	5	8	2.75	26	25	1	0	137	99	12	43	176	11.5	1.03	.197
Minor League Totals			15	16	2.72	66	54	1	4	295	203	19	100	364	11.1	1.03	.193

8 ALEK THOMAS, OF

Born: April 28, 2000. **B-T:** L-L. **HT:** 5-11. **WT:** 175. **Drafted:** HS—Chicago, 2018 (2nd round). **Signed by:** Nate Birtwell.

TRACK RECORD: The son of White Sox strength coach Allen Thomas, Alek bypassed a commitment to Texas Christian to sign with the Diamondbacks for $1.2 million as the 63rd overall pick. He quickly won over fans inside and outside the organization with his athleticism, aggressiveness and ability to hit at his first two stops as a pro.

SCOUTING REPORT: Thomas is undersized—he's generously listed at 5-foot-11—but has a strong build and is likely one of the best pure athletes in the system. His swing can get long and he might need to tone down some aspects of it, but he has an innate ability to find the barrel. Projections on his power were mixed but some believe he could eventually reach 10-15 home runs. Scouts believe he should stick in center field, where he has above-average range. His arm is fringe-average at best. He's a good runner with solid instincts on the bases, though he needs to work on his basestealing.

BA GRADE
55 Risk: Extreme
Hit: 55. Power: 45.
Run: 60. Field: 55.
Arm: 40.

THE FUTURE: Thomas' size might have been the biggest reason he wasn't drafted higher. It's the main reason some scouts are reluctant to build in too much projection in his game. That said, those who really like him draw comparisons with Adam Eaton, Brett Gardner and Ender Inciarte. Thomas has a chance to open 2019 with low Class A Kane County.

Year	Club (League)	Class	AVG	G	AB	R	H	2B	3B	HR	RBI	BB	SO	SB	CS	OBP	SLG
2018	Diamondbacks (AZL)	R	.325	28	123	24	40	3	5	0	10	13	18	8	2	.394	.431
	Missoula (PIO)	R	.341	28	123	26	42	11	1	2	17	11	19	4	3	.396	.496
Minor League Totals			.333	56	246	50	82	14	6	2	27	24	37	12	5	.395	.463

9 JAKE McCARTHY, OF

Born: July 30, 1997. **B-T:** L-L. **HT:** 6-3. **WT:** 195. **Drafted:** Virginia, 2018 (1st round supplemental). **Signed by:** Rick Matsko.

TRACK RECORD: A wrist injury limited McCarthy to just 20 games during his junior season, but his strong track record allowed him to maintain his draft status. He signed with the Diamondbacks for $1.65 million as the 39th overall pick, following his older brother, Joe, on the same path to the pros from the University of Virginia. He showed off a well-rounded skill set during a 55-game pro debut in the short-season Northwest League.

SCOUTING REPORT: McCarthy has an athletic frame with room to add strength. He has had success using a simple, contact-oriented swing, but it's somewhat stiff and upper-body driven, and the D-backs would like to see him become looser and more rhythmic while using his lower half more. He runs well and takes good routes to balls, and some scouts believe he'll easily stick in center field with a chance to be a plus defender there. His arm is fringe-average. He is considered a hard worker and excellent teammate and is said to have great makeup.

BA GRADE
50 Risk: High
Hit: 55. Power: 40.
Run: 60. Field: 60.
Arm: 45.

THE FUTURE: Though McCarthy is lefthanded, he has an all-around game that's reminiscent of A.J. Pollock when he was drafted. Most see McCarthy's floor as a fourth outfielder, and if, like Pollock, he can make adjustments and learn to tap into more power, he could develop into an everyday player. He likely will start the 2019 season at high Class A Visalia.

Year	Club (League)	Class	AVG	G	AB	R	H	2B	3B	HR	RBI	BB	SO	SB	CS	OBP	SLG
2018	Diamondbacks (AZL)	R	.273	3	11	1	3	0	1	0	4	1	1	1	0	.333	.455
	Hillsboro (NWL)	SS	.288	55	208	33	60	17	3	3	18	22	40	20	8	.378	.442
Minor League Totals			.288	58	219	34	63	17	4	3	22	23	41	21	8	.375	.443

10 BLAZE ALEXANDER, SS

Born: June 19, 1999. **B-T:** R-R. **HT:** 6-0. **WT:** 160. **Drafted:** HS—Bradenton, Fla., 2018 (11th round). **Signed by:** Luke Wrenn.

TRACK RECORD: Alexander slipped in the 2018 draft, perhaps due to some combination of a high asking price as well as concerns about how often he swung and missed his senior year at IMG Academy. After signing with the Diamondbacks for $500,000, he quickly quieted any worries about his bat, performing so well in his pro debut he helped ease the sting of the club's inability to sign top pick Matt McLain.

SCOUTING REPORT: Alexander, whose dad Charles pitched parts of three seasons in the Indians' system and whose older brother C.J. is in the Braves organization, has a lean, athletic frame and an arm that rates near the top of the scouting scale. His swing is consistent and under control, with no wasted movement, and he has good finish at the end, prompting some scouts to envision him growing into power to all fields, though he does tend to roll over on pitches with his top hand. He has good instincts in the field but isn't as fluid and easy as shortstops often are, leading some to envision a shift to third or second base.

THE FUTURE: Alexander has a chance to open next season in low Class A Kane County and could develop into an infielder in the J.J. Hardy or Chris Taylor mold.

BA GRADE

55 Risk: Extreme

Hit: 50. **Power:** 45.
Run: 45. **Field:** 55.
Arm: 65.

Year	Club (League)	Class	AVG	G	AB	R	H	2B	3B	HR	RBI	BB	SO	SB	CS	OBP	SLG
2018	Diamondbacks (AZL)	R	.362	27	94	25	34	10	2	2	25	19	21	7	3	.475	.574
	Missoula (PIO)	R	.302	28	116	27	35	9	3	3	17	12	31	3	0	.364	.509
Minor League Totals			.329	55	210	52	69	19	5	5	42	31	52	10	3	.417	.538

11 TAYLOR CLARKE, RHP

BA GRADE

45 Risk: Medium

Born: May 13, 1993. **B-T:** R-R. **HT:** 6-4. **WT:** 200. **Drafted:** College of Charleston, 2015 (3rd round). **Signed by:** George Swain.

TRACK RECORD: Clarke continued his steady, consistent progression through the system in 2018, logging a career-high 152 innings while pitching in a difficult Triple-A Pacific Coast League environment. He has thrown at least 145 innings in each of the past three seasons. He was in consideration for a callup at multiple points in 2018, but the club opted for more veteran options.

SCOUTING REPORT: Clarke is much the same pitcher as always: a strike-thrower with good pitchability and solid, if unspectacular, stuff. His fastball velocity ticked up a bit in 2018, topping out around 95 mph and sitting closer to 93, and coaches say his changeup improved, though still remains his second-best secondary offering behind his slider. Clarke took his preparation and game-planning seriously, and with his above-average command was able to attack hitters with a purpose. He could benefit even further from the more-detailed data he would receive in the majors.

THE FUTURE: Depending on how things shake out, Clarke could have a chance to compete for a big league rotation spot and is knocking on the door after being added to the 40-man roster in November.

Year	Club (League)	Class	W	L	ERA	G	GS	CG	SV	IP	H	HR	BB	SO	K/9	WHIP	AVG
2016	Kane County (MWL)	LoA	3	2	2.83	6	6	0	0	29	24	1	5	24	7.5	1.01	.222
	Visalia (CAL)	HiA	1	1	2.74	4	4	0	0	23	19	3	7	22	8.6	1.13	.221
	Mobile (SL)	AA	8	6	3.59	17	17	0	0	98	99	9	21	72	6.6	1.23	.261
2017	Jackson (SL)	AA	9	7	2.91	21	21	0	0	111	94	7	39	107	8.6	1.19	.232
	Reno (PCL)	AAA	3	2	4.81	6	6	0	0	34	29	8	13	31	8.3	1.25	.225
2018	Reno (PCL)	AAA	13	8	4.03	27	27	0	0	152	149	12	44	125	7.4	1.27	.254
Minor League Totals			37	26	3.41	94	81	0	3	467	422	40	133	408	7.9	1.19	.239

12 ANDY YOUNG, 2B

BA GRADE

50 Risk: High

Born: May 10, 1994. **B-T:** R-R. **HT:** 6-0. **WT:** 195. **Drafted:** Indiana State, 2016 (37th round). **Signed by:** Jason Bryans (Cardinals).

TRACK RECORD: Just 17 players born in North Dakota have ever reached the majors. Young is hard-charging toward becoming No. 18. The Cardinals picked Young in the 37th round in 2016, signed him for just $3,000 and quickly realized they had a steal. He mashed his way up three levels in his first full season, and he followed in 2018 by finishing fourth in the Cardinals' system in home runs (21) as he moved to Double-A. The Diamondbacks acquired him in the Paul Goldschmidt trade after the season.

THE FUTURE: Young is a second baseman, but his best position is "hitter." He's a physical specimen with a chiseled core, strong wrists, thick forearms and big legs that give him a strong base and make him a powerful runner. He has a short, compact swing that packs a punch, and he uses the entire field with average raw power. He jumps on fastballs early and doesn't walk much, but he doesn't strike out much, either. Reports on Young's athleticism vary widely. The D-backs envision him at either second or third base and see a David Bote-type player; others believe he'll have to move to left field.

THE FUTURE: Young will go as far as his bat takes him, and there's a growing consensus that will be the majors. He'll likely open the season in Double-A Jackson.

Year	Club (League)	Class	AVG	G	AB	R	H	2B	3B	HR	RBI	BB	SO	SB	CS	OBP	SLG
2016	Cardinals (GCL)	R	.323	11	31	7	10	2	1	0	5	7	3	0	0	.500	.452
	State College (NYP)	SS	.261	42	161	26	42	3	5	3	19	10	44	3	0	.322	.398
2017	Peoria (MWL)	LoA	.284	58	211	31	60	11	4	12	38	22	54	5	2	.379	.545
	Palm Beach (FSL)	HiA	.265	57	196	24	52	9	0	5	20	10	49	3	0	.327	.388
	Springfield, MO (TL)	AA	.667	2	3	2	2	0	0	0	1	1	1	0	0	.800	.667
2018	Palm Beach (FSL)	HiA	.276	84	297	43	82	10	2	12	34	31	59	4	0	.372	.444
	Springfield, MO (TL)	AA	.319	35	135	18	43	3	1	9	24	7	26	0	2	.395	.556
Minor League Totals			.281	289	1034	151	291	38	13	41	141	88	236	15	4	.367	.462

13 ANDY YERZY, C/1B

Born: July 5, 1998. **B-T:** L-R. **HT:** 6-3. **WT:** 215. **Drafted:** HS—Toronto, 2016 (2nd round). **Signed by:** Dennis Sheehan.

TRACK RECORD: Yerzy opened the year in extended spring training before heading to short-season Northwest League, where he put together a second consecutive strong year at the plate. But he again left evaluators unsure about where his future lies; few doubt his bat, but no one seems overly confident he can stick at catcher.

SCOUTING REPORT: Yerzy has good bat speed, a powerful swing and an advanced approach that's aided by his studious commitment to learning the craft. After he lowered his hands and started using his lower half more, he began driving balls more consistently. Coaches say he might have finished with twice as many homers if Hillsboro were more hitter-friendly. Yerzy continues to improve defensively but has a ways to go to become a consistent, average receiver and thrower, and it appears the bat is developing much faster than his defense. He started eight games at first base in Hillsboro and played the position exclusively in instructional league, though the organization says he's still being viewed as a catcher.

THE FUTURE: The club likely will continue to give Yerzy every chance to catch because of the value he would provide there, but if the bat continues its trajectory first base could make more sense.

Year	Club (League)	Class	AVG	G	AB	R	H	2B	3B	HR	RBI	BB	SO	SB	CS	OBP	SLG
2016	Diamondbacks (AZL)	R	.196	27	102	5	20	3	0	1	15	4	22	0	0	.220	.255
	Missoula (PIO)	R	.250	18	60	2	15	2	0	0	1	0	16	0	1	.274	.283
2017	Missoula (PIO)	R	.298	54	225	36	67	12	0	13	45	24	45	0	0	.365	.524
2018	Hillsboro (NWL)	SS	.297	63	239	30	71	11	1	8	34	28	67	0	0	.382	.452
Minor League Totals			.276	162	626	73	173	28	1	22	95	56	150	0	1	.341	.430

14 MATT TABOR, RHP

Born: July 14, 1998. **B-T:** R-R. **HT:** 6-2. **WT:** 180. **Drafted:** HS—Milton, Mass., 2017 (3rd round). **Signed by:** Dennis Sheehan.

TRACK RECORD: Tabor didn't have a breakout performance in his first full season as a pro, but coaches say he might have improved from start to finish more than any pitcher in the organization, and he continues to give the club hope he can develop into a big league starter. He didn't miss a ton of bats in the short-season Northwest League, but his clean, repeatable delivery allowed him to fill up the strike zone and he showed good pitchability.

SCOUTING REPORT: Tabor doesn't have overpowering stuff, but his fastball improved as the season progressed, going from sitting 90-91 mph to about 93. His changeup is his best secondary offering, a pitch that some say is the best in the organization. The fastball/changeup combo draws comparisons with former Diamondbacks pitcher Chase Anderson. Tabor's breaking ball remains a work in progress. For now, it's a slider, but there are some who would like to see him go back to a curveball, which might work better given his ability to pitch north-south with the fastball.

THE FUTURE: Tabor matured as a pitcher in 2018 but still has work to do if he's going to reach his mid-rotation ceiling. He's in line to open the year in low Class A Kane County.

Year	Club (League)	Class	W	L	ERA	G	GS	CG	SV	IP	H	HR	BB	SO	K/9	WHIP	AVG
2017	Diamondbacks (AZL)	R	0	1	1.93	4	4	0	0	5	8	0	0	9	17.4	1.71	.348
2018	Hillsboro (NWL)	SS	2	1	3.26	14	14	0	0	61	59	4	13	46	6.8	1.19	.251
Minor League Totals			2	2	3.17	18	18	0	0	65	67	4	13	55	7.6	1.22	.260

15 MERRILL KELLY

Born: Oct. 14, 1988. **B-T:** R-R. **HT:** 6-2. **WT:** 190. **Drafted:** Arizona State, 2010 (8th round). **Signed by:** Jayson Durocher (Rays).

TRACK RECORD: After two years at Yavapai (Ariz.) JC and one at Arizona State, Kelly climbed steadily through the Rays system, posting strong numbers for Triple-A Durham in 2014. Trouble was, he was buried in a pitching-rich organization. Believing his best bet would be to get out of the Rays' control, he headed to Korea, expecting to be there for one or two years before returning home. He stayed for four. After helping SK Wyverns win a Korea Baseball Organization championship in 2018, he signed a two-year, $5.5 million deal with the D-backs in December.

SCOUTING REPORT: Kelly, who twice ranked in the KBO's top 10 in ERA, has the makings of a No. 5 starter. He has a five-pitch mix, starting with a fastball that sits 92-93 mph and can touch 97. His velocity is up from his days with the Rays, when he sat 88-90 mph. Scouts see his hard, tight curveball as his best secondary pitch, followed by his changeup. He also throws a slider and a cutter. He has above-average control and average command.

THE FUTURE: Unlike most pitchers who leave for Asia, Kelly has never pitched in the majors. He'll get a chance to compete for a rotation spot with the Diamondbacks this spring.

Year	Club (League)	Class	W	L	ERA	G	GS	CG	SV	IP	H	HR	BB	SO	K/9	WHIP	AVG
2016	SK (KBO)	KOR	9	8	3.68	31	31	0	0	200	205	15	60	152	6.8	1.33	—
2017	SK (KBO)	KOR	16	7	3.60	30	30	0	0	190	204	16	45	189	9.0	1.31	—
2018	SK (KBO)	KOR	12	7	4.09	28	28	0	0	158	152	18	47	161	9.2	1.26	—
Korean League Totals			48	32	3.86	119	118	1	0	730	749	65	206	641	7.9	1.31	—
Minor League Totals			39	26	3.40	125	76	0	0	527	467	28	194	379	6.5	1.25	.237

16 YOAN LOPEZ, RHP

Born: Jan. 2, 1993. **B-T:** R-R. **HT:** 6-3. **WT:** 185. **Signed:** Cuba, 2015. **Signed by:** De Jon Watson.

TRACK RECORD: Lopez's jagged path through the minors culminated with his first trip to the majors in September, and after an ugly debut that went homer, triple, homer, he rebounded during the rest of the month to show the sort of dominant stuff that looks like it could be right at home in a late-inning role.

SCOUTING REPORT: Originally signed for a bonus of more than $8 million in January 2015, Lopez left his Double-A team without permission in each of his first two seasons as a pro. He has never spoken publicly about the reasons why, but the departures raised concerns about his makeup. He has gone about reshaping opinions and is no longer viewed as a bad teammate. Lopez has some of the best stuff of any reliever in the organization, featuring a fastball that touched 99 mph and sat 97 in September to go with a swing-and-miss slider that sits in the mid-80s. He also appears to have the mentality for the ninth; during an outing against the Dodgers he escaped a jam and glared at Manny Machado on his way off the field.

THE FUTURE: Lopez's pure stuff and reshaped attitude give him a chance to win a roster spot in the spring. He could work his way into a prominent bullpen role.

Year	Club (League)	Class	W	L	ERA	G	GS	CG	SV	IP	H	HR	BB	SO	K/9	WHIP	AVG
2016	Mobile (SL)	AA	4	7	5.52	14	14	1	0	62	67	10	32	36	5.2	1.60	.277
	Diamondbacks (AZL)	R	0	0	0.00	2	2	0	0	3	3	0	0	4	12.0	1.00	.250
2017	Diamondbacks (AZL)	R	0	0	0.00	1	0	0	1	1	1	0	0	1	3	27.0	1.00	.000
	Visalia (CAL)	HiA	2	0	0.88	20	0	0	4	31	16	2	9	56	16.4	0.82	.152
2018	Jackson (SL)	AA	2	6	2.92	45	0	0	12	62	38	4	26	87	12.7	1.04	.174
	Arizona (NL)	MAJ	0	0	3.00	10	0	0	0	9	7	2	1	11	11.0	0.89	.212
Major League Totals			0	0	3.00	10	0	0	0	9	7	2	1	11	11.0	0.89	.212
Minor League Totals			10	19	3.65	93	26	1	17	212	173	20	92	224	9.5	1.25	.223

17 PAVIN SMITH, 1B

Born: Feb. 6, 1996. **B-T:** L-L. **HT:** 6-2. **WT:** 210. **Drafted:** Virginia, 2017 (1st round). **Signed by:** Rick Matsko.

TRACK RECORD: Regarded as one of the best pure hitters in the 2017 draft class, Smith was the seventh overall pick, then turned in a solid pro debut, hitting for average if not power at the short-season level. His first full season did not go as well. In the hitter-friendly California League, he hit just .156 in April and was at .223 at the end of June. He finished strong, but his year raised concerns about his upside and future role.

SCOUTING REPORT: Smith has a pretty swing and excellent plate discipline, but detractors see just average bat speed and say he's a below-average athlete. He's also a below-average runner, and the consensus is he's a first baseman only, putting even more pressure on the bat. He shows off plus raw power in BP but has trouble tapping into it. Many believe Smith was too passive at the plate and the organization was working with him on being more aggressive early in counts.

THE FUTURE: Some scouts project Smith as a bat off the bench, and even most of those who like him are cautious in their comparisons. He'll likely open 2019 at Double-A Jackson.

Year	Club (League)	Class	AVG	G	AB	R	H	2B	3B	HR	RBI	BB	SO	SB	CS	OBP	SLG
2017	Hillsboro (NWL)	SS	.318	51	195	34	62	15	2	0	27	27	24	2	1	.401	.415
2018	Visalia (CAL)	HiA	.255	120	439	63	112	25	1	11	54	57	65	3	2	.343	.392
Minor League Totals			.274	171	634	97	174	40	3	11	81	84	89	5	3	.361	.399

18 RYAN WEISS, RHP

BA GRADE
45 Risk: High

Born: Dec. 10, 1996. **B-T:** R-R. **HT:** 6-4. **WT:** 210. **Drafted:** Wright State, 2018 (4th round). **Signed by:** Jeremy Kehrt.

TRACK RECORD: Weiss helped Wright State win the Horizon League championship in 2018 and reach the NCAA Tournament for the third time in four years. In two years there, he logged a 2.80 ERA with 172 strikeouts in 186.2 innings. They D-backs felt fortunate they got him in the fourth round, believing he might have gone higher had he been pitching at a bigger school. He signed for $400,000.

SCOUTING REPORT: Weiss checks all the boxes for a future starter. He has a prototypical pitcher's frame, tremendous athleticism, a clean delivery and smooth arm action. He has the ability to fill the strike zone and a deep repertoire of pitches fronted by a fastball that sits 92-93 mph and touches 95. Weiss has both a slider and a curveball, though he might need to pick one because the two can bleed together. He also has a changeup that can act like a splitter, diving down and to his arm side. He's shown he can overcome unthinkable adversity: He lost both of his parents during a six-year span, his father to suicide, his mother to a heart attack in January 2018.

THE FUTURE: In Weiss, the D-backs have starter who should fit in the back end of a rotation and could very well grow into more. He will begin 2019 at high Class A Visalia.

Year	Club (League)	Class	W	L	ERA	G	GS	CG	SV	IP	H	HR	BB	SO	K/9	WHIP	AVG
2018	Diamondbacks (AZL)	R	0	0	9.00	1	0	0	0	1	2	0	0	2	18.0	2.00	.400
	Hillsboro (NWL)	SS	0	1	3.68	12	12	0	0	29	27	3	3	27	8.3	1.02	.241
Minor League Totals			0	1	3.86	13	12	0	0	30	29	3	3	29	8.6	1.05	.248

19 BUDDY KENNEDY, 3B

BA GRADE
45 Risk: High

Born: Oct. 5, 1998. **B-T:** R-R. **HT:** 6-1. **WT:** 190. **Drafted:** HS—Millville, N.J., 2017 (5th round). **Signed by:** Rick Matsko.

TRACK RECORD: The grandson of four-time all-star Don Money and a product of the same high school as Mike Trout, Kennedy swung the bat well in the Rookie-level Pioneer League in 2018, winning over some onlookers who see a chance for him to develop into a big leaguer, perhaps even an everyday player.

SCOUTING REPORT: Kennedy does not particularly look the part. He has the build of a fire hydrant, and while he's more athletic than that suggests, scouts believe he's going to have to work to maintain that athleticism. He seems to have a natural ability to find the barrel with a short, controlled swing, and he avoids expanding the strike zone and rarely strikes out. He may never be a big power guy, but scouts believe his gap-to-gap power could grow into double-digit home runs. He showed improvement at third base but his future could be all over the infield or even on an outfield corner, assuming the bat continues to develop. His arm is average, both in strength and accuracy, and he's said to be an average runner, perhaps slightly above-average once underway.

THE FUTURE: Kennedy figures to be part of the crew of interesting prospects bound for low Class A Kane County in 2019.

Year	Club (League)	Class	AVG	G	AB	R	H	2B	3B	HR	RBI	BB	SO	SB	CS	OBP	SLG
2017	Diamondbacks (AZL)	R	.270	50	178	29	48	9	8	0	20	19	47	7	2	.343	.410
2018	Missoula (PIO)	R	.327	57	226	46	74	17	1	4	32	26	34	2	0	.396	.465
Minor League Totals			.302	107	404	75	122	26	9	4	52	45	81	9	2	.373	.441

20 MARCUS WILSON, OF

BA GRADE
45 Risk: High

Born: Aug. 15, 1996. **B-T:** R-R. **HT:** 6-3. **WT:** 175. **Drafted:** HS—Gardena, Calif., 2014 (2nd round supplemental). **Signed by:** Hal Kurtzman.

TRACK RECORD: Wilson put together one of the better seasons of any position prospect in the system in 2017, but he struggled to follow it up in 2018, posting alarming strikeout totals and getting chewed up by righthanded pitchers at high Class A Visalia.

SCOUTING REPORT: Facing better pitchers than he ever had, Wilson's timing appeared to be off for much of 2018, some of which could be attributed to an inability to sync up his pre-pitch movements and his swing. A year ago, he drew praise for his plate discipline, but his approach backed up on him. He tried to stay patient and often wound up working deep counts, then got beat or chased with two strikes. His season might not have been as bad as the numbers show; Wilson's batted-ball data suggest he hit into tough luck. Opinions are split on his ability to remain in center field, though he has a solid-average arm that would play on a corner. He still earns good marks for his athleticism and coaches say he works as hard as anyone.

THE FUTURE: Always viewed as a slow developer, Wilson might have to prove in spring he's ready for Double-A or else return to Visalia to begin 2019.

Year	Club (League)	Class	AVG	G	AB	R	H	2B	3B	HR	RBI	BB	SO	SB	CS	OBP	SLG
2016	Hillsboro (NWL)	SS	.252	43	135	24	34	5	2	0	15	38	40	18	3	.418	.319
	Kane County (MWL)	LoA	.253	26	99	11	25	8	1	1	5	13	32	7	2	.357	.384
2017	Kane County (MWL)	LoA	.295	103	383	56	113	21	5	9	54	55	90	15	7	.383	.446
2018	Visalia (CAL)	HiA	.235	111	447	60	105	26	2	10	48	44	141	16	6	.309	.369
Minor League Totals			.255	379	1408	208	359	74	13	22	166	199	404	67	24	.350	.373

21 DREW ELLIS, 3B

Born: Dec. 1, 1995. **B-T:** R-R. **HT:** 6-3. **WT:** 210. **Drafted:** Louisville, 2017 (2nd round). **Signed by:** Nate Birtwell.

TRACK RECORD: After enjoying a strong junior year at the plate for Louisville and being selected with the 44th overall pick in 2017, Ellis left college with more questions about his defense than his offense. The opposite appears true after his first full year as a pro. Ellis had just a so-so season at the plate in the California League, collecting 50 extra-base hits and posting a solid 10.4 percent walk rate.

SCOUTING REPORT: Ellis hit for a low average and exhibited various red flags for scouts, including what some believed was a long swing with mediocre bat speed and a penchant for chasing offspeed stuff. Ellis went to the Arizona Fall League to work on driving the ball more consistently to all fields. Reports on his defense at third base were largely positive, with scouts putting plus grades on his hands and arm strength and saying his average range plays up thanks to good instincts and anticipation. He's not a good runner, grading out as below-average.

THE FUTURE: Rival scouts were hesitant to project Ellis as an everyday player, with many seeing him as a bench bat or the righthanded half of a platoon in the mold of a late-career David Freese.

Year	Club (League)	Class	AVG	G	AB	R	H	2B	3B	HR	RBI	BB	SO	SB	CS	OBP	SLG
2017	Hillsboro (NWL)	SS	.227	48	181	35	41	8	0	8	23	24	45	3	1	.327	.403
2018	Visalia (CAL)	HiA	.246	120	443	57	109	34	1	15	71	52	98	2	6	.331	.429
Minor League Totals			.240	168	624	92	150	42	1	23	94	76	143	5	7	.330	.421

22 LUIS FRIAS, RHP

Born: May 23, 1998. **B-T:** R-R. **HT:** 6-3. **WT:** 240. **Signed:** Dominican Republic, 2015. **Signed by:** Jose Ortiz/Junior Noboa.

TRACK RECORD: Diamondbacks executive Junior Noboa, the team's vice president of Latin operations, never shies away from signing prospects from Latin America, even if they're older than 16. Frias was about 17 and a half when the club signed him for $50,000 in November 2015, and he's proceeded to add size, strength and velocity to make himself into one of the organization's most enticing young arms.

SCOUTING REPORT: Frias is still raw, but he has a fastball that sits in the mid-90s and touches 100 mph along with a breaking ball that has the potential to be a putaway pitch. His command is erratic and his delivery inconsistent because he can struggle to maintain direction to the plate. Coaches believe he is too reliant on being overpowering and needs to learn the times he can benefit from taking a little off. He has added more than 40 pounds to his frame since signing and will need to stay on top of his conditioning.

THE FUTURE: Frias' development has a long way to go, and more avenues point toward the bullpen than the rotation, but he's still young and the Diamondbacks will take their time to see how things come together.

Year	Club (League)	Class	W	L	ERA	G	GS	CG	SV	IP	H	HR	BB	SO	K/9	WHIP	AVG
2016	D-backs (DSL)	R	3	2	3.83	13	11	0	0	52	45	0	28	47	8.2	1.41	.231
2017	Did not play																
2018	Diamondbacks (AZL)	R	1	1	2.48	7	6	0	0	29	17	1	11	31	9.6	0.97	.167
	Hillsboro (NWL)	SS	0	4	3.16	7	7	0	0	26	21	0	15	27	9.5	1.40	.221
Minor League Totals			4	7	3.30	27	24	0	0	106	83	1	54	105	8.9	1.29	.212

23 DOMINIC MIROGLIO, C

BA GRADE

45 Risk: High

Born: March 10, 1995. **B-T:** R-R. **HT:** 6-0. **WT:** 203. **Drafted:** San Francisco, 2017 (20th round). **Signed by:** Orsino Hill.

TRACK RECORD: Miroglio missed most of his junior year at San Francisco following a hand injury, and after being drafted in the 16th round by the Rays, he opted to return to school as a redshirt junior. The Diamondbacks took him the following year, and Miroglio has proceeded to hit a combined .309 in his first two years as a pro, rapidly advancing to Double-A in his second pro season.

SCOUTING REPORT: Miroglio has solid pitch-recognition and bat-to-ball skills and the ability to use the whole field. His power is somewhat limited, but since he began incorporating his lower half more in pro ball, he's been able to drive the ball with more authority. He gets good marks for his receiving and ability to work with pitchers, and he makes up for average arm strength with a quick release. He has great makeup and a high-energy personality.

THE FUTURE: Miroglio has the ingredients to carve out a career as a backup, but since he continues to perform the D-backs aren't putting a limit on his ceiling. He'll likely open 2019 back with Double-A Jackson.

Year	Club (League)	Class	AVG	G	AB	R	H	2B	3B	HR	RBI	BB	SO	SB	CS	OBP	SLG
2017	Missoula (PIO)	R	.317	37	142	18	45	13	0	1	16	14	8	0	0	.384	.430
2018	Visalia (CAL)	HiA	.327	76	278	41	91	23	1	4	42	20	42	5	2	.394	.460
	Jackson (SL)	AA	.231	21	78	3	18	4	1	0	10	1	12	0	1	.259	.308
Minor League Totals			.309	134	498	62	154	40	2	5	68	35	62	5	3	.371	.428

24 DOMINGO LEYBA, 2B

BA GRADE

40 Risk: Medium

Born: Sept. 11, 1995. **B-T:** B-R. **HT:** 5-11. **WT:** 160. **Signed:** Dominican Republic, 2012. **Signed by:** Miguel Rodriguez/Carlos Santana/Ramon Perez/Miguel Garcia (Tigers).

TRACK RECORD: Acquired as part of the three-team deal in December 2014 that brought Robbie Ray to the Diamondbacks, Leyba missed much of the 2017 season due to shoulder surgery. He returned in 2018 and had just a so-so season from a results perspective, showing good bat-to-ball skills and a slightly above-average walk rate but not providing much of an impact with the bat.

SCOUTING REPORT: Leyba is a difficult player for some scouts to evaluate. Many see him only as a second baseman—particularly with his arm strength backing up after surgery—and with below-average power and average speed he could be a second-division regular at best. Still, he has such good feel for hitting some believe he has more power to tap into than he's shown. Leyba has the glove for both middle infield positions and the athleticism to serve as a utility infielder if not a true everyday player.

THE FUTURE: This will be Leyba's third year on the 40-man roster, though he has yet to appear close to a big league callup. That could change in 2019, when he is likely to open the season in Triple-A Reno.

Year	Club (League)	Class	AVG	G	AB	R	H	2B	3B	HR	RBI	BB	SO	SB	CS	OBP	SLG
2016	Visalia (CAL)	HiA	.294	86	340	48	100	25	1	6	40	29	62	5	1	.346	.426
	Mobile (SL)	AA	.301	44	156	21	47	7	1	4	20	17	22	4	2	.374	.436
2017	Hillsboro (NWL)	SS	.286	6	28	4	8	1	0	1	6	4	2	0	0	.375	.429
	Jackson (SL)	AA	.276	17	58	11	16	4	0	2	9	5	6	0	0	.344	.448
2018	Jackson (SL)	AA	.269	83	320	43	86	17	2	5	30	35	46	5	2	.344	.381
Minor League Totals			.284	484	1877	278	533	108	18	27	208	164	284	42	23	.343	.404

25 EMILIO VARGAS, RHP

BA GRADE

45 Risk: High

Born: Aug. 12, 1996. **B-T:** R-R. **HT:** 6-3. **WT:** 200. **Signed:** Dominican Republic, 2013. **Signed by:** Rafael Mateo/Junior Noboa/Jose Ortiz.

TRACK RECORD: Signed for $80,000 in January 2013, Vargas has long been on the organization's prospect radar, with player development personnel anticipating a breakout season for years. He showed occasional flashes, including a 16-strikeout game in 2016, but it wasn't until 2018 that he managed to put together a strong season from start to finish. He reported to high Class A Visalia and led the California League in ERA (2.50) and strikeouts (140) through August before earning a promotion to Double-A

SCOUTING REPORT: Vargas has a strong, durable build and a clean arm stroke. He throws a low-90s fastball with a high spin rate, allowing it to play as though it's in the mid-90s. His changeup turned into his best secondary pitch once he started using it more in Double-A, moving ahead of a slider that became less slurvy as the season progressed. He struggled with control early, but his strike-throwing improved significantly. Still, without a plus pitch, scouts aren't sure the command is where it needs to be.

THE FUTURE: Vargas' command questions leave some wondering about his future role, but he'll get a chance to keep getting outs as a starter, likely beginning in Double-A in 2019.

Year	Club (League)	Class	W	L	ERA	G	GS	CG	SV	IP	H	HR	BB	SO	K/9	WHIP	AVG
2016	Kane County (MWL)	LoA	5	6	3.31	13	13	1	0	71	63	7	18	69	8.8	1.15	.234
	Visalia (CAL)	HiA	0	0	7.80	4	3	0	0	15	20	2	7	15	9.0	1.80	.313
2017	Kane County (MWL)	LoA	5	7	4.02	21	20	0	1	101	85	8	43	98	8.8	1.27	.232
2018	Visalia (CAL)	HiA	8	5	2.50	20	19	0	0	108	92	7	41	140	11.7	1.23	.230
	Jackson (SL)	AA	1	3	4.04	6	6	0	0	36	31	6	8	30	7.6	1.09	.225
Minor League Totals			30	28	3.40	107	79	1	2	474	425	31	157	472	9.0	1.23	.237

26 MATT MERCER, RHP

BA GRADE
45 Risk: High

Born: Sept. 1, 1996. **B-T:** R-R. **HT:** 6-2. **WT:** 180. **Drafted:** Oregon, 2018 (5th round). **Signed by:** Donnie Reynolds.

TRACK RECORD: Mercer was undrafted out of high school after needing Tommy John the summer before his senior year and went 635 days—he counted—before pitching in his next game. After three years at Oregon, he finally got the call in the fifth round in 2018, then proceeded to turn in an impressive pro debut, capped by a dominant 12-up, 12-down performance in a Northwest League playoff start.

SCOUTING REPORT: Mercer uncoils an aggressive delivery from an undersized but athletic frame, using a short arm action with an extremely fast arm stroke. His fastball sits in the 93-95 mph range, topping at 97. His high spin rate allows him to use his fastball effectively up in the zone, something he was discouraged from doing at Oregon but began incorporating more often in pro ball. His changeup, a potential plus pitch, comes out of the same slot and has downward action with armside run. His curveball shows flashes of developing into an above-average pitch. Mercer's delivery and size raise questions about whether he can maintain his stuff throughout a long season as a starter.

THE FUTURE: Mercer should be in the mix for a rotation spot in high Class A Visalia to start 2019.

Year	Club (League)	Class	W	L	ERA	G	GS	CG	SV	IP	H	HR	BB	SO	K/9	WHIP	AVG
2018	Diamondbacks (AZL)	R	0	0	4.50	1	1	0	0	2	2	1	1	1	4.5	1.50	.250
	Hillsboro (NWL)	SS	0	0	3.00	12	12	0	0	27	19	1	6	37	12.3	0.93	.192
Minor League Totals			0	0	3.10	13	13	0	0	29	21	2	7	38	11.8	0.97	.196

27 HARRISON FRANCIS, RHP

BA GRADE
50 Risk: Extreme

Born: Oct. 26, 1998. **B-T:** R-R. **HT:** 6-2. **WT:** 195. **Drafted:** HS—Tallahassee, Fla., 2017 (4th round). **Signed by:** Luke Wrenn.

TRACK RECORD: Francis, whose older brother Bowden is a Brewers prospect, opened his first full pro season in extended spring training and made significant improvement throughout the year, showing better stuff across the board than when the D-backs signed him as a fourth-rounder in 2017.

SCOUTING REPORT: Francis has a strong frame and an aggressive delivery. He gets a high number of swinging strikes on his fastball, a pitch with sink and run that ranged from 90-94 mph, averaging 92. His changeup isn't just his best secondary offering, it's one of the best changeups in the organization, and he had to scale back his use of it to work on his curveball, which showed improvement. There is a fair amount of effort in his delivery, including a head snap, leading some to believe the bullpen could be in his future, but if he continues throwing strikes, refining his pitch mix and missing bats, the Diamondbacks will give him every chance to start.

THE FUTURE: Once viewed as a pitcher whose development could be gradual, Francis made big strides and showed excellent aptitude in 2018. He likely will open the 2019 season as part of a loaded low Class A Kane County team.

Year	Club (League)	Class	W	L	ERA	G	GS	CG	SV	IP	H	HR	BB	SO	K/9	WHIP	AVG
2017	Diamondbacks (AZL)	R	0	1	9.00	3	3	0	0	3	5	0	2	5	15.0	2.33	.333
2018	Diamondbacks (AZL)	R	5	0	3.03	9	4	0	0	36	36	0	11	39	9.8	1.32	.255
	Hillsboro (NWL)	SS	3	0	1.53	5	0	0	0	18	15	0	8	21	10.7	1.30	.231
Minor League Totals			8	1	2.88	17	7	0	0	56	56	0	21	65	10.4	1.37	.253

28 JACKSON GODDARD, RHP

BA GRADE
45 Risk: High

Born: Dec. 12, 1996. **B-T:** R-R. **HT:** 6-3. **WT:** 220. **Drafted:** Kansas, 2018 (3rd round). **Signed by:** Jake Williams.

TRACK RECORD: Goddard, who spent three seasons in Kansas' weekend rotation, battled through an oblique injury that cost him six weeks in the middle of his junior season. Still, the Diamondbacks selected him with the 99th overall pick, the third-highest selection in school history, and signed him for $550,000.

SCOUTING REPORT: Goddard had an inconsistent track record in college, but the D-backs believe he has the makings of a power starter. With a strong, athletic build, he has a fastball that sits in the low-to-mid-

90s, and he's able to hold that velocity deep into games. He throws both a slider and a changeup, either of which could be his best secondary offering depending on the day. He sometimes has issues throwing strikes, but the D-backs think that will improve as he becomes more consistent with his delivery. He didn't look quite like himself after signing—his velocity was down, as was the bite on his slider and action on his changeup—perhaps the result of being tired from a long season.

THE FUTURE: Depending on his camp performance, Goddard will open 2019 at either low Class A Kane County or high Class A Visalia.

Year	Club (League)	Class	W	L	ERA	G	GS	CG	SV	IP	H	HR	BB	SO	K/9	WHIP	AVG
2018	Diamondbacks (AZL)	R	0	0	0.00	1	1	0	0	1	0	0	0	0	0.0	0.00	.000
	Hillsboro (NWL)	SS	1	3	4.18	13	12	0	0	28	19	1	12	27	8.7	1.11	.204
Minor League Totals			1	3	4.03	14	13	0	0	29	19	1	12	27	8.4	1.07	.198

29 JIMMIE SHERFY, RHP

BA GRADE

40 Risk: Medium

Born: Dec. 27, 1991. **B-T:** R-R. **HT:** 6-0. **WT:** 175. **Drafted:** Oregon, 2013 (10th round). **Signed by:** Donnie Reynolds.

TRACK RECORD: Sherfy has always been one of the smaller players on every team he's been on. But he's also always had a lightning quick arm, which he used to reach the big leagues in 2017 and 2018.

SCOUTING REPORT: Sherfy has a mid-90s fastball and a sharp-breaking curveball. His fastball can be straight and he doesn't always command it, but when he does he can consistently put hitters away with the curve, a pitch that grades as plus. Sherfy's easygoing, laid-back nature seems to serve him well in pressure situations. His walk rate more than doubled from 2017 to 2018, but team officials point to the success of righthander Silvino Bracho as the reason Sherfy spent most of 2018 at Triple-A Reno.

THE FUTURE: Sherfy figures to again have a chance to pitch his way into a big league role—even a prominent one given the uncertainty in the D-backs' bullpen.

Year	Club (League)	Class	W	L	ERA	G	GS	CG	SV	IP	H	HR	BB	SO	K/9	WHIP	AVG
2016	Visalia (CAL)	HiA	0	0	0.00	12	0	0	8	12	5	0	6	21	15.3	0.89	.128
	Mobile (SL)	AA	2	0	0.46	16	0	0	10	20	6	1	5	31	14.2	0.56	.092
	Reno (PCL)	AAA	1	4	6.17	24	0	0	12	23	20	5	13	27	10.4	1.41	.247
2017	Reno (PCL)	AAA	2	1	3.12	44	0	0	20	49	37	6	10	61	11.2	0.96	.211
	Arizona (NL)	MAJ	2	0	0.00	11	0	0	1	11	5	0	2	9	7.6	0.66	.143
2018	Reno (PCL)	AAA	5	1	1.60	38	0	0	15	45	31	1	20	58	11.6	1.13	.190
	Arizona (NL)	MAJ	0	0	1.65	15	0	0	16	8	1	10	17	9.4	1.10	.145
Major League Totals			2	0	1.00	26	0	0	1	27	13	1	12	26	8.7	0.93	.144
Minor League Totals			17	14	3.56	244	0	0	81	265	202	22	109	345	11.7	1.17	.211

30 KEVIN GINKEL, RHP

BA GRADE

40 Risk: High

Born: March 24, 1994. **B-T:** R-R. **HT:** 6-4. **WT:** 210. **Drafted:** Arizona, 2016 (22nd round). **Signed by:** Doyle Wilson.

TRACK RECORD: Ginkel had an inconsistent 2017 that left him on the periphery of the Diamondbacks' prospect radar. He found his way back on the map in a big way in 2018, finishing an impressive season with a strong showing in the Arizona Fall League.

SCOUTING REPORT: A year ago, Ginkel's fastball topped out in the low 90s and he was having trouble bouncing back from outing to outing. In the offseason, he worked to revamp his pitching mechanics, trying to become more athletic by incorporating his lower half more. He began to get extreme extension of nearly seven feet. His velocity picked up, sitting in the low-to-mid-90s, which allowed him to challenge hitters with his fastball. His excellent spin rate allowed him to pitch aggressively up in the zone. He also mixed in his slider and changeup effectively. He surprised even himself with his results, posting a miniscule ERA along with a strikeout rate of 12.9 per nine innings.

THE FUTURE: Ginkel won't need to be added to the 40-man roster until after the 2019 season. He'll likely open 2019 back in Double-A Jackson and could turn himself into a candidate for the big leagues.

Year	Club (League)	Class	W	L	ERA	G	GS	CG	SV	IP	H	HR	BB	SO	K/9	WHIP	AVG
2016	Hillsboro (NWL)	SS	1	0	2.61	18	0	0	2	21	17	0	6	22	9.6	1.11	.224
2017	Kane County (MWL)	LoA	1	1	14.85	6	0	0	0	7	8	1	9	5	6.8	2.55	.308
	Hillsboro (NWL)	SS	0	1	3.48	20	0	0	0	34	26	1	11	49	13.1	1.10	.213
2018	Visalia (CAL)	HiA	1	1	0.99	20	0	0	4	27	20	2	3	40	13.2	0.84	.200
	Jackson (SL)	AA	5	0	1.69	34	0	0	5	43	26	3	9	60	12.7	0.82	.176
Minor League Totals			8	3	2.82	98	0	0	11	131	97	7	38	176	12.1	1.03	.206

Atlanta Braves

BY J.J. COOPER

Success arrived a little early in Atlanta. Expected to battle for a wild card spot at best in 2018, the Braves instead ran away with the National League East division title, taking advantage of a year when the Nationals (82-80) were the only other team to finish with a winning record.

Talent-wise, the Braves should be better in 2019. That should also be true for much of the rest of the division. Atlanta's combination of a young, established big league lineup and waves of upper-level pitching prospects gives it more flexibility than the rest of the division. While the Phillies lack any young position player who has established himself as a star, the Braves have three hitters who produced 3.5 wins above replacement (WAR) or more last season who are 25 or younger.

The Braves' depth of young and inexpensive hitters allowed general manager Alex Anthopoulos to sign third baseman Josh Donaldson to a clever one-year, $23 million deal. If healthy, he gives Atlanta another lineup cornerstone, but the deal is constructed in a way that allows Atlanta to shift to Austin Riley at third base in 2020 and beyond, when the pitching staff and eventually the lineup will start to get more expensive.

Atlanta's pitching depth in Double-A and Triple-A leaves the team with more starting pitching options than spots over the next couple of seasons. Some of these young arms will move to the bullpen. Others will wait in Triple-A for an opportunity (which may be hard to come by with an organization that is trying to contend), but some will likely be used in trades to help the big league club.

In his first year as Braves' GM, Anthopoulos held onto the vast majority of his best prospects, deciding to get to know what he had before making any big moves. There's no reason to be as cautious in year two with 10 legitimate pitching prospects penciled to start the season in Double-A or higher. Atlanta will have plenty of inventory to improve its team at the trade deadline.

What the Braves do not have is depth at the lower levels of the minor leagues. MLB's sanctions are already starting to make themselves known and it will only get worse over the next few seasons. The Braves lost almost an entire signing class when its top 2016 signees were declared free agents. The club has been limited to spending $300,000 internationally in the 2017-2018 and 2018-2019 signing periods. It will be limited to signing players for $10,000 or less in 2019-2020 and then will see its bonus pool cut in half in 2020-2021.

The team's lower-level depth was also hurt when

Ronald Acuña Jr. showed all five tools as a rookie and looks like a future MVP candidate.

PROJECTED 2022 LINEUP

Catcher	William Contreras (24)
First Base	Freddie Freeman (33)
Second Base	Ozzie Albies (26)
Third Base	Austin Riley (24)
Shortstop	Dansby Swanson (29)
Left Field	Drew Waters (23)
Center Field	Ender Inciarte (32)
Right Field	Ronald Acuña Jr. (24)
No. 1 Starter	Ian Anderson (24)
No. 2 Starter	Mike Soroka (25)
No. 3 Starter	Mike Foltynewicz (30)
No. 4 Starter	Kyle Wright (26)
No. 5 Starter	Sean Newcomb (28)
Closer	Touki Toussaint (25)

it failed to sign righthander Carter Stewart, the team's first-round pick in 2018. The Braves will get a compensation pick in 2019, but the void created by Stewart will hurt in the immediate term.

For a team that has long relied on a productive international program, those sanctions will leave holes that are hard to fill. The Braves continue to draft well, but they also expect to pick at the back of the first round for several years to come while they contend for division titles.

That combination will be tough to overcome eventually for a team that has heavily relied on its farm system for the past 25 years. But that's a long-term issue for a team whose big league future looks quite bright.

SCOTT CUNNINGHAM/GETTY IMAGES

ATLANTA BRAVES

TOP 2019 ROOKIE: Austin Riley, 3B/OF. Josh Donaldson's signing will take the pressure off Riley, but he has the power to still provide a boost to the Braves at some point in 2019.
BREAKOUT PROSPECT: Huascar Ynoa, RHP. Ynoa may be a couple of years away from putting it all together, but already in flashes he shows he can dominate hitters.
SLEEPER: Corbin Clouse, LHP. He could earn some innings in Atlanta's bullpen thanks to his ability to handle righthanded hitters as well as lefties.

SOURCE OF TOP 30 TALENT

Homegrown	26	Acquired	4
College	7	Trade	4
High School	9	Rule 5 draft	0
Junior College	3	Independent leagues	0
Nondrafted free agent	1	Free agents/waivers	0
International	6		

LF
Jeffrey Ramos (26)

CF
Drew Waters (7)
Cristian Pache (8)
Justin Dean

RF
Greyson Jenista (15)
Israel Wilson (28)

3B
Austin Riley (1)
C.J. Alexander (18)

SS
A.J. Graffanino (25)
Ray-Patrick Didder (30)
Derian Cruz
Riley Delgado

2B
Riley Unroe

1B
Braxton Davidson

C
William Contreras (9)
Alex Jackson (23)
Lucas Herbert
Drew Lugbauer

LHP

LHSP	LHRP
Luiz Gohara (10)	Corbin Clouse
Kyle Muller (11)	Thomas Burrows
Joey Wentz (13)	Tanner Allison
Kolby Allard (14)	Jake Higginbotham
Tucker Davidson (21)	
Dilmer Mejia	

RHP

RHSP	RHRP
Ian Anderson (2)	Patrick Weigel (12)
Mike Soroka (3)	Freddy Tarnok (16)
Kyle Wright (4)	Tristan Beck (17)
Touki Toussaint (5)	Huascar Ynoa (19)
Bryse Wilson (6)	Jacob Webb (20)
Wes Parsons (24)	Chad Sobotka (22)
Nolan Kingham	Trey Riley (27)
	Jasseel de la Cruz (29)
	Josh Graham
	Grant Dayton
	Victor Vodnik
	Luis Mora
	Matt Rowland
	Troy Bacon

DRAFT ANALYSIS

2018

BEST PURE HITTER: 3B C.J. Alexander (20) didn't look like a typical 20th-round pick in his pro debut. He showed a pull-heavy approach at State JC of Florida, but as a pro he was very comfortable driving the ball to center field and left-center. He's a plus hitter with the willingness to adapt to how pitchers are pitching to him. OF Greyson Jenista (2) has a pure swing that is prettier than Alexander's. He's an above-average hitter.

BEST POWER: Jenista posted modest power numbers at Wichita State and hit just four home runs in his pro debut, but the Braves believe that he will eventually start turning plus-plus raw power into at least plus productive power. His swing has natural loft to it and he has impressive strength

FASTEST RUNNER: OF Justin Dean (17) can post plus-plus run times or better in a 60-yard dash. He averaged 11 steals a year at Lenoir-Rhyne (N.C.) but swiped 16 bags in just 60 pro games.

BEST DEFENSIVE PLAYER: SS A.J. Graffanino (8) is a plus defender with the range scouts look for in a shortstop. He has an above-average arm.

BEST ATHLETE: Graffanino is the twitchiest, most athletic player the Braves drafted. He battled hamstring injuries at Washington but has above-average speed.

BEST FASTBALL: RHP Trey Riley (5) has run his fastball up to 97 mph at his best and has sat 93-95. RHP Tristan Beck (4) has touched 97 on his best days, but his fastball backed up during his junior season at Stanford. He pitched sparingly in his pro debut. RHP Victor Vodnik (14) has to work on his consistency, but he can touch 97.

BEST SECONDARY PITCH: Beck's curveball and slider have both flashed plus, but they weren't as consistent in his return in 2018 from a back injury that sidelined him for the entire 2017 season. Riley's slider is a plus-plus pitch when he's locked in, though it is inconsistent.

BEST PRO DEBUT: Alexander hit .352/.429/.425

TOP DRAFT PICKS OF THE DECADE

Year	Player, Pos.	2018 Org
2009	Mike Minor, LHP	Rangers
2010	Matt Lipka, SS (1st round supplemental)	Giants
2011	Sean Gilmartin, LHP	Orioles
2012	Lucas Sims, RHP	Reds
2013	Jason Hursh, RHP	Braves
2014	Braxton Davidson, OF	Braves
2015	Kolby Allard, LHP	Braves
2016	Ian Anderson, RHP	Braves
2017	Kyle Wright, RHP	Braves
2018	*Carter Stewart, RHP	—
* Did not sign		

between the Gulf Coast, Appalachian and Florida State leagues.

MOST INTRIGUING BACKGROUND: Graffanino is the son of Tony Graffanino, a 10th-round pick of the Braves in 1990. The elder Graffanino made it to the major leagues with Atlanta from 1996-1998 as a second baseman. It was the start of a 13-year major league career that included four trips to the playoffs.

CLOSEST TO THE MAJORS: If he can stay healthy, Beck could move quickly as a polished college pitcher. Jenista likely won't move as quickly as Beck, but he is a polished college hitter who could be on a relatively speedy path up the minor league ladder.

BEST-LATE ROUND PICK: LHP Gabriel Rodriguez (31) was an outfielder at Miami-Dade JC but he has shown a 96-99 mph fastball off the mound as he begins a conversion to pitching. While raw, Rodriguez has the arm to be an interesting pitching prosepct.

THE ONE WHO GOT AWAY: RHP Carter Stewart (1) did not sign after the Braves reduced his bonus offer after not liking what they found on his medical exam. The Braves will receive the ninth pick in the 2019 draft as compensation for not signing him the Florida high school righthander.

—J.J. COOPER

2017

RHP Kyle Wright (1) shot through the minors to reach the big leagues in September. OF Drew Waters (2) and RHP Freddy Tarnok (3) are off to promising starts after being picked from the prep ranks.

GRADE: B

2016

The Braves loading up on prep arms paid off. RHP Bryse Wilson (4) has reached Atlanta. RHP Ian Anderson (1) has one of the system's highest ceilings and LHPs Joey Wentz (1s) and Kyle Muller (2) have impressed.

GRADE: A

2015

The Braves added plenty of talent with this draft. 3B Austin Riley (1s) is their top prospect. LHP Kolby Allard (1) and Mike Soroka (1) project as starters and RHP A.J. Minter (2s) has established himself in the bullpen.

GRADE: A

1 AUSTIN RILEY, 3B

Born: April 2, 1997. **B-T:** R-R. **Ht.:** 6-2. **Wt.:** 220.
Drafted: HS—Southaven, Miss., 2015 (1st round supplemental). **Signed by:** Don Thomas.

In high school, Riley was a thick-bodied, strong-armed pitcher/third baseman. Because of Riley's thick trunk and arm strength, most scouts viewed him as a pitching prospect, and he would have played both ways if he had made it to Mississippi State. But the Braves believed in his bat and his work ethic and drafted him as a hitter. Riley has cut out junk food and focused on conditioning as a pro. As a result, he has slimmed down and is more athletic and nimble. After hitting 20 home runs in his first full season and 20 again in 2017, he had to settle for 19 in 2018. He would have likely topped his previous career high if not for a knee injury he suffered at Triple-A Gwinnett when diving for a ball. He missed almost all of June and saw his power sapped for another month. But in August, he finished by hitting eight home runs in a 13-game stretch.
SCOUTING REPORT: Riley's plus-plus raw power has always been his best attribute. He has the potential to hit 25-30 home runs regularly in the majors. He has a pull-heavy approach when he gets into advantageous counts but has the strength and power to drive the ball out to right and right-center field. Riley's approach leads to strikeouts, but he has always managed to stay on the right side of the line that separates free-swingers who can't hit from those who hit enough to get to their power. Riley's bat-to-ball skills give him a chance to be an average hitter to go with his excellent power. He's shown an ability to make adjustments. His swing is now more direct to the ball, and he has sped up his hands as a pro. Defensively, Riley's conditioning and work has helped him turn himself into a plus defender. His plus-plus arm is a key to his success at third base, but he also has developed the quick feet and quick hands scouts look for at third base. His quickness is more of the first-step variety because his raw speed is below-average and will likely get worse as he ages.
THE FUTURE: Riley should factor in the Braves' big league plans in 2019, but the emergence of Johan Camargo and the free agent signing of Josh Donaldson cloud the picture. The Braves could be patient and let Riley get additional time at Triple-A, but they have said he will get a look in the outfield at spring training.

MIKE JANES/FOUR SEAM

BA GRADE	SCOUTING GRADES
60 Risk: Medium	Hit: 50. Power: 70. Run: 40. Field: 60. Arm: 70.

Projected future grades on 20-80 scouting scale.

TOP PROSPECTS OF THE DECADE

Year	Player, Pos.	2018 Org
2009	Tommy Hanson, RHP	Deceased
2010	Jason Heyward, OF	Cubs
2011	Julio Teheran, RHP	Braves
2012	Julio Teheran, RHP	Braves
2013	Julio Teheran, RHP	Braves
2014	Lucas Sims, RHP	Reds
2015	Jose Peraza, 2B	Reds
2016	Sean Newcomb, LHP	Braves
2017	Dansby Swanson, SS	Braves
2018	Ronald Acuña Jr., OF	Braves

BEST TOOLS

Best Hitter for Average:	Austin Riley
Best Power Hitter	Austin Riley
Best Strike-Zone Discipline	Greyson Jenista
Fastest Baserunner	Cristian Pache
Best Athlete	Cristian Pache
Best Fastball	Ian Anderson
Best Curveball	Touki Toussaint
Best Slider	Mike Soroka
Best Changeup	Touki Toussaint
Best Control	Kolby Allard
Best Defensive Catcher	Lucas Herbert
Best Defensive Infielder	Austin Riley
Best Infield Arm	Austin Riley
Best Defensive Outfielder	Cristian Pache
Best Outfield Arm	Cristian Pache

Year	Club (League)	Class	AVG	G	AB	R	H	2B	3B	HR	RBI	BB	SO	SB	CS	OBP	SLG
2016	Rome (SAL)	LoA	.271	129	495	68	134	39	2	20	80	39	147	3	3	.324	.479
2017	Florida (FSL)	HiA	.252	81	306	43	77	10	1	12	47	23	74	0	2	.310	.408
	Mississippi (SL)	AA	.315	48	178	28	56	9	1	8	27	20	50	2	0	.389	.511
2018	Mississippi (SL)	AA	.333	27	99	17	33	10	3	6	20	8	28	0	0	.394	.677
	Braves (GCL)	R	.278	6	18	3	5	3	0	1	3	3	6	0	0	.409	.611
	Gwinnett (IL)	AAA	.282	74	287	40	81	17	0	11	46	26	93	1	0	.347	.456
Minor League Totals			.283	425	1600	235	452	102	8	70	263	145	463	8	7	.347	.488

2 IAN ANDERSON, RHP

Born: May 2, 1998. **B-T:** R-R. **Ht.:** 6-3. **Wt.:** 170. **Drafted:** HS—Clinton Park, N.Y., 2016 (1st round). **Signed by:** Greg Morhardt.

TRACK RECORD: As the third pick in the 2016 draft, Anderson tied Steve Avery and Ken Dayley as the highest-drafted pitcher in club history. Given a chance to throw more innings in 2018, Anderson made every start. He finished his season at Double-A Mississippi with two of his best outings of the year, including a 10-strikeout outing in his season finale.

SCOUTING REPORT: Anderson has the pieces to be a frontline ace if his control and command catch up to his stuff. He has a n excellent pitcher's frame with further room to fill out and a fluid, fast arm. His foundation is a plus-plus 92-97 mph four-seam fastball. Working from an over-the-top delivery, when he's on he can consistently get plenty of plane on a fastball that tickles the bottom of the zone and he has enough life to elevate for swings and misses. His 75-79 mph curveball is a plus pitch with 12-to-6 movement. He also throws an 86-88 mph changeup that flashes above-average with decep-

BA GRADE

65 Risk: High

Fastball: 70.
Cuveball: 60.
Change: 55. CTL: 50.

tion and occasional late drop. Anderson has started to feel comfortable enough to throw his changeup to righthanders as well as lefties. He stays direct to the plate in his delivery, but his fastball command is scattershot. There's nothing in his delivery that indicates long-term control concerns, but his currently below-average control needs to improve by more than a grade to reach his lofty ceiling.

THE FUTURE: Anderson will head back to Double-A in 2019. He could be ready for a September callup, but the Braves have a full rotation of starting candidates ticketed for Triple-A who will be ahead of him.

Year	Club (League)	Class	W	L	ERA	G	GS	CG	SV	IP	H	HR	BB	SO	K/9	WHIP	AVG
2016	Braves (GCL)	R	1	0	0.00	5	5	0	0	18	14	0	4	18	9.0	1.00	.222
	Danville (APP)	R	0	2	3.74	5	5	0	0	22	19	1	8	18	7.5	1.25	.244
2017	Rome (SAL)	LoA	4	5	3.14	20	20	0	0	83	69	0	43	101	11.0	1.35	.232
2018	Florida (FSL)	HiA	2	6	2.52	20	20	0	0	100	73	2	40	118	10.6	1.13	.198
	Mississippi (SL)	AA	2	1	2.33	4	4	0	0	19	14	0	9	24	11.2	1.19	.203
Minor League Totals			9	14	2.64	54	54	0	0	242	189	3	104	279	10.4	1.21	.216

3 MIKE SOROKA, RHP

Born: Aug. 4, 1997. **B-T:** R-R. **Ht.:** 6-4. **Wt.:** 195. **Drafted:** HS—Calgary, 2015 (1st round). **Signed by:** Brett Evert.

TRACK RECORD: Wherever he has gone, Soroka has been the youngest player on the field. And when he made his MLB debut in early May he was the youngest player in the majors. Less than three years after he was drafted, Soroka was in the big leagues holding the Mets to one run over six innings. He made four more starts for the Braves before being shut down with shoulder soreness. He didn't return until a brief instructional league outing.

SCOUTING REPORT: Soroka attacks hitters with a sinker/slider combination that generates more weak contact than strikeouts. He mixes a plus 92-94 mph two-seamer that he works down and in to righthanded hitters (and down and away from lefthanders) with a 92-94 mph four-seamer that he elevates. He is at his best when he's keeping the ball down, which sets up his above-average 85-87 mph slider that he turned into a harder, sharper pitch in 2018. Soroka mixes in an average changeup sporadically against lefthanded hitters. What makes it all work is Soroka's plus control and above-average command. He has a clean delivery and has long impressed with his competitive, mature makeup.

BA GRADE

60 Risk: Medium

Fastball: 60.
Slider: 55.
Change: 50. CTL: 60.

THE FUTURE: Soroka showed his normal velocity at instructs, and the Braves expect he will be at full strength for spring training. But Soroka's shoulder injury was a first hiccup for a pitcher who had never suffered a setback as a pro. He should pitch in the Braves rotation in 2019. His command, stuff and outstanding makeup fit the mold of a mid-rotation starter.

Year	Club (League)	Class	W	L	ERA	G	GS	CG	SV	IP	H	HR	BB	SO	K/9	WHIP	AVG
2016	Rome (SAL)	LoA	9	9	3.02	25	24	1	0	143	130	3	32	125	7.9	1.13	.244
2017	Mississippi (SL)	AA	11	8	2.75	26	26	0	0	154	133	10	34	125	7.3	1.09	.233
2018	Rome (SAL)	LoA	0	0	0.00	1	1	0	0	4	0	0	0	3	7.4	0.00	.000
	Gwinnett (IL)	AAA	2	1	2.00	5	5	1	0	27	20	0	6	31	10.3	0.96	.204
	Atlanta (NL)	MAJ	2	1	3.51	5	5	0	0	26	30	1	7	21	7.4	1.44	.288
Major League Totals			2	1	3.51	5	5	0	0	26	30	1	7	21	7.4	1.44	.288
Minor League Totals			22	20	2.81	67	65	2	0	361	316	13	77	321	8.0	1.09	.235

4 KYLE WRIGHT, RHP

Born: Oct. 2, 1995. **B-T:** R-R. **Ht.:** 6-4. **Wt.:** 200. **Drafted:** Vanderbilt, 2017 (1st round). **Signed by:** Dustin Evans.

TRACK RECORD: The top college pitcher in his draft class, Wright became just the fourth college pitcher the Braves have selected with a top-10 pick in the June draft and the first since fellow Vanderbilt Commodore Mike Minor in 2009. He became the first player from the 2017 draft to reach the big leagues when he was called up in September. The Braves moved him to the bullpen at Triple-A Gwinnett in August to see if he could help in Atlanta, but he pitched only sporadically in September and was not added to the postseason roster.

SCOUTING REPORT: Wright has the most varied arsenal of the Braves' top-tier pitching prospects. His fastball and curveball are both plus pitches, and he mixes in a slider that flashes above-average potential as well as an average changeup. His slider and curve sometimes merge together, but his power 82-85 mph breaking ball is a downer out pitch. His 92-96 mph fastball has excellent armside run. Scouts like his delivery, but Wright has yet to show the above-average control that many scouts expect him to develop.

THE FUTURE: Wright has already reached Atlanta, but he could use further time in Triple-A as he works to refine his control. He heads to spring training with a shot to break camp with the big league club, but more likely he's a midseason callup. Wright projects as a future mid-rotation starter.

BA GRADE

55 Risk: Medium

Fastball: 60.
Curveball: 60.
Slider: 55. **CTL:** 55.

Year	Club (League)	Class	W	L	ERA	G	GS	CG	SV	IP	H	HR	BB	SO	K/9	WHIP	AVG
2017	Braves (GCL)	R	0	0	1.59	3	3	0	0	6	3	0	2	8	12.7	0.88	.150
	Florida (FSL)	HiA	0	1	3.18	6	6	0	0	11	8	0	4	10	7.9	1.06	.205
2018	Mississippi (SL)	AA	6	8	3.70	20	20	0	0	109	103	6	43	105	8.6	1.34	.249
	Gwinnett (IL)	AAA	2	1	2.51	7	4	0	0	29	15	2	8	28	8.8	0.80	.152
	Atlanta (NL)	MAJ	0	0	4.50	4	0	0	0	6	4	2	6	5	7.5	1.67	.182
Major League Totals			0	0	4.50	4	0	0	0	6	4	2	6	5	7.5	1.67	.182
Minor League Totals			8	10	3.37	36	33	0	0	155	129	8	57	151	8.8	1.20	.226

5 TOUKI TOUSSAINT, RHP

Born: June 26, 1996. **B-T:** R-R. **Ht.:** 6-3. **Wt.:** 185. **Drafted:** HS—Coral Springs, Fla., 2014 (1st round). **Signed by:** Frankie Thon Jr. (D-backs).

TRACK RECORD: The Braves essentially paid for an extra first-round pick when they acquired Toussaint in 2015 because of their willingness to take on the $9 million salary of the injured Bronson Arroyo. Toussaint has taken a little longer to develop than some of his fellow Braves prep pitching prospects, but he still reached the majors at age 22.

SCOUTING REPORT: Below-average control has always been Toussaint's biggest hiccup. He has consistently struggled to locate his fastball. It's a quality pitch as it sits 93-97 mph and earns plus grades. He generally works his sinker down in the zone to his arm side, but to succeed he needs to be able to spot his four-seamer to his glove side. If Toussaint can develop even average control and command, he could dominate because of his plus curveball that has long been a weapon and a more recently developed plus split-changeup. He has steadily improved his control, but he still lands hard in his finish and struggles to maintain his direction to the plate. Toussaint is extremely athletic, so there is reason to believe that he can add the final refinements to reach his high ceiling.

BA GRADE

60 Risk: High

Fastball: 60.
Curveball: 60.
Change: 60. **CTL:** 45.

THE FUTURE: Toussaint made big strides in 2018, and he could develop into a mid-rotation starter. His stuff would play up even more in the bullpen, which may be a useful short-term role for the Braves since they have a surplus of quality big league ready starting pitchers.

Year	Club (League)	Class	W	L	ERA	G	GS	CG	SV	IP	H	HR	BB	SO	K/9	WHIP	AVG
2016	Rome (SAL)	LoA	4	8	3.88	27	24	0	0	132	105	13	71	128	8.7	1.33	.217
2017	Florida (FSL)	HiA	3	9	5.04	19	19	0	0	105	101	8	42	123	10.5	1.36	.245
	Mississippi (SL)	AA	3	4	3.18	7	7	1	0	40	30	3	22	44	10.0	1.31	.207
2018	Mississippi (SL)	AA	4	6	2.93	16	16	0	0	86	66	7	36	107	11.2	1.19	.208
	Gwinnett (IL)	AAA	5	0	1.43	8	8	0	0	50	35	0	17	56	10.0	1.03	.193
	Atlanta (NL)	MAJ	2	1	4.03	7	5	0	0	29	18	1	21	32	9.9	1.34	.182
Major League Totals			2	1	4.03	7	5	0	0	29	18	1	21	32	9.9	1.34	.182
Minor League Totals			26	38	4.08	106	101	2	0	530	446	46	254	557	9.5	1.32	.225

6 BRYSE WILSON, RHP

Born: Dec. 20, 1997. **B-T:** R-R. **Ht.:** 6-1. **Wt.:** 215. **Drafted:** HS—Hillsborough, N.C., 2016 (4th round). **Signed:** Billy Best.

TRACK RECORD: The Braves move their pitchers fast, but no one has moved faster than Wilson. He was an excellent high school football player as a wide receiver, quarterback, running back and linebacker. In 2018, Wilson began the season by allowing one run in five starts at high Class A. He blitzed through Double-A, dominated Triple-A (including an eight-inning, one-hit, 13-strike-out gem) and threw five scoreless innings in his major league debut.

SCOUTING REPORT: Wilson's success depends on his 92-98 mph fastball, which is one of the best in an organization filled with quality fastballs. It's a future plus-plus pitch, largely because of its late life and his above-average control. It can sink or cut it as needed. He can locate it armside and glove-side. When he's on, Wilson can dominate with just his fastball, and that's often what he did in 2018. That may be to his minor detriment developmentally, because he's yet to find a need to develop his less advanced secondary offerings. His slurvy curveball flashes plus when he tightens it, but some scouts believe his arm action will prevent the pitch from ever being consistent. His fringe-average changeup needs to improve. It has some fade, but he tips it at times.

THE FUTURE: It's hard not to enjoy watching Wilson pitch because he attacks hitters with ferocious competitiveness and self-confidence. The Braves have pitchers with better secondary pitches, but Wilson's strength, fastball and makeup give him a shot to be a durable No. 4 starter for a long time.

BA GRADE
50 Risk: Medium
Fastball: 70.
Curveball: 55.
Change: 50. CTL: 55.

Year	Club (League)	Class	W	L	ERA	G	GS	CG	SV	IP	H	HR	BB	SO	K/9	WHIP	AVG
2016	Braves (GCL)	R	1	1	0.68	9	6	0	0	27	16	0	8	29	9.8	0.90	.172
2017	Rome (SAL)	LoA	10	7	2.50	26	26	1	0	137	105	8	37	139	9.1	1.04	.211
2018	Florida (FSL)	HiA	2	0	0.34	5	5	0	0	27	16	0	7	26	8.8	0.86	.167
	Mississippi (SL)	AA	3	5	3.97	15	15	0	0	77	77	3	26	89	10.4	1.34	.258
	Gwinnett (IL)	AAA	3	0	5.32	5	3	0	0	22	20	6	3	28	11.5	1.05	.238
	Atlanta (NL)	MAJ	1	0	6.43	3	1	0	0	7	8	0	6	6	7.7	2.00	.308
Major League Totals			1	0	6.43	3	1	0	0	7	8	0	6	6	7.7	2.00	.308
Minor League Totals			19	13	2.74	60	55	1	0	289	234	17	81	311	9.7	1.09	.219

7 DREW WATERS, OF

Born: Dec. 30, 1998. **B-T:** B-R. **Ht.:** 6-2. **Wt.:** 183. **Drafted:** HS—Woodstock, Ga., 2017 (2nd round). **Signed by:** Dustin Evans.

TRACK RECORD: Waters comes from an athletic family. His father played on the offensive line at Georgia Tech in the mid-1980s. Drew is more of a quick-twitch athlete. He was the first prep outfielder the Braves have signed out of Georgia since they drafted Jason Heyward in 2007. In 2018, he was one of the best hitters in the South Atlantic League. He would have ranked in the top five in the league in batting average (.303) and slugging (.513) if not for an August promotion to the Florida State League.

SCOUTING REPORT: Waters has the tools to be an above-average or even plus hitter as a switch-hitter with a loose, handsy swing, especially from the left side. He uses the entire field and consistently squares up balls. But he has a good bit of work to do to become a mature, refined hitter. Right now, he too often looks to ambush the first hittable fastball he can find, leading to too many quick at-bats. It's worked so far, but pitchers working backwards can take advantage of his aggressiveness. Waters might eventually outgrow center field, but he's an above-average defender for now. His plus arm would fit in right field if he fills out too much to stay in center field. He's a plus runner and knows how to pick his spots to steal.

BA GRADE
55 Risk: High
Hit: 55. Power: 60.
Run: 60. Field: 55
Arm: 60.

THE FUTURE: The Braves have two center field prospects moving up in lockstep, with Cristian Pache one level ahead of Waters. Waters has more offensive potential and Pache has more defensive aptitude.

Year	Club (League)	Class	AVG	G	AB	R	H	2B	3B	HR	RBI	BB	SO	SB	CS	OBP	SLG
2017	Braves (GCL)	R	.347	14	49	13	17	3	1	2	10	7	11	2	1	.448	.571
	Danville (APP)	R	.255	36	149	20	38	11	1	2	14	16	59	4	2	.331	.383
2018	Rome (SAL)	LoA	.303	84	337	58	102	32	6	9	36	21	72	20	5	.353	.513
	Florida (FSL)	HiA	.268	30	123	14	33	7	3	0	3	8	33	3	0	.316	.374
Minor League Totals			.289	164	658	105	190	53	11	13	63	52	175	29	8	.349	.462

8 CRISTIAN PACHE, OF

Born: Nov. 18, 1998. **B-T:** R-R. **Ht. 6-2. Wt.:** 185. **Signed:** Dominican Republic, 2015. **Signed by:** Matias Laureano.

TRACK RECORD: When the Braves' futures stars played the big league club in an exhibition game, Pache gave a hint of what was to come by hitting a pair of home runs off Sean Newcomb. Before that, he had gone homerless in his first 176 pro games. Pache demonstrated that newfound power during the season with nine home runs and a late-season promotion to Double-A Mississippi.

SCOUTING REPORT: Pache can make a case that he's the best defensive center fielder in the minor leagues. He is a plus-plus defender who combines plus-plus speed with a belief that every ball is his to catch. He's especially good at running down balls hit over his head. He has a great first step, though his routes can meander at times. Scouts are more mixed on whether Pache is going to hit. He showed improved power and he can now punish pitchers for their mistakes, but he's too aggressive for a potential top-of-the-order hitter and has become pull-focused, while his skills are more suited to using the whole field. He could become an average hitter with 10-12 home run pop, but he strikes out too much and doesn't draw the walks needed to lead off. His speed hasn't paid off as much on the basepaths, as he is not an effective basestealer.

THE FUTURE: Pache's age and athleticism give him plenty of potential. Scouts generally see him as a future regular, but not a future star, because they don't see an impact bat. He'll return to Double-A Mississippi to begin the season, but with his defensive ability, he could fill a big league role at any point in 2019 if the Braves needed a fill-in. Ender Inciarte's contract (he's signed through 2021 with a team option for 2022) means either Inciarte or Pache will likely need to be moved at some point.

BA GRADE	
55	**Risk:** High
Hit: 50. **Power:** 40.	
Run: 70. **Field:** 70.	
Arm: 70	

Year	Club (League)	Class	AVG	G	AB	R	H	2B	3B	HR	RBI	BB	SO	SB	CS	OBP	SLG
2016	Braves (GCL)	R	.283	27	106	16	30	2	4	0	11	6	11	7	3	.325	.377
	Danville (APP)	R	.333	30	114	12	38	2	3	0	10	7	13	4	2	.372	.404
2017	Rome (SAL)	LoA	.281	119	469	60	132	13	8	0	42	39	104	32	14	.335	.343
2018	Florida (FSL)	HiA	.285	93	369	46	105	20	5	8	40	15	69	7	6	.311	.431
	Mississippi (SL)	AA	.260	29	104	10	27	3	1	1	7	5	28	0	2	.294	.337
Minor League Totals			.286	298	1162	144	332	40	21	9	110	72	225	50	27	.327	.380

9 WILLIAM CONTRERAS, C

Born: Dec. 24, 1997. **B-T:** R-R. **Ht.:** 6-0. **Wt.:** 180. **Signed:** Venezuela, 2015. **Signed by:** Rolando Petit.

TRACK RECORD: Contreras is the younger brother of Cubs catcher Willson Contreras. While the older Contreras didn't make it to full-season ball until he was 21, William was one of the best catchers in the South Atlantic League as a 20-year-old. He shared the job at low Class A Rome with Drew Lugbauer, and the Braves ensured he didn't wear down by playing him at DH, too. He received a late-season bump to high Class A Florida.

SCOUTING REPORT: Contreras has plus raw power that he already turns into productive power, and his hands work well enough that he can also drive the ball to right-center field. That gives him a chance to hit .270 or so. He has some young player hitting habits he must break. He tends to pull off the ball and step in the bucket, leaving him vulnerable to being pitched away, but those are correctable flaws and he shows solid strike-zone awareness. Defensively, he has good hands, moves well and shows more athleticism than most catchers. He has a plus arm but sometimes struggles with his transfer when he rushes.

BA GRADE	
55	**Risk:** High
Hit: 50. **Power:** 55.	
Run: 40. **Field:** 50.	
Arm: 60.	

THE FUTURE: The Braves position player prospect depth is much thinner now than it was a couple of years, which makes Contreras' development even more important. Contreras is still multiple years away from being big league-ready, but he has all the tools to be the rare catcher who can handle the job defensively while producing offensively.

Year	Club (League)	Class	AVG	G	AB	R	H	2B	3B	HR	RBI	BB	SO	SB	CS	OBP	SLG
2016	Braves (GCL)	R	.264	30	72	8	19	5	0	1	8	7	15	0	1	.346	.375
2017	Danville (APP)	R	.290	45	169	29	49	10	1	4	25	24	30	1	0	.379	.432
2018	Rome (SAL)	LoA	.293	82	307	54	90	17	1	11	39	29	73	1	1	.360	.463
	Florida (FSL)	HiA	.253	23	83	3	21	7	0	0	10	6	16	0	0	.300	.337
Minor League Totals			.290	229	803	115	233	48	6	16	114	81	155	4	4	.359	.425

10 LUIZ GOHARA, LHP

Born: July 31, 1996. **B-R:** L-L. **Ht.:** 6-3. **Wt.:** 265. **Signed:** Brazil, 2012.
Signed by: Emilio Carrasquel/Hide Sueyoshi (Mariners).

TRACK RECORD: Few players had a rougher 2018 than Gohara. Acquired from the Mariners for Shae Simmons and Mallex Smith, Gohara climbed from high Class A to make five major league starts in 2017. His father died in his arms during the offseason, and he left with team permission during the season to be with his mother as she had heart surgery. He missed most of spring training with an ankle injury and finished the season on the disabled list with a shoulder injury.

SCOUTING REPORT: Gohara's conditioning was a problem in 2018. It affected his arm speed, and his fastball dipped from 95-99 mph to 91-95. His slider also backed up. It's impossible to know if his previously top-of-the-scale fastball and plus-plus slider will return, but even if he finds a midpoint between 2017 and 2018, he would have a pair of plus pitches. He needs to improve his below-average changeup if he's going to work as a starte.

BA GRADE

55 Risk: High

Fastball: 60.
Slider: 60.
Change: 40. **CTL:** 45.

THE FUTURE: The Braves said that Gohara lost 35 pounds while working out in Orlando after the season. When everything is working properly, He has one of the best arms in baseball. He rarely showed his best stuff in 2018, but between the injuries and off-field tragedy, there is reason to hope he can return to form in 2019. With so many pitching prospects in the upper minors, 2019 may be Gohara's last chance to show the Braves what he can do.

Year	Club (League)	Class	W	L	ERA	G	GS	CG	SV	IP	H	HR	BB	SO	K/9	WHIP	AVG
2016	Everett (NWL)	SS	2	0	1.76	3	3	0	0	15	13	1	3	21	12.3	1.04	.224
	Clinton (MWL)	LoA	5	2	1.82	10	10	0	0	54	44	1	20	60	9.9	1.18	.223
2017	Florida (FSL)	HiA	3	1	1.98	7	7	0	0	36	33	0	10	39	9.7	1.18	.243
	Mississippi (SL)	AA	2	1	2.60	12	11	0	0	52	42	2	18	60	10.4	1.15	.218
	Gwinnett (IL)	AAA	2	2	3.31	7	7	0	0	35	31	4	16	48	12.2	1.33	.230
	Atlanta (NL)	MAJ	1	3	4.91	5	5	0	0	29	32	2	8	31	9.5	1.36	.283
2018	Mississippi (SL)	AA	0	1	2.70	1	1	0	0	3	5	0	3	4	10.8	2.40	.357
	Atlanta (NL)	MAJ	0	1	5.95	9	1	0	1	20	16	3	8	18	8.2	1.22	.222
	Gwinnett (IL)	AAA	3	4	4.94	12	12	0	0	55	54	9	15	55	9.1	1.26	.263
Major League Totals			1	4	5.33	14	6	0	1	49	48	5	16	49	9.0	1.31	.259
Minor League Totals			22	28	3.89	87	86	0	0	386	378	28	158	434	10.1	1.39	.255

11 KYLE MULLER, LHP

BA GRADE

50 Risk: Medium

Born: Oct. 7, 1997. **B-T:** R-L. **Ht.:** 6-7. **Wt.:** 250. **Drafted:** HS—Dallas, Texas, 2016 (2nd round). **Signed by:** Nate Dion.

TRACK RECORD: A year ago, Muller seemed on his way to becoming the rare whiff among Braves' high-dollar prep pitching picks. He lost 4-5 mph off his fastball and was put on a much slower track than the typical Braves pitcher. Muller responded by paying his way to spend part of the offseason working at Driveline Baseball in Washington. It paid off when he regained his fastball and flew through the system, pitching successfully at three levels.

SCOUTING REPORT: Muller was an entirely different pitcher in 2018 thanks to his recovered velocity. He still lacks a true plus weapon, but he now has the chance to have a lot of average to above-average offerings. He attacked hitters with his 92-95 mph fastball that was an above-average pitch. His improved arm speed helped his slider flash above-average more regularly, and he'll mix in a fringe-average curveball that works as a get-more pitch. His changeup shows some late tumble at times and is a future average pitch. Muller has more control than command.

THE FUTURE: As a lefthander with a lot of options to attack hitters, Muller projects as a solid mid-rotation starter. He's headed back to Double-A, where he'll be part of a very talented rotation stuck behind a similarly talented Triple-A rotation.

Year	Club (League)	Class	W	L	ERA	G	GS	CG	SV	IP	H	HR	BB	SO	K/9	WHIP	AVG
2016	Braves (GCL)	R	1	0	0.65	10	9	0	0	28	14	0	12	38	12.4	0.94	.144
2017	Danville (APP)	R	1	1	4.15	11	11	0	0	48	43	5	18	49	9.3	1.28	.232
2018	Rome (SAL)	LoA	3	0	2.40	6	6	0	0	30	24	3	8	23	6.9	1.07	.222
	Florida (FSL)	HiA	4	2	3.24	14	14	0	0	81	80	2	32	79	8.8	1.39	.26
	Mississippi (SL)	AA	4	1	3.10	5	5	1	0	29	22	3	6	27	8.4	0.97	.206
Minor League Totals			13	4	2.97	46	45	1	0	215	183	13	76	216	9.0	1.20	.230

12 JOEY WENTZ, LHP

BA GRADE

50 Risk: Medium

Born: Oct. 6, 1997. **B-T:** L-L. **Ht.:** 6-5. **Wt.:** 220. **Drafted:** HS—Shawnee Mission, Kan., 2016 (1st round supplemental). **Signed by:** Nate Dion.

TRACK RECORD: About the only thing that slowed down Wentz in 2018 was the disabled list. He missed significant time with an oblique injury, but when he was on the mound he was among the most effective pitchers in the Florida State League. He had a 29-inning scoreless streak at one point in 2018.

SCOUTING REPORT: Wentz lost a little velocity in the adjustment to the five-day schedule of pro ball, but he's regained it. His 90-95 mph fastball plays even better than its radar gun reading because he gets good plane from his high overhand release point. Wentz spots his fastball precisely with above-average command even if he has only average control because he doesn't give in. Wentz mixes in a future above-average curveball and plus changeup. He's a solid fielder and limits the running game.

THE FUTURE: Wentz would have likely made it to Double-A last year if not for his oblique injury. There are many, many starting pitchers in the farm system between Wentz and the big leagues, but it's hard not to be impressed with his feel and solid stuff. His ceiling is as a solid mid-rotation starter.

Year	Club (League)	Class	W	L	ERA	G	GS	CG	SV	IP	H	HR	BB	SO	K/9	WHIP	AVG
2016	Braves (GCL)	R	0	0	0.00	4	4	0	0	12	3	0	5	18	13.5	0.67	.083
	Danville (APP)	R	1	4	5.06	8	8	0	0	32	31	0	20	58	15.9	1.59	.265
2017	Rome (SAL)	LoA	8	3	2.60	26	26	0	0	132	99	4	46	152	10.4	1.10	.209
2018	Florida (FSL)	HiA	3	4	2.28	16	16	0	0	67	49	3	24	53	7.1	1.09	.206
Minor League Totals			12	11	2.71	54	54	0	0	243	182	7	95	258	9.6	1.14	.211

13 PATRICK WEIGEL, RHP

BA GRADE

55 Risk: Extreme

Born: July 8, 1994. **B-T:** R-R. **Ht.:** 6-6. **Wt.:** 230. **Drafted:** Houston, 2015 (7th round). **Signed by:** Darin Vaughn.

TRACK RECORD: After pitching for three colleges in three seasons, the strong-armed Weigel leapt through the Braves' farm system and was not far away from Atlanta when he blew out his elbow in June 2017. He spent a year and a half rehabbing, but should be at full speed for the 2019 season.

SCOUTING REPORT: Weigel's delivery is never pretty and sometimes his arm works to catch up to his lower half, but he's strong enough that he makes it work. He got back on the mound during instructional league and he showed plenty of signs that he was rusty. He showed solid velocity (91-95 mph) but he struggled to throw strikes and his slider didn't have its usual break, but that was just a chance to get back on the mound. Pre-injury, Weigel touched up to 98 with a plus fastball, generally sitting 92-95 mph over the course of an outing. His slider flashed above-average and he showed he could manipulate its break and work it to both sides of the plate. His changeup was a below-average pitch that was often too firm.

THE FUTURE: Weigel's injury might end up pushing him to the bullpen because the Braves have so many starting pitching prospects. He has a starter's frame, but his stuff could play even better in short stints.

Year	Club (League)	Class	W	L	ERA	G	GS	CG	SV	IP	H	HR	BB	SO	K/9	WHIP	AVG
2016	Rome (SAL)	LoA	10	4	2.51	22	21	1	0	129	92	7	47	135	9.4	1.08	.203
	Mississippi (SL)	AA	1	2	2.18	3	3	0	0	21	9	2	8	17	7.4	0.82	.132
2017	Mississippi (SL)	AA	3	0	2.89	7	7	0	0	37	32	2	11	38	9.2	1.15	.234
	Gwinnett (IL)	AAA	3	2	5.27	8	8	0	0	41	42	5	17	30	6.6	1.44	.269
2018	Braves (GCL)	R	0	0	0.00	4	3	0	0	4	2	0	0	6	13.5	0.50	.167
Minor League Totals			17	11	3.27	58	56	1	0	284	230	18	109	275	8.7	1.20	.223

14 KOLBY ALLARD, LHP

BA GRADE

45 Risk: Medium

Born: Aug. 13, 1997. **B-T:** L-L. **Ht.:** 6-1. **Wt.:** 190. **Drafted:** HS—San Clemente, Calif., 2015 (1st round). **Signed by:** Dan Cox.

TRACK RECORD: Wherever Allard has pitched, he's been one of the youngest players, if not the youngest, in the league he's pitching. And until he reached Atlanta, he's always been one of the best pitchers in wherever he's pitched. But Allard's lack of velocity makes it hard to be confident in lasting big league success, even though he's posted a 2.93 ERA in 65 career minor league starts.

SCOUTING REPORT: Allard made his major league debut in August 2018 and in doing so confirmed some of the fears that dogged him even when he was having success in Triple-A. Allard's fastball is a below-average pitch. It sits 88-90 and rarely bumps 91-92. He locates it well and pitches backward, allowing him to try to sneak a fastball by a hitter after slowing their eyes with his curveball or changeup. But against big league hitters, Allard's margins of error are so small that he has to do everything almost perfectly to have success. He has an above-average curveball and an average changeup, but he has has to nibble with all of them because he lacks a pitch to get swings and misses in the strike zone.

THE FUTURE: Allard doesn't have much more to prove in Triple-A. He was third in the International

League in ERA in 2018. Still, he needs to find 2-3 extra mph that he's been losing in pro ball. Unless he adds more oomph, his ceiling is as a No. 5 starter.

Year	Club (League)	Class	W	L	ERA	G	GS	CG	SV	IP	H	HR	BB	SO	K/9	WHIP	AVG
2016	Danville (APP)	R	3	0	1.32	5	5	0	0	27	18	0	5	33	10.9	0.84	.186
	Rome (SAL)	LoA	5	3	3.73	11	11	1	0	60	54	5	20	62	9.2	1.23	.244
2017	Mississippi (SL)	AA	8	11	3.18	27	27	2	0	150	146	11	45	129	7.7	1.27	.258
2018	Atlanta (NL)	MAJ	1	1	12.38	3	1	0	0	8	19	3	4	3	3.4	2.88	.463
	Gwinnett (IL)	AAA	6	4	2.72	19	19	0	0	112	102	6	34	89	7.1	1.21	.249
Major League Totals			1	1	12.38	3	1	0	0	8	19	3	4	3	3.4	2.88	.463
Minor League Totals			22	18	2.93	65	65	3	0	356	321	22	104	325	8.2	1.19	.245

15 GREYSON JENISTA, OF

BA GRADE
50 Risk: High

Born: Dec. 7, 1996. **B-T:** L-R. **Ht.:** 6-4. **Wt.:** 210. **Drafted:** Wichita State, 2018 (2nd round). **Signed by:** Nate Dion.

TRACK RECORD: Jenista was a career .318/.430/.487 hitter for the Shockers, and his stat line didn't change much from his freshman season through his junior year. He also was the Cape Cod League MVP in the summer before his junior season. Primarily a first baseman in his first two college seasons, he played center field as a junior before moving to right field in pro ball.

SCOUTING REPORT: Scouts have long believed that Jenista will hit and have seen him put on impressive power displays in batting practice, but there are plenty of questions about how easily Jenista can translate that power into actual games. Braves officials say they believe that he will eventually learn to loft the ball more frequently. His bat path is pretty level through the zone right now, emphasizing contact over lift and power. He'll likely have to trade away some of that contact ability to reach his 20-plus home run potential, but he'll need to make that trade as a corner outfielder. Jenista is an average runner now, but will likely slow down as he matures. He's fine in right fielder as a fringe-average defender with an average arm.

THE FUTURE: Jenista will return to high Class A Florida to begin 2019. Jenista has gotten stronger, but his biggest focus for 2019 will be to start driving the ball in the air more consistently.

Year	Club (League)	Class	AVG	G	AB	R	H	2B	3B	HR	RBI	BB	SO	SB	CS	OBP	SLG
2018	Danville (APP)	R	.250	10	40	10	10	1	0	3	7	6	9	0	1	.348	.500
	Rome (SAL)	LoA	.333	32	117	20	39	5	3	1	23	10	17	4	1	.377	.453
	Florida (FSL)	HiA	.152	19	66	3	10	3	1	0	4	7	15	0	0	.230	.227
Minor League Totals			.265	61	223	33	59	9	4	4	34	23	41	4	2	.328	.395

16 FREDDY TARNOK, RHP

BA GRADE
50 Risk: High

Born: Nov. 24, 1998. **B-T:** R-R. **Ht.:** 6-3. **Wt.:** 185. **Drafted:** HS—Riverview, Fla., 2017 (3rd round). **Signed by:** Justin Clark.

TRACK RECORD: It's been quite a transition for Tarnok. Until his senior year in high school he was a shortstop who barely pitched, but a well-timed move to the mound had turned him into a top 100 pick.

SCOUTING REPORT: The Braves slowly stretched Tarnok into a starting role over the course of the season, but his long-term role is very much up in the air. His lack of pitching experience is apparent at times as he has further work to do to repeat his delivery more consistently and his secondary offerings are often immature. Tarnok will show flashes of potential with his 85-87 mph slider and his 84-86 mph changeup, but neither are consistent at this point and both rarely flash better than average. His 91-94 mph average fastball can generate swings and misses. His command and control are both below-average as well.

THE FUTURE: Tarnok's prospect status is all about projection. If he fills out, gets stronger and adds polish he could end up as a high-leverage reliever. He's ready to move up to high Class A Florida.

Year	Club (League)	Class	W	L	ERA	G	GS	CG	SV	IP	H	HR	BB	SO	K/9	WHIP	AVG
2017	Braves (GCL)	R	0	3	2.57	9	9	0	0	14	11	0	3	10	6.4	1.00	.208
2018	Rome (SAL)	LoA	5	5	3.96	27	11	0	0	77	70	5	41	83	9.7	1.44	.235
Minor League Totals			5	8	3.74	36	20	0	0	91	81	5	44	93	9.2	1.37	.231

17 TRISTAN BECK, RHP

BA GRADE
50 Risk: High

Born: June 24, 1996. **B-T:** R-R. **Ht.:** 6-4. **Wt.:** 165. **Drafted:** Stanford, 2018 (4th round). **Signed by:** Jim Blueberg.

TRACK RECORD: The Braves targeted Beck when he was a high school senior at Corona (Calif.) HS, but moved on when it was clear he wanted to head to Stanford. He was a draft-eligible sophomore but fell to the 29th round after he didn't pitch all season while recovering from a stress fracture in his back. Beck got on the mound for an effective junior season (8-4, 2.98), but concerns over his back and his durability meant the Braves got him several rounds later than they hoped to pick him in 2015.

SCOUTING REPORT: Beck's stuff was not as consistent in 2018. He can still touch 96-97 mph early in games and he can snap off an above-average slider or curve, but he has significant trouble maintaining that velocity. He normally quickly slides back to 90-92 mph and his fastball flattens out. The Braves were very cautious with his innings in his pro debut. Beck has always been a craftsman more than a power pitcher, but his slider and curveball also backed up this year. At his best he has four average or better pitches, but early in his pro career, he's lacking a plus pitch. If his stuff can come close to what it is at its best and he maintains his average control, he's a mid-rotation starter. But that's a big if.

THE FUTURE: A healthy Beck could move quickly. He should be ready for high Class A Florida in 2019.

Year	Club (League)	Class	W	L	ERA	G	GS	CG	SV	IP	H	HR	BB	SO	K/9	WHIP	AVG
2018	Braves (GCL)	R	0	0	0.00	3	1	0	0	5	4	0	2	7	13.5	1.29	.235
Minor League Totals			0	0	0.00	3	1	0	0	5	4	0	2	7	13.5	1.29	.235

18 C.J. ALEXANDER, 3B

BA GRADE

50 Risk: High

Born: July 17, 1996. **B-T:** L-R. **Ht.:** 6-5. **Wt.:** 215. **Drafted:** State JC of Florida, 2018 (20th round). **Signed by:** Justin Clark.

TRACK RECORD: The track record of junior college hitters is not good. While there are some draft finds, there are also plenty of high draft picks whose success at the plate did not translate to pro ball. Alexander, the older brother of D-backs shortstop Blaze Alexander, was collateral damage for that. Even after hitting .405/.488/.785, he had to wait until the 20th round to hear his name called.

SCOUTING REPORT: From the day he became a pro, Alexander has shown that his hitting ability translates to pro ball and a wood bat. He adjusted his approach in pro ball as he went from a pull-heavy hitter to one who can wear out the left-center field gap. He's an above-average hitter and there's average power potential as well, although he's yet to show he can hit for average and power at the same time with a wood bat. His swing is designed to lift the ball and it is short and compact. Defensively, Alexander is fine at third with average range and a plus arm and he's an average runner.

THE FUTURE: Alexander was a revelation. He'll head to low Class A Rome to prove he can keep hitting against more advanced pitching. If his 2019 season comes close to matching his 2018 production he'll quickly climb these rankings. He has the pieces to be an everyday third baseman.

Year	Club (League)	Class	AVG	G	AB	R	H	2B	3B	HR	RBI	BB	SO	SB	CS	OBP	SLG
2018	Braves (GCL)	R	.412	9	34	6	14	0	2	1	8	6	4	0	0	.500	.618
	Danville (APP)	R	.354	22	82	10	29	3	4	0	12	13	21	1	1	.439	.488
	Florida (FSL)	HiA	.325	21	80	5	26	5	1	1	7	8	17	3	1	.386	.450
Minor League Totals			.352	52	196	21	69	8	7	2	27	27	42	4	2	.429	.495

19 HUASCAR YNOA, RHP

BA GRADE

50 Risk: High

Born: May 28, 1998. **B-T:** R-R. **Ht.:** 6-2. **Wt.:** 220. **Signed:** Dominican Republic, 2014. **Signed by:** Fred Guerrero (Twins).

TRACK RECORD: The Braves' farm system is top-heavy. The vast majority of the team's best pitching prospects are ticketed for Double-A or Triple-A in 2019. Ynoa is one Class A arm with a sky-high ceiling.

SCOUTING REPORT: Ynoa has some of the best pure stuff in the Braves system. He sits 92-96 mph and has touched 100 mph at his best, and both his slider and changeup have at least average potential. Ynoa's changeup is inconsistent but at its best it has excellent late fade and sink, and it dives away from lefthanded hitters' bats. Ynoa's 83-86 mph slider has potential as well, with solid tilt. Too often at this point it is just a chase pitch. Ynoa has a strong frame and he's gotten more direct to the plate, but he still has below-average control and command. He is really aiming at this point to just get his fastball over the plate rather than trying to hit spots.

THE FUTURE: Ynoa needs plenty of further refinement, but he has the stuff and durability to be a mid-rotation starter and he has a solid fallback option as a power reliever. He's set to return to high Class A Florida.

Year	Club (League)	Class	W	L	ERA	G	GS	CG	SV	IP	H	HR	BB	SO	K/9	WHIP	AVG
2016	Twins (GCL)	R	3	5	3.18	11	11	0	0	51	44	1	12	51	9.0	1.10	.228
2017	Elizabethton (APP)	R	0	1	5.26	6	6	0	0	26	28	1	14	23	8.1	1.64	.277
	Danville (APP)	R	0	3	5.26	7	7	0	0	26	24	1	15	27	9.5	1.52	.238
2018	Rome (SAL)	LoA	7	8	3.63	18	18	0	0	92	69	7	42	100	9.8	1.21	.205
	Florida (FSL)	HiA	1	4	8.03	6	6	0	0	25	33	1	12	31	11.3	1.82	.317
Minor League Totals			13	26	4.05	62	62	0	0	275	241	12	125	279	9.1	1.33	.231

20 JACOB WEBB, RHP

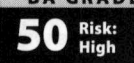

BA GRADE	
50	**Risk:** High

Born: Aug. 15, 1993. **B-T:** R-R. **Ht.:** 6-2. **Wt.:** 215. **Drafted:** Tabor (Kan.), 2014 (18th round). **Signed by:** Terry Tripp Jr.

TRACK RECORD: A high school outfielder/infielder, Webb moved to the mound while playing for the NAIA's Tabor (Kan.) College. He quickly became the school's ace and its second-ever draftee. He missed all of 2015 recovering from Tommy John surgery. He's steadily improved his fringy control since and cemented a spot on the 40-man roster with a dominant start to the Dominican Winter League season.

SCOUTING REPORT: Webb's 95-97 mph fastball and tight 80-83 mph curveball give him a pair of plus pitches, with some scouts giving his fastball plus-plus grades. The two pitches work well together as uses the full height of the strike zone. He likes to work his fastball up and down in the strike zone, while his curve has a short, tight 12-to-6 break. He's shown he can bury it or throw it in the zone. Webb hides the ball well with a hip turn to help begin a compact delivery. He rarely mixes in a changeup. Webb's control is fringe-average. His stuff is good enough that he just has to be around the zone.

THE FUTURE: Webb should fit in the Braves' bullpen at some point in 2018. If he can continue to improve his control, he has the stuff to pitch in the late innings.

Year	Club (League)	Class	W	L	ERA	G	GS	CG	SV	IP	H	HR	BB	SO	K/9	WHIP	AVG
2016	Rome (SAL)	LoA	0	0	16.20	2	0	0	0	2	3	0	2	3	16.2	3.00	.429
	Danville (APP)	R	0	0	3.18	12	0	0	2	11	7	1	7	28	22.2	1.24	.171
2017	Florida (FSL)	HiA	2	1	1.74	22	0	0	2	41	29	1	22	48	10.5	1.23	.203
	Mississippi (SL)	AA	3	1	2.63	16	0	0	0	24	17	1	14	26	9.8	1.29	.202
2018	Mississippi (SL)	AA	1	2	3.18	21	0	0	7	23	16	4	12	35	13.9	1.24	.195
	Gwinnett (IL)	AAA	2	2	3.13	30	0	0	11	32	20	3	11	34	9.7	0.98	.175
Minor League Totals			10	7	2.65	114	6	0	22	166	122	12	76	205	11.1	1.19	.203

21 TUCKER DAVIDSON, LHP

BA GRADE	
45	**Risk:** High

Born: March 25, 1996. **B-T:** L-L. **Ht.:** 6-2. **Wt.:** 215. **Drafted:** Midland (Texas) JC, 2016 (19th round). **Signed by:** Nate Dion.

TRACK RECORD: Davidson was one of the Braves' biggest breakout prospects in 2017, but in 2018 his control took two steps backward. His attempts to fix the problems didn't pay off until late in the season.

SCOUTING REPORT: Davidson's fastball lacked the high-end pop it showed at times in 2017, when he touched 95-97 mph in shorter stints. More often in 2018 he was 91-94, but that is still plenty of fastball if he can locate it like he did in 2017. Davidson's control and command of his fastball backed up, which left him too often behind in counts. His 12-to-6 curveball is a potentially plus weapon, but he didn't rely on it enough, as he wasn't comfortable enough to throw it for strikes when behind in counts. Similarly, he tried to muscle up with a fastball at times when his average changeup would have likely been more effective.

THE FUTURE: Davidson took a step back, but he still has the three-pitch arsenal that gives him a chance to start. His delivery has some effort, leading some scouts to believe he'll eventually be a power reliever.

Year	Club (League)	Class	W	L	ERA	G	GS	CG	SV	IP	H	HR	BB	SO	K/9	WHIP	AVG
2016	Braves (GCL)	R	0	3	1.52	11	1	0	0	30	32	1	4	32	9.7	1.21	.271
2017	Rome (SAL)	LoA	5	4	2.60	31	12	0	2	104	96	4	30	101	8.8	1.22	.248
2018	Florida (FSL)	HiA	7	10	4.18	24	24	1	0	118	120	5	58	99	7.5	1.50	.270
Minor League Totals			12	17	3.22	66	37	1	2	252	248	10	92	232	8.3	1.35	.261

22 CHAD SOBOTKA, RHP

BA GRADE	
45	**Risk:** High

Born: July 10, 1993. **B-T:** R-R. **Ht.:** 6-7. **Wt.:** 230. **Drafted:** South Carolina-Upstate, 2014 (4th round). **Signed by:** Billy Best.

TRACK RECORD: The Braves showed plenty of patience with Sobotka. They picked him in 2014 despite the fact that he'd missed the entire season with a back injury. Then, when he got back on the mound, he struggled. But after three up-and-down seasons in the minors, Sobotka put it all together in 2018, jumping from Double-A Mississippi to a spot on the Braves' playoff roster.

SCOUTING REPORT: Sobotka's delivery is designed to give him the best chance possible to throw strikes. He sets up as far to the first-base side of the rubber as he can to give him a shot to locate his fastball armside as well as gloveside. He also uses a very simple delivery from the stretch at all times. Even with that, Sobotka struggles to throw strikes. When it all works, he can blow hitters away with a lively, 96-99 mph fastball with modest run and a hard, 86-88 plus slider that is short and tight with more depth than sweep. When it doesn't, his well below-average command leads to long counts and walks, although his stuff is still good enough that his problem is more walks than hits—righthanders had just seven extra-base hits against him all season. Sobotka thrived in 2018 despite well below-average control, and his stuff is good enough for him to survive fringe-average control. But he has work to do to get there.

THE FUTURE: Sobotka will be part of the Braves' bullpen plans in 2019. His control will determine whether he's a low-leverage arm guy or someone who can eventually be trusted with high-leverage work.

Year	Club (League)	Class	W	L	ERA	G	GS	CG	SV	IP	H	HR	BB	SO	K/9	WHIP	AVG
2016	Rome (SAL)	LoA	1	2	4.26	15	0	0	0	19	23	1	12	19	9.0	1.84	.303
	Carolina (CAR)	HiA	1	1	2.04	13	0	0	3	18	12	0	3	24	12.2	0.85	.197
	Mississippi (SL)	AA	0	0	0.00	2	0	0	0	2	0	0	0	2	9.0	0.00	.000
2017	Mississippi (SL)	AA	3	1	5.23	18	0	0	0	31	29	1	19	23	6.7	1.55	.252
	Florida (FSL)	HiA	1	4	6.75	16	0	0	2	27	32	3	13	29	9.8	1.69	.314
2018	Florida (FSL)	HiA	2	0	2.21	13	1	0	2	20	9	0	7	28	12.4	0.79	.132
	Mississippi (SL)	AA	2	3	1.93	22	0	0	6	28	16	1	13	37	11.9	1.04	.170
	Gwinnett (IL)	AAA	0	0	1.93	9	0	0	3	9	5	0	9	12	11.6	1.50	.152
	Atlanta (NL)	MAJ	1	0	1.88	14	0	0	0	14	5	2	9	21	13.2	0.98	.104
Major League Totals			1	0	1.88	14	0	0	0	14	5	2	9	21	13.2	0.98	.104
Minor League Totals			11	17	4.24	123	10	0	16	191	172	11	98	196	9.2	1.41	.246

23 ALEX JACKSON, C

Born: Dec. 25, 1995. **B-T:** R-R. **Ht.:** 6-2. **Wt.:** 250. **Drafted:** HS—San Diego, 2014 (1st round). **Signed by:** Gary Patchett (Mariners).

TRACK RECORD: Jackson was once considered the best high school bat in the 2014 draft class. Seattle moved him from catcher to right field, but that swing never translated to pro ball. The Braves acquired him in a buy-low trade (sending Rob Whalen and Max Povse to Seattle) and moved him back to catcher.

SCOUTING REPORT: Jackson still hasn't proven he can hit, but more disturbingly his power largely disappeared in 2018. Jackson has plus-plus raw power, but his all-pull all-the-time approach was an easy mark for a pitcher with a plan. Every one of Jackson's home runs last season was hit to left field. When he was in high school Jackson was known for loose hands and a fast bat, but he's tightened up and now has modest bat speed. Defensively, Jackson is catching up for lost time as a receiver, but his biggest hurdle is getting more flexible and improving his game calling. One of the reasons the Braves promoted him to Triple-A was to get him acclimated to more in-depth scouting reports. He does have a plus arm.

THE FUTURE: Jackson was added to the 40-man roster. He has a long way to go to prove he can fill a backup role. He'll get to work at Triple-A Gwinnett.

Year	Club (League)	Class	AVG	G	AB	R	H	2B	3B	HR	RBI	BB	SO	SB	CS	OBP	SLG
2016	Clinton (MWL)	LoA	.243	92	333	43	81	20	1	11	55	34	103	2	1	.332	.408
2017	Florida (FSL)	HiA	.272	66	257	44	70	17	0	14	45	13	74	0	1	.333	.502
	Mississippi (SL)	AA	.255	30	110	12	28	4	0	5	20	10	32	0	0	.317	.427
2018	Mississippi (SL)	AA	.200	64	225	27	45	12	1	5	24	20	78	0	0	.282	.329
	Gwinnett (IL)	AAA	.204	35	108	15	22	11	2	3	17	12	42	0	0	.296	.426
Minor League Totals			.234	386	1386	193	325	87	7	48	215	125	449	5	8	.318	.411

24 WES PARSONS, RHP

Born: Sept. 6, 1992. **B-T:** R-R. **Ht.:** 6-5. **Wt.:** 210. **Signed:** Jackson State (Tenn.) JC, 2012 (NDFA). **Signed by:** Terry Tripp Jr.

TRACK RECORD: Parsons had been ignored in back-to-back drafts before the Braves liked his work in the Northwoods League and signed him as a nondrafted free agent.

SCOUTING REPORT: There is nothing sexy about Parsons' approach or stuff, but he's crafty, consistent and durable. Parsons doesn't have an above-average pitch, but his 91-93 mph fastball and 85-87 mph slider are both average offerings and his changeup is fringe-average. He gets armside run on his fastball. It doesn't lead to swings-and-misses as much as poor contact. His slider trades depth for power, and gets under the hands of lefthanded hitters.

THE FUTURE: The Braves are so loaded in starting pitching prospects that Parsons will be fighting to make the Triple-A rotation out of spring training. He just may have to contribute in another organization.

Year	Club (League)	Class	W	L	ERA	G	GS	CG	SV	IP	H	HR	BB	SO	K/9	WHIP	AVG
2016	Braves (GCL)	R	0	0	2.70	4	1	0	0	7	8	0	0	9	12.2	1.20	.296
	Mississippi (SL)	AA	0	0	0.00	1	1	0	0	4	1	0	2	2	4.5	0.75	.091
	Carolina (CAR)	HiA	0	2	3.86	16	7	0	0	56	56	0	18	44	7.1	1.32	.264
2017	Gwinnett (IL)	AAA	0	0	8.64	4	1	0	0	8	18	0	6	10	10.8	2.88	.429
	Mississippi (SL)	AA	3	3	2.71	26	10	0	3	103	83	5	33	98	8.6	1.13	.219
2018	Mississippi (SL)	AA	1	2	1.23	8	7	0	0	29	24	1	10	28	8.6	1.16	.216
	Atlanta (NL)	MAJ	0	1	7.20	1	0	0	0	5	6	1	3	3	5.4	1.80	.316
	Gwinnett (IL)	AAA	7	3	3.29	15	13	0	1	82	70	7	23	69	7.6	1.13	.212
Major League Totals			0	1	7.20	1	0	0	0	5	6	1	3	3	5.4	1.80	.316
Minor League Totals			24	24	3.38	121	86	1	4	532	487	29	148	473	8.0	1.19	.243

25 A.J. GRAFFANINO, SS

BA GRADE

45 Risk: High

Born: July 16, 1997. **B-T:** L-R. **Ht.:** 6-2. **Wt.:** 170. **Drafted:** Washington, 2018 (8th round). **Signed by:** Brett Evert.

TRACK RECORD: Graffanino, the son of former big leaguer Tony Graffanino, immediately became the team's best minor league shortstop the day he was drafted, after impressing with his glove for three years at Washington.

SCOUTING REPORT: Graffanino missed two months during the college season with a hamstring injury, but he showed a significantly better bat when he was healthy. Graffanino showed a pesky approach focused on putting the ball in play with very few attempts to drive the ball. A former switch-hitter, Graffanino now hits exclusively from the left side. He has bottom-of-the-scale power. He's still a better glove than bat. Defensively, Graffanino has a shortstop's twitchy range and an above-average arm.

THE FUTURE: Graffanino is the only player in full-season ball for the Braves who projects as a potential big league shortstop, although his light bat limits his upside. He's ready for high Class A Florida.

Year	Club (League)	Class	AVG	G	AB	R	H	2B	3B	HR	RBI	BB	SO	SB	CS	OBP	SLG
2018	Danville (APP)	R	.407	6	27	2	11	0	0	0	6	1	3	1	0	.400	.407
	Rome (SAL)	LoA	.301	37	143	19	43	8	0	1	11	8	24	4	3	.333	.378
Minor League Totals			.318	43	170	21	54	8	0	1	17	9	27	5	3	.344	.382

26 JEFFREY RAMOS, OF

BA GRADE

45 Risk: High

Born: Feb. 10, 1999. **B-T:** R-R. **Ht.:** 6-1. **Wt.:** 185. **Signed:** Dominican Republic, 2016. **Signed by:** Jonathan Cruz.

TRACK RECORD: The Braves' 2016 international class was supposed be a foundation of the farm system. After sanctions, Ramos as one of the few remaining players from that class who could reach Atlanta.

SCOUTING REPORT: Ramos' path to the big leagues is difficult because he's a free-swinging left fielder who is limited defensively. Ramos' selectivity needs to improve, but he makes solid contact and his simple swing gives him a path to being a fringe-average hitter. That may be enough if he can get to all of his 20-25 home run power potential. Ramos is limited to left by a below-average arm. Ramos has improved defensively, but he's limited by fringe-average speed and poor jumps. He's a below-average left fielder.

THE FUTURE: Ramos will move up to high Class A Florida. He has to keep a close watch on his conditioning, but if he can figure out a better plan at the plate, he could be a big league regular.

Year	Club (League)	Class	AVG	G	AB	R	H	2B	3B	HR	RBI	BB	SO	SB	CS	OBP	SLG
2016	Braves (DSL)	R	.230	33	126	19	29	8	1	1	12	9	27	3	2	.283	.333
2017	Braves (GCL)	R	.325	30	117	22	38	7	1	6	30	8	27	1	0	.374	.556
	Danville (APP)	R	.278	20	72	7	20	6	0	1	8	3	15	0	0	.308	.403
2018	Rome (SAL)	LoA	.245	122	469	57	115	24	6	16	69	27	89	2	0	.290	.424
Minor League Totals			.258	205	784	105	202	45	8	24	119	47	158	6	2	.304	.427

27 TREY RILEY, RHP

BA GRADE

50 Risk: Extreme

Born: April 21, 1998. **B-T:** R-R. **Ht.:** 6-2. **Wt.:** 200. **Drafted:** John A. Logan (Ill.) JC, 2018 (5th round). **Signed by:** Kevin Barry.

TRACK RECORD: Riley transferred to John A. Logan (Ill.) JC after throwing one game at Oklahoma State. His career with the Vols went much better as he struck out 117 in only 77.2 innings at Logan.

SCOUTING REPORT: Riley's best is really impressive. He sits 92-94 mph and touches 96-97 with a plus fastball that has above-average life. Riley's slider is also a plus pitch and he's quickly refined his curveball into a potentially above-average downer as well. He has toyed with a below-average changeup. Riley struggled to throw strikes in his pro debut and he's prone to spinning off toward first base, but he has solid athleticism and a relatively clean delivery.

THE FUTURE: Riley is one of the higher-upside, but riskiest arms in the low minors for the Braves.

Year	Club (League)	Class	W	L	ERA	G	GS	CG	SV	IP	H	HR	BB	SO	K/9	WHIP	AVG
2018	Danville (APP)	R	0	0	8.00	6	2	0	0	9	10	1	10	13	13.0	2.22	.278
Minor League Totals			0	0	8.00	6	2	0	0	9	10	1	10	13	13.0	2.22	.278

28 ISRAEL WILSON, OF

BA GRADE

45 Risk: Extreme

Born: March 3, 1998. **B-T:** L-R. **Ht.:** 6-3. **Wt.:** 185. **Signed:** Dominican Republic, 2014. **Signed by:** Luis Ortiz.

TRACK RECORD: Wilson has the kind of tools that make scouts dream. He and White Sox outfielder

Micker Adolfo grew up together in St. Thomas but moved to the Dominican Republic to train in preparation for their baseball careers. Wilson has long had athleticism, strength and speed, but his immature approach was readily apparent when he struggled after a promotion to high Class A Florida.

SCOUTING REPORT: Wilson was a shortstop when he signed, but he quickly moved to center field as a pro and now plays right field predominantly, where he's an average defender who is limited by his routes. His tools are excellent. He's an above-average runner with a plus arm and plus raw power. But his hitting approach is simplistic to the extreme and leads scouts to project him as a below-average hitter. He is looking to attack and pull a fastball whatever the count, which leads him too often hacking at three pitches and then heading back to the dugout. If he can develop selectivity, he has the tools to be a useful big leaguer.

THE FUTURE: Wilson is a high-risk prospect, but one who has the tools to be a regular if he puts it all together. A return to high Class A Florida will be a big test.

Year	Club (League)	Class	AVG	G	AB	R	H	2B	3B	HR	RBI	BB	SO	SB	CS	OBP	SLG
2016	Danville (APP)	R	.192	38	130	19	25	8	1	2	12	14	51	6	2	.276	.315
2017	Danville (APP)	R	.250	17	68	11	17	2	3	4	12	9	18	2	0	.338	.544
	Rome (SAL)	LoA	.262	43	168	28	44	3	3	2	20	18	52	9	3	.340	.351
2018	Rome (SAL)	LoA	.229	68	223	38	51	10	2	6	25	28	77	11	4	.316	.372
	Florida (FSL)	HiA	.215	40	135	16	29	5	1	2	10	14	43	5	1	.287	.311
Minor League Totals			.228	254	868	141	198	33	11	26	101	109	297	36	14	.318	.381

29 JASSEEL DE LA CRUZ, RHP

BA GRADE
45 Risk: Extreme

Born: June 26, 1997. **B-T:** R-R. **Ht.:** 6-1. **Wt.:** 175. **Signed:** Dominican Republic, 2015. **Signed by:** Matias Laureano.

TRACK RECORD: The Braves found the late-blooming de la Cruz as an 18-year-old in 2015. He's developed into one of the best arms the Braves have in the low minors.

SCOUTING REPORT: All too often when the going gets tough, de la Cruz rears back and hopes for the best. His 90-96 mph fastball is hard enough to blow hitters away, but it's much more effective when hitters aren't waiting for it. Too often in 2018, de la Cruz fell behind in counts and then got away from mixing pitches, become too predictably fastball-reliant. He also would get into habits of overthrowing. But when he's cruising, he has an above-average fastball and a slider that flashes plus. His control is below-average. His delivery is long in the back, but he uses his legs well in his delivery.

THE FUTURE: Understandably de la Cruz is developmentally behind many of his peers because he got a late start to pitching in pro ball. But he has the pieces of a future power reliever thanks to two pitches with plus potential.

Year	Club (League)	Class	W	L	ERA	G	GS	CG	SV	IP	H	HR	BB	SO	K/9	WHIP	AVG
2016	Braves (DSL)	R	2	0	3.42	12	3	0	0	26	23	1	14	20	6.8	1.41	.247
	Braves (GCL)	R	2	0	0.00	6	0	0	0	15	4	0	1	12	7.2	0.33	.085
2017	Braves (GCL)	R	2	1	1.89	4	4	0	0	19	13	1	7	17	8.1	1.05	.188
	Danville (APP)	R	0	2	5.32	7	6	0	0	24	25	1	11	19	7.2	1.52	.260
2018	Rome (SAL)	LoA	3	4	4.83	15	13	0	0	69	65	6	34	65	8.5	1.43	.250
Minor League Totals			9	8	3.95	51	26	0	0	159	136	9	75	139	7.9	1.32	.231

30 RAY-PATRICK DIDDER, SS

BA GRADE
40 Risk: Medium

Born: Oct. 1, 1994. **B-T:** R-R. **Ht.:** 6-0. **Wt.:** 180. **Signed:** Aruba, 2013. **Signed by:** Dargello Lodowica.

TRACK RECORD: As a pro, Didder has played five different positions and could plausibly play anywhere other than catcher or pitcher. And with a plus arm, he'd even be credible in a mop-up role on the mound.

SCOUTING REPORT: Didder is an excellent athlete. The Braves moved him to center field full-time in 2016, but started playing him at shortstop again in 2017. He's a plus defender in center or either outfield corner and he's an average defender at shortstop, second or third base. His plus arm is handy wherever he plays. His plus speed also plays well on the basepaths. The limiting factor for Didder is his bat. Didder has below-average pitch recognition and his barrel control is unexceptional. Didder doesn't get the bat knocked out of his hand, but he's a below-average hitter with well-below-average power.

THE FUTURE: Didder will likely never hit enough to be a regular, but his speed and defense makes him a potentially useful player for the back spot on the roster.

Year	Club (League)	Class	AVG	G	AB	R	H	2B	3B	HR	RBI	BB	SO	SB	CS	OBP	SLG
2016	Rome (SAL)	LoA	.274	132	478	95	131	15	9	6	35	50	100	37	12	.387	.381
2017	Florida (FSL)	HiA	.230	118	418	51	96	17	5	5	44	44	123	25	13	.331	.330
2018	Florida (FSL)	HiA	.209	76	244	37	51	3	5	3	22	28	77	18	3	.309	.299
	Mississippi (SL)	AA	.275	46	131	17	36	6	2	1	17	16	37	9	2	.373	.374
Minor League Totals			.250	526	1786	287	447	54	34	15	162	204	455	111	44	.357	.344

Baltimore Orioles

BY JON MEOLI

However this past era of Orioles baseball will be described—a return to relevance, or a period of playoff baseball—it will be remembered perhaps most of all for how spectacularly poor its coda was in 2018.

The Orioles lost a club-record 115 games, tied for fourth-most in baseball history, and once they began trading away their expensive stars in July, executive vice president Dan Duquette and the rest of the organization were forced to confront how things got so bad so quickly.

When Duquette traded Manny Machado to the Dodgers in a five-player deal during the all-star break, he said the organization would divert  resources saved in shedding major league payroll to areas the club has neglected in pursuit of a championship: "technology, international scouting, facilities, the draft, strengthening our analytics, investing in more front office staff to be more in line with our competitors (and) expanding our nutrition and wellness resources at every level of the organization."

It's a long and damning list. The Orioles didn't invest significantly in Latin America, a rich talent base that produces some of the impact arms and up-the-middle stars the Orioles lack, because of an ownership directive.

Their pro scouting staff is one of the game's smallest, and though they have improved of late in the draft, especially in terms of stocking the pitching ranks with high-floor talent and some impact mixed in, their pro assessment limitations were laid bare in the July trades, where some pieces were clearly acquired based on statistics.

On the analytics front, the work the club's staff does is limited in impact because of how separated the operation is from the major league club and the player development side.

Though Duquette laid out those intentions and executed phase one of a rebuild while cutting future payroll obligations, neither he nor manager Buck Showalter will be around for the rest of it. The club let them go when their contracts expired at the end of the season.

Baltimore held true to its word when it hired Mike Elias as executive vice president and general manager in mid-November. Elias had served as an assistant GM and scouting director for the Astros as Houston rose from doormats to World Series champions in 2017. Elias brought with him former Astros compatriot Sig Mejdal as assistant GM for analytics.

Managing partner Peter Angelos, 89, has ceded most day-to-day control to his sons, Louis and John, who hold the titles of ownership representa-

Outfielder Cedric Mullins raised his profile with a big 2018 for the rebuilding Orioles.

PROJECTED 2022 LINEUP

Catcher	Chance Sisco (27)
First Base	Trey Mancini (30)
Second Base	Jonathan Villar (31)
Third Base	Renato Nunez (28)
Shortstop	Richie Martin (27)
Left Field	Cedric Mullins (27)
Center Field	Yusniel Diaz (26)
Right Field	Austin Hays (26)
Designated Hitter	Ryan Mountcastle (25)
No. 1 Starter	Dylan Bundy (29)
No. 2 Starter	DL Hall (23)
No. 3 Starter	Keegan Akin (27)
No. 4 Starter	Dean Kremer (26)
No. 5 Starter	Grayson Rodriguez (22)
Closer	Hunter Harvey (27)

tive and executive VP, respectively.

Elias and his front office must bridge some of the vast gaps in the organization's structure. Baltimore has chosen well at the top of recent drafts, including 2017 first-rounder DL Hall and 2016 third-rounder Austin Hays, but a seeming preference for baseball talent over projectable tools limits some upside. The club's issues developing impact starting pitchers are well-documented and must change if the Orioles are to succeed.

There's some talent on the farm, but the new front office will probably be given a blank slate to try to build the organization as it sees fit. It will be a daunting task, but there's nowhere to go but up.

DEPTH CHART

BALTIMORE ORIOLES

TOP 2019 ROOKIE: Branden Kline, RHP. A dynamic arm like Kline with three potential plus pitches has plenty of room to grow into a major league contributor.

BREAKOUT PROSPECT: Jean Carlos Encarnacion, 3B. He has the pop to do serious damage in the small confines of Frederick's Nymeo Field.

SLEEPER: Zach Jarrett, OF. The son of NASCAR legend Dale Jarrett, he improved vastly in his first full season at low Class A Delmarva and could hit his way onto the radar with a repeat performance.

SOURCE OF TOP 30 TALENT			
Homegrown	18	Acquired	12
College	8	Trade	9
Junior college	1	Rule 5 draft	3
High school	8	Independent league	0
Nondrafted free agent	0	Free agent/waivers	0
International	1		

LF
Ryan Mountcastle (4)
John Andreoli
Zach Jarrett
Jacob Brown
Jaylen Ferguson

CF
Yusniel Díaz (1)
Ryan McKenna (8)
T.J. Nichting
Cole Billingsley
Nick Horvath

RF
Austin Hays (3)
DJ Stewart (15)
Robert Neustrom
Jake Ring

3B
Jean Carlos Encarnacion (17)
Drew Dosch
Jomar Reyes

SS
Richie Martin (14)
Adam Hall (18)
Cadyn Grenier (19)
Jean Carmona (26)
Mason McCoy

2B
Rylan Bannon (23)
Drew Jackson (30)
Preston Palmeiro

1B
J.C. Escarra
Seamus Curran

C
Austin Wynns
Martin Cervenka
Brett Cumberland
Cody Roberts

LHP

LHSP	LHRP
DL Hall (2)	Tyler Erwin
Keegan Akin (6)	
Zac Lowther (16)	
Alex Wells (20)	
Drew Rom (25)	
Josh Rogers (28)	
John Means	
Bruce Zimmermann	

RHP

RHSP	RHRP
Grayson Rodriguez (5)	Branden Kline (22)
Hunter Harvey (7)	Zach Pop (24)
Dean Kremer (9)	Pedro Araujo (27)
Blaine Knight (10)	Matthias Dietz (29)
Brenan Hanifee (11)	Cody Carroll
Dillon Tate (12)	Evan Phillips
Luis Ortiz (13)	Ryan Meisinger
Mike Baumann (21)	Jay Flaa
Gray Fenter	

DRAFT ANALYSIS

2018

BEST PURE HITTER: Known for his defensive prowess, SS Cadyn Grenier (1s) had a career year as a junior with Oregon State, hitting .319/.408/.462 with 17 doubles. His pro debut wasn't as encouraging with the bat—he hit .217/.298/.335 in the South Atlantic League—but Grenier started to figure things out towards the end of the season and hit .300/.328/.450 over his last 15 games.

BEST POWER HITTER: OF Robert Neustrom (5) has plus raw power to all fields. He hit 11 home runs with Iowa this spring before heading to the New York-Penn League, where he homered four times in 61 games, with 16 doubles.

FASTEST RUNNER: The Orioles see Grenier as a plus-plus runner and believe that speed will play on the bases, though most amateur scouts hesitated to throw a plus tool on him prior to the draft.

BEST DEFENSIVE PLAYER: No one doubts that Grenier is an immensely capable defender at shortstop, as one of the most consistent and reliable defenders in college last year. He slows the game down well and has an extremely accurate arm, with advanced footwork and reliable hands.

BEST ATHLETE: Grenier's athleticism helps his impressive defensive toolset, with body control that allows him to make difficult plays on the run and throw accurately while off-balance.

BEST FASTBALL: After overhauling his body last winter, RHP Grayson Rodriguez (1) was the pop-up player of the draft and went from a low-90s fastball to a heater that was regularly in the 97-98 mph range, with some scouts citing 99 mph.

BEST SECONDARY PITCH: Rodriguez throws a plus curveball in the 77-80 mph range with standard three-quarter shape and solid depth.

BEST PRO DEBUT: Rodriguez began his career with 12 shutout innings and had a solid 20-7 strikeout-to-walk ratio. LHP Drew Rom (4) posted a 1.76 ERA over 30.2 innings in the Gulf Coast League, struck out 28 batters and walked just six.

TOP DRAFT PICKS OF THE DECADE

Year	Player, Pos.	2018 Org
2009	Matt Hobgood, RHP	Did not play
2010	Manny Machado, SS	Dodgers
2011	Dylan Bundy, RHP	Orioles
2012	Kevin Gausman, RHP	Braves
2013	Hunter Harvey, RHP	Orioles
2014	Brian Gonzalez, LHP (3rd round)	Orioles
2015	D.J. Stewart, OF	Orioles
2016	Cody Sedlock, RHP	Orioles
2017	D.L. Hall, LHP	Orioles
2018	Grayson Rodriguez, RHP	Orioles

MOST INTRIGUING BACKGROUND: The Orioles loved watching the progression of Rodriguez throughout 2018. The Texas righthander went from throwing in the lower 90s during the summer of 2017 with a dumpy body to a completely different arm during the spring.

CLOSEST TO THE MAJORS: RHP Blaine Knight (3) could move through the system quickly given his proclivity for throwing strikes and his track record on the mound in the SEC with Arkansas—where he posted a 3.01 ERA with an 8.74 K/9.

BEST LATE-ROUND PICK: RHP Jake Zebron (18) signed for $125,000 in the 18th round and had a strong debut in the Gulf Coast League, posting a 2.97 ERA over 30.1 innings. He has a solid, 6-foot-3, 180-pound frame with a lean muscular body who was up to as high as 96 mph during the spring with feel to spin a breaking ball as well.

THE ONE WHO GOT AWAY: RHP Caleb Killian (20) has a sinking fastball up to 95 mph and two solid secondaries in a curveball and changeup. The Orioles liked the starter attributes he showed—including improved strike-throwing from his freshman to draft-eligible sophomore season—but he'll head back to Texas Tech for a junior campaign in a more shallow 2019 pitching class.

—CARLOS COLLAZO

2017

LHP D.L. Hall (1) had a strong first full professional season and already is the top pitcher in the system. SS Adam Hall (2) is off to a fine start. LHP Zac Lowther (2s) and RHP Michael Baumann give the class a pair of advanced arms.

GRADE: B

2016

OF Austin Hays (3) shot to the big leagues in his first full pro season but didn't repeat that success in 2018. RHP Cody Sedlock (1) has struggled, but LHP Keegan Akin (2) has been solid and is closing in on the big league rotation.

GRADE: C

2015

OF D.J. Stewart (1) made his big league debut and 3B Ryan Mountcastle (1) will soon reach Baltimore as well, though both have defensive questions. OF Cedric Mullins (13) has emerged as the class' surprise standout.

GRADE: C

1 YUSNIEL DIAZ, OF

Born: Oct. 7, 1996. **B-T:** R-R. **Ht:** 6-1. **Wt:** 195.
Signed: Cuba, 2015. **Signed by:** Ismael Cruz/
Miguel Tosar/Roman Barinas (Dodgers).

An impressive prospect as a teenager in Cuba, Diaz, signed with the Dodgers for $15.5 million after the 2015 season. He began 2018 with Double-A Tulsa, put together a strong first half, and was fresh off a two-homer performance at the Futures Game in July when the Orioles made him the centerpiece of the Manny Machado trade. Diaz overdid it a bit trying to show he was worthy of that distinction at Double-A Bowie, but his low batting average did little to dampen expectations.

SCOUTING REPORT: Diaz has a pretty well-rounded skill set, but the Orioles are working to continue the refinements he was making as a Dodger. He has fast hands and all-fields power, but is working to iron out his lower half. The Orioles observed that his back foot was pointed at the umpire; others saw his front half causing him to pull his hands through to quickly, taking away the opposite-field power that comes naturally to him. His ability to rein his swing in and hit the ball the other way late in counts, plus Diaz's ability to work a walk, indicate a strong approach that should allow him to continue to post high on-base percentages. He's proven capable of making adjustments both with the Dodgers and with the Orioles, and must realize that his bat speed and strength will supply plenty of power as he matures. He doesn't need to rush and get pull-happy to create holes in his swing. Defensively, Diaz showed the Orioles he can handle all three outfield positions, with enough range for center field but an arm that fits in right. His twitchy athleticism allows for plenty of projection to add to his above-average speed, but his career 44.4 percent stolen base rate shows he has work to do to turn his speed into an offensive weapon.

THE FUTURE: In terms of ceiling and present pedigree, Diaz is a peerless talent among position players in the Orioles' system. He's the closest thing to an everyday impact player that the farm system boasts, and even if he doesn't show his entire range of skills immediately upon his arrival to the majors—which could be as soon as early 2019—Diaz is the type of player who will contribute enough to stick and grow into an above-average everyday player. He may push for a roster spot out of spring training, but with several other young outfielders on the roster already, Diaz may have to wait his turn at Triple-A Norfolk.

ROB TRINGALI/MLB PHOTOS VIA GETTY

BA GRADE	SCOUTING GRADES
55 Risk: Medium	Hit: 55. Power: 55. Run: 55. Field: 55. Arm: 60.

Projected future grades on 20-80 scouting scale

TOP PROSPECTS OF THE DECADE

Year	Player, Pos.	2018 Org
2009	Matt Wieters, C	Nationals
2010	Brian Matusz, LHP	Did not play
2011	Manny Machado, SS	Dodgers
2012	Dylan Bundy, RHP	Orioles
2013	Dylan Bundy, RHP	Orioles
2014	Dylan Bundy, RHP	Orioles
2015	Dylan Bundy, RHP	Orioles
2016	Dylan Bundy, RHP	Orioles
2017	Chance Sisco, C	Orioles
2018	Austin Hays, OF	Orioles

BEST TOOLS

Best Hitter for Average	Yusniel Diaz
Best Power Hitter	Austin Hays
Best Strike-Zone Discipline	Ryan McKenna
Fastest Baserunner	Kirvin Moesquit
Best Athlete	Austin Hays
Best Fastball	DL Hall
Best Curveball	DL Hall
Best Slider	Branden Kline
Best Changeup	Alex Wells
Best Control	Zac Lowther
Best Defensive Catcher	Austin Wynns
Best Defensive Infielder	Cadyn Grenier
Best Infield Arm	Jean Carlos Encarnacion
Best Defensive Outfielder	Ryan McKenna
Best Outfield Arm	Austin Hays

Year	Club (League)	Class	AVG	G	AB	R	H	2B	3B	HR	RBI	BB	SO	SB	CS	OBP	SLG
2016	Dodgers (AZL)	R	.143	3	14	2	2	0	0	1	3	0	3	0	0	.143	.357
	R. Cucamonga (CAL)	HiA	.272	82	316	47	86	8	7	8	54	29	71	7	8	.333	.418
2017	R. Cucamonga (CAL)	HiA	.278	83	331	42	92	15	3	8	39	35	73	7	9	.343	.414
	Tulsa (TL)	AA	.333	31	108	15	36	8	0	3	13	10	29	2	5	.390	.491
2018	Tulsa (TL)	AA	.314	59	220	36	69	10	4	6	30	40	39	8	8	.428	.477
	Bowie (EL)	AA	.239	38	134	23	32	5	1	5	15	18	28	4	5	.329	.403
Minor League Totals			.282	296	1123	165	317	46	15	31	154	133	243	28	35	.359	.433

2 DL HALL, LHP

Born: Sept. 19, 1998. **B-T:** L-L. **Ht.:** 6-0. **Wt.:** 180. **Drafted:** HS—Valdosta, Ga., 2017 (1st round). **Signed by:** Arthur McConnehead.

BA GRADE

60 Risk: High

Fastball: 60.
Curveball: 60.
Change: 60. CTL: 55.

TRACK RECORD: A baseball/basketball start in high school, Hall was touted as perhaps the premier prep lefthander in the 2017 draft, and the Orioles were thrilled when he fell to the 21st pick. After bypassing a Florida State commitment for $3 million, he has lived up to expectations so far. After struggling some with his delivery upon his debut in 2017, Hall turned in a full, healthy season in 2018. Over the second half of the season he was arguably the best pitcher in the South Atlantic League. Hall allowed only 32 hits in 53.2 innings while posting a 0.82 ERA in 11 appearances after the all-star break.
SCOUTING REPORT: Hall got better as the season went on for low Class A Delmarva, and held his fastball velocity throughout the season, topping out at 97 mph and sitting 92-95 mph from an effortless, balanced delivery with excellent arm speed. His changeup, which came into the season as a below-average pitch, improved significantly and joins his fastball and breaking ball as future plus pitches. Hall learned to pitch without his best stuff at times in 2018, and his mental development with his natural athleticism bode well for the future. Hall ate up righthanded hitters, holding them to a .180/.292/.276 stat line, which also is a positive indicator for future success as his fastball and changeup kept righthanded hitters from ever getting comfortable.
THE FUTURE: Hall's early success and health put him in position to break the Orioles' developmental struggles when it comes to high school pitchers. He projects as a mid-rotation starter at worst, with the only caveat that he needs to stay healthy. He'll get a chance to do that at high Class A Frederick in 2019.

Year	Club (League)	Class	W	L	ERA	G	GS	CG	SV	IP	H	HR	BB	SO	K/9	WHIP	AVG
2017	Orioles (GCL)	R	0	0	6.97	5	5	0	0	10	10	1	10	12	10.5	1.94	.263
2018	Delmarva (SAL)	LoA	2	7	2.10	22	20	0	0	94	68	6	42	100	9.5	1.17	.203
Minor League Totals			2	7	2.58	27	25	0	0	105	78	7	52	112	9.6	1.24	.209

3 RYAN MOUNTCASTLE, 3B

Born: Feb. 18, 1997. **B-T:** R-R. **Ht.:** 6-3. **Wt.:** 195. **Drafted:** HS—Oviedo, Fla., 2015 (1st round). **Signed by:** Kelvin Colon.
TRACK RECORD: It's fitting that the Orioles' compensatory pick for losing Nelson Cruz to free agency after the 2014 season resulted in another pure hitter. Mountcastle won the Carolina League batting title in 2017, and showed few ill effects from a fractured wrist once he settled in at Double-A Bowie.
SCOUTING REPORT: Mountcastle's fluid hands and developed frame make him a hitter with power, not the other way around. Both can be plus skills going forward, and he'll need every bit of his bat to boost a defensive profile that's below-average anywhere on the diamond. Mountcastle has made a specific effort to get himself into counts where he can drive the ball, and so far it's paid off. A shortstop when he signed, Mountcastle slid over to third base in 2017. Even with improvement there in 2018, Mountcastle remains well below-average there and projects to left field or first base. Mountcastle's biggest hurdle to a defensive home is his well below-average arm. Scouts don't believe he can handle any position in the dirt that requires him to throw regularly. Left field or first base is his most likely long-term home, but even left field will be a stretch because of his arm.

BA GRADE

55 Risk: High

Hit: 55. Power: 55.
Run: 50. Field: 30.
Arm: 30.

THE FUTURE: Mountcastle's bat will make him an everyday big leaguer, but his value will be tied to where he plays. The farther down the defensive spectrum he goes—and scouts believe his arm would be a liability even in left field—the more pressure he'll have on the bat. He can hit his way into the major league conversation in 2019 from Triple-A Norfolk.

Year	Club (League)	Class	AVG	G	AB	R	H	2B	3B	HR	RBI	BB	SO	SB	CS	OBP	SLG
2016	Delmarva (SAL)	LoA	.281	115	455	53	128	28	4	10	51	25	95	5	4	.319	.426
2017	Frederick (CAR)	HiA	.314	88	360	63	113	35	1	15	47	14	61	8	2	.343	.542
	Bowie (EL)	AA	.222	39	153	18	34	13	0	3	15	3	35	0	0	.239	.366
2018	Bowie (EL)	AA	.297	102	394	63	117	19	4	13	59	26	79	2	0	.341	.464
Minor League Totals			.289	397	1558	220	450	102	9	45	191	77	316	25	11	.323	.453

4 AUSTIN HAYS, OF

Born: July 5, 1995. **B-T:** R-R. **Ht.:** 6-1. **Wt.:** 195. **Drafted:** Jacksonville, 2016 (3rd round). **Signed by:** Arthur McConnehead.

TRACK RECORD: Hays became the first member of the 2016 draft class to make the majors in 2017, establishing himself as the Orioles' top prospect in the process. But his candidacy to win the starting right field job never took off in 2018 after spring shoulder soreness. He scuffled upon his return to Double-A Bowie and missed two months with a stress fracture in his ankle. He bounced back with a decent August (.267/.287/.500) but had ankle surgery in September.

SCOUTING REPORT: Hays got away from his all-fields approach, appearing to sell out for pull power and get through the zone too quickly. His naturally quick hands and solid approach allow him to catch up to heat and recognize spin, but he only did that in August when he closed off his stance, and even then, his over-aggressive approach meant that he rarely got on base other than when he cracked an extra-base hit. When his above-average power is a symptom of his fluid, adaptable swing instead of the end goal, Hays has an above-average hit tool, although his on-base percentage is largely tied to his batting average. His plus arm projects best in right, but he can also play center.

THE FUTURE: Hays hit the reset button once he returned in August and showed his immense talent and everyday outfield ceiling was still in there. He'll get another crack at the Opening Day roster in what's expect to be a crowded outfield.

BA GRADE

55 Risk: High

Hit: 55. Power: 55.
Run: 50. Field: 55.
Arm: 60.

Year	Club (League)	Class	AVG	G	AB	R	H	2B	3B	HR	RBI	BB	SO	SB	CS	OBP	SLG
2016	Aberdeen (NYP)	SS	.336	38	140	14	47	9	2	4	21	11	32	4	3	.386	.514
2017	Frederick (CAR)	HiA	.324	64	262	42	85	15	3	16	41	12	40	4	6	.361	.588
	Bowie (EL)	AA	.330	64	261	39	86	17	2	16	54	13	45	1	1	.367	.594
	Baltimore (AL)	MAJ	.217	20	60	4	13	3	0	1	8	2	16	0	0	.238	.317
2018	Aberdeen (NYP)	SS	.189	9	37	6	7	2	0	0	3	2	7	0	0	.231	.243
	Bowie (EL)	AA	.242	66	273	34	66	12	2	12	43	12	59	6	3	.271	.432
Major League Totals			.217	20	60	4	13	3	0	1	8	2	16	0	0	.238	.317
Minor League Totals			.299	241	973	135	291	55	9	48	162	50	183	15	13	.336	.522

5 GRAYSON RODRIGUEZ, RHP

Born: Nov. 16, 1999. **B-T:** L-R. **Ht.:** 6-5. **Wt.:** 220. **Drafted:** HS—Nacogdoches, Texas, 2018 (1st round). **Signed by:** Thom Dreier.

TRACK RECORD: Rodriguez pitched his way into the first round of the 2018 draft after transforming his body by adding 20 pounds of muscle and reworking his delivery to use his strapping frame last winter. That made him the biggest pop-up name in the draft, and led the Orioles to sign him to a $4.3 million bonus. Rodriguez didn't allow a run until his seventh outing in the Rookie-level Gulf Coast League in outings that were limited to three innings or less.

SCOUTING REPORT: Though his fastball was up to 97 mph as an amateur, Rodriguez generally worked at 91-94 mph as a pro with good angle and life down in the zone. It's not uncommon for prep pitchers to see their velocity back up a little while they adjust to pitching on a five-day schedule, and Rodriguez has the strength to gain back some of that velo. His slider, which sits in the low 80s with tilt, is the newest of his secondary pitches, though his two-plane, mid-70s curveball might fit better from his high arm slot. His fringy changeup wasn't necessary in high school, but is developing. He's able to get down the mound well with a big frame and repeatable delivery, allowing him to locate down in the zone.

THE FUTURE: Rodriguez has all the makings of a physical workhorse starter who can slot into a rotation and provide quality innings with a ceiling as high as a No. 3 starter. The Orioles have made a big investment in developing both reliable back-end starters among college draftees to blend with higher-ceiling high school pitchers. Rodriguez and Hall are vital cogs to that approach. Rodriguez could get his first taste of full-season ball at low Class A Delmarva to begin 2019.

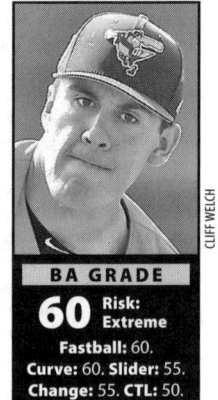

CLIFF WELCH

BA GRADE

60 Risk: Extreme

Fastball: 60.
Curve: 60. Slider: 55.
Change: 55. CTL: 50.

Year	Club (League)	Class	W	L	ERA	G	GS	CG	SV	IP	H	HR	BB	SO	K/9	WHIP	AVG
2018	Orioles (GCL)	R	0	2	1.40	9	8	0	0	19	17	0	7	20	9.3	1.24	.236
Minor League Totals			0	2	1.40	9	8	0	0	19	17	0	7	20	9.3	1.24	.236

6 KEEGAN AKIN, LHP

Born: April 1, 1995. **B-T:** L-L. **Ht.:** 6-0. **Wt.:** 225. **Drafted:** Western Michigan, 2016 (2nd round). **Signed by:** Dan Durst.

TRACK RECORD: Akin is the most advanced arm to develop from the Orioles' increased focus on college pitching that began in the 2016 draft. He battled conditioning and mechanical issues in 2017, but had no such troubles in 2018 as he won the organization's minor league pitcher of the year award.

SCOUTING REPORT: In 2017, Akin battled an oblique injury and a dip in his velocity. He saw his fastball velocity creep back up a bit in 2018. He touched 95 mph and held 91-94 deep into outings at Double-A Bowie while keeping the deception that makes the pitch effective. Hitters have trouble picking up his above-average fastball out of his hand and have to honor the fact that Akin is fearless throwing it to either side of the plate. The same goes for his plus low-80s slider, which he throws to both left- and righthanded hitters, as well as his average low-80s changeup.

THE FUTURE: The Orioles mulled adding Akin to the major league roster at times in 2018, because his consistent success won over some doubters in the organization. But with so many other players to add to the roster, Akin's arrival was put off until 2019, when he'll likely be a candidate for the rotation in spring training. Even if he doesn't make the Opening Day roster, he will likely pitch in Baltimore in 2019.

BA GRADE
50 Risk: Medium
Fastball: 55.
Slider: 60.
Change: 50. CTL: 55.

Year	Club (League)	Class	W	L	ERA	G	GS	CG	SV	IP	H	HR	BB	SO	K/9	WHIP	AVG
2016	Aberdeen (NYP)	SS	0	1	1.04	9	9	0	0	26	15	0	7	29	10.0	0.85	.161
2017	Frederick (CAR)	HiA	7	8	4.14	21	21	0	0	100	89	12	46	111	10.0	1.35	.240
2018	Bowie (EL)	AA	14	7	3.27	25	25	0	0	138	114	16	58	142	9.3	1.25	.225
Minor League Totals			21	16	3.38	55	55	0	0	264	218	28	111	282	9.6	1.25	.225

7 HUNTER HARVEY, RHP

Born: Dec. 9, 1994. **B-T:** R-R. **Ht.:** 6-3. **Wt.:** 175. **Drafted:** HS—Catawba, N.C., 2013 (1st round). **Signed by:** Chris Gale.

TRACK RECORD: Harvey quickly established himself as one of the Orioles' most talented pitchers, but in six pro seasons, his career has been totally derailed by injuries. It includes elbow soreness in 2014, a fractured leg in 2015 and groin surgery in 2016 before Tommy John surgery later that summer. From 2015 to 2017, he threw a total of 32.2 innings over three seasons. Despite that, the Orioles added Harvey to their 40-man roster before the 2018 season. He impressed in spring training, leading the Orioles to consider adding him to the big league roster. But after nine starts for Double-A Bowie he went back to the disabled list again with a shoulder injury. Harvey has spent time on the disabled list in five of his six pro seasons.

SCOUTING REPORT: Harvey's stuff has never been an issue, but it won't matter if he can't pitch. Coming from a crossfire delivery that could be problematic for his command at the highest level, Harvey' plus fastball sits 92-95

BA GRADE
55 Risk: Extreme
Fastball: 70.
Curveball: 60.
Change: 50. CTL: 50.

mph and has reached 97 with run and angle, and his two-plane curveball still impresses. His changeup is still a developing pitch, and he added a cutter in 2018, though not in games. There's some effort in Harvey's delivery, and while his frame has filled out, it hasn't shown in an improved ability to be able to handle a workload.

THE FUTURE: The Orioles constantly point to another injury-beset top pick—Dylan Bundy—in not discounting Harvey's promise to be a No. 3 starter. It's a big ask for a pitcher who has never thrown 100 innings in a pro season to ramp up to such a heavier workload. If he can't hold up, he has an electric high-leverage relief arsenal.

Year	Club (League)	Class	W	L	ERA	G	GS	CG	SV	IP	H	HR	BB	SO	K/9	WHIP	AVG
2016	Orioles (GCL)	R	0	0	0.00	2	2	0	0	5	3	0	0	11	19.8	0.60	.167
	Aberdeen (NYP)	SS	0	1	3.52	3	3	0	0	8	9	0	6	7	8.2	1.96	.310
2017	Orioles (GCL)	R	0	0	0.00	3	3	0	0	5	6	0	0	6	10.8	1.20	.300
	Aberdeen (NYP)	SS	0	0	0.00	2	2	0	0	5	1	0	3	10	18.0	0.80	.063
	Delmarva (SAL)	LoA	0	1	2.08	3	3	0	0	9	4	0	3	14	14.5	0.81	.133
2018	Bowie (EL)	AA	1	2	5.57	9	9	0	0	32	36	3	9	30	8.4	1.39	.290
Minor League Totals			8	10	3.11	47	47	0	0	177	146	8	60	217	11.1	1.17	.226

8 RYAN McKENNA, OF

Born: Feb. 14, 1997. **B-T:** R-R. **Ht.:** 5-11. **Wt.:** 185. **Drafted:** HS—Dover, N.H.,
2015 (4th round). **Signed by:** Kirk Fredriksson.

TRACK RECORD: The top prep player in New England in his draft year was
snatched away from the hometown Red Sox when the Orioles drafted him
and signed him away from a Liberty commitment. McKenna exploded with
28 extra-base hits in 67 games in 2018 at high Class A Frederick, earning a
Carolina League all-star nod before struggling after a promotion to Double-A
Bowie.

SCOUTING REPORT: McKenna refined his approach to be on time for the
fastball and adjust to breaking balls, helping his bat speed and barrel control
play up into what projects as an average hit tool with fringe pop, but plenty
of gap power for extra-base hits. Conversely, his ability to bunt for base hits
was lauded as he dealt with his late-season slump, and he still was able to work
a walk even when it wasn't going well. His above-average speed plays up and
makes him the best bet in the Orioles' minor league system to stick in center
field, where he projects as an average defender with an average arm.

BA GRADE

50 Risk:
High

Hit: 50. Power: 45.
Run: 55. Field: 50.
Arm: 50.

THE FUTURE: McKenna is the type of player for whom the sum may exceed the parts. He improved to
the point that an everyday major league role is possible. His ability to play all three outfield positions gives
him a path to being a fourth outfielder as well, but he'll need to prove he can hit at the higher levels of
the minors. A return to Double-A Bowie is the first step on that path to Baltimore.

Year	Club (League)	Class	AVG	G	AB	R	H	2B	3B	HR	RBI	BB	SO	SB	CS	OBP	SLG
2016	Aberdeen (NYP)	SS	.241	62	220	29	53	10	1	1	26	22	59	17	6	.320	.309
2017	Delmarva (SAL)	LoA	.256	126	468	62	120	33	2	7	42	43	128	20	2	.331	.380
2018	Frederick (CAR)	HiA	.377	67	257	60	97	18	2	8	37	37	45	5	6	.467	.556
	Bowie (EL)	AA	.239	60	213	35	51	8	2	3	16	29	56	4	1	.341	.338
Minor League Totals			.277	325	1192	191	330	69	8	19	124	137	294	47	16	.362	.396

9 DEAN KREMER, RHP

Born: Jan. 7, 1996. **B-T:** R-R. **Ht.:** 6-3. **Wt.:** 180. **Drafted:** Nevada-Las Vegas,
2016 (14th round). **Signed by:** Brian Compton (Dodgers).

TRACK RECORD: A late-bloomer who wasn't drafted out of high school,
Kremer has progressed tremendously since the Dodgers made him the first
Israeli citizen selected by a major league club (Kremer was born in California
to Israeli parents and holds Israeli citizenship). Kremer struggled as a swingman in 2017, but adjusted his repertoire with the Dodgers analytics staff's
help to emphasize his curveball. Acquired in the Manny Machado trade, he
led the minors with 178 strikeouts in 2018.

SCOUTING REPORT: Kremer's ability to miss bats comes through a well-
balanced four-pitch mix, highlighted by a 91-94 mph fastball that touches 95.
His biting 74-76 mph curveball both misses bats and gets weak contact, and
he uses it in all situations, while his slider still could develop into a putaway
pitch and his changeup is coming along. He has an advanced feel for pitching and sequencing and has distinguished himself already in the system by

BA GRADE

50 Risk:
High

Fastball: 60.
Curve: 60. Slider: 55.
Change: 45. CTL: 50.

showing an aptitude for learning and an ability to process and carry out plans to refine his arsenal and
approach.

THE FUTURE: Kremer might not have more than a No. 4 starter ceiling. But he's had success in the upper
level of the minors and has a clear path to a big league job in the not-to-distant future for a team that will
be in dire need of young, durable starting pitchers. Kremer could push to Triple-A Norfolk in his first
full year in the Orioles system.

Year	Club (League)	Class	W	L	ERA	G	GS	CG	SV	IP	H	HR	BB	SO	K/9	WHIP	AVG
2016	Ogden (PIO)	R	0	1	3.86	6	6	0	0	16	15	0	3	13	7.2	1.10	.250
	Great Lakes (MWL)	LoA	2	0	0.59	6	0	0	0	15	4	0	4	22	12.9	0.52	.083
2017	R. Cucamonga (CAL)	HiA	1	4	5.18	33	6	0	3	80	86	6	34	96	10.8	1.50	.274
2018	R. Cucamonga (CAL)	HiA	5	3	3.30	16	16	0	0	79	67	7	26	114	13.0	1.18	.230
	Tulsa (TL)	AA	1	0	0.00	1	1	1	0	7	3	0	3	11	14.1	0.86	.130
	Bowie (EL)	AA	4	2	2.58	8	8	0	0	45	38	3	17	53	10.5	1.21	.228
Minor League Totals			13	10	3.56	70	37	1	3	243	213	16	87	309	11.4	1.23	.236

10 BLAINE KNIGHT, RHP

Born: June 28, 1996. **B-T:** R-R. **Ht.:** 6-3. **Wt.:** 165. **Drafted:** Arkansas, 2018 (3rd round). **Signed by:** Ken Guthrie.

TRACK RECORD: Once Knight was done with an All-American junior year that included beating every top pitcher and going undefeated in the Southeastern Conference, then pitching Arkansas to the finals of the College World Series, the Orioles signed him to an above-slot $1.1 million bonus as a third-round pick. They gave him a break before sending him to short-season Aberdeen, where he essentially continued working as a Friday starter on a pitch count before he went back to finish his degree.

SCOUTING REPORT: Knight worked 91-95 mph at Aberdeen after a long college season, showing an elite spin rate on both an 82-84 mph slider and his slower curveball, plus a potential above-average changeup. What stood out to the Orioles in their brief look was his aptitude for mixing his pitches and the purpose with which he threw each pitch. Knight's lean frame shows some projection, as does his athleticism and his loose arm action.

THE FUTURE: Such a feel for pitching and the weapons Knight has means there won't be much resistance on his path to a No. 3 starter ceiling in the low minors, though his heavy workload at Arkansas and his slight build will naturally cause durability concerns.

BA GRADE
50 Risk: High
Fastball: 60.
Curve: 55. SL: 55.
Change: 55. CTL: 50.

Year	Club (League)	Class	W	L	ERA	G	GS	CG	SV	IP	H	HR	BB	SO	K/9	WHIP	AVG
2018	Aberdeen (NYP)	SS	0	1	2.61	4	4	0	0	10	13	1	3	8	7.0	1.55	.302
Minor League Totals			0	1	2.61	4	4	0	0	10	13	1	3	8	7.0	1.55	.302

11 BRENAN HANIFEE, RHP

BA GRADE
50 Risk: High

Born: May 29, 1998. **B-T:** R-R. **Ht.:** 6-5. **Wt.:** 180. **Drafted:** HS— Bridgewater, Va., 2016 (4th round). **Signed by:** Rich Morales.

TRACK RECORD: Hanifee signed for an above-slot $500,000 after jumping onto the 2016 draft radar, but he didn't debut until 2017 at short-season Aberdeen. His 2018 at low Class A Delmarva was a master class in efficiency, with Hanifee presenting himself as a throwback starter who pitched to contact and worked deep into games. He gave the Shorebirds 11 quality starts in 16 outings before workload restrictions.

SCOUTING REPORT: Hanifee was a favorite of scouts during in 2018, with one remarking that he pitches like he's 35 years old. His 91-94 mph fastball has tremendous sink and helped him to an above-average groundball rate, though he can command it well and change eye levels with it as well. He throws his slider for strikes with plus potential, and his changeup can get to average or a tick above. Everything plays up because it's down in the zone.

THE FUTURE: Hanifee reaching his No. 4 stater potential will hinge on his secondary pitches and continued ability to locate. His athleticism and advanced approach make that more likely than a typical high school draftee. He'll try to continue his progress at high Class A Frederick in 2019.

Year	Club (League)	Class	W	L	ERA	G	GS	CG	SV	IP	H	HR	BB	SO	K/9	WHIP	AVG
2017	Aberdeen (NYP)	SS	7	3	2.75	12	12	0	0	69	65	2	12	44	5.8	1.12	.249
2018	Delmarva (SAL)	LoA	8	6	2.86	23	23	1	0	132	120	8	22	85	5.8	1.08	.244
Minor League Totals			15	9	2.83	35	35	1	0	201	185	10	34	129	5.8	1.09	.246

12 DILLON TATE, RHP

BA GRADE
50 Risk: High

Born: May 1, 1994. **B-T:** R-R. **Ht.:** 6-2. **Wt.:** 195. **Drafted:** UC Santa Barbara, 2015 (1st round). **Signed by:** Todd Guggiana (Rangers).

TRACK RECORD: Tate was a breakout star for UC Santa Barbara and the top college pitcher in the 2015 draft class. He went fourth overall to the Rangers and signed for $4.2 million before being dealt to the Yankees for Carlos Beltran. He made strides with New York and was an Eastern League all-star at Double-A Trenton when he became the top piece in the Zach Britton trade at the 2018 deadline.

SCOUTING REPORT: Tate works from a deliberate but athletic delivery, and he saw recent improvement by coming more set with his hands and allowing himself to stay tall over the rubber longer. His fastball has sinking life at 92-94 mph when he gets through it, but it flattens out at times. Likewise, his mid-80s slider and changeup have plus potential on their best days, but Tate struggles to harness them consistently.

THE FUTURE: The Orioles added Tate to the 40-man roster after the year to protect him from the Rule 5 draft. He could reach a No. 4 starter ceiling with repetitions and consistent innings, but an impact set-up man in short stints is most likely.

Year	Club (League)	Class	W	L	ERA	G	GS	CG	SV	IP	H	HR	BB	SO	K/9	WHIP	AVG
2016	Hickory (SAL)	LoA	3	3	5.12	17	16	0	0	65	78	5	27	55	7.6	1.62	.311
	Charleston, SC (SAL)	LoA	1	0	3.12	7	0	0	0	17	21	1	6	15	7.8	1.56	.292
2017	Tampa (FSL)	HiA	6	0	2.62	9	9	0	0	58	48	4	15	46	7.1	1.08	.221
	Trenton (EL)	AA	1	2	3.24	4	4	1	0	25	23	3	9	17	6.1	1.28	.253
2018	Trenton (EL)	AA	5	2	3.38	15	15	0	0	83	67	7	25	75	8.2	1.11	.218
	Bowie (EL)	AA	2	3	5.75	7	7	0	0	41	48	3	9	21	4.6	1.40	.302
Minor League Totals			18	10	3.84	65	57	1	0	298	288	24	94	237	7.2	1.28	.256

13   LUIS ORTIZ, RHP

BA GRADE

50 Risk: High

Born: Sept. 22, 1995. **B-T:** R-R. **Ht.:** 6-3. **Wt.:** 230. **Drafted:** HS—Sanger, Calif., 2014 (1st round). **Signed by:** Butch Metzger (Rangers).

TRACK RECORD: Ortiz presented an intriguing amateur skill set but fell to the 30th overall pick in 2014 because of arm tightness, signing for $1.75 million. Undeniable talent and health questions followed him from the Rangers to the Brewers then to the Orioles in the 2018 trade-deadline deal for Jonathan Schoop. Durability issues and conditioning are holding him back. A hamstring injury covering first base ended his first major league start in September, and thereby his season.

SCOUTING REPORT: Ortiz's upside mostly resides in his arm strength, with a plus fastball up to 96 mph in shorter stints and a potentially above-average slider when he stays behind it. He also shows feel for a changeup, but Ortiz didn't show the ability to repeat his delivery or command his pitches at the major league level. He is listed at 230 pounds but is significantly heavier, with a plump physique that has produced questions as to whether he'd be able to stay healthy or control his delivery.

THE FUTURE: Ortiz has previously been touted as a starter with No. 3 potential, but it's more a back-end rotation ceiling with a higher likelihood to end up in the bullpen after what he showed in 2018.

Year	Club (League)	Class	W	L	ERA	G	GS	CG	SV	IP	H	HR	BB	SO	K/9	WHIP	AVG
2016	High Desert (CAL)	HiA	3	2	2.60	7	6	0	0	28	23	4	6	28	9.1	1.05	.221
	Frisco (TL)	AA	1	4	4.08	9	8	0	1	40	47	3	7	34	7.7	1.36	.296
	Biloxi (SL)	AA	2	2	1.93	6	6	0	0	23	26	2	10	16	6.2	1.54	.280
2017	Biloxi (SL)	AA	4	7	4.01	22	20	1	0	94	79	12	37	79	7.5	1.23	.227
2018	Biloxi (SL)	AA	3	4	3.71	16	11	0	2	68	63	7	18	65	8.6	1.19	.240
	Norfolk (IL)	AAA	2	1	3.69	6	6	0	0	32	34	4	8	21	6.0	1.33	.274
	Baltimore (AL)	MAJ	0	1	15.43	2	1	0	0	2	7	0	3	0	0.0	4.29	.500
Major League Totals			0	1	15.43	2	1	0	0	2	7	0	3	0	0.0	4.29	.500
Minor League Totals			20	22	3.25	88	76	1	4	355	333	34	101	308	7.8	1.22	.246

14   RICHIE MARTIN, SS/2B

BA GRADE

45 Risk: Medium

Born: Dec. 22, 1994. **B-T:** R-R. **Ht.:** 5-11. **Wt.:** 190. **Drafted:** Florida, 2015 (1st round). **Signed by:** Trevor Schaffer (Athletics).

TRACK RECORD: A well-regarded college shortstop at Florida, Martin came as advertised defensively in pro ball, yet he had failed to produce offensively in his first three seasons in the Athletics' system. That changed at Double-A Midland in 2018, when Martin hit .300 to rank third in the Texas League batting race. He also established career highs for home runs (six), doubles (29), stolen bases (25) and walks (44). The Orioles selected him with the first pick in the 2018 Rule 5 draft.

SCOUTING REPORT: After years of tinkering with his swing, Martin found a setup that worked for him and he stuck with it. He also updated his contact lens prescription in the offseason. The timing of Martin's breakout season was unusual because he missed spring training while recovering from meniscus surgery on his right knee, and then he missed time in April with a lower back strain. He certainly didn't seem restricted at the plate or in the field. Martin tends to chase breaking pitches too often, and his batting average figures to come down in future seasons when the hits don't fall as frequently, but even as a fringe hitter with below-average power he could help a team. That's because he is a lockdown shortstop with plus range, plus speed and a plus arm. His fundamentals are strong and he converts nearly all routine plays.

THE FUTURE: Martin's energetic style endears him with teammates and his work ethic should carry him to a big league role as a probable second-division shortstop or utility infielder. Given Baltimore's shallow middle infield depth, he seems like a good bet to stick with the major league club.

Year	Club (League)	Class	AVG	G	AB	R	H	2B	3B	HR	RBI	BB	SO	SB	CS	OBP	SLG
2016	Stockton (CAL)	HiA	.230	86	330	46	76	14	2	3	31	36	73	12	8	.322	.312
	Midland (TL)	AA	.333	5	15	1	5	1	1	0	7	3	2	2	1	.444	.533
2017	Midland (TL)	AA	.226	86	287	43	65	11	3	4	29	23	57	12	3	.306	.328
	Stockton (CAL)	HiA	.266	23	94	16	25	2	3	1	6	8	21	1	1	.330	.383
2018	Midland (TL)	AA	.300	118	453	68	136	29	8	6	42	44	86	25	10	.368	.439
Minor League Totals			.257	369	1369	205	352	63	21	16	131	139	286	59	30	.340	.369

15 DJ STEWART, OF

Born: Nov. 30, 1993. **B-T:** L-R. **Ht.:** 6-0. **Wt.:** 230. **Drafted:** Florida State, 2015 (1st round). **Signed by:** Arthur McConnehead.

BA GRADE 45 Risk: Medium

TRACK RECORD: Stewart's potential to develop into a lefthanded-hitting power bat, plus his background as the 2014 Atlantic Coast Conference player of the year, made him attractive to the Orioles with their top pick in 2015 and earned him a $2.06 million bonus. He finally showed why with a 20 homer-20 steal season at Double-A Bowie in 2017 before a hamstring injury knocked him off track in 2018. He made his major league debut in September anyway.

SCOUTING REPORT: Stewart's total package may be one of a big leaguer, even if the parts don't seem it. His swing, while improved of late, can be one-plane still, sapping some of the utility of his above-average power and leaving potential holes going forward. He makes strong contact when he gets the barrel to the ball. He runs well underway and plays a capable corner outfield, though neither tool is more than average.

THE FUTURE: Stewart faces an ideal situation in Baltimore to break in and try and realize his fringe everyday potential. He could very well thrive in a platoon role or as a bench bat.

Year	Club (League)	Class	AVG	G	AB	R	H	2B	3B	HR	RBI	BB	SO	SB	CS	OBP	SLG
2016	Delmarva (SAL)	LoA	.230	62	213	27	49	12	1	4	25	42	58	16	6	.366	.352
	Frederick (CAR)	HiA	.279	59	201	41	56	12	2	6	30	36	46	10	3	.389	.448
2017	Bowie (EL)	AA	.278	126	457	80	127	26	2	21	79	65	87	20	4	.378	.481
2018	Norfolk (IL)	AAA	.235	116	421	59	99	24	2	12	55	54	103	11	4	.329	.387
	Baltimore (AL)	MAJ	.250	17	40	8	10	3	0	3	10	4	12	2	1	.340	.550
Major League Totals			.250	17	40	8	10	3	0	3	10	4	12	2	1	.340	.550
Minor League Totals			.250	425	1530	232	383	82	9	49	213	220	346	61	18	.351	.412

16 ZAC LOWTHER, LHP

Born: April 30, 1996. **B-T:** L-L. **Ht.:** 6-2. **Wt.:** 235. **Drafted:** Xavier, 2017 (2nd round supplemental). **Signed by:** Adrian Dorsey.

BA GRADE 45 Risk: High

TRACK RECORD: Lowther struck out a school-record 123 batters as a junior at Xavier, and after signing for slot ($779,500) in 2017, he continued to baffle hitters in the low minors in 2018. He was drafted in part because he had elite extension in his delivery, and the deception continued at two Class A levels in 2018, when he struck out 11 batters per nine innings to lead all Orioles minor league starters.

SCOUTING REPORT: Lowther throws from a low three-quarters delivery with quick, whippy arm action. He has fringe-average fastball velocity at 88-92 mph, but hitters simply can't see it, and he locates the pitch well in the zone. His delivery helps his low-80s changeup and slurvy breaking ball play up, with each pitch showing average potential, though his whole arsenal dips as he gets deep into games.

THE FUTURE: Lowther's ability to sustain his above-average command and keep hitters off his fastball will be his separator once he hits the high minors. Lowther has shown he can make adjustments at new levels quickly and will get that chance at Double-A Bowie in 2019.

Year	Club (League)	Class	W	L	ERA	G	GS	CG	SV	IP	H	HR	BB	SO	K/9	WHIP	AVG
2017	Aberdeen (NYP)	SS	2	2	1.66	12	11	0	0	54	35	1	11	75	12.4	0.85	.182
2018	Delmarva (SAL)	LoA	3	1	1.16	6	6	0	0	31	12	2	9	51	14.8	0.68	.115
	Frederick (CAR)	HiA	5	3	2.53	17	16	0	0	93	74	6	26	100	9.7	1.08	.220
Minor League Totals			10	6	2.02	35	33	0	0	178	121	9	46	226	11.4	0.94	.191

17 JEAN CARLOS ENCARNACION, 3B

Born: Jan. 17, 1998. **B-T:** R-R. **Ht.:** 6-3. **Wt.:** 195. **Signed:** Dominican Republic, 2016. **Signed by:** Jonathan Cruz (Braves).

BA GRADE 50 Risk: Extreme

TRACK RECORD: As the Orioles get back into the international market, Encarnacion is an example of the talents they can find there. Signed for $10,000 by the Braves and acquired in the July 2018 trade for Kevin Gausman and Darren O'Day, Encarnacion has hit at every level since making his U.S. debut in 2017. He earned postseason South Atlantic League all-star honors for his efforts between low Class A Rome and Delmarva in 2018.

SCOUTING REPORT: A strapping athlete with good bat speed and leverage in his righthanded swing, Encarnacion shows potential for at least an average hit tool and plus power, with a loose swing and average bat control. His approach, however, is extremely aggressive and will need to be refined significantly to allow him to reach his ceiling. He shows a plus arm at third base and is presently average there, though he could also play a corner outfield spot.

THE FUTURE: Encarnacion is the type of potential impact everyday bat that the Orioles' international philosophy has made scarce in their system. He likely will go to high Class A Frederick in 2019 with an eye on shoring up his approach.

Year	Club (League)	Class	AVG	G	AB	R	H	2B	3B	HR	RBI	BB	SO	SB	CS	OBP	SLG
2016	Braves (DSL)	R	.264	37	140	19	37	3	3	0	16	11	30	4	0	.340	.329
2017	Braves (GCL)	R	.350	27	103	16	36	8	4	2	16	4	22	4	2	.374	.563
	Danville (APP)	R	.290	23	93	14	27	3	0	1	6	3	21	3	5	.316	.355
2018	Rome (SAL)	LoA	.288	97	361	45	104	23	5	10	57	13	100	5	5	.314	.463
	Delmarva (SAL)	LoA	.218	26	101	10	22	4	2	2	7	3	34	0	0	.240	.356
Minor League Totals			.283	210	798	104	226	41	14	15	102	34	207	16	12	.318	.426

18 ADAM HALL, SS

BA GRADE
50 Risk: Extreme

Born: May 22, 1999. **B-T:** R-R. **Ht.:** 6-0. **Wt.:** 170. **Drafted:** HS—London, Ont., 2017 (2nd round). **Signed by:** Chris Reitsma.

TRACK RECORD: Hall put himself on the map with the Canadian junior national team in games and showcases, showing enough to earn an above-slot $1.3 million bonus as a 2017 second-round pick. An oblique injury limited him to two games in the Rookie-level Gulf Coast League season in his pro debut, and things came slowly for him at short-season Aberdeen in 2018 before a 19-game hitting streak in August won him New York-Penn League player of the month honors.

SCOUTING REPORT: Hall came into the system as a below-average fielder and thrower but built those tools up to the point where they project as above-average. His approach improved as he stopped trying to hit for power and let his quick bat do the work, and with the defensive profile, an average hit tool would be plenty even with below-average power. He's already one of the best baserunners in the system.

THE FUTURE: Hall has developed quicker than the Orioles thought and should make his full-season debut at age 19 in 2019 at low Class A Delmarva. Continued progress defensively will lessen the pressure on his bat and help him to an average everyday ceiling at a middle infield position.

Year	Club (League)	Class	AVG	G	AB	R	H	2B	3B	HR	RBI	BB	SO	SB	CS	OBP	SLG
2017	Orioles (GCL)	R	.667	2	9	4	6	1	1	0	2	0	2	1	0	.667	1.000
2018	Aberdeen (NYP)	SS	.293	62	222	35	65	9	3	1	24	17	58	22	5	.368	.374
Minor League Totals			.307	64	231	39	71	10	4	1	26	17	60	23	5	.378	.398

19 CADYN GRENIER, SS

BA GRADE
45 Risk: High

Born: Oct. 31, 1996. **B-T:** R-R. **Ht.:** 5-11. **Wt.:** 188. **Drafted:** Oregon State, 2018 (1st round supplemental). **Signed by:** Brandon Verley.

TRACK RECORD: Grenier passed up a chance to sign with the Cardinals as a 21st-rounder in 2015 to go to Oregon State, where the Beavers won the College World Series and Grenier won the Brooks Wallace Award as the nation's top shortstop in 2018. He signed for $1.8 million as the 37th overall pick and went straight to low Class A Delmarva.

SCOUTING REPORT: With the Shorebirds, Grenier showed much of the profile he carried out of the draft. He's a plus defender with plus range and above-average hands who can make all the throws at shortstop, but his major league value will hinge on his bat. The Orioles already began calming down his swing to get him to the best version of it more often, but the hope that it can be an average hit tool doesn't have the brightest outlook after he hit .216/.297/.333 in his pro debut.

THE FUTURE: Grenier's defense will carry him quickly through the system, regardless of his bat, even if it's a long way where he is now and a second-division, glove-first regular role. He may bump up to high Class A Frederick for 2019.

Year	Club (League)	Class	AVG	G	AB	R	H	2B	3B	HR	RBI	BB	SO	SB	CS	OBP	SLG
2018	Delmarva (SAL)	LoA	.216	43	162	23	35	12	2	1	13	17	53	3	2	.297	.333
Minor League Totals			.216	43	162	23	35	12	2	1	13	17	53	3	2	.297	.333

20 ALEX WELLS, LHP

BA GRADE
40 Risk: Medium

Born: Feb. 27, 1997 **B-T:** L-L. **Ht.:** 6-1. **Wt.:** 190. **Signed:** Australia, 2015. **Signed by:** Brett Ward/Mike Snyder.

TRACK RECORD: An Australian who signed for $300,000 in 2015, Wells has succeeded at every level since his pro debut in 2016. He won the Jim Palmer minor league pitcher of the year award for the Orioles in 2017, has been an all-star at every level–most recently at high Class A Frederick–and represented the Orioles in the 2018 Futures Game.

SCOUTING REPORT: As a pitchability lefthander with a light fastball at 87-91 mph, Wells needs his command to be perfect, which it only was at times this year. At his best, he shows plus command with a feel for three pitches, including a changeup and curveball that each have average potential. There's not much physical projection, but Wells has a simple, repeatable delivery and knows how to pitch with what he has. The concern is that even exceptional command won't be enough at more advanced levels because of Wells lack of any one overpowering pitch.

THE FUTURE: Even a tick more velocity would raise Wells' ceiling a bit, but at this point, he is a No. 5 starter or swingman at best. If he can command and get outs at Double-A Bowie in 2019, that outlook could be solidified.

Year	Club (League)	Class	W	L	ERA	G	GS	CG	SV	IP	H	HR	BB	SO	K/9	WHIP	AVG
2016	Aberdeen (NYP)	SS	4	5	2.15	13	13	0	0	63	48	1	9	50	7.2	0.91	.216
2017	Delmarva (SAL)	LoA	11	5	2.38	25	25	0	0	140	118	16	10	113	7.3	0.91	.222
2018	Frederick (CAR)	HiA	7	8	3.47	24	24	0	0	135	142	19	33	101	6.7	1.30	.270
Minor League Totals			22	18	2.77	62	62	0	0	338	308	36	52	264	7.0	1.07	.241

21 MICHAEL BAUMANN, RHP

BA GRADE

45 Risk: High

Born: Sept. 10, 1995. **B-T:** R-R. **Ht.:** 6-4. **Wt.:** 225. **Drafted:** Jacksonville, 2017 (3rd round). **Signed by:** Arthur McConnehead.

TRACK RECORD: After getting great returns from Austin Hays in the third round out of Jacksonville in 2016, they went back to the Dolphins roster for Baumann in 2017, signing him for a below-slot $500,000 as a third-round pick. Baumann cruised to high Class A Frederick within a year of signing, where he was challenged as a power pitcher despite his college pedigree.

SCOUTING REPORT: Baumann has a plus fastball in every sense, from its 92-96 mph velocity to its present sink and command potential. He fills up the zone with the pitch, but has been punished for leaving it over the plate at higher levels and must keep it down in the zone. The same goes for his slider, which he sometimes struggles to get behind. Baumann also throws a changeup that's a clear third pitch from a balanced delivery and boasts a sturdy pitcher's frame. His control is below-average, pushing the quality of his stuff down and limiting his strikeouts.

THE FUTURE: Baumann's starter track will be vital to him being able to develop the secondary pitches necessary to reach a back-end starter's ceiling. He could prove more useful as a high-leverage set-up man down the road, but he will likely begin 2019 at Double-A Bowie in the rotation.

Year	Club (League)	Class	W	L	ERA	G	GS	CG	SV	IP	H	HR	BB	SO	K/9	WHIP	AVG
2017	Orioles (GCL)	R	0	0	0.00	1	1	0	0	1	2	0	0	2	18.0	2.00	.400
	Aberdeen (NYP)	SS	4	2	1.31	10	9	0	0	41	25	2	19	41	8.9	1.06	.168
2018	Delmarva (SAL)	LoA	5	0	1.42	7	7	0	0	38	23	0	13	47	11.1	0.95	.180
	Frederick (CAR)	HiA	8	5	3.88	17	17	2	0	93	82	9	40	59	5.7	1.32	.238
Minor League Totals			17	7	2.71	35	34	2	0	173	132	11	72	149	7.8	1.18	.211

22 BRANDEN KLINE, RHP

BA GRADE

45 Risk: High

Born: Sept. 29, 1991. **B-T:** R-R. **Ht.:** 6-3. **Wt.:** 210. **Drafted:** Virginia, 2012 (2nd round). **Signed by:** Chris Gale.

TRACK RECORD: Kline appeared to be on the verge of a breakout in 2015 when a weighted ball program brought him a bump in fastball velocity, but an elbow injury that summer eventually required Tommy John surgery. He rehabbed through 2016 and required two cleanup procedures in 2017 before returning as an electric reliever in 2018.

SCOUTING REPORT: As a starter, Kline had a diverse and effective mix, but no true putaway pitch to complement his mid-90s fastball. But the corresponding jump in his arsenal out of the bullpen means he has a dynamic three-pitch mix. His 94-96 mph fastball explodes out of his hand and is a plus-plus pitch when up in the zone, while his mid-80s slider and mid-80s changeup can be thrown in any count and get swinging strikes. Each has plus potential, and Kline held his stuff on a reliever's schedule.

THE FUTURE: Kline turned 26 in September and would have been in the majors if he had innings left after so long off the mound. He was added to the 40-man roster in the offseason and will compete for a spot with the Orioles in spring training.

Year	Club (League)	Class	W	L	ERA	G	GS	CG	SV	IP	H	HR	BB	SO	K/9	WHIP	AVG
2016	Did not play—Injured																
2017	Did not play—Injured																
2018	Frederick (CAR)	HiA	1	0	1.31	12	0	0	2	21	20	0	3	23	10.0	1.11	.253
	Bowie (EL)	AA	4	4	1.80	32	0	0	15	45	32	3	15	48	9.6	1.04	.199
Minor League Totals			17	17	3.71	89	45	0	17	296	301	22	98	246	7.5	1.35	.267

23 RYLAN BANNON, 2B

BA GRADE

45 Risk: High

Born: April 22, 1996. **B-T:** R-R. **Ht.:** 5-10. **Wt.:** 180. **Drafted:** Xavier, 2017 (8th round). **Signed by:** Marty Lamb (Dodgers).

TRACK RECORD: Bannon was the Big East Conference player of the year at Xavier in 2017 and he showed increased power in his pro debut. The Dodgers skipped him to high Class A Rancho Cucamonga in 2018, and he hit 20 home runs in half a season to win California League MVP despite being sent to the Orioles in the Manny Machado trade in July. He struggled upon a jump to Double-A Bowie in his Orioles debut.
SCOUTING REPORT: Bannon moved from third base to second base with the Baysox, where his smaller frame and low arm swing play as part of an average defensive profile. His swing was exposed some after the trade, with his high leg kick from an open stance limiting his barrel control and disrupting his timing. His swing feasts on low pitches when he's on them, and his advanced approach has helped him hit at every level he's played in save for the Eastern League.
THE FUTURE: Bannon's track record shows he's liable to hit in Bowie when he returns there next spring, and that's what will have to carry him to a fringe everyday role in the majors.

Year	Club (League)	Class	AVG	G	AB	R	H	2B	3B	HR	RBI	BB	SO	SB	CS	OBP	SLG
2017	Ogden (PIO)	R	.336	40	149	39	50	8	0	10	30	19	29	5	0	.425	.591
2018	R. Cucamonga (CAL)	HiA	.296	89	338	58	100	17	6	20	61	59	103	4	4	.402	.559
	Bowie (EL)	AA	.204	32	98	16	20	6	0	2	11	22	24	0	0	.344	.327
Minor League Totals			.291	161	585	113	170	31	6	32	102	100	156	9	4	.398	.528

24 ZACH POP, RHP

BA GRADE

45 Risk: High

Born: Sept. 20, 1996. **B-T:** R-R. **Ht.:** 6-4. **Wt.:** 220. **Drafted:** Kentucky, 2017 (7th round). **Signed by:** Marty Lamb (Dodgers).

TRACK RECORD: Pop, a product of the Canadian National Team system, dealt with an arm injury in his junior year at Kentucky that hurt him in the draft, but he's shown no issues as a pro. He climbed three levels in 2018 between his time with the Dodgers and Orioles after he was part of the Manny Machado trade. All told, Pop generated an elite groundball rate while striking out 8.9 per nine innings.
SCOUTING REPORT: Pop may have a typical reliever's fastball/slider arsenal, but his heater has atypical life. It's a heavy 92-96 mph sinker from a low arm slot, but he'll need his mid-80s slider to reach its above-average potential to keep hitters off his fastball. His heater has a plus-plus ceiling, and Pop showed enough command for the Orioles to believe he profiles as a potential impact reliever.
THE FUTURE: Pop might have the best pure stuff of anyone acquired by the Orioles in their five July trades, and he has both the mentality and the arsenal to be an effective bridge reliever to get his team to the back-end of the bullpen.

Year	Club (League)	Class	W	L	ERA	G	GS	CG	SV	IP	H	HR	BB	SO	K/9	WHIP	AVG
2017	Dodgers (AZL)	R	0	0	0.00	5	0	0	0	5	2	0	2	5	9.0	0.80	.125
2018	Great Lakes (MWL)	LoA	0	2	2.20	11	0	0	0	16	12	1	7	24	13.2	1.16	.194
	R. Cucamonga (CAL)	HiA	1	0	0.33	19	0	0	7	27	13	0	6	23	7.7	0.70	.149
	Bowie (EL)	AA	1	1	2.53	14	0	0	1	21	14	0	6	17	7.2	0.94	.189
Minor League Totals			2	3	1.42	49	0	0	8	70	41	1	21	69	8.9	0.89	.172

25 DREW ROM, LHP

BA GRADE

50 Risk: Extreme

Born: Dec. 15, 1999. **B-T:** L-L. **Ht.:** 6-2. **Wt.:** 170. **Drafted:** HS—Fort Thomas, Ky., 2018 (4th round). **Signed by:** Adrian Dorsey.

TRACK RECORD: Rom signed for an above-slot $650,000 as a 2018 fourth-rounder to forgo a commitment to Michigan. He got his first taste of the pro game in the Rookie-level Gulf Coast League, where he struck out 8.2 per nine innings and dominated lefthanded hitters.
SCOUTING REPORT: Rom's fastball sat 89-91 mph ahead of the draft, but dipped down after he signed following a long high school season. What he lacks in fastball velocity, he makes up with bite and shape on a potential plus slider at 77-80 mph, and his split-changeup has above-average potential. The fact Rom has shown velocity before and has a projectable pitcher's frame with room to add muscle and arm strength from a clean, easy three-quarters arm slot should ease his transition into full-season ball.
THE FUTURE: Rom has a back-end rotation ceiling, and his slider could play well in relief. He could get a crack at the low Class A Delmarva rotation in 2019.

Year	Club (League)	Class	W	L	ERA	G	GS	CG	SV	IP	H	HR	BB	SO	K/9	WHIP	AVG
2018	Orioles (GCL)	R	0	2	1.76	10	9	0	0	31	20	1	6	28	8.2	0.85	.183
Minor League Totals			0	2	1.76	10	9	0	0	31	20	1	6	28	8.2	0.85	.183

26 JEAN CARMONA, SS/2B

Born: Oct. 31, 1999. **B-T:** S-R. **Ht.:** 6-1. **Wt.:** 183. **Signed:** Dominican Republic, 2016. **Signed by:** Julio de la Cruz (Brewers).

TRACK RECORD: Carmona was a top player in the 2016 international class when the Brewers signed him for $725,000. He hit well in the Dominican Summer League in 2017 before coming to the U.S. He spent 2018 in Rookie ball both before and after he was part of the Jonathan Schoop trade in July.

SCOUTING REPORT: Carmona's current promise is inflated by the fact that there's no one skill that can't be dreamt on at this point. He's a big for a shortstop but handles the position well. His physical projection creates the possibility that he could be a switch-hitter with at least an average hit tool and above-average power with bat speed. That same projection could take him off shortstop, however. He has the arm for either shortstop or third base. He has played second base as well.

THE FUTURE: Carmona will get every chance to develop into a reliable everyday player at shortstop, and he may not have much impediment in the Orioles' system. He could be challenged with his full-season debut at low Class A Delmarva in 2019.

Year	Club (League)	Class	AVG	G	AB	R	H	2B	3B	HR	RBI	BB	SO	SB	CS	OBP	SLG
2017	Brewers (DSL)	R	.302	47	159	37	48	9	7	0	18	22	39	8	7	.406	.447
	Brewers (AZL)	R	.146	13	48	5	7	1	1	1	6	6	12	2	1	.232	.271
2018	Helena (PIO)	R	.239	39	155	28	37	8	3	4	24	13	45	5	3	.298	.406
	Aberdeen (NYP)	SS	.226	24	93	9	21	7	0	0	7	6	25	0	1	.280	.301
Minor League Totals			.248	123	455	79	113	25	11	5	55	47	121	15	12	.328	.385

27 PEDRO ARAUJO, RHP

Born: July 2, 1993. **B-T:** R-R. **Ht.:** 6-3. **Wt.:** 215. **Signed:** Dominican Republic, 2011. **Signed by:** Jose Serra/Carlos Reyes (Cubs).

TRACK RECORD: A late-bloomer who was never exactly on the fast track, Araujo signed with the Cubs for $100,000 as a 17-year-old in 2011 and didn't make it out of the Dominican Summer League until 2014. He wasn't in full-season ball until 2016, and he made one appearance in Double-A in 2017 before the Orioles took him in the Rule 5 draft. He made 20 appearances for Baltimore and struck out a batter per inning in his major league debut in 2018, but he struggled with his command suffering a season-ending elbow injury in mid-June.

SCOUTING REPORT: Araujo features a low-90s fastball that tops out at 95 mph with sink and was able to get swinging strikes in the big leagues on both his slider and changeup. Opposing hitters whiffed on 33.9 percent of his pitches, but he pitched his way into bad counts. His command, while no better than average, wasn't an issue as much as a lack of conviction at a level far advanced than what he was used to.

THE FUTURE: The Orioles kept Araujo around in the hopes that he can be a useful middle reliever once his Rule 5 roster restrictions expire. He will be back in the Orioles' bullpen in 2019.

Year	Club (League)	Class	W	L	ERA	G	GS	CG	SV	IP	H	HR	BB	SO	K/9	WHIP	AVG
2016	Myrtle Beach (CAR)	HiA	0	2	5.21	13	0	0	1	19	18	2	13	22	10.4	1.63	.247
	South Bend (MWL)	LoA	3	0	1.59	16	0	0	3	34	19	1	11	45	11.9	0.88	.161
2017	Tennessee (SL)	AA	0	0	0.00	1	0	0	0	2	1	0	1	4	18.0	1.00	.125
	Myrtle Beach (CAR)	HiA	6	1	1.81	44	0	0	10	65	42	3	17	83	11.6	0.91	.177
2018	Baltimore (AL)	MAJ	1	3	7.71	20	0	0	0	28	29	9	18	29	9.3	1.68	.264
Major League Totals			1	3	7.71	20	0	0	0	28	29	9	18	29	9.3	1.68	.264
Minor League Totals			26	9	2.63	145	22	0	16	342	269	12	105	394	10.4	1.09	.213

28 JOSH ROGERS, LHP

Born: July 10, 1994. **B-T:** L-L. **Ht.:** 6-3. **Wt.:** 220. **Drafted:** Louisville, 2015 (11th round). **Signed by:** Mike Gibbons (Yankees).

TRACK RECORD: Rogers pitched as a freshman at Louisville despite Tommy John surgery as a senior in high school, and he signed with the Yankees for an above-slot $485,000 as a draft-eligible sophomore. He was surprised to start 2018 at Triple-A, but more than held his own there before joining the Orioles in the Zach Britton trade. His first major league start came a month later.

SCOUTING REPORT: Rogers has been effective at every level in pro ball because of how he spots his 88-92 mph fastball and uses two offspeed pitches, including an average slider and plus changeup to keep hitters off balance. But without a go-to out pitch among them, Rogers needs to be precise down in the strike zone and hit his spots to generate weak contact. He had shown the ability to do that up until he reached the majors with average command from a three-quarters arm slot.

THE FUTURE: Rogers reached the majors in the role that he may ultimately fill: spot starter. He could peak as a No. 5 starter or carve a useful role as a swingman or up-and-down rotation depth option.

Year	Club (League)	Class	W	L	ERA	G	GS	CG	SV	IP	H	HR	BB	SO	K/9	WHIP	AVG
2016	Charleston, SC (SAL)	LoA	2	1	1.59	4	4	0	0	23	14	1	2	25	9.9	0.71	.171
	Tampa (FSL)	HiA	10	5	2.53	20	20	2	0	114	111	5	20	90	7.1	1.15	.256
2017	Tampa (FSL)	HiA	4	3	2.22	8	8	0	0	53	45	3	8	51	8.7	1.01	.231
	Trenton (EL)	AA	4	2	4.62	7	7	0	0	39	35	5	8	29	6.7	1.10	.240
2018	Scranton/W-B (IL)	AAA	6	8	3.95	19	19	1	0	109	118	13	29	83	6.8	1.34	.273
	Norfolk (IL)	AAA	2	1	2.08	5	5	0	0	30	26	3	7	18	5.3	1.09	.226
	Baltimore (AL)	MAJ	1	2	8.49	3	3	0	0	12	17	2	5	6	4.6	1.89	.340
Major League Totals			1	2	8.49	3	3	0	0	12	17	2	5	6	4.6	1.89	.340
Minor League Totals			30	20	3.07	68	63	3	1	381	363	30	77	312	7.4	1.15	.250

29 MATTHIAS DIETZ, RHP

BA GRADE

45 Risk: Very High

Born: Sept. 20, 1995. **B-T:** R-R. **Ht.:** 6-5. **Wt.:** 220. **Drafted:** John A. Logan (Ill.), JC. 2016 (2nd round). **Signed by:** Dan Durst.

TRACK RECORD: Dietz was the top junior college pitcher in the 2016 draft thanks to a growth spurt between seasons, and he signed for an above-slot $1.3 million as the 69th overall pick. A big-armed but raw pitcher, Dietz didn't start getting results until he repeated low Class A Delmarva in 2018. He was a South Atlantic League all-star but stumbled upon a promotion to high Class A Frederick, where he walked more than a batter per inning with a 2.06 WHIP.

SCOUTING REPORT: Even when effective, Dietz struggles with both command and control, which limits his entire package. His fastball sits 92-96 mph with run and is a touch firmer in shorter stints, with his mid-80s slider far ahead of his firm, below-average changeup. He struggles to put all the pieces of his delivery together consistently, and thus can't consistently command any of his pitches.

THE FUTURE: Anyone with Dietz's arm will get plenty of chances. The Orioles feel it suits his development to start so he can hone his delivery and secondary pitches. His future is almost certainly in the bullpen, where he has a middle-relief profile—if he can rein in his control. He could be back in Frederick to open 2019.

Year	Club (League)	Class	W	L	ERA	G	GS	CG	SV	IP	H	HR	BB	SO	K/9	WHIP	AVG
2016	Aberdeen (NYP)	SS	0	3	4.82	7	7	0	0	19	22	0	10	8	3.9	1.71	.306
2017	Delmarva (SAL)	LoA	3	10	4.93	26	26	0	0	130	144	6	50	92	6.4	1.50	.282
2018	Delmarva (SAL)	LoA	6	2	3.56	13	13	0	0	66	56	2	36	67	9.2	1.40	.236
	Frederick (CAR)	HiA	1	6	7.98	11	9	0	0	38	40	6	39	27	6.3	2.06	.274
Minor League Totals			10	21	5.03	57	55	0	0	252	262	14	135	194	6.9	1.57	.272

30 DREW JACKSON, 2B/SS

BA GRADE

40 Risk: High

Born: July 28, 1993. **B-T:** R-R. **Ht.:** 6-2. **Wt.:** 200. **Drafted:** Stanford, 2015 (5th round). **Signed by:** Stacey Pettis (Mariners).

TRACK RECORD: The athletic Jackson struggled to hit until he got contact lenses his junior year at Stanford, and his increased offensive production got him drafted by the Mariners in the fifth round in 2015. The Dodgers acquired him from Seattle for righthander Chase De Jong just before the start of the 2017 season. After injuries sidetracked Jackson's first year in the Dodgers' system, he emerged as versatile threat during Double-A Tulsa's Texas League title run, finishing with 20 doubles, 15 homers, 22 stolen bases and an .804 OPS while playing shortstop, second base and center field. The Orioles acquired him in the 2018 Rule 5 draft and must keep him on the 25-man roster to retain his rights.

SCOUTING REPORT: Jackson's athleticism has long been his calling card. He is a plus-plus runner with a plus-plus arm, two attributes that allow him to play in the middle of the diamond. His footwork and approach on ground balls are inconsistent, making him more reliable at second base than shortstop. Jackson's modest natural timing in the batter's box makes him a fringe-average hitter at best, but he found new power with physical maturity to enhance his overall impact.

THE FUTURE: Jackson is being groomed for a utility future with his up-the-middle-athleticism. He'll try to show he can keep hitting at the big league level in 2019.

Year	Club (League)	Class	AVG	G	AB	R	H	2B	3B	HR	RBI	BB	SO	SB	CS	OBP	SLG
2016	Bakersfield (CAL)	HiA	.258	124	524	87	135	24	2	6	47	50	105	16	8	.332	.345
2017	Dodgers (AZL)	R	.200	3	10	1	2	0	2	0	4	1	4	0	0	.273	.600
	R. Cucamonga (CAL)	HiA	.254	66	252	48	64	16	2	8	30	34	67	14	6	.367	.429
	Tulsa (TL)	AA	.234	29	111	22	26	5	1	1	10	11	28	7	2	.346	.324
2018	Tulsa (TL)	AA	.251	103	342	57	86	20	1	15	46	45	93	22	7	.356	.447
Minor League Totals			.269	384	1465	279	394	77	9	32	163	171	332	106	27	.360	.399

Boston Red Sox

BY ALEX SPEIER

En route to a franchise-record 108 wins in the regular season and their fourth championship this century, the Red Sox added to the growing list of champions built upon the foundation of a standout homegrown core. Mookie Betts, Xander Bogaerts, Andrew Benintendi, Rafael Devers, and Christian Vazquez all played key roles in the team's title run. So did Chris Sale and Craig Kimbrel, players who were acquired with high-end prospects in recent years.

Yet while the Red Sox have a group of young stars in the big leagues and their current core has at least a couple more years of championship contention, the farm system remains in a rebuilding stage. Even in their championship run, the Red Sox remained mindful of the challenge that lies in front of them as they try to work toward the restoration of high-end minor league depth. For the second straight season, the team carefully preserved its high-end prospects in trade talks during the season in deference to the need to balance present and future interests.

Even so, early in 2018, those preservation efforts seemed anything but promising during a start to the minor league season that was little short of disastrous. Jay Groome (who entered the year as the organization's top pitching prospect) had Tommy John surgery, Michael Chavis (the top position player to start the year) got suspended for a positive PED test, and several of the system's top pitching prospects endured early control issues.

Yet as the year progressed, the Red Sox saw an increasing number of glimpses that suggested promise moving forward. Among full-season players, Bobby Dalbec showed huge tools—top-of-the-scale power and strong defense—and Chavis returned with a solid performance down the stretch to give the Sox a pair of promising upper-level prospects. Players who struggled early—particularly high Class A Salem teammates Darwinzon Hernandez, Tanner Houck and Bryan Mata—re-established their prospect credentials.

Beneath that surface of players who will start 2019 in the upper levels, the Red Sox continued to accumulate high school draftees and international amateurs with a chance to reshape the perception of the system in the coming years. Three members of the international class of 2017-18 —shortstop Antoni Flores, third baseman Danny Diaz, and outfielder Gilberto Jimenez—offered evidence of high-ceiling potential. So did several of the team's 2018 draftees, including first-rounder Triston Casas, second-rounder Nick Decker, seventh-round selection Jarren Duran, 11th-rounder

Andrew Benintendi flourished as the primary No. 2 hitter with 16 homers and 41 doubles.

PROJECTED 2022 LINEUP

Catcher	Christian Vazquez (31)
First Base	Triston Casas (22)
Second Base	Michael Chavis (26)
Third Base	Rafael Devers (25)
Shortstop	Xander Bogaerts (29)
Left Field	Bobby Dalbec (27)
Center Field	Andrew Beintendi (27)
Right Field	Mookie Betts (29)
Designated Hitter	J.D. Martinez (34)
No. 1 Starter	Chris Sale (33)
No. 2 Starter	David Price (36)
No. 3 Starter	Rick Porcello (33)
No. 4 Starter	Jay Groome (23)
No. 5 Starter	Bryan Mata (23)
Closer	Darwinzon Hernandez (25)

Nick Northcut, and 21st-round selection Brandon Howlett.

Of course, a system in which the highest-ceiling players are concentrated in the lower levels (particularly short-season ball) is inherently is subject to volatility. A handful of performance breakthroughs by a growing population of players who have yet to progress beyond short-season ball would change the reputation of the farm system significantly. But if key lower-level players fail to deliver, the view of the farm system as thin will be difficult to shake.

The Red Sox remain amidst a title-contention window thanks to the players who they've already developed. How long that window remains open will be determined, at least in part, by the progress of players who are closer to the start of their professional careers than they are to the big leagues.

DEPTH CHART

BOSTON RED SOX

TOP 2019 ROOKIE: Durbin Feltman, RHP. Though drafted in 2018, he has a chance to be a key late-innings contributor by the end of 2019.
BREAKOUT PROSPECT: Gilberto Jimenez, OF. His strong, balanced skill set gives him a chance to emerge quickly as one of the top Red Sox prospects.
SLEEPER: Kole Cottam, C. Though his pro debut ended early after surgery to repair a torn meniscus, Cottam showed power and strong leadership traits behind the plate.

SOURCE OF TOP 30 TALENT			
Homegrown	29	Acquired	1
College	12	Trade	1
Junior college	0	Rule 5 draft	0
High school	8	Independent league	0
Nondrafted free agent	0	Free agent/waivers	0
International	9		

LF
Tyler Esplin
Devlin Granberg

CF
Jarren Duran (12)
Gilberto Jimenez (20)
Eduardo Lopez (25)
Kervin Suarez
Cole Brannen
Tate Matheny

RF
Nick Decker (16)
Tyler Dearden

3B
Bobby Dalbec (1)
Danny Diaz (13)
Brandon Howlett (14)
Nick Northcut (19)

SS
Antoni Flores (9)
C.J. Chatham (10)
Ceddanne Rafaela

2B
Brett Netzer (29)
Everlouis Lozada

1B
Michael Chavis (2)
Triston Casas (5)
Josh Ockimey (21)
Pedro Castellanos (27)
Sam Travis (28)
Garrett Benge

C
Roldani Baldwin
Kole Cottam
Elih Marrero
Dan Butler

LHP

LHSP	LHRP
Darwinzon Hernandez (3)	Yoan Aybar (30)
Jay Groome (4)	Bobby Poyner
Jhonathan Diaz	Jhonathan Diaz
Matt Kent	Daniel McGrath
	Josh Taylor

RHP

RHSP	RHRP
Bryan Mata (6)	Durbin Feltman (11)
Tanner Houck (7)	Colten Brewer (15)
Mike Shawaryn (8)	Travis Lakins (17)
Denyi Reyes (18)	Zach Schellenger (23)
Kutter Crawford (22)	Joan Martinez
Chase Shugart (24)	Eduard Bazardo
Alex Scherff (26)	Brayan Bello
Chandler Shepherd	
Alexander Montero	
Thad Ward	

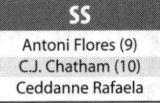
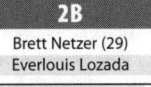

DRAFT ANALYSIS

2018

BEST PURE HITTER: 3B Triston Casas (1) didn't get much time to prove himself after enduring a season-ending injury in just his second game, but the Red Sox drafted him in the first round thanks to a very advanced lefthanded bat.

BEST POWER HITTER: Casas has a large, 6-foot-4, 238-pound frame and 70-grade raw power. His immense strength gives him a bigger margin for error than most hitters and gives him tremendous offensive upside when paired with his feel to hit and professional approach.

FASTEST RUNNER: Duran's loudest tool is his speed, as an 80-grade runner who has posted 3.95-second times from home to first. Duran stole 49 bags in 68 tries over three seasons with Long Beach State and went 24-for-34 in his pro debut.

BEST DEFENSIVE PLAYER: C Elih Marrero (8) is athletic with reliable hands and an accurate arm, though he's still figuring out the more intricate parts of the game like managing a full pitching staff. He threw out 52 percent of base runners this summer, and also has his father, 10-year major leaguer Eli, to go to for pointers.

BEST FASTBALL: RHP Durbin Feltman (3) touched 99 mph as a reliever across three different levels, getting as far as the Carolina League.

BEST SECONDARY PITCH: Feltman has a powerful, downer slider that has some depth and comes in in the mid-80s. It's an unorthodox pitch because it's thrown with typical slider velocity, but has a more traditional curveball shape with downer action than late, lateral tilt seen by most sliders.

BEST PRO DEBUT: 3B Brandon Howlett (21) seems to have put some vision issues that hampered him during the spring behind him, and he hit .289/.402/.513 between the Gulf Coast and New York-Penn leagues with 22 extra-base hits.

TOP DRAFT PICKS OF THE DECADE

Year	Player, Pos.	2018 Org
2009	Reymond Fuentes, OF	D-backs
2010	Kolbrin Vitek, 2B	Did not play
2011	Matt Barnes, RHP	Red Sox
2012	Deven Marrero, SS	D-backs
2013	Trey Ball, LHP	Red Sox
2014	Michael Chavis, SS	Red Sox
2015	Andrew Benintendi, OF	Red Sox
2016	Jay Groome, LHP	Red Sox
2017	Tanner Houck, RHP	Red Sox
2018	Triston Casas, 3B	Red Sox

BEST ATHLETE: Duran is quite the runner, but he's also got plenty of quick-twitch athleticism that shows up defensively and in the box.

MOST INTRIGUING BACKGROUND: Marrero following the path of his father is a good choice, as is SS/3B Korby Batesole (26), whose father Mike has been the head coach at Fresno State for 15 years and won the College World Series in 2008.

CLOSEST TO THE MAJORS: Having already reached high Class A in his first taste of pro ball, it would be hard to see any player in the 2018 Red Sox draft class reaching the majors before Feltman.

BEST LATE-ROUND PICK: Howlett has exceeded the Red Sox's expectations with how advanced he is at the plate, and with how frequently he's already able to get to his power in-game. He and already looks like a steal for $185,000 in the 21st round.

THE ONE WHO GOT AWAY: Boston signed each of its draft picks through the 13th round before missing with 2B Nick Lucky (14), who will take a smooth, lefthanded bat to Coastal Carolina. He's also solid runner and defender, but the coaching staff at Coastal believes he's one of the most advanced freshman hitters they've had in a decade.

—CARLOS COLLAZO

2017

Collectively, this class scuffled in its first full pro season but also flashed promise. RHPs Tanner Houck (1), Alex Scherff (5) and Zach Schellenger (6) have the most upside of the group. RHP Kutter Crawford (16) has been a late-round success.

GRADE: C

2016

3B Bobby Dalbec (4) hit 32 home runs in 2018 as he rose to become the Red Sox's top prospect. RHP Mike Shawaryn (5) is closing in on Boston. LHP Jay Groome (1) underwent Tommy John surgery, leaving this grade somewhat incomplete.

GRADE: B

2015

OF Andrew Benintendi (1) played a key role in helping Boston to the World Series title. RHP Ben Taylor (7) and LHP Bobby Poyner (14) give the class two more big leaguers and LHP Logan Allen (8) continues to progress with the Padres.

GRADE: A

1 BOBBY DALBEC, 3B

Born: June 29, 1995. **B-T:** R-R. **Ht:** 6-4. **Wt:** 225. **Drafted:** Arizona, 2016 (4th round). **Signed by:** Vaughn Williams.

A two-way player at Arizona who dominated on the mound in the 2016 College World Series, Dalbec has had a pro career of extremes. He had a tremendous pro debut with short-season Lowell in 2016, then struggled severely in his first full season in 2017, which was interrupted by surgery to remove a broken hamate. With health in 2018, Dalbec turned heads with top-of-the-charts power to all fields as well as plus defense at third base. He set a high Class A Salem record with 26 home runs before his promotion to Double-A Portland.

SCOUTING REPORT: Between his power, glove and arm, Dalbec has a combination of plus or better tools that few others in the system possess. Yet early in 2018, some scouts thought that it was a matter of time before he moved to the mound. Then Dalbec got on a roll in which he not only made more frequent contact but destroyed baseballs with eye-opening consistency. "My God, what power," exclaimed one scout. To get to that elite power, he will need to control his strikeout rate, which ballooned to 37 percent at Double-A. It's a challenge made greater by a hand hitch in his swing. But some believe that Dalbec's hitting intellect will allow him to hit enough to make an impact, particularly given that (A) he handled good fastballs in the zone this year, (B) he may benefit from a more consistent strike zone as he moves up, and (C) he has the ability to stay back on pitches rather than selling out for power. He can hit line drives to right-center field that carry over the fence. Still, some evaluators view his profile as risky given the frequency with which he chases secondary pitches out of the strike zone. Though a 6-foot-4 frame sometimes works against third basemen, Dalbec shows surprising quickness and range, excellent hands and a cannon arm that delivered mid-90s fastballs from the mound. While he has the skills to play third, he also saw time at first base in the Arizona Fall League to open more potential pathways to the big leagues.

THE FUTURE: If Dalbec can't control his strikeout rate, his future role would be limited to that of a platoon corner bat with good defensive skills. But his power is so significant that if he can hit .250 while maintaining a high walk rate, he could be an above-average or better third baseman who offers ample run production as a five- or six-hole type of hitter.

MIKE JANES/FOUR SEAM

BA GRADE	SCOUTING GRADES
55 Risk: High	Hit: 45. Power: 70. Run: 40. Field: 60. Arm: 70.

Projected future grades on 20-80 scouting scale

TOP PROSPECTS OF THE DECADE

Year	Player, Pos.	2018 Org
2009	Lars Anderson, 1B	Germany
2010	Ryan Westmoreland, OF	Did not play
2011	Jose Iglesias, SS	Tigers
2012	Will Middlebrooks, 3B	Did not play
2013	Xander Bogaerts, SS	Red Sox
2014	Xander Bogaerts, SS/3B	Red Sox
2015	Blake Swihart, C	Red Sox
2016	Yoan Moncada, 3B	White Sox
2017	Andrew Benintendi, OF	Red Sox
2018	Jay Groome, LHP	Red Sox

BEST TOOLS

Best Hitter for Average	C.J. Chatham
Best Power Hitter	Bobby Dalbec
Best Strike-Zone Discipline	Bobby Dalbec
Fastest Baserunner	Jarren Duran
Best Athlete	Jarren Duran
Best Fastball	Darwinzon Hernandez
Best Curveball	Jay Groome
Best Slider	Durbin Feltman
Best Changeup	Bryan Mata
Best Control	Denyi Reyes
Best Defensive Catcher	Kole Cottam
Best Defensive Infielder	Bobby Dalbec
Best Infield Arm	Bobby Dalbec
Best Defensive Outfielder	Tate Matheny
Best Outfield Arm	Gilberto Jimenez

Year	Club (League)	Class	AVG	G	AB	R	H	2B	3B	HR	RBI	BB	SO	SB	CS	OBP	SLG
2016	Lowell (NYP)	SS	.386	34	132	25	51	13	2	7	33	9	33	2	2	.427	.674
2017	Red Sox (GCL)	R	.259	7	27	3	7	1	0	0	2	5	9	1	0	.375	.296
	Greenville (SAL)	LoA	.246	78	284	48	70	15	0	13	39	36	123	4	5	.345	.437
2018	Salem (CAR)	HiA	.256	100	344	59	88	27	2	26	85	60	130	3	1	.372	.573
	Portland (EL)	AA	.261	29	111	14	29	8	1	6	24	6	46	0	0	.323	.514
Minor League Totals			.273	248	898	149	245	64	5	52	183	116	341	10	8	.365	.529

2 MICHAEL CHAVIS, 3B/1B

Born: Aug. 11, 1995. **B-T:** R-R. **Ht.:** 5-10. **Wt.:** 190. **Drafted:** HS—Marietta, Ga., 2014 (1st round). **Signed by:** Brian Moehler.

TRACK RECORD: Chavis struggled early in his pro career before a breakout 2017 campaign in which he hit 31 homers to vault near the top of the system. However, an 80-game suspension for a positive PED test in 2018 raised significant questions. Once on the field, Chavis looked like a better prospect than he had in 2017, showing both better defense at third base and a more controlled effort level at the plate.

SCOUTING REPORT: Early in his career, Chavis would sell out to get to his significant pull power, but he has learned to stay back on pitches and drive the ball from right-center field to the left-field foul line. He generates considerable power from his compact frame even while continuing to live with swing-and-miss in order to get there. Chavis has improved his conditioning and athleticism since turning pro, allowing him to stay at third base, though evaluators express uncertainty about his future position. He could see time in left field, and some in the organization want him to try second base.

THE FUTURE: Profile remains the big question for Chavis. He appears capable of playing the corners and delivering platoon impact—if not more. He likely will open 2019 at Triple-A Pawtucket.

BA GRADE
55 Risk: High
Hit: 50. **Power:** 60.
Run: 45. **Field:** 45.
Arm: 50.

Year	Club (League)	Class	AVG	G	AB	R	H	2B	3B	HR	RBI	BB	SO	SB	CS	OBP	SLG
2016	Greenville (SAL)	LoA	.244	74	279	30	68	11	3	8	35	22	74	3	1	.321	.391
	Salem (CAR)	HiA	.160	7	25	5	4	0	0	0	1	2	7	1	0	.222	.160
2017	Salem (CAR)	HiA	.323	59	223	50	72	18	2	17	56	19	57	1	0	.392	.650
	Portland (EL)	AA	.250	67	248	39	62	18	0	14	39	20	56	1	0	.310	.492
2018	Lowell (NYP)	SS	.313	5	16	5	5	4	0	1	3	5	5	0	0	.476	.750
	Portland (EL)	AA	.303	33	122	23	37	7	0	6	17	13	35	3	1	.388	.508
	Pawtucket (IL)	AAA	.273	8	33	8	9	3	0	2	7	1	12	0	0	.294	.545
Minor League Totals			.257	401	1515	237	390	102	9	65	232	126	428	22	10	.325	.465

3 DARWINZON HERNANDEZ, LHP

Born: Dec. 17, 1996. **B-T:** L-L. **Ht.:** 6-2. **Wt.:** 185. **Signed:** Venezuela, 2013. **Signed by:** Rolando Pino/Ramon Mora.

TRACK RECORD: An elbow injury just before the opening of the 2013 signing period scared some teams off Hernandez, but the Red Sox signed him for $7,500. His stuff has improved steadily and he has dominated at times. He struggled badly with his control at high Class A Salem early in 2018, prompting questions about whether he could remain in the rotation. A dominant second half resulted in a promotion to Double-A Portland.

SCOUTING REPORT: Hernandez works from a low three-quarters arm slot with a mid-to-upper-90s fastball, a slider that shows plus potential and a curveball that is solid when in the strike zone. He loses his delivery and release point at times, resulting in control struggles and pitch inefficiency that have convinced some that he will be a reliever, where he worked in Double-A and the Arizona Fall League. The Red Sox want to see if Hernandez can mix in a few changeups for strikes, which could help him excel for a couple turns through a lineup.

THE FUTURE: If Hernandez clicks, he could be a potential Jake McGee-type reliever who can blow away opponents with his fastball. Others see a Robbie Ray-type starter—if he can cut down his walk rate. Hernandez will return to Double-A, this time as a starter.

BA GRADE
50 Risk: High
Fastball: 60.
Slider: 60. **Change:** 40.
Curve: 50. **CTL:** 45.

Year	Club (League)	Class	W	L	ERA	G	GS	CG	SV	IP	H	HR	BB	SO	K/9	WHIP	AVG
2016	Lowell (NYP)	SS	3	5	4.10	14	14	0	0	48	39	1	36	58	10.8	1.55	.217
2017	Greenville (SAL)	LoA	4	5	4.01	23	23	0	0	103	85	8	49	116	10.1	1.30	.221
2018	Salem (CAR)	HiA	9	5	3.56	23	23	0	0	101	80	1	60	124	11.0	1.39	.220
	Portland (EL)	AA	0	0	3.00	5	0	0	0	6	6	0	6	10	15.0	2.00	.250
Minor League Totals			23	17	3.25	95	74	0	0	352	289	10	200	389	9.9	1.39	.223

4 JAY GROOME, LHP

Born: Aug. 23, 1998. **B-T:** L-L. **Ht.:** 6-6. **Wt.:** 220. **Drafted:** HS—Barnegat, N.J., 2016 (1st round). **Signed by:** Ray Fagnant.

TRACK RECORD: In the two years since the Red Sox jumped when Groome fell to them at No. 12 overall, the lefthander has shown glimpses of why he was viewed as perhaps the most talented high school pitcher in his draft. After a difficult first pro season in 2017, he appeared poised for a leap forward after an offseason spent in Fort Myers, Fla.,working out frequently with Chris Sale. Yet at the end of a dominant spring training he suffered an ulnar collateral ligament tear and had Tommy John surgery in May.

SCOUTING REPORT: When healthy, Groome showed a strong mix of three average to plus pitches and a tremendous ability to manipulate the ball with an easy delivery that augurs well for the ability to command a complete mix. In spring training, his fastball sat regularly in the mid-90s, and his sharp, two-plane curveball got plenty of swings and misses. He also showed improvement with his changeup. Down the road, his feel for the ball suggests that a cutter could be added to the mix.

THE FUTURE: If all goes well, Groome will join an affiliate by the middle of the 2019 season. He still has No. 2 starter ceiling, but with concerns throughout the industry about how close he'll come to reaching it.

BA GRADE
55 Risk: Extreme
Fastball: 60.
Curve: 60. Change: 50.
Cutter: 55. CTL: 55.

Year	Club (League)	Class	W	L	ERA	G	GS	CG	SV	IP	H	HR	BB	SO	K/9	WHIP	AVG
2016	Red Sox (GCL)	R	0	0	2.25	2	2	0	0	4	3	0	0	8	18.0	0.75	.200
	Lowell (NYP)	SS	0	0	3.38	1	1	0	0	3	0	0	4	2	6.8	1.50	.000
2017	Lowell (NYP)	SS	0	2	1.64	3	3	0	0	11	5	0	5	14	11.5	0.91	.132
	Greenville (SAL)	LoA	3	7	6.70	11	11	0	0	44	44	6	25	58	11.8	1.56	.257
2018	Did not play—Injured																
Minor League Totals			3	9	5.37	17	17	0	0	62	52	6	34	82	11.9	1.39	.223

5 TRISTON CASAS, 1B/3B

Born: Jan. 15, 2000. **B-T:** L-R. **Ht.:** 6-4. **Wt.:** 238. **Drafted:** HS—Plantation, Fla., 2018 (1st round). **Signed by:** Willie Romay.

TRACK RECORD: Area scout Willie Romay started following Casas as a high school freshman, mesmerized by his exceptional ability to drive the ball to all fields—a skill also evident in summer wood-bat leagues, including his time with Team USA. Shortly after Casas signed as the 26th overall pick, he suffered a torn ligament in his thumb while making a diving play in the field; the subsequent surgery ended his pro debut, but he was back on the field by instructional league.

SCOUTING REPORT: Casas shows light-tower power, a trait made evident in workouts where he deposited balls into the center-field bleachers and the distant bullpen in right-center. Yet his ability to stay inside the ball, cover holes and drive pitches to the opposite field suggests the potential for a strong hit tool. Given Casas' size, there are likely to be holes in his swing as he adjusts to pro ball in 2019. He split time between first and third base in instructional league, but he most likely profiles at first, where his surprising athleticism and large wingspan could make him stand out.

BA GRADE
55 Risk: Extreme
Hit: 60. Power: 60.
Run: 40. Field: 60.
Arm: 50.

THE FUTURE: Casas has upside on par with any other Red Sox prospect, and if he performs at low Class A Greenville in 2019 he could vault to the top of this list.

Year	Club (League)	Class	AVG	G	AB	R	H	2B	3B	HR	RBI	BB	SO	SB	CS	OBP	SLG
2018	Red Sox (GCL)	R	.000	2	4	0	0	0	0	0	0	1	2	0	0	.200	.000
Minor League Totals			.000	2	4	0	0	0	0	0	0	1	2	0	0	.200	.000

6 BRYAN MATA, RHP

Born: May 3, 1999. **B-T:** R-R. **Ht.:** 6-3. **Wt.:** 220. **Signed:** Venezuela, 2016.
Signed by: Alex Requena/Eddie Romero.

TRACK RECORD: In January 2016, the Red Sox rushed Mata to the mound at a workout organized by Alex Requena to get a one-inning look before the skies opened in a downpour. It was enough to convince the team to sign him for $25,000 that day. Since then he has consistently held his own as one of the youngest players at his levels.

SCOUTING REPORT: Mata struggled to throw strikes early in 2018 while moving from being chiefly a four-seam fastball pitcher to learning how to use a two-seamer in order to generate more ground balls. He has a starter's mix, with above-average velocity—he averages roughly 94 mph and tops out at 97—and the ability both to spin a breaking ball and slow bats with a changeup that gets some swings and misses. The key for Mata will be reclaiming his control after struggling at times to maintain his delivery in 2018. His struggles were at least partly a result of his physical growth.

BA GRADE

50 Risk: High

Fastball: 55.
Curveball: 50.
Change: 55. **CTL:** 45.

THE FUTURE: Though Mata's 2018 season was cut short in July, shortly after the Futures Game, by growth-related back discomfort, he will compete for a spot in the Double-A rotation to remain on an aggressive development track. He has the upside of a No. 3 or No. 4 starter.

Year	Club (League)	Class	W	L	ERA	G	GS	CG	SV	IP	H	HR	BB	SO	K/9	WHIP	AVG
2016	Red Sox2 (DSL)	R	4	4	2.80	14	14	0	0	61	54	2	19	61	9.0	1.20	.242
2017	Greenville (SAL)	LoA	5	6	3.74	17	17	1	0	77	75	3	26	74	8.6	1.31	.259
2018	Salem (CAR)	HiA	6	3	3.50	17	17	0	0	72	58	1	58	61	7.6	1.61	.229
Minor League Totals			15	13	3.39	48	48	1	0	210	187	6	103	196	8.4	1.38	.244

7 TANNER HOUCK, RHP

Born: June 29, 1996. **B-T:** R-R. **Ht.:** 6-5. **Wt.:** 220. **Drafted:** Missouri, 2017 (1st round). **Signed by:** Todd Gold.

TRACK RECORD: The Red Sox were thrilled that a pitcher with Houck's Southeastern Conference and Team USA pedigree remained on the board at No. 24 overall. Yet in his first spring training, Houck raised his arm slot and changed from a two-seam/slider mix to more of a four-seam/curveball combination that he struggled to command. He went back to a more familiar arm slot and mix in the second half of 2018, with strong results down the stretch.

SCOUTING REPORT: Houck's flexibility permits him to have excellent extension from a low three-quarters arm slot, though he has a lot of moving parts and sometimes struggles to hold his release point. Moving forward, he has the potential to employ both a sinking two-seamer with armside run and a four-seamer that stays true to his glove side to spread the strike zone for swings and misses at the top of it and grounders at the bottom. He also throws a potential wipeout slider. His changeup needs to make progress for him to stay in the rotation, even if he only lands it for occasional strikes.

BA GRADE

50 Risk: High

Fastball: 60.
Slider: 60.
Change: 45. **CTL:** 45.

THE FUTURE: Houck is determined to prove he can start, though many feel his future is in the bullpen unless he improves effectiveness against lefthanded hitters. He has No. 4 starter potential if he starts.

Year	Club (League)	Class	W	L	ERA	G	GS	CG	SV	IP	H	HR	BB	SO	K/9	WHIP	AVG
2017	Lowell (NYP)	SS	0	3	3.63	10	10	0	0	22	21	0	8	25	10.1	1.30	.239
2018	Salem (CAR)	HiA	7	11	4.24	23	23	0	0	119	110	11	60	111	8.4	1.43	.245
Minor League Totals			7	14	4.14	33	33	0	0	141	131	11	68	136	8.7	1.41	.244

8 MIKE SHAWARYN, RHP

Born: Sept. 17, 1994. **B-T:** R-R. **Ht.:** 6-2. **Wt.:** 200. **Drafted:** Maryland, 2016 (5th round). **Signed by:** Chris Calciano.

TRACK RECORD: Shawaryn has moved steadily through the system, offering the sort of consistent performance that has permitted him to deliver solid performances as a starter across four levels in two years.

SCOUTING REPORT: Shawaryn is a physical strike-thrower who attacks the zone with a low-90s fastball that has natural cut and a swing-and-miss slider whose speed and break he varies, with some evaluators coming away describing it as a cutter. At Triple-A Pawtucket, he showed an increased willingness to employ a changeup that grades as below-average now but has the potential to improve. If it doesn't, Shawaryn has the potential to be a solid medium-leverage reliever who can be trusted to throw strikes out of the bullpen. He has shown flyball tendencies that suggest home run vulnerability, a trait that would be a concern at Fenway Park. Still, Shawaryn receives high marks for his work ethic, makeup and aptitude, giving evaluators confidence that he has a good chance of emerging as a solid big league contributor.

THE FUTURE: Shawaryn will open 2019 back in Pawtucket as a depth option, either for the rotation or bullpen. In preparation for the possibility of a relief role, he worked out of the pen in the Arizona Fall League.

BA GRADE

45 Risk: Medium

Fastball: 55.
Slider: 60.
Change: 45. **CTL:** 45.

Year	Club (League)	Class	W	L	ERA	G	GS	CG	SV	IP	H	HR	BB	SO	K/9	WHIP	AVG
2016	Lowell (NYP)	SS	0	1	2.87	6	6	0	0	16	15	0	7	22	12.6	1.40	.254
2017	Greenville (SAL)	LoA	3	2	3.88	10	10	0	0	53	44	5	13	78	13.2	1.07	.222
	Salem (CAR)	HiA	5	5	3.76	16	16	0	0	81	71	10	35	91	10.1	1.30	.232
2018	Portland (EL)	AA	6	8	3.28	19	19	1	0	113	100	7	27	99	7.9	1.13	.238
	Pawtucket (IL)	AAA	3	2	3.93	7	6	1	0	37	30	6	11	33	8.1	1.12	.221
Minor League Totals			17	18	3.57	58	57	2	0	300	260	28	93	323	9.7	1.18	.232

9 ANTONI FLORES, SS

Born: Oct. 14, 2000. **B-T:** R-R. **Ht.:** 6-1. **Wt.:** 190. **Signed:** Venezuela, 2017. **Signed by:** Angel Escobar/Eddie Romero.

TRACK RECORD: The Red Sox signed Flores out of Venezuela for $1.4 million in 2017 based on the attraction of his all-around tools as well as his feel for the game. He stood out in the Dominican Summer League enough to convince the Red Sox to promote him to the Rookie-level Gulf Coast League after just 13 games, but a conservative course with lower-half injuries limited him to just two games in the GCL.

SCOUTING REPORT: Flores has shown the Red Sox a consistently strong feel for hitting with advanced plate discipline and a good feel for getting the barrel on the ball, with strength gains allowing him to post higher-than-expected exit velocities. He was wiry at the time he signed, somewhat akin to a young Alcides Escobar, but Flores has already filled out quite a bit. As he continues to do so, there's a chance he will outgrow shortstop and move to third base. Still, his potential to develop into an above-average shortstop stood out in a system that is light up the middle. At least one rival evaluator viewed Flores as the best prospect in the entire system.

THE FUTURE: Flores seems like a candidate to join short-season Lowell in June, though he has a chance to push for low Class A Greenville at some point in 2019.

BA GRADE

50 Risk: Extreme

Hit: 55. **Power:** 50.
Run: 50. **Field:** 50.
Arm: 60.

Year	Club (League)	Class	AVG	G	AB	R	H	2B	3B	HR	RBI	BB	SO	SB	CS	OBP	SLG
2018	Red Sox2 (DSL)	R	.347	13	49	10	17	3	1	1	14	8	7	0	1	.439	.510
	Red Sox (GCL)	R	.250	2	4	0	1	0	1	0	0	1	1	0	0	.400	.750
Minor League Totals			.340	15	53	10	18	3	2	1	14	9	8	0	1	.435	.528

10 C.J. CHATHAM, SS

Born: Dec. 22, 1994. **B-T:** R-R. **Ht.:** 6-4. **Wt.:** 185. **Drafted:** Florida Atlantic, 2016 (2nd round). **Signed by:** Willie Romay.

TRACK RECORD: After he missed almost all of his first full pro season in 2017 with a recurring hamstring injury, Chatham returned with a strong performance across two levels in 2018, competing for the Carolina League batting title until the final days of the season while showing solid defensive skills.

SCOUTING REPORT: Chatham showed a knack for getting the bat on the ball, sometimes demonstrating doubles power and sometimes by flipping singles to right field. His feel for hitting suggests a solid hit tool that should allow him—in concert with his defense—to reach the big leagues. Though Chatham hit for power in college, he hasn't done so as a pro. Now that he has a healthy season to his name, he is spending his offseason in a strengthening program to try to tap into more power. Defensively, Chatham lacks explosive actions but has good footwork and body control. Though he lacks standout tools, he showed a solid all-around game to project as a potential everyday up-the-middle player with the floor of a utility player.

THE FUTURE: Chatham seems likely to open 2019 at Double-A Portland, and he may not be far from offering the Red Sox a righthanded infield depth option.

BA GRADE	
45	**Risk:** High

Hit: 55. **Power:** 40.
Run: 45. **Field:** 50.
Arm: 55.

Year	Club (League)	Class	AVG	G	AB	R	H	2B	3B	HR	RBI	BB	SO	SB	CS	OBP	SLG
2016	Red Sox (GCL)	R	.167	8	24	2	4	2	0	1	2	0	7	0	0	.200	.375
	Lowell (NYP)	SS	.259	27	108	19	28	4	1	4	19	8	20	0	1	.319	.426
2017	Greenville (SAL)	LoA	.333	1	3	0	1	0	0	0	2	0	0	0	1	.333	.333
	Red Sox (GCL)	R	.313	6	16	5	5	0	0	1	3	2	1	0	0	.389	.500
2018	Greenville (SAL)	LoA	.307	19	75	13	23	6	1	0	9	3	14	1	1	.329	.413
	Salem (CAR)	HiA	.315	95	362	42	114	14	1	3	43	21	72	10	4	.355	.384
Minor League Totals			.298	156	588	81	175	26	3	9	78	34	114	11	7	.340	.398

11 DURBIN FELTMAN, RHP

BA GRADE	
45	**Risk:** High

Born: April 18, 1997. **B-T:** R-R. **Ht.:** 6-0. **Wt.:** 205. **Drafted:** Texas Christian, 2018 (3rd round). **Signed by:** Brandon Agamennone.

TRACK RECORD: Feltman split time between pitching and catching in high school, but with a full-time move to the mound at Texas Christian, his velocity exploded. He went from the upper-80s to the upper-90s as a freshman and emerged as TCU's closer. He punctuated a great college career with a dominant junior campaign (0.74 ERA, 43 strikeouts and 6 walks in 24 innings) and signed with the Red Sox for $559,600 as the 100th overall pick. He continued to dominate in his pro debut, posting a 1.93 ERA with 36 strikeouts and five walks in 23 innings while jumping to high Class A Salem.

SCOUTING REPORT: Despite a max-effort delivery that creates durability questions, Feltman commands two swing-and-miss pitches. His high-spin, 95-99 mph fastball has two-plane movement, seeming to rise above bats with cut to generate tons of swings and misses. He also features a wipeout mid-80s slider. Those offerings are so sufficiently developed that, entering the draft, there were questions whether Felltman might be in the big leagues in 2018. While the Red Sox decided to tap the brakes on such hype by keeping him in the low minors, there's a good chance that he will stay on an aggressive path in 2019.

THE FUTURE: Feltman might open 2019 in Double-A Portland, and there's a strong likelihood that he will be in the big league bullpen by next year. He could be an important late-innings factor—either as a setup man or closer—in the near future.

Year	Club (League)	Class	W	L	ERA	G	GS	CG	SV	IP	H	HR	BB	SO	K/9	WHIP	AVG
2018	Lowell (NYP)	SS	0	0	0.00	4	0	0	0	4	0	0	0	7	15.8	0.00	.000
	Greenville (SAL)	LoA	0	1	2.57	7	0	0	3	7	6	0	1	14	18.0	1.00	.214
	Salem (CAR)	HiA	1	0	2.19	11	0	0	1	12	12	0	4	15	10.9	1.30	.261
Minor League Totals			1	1	1.93	22	0	0	4	23	18	0	5	36	13.9	0.99	.207

12 JARREN DURAN, OF/2B

BA GRADE	
45	**Risk:** High

Born: Sept. 5, 1996. **B-T:** L-R. **Ht.:** 6-2. **Wt.:** 200. **Drafted:** Long Beach State, 2018 (7th round). **Signed by:** Justin Horowitz.

TRACK RECORD: Duran combined solid bat-to-ball skills and a good feel for the strike zone with standout speed at Long Beach State. The Red Sox drafted him in the seventh round and signed him for $189,800 with the hope of seeing how the college second baseman might fare in the outfield. In his pro debut,

Duran showed not only those traits but also surprising gap power, hitting .357/.394/.516 with 28 extra-base hits in 67 games—one more than he had in his sophomore and junior years combined.

SCOUTING REPORT: Duran shows an above-average hit tool, keeping the bat in the zone for a long time and getting the barrel on all pitch types. He also showed the ability to backspin the ball in unexpected fashion in his pro debut to both the pull-side and opposite field. His 70-grade speed allows him to make an impact on the bases and to take advantage of mis-hits, and ultimately should serve him well in center and right field.

THE FUTURE: While Duran in college looked like a potential role player, the skill set he showed in a dazzling pro debut suggested a player with the ceiling of a Brett Gardner-type.

Year	Club (League)	Class	AVG	G	AB	R	H	2B	3B	HR	RBI	BB	SO	SB	CS	OBP	SLG
2018	Lowell (NYP)	SS	.348	37	155	28	54	5	10	2	20	11	26	12	4	.393	.548
	Greenville (SAL)	LoA	.367	30	128	24	47	9	1	1	15	5	22	12	6	.396	.477
Minor League Totals			.357	67	283	52	101	14	11	3	35	16	48	24	10	.394	.516

13 DANNY DIAZ, 3B

BA GRADE

50 Risk: Extreme

Born: Jan. 2, 2001. **B-T:** 6-4. **Ht.:** 6-4. **Wt.:** 222. **Signed:** Dominican Republic, 2017. **Signed by:** Ernesto Gomez/Eddie Romero.

TRACK RECORD: In his DSL pro debut, Diaz—who grew three inches and added roughly 50 pounds in his first year in the Red Sox system—showed the standout power that led the Red Sox to sign him for $1.6 million in 2017. He blasted six homers in 26 games before surgery to remove a broken hamate ended his season.

SCOUTING REPORT: Diaz has the size and strength of a middle-of-the-order hitter, but with the swing-and-miss and aggressive approach (23.9 percent strikeout rate, 4.4 percent walk rate) to create risk in his profile. Diaz moved from short to third once in pro ball, and he shows soft hands and good arm strength at the position. His size raises long-term questions about whether he'll move off the position, and the Sox plan to give him time at both third and first.

THE FUTURE: If everything clicks, Diaz could emerge in several years as a third baseman with top-end power, but with his size and his struggles to make contact, his development track may prove deliberate.

Year	Club (League)	Class	AVG	G	AB	R	H	2B	3B	HR	RBI	BB	SO	SB	CS	OBP	SLG
2018	Red Sox2 (DSL)	R	.238	26	105	17	25	7	0	6	27	5	27	0	3	.283	.476
Minor League Totals			.238	26	105	17	25	7	0	6	27	5	27	0	3	.283	.476

14 BRANDON HOWLETT, 3B

BA GRADE

50 Risk: Extreme

Born: Sept. 12, 1999. **B-T:** R-R. **Ht.:** 6-1. **Wt.:** 205. **Drafted:** HS—Lakeland, Fla., 2018 (21st round). **Signed by:** Stephen Hargett.

TRACK RECORD: The Red Sox believed Howlett possessed an advanced approach and intriguing upside for a 21st-round selection, but didn't realize those traits would become so quickly apparent in pro ball. After signing for $185,000 to pass up a Florida State commitment, Howlett had a standout debut backed by a new contact lens prescription.

SCOUTING REPORT: Howlett squared up balls frequently in his debut, showing easy home run power to the pull side and driving doubles to right-center. The ability to use all fields suggests a player who has the ability to post high averages, and Howlett has also shown considerable plate discipline, even with some swing and miss. Evaluators are split on whether he'll stay at third or move to first base or left field, but he showed well at third in his debut and will continue to get time there.

THE FUTURE: Howlett has the upside of a middle-of-the-order run-producer, potentially at a premium position, thus making the teenager one of the potential steals of the draft thanks to his improved vision. He will be in the conversation to open 2019 at low Class A Greenville.

Year	Club (League)	Class	AVG	G	AB	R	H	2B	3B	HR	RBI	BB	SO	SB	CS	OBP	SLG
2018	Red Sox (GCL)	R	.307	39	137	24	42	15	0	5	25	22	38	0	1	.405	.526
	Lowell (NYP)	SS	.133	5	15	5	2	1	0	1	2	6	3	1	0	.381	.400
Minor League Totals			.289	44	152	29	44	16	0	6	27	28	41	1	1	.402	.513

15 COLTEN BREWER, RHP

BA GRADE

40 Risk: Medium

Born: Oct. 29, 1992. **B-T:** R-R. **Ht.:** 6-4. **Wt.:** 230. **Drafted:** HS—Canton, Texas, 2011 (4th round). **Signed by:** Mike Leuzinger (Pirates).

TRACK RECORD: The Red Sox are Brewer's fourth organization in as many years, as he's gone from the

Pirates to the Yankees to the Padres to Boston after being traded for Esteban Quiroz in November. The big righthander had a 3.75 ERA with 11.8 strikeouts and 2.8 walks per nine inning and strong groundball rates in Triple A in 2018.

SCOUTING REPORT: Brewer relies heavily on one of the hardest cutters in the game. His 92.4 mph average cutter velocity was the sixth-highest in MLB in 2018 by a pitcher who threw at least 50 cutters. He complements that pitch with a low-80s curve and high-80s slider, both of which demonstrate a strong ability to spin the ball. The Red Sox believe that between his velocity and spin, that there are a lot of raw materials that can yield a solid middle-innings option, although his command and control need work.

THE FUTURE: Brewer should represent one of the Red Sox's top bullpen depth options in 2019. He has two options remaining and will get plenty of chances.

Year	Club (League)	Class	W	L	ERA	G	GS	CG	SV	IP	H	HR	BB	SO	K/9	WHIP	AVG
2016	Bradenton (FSL)	HiA	3	7	4.09	18	13	0	2	70	82	5	27	66	8.4	1.55	.285
2017	Tampa (FSL)	HiA	0	0	0.00	6	0	0	2	9	3	0	1	15	14.5	0.43	.091
	Scranton/W-B (IL)	AAA	0	0	11.70	6	0	0	1	10	17	2	4	11	9.9	2.10	.347
	Trenton (EL)	AA	3	1	1.31	29	0	0	11	41	37	0	11	43	9.4	1.16	.231
2018	El Paso (PCL)	AAA	3	4	3.75	37	0	0	3	48	40	3	15	63	11.8	1.15	.229
	San Diego (NL)	MAJ	1	0	5.59	11	0	0	0	10	15	0	7	10	9.3	2.28	.357
Major League Totals			1	0	5.59	11	0	0	0	10	15	0	7	10	9.3	2.28	.357
Minor League Totals			17	24	4.01	129	44	0	19	337	337	23	109	321	8.6	1.32	.257

16 NICK DECKER, OF

BA GRADE
50 Risk: Extreme

Born: Oct. 2, 1999. **B-T:** L-L. **Ht.:** 6-0. **Wt.:** 200. **Drafted:** HS—Tabernacle, N.J., 2018 (2nd round). **Signed by:** Ray Fagnant.

TRACK RECORD: Decker dominated his New Jersey high school peers while also impressing the Red Sox with his makeup—an impression formed in no small part by the opportunity for scout Ray Fagnant to coach Decker at East Coast Pro. The Red Sox selected Decker with the 64th overall pick and signed him for $1.25 million to forgo a Maryland commitment. Decker got into just two games in the Rookie-level Gulf Coast League before a non-displaced wrist fracture forced him to miss the rest of the season.

SCOUTING REPORT: Decker has the hand strength and bat speed to generate all-fields power. There's the potential for a fair amount of swing-and-miss in his game, though during instructional league he showed a hit tool that was more advanced than expected. For now, he'll likely develop in center and right field. While he has the arm for right, it remains to be seen whether he maintains the range to stay out of left.

THE FUTURE: As a player who contended with the abbreviated high school schedules of the Northeast, Decker may take some time to develop. There are likely to be periods of struggle in his game, interspersed with some prodigious shows of power that suggest the upside of a power-hitting corner outfielder.

Year	Club (League)	Class	AVG	G	AB	R	H	2B	3B	HR	RBI	BB	SO	SB	CS	OBP	SLG
2018	Red Sox (GCL)	R	.250	2	4	1	1	1	0	0	0	1	1	0	0	.400	.500
Minor League Totals			.250	2	4	1	1	1	0	0	0	1	1	0	0	.400	.500

17 TRAVIS LAKINS, RHP

BA GRADE
40 Risk: Medium

Born: June 29, 1994. **B-T:** R-R. **Ht.:** 6-1. **Wt.:** 180. **Drafted:** Ohio State, 2015 (6th round). **Signed by:** John Pyle.

TRACK RECORD: Though Lakins showed some of the best stuff of any Red Sox starting pitching prospect, both of his first two pro seasons ended with stress fractures in his right elbow tip, prompting the team to move him to the bullpen in 2018.

SCOUTING REPORT: Lakins still uses the entire four-pitch repertoire that he employed as a starter, though he relies chiefly on his fastball that reaches 96 mph and a plus cutter. Even so, the breadth of pitches gives him a chance to be more than a single-inning reliever. Lakins' fastball is straight, so velocity and location are essential for its effectiveness. His the ability to shape his cutter played off his fastball well and showed the ability to generate swings and misses.

THE FUTURE: Lakins likely will open the year in Triple-A. He should be a big league depth option in 2019 with a middle-innings future.

Year	Club (League)	Class	W	L	ERA	G	GS	CG	SV	IP	H	HR	BB	SO	K/9	WHIP	AVG
2016	Salem (CAR)	HiA	6	3	5.93	19	18	0	0	91	111	8	36	79	7.8	1.62	.299
2017	Salem (CAR)	HiA	5	0	2.61	7	7	0	0	38	32	2	13	43	10.2	1.18	.225
	Portland (EL)	AA	0	4	6.23	8	8	0	0	30	34	2	21	19	5.6	1.81	.301
2018	Portland (EL)	AA	2	2	2.61	26	6	0	1	38	27	3	13	42	9.9	1.05	.191
	Pawtucket (IL)	AAA	1	0	1.65	10	0	0	2	16	11	0	5	15	8.3	0.98	.186
Minor League Totals			14	9	4.42	71	40	0	3	216	215	15	89	201	8.4	1.41	.258

18 DENYI REYES, RHP

BA GRADE

45 Risk: High

Born: Nov. 2, 1996. **B-T:** R-R. **Ht.:** 6-4. **Wt.:** 209. **Signed:** Dominican Republic, 2014. **Signed by:** Manny Nanita/Eddie Romero.

TRACK RECORD: Reyes converted to the pitching from shortstop after signing out of the Dominican Republic in 2014. While he lacks big stuff, his superb command and pitchability have allowed him to dominate the lower levels. Reyes posted a miniscule 1.97 ERA at the Class A levels in 2018, with 145 strikeouts and 19 walks in 155.2 innings.

SCOUTING REPORT: Taken on their own, none of Reyes' four pitches grades average, but he embodies the art of pitching. Reyes has plus command and creative sequencing along with some deception to his 89-92 mph fastball, a combination of traits that has befuddled low-level hitters. He'll mix in a slider, curveball and changeup, with the slider he can backdoor his best secondary. While some note that the big-bodied righthander could add velocity, his present ability to sequence and mix gives him back-end starter potential. His lack of stuff may make it hard for him to turn over a lineup more than once or twice, but he can pitch to a game plan.

THE FUTURE: Some evaluators believe Reyes' sophistication on the mound could allow him to serve as a big league depth option relatively soon, with a chance to emerge as more than that.

Year	Club (League)	Class	W	L	ERA	G	GS	CG	SV	IP	H	HR	BB	SO	K/9	WHIP	AVG
2016	Red Sox (GCL)	R	4	1	2.34	9	3	0	0	35	30	3	4	25	6.5	0.98	.222
2017	Lowell (NYP)	SS	9	0	1.45	15	0	0	0	62	52	3	7	53	7.7	0.95	.221
2018	Greenville (SAL)	LoA	10	3	1.89	21	18	2	0	124	92	11	13	122	8.9	0.85	.201
	Salem (CAR)	HiA	2	2	2.25	6	6	0	0	32	30	2	6	23	6.5	1.13	.242
Minor League Totals			32	7	2.12	66	41	2	0	327	277	19	33	286	7.9	0.95	.224

19 NICK NORTHCUT, 3B

BA GRADE

50 Risk: Extreme

Born: June 13, 1999. **B-T:** R-R. **Ht.:** 6-1. **Wt.:** 200. **Drafted:** HS—Mason, Ohio, 2018 (11th round). **Signed by:** John Pyle.

TRACK RECORD: Though the Red Sox didn't prioritize the addition of power-hitting corners in the 2018 draft, Northcut represented the continuation of a run on such players when the Red Sox took him in the 11th round and signed him away from a Vanderbilt commitment for $565,500. In his pro debut, the 19-year-old hit .223/.303/.319 between Rookie ball and short-season Lowell.

SCOUTING REPORT: Northcut showed the flashes of plus power in his pro debut that drew the Red Sox to him, though he also endured some periods of swings and misses that are typical of righthanded hitters out of high school. Defensively, he has the hands and arm for third. Both his instincts and makeup are considered strong. He has a thick, high-maintenance body that will need to be maintained.

THE FUTURE: Northcut has the upside of a power-hitting everyday third baseman. He'll enter a crowded mix in the lower levels of the Red Sox system at that position.

Year	Club (League)	Class	AVG	G	AB	R	H	2B	3B	HR	RBI	BB	SO	SB	CS	OBP	SLG
2018	Red Sox (GCL)	R	.232	41	142	13	33	9	0	1	20	15	45	0	0	.319	.317
	Lowell (NYP)	SS	.167	6	24	3	4	1	0	1	5	1	10	0	0	.200	.333
Minor League Totals			.223	47	166	16	37	10	0	2	25	16	55	0	0	.303	.319

20 GILBERTO JIMENEZ, OF

BA GRADE

50 Risk: Extreme

Born: July 8, 2000. **B-T:** B-R. **Ht.:** 5-11. **Wt.:** 160. **Signed:** Dominican Republic, 2017. **Signed by:** Eddie Romero/Manny Nanita.

TRACK RECORD: Jimenez slipped through the cracks in the 2017-18 interantional signing period, permitting the Red Sox to sign him for just $10,000. He stood out as a dynamic top-of-the-order hitter with a balanced skill set while hitting .319/.384/.420 in the Dominican Summer League in 2018.

SCOUTING REPORT: A natural righthanded hitter, Jimenez posted much better numbers batting lefthanded (.350/.416/.478) than righthanded (.204/.259/.204) in his first year as a switch-hitter. He showed the speed to impact the game both as a true center fielder and on the bases, though his 16 steals came with 14 times getting thrown out. He shows an across-the-board tool set that grades as average or better except for his power, though it's possible that he could grow into the ability to drive the ball.

THE FUTURE: Jimenez has as much upside as nearly any outfielder in the system, though years remain to show whether that promise takes shape as eventual big league production.

Year	Club (League)	Class	AVG	G	AB	R	H	2B	3B	HR	RBI	BB	SO	SB	CS	OBP	SLG
2018	Red Sox1 (DSL)	R	.319	67	257	42	82	10	8	0	22	19	40	20	15	.384	.420
Minor League Totals			.319	67	257	42	82	10	8	0	22	19	40	20	15	.384	.420

21 JOSH OCKIMEY, 1B

BA GRADE

45 Risk: High

Born: Oct. 18, 1995. **B-T:** L-L. **Ht.:** 6-1. **Wt.:** 215. **Drafted:** HS—Philadelphia, 2014 (5th round). **Signed by:** Chris Calciano.

TRACK RECORD: In five pro seasons since signing for $450,000, Ockimey has shown an ability to drive balls out of the park from line to line, work counts en route to a high volume of walks, and pulverize righties, whom he tagged at a .273/.393/.531 clip in 2018. However, his swings and misses have grown at every level he's climbed, culminating in a concerning 31-percent strikeout rate at Double-A and Triple-A.

SCOUTING REPORT: Ockimey possesses raw power and the ability to drive the ball in the air to all fields, favorable traits for a potential resident of Fenway Park. Yet while he does a good job with pitch recognition, his lack of rhythm at the plate contributes to a high-volume of swings and misses, especially against lefties. He's also defensively limited. Despite a tremendous work ethic, most view him as a future DH with the ability to spend time at first base rather than an ideal everyday first base option.

THE FUTURE: While Ockimey concluded 2018 in Triple-A, his profile—lefthanded platoon DH/first baseman—creates a challenging path to the big leagues. Even so, some believe that he still has the ability to emerge as a more consistent hitter with significant power, with a best-case scenario of an Adam Lind-like role.

Year	Club (League)	Class	AVG	G	AB	R	H	2B	3B	HR	RBI	BB	SO	SB	CS	OBP	SLG
2016	Greenville (SAL)	LoA	.226	117	407	60	92	25	1	18	62	88	129	3	1	.367	.425
2017	Salem (CAR)	HiA	.275	100	349	56	96	20	2	11	63	66	110	1	4	.388	.438
	Portland (EL)	AA	.272	31	103	12	28	7	0	3	11	17	33	0	0	.372	.427
2018	Portland (EL)	AA	.254	90	311	43	79	19	2	15	56	59	112	0	1	.370	.473
	Pawtucket (IL)	AAA	.215	27	93	10	20	2	0	5	15	11	37	1	0	.305	.398
Minor League Totals			.247	457	1574	228	389	89	9	56	255	280	536	8	8	.362	.422

22 KUTTER CRAWFORD, RHP

BA GRADE

45 Risk: High

Born: April 1, 1996. **B-T:** R-R. **Ht.:** 6-1. **Wt.:** 192. **Drafted:** Florida Gulf Coast, 2017 (16th round). **Signed by:** Willie Romay.

TRACK RECORD: After transferring from Indian River (Fla.) to Florida Gulf Coast as a junior, Crawford posted a 1.71 ERA that ranked eighth in NCAA in 2017. But the fact that he did it in the mid-tier Atlantic Sun Conference and the absence of a clear plus offering left him on the board on day three of the draft, when the Red Sox picked him in the 16th round. In 2018, Crawford's performance became harder to overlook. He had a 3.26 ERA, 9.8 strikeouts and 3.0 walks per nine in 27 starts at the Class A levels.

SCOUTING REPORT: Yes, he has a cutter, and it's the best offering in Crawford's four-pitch mix, projecting as a potential average to above-average big league pitch. He also features a fastball that averaged 92 mph early in the year but ticked down a bit later. He mixes in a curveball and changeup, with everything seemingly coming out of the same tunnel. Crawford helps his stuff play up by being a competitor who has an aggressive tempo and mixes his pitches.

THE FUTURE: Crawford's four-pitch mix suggests a potential depth starter. It remains to be seen if he can develop another pitch to the point of surpassing that outlook.

Year	Club (League)	Class	W	L	ERA	G	GS	CG	SV	IP	H	HR	BB	SO	K/9	WHIP	AVG
2017	Lowell (NYP)	SS	0	0	0.00	1	1	0	0	1	1	0	1	2	18.0	2.00	.250
2018	Greenville (SAL)	LoA	5	4	2.96	21	21	0	0	112	104	6	34	120	9.6	1.23	.243
	Salem (CAR)	HiA	2	3	4.31	6	6	0	0	31	28	0	14	37	10.6	1.34	.239
Minor League Totals			7	7	3.24	28	28	0	0	145	133	6	49	159	9.9	1.26	.242

23 ZACH SCHELLENGER, RHP

BA GRADE

50 Risk: Extreme

Born: Jan. 9, 1996. **B-T:** R-R. **Ht.:** 6-5. **Wt.:** 210. **Drafted:** Seton Hall, 2017 (6th round). **Signed by:** Ray Fagnant.

TRACK RECORD: Schellenger showed overpowering late-inning stuff at Seton Hall and especially in the 2016 Cape Cod League but health and durability issues have persisted in pro ball. He forged a 1.65 ERA with big strikeout (38 percent) and groundball (71 percent) rates in 2018, but it came in just 16 innings against Rookie-level and low Class A opponents due to a shoulder impingement and back soreness.

SCOUTING REPORT: Though Schellenger lacks fluidity in his delivery, he repeats from a low three-quarters arm slot that's uncomfortable for hitters, particularly righties. While he touched the upper 90s in college, he's worked more in the mid 90s as a pro with his two-seamer, a pitch that features both sink and armside run, and a wipeout slider. Both pitches show plus potential.

THE FUTURE: Schellenger is hard to forecast. He's got the stuff to fly to the big leagues in a late-innings role, but he hasn't been on the mound enough. Though he's spent little time in Greenville, his stuff may allow the Red Sox to push him to high Class A Salem if he's healthy to start 2019.

Year	Club (League)	Class	W	L	ERA	G	GS	CG	SV	IP	H	HR	BB	SO	K/9	WHIP	AVG
2017	Red Sox (GCL)	R	0	0	6.00	3	1	0	0	3	1	0	6	4	12.0	2.33	.100
2018	Red Sox (GCL)	R	0	0	1.50	6	1	0	0	6	2	0	1	8	12.0	0.50	.105
	Greenville (SAL)	LoA	0	0	1.74	9	0	0	0	10	7	0	3	17	14.8	0.97	.189
Minor League Totals			0	0	2.33	18	2	0	0	19	10	0	10	29	13.5	1.03	.152

24 CHASE SHUGART, RHP

BA GRADE
45 Risk: High

Born: Oct. 24, 1996. **B-T:** R-R. **Ht.:** 5-10. **Wt.:** 180. **Drafted:** Texas, 2018 (12th round). **Signed by:** Brandon Agamennone.

TRACK RECORD: After Shugart spent two years pitching out of Texas' bullpen, the Longhorns moved him into the rotation as a junior. He showed the ability to mix four pitches while working to a 4.36 ERA in 84 innings, but then showed surprisingly impressive stuff in his pro debut after the Red Sox took him in the 12th round and signed him for $125,000.

SCOUTING REPORT: In bursts, Shugart has shown arm strength with a fastball up to 97 mph and an athletic delivery that allows him to work to both sides of the plate with a four-pitch mix. His diminutive stature raises questions about whether he will have the durability to sustain mid-90s velocity as a starter or if he's more likely to work in the low 90s as he did at Texas. He mixes in a changeup, slider and curveball to round out his arsenal, though none stand out as plus.

THE FUTURE: Shugart's mix permits him to project as a multi-inning reliever if not a starter. He'll get a chance in spring training to compete for a rotation spot at high Class A Salem in 2017.

Year	Club (League)	Class	W	L	ERA	G	GS	CG	SV	IP	H	HR	BB	SO	K/9	WHIP	AVG
2018	Red Sox (GCL)	R	0	1	1.80	3	3	0	0	5	4	0	1	6	10.8	1.00	.211
	Lowell (NYP)	SS	0	0	0.00	1	1	0	0	3	0	0	0	3	9.0	0.00	.000
Minor League Totals			0	1	1.13	4	4	0	0	8	4	0	1	9	10.1	0.63	.138

25 EDUARDO LOPEZ, CF

BA GRADE
50 Risk: Extreme

Born: May 8, 2002. **B-T:** B-R. **Ht.:** 6-0. **Wt.:** 170. **Signed:** Dominican Republic, 2018. **Signed by:** Eddie Romero/Esau Medina.

TRACK RECORD: Lopez emerged as one of the top hitters in the 2018 international class despite lacking huge tools. The Red Sox committed $1.15 million to him based on the combination of his up-the-middle athleticism and advanced instincts and polish in games throughout the scouting process.

SCOUTING REPORT: The switch-hitting Lopez features a swing that is similar from both sides, one with which he consistently squares the ball while laying off pitches outside of the strike zone. He projects to be an above-average to plus hitter with the potential for power as he gains strength. Though an average runner, his instincts are strong enough that the Red Sox project him to stay in center field.

THE FUTURE: Lopez will make his pro debut in the Dominican Summer League in 2019, but there's a chance he could move fast given the unusual advancement of his game.

Year	Club (League)	Class	AVG	G	AB	R	H	2B	3B	HR	RBI	BB	SO	SB	CS	OBP	SLG
2018	Did not play—Signed 2019 contract																

26 ALEX SCHERFF, RHP

BA GRADE
50 Risk: Extreme

Born: Feb. 5, 1998. **B-T:** S-R. **Ht.:** 6-3. **Wt.:** 205. **Drafted:** HS—Colleyville, Texas, 2017 (5th round). **Signed by:** Brandon Agamennone.

TRACK RECORD: Scherff, the 2017 Gatorade High School Player of the Year in Texas, got off to a dreadful start at low Class A Greenville in 2018 while attempting to make some delivery adjustments. But after forging a 9.35 ERA with more walks than strikeouts through four starts, he recovered to post a 3.25 ERA with 7.3 strikeouts and 1.9 walks per nine the rest of the way while showing improved stuff and command. He missed two months in the middle of the year with an intercostal strain.

SCOUTING REPORT: Once Scherff restored his mechanics, he frequently worked at 93-95 mph on his fastball with a good feel for a solid changeup that misses barrels. His fastball lacks deception, but he should have the velocity and command to compensate. His third pitch is a work in progress. In high school he threw a curveball, but he worked during instructional league to shift to a slider, and it's possible that he'll refine that to more of a cutter.

THE FUTURE: If Scherff finds an average or better third pitch, he has the makings of a starter. If not, his future is in the bullpen. His spring training performance will determine whether he opens 2019 at high

Class A Salem or back in Greenville.

Year	Club (League)	Class	W	L	ERA	G	GS	CG	SV	IP	H	HR	BB	SO	K/9	WHIP	AVG
2018	Red Sox (GCL)	R	0	0	1.80	2	1	0	0	5	5	0	1	3	5.4	1.20	.294
	Greenville (SAL)	LoA	1	5	4.98	15	15	0	0	65	68	7	23	51	7.1	1.40	.279
Minor League Totals			1	5	4.76	17	16	0	0	70	73	7	24	54	6.9	1.39	.280

27 PEDRO CASTELLANOS, 1B/OF

BA GRADE

45 Risk: Very High

Born: Dec. 11, 1997. **B-T:** R-R. **Ht.:** 6-3. **Wt.:** 195. **Signed:** Venezuela, 2015.
Signed by: Rolando Pino/Ernesto Gomez.

TRACK RECORD: Castellanos has done nothing but hit since entering the Red Sox's system, posting a .319/.365/.437 slash line in three seasons and batting over .300 every year. That line was held down by back injuries that limited him in the first half at low Class A Greenville in 2018. Once healthy, he posted a .330/.360/.427 line in the second half.

SCOUTING REPORT: Castellanos defies expectations. He's a big man who looks like he should feature plenty of power while having holes in his swing. Instead, he has miniscule strikeout rates (13.2 percent in 2018) and sprays the ball to all fields. For now, he features an atypical corner profile of a potential plus hit tool with well below-average in-game power. Castellanos does have the size and strength to suggest an uptick in doubles and homers if he starts lofting the ball. He's hit .370 in his career with more power against lefties.

THE FUTURE: Castellanos has a track record that suggests he can hit, and if he continues to post huge averages against lefties, he'll keep moving up as a potential platoon bat. If he taps into his reservoir of raw power without severely compromising his sound offensive approach, he has a chance to emerge as a regular. He will open 2019 at high Class A Salem.

Year	Club (League)	Class	AVG	G	AB	R	H	2B	3B	HR	RBI	BB	SO	SB	CS	OBP	SLG
2016	Red Sox2 (DSL)	R	.325	62	237	28	77	23	4	3	47	20	25	2	5	.392	.494
2017	Red Sox (GCL)	R	.339	52	186	27	63	14	1	2	30	10	15	0	0	.385	.457
	Greenville (SAL)	LoA	.333	2	9	1	3	1	0	0	1	0	2	0	0	.333	.444
2018	Greenville (SAL)	LoA	.302	88	344	39	104	20	3	1	34	12	50	1	3	.334	.387
Minor League Totals			.318	204	776	95	247	58	8	6	112	42	92	3	8	.365	.437

28 SAM TRAVIS, 1B/OF

BA GRADE

40 Risk: High

Born: Aug. 27, 1993. **B-T:** R-R. **Ht.:** 6-0. **Wt.:** 205. **Drafted:** Indiana, 2014 (2nd round). **Signed by:** Blair Henry.

TRACK RECORD: For years Travis looked like one of the best pure hitters in Boston's system, but his performance has gotten progressively worse over three seasons in Triple-A. He hit .258/.317/.360 with Pawtucket in 2018, posting his highest strikeout rate (22.4 percent) and lowest isolated power (.102) at any minor league level of his career.

SCOUTING REPORT: Travis tried to overhaul his direct-to-the-ball approach with an eye toward turning his considerable strength into more extra-base impact. The opposite occurred, with Travis seeing his groundball and strikeout rates go up, particularly against righties. Down the stretch he got back to a more contact-oriented, all-fields approach, slashing his strikeout rate roughly in half (from 27.8 percent to 14.8 percent) and hitting .299/.345/.383. He's made significant defensive strides at first, while delivering below-average defense in left.

THE FUTURE: It's become increasingly difficult to see Travis as an everyday first baseman, but even in his difficult 2018, he hit well enough against lefties (.284/.367/.432) to suggest a decent shot at a platoon role. He'll likely open 2019 back in Pawtucket.

Year	Club (League)	Class	AVG	G	AB	R	H	2B	3B	HR	RBI	BB	SO	SB	CS	OBP	SLG
2016	Pawtucket (IL)	AAA	.272	47	173	26	47	10	0	6	29	15	40	1	0	.332	.434
2017	Pawtucket (IL)	AAA	.270	82	304	40	82	14	0	6	24	37	57	6	2	.351	.375
	Boston (AL)	MAJ	.263	33	76	13	20	6	0	0	1	6	23	1	0	.325	.342
2018	Pawtucket (IL)	AAA	.258	97	361	35	93	13	0	8	43	29	89	1	2	.317	.360
	Boston (AL)	MAJ	.222	19	36	5	8	3	0	1	7	2	10	0	0	.263	.389
Major League Totals			.250	52	112	18	28	9	0	1	8	8	33	1	0	.306	.357
Minor League Totals			.286	424	1599	211	458	85	8	36	218	151	295	32	18	.351	.417

29 BRETT NETZER, 2B

BA GRADE

40 Risk: High

Born: June 4, 1996. **B-T:** L-R. **Ht.:** 6-0. **Wt.:** 195. **Drafted:** Charlotte, 2017 (3rd round). **Signed by:** Pat Portugal.

TRACK RECORD: Netzer played his first full pro season in 2018 under challenging circumstances after his father passed away from colon cancer in the spring. By the end of the year at high Class A Salem, Netzer seemed understandably drained while posting a .235/.292/.329 line down the stretch. But some evaluators believed a strong first half in which he hit .308/.361/.396 while showing good strike-zone judgment, may be more representative of his skill set.

SCOUTING REPORT: Netzer swings at strikes and shoots line drives to all fields. The approach serves him well against righties (.288/.344/.377 in 2018) but he struggles against lefties (.229/.278/.319) and has little power present or projectable. Defensively, he projects as average or a tick below at second.

THE FUTURE: Netzer's contact ability from the left side is a good starting point, but he needs to make more impact and improve his defense. He stands to open 2019 at Double-A Portland.

Year	Club (League)	Class	AVG	G	AB	R	H	2B	3B	HR	RBI	BB	SO	SB	CS	OBP	SLG
2017	Lowell (NYP)	SS	.317	22	82	11	26	6	0	0	14	9	20	0	3	.376	.390
	Greenville (SAL)	LoA	.260	26	100	15	26	4	0	0	13	9	24	5	1	.327	.300
2018	Salem (CAR)	HiA	.270	124	481	50	130	31	3	2	50	37	115	3	8	.325	.360
Minor League Totals			.275	172	663	76	182	41	3	2	77	55	159	8	12	.332	.354

30 YOAN AYBAR, LHP

BA GRADE

45 Risk: Extreme

Born: July 3, 1997. **B-T:** L-L. **Ht.:** 6-2. **Wt.:** 165. **Signed:** Dominican Republic, 2013. **Signed by:** Jonathan Cruz/Eddie Romero

TRACK RECORD: Signed as a potential five-tool outfielder out of the Dominican Republic in 2013, Aybar didn't hit enough in four pro seasons to progress beyond A-ball, and so the decision was made to see how his rocket of an arm would translate to the mound. Despite modest numbers (4.13 ERA, 8.6 strikeouts and 4.4 walks per nine), he showed standout flashes in Rookie ball and short-season Lowell in his pitching debut.

SCOUTING REPORT: Aybar has shown the ability to work at 96-98 mph with his fastball, and both his changeup and slider have gotten swings and misses. His mechanics remain inconsistent, which isn't a surprise given his long limbs and lack of prior pitching experience, but in flashes he shows the makings of a lefthanded power arm out of the bullpen.

THE FUTURE: Though raw, Aybar showed plenty of promise in his initial work off a mound. His inexperience suggests a slow progression would be beneficial.

Year	Club (League)	Class	W	L	ERA	G	GS	CG	SV	IP	H	HR	BB	SO	K/9	WHIP	AVG
2018	Red Sox (GCL)	R	1	1	4.10	15	0	0	0	26	23	0	12	27	9.2	1.33	.232
	Lowell (NYP)	SS	1	0	4.50	2	0	0	0	2	2	0	2	0	0.0	2.00	.250
Minor League Totals			2	1	4.13	17	0	0	0	28	25	0	14	27	8.6	1.38	.234

Chicago Cubs

BY JOSH NORRIS

The Cubs' 2018 season boiled down to two painful days.

Their loss to the Brewers on Oct. 1 ceded the NL Central to Milwaukee, and their loss to the Rockies a night later in the wild card game bounced them from the playoffs. Just like that, a team that held a five-game division as late as Sept. 2 ended its season with a whimper.

The problems that led to that early exit presented themselves early. The team's marquee addition in free agency, Yu Darvish, was equal parts ineffective and injured, and had to be replaced down the stretch through a trade for lefthander Cole Hamels. Cornerstone third baseman Kris Bryant, too, was stung by the injury bug and missed 60 games.

The bright side for the Cubs, however, is that their youthful core of position players could easily turn the team's fortunes in 2019. MVP contender Javier Baez, buttressed by a refreshed Bryant and Willson Contreras, could mash the team back to the top of the division. Continued mashing from cornermen Anthony Rizzo and Kyle Schwarber should figure into that equation as well.

The problem now is not the near future, but the long term. Trades of Gleyber Torres to the Yankees and Eloy Jimenez and Dylan Cease to the White Sox have stripped the Cubs' farm system of its most precious jewels. The Torres trade brought a World Series to Chicago, so there's little regret there, but Jimenez and Cease returned only lefthander Jose Quintana, who was underwhelming in his first full season with the Cubs. Jimenez ranks as one of the finest prospects in the game, and Cease is trending toward a middle-of-the-rotation future.

To remedy looming deficits, the Cubs, led by scouting director Matt Dorey, went hitter-heavy in the 2018 draft. Four of the club's first five picks were hitters. That group was led by Stanford middle infielder Nico Hoerner, whose pro debut was cut short by injury though he recovered in time to tear up the Arizona Fall League. Hoerner was followed by high-end high school talents Brennen Davis and Cole Roederer, who wowed scouts with their performances in the Rookie-level Arizona League.

The team also got a breakout year from catcher Miguel Amaya, whose scorching first half propelled him to a spot in the Futures Game. Lefthander Brailyn Marquez also impressed evaluators with a mid-90s fastball and ranked among the top prospects in the short-season Northwest League.

The Cubs' main objective now should be to acquire the pitching to back up their array of fear-

Javier Baez made the all-star team in 2018 and finished runner-up for National League MVP.

PROJECTED 2022 LINEUP

Catcher	Willson Contreras (29)
First Base	Anthony Rizzo (32)
Second Base	Javier Baez (29)
Third Base	Kris Bryant (30)
Shortstop	Nico Hoerner (25)
Left Field	Kyle Schwarber (29)
Center Field	Albert Almora Jr. (29)
Right Field	Ian Happ (27)
No. 1 Starter	Jose Quintana (33)
No. 2 Starter	Yu Darvish (35)
No. 3 Starter	Kyle Hendricks (32)
No. 4 Starter	Brailyn Marquez (23)
No. 5 Starter	Adbert Alzolay (27)
Closer	Carl Edwards Jr. (30)

some hitters. Hamels and Jon Lester will be 35 come Opening Day, while Darvish and Quintana didn't provide any evidence that they could front a rotation with designs on the ultimate prize.

The rise of the Brewers presents another problem for the Cubs. Milwaukee signed outfielder Lorenzo Cain then dealt for MVP Christian Yelich, who lifted the team across the finish line in the second half. Cain is signed through 2022, and Yelich is under team control for the same term.

All this means the Cubs will have to be creative in their pursuit of pitching as they attempt to return to the World Series before their core of sluggers gets too expensive to keep together for the long-term.

CHICAGO CUBS

TOP 2019 ROOKIE: Adbert Alzolay, RHP. After recovering from injury, Alzolay should get a chance to make an impact in the rotation.
BREAKOUT PROSPECT: Richard Gallardo, RHP. The Cubs' top international signee from 2018 could leap up the ranks with a strong debut.
SLEEPER: Yunior Perez, RHP. The 20-year-old already brings his fastball up to 99 mph.

SOURCE OF TOP 30 TALENT

Homegrown	29	Acquired	1
College	10	Trade	1
Junior college	2	Rule 5 draft	0
High school	7	Independent league	0
Nondrafted free agent	0	Free agent/waivers	0
International	10		

LF
Cole Roederer (4)
Jimmy Herron (26)
Mark Zagunis

CF
Brennen Davis (5)
Edmond Americaan (16)
D.J. Wilson (25)
D.J. Artis
Fernando Kelli
Charcer Burks
Chris Singleton

RF
Nelson Velazquez (13)
Jonathan Sierra
Eddy Martinez
Jose Gutierrez

3B
Luke Reynolds
Austin Filiere

SS
Nico Hoerner (1)
Aramis Ademan (10)
Luis Verdugo (12)
Zack Short (19)
Reivaj Garcia (23)
Christopher Morel
Luis Vazquez

2B
Andy Weber
Trent Giambrone

1B
Jared Young (24)
Fidel Mejia
Austin Upshaw

C
Miguel Amaya (2)
Jhonny Pereda (26)
P.J. Higgins

LHP

LHSP	LHRP
Brailyn Marquez (3)	Manuel Rondon
Justin Steele (9)	Wyatt Short
Brendon Little (17)	
Bryan Hudson	

RHP

RHSP	RHRP
Adbert Alzolay (6)	Dillon Maples (18)
Paul Richan (7)	James Norwood
Cory Abbott (8	Yunior Perez
Richard Gallardo (11)	Duane Underwood
Alex Lange (14)	Dakota Mekkes
Jose Albertos (15)	
Riley Thompson (20)	
Oscar De La Cruz (21)	
Thomas Hatch (22)	
Trevor Clifton (27)	
Keegan Thompson (29)	
Erick Leal (30)	
Jeremiah Estrada	
Yovanny Cruz	
Javier Assad	
Erich Uelmen	
Alec Mills	
Tyson Miller	
Matt Swarmer	
Alexander Vargas	

DRAFT ANALYSIS

2018

BEST PURE HITTER: OF Cole Roederer (2s) showed an advanced feel to hit for a prep player, including an ability to use the whole field and hang in against lefthanders. The Cubs liked Stanford SS Nico Hoerner (1) for his ability to put bat on ball. He whiffed no more than 29 times in each of his three seasons, and he showed an his ability to make every at-bat competitive.

BEST POWER: Southern Miss 3B Luke Reynolds (10) took a circuitous path to the draft, but he has plus raw power now and put forth a 1.250 OPS in his final season in college. OF Brennen Davis' (2) strength, athleticism and lofted swing path gives him chance to develop above-average power.

FASTEST RUNNER: OF Edmond Americaan (35) greatly improved his game with one year at Chipola JC. His toolset includes 70-grade speed, which he used to steal 11 bases in a 30-game pro debut in the Rookie-level Arizona League. Liberty OF D.J. Artis (7) isn't far behind Americaan, clocking in with plus speed.

BEST DEFENSIVE PLAYER: The Cubs got a polished infielder when they took INF Andy Weber (5) out of Virginia. Weber, who spent time at shortstop, third base and second base during his time with the Cavaliers, has smooth hands, a quick transfer and an accurate, plus arm.

BEST ATHLETE: Davis also starred in basketball in high school, earning defensive player of the year honors in Arizona. His mother, Jakki, was a long jumper at the University of Washington.

BEST FASTBALL: Louisville RHP Riley Thompson (11) ran his fastball up to 98 mph and sat in the 93-94 mph range in his pro debut. The Cubs say the pitch showed the carry and ride through the zone that makes the pitch play better when it's thrown in the upper part of the zone.

BEST SECONDARY PITCH: RHP Paul Richan (2s) has a full four-pitch arsenal and earns high marks for his ability to vary the shape and velocity on his

TOP DRAFT PICKS OF THE DECADE

Year	Player, Pos	2018 Org
2009	Brett Jackson, OF	Did not play
2010	Hayden Simpson, RHP	Did not play
2011	Javier Baez, SS	Cubs
2012	Albert Almora, OF	Cubs
2013	Kris Bryant, 3B	Cubs
2014	Kyle Schwarber, C	Cubs
2015	Ian Happ, OF	Cubs
2016	Thomas Hatch, RHP (3rd round)	Cubs
2017	Brendon Little, LHP	Cubs
2018	Nico Hoerner, SS	Cubs

slider. He can throw the pitch for strikes and chases and will do so to both sides of the plate.

BEST PRO DEBUT: Hoerner was trending this way before his season was cut short, but Roederer takes the honor for his excellent turn in the AZL. Roederer ranked No. 7 on BA's AZL Top 20 Prospects list for his all-around blend of skills.

MOST INTRIGUING BACKGROUND: Both of Weber's parents are violinists, and his father plays professionally with the Cleveland Orchestra. In addition to his basketball background and athletic bloodlines, Davis also owns a pet goat and two pet llamas named Marco and Polo.

CLOSEST TO THE MAJORS: Hoerner spent three years in the Pacific-12 Conference, and he showed well in the Arizona Fall League against some of the best competition in the minor leagues in his first taste of pro ball. He has a chance to hit his way to Chicago in short order.

BEST LATE-ROUND PICK: The Cubs had long been intrigued by Americaan, whom they nabbed in the 35th round and signed for a round-high $208,950. The figure was also the highest bonus in their class after the seventh round.

THE ONE WHO GOT AWAY: LHP Mitchell Parker (28) and RHP Tyler Ras (33) are a pair of projectable pitchers who may blossom in college.

—JOSH NORRIS

2017

The Cubs went heavy on college pitching and landed some intriguing arms. RHP Cory Abbott (2) led the organization in ERA in 2018. OF Nelson Velazquez (5) has been the best of the position players so far.

GRADE: C

2016

The Cubs didn't have a pick in the first two rounds and then focused on college pitching. RHP Thomas Hatch (3) is the best of that group, while SS Zack Short (17) has been a late-round surprise.

GRADE: F

2015

This class is largely riding on OF Ian Happ (1), who had an up-and-down season. OF D.J. Wilson (4) still offers upside, and OF Donnie Dewees (2) and 3B Matt Rose (11) were used as trade chips.

GRADE: B

1 NICO HOERNER, SS

Born: May 13, 1997. **B-T:** R-R. **HT:** 6-1. **WT:** 200. **Drafted:** Stanford, 2018 (1st round). **Signed by:** Gabe Zappin.

While he was never a thumper during his three seasons at Stanford, Hoerner stood out for his ability to make consistent quality contact. He never had a strikeout rate higher than 12.5 percent in any season. He also showed aptitude with wood bats by hitting better than .300 in both the Northwoods and Cape Cod leagues. Combine those skills with his leadership qualities up the middle, and it was an easy call for the Cubs to draft Hoerner 24th overall and sign him for $2,724,000. His pro career started with a bang when he hit the first pitch he saw in the Rookie-level Arizona League for a triple. He moved quickly through the AZL and short-season Eugene before arriving at the low Class A South Bend. His regular season stopped there when he strained a ligament in his left elbow. He recovered in time for an assignment to the Arizona Fall League, where he produced an .867 OPS over 21 games.

SCOUTING REPORT: In an era where big strikeout totals are common, Hoerner's knack for putting the bat on the ball stands out, but that contact did not come with a significant skew toward one side of the field. He sprayed line drives from gap to gap, though most of his power was to his pull side. As suggested by his contact skills, Hoerner also showed an excellent approach with two strikes and did not give away at-bats. Those skills give him a chance to be a plus hitter with below-average power. Defensively, he's not going to wow evaluators with highlight reel plays or extraordinary range, but he's not going to make many foolish mistakes, either. The Cubs compare him with the Cardinals' Paul DeJong, who doesn't jump off the page at shortstop but has managed to stick there because of his instincts. Hoerner has the arm strength to stick at shortstop but needs to become more consistent with his mechanics. Specifically, the Cubs want him to work through the ball more often when he throws and use his momentum to keep the ball true to his target. The Cubs see a scenario where Hoerner's athleticism would allow him to move around the diamond, like Ian Happ.

THE FUTURE: Though Hoerner's time in South Bend was short, his college pedigree and successful stint in the AFL will likely allow the Cubs to move him to high Class A Myrtle Beach in 2019. He will continue to try to solidify a permanent role at shortstop while further proving his hit tool against more experienced pitchers.

ZACHARY LUCY/FOUR SEAM

BA GRADE	SCOUTING GRADES
55 Risk: High	Hit: 60. Power: 40. Run: 55. Field: 50. Arm: 50.

Projected future grades on 20-80 scouting scale.

TOP PROSPECTS OF THE DECADE

Year	Player, Pos	2018 Org
2009	Josh Vitters, 3B	Can-Am League
2010	Starlin Castro, SS	Marlins
2011	Chris Archer, RHP	Pirates
2012	Brett Jackson, OF	Did not play
2013	Javier Baez, SS	Cubs
2014	Javier Baez, SS	Cubs
2015	Kris Bryant, 3B	Cubs
2016	Gleyber Torres, SS	Yankees
2017	Eloy Jimenez, OF	White Sox
2018	Aramis Ademan, SS	Cubs

BEST TOOLS

Best Hitter for Average	Nico Hoerner
Best Power Hitter	Brennen Davis
Best Strike-Zone Discipline	Mark Zagunis
Fastest Baserunner	D.J. Wilson
Best Athlete	Brennen Davis
Best Fastball	Brailyn Marquez
Best Curveball	Alex Lange
Best Slider	Dillon Maples
Best Changeup	Duane Underwood Jr.
Best Control	Cory Abbott
Best Defensive Catcher	Miguel Amaya
Best Defensive Infielder	Zack Short
Best Infield Arm	Luis Verdugo
Best Defensive Outfielder	D.J. Wilson
Best Outfield Arm	Eddy Martinez

Year	Club (League)	Class	AVG	G	AB	R	H	2B	3B	HR	RBI	BB	SO	SB	CS	OBP	SLG
2018	Cubs 1 (AZL)	R	.250	3	12	3	3	1	1	0	1	2	0	2	0	.400	.500
	Eugene (NWL)	SS	.318	7	22	6	7	0	1	1	2	5	3	4	1	.464	.545
	South Bend (MWL)	LoA	.400	4	15	1	6	1	0	1	3	2	1	0	0	.471	.667
Minor League Totals			.327	14	49	10	16	2	2	2	6	9	4	6	1	.450	.571

2 MIGUEL AMAYA, C

Born: March 9, 1999. **B-T:** R-R. **HT:** 6-1. **WT:** 200. **Signed:** Panama, 2015.
Signed by: Cirillo Cumberbatch/Hector Ortega/Louie Eljaua.
TRACK RECORD: After a strong showing in 15U tournaments for Panama, t
The Cubs liked Amaya's combination of advanced defensive skills and hitting
ability and signed him for $1 million out of Panama in 2015. They skipped
him over the Rookie-level Arizona League straight to short-season Eugene in
2017, where he ranked as the league's No. 16 prospect. He broke out during
the first half of 2018 at low Class A South Bend, when he hit .288/.365/.500
with nine home runs and earned a spot in the annual Futures Game. but his
production tailed off in the second half because of his jump in workload. His
116 games played in 2018 matched his totals from the previous two seasons
combined.

BA GRADE

55 Risk:
High

Hit: 50. **Power:** 50.
Run: 20. **Field:** 60.
Arm: 60.

SCOUTING REPORT: Before wearing down in the Midwest League, Amaya
used a loose, compact swing to spray line drives from gap to gap. He showed
the typical weaknesses expected from a 19-year-old getting his first test at
full-season ball, including a need to better recognize spin. He hit fastballs well, and showed home run
power mainly to his pull side, though not exclusively. Evaluators expect above-average power in the future,
though that forecast could change as his pitch recognition improves. He's a calm receiver and with strong
hands that help him steal strikes for his pitchers. He does especially well bringing low pitches back into
the bottom part of the zone. He's got above-average arm strength but needs to clean up his footwork,
though he still threw out 34 percent of runners in the Midwest League.
THE FUTURE: After a career-high workload, Amaya will begin 2019 with high Class A Myrtle Beach,
where he'll try to prove that his first half in 2018 wasn't a fluke.

Year	Club (League)	Class	AVG	G	AB	R	H	2B	3B	HR	RBI	BB	SO	SB	CS	OBP	SLG
2016	Cubs2 (DSL)	R	.245	58	208	29	51	12	0	1	22	21	27	9	3	.344	.317
2017	Eugene (NWL)	SS	.228	58	228	21	52	14	1	3	26	11	49	1	0	.266	.338
2018	South Bend (MWL)	LoA	.256	116	414	54	106	21	2	12	52	50	91	1	0	.349	.403
Minor League Totals			.246	232	850	104	209	47	3	16	100	82	167	11	3	.327	.365

3 BRAILYN MARQUEZ, LHP

Born: Jan. 30, 1999. **B-T:** L-L. **HT:** 6-4. **WT:** 185. **Signed:** Dominican Republic,
2015. **Signed by:** Marino Encarnacion/Jose Serra/Alex Suarez/Louie Eljaua.
TRACK RECORD: Marquez's $600,000 bonus was the biggest for any lefthand-
er in the 2015 international class. He earned that bonus by showing a present
low-90s fastball along with projection to spare. He followed a strong pro
debut in the Dominican Summer League with a rocky turn in the Rookie-
level Arizona League before breaking out at short-season Eugene in 2018. He
ranked No. 3 on the Northwest League's Top 20 prospect list.
SCOUTING REPORT: Marquez stands out immediately for his power fastball
from the left side. The pitch sits in the mid-90s, touches 98 mph and shows
riding life through the zone. He backs it up with a pair of offspeed pitches
that need refinement but project as above-average or better. His mid-80s slider
snaps out of the zone at its best, but he needs to find more consistent spin
to keep it from becoming loose and looking like a bad curveball. Marquez's
changeup, thrown around 86-91 mph, shows hard lateral movement like a

BA GRADE

55 Risk:
Very High

Fastball: 70.
Change: 60.
Slider: 55. **CTL:** 50.

two-seam fastball away from righthanded hitters. He also showed a strong idea of how to set hitters up
and continue to throw his best stuff with men on base. He needs to get stronger to maintain his velocity
through the later innings and repeat his delivery, which would help improve his fringy command.
THE FUTURE: Marquez finished 2018 at low Class A South Bend and should return there to begin 2019.
He has the ceiling of a mid-rotation starter.

Year	Club (League)	Class	W	L	ERA	G	GS	CG	SV	IP	H	HR	BB	SO	K/9	WHIP	AVG
2016	Cubs (DSL)	R	4	2	1.48	12	12	0	0	55	44	1	23	48	7.9	1.23	.222
2017	Cubs (AZL)	R	2	1	5.52	11	9	0	0	44	50	3	12	52	10.6	1.41	.275
2018	Eugene (NWL)	SS	1	4	3.21	10	10	0	0	48	46	5	14	52	9.8	1.26	.257
	South Bend (MWL)	LoA	0	0	2.57	2	2	0	0	7	7	0	2	7	9.0	1.29	.259
Minor League Totals			7	7	3.23	35	33	0	0	153	147	9	51	159	9.3	1.29	.251

4 COLE ROEDERER, OF

BILL MITCHELL

Born: Sept. 24, 1999. **B-T:** L-L. **HT:** 6-0. **WT:** 175. **Drafted:** HS—Santa Clarita, Calif, 2018 (2nd round supplemental). **Signed by:** Tom Myers.

TRACK RECORD: Roederer vaulted up draft boards in 2018 after getting stronger and retooling his swing to add more power. He lost part of his season at Hart High with a separated right shoulder and a pulled hamstring. He was listed on BA's High School All-America third team, and The Cubs used a $1.2 million bonus to pry him away from a commitment to UCLA. He performed well in the Rookie-level Arizona League and ranked No. 7 on the circuit's prospect list.

SCOUTING REPORT: Roederer had always been an interesting prospect, but the enhanced power sealed the deal. Before the draft, scouts saw enough sock in his bat to project a ceiling of 20-25 home runs. Scouts saw a short, compact swing with plenty of bat speed and hands skilled enough to find the barrel often to project a plus hit tool with above-average power. Roederer has the instincts to play center field, but his fringe-average speed might push him to a corner. His arm is fringe-average, but he releases the ball quickly and his throws are accurate. Scouts on both the amateur and pro side saw hints of the same type of skill set that made Andrew Benintendi a star for the Red Sox.

THE FUTURE: After an excellent summer in Arizona, Roederer is likely to begin 2019 at low Class A South Bend, where he'll be tested by the jump in pitching and the bitter cold of the early-season Midwest League.

BA GRADE
55 Risk: Extreme
Hit: 60. Power: 55.
Run: 50. Field: 50.
Arm: 45.

Year	Club (League)	Class	AVG	G	AB	R	H	2B	3B	HR	RBI	BB	SO	SB	CS	OBP	SLG
2018	Cubs 2 (AZL)	R	.275	36	142	30	39	4	4	5	24	18	37	13	4	.354	.465
Minor League Totals			.275	36	142	30	39	4	4	5	24	18	37	13	4	.354	.465

5 BRENNEN DAVIS, OF

BILL MITCHELL

Born: Nov. 2, 1999. **B-T:** R-R. **HT:** 6-4. **WT:** 175. **Drafted:** HS—Chandler, Ariz., 2018 (2nd round). **Signed by:** Steve McFarland.

TRACK RECORD: Davis was a two-sport star in high school and earned defensive player of the year honors for his work on the basketball court. He came to baseball relatively late, which, along with his enviable frame, gives him a large amount of projection. Despite struggles with a hamstring injury, Davis translated enough of his raw talents into skills over the course of his senior year to warrant a second-round pick and a $1.1 million bonus to pry him from a commitment to Miami.

SCOUTING REPORT: The Cubs eased Davis into pro ball with the expectation that his talent would gradually show itself. He has a bit of a grooved swing that might prevent him from hitting for a high average, but he has enough loft to combine with his natural strength to produce at least above-average power. Scouts who saw him in the Rookie-level Arizona League believe his speed—which grades out as at least plus—average arm and instincts should help him stay in center field. He has to catch up with other players his age, but his raw tools give him a chance to become an impact player.

THE FUTURE: Davis will begin the 2019 season back in extended spring training before heading to either the AZL or the short-season Northwest League, where he'll be tested by advanced pitching.

BA GRADE
50 Risk: Very High
Hit: 45. Power: 60.
Run: 60. Field: 55.
Arm: 50.

Year	Club (League)	Class	AVG	G	AB	R	H	2B	3B	HR	RBI	BB	SO	SB	CS	OBP	SLG
2018	Cubs 2 (AZL)	R	.298	18	57	9	17	2	0	0	3	10	12	6	1	.431	.333
Minor League Totals			.298	18	57	9	17	2	0	0	3	10	12	6	1	.431	.333

6 ADBERT ALZOLAY, RHP

Born: March 1, 1995. **B-T:** R-R. **HT:** 6-1. **WT:** 175. **Signed:** Dominican Republic, 2012. **Signed by:** Julio Figueroa/Hector Ortega.

TRACK RECORD: Alzolay was a fairly anonymous addition when the Cubs signed him as a 17-year-old, but he burst up the prospect rankings with a strong 2017 season split between high Class A Myrtle Beach and Double-A Tennessee. He achieved those results with a fastball that had jumped a grade—from the low to mid-90s—thanks to a commitment to the Cubs' throwing program and better incorporation of his lower half. He appeared on the cusp of the big leagues in 2018 before a lat injury halted his season.

SCOUTING REPORT: Before the injury, Alzolay was continuing to build on the progress he made in 2017. He continued to show a mid-90s fastball and an average curveball in the low 80s and, to the Cubs' delight, had begun to show more feel for his changeup, which had ranked as a below-average pitch entering the season. He was still as aggressive on the mound as ever, and had ramped up his efforts to learn English and keep himself in peak physical shape. To accomplish the latter goal, he had taken to hiking Camelback Mountain on days off.

THE FUTURE: Alzolay will head back to Triple-A Iowa with a goal of making his major league debut in 2019. He has the upside of a mid-rotation starter.

BA GRADE

45 Risk: High

Fastball: 60.
Curveball: 55.
Change: 50. CTL: 45.

Year	Club (League)	Class	W	L	ERA	G	GS	CG	SV	IP	H	HR	BB	SO	K/9	WHIP	AVG
2016	South Bend (MWL)	LoA	9	4	4.34	22	20	0	0	120	119	9	28	81	6.1	1.22	.260
2017	Myrtle Beach (CAR)	HiA	7	1	2.98	15	15	1	0	82	65	8	22	78	8.6	1.07	.217
	Tennessee (SL)	AA	0	3	3.03	7	7	0	0	33	27	0	12	30	8.3	1.19	.229
2018	Iowa (PCL)	AAA	2	4	4.76	8	8	0	0	40	43	4	13	27	6.1	1.41	.281
Minor League Totals			31	22	3.44	89	68	1	0	422	365	30	112	354	7.6	1.13	.232

7 PAUL RICHAN, RHP

Born: March 26, 1997. **B-T:** R-R. **HT:** 6-2. **WT:** 200. **Drafted:** San Diego, 2018 (2nd round supplemental). **Signed by:** Alex Lontayo.

TRACK RECORD: Richan's draft year started strong when he tossed eight innings of one-run ball against Michigan in an early-season tournament. He faded down the stretch a bit, but the Cubs were undeterred and popped him with their pick in the supplemental second round. Because he was so advanced, the Cubs moved Richan immediately to short-season Eugene, where he was part of the Emeralds' improbable run to the Northwest League title.

SCOUTING REPORT: Richan's arsenal is by no means flashy, but he pounds the zone with four pitches for strikes. He starts his arsenal with a low-90s fastball that touched up to 94 mph as an amateur and couples the pitch with a potentially plus slider that he can throw for called strikes or bury for chases. He also throws a changeup and curveball that each project to be average or a tick above. Scouts who saw him at San Diego also noted a late-breaking two-seamer. Richan gets a little bit of a boost from deception caused by hiding the ball in the back of his delivery.

THE FUTURE: Richan profiles as a classic innings-eater toward the back of a rotation. He has the pedigree to jump directly to high Class A Myrtle Beach if the Cubs decided that's the best place for his development.

BA GRADE

45 Risk: High

Fastball: 50.
Slider: 55. Change: 50.
Curve: 50. CTL: 60.

Year	Club (League)	Class	W	L	ERA	G	GS	CG	SV	IP	H	HR	BB	SO	K/9	WHIP	AVG
2018	Eugene (NWL)	SS	0	2	2.12	10	9	0	0	30	19	2	5	31	9.4	0.81	.183
Minor League Totals			0	2	2.12	10	9	0	0	30	19	2	5	31	9.4	0.81	.183

8 CORY ABBOTT, RHP

Born: Sept. 20, 1995. **B-T:** R-R. **HT:** 6-2. **WT:** 210. **Drafted:** Loyola Marymount, 2017 (2nd round). **Signed by:** Tom Myers.

TRACK RECORD: Abbott's stock rose during his junior year at Loyola Marymount after watching a video of Noah Syndergaard explaining how he throws his slider. He copied those instructions and saw his own slider take off as a result. He threw a perfect game on March 25, and shot all the way to the second round. He got his feet wet at short-season Eugene in 2017 before earning the organization's pitcher of the year honors in 2018.

SCOUTING REPORT: Abbott starts his mix with a low-90s fastball with heavy sink that he commands to all sectors of the zone. He pairs the pitch with a short, late-breaking slider in the mid-80s that he uses to get the bulk of his swings and misses. The pitch grades as a 60 on the 20-to-80 scouting scale. His changeup, which he throws in the 83-85 mph range, shows flashes of a plus offering as well. He also throws a below-average curveball that's more of a get-me-over pitch at this point. He throws all four pitches for strikes and fills up the zone with aplomb. His 2.50 ERA was the best in the organization and his 131 strikeouts were second behind Matt Swarmer.

BA GRADE
45 Risk: High
Fastball: 60.
Slider: 60. Change: 50.
Curve: 45. CTL: 55.

THE FUTURE: Abbott should head to Double-A Tennessee in 2019 and has the upside of a No. 4 starter.

Year	Club (League)	Class	W	L	ERA	G	GS	CG	SV	IP	H	HR	BB	SO	K/9	WHIP	AVG
2017	Eugene (NWL)	SS	0	0	3.86	5	5	0	0	14	14	1	3	18	11.6	1.21	.269
2018	South Bend (MWL)	LoA	4	1	2.47	9	9	0	0	47	35	5	13	57	10.8	1.01	.207
	Myrtle Beach (CAR)	HiA	4	5	2.53	13	13	0	0	68	59	3	26	74	9.8	1.26	.234
Minor League Totals			8	6	2.65	27	27	0	0	129	108	9	42	149	10.4	1.16	.228

9 JUSTIN STEELE, LHP

Born: July 11, 1995. **B-T:** L-L. **HT:** 6-2. **WT:** 195. **Drafted:** HS—Lucedale, Miss., 2014 (5th round). **Signed by:** J.P. Davis.

TRACK RECORD: The Cubs signed four pitchers to seven-figure bonuses in the 2014 draft. That haul included Steele, whose combination of athleticism and a low-90s fastball from the left side convinced the Cubs to sign him for $1 million, the highest bonus awarded in the fifth round that year. He ranked No. 12 on the Northwest League Top 20 during his pro debut, and had turned in a Carolina League all-star season at high Class A Myrtle Beach in 2017 before requiring Tommy John surgery that kept him out until early-July 2018.

SCOUTING REPORT: Steele returned from surgery in 11 months and looked as strong as ever. With Myrtle Beach he showed a fastball that sat in the low 90s and touched 95 mph with sink and finish. He backed it up with a sharp slider in the mid-80s as well as a downer curveball that flashed plus in the 76-80 mph range. He was just beginning to regain the feel for his changeup. He repeats his delivery thanks to plus athleticism and also boasts excellent arm speed.

BA GRADE
45 Risk: High
Fastball: 60.
Slider: 55.
Change: 50. CTL: 50.

THE FUTURE: After building innings in the Arizona Fall League, Steele appears headed for Double-A Tennessee to begin 2019. He has the upside of a No. 4 starter. Steele was added to the 40-man roster in December to protect him from the Rule 5 draft.

Year	Club (League)	Class	W	L	ERA	G	GS	CG	SV	IP	H	HR	BB	SO	K/9	WHIP	AVG
2016	South Bend (MWL)	LoA	5	7	5.00	19	19	0	0	77	93	3	39	76	8.8	1.71	.305
2017	Myrtle Beach (CAR)	HiA	6	7	2.92	20	20	0	0	99	100	6	36	82	7.5	1.38	.265
2018	Cubs 1 (AZL)	R	0	0	1.47	5	5	0	0	18	9	1	4	27	13.3	0.71	.143
	Myrtle Beach (CAR)	HiA	2	1	2.45	4	4	0	0	18	12	0	6	19	9.3	0.98	.185
	Tennessee (SL)	AA	0	1	3.60	2	2	0	0	10	8	1	3	7	6.3	1.10	.216
Minor League Totals			16	17	3.35	69	64	0	0	282	275	11	111	274	8.7	1.37	.257

10 ARAMIS ADEMAN, SS

Born: Sept. 13, 1998. **B-T:** L-R. **HT:** 5-11. **WT:** 160. **Signed:** Dominican Republic, 2015. **Signed by:** Jose Estevez/Gian Guzman/Jose Serra/Louis Eljaua.

TRACK RECORD: After playing with the Dominican Republic 15U team and training with Amaurys Nina, who also trained former Cubs prospect Eloy Jimenez, Ademan signed with the Cubs for $2 million. The Cubs skipped Ademan and fellow 2015 signee Miguel Amaya over the Rookie-level Arizona League and instead sent both to short-season Eugene in 2017, when Ademan ranked as the Northwest League's No. 7 prospect. The Cubs moved Ademan aggressively again in 2018, jumping him to high Class A Myrtle Beach after just 29 games in the Midwest League to close the previous season.

SCOUTING REPORT: Ademan opened 2018 as the Carolina League's second-youngest player, and it showed. He still boasts a smooth, sound swing, but desperately needs to get more oomph behind the ball. His gap power is exclusively to the pull side, though his singles were spread evenly around the outfield. He's unlikely to have better than gap power, but the strength gains need to come before he reaches even that mark. The Cubs see Ademan as a potential above-average defender at shortstop on the 20-to-80 scouting scale with an average arm that needs to be refined. They have worked with Ademan to keep his upper and lower body in sync to improve his throws.

THE FUTURE: The Cubs preached process over results with Ademan and hope that a down 2018 will provide a chance for a big rebound in 2019, when he likely returns to Myrtle Beach and will play the entire season at 20 years old.

BA GRADE
50 Risk: Very High
Hit: 50. Power: 40.
Run: 50. Field: 55.
Arm: 50.

Year	Club (League)	Class	AVG	G	AB	R	H	2B	3B	HR	RBI	BB	SO	SB	CS	OBP	SLG
2016	Cubs2 (DSL)	R	.254	59	209	37	53	5	4	0	16	34	28	17	9	.366	.316
2017	Eugene (NWL)	SS	.286	39	161	23	46	9	4	4	27	14	30	10	6	.365	.466
	South Bend (MWL)	LoA	.244	29	127	13	31	6	1	3	15	4	24	4	2	.269	.378
2018	Myrtle Beach (CAR)	HiA	.207	114	396	49	82	11	3	3	38	38	95	9	5	.291	.273
Minor League Totals			.237	241	893	122	212	31	12	10	96	90	177	40	22	.319	.333

11 RICHARD GALLARDO, RHP

BA GRADE
50 Risk: Extreme

Born: Sept. 6, 2001. **B-T:** R-R. **HT:** 6-1. **WT:** 185. **Signed:** Venezuela, 2018. **Signed by:** Hector Ortega/Louie Eljaua.

TRACK RECORD: After pitching for Venezuela at the 15U World Cup in Japan, Gallardo put himself in contention to be the best prospect available in the 2018 international class. One of the top international arms available, he ranked just behind Cuban righty Osiel Rodriguez as the best pitcher. He struck out six of the seven batters he faced at MLB's international showcase in 2018, then signed with the Cubs in July.

SCOUTING REPORT: Gallardo earned his ranking thanks to a combination of present stuff, projection and a fluid delivery. His fastball sat between 89-93 mph with carry up in the zone. He paired the pitch with a sharp-breaking 70-75 mph curveball that flashed plus. His body is ready to carry more strength, and his delivery is sound enough to let him command his fastball at a rate that belies his youth.

THE FUTURE: Gallardo will make his professional debut in 2019 and will be with one of the Cubs' two affiliates in the Rookie-level Arizona League. He has the upside of a mid-rotation starter.

Year	Club (League)	Class	W	L	ERA	G	GS	CG	SV	IP	H	HR	BB	SO	K/9	WHIP	AVG
2018	Did not play—Signed 2019 contract																

12 LUIS VERDUGO, SS

BA GRADE
50 Risk: Extreme

Born: Oct. 12, 2000. **B-T:** R-R. **HT:** 6-0. **WT:** 172. **Signed:** Mexico, 2017. **Signed by:** Sergio Hernandez /Louie Eljaua.

TRACK RECORD: The Cubs have dipped into Mexico frequently recently, signing lefty Jose Albertos in 2015 and then again in 2017 to nab Verdugo for $1.2 million. Verdugo played on the Mexican national team as a 15-year-old, and performed well as a member of the Mexico City Red Devils against older competition. He ranked No. 17 among the Arizona League's Top 20 prospects.

SCOUTING REPORT: Despite poor numbers, scouts in the Arizona League loved Verdugo for his athleticism and projection. His swing has a busy load and a bit of hitch with his hands, but he's showed the ability to get the barrel to the baseball when his swing is on time. He shows power in batting practice, and evaluators believe it will start to show up more often in games thanks to his ability to whip the bat through the zone with above-average speed, the natural loft to his swing and the likelihood that he will get stronger. He's a sound defender at shortstop already with a strong internal clock and quick reactions.

He's got a plus throwing arm but below-average speed.

THE FUTURE: Verdugo played all year at 17 years old and will likely return to the AZL for more seasoning in 2019. He has the upside of an everyday regular at shortstop with above-average power.

Year	Club (League)	Class	AVG	G	AB	R	H	2B	3B	HR	RBI	BB	SO	SB	CS	OBP	SLG
2018	Cubs 2 (AZL)	R	.193	47	176	28	34	4	1	4	20	17	45	5	3	.264	.295
Minor League Totals			.193	47	176	28	34	4	1	4	20	17	45	5	3	.264	.295

13 NELSON VELAZQUEZ, OF

BA GRADE

50 Risk: Extreme

Born: Dec. 26, 1998. **B-T:** R-R. **HT:** 6-0. **WT:** 190. **Drafted:** HS—Carolina, P.R., 2017 (5th round). **Signed by:** Edwards Guzman.

TRACK RECORD: The Cubs became sold on Velazquez's talent in May 2017, when he starred at the Excellence Games. He showed off 70-grade speed at that event as well as a strong arm and above-average raw power. His eight home runs tied him for third in the Rookie-level Arizona League in his debut, and his 11 homers in the Northwest League in 2018 tied him for fifth on the college-heavy circuit.

SCOUTING REPORT: The most troubling part of Velazquez's season was his inability to adjust to the way he was pitched. He didn't budge from a pull-happy approach, choosing instead to sell out for power at Eugene's pitcher-friendly PK Park. The most frustrating part was that Velazquez shows plenty of opposite-field power in batting practice, but hasn't made the adjustments to use it. His lower half has thickened up some, degrading some of the speed that he showed as an amateur. Scouts have gotten run times that range from a tick below-average to plus, helping to make him an average defender in both corners and usable in center field. His plus throwing arm would serve him well in right field.

THE FUTURE: Velazquez flunked his initial test at low Class A South Bend in 2018, so he'll likely head back to the Midwest League in 2019. He's got a high ceiling, but a long way to go to make it a reality.

Year	Club (League)	Class	AVG	G	AB	R	H	2B	3B	HR	RBI	BB	SO	SB	CS	OBP	SLG
2017	Cubs (AZL)	R	.236	32	110	26	26	5	2	8	17	15	39	5	2	.333	.536
2018	South Bend (MWL)	LoA	.188	31	112	6	21	1	0	0	7	7	43	3	0	.242	.196
	Eugene (NWL)	SS	.250	72	264	35	66	18	2	11	33	23	81	12	4	.322	.458
Minor League Totals			.233	135	486	67	113	24	4	19	57	45	163	20	6	.307	.416

14 ALEX LANGE, RHP

BA GRADE

45 Risk: High

Born: Oct. 2, 1995. **B-T:** R-R. **HT:** 6-3. **WT:** 197. **Drafted:** Louisiana State, 2017 (1st round). **Signed by:** Kevin Ellis.

TRACK RECORD: Lange was stellar in college, amassing a 30-9, 2.91 mark over three seasons at Louisiana State and reaching the College World Series finals in 2017. He was eased slowly into pro ball at short-season Eugene before getting his first full workload in 2018.

SCOUTING REPORT: The biggest problem with Lange's season was that his fastball was down a notch from his college days, instead settling in at 89-92 mph. Moreover, the pitch wasn't thrown with much move-ment or life. Some scouts went as far as describing the pitch as a batting practice fastball. He backed the pitch up with a changeup that showed sink and fade and projected as plus, and a power curveball with bite and depth. The curve was inconsistent at times, and projects as average. He throws from a hurried, funky delivery that includes a head whack and can hamper his control and command. Evaluators suggest slowing down and making an effort to separate his hands over the rubber might better serve him.

THE FUTURE: Lange will move to Double-A Tennessee in 2019, and has a ceiling of a back-end starter.

Year	Club (League)	Class	W	L	ERA	G	GS	CG	SV	IP	H	HR	BB	SO	K/9	WHIP	AVG
2017	Eugene (NWL)	SS	0	1	4.82	4	4	0	0	9	9	0	3	13	12.5	1.29	.243
2018	Myrtle Beach (CAR)	HiA	6	8	3.74	23	23	0	0	120	104	6	38	101	7.6	1.18	.234
Minor League Totals			6	9	3.82	27	27	0	0	130	113	6	41	114	7.9	1.19	.235

15 JOSE ALBERTOS, RHP

BA GRADE

50 Risk: Extreme

Born: Nov. 7, 1998. **B-T:** R-R. **HT:** 6-1. **WT:** 185. **Signed:** Mexico, 2015. **Signed by:** Sergio Hernandez/Louie Eljaua.

TRACK RECORD: After signing out of Mexico for $1.5 million, Albertos' track record as a pro has been checkered to say the least. He pitched just four innings in his debut season, then put together a standout campaign between the Rookie-level Arizona League and short-season Northwest League in 2017. That year gave the Cubs hope that Albertos would be their first high-end homegrown pitcher in some time.

SCOUTING REPORT: Albertos' 2018 season was disastrous. He was jumped to low Class A South Bend, where he was hit hard and showed little control. He was then sent back to Eugene, where it didn't get much better. Some scouts saw him operating with a 96-97 mph fastball, while others saw him working hard to throw a low-90s version in the zone. He still shows flashes of an above-average curveball and changeup, but his biggest problem is getting to the best versions of his pitches consistently. Evaluators inside and outside the organization saw a pitcher who needs to find some sort of harmony in his delivery. Whether that involves slowing down, getting downhill more often, finding a consistent landing point, staying balanced or a combination of all four, things need to change to help him throw strikes more often. **THE FUTURE:** The 2018 season weighed on Albertos' confidence. He will need to return to low Class A in 2019. The Cubs still believe in his stuff, but there are miles to go before he comes close to realizing his ceiling.

Year	Club (League)	Class	W	L	ERA	G	GS	CG	SV	IP	H	HR	BB	SO	K/9	WHIP	AVG
2016	Cubs (AZL)	R	0	0	0.00	1	1	0	0	4	1	0	1	7	15.8	0.50	.077
2017	Cubs (AZL)	R	0	0	4.32	2	2	0	0	8	6	0	3	6	6.5	1.08	.200
	Eugene (NWL)	SS	2	1	2.86	8	8	0	0	35	24	0	14	42	10.9	1.10	.181
2018	South Bend (MWL)	LoA	0	5	18.69	9	4	0	0	13	17	1	32	17	11.8	3.77	.321
	Eugene (NWL)	SS	0	4	11.94	11	6	0	0	17	19	0	33	21	10.9	3.00	.284
Minor League Totals			2	10	7.56	31	21	0	0	77	67	1	83	93	10.8	1.94	.226

16 EDMOND AMERICAAN, OF

BA GRADE

50 Risk: Extreme

Born: March 26, 1997. **B-T:** L-L. **HT:** 6-1. **WT:** 170. **Drafted:** Chipola (Fla.) JC, 2018 (35th round). **Signed by:** Tom Clark.

TRACK RECORD: Americaan has long been attractive to pro teams, having been drafted by the Diamondbacks out of high school and then again by the Rangers after his freshman season at Chipola. The Cubs came calling again, this time in the 35th round, and signed him for $208,950. The bonus was the second-highest after the 34th round.

SCOUTING REPORT: Americaan showed more power in his second season at Chipola, and his home runs jumped from one in 2017 to eight in 2018. He accomplished this by adding more loft to his swing and consciously aiming to hit the ball in the air more often. The new power jumps his profile a bit, from table-setter type of player to possibly a little more. He's a plus runner, which will help him stick in center field, though he needs to sharpen his routes and jumps. He's also got an above-average throwing arm, meaning he could play right field if necessary.

THE FUTURE: The Cubs have been fairly aggressive sending players to low Class A South Bend in their first full pro seasons, so it seems likely that Americaan could start there in 2019.

Year	Club (League)	Class	AVG	G	AB	R	H	2B	3B	HR	RBI	BB	SO	SB	CS	OBP	SLG
2018	Cubs 1 (AZL)	R	.295	30	112	22	33	5	2	0	9	13	30	11	6	.373	.375
Minor League Totals			.295	30	112	22	33	5	2	0	9	13	30	11	6	.373	.375

17 BRENDON LITTLE, LHP

BA GRADE

45 Risk: High

Born: Aug. 11, 1996. **B-T:** L-L. **HT:** 6-1. **WT:** 195. **Drafted:** State JC of Florida, 2017 (1st round). **Signed by:** John Koronka.

TRACK RECORD: After pitching just four innings as a freshman at North Carolina, Little transferred to the State JC of Florida after wowing evaluators in the Cape Cod League. His draft stock shot up as a result, and the Cubs gave him $2.2 million to turn professional. He struggled at short-season Eugene after being drafted, then spent all of 2018 at low Class A South Bend proving surprisingly hittable for a pitcher with excellent stuff.

SCOUTING REPORT: Little's biggest appeal still comes from his fastball, which sits in the low 90s and can touch up to 95 when he needs a strikeout. He couples it with a future plus curveball in the mid-70s with 12-to-6 break as well as a changeup that is fringe-average now but could get to average because of the conviction with which it's thrown. The biggest issue now is getting Little to repeat his delivery, which so far has cost him enough control to serve up four walks per nine innings.

THE FUTURE: After a full year at South Bend, Little should move up to high Class A Myrtle Beach in 2019. He has the ceiling of a back-end starter.

Year	Club (League)	Class	W	L	ERA	G	GS	CG	SV	IP	H	HR	BB	SO	K/9	WHIP	AVG
2017	Eugene (NWL)	SS	0	2	9.37	6	6	0	0	16	21	2	9	12	6.6	1.84	.300
2018	South Bend (MWL)	LoA	5	11	5.15	22	21	0	0	101	106	8	43	90	8.0	1.47	.264
Minor League Totals			5	13	5.74	28	27	0	0	118	127	10	52	102	7.8	1.52	.270

18 DILLON MAPLES, RHP

Born: May 9, 1992. **B-T:** R-R. **HT:** 6-2. **WT:** 225. **Drafted:** HS—Southern Pines, N.C., 2011 (14th round). **Signed by:** Billy Swoope.

BA GRADE
45 Risk: High

TRACK RECORD: In the last draft before the pool era, Maples got $2.5 million to sign with the Cubs even though he was the 429th overall pick. Injuries marred the early stages of his career, but Maples was healthy for all of 2017 and rocketed through three levels of the minor leagues before reaching Chicago.
SCOUTING REPORT: Maples is among the most slider-heavy pitchers. When he was in the big leagues, he threw the pitch 69 percent of the time, nearly three times more often than he threw his four-seam fastball. That's particularly notable, considering his fastball sits in the upper 90s and touched 100 in 2018. He mixes in a curveball, but doesn't throw a changeup. Now he needs to figure out command because even with two pitches that grade as 70 or better on the 20-to-80 scouting scale, Maples was still hit hard in the big leagues. Maples near bottom-of-the-scale control is his biggest hurdle. He simply doesn't throw enough strikes–he failed to throw strikes on 60 percent of his pitches in any month last season.
THE FUTURE: Maples will get a long look in spring training and should compete for a spot in Chicago's bullpen on Opening Day. If not, it's back to Triple-A Iowa for more seasoning.

Year	Club (League)	Class	W	L	ERA	G	GS	CG	SV	IP	H	HR	BB	SO	K/9	WHIP	AVG
2016	Myrtle Beach (CAR)	HiA	0	1	7.71	9	0	0	0	7	9	0	7	6	7.7	2.29	.281
	South Bend (MWL)	LoA	1	2	3.24	19	0	0	9	25	18	1	10	17	6.1	1.12	.198
2017	Myrtle Beach (CAR)	HiA	4	0	2.01	21	0	0	3	31	21	2	15	44	12.6	1.15	.188
	Tennessee (SL)	AA	1	1	3.29	14	0	0	6	14	11	0	11	28	18.4	1.61	.212
	Iowa (PCL)	AAA	1	2	1.96	17	0	0	4	18	12	1	11	28	13.7	1.25	.185
	Chicago (NL)	MAJ	0	0	10.13	6	0	0	0	5	6	0	6	11	18.6	2.25	.286
2018	Iowa (PCL)	AAA	2	3	2.79	41	0	0	10	39	22	1	39	75	17.5	1.58	.162
	Chicago (NL)	MAJ	1	0	11.81	9	0	0	0	5	7	2	5	9	15.2	2.25	.318
Major League Totals			1	0	10.97	15	0	0	0	11	13	2	11	20	16.9	2.25	.302
Minor League Totals			15	20	4.30	176	30	0	34	284	239	8	192	335	10.6	1.52	.225

19 ZACK SHORT, SS

Born: May 29, 1995. **B-T:** R-R. **HT:** 5-10. **WT:** 175. **Drafted:** Sacred Heart, 2016 (17th round). **Signed by:** Matt Sherman.

BA GRADE
45 Risk: High

TRACK RECORD: Short hit just .241/.352/.399 in his final season at Sacred Heart, but the Cubs took a flyer on him in the 17th round. He helped short-season Eugene win a championship in 2016 and saw a power spike in his first full season as a pro. His 13 home runs in 2017 were just two fewer than he'd hit in his three college seasons combined.
SCOUTING REPORT: Short's power spike continued in 2018, when he set a new career high with 17 homers over a full season at Double-A Tennessee. Evaluators who saw him believed the uptick was because Short was hunting inside fastballs he could pull over the left-field wall. Indeed, all but one of Short's homers was hit to the pull side. Those same evaluators suggested Short could increase his profile a little bit by toning down the all-or-nothing approach and using more of the whole field. They also noted a tendency to chase pitches. In the field, Short is big league ready. He's sure-handed with a quick first step and solid instincts for shortstop, and his double-plus arm will keep him at the position. Short is a below-average runner.
THE FUTURE: Short will move to Triple-A in 2019 and could make a big league cameo by year's end. If his offensive profile doesn't change, he's at least a solid backup infielder with power.

Year	Club (League)	Class	AVG	G	AB	R	H	2B	3B	HR	RBI	BB	SO	SB	CS	OBP	SLG
2016	Cubs (AZL)	R	.318	14	44	12	14	3	0	0	8	14	9	5	1	.500	.386
	Eugene (NWL)	SS	.236	39	127	22	30	6	1	1	23	33	24	10	5	.401	.323
2017	South Bend (MWL)	LoA	.237	66	236	50	56	17	3	7	26	54	54	15	5	.393	.424
	Myrtle Beach (CAR)	HiA	.263	65	232	34	61	11	3	6	21	40	50	3	5	.372	.414
2018	Tennessee (SL)	AA	.227	124	436	68	99	28	2	17	59	82	136	8	3	.356	.417
Minor League Totals			.242	308	1075	186	260	65	9	31	137	223	273	41	19	.380	.406

20 RILEY THOMPSON, RHP

Born: July 9, 1996. **B-T:** L-R. **HT:** 6-3. **WT:** 205. **Drafted:** Louisville, 2018 (11th round). **Signed by:** Jacob Williams.

BA GRADE
45 Risk: High

TRACK RECORD: Thompson was drafted twice before signing with the Cubs—in the 37th round out of high school by the Reds and again a year later by the Yankees as the rare draft-eligible redshirt freshman. He had Tommy John surgery in 2016, then missed part of his redshirt freshman season with a sore arm. Thompson performed poorly in his final collegiate season, but his pure stuff was too good to pass up.

SCOUTING REPORT: In the spring, Thompson lit up radar guns with a fastball that sat in the mid-90s and touched triple digits. He paired the pitch with a powerful curveball that he used for strikeouts. At their best, both pitches earned 70 grades on the 20-to-80 scouting scale. He also mixed in a potentially average changeup. Well below-average control hampered him in college, but he calmed down some to walk nine hitters in his first 25 innings. The Cubs believe that smoothing out his delivery to make it more repeatable will help Thompson get the most out of his premium arsenal.

THE FUTURE: Given that he already shows three pitches, the Cubs will continue to use Thompson as a starter. If that fails, his fastball and curveball—with improved control—could help him move quickly to the big league bullpen in a reliever's role. He should move to low Class A South Bend in 2019.

Year	Club (League)	Class	W	L	ERA	G	GS	CG	SV	IP	H	HR	BB	SO	K/9	WHIP	AVG
2018	Eugene (NWL)	SS	0	2	2.84	9	8	0	0	25	24	1	9	25	8.9	1.30	.253
Minor League Totals			0	2	2.84	9	8	0	0	25	24	1	9	25	8.9	1.30	.253

21 OSCAR DE LA CRUZ, RHP

BA GRADE

45 Risk: Very High

Born: March 4, 1995. **B-T:** R-R. **HT:** 6-4. **WT:** 200. **Signed:** Dominican Republic, 2012. **Signed by:** Mario Encarnacion/Jose Serra.

TRACK RECORD: Since signing for $85,000, De La Cruz has shown plenty of potential but has had his progress waylaid over the years by injuries and an 80-game suspension to begin 2018 after testing positive for a masking agent. His suspension occurred toward midseason, and he'll be eligible to get back on the mound early in 2019.

SCOUTING REPORT: Those who saw De La Cruz in 2018 still came away impressed with his stuff. Evaluators saw a fastball that sat in the low 90s but could reach as high as 96 when he needed a whiff. His changeup was inconsistent but flashed plus at times. Less impressive was the curveball, which needed tightening and showed a visible hump out of De La Cruz's hand. Scouts outside the organization also noted that his arm slot on the curveball was different than on his fastball or changeup, and the Cubs acknowledged that he was working to find a consistent slot for all his pitches. All of this, of course, was before his suspension, making his 2019 season a bit of a wild card.

THE FUTURE: Once he returns, De La Cruz could return to Double-A for more seasoning or move to Triple-A Iowa to speed up his development a bit.

Year	Club (League)	Class	W	L	ERA	G	GS	CG	SV	IP	H	HR	BB	SO	K/9	WHIP	AVG
2016	Cubs (AZL)	R	0	1	6.00	1	1	0	0	3	3	1	1	2	6.0	1.33	.250
	Eugene (NWL)	SS	0	0	1.08	2	2	0	0	8	5	1	2	14	15.1	0.84	.167
	South Bend (MWL)	LoA	1	2	3.25	6	6	0	0	28	22	0	8	35	11.4	1.08	.218
2017	Cubs (AZL)	R	0	0	0.00	1	0	0	0	2	0	0	0	1	4.5	0.00	.000
	Myrtle Beach (CAR)	HiA	4	3	3.46	12	12	1	0	55	55	6	13	47	7.7	1.24	.263
2018	Tennessee (SL)	AA	6	7	5.24	16	16	1	0	77	76	8	31	73	8.5	1.38	.259
Minor League Totals			26	17	3.39	69	65	2	0	332	289	24	96	321	8.7	1.16	.233

22 THOMAS HATCH, RHP

BA GRADE

40 Risk: High

Born: Sept. 29, 1994. **B-T:** R-R. **HT:** 6-1. **WT:** 190. **Drafted:** Oklahoma State, 2016 (3rd round). **Signed by:** Ty Nichols.

TRACK RECORD: Hatch missed a season at Oklahoma State with a strained ulnar collateral ligament. A platelet-rich plasma injection helped him get back on the mound without surgery, however, and he went 9-3, 2.14 in his junior season to help lead the Cowboys to the College World Series. He got on the mound as a pro for the first time in 2017, to mixed results, and was inconsistent again in 2018.

SCOUTING REPORT: Hatch has a solid three-pitch mix, but nothing that would qualify as a knockout. He sinks his low-90s fastball to both sides of the plate and can run the pitch up to 95 at times. He pairs it with a low-80s slider that he can manipulate for called strikes or sharpen for chases. The pitch projects as a 55 on the 20-to-80 scouting scale. He also throws an 80-82 mph changeup that is below-average now and projects to be a tick better with repetition.

THE FUTURE: After a year in Double-A, Hatch is likely to move to Triple-A Iowa in 2019. He has the ceiling of a No. 5 starter or a long reliever.

Year	Club (League)	Class	W	L	ERA	G	GS	CG	SV	IP	H	HR	BB	SO	K/9	WHIP	AVG
2017	Myrtle Beach (CAR)	HiA	5	11	4.04	26	26	0	0	125	126	2	50	126	9.1	1.41	.264
2018	Tennessee (SL)	AA	8	6	3.82	26	26	2	0	144	127	16	61	117	7.3	1.31	.245
Minor League Totals			13	17	3.92	52	52	2	0	268	253	18	111	243	8.2	1.36	.254

23 REIVAJ GARCIA, SS

BA GRADE

45 Risk: Extreme

Born: Aug. 12, 2001. **B-T:** S-R. **HT:** 5-11. **WT:** 175. **Signed:** Mexico, 2017.
Signed by: Sergio Hernandez/Louie Eljaua.

TRACK RECORD: Garcia was signed away from the Yucatan Lions just after turning 16 and received a $500,000 bonus. He joins fellow Mexican prospects Jose Albertos and Luis Verdugo among the Cubs' best minor leaguers. He was lauded for his overall game awareness and savvy at a young age.

SCOUTING REPORT: Garcia opened his professional career by showing an impressive feel to hit for someone his age. He struck out just 18.8 percent of the time and walked at nearly an eight percent clip, impressive numbers for someone his age. He was a much better hitter from the left side, where he put up a .771 OPS over 118 at-bats. Scouts who saw him in the Rookie-level Arizona League felt comfortable projecting Garcia's hit tool all the way to plus. He's not going to produce much power, so the hit tool will have to reach that level to have much offensive value. He's an average runner and has an average throwing arm, which gives him a chance to stick at shortstop.

THE FUTURE: Garcia won't turn 18 until August 2019, so a return to the Rookie-level Arizona League seems to be in the cards.

Year	Club (League)	Class	AVG	G	AB	R	H	2B	3B	HR	RBI	BB	SO	SB	CS	OBP	SLG
2018	Cubs 2 (AZL)	R	.302	40	172	28	52	9	0	0	13	15	36	7	3	.362	.355
Minor League Totals			.302	40	172	28	52	9	0	0	13	15	36	7	3	.362	.355

24 JARED YOUNG, 1B

BA GRADE

40 Risk: High

Born: July 9, 1995. **B-T:** L-R. **HT:** 6-2. **WT:** 185. **Drafted:** Old Dominion, 2017 (15th round). **Signed by:** Billy Swoope.

TRACK RECORD: Young played for three colleges in three years, starting at Division II Minot State before moving to Connors State (Okla.) JC and then to Old Dominion for his draft season. He hit well at all three stops, leading the Cubs to take a flyer on him with the hope that he would develop in the same way many of their hitters have over the years.

SCOUTING REPORT: Young was the best pure hitter on his high Class A Myrtle Beach team, and his numbers followed accordingly. He finished fourth in the organization in home runs (16), second in RBIs (76) and first in batting average among players at full-season affiliates (.300). He produces above-average raw power from his lefthanded stroke, though most of his home runs came to the pull side. He's an average runner and a competent defender at first base with enough athleticism to make some believe he could hack it in the outfield.

THE FUTURE: After a full season at Myrtle Beach, Young should get his first taste of the upper levels at Double-A Tennessee. He's got a tough profile and will have to hit his way to the big leagues.

Year	Club (League)	Class	AVG	G	AB	R	H	2B	3B	HR	RBI	BB	SO	SB	CS	OBP	SLG
2017	Eugene (NWL)	SS	.257	39	140	23	36	6	1	1	15	11	29	6	2	.311	.336
2018	South Bend (MWL)	LoA	.313	69	259	41	81	13	6	10	53	20	47	1	0	.368	.525
	Myrtle Beach (CAR)	HiA	.282	51	188	20	53	6	2	6	23	11	40	6	1	.341	.431
Minor League Totals			.290	159	587	84	170	25	9	17	91	42	116	13	3	.346	.450

25 D.J. WILSON, OF

BA GRADE

45 Risk: Very High

Born: Oct. 8, 1996. **B-T:** L-L. **HT:** 5-8. **WT:** 177. **Drafted:** HS—Canton, Ohio, 2015 (4th round). **Signed by:** Daniel Carte.

TRACK RECORD: Until this past draft, Wilson was the Cubs' highest drafted prep player since Albert Almora in 2012. His time at low Class A South Bend was cut short in 2017 because of a fractured fibula, and he was limited to 64 games at high Class A Myrtle Beach in 2018 because of wrist and hamstring injuries. He made up some of that time with six weeks in the Arizona Fall League.

SCOUTING REPORT: Wilson struggled at the plate in both the regular season and the AFL partly due to issues with pitch recognition and partly because of the way he sets up at the plate. He sets his hands low in his stance, then struggles to get them separated from his body. He's got gap power and above-average speed that gets to plus underway. The speed helps him in center field, where some scouts give him a chance at being a double-plus defender. His throwing arm has improved from 2017 and now ranks as average.

THE FUTURE: Wilson will play all of the 2019 season at 22 years old, so a return to high Class A with a chance at Double-A later in the season wouldn't be the worst thing for his development.

Year	Club (League)	Class	AVG	G	AB	R	H	2B	3B	HR	RBI	BB	SO	SB	CS	OBP	SLG
2016	Eugene (NWL)	SS	.257	64	245	37	63	15	2	3	29	20	56	21	8	.320	.371
2017	Cubs (AZL)	R	.500	3	8	5	4	1	0	3	5	2	1	1	0	.583	1.750
	South Bend (MWL)	LoA	.229	88	310	56	71	16	8	9	45	33	89	15	7	.309	.419
2018	Myrtle Beach (CAR)	HiA	.219	64	237	27	52	9	2	1	13	32	71	10	6	.315	.287
Minor League Totals			.240	241	879	137	211	44	14	16	98	93	232	52	22	.318	.377

26 JHONNY PEREDA, C

BA GRADE
40 Risk: High

Born: April 18, 1996. **B-T:** R-R. **HT:** 6-1. **WT:** 170. **Signed:** Venezuela, 2013. **Signed by:** Hector Ortega.

TRACK RECORD: Pereda was an unheralded signing in 2013, but has slowly started to open eyes in the system. He was given his biggest workload in 2018—122 games in the regular season plus eight more in the Arizona Fall League—and performed respectably from open to close.

SCOUTING REPORT: Pereda showed a strong approach to the strike zone in 2018, as shown by a lack of strikeouts and a respectable 10.3 percent walk rate which was identical to the figure he produced in 2017. He shows almost no power now, but could add a little punch with necessary strength gain. Even with a smallish frame, Pereda caught 83 games throughout the course of the season. He's got a strong arm and caught 38 percent of potential basestealers, though he could stand to clean up his throwing mechanics a bit to streamline his momentum toward second base. He's a bottom-of-the-scale runner.

THE FUTURE: Pereda will move to Double-A Tennessee in 2019 and has a ceiling as a backup catcher with a bit of offensive upside.

Year	Club (League)	Class	AVG	G	AB	R	H	2B	3B	HR	RBI	BB	SO	SB	CS	OBP	SLG
2016	Cubs (AZL)	R	.289	41	128	17	37	7	1	2	23	16	21	0	2	.376	.406
2017	South Bend (MWL)	LoA	.246	92	317	33	78	13	0	0	30	37	60	2	3	.332	.287
2018	Myrtle Beach (CAR)	HiA	.272	122	441	51	120	12	2	8	57	51	68	4	2	.347	.363
Minor League Totals			.248	388	1324	149	329	50	4	13	146	152	207	7	11	.330	.322

27 JIMMY HERRON, OF

BA GRADE
45 Risk: Very High

Born: July 27, 1996. **B-T:** R-L. **HT:** 6-1. **WT:** 195. **Drafted:** Duke, 2018 (3rd round). **Signed by:** Billy Swoope.

TRACK RECORD: Herron turned down the Yankees when the club drafted him as a sophomore and instead went to the Cape Cod League, where he showed the compact, pure hitting stroke that served him so well as a collegian. He struggled a bit in his junor season, but the Cubs still believed enough in the bat and their own player-development program to take him with the 98th overall pick.

SCOUTING REPORT: At his best, Herron produces a smooth swing from the right side that is geared toward line drives. He got a little homer-happy in his final season at Duke, utilizing a path that was noticeably more uphill than what he'd shown previously. When the season was over, though, his numbers were roughly in line with what he'd produced over the first two years. He's a plus runner, which helps him play center field capably. He has a below-average arm, however, and would be limited to left field.

THE FUTURE: Herron finished his first pro year at low Class A South Bend, and has enough of a college pedigree that he could move to high Class A Myrtle Beach in 2019.

Year	Club (League)	Class	AVG	G	AB	R	H	2B	3B	HR	RBI	BB	SO	SB	CS	OBP	SLG
2018	Cubs 1 (AZL)	R	.310	9	29	6	9	3	0	1	2	8	2	0	0	.459	.517
	South Bend (MWL)	LoA	.245	33	110	12	27	2	0	3	17	12	24	1	3	.333	.345
Minor League Totals			.259	42	139	18	36	5	0	4	19	20	26	1	3	.361	.381

28 TREVOR CLIFTON, RHP

BA GRADE
40 Risk: High

Born: May 11, 1995. **B-T:** R-R. **HT:** 6-4. **WT:** 225. **Drafted:** HS—Maryville, Tenn., 2013 (12th round). **Signed by:** Keith Rymon.

TRACK RECORD: After an up-and-down season at Double-A Tennessee in 2017, Clifton mastered the level in 2018 and then put forth a 3.89 ERA in the hitter-friendly Pacific Coast League. If he'd pitched enough innings, the figure would have put him in a tie for sixth place in the league.

SCOUTING REPORT: Scouts who saw Clifton this year noted four pitches that were average at best, starting with a fastball in the low 90s that touched 94. The pitch had two-seam movement at the end of the velo band. His best offspeed pitch was an average slider thrown in the low 80s, and he backed it up with a changeup in the high 70s that he was unafraid to throw in right-on-right matchups. He has a curveball as well, but scouts noted its visibly different slot from his other pitches.

THE FUTURE: Clifton is likely to return to Triple-A Iowa. His ceiling is in the back of a rotation, but as a pitcher who has been unprotected and unpicked in back-to-back Rule 5 drafts, there is still a ways to go to get to that ceiling.

Year	Club (League)	Class	W	L	ERA	G	GS	CG	SV	IP	H	HR	BB	SO	K/9	WHIP	AVG
2016	Myrtle Beach (CAR)	HiA	7	7	2.72	23	23	0	0	119	97	4	41	129	9.8	1.16	.225
2017	Tennessee (SL)	AA	5	8	5.20	21	21	0	0	100	112	8	45	86	7.7	1.56	.286
2018	Tennessee (SL)	AA	3	4	2.86	12	12	0	0	57	41	0	23	45	7.1	1.13	.200
	Iowa (PCL)	AAA	4	3	3.89	14	12	0	0	69	65	8	29	56	7.3	1.36	.258
Minor League Totals			31	34	3.82	114	104	0	0	525	478	30	223	488	8.4	1.33	.246

29 KEEGAN THOMPSON, RHP

BA GRADE

40 Risk: High

Born: March 13, 1995. **B-T:** R-R. **HT:** 6-0. **WT:** 193. **Drafted:** Auburn, 2017 (3rd round). **Signed by:** Alex McClure.

TRACK RECORD: Thompson and system-mate Trevor Clifton combined to help USA Baseball's 16U team win a gold medal in 2011 and repeated the feat two years later with the 18U squad. After four years with Auburn (including a Tommy John surgery), Thompson was drafted and made quick work of the competition in the short-season Northwest League.

SCOUTING REPORT: Thompson doesn't have a knockout pitch, so he relies on pitchability to get his outs. His fastball sits at around 91 mph and touches 93, but it doesn't have a whole lot of movement. That's especially true if he misses up with the pitch, though it does have some carry through the zone. Scouts pegged both breaking balls as potential above-average pitches because of his ability to spin them, though he needs to be more consistent with their release points. His changeup is a fringe-average pitch.

THE FUTURE: Thompson made it to Double-A in his first full season as a pro and has the ceiling of a back-end starter.

Year	Club (League)	Class	W	L	ERA	G	GS	CG	SV	IP	H	HR	BB	SO	K/9	WHIP	AVG
2017	Eugene (NWL)	SS	1	2	2.37	7	1	0	0	19	15	1	4	23	10.9	1.00	.214
2018	Myrtle Beach (CAR)	HiA	3	3	3.19	12	12	0	0	68	49	6	13	61	8.1	0.92	.202
	Tennessee (SL)	AA	6	3	4.06	13	13	0	0	62	66	3	21	54	7.8	1.40	.273
Minor League Totals			10	8	3.45	32	26	0	0	149	130	10	38	138	8.4	1.13	.234

30 ERICK LEAL, RHP

BA GRADE

40 Risk: High

Born: March 17, 1995. **B-T:** R-R. **HT:** 6-3. **WT:** 180. **Signed:** Venezuela, 2011. **Signed by:** Marlon Urdaneta (Diamondbacks).

TRACK RECORD: Leal was signed by the Diamondbacks in 2011, then shipped to the Cubs for outfielder Tony Campana. He missed the 2017 season while recovering from Tommy John surgery, but boosted his stock with a strong year at high Class A Myrtle Beach and an encore performance in the Arizona Fall League.

SCOUTING REPORT: Leal typically operates with a fastball that sits at 88-92 mph with a bit of tail, but he really makes his money with a plus changeup. The pitch comes in at 82-84 mph, is thrown with the same conviction as his fastball and shows excellent tumble away from lefthanders. He's got a feel for spinning his curveball as well, though it doesn't quite show the snap needed to be a true out pitch. All of his offerings are boosted a touch by a superb delivery and arm action.

THE FUTURE: Leal should get his first taste of the upper levels in 2019 and has a ceiling as a back-end starter or swingman.

Year	Club (League)	Class	W	L	ERA	G	GS	CG	SV	IP	H	HR	BB	SO	K/9	WHIP	AVG
2016	Cubs (AZL)	R	1	0	0.00	2	1	0	0	3	1	0	1	5	15.0	0.67	.111
	Myrtle Beach (CAR)	HiA	10	4	3.23	19	18	0	0	95	92	5	22	66	6.3	1.20	.253
2017	Did not play—Injured																
2018	Myrtle Beach (CAR)	HiA	1	1	1.41	21	8	0	1	64	35	2	17	61	8.6	0.82	.156
Minor League Totals			37	19	3.04	105	81	1	2	471	442	28	109	371	7.1	1.17	.245

Chicago White Sox

BY JOSH NORRIS

From the outset of their rebuild, the White Sox knew there would be growing pains. The teardown began in earnest in the winter of 2016, when ace lefthander Chris Sale and center fielder Adam Eaton were shipped to the Red Sox and Nationals, respectively, for a haul of prospects that included four members of the Top 100 prospects, including two of the top 10 in infielder Yoan Moncada and righthander Lucas Giolito.

Plenty more trades followed, including a swap of Jose Quintana to the Cubs that landed two of their current top three prospects in outfielder Eloy Jimenez and righthander Dylan Cease. The result is one of the best farm systems in the game, stocked with plenty of players on the cusp of their big league debuts.

The first wave of new blood debuted to mixed results in Chicago in 2018, including Giolito and fellow righthander Reynaldo Lopez, who were part of the big league rotation all season. Lopez was solid, but Giolito's 6.13 ERA, 5.56 FIP and 4.67 walks-per-nine innings were the worst among qualified starters. Moncada, the jewel of the Sale trade, didn't fare well either. His 217 strikeouts led the major leagues.

Righthander Michael Kopech, who also came over in the Sale trade, showed spurts of dominance dampened by rain, but tore his ulnar collateral ligament in his final outing and had Tommy John surgery that will keep him out of action until the middle of 2020. Kopech was expected to be a major player in the team's return to prominence, so the surgery was a particularly sharp blow.

The failure of their young players precipitated a move backward in the win-loss column. Chicago finished 62-100, five games worse than 2017.

Things were much brighter on the farm, where Jimenez was everything the White Sox expected and more. Aside from a couple of minor injuries, Jimenez terrorized pitchers at both of his upper-level stops. He finished in the top two in the system in average, home runs and RBIs, and should make his big league debut a few weeks into 2019.

Kopech broke through in the middle of 2018, but the biggest jump forward on the mound belonged to Dylan Cease. The righthander was dominant from Opening Day until season's end between high Class A Winston-Salem and Double-A Birmingham, and tied for the system lead in wins (12), while finishing second in ERA (2.40) and strikeouts (160).

Perennial losing means high picks in the draft, and in 2018 the White Sox used the fourth overall

Yoan Moncada has shown power and patience but has hit just .235 in his big league career.

PROJECTED 2022 LINEUP

Catcher	Zack Collins (27)
First Base	Jose Abreu (35)
Second Base	Nick Madrigal (25)
Third Base	Yoan Moncada (27)
Shortstop	Tim Anderson (29)
Left Field	Eloy Jimenez (25)
Center Field	Luis Robert (24)
Right Field	Micker Adolfo (25)
Designated Hitter	Daniel Palka (30)
No. 1 Starter	Michael Kopech (26)
No. 2 Starter	Reynaldo Lopez (28)
No. 3 Starter	Dylan Cease (26)
No. 4 Starter	Carlos Rodon (29)
No. 5 Starter	Dane Dunning (27)
Closer	Ian Hamilton (27)

pick to add Oregon State second baseman Nick Madrigal, who is arguably the best pure hitter in the class.

Through draft picks and trades, the White Sox have assembled an enviable collection of minor league talent. They have elite prospects both at the plate and on the mound, and have spread them out across the tiers of their system.

Now comes the hard part: developing them into major league impact players who can help the team rise out of the AL Central cellar and begin challenging the Indians for the top spot in the division. Between the continued maturation of the first wave and the debuts of the second wave, 2019 will be a fulcrum on which the rebuild swings.

DEPTH CHART

CHICAGO WHITE SOX

TOP 2019 ROOKIE: Eloy Jimenez, OF. After a few weeks of seasoning, he should entrench himself in the middle of the lineup.

BREAKOUT PROSPECT: Luis Basabe, OF. A star turn in the Futures Game showed how impactful Basabe can be when everything clicks.

SLEEPER: Lane Ramsey, RHP. The college reliever has a huge frame and an upper-90s fastball that could help him move quickly.

SOURCE OF TOP 30 TALENT			
Homegrown	23	Acquired	7
College	17	Trade	7
Junior college	0	Rule 5 draft	0
High school	0	Independent league	0
Nondrafted free agent	0	Free agent/waivers	0
International	3		

LF
Eloy Jimenez (1)
Blake Rutherford (8)
Steele Walker (8)
Joel Booker (27)

CF
Luis Robert (5)
Luis Basabe (11)
Cabera Weaver (25)
Romy Gonzalez
Luis Mieses

RF
Micker Adolfo (6)
Luis Gonzalez (9)
Alexander Comas (24)
Tito Polo
Alex Call

3B
Bryce Bush (21)
Jake Burger (23)
Johan Cruz
Ti'Quan Forbes

SS
Laz Rivera (16)
Lency Delgado
Lenyn Sosa
Luis Curbelo
Yeyson Yrizarri

2B
Nick Madrigal (4)
Amado Nunez
Danny Mendick

1B
Gavin Sheets (14)
Corey Zangari

C
Zack Collins (12)
Seby Zavala (15)
Gunnar Troutwine

LHP

LHSP	LHRP
Konnor Pilkington (22)	Kodi Medeiros (30)
Ian Clarkin	Caleb Frare
Bernardo Flores	Bennett Sousa
Andre Davis	
Tanner Banks	
Jordan Guerrero	

RHP

RHSP	RHRP
Michael Kopech (2)	Ian Hamilton (13)
Dylan Cease (3)	Zack Burdi (18)
Dane Dunning (7)	Zach Thompson (28)
Alec Hansen (17)	Tyler Johnson (29)
Jordan Stephens (19)	Lane Ramsey
Spencer Adams (20)	Connor Walsh
Lincoln Henzman (26)	Thyago Vieira
Kade McClure	Jake Elliott
Blake Battenfield	
Jonathan Stiever	
Isaiah Carranza	

DRAFT ANALYSIS

2018

BEST PURE HITTER: 2B Nick Madrigal (1) was arguably the best hitter in the class, thanks to extraordinary hand-eye coordination and an incredible knack for finding the barrel. He hit pretty much everything, both in college and as a pro. That's both good and bad, as he also rarely walked in his pro debut. He walked and struck out a combined 12 times after signing.

BEST POWER HITTER: OF Romy Gonzalez (18) cracked 10 home runs in 201 at-bats with Rookie-level Great Falls in his pro debut. There are other players who earn higher grades for raw power, but Gonzalez's 55 power is the best in games.

FASTEST RUNNER: Madrigal is a plus runner, turning in run times under 4.2 seconds from home to first. He is a little faster underway, too.

BEST DEFENSIVE PLAYER: Madrigal has well above-average hands, which benefited even further from his time with former Gold Glove shortstop and Winston-Salem manager Omar Vizquel. He also showed an accurate throwing arm that he can crank up to plus when he really uncorks one.

BEST ATHLETE: OF Caberea Weaver (7) cuts an impressive physique at 6-foot-3, 180 pounds, and he shows plenty of looseness and athleticism on defense and on the bases. He doesn't get great run times out of the box, but he can show plus or better speed underway.

BEST FASTBALL: RHP Lane Ramsey (23) sits in the mid-90s and cranks it up to 97 mph. At 6-foot-9, he gets excellent extension on the pitch.

BEST SECONDARY PITCH: Drafted out of Virginia, LHP Bennett Sousa (10) throws a slider with high enough spin that TrackMan classifies the pitch as a curveball. He used the pitch to strike out 42 hitters in 35.1 innings in his pro debut.

BEST PRO DEBUT: Madrigal played at three levels and didn't strike out until his 20th game. He struck out just five times all year, and hit .303 for the abbreviated season.

TOP DRAFT PICKS OF THE DECADE

Year	Player, Pos.	2018 Org
2009	Jared Mitchell, OF	Atlantic League
2010	Chris Sale, LHP	Red Sox
2011	Keenyn Walker, OF (1st round supp.)	Atlantic Lge
2012	Courtney Hawkins, OF	Reds
2013	Tim Anderson, SS	White Sox
2014	Carlos Rodon, LHP	White Sox
2015	Carson Fulmer, RHP	White Sox
2016	Zack Collins, C	White Sox
2017	Jake Burger, 3B	White Sox
2018	Nick Madrigal, SS	White Sox

MOST INTRIGUING BACKGROUND: Though they didn't sign him, the White Sox gained national attention for their selection of Matt Klug (38), whose parents and childhood best friend all died during his high school career. The White Sox selected Klug as a way to honor him for all that he'd gone through while continuing to play baseball at Brookwood HS, in Snellville, Ga.

CLOSEST TO THE MAJORS: Madrigal carries a strong college pedigree that includes a College World Series championship, and he succeeded at high Class A Winston-Salem in his pro debut. He should move quickly.

BEST LATE-ROUND PICK: Bryce Bush (33) was drafted as an outfielder, but the White Sox are trying him at third base. He's understandably raw at the position, but the team believes he has the arm strength and athleticism to make it work. If not, he could move back to right field. His $290,000 bonus was the second largest of anyone taken after the 20th round.

THE ONE WHO GOT AWAY: The White Sox's first unsigned pick didn't come until the 34th round, so they didn't miss on many targets. LHP Mason Montgomery (39) has flashed 94-96 mph velocity and may develop into an excellent prospect at Texas Tech.

—JOSH NORRIS

2017

3B Jake Burger (1) twice tore his left Achilles tendon and he was sidelined all of 2018, leaving this grade incomplete. OF Luis Gonzalez (3) and RHP Lincoln Henzmen (4) have found success at the outset of their pro careers.

GRADE: C

2016

RHP Ian Hamilton (11) moved quickly and this season made his big league debut in the White Sox bullpen. C Zack Collins (1) is still progressing in the upper minors, but RHP Alec Hansen (2) regressed in 2018 after a strong start as a pro.

GRADE: C

2015

RHP Carson Fulmer (1) raced to the big leagues but hasn't been able to stick in Chicago. RHP Jordan Stephens (5) and C Seby Zavela (12) are most likely to join him as big leaguers from this class but neither offers significant upside.

GRADE: D

1 ELOY JIMENEZ, OF

Born: Nov. 27, 1996. **B-T:** R-R. **HT:** 6-4. **WT:** 205.
Signed: Dominican Republic, 2013.
Signed by: Jose Serra/Carlos Reyes (Cubs).

Baseball America ranked Jimenez as the No. 1 prospect in the 2013 international class, and the Cubs signed both him and No. 2 prospect Gleyber Torres. The Cubs dealt Jimenez to the White Sox along with right-hander Dylan Cease as part of the four-player package for Jose Quintana in July 2017. Jimenez missed two weeks early in 2018 with a strained left pectoral muscle, and then two more weeks at midseason with a strained left adductor muscle. He spent the summer tearing apart the upper levels and finished the season ranked inside the top 10 in the minors in both batting average (.337) and slugging (.577). He also ranked as the No. 1 prospect in both the Southern and International leagues. Jimenez was not called up by the White Sox in September, even though he was already on the 40-man roster. The White Sox explained that he still has work to do on his defense in left field, but more notably it kept Jimenez from starting his service time clock.

SCOUTING REPORT: For as long as he's been a prospect, Jimenez has projected as an elite hitter who can hit for average and power. Five seasons into his minor league career, he's done nothing to dissuade evaluators in that regard. He has at least double-plus power to all sectors now, and he hit a system-best 22 home runs in 2018. He has shown he can hit the ball out to all fields. His coiled lower half and rubber band-like takeaway in his swing remind some evaluators of Miguel Cabrera. He also shows an impressive knack for learning how pitchers plan to attack him, and then adjusting to the strategy within the same game. These qualities should allow Jimenez to be a plus hitter with plus-plus power. Defensively, he's unlikely to ever be a standout. His range and throwing arm are both below-average. Because of this, he will be limited to left field. He's not necessarily going to be a liability in the outfield, but he's unlikely to be an asset out there either. Jimenez is a below-average runner as well. His value as a big leaguer is going to be largely limited to his bat, but it's a special bat.

THE FUTURE: Barring injury, Jimenez should be a major leaguer very early in 2019. He has very little left to prove in the minor leagues, and the White Sox are in a position to let him develop defensively in the big leagues with a rebuilding White Sox club.

BRIAN WESTERHOLT/FOUR SEAM

BA GRADE	SCOUTING GRADES
70 Risk: Medium	Hit: 60. Power: 70. Run: 40. Field: 45. Arm: 40.

Projected future grades on 20-80 scouting scale

TOP PROSPECTS OF THE DECADE

Year	Player, Pos.	2018 Org
2009	Gordon Beckham, SS	Mariners
2010	Jared Mitchell, OF	Atlantic League
2011	Chris Sale, LHP	Red Sox
2012	Addison Reed, RHP	Twins
2013	Courtney Hawkins, OF	Reds
2014	Jose Abreu, 1B	White Sox
2015	Carlos Rodon, LHP	White Sox
2016	Tim Anderson, SS	White Sox
2017	Yoan Moncada, 2B/3B	White Sox
2018	Eloy Jimenez, OF	White Sox

BEST TOOLS

Best Hitter for Average	Eloy Jimenez
Best Power Hitter	Eloy Jimenez
Best Strike-Zone Discipline	Zack Collins
Fastest Baserunner	Joel Booker
Best Athlete	Luis Robert
Best Fastball	Michael Kopech
Best Curveball	Dylan Cease
Best Slider	Michael Kopech
Best Changeup	Jordan Guerrero
Best Control	Lincoln Henzman
Best Defensive Catcher	Nate Nolan
Best Defensive Infielder	Nick Madrigal
Best Infield Arm	Yeyson Yrizarri
Best Defensive Outfielder	Luis Alexander Basabe
Best Outfield Arm	Micker Adolfo

Year	Club (League)	Class	AVG	G	AB	R	H	2B	3B	HR	RBI	BB	SO	SB	CS	OBP	SLG
2016	South Bend (MWL)	LoA	.329	112	432	65	142	40	3	14	81	25	94	8	3	.369	.532
2017	Myrtle Beach (CAR)	HiA	.271	42	155	23	42	6	2	8	32	18	35	0	0	.351	.490
	Winston-Salem (CAR)	HiA	.345	29	110	20	38	11	1	8	26	12	21	0	2	.410	.682
	Birmingham (SL)	AA	.353	18	68	11	24	5	0	3	7	5	16	1	1	.397	.559
2018	Birmingham (SL)	AA	.317	53	205	36	65	15	2	10	42	18	39	0	0	.368	.556
	Charlotte (IL)	AAA	.343	54	207	27	71	13	1	12	33	14	30	0	1	.388	.589
Minor League Totals			.309	407	1559	231	482	108	11	65	281	117	310	15	10	.358	.518

2 MICHAEL KOPECH, RHP

Born: April 30, 1996. **B-T:** R-R. **HT:** 6-3. **WT:** 205. **Drafted:** HS—Mount Pleasant, Texas, 2014 (1st round). **Signed by:** Tim Collinsworth (Red Sox).

TRACK RECORD: Acquired in the Chris Sale trade, Kopech made big strides to earn his first big league callup. After battling massive control problems early in the season, he rectified them by early July. Over his final seven starts, including four big league outings he struck out 42 and walked two in 34.1 innings. His only bad big league outing was his last one, and with good reason: he had a torn elbow ligament that required Tommy John surgery.

SCOUTING REPORT: Even after learning to use his whole arsenal to get hitters out, Kopech's signature pitch is still his blazing fastball that touches as high as 102 mph. As the season went along, he throttled down to a still-blazing 95-98 and showed improved command. He started to do a better job of repeating his delivery and finding a consistent arm path. His slider has always been his best secondary pitch, flashing plus grades and working as a true finisher. Improved fastball command made Kopech's slider more effective because hitters were less able to lay off of it. He added a fringy curveball in 2018. While it is a barely usable pitch, throwing it helped improve his still-inconsistent changeup into a pitch that flashes average. In the past, his changeup was often much too firm.

THE FUTURE: Kopech had Tommy John surgery in September, meaning his 2019 season is wiped out. If everything goes according to plan, he should be back in the rotation some time in the middle of 2020. He has front-of-the-rotation potential.

	BA GRADE	
65	**Risk:** Very High	
	Fastball: 80.	
	Slider: 60. **Curve:** 50.	
	Change: 50. **CTL:** 50.	

Year	Club (League)	Class	W	L	ERA	G	GS	CG	SV	IP	H	HR	BB	SO	K/9	WHIP	AVG
2016	Lowell (NYP)	SS	0	0	0.00	1	1	0	0	4	4	0	4	4	8.3	1.85	.250
	Salem (CAR)	HiA	4	1	2.25	11	11	0	0	52	25	1	29	82	14.2	1.04	.147
2017	Birmingham (SL)	AA	8	7	2.87	22	22	0	0	119	77	6	60	155	11.7	1.15	.184
	Charlotte (IL)	AAA	1	1	3.00	3	3	0	0	15	15	0	5	17	10.2	1.33	.263
2018	Charlotte (IL)	AAA	7	7	3.70	24	24	0	0	126	101	9	60	170	12.1	1.27	.219
	Chicago (AL)	MAJ	1	1	5.02	4	4	0	0	14	20	4	2	15	9.4	1.53	.328
Major League Totals			1	1	5.02	4	4	0	0	14	20	4	2	15	9.4	1.53	.328
Minor League Totals			24	22	3.05	85	84	0	0	396	286	18	194	514	11.7	1.21	.203

3 DYLAN CEASE, RHP

Born: Dec. 28, 1995. **B-T:** R-R. **HT:** 6-2. **WT:** 190. **Drafted:** HS—Milton, Ga., 2014 (6th round). **Signed by:** Keith Lockhart (Cubs).

TRACK RECORD: After recovering from Tommy John surgery, Cease came over to the White Sox along with slugger Eloy Jimenez as part of the Jose Quintana trade in July 2017. At high Class A Winston-Salem and Double-A Birmingham in 2018, Cease notched 160 strikeouts, 10 behind Kopech for the system lead.

SCOUTING REPORT: Cease's top-of-the-scale fastball sits in the mid-90s and has touched triple digits. He comes by that velocity almost effortlessly, from a high-slot delivery that features whip-quick arm speed. The fastball doesn't show a whole lot of side-to-side life, though there is some sink and tail when he works it toward the bottom of the zone. More often, the pitch features riding life up in the zone. He complements the pitch with a plus 12-to-6 curveball in the mid-70s. He doesn't always land the pitch for a strike, but it induces chases when buried. His third pitch is an average low-to-mid-80s changeup that features moderate sink. He also throws a developing slider. Cease's fringe-average control has shown improvement, but he still needs to refine it.

THE FUTURE: Cease will likely return to Double-A to refine his offspeed pitches. He has the ceiling of a mid-rotation starter or a dominant closer.

	BA GRADE	
60	**Risk:** High	
	Fastball: 80.	
	Curve: 60. **Slider:** 50.	
	Change: 50. **CTL:** 50.	

Year	Club (League)	Class	W	L	ERA	G	GS	CG	SV	IP	H	HR	BB	SO	K/9	WHIP	AVG
2016	Eugene (NWL)	SS	2	0	2.22	12	12	0	0	45	27	1	25	66	13.3	1.16	.175
2017	South Bend (MWL)	LoA	1	2	2.79	13	13	0	0	52	39	2	26	74	12.9	1.26	.214
	Kannapolis (SAL)	LoA	0	8	3.89	9	9	0	0	42	35	1	18	52	11.2	1.27	.229
2018	Winston-Salem (CAR)	HiA	9	2	2.89	13	13	0	0	72	52	5	28	82	10.3	1.12	.204
	Birmingham (SL)	AA	3	2	1.72	10	10	0	0	52	30	3	22	78	13.4	0.99	.168
Minor League Totals			16	14	2.67	68	65	0	0	286	195	12	135	377	11.9	1.15	.194

4 NICK MADRIGAL, 2B

Born: March 5, 1997. **B-T:** R-R. **HT:** 5-8. **WT:** 160. **Drafted:** Oregon State, 2018 (1st round). **Signed by:** Mike Gange.

TRACK RECORD: Madrigal's Beavers won the College World Series, Oregon State's first title since going back-to-back in 2006 and 2007. He missed much of the college season with a broken left wrist, but he was back on the field for the CWS and the draft, when Chicago selected him fourth overall.

SCOUTING REPORT: Madrigal's carrying tool is his uncanny ability to put the barrel on the ball while avoiding chasing out of the strike zone. He owes his contact ability to excellent hand-eye coordination that helps in the field as well. At 5-foot-8, Madrigal is not an imposing player, and he faces concerns about his below-average power. He hit just eight home runs in three seasons at Oregon State, and carded just seven extra-base hits (all doubles) as a pro. His opposite-field approach will require tweaks for him to ever hit for significant power. The White Sox plan to work with him to add a little more loft to his swing in an effort to maximize his power without sacrificing his contact skills.

BA GRADE

60 Risk: High

Hit: 60. Power: 40.
Run: 60. Field: 60.
Arm: 50.

In the field, Madrigal will be tried at shortstop. He could be serviceable there and projects as an outstanding second baseman. Evaluators who watched Madrigal take grounders with Winston-Salem manager Omar Vizquel were impressed with how his hands compared with the 11-time Gold Glover's. Madrigal's accurate, average arm ticked up to above-average and even plus at times as he became more comfortable letting throws rip. He's a plus runner whose speed should add to the value of his on-base skills.

THE FUTURE: Madrigal will likely jump to Double-A in 2019 in his first full season. He has the ceiling of a middle infielder who could eventually compete for batting titles.

Year	Club (League)	Class	AVG	G	AB	R	H	2B	3B	HR	RBI	BB	SO	SB	CS	OBP	SLG
2018	White Sox (AZL)	R	.154	5	13	2	2	0	0	0	1	1	0	0	1	.353	.154
	Kannapolis (SAL)	LoA	.341	12	44	9	15	3	0	0	6	1	0	2	2	.347	.409
	Winston-Salem (CAR)HiA		.306	26	98	14	30	4	0	0	9	5	5	6	3	.355	.347
Minor League Totals			.303	43	155	25	47	7	0	0	16	7	5	8	6	.353	.348

5 LUIS ROBERT, OF

Born: Aug. 3, 1997. **B-T:** R-R. **HT:** 6-3. **WT:** 185. **Signed:** Cuba, 2017. **Signed by:** Kenny Williams/Marco Paddy.

TRACK RECORD: After signing for $26 million, a franchise record for an international signee, in the summer of 2017 and spending his pro debut in the Dominican Summer League, hopes were high for Robert's stateside debut. He provided glimpses of his massive potential during his appearances in big league spring training in 2018, but a torn ligament in his left thumb cost him the first two months of the season. He made his debut in the Rookie-level Arizona League, but re-injured the same thumb four games into his time with high Class A Winston-Salem.

SCOUTING REPORT: Robert came into the season with a tantalizing but raw skill set that needed time to mature into full-on skills. He's got one of the best bodies in the system, along with Micker Adolfo, and one of the highest upsides as well. His bat speed and plus-plus raw power are among the best in the system, and he put on impressive batting practice shows. He's got well

BA GRADE

60 Risk: Extreme

Hit: 55. Power: 60.
Run: 70. Field: 60.
Arm: 50.

above-average bat speed, and he improved his swing path. He needs to improve his strike-zone discipline, as evidenced by his 26.4 percent strikeout rate and 5.7 percent walk rate during his time with Winston-Salem. He's got the double-plus speed necessary to stay in center field, but he needs to refine his routes and jumps. If he did have to move to a corner, his plus arm would make him a natural fit for right field.

THE FUTURE: As was the case entering 2018, Robert's tools are among the best in the system. He'll work to refine them in 2019, likely back at Winston-Salem. Robert has all-star potential.

Year	Club (League)	Class	AVG	G	AB	R	H	2B	3B	HR	RBI	BB	SO	SB	CS	OBP	SLG
2016	Ciego de Avila (CNS)CNS		.401	53	182	51	73	12	2	12	40	38	30	11	6	.526	.687
	Cuban Team (C-A)	IND	.286	16	63	12	18	2	1	1	8	4	15	3	0	.319	.397
2017	White Sox (DSL)	R	.310	28	84	17	26	8	1	3	14	22	23	12	3	.491	.536
2018	Kannapolis (SAL)	LoA	.289	13	45	5	13	3	1	0	4	4	12	4	2	.360	.400
	White Sox (AZL)	R	.389	5	18	5	7	2	1	0	2	0	3	3	0	.389	.611
	Winston-Salem (CAR)HiA		.244	32	123	21	30	6	1	0	11	8	37	8	2	.317	.309
Minor League Totals			.281	78	270	48	76	19	4	3	31	34	75	27	7	.389	.415

6 MICKER ADOLFO, OF

Born: Sept. 11, 1996. **B-T:** R-R. **HT:** 6-3. **WT:** 200. **Signed:** Dominican Republic, 2013. **Signed by:** Marco Paddy.

TRACK RECORD: Adolfo signed with the White Sox in 2013 primarily on the strength of his plus-plus raw power. He took time to develop at the plate, but showed significant improvement in 2017 and was impressive in an injury-plagued 2018. A strained elbow limited Adolfo to DH at high Class A Winston-Salem, and he had Tommy John surgery in July.

SCOUTING REPORT: Adolfo's calling card is his plus-plus power to all fields. He has shown steady improvement as a hitter, which has helped his power play in games. Adolfo's swing is geared toward power. He sets up with a wide base and then coils his body with a significant timing step. He projects as a low-average slugger, but he's showing better pitch recognition. His strikeout rate fell below 30 percent and his walk rate reached double digits for the first time in his career in 2018. When healthy, Adolfo's throwing arm is among the best in the minors. Even if surgery saps some of that arm strength, it should still be plus. He's an above-average runner now, though he likely will slow down. He should be an average defender in right field.

THE FUTURE: Once Adolfo recovers from surgery, he should head back to the Carolina League to continue working on plate discipline while kicking off the rust.

BA GRADE

55 Risk: High

Hit: 40. **Power:** 60.
Run: 55. **Field:** 50.
Arm: 70.

Year	Club (League)	Class	AVG	G	AB	R	H	2B	3B	HR	RBI	BB	SO	SB	CS	OBP	SLG
2016	White Sox (AZL)	R	.250	4	16	2	4	2	0	1	2	1	8	0	0	.333	.563
	Kannapolis (SAL)	LoA	.219	65	247	30	54	13	1	5	21	14	88	0	1	.269	.340
2017	Kannapolis (SAL)	LoA	.264	112	424	60	112	28	2	16	68	31	149	2	0	.331	.453
2018	Winston-Salem (CAR)	HiA	.282	79	291	48	82	18	1	11	50	34	92	2	1	.369	.464
Minor League Totals			.252	328	1240	181	312	74	7	38	172	100	447	7	4	.321	.415

7 DANE DUNNING, RHP

Born: Dec. 20, 1994. **B-T:** R-R. **HT:** 6-4. **WT:** 200. **Drafted:** Florida, 2016 (1st round). **Signed by:** Buddy Hernandez (Nationals).

TRACK RECORD: Dunning, Lucas Giolito and Reynaldo Lopez joined the White Sox in the December 2016 Adam Eaton trade. Lopez and Giolito spent the season in the big league rotation, while Dunning impressed in the minors, reaching Double-A Birmingham. A strained right elbow cost him two months, but he returned for instructional league.

SCOUTING REPORT: Dunning's go-to pitches are his above-average low-90s sinker and plus slider. The righthander has worked hard over the past two seasons to consistently get full extension in his delivery, which imparts maximum action on his sinker. His slider is thrown in the low-to-mid-80s and shows 10-to-4 break. His above-average curveball, which he reintroduced after shelving it early in his career, is coming along quickly. Dunning tinkered with the grip on the pitch until he settled on a spike grip, which gives the pitch a sharper break. He also moved to the center of the rubber in 2018, which gives him a little more margin for error when it comes to working to his glove side. His changeup, which is thrown in the same velocity band as his slider, projects as above-average.

THE FUTURE: Dunning is likely headed back to Birmingham. He projects as a No. 4 starter.

BA GRADE

55 Risk: High

Fastball: 55.
Slider: 60. **Curve:** 60.
Change: 55. **CTL:** 55.

Year	Club (League)	Class	W	L	ERA	G	GS	CG	SV	IP	H	HR	BB	SO	K/9	WHIP	AVG
2016	Nationals (GCL)	R	0	0	0.00	1	1	0	0	2	0	0	0	3	13.5	0.00	.000
	Auburn (NYP)	SS	3	2	2.14	7	7	1	0	34	26	1	7	29	7.8	0.98	.208
2017	Kannapolis (SAL)	LoA	2	0	0.35	4	4	0	0	26	13	0	2	33	11.4	0.58	.143
	Winston-Salem (CAR)	HiA	6	8	3.51	22	22	0	0	118	114	15	36	135	10.3	1.27	.250
2018	Winston-Salem (CAR)	HiA	1	1	2.59	4	4	0	0	24	20	2	3	31	11.5	0.95	.215
	Birmingham (SL)	AA	5	2	2.76	11	11	0	0	62	57	0	23	69	10.0	1.29	.243
Minor League Totals			17	13	2.74	49	49	3	0	266	230	18	71	300	10.2	1.13	.229

8 BLAKE RUTHERFORD, OF

Born: May 2, 1997. **B-T:** L-L. **HT:** 6-3. **WT:** 195. **Drafted:** HS—Canoga Park, Calif., 2016 (1st round). **Signed by:** Bobby DeJardin (Yankees).

TRACK RECORD: Rutherford was part of a four-player package the White Sox received for third baseman Todd Frazier and relievers David Robertson and Tommy Kahnle in July 2017. Rutherford led the system with 78 RBIs in 2018.

SCOUTING REPORT: Rutherford's blend of 50 and 55 tools on the 20-to-80 scouting scale give him a chance to be at least an average regular. On a high Class A Winston-Salem team filled with bat-first prospects, Rutherford's smooth swing stood out to scouts. His above-average raw power hasn't turned into many home runs, and those he has hit are all pulled. Some scouts attribute this to a lack of "snap" in Rutherford's wrists, though the White Sox believe his power will grow. He shows the ability to impact the ball both early and late in the hitting zone, giving him an ability to hit to all fields. He is adept at all three outfield spots, though he plays mostly right field. He's a tick below-average runner, though he makes up for it with plus instincts. He has an average, accurate arm.

THE FUTURE: Rutherford will likely move to Double-A Birmingham in 2019. Though scouts debate his impact potential, they see a future big league regular.

BA GRADE
50 Risk: High
Hit: 55. Power: 50.
Run: 45. Field: 50.
Arm: 50.

Year	Club (League)	Class	AVG	G	AB	R	H	2B	3B	HR	RBI	BB	SO	SB	CS	OBP	SLG
2016	Yankees2 (GCL)	R	.240	8	25	3	6	1	0	1	3	4	6	0	0	.333	.400
	Pulaski (APP)	R	.382	25	89	13	34	7	4	2	9	9	24	0	2	.440	.618
2017	Charleston, SC (SAL)	LoA	.281	71	274	41	77	20	2	2	30	25	55	9	4	.342	.391
	Kannapolis (SAL)	LoA	.213	30	122	11	26	5	0	0	5	13	21	1	0	.289	.254
2018	Winston-Salem (CAR)	HiA	.293	115	447	67	131	25	9	7	78	34	90	15	8	.345	.436
Minor League Totals			.286	249	957	135	274	58	15	12	125	85	196	25	14	.346	.416

9 LUIS GONZALEZ, OF

Born: Sept. 10, 1995. **B-T:** L-L. **HT:** 6-1. **WT:** 190. **Drafted:** New Mexico, 2017 (3rd round). **Signed by:** John Kazanas.

TRACK RECORD: Gonzalez was a pitcher and hitter at New Mexico. The White Sox believed there was even more potential to be unlocked once he concentrated exclusively on hitting. He put together an excellent all-around 2018 season at two Class A levels.

SCOUTING REPORT: Gonzalez is a well-rounded prospect who has shown he's capable of putting up solid, professional at-bats with a modicum of power. His home run power is almost exclusively to his pull side. He does line doubles to all fields, so there is hope some of those doubles will turn into home runs. He showed little trouble handling lefthanders in 2018. He took it upon himself to make adjustments within the season, including using his lower half more in his swing and improving his bat path to keep it in the hitting zone more often. Gonzalez moved around the outfield for high Class A Winston-Salem, but the majority of his time came in center field. He's a capable defender at that position, but his above-average range and plus arm make him a more likely right fielder. Whether he'll have the power to profile there is a question for 2019.

THE FUTURE: After a strong 2018 Gonzalez is likely headed for Double-A Birmingham.

BA GRADE
50 Risk: High
Hit: 60. Power: 45.
Run: 50. Field: 50.
Arm: 60.

Year	Club (League)	Class	AVG	G	AB	R	H	2B	3B	HR	RBI	BB	SO	SB	CS	OBP	SLG
2017	Great Falls (PIO)	R	.118	4	17	3	2	1	0	0	3	4	3	0	0	.286	.176
	Kannapolis (SAL)	LoA	.245	63	233	26	57	13	4	2	12	38	50	2	3	.356	.361
2018	Kannapolis (SAL)	LoA	.300	55	230	35	69	16	2	8	26	21	57	7	2	.358	.491
	Winston-Salem (CAR)	HiA	.313	62	252	50	79	24	3	6	45	27	46	3	5	.376	.504
Minor League Totals			.283	184	732	114	207	54	9	16	86	90	156	12	10	.362	.447

10 STEELE WALKER, OF

Born: July 30, 1996. **B-T:** L-L. **HT:** 5-11. **WT:** 190. **Drafted:** Oklahoma, 2018 (2nd round). **Signed by:** Rob Cummings.

TRACK RECORD: Throughout his amateur career, Walker established himself as a talented, professional hitter. After successful turns in the Northwoods and Cape Cod League, Walker was among the standouts on the 2017 Collegiate National Team. He finished second in batting average and slugging percentage on Team USA and tied for the team lead in home runs. He set collegiate highs in all three triple-slash categories in his junior year at Oklahoma (.352/.441/.606) before a late-season oblique injury forced him to sit out the Sooners' postseason. That oblique injury lingered, which helped explain a lackluster pro debut.

BA GRADE

50 Risk: High

Hit: 55. **Power:** 55.
Run: 50. **Field:** 55.
Arm: 50.

SCOUTING REPORT: Walker's value is tied to his bat, which the White Sox believe is capable of producing both average and power. He has strong wrists and a smooth, rhythmic swing from the left side that features a lofted swing path that could help him hit for above-average power. He showed clear pull-side tendencies in his brief pro debut. The White Sox were pleased with how he handled center field as a pro, and his average foot speed and arm strength should give him a chance to stick there for the foreseeable future thanks to solid routes and reads. If he does have to move to a corner outfield spot, his arm strength and power potential would give him a fair shot to profile in right field.

THE FUTURE: After a tune-up in Rookie ball and low Class A Kannapolis in 2018, Walker should begin his first full pro season at high Class A Winston-Salem.

Year	Club (League)	Class	AVG	G	AB	R	H	2B	3B	HR	RBI	BB	SO	SB	CS	OBP	SLG
2018	White Sox (AZL)	R	.455	4	11	0	5	0	0	0	0	1	1	0	0	.538	.455
	Great Falls (PIO)	R	.206	9	34	4	7	1	0	2	4	1	7	1	1	.263	.412
	Kannapolis (SAL)	LoA	.186	31	113	13	21	5	0	3	17	8	29	5	1	.246	.310
Minor League Totals			.209	44	158	17	33	6	0	5	21	10	37	6	2	.271	.342

11 LUIS ALEXANDER BASABE, OF

BA GRADE

50 Risk: High

Born: Aug. 22, 1996. **B-T:** S-R. **HT:** 6-0. **WT:** 160. **Signed:** Venezuela, 2012. **Signed by:** Eddie Romero/Luis Segovia (Red Sox).

TRACK RECORD: The Red Sox signed Basabe and his identical twin brother in 2012, but shipped both players out in separate deals in 2016. Luis Alexander was included as part of the four-player deal Boston used to acquire ace lefthander Chris Sale, but his tools were muted in his first season with his new team because of a nagging knee injury that required surgery in the offseason.

SCOUTING REPORT: Basabe has a chance to be a true five-tool player. His hit tool is the least polished at this point, but projects as average with further refinement. The White Sox worked with him this year on his hand position at the plate and made his swing more direct to the ball. Evaluators noted that he saw spin well, but was vulnerable to changeups. He shows the ability to get the barrel to hard fastballs, and uses plus bat speed to generate above-average raw power. Those skills were evident in the Futures Game, where he turned around a 102-mph pitch for a home run against Reds fireballer Hunter Greene. Basabe has all the tools to stick in center field, including plus footspeed that helps him get excellent jumps on balls and a plus throwing arm.

THE FUTURE: After a stint in the Arizona Fall League, Basabe is likely to return to Double-A Birmingham to continue working on his hit tool and adding polish to his overall game.

Year	Club (League)	Class	AVG	G	AB	R	H	2B	3B	HR	RBI	BB	SO	SB	CS	OBP	SLG
2016	Greenville (SAL)	LoA	.258	105	403	61	104	24	8	12	52	40	116	25	5	.325	.447
	Salem (CAR)	HiA	.364	5	22	5	8	2	1	0	1	1	3	0	0	.391	.545
2017	Winston-Salem (CAR)	HiA	.221	107	375	52	83	12	5	5	36	49	104	17	6	.320	.320
2018	Winston-Salem (CAR)	HiA	.266	58	207	36	55	12	5	9	30	34	64	7	8	.370	.502
	Birmingham (SL)	AA	.251	61	231	41	58	9	3	6	26	30	76	9	4	.340	.394
Minor League Totals			.248	524	1922	333	477	92	38	41	226	278	547	106	38	.347	.400

12 ZACK COLLINS, C

BA GRADE

50 Risk: High

Born: Feb. 6, 1995. **B-T:** L-R. **HT:** 6-3. **WT:** 220. **Drafted:** Miami, 2016 (1st round). **Signed by:** Jose Ortega.

TRACK RECORD: After three stellar seasons at Miami, the White Sox selected Collins in the first round in 2016 and signed him for $3,380,600. He quickly jumped to high Class A Winston-Salem, and spent 137 of his first 140 pro games with the Dash before moving to Double-A late in 2017. He spent all of 2018 in Birmingham, where he showed flashes of his potential in between fallow stretches.

SCOUTING REPORT: Collins' best tool is his batting eye. His 101 walks in 2018 were the second-most in the minors, and his knowledge of the strike zone has helped him boost his on-base percentage significantly. His hit tool is not likely to be average and still needs refinement both in approach and mechanics. His swing starts with a deep, exaggerated load that can leave him vulnerable to hard fastballs. He also has a tendency to get out of a natural opposite-field swing and instead try to pull everything with his double-plus raw power. The White Sox are committed to developing Collins as a catcher, but outside evaluators wonder if he might need to move to first base. He made strides as a game-caller, but needs serious improvement as a receiver. He struggles simply catching the ball at times, and his poor footwork forces his above-average arm strength to play down.

THE FUTURE: After an entire season at Double-A Birmingham, Collins is likely to move to Triple-A Charlotte in 2019. With serious improvements to his defense, he could be an offensive-minded catcher.

Year	Club (League)	Class	AVG	G	AB	R	H	2B	3B	HR	RBI	BB	SO	SB	CS	OBP	SLG
2016	White Sox (AZL)	R	.091	3	11	1	1	0	0	0	0	0	7	0	0	.091	.091
	Winston-Salem (CAR)HiA		.258	36	120	24	31	7	0	6	18	33	39	0	0	.418	.467
2017	Winston-Salem (CAR)HiA		.223	101	341	63	76	18	3	17	48	76	118	0	2	.365	.443
	Birmingham (SL)	AA	.235	12	34	7	8	2	0	2	5	11	11	0	0	.422	.471
2018	Birmingham (SL)	AA	.234	122	418	58	98	24	1	15	68	101	158	5	0	.382	.404
Minor League Totals			.232	274	924	153	214	51	4	40	139	221	333	5	2	.379	.425

13 IAN HAMILTON, RHP

BA GRADE

50 Risk: High

Born: June 16, 1995. **B-T:** R-R. **HT:** 6-0. **WT:** 200. **Drafted:** Washington State, 2016 (11th round). **Signed by:** Robbie Cummings.

TRACK RECORD: Hamilton spent his final college season in the rotation at Washington State, but he missed the late-innings adrenaline and moved back to the bullpen immediately upon turning pro. He made his major league debut on Aug. 31.

SCOUTING REPORT: Hamilton's signature is his high-octane heat. He averaged close to 97 mph in his major league time, and touched triple digits regularly in the minor leagues. The pitch also spins at roughly 2,300 rpm, close to the major league average for four-seam fastballs. He pairs the fastball with a sharp-biting, plus slider in the low 90s that he can use both as a called strike or a chase pitch for a strikeout. He also has a changeup, but it is below-average and a distant third pitch. Hamilton has shown excellent control in the minors, but worked in 2018 to polish his command. He also worked to stay behind the fastball to get the most out of the pitch when he throws it in the upper part of the strike zone.

THE FUTURE: Hamilton should be in the mix for a bullpen spot out of spring training, but could also head back to Triple-A Charlotte for more seasoning. He has the ceiling of a late-inning reliever.

Year	Club (League)	Class	W	L	ERA	G	GS	CG	SV	IP	H	HR	BB	SO	K/9	WHIP	AVG
2016	White Sox (AZL)	R	0	0	0.00	1	0	0	0	1	0	0	1	2	18.0	1.00	.000
	Kannapolis (SAL)	LoA	1	1	3.69	21	0	0	8	32	22	3	14	27	7.7	1.14	.202
2017	Birmingham (SL)	AA	1	3	5.50	13	0	0	1	18	24	0	8	21	10.5	1.78	.317
	Winston-Salem (CAR)	HiA	3	3	1.71	30	0	0	6	53	32	1	8	52	8.9	0.76	.179
2018	Birmingham (SL)	AA	2	1	1.78	21	0	0	12	25	20	0	12	34	12.1	1.26	.211
	Charlotte (IL)	AAA	1	1	1.85	21	0	0	9	24	17	2	4	26	9.6	0.86	.187
	Chicago (AL)	MAJ	0	0	4.50	10	0	0	0	8	6	2	5	5	5.6	1.00	.207
Major League Totals			1	2	4.50	10	0	0	0	8	6	2	5	5	5.6	1.00	.207
Minor League Totals			8	9	2.59	107	0	0	36	153	115	6	47	162	9.5	1.06	.211

14 GAVIN SHEETS, 1B

BA GRADE

50 Risk: High

Born: April 23, 1996. **B-T:** L-L. **HT:** 6-4. **WT:** 230. **Drafted:** Wake Forest, 2017 (2nd round). **Signed by:** Abe Fernandez.

TRACK RECORD: After hitting 11 home runs in his freshman and sophomore seasons at Wake Forest, Sheets nearly doubled that total by swatting 21 in his junior season. That power surge prompted the White Sox to draft him in the second round and sign him for $2 million. He did not meet expectations as a pro, and his .397 slugging percentage was a bit eyebrow-raising considering what he'd done in college.

SCOUTING REPORT: Sheets' rough pro debut was a precursor to his first full year. He hit just six home runs in 2018, none of which came after May 23. The White Sox worked with Sheets on his mechanics at the plate, including adjustments to the way his hands worked through the zone and some tweaks designed to incorporate his lower half more so his bat path can become more uphill. Opposing scouts saw plus raw power in batting practice, but also noticed exploitable holes in his swing inside and up during games. He's an average defender at first base with an average arm, but is also a well below-average runner.

THE FUTURE: Sheets is likely to move to Double-A Birmingham in 2019, where he'll continue to work to unlock the power he'll need to profile at first base.

Year	Club (League)	Class	AVG	G	AB	R	H	2B	3B	HR	RBI	BB	SO	SB	CS	OBP	SLG
2017	White Sox (AZL)	R	.500	4	12	3	6	2	0	1	3	3	0	0	0	.625	.917
	Kannapolis (SAL)	LoA	.266	52	192	16	51	10	0	3	25	20	34	0	0	.346	.365
2018	Winston-Salem (CAR)HiA		.293	119	437	58	128	28	2	6	61	52	81	1	0	.368	.407
Minor League Totals			.289	175	641	77	185	40	2	10	89	75	115	1	0	.367	.404

15 SEBY ZAVALA, C

BA GRADE
45 Risk: Medium

Born: Aug. 28, 1993. **B-T:** R-R. **HT:** 5-11. **WT:** 205. **Drafted:** San Diego State, 2015 (12th round). **Signed by:** George Kachigan.

TRACK RECORD: Zavala's career at San Diego State included a Tommy John surgery, a switch to left field and a breakout in power that boosted his draft stock. As a professional, Zavala has moved more or less in lockstep with the organization's other high-profile catching prospect, Zack Collins.

SCOUTING REPORT: Zavala started strong at Birmingham, swatting 11 home runs (which placed him fifth on the team despite playing just 56 games) and showing the power that put him on the map in 2017. His offense took a dip in Triple-A, but recurring left wrist irritation may have played a significant role. He's a borderline average defender who blocks well but needs to do better at smothering balls in the dirt. He's got an average throwing arm, which he used to throw out 33 percent of runners between both levels.

THE FUTURE: The White Sox placed Zavala on their 40-man roster after the season, and he has a good shot of making his big league debut at some point in 2019. He's likely to start back at Triple-A Charlotte.

Year	Club (League)	Class	AVG	G	AB	R	H	2B	3B	HR	RBI	BB	SO	SB	CS	OBP	SLG
2016	Kannapolis (SAL)	LoA	.253	93	360	40	91	19	3	7	49	35	108	1	1	.330	.381
2017	Kannapolis (SAL)	LoA	.259	52	185	32	48	8	0	13	34	13	52	0	0	.327	.514
	Winston-Salem (CAR)HiA		.302	55	202	31	61	13	0	8	38	24	52	1	0	.376	.485
2018	Birmingham (SL)	AA	.271	56	199	32	54	7	0	11	31	27	65	0	0	.358	.472
	Charlotte (IL)	AAA	.247	47	178	18	44	15	0	2	20	5	43	0	2	.267	.365
Minor League Totals			.271	338	1253	186	340	79	8	45	207	119	347	4	3	.341	.455

16 LAZ RIVERA, SS

BA GRADE
50 Risk: High

Born: Sept. 20, 1994. **B-T:** R-R. **HT:** 6-1. **WT:** 185. **Drafted:** Tampa, 2017 (28th round). **Signed by:** Steve Nichols.

TRACK RECORD: Rivera's college career saw him bounce from Miami as a freshman to Chipola (Fla.) JC as a sophomore and then to Tampa for his next two seasons before the White Sox popped him in 2017. He hit well wherever he went, posting a .988 OPS among his three schools before turning professional.

SCOUTING REPORT: Rivera is part of the new breed of infield prospect who hits first and asks questions later, a la Brandon Lowe and Nick Solak with the Rays. He brings above-average bat speed and a short path to the ball, which he used to post excellent numbers at both Class A levels. He's an aggressive hitter who crushes fastballs but needs to work on not chasing offspeed pitches. He played almost exclusively at shortstop, though his 40-grade arm profiles better at second base. He has the hands and actions to stay up the middle, but his arm and fringe-average speed will probably push him to the right side of the diamond.

THE FUTURE: After a stint in the Arizona Fall League, Rivera is likely headed to Double-A Birmingham.

Year	Club (League)	Class	AVG	G	AB	R	H	2B	3B	HR	RBI	BB	SO	SB	CS	OBP	SLG
2017	White Sox (AZL)	R	.296	47	186	37	55	12	5	2	24	8	26	3	4	.374	.446
2018	Kannapolis (SAL)	LoA	.346	63	237	42	82	15	2	6	24	6	48	7	3	.395	.502
	Winston-Salem (CAR)HiA		.280	61	225	38	63	15	2	7	37	7	44	10	7	.325	.458
Minor League Totals			.309	171	648	117	200	42	9	15	85	21	118	20	14	.365	.471

17 ALEC HANSEN, RHP

BA GRADE
50 Risk: Very High

Born: Oct. 10, 1994. **B-T:** R-R. **HT:** 6-7. **WT:** 235. **Drafted:** Oklahoma, 2016 (2nd round). **Signed by:** Clay Overcash.

TRACK RECORD: Entering his junior season at Oklahoma, Hansen was in play for the No. 1 overall pick in the draft. From there, he lost the strike zone and his spot in the rotation. The White Sox scooped him up in the second round and signed him for $1.2 million. His first two seasons as a pro showed immense potential, highlighted by a dominant season in which his 191 strikeouts were second in the minor leagues.

SCOUTING REPORT: From the outset, Hansen's 2018 season was a disaster. His season was delayed until mid-June by tightness in his right forearm, and he pitched so poorly at Double-A Birmingham that he was sent back to high Class A Winston-Salem less than a month later. He finished the season with more walks (59) than strikeouts (55), but his stuff was clearly down. He was pitching with a low-90s fastball and still didn't regain his command when he returned to Winston-Salem, where he'd dominated in 2017. Beyond the injuries, the White Sox continued working with Hansen to keep his big body in sync and over the rubber throughout his delivery.

THE FUTURE: Hansen clearly has the stuff to dominate, but he needs to find the mental toughness to put 2018 in the rearview mirror. He is likely to return to Double-A in 2019.

Year	Club (League)	Class	W	L	ERA	G	GS	CG	SV	IP	H	HR	BB	SO	K/9	WHIP	AVG
2016	White Sox (AZL)	R	0	0	0.00	3	3	0	0	7	1	0	4	11	14.1	0.71	.048
	Great Falls (PIO)	R	2	0	1.23	7	7	0	0	37	12	3	12	59	14.5	0.65	.102
	Kannapolis (SAL)	LoA	0	1	2.45	2	2	0	0	11	11	0	4	11	9.0	1.36	.262
2017	Kannapolis (SAL)	LoA	7	3	2.48	13	13	0	0	73	57	3	23	92	11.4	1.10	
.207	Winston-Salem (CAR)	HiA	4	5	2.93	11	11	1	0	58	42	5	25	82	12.7	1.15	.203
	Birmingham (SL)	AA	0	0	4.35	2	2	0	0	10	15	0	3	17	14.8	1.74	.333
2018	Birmingham (SL)	AA	0	4	6.56	9	9	0	0	36	30	3	42	35	8.8	2.02	.238
	Winston-Salem (CAR)	HiA	0	1	5.74	5	5	0	0	16	14	0	17	20	11.5	1.98	.250
Minor League Totals			13	14	3.20	52	52	1	0	247	182	14	130	327	11.9	1.26	.204

18 ZACK BURDI, RHP

BA GRADE

50 Risk: Very High

Born: March 9, 1995. **B-T:** R-R. **HT:** 6-3. **WT:** 205. **Drafted:** Louisville, 2016 (1st round). **Signed by:** Phil Gulley.

TRACK RECORD: In three seasons as Louisville's closer, Burdi was dominant. He struck out 83 in 70 innings and racked up 20 saves over three seasons before the White Sox took him with their first-round pick in 2016. He signed for $2,128,500 then zoomed to Triple-A Charlotte and seemed to be on the cusp of the major leagues before he tore his ulnar collateral ligament in 2017 and had Tommy John surgery. The operation kept him out all of the 2018 regular season before he returned in the Arizona Fall League.

SCOUTING REPORT: Before the surgery, Burdi's calling card was his hard fastball. The pitch sat in the upper 90s and touched triple digits with regularity. Paired with a slider that flashed plus, Burdi had the earmarks of a late-inning reliever. In the AFL, though, roughly 15 months after the surgery, his velocity ranged anywhere from 91-97 mph. He still showed an 82-86 mph slider that flashed plus, and an 85-88 mph changeup that projects as above-average. He has never pitched on back-to-back days in his pro career.

THE FUTURE: Simply getting back on the mound was a good sign, and his ceiling can't be properly assessed until it's certain where his fastball is going to park, but a return to full health would give him a future in the back of a bullpen. He should head back to Triple-A in 2019.

Year	Club (League)	Class	W	L	ERA	G	GS	CG	SV	IP	H	HR	BB	SO	K/9	WHIP	AVG
2016	White Sox (AZL)	R	0	0	0.00	1	0	0	0	1	1	0	0	1	9.0	1.00	.250
	Winston-Salem (CAR)	HiA	0	0	5.40	4	0	0	0	5	6	1	0	4	7.2	1.20	.316
	Birmingham (SL)	AA	0	0	3.94	12	0	0	0	16	7	2	9	24	13.5	1.00	.132
	Charlotte (IL)	AAA	1	0	2.25	9	0	0	1	16	9	0	11	22	12.4	1.25	.161
2017	Charlotte (IL)	AAA	0	4	4.05	29	0	0	7	33	30	2	17	51	13.8	1.41	.231
2018	White Sox (AZL)	R	0	1	2.84	7	1	0	0	6	5	0	4	7	9.9	1.42	.217
Minor League Totals			1	5	3.59	62	1	0	8	78	58	5	41	109	12.6	1.27	.204

19 JORDAN STEPHENS, RHP

BA GRADE

45 Risk: Medium

Born: Sept. 12, 1992. **B-T:** R-R. **HT:** 6-1. **WT:** 190. **Drafted:** Rice, 2015 (5th round). **Signed by:** Chris Walker.

TRACK RECORD: Stephens had Tommy John surgery in his junior year at Rice, took a medical redshirt and rebounded to be a fifth round pick. He ranked third in the system with 139 strikeouts in 2018.

SCOUTING REPORT: Stephens gets his outs with a fairly standard four-pitch arsenal, fronted by a low 90s fastball with cutter action and a mid-80s slider. He throws a mid-70s curveball and a firm mid-80s changeup as well. He throws all four from a simple, repeatable delivery that gives him average control.

THE FUTURE: There has been talk in the organization that Stephens' stuff might play better in the bullpen. In the bullpen he might fit in the seventh or eighth inning. The White Sox added him to their 40-man roster during the offseason.

Year	Club (League)	Class	W	L	ERA	G	GS	CG	SV	IP	H	HR	BB	SO	K/9	WHIP	AVG
2016	Winston-Salem (CAR)	HiA	7	10	3.45	27	27	0	0	141	129	12	48	155	9.9	1.26	.243
2017	Birmingham (SL)	AA	3	7	3.14	16	16	0	0	92	84	4	35	83	8.1	1.30	.249
2018	Birmingham (SL)	AA	4	3	2.95	7	7	0	0	40	37	1	12	40	9.1		.259
	Charlotte (IL)	AAA	4	7	4.71	21	21	0	0	107	114	11	42	99	8.3	1.46	.271
Minor League Totals			18	27	3.54	82	72	0	0	397	373	28	140	398	9.0	1.29	.250

20 SPENCER ADAMS, RHP

Born: April 13, 1996. **B-T:** R-R. **HT:** 6-3. **WT:** 171. **Drafted:** HS—Cleveland, Ga., 2014 (2nd round). **Signed by:** Kevin Burrell.

BA GRADE	
45	Risk: Medium

TRACK RECORD: Adams was an attractive draft prospect because of his athleticism and projection, and a fastball that had run its way up to 96 mph. That fastball took a step back once he turned pro, though he still had enough velocity and sink to perform well at the lower levels.
SCOUTING REPORT: Adams still hasn't recovered the mid-90s velocity that he had as an amateur, and scouts saw the pitch more often in the 89-91 mph range in 2018. The fastball fronted a four-pitch mix completed by a slider and changeup in the low 80s and a curveball in the high 70s. The slider was the best of his offspeed pitches, rating as a touch above-average offering. His changeup and curve are both fringe-average. His lack of an out pitch was made plain in 2018 by a scant 5.4 strikeouts per nine innings.
THE FUTURE: To succeed in the big leagues, Adams will need to mix and match and pitch to contact, giving him a ceiling of a fifth starter who more likely is an up-and-down arm. The White Sox's left him off their 40-man roster and he went unpicked in the Rule 5 draft. He's likely to head back to Triple-A Charlotte.

Year	Club (League)	Class	W	L	ERA	G	GS	CG	SV	IP	H	HR	BB	SO	K/9	WHIP	AVG
2016	Winston-Salem (CAR)	HiA	8	7	4.01	18	18	1	0	108	120	7	21	74	6.2	1.31	.275
	Birmingham (SL)	AA	2	5	3.90	9	9	0	0	55	59	2	10	26	4.2	1.25	.274
2017	Birmingham (SL)	AA	7	15	4.42	26	26	2	0	153	171	19	40	113	6.7	1.38	.281
2018	Birmingham (SL)	AA	3	6	4.59	13	13	0	0	69	80	10	20	53	6.9	1.46	.290
	Charlotte (IL)	AAA	4	7	3.19	15	15	0	0	90	82	10	38	42	4.2	1.33	.248
Minor League Totals			39	48	3.82	115	114	4	0	646	703	60	151	463	6.5	1.32	.275

21 BRYCE BUSH, 3B

Born: Dec. 14, 1999. **B-T:** R-R. **HT:** 6-0. **WT:** 200. **Drafted:** HS—Warren, Mich., 2018 (33rd round). **Signed by:** Justin Wechsler.

BA GRADE	
50	Risk: Extreme

TRACK RECORD: Bush was lauded for having some of the best bat speed in the 2018 draft class, but fell due to signability concerns surrounding his commitment to Mississippi State. The White Sox gambled, however, and signed him for a bonus of $290,000, sixth-highest in Chicago's class.
SCOUTING REPORT: Bush's top-notch bat speed is part of an unorthodox swing that includes a low hand-set before launching into a steep uphill path. Those two elements make scouts believe he'll ultimately hit for more power than average. He also needs to adjust his swing to keep him from drifting away from the ball. He's a work in progress at third base who will need reps to continue to master the intricacies of the position. He needs to learn to slow the game down, improve his reaction time and learn the angles required. He's got solid reaction time and a strong arm over at third base, and scouts see the necessary athleticism for the position as well. He's a fringe-average runner.
THE FUTURE: Bush bullied his way out of the Rookie-level Arizona League before running into more resistance in the Pioneer League. He could return there in 2019, or start out at low Class A Kannapolis.

Year	Club (League)	Class	AVG	G	AB	R	H	2B	3B	HR	RBI	BB	SO	SB	CS	OBP	SLG
2018	White Sox (AZL)	R	.442	14	43	8	19	4	0	1	8	8	4	1	2	.538	.605
	Great Falls (PIO)	R	.250	24	96	16	24	5	1	2	10	10	21	3	0	.327	.385
Minor League Totals			.309	38	139	24	43	9	1	3	18	18	25	4	2	.396	.453

22 KONNOR PILKINGTON, LHP

Born: Sept. 12, 1997. **B-T:** L-L. **HT:** 6-3. **WT:** 225. **Drafted:** Mississippi State, 2018 (3rd round). **Signed by:** Warren Hughes.

BA GRADE	
45	Risk: High

TRACK RECORD: Pilkington comes with plenty of pedigree. He pitched for three seasons in the Southeastern Conference, ranked as the No. 14 prospect in the 2016 Cape Cod League and pitched to a 2.65 ERA on the 2017 Collegiate National Team. He was also one of the youngest collegiate players available in the draft.
SCOUTING REPORT: Pilkington is by no means overpowering, pitching with a fastball that usually settles in around 89-92 but has touched up to 94. His 76-78 mph curveball flashes above-average potential, and Pilkington can vary the break on the pitch to make it look like a slider as well. His changeup, which he throws around 79-83 mph, also got potential plus grades from scouts. He sometimes rushes through his delivery and finishes stiff and upright, but it hasn't been a problem for him so far.
THE FUTURE: Pilkington pitched mostly at Rookie-level Great Falls in 2018, but because of his pedigree could go to either low Class A Kannapolis or high Class A Winston-Salem.

Year	Club (League)	Class	W	L	ERA	G	GS	CG	SV	IP	H	HR	BB	SO	K/9	WHIP	AVG
2018	White Sox (AZL)	R	0	0	18.00	2	1	0	0	2	7	0	1	2	9.0	4.00	.538
	Great Falls (PIO)	R	0	1	5.25	6	6	0	0	12	14	1	4	9	6.8	1.50	.292
Minor League Totals			0	1	7.07	8	7	0	0	14	21	1	5	11	7.1	1.86	.344

23 JAKE BURGER, 3B

BA GRADE
50 Risk: Extreme

Born: April 10, 1996. **B-T:** R-R. **HT:** 6-2. **WT:** 210. **Drafted:** Missouri State, 2017 (1st round). **Signed by:** Clay Overcash.

TRACK RECORD: After three thunderous years at Missouri State, which included a cumulative 47 home runs and a 1.040 OPS, the White Sox drafted Burger with their first-round pick and let him get his feet wet at low Class A Kannapolis for the bulk of his pro debut. He's torn his left Achilles tendon twice since then; once in February 2018 and then again in May while rehabbing the original injury.

SCOUTING REPORT: Before the injuries, scouts were counting on Burger to be a solid-average hitter with plenty of potential for power production. That aspect of his game will likely remain the same once he returns. The bigger question will revolve around where Burger fits on a diamond. Even before he got hurt there were concerns about whether his size and mobility would allow him to stick at third base. The White Sox pointed to his exemplary makeup as reason to believe he'd get his body in the necessary shape to stay at third. With two major surgeries since then, the questions are only going to get louder.

THE FUTURE: Achilles repair typically takes about a year, meaning the earliest Burger would get back on the field would be at midseason 2019.

Year	Club (League)	Class	AVG	G	AB	R	H	2B	3B	HR	RBI	BB	SO	SB	CS	OBP	SLG
2017	White Sox (AZL)	R	.154	4	13	4	2	1	0	1	2	1	2	0	0	.353	.462
	Kannapolis (SAL)	LoA	.271	47	181	21	49	9	2	4	27	13	28	0	1	.335	.409
2018	Did not play—Injured																
Minor League Totals			.263	51	194	25	51	10	2	5	29	14	30	0	1	.336	.412

24 ANDERSON COMAS, OF

BA GRADE
50 Risk: Extreme

Born: Feb. 10, 2000. **B-T:** L-L. **HT:** 6-3. **WT:** 185. **Signed:** Dominican Republic, 2016. **Signed by:** Marino De Leon.

TRACK RECORD: Comas has put up solid numbers in his first two professional seasons, including a .306 batting average in 2018 that ranked fourth in the organization. He will require time and patience as he grows into his frame.

SCOUTING REPORT: Comas has produced solid averages and plenty of contact in his first two seasons thanks to a smooth, controlled swing from the left side. He's got long levers, which will take some development time to learn to get in sync consistently. A slight uppercut paired with the ability to keep his barrel in the zone gives scouts reason to believe he'll develop at least average power. He's got natural instincts in the outfield along with an average throwing arm and slightly above-average footspeed.

THE FUTURE: Comas will be a project to develop, but his projectable body and present skills suggest a player who might be worth the wait. He'll play all of 2019 as a 19-year-old, and should move to Rookie-level Great Falls in June.

Year	Club (League)	Class	AVG	G	AB	R	H	2B	3B	HR	RBI	BB	SO	SB	CS	OBP	SLG
2017	White Sox (DSL)	R	.291	63	237	29	69	5	2	0	17	8	45	1	1	.316	.329
2018	White Sox (AZL)	R	.306	41	160	17	49	6	2	1	22	7	26	5	1	.339	.388
Minor League Totals			.297	104	397	46	118	11	4	1	39	15	71	6	2	.325	.353

25 CABEREA WEAVER, OF

BA GRADE
50 Risk: Extreme

Born: Dec. 1, 1999. **B-T:** R-R. **HT:** 6-2. **WT:** 150. **Drafted:** HS—Snellville, Ga., 2018 (7th round). **Signed by:** Kevin Burrell.

TRACK RECORD: Weaver's appeal was based on his athleticism, projectable frame and wiry strength. He's particularly raw, but showed a well-rounded set of skills while playing at South Gwinnett HS, which he helped lead to the second round of the state playoffs. His $226,200 bonus was among the highest handed out in the seventh round.

SCOUTING REPORT: Weaver has a bit of a longer swing with a fair amount of moving parts, but he compensates with a whippy stroke with above-average bat speed. He showed a better sense of timing during batting practice, and showed a solid feel for the zone in games. His next best tool is his speed, though he has trouble getting out of the box at times and doesn't show his true, double-plus quickness until he gets underway. Scouts believe his speed and instincts will keep him in center field.

THE FUTURE: Weaver typically batted at the top or bottom of lineups, which is where his skill set dictates. He projects as a slash-and-burn type of player who causes havoc on the bases. He's likely to land at Rookie-level Great Falls in 2019.

Year	Club (League)	Class	AVG	G	AB	R	H	2B	3B	HR	RBI	BB	SO	SB	CS	OBP	SLG
2018	White Sox (AZL)	R	.248	50	149	26	37	5	3	1	11	18	52	8	1	.367	.342
Minor League Totals			.248	50	149	26	37	5	3	1	11	18	52	8	1	.367	.342

26 LINCOLN HENZMAN, RHP

BA GRADE
45 Risk: High

Born: July 4, 1995. **B-T:** R-R. **HT:** 6-2. **WT:** 200. **Drafted:** Louisville, 2017 (4th round). **Signed by:** Phil Gulley.

TRACK RECORD: Henzman pitched almost exclusively as a reliever at Louisville, including a turn as the team's closer in 2017. He saved 16 games that spring, but the White Sox liked him as a potential starter and popped him with their fourth-round pick. Since transitioning to pro ball, Henzman has moved into a starter's role for nearly all of his appearances.

SCOUTING REPORT: Henzman isn't going to blow hitters away with his fastball, which sits in the 90-92 mph range with cutting action. He pairs the pitch with an above-average slider in the mid 80s and an average changeup in the low 80s. He controls the strike zone, with a combined rate of 1.5 walks per nine innings between two Class A levels.

THE FUTURE: As a pitcher with an Atlantic Coast Conference pedigree, it was no surprise that Henzman was successful at the lower levels. He'll get a real test in 2019 when he moves up to Double-A Birmingham against more advanced hitters.

Year	Club (League)	Class	W	L	ERA	G	GS	CG	SV	IP	H	HR	BB	SO	K/9	WHIP	AVG
2017	White Sox (AZL)	R	0	0	0.00	1	0	0	0	1	0	0	0	1	9.0	0.00	.000
	Great Falls (PIO)	R	0	3	4.00	10	7	0	0	27	27	0	9	16	5.3	1.33	.270
2018	Kannapolis (SAL)	LoA	6	3	2.23	13	13	1	0	73	68	5	8	60	7.4	1.05	.241
	Winston-Salem (CAR)	HiA	0	1	2.60	14	9	0	0	35	34	1	10	20	5.2	1.27	.256
Minor League Totals			6	7	2.66	38	29	1	0	135	129	6	27	97	6.5	1.15	.249

27 JOEL BOOKER, OF

BA GRADE
45 Risk: High

Born: Nov. 1, 1993. **B-T:** R-R. **HT:** 6-1. **WT:** 190. **Drafted:** Iowa, 2016 (22nd round). **Signed by:** J.J. Lally.

TRACK RECORD: After spending his first two collegiate seasons at Indian Hills (Iowa) JC, Booker transferred to Iowa for his junior and senior seasons. He showed contact and speed with the Hawkeyes, which led the White Sox to take a flyer on him as a senior sign. He's displayed a similar set of skills as a pro and in 2018 started to tap into a bit more power.

SCOUTING REPORT: Booker spent the offseason overhauling his swing, including eliminating a bat wrap and re-learning how to use his upper and lower body. The results were stark. He stood out among a prospect-filled outfield at high Class A Winston-Salem, earned the Carolina League's All-Star Game MVP and then moved to the upper levels for the first time. Booker unlocked some power at Winston-Salem, but the White Sox would prefer he spray the ball around the park and use his plus speed on the basepaths. He plays solid defense in the outfield, and can use his speed to make up for any mistakes he makes on routes.

THE FUTURE: Booker will likely return to Double-A Birmingham to start 2019, though the arrivals of Blake Rutherford, Luis Robert and possibly Micker Adolfo might mean a move to Triple-A Charlotte.

Year	Club (League)	Class	AVG	G	AB	R	H	2B	3B	HR	RBI	BB	SO	SB	CS	OBP	SLG
2016	White Sox (AZL)	R	.296	33	135	30	40	8	1	1	18	13	27	26	1	.387	.393
	Great Falls (PIO)	R	.328	32	125	21	41	8	0	1	13	14	22	15	2	.421	.416
2017	Winston-Salem (CAR)	HiA	.233	52	189	23	44	6	0	2	15	10	41	9	3	.284	.296
	Kannapolis (SAL)	LoA	.301	71	286	53	86	11	2	3	29	17	66	14	5	.359	.385
2018	Winston-Salem (CAR)	HiA	.297	53	192	39	57	14	2	5	21	22	42	14	9	.389	.469
	Birmingham (SL)	AA	.266	66	267	43	71	12	2	2	17	22	77	12	8	.338	.348
Minor League Totals			.284	307	1194	209	339	59	7	14	113	98	275	90	28	.358	.380

28 ZACH THOMPSON, RHP

BA GRADE
40 Risk: Medium

Born: Oct. 23, 1993. **B-T:** R-R. **HT:** 6-7. **WT:** 230. **Drafted:** Texas-Arlington, 2014 (5th round). **Signed by:** Keith Staab.

TRACK RECORD: At 6-foot-7, Thompson was projectable coming out of college. He scuffled somewhat in his junior year at Texas-Arlington, causing him to drop to the White Sox in the fifth round. He transitioned to the bullpen full time in the middle of the 2017 season.

SCOUTING REPORT: Thompson uses his massive frame to pump mid-90s fastballs, though his low-90s cutter might be his best offering. He commands the cutter, which grades as a plus pitch, better than his four-seamer. He sometimes has to back off his fastball to keep it in the zone, and command will be an issue he has to keep in check as he advances. He mixes in a below-average curveball as well.

THE FUTURE: Thompson finished the year with a solid stint in the Arizona Fall League and should start next season in Triple-A. He went unpicked in the Rule 5 draft but could make it to Chicago in 2019.

Year	Club (League)	Class	W	L	ERA	G	GS	CG	SV	IP	H	HR	BB	SO	K/9	WHIP	AVG
2016	Kannapolis (SAL)	LoA	6	3	2.62	16	16	0	0	86	58	5	39	88	9.2	1.13	.193
	Winston-Salem (CAR)	HiA	3	5	5.60	10	10	0	0	55	66	7	15	40	6.6	1.48	.292
2017	Winston-Salem (CAR)	HiA	2	7	5.59	33	14	0	0	93	103	8	50	73	7.0	1.64	.281
2018	Winston-Salem (CAR)	HiA	2	1	1.78	22	0	0	1	35	29	1	11	36	9.2	1.13	.218
	Birmingham (SL)	AA	4	0	1.35	21	0	0	1	40	28	3	18	40	9.0	1.15	.194
Minor League Totals			22	27	3.85	129	67	0	2	428	404	32	184	367	7.7	1.37	.249

29 TYLER JOHNSON, RHP

BA GRADE

45 Risk: High

Born: Aug. 21, 1995. **B-T:** R-R. **HT:** 6-3. **WT:** 205. **Drafted:** South Carolina, 2017 (5th round). **Signed by:** Kevin Burrell.

TRACK RECORD: At South Carolina, Johnson was one of the most dominant relievers in college. Limited to 85.1 innings because of inflammation in his biceps and triceps and a stress reaction in his back, Johnson still found time to whiff 107 hitters. The White Sox used their fifth-round pick plus a $390,000 bonus to keep him from a senior season with the Gamecocks.

SCOUTING REPORT: Johnson's most overwhelming tool is his fastball, which sits in the mid 90s with angle and armside life. He used the pitch to whiff 89 hitters in just 58 innings between two Class A levels. Impressively, Johnson accomplished that dominance without a knockout secondary pitch. Scouts rated his slider as a 40-grade offering on the 20-to-80 scouting scale, and his command was a tick below-average as well. The lack of a wipeout offspeed pitch and shaky command gives evaluators pause when considering how Johnson will fare at the upper levels.

THE FUTURE: After an excellent season at Kannapolis and Winston-Salem, Johnson is likely to move to Double-A Birmingham in 2019.

Year	Club (League)	Class	W	L	ERA	G	GS	CG	SV	IP	H	HR	BB	SO	K/9	WHIP	AVG
2017	Great Falls (PIO)	R	1	1	0.90	8	0	0	0	10	7	0	7	16	14.4	1.40	.194
	Kannapolis (SAL)	LoA	0	0	5.74	14	0	0	2	16	19	0	12	21	12.1	1.98	.302
2018	Kannapolis (SAL)	LoA	5	0	1.33	20	0	0	7	27	16	1	10	46	15.3	0.96	.170
	Winston-Salem (CAR)	HiA	4	0	1.45	21	0	0	7	31	19	1	6	43	12.5	0.81	.174
Minor League Totals			10	1	2.15	63	0	0	16	84	61	2	35	126	13.6	1.15	.202

30 KODI MEDEIROS, LHP

BA GRADE

45 Risk: High

Born: May 25, 1996. **B-T:** L-L. **HT:** 6-2. **WT:** 180. **Drafted:** HS—Hilo, Hawaii, 2014 (1st round). **Signed by:** Josh Belovsky (Brewers).

TRACK RECORD: Mid-90s fastballs from the left side made Medeiros one of the most talked-about prospects heading into the 2014 draft, and the Brewers saw enough from the young Hawaiian to draft him in the first round and steer him away from a commitment to Pepperdine with a $2.5 million bonus. There have long been questions about whether his stuff would play better out of the bullpen, but Milwaukee kept him in a starter's role until they dealt him to Chicago for Joakim Soria in July 2018.

SCOUTING REPORT: Medeiros brings an 88-92 mph fastball from a tough, low-slot angle and pairs it with a sweeping slider in the upper 70s that was undercut by poor command. He also throws a changeup in the mid 80s that grades out better than the slider, though none of his three offerings grades out as better than average, and his command is still poor.

THE FUTURE: Medeiros will likely head to Triple-A Charlotte in his first full season with his new organization, and could make his first foray into a relief role.

Year	Club (League)	Class	W	L	ERA	G	GS	CG	SV	IP	H	HR	BB	SO	K/9	WHIP	AVG
2016	Brevard County (FSL)	HiA	4	12	5.93	23	22	0	0	85	102	4	63	64	6.8	1.94	.300
2017	Carolina (CAR)	HiA	8	9	4.98	27	18	0	1	128	114	7	53	121	8.5	1.30	.241
2018	Biloxi (SL)	AA	7	5	3.14	20	15	0	0	103	90	9	45	107	9.3	1.31	.234
	Birmingham (SL)	AA	0	2	4.98	7	7	0	0	34	31	4	22	34	8.9	1.54	.250
Minor League Totals			23	35	4.71	111	82	0	3	462	440	26	236	446	8.7	1.46	.252

Cincinnati Reds

BY JUSTIN COLEMAN

The Reds have been in rebuild mode since 2015, and their 67-95 record confirms that this year was another step in that direction. It was their second-worst record of the decade, falling just short of the 64-98 2015 Reds club. Nine players made their debut in 2018, after a total of 29 rookies took the field for them between the 2016 and 2017 seasons. While there is plenty of opportunity for the players, it hasn't become clear who will step up and take advantage.

The season got off to a rocky start, going 3-15 to open the season. This prompted Cincinnati to dismiss manager Bryan Price and tab Jim Riggleman as skipper for the rest of the season. The rebuilding club went into the season without former sluggers Todd Frazier and Jay Bruce while trading OF Adam Duvall midseason to Atlanta for prospects.

An aging Joey Votto and rising star Eugenio Suarez were left to carry the offense for much of the season. Infielder Scooter Gennett broke a Reds record, hitting the most grand slams (4) in a single season while posting the second highest batting average (.310) in the national league.

The club posted the second-worst ERA (4.63) in the National league, only behind the Marlins (4.76). The team has seen some positive steps from Luis Castillo, whom they received from Miami in exchange for righthander Dan Straily. He was the only Reds pitcher to amass more than 30 starts, pitching to a 4.30 ERA. Righthanders Sal Romano, Anthony Desclafani and Tyler Mahle each made over 20 starts, but their seasons were not very productive. Highly touted lefty Amir Garrett spent his entire season with the big league club after suffering from nagging injuries in 2017. He did not make any starts, and appeared in 66 games out the bullpen.

Losing records over the past few seasons have positioned Cincinnati to land marquee amateur talent in the draft. Top prospect Nick Senzel has lived up to his reputation, and looks to rebound in 2019 after an injury-riddled season. The team has loaded up on impactful infielders with Jeter Downs and Shed Long, both of whom have the capability to hit in the big leagues. 2018 First-rounder Jonathan India acquitted himself nicely after signing an under-slot deal as the fifth overall pick in the draft.

President Dick Williams has used a myriad of avenues to add pitching to the farm system. The 2017 draft produced righthander Hunter Greene, who has star potential but was shut down due to an elbow injury. Cincinnati took two promising arms in the second and third rounds, respectfully, of

A shoulder injury cut short what had been a promising rookie season for Jesse Winker.

JOE ROBBINS-GETTY IMAGES

PROJECTED 2022 LINEUP

Catcher	Tyler Stephenson (25)
First Base	Joey Votto (38)
Second Base	Jonathan India (25)
Third Base	Eugenio Suarez (30)
Shortstop	Jose Peraza (28)
Left Field	Nick Senzel (27)
Center Field	Taylor Trammell (24)
Right Field	Jesse Winker (28)
No. 1 Starter	Luis Castillo (29)
No. 2 Starter	Hunter Greene (23)
No. 3 Starter	Tony Santillan (25)
No. 4 Starter	Tyler Mahle (27)
No. 5 Starter	Vladimir Gutierrez (26)
Closer	Raisel Iglesias (32)

the 2018 draft, signing athletic righthanders Lyon Richardson and Josiah Gray. 2016 international signee Vladimir Gutierrez is trending positively after making 27 starts for Double-A Pensacola. The lower minors is also littered with interesting arms, such as newly acquired righthander James Marinan, but none of them will impact the big league team anytime soon.

None of the rookies who appeared in 2018 appears capable of impacting the ballclub in 2019. The Reds' touted minor leaguers are either returning from injury or are in the lower minors, making this an interesting time for Cincinnati as it looks to see who steps up and takes advantage of big league opportunities.

DEPTH CHART

CINCINNATI REDS

TOP 2019 ROOKIE: Nick Senzel, 3B/2B. Injuries hurt his trajectory, but his power and versatility should impact the big league club in 2019.
BREAKOUT PROSPECT: Jose Israel Garcia, SS. He is a superb defender whose bat is trending in the right direction.
SLEEPER: Ryan Hendrix, RHP. The righthander dominated the Florida State League to the tune of a 1.76 ERA with a power fastball/curveball combo.

SOURCE OF TOP 30 TALENT

Homegrown	25	Acquired	5
College	7	Trade	4
Junior college	0	Rule 5 draft	1
High school	9	Independent league	0
Nondrafted free agent	1	Free agent/waivers	0
International	8		

LF
Taylor Trammell (3)
T.J Friedl (17)
Brian O'Grady

CF
Mike Siani (10)
Jose Siri (11)
Stuart Fairchild (12)
Mariel Bautista (20)
Danny Lantigua (26)
Miles Gordon

RF
Aristides Aquino (21)
Michael Beltre
Gabby Guerrero

3B
Nick Senzel (1)
Jonathan India (4)
Juan Martinez (22)
Rylan Thomas
D.J Peterson

SS
Jeter Downs (8)
Jose Israel Garcia (14)
Alfredo Rodriguez (25)
Blake Trahan

2B
Shed Long (7)
Alex Blandino
Juan Perez
Jonathan Willems

1B
Ibandel Isabel (27)
Connor Joe (29)
Bren Spillane (30)
Gavin LaValley
Nick Longhi
Montreal Marshall

C
Tyler Stephenson (6)
Hendrik Clementina (24)
Chris Okey
Stuart Turner
Victor Ruiz

LHP

LHSP	LHRP
Jacob Heatherly (23)	Juan Martinez
Scott Moss (28)	Joel Bender
Packy Naughton	Victor Payano
Seth Varner	

RHP

RHSP	RHRP
Hunter Greene (2)	Keury Mella (16)
Tony Santillan (5)	Jimmy Herget (19)
Vladimir Gutierrez (9)	Joel Kuhnel
Josiah Gray (13)	Ryan Hendrix
Lyon Richardson (15)	Wendolyn Bautista
James Marinan (18)	

DRAFT ANALYSIS

2018

BEST PURE HITTER: 3B Jonathan India (1) has all the ingredients of a well-balanced hitter. He has good power and a feel for the strike zone, which helps him to drive the ball all over the field. He hit .350/.497/.717 for Florida last spring and made it to low Class A Dayton in his pro debut.

BEST POWER HITTER: 1B/OF Bren Spillane (3) smacked 23 home runs for Illinois before being selected by Cincinnati in the third round. He has a big frame and has leverage in his swing, featuring future plus power. The swing creates excellent power to the opposite field. Scouts were worried about his strikeouts at Illinois, and those fears were realized in his pro debut, as he struck out 75 times in only 47 games.

FASTEST RUNNER: OF Mike Siani (4) features plus speed that helps him be a threat on both sides of the ball. He has excellent foot speed and a very good feel for stealing bases.

BEST DEFENSIVE PLAYER: Athleticism, excellent speed and a good throwing arm create a plus defensive profile for Siani. His routes and reads are advanced, and he will remain in center field moving forward.

BEST ATHLETE: Siani makes the most of his athletic body, profiling as a quick-twitch outfielder. His athleticism helps him to provide value defensively in center field, on the basepaths and at the plate.

BEST FASTBALL: RHP Lyon Richardson (2), a converted shortstop, has plenty of velocity. In high school, he touched 97 mph with his fastball. It has good plane and is a future plus pitch.

BEST SECONDARY PITCH: RHP Josiah Gray (2s) showed advanced feel for a changeup. Another converted infielder, Gray throws his changeup with sink and fade. It projects as a plus pitch.

BEST PRO DEBUT: With his advanced changeup and plenty of fastball, Gray (2s) dominated the Appalachian league. The 20-year-old struck out

TOP DRAFT PICKS OF THE DECADE

Year	Player, Pos	2018 Org
2009	Mike Leake, RHP	Mariners
2010	Yasmani Grandal, C	Dodgers
2011	Robert Stephenson, RHP	Reds
2012	Nick Travieso, RHP	Reds
2013	Phillip Ervin, OF	Reds
2014	Nick Howard, RHP	Reds
2015	Tyler Stephenson, C	Reds
2016	Nick Senzel, 3B	Reds
2017	Hunter Greene, RHP	Reds
2018	Jonathan India, 3B	Reds

over a batter per inning, giving up just 29 hits across 52.1 innings.

MOST INTRIGUING BACKGROUND: While many prospects do come from bigger schools, Gray comes from Division II Le Moyne (N.Y.) College. The righty burst onto the scene in the Cape Cod league, striking out 21 batters in 12 innings for the Chatham Anglers the previous summer.

CLOSEST TO THE MAJORS: The 2018 Southeastern Conference player of the year, India (1) comes with a polished skillset. With an advanced feel for hitting and the ability to move around the diamond as a polished defender, he should fly up the minor league levels, much like other recent SEC top draft picks like Alex Bregman, Dansby Swanson and Andrew Benintendi.

BEST LATE-ROUND PICK: Selected in the 27th round, RHP Eddy Demurias (27) looks the part of a future bullpen piece for Cincinnati. The aggressive pitcher throws his fastball in the low to mid 90's with a quality slider that should hold value in the bullpen.

THE ONE WHO GOT AWAY: OF Josiah Sightler (12) opted to head to South Carolina. Sightler can pitch as well as play first base and outfield. He has a plus arm, good hit tool and profiles well as a corner bat.

—JUSTIN COLEMAN

2017

RHP Hunter Greene (1) had an up-and-down season but his promise remains immense. SS Jeter Downs (1s) and OF Stuart Fairchild (2) showed well in their first full pro seasons. LHP Jacob Heatherly (3) isn't as advanced but flashed his upside.

GRADE: B

2016

The combination of 3B Nick Senzel (1) and OF Taylor Trammell (1s) give this class plenty of star power. Senzel has had some injury issues but should soon arrive in Cincinnati. Trammell was named MVP of the 2018 Futures Game.

GRADE: A

2015

C Tyler Stephenson (1) bounced back after injuries sidelined him in 2017. RHP Tony Santillan (2) took a step forward while reaching Double-A. RHP Tanner Rainey (2s) made his MLB debut and was later traded for Tanner Roark.

GRADE: B

1 NICK SENZEL, 3B/2B

Born: June 29, 1995. **B-T:** R-R. **HT:** 6-1. **WT:** 205. **Drafted:** Tennessee, 2016 (1st round). **Signed by:** Brad Meador.

From the day he arrived at Tennessee, Senzel showed he was special. He batted cleanup for the Volunteers from his first game as a freshman, starred for three years there and in the Cape Cod League and became the highest drafted player in school history. Senzel's fast track to the big leagues has been slowed by position switches and ailments. Vertigo ended his 2017 season early. With Eugenio Suarez signed to an extension, the Reds tried Senzel at shortstop and second base in spring training 2018 before junking the shortstop plan when he reported to Triple-A Louisville. A further bout of vertigo cost Senzel much of May. A torn ligament in his throwing hand ended his season in late June. Elbow surgery for bone spurs ruined plans to send him to the Arizona Fall League.

SCOUTING REPORT: The Reds have moved Senzel around the field because they know his bat should play anywhere and he has the kind of easy athleticism that allows him to handle various defensive challenges. He features quick hands and a disciplined knowledge of the strike zone. A plus hitter, Senzel stays balanced with ease and stays short to the ball, allowing him to get the barrel on pitches in all areas of the strike zone. He makes consistent contact and has plus power that would profile at his natural position of third base. Senzel's approach is aimed toward making hard contact to all fields. He is an above-average runner who runs the bases well. His good instincts and plus arm will be suited to play third base long term, but with that position manned by Suarez in Cincinnati, Senzel could pursue second base, center field or left field in the big leagues. He showed he can be at least an above-average defensive second baseman. Senzel tried both outfield spots at instructional league. His athleticism and understanding of the game should help him grow to be a solid defender at multiple positions.

THE FUTURE: While the Reds will play it safe with Senzel and his injury-riddled past, he should be playing in Cincinnati before long. His maturity and advanced approach both offensively and defensively should allow him to have an immediate impact on the big league club. When the Reds non-tendered Billy Hamilton, Senzel's path to an outfield job in 2019 cleared, but second base is a logical landing spot once Scooter Gennett's contract expires after the 2019 season.

BRIAN WESTERHOLT/FOUR SEAM

BA GRADE	SCOUTING GRADES
65 Risk: High	Hit: 60. Power: 60. Run: 55. Field: 60. Arm: 60.

Projected future grades on 20-80 scouting scale.

TOP PROSPECTS OF THE DECADE

Year	Player, Pos	2018 Org
2009	Yonder Alonso, 1B	Indians
2010	Todd Frazier, 3B	Mets
2011	Aroldis Chapman, LHP	Yankees
2012	Devin Mesoraco, C	Mets
2013	Billy Hamilton, OF	Reds
2014	Robert Stephenson, RHP	Reds
2015	Robert Stephenson, RHP	Reds
2016	Robert Stephenson, RHP	Reds
2017	Nick Senzel, 3B/2B	Reds
2018	Nick Senzel, 3B/2B	Reds

BEST TOOLS

Best Hitter for Average	Nick Senzel
Best Power Hitter	Ibandel Isabel
Best Strike-Zone Discipline	Nick Senzel
Fastest Baserunner	Jose Siri
Best Athlete	Taylor Trammell
Best Fastball	Hunter Greene
Best Curveball	Ryan Hendriks
Best Slider	Vladimir Gutierrez
Best Changeup	Vladimir Gutierrez
Best Control	Vladimir Gutierrez
Best Defensive Catcher	Mark Kolozsvary
Best Defensive Infielder	Blake Trahan
Best Infield Arm	Taylor Sparks
Best Defensive Outfielder	Jose Siri
Best Outfield Arm	Aristides Aquino

Year	Club (League)	Class	AVG	G	AB	R	H	2B	3B	HR	RBI	BB	SO	SB	CS	OBP	SLG
2016	Billings (PIO)	R	.152	10	33	3	5	1	0	0	4	6	5	3	0	.293	.182
	Dayton (MWL)	LoA	.329	58	210	38	69	23	3	7	36	32	49	15	7	.415	.567
2017	Daytona (FSL)	HiA	.305	62	246	41	75	26	2	4	31	23	54	9	2	.371	.476
	Pensacola (SL)	AA	.340	57	209	40	71	14	1	10	34	26	43	5	4	.413	.560
2018	Louisville (IL)	AAA	.310	44	171	23	53	12	2	6	25	19	39	8	2	.378	.509
Minor League Totals			.314	231	869	145	273	76	8	27	130	106	190	40	15	.390	.513

2 HUNTER GREENE, RHP

Born: Aug. 6, 1999. **B-T:** R-R. **HT:** 6-4. **WT:** 215. **Drafted:** HS—Sherman Oaks, Calif., 2017 (1st round). **Signed by:** Rick Ingalls.

TRACK RECORD: The second pick in the 2017 draft, Greene had a rough introduction to low Class A Dayton. He posted a 14.63 ERA in four April starts but turned around his season by throwing more strikes and getting better luck on balls in play. He had to be shut down in late July because of a sprained ulnar collateral ligament in his elbow. He resumed throwing off a mound in mid-December and is expected to be full speed for spring training. **SCOUTING REPORT:** Greene topped out at 103 mph in the Futures Game and regularly sat 97-100 in 2018. The righthander throws both a heavy two-seam fastball as well as a four-seamer. Evaluators have worried that Greene's clean delivery and straight fastball make it too easy for opponents to pick up the ball out of his hand. His mid-80s slider has three-quarters break that features good plane and downward bite. It projects as a plus pitch. Greene has the arm action to be able to throw a future average changeup, but it's generally his worst pitch and explains in part why lefties hit .298/.397/.567.

THE FUTURE: The Reds will be cautious with Greene, but if he shows he's fully healthy in spring training, he's ready for high Class A.

BA GRADE
65 Risk: Extreme
Fastball: 80.
Slider: 60.
Change: 50. CTL: 50.

Year	Club (League)	Class	W	L	ERA	G	GS	CG	SV	IP	H	HR	BB	SO	K/9	WHIP	AVG
2017	Billings (PIO)	R	0	1	12.46	3	3	0	0	4	8	0	1	6	12.5	2.08	.400
2018	Dayton (MWL)	LoA	3	7	4.48	18	18	0	0	68	66	6	23	89	11.7	1.30	.251
Minor League Totals			3	8	4.95	21	21	0	0	73	74	6	24	95	11.8	1.35	.261

3 TAYLOR TRAMMELL, OF

Born: Sept. 13, 1997. **B-T:** L-L. **HT:** 6-2. **WT:** 195. **Drafted:** HS—Kennesaw, Ga., 2016 (1st round supplemental). **Signed by:** Jon Poloni.

TRACK RECORD: A star running back in high school, Trammell has made a smooth transition to pro ball. He has hit at every level and he starred on the big stage in 2018, earning MVP honors at the Futures Game with a 2-for-2 game with a triple and a 438-foot home run. He ranked among the Florida State League leaders in on-base percentage and stolen bases.

SCOUTING REPORT: Trammell's athleticism has helped him become an impact player on both sides of the ball. He is a plus hitter. There will always be swing-and-miss to his game, but he gets to his power even with a simple setup that allows him to stay balanced at the plate. Trammell doesn't try to do too much, making the most of his skill set while understanding game situations. A strong upper body and quick hands will develop into above-average power. Trammell is a plus runner who is aggressive on the basepaths while also showing plus range in center field. He has improved his defensive play but has a below-average arm.

THE FUTURE: Trammell's bat and athleticism should help him become an offensive-minded, first-division outfielder before too long. He fits best in center field, but his bat could profile in left field.

BA GRADE
60 Risk: High
Hit: 60. Power: 55.
Run: 60. Field: 55.
Arm: 45.

Year	Club (League)	Class	AVG	G	AB	R	H	2B	3B	HR	RBI	BB	SO	SB	CS	OBP	SLG
2016	Billings (PIO)	R	.303	61	228	39	69	9	6	2	34	23	57	24	7	.374	.421
2017	Dayton (MWL)	LoA	.281	129	491	80	138	24	10	13	77	71	123	41	12	.368	.450
2018	Daytona (FSL)	HiA	.277	110	397	71	110	19	4	8	41	58	105	25	10	.375	.406
Minor League Totals			.284	300	1116	190	317	52	20	23	152	152	285	90	29	.372	.428

4 JONATHAN INDIA, 3B

Born: Dec. 15, 1996. **B-T:** R-R. **HT:** 6-1. **WT:** 200. **Drafted:** Florida, 2018 (1st round). **Signed by:** Sean Buckley.

TRACK RECORD: India was part of one the best high school infields ever. At American Heritage High in Delray Beach, Fla., he played with Tyler Frank (a Rays second-round pick) and $6 million signee Lucius Fox. Drafted fifth overall in 2018, India blasted 21 home runs as a junior at Florida after hitting 10 home runs in his first two years combined.

SCOUTING REPORT: Coming from a top college program, India has a advanced hitting skills and a polished defensive approach. The game doesn't speed up on him, and he controls his at-bats like a veteran. He has a sound setup at the plate, allowing him to sync his lower and upper halves. His above-average power and above-average hit tool are excellent fits at third base. His footwork and average arm are stretched at shortstop, where he played some in his pro debut, but he can be an above-average defender at second or third. India has average speed but isn't considered much of a stolen base threat.

BA GRADE

60 Risk: High

Hit: 55. **Power:** 55.
Run: 50. **Field:** 55.
Arm: 55.

THE FUTURE: Nick Senzel jumped straight to high Class A in his first full pro season, and it makes sense for India to be on a similar timetable. The Reds will have to determine India's ultimate position with Eugenio Suarez, Senzel and him all sharing similar defensive profiles. India's bat should play regardless of position.

Year	Club (League)	Class	AVG	G	AB	R	H	2B	3B	HR	RBI	BB	SO	SB	CS	OBP	SLG
2018	Greeneville (APP)	R	.261	14	46	11	12	2	1	3	12	15	12	1	0	.452	.543
	Billings (PIO)	R	.250	3	8	1	2	0	0	0	0	0	4	0	1	.400	.250
	Dayton (MWL)	LoA	.229	27	96	17	22	7	0	3	11	13	28	5	0	.339	.396
Minor League Totals			.240	44	150	29	36	9	1	6	23	28	44	6	1	.380	.433

5 TONY SANTILLAN, RHP

Born: April 15, 1997. **B-T:** R-R. **HT:** 6-3. **WT:** 240. **Drafted:** HS—Seguin, Texas, 2015 (2nd round). **Signed by:** Byron Ewing.

TRACK RECORD: Santillan geared down his fastball in 2018 and the decision yielded excellent results. He nearly halved his walk rate to 2.3 per nine innings in 2018, showing significantly improved control with little degradation in the quality of his stuff. Santillan has also proved durable. After throwing 128 innings in 2017, he tossed 149 more in 2018.

SCOUTING REPORT: Santillan has a big, athletic body and attacks hitters with an approach that is all about power—even his changeup is hard. There's some effort to his delivery, but Santillan maintains his stuff for six to seven innings and throws strikes, projecting to have average control if not average command. His plus-plus fastball sits 94-98 mph with late life. It can be a heavy fastball that is difficult for hitters to square. He works off his fastball with a future plus slider that has good plane and tight break, though it morphs into a cutter at times. While his firm 85-88 mph changeup lags behind the other two offerings, he does show some feel for it and throws it with deception and fade.

BA GRADE

60 Risk: High

Fastball: 70.
Slider: 55.
Change: 55. **CTL:** 50.

THE FUTURE: Santillan has put in the work to better control his front side. That improved control is important for him to reach his ceiling as a mid-rotation starter.

Year	Club (League)	Class	W	L	ERA	G	GS	CG	SV	IP	H	HR	BB	SO	K/9	WHIP	AVG
2016	Billings (PIO)	R	1	0	3.92	8	8	0	0	39	32	4	16	46	10.6	1.23	.221
	Dayton (MWL)	LoA	2	3	6.82	7	7	0	0	30	27	3	24	38	11.3	1.68	.245
2017	Dayton (MWL)	LoA	9	8	3.38	25	24	0	0	128	104	9	56	128	9.0	1.25	.222
2018	Daytona (FSL)	HiA	6	4	2.70	15	15	1	0	87	81	5	22	73	7.6	1.19	.245
	Pensacola (SL)	AA	4	3	3.61	11	11	0	0	62	65	8	16	61	8.8	1.30	.264
Minor League Totals			22	20	3.69	74	72	1	0	366	324	30	145	365	9.0	1.28	.237

6 TYLER STEPHENSON, C

Born: Aug. 16, 1996. **B-T:** R-R. **HT:** 6-4. **WT:** 225. **Drafted:** HS—Kennesaw, Ga., 2015 (1st round). **Signed by:** John Poloni.

TRACK RECORD: The most important statistic for Stephenson in 2018 was his total of 97 games caught. His 2016 season was derailed by a concussion and sore left wrist, which ultimately required surgery. He missed much of the second half of 2017 with a sprained thumb. So he and the Reds were thrilled to see Stephenson lead the high Class A Florida State League in games caught, putouts and fielding percentage (.996).

SCOUTING REPORT: Stephenson's big frame works behind the plate because of his strength and athleticism, though his size means he's less nimble than a smaller backstop. He still has work to do with his game-calling. His arm grades out as plus, even though his footwork and release can hinder his throwing from time to time—he threw out 24 percent of basestealers in 2018. At the plate, Stephenson has the potential to be an average hitter with average power. His swing starts with a minor leg kick leading into a modest load of the hands before driving the barrel through the zone.

THE FUTURE: With a big arm and enough athleticism to play every day at catcher, Stephenson is one of the rare prospects who can contribute both offensively and defensively as a catcher.

BA GRADE

50 Risk: High

Hit: 50. Power: 50.
Run: 40. Field: 50.
Arm: 60.

Year	Club (League)	Class	AVG	G	AB	R	H	2B	3B	HR	RBI	BB	SO	SB	CS	OBP	SLG
2016	Reds (AZL)	R	.250	5	20	4	5	1	0	1	2	2	7	0	0	.348	.450
	Dayton (MWL)	LoA	.216	39	139	17	30	4	1	3	16	12	45	0	0	.278	.324
2017	Dayton (MWL)	LoA	.278	80	295	39	82	22	0	6	50	44	58	2	1	.374	.414
2018	Daytona (FSL)	HiA	.250	109	388	60	97	20	1	11	59	45	98	1	0	.338	.392
Minor League Totals			.257	287	1036	148	266	62	2	22	143	125	250	3	3	.343	.384

7 SHED LONG, 2B

Born: Aug. 22, 1995. **B-T:** L-R. **HT:** 5-8. **WT:** 184. **Drafted:** HS—Jacksonville, Ala., 2013 (12th round). **Signed by:** Ben Jones.

TRACK RECORD: Long's pro career got off to a slow start, but he took off at the plate once he moved from catcher to second base, where his athleticism plays better. He has steadily worked to improve his defense at second while consistently providing solid-average power and a discerning batting eye.

SCOUTING REPORT: Long is a bat-first player, using special bat speed and barrel manipulation to hit the ball to all fields. While he has had some issues with making consistent contact, his lefthanded bat shows signs of being above-average with future average power. His hands are very strong, which allows him to generate his bat speed. Long's actions in the field need work, but his athleticism and average arm have helped him improve to the point where he's a fringe-average defender. He is an average runner.

THE FUTURE: Long should see regular at-bats at Triple-A Louisville in 2019, when he will face pressure to produce because of a probable glut at second base in Cincinnati. The Reds' deep inventory of infielders includes recent first-rounders Nick Senzel and Jonathan India, both of whom could be forced off third base to second base once Scooter Gennett leaves the Reds.

BA GRADE

50 Risk: High

Hit: 55. Power: 50.
Run: 55. Field: 45.
Arm: 50.

Year	Club (League)	Class	AVG	G	AB	R	H	2B	3B	HR	RBI	BB	SO	SB	CS	OBP	SLG
2016	Dayton (MWL)	LoA	.281	94	335	47	94	24	1	11	45	44	85	16	3	.371	.457
	Daytona (FSL)	HiA	.322	38	143	22	46	6	4	4	30	10	35	5	1	.371	.503
2017	Daytona (FSL)	HiA	.312	62	247	37	77	16	1	13	36	27	63	6	3	.380	.543
	Pensacola (SL)	AA	.227	42	141	13	32	6	2	3	14	19	31	3	1	.319	.362
2018	Pensacola (SL)	AA	.261	126	452	75	118	22	5	12	56	57	123	19	6	.353	.412
Minor League Totals			.272	457	1635	231	445	86	15	50	211	188	403	54	19	.353	.435

8 JETER DOWNS, 2B/SS

Born: July 27, 1998. **B-T:** R-R. **HT:** 5-11. **WT:** 180. **Drafted:** HS—Miami Gardens, Fla., 2017 (1st round supplemental). **Signed by:** Hector Otero.

TRACK RECORD: Downs comes from a baseball family. His father, Jerry Sr., pitched in Colombia. His older brother Jerry is a first baseman in the Red Sox organization. And Jeter was named after Yankees shortstop Derek Jeter. Downs' adjustment to pro ball continued at low Class A Dayton in 2018 and has been relatively.

SCOUTING REPORT: Downs wasn't fazed by the Midwest League, showing off a future above-average hit tool and racking up extra-base hits. He uses a simple setup and sound mechanics to generate loud contact, showing the ability to hit to all fields with average power. Downs has the tools to stay in the infield, though evaluators believe his modest range and above-average arm will fit better at third base or second base. Of course, the Reds are loaded with promising infield prospects, so they have plenty of incentive to work with Downs to help him improve at shortstop. He's an above-average runner who is a constant threat to steal because of good reads and jumps.

BA GRADE
50 Risk: High
Hit: 55. Power: 50.
Run: 55. Field: 50.
Arm: 55.

THE FUTURE: Downs has done plenty to impress the Reds so far and is ready for a jump to high Class A. He profiles as a future infield regular.

Year	Club (League)	Class	AVG	G	AB	R	H	2B	3B	HR	RBI	BB	SO	SB	CS	OBP	SLG
2017	Billings (PIO)	R	.267	50	172	31	46	3	3	6	29	27	32	8	5	.370	.424
2018	Dayton (MWL)	LoA	.257	120	455	63	117	23	2	13	47	52	103	37	10	.351	.402
Minor League Totals			.260	170	627	94	163	26	5	19	76	79	135	45	15	.356	.408

9 VLADIMIR GUTIERREZ, RHP

Born: Sept. 18,1995. **B-T:** R-R. **HT:** 6-0. **WT:** 190. **Signed:** Cuba, 2016. **Signed by:** Tony Arias/Chris Buckley.

TRACK RECORD: Cincinnati signed Gutierrez for $4.7 million in September 2016. Since then, he has developed a little slower than expected for a pitcher with experience in Cuba's top league, Serie Nacional. At the time of his signing, Gutierrez was seen as a potential power reliever, but he has proven to have more feel and a little less stuff than expected.

SCOUTING REPORT: Gutierrez isn't overpowering but gets hitters out using an effective three-pitch mix that he throws from a three-quarters arm slot with future above-average control. His delivery adds some deception with a slight turn of his back before exploding toward the plate. His average fastball sits comfortably in the low 90s while touching 96 mph. He flashes a future above-average 12-to-6 curveball that ranges from 78-83 mph. It has very good break and he can land it for strikes while also bending it out of the strike zone. His low-80s changeup is also a solid-average pitch. It has deception and fade.

BA GRADE
50 Risk: High
Fastball: 55.
Curveball: 55.
Change: 50. CTL: 55.

THE FUTURE: Gutierrez is ready for Triple-A Louisville. With his stuff and control, he has shown that he can reach the big leagues as a back-of-the-rotation starter in late 2019 or 2020.

Year	Club (League)	Class	W	L	ERA	G	GS	CG	SV	IP	H	HR	BB	SO	K/9	WHIP	AVG
2016	Did not play																
2017	Daytona (FSL)	HiA	7	8	4.46	19	19	0	0	103	108	10	19	94	8.2	1.23	.267
2018	Pensacola (SL)	AA	9	10	4.35	27	27	0	0	147	139	18	38	145	8.9	1.20	.246
Minor League Totals			16	18	4.39	46	46	0	0	250	247	28	57	239	8.6	1.22	.255

10 MIKE SIANI, OF

Born: July 16, 1999. **B-T:** L-L. **HT:** 6-1. **WT:** 180. **Drafted:** HS—Philadelphia, 2018 (4th round). **Signed by:** Jeff Brookens.

TRACK RECORD: The Reds went over slot to ink Siani in 2018, signing him for $2 million—a full $1 million more than any other fourth-round pick. He highlighted his 2017 amateur season by helping USA Baseball win gold at the 18U World Cup. He showed a well-rounded game in his pro debut at Rookie-level Greeneville, hitting .288/.351/.386.

SCOUTING REPORT: For a recent high school pick, Siani shows an advanced understanding of the game, especially when he roams center field. He stays under control and shows poise. He gets a good first step on his reads and takes solid routes. He is very athletic, and it shows on both sides of the ball. Siani's plus arm and speed make him a safe bet to remain in center field. He uses a small leg kick with minimal loading to stay short to the ball, though his contact ability suffers from a tendency to get big and swing for the fences. Siani's bat is relatively well refined for a young hitter and he projects to have average productive power to go with an average bat.

THE FUTURE: Siani will head to low Class A Dayton in 2019. Center field is one of the thinnest positions in the Reds' system, so the path is clear for his advancement. He's more solid than spectacular, but he has few glaring flaws.

BA GRADE
50 Risk: High
Hit: 50. **Power:** 50.
Run: 60. **Field:** 60.
Arm: 60.

Year	Club (League)	Class	AVG	G	AB	R	H	2B	3B	HR	RBI	BB	SO	SB	CS	OBP	SLG
2018	Greeneville (APP)	R	.288	46	184	24	53	6	3	2	13	16	35	6	4	.351	.386
Minor League Totals			.288	46	184	24	53	6	3	2	13	16	35	6	4	.351	.386

11 JOSE SIRI, OF

BA GRADE
50 Risk: High

Born: July 22, 1995. **B-T:** R-R. **HT:** 6-2. **WT:** 175. **Signed:** Dominican Republic, 2012. **Signed by:** Richard Jimenez.

TRACK RECORD: Siri has long flashed exceptional tools that have been hindered by poor plate discipline. His 2018 season was more of the same. He started the season on the disabled list with a thumb injury after crashing into a wall during a spring training game, which affected his power early in his return. Siri earned a promotion to Double-A Pensacola, where he showed the plus tools that have long enticed scouts and the below-average approach that leads to too many empty at-bats.

SCOUTING REPORT: Siri is unlikely to ever be better than a below-average hitter as he tends to swing and miss outside of the strike zone–his 32.2 percent strikeout rate was among the worst in the Southern League. When he does make contact, he does drive the ball, which is why there is still reason for hope. Siri is an excellent defender and has a plus arm that will help him in center field. He is also a plus runner, which helps him to have good range in the outfield. His mentality is aggressive, as he is always looking to push the envelope and take the extra base when possible.

THE FUTURE: Siri saw his batting average and on-base percentage take a dip at Double-A, so it's likely he returns there to get some more at-bats. But he should make it to Triple-A Louisville this year. Siri has the tools to be an everyday outfielder, but unless his selectivity improves he's unlikely to live up to those hopes.

Year	Club (League)	Class	AVG	G	AB	R	H	2B	3B	HR	RBI	BB	SO	SB	CS	OBP	SLG
2016	Dayton (MWL)	LoA	.145	27	83	5	12	3	0	0	3	2	34	3	2	.163	.181
	Billings (PIO)	R	.320	59	241	52	77	12	8	10	35	8	66	17	4	.348	.560
2017	Dayton (MWL)	LoA	.293	126	498	92	146	24	11	24	76	33	130	46	12	.341	.530
2018	Daytona (FSL)	HiA	.261	30	119	15	31	9	2	1	9	4	32	9	1	.280	.395
	Pensacola (SL)	AA	.229	66	253	42	58	8	9	12	34	24	91	14	5	.300	.474
Minor League Totals			.271	463	1765	312	478	79	52	57	217	105	510	129	38	.316	.471

12 STUART FAIRCHILD, OF

BA GRADE
45 Risk: High

Born: March 17, 1996. **B-T:** R-R. **HT:** 6-0. **WT:** 190. **Drafted:** Wake Forest, 2017 (2nd round). **Signed by:** Perry Smith.

TRACK RECORD: After a productive career at Wake Forest, Fairchild has acquitted himself nicely in his first two pro seasons. He's shown he can get on base while playing a solid center field, but the righthanded hitter has yet to show as much pop as he demonstrated with the Demon Deacons.

SCOUTING REPORT: Although he has solid-average tools, Fairchild is known for performing above them. He takes an advanced approach to hitting, showing both patience and the ability to drive the ball. He has a strong build and clean swing, which should lead to roughly average power. Fairchild is a plus runner and plays center field well. He has good feel for roaming the outfield, although his arm is considered below-average.

THE FUTURE: Fairchild will likely begin the season at high Class A Daytona, but will end up playing most of the season in Double-A. His offensive adjustments and ability to play quality defense in the outfield give him a chance to be a big league regular, but he'll have to hit for more power or average to avoid a fourth outfielder tag.

Year	Club (League)	Class	AVG	G	AB	R	H	2B	3B	HR	RBI	BB	SO	SB	CS	OBP	SLG
2017	Billings (PIO)	R	.304	56	204	36	62	5	4	3	23	19	35	12	4	.393	.412
2018	Dayton (MWL)	LoA	.277	67	235	40	65	12	5	7	37	31	65	17	4	.377	.460
	Daytona (FSL)	HiA	.250	63	220	25	55	14	1	2	20	17	63	6	2	.306	.350
Minor League Totals			.276	186	659	101	182	31	10	12	80	67	163	35	10	.359	.408

13 JOSIAH GRAY, RHP

BA GRADE

50 Risk: High

Born: December 21, 1997. **B-T:** R-R. **HT:** 6-1. **WT:** 190. **Drafted:** Le Moyne (N.Y.), 2018 (2nd round supplemental). **Signed by:** Lee Seras.

TRACK RECORD: When Gray arrived at Le Moyne (N.Y.) College he was a shortstop whose arm was his best tool. He began pitching significantly in the summer before his sophomore year and transitioned to being a starting pitcher for his junior season. He dominated Division II, going 11-0, 1.25 and he proved equally impossible to hit in the Appalachian League, where he would have led the league in ERA and opponent's average if he had not fallen two innings short of qualifying.

SCOUTING REPORT: Gray has a lively arm, athletic body and excellent arm strength. His 91-95 mph fastball is a plus pitch because of its life, his command of it and his ability to generate swings and misses up in the zone. His 84-87 mph slider could use further refinement. It's somewhat slurvy for now, but it shows late tilt at its best and projects as an above-average pitch. Gray also mixes in a developing changeup that needs to improve. Gray shows advanced fastball command and average control for his age.

THE FUTURE: Gray has plenty of room to continue to develop as a pitcher, but his athleticism, strong lower half and his feel for pitching gives him a strong base to begin with as a pitcher. He's ready for full-season ball. Whether he ends up as a two-pitch reliever or an athletic mid-rotation starter is still to be determined.

Year	Club (League)	Class	W	L	ERA	G	GS	CG	SV	IP	H	HR	BB	SO	K/9	WHIP	AVG
2018	Greeneville (APP)	R	2	2	2.58	12	12	0	0	52	29	1	17	59	10.1	0.88	.155
Minor League Totals			2	2	2.58	12	12	0	0	52	29	1	17	59	10.1	0.88	.155

14 JOSE ISRAEL GARCIA, SS

BA GRADE

45 Risk: High

Born: April 5, 1998. **B-T:** R-R. **HT:** 6-2. **WT:** 205. **Signed:** Cuba, 2017. **Signed by:** Chris Buckley/Tony Arias/Miguel Machado/Jim Stoeckel/Bob Engle/Hector Otero.

TRACK RECORD: The Reds went over their international spending limit to sign Garcia in June of 2017, shelling out $5 million. The organization challenged Garcia immediately, assigning him to play with low Class A Dayton. He took a while to get settled in and had plenty of rust to shake off, but once the weather warmed up, he hit .277/.322/.398 in the second half. Garcia played both shortstop and second base in 2018 for Dayton, sharing the positions with Jeter Downs.

SCOUTING REPORT: While scouts are comfortable that Garcia will be a solid fielder, there's much less confidence in his bat. He is a gap-to-gap hitter who could develop average power as he matures. He stays balanced with his swing but needs to refine his understanding of the strike zone to make the most of his fringe-average hit tool. Garcia has gotten significantly bigger and stronger since arriving from Cuba, which adds hope that he'll start driving the ball. Primarily a second baseman in Cuba, Garcia showed that he can be above-average defender at shortstop with plus speed, a plus arm and the range scouts look for in a shortstop. Garcia has good hands, but with Dayton he committed 28 errors, almost equally divided between fielding and throwing. He has to figure out how to slow the game down at shortstop.

THE FUTURE: The Reds have a lot of middle infielders in the system, but Garcia has one of the clearest paths to being a big league shortstop because he has a better glove than Downs and a better bat than Alfredo Rodriguez.

Year	Club (League)	Class	AVG	G	AB	R	H	2B	3B	HR	RBI	BB	SO	SB	CS	OBP	SLG
2018	Dayton (MWL)	LoA	.245	125	482	61	118	22	4	6	53	19	112	13	9	.290	.344
Minor League Totals			.245	125	482	61	118	22	4	6	53	19	112	13	9	.290	.344

15 T.J. FRIEDL, OF

Born: August 14, 1995. **B-T:** L-L. **HT:** 5-10. **WT:** 170. **Drafted:** Nevada, 2016 (NDFA). **Signed by:** Rich Bordi/Sam Grossman.

BA GRADE

40 Risk: Medium

TRACK RECORD: After most teams failed to notice that Friedl was a draft-eligible sophomore, he went out and starred for Team USA's Collegiate National Team that summer, which set off a bidding war when teams realized he eligible to sign. Cincinnati signed Friedl for $735,000, the largest signing bonus ever given to an undrafted free agent. Friedl missed time in 2017 with a thumb injury, but he was fully healthy in 2018 as he bounced between left and center field.

SCOUTING REPORT: Freidl has a feel for making contact with a high-contact, low-power approach. He has transitioned from using a slightly open stance with a leg-kick stride to using no stride. This change has allowed him to wait and not commit so early on pitches, which has helped his on-base percentage and his contract rate. He projects as an above-average hitter. He's an above-average defender in center field and plus in the corners with an average arm. He is also a plus runner who can handle all three outfield positions effectively. Friedl is a high-energy player who plays with plenty of intensity.

THE FUTURE: Friedl doesn't have enough bat or power to be a big league regular, but he's a good fit as a backup outfielder thanks to his speed, defense, contact ability and hustle.

Year	Club (League)	Class	AVG	G	AB	R	H	2B	3B	HR	RBI	BB	SO	SB	CS	OBP	SLG
2016	Billings (PIO)	R	.347	29	121	24	42	11	2	3	17	13	25	7	2	.423	.545
2017	Dayton (MWL)	LoA	.284	66	250	47	71	20	6	5	25	29	46	14	7	.378	.472
	Daytona (FSL)	HiA	.257	48	179	15	46	6	2	2	13	10	39	2	1	.313	.346
2018	Daytona (FSL)	HiA	.294	64	228	40	67	10	4	3	35	38	44	11	4	.405	.412
	Pensacola (SL)	AA	.276	67	261	47	72	10	3	2	16	28	56	19	5	.359	.360
Minor League Totals			.287	274	1039	173	298	57	17	15	106	118	210	53	19	.374	.418

16 MARIEL BAUTISTA, OF

Born: Oct. 15, 1997. **B-T:** R-R. **HT:** 6-2. **WT:** 170. **Signed:** Dominican Republic, 2014. **Signed by:** Richard Jimenez.

BA GRADE

50 Risk: Extreme

TRACK RECORD: The Reds have moved Bautista conservatively since signing him in 2014, but he's hit everywhere he's played. Bautista's .330 average led all Reds minor leaguers and marked the third straight season he's hit .320 or better. Even more encouragingly, Bautista started to drive the ball in 2018 with eight home runs in the power-friendly Pioneer League.

SCOUTING REPORT: Bautista is a toolsy outfielder who has a loose body and above-average bat speed. He has a wiry body and a frame that should be able to add strength, with some scouts projecting future plus power once he fills out. For now, the 20-year-old struggles to maintain his weight during the season. He doesn't walk much and has a tendency to expand the strike zone with a pull-heavy approach he will need to adjust as he climbs the ladder. His bat speed and hand-eye coordination give him the tools to make those adjustments. Bautista is a plus runner and has an average arm. He'll likely slow down a little as he fills out, which leads to healthy debates about whether he can stay in center field.

THE FUTURE: After a surge in power during his time in the Pioneer League, Bautista is ready for full-season ball. He'll need to make adjustments, but he has the tools to be a regular in the outfield.

Year	Club (League)	Class	AVG	G	AB	R	H	2B	3B	HR	RBI	BB	SO	SB	CS	OBP	SLG
2016	Rojos (DSL)	R	.333	62	237	40	79	16	4	3	35	22	36	13	4	.408	.473
2017	Reds (AZL)	R	.320	36	147	29	47	9	1	0	20	5	24	16	1	.353	.395
2018	Billings (PIO)	R	.330	56	209	43	69	12	4	8	37	16	29	16	3	.386	.541
Minor League Totals			.313	205	763	145	239	47	12	13	117	63	132	51	10	.379	.457

17 LYON RICHARDSON, RHP

Born: Jan. 18, 2000. **B-T:** B-R. **HT:** 6-2. **WT:** 175. **Drafted:** HS—Jensen Beach, Fla., 2018 (2nd round). **Signed by:** Stephen Hunt.

BA GRADE

50 Risk: Extreme

TRACK RECORD: Richardson was one of the fastest risers in the 2018 draft class after some electric outings helped him rise out of sleeper status. Richardson was slated to head to Florida as a righthander and outfielder before he blew up last spring. He flashed a 97-98 mph fastball at his best, but his velocity and the quality of his stuff varied significantly. In his pro debut, the Reds rarely saw the dominating stuff he showed in the spring. Scouts said he looked raw and worn down in the Appalachian League.

SCOUTING REPORT: Richardson is athletic and has plenty of arm strength with a projectable frame that is built for innings. He showed little ability to locate his fastball gloveside in his pro debut and his curveball flashed average, rather than the plus breaker he would land occasionally in high school. Richardson has a very fast, live arm and gets downhill plane on his 92-94 mph fastball that touches 97. Richardson's delivery is a little stiff, but he has the athleticism and strength to develop average control. Like many young pitchers, Richardson's changeup needs development, but he throws it with similar arm speed and it grades as future average.

THE FUTURE: Richardson is still very raw and may not be ready for the jump to the Midwest League. His frame, athleticism and fast arm give him a chance to develop into a back-end starter.

Year	Club (League)	Class	W	L	ERA	G	GS	CG	SV	IP	H	HR	BB	SO	K/9	WHIP	AVG
2018	Greeneville (APP)	R	0	5	7.14	11	11	0	0	29	37	3	16	24	7.4	1.83	.308
Minor League Totals			0	5	7.14	11	11	0	0	29	37	3	16	24	7.4	1.83	.308

18 KEURY MELLA, RHP

BA GRADE

45 Risk: High

Born: August 2, 1993. **B-T:** R-R. **HT:** 6-2. **WT:** 200. **Signed:** Dominican Republic, 2012. **Signed by:** Pablo Peguero (Giants).

TRACK RECORD: Mella was acquired in 2015 from the Giants alongside outfielder Adam Duvall in exchange for righthander Mike Leake. The Reds added him to the 40-man roster before the 2017 season and have been patient. They have continued to work Mella as a starter in the minors, but when they called him up to the majors he moved to the bullpen, which has long been his expected big league role. He has struggled in two brief big league stints and he finished the season on the 60-day disabled list with an oblique strain.

SCOUTING REPORT: Mella's main weapon is his plus fastball, which sits 94-96 mph and can touch 97 mph. He generates velocity from a fairly compact, explosive delivery. His fastball is a solid pitch, but he has yet to figure out a true offspeed weapon. His average, low-80s slider had late downward movement but it's not a true bat-missing pitch and his changeup has never rounded into form as a pitch he can trust. When he reached the majors last year, Mella relied much too heavily on his fastball. While he scattered pitches all around the zone in the majors, he's shown average control in the minors.

THE FUTURE: Even after seven pro seasons, Mella's ultimate role is still unclear. He doesn't miss enough bats to be a high-leverage reliever and his secondary offerings aren't good enough to turn over the lineup a couple of times. Mella has only one option remaining, so 2019 will be a make-or-break year.

Year	Club (League)	Class	W	L	ERA	G	GS	CG	SV	IP	H	HR	BB	SO	K/9	WHIP	AVG
2016	Daytona (FSL)	HiA	8	9	3.90	25	24	0	0	132	150	7	56	95	6.5	1.56	.290
	Louisville (IL)	AAA	1	0	1.29	1	1	0	0	7	3	1	1	6	7.7	0.57	.130
2017	Pensacola (SL)	AA	4	10	4.30	27	26	1	1	134	135	14	43	109	7.3	1.33	.260
	Cincinnati (NL)	MAJ	0	0	6.75	2	0	0	0	4	5	1	2	1	2.3	1.75	.294
2018	Pensacola (SL)	AA	7	3	3.07	16	16	0	0	85	70	8	31	87	9.2	1.19	.222
	Cincinnati (NL)	MAJ	0	0	8.68	4	0	0	0	9	13	4	8	8	7.7	2.25	.351
	Louisville (IL)	AAA	2	1	2.74	5	5	0	0	23	20	1	6	14	5.5	1.13	.244
Major League Totals			0	0	8.10	6	0	0	0	13	18	5	10	9	6.1	2.10	.333
Minor League Totals			40	36	3.41	136	133	2	1	675	633	42	236	616	8.2	1.29	.247

19 JAMES MARINAN, RHP

BA GRADE

50 Risk: Extreme

Born: Oct. 10, 1998. **B-T:** R-R. **HT:** 6-5. **WT:** 220. **Drafted:** HS—Lake Worth, Fla., 2017 (4th round). **Signed by:** Adrian Casanova (Dodgers).

TRACK RECORD: Marinan went from being an interesting two-way prospect to a much harder throwing pitching prospect as a high school senior. The Dodgers spent big to land Marinan, and signed him for $822,500, which was more than double the slot amount for the fourth-round pick. Los Angeles then turned him quickly into a big leaguer by trading him in a package that landed reliever Dylan Floro.

SCOUTING REPORT: Marinan throws from a three quarter arm slot, which helps him get some sink on his low-90s fastball. He also showed he can get some arm-side run on his above-average. He gets some swing and miss with his promising curveball which has good spin, although it needs more refining. His third pitch is a changeup which he shows some feel for and has a chance to be at least average down the road. Like many tall pitchers, he struggles to consistently repeat his delivery, which leads to control problems.

THE FUTURE: As a pitcher who is still figuring out how to pitch with premium velocity, Marinan will be on a slower developmental track. He's ready to jump to low Class A Dayton. His frame and stuff makes him a promising starting pitcher, but one who has a long way to go.

Year	Club (League)	Class	W	L	ERA	G	GS	CG	SV	IP	H	HR	BB	SO	K/9	WHIP	AVG
2017	Dodgers (AZL)	R	2	0	1.59	9	6	0	0	17	14	0	14	14	7.4	1.65	.250
2018	Dodgers (AZL)	R	0	0	0.84	3	3	0	0	11	11	0	4	11	9.3	1.41	.289
	Billings (PIO)	R	3	2	3.98	11	11	0	0	43	49	1	19	39	8.2	1.58	.287
Minor League Totals			5	2	2.93	23	20	0	0	71	74	1	37	64	8.2	1.57	.279

20 JIMMY HERGET, RHP

BA GRADE

40 Risk: Medium

Born: September 9,1993. **B-T:** R-R. **HT:** 6-3. **WT:** 170. **Drafted:** South Florida, 2015 (6th round). **Signed by:** Greg Zunino.

TRACK RECORD: Herget brings the funk as much as George Clinton. He is never a comfortable at-bat, especially for righthanded hitters, but after making it to the Futures Game in 2017, he struggled more in 2018 as too often Triple-A hitters found him catching too much of the plate with his fastball and slider.

SCOUTING REPORT: Herget mixes arm slots, but he generally throws from a true sidearm slot with an almost whippy arm action. Few sidearmers throw as hard as Herget, as he'll sit 92-94 and touch 96. His arm slot means his fastball generaly runs in on righthanded hitters and away from lefthanded hitters, but he's shown that he can also work in on lefties' hands at times. He mixes in a plus slider that sits in the low 80s with good tilt. His third pitch is a below-average changeup that is only a change of pace for lefties. Herget's control wasn't as good as it has been in 2018, but he projects to have average control and command.

THE FUTURE: Herget should be a bullpen option in 2019 for Cincinnati. His two-pitch mix and deception against righthanders should help him get work as a middle reliever.

Year	Club (League)	Class	W	L	ERA	G	GS	CG	SV	IP	H	HR	BB	SO	K/9	WHIP	AVG
2016	Daytona (FSL)	HiA	4	4	1.78	50	0	0	24	61	47	3	22	83	12.3	1.14	.208
2017	Pensacola (SL)	AA	1	3	2.73	24	0	0	16	30	22	1	12	44	13.3	1.15	.202
	Louisville (IL)	AAA	3	1	3.06	28	0	0	9	32	30	4	9	28	7.8	1.21	.248
2018	Louisville (IL)	AAA	1	3	3.47	50	0	0	0	60	59	5	21	65	9.8	1.34	.253
Minor League Totals			12	11	2.77	176	0	0	64	208	174	14	75	246	10.7	1.20	.225

21 ARISTIDES AQUINO, OF

BA GRADE

40 Risk: Medium

Born: April 22,1994. **B-T:** R-R. **HT:** 6-4. **WT:** 220. **Signed:** Dominican Republic, 2011. **Signed by:** Richard Jimenez.

TRACK RECORD: Aquino has long had prototypical right field tools, but he's struggled to fully take advantage. He did get his first big league at-bat in October. But the Reds then non-tendered him to drop him from the 40-man roster. He then returned to the Reds on a minor league contract. Over-aggressiveness has long been Aquino's biggest issue.

SCOUTING REPORT: Aquino is a sturdy, athletic outfielder who has plus raw power to all fields. His power in games will be above-average in the future. He doesn't make a lot of quality contact, mostly because he has a tendency to chase and expand the strike zone. He has a very good arm, but his below-average speed limits him to a corner spot. His outfield defense is average, and fits well in the corner.

THE FUTURE: In need of strike zone refinement, Aquino will play quite a lot of right field for Triple-A Louisville. Aquino most likely ends up as a long-time Triple-A outfielder with occasional stints in the big leagues, but he's still young enough to have a hope for a larger role.

Year	Club (League)	Class	AVG	G	AB	R	H	2B	3B	HR	RBI	BB	SO	SB	CS	OBP	SLG
2016	Daytona (FSL)	HiA	.273	125	484	69	132	26	12	23	79	34	104	11	7	.327	.519
2017	Pensacola (SL)	AA	.216	131	459	54	99	20	6	17	56	39	145	9	3	.282	.397
2018	Cincinnati (NL)	MAJ	.000	1	1	0	0	0	0	0	0	0	1	0	0	.000	.000
	Pensacola (SL)	AA	.240	114	404	49	97	20	2	20	55	35	112	4	5	.306	.448
Major League Totals			.000	1	1	0	0	0	0	0	0	0	1	0	0	.000	.000
Minor League Totals			.242	701	2615	357	634	130	42	96	389	193	679	65	44	.303	.434

22 JUAN MARTINEZ, 3B

BA GRADE

45 Risk: Extreme

Born: Nov. 8, 1998. **B-T:** R-R. **HT:** 6-0. **WT:** 179. **Signed:** Dominican Republic, 2015. **Signed by:** Richard Jimenez.

TRACK RECORD: It took Martinez three seasons to hit his first professional home run, but once he'd done so, he went on a power tear. Playing in the power-friendly Pioneer League, Martinez ended up hitting eight home runs. Martinez hit his first professional home run on July 6 and tallied seven more on the season. He did so while showing better contact ability.

SCOUTING REPORT: Martinez will have to make steady improvement at the plate. He puts together good at-bats, but his swing has an arm bar to it and emphasizes power over feel for hitting. He has to work on his barrel awareness. Martinez has the defense to stick at third base as he has soft hands and an average arm. His footwork will need to improve.

THE FUTURE: Martinez is still young and has plenty of potential, but he also has a lot of work to do. Martinez is ready to jump to low Class A Dayton. If he can improve his swing and continue to refine his defense, Martinez has a chance to develop a big league third baseman.

Year	Club (League)	Class	AVG	G	AB	R	H	2B	3B	HR	RBI	BB	SO	SB	CS	OBP	SLG
2016	Rojos (DSL)	R	.281	19	64	10	18	5	0	0	9	9	13	0	1	.415	.359
2017	Reds (AZL)	R	.220	40	141	25	31	10	1	0	19	13	43	2	1	.323	.305
2018	Greeneville (APP)	R	.240	9	25	9	6	4	0	0	1	8	5	0	0	.441	.400
	Billings (PIO)	R	.274	47	164	22	45	6	1	8	33	12	39	0	1	.322	.470
Minor League Totals			.254	115	394	66	100	25	2	8	62	42	100	2	3	.348	.388

23 JACOB HEATHERLY, LHP

BA GRADE
45 Risk: Extreme

Born: May 20,1998. **B-T:** L-L. **HT:** 6-2. **WT:** 208. **Drafted:** HS—Cullman, Ala., 2017 (3rd round). **Signed by:** Jim Moran.

TRACK RECORD: When the Reds drafted Heatherly in the third round and paid him an above-slot $1.047 million, they knew they were acquiring a high-ceiling project. After a solid pro debut in the Rookie-level Arizona League, Heatherly reminded everyone how far he has to go with a very difficult start to the 2018 season. He walked 11 batters in just 3.2 innings over his first two starts with Rookie-level Greeneville. He settled down afterward but still battled significant control issues all season.

SCOUTING REPORT: Heatherly is physical and has a relatively clean delivery, but that hasn't helped him throw strikes so far. Heathlerly sits 92-93 mph and touches 95 with a heavy fastball that he can command to both sides of the plate at his best. His best secondary offering is his future plus curveball, which has good spin and works against both lefties and righties. He also throws a slider that tends to blend from time to time with his curveball. He has worked on a low-80s changeup that he doesn't yet show much confidence in.

THE FUTURE: Heatherly is learning how to pitch more aggressively and how to throw strikes. Much like last year, he'll compete for a spot in low Class A Dayton, but he'll have to show significant improvement to survive in the Midwest League.

Year	Club (League)	Class	W	L	ERA	G	GS	CG	SV	IP	H	HR	BB	SO	K/9	WHIP	AVG
2017	Reds (AZL)	R	2	1	2.93	9	6	0	0	31	26	3	16	26	7.6	1.37	.224
	Billings (PIO)	R	0	1	12.00	3	3	0	0	9	17	0	4	5	5.0	2.33	.405
2018	Greeneville (APP)	R	1	5	5.82	11	11	0	0	39	34	3	40	49	11.4	1.91	.241
Minor League Totals			3	7	5.40	23	20	0	0	78	77	6	60	80	9.2	1.75	.258

24 HENDRIK CLEMENTINA, C

BA GRADE
45 Risk: Extreme

Born: June 17, 1997. **B-T:** R-R. **HT:** 6-0. **WT:** 250. **Signed:** Curacao, 2013. **Signed by:** Rolando Chirino/Patrick Guerrero/Bob Engle (Dodgers).

TRACK RECORD: Acquired in the 2017 trade that sent lefthander Tony Cingrani to the Dodgers, Clementina has performed well in the Reds' system. After spending all of last season in rookie ball, he adjusted well to full-season competition.

SCOUTING REPORT: Clementina shows plus-plus raw power that should translate into 16-20 home runs a year eventually. His hit tool is below-average but he still manages to grind out quality at-bats. Defensively he has to work on pitch calling and staying focused from pitch to pitch, but there are the tools and desire to catch. Clementina is a big-bodied catcher who is a little limited by his size. He's raw defensively, but he's shown steady improvement. His body works behind the plate and his arm grades as average. Good hands allow him to be an above-average pitch framer.

THE FUTURE: Clementina is big for a catcher, so he'll have to work hard to stay on top of his body. He has the ability to be a future backup catcher with power potential.

Year	Club (League)	Class	AVG	G	AB	R	H	2B	3B	HR	RBI	BB	SO	SB	CS	OBP	SLG
2016	Dodgers (AZL)	R	.217	44	157	22	34	4	1	6	23	14	42	2	0	.286	.369
2017	Ogden (PIO)	R	.370	24	92	17	34	5	0	4	25	10	16	0	0	.439	.554
	Billings (PIO)	R	.240	27	96	13	23	6	0	2	10	7	25	0	0	.302	.365
2018	Dayton (MWL)	LoA	.268	96	340	38	91	22	1	18	59	30	99	1	0	.327	.497
Minor League Totals			.269	266	948	124	255	53	3	32	145	74	236	7	4	.329	.432

25 ALFREDO RODRIGUEZ, SS

BA GRADE
40 Risk: High

Born: June 17, 1994. **B-T:** R-R. **HT:** 6-0. **WT:** 190. **Signed:** Cuba, 2016. **Signed by:** Tony Arias/Chris Buckley.

TRACK RECORD: The Reds shelled out $7 million to sign Rodriguez in July of 2016. While many scouts believed that Rodriguez's bat would be too light in pro ball, the Reds believed he would develop at the plate. So far, other team's scouts have been right. Rodriguez struggles to hit the ball over outfielders' heads. His 2018 season was also derailed by a hamate injury.

SCOUTING REPORT: Rodriguez is a gifted defensive player who is polished at shortstop. He has a good internal clock and feel for the position. While he has below-average speed, that doesn't hurt him in the field. His arm is plus and has the footwork to be an above-average defender. At the plate, Rodriguez has much further to go. While he controls the barrel well, he lacks bat speed and his bottom-of-the-scale power allows teams to position the outfield to cut off bloopers.

THE FUTURE: After dealing with some injuries, Rodriguez will get more at-bats in the lower minors to work on his offensive tools. The skills are there to be a superb defender up the middle, but his bat will make it hard for him to even handle a bench role.

Year	Club (League)	Class	AVG	G	AB	R	H	2B	3B	HR	RBI	BB	SO	SB	CS	OBP	SLG
2016	Reds (DSL)	R	.234	22	77	12	18	5	0	0	8	9	16	9	0	.333	.299
2017	Daytona (FSL)	HiA	.253	118	483	52	122	14	0	2	36	25	79	11	9	.294	.294
2018	Pensacola (SL)	AA	.192	9	26	4	5	0	0	0	0	2	7	0	0	.276	.192
	Reds (AZL)	R	.250	6	20	3	5	3	0	0	3	1	3	0	0	.286	.400
	Daytona (FSL)	HiA	.207	31	111	12	23	5	1	2	12	8	22	4	0	.270	.324
Minor League Totals			.241	186	717	83	173	27	1	4	59	45	127	24	9	.294	.298

26 DANNY LANTIGUA, OF

BA GRADE

45 Risk: Extreme

Born: March 7, 1999. **B-T:** B-R. **HT:** 6-1. **WT:** 165. **Signed:** Dominican Republic, 2016. **Signed by:** Richard Jimenez.

TRACK RECORD: After going homer-less in 2017, Lantigua proved to be one of the better power hitters in the Rookie-level Arizona League in 2018, when he finished with a league-best 26 extra-base hits and was third in the league with eight home runs.

SCOUTING REPORT: Lantigua is an athletic switch-hitter who has plus raw power. The raw power should translate to above-average productive power from both sides of the plate. His swing gets long from time to time, making it difficult to generate consistent contact. His above-average speed gives him a chance to stay in center field. His plus arm would also fit in right, with some scouts believing he'll end up outgrowing center field and sliding over.

THE FUTURE: Playing more games at the rookie level would be beneficial, as more consistent contact is needed before making the next jump. His defensive tools and intriguing power give him a chance to be an everyday corner outfielder on a second-division team.

Year	Club (League)	Class	AVG	G	AB	R	H	2B	3B	HR	RBI	BB	SO	SB	CS	OBP	SLG
2017	Reds (DSL)	R	.200	17	60	6	12	3	2	0	7	4	22	1	0	.250	.317
2018	Reds (AZL)	R	.223	52	197	26	44	12	6	8	37	13	75	5	4	.274	.467
Minor League Totals			.218	69	257	32	56	15	8	8	44	17	97	6	4	.269	.432

27 IBANDEL ISABEL, 1B/OF

BA GRADE

45 Risk: Extreme

Born: June 20, 1995. **B-T:** R-R. **HT:** 6-4. **WT:** 225. **Signed:** Dominican Republic, 2013. **Signed by:** Bob Engle/Patrick Guerrero (Dodgers).

TRACK RECORD: Isabel was dealt to Cincinnati from the Dodgers as a part of a package for reliever Ariel Hernandez. Originally signed at age 17, Ibandel has spent time in the outfield as well as first base. Isabel has some of the best power in the minors. He set a Florida State League record with 35 homers in 2018 and with 36 overall tied the Mets' Peter Alonso for the overall minor league lead.

SCOUTING REPORT: Isabel is well known for having top-shelf raw power. He generates excellent loft and can hit it out of the park to any field. He slots his hands into a lower position before taking a big stride, which has caused him to swing and miss with frightening frequency. When he connects, he can clear the wall in any park. Ibandel is athletic enough and has a solid arm. His footwork around the bag is passable and works well enough to stick there defensively.

THE FUTURE: Double-A is going to be a big test for Isabel. He was left unprotected and unpicked in the Rule 5 draft, and teams are skeptical that his approach will allow him to make enough contact.

Year	Club (League)	Class	AVG	G	AB	R	H	2B	3B	HR	RBI	BB	SO	SB	CS	OBP	SLG
2016	Ogden (PIO)	R	.351	32	114	19	40	6	2	5	29	15	36	0	2	.432	.570
	Great Lakes (MWL)	LoA	.273	24	88	17	24	5	1	7	15	9	41	1	2	.347	.591
2017	R. Cucamonga (CAL)	HiA	.259	122	444	62	115	16	1	28	87	40	172	0	2	.327	.489
2018	R. Cucamonga (CAL)	HiA	.238	6	21	1	5	2	0	1	3	2	9	0	0	.304	.476
	Daytona (FSL)	HiA	.258	104	376	62	97	11	0	35	75	36	152	1	1	.333	.566
Minor League Totals			.277	430	1518	231	420	69	14	87	286	145	565	9	11	.348	.513

28 SCOTT MOSS, LHP

Born: Oct. 6, 1994. **B-T:** L-L. **HT:** 6-5. **WT:** 215. **Drafted:** Florida, 2016 (4th round). **Signed by:** Greg Zunino.

BA GRADE
40 Risk: High

TRACK RECORD: After sitting out his first two years at Florida recovering from Tommy John surgery, Moss was dominating in his only year on the mound for the Gators. After posting a 1.57 ERA with only two extra-base hits allowed in 23 innings, Moss was nearly as effective with low Class A Dayton in 2017. The crafty lefty was still effective and durable but not nearly as dominating in the Florida State League.
SCOUTING REPORT: Moss relies on feel for pitching, locating and messing with hitters' timing because he lacks a plus pitch. His 88-92 mph fastball is effective because he spots it well to the four corners of the strike zone. His slider flashes above-average and he mixes in a fringe-average changeup. Moss repeats his delivery well and throws consistent strikes, showing future average control and above-average command.
THE FUTURE: After starting 25 games in the high Class A Florida State league, Moss will be ticketed Double-A Chattanooga in 2019. With more seasoning of his changeup, Moss could fit as a swingman.

Year	Club (League)	Class	W	L	ERA	G	GS	CG	SV	IP	H	HR	BB	SO	K/9	WHIP	AVG
2016	Billings (PIO)	R	3	1	2.35	10	10	0	0	38	35	2	14	29	6.8	1.28	.241
2017	Dayton (MWL)	LoA	13	6	3.45	26	26	0	0	136	114	11	48	156	10.3	1.19	.224
2018	Daytona (FSL)	HiA	15	4	3.68	25	25	0	0	132	135	13	41	112	7.6	1.33	.262
Minor League Totals			31	11	3.41	61	61	0	0	306	284	26	103	297	8.7	1.26	.243

29 CONNOR JOE, 1B/3B

Born: Aug. 16, 1992. **B-T:** R-R. **HT:** 6-0. **WT:** 205. **Drafted:** San Diego, 2014 (1st round supplemental). **Signed by:** Brian Tracy (Pirates).

BA GRADE
40 Risk: High

TRACK RECORD: The Pirates drafted Joe 39th overall in 2014 and signed him for $1.25 million, but injuries and constant position changes kept him from getting settled. The Pirates traded him to the Braves in August 2017, and Atlanta flipped him to the Dodgers a month later for international bonus money.
SCOUTING REPORT: Joe had an open stance in college at San Diego but was told to shelve it by the Pirates. He re-opened his stance with the Dodgers and found himself in a more athletic position to hit, resulting in consistently better swings and harder contact. With advanced strike zone discipline, Joe's re-tooled setup allowed him to realize his initial projection of a solid-average hitter with average power. Joe is an average defender at first base and below-average at third base. During instructional league the Dodgers mixed him in at catcher, a position he briefly played in college.
THE FUTURE: Joe may be the Dodgers' next late-career success story brought about by a swing change, although that success may come in Cincinnati. As a Rule 5 pick, he'll battle for a spot on the Reds' bench.

Year	Club (League)	Class	AVG	G	AB	R	H	2B	3B	HR	RBI	BB	SO	SB	CS	OBP	SLG
2016	Bradenton (FSL)	HiA	.277	107	390	49	108	26	2	5	52	45	84	2	4	.351	.392
2017	West Virginia (NYP)	SS	.250	3	12	2	3	1	0	0	0	1	4	0	0	.308	.333
	Altoona (EL)	AA	.240	74	242	29	58	11	4	5	30	34	40	2	4	.338	.380
	Mississippi (SL)	AA	.135	20	52	2	7	1	0	0	4	6	18	0	1	.233	.154
2018	Tulsa (TL)	AA	.304	57	204	35	62	16	1	11	30	38	57	1	2	.425	.554
	Okla. City (PCL)	AAA	.294	49	160	34	47	10	2	6	25	22	31	2	0	.385	.494
Minor League Totals			.264	390	1350	189	356	77	10	28	161	196	268	7	15	.363	.398

30 BREN SPILLANE, OF/1B

Born: Sept. 21, 1996. **B-T:** R-R. **HT:** 6-4. **WT:** 210. **Drafted:** Illinois, 2018 (3rd round). **Signed by:** Andy Stack.

BA GRADE
45 Risk: Extreme

TRACK RECORD: Spillane was the 2018 Big Ten Player of the Year with Illinois, where he slugged a .903 his final season. His 23 home runs were a career high, besting his previous career high of five. He was promptly selected by Cincinnati and signed an under-slot deal.
SCOUTING REPORT: Spillane has plus raw power and has the ability to drive the ball to all fields, but his swing is a bit unorthodox due to the setup of his hands and elbows. He starts with his hands well separated from his body, which makes it hard to get the bat on plane. Spillane He has an average arm and projects to be an average defender in right field and has a chance to be an above-average defender at first base.
THE FUTURE: Spillane will jump to low Class A Dayton. His power is rare and could put him among the Midwest League's home run leaders, but he's also likely to rank among the league's strikeout leaders.

Year	Club (League)	Class	AVG	G	AB	R	H	2B	3B	HR	RBI	BB	SO	SB	CS	OBP	SLG
2018	Billings (PIO)	R	.236	48	148	28	35	9	3	5	22	30	76	2	2	.375	.439
Minor League Totals			.236	48	148	28	35	9	3	5	22	30	76	2	2	.375	.439

Cleveland Indians

BY TEDDY CAHILL

The Indians again won the AL Central in 2018, giving them three straight division titles for the first time since the club's 1990s heydays. But there was no postseason magic in Cleveland as the Indians were swept out of the playoffs by the Astros in the ALDS.

The season had many of the same hallmarks that have come to define this current run of Indians' dominance in the division. Corey Kluber finished third in the Cy Young voting and Jose Ramirez matched that finish in the MVP race. Francisco Lindor continued to electrify crowds—never more so than when he homered in an Indians' win in his native Puerto Rico—and the team made a big trade (top prospect Francisco Mejia for Brad Hand and Adam Cimber) to shore up the bullpen.

The season came to an ignominious end, however, as the Indians were swept in the playoffs for the first time since 1954. That ending, combined with key players such as Cody Allen, Michael Brantley and Adam Miller headed for free agency and the continued aging of the team's core, made for an angsty fall as the Indians try to plot a course to snap their 71-year title drought—the longest in the sport.

But the club remains well-positioned under the leadership of president Chris Antonetti and general manager Mike Chernoff, who extended his contract in Cleveland amid reported interest this year from multiple teams with GM openings. The AL Central, loaded with rebuilding teams, still gives the Tribe an advantageous path to the postseason, and their starting rotation and infield pairing of Lindor and Ramirez remain among the best in the game.

Cleveland's farm system is short on upper-level talent after the club has made several trades in recent years to reinforce the big league team. But it has remained productive, and in 2018 churned out another solid starting pitcher in Shane Bieber, who went 11-5, 4.55 during his debut.

Righthander Triston McKenzie, now the team's top prospect, has reached the upper levels of the minor leagues and has a chance to be the best pitcher drafted by the Indians since CC Sabathia. He should soon be ready to join Bieber in the Indians' big league rotation.

The system's next wave of prospects is building in the lower levels of the system. Shortstop Tyler Freeman won the New York-Penn League batting title as a 19-year-old. Shortstop Brayan Rocchio opened eyes as 17-year-old in the Arizona League during his professional debut. The club took advantage of holding three of the first 41 draft picks in June to add more premium talent to the

Rookie Shane Bieber showcased elite control but proved too hittable and ran up a 4.55 ERA.

PROJECTED 2022 LINEUP

Catcher	Roberto Perez (33)
First Base	Jake Bauers (26)
Second Base	Jose Ramirez (29)
Third Base	Nolan Jones (24)
Shortstop	Francisco Lindor (28)
Left Field	Daniel Johnson (27)
Center Field	Greg Allen (29)
Right Field	Bradley Zimmer (29)
Designated Hitter	Bobby Bradley (26)
No. 1 Starter	Trevor Bauer (31)
No. 2 Starter	Triston McKenzie (24)
No. 3 Starter	Corey Kluber (33)
No. 4 Starter	Mike Clevinger (31)
No. 5 Starter	Shane Bieber (27)
Closer	Sam Hentges (25)

system and its international program continues to land impactful players.

The Indians will spend the summer of 2019 on MLB's main stage as they host the All-Star Game. It will be their first time hosting the Midsummer Classic since 1997—when their time in the spotlight extended to the end of October with a World Series appearance.

To follow 1997's script again in 2019 won't be easy for the Tribe. But with a strong on-field core and stable, successful front office in place, Cleveland can dare to dream that the magic will return.

DEPTH CHART

CLEVELAND INDIANS

TOP 2019 ROOKIE: Aaron Civale, RHP. It won't be easy for any rookie to break into a veteran-laden team in 2019, but Civale could make an impact in the bullpen.

BREAKOUT PROSPECT: Carlos Vargas, RHP. Vargas is in a similar spot as Luis Oviedo was a year ago and could take a similar jump as he advances to short-season Mahoning Valley.

SLEEPER: Raymond Burgos, LHP. The Puerto Rican native has seen his velocity jump as he's filled out his 6-foot-5 frame and he's now consistently throwing his fastball in the low to mid 90s.

SOURCE OF TOP 30 TALENT			
Homegrown	28	Acquired	2
College	5	Trades	2
Junior college	0	Rule 5 draft	0
High school	13	Independent leagues	0
Nondrafted free agents	0	Free agents/waivers	0
International	10		

LF
George Valera (5)
Daniel Johnson (14)
Oscar Gonzalez (22)
Andrew Calica

CF
Oscar Mercado (16)
Quentin Holmes (27)
Korey Holland
Austen Wade

RF
Will Benson (21)
Jonathan Rodriguez (29)
Ka'ai Tom

3B
Nolan Jones (2)
Raynel Delgado (23)
Junior Sanquintin (26)
Henry Pujols

SS
Tyler Freeman (3)
Brayan Rocchio (9)
Yu-Cheng Chang (11)
Gabriel Rodriguez (12)
Ernie Clement (18)
Marcos Gonzalez

2B
Aaron Bracho (19)
Richie Palacios (28)
Jose Fermin
Jesus Lara

1B
Bobby Bradley (7)
Mike Papi
Miguel Jerez

C
Bo Naylor (4)
Eric Haase (25)
Logan Ice
Mike Rivera

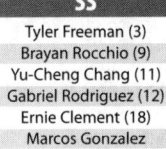
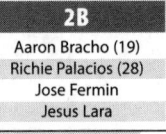

LHP

LHSP	LHRP
Sam Hentges (6)	Kyle Nelson
Kirk McCarty (30)	R.C. Orlan
Adam Scott	Rob Kaminsky
Raymond Burgos	Ben Krauth
Matt Turner	
Sean Brady	
Brady Aiken	
Juan Hillman	

RHP

RHSP	RHRP
Triston McKenzie (1)	Nick Sandlin (24)
Luis Oviedo (8)	Henry Martinez
Ethan Hankins (10)	Dalbert Siri
Carlos Vargas (13)	Robert Broom
Aaron Civale (15)	Jonathan Teaney
Jean Carlos Mejia (17)	
Lenny Torres (20)	
Eli Morgan	
Zach Plesac	
Chih-Wei Hu	
Walker Lockett	

DRAFT ANALYSIS

2018

BEST PURE HITTER: There were some scouts who believed C Bo Naylor (1) was the best pure hitter in the high school class. He does a good job controlling the strike zone and uses the whole field to hit. 2B Richie Palacios (3) and SS Raynel Delgado (6) also stand out for their hittability.

BEST POWER HITTER: Naylor isn't just a contact hitter. He also has plus raw power that plays as solid-average in games. OF Billy Wilson (28) wasn't known as a slugger during his career at Loyola Marymount, but he hit 10 home runs this summer, albeit in the Rookie-level Arizona League.

FASTEST RUNNER: The Indians didn't draft any true burners, but Palacios, OF Steven Kwan (5), OF Korey Holland (14) and SS Gionti Turner (27) all show plus run times.

BEST DEFENSIVE PLAYER: Kwan is an above-average defender in center field thanks to his speed and outfield instincts.

BEST FASTBALL: RHP Ethan Hankins (1) has run his fastball up to 98 mph though he didn't show that velocity in the spring when he was slowed by a shoulder injury. RHP Lenny Torres (1s) touched 97 mph this spring and sat 94 mph this summer. RHP Liam Jenkins (17) has touched 99 mph from a big, 6-foot-8 frame.

BEST SECONDARY PITCH: RHP Nick Sandlin (2) this spring at Southern Mississippi used his wipeout slider to help him pile up 144 strikeouts, fifth most in the country, and lead the nation with a 1.06 ERA. LHP Adam Scott (4) also has shown he is adept at landing his slider for strikes.

BEST PRO DEBUT: Sandlin built on his All-American spring with a phenomenal professional debut. He rocketed up the ladder, reaching Double-A Akron, posting a 36-to-3 strikeout-to-walk ratio in 24 innings along the way.

BEST ATHLETE: Naylor moves well for a catcher and is an above-average runner. He also has a lot of experience in the infield and could man the hot corner if catching doesn't work out. Holland's speed and athleticism play well in the outfield.

TOP DRAFT PICKS OF THE DECADE

Year	Player, Pos.	2018 Org
2009	Alex White, RHP	Atlantic League
2010	Drew Pomeranz, LHP	Red Sox
2011	Francisco Lindor, SS	Indians
2012	Tyler Naquin, OF	Indians
2013	Clint Frazier, OF	Yankees
2014	Bradley Zimmer, OF	Indians
2015	Brady Aiken, LHP	Indians
2016	Will Benson, OF	Indians
2017	Quentin Holmes, OF (2nd round)	Indians
2018	Bo Naylor, C	Indians

MOST INTRIGUING BACKGROUND: The Indians drafted a handful of players with baseball bloodlines, starting with Naylor, whose brother Josh is in the Padres' organization. Sandlin not only stood out on the field this spring but also in the classroom, where he had a 3.9 GPA as an engineering major.

CLOSEST TO THE MAJORS: For a time, it looked like Sandlin might reach the major leagues in September. If he stays in the bullpen, he'll soon be in the mix for the Indians. Even if he goes back to starting, his rise won't be dramatically slowed as he's already shown he can handle advanced competition.

BEST LATE-ROUND PICK: Holland signed a well-above slot deal in the 14th round but still could provide good value thanks to his feel for hitting to go along with his speed and athleticism. OF Jonathan Engelmann (31) has some intriguing tools and put together a solid pro debut.

THE ONE WHO GOT AWAY: OF Antoine Duplantis (19) opted to return for his senior season at Louisiana State, where he's been a three-year starter and integral part of the lineup. The Indians also took SS Gunnar Halter (26) and OF Andrew Eyster (32) out of the junior college ranks, but both opted to uphold their commitments to Southeastern Conference schools, where they figure to play key roles in 2019.

—TEDDY CAHILL

2017

SS Tyler Freeman (2s) has impressed early and won the New York-Penn League batting title. SS Ernie Clement (4) and LHP Kirk McCarty (7), both picked from the college ranks, have also had early success.

GRADE: C

2016

RHP Shane Bieber (4) made plenty of believers as he raced to Cleveland. 3B Nolan Jones (2) has become one of the system's top prospects. OF Will Benson (1) remains an enigma but led the Midwest League in homers.

GRADE: B

2015

The Indians took a risk when they drafted LHPs Brady Aiken (1) and Juan Hillman (2), and RHP Triston McKenzie (1s). Aiken and Hillman haven't panned out but McKenzie can carry this class' banner alone.

GRADE: B

1 TRISTON McKENZIE, RHP

Born: Aug. 2, 1997. **B-T:** R-R. **Ht.:** 6-5. **Wt.:** 165.
Drafted: HS—Royal Palm Beach, Fla., 2015 (1st round supplemental). **Signed by:** Juan Alvarez.

MIKE JANES/FOUR SEAM

In the spring of 2015, McKenzie presented scouts with a difficult assignment. He had an excellent amateur track record and impressive present stuff, but he was listed at a rail-thin 6-foot-5, 165 pounds. While some questioned how much weight his frame would ever carry, the Indians drafted McKenzie 42nd overall and have been rewarded for the decision. He has built an impressive track record of success in pro ball. In 2017 alone, he pitched in the Futures Game, was named Carolina League pitcher of the year and ranked second in the minors with 186 strikeouts. He was slowed by forearm soreness in 2018 that the Indians took a very conservative approach with, delaying his debut until June. Still, he was pitching in Double-A Akron as a 20-year-old and put together a strong summer. The concerns about his thin frame remain today, but his track record and stuff are such that they have been lessened.

SCOUTING REPORT: McKenzie's fastball can get up to 95 mph and in each of the last two years it averaged about 92 mph. He held that velocity throughout the season and while it would dip during starts, he also showed the ability to reach back for more and finish strong. His plus fastball plays up and gets swings and misses thanks to the extension in his delivery and the high spin rate he generates. He also has a good feel for spinning his plus curveball and gets good depth on the offering. McKenzie's changeup continues to develop and has the potential to be an above-average offering. He is starting to learn how to sequence and attack hitters with his full arsenal. He commands the ball well and earns praise for his makeup and understanding of his craft. McKenzie's biggest area for development remains improving his physique to allow him to manage a starter's workload.

THE FUTURE: McKenzie will pitch nearly all of 2019 as a 21-year-old and is speeding toward the big leagues, where he has the upside to be a frontline starter. To this point he hasn't been challenged much and he has a chance to earn a spot in the big leagues in 2019. But with Cleveland's crowded big league rotation, the Indians can afford to let McKenzie force the issue with a strong showing in the upper levels of the minors.

BA GRADE	SCOUTING GRADES
60 Risk: Medium	Fastball: 60. Curveball: 60. Changeup: 55. Control: 60.

Projected future grades on 20-80 scouting scale

TOP PROSPECTS OF THE DECADE

Year	Player, Pos.	2018 Org
2009	Carlos Santana, C	Phillies
2010	Carlos Santana, C	Phillies
2011	Lonnie Chisenhall, 3B	Indians
2012	Francisco Lindor, SS	Indians
2013	Francisco Lindor, SS	Indians
2014	Francisco Lindor, SS	Indians
2015	Francisco Lindor, SS	Indians
2016	Bradley Zimmer, OF	Indians
2017	Francisco Mejia, C	Padres
2018	Francisco Mejia, C	Padres

BEST TOOLS

Best Hitter for Average	Tyler Freeman
Best Power Hitter	Bobby Bradley
Best Strike-Zone Discipline	Ernie Clement
Fastest Baserunner	Quentin Holmes
Best Athlete	Will Benson
Best Fastball	Luis Oviedo
Best Curveball	Triston McKenzie
Best Slider	Kyle Nelson
Best Changeup	Eli Morgan
Best Control	Aaron Civale
Best Defensive Catcher	Eric Haase
Best Defensive Infielder	Jose Fermin
Best Infield Arm	Nolan Jones
Best Defensive Outfielder	Oscar Mercado
Best Outfield Arm	Jonathan Rodriguez

Year	Club (League)	Class	W	L	ERA	G	GS	CG	SV	IP	H	HR	BB	SO	K/9	WHIP	AVG
2016	Mahoning Valley (NYP)	SS	4	3	0.55	9	9	1	0	49	31	2	16	55	10.0	0.95	.180
	Lake County (MWL)	LoA	2	2	3.18	6	6	0	0	34	27	2	6	49	13.0	0.97	.214
2017	Lynchburg (CAR)	HiA	12	6	3.46	25	25	0	0	143	105	14	45	186	11.7	1.05	.204
2018	Akron (EL)	AA	7	4	2.68	16	16	0	0	91	63	8	28	87	8.6	1.00	.191
Minor League Totals			26	16	2.68	60	59	1	0	329	230	26	98	394	10.8	1.00	.194

2 NOLAN JONES, 3B

Born: May 7, 1998. **B-T:** L-L. **Ht.:** 6-3. **Wt.:** 195. **Drafted:** HS—Bensalem, Pa., 2016 (2nd round). **Signed by:** Mike Kanen.

TRACK RECORD: Jones was regarded as one of the best prep hitters in the 2016 draft class and while he slipped to the second round on draft day, he's lived up to his amateur reputation in pro ball. After leading the New York-Penn League in OPS (.912) in 2017, he followed that up with a strong year at two Class A stops in his first taste of full-season ball, ending the year in high Class A Lynchburg.

SCOUTING REPORT: Jones has an easy lefthanded swing and uses the whole field to hit. He is a patient hitter who led all Indians minor leaguers in walks (89), though his patience also means plenty of deep counts. He will always strike out fairly often as a result. He has plus raw power and in 2018 began to turn what had previously been doubles pop into over-the-fence strength. Jones fits the third base profile, but he will need to improve defensively to stay at the hot corner. He has a plus arm but needs to improve his glove work and

BA GRADE
55 Risk: High
Hit: 55. **Power:** 60.
Run: 50. **Field:** 50.
Arm: 60.

infield actions, especially when ranging to his right. If he did need to move, his athleticism and average speed should play in the outfield, though some believe he is destined for first base.

THE FUTURE: Jones has established himself as the system's top position player prospect and has the potential to be an impact bat in the future. He's impressed the Indians with his all-around offensive game and work ethic. He likely will return to high Class A Lynchburg to begin 2019.

Year	Club (League)	Class	AVG	G	AB	R	H	2B	3B	HR	RBI	BB	SO	SB	CS	OBP	SLG
2016	Indians (AZL)	R	.257	32	109	10	28	5	2	0	9	23	49	3	1	.388	.339
2017	Mahoning Valley (NYP)	SS	.317	62	218	41	69	18	3	4	33	43	60	1	0	.430	.482
2018	Lake County (MWL)	LoA	.279	90	323	46	90	12	0	16	49	63	97	2	1	.393	.464
	Lynchburg (CAR)	HiA	.298	30	104	23	31	9	0	3	17	26	34	0	0	.438	.471
Minor League Totals			.289	214	754	120	218	44	5	23	108	155	240	6	2	.410	.452

3 TYLER FREEMAN, SS

Born: May 21, 1999. **B-T:** R-R. **Ht.:** 6-0. **Wt.:** 170. **Drafted:** HS—Rancho Cucamonga, Calif., 2017 (2nd round supp). **Signed by:** Mike Bradford.

TRACK RECORD: Freeman this summer starred for short-season Mahoning Valley in his first full professional season. He led the New York-Penn League in batting (.352), slugging (.511), runs (49), hits (95) and doubles (29), while playing the whole summer as a 19-year-old.

SCOUTING REPORT: Freeman stands out most for his hitting and excellent feel for the barrel. He has a very aggressive approach at the plate and rarely walks as a result, but when he swings he makes contact. Thanks to his ability to consistently square balls up, he produces plenty of doubles—he hit the most doubles in the New York-Penn League since 1999—and he may be able to develop fringe-average power as he physically matures. Freeman was drafted as a shortstop and the Indians are developing him there, though he's also gotten time at second base in each of the last two years. He's already improved his

BA GRADE
55 Risk: High
Hit: 60. **Power:** 45.
Run: 50. **Field:** 50.
Arm: 55.

hands, infield actions and instincts but he's still an average runner with average arm strength, which may mean a move to second base is still in his future.

THE FUTURE: Regardless of where Freeman ends up defensively, his bat will be the main attraction. He'll advance to full-season ball in 2019 with low Class A Lake County in 2019 and look to continue his impressive performance at the plate.

Year	Club (League)	Class	AVG	G	AB	R	H	2B	3B	HR	RBI	BB	SO	SB	CS	OBP	SLG
2017	Indians (AZL)	R	.297	36	128	19	38	9	0	2	14	7	12	5	1	.364	.414
2018	Mahoning Valley (NYP)	SS	.352	72	270	49	95	29	4	2	38	8	22	14	3	.405	.511
Minor League Totals			.334	108	398	68	133	38	4	4	52	15	34	19	4	.392	.480

4 BO NAYLOR, C

BILL MITCHELL

Born: Feb. 21, 2000. **B-T:** L-R. **Ht.:** 6-0. **Wt.:** 195. **Drafted:** HS—Mississauga, Ont., 2018 (1st round). **Signed by:** Mike Kanen.

TRACK RECORD: Naylor, the younger brother of Padres' prospect Josh Naylor, starred on the showcase circuit and with the Canadian Junior National Team, compiling a long track record of success. The Indians drafted him 29th overall and sent him to the Rookie-level Arizona League, where he had a solid summer.

SCOUTING REPORT: Naylor, like his older brother, stands out for his offensive skills, but he's a different kind of hitter. He's a plus hitter with average power. There were some scouts who believed Naylor had the best hit tool among all prep hitters in his draft class thanks to his smooth swing, pitch recognition and approach. His power hasn't always played in games, but he makes consistent hard contact and has the ability to drive the ball. Naylor is an above-average runner and his athleticism plays well behind the plate, as does his plus arm. Like all high school catchers, he'll need to refine his catching skills. He also played a lot of third base as an amateur and he profiles well at the hot corner, but the Indians are committed to him catching.

THE FUTURE: The Indians in recent years have taken a conservative approach with their highly drafted prep bats. That means Naylor probably will head to short-season Mahoning Valley as a 19-year-old.

BA GRADE
60 Risk: Extreme
Hit: 60. Power: 50.
Run: 55. Field: 50.
Arm: 60.

Year	Club (League)	Class	AVG	G	AB	R	H	2B	3B	HR	RBI	BB	SO	SB	CS	OBP	SLG
2018	Indians 2 (AZL)	R	.274	33	117	17	32	3	3	2	17	21	28	5	1	.381	.402
Minor League Totals			.274	33	117	17	32	3	3	2	17	21	28	5	1	.381	.402

5 GEORGE VALERA, OF

BILL MITCHELL

Born: Nov. 13, 2000. **B-T:** L-L. **Ht.:** 5-10. **Wt.:** 160. **Signed:** Dominican Republic, 2017. **Signed by:** Jhonathan Leyba/ Domingo Toribio.

TRACK RECORD: The Indians in 2017 took advantage of their recently revamped international scouting department and the rule changes in the latest Collective Bargaining Agreement to make a splash on the international market. Valera, the fifth-ranked player in the 2017 international singing class, headlined the Indians' big haul, inking a deal worth $1.3 million. He was born in New York and lived there until his family moved to the Dominican Republic when he was 13. He made his professional debut in 2018 in the Rookie-level Arizona League as a 17-year-old, but he was limited to just six games before a broken hamate ended his season.

SCOUTING REPORT: Valera has a loose, compact swing and keeps his bat in the hitting zone for a long time. His feel for the barrel, bat-to-ball skills, pitch recognition and discipline all help him make consistent, hard contact and give him the kind of hitting ability the Indians covet. He has above-average raw power and gets to it in games well, though he has more of a hit-over-power profile. Valera profiles as a corner outfielder with average speed and arm strength.

THE FUTURE: Valera as an amateur drew comparisons with the Nationals' Juan Soto, and while he's unlikely to mimic Soto's meteoric rise through the minor leagues, he is advanced enough that an assignment to low Class A Lake County is possible in 2019.

BA GRADE
60 Risk: Extreme
Hit: 60. Power: 50.
Run: 50. Field: 50.
Arm: 50.

Year	Club (League)	Class	AVG	G	AB	R	H	2B	3B	HR	RBI	BB	SO	SB	CS	OBP	SLG
2018	Indians 2 (AZL)	R	.333	6	18	4	6	1	0	1	6	3	3	1	1	.409	.556
Minor League Totals			.333	6	18	4	6	1	0	1	6	3	3	1	1	.409	.556

6 SAM HENTGES, LHP

Born: July 18, 1996. **B-T:** R-R. **Ht.:** 6-6. **Wt.:** 245. **Drafted:** HS—Arden Hills, Minn., 2014 (4th round). **Signed by:** Les Pajari.

TRACK RECORD: Hentges was raw even for a prep player from Minnesota when the Indians drafted him in 2014. He was one of the youngest players in the 2014 draft class and didn't pitch much until late in his junior year of high school. He started his pro career slowly, in part because he needed Tommy John surgery in 2016. Back to full health in 2018, he took a big step forward with high Class A Lynchburg, where he ranked third in the Carolina League in strikeouts (122).

SCOUTING REPORT: Hentges has a big, physical frame that he has grown into since signing and he has the powerful fastball to match. His fastball averages about 93 mph and he can run it up to 97. Because his fastball is so good, he can overpower lower-level hitters with it, but as he advances, he'll have to refine his secondary offerings. The good news is he has the makings of three good offspeed pitches. His curveball flashes plus—he just needs to throw it more consistently. This year he added a cutter to give him another weapon and he also mixes in a promising changeup. Like many big, young pitchers, Hentges needs to improve his control and take better advantage of his height to pitch down in the zone.

THE FUTURE: Having shown he can handle a full-season's workload, Hentges can now focus on refining some of the more detailed areas of his game. He has mid-rotation potential and will likely begin the 2019 season with Double-A Akron.

BA GRADE

55 Risk: High

Fastball: 60. Curve: 55. Cutter: 50. Change: 50. CTL: 50

Year	Club (League)	Class	W	L	ERA	G	GS	CG	SV	IP	H	HR	BB	SO	K/9	WHIP	AVG
2016	Lake County (MWL)	LoA	2	4	6.12	14	14	0	0	60	71	8	29	73	10.9	1.66	.296
2017	Indians (AZL)	R	0	3	4.85	6	6	0	0	13	16	2	3	18	12.5	1.46	.296
	Mahoning Valley (NYP)	SS	0	1	2.04	5	5	0	0	18	5	1	12	23	11.7	0.96	.088
2018	Lynchburg (CAR)	HiA	6	6	3.27	23	23	0	0	118	114	4	53	122	9.3	1.41	.260
Minor League Totals			12	19	3.98	69	59	0	0	278	272	19	129	307	9.9	1.44	.258

7 BOBBY BRADLEY, 1B

Born: May 29, 1996. **B-T:** L-R. **Ht.:** 6-1. **Wt.:** 225. **Drafted:** HS—Gulfport, Miss., 2014 (3rd round). **Signed by:** Mike Bradford.

TRACK RECORD: Bradley has been one of the most productive players in the Indians' farm system since they drafted him in 2014. He won the Rookie-level Arizona League triple crown that summer by hitting .361 with eight home runs and 50 RBIs. He led the Midwest League with 27 home runs in 2015 and the Carolina League with 29 home runs in 2016, while also collecting MVP honors. He has hit 50 homers over the last two years and in 2018 reached Triple-A Columbus as a 22-year-old.

SCOUTING REPORT: Bradley's raw power is the best in the system and he has shown he is adept at getting to it in games. He has a strong, physical frame and creates excellent bat speed that allows him to drive the ball out to all fields. That power comes with a lot of swing and miss, and he has struck out in 25 percent of his plate appearances at Double-A and Triple-A. Bradley is a well-below average runner with an average arm, limiting him to first base.

BA GRADE

50 Risk: High

Hit: 40. Power: 70. Run: 20. Field: 45. Arm: 50.

THE FUTURE: After reaching Triple-A Columbus in the second half of 2018, Bradley will return there to start 2019. While the Indians in December traded away Yonder Alonso and Edwin Encarnacion, they also acquired Jake Bauers and Carlos Santana, who both figure to see time at first base. Still, Bradley's opportunity in Cleveland is fast approaching.

Year	Club (League)	Class	AVG	G	AB	R	H	2B	3B	HR	RBI	BB	SO	SB	CS	OBP	SLG
2016	Lynchburg (CAR)	HiA	.235	131	485	82	114	23	1	29	102	75	170	3	0	.344	.466
2017	Akron (EL)	AA	.251	131	467	66	117	25	3	23	89	55	122	3	3	.331	.465
2018	Akron (EL)	AA	.214	97	369	49	79	19	3	24	64	45	105	1	0	.304	.477
	Columbus (IL)	AAA	.254	32	114	11	29	7	2	3	19	11	43	0	0	.323	.430
Minor League Totals			.252	540	1999	309	503	102	17	114	416	259	626	13	3	.342	.491

MIKE JANES/FOUR SEAM IMAGES

8 LUIS OVIEDO, RHP

Born: May 15, 1999. **B-T:** R-R. **Ht.:** 6-4. **Wt.:** 250. **Signed:** Venezuela, 2015.
Signed by: Koby Perez/Luis Camacho.
TRACK RECORD: Oviedo, the top pitcher in the Indians' 2015 international signing class, stood out in 2017 for his tools despite his unsightly 7.14 ERA during his U.S. debut in the Rookie level Arizona League. The next year at short-season Mahoning Valley, Oviedo's considerable talent and his stats began to line up and he earned a late promotion to low Class A Lake County.
SCOUTING REPORT: Oviedo has filled out his big frame and refined his body since signing, and his velocity has grown as a result. His fastball now sits 94-98 mph with sinking action, up from the upper-80s when he signed. He got back to throwing his big curveball this year, which, along with his slider, gives him two distinct breaking balls that can induce swings and misses. He also has good feel for his changeup, which is advanced for his age. In the end, Oviedo could have four average or better offerings. He did a good job refining his delivery to get it to be more controllable and allow him to throw strikes more consistently.
THE FUTURE: With his power stuff, Oviedo has considerable upside. He'll return to the Midwest League in 2019 and look to show that he can handle the workload of a full season.

BA GRADE
55 Risk: Very High
Fastball: 60. Curve: 50.
Slider: 55. Change: 50.
CTL: 50.

Year	Club (League)	Class	W	L	ERA	G	GS	CG	SV	IP	H	HR	BB	SO	K/9	WHIP	AVG
2016	Indians (DSL)	R	2	8	4.00	14	14	0	0	63	67	1	17	56	8.0	1.33	.276
2017	Indians (AZL)	R	4	2	7.14	14	7	0	0	52	62	2	22	70	12.2	1.63	.286
2018	Mahoning Valley (NYP)	SS	4	2	1.88	9	9	0	0	48	34	3	10	61	11.4	0.92	.192
	Lake County (MWL)	LoA	1	0	3.00	2	2	0	0	9	5	0	7	6	6.0	1.33	.179
Minor League Totals			11	12	4.30	39	32	0	0	172	168	6	56	193	10.1	1.30	.253

9 BRAYAN ROCCHIO, SS

Born: Jan. 13, 2001. **B-T:** B-R. **Ht.:** 5-10. **Wt.:** 150. **Signed:** Venezuela. **Signed by:** Jhonathan Leyba.
TRACK RECORD: Rocchio joined George Valera and Aaron Bracho in the Indians' deep 2017 international signing class, who both ranked among the top 20 prospects in the class. They were sidelined by injuries in 2018, but Rocchio advanced to the Rookie-level Arizona League in 2018, where he ranked third in batting (.343).
SCOUTING REPORT: Rocchio doesn't stand out physically but was quickly nicknamed "The Professor" because of his high baseball IQ and game awareness. A switch-hitter, he has a smooth, consistent swing from both sides of the plate and excellent pitch recognition. He's an aggressive hitter and consistently barrels the ball. His size means power isn't a part of his game now, but as he physically matures he'll start sending some of his line drives over the fence. He likely will always be a hit-over-power player, however. While there were questions when he signed about his ability to stick at shortstop, Rocchio did his best to show he can play the position in 2018. He's a plus runner, and his hands and arm are good enough for the position, especially because his instincts and baseball IQ help his tools play up.
THE FUTURE: Rocchio has already put himself on an accelerated track with his impressive professional debut. The Indians have a logjam of lower-level middle infielders reminiscent of half a dozen years ago when Jose Ramirez, Francisco Lindor and Erik Gonzalez were beginning their careers. But it will be hard to slow Rocchio down now, and he will likely go to short-season Mahoning Valley in 2019 , where he'll be one of the youngest players in the New York-Penn League.

BILL MITCHELL

BA GRADE
55 Risk: Extreme
Hit: 55. Power: 30.
Run: 60. Field: 55.
Arm: 50.

Year	Club (League)	Class	AVG	G	AB	R	H	2B	3B	HR	RBI	BB	SO	SB	CS	OBP	SLG
2018	Indians (DSL)	R	.323	25	99	19	32	2	3	1	12	5	14	8	5	.391	.434
	Indians 2 (AZL)	R	.343	35	143	21	49	10	1	1	17	10	17	14	8	.389	.448
Minor League Totals			.335	60	242	40	81	12	4	2	29	15	31	22	13	.390	.442

10 ETHAN HANKINS, RHP

Born: May 23, 2000. **B-T:** R-R. **Ht.:** 6-6. **Wt.:** 200. **Drafted:** HS—Gainesville, Ga., 2018 (1st round). **Signed by:** C.T. Bradford.

TRACK RECORD: Following Hankins' performance on the showcase circuit during the summer and a stellar showing for USA Baseball in the 18U World Cup, Hankins was considered the best prep player in the 2018 draft class. But he suffered a shoulder injury in February and while he returned to the mound before the draft, his stuff was not as crisp as it had been. That led Hankins to slide to the last pick of the first round.

SCOUTING REPORT: Hankins has a long, lean frame and uncommon athleticism for a pitcher of his size. He runs his fastball up to 97 mph and typically sits in the mid-90s with plus life. He has the makings of quality secondary pitches, but they'll need to become more consistent offerings. His slider and changeup both have the ability to be above-average, and he also throws a bigger curveball, though it lags behind his other pitches. Hankins controls his arsenal well, but it will be important for him to maintain his delivery as he grows into his large frame.

THE FUTURE: The Indians are confident Hankins' shoulder issues are behind him. If he's able to get back to the level he showed in 2017, he has high-end upside. He'll likely start 2019 with short-season Mahoning Valley.

BILL MITCHELL

BA GRADE
55 Risk: Extreme
Fastball: 60. Slider: 55. Change: 50. CTL: 50.

Year	Club (League)	Class	W	L	ERA	G	GS	CG	SV	IP	H	HR	BB	SO	K/9	WHIP	AVG
2018	Indians 2 (AZL)	R	0	0	6.00	2	2	0	0	3	4	0	0	6	18.0	1.33	.308
Minor League Totals			0	0	6.00	2	2	0	0	3	4	0	0	6	18.0	1.33	.308

11 YU CHANG, SS/3B

BA GRADE
50 Risk: High

Born: Aug. 18, 1995. **B-T:** R-R. **Ht.:** 6-1. **Wt.:** 175. **Signed:** Taiwan, 2013. **Signed by:** Allen Lin/Jayson Lynn.

TRACK RECORD: Chang was a prominent prep player in Taiwan and was one of the top amateur free agents to sign out of Asia in 2013. His profile has risen in the last few seasons as his power has developed and he has reportedly received heavy interest in trade talks.

SCOUTING REPORT: Chang has solid all-around offensive tools, and while he didn't hit 24 home runs again in 2018 like he did the year before, he still had solid production as a 22-year-old in Triple-A. After getting pull-happy in 2017, he got back to using the whole field more effectively. He is a patient hitter, but his willingness to work deep in counts has led to strikeout rates in excess of 25 percent the last two years. Though Chang may not pass the eye test at shortstop, he can make all the plays at the position and is an average defender with average or better speed and arm strength. The Indians this year began to work to increase his versatility, giving him time at both second and third base, and in the Arizona Fall League he exclusively played those positions.

THE FUTURE: Francisco Lindor is entrenched at shortstop in Cleveland and the Indians' next wave of exciting, athletic shortstops is likely to reach the big leagues by the time he reaches free agency. So, while Chang is a capable shortstop, he's unlikely to ever regularly play it in Cleveland. The Indians will have a spring training competition for at least their utility infielder job and possibly one everyday infield role and Chang will be in the mix.

Year	Club (League)	Class	AVG	G	AB	R	H	2B	3B	HR	RBI	BB	SO	SB	CS	OBP	SLG
2016	Lynchburg (CAR)	HiA	.259	109	417	78	108	30	8	13	70	45	110	11	3	.332	.463
2017	Akron (EL)	AA	.220	126	440	72	97	24	5	24	66	52	134	11	4	.312	.461
2018	Columbus (IL)	AAA	.256	127	457	56	117	28	2	13	62	44	144	4	3	.330	.411
Minor League Totals			.251	509	1866	297	468	107	23	65	275	186	519	37	17	.326	.437

12 GABRIEL RODRIGUEZ, SS

BA GRADE
55 Risk: Extreme

Born: Feb. 22, 2002. **B-T:** R-R. **Ht.:** 6-2. **Wt.:** 175. **Signed:** Venezuela, 2018. **Signed by:** Hernan Albornoz.

TRACK RECORD: Rodriguez was the shortstop on Venezuela's 15U national team at the 2016 Pan American Championships and established himself as one of the best hitters in the 2018 international signing class. He was the eighth-ranked player in the class and headlined the Indians' international signings over the summer.

SCOUTING REPORT: Rodriguez stands out for his consistency and all-around tools. He has a short, simple swing and an advanced approach at the plate. As he physically matures, he figures to develop average power and he has already shown the ability to drive balls to all fields. Rodriguez has a bigger frame and he may eventually outgrow shortstop. He has a strong arm and smooth actions that will allow him to stay in the infield, likely at third base, if he needs to move.

THE FUTURE: The Indians have shown a willingness to be aggressive with their top international signings and if Rodriguez follows that path, he'll likely make his professional debut in the Rookie-level Arizona League.

Year	Club (League)	Class	AVG	G	AB	R	H	2B	3B	HR	RBI	BB	SO	SB	CS	OBP	SLG
2018	Did not play—Signed 2019 contract																

13 CARLOS VARGAS, RHP

BA GRADE
55 Risk: Extreme

Born: Oct. 13, 1999. **B-T:** R-R. **Ht.:** 6-3. **Wt.:** 180. **Signed:** Dominican Republic, 2016. **Signed by:** Rafael Espinal.

TRACK RECORD: The Indians' international department went through a transition in 2016 and their biggest signing in that class was Vargas, who signed for just $275,000. Though he wasn't a particularly high-profile prospect at the time, the Indians landed a premium arm. He made his professional debut in 2018 in the Rookie-level Arizona League, where his big arm stood out.

SCOUTING REPORT: Vargas in 2016 had an ultra-projectable frame when he signed as a 17-year old throwing a fastball that reached 93 mph. The anticipated uptick in his velocity has come to pass and his fastball now reaches 100 mph and sits in the upper 90s. His slider sits around 90 mph and is a plus pitch at its best. Vargas has an electric arm and the next stage of his development will be about harnessing his stuff, consistently throwing strikes and developing a third pitch.

THE FUTURE: Vargas is on a similar developmental path as Luis Oviedo, who has delivered positive early returns. If Vargas can harness his stuff, he has as much upside as nearly anyone in the system. He'll follow in 2019 in Oviedo's footsteps at short-season Mahoning Valley.

Year	Club (League)	Class	W	L	ERA	G	GS	CG	SV	IP	H	HR	BB	SO	K/9	WHIP	AVG
2018	Indians 2 (AZL)	R	1	2	3.93	10	9	0	0	34	33	2	24	41	10.7	1.66	.256
Minor League Totals			1	2	3.93	10	9	0	0	34	33	2	24	41	10.7	1.66	.256

14 DANIEL JOHNSON, OF

BA GRADE
50 Risk: High

Born: July 11, 1995. **B-T:** L-L. **HT:** 5-10. **WT:** 185. **Drafted:** New Mexico State, 2016 (5th round). **Signed by:** Mitch Sokol (Nationals).

TRACK RECORD: Johnson has continued to refine his game every year since being drafted in the fifth round in 2016 out of New Mexico State. After a mediocre debut in the New York Penn League in 2016, Johnson had a strong offensive campaign in the South Atlantic and Carolina Leagues in 2017, hitting 22 home runs and stealing 22 bases. The toolsy outfielder had a slow March to start 2018, but began heating up in May and hit .327/.406/.451 during the month before his season was derailed by a broken hamate bone. After the season, the Indians acquired Johnson, Jefry Rodriguez and Andruw Monasterio from the Nationals for Yan Gomes.

SCOUTING REPORT: A fringe-average hitter, Johnson was starting to come into his own offensively before his injury, and scouts believe he has at least above-average raw power thanks to his quick hands and natural strength. While he lost a month of valuable at-bats, the Nationals were excited about the progress that he made in 2018 defensively, improving his jumps, route-running and throwing accuracy. Johnson has 70-grade arm strength and is starting to take advantage of it with better decision making. His plus speed allows him to play every outfield position, though his arm strength makes right field the best fit—and that's where he played the majority of his innings in 2018.

THE FUTURE: A full season of health in the upper minors will give a more clear picture of what sort of offensive player Johnson really is, and with his defensive strides he could wind up debuting at some point late in 2019.

Year	Club (League)	Class	AVG	G	AB	R	H	2B	3B	HR	RBI	BB	SO	SB	CS	OBP	SLG
2016	Auburn (NYP)	SS	.265	62	245	25	65	9	4	1	14	7	42	13	3	.312	.347
2017	Hagerstown (SAL)	LoA	.300	88	327	61	98	16	4	17	52	22	70	12	9	.361	.529
	Potomac (CAR)	HiA	.294	42	170	22	50	13	0	5	20	13	30	10	2	.346	.459
2018	Nationals (GCL)	R	.300	7	20	3	6	0	0	1	4	2	2	1	0	.417	.450
	Harrisburg (EL)	AA	.267	89	356	48	95	19	7	6	31	23	90	21	4	.321	.410
Minor League Totals			.281	288	1118	159	314	57	15	30	121	67	234	57	18	.337	.439

15 AARON CIVALE, RHP

BA GRADE

45 Risk: High

Born: June 12, 1995. **B-T:** R-R. **Ht.:** 6-2. **Wt.:** 215. **Drafted:** Northeastern, 2016 (3rd round). **Signed by:** Mike Kanen.

TRACK RECORD: Civale moved to the rotation as a junior at Northeastern and delivered phenomenal results in 2016, ranking in the top 15 nationally in ERA (1.73), strikeouts (121) and WHIP (0.93). He's taken off since that move and in 2018 reached Double-A Akron. He was sidelined in May for about a month due to a right lat strain but was able to get back on track down the stretch.

SCOUTING REPORT: Civale's above-average control is his best tool, and he also mixes in solid stuff. His fastball sits in the low 90s and his feel for spin enables him to throw a cutter, slider and curveball. His curveball is the best of the group, but they all work well in concert to give the effect of an above-average breaking ball that changes angles and power and about half of his pitches are a breaking ball of some kind. Civale has worked to improve his changeup after not needing it as an amateur.

THE FUTURE: Civale's stuff, size and makeup give him a chance to be a workhorse starter and the Indians have never been eager to return him to the bullpen. But breaking into their rotation is no easy task and the Tribe's need for bullpen help may mean his first chance in the big leagues comes as a reliever. Civale is likely to open the season in the rotation for Triple-A Columbus.

Year	Club (League)	Class	W	L	ERA	G	GS	CG	SV	IP	H	HR	BB	SO	K/9	WHIP	AVG
2016	Mahoning Valley (NYP)	SS	0	2	1.67	13	13	0	0	38	23	0	8	28	6.7	0.82	.180
2017	Lake County (MWL)	LoA	2	4	4.58	10	10	0	0	57	64	2	5	53	8.4	1.21	.284
	Lynchburg (CAR)	HiA	11	2	2.59	17	17	0	0	108	96	11	9	88	7.4	0.98	.238
2018	Akron (EL)	AA	5	7	3.89	21	21	0	0	106	115	12	21	78	6.6	1.28	.276
Minor League Totals			18	15	3.29	61	61	0	0	309	298	25	43	247	7.2	1.10	.254

16 OSCAR MERCADO, OF

BA GRADE

45 Risk: High

Born: Dec. 16, 1994. **B-T:** R-R. **Ht.:** 6-2. **Wt.:** 175. **Drafted:** HS—Tampa, 2013 (2nd round). **Signed by:** Charlie Gonzalez (Cardinals).

TRACK RECORD: Mercado, a native of Colombia, moved to Florida with his family when he was 8 years old and eventually developed into one of the top shortstops in the country. He struggled at the outset of his professional career but got back on track following a full-time move to the outfield in 2017 at Double-A Springfield. He was putting together another solid season the following year when he was dealt to the Indians at the trade deadline in exchange for two minor league outfielders.

SCOUTING REPORT: The Indians liked Mercado's all-around skill set and his ability to fill an organizational need for a righthanded center fielder, because nearly all their upper-level outfielders are lefthanded hitters. Mercado has wiry strength and produces good bat speed. After his strikeout rate spiked in 2017, he did a much better job in 2018 of controlling the strike zone. His average raw power mostly plays as doubles pop and he does a good job of using his plus speed on the bases. His speed also plays well in the outfield, where he covers ground well. He has average arm strength.

THE FUTURE: The Indians entered the offseason with a muddled outfield picture due to potential free agent losses and injuries. No matter how the winter plays out, Mercado figures to compete for a big-league job in spring training, either as a regular or a fourth outfielder.

Year	Club (League)	Class	AVG	G	AB	R	H	2B	3B	HR	RBI	BB	SO	SB	CS	OBP	SLG
2016	Palm Beach (FSL)	HiA	.215	125	442	50	95	23	1	0	27	44	71	33	20	.296	.271
2017	Springfield, MO (TL)	AA	.287	120	477	76	137	20	4	13	46	32	112	38	19	.341	.428
2018	Memphis (PCL)	AAA	.285	100	382	73	109	21	1	8	42	36	64	31	8	.351	.408
	Columbus (IL)	AAA	.252	32	103	12	26	5	1	0	5	13	23	6	4	.342	.320
Minor League Totals			.252	596	2284	340	576	106	15	29	203	185	407	196	81	.317	.350

17 JEAN CARLOS MEJIA, RHP

BA GRADE

50 Risk: Extreme

Born: Aug. 26, 1996. **B-T:** R-R. **Ht.:** 6-4. **Wt.:** 205. **Signed:** Dominican Republic, 2013. **Signed by:** Rafael Espinal/Ramon Pena.

TRACK RECORD: The Indians in 2013 signed Mejia as a 17-year-old out of the Dominican Republic. He started his professional career slowly, spending three years in the Dominican Summer League. He made his U.S. debut in 2017 and started to build some buzz before breaking out in 2018. His performance this year, mostly at low Class A Lake County, led him to be a popular name at the trade deadline and he was eventually added to the 40-man roster to protect him from the Rule 5 draft.

SCOUTING REPORT: Mejia has a big, 6-foot-4 frame with a chance to develop into a solid starting pitcher. His fastball has been up to 96 mph and sits at 93. He has a good feel for spin and his curveball and slider both have plus potential. He also can generate swings-and-misses with his changeup. He pitches with above-average control. With a big frame and a solid four-pitch arsenal that he can throw for strikes, Mejia offers considerable upside. But he is also short on experience. Already 22, he has only started 17 games and thrown 241.1 innings in his career.

THE FUTURE: In 2019 Mejia will look to build on his breakout performance with high Class A Lynchburg. If he does, he should start advancing more quickly and could soon establish himself as one of the Indians' top pitching prospects.

Year	Club (League)	Class	W	L	ERA	G	GS	CG	SV	IP	H	HR	BB	SO	K/9	WHIP	AVG
2016	Indians (DSL)	R	2	4	3.48	17	1	0	5	34	33	0	5	22	5.9	1.13	.239
2017	Indians (AZL)	R	1	0	3.14	10	0	0	6	14	13	0	5	19	11.9	1.26	.228
	Mahoning Valley (NYP)	SS	1	0	0.00	11	0	0	3	23	6	0	5	31	12.3	0.49	.083
2018	Lake County (MWL)	LoA	4	8	3.13	17	15	0	0	92	84	3	20	97	9.5	1.13	.241
	Lynchburg (CAR)	HiA	0	1	6.00	1	1	0	0	6	5	0	1	3	4.5	1.00	.227
Minor League Totals			**15**	**16**	**2.61**	**91**	**17**	**0**	**16**	**241**	**193**	**4**	**63**	**226**	**8.4**	**1.06**	**.215**

18 ERNIE CLEMENT, SS

Born: March 22, 1996. **B-T:** R-R. **Ht.:** 6-0. **Wt.:** 170. **Drafted:** Virginia, 2017 (4th round). **Signed by:** Bob Mayer.

BA GRADE
45 Risk: High

TRACK RECORD: Clement developed a reputation as a pure hitter during college. He was a career .306 hitter at Virginia, whiffed just 31 times in three seasons with the Cavaliers and in 2016 earned MVP honors in the Cape Cod League after leading the circuit in hits and stolen bases. His college success has translated to the professional ranks and Clement zipped through the lower levels of the minor leagues to reach Double-A Akron in his first full professional season.

SCOUTING REPORT: Clement embodies the notion that good things happen when you put the ball in play. He has an aggressive approach and an uncanny knack for putting the bat on the ball. He doesn't walk much, but such is his bat control that this season he still walked more than he struck out (41 walks to 35 strikeouts). He has minimal power and instead sprays the ball all over the field and takes advantage of his plus speed to get on base. Clement was a versatile defender in college but in 2018 exclusively played shortstop. He has above-average instincts defensively and good hands. The biggest concern about his ability to stay at the position is his arm strength, which is fringy for a shortstop.

THE FUTURE: The Indians have toolsier shortstops than Clement and his future in Cleveland is still likely as a super-utility player, where his speed, instincts and bat-to-ball skills would play well. The early returns indicate Clement may still be able to be an everyday player. He'll start 2019 back in Akron as the regular shortstop.

Year	Club (League)	Class	AVG	G	AB	R	H	2B	3B	HR	RBI	BB	SO	SB	CS	OBP	SLG
2017	Mahoning Valley (NYP)	SS	.280	45	175	32	49	9	1	0	13	6	12	6	2	.315	.343
2018	Lake County (MWL)	LoA	.267	54	221	34	59	14	1	1	15	23	21	11	6	.337	.353
	Lynchburg (CAR)	HiA	.346	33	133	29	46	7	0	1	13	15	7	5	3	.425	.421
	Akron (EL)	AA	.246	15	65	9	16	5	1	0	5	3	7	2	1	.279	.354
Minor League Totals			**.286**	**147**	**594**	**104**	**170**	**35**	**3**	**2**	**46**	**47**	**47**	**24**	**12**	**.346**	**.365**

19 AARON BRACHO, SS

Born: April 24, 2001. **B-T:** B-R. **Ht.:** 5-11. **Wt.:** 175. **Signed:** Venezuela, 2017. **Signed by:** Hernan Albornoz/Rafael Cariel.

BA GRADE
50 Risk: Extreme

TRACK RECORD: Bracho, the 17th ranked player in the overall class, joined George Valera in headlining the Indians' 2017 international signees. Like Valera, Bracho in 2018 was sidelined by injury, in his case a right arm injury.

SCOUTING REPORT: Bracho stood out for his offensive performance in games before signing. He is a switch-hitter with a mature approach and a smooth, compact swing from both sides of the plate. He has good bat speed, helping him produce a surprising amount of power for his size that could develop into average pop. Bracho was signed as a shortstop and will get a chance to develop there, but many scouts are not convinced he will stay at the position. He is an above-average runner and has good hands, but his infield actions and arm strength will likely profile better at second base. The silver lining of his injury is that Bracho is throwing better since getting healthy.

THE FUTURE: Being sidelined for a year also gave Bracho a chance to grow off the field, an important development for any teenager. He is in line to make his professional debut in 2019.

Year	Club (League)	Class	AVG	G	AB	R	H	2B	3B	HR	RBI	BB	SO	SB	CS	OBP	SLG
2017	Did not play—Signed 2018 contact																
2018	Did not play—Injured																

20 LENNY TORRES, RHP

BA GRADE

50 Risk: Extreme

Born: Oct. 15, 2000. **B-T:** R-R. **Ht.:** 6-1. **Wt.:** 190. **Drafted:** HS—Beacon, N.Y., 2018 (1st round supplemental). **Signed by:** Mike Kanen.

TRACK RECORD: Torres, a New York City native, didn't pitch much growing up but after starting to focus on it in the last few years quickly showed big upside on the mound. The Indians made him the 41st overall pick the following June and he made a smooth transition to pro ball, excelling in the Rookie-level Arizona League.

SCOUTING REPORT: Torres doesn't have a big frame at a listed 6-foot-1, but he has a quick arm and can run his fastball up to 97 mph. His fastball typically sits 94 mph and he pairs it with a slider that has plus potential. He is working to implement a changeup, which at its best has hard downer action, but is still a work in progress. His control is also an area of focus, though he surprised with his strike-throwing ability during his debut.

THE FUTURE: Before the draft, Torres faced lots of questions about whether he could be a starter in pro ball because of his size and lack of a third pitch. The Indians are optimistic that he'll be able to take the necessary developmental steps to start thanks to his athleticism, youth and relative inexperience on the mound. The early returns were good, and Torres will look to build on them in 2019 as he advances to short-season Mahoning Valley.

Year	Club (League)	Class	W	L	ERA	G	GS	CG	SV	IP	H	HR	BB	SO	K/9	WHIP	AVG
2018	Indians 2 (AZL)	R	0	0	1.76	6	5	0	0	15	14	0	4	22	12.9	1.17	.246
Minor League Totals			0	0	1.76	6	5	0	0	15	14	0	4	22	12.9	1.17	.246

21 WILL BENSON, OF

BA GRADE

50 Risk: Extreme

Born: June 16, 1998. **B-T:** L-L. **Ht.:** 6-5. **Wt.:** 215. **Drafted:** HS—Atlanta, 2016 (1st round). **Signed by:** C.T. Bradford.

TRACK RECORD: Benson was a highly-touted player in 2016 coming out of the Atlanta prep ranks and has long stood out for his big tools, especially his power. Both the good and bad in his game has been exposed in the minor leagues, most starkly in 2018 when he reached full-season ball for the first time.

SCOUTING REPORT: Benson produces exceptional bat speed thanks to his strength and quick hands and turns that bat speed into tremendous lefthanded raw power, rivaling Bobby Bradley for the best in the system. That power helped Benson hit 22 home runs to lead the Midwest League. It also comes with a hefty amount of swing-and-miss, however, and he whiffed in 30 percent of his plate appearances. Benson has a patient, bordering on passive, approach at the plate. He ranked third in the league in walks (82) but he also often works deep in counts, contributing to his high strikeout rate. While he may just be on his way to becoming a three true outcome player, Benson's athleticism and peripheral numbers—especially a low BABIP and consistently high exit velocities—provide optimism if he can make necessary adjustments at the plate to become more consistent and hit more line drives. He profiles well in right field thanks to his plus arm and solid speed that plays better underway.

THE FUTURE: Benson won't turn 21 until June but he is eventually going to have to demonstrate more hittability to reach his considerable ceiling. He'll try to take steps toward that in 2019 as he advances to high Class A Lynchburg.

Year	Club (League)	Class	AVG	G	AB	R	H	2B	3B	HR	RBI	BB	SO	SB	CS	OBP	SLG
2016	Indians (AZL)	R	.215	44	158	31	34	10	3	6	27	22	60	10	2	.326	.430
2017	Mahoning Valley (NYP)SS		.238	56	202	29	48	8	5	10	36	31	80	7	1	.347	.475
2018	Lake County (MWL)	LoA	.180	123	416	54	75	11	1	22	58	82	152	12	6	.324	.370
Minor League Totals			.202	223	776	114	157	29	9	38	121	135	292	29	9	.330	.410

22 OSCAR GONZALEZ, OF

BA GRADE

45 Risk: High

Born: Jan. 10, 1998. **B-T:** R-R. **Ht.:** 6-2. **Wt.:** 180. **Signed:** Dominican Republic, 2014. **Signed by:** Ramon Pena/Felix Nivar.

TRACK RECORD: Gonzalez, the Indians' top target in the 2014 international class, made a resounding U.S. debut in 2016, when he won MVP honors in the Arizona League. He reached full-season ball in 2018 with low Class A Lake County, where he produced a solid season.

SCOUTING REPORT: Gonzalez stands out most for his well above-average raw power, and he does a good job of getting to it in games. He is very aggressive at the plate and he'll need to improve his plate discipline as he advances, but his bat-to-ball skills are better than his strikeout rate (22.3 percent) indicates and he ranked fifth in the Midwest League in hits (135). Gonzalez is an average runner and has plus arm strength, giving him a chance to play right field, though he has mostly played left field since leaving the Dominican

Summer League, partially in deference to Will Benson.

THE FUTURE: Whatever outfield corner Gonzalez ends up in, it will be up to his bat to push him through the minor leagues. He will advance in 2019 to high Class A Lynchburg, where he and Benson will again be paired together.

Year	Club (League)	Class	AVG	G	AB	R	H	2B	3B	HR	RBI	BB	SO	SB	CS	OBP	SLG
2016	Indians (AZL)	R	.303	40	145	30	44	10	2	8	26	8	57	4	0	.342	.566
	Mahoning Valley (NYP)	SS	.000	1	3	0	0	0	0	0	0	1	1	0	0	.250	.000
2017	Mahoning Valley (NYP)	SS	.283	55	237	20	67	16	0	3	34	5	61	0	0	.301	.388
2018	Lake County (MWL)	LoA	.292	114	462	52	135	25	1	13	52	12	107	5	6	.310	.435
Minor League Totals			.270	280	1103	127	298	68	4	28	150	45	291	10	9	.301	.415

23 RAYNEL DELGADO, SS

BA GRADE

50 Risk: Extreme

Born: April 4, 2000. **B-T:** B-R. **Ht.:** 6-2. **Wt.:** 185. **Drafted:** HS—Fort Lauderdale, 2018 (6th round). **Signed by:** Andrew Krause.

TRACK RECORD: Delgado was born in Cuba and came to the United States with his mother as a 7-year-old. He developed into one of the top infielders in the country and in 2017 played for USA Baseball's 18U national team that won the gold medal at the World Cup, beating the Cuban national team along the way. He slipped the next June to the sixth round, but the Indians signed him to an above-slot bonus of $900,000.

SCOUTING REPORT: Delgado is more advanced from both sides than many young switch-hitters and he has a long track record of hitting against strong competition. He has a solid swing and a calm approach that served him well as he transitioned to pro ball. He has above-average power potential, especially as he fills out his 6-foot-2 frame. Delgado doesn't jump out as much defensively but is still solid in the infield. His advanced instincts help his tools play up and his hands and infield actions work well. He split time between shortstop, second and third base, and the development of his athleticism and arm strength will determine where he settles.

THE FUTURE: The Indians have a crowded shortstop depth chart in the lower levels of their system and that may mean Delgado moves off the position sooner than later so that they can keep challenging him offensively. He'll advance in 2019 to short-season Mahoning Valley, where he'll probably continue moving around the infield.

Year	Club (League)	Class	AVG	G	AB	R	H	2B	3B	HR	RBI	BB	SO	SB	CS	OBP	SLG
2018	Indians 2 (AZL)	R	.306	46	173	34	53	10	0	1	21	30	44	10	2	.409	.382
Minor League Totals			.306	46	173	34	53	10	0	1	21	30	44	10	2	.409	.382

24 NICK SANDLIN, RHP

BA GRADE

45 Risk: High

Born: Jan. 11, 1997. **B-T:** R-R. **Ht.:** 5-11. **Wt.:** 175. **Drafted:** Southern Mississippi, 2018 (2nd round). **Signed by:** Chuck Bartlett.

TRACK RECORD: In 2018, Sandlin moved from closing to the front of Southern Mississippi's rotation with great success and won the nation's ERA title (1.06). His All-American season sent him shooting up draft boards despite his unusual profile. His ascension continued in pro ball and he pitched at four levels after signing, finishing the season with Double-A Akron.

SCOUTING REPORT: Listed at 5-foot-11, 175 pounds, Sandlin is undersized and typically throws from a sidearm slot, though he'll also raise it to more of a three-quarters look. In 2018, he showed the ability to hold his stuff deep in games and proved effective against righties and lefties. His fastball sits in the low 90s with plenty of run and sink. He can manipulate his slider to make it a big, wipeout pitch or to land it for a strike. His changeup isn't as good as his sinker-slider combination, but it is a viable third offering. He has above-average command and stands out for his athleticism.

THE FUTURE: Sandlin has tremendous feel for pitching and made a compelling case that he can be a starter, although he pitched exclusively out of the bullpen after signing, in part to limit his workload after he threw 102 innings for Southern Miss. As a reliever, he'll likely soon be in the big leagues. Even if he goes back to starting, his rise won't be dramatically slowed because he's already shown he can handle advanced competition.

Year	Club (League)	Class	W	L	ERA	G	GS	CG	SV	IP	H	HR	BB	SO	K/9	WHIP	AVG
2018	Indians 1 (AZL)	R	0	0	0.00	3	0	0	0	3	2	0	0	4	12.0	0.67	.200
	Lake County (MWL)	LoA	0	0	1.74	10	0	0	1	10	9	0	0	15	13.1	0.87	.237
	Lynchburg (CAR)	HiA	1	0	1.42	7	0	0	4	6	2	0	2	10	14.2	0.63	.091
	Akron (EL)	AA	1	0	10.38	5	0	0	0	4	8	0	1	7	14.5	2.08	.400
Minor League Totals			2	0	3.00	25	0	0	5	24	21	0	3	36	13.5	1.00	.233

25 ERIC HAASE, C

BA GRADE

40 Risk: Medium

Born: Dec. 18, 1992. **B-T:** R-R. **Ht.:** 5-10. **Wt.:** 180. **Drafted:** HS—Dearborn, Mich., 2011 (7th round). **Signed by:** Junie Melendez.

TRACK RECORD: The Indians went over slot to sign Haase in 2011 but he looked to be more org player than prospect much of his professional career. He challenged that evaluation with a breakout 2017 season with Double-A Akron. In 2018, he hit 20 home runs with Triple-A Columbus and was rewarded with a September callup to make his big league debut at 25.

SCOUTING REPORT: Haase had long shown strength in his swing but after the 2016 season made some changes to improve his launch angle. His power comes with a hefty amount of swing and miss, but his strikeout rate of 30 percent has remained steady. Haase caught a career-high 90 games in 2018 because he was able to stay healthy and was decoupled from Francisco Mejia, with whom he often shared catching duties. He earns praise for his receiving and has solid arm strength.

THE FUTURE: The Indians in July traded Mejia, relieving their catching logjam in the upper levels. The trade of Yan Gomes to the Nationals gives Haase a better shot at playing time in Cleveland in 2019.

Year	Club (League)	Class	AVG	G	AB	R	H	2B	3B	HR	RBI	BB	SO	SB	CS	OBP	SLG
2016	Akron (EL)	AA	.208	63	226	28	47	14	1	12	33	17	75	0	2	.265	.438
2017	Akron (EL)	AA	.258	95	333	59	86	17	5	26	59	44	116	4	2	.349	.574
	Columbus (IL)	AAA	.333	2	6	1	2	0	0	1	2	1	2	0	0	.500	.833
2018	Columbus (IL)	AAA	.236	120	433	54	102	24	3	20	71	31	143	3	1	.288	.443
	Cleveland (AL)	MAJ	.125	9	16	0	2	0	0	0	1	0	6	0	0	.176	.125
Major League Totals			.125	9	16	0	2	0	0	0	1	0	6	0	0	.176	.125
Minor League Totals			.246	602	2179	308	535	135	25	102	339	209	704	14	12	.316	.471

26 JUNIOR SANQUINTIN, SS

BA GRADE

50 Risk: Extreme

Born: Jan. 8, 2002. **B-T:** B-R. **Ht.:** 6-0. **Wt.:** 185. **Signed:** Dominican Republic, 2018. **Signed by:** Rigoberto De Los Santos/Jhonathan Leyba.

TRACK RECORD: Sanquintin grew up playing against older competition in his native Dominican Republic. Ranked No. 21 in the 2018 international class, he signed in July with the Indians.

SCOUTING REPORT: Sanquintin is a switch-hitter who produces plenty of bat speed. The Indians bring their international free agents to Progressive Field, where they take batting practice and are honored. Sanquintin put on a show, consistently driving balls out to the opposite field from both sides of the plate. His above-average raw power comes with some swing-and-miss and he's an aggressive hitter. He has a good feel for the barrel and more hittability than his profile suggests. Sanquintin was signed as a shortstop but most evaluators expect he will move off the position sooner than later. If he can smooth out some rough edges defensively, he would profile at third base, though some believe he's destined for an outfield corner.

THE FUTURE: Sanquintin will make his professional debut in 2018 and with his advanced offensive skills, he figures to advance to the Rookie-level Arizona League.

Year	Club (League)	Class	AVG	G	AB	R	H	2B	3B	HR	RBI	BB	SO	SB	CS	OBP	SLG
2018	Did not play—Signed 2019 contract																

27 QUENTIN HOLMES, OF

BA GRADE

50 Risk: Extreme

Born: July 7, 1999. **B-T:** R-R. **Ht.:** 6-3. **Wt.:** 175. **Drafted:** HS—East Elmhurst, N.Y., 2017 (2nd round). **Signed by:** Mike Kanen.

TRACK RECORD: Holmes starred on the showcase circuit in the summer of 2016, establishing himself as one of the best athletes in the draft class. But he fell to the back of the second round, where the Indians were happy to take a player with his upside. His professional career has started slowly and 2018 amounted to a lost summer due to a hamstring injury that sidelined him for all but seven games.

SCOUTING REPORT: Holmes' game is geared around his top-of-the-scale speed. His feel for the barrel helps him shoot balls into the gaps before letting his speed take over. But he also generates good bat speed and can hit for power, especially when he turns on the ball. His speed helps him cover lots of ground in center field, where he could develop into a plus defender.

THE FUTURE: Holmes was young for his class, which in some ways lessens the impact of his lost summer. He just needs to get game reps, which he'll likely do in 2019 with short-season Mahoning Valley.

Year	Club (League)	Class	AVG	G	AB	R	H	2B	3B	HR	RBI	BB	SO	SB	CS	OBP	SLG
2017	Indians (AZL)	R	.182	41	159	22	29	5	3	2	15	8	61	5	4	.220	.289
2018	Indians 1 (AZL)	R	.000	1	2	0	0	0	0	0	0	0	1	0	0	.000	.000
	Indians 2 (AZL)	R	.158	6	19	5	3	1	0	0	1	4	7	2	1	.304	.211
Minor League Totals			.178	48	180	27	32	6	3	2	16	12	69	7	5	.228	.278

28 RICHIE PALACIOS, 2B

Born: May 16, 1997. **B-T:** L-R. **Ht.:** 5-11. **Wt.:** 180. **Drafted:** Towson, 2018 (3rd round). **Signed by:** Aaron Etchison.

BA GRADE

45 Risk: High

TRACK RECORD: Palacios had a decorated college career at Towson. Drafted in the third round, he followed the footsteps of his uncle, Rey, and older brother, Joshua, into pro ball and had a solid debut.
SCOUTING REPORT: Palacios has a good feel for the barrel and produces excellent bat speed. He worked this spring to cut down on his strikeouts and hit the ball the other way more often. He improved in both areas, while getting to his average power more frequently. He's a good athlete and a plus runner. Palacios has a high ceiling offensively, but questions remain about his defense. He played shortstop for Towson, but his infield actions and arm strength are not good enough to stay there. His athleticism and work ethic may help him stay in the infield at second base, but his speed would also play well in the outfield.
THE FUTURE: Wherever Palacios ends up defensively, he'll likely always be bat over glove. He's advanced enough to handle an assignment to high Class A Lynchburg, where he'll continue to work on his defense.

Year	Club (League)	Class	AVG	G	AB	R	H	2B	3B	HR	RBI	BB	SO	SB	CS	OBP	SLG
2018	Indians 1 (AZL)	R	.438	5	16	4	7	1	0	2	6	6	2	2	0	.591	.875
	Mahoning Valley (NYP)	SS	.411	20	73	12	30	5	1	2	17	11	12	2	1	.477	.589
	Lake County (MWL)	LoA	.300	20	80	10	24	2	1	2	7	2	13	3	0	.317	.425
Minor League Totals			.361	45	169	26	61	8	2	6	30	19	27	7	1	.421	.538

29 JOHNATHAN RODRIGUEZ, OF

Born: Nov. 4, 1999. **B-T:** B-R. **Ht.:** 6-3. **Wt.:** 180. **Drafted:** HS—Florida, P.R., 2017 (3rd round). **Signed by:** Juan Alvarez.

BA GRADE

50 Risk: Extreme

TRACK RECORD: Rodriguez was one of the youngest players in the 2017 draft class. He is more of a long-term developmental bet, but adjusted faster to professional baseball than some had expected.
SCOUTING REPORT: Rodriguez, a switch-hitter, has a smooth swing and showed he has some feel for the strike zone. He has plus raw power and projects to hit for power as he fills out his projectable frame. While his power hasn't translated into many home runs in pro ball, he has driven the ball well into gaps and played all season as an 18-year-old. Rodriguez has below-average speed, but his plus arm plays well in right field, where he can be a solid defender.
THE FUTURE: Rodriguez's age has allowed the Indians to take a conservative approach in his development and he'll still reach short-season Mahoning Valley in 2019 as a 19-year-old. He is raw, but he has the tools and work ethic to, in time, develop into a prototypical right fielder.

Year	Club (League)	Class	AVG	G	AB	R	H	2B	3B	HR	RBI	BB	SO	SB	CS	OBP	SLG
2017	Indians (AZL)	R	.250	31	96	13	24	4	2	0	11	21	23	0	1	.381	.333
2018	Indians 1 (AZL)	R	.294	47	187	36	55	10	4	1	22	22	44	8	3	.370	.406
Minor League Totals			.279	78	283	49	79	14	6	1	33	43	67	8	4	.374	.382

30 KIRK McCARTY, LHP

Born: Oct. 12, 1995. **B-T:** L-L. **Ht.:** 5-10. **Wt.:** 185. **Drafted:** Southern Mississippi, 2017 (7th round). **Signed by:** Chuck Bartlett.

BA GRADE

45 Risk: High

TRACK RECORD: McCarty had a prolific high school career and went on to have a strong career at Southern Mississippi. The Indians drafted him in the seventh round in 2017. He had a breakout 2018 and led all Indians minor leaguers with 161 strikeouts.
SCOUTING REPORT: At a listed 5-foot-10, 180 pounds, McCarty isn't imposing on the mound and was viewed more as a pitchability lefty coming out of college. The Indians helped him boost his fastball from the upper 80s into the low 90s with riding life by encouraging him to pitch more off his four-seamer. He has a refined four-pitch arsenal with a bigger curveball, a tight slider and a changeup that he disguises well. His secondary offerings are all solid and they play well off each other. He has above-average control and does a good job throwing his fastball to both sides of the plate.
THE FUTURE: McCarty has taken a step forward and opened some eyes with his performance in 2018. He'll face a challenge when he advances to Double-A Akron, but he has all the tools to be a solid back-of-the-rotation starter.

Year	Club (League)	Class	W	L	ERA	G	GS	CG	SV	IP	H	HR	BB	SO	K/9	WHIP	AVG
2017	Mahoning Valley (NYP)	SS	2	2	1.85	13	6	0	0	34	27	3	10	33	8.7	1.09	.213
2018	Lake County (MWL)	LoA	4	9	4.29	22	22	0	0	115	120	14	34	132	10.3	1.34	.270
	Lynchburg (CAR)	HiA	1	2	3.19	5	5	0	0	31	26	2	4	29	8.4	0.97	.234
Minor League Totals			7	13	3.64	40	33	0	0	180	173	19	48	194	9.7	1.23	.253

Colorado Rockies

BY TRACY RINGOLSBY

The Rockies are coming off back-to-back postseason appearances for the first time in franchise history. They finished the 162-game schedule in 2018 tied with the Dodgers for first place in the National League West, only to have their hopes for the first division title in franchise history fall apart when they lost Game 163 to the Dodgers.

And the Rockies did it the old-fashioned way by building from within. True, Colorado spent money on free agents, plugging the holes that were visible last offseason.

The core of the team, however, was developed from within, an exclamation point on the way

the scouting department, under Bill Schmidt, and farm department, under Zach Wilson, have worked together in recent years. The Rockies had 12 homegrown players on their postseason roster—the most of any of the 10 teams that advanced into October.

That included six pitchers combining to start 162 of their 163 regular season games, five of whom originally signed with the Rockies. They relied on first-round picks Kyle Freeland (2014), Tyler Anderson (2011) and Jon Gray (2013); 2010 second-rounder Chad Bettis, Venezuelan signee Antonio Senzatela and German Marquez, who arrived in a trade with the Rays and spent a year in the Rockies' farm system. They joined a rotation that led all NL tams in innings.

And there is more where they came from. Righthanders Peter Lambert and Ryan Castellani could be ready by midseason 2019 if not sooner.

The Rockies' lineup was anchored by draft choices Nolan Arenado at third base, Trevor Story at shortstop, Charlie Blackmon in center field, and Chris Iannetta behind the plate, albeit after a career path that took him from Colorado to the Angels, Mariners and Diamondbacks before returning to the Rockies.

While the Rockies' offseason focus was to try and beef up the offense, it is not out of the question that seven of the eight regular spots in the lineup could be filled by homegrown hitters.

Ian Desmond, a December 2016 free agent signee, could wind up at first base or in left field, but he would be the exception to the possibility of Iannetta, Story, Arenado and Blackmon being joined on Opening Day by Ryan McMahon at first base, Garrett Hampson at second base and David Dahl in center field, with Blackmon moving to right.

And that's without the likes of Arenado's cousin, third baseman Josh Fuentes, who was the MVP and rookie of the year in the Triple-A Pacific

Drafted eighth overall in 2014, Kyle Freeland developed into the Rockies' ace in 2018.

PROJECTED 2022 LINEUP

Catcher	Tom Murphy (31)
First Base	Tyler Nevin (25)
Second Base	Brendan Rodgers (25)
Third Base	Nolan Arenado (31)
Shortstop	Trevor Story (29)
Left Field	Charlie Blackmon (35)
Center Field	David Dahl (28)
Right Field	Ryan McMahon (27)
No. 1 Starter	Kyle Freeland (29)
No. 2 Starter	German Marquez (27)
No. 3 Starter	Jon Gray (30)
No. 4 Starter	Antonio Senzatela (27)
No. 5 Starter	Peter Lambert (25)
Closer	Jesus Tinoco (27)

Coast League. Shortstop Brendan Rodgers, the organization's top prospect for the second year in a row, is ticketed for Triple-A Albuquerque but could force the issue at some point in the spring or early summer.

The Rockies' success in 2017 and 2018 is the product of homegrown pitchers, who take pitching in Coors Field as a challenge, not a fear. They live with their curveballs, understanding that the ball might not break as sharply at altitude as it does at sea level. Yet the curveball is effective in any context because its lower velocity (than a slider) upsets batters' timing while also benefitting from the element of surprise. That makes the prospect of a return to the postseason a distinct possibility.

DUSTIN BRADFORD/GETTY IMAGES

COLORADO ROCKIES

TOP 2019 ROOKIE: Garrett Hampson, 2B. Versatility and speed showed up in brief big league opportunity in 2018.
BREAKOUT PROSPECT: Mike Nikorak, RHP. After missing 16 months with Tommy John surgery, he returned to the mound in August and showed signs of being ready to move quickly.
SLEEPER: Eddy Diaz, SS: The Rockies' first Cuban signee is a teenager with explosive athleticism, plus-plus speed, hitting ability and plate discipline.

SOURCE OF TOP 30 TALENT			
Homegrown	29	Acquired	1
College	14	Trades	1
Junior college	2	Rule 5 draft	0
High school	9	Independent leagues	0
Nondrafted free agents	1	Free agents/waivers	0
International	3		

LF
Daniel Montana (21)
Vince Fernandez (24)
Will Goslan
Walking Cabrera

CF
Yonathan Daza (19)
Wes Rogers
Mylz Jones

RF
Sam Hilliard (10)
Niko Decolati (29)

3B
Colton Welker (4)
Josh Fuentes (12)
Coco Montes

SS
Brendan Rodgers (1)
Ryan Vilade (9)
Terrin Vavra (14)
Eddy Diaz

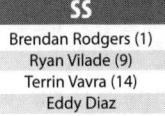

2B
Garrett Hampson (2)
Bret Boswell (28)

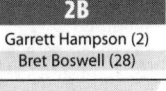

1B
Grant Lavigne (5)
Tyler Nevin (6)
Brian Mundell (25)
Roberto Ramos (27)
Daniel Jipping

C
Willie MacIver (30)
Tom Murphy
Dom Nunez

LHP
LHSP	LHRP
Ryan Rolison (7)	Ben Bowden (17)
Breiling Eusebio (26)	Mitch Horacek

RHP
RHSP	RHRP
Peter Lambert (3)	Jesus Tinoco (13)
Riley Pint (8)	Robert Tyler (18)
Ryan Castellani (11)	Justin Lawrence (15)
Ryan Feltner (20)	Reid Humphreys (16)
Rico Garcia (22)	Tommy Doyle
Mike Nikorak (23)	Logan Cozart
Will Gaddis	Hayden Roberts
Antonio Santos.	Tommy Doyle

DRAFT ANALYSIS

2018

BEST PURE HITTER: 1B Grant LaVigne (1s) was a risky pick as a high school first baseman out of New Hampshire, but the Rockies loved the big lefthander's feel to hit and hit with power.

BEST POWER: Both Lavigne and OF Niko Decolati (6) have plus raw power. Lavigne homered six times with Grand Junction in 59 games, while Decolati hit .327/.414/.532 with 11 home runs in 69 games with the same team after hitting six with Loyola Marymount as a junior in college.

FASTEST RUNNER: Decolati is a plus runner, as is OF Luke Morgan (20). Decolati went 17-for-22 (77 percent) in stolen base attempts in rookie ball this summer, while Morgan went 16-for-19 (84 percent) with Boise in the Northwest League.

BEST DEFENSIVE PLAYER: SS Terrin Vavra (3) stood out more for his offensive production in college, but the Rockies were impressed with his defensive ability up the middle. Vavra split time at shortstop and second base in the Northwest League, and likely fits better at the keystone moving forward, but he is solid at both spots.

BEST ATHLETE: Decolati is tooled up with plus power and speed, but also brings an athleticism that will help him on the bases, in the batter's box and as he transitions to the outfield with Colorado.

BEST FASTBALL: RHP Ryan Feltner (4) has run his fastball up to 97 mph in the past but was mostly in the 90-95 mph range. RHP Shelby Lackey (18) saw a bit more velocity out of the bullpen, reaching back for 96-97 mph regularly working out of a relief role.

BEST SECONDARY PITCH: LHP Ryan Rolison (1) was one of the top college lefthanders in the 2018 draft class and was the first player of that demographic selected when the Rockies called his name at No. 22. Rolison throws an above-average curveball that routinely generated whiffs, and the pitch plays up with Rolison's crossfire delivery.

TOP DRAFT PICKS OF THE DECADE

Year	Player, Pos.	2018 Org
2009	Tyler Matzek, LHP	American Association
2010	Kyle Parker, OF	Did not play
2011	Tyler Anderson, LHP	Rockies
2012	David Dahl, OF	Rockies
2013	Jon Gray, RHP	Rockies
2014	Kyle Freeland, LHP	Rockies
2015	Brendan Rodgers, SS	Rockies
2016	Riley Pint, RHP	Rockies
2017	Ryan Vilade, 3B (2nd round)	Rockies
2018	Ryan Rolison, LHP	Rockies

BEST PRO DEBUT: Lavigne finished second in the Pioneer League with a .481 on-base percentage and showed that he could more than hold his own against low-level minor league arms.

MOST INTRIGUING BACKGROUND: Vavra's father Joe was drafted by the Dodgers in the eighth round in 1982 and played five seasons in the minors, reaching Triple-A. Vavra then became the coach of the GCL Dodgers, served as a minor league field coordinator for both the Dodgers and Twins and also served as a hitting coach with Minnesota. He is currently a quality assurance coach with the Tigers.

CLOSEST TO THE MAJORS: Rolison has two years of solid track record in the SEC, impressive strike-throwing ability and a solid three-pitch mix that should allow him to move quickly.

BEST LATE-ROUND PICK: SS Coco Montes (15) was named the MVP of the Pioneer League after hitting .333/.413/.513 with eight home runs while logging time at second base, shortstop and third.

THE ONE WHO GOT AWAY: The Rockies knew they weren't going to sign RHP Kumar Rocker (38), as the physical pitcher could have easily gone in the first round. Rocker will take his three-pitch repertoire of plus offerings to Vanderbilt.

—CARLOS COLLAZO

2017

The this class got off to a slow start in pro ball. 3B Ryan Vilade (2) has the most upside of the group. OF Casey Golden (20) in 2018 won South Atlantic League MVP, though he was old for the level.

GRADE: D

2016

While RHP Riley Pint (1) had a disappointing, injury-plagued season, SS Garret Hampson (3) made his big league debut and was a part of the Rockies' post-season roster. 3B Colton Welker provides solid upside.

GRADE: B

2015

SS Brendan Rodgers (1) has lived up to expectations and has developed into one of the game's best prospects. Fellow prep draftees 3B Tyler Nevin (1s) and RHP Peter Lambert (2) are also making strong progress.

GRADE: B

1 BRENDAN RODGERS, SS/2B

Born: Aug. 9, 1996. **B-T:** R-R. **HT:** 6-0. **WT.:** 185.
Drafted: HS—Lake Mary, Fla., 2015 (1st round).
Signed by: John Cedarburg

Just what the Rockies think of Rodgers is as obvious as the franchise-record $5.5 million bonus he received after being selected third overall in the 2015 draft, behind shortstops Dansby Swanson and Alex Bregman. They both came out of college and have made the big leagues. Rodgers, a high school sign, is now on the verge of getting his own opportunity at the highest level. Selected to play in the Futures Game in 2018, he was promoted late in the season to Triple-A Albuquerque. He struggled there not only with shoulder tightness, but also a slight hamstring issue, which led to the Rockies deciding against a plan to send him to the Arizona Fall League.

SCOUTING REPORT: Rodgers has worked to maintain consistency with the lower half of his body when he is hitting, helping him improve his ability to stay on breaking pitches, which at each level become more challenging because the pitchers are more refined. He is an active hitter, who is in attack mode, and his brief time in Triple-A underscored to him that veteran pitchers will exploit that aggressiveness with their mixture of pitches. Still, he shows the potential to be a plus hitter with above-average power. He was drafted as a shortstop and has shown the ability to remain at that position. The Rockies, however, in their organizational approach, also worked him at second base in his first three years, and in 2018 added third base as an option. He has shown an aptitude for all three thanks to above-average range and a plus arm. Crucially, he has recognized the importance of defense, which wasn't as big an issue in high school when he was such a dominant hitter. There is a growing feeling that he could wind up being a shortstop, though second or third base could provide a quick promotion in light of the recent loss of DJ LeMahieu to free agency, not to mention third baseman Nolan Arenado's potential free agency following the 2019 season.

THE FUTURE: Given his power, Rodgers will be a plus offensive weapon as a middle infielder. He has shown the ability to adapt to the higher quality of pitching at each level, getting an education in his brief exposure at Albuquerque. Veteran pitchers at Triple-A have more thorough scouting reports on how to attack hitters and sharper pitches that will require ongoing adjustment by Rodgers.

TOMASSO DeROSA

BA GRADE	SCOUTING GRADES
60 Risk: Medium	Hit: 60. Power: 55. Run: 50. Field: 55. Arm: 60.

Projected future grades on 20-80 scouting scale

TOP PROSPECTS OF THE DECADE

Year	Player, Pos.	2018 Org
2009	Dexter Fowler, OF	Cardinals
2010	Tyler Matzek, LHP	American Association
2011	Tyler Matzek, LHP	American Association
2012	Drew Pomeranz, LHP	Red Sox
2013	Nolan Arenado, 3B	Rockies
2014	Jon Gray, RHP	Rockies
2015	David Dahl, OF	Rockies
2016	Jon Gray, RHP	Rockies
2017	Brendan Rodgers, SS	Rockies
2018	Brendan Rodgers, SS	Rockies

BEST TOOLS

Best Hitter for Average	Colton Welker
Best Power Hitter	Roberto Ramos
Best Strike-Zone Discipline	Grant Lavigne
Fastest Baserunner	Garrett Hampson
Best Athlete	Garrett Hampson
Best Fastball	Riley Pint
Best Curveball	Riley Pint
Best Slider	Ryan Castellani
Best Changeup	Peter Lambert
Best Control	Peter Lambert
Best Defensive Catcher	Dom Nunez
Best Defensive Infielder	Brendan Rodgers
Best Infield Arm	Colton Welker
Best Defensive Outfielder	Yonathan Daza
Best Outfield Arm	Yonathan Daza

Year	Club (League)	Class	AVG	G	AB	R	H	2B	3B	HR	RBI	BB	SO	SB	CS	OBP	SLG
2016	Asheville (SAL)	LoA	.281	110	442	73	124	31	0	19	73	35	98	6	3	.342	.480
2017	Hartford (EL)	AA	.260	38	150	20	39	5	0	6	17	8	36	0	2	.323	.413
	Lancaster (CAL)	HiA	.383	51	222	44	85	21	3	12	46	6	35	2	1	.403	.667
2018	Hartford (EL)	AA	.275	95	357	49	98	23	2	17	62	30	76	12	3	.342	.493
	Albuquerque (PCL)	AAA	.232	19	69	5	16	4	0	0	5	1	16	0	0	.264	.290
Minor League Totals			.290	350	1383	213	401	92	7	57	223	95	298	24	12	.345	.490

2 GARRETT HAMPSON, 2B/SS

Born: Oct. 10, 1994. **B-T:** R-R. **HT:** 5-11. **WT:** 185. **Drafted:** Long Beach State, 2016 (3rd round). **Signed by:** Matt Hattabaugh.

TRACK RECORD: Hampson gets lost in the shuffle with the likes of shortstops Brendan Rodgers and third baseman Colton Welker in the organization, but what can't be overlooked is that Hampson made his big league debut in just his third pro season and was part of the Rockies' postseason roster. He has hit .300 at each stop in the minor leagues, skipping low Class A and spending just two months at Double-A in his rise to the Rockies.

SCOUTING REPORT: Hampson's plus speed and consistency in making contact are the foundation for his success. He has struck out just 15 percent of the time in his minor league career, despite being fast-tracked to the big leagues, and has hit a composite .317 in his three minor league stops. His arm is best suited for second base and center field, but he is an alternative when a need arises at shortstop. He will unload an occasional home run, but his well below-average power is a sidelight to his game. His offensive approach is to hit the ball on the ground or on a line, trying to avoid lazy fly balls.

BA GRADE

50 Risk: Medium

Hit: 55. **Power:** 40.
Run: 60. **Field:** 50.
Arm: 50

THE FUTURE: Versatility is a key for Hampson. Signed as a shortstop, he has been most comfortable at second base, but also has shown the skills to play center field. The infield depth in Colorado's system makes his ability to play multiple positions critical.

Year	Club (League)	Class	AVG	G	AB	R	H	2B	3B	HR	RBI	BB	SO	SB	CS	OBP	SLG
2016	Boise (NWL)	SS	.301	68	256	43	77	14	8	2	44	48	56	36	4	.404	.441
2017	Lancaster (CAL)	HiA	.326	127	533	113	174	24	12	8	70	56	77	50	14	.387	.462
2018	Hartford (EL)	AA	.304	38	148	28	45	8	2	4	15	21	17	19	1	.391	.466
	Albuquerque (PCL)	AAA	.314	72	296	53	93	17	4	6	25	30	58	17	4	.377	.459
	Colorado (NL)	MAJ	.275	24	40	3	11	3	1	0	4	7	12	2	0	.396	.400
Major League Totals			.275	24	40	3	11	3	1	0	4	7	12	2	0	.396	.400
Minor League Totals			.315	305	1233	237	389	63	26	20	154	155	208	122	23	.389	.457

3 PETER LAMBERT, RHP

Born: April 18, 1997 **B-T:** R-R. **HT:** 6-2. **WT:** 200. **Drafted:** HS—Sam Dimas, Calif., 2015 (2nd round). **Signed by:** Jon Luekens.

TRACK RECORD: The Rockies jumped Lambert to Triple-A Albuquerque at midseason and he struggled for the first time in his career. That was a major step forward because it led to Lambert realizing adjustments needed to be made to offset the impact of altitude. It's promising, however, that he continued to throw strikes even as other numbers deteriorated.

SCOUTING REPORT: Lambert has a legitimate four-pitch mix to work in a major league rotation. He is not going to overpower, but he understands the art of pitching. He mixes his repertoire, moves the ball around and has pinpoint control. His go-to pitch off his fastball is a legitimate plus curveball. He works his plus changeup in regularly. His fringy slider is a definite fourth pitch. He works off a fastball that sits in the low 90s, but with his feel for locating and deception in his delivery, hitters have trouble catching up to his heater.

BA GRADE

50 Risk: Medium

Fastball: 50.
Curve: 60. **Change:** 60.
Slider: 45. **CTL:** 60.

THE FUTURE: The Rockies have a young core at the big league level, so it will be easy to send Lambert back to Albuquerque, which is the same altitude as Denver. He can adjust there. Lambert is on a fast track to move into the rotation when a need arises and is seen as a No. 3 or 4 starter type because of his command and moxie.

Year	Club (League)	Class	W	L	ERA	G	GS	CG	SV	IP	H	HR	BB	SO	K/9	WHIP	AVG
2016	Asheville (SAL)	LoA	5	8	3.93	26	26	0	0	126	125	7	33	108	7.7	1.25	.264
2017	Lancaster (CAL)	HiA	9	8	4.17	26	26	0	0	142	147	18	30	131	8.3	1.24	.267
2018	Hartford (EL)	AA	8	2	2.23	15	15	1	0	93	80	6	12	75	7.3	0.99	.236
	Albuquerque (PCL)	AAA	2	5	5.04	11	11	0	0	55	72	5	15	31	5.0	1.57	.320
Minor League Totals			24	27	3.76	86	86	1	0	448	453	39	101	371	7.5	1.24	.264

4 COLTON WELKER, 3B

Born: Oct. 9, 1997. **B-T:** R-R. **HT:** 6-2. **WT:** 195. **Drafted:** HS—Parkland, Fla., 2016 (4th round). **Signed by:** Rafael Reyes.

TRACK RECORD: In his third pro season, Welker continued to establish the fact he has an impact bat. An injury kept him from qualifying for a batting title in the South Atlantic League in 2017. He was healthy throughout the 2018 season and claimed the batting championship in the high Class A California League. He has hit a composite .335 in his professional career.

SCOUTING REPORT: Welker has natural leverage to hit for above-average power in his swing. As he fills out and gets stronger there is the expectation he will develop middle-of-the-lineup power, a lot like Nolan Arenado, who never hit more than 18 home runs in a minor league season. He has that hitting instinct, using the entire field. As part of the Rockies' versatility push, he put in some time at first base in the second half of 2018 at Lancaster. Third base, though, is his future. He has the reactions, soft hands and arm strength to handle both corners with an accurate arm.

BA GRADE

55 Risk: High

Hit: 60. Power: 55.
Run: 50. Field: 55.
Arm: 55.

THE FUTURE: Welker should be big league ready some time in 2020. The expectation is he will settle in quickly at Double-A and be moved up to Albuquerque at some point in 2019, which could facilitate his rise to the big leagues. He remains the focus of the Rockies' future at third base.

Year	Club (League)	Class	AVG	G	AB	R	H	2B	3B	HR	RBI	BB	SO	SB	CS	OBP	SLG
2016	Grand Junction (PIO)	R	.329	51	210	38	69	15	2	5	36	13	28	6	4	.366	.490
2017	Asheville (SAL)	LoA	.350	67	254	32	89	18	1	6	33	18	42	5	7	.401	.500
2018	Lancaster (CAL)	HiA	.333	114	454	74	151	32	0	13	82	42	103	5	1	.383	.489
Minor League Totals			.337	232	918	144	309	65	3	24	151	73	173	16	12	.384	.492

5 GRANT LAVIGNE, 1B

Born: Aug. 27, 1999. **B-T:** L-R. **HT:** 6-4. **WT:** 220. **Drafted:** HS—Bedford, N.H., 2018 (1st round supplemental). **Signed by:** Mike Garlatti.

TRACK RECORD: There has never been a position player from New Hampshire who turned pro out of high school and made it to the big leagues. And now, along comes Lavigne, the highest-drafted high school player (42nd overall) ever out of the Granite State. He hit .400 or better each of his four years in high school, and as a senior walked 30 times in 90 plate appearances and struck out just six times, showing excellent plate discipline. He developed a feel for the wood bat when he played three summers in a wood bat league in New England.

SCOUTING REPORT: Lavigne's strike-zone discipline and knowledge are upper echelon, particularly for a big-time power threat. Scouts talk about seeing him battle from an 0-2 count to 3-2 and hitting an opposite field home run. He ranked as the No. 1 prospect in the Rookie-level Pioneer League in his pro debut after leading the league with 45 walks and a .477 on-base percentage.

BA GRADE

55 Risk: Very High

Hit: 60. Power: 60.
Run: 50. Field: 55.
Arm: 50.

He also hit .350 with six home runs as an 18-year-old. Given his size, he is a first baseman all the way, and shows the fire to be elite. He has soft hands and agility, moving well around the base. He answered some questions about his lack of competition in high school quickly in Rookie ball.

THE FUTURE: Lavigne has the type of bat that will put him on the fast track. He is a prototype for a Gold Glove, Silver Slugger-caliber first baseman. He is a big man but already has the work and dietary habits necessary to keep himself in check.

Year	Club (League)	Class	AVG	G	AB	R	H	2B	3B	HR	RBI	BB	SO	SB	CS	OBP	SLG
2018	Grand Junction (PIO)	R	.350	59	206	45	72	13	2	6	38	45	40	12	7	.477	.519
Minor League Totals			.350	59	206	45	72	13	2	6	38	45	40	12	7	.477	.519

6 TYLER NEVIN, 1B/3B

Born: May 29, 1997. **B-T:** R-R. **HT:** 6-4. **WT:** 200. **Drafted:** HS—Poway, Calif., 2015 (1st round supplement). **Signed by:** Jon Luekens.

TRACK RECORD: The son of Phil Nevin, who was the No. 1 pick in the 1992 draft, Tyler battled injuries his first three pro seasons, limiting him to a combined 518 at-bats. In 2018, however, the potential began to turn into results. He hit for average and power at high Class A Lancaster. And he followed that up with a breakout effort in the Arizona Fall League, where he won the batting title despite coming out of Class A ball.
SCOUTING REPORT: Nevin is a taller, sleeker build than his father but has the bat speed that promises a productive offensive career. He showed developing plate discipline at Lancaster, giving him the potential for a plus bat with above-average power. Projected as a third baseman at the time of his draft, he has seen considerable time at first base as a consequence of spending the 2018 season on the same roster as Welker. He has the soft hands to be a plus first baseman, but given his athleticism, the Rockies will give him a look in the outfield as well. Plate discipline came over the course of 2018, capped off by the AFL effort in which he drew 15 walks and struck out just five times.
THE FUTURE: Nevin's statement in 2018 underscores he has impact potential in the big leagues. He has the physical skills and work ethic to be a middle-of-the-lineup corner infielder on a contending team.

BA GRADE
50 Risk: High
Hit: 60. **Power:** 55.
Run: 40. **Field:** 55.
Arm: 45.

Year	Club (League)	Class	AVG	G	AB	R	H	2B	3B	HR	RBI	BB	SO	SB	CS	OBP	SLG
2016	Boise (NWL)	SS	1.000	1	1	1	1	1	0	0	0	0	0	0	0	1.000	2.000
2017	Boise (NWL)	SS	.233	6	30	4	7	3	0	1	5	0	9	0	1	.233	.433
	Asheville (SAL)	LoA	.305	76	298	45	91	18	3	7	47	27	56	10	5	.364	.456
2018	Lancaster (CAL)	HiA	.328	100	378	59	124	25	1	13	62	34	77	4	3	.386	.503
Minor League Totals			.305	236	896	138	273	62	5	23	132	90	184	17	16	.371	.462

7 RYAN ROLISON, LHP

Born: July 11, 1997. **B-T:** R-L. **HT:** 6-2. **WT:** 195. **Drafted:** Mississippi, 2018 (1st round). **Signed by:** Zack Zulli.

TRACK RECORD: Rolison has been on the radar for some time. He was a second-team All-American out of high school, but he slipped in the 2016 draft because of a strong commitment to Mississippi. He became the third pitcher in Ole Miss history to have at least 10 wins and 100 strikeouts in a season. Keeping with Colorado's philosophy in the draft, Rolison's workload in his pro debut was limited so the organization could get to know him and not overextend him after a heavy workload in the spring. He impressed enough in his nine appearances that he was held back to pitch a game in the Pioneer League championship series, only to see Grand Junction eliminated in the semi-finals.
SCOUTING REPORT: Rolison is a Kyle Freeland type. He pitches at 92-93 mph with his fastball and commands a breaking ball that is more of a curveball than slider. His breaking pitch needs refinement. Rolison also has a changeup but was limited in using it at the college level. He commands both sides of the plate and repeats his delivery.
THE FUTURE: Rolison figures to move quickly through the development process considering his awareness and willingness to adjust to situations. He has strong fastball command. The key now is refining the curveball and becoming more comfortable with usage of his changeup, which is a critical pitch at Coors Field. He has a No. 4 starter type of profile.

BA GRADE
50 Risk: High
Fastball: 55.
Curveball: 50.
Change: 55. **CTL:** 55.

Year	Club (League)	Class	W	L	ERA	G	GS	CG	SV	IP	H	HR	BB	SO	K/9	WHIP	AVG
2018	Grand Junction (PIO)	R	0	1	1.86	9	9	0	0	29	15	2	8	34	10.6	0.79	.149
Minor League Totals			0	1	1.86	9	9	0	0	29	15	2	8	34	10.6	0.79	.149

8 RILEY PINT, RHP

Born: Nov. 6, 1997. **B-T:** R-R. **HT:** 6-4. **WT:** 230. **Drafted:** HS—Overland Park, Kan., 2016 (1st round). **Signed by:** Bret Baldwin.

TRACK RECORD: It's time for Pint to make a move. One of the most over-powering pitchers in the 2016 draft class, his results and durability in pro ball haven't been there. Able to get away with hitters chasing pitches when he was in high school because of his dominating velocity, Pint has had to work on his control. Hopes for a breakthrough season in 2018 weren't met because he was limited to just 8.1 innings of work in four appearances.

SCOUTING REPORT: Pint can simply overpower hitters when he throws strikes. He is a starting pitcher who sits 97-99 mph and can run it up to 102 without any stress. He also has one of the better curveballs in the organization. It is all about consistency. If the pieces of the puzzle fit together he's a legit No. 1 starter—but that is a giant if because he hasn't gotten out of low Class A ball. He showed promise in 2018 but then came the injuries that flared up in the first inning of his first South Atlantic League start and kept him from getting back on the mound most of the summer, limiting him to three starts at short-season Boise.

THE FUTURE: Pint's 2019 season has plenty of promise, but it is critical for him to take a step up and get in a full season to start answering the questions and concerns that have grown out of his history of injuries. Given Pint's size and ability to simply intimidate hitters in high school, the Rockies have shown a willingness to be patient, but this will be his fourth year in pro ball and an uptick is vital.

TONY FARLOW/ASHEVILLE TOURISTS

BA GRADE

55 Risk: Extreme

Fastball: 70.
Curve: 60. **Slider:** 50.
Change: 60. **CTL:** 40.

Year	Club (League)	Class	W	L	ERA	G	GS	CG	SV	IP	H	HR	BB	SO	K/9	WHIP	AVG
2016	Grand Junction (PIO)	R	1	5	5.35	11	11	0	0	37	43	2	23	36	8.8	1.78	.307
2017	Asheville (SAL)	LoA	2	11	5.42	22	22	0	0	93	96	3	59	79	7.6	1.67	.264
2018	Asheville (SAL)	LoA	0	1	81.00	1	1	0	0	0	2	0	2	0	0.0	12.00	.500
	Boise (NWL)	SS	0	2	1.13	3	3	0	0	8	4	0	9	8	9.0	1.63	.167
Minor League Totals			3	19	5.33	37	37	0	0	138	145	5	93	123	8.0	1.72	.273

9 RYAN VILADE, SS

Born: Feb. 18, 1999. **B-T:** R-R. **HT:** 6-2. **WT:** 198. **Drafted:** HS—Stillwater, Okla., 2017 (2nd round). **Signed by:** Jesse Retzlaf.

TRACK RECORD: Vilade was faced with failure on the field for the first time in 2018 and responded impressively. Hitting .209 on May 23 in his first full-season challenge, he was still hitting just .237 on July 9. From that point on, however, he hit .326 and cut his strikeout ratio from one every 3.6 at-bats through July 8 to once every 8.9 at-bats the rest of the season. His father is Oklahoma State assistant coach James Vilade, who has a long history of coaching at the minor league level.

SCOUTING REPORT: Don't be deceived by Vilade's total of 10 home runs in his first two pro seasons. He can lift and drive the ball, which was apparent when he won the Under Armor All-America home run derby at Wrigley Field prior to his senior year in high school. The key for Vilade is making adjustments, which he showed in that late-season revival at Asheville. He has the defensive instincts to play shortstop, but there are some who question his range.

THE FUTURE: Vilade is going to be given every opportunity to prove he is a shortstop, but given Colorado's approach with minor league players, he will also see time at third base and first base in the team's effort to create depth at multiple positions. His bat profiles a little lower down the lineup, and he could be one of those guys lurking in the No. 6 or No. 7 hole.

BA GRADE

50 Risk: High

Hit: 50. **Power:** 55.
Run: 50. **Field:** 50.
Arm: 60.

Year	Club (League)	Class	AVG	G	AB	R	H	2B	3B	HR	RBI	BB	SO	SB	CS	OBP	SLG
2017	Grand Junction (PIO)	R	.308	33	117	23	36	3	2	5	21	27	31	5	5	.438	.496
2018	Asheville (SAL)	LoA	.274	124	457	77	125	20	4	5	44	49	96	17	13	.353	.368
Minor League Totals			.280	157	574	100	161	23	6	10	65	76	127	22	18	.371	.394

10 SAM HILLIARD, OF

Born: Feb. 21, 1994. **B-T:** L-L. **HT:** 6-5. **WT:** 235. **Drafted:** Wichita State, 2015 (15th round). **Signed by:** Bret Baldwin.

BA GRADE

50 Risk: High

Hit: 55. **Power:** 55. **Run:** 45. **Field:** 50. **Arm:** 55.

TRACK RECORD: Hilliard faced an emotional challenge in 2018, dealing with his father being diagnosed with Lou Gehrig's disease. He, however, showed mental strength and rebounded in the Arizona Fall League, where he hit .328. Hilliard was a highly touted pitcher out of junior college but struggled early at Wichita State and made his mark as a hitter. Rockies area scout Bret Baldwin said he was fortunate to be a first-year scout and wasn't turned off by Hilliard's mound struggles.
SCOUTING REPORT: During the 2018 season, Hilliard adopted a bit of a leg kick that helped him keep his weight back and see the ball longer, which was a big help in starting to handle breaking pitches and show signs of cutting down a strikeout rate that was close to 30 percent. His size and physical skills profile perfectly in right field. His hit tool, power and arm all grade as above-average. Hilliard is a plus runner who could play center field, but due to his size and the demands of the outfield at Coors Field, the plan is for him to stay in right field.
THE FUTURE: Given that Hilliard did not make the move to the outfield until 2015, he is more raw than a typical college bat. He has proven to be a quick learner and is pushing aside a label earlier in his career that he would wind up in a platoon role.

Year	Club (League)	Class	AVG	G	AB	R	H	2B	3B	HR	RBI	BB	SO	SB	CS	OBP	SLG
2016	Asheville (SAL)	LoA	.267	127	461	71	123	23	5	17	83	56	150	30	12	.348	.449
2017	Lancaster (CAL)	HiA	.300	133	536	95	161	23	7	21	92	50	154	37	17	.360	.487
2018	Hartford (EL)	AA	.262	121	435	58	114	22	3	9	40	41	151	23	14	.327	.389
Minor League Totals			.282	441	1654	269	466	81	23	54	257	183	510	102	47	.353	.456

11 RYAN CASTELLANI, RHP

BA GRADE

50 Risk: High

Born: April 1,1996. **B-T:** R-R. **HT:** 6-3. **WT:** 190. **Drafted:** HS—Phoenix, 2014 (2nd round). **Signed by:** Chris Forbes.

TRACK RECORD: Sent back to Double-A Hartford in 2018, Castellani struggled and finally realized he was delivering the ball too much over the top, losing the action and velocity on his pitches. By the end of the Arizona Fall League he had dropped back to a three-quarters arm slot, regaining velocity, movement and command. He allowed one run in five innings in three of his final four AFL appearances.
SCOUTING REPORT: Signed at age 18 out of high school, Castellani has a three-pitch mix built around a fastball that can hit 98 mph, but he sits at 93 mph. He has a curveball, but it takes a back seat to a slider that is a separator. Castellani isn't worried about pitching to contract because the sinking action on his fastball induces ground balls.
THE FUTURE: Castellani can climb on the express lane to the big leagues if he builds off his success in the final weeks of the AFL. He has the competitive nature, and when he is right, his pitch assortment makes it difficult for hitters to sit on a particular pitch.

Year	Club (League)	Class	W	L	ERA	G	GS	CG	SV	IP	H	HR	BB	SO	K/9	WHIP	AVG
2016	Modesto (CAL)	HiA	7	8	3.81	26	26	1	0	168	156	8	50	142	7.6	1.23	.248
2017	Hartford (EL)	AA	9	12	4.81	27	27	1	0	157	163	16	47	132	7.6	1.33	.264
2018	Hartford (EL)	AA	7	9	5.49	26	26	0	0	134	135	15	70	91	6.1	1.53	.265
Minor League Totals			26	38	4.55	116	116	2	0	610	623	46	205	484	7.1	1.36	.264

12 JOSH FUENTES, 3B

BA GRADE

45 Risk: Medium

Born: Feb. 19, 1993. **B-T:** R-R. **HT:** 6-2. **WT:** 215. **Signed:** Missouri Baptist, 2014 (NDFA). **Signed by:** Jon Luekens.

TRACK RECORD: Fuentes is the cousin of Rockies third baseman Nolan Arenado, which gave Colorado an edge to sign him as a nondrafted free agent. In the last two seasons, Fuentes has created his own identity. After hitting .307 at Double-A Hartford in 2017, he brought home all the honors in the Triple-A Pacific Coast League in 2018. He was a midseason and postseason PCL all-star and both the league's MVP and rookie of the year. He also claimed MVP honors at the Triple-A all-star game. The key to his success? Fuentes quit trying to be Nolan Arenado and blossomed as Josh Fuentes.
SCOUTING REPORT: As he has moved up in the Rockies' system, Fuentes has responded to the challenge, improving his stock each year. He hit .327 at Triple-A Albuquerque with 65 extra-base hits, and a team-

high 95 RBIs. He welcomes the challenge of getting better, but unlike the always-serious nature of his all-star cousin, Fuentes has allowed his laid-back approach and sense of humor emerge as he has become more relaxed and successful. He has the hands and arm strength to be an elite defensive third baseman. Critics will point to the fact Fuentes has reached double figures in home runs just twice in five minor league seasons, including 14 in the PCL in 2018. But for the record, cousin Nolan never hit more than 18 home runs in any minor league season.

THE FUTURE: Fuentes established himself as a player to watch with his consistent effort and all-around strong play in 2018. His big year has positioned him to be a candidate to replace Arenado at third base if he departs as a free agent after the 2019 season.

Year	Club (League)	Class	AVG	G	AB	R	H	2B	3B	HR	RBI	BB	SO	SB	CS	OBP	SLG
2016	Asheville (SAL)	LoA	.398	28	93	18	37	14	0	4	20	4	22	2	4	.442	.677
	Modesto (CAL)	HiA	.278	77	291	44	81	15	4	9	44	16	54	1	1	.342	.450
2017	Hartford (EL)	AA	.307	122	414	48	127	28	7	15	72	24	92	8	5	.352	.517
2018	Albuquerque (PCL)	AAA	.327	135	551	93	180	39	12	14	95	21	103	3	5	.354	.517
Minor League Totals			.299	496	1836	268	549	127	24	49	289	107	374	27	23	.348	.474

13 JESUS TINOCO, RHP

BA GRADE
50 Risk: High

Born: April 30, 1995. **B-T:** R-R. **HT:** 6-4. **WT:** 190. **Signed:** Venezuela, 2011. **Signed by:** Marco Paddy/Rafael Moncada (Blue Jays).

TRACK RECORD: In the five-player trade that sent Troy Tulowitzki to the Blue Jays, Tinoco was the low-level throw-in from Toronto to the Rockies. He has pitched his way into being the one with most potential impact. He has had dominant moments as a starter but has been inconsistent. Then came his trip to the Arizona Fall League, and his role in the bullpen, where he compiled a 1.72 ERA.

SCOUTING REPORT: Tinoco's big pitch is a fastball that jumps from the 92-95 mph range when he is starting to 94-97 out of the bullpen. He is solid-average with both a curveball and slider but tends to be more comfortable with the curveball and its velocity differential. Tinoco is still working on a changeup, but if he becomes a reliever, his third pitch is more the cherry on top than the ice cream in his sundae.

THE FUTURE: The Rockies say Tinoco could still become a starter, but the 23-year-old would seem a perfect fit in the bullpen, where his power arm dominates, and his AFL success gave him a confidence boost. He is headed to Triple-A to open 2019, which would seem a good place to give him an extended look in the pen considering the mile-high altitude of Albuquerque.

Year	Club (League)	Class	W	L	ERA	G	GS	CG	SV	IP	H	HR	BB	SO	K/9	WHIP	AVG
2016	Modesto (CAL)	HiA	0	3	14.85	4	4	0	0	13	37	3	3	8	5.4	3.00	.536
	Asheville (SAL)	LoA	3	8	5.63	16	16	0	0	86	118	10	25	53	5.5	1.66	.324
2017	Lancaster (CAL)	HiA	11	4	4.67	24	24	0	0	141	157	19	50	107	6.8	1.47	.285
2018	Hartford (EL)	AA	9	12	4.79	26	26	1	0	141	149	23	38	132	8.4	1.33	.269
Minor League Totals			32	52	4.75	131	120	1	2	648	740	62	200	531	7.4	1.45	.286

14 TERRIN VAVRA, SS

BA GRADE
50 Risk: High

Born: May 12, 1997. **B-T:** L-R. **HT:** 6-1. **WT:** 185. **Drafted:** Minnesota, 2018 (3rd round). **Signed by:** Brett Baldwin.

TRACK RECORD: Vavra grew up around big league clubhouses. His father Joe is currently the quality control coach for the Tigers, but previously was a bench coach with the Twins. Growing up Vavra spent time at the ballpark and learned from big league players like Joe Mauer. He is more advanced than two older brothers, both of whom reached high Class A in their playing careers.

SCOUTING REPORT: Vavra has feel for the game. Scouts compare him with current Rockies middle infield prospect Garrett Hampson, but without Hampson's speed. Vavra has been a shortstop, but his range and arm strength are issues that will need to be addressed. He hits for average and will surprise with his pop. He drove a grand slam out to dead center field at short-season Boise, which is not exactly a hitter-friendly park. Vavra's intangibles stick out. He was a leader in college and quickly assumed that role at short-season Boise in his debut.

THE FUTURE: Vavra has the "it" factor. He has a long way to go to get to the big leagues, but his bat and versatility in the infield make it likely. He figures to wind up at second base as an everyday player or a utility infielder. He has the arm and instincts to handle that challenge.

Year	Club (League)	Class	AVG	G	AB	R	H	2B	3B	HR	RBI	BB	SO	SB	CS	OBP	SLG
2018	Boise (NWL)	SS	.302	44	169	22	51	8	4	4	26	26	40	9	1	.396	.467
Minor League Totals			.302	44	169	22	51	8	4	4	26	26	40	9	1	.396	.467

15 JUSTIN LAWRENCE, RHP

BA GRADE

50 Risk: High

Born: Nov. 5, 1994. **B-T:** R-R. **HT:** 6-4. **WT:** 220. **Drafted:** Daytona State (Fla.) JC, 2015 (12th round). **Signed by:** John Cedarburg.

TRACK RECORD: After adopting a lower arm slot his freshman year at Jacksonville, Lawrence transferred to Daytona State JC and refined his delivery. He has worked periodically with former Rockies submariner Steve Reed in refining his delivery. Lawrence suffered a setback in 2017 with a torn latissimus dorsi and teres minor, which sidelined him in late May for the remainder of the season, but he bounced back in 2018, earning selection to the high Class A California League all-star game.

SCOUTING REPORT: Lawrence is the exception to the rule for a sidearmer. He has the typical sinking action on his pitches but did not suffer a loss in velocity. His fastball ranges from 97-101 mph. In fact, threw more 100 mph pitches (seven) than any pitcher in the Arizona Fall League. Lawrence also commands a slider. He's particularly tough on righthanded hitters, who can't help but feel that Lawrence's fastball is headed for their rib cage. He stays on the outer third of the plate versus lefthanded hitters, rarely coming inside.

THE FUTURE: Lawrence is at worst a matchup righthanded reliever. As his confidence grows and he becomes more aggressive against opposite-hand hitters, he has closer potential considering the combination of velocity and movement.

Year	Club (League)	Class	W	L	ERA	G	GS	CG	SV	IP	H	HR	BB	SO	K/9	WHIP	AVG
2016	Asheville (SAL)	LoA	2	5	7.18	26	0	0	0	36	48	4	14	23	5.7	1.71	.327
	Boise (NWL)	SS	2	1	2.20	23	0	0	8	29	27	0	6	40	12.6	1.15	.243
2017	Asheville (SAL)	LoA	0	2	1.65	16	0	0	6	16	10	1	4	20	11.0	0.86	.172
2018	Lancaster (CAL)	HiA	0	2	2.65	55	0	0	11	54	36	2	27	62	10.3	1.16	.188
Minor League Totals			4	13	4.38	142	0	0	25	160	152	11	67	163	9.1	1.37	.248

16 REID HUMPHREYS, RHP

BA GRADE

45 Risk: Medium

Born: Nov. 21, 1994. **B-T:** R-R. **HT:** 6-1. **WT:** 205. **Drafted:** Mississippi State, 2016 (7th round). **Signed by:** Zach Zulli.

TRACK RECORD: Humphreys is the younger brother of former Mississippi State and then big league first baseman Tyler Moore. Humphreys, who was the Gatorade player of the year for Mississippi his senior year in high school, made the conversion from a light-hitting infielder to pitcher his junior year at MSU, when he became the team's closer. By season's end he made a strong enough impression to be drafted.

SCOUTING REPORT: Humphreys offers an aggressive three-pitch mix. His four-seam fastball is consistent in the 94-96 mph range with a cutter that registers at 90-93. The change of speeds comes with a slider that is in the 82-84 mph range. He walked just 13 batters and struck out 51 in 34.1 innings at high Class A Lancaster, showing no hesitation to challenge hitters in the strike zone.

THE FUTURE: Humphreys has a closer mentality. He converted all 22 of his save opportunities despite spending four months at hitter-friendly Lancaster. He closed the season with a glimpse of Double-A and most likely will return to Hartford to open 2019, but he could wind up in the big leagues at some point in 2019 in the first step toward a possible career in the ninth inning.

Year	Club (League)	Class	W	L	ERA	G	GS	CG	SV	IP	H	HR	BB	SO	K/9	WHIP	AVG
2016	Grand Junction (PIO)	R	1	0	3.48	9	0	0	0	10	11	0	5	9	7.8	1.55	.250
2017	Asheville (SAL)	LoA	1	3	2.56	43	0	0	13	46	32	3	6	47	9.3	0.83	.194
2018	Lancaster (CAL)	HiA	2	0	1.83	35	0	0	22	34	22	1	13	51	13.4	1.02	.179
	Hartford (EL)	AA	0	1	3.18	7	0	0	4	6	3	0	7	7	11.1	1.76	.167
Minor League Totals			4	4	2.44	94	0	0	39	96	68	4	31	114	10.7	1.03	.194

17 BEN BOWDEN, LHP

BA GRADE

45 Risk: High

Born: Oct. 21, 1994. **B-T:** L-L. **HT:** 6-4. **WT:** 235. **Drafted:** Vanderbilt, 2016 (2nd round). **Signed by:** Scott Corman.

TRACK RECORD: After missing 2017 because of a hamstring strain and then a back strain, which he suffered helping a passenger place a bag in the overhead compartment on a plane, Bowden enjoyed a full-season return. He split 2018 between low Class A Asheville and high Class A Lancaster. The 45th player selected in 2016, Bowden was the closer on Vanderbilt's national championship team that year.

SCOUTING REPORT: Bowden has a closer's mentality. He comes at hitters with a fastball in the 93-95 mph range and a decent changeup that keeps hitters off balance. At the Class A level, his command was evident. He walked 20 and struck out 78 in 52 innings, basically using a two-pitch mix. Bowden is working on a breaking ball but needs to firm up a what so far has been more of a slurve. If he can create more consistency with that pitch it would add a swing-and-miss pitch to his mix.

THE FUTURE: With a third pitch, Bowden has closer potential. Without a third pitch, he provides a power lefthander to handle late innings. He is an intimidating figure on the mound and doesn't back down from difficult situations.

Year	Club (League)	Class	W	L	ERA	G	GS	CG	SV	IP	H	HR	BB	SO	K/9	WHIP	AVG
2016	Asheville (SAL)	LoA	0	1	3.04	26	0	0	0	24	23	1	15	29	11.0	1.61	.261
2017	Did not play—Injured																
2018	Asheville (SAL)	LoA	3	0	3.52	15	0	0	0	15	17	2	5	25	14.7	1.43	.274
	Lancaster (CAL)	HiA	4	2	4.17	34	0	0	0	37	35	6	15	53	13.0	1.36	.245
Minor League Totals			7	3	3.69	75	0	0	0	76	75	9	35	107	12.7	1.45	.256

18 ROBERT TYLER, RHP

BA GRADE

45 Risk: High

Born: June 18, 1995. **B-T:** R-R. **HT:** 6-4. **WT:** 225. **Drafted:** Georgia, 2016 (1st round supplemental). **Signed by:** Sean Gamble.

TRACK RECORD: Tyler's pro career had a one-year detour. After making his short-season debut in 2016, he was sidelined in 2017 by lingering shoulder soreness. He was fine in 2018, and after an impressive effort at low Class A Asheville that included 52 strikeouts and seven walks in 38.1 innings, he was promoted to high Class A Lancaster. Like many pitchers, he struggled in the California League.

SCOUTING REPORT: Tyler can dominate with two pitches—fastball and changeup. He has consistent velocity in the 98-101 mph range on his fastball. His changeup is typically about 10 mph slower, creating great separation. His changeup comes out of the same arm slot as his fastball. Tyler is working on a slider that would give him a change of location option to go with the other two pitches.

THE FUTURE: Tyler has a big arm that has him destined for a bullpen role. He has that "here it is—hit it" mentality that is a part of successful late-inning pitchers. He is not afraid to come inside with his fastball to lefthanded hitters as well as righthanded hitters.

Year	Club (League)	Class	W	L	ERA	G	GS	CG	SV	IP	H	HR	BB	SO	K/9	WHIP	AVG
2016	Boise (NWL)	SS	0	2	6.43	5	5	0	0	7	2	0	16	5	6.4	2.57	.083
2017	Did not play																
2018	Asheville (SAL)	LoA	4	2	3.99	34	0	0	8	38	37	5	7	52	12.2	1.15	.243
	Lancaster (CAL)	HiA	0	1	9.64	12	0	0	0	9	17	2	5	5	4.8	2.36	.425
Minor League Totals			4	5	5.27	51	5	0	8	55	56	7	28	62	10.2	1.54	.259

19 YONATHAN DAZA, OF

BA GRADE

45 Risk: High

Born: Feb. 28, 1994. **B-T:** R-R. **HT:** 6-2. **WT:** 190. **Drafted:** Venezuela, 2010. **Signed by:** Rolando Fernandez/Carlos Gomez/Orlando Medina.

TRACK RECORD: Signed as a 16-year-old, Daza spent three years in the Dominican Summer League before coming to the U.S. in 2015. He responded to the new environment and has hit better than .300 in each of his four seasons since debuting at short-season Boise. His 2018 season at Double-A Hartford was limited to 54 games because of a hamstring injury that he re-aggravated. That kept him out of action for the final three months of the season.

SCOUTING REPORT: Daza is arguably the best defensive center field in the organization—including the big league team. He has speed, a plus-plus arm with accuracy. He isn't a power hitter, but he creates offense. Despite not being a home run hitter, he has shown an ability to drive in runs. He had 87 RBIs at high Class A Lancaster when he won the California League batting title in 2017. In an organization loaded with lefthanded hitters, Daza provides the potential of an interesting righthanded bat.

THE FUTURE: Daza has a clean bill of health for 2019, and it's not out of the question his big league debut will come at some point during the year. The presence of Daza is a factor the Rockies have already discussed with Charlie Blackmon, as in Daza could push Blackmon to an outfield corner.

Year	Club (League)	Class	AVG	G	AB	R	H	2B	3B	HR	RBI	BB	SO	SB	CS	OBP	SLG
2016	Asheville (SAL)	LoA	.307	119	475	63	146	35	2	3	58	23	78	2	7	.341	.408
	Modesto (CAL)	HiA	.242	8	33	1	8	2	0	0	3	1	7	1	1	.306	.303
2017	Lancaster (CAL)	HiA	.341	125	519	93	177	34	11	3	87	30	88	31	8	.376	.466
2018	Hartford (EL)	AA	.306	54	219	27	67	18	2	4	29	7	24	4	5	.330	.461
Minor League Totals			.310	594	2237	334	693	140	24	19	317	108	326	84	52	.351	.419

20 RYAN FELTNER, RHP

BA GRADE

45 Risk: High

Born: Sept. 2, 1996. **B-T:** R-R. **HT:** 6-4. **WT:** 190. **Drafted:** Ohio State, 2018 (4th round). **Signed by:** Ed Santa.

TRACK RECORD: The Ohio Gatorade player of the year his senior year in high school, Feltner split time between the bullpen and rotation at Ohio State. He struggled with command early in his 2018 junior season but finished strong, working six shutout innings against Iowa in the Big Ten Conference elimination game. He started in his pro debut at Rookie-level Grand Junction but was limited to 30.2 innings in nine starts, which was part of the Rockies' plan to limit work in pitchers' first years of pro ball.

SCOUTING REPORT: Feltner has a three-pitch mix with his fastball, slider and changeup. He showed the ability at Grand Junction to consistently throw strikes. He sits at 94-95 mph with his fastball but projects to add some velocity in pro ball. The breaking pitch is a bit of a cross between a curve and slider, but the focus will be on creating a true slider to supplement his fastball/changeup mix.

THE FUTURE: Some scouts speculated last spring that Feltner would wind up in the bullpen, but the Rockies saw enough in his time at Grand Junction to give him every chance to be a mid-rotation starter. He has the size and durability. The key will be the development of his breaking pitch.

Year	Club (League)	Class	W	L	ERA	G	GS	CG	SV	IP	H	HR	BB	SO	K/9	WHIP	AVG
2018	Grand Junction (PIO)	R	0	0	0.88	9	9	0	0	31	16	1	4	39	11.4	0.65	.157
Minor League Totals			0	0	0.88	9	9	0	0	31	16	1	4	39	11.4	0.65	.157

21 DANIEL MONTANO, OF

BA GRADE
50 Risk: Extreme

Born: March 31, 1999. **B-T:** L-R. **HT:** 6-1. **WT:** 170. **Signed:** Venezuela, 2015. **Signed by:** Rolando Fernandez/Carlos Gomez/Orlando Medina.

TRACK RECORD: A 16-year-old Montano received the largest international bonus ever given by the Rockies when he signed in 2015: $2 million. He spent two years in the Dominican Summer League, then came to the U.S. in 2018 to play at Rookie-level Grand Junction, where he hit .279 in 62 games.

SCOUTING REPORT: The Rockies initially felt Montano would wind up in left field, but he responded well to center field in the Pioneer League. With instruction, he showed an above-average arm and will get stronger as he began to physically mature. Montano gets a good read on the ball off the bat. He has a quick bat and—for his age—a good feel for the strike zone. He forces pitchers to come to him instead of chasing pitches out of the zone. He has the speed to steal bases, but he's learning his jumps and reads.

THE FUTURE: Montano has matured on the field to the point he well could find himself in center field, and he has the range to cover the vast territory at Coors Field. He most likely will hit at the top of the lineup or could fit into the seventh slot, where his speed could force pitchers to be more aggressive to the hitter behind him.

Year	Club (League)	Class	AVG	G	AB	R	H	2B	3B	HR	RBI	BB	SO	SB	CS	OBP	SLG
2016	Rockies (DSL)	R	.228	65	241	41	55	17	2	9	32	31	65	8	3	.325	.427
2017	Rockies (DSL)	R	.270	52	189	32	51	14	3	3	39	24	39	9	7	.355	.423
2018	Colorado (DSL)	R	.182	11	44	4	8	2	0	1	8	5	5	2	0	.275	.295
	Grand Junction (PIO)	R	.279	62	240	32	67	15	5	4	29	21	57	9	5	.338	.433
Minor League Totals			.254	190	714	109	181	48	10	17	108	81	166	28	15	.334	.420

22 RICO GARCIA, RHP

BA GRADE
45 Risk: High

Born: Jan. 10, 1994. **B-T:** R-R. **HT:** 5-11. **WT:** 190. **Drafted:** Hawaii Pacific, 2016 (30th round). **Signed by:** Matt Hattabaugh.

TRACK RECORD: After spending the previous two seasons mostly at short-season Boise, Garcia made an emphatic impression in 2018 when he started at high Class A Lancaster. He earned midseason and postseason all-star honors in the California League and finished the year at Double-A Hartford. Going a combined 13-9, 2.96 and striking out 162 while walking 42 in 167 innings, Garcia became more than an organization player. The stronger the competition, the better Garcia has pitched.

SCOUTING REPORT: Garcia has responded to coaching and a regular throwing program. He has worked on his delivery to provide better balance, which allows him to use his legs better. Garcia's fastball improved to an average of 92 mph with a peak of 96 on a regular basis. The uptick on his fastball combined with a quality changeup and solid curveball has elevated his prospect status. His curveball has good downward break that disrupts hitters' timing.

THE FUTURE: Garcia is coming in a hurry, but only after he got the chance. In two full seasons, he already has put together an impressive effort at Double-A. Area scout Matt Hattabaugh deserves credit for staying with Garcia, even though he was at a smaller school in Hawaii.

Year	Club (League)	Class	W	L	ERA	G	GS	CG	SV	IP	H	HR	BB	SO	K/9	WHIP	AVG
2016	Boise (NWL)	SS	0	4	6.37	16	8	0	0	35	50	1	17	35	8.9	1.90	.329
2017	Boise (NWL)	SS	0	4	3.95	8	8	0	0	41	50	2	11	35	7.7	1.49	.305
	Asheville (SAL)	LoA	2	2	2.57	8	4	0	0	28	27	2	7	30	9.6	1.21	.246
2018	Lancaster (CAL)	HiA	7	7	3.42	16	15	0	0	100	99	12	22	101	9.1	1.21	.255
	Hartford (EL)	AA	6	2	2.28	11	11	0	0	67	54	8	20	61	8.2	1.10	.223
Minor League Totals			15	19	3.52	59	46	0	0	271	280	25	77	262	8.7	1.32	.265

23 MIKE NIKORAK, RHP

BA GRADE

50 Risk: Extreme

Born: Sept. 16, 1996. **B-T:** R-R. **HT:** 6-5. **WT:** 220. **Drafted:** HS— Stroudsburg, Pa., 2015 (1st round). **Signed by:** Mike Garlatti.

TRACK RECORD: The 27th overall pick in 2015, Nikorak signed for $2.3 million out of high school. He had Tommy John surgery in 2016 that led to a 16-month rehab that culminated in a return to the mound late in 2018 at short-season Boise. Nikorak went to instructional league in 2018 and made impressive strides with his command.

SCOUTING REPORT: Nikorak's pitch mix is there. His four-seam fastball hits 97 mph, and his two-seamer can generate ground balls. His low-80s curveball provides an offspeed pitch with movement, and he has worked to refine his changeup. Pitching coaches Ryan Kibler and Bob Apodaca have worked with Nikorak to clean up his mechanics, knowing he has to be more consistent in the delivery to clean up his control problems. He has issued 62 walks in 55.1 pro innings, all in short-season ball.

THE FUTURE: The Rockies plan to get Nikorak on the mound in 2019 and have him take regular turns, most likely at low Class A Asheville. The potential that made him a high draft pick is there, but after the lengthy absence from the field following the Tommy John surgery, Nikorak has not moved up the ladder as quickly as anticipated. This will be a major year for his development.

Year	Club (League)	Class	W	L	ERA	G	GS	CG	SV	IP	H	HR	BB	SO	K/9	WHIP	AVG
2015	Grand Junction (PIO)	R	0	4	11.72	8	8	0	0	18	26	1	32	14	7.1	3.28	.347
2016	Grand Junction (PIO)	R	1	0	3.68	7	7	0	0	29	33	2	19	20	6.1	1.77	.287
2017	Did not play—Injured																
2018	Boise (NWL)	SS	0	0	4.32	9	2	0	0	8	7	0	11	10	10.8	2.16	.233
Minor League Totals			1	4	6.34	24	17	0	0	55	66	3	62	44	7.2	2.31	.300

24 VINCE FERNANDEZ, OF

BA GRADE

45 Risk: High

Born: July 25, 1995. **B-T:** L-R. **HT:** 6-3. **WT:** 210. **Drafted:** UC Riverside, 2016 (10th round). **Signed by:** Jon Lukens.

TRACK RECORD: The Big West Conference player of the year in 2016, Fernandez has proven to be a productive hitter in pro ball. He followed up 16 home runs in his first full season, at low Class A Asheville in 2017, with 25 doubles, eight triples and 24 home runs at high Class A Lancaster in 2018.

SCOUTING REPORT: Fernandez is a legitimate hitter who still figures to get stronger. He has a consistent power swing and uses his hands well. He shows above-average power to all fields but gets himself in trouble when he gets too aggressive, which is underscored by 172 strikeouts in 2018 and a career strikeout rate of 31 percent. Fernandez's bat will determine how far he goes. He is best suited to left field and can catch what he gets to, but his range is merely adequate. He does have above-average arm strength.

THE FUTURE: After his first two full seasons were spent in hitter-friendly ballparks, Fernandez faces a big test in 2019 with his likely move to Double-A Hartford. This will be a good test of how well he adapts, and his ability to make some adjustments to ensure more consistent contact.

Year	Club (League)	Class	AVG	G	AB	R	H	2B	3B	HR	RBI	BB	SO	SB	CS	OBP	SLG
2016	Grand Junction (PIO)	R	.310	51	203	36	63	17	6	5	31	20	61	6	2	.370	.527
2017	Asheville (SAL)	LoA	.269	100	375	57	101	23	1	16	59	44	122	12	8	.352	.464
2018	Lancaster (CAL)	HiA	.265	117	423	82	112	25	8	24	75	65	172	10	5	.370	.532
Minor League Totals			.276	268	1001	175	276	65	15	45	165	129	355	28	15	.363	.505

25 BRIAN MUNDELL, 1B

BA GRADE

40 Risk: Medium

Born: Feb. 28, 1994. **B-T:** R-R. **HT:** 6-3. **WT:** 230. **Drafted:** Cal Poly, 2015 (7th round). **Signed by:** Matt Hattabaugh.

TRACK RECORD: The first college player the Rockies drafted in 2015, Mundell has shed the DH label he carried in college, settling in at first base in pro ball. After splitting his 2017 season between high Class A Lancaster and Double-A Hartford in 2017, Mundell put in a full season at Hartford in 2018. As much as he is a factor in the lineup, Mundell is big in the clubhouse, where he takes on an elder statesmen role that belies the fact he is still 25.

SCOUTING REPORT: The biggest surprise from Mudnell's college days is how well he has handled the defensive chores at first base. He has a good feel at the plate but has yet to make that next adjustment to turn his ability to make contact into home run power, having hit just 40 home runs in four pro seasons that included seven to go with a .372 slugging percentage at Double-A in 2018.

THE FUTURE: Mundell needs to make the next step in terms of power. To get a regular shot in the big leagues, particularly in Coors Field, home runs are a part of the package. He makes enough contract and drives the ball into allies, so the adjustment to turn on a pitch should be something he can handle.

Year	Club (League)	Class	AVG	G	AB	R	H	2B	3B	HR	RBI	BB	SO	SB	CS	OBP	SLG
2016	Asheville (SAL)	LoA	.313	136	537	94	168	59	1	14	83	56	83	7	8	.383	.505
2017	Lancaster (CAL)	HiA	.295	67	264	44	78	16	1	12	59	35	44	0	1	.375	.500
	Hartford (EL)	AA	.302	52	172	30	52	12	0	3	19	25	26	1	1	.394	.424
2018	Hartford (EL)	AA	.263	128	441	49	116	25	1	7	41	53	77	1	3	.345	.372
Minor League Totals			.290	452	1658	252	481	131	4	40	238	201	275	16	14	.369	.446

26 BREILING EUSEBIO, LHP

BA GRADE

50 Risk: Extreme

Born: Nov. 21, 1996. **B-T:** L-L. **HT:** 6-1. **WT:** 175. **Signed:** Dominican Republic, 2013. **Signed by:** Roland Fernandez/Martin Cabrera/Frank Roa.

TRACK RECORD: The Rockies hoped that Eusebio, in his fifth pro season in 2018 and third in the U.S., would have a breakout season. Three starts into the year at low Class A Asheville and Eusebio was done for the season with Tommy John surgery. That comes on the heels of making just 11 starts in 2017 before having his season cut short by an oblique strain in early August.

SCOUTING REPORT: Eusebio is an aggressive lefthander who pitches down in the zone. He has a quality fastball with the appearance of more velocity than the 91-93 mph range that shows up on the radar guns. That is because he has a strong stride, which allows him to get extended way out front and keep the ball down. He also has a quality changeup but needs to refine his curveball.

THE FUTURE: The Rockies hope Eusebio will be able to be activated in the spring and open the season with a full-season team, or at least be ready by the end of April. Given his ailments the last two years, he needs regular time on the mound to get the kinks worked out and put him back on track.

Year	Club (League)	Class	W	L	ERA	G	GS	CG	SV	IP	H	HR	BB	SO	K/9	WHIP	AVG
2016	Boise (NWL)	SS	2	5	5.26	13	13	0	0	63	78	6	30	42	6.0	1.71	.305
2017	Boise (NWL)	SS	3	0	1.59	3	3	0	0	17	10	0	4	22	11.6	0.82	.175
	Asheville (SAL)	LoA	3	3	4.46	8	8	0	0	40	44	3	16	31	6.9	1.49	.280
2018	Asheville (SAL)	LoA	0	1	4.82	3	3	0	0	9	12	1	3	11	10.6	1.61	.316
Minor League Totals			13	15	3.58	52	46	0	0	231	232	13	80	215	8.4	1.35	.260

27 ROBERTO RAMOS, 1B

BA GRADE

45 Risk: High

Born: Dec. 28, 1994. **B-T:** L-R. **HT:** 6-5. **WT:** 220. **Drafted:** JC of the Canyons (Calif.), 2014 (16th round). **Signed by:** Matt Hattabaugh.

TRACK RECORD: Ramos has shown an ability to make adjustments and catch up with each league he has been assigned to. He was considered to have decent power potential, and it came through in 2018 when he hit a combined 32 home runs at high Class A Lancaster and Double-A Hartford. In three of the last four years, his first-half performance has resulted in a promotion to the next level in the second half. A native of Hermosillo, Mexico, Ramos returned there in the offseason to play in the Mexican Pacific League, but after an impressive start suffered a broken finger that ended his winter activity.

SCOUTING REPORT: Ramos has legitimate power, but he also has a propensity to strike out, which is a focus for his ability to reach that next level. He is not quick-footed but has soft hands, which is important for a first baseman. He is a solid candidate to fill that spot and has worked to improve each year. Ramos is going to have to stay focused on cutting down his strikeout rate, which bumped 30 percent in 2018.

THE FUTURE: Ramos' power potential is his ticket to the big leagues, but he can negate it by failing to make contact.

Year	Club (League)	Class	AVG	G	AB	R	H	2B	3B	HR	RBI	BB	SO	SB	CS	OBP	SLG
2016	Modesto (CAL)	HiA	.231	19	78	7	18	7	0	2	9	10	26	0	0	.315	.397
	Grand Junction (PIO)	R	.404	13	57	12	23	5	1	5	23	2	13	3	1	.424	.789
2017	Lancaster (CAL)	HiA	.297	122	478	72	142	29	1	13	68	41	124	3	2	.351	.444
2018	Lancaster (CAL)	HiA	.304	60	214	44	65	15	3	17	43	32	65	3	1	.411	.640
	Hartford (EL)	AA	.231	61	199	26	46	9	0	15	34	26	75	2	1	.320	.503
Minor League Totals			.287	369	1350	216	387	87	5	68	244	143	393	16	6	.360	.510

28 BRET BOSWELL, 2B

BA GRADE

45 Risk: High

Born: Oct. 4, 1994. **B-T:** L-R. **HT:** 6-1. **WT:** 180. **Drafted:** Texas, 2017 (8th round). **Signed by:** Jeff Edwards.

TRACK RECORD: Boswell has been a postseason all-star in both of his pro seasons, first in the short-season Northwest League in 2017 and then the low Class A South Atlantic League in 2018. He had a strong enough season at Asheville in 2018 that he was promoted to high Class A Lancaster for the final five weeks of the season. He hit a combined .296 with 27 home runs.

SCOUTING REPORT: Boswell has plus pop for a middle infielder and has shown the ability to hit for average. Originally a shortstop in college, he was moved to second base the year he was drafted and has above-average range and arm strength for that position. He hangs in well on the double-play pivot.

THE FUTURE: Boswell could return to Lancaster to open 2019, but if he maintains his results he will be moving to Double-A Hartford quickly. Things could get crowded in the Rockies' second base derby the next few years with the likes of Garrett Hampson, Brendan Rodgers and Boswell all candidates.

Year	Club (League)	Class	AVG	G	AB	R	H	2B	3B	HR	RBI	BB	SO	SB	CS	OBP	SLG
2017	Boise (NWL)	SS	.293	54	229	46	67	8	5	11	42	15	55	3	3	.339	.515
2018	Asheville (SAL)	LoA	.288	97	379	69	109	20	4	17	50	21	103	7	5	.331	.496
	Lancaster (CAL)	HiA	.322	30	118	28	38	5	1	10	28	13	41	2	0	.388	.636
Minor League Totals			.295	181	726	143	214	33	10	38	120	49	199	12	8	.343	.525

29 NIKO DECOLATI, OF

Born: Aug. 12, 1997. **B-T:** R-R. **HT:** 6-1. **WT:** 215. **Drafted:** Loyola Marymount, 2018 (6th round). **Signed by:** Matt Hattabaugh.

TRACK RECORD: A native of Boulder, Colo., whose father played at Northern Colorado, Decolati was a third baseman and shortstop at Loyola Marymount, but he made the quick transition to the outfield at Rookie-level Grand Junction after signing with the Rockies. He admits he put pressure on himself going into the college season because there had been talk of him being selected in the first three rounds. He slipped to sixth but quickly adapted to pro ball. Decolati led Grand Junction with 56 RBIs and 17 stolen bases and tied for the team lead with 11 home runs.

SCOUTING REPORT: Decolati's athleticism was apparent by how easily he adapted to the move to the outfield. He also put to rest fears of putting too much pressure on himself with his impressive pro debut. He has plus speed, a strong arm and tracks the ball well. At the plate, he is aggressive, looking to drive the ball to all fields. He welcomes the clutch situations.

THE FUTURE: Decolati's goal is to make his big league home in Coors Field, where he grew up watching the Rockies play before his father's job took the family to Las Vegas. He has the versatility that opens the door for him to fit multiple roles, which adds to the chance of fulfilling the big league dream.

Year	Club (League)	Class	AVG	G	AB	R	H	2B	3B	HR	RBI	BB	SO	SB	CS	OBP	SLG
2018	Grand Junction (PIO)	R	.327	69	263	55	86	15	3	11	56	34	56	17	5	.414	.532
Minor League Totals			.327	69	263	55	86	15	3	11	56	34	56	17	5	.414	.532

30 WILLIE MACIVER, C

Born: Oct. 28, 1996. **B-T:** R-R. **HT:** 6-2. **WT:** 205. **Drafted:** Washington, 2018 (9th round). **Signed by:** Matt Pignataro.

TRACK RECORD: A third baseman his sophomore year at Washington, MacIver assumed more catching duties as a junior, which caught the Rockies' attention. He went into his junior year in 2018 projected to be one of the top 100 college players off the draft board. However, MacIver suffered a hamate injury in late March and missed nearly two months. He finished with a .232 average, three home runs and 24 RBIs. Rockies scouting director Bill Schmidt never forgot what he saw from MacIver in the Cape Cod League in the summer of 2017 and didn't hesitate when the catcher was still on the board in the ninth round.

SCOUTING REPORT: MacIver is athletic enough and has a strong enough arm to catch in the big leagues. He has adapted well to the full-time challenge. He appeared in 31 games at short-season Boise behind the plate, and 23 others at DH. He has the offensive potential to be an impact player, which he showed in the Northwest League by hitting .284 with 30 RBIs in 213 at-bats.

THE FUTURE: The Rockies have a lack of depth at catcher. MacIver has a chance to move quickly through the system if he shows the ability to handle the receiving chores. Having played first base and third base as well as catching at Washington, he is more agile than most catchers.

Year	Club (League)	Class	AVG	G	AB	R	H	2B	3B	HR	RBI	BB	SO	SB	CS	OBP	SLG
2018	Boise (NWL)	SS	.284	54	194	25	55	10	3	5	30	18	44	4	6	.358	.443
Minor League Totals			.284	54	194	25	55	10	3	5	30	18	44	4	6	.358	.443

Detroit Tigers

BY JUSTIN COLEMAN

The Tigers have spent most of the past decade infusing their club with high-priced superstars in an effort to win the World Series. They dished out large contracts, north of $180 million, to Miguel Cabrera, Justin Verlander and Prince Fielder. The roster was filled out with a veteran bullpen and other veteran position players, including Ian Kinsler and Victor Martinez. Detroit won the 2012 American League pennant and fell in the Championship Series in 2011 and 2013. Unfortunately, they weren't able to hoist the World Series trophy in any of those campaigns.

The effort to win fell short and owner Mike Illitch passed away in February 2017. With it, the Tigers took on a new longer-term mindset.

Before departing, previous GM Dave Dombrowski had traded veterans Yoenis Cespedes and David Price in an effort to infuse the farm system with much-needed talent. But those were moves hoped to help return the team to contention almost immediately. It didn't work. While the 2016 season ended with 86 wins, 2017 and 2018 both ended with the same record: 64-98.

Now, the Tigers are in the midst of their first full-bore rebuild in years. They let go of veterans Kinsler, Justin Upton and Verlander with an eye on accruing young minor league talent. The contracts of Cabrera and righthander Jordan Zimmermann are untradeable at this point, each with significant injury history attached to their names.

This period in franchise history has been a time of serious focus on the draft and international market as Detroit aims to build a farm system that creates sustained success in the future.

The Tigers' minor league system saw an uptick in 2018, with quality performances from a group of young and talented arms. Matt Manning, Beau Burrows and Franklin Perez are making cases as the future of the big league rotation. The 2018 draft yielded a potential superstar talent in Casey Mize, the top-ranked prospect in the 2018 draft class. In addition, there are some interesting bullpen arms who have surfaced, though their profiles don't fit the mold of future closers.

While the position talent isn't as strong, there are some athletic outfielders on the horizon. Detroit was able to acquire Daz Cameron, who came over in the Verlander trade, and Parker Meadows, a high school pick taken at the top of the second round of the 2018 draft.

With pitching and young, athletic outfielders leading the next wave of Tigers, it would be easy to overlook a cluster of impressive young infielders. The middle of the diamond has talent, with

Reliever Joe Jimenez made the all-star team in 2018, his first full season in the big leagues.

PROJECTED 2022 LINEUP

Catcher	Jake Rogers (27)
First Base	Jeimer Candelario (28)
Second Base	Willi Castro (25)
Third Base	Isaac Paredes (23)
Shortstop	Sergio Alcantara (25)
Left Field	Parker Meadows (22)
Center Field	Daz Cameron (25)
Right Field	Nick Castellanos (30)
Designated Hitter	Christin Stewart (28)
No. 1 Starter	Casey Mize (25)
No. 2 Starter	Michael Fulmer (29)
No. 3 Starter	Matt Manning (24)
No. 4 Starter	Franklin Perez (24)
No. 5 Starter	Alex Faedo (26)
Closer	Beau Burrows (25)

the likes of Isaac Paredes, Sergio Alcantara, Willi Castro and Wenceel Perez. Each of these players is athletic, with Paredes having the highest impact potential with the bat. The group of infielders have come mostly via trade and international signings.

Trades have helped to replenish the Tigers' system, accounting for roughly one-third of the system's Top 30 Prospects. The homegrown talent has stemmed mostly from college picks, which has helped to create the rich pitching foundation that Detroit has built.

The organization will look to continue its rebuild with the No. 5 overall pick in the 2019 draft.

DETROIT TIGERS

TOP 2019 ROOKIE: Christin Stewart, OF. Stewart should supply some power in the middle of Detroit's lineup in 2019 after hitting 25 home runs in the minors before his 2018 callup.
BREAKOUT PROSPECT: Sergio Alcantara, SS. The defensive standout has had flashes of offensive impact, particularly with a hot month of June in his first taste of Double-A ball.
SLEEPER: Ethan DeCaster, RHP. He posted a 0.84 ERA in 32 innings after being drafted out of Duke in 2018.

SOURCE OF TOP 30 TALENT			
Homegrown	21	Acquired	9
College	11	Trade	9
Junior college	0	Rule 5 draft	0
High school	4	Independent league	0
Nondrafted free agent	1	Free agent/waivers	0
International	5		

LF
Christin Stewart (8)
Brock Deatherage (28)
Cam Gibson

CF
Daz Cameron (5)
Parker Meadows (7)
Jacob Robson (24)
Daniel Woodrow (25)
Derek Hill
Kingston Liniak

RF
Jose Azocar (30)

3B
Isaac Paredes (3)
Kody Eaves
Chad Sedio

SS
Willi Castro (9)
Wenceel Perez (11)
Sergio Alcantara (14)
Jose King

2B
Kody Clemens (12)
Dawel Lugo (17)

1B
Josh Lester
Reynaldo Rivera

C
Jake Rogers (13)
Sam McMillan (27)
Joey Morgan
Grayson Greiner

LHP

LHSP	LHRP
Gregory Soto (15)	Matt Hall (23)
Austin Sodders (20)	Tarik Skubal
Adam Wolf	Evan Hill
Tyler Alexander	

RHP

RHSP	RHRP
Casey Mize (1)	Sandy Baez (19)
Matt Manning (2)	Spencer Turnbull (21)
Franklin Perez (4)	Bryan Garcia (22)
Beau Burrows (6)	Anthony Castro (26)
Alex Faedo (10)	Jason Foley (29)
Kyle Funkhouser (16)	Wilkel Hernandez (30)
Logan Shore (18)	Reed Garrett
Grayson Long	Wladimir Pinto
	Gerson Moreno
	Elvin Rodriguez
	Mark Ecker
	Ethan DeCaster
	Gio Arriera

DRAFT ANALYSIS

2018

BEST PURE HITTER: 2B Kody Clemens (3) had a breakout year at the plate for Texas in 2018, as he hit .351. He followed it up with an impressive pro debut, when he hit .288/.365/.450 while making it to high Class A. He handles the bat very well and has feel for the strike zone, giving him a chance to be a plus hitter.

BEST POWER: OF Brock Deatherage (10) showed solid power at N.C. State, where he hit 14 home runs in 60 games. His above-average power (and plus raw power) didn't disappoint in his first cameo in the minors, as he hit four home runs in just two games in the Gulf Coast League. His power tailed off as he moved up (he hit three home runs in 58 subsequent games), but he looks to be an excellent senior sign as a center fielder with juice.

FASTEST RUNNER: OF Parker Meadows (2) is a plus runner who uses that speed to cover plenty of ground in center field.

BEST DEFENSIVE PLAYER: Meadows should be able to stick in center field as a rangy defender. He has a plus arm and takes solid routes.

BEST ATHLETE: OF Kingston Liniak (4) is an above-average runner with a loose, athletic body that has room for projection. Meadows is also in the running for this category with long strides.

BEST FASTBALL: RHP Casey Mize (1) has a plus fastball that gets some plus-plus grades thanks to his ability to locate it with above-average control. RHP Hugh Smith (6) has a plus fastball that touches 97 mph. At 6-foot-10, he gets excellent extension, which helps the pitch play up.

BEST SECONDARY PITCH: Not many pitchers throw a splitter any more, and even fewer can use it as a weapon. Mize has a plus-plus splitter that was the key to his domination of the Southeastern Conference when he was at Auburn.

BEST PRO DEBUT: LHP Tarik Skubal (9) had control problems at Seattle, but he had no problems in his pro debut. He went 3-0, 0.40 in 22.1 innings

TOP DRAFT PICKS OF THE DECADE

Year	Player, Pos.	2018 Org
2009	Jacob Turner, RHP	Tigers
2010	Nick Castellanos, 3B (1st round supp.)	Tigers
2011	James McCann, C (2nd round)	Tigers
2012	Jake Thompson, RHP (2nd round)	Brewers
2013	Jonathon Crawford, RHP	Did not play
2014	Derek Hill, OF	Tigers
2015	Beau Burrows, RHP	Tigers
2016	Matt Manning, RHP	Tigers
2017	Alex Faedo, RHP	Tigers
2018	Casey Mize, RHP	Tigers

across three stops, and his 92-95 mph fastball helped him rack up 33 strikeouts.

MOST INTRIGUING BACKGROUND: While he isn't a pitcher like his father, Kody Clemens (3) hopes to have his own impactful career in baseball. Coming from a baseball family, Kody is known for having a great feel at second base. Smith was not seen as a prospect in high school, but he went from 5-foot-11, 145 pounds as a 16-year-old to 6-foot-10, 215 pounds as a college junior, which is why he was the top prospect in Division III baseball.

CLOSEST TO THE MAJORS: After having major success at Auburn, Mize figures to advance through the minors quickly. With quality control and a good mix of pitches, the righty figures to be a big factor in the Tigers rotation before too long.

BEST LATE-ROUND PICK: RHP Ethan DeCaster (18) pitched well across four levels of the minors after being drafted out of Duke. He only walked six batters in 39 innings while striking out 39 and advancing to high Class A.

THE ONE WHO GOT AWAY: The Tigers signed all but two picks. RHP Cole Henry (38) did not sign with Detroit, choosing to attend Louisiana State instead. The big-bodied righty features a three-pitch mix and a low to mid-90's fastball that he will continue polishing in college.

—JUSTIN COLEMAN

2017

The early returns weren't outstanding for this class, but RHP Alex Faedo (1) made his pro debut and quickly reached Double-A. 1B Rey Rivera and (2) C Sam McMillan (5) have work to do but showed upside in thier first full pro seasons.

GRADE: C

2016

RHP Matt Manning (1) rose through three levels to reach Double-A. RHP Kyle Funkhouser (4) is closing in on Detroit, and RHP Bryan Garcia (6) should be as well despite missing 2018 due to Tommy John surgery.

GRADE: B

2015

This class has already produced a trio of big leaguers - OF Christin Stewart (1), RHP Drew Smith (3) and LHP Matt Hall (6). RHP Beau Burrows (1) could soon make it four after a solid year in Double-A. He projects as the best of the class.

GRADE: C

1 CASEY MIZE, RHP

Born: May 1, 1997. **B-T:** R-R. **HT:** 6-3. **WT:** 220.
Drafted: Auburn, 2018 (1st). **Signed By:** Justin Henry.

The Tigers had not picked first overall since 1997, when they selected Rice closer Matt Anderson. They hope that picking a college righthander works out better this time. Mize signed for $7.5 million, which set a bonus record for any player since the current draft format was adopted in 2012. Mize came into his junior season at Auburn facing questions about his durability. He had missed time as a sophomore with a flexor strain and did not pitch that summer. But he had no problems fronting Auburn's rotation in 2018 and reinforced the conviction that he was the clear top player in the 2018 draft class. Using his signature splitter, Mize held hitters to a .217 average in college. After tossing a career-high 114.2 innings in his junior season, Mize made just five starts in pro ball before shutting things down for the year.
SCOUTING REPORT: Mize features a 91-95 mph fastball that touches 97. It's a plus-plus pitch that plays up because of how well he locates it. His fastball sets up his other offerings, all of which are above-average across the board. Mize's 80-86 mph slider is almost two pitches in one. He can make it bigger and slower when he's looking for an early-count strike, but he can also throw it harder and tighter as a later-count out pitch. His best weapon is his plus-plus, mid-80s splitter. While many pitchers struggle to command and control their splitter, he commands his nearly as well as his fastball. It looks like his fastball out of his hand and then dives out of the zone as it nears the plate. Additionally, Mize has started to throw a cutter that flashes above-average. Everything he throws is hard, and he uses his splitter in lieu of a changeup. As good as his stuff is, Mize's plus control is equally noteworthy. He ranked among the top 20 in walk rate in Division I as both a sophomore and junior and led D-I in strikeout-to-walk rate in 2017. The intangibles will also play a role for the righty, and Tigers coaches love his approach to the game.
THE FUTURE: As he works to repeat his delivery with more consistency, Mize should fly through the minors. The 2019 season will be his first full campaign in the minors, and he should have no trouble reaching Double-A Erie by the end of it. Mize's ability to command his offerings and throw a plus-plus splitter and two additional plus pitches put him in an excellent position to be a potential front-of-the-rotation starter.

TOM DIPACE

BA GRADE	SCOUTING GRADES	
65 Risk: High	**Fastball:** 70. **Splitter:** 70.	
	Slider: 55. **Cut:** 55. **Control:** 60.	

Projected future grades on 20-80 scouting scale

TOP PROSPECTS OF THE DECADE

Year	Player, Pos.	2018 Org
2009	Rick Porcello, RHP	Red Sox
2010	Jacob Turner, RHP	Tigers
2011	Jacob Turner, RHP	Tigers
2012	Jacob Turner, RHP	Tigers
2013	Nick Castellanos ,3B/OF	Tigers
2014	Nick Castellanos, 3B/OF	Tigers
2015	Steven Moya, OF	Japan
2016	Michael Fulmer, RHP	Tigers
2017	Matt Manning, RHP	Tigers
2018	Franklin Perez, RHP	Tigers

BEST TOOLS

Best Hitter For Average	Isaac Paredes
Best Power Hitter	Christin Stewart
Best Strike-Zone Discipline	Isaac Paredes
Fastest Baserunner	Derek Hill
Best Athlete	Parker Meadows
Best Fastball	Matt Manning
Best Curveball	Matt Hall
Best Slider	Spencer Turnbull
Best Changeup	Franklin Perez
Best Control	Austin Soders
Best Defensive Catcher	Jake Rogers
Best Defensive Infielder	Sergio Alcantara
Best Infield Arm	Sergio Alcantara
Best Defensive Outfielder	Derek Hill
Best Outfield Arm	Jose Azocar

Year	Club (League)	Class	W	L	ERA	G	GS	CG	SV	IP	H	HR	BB	SO	K/9	WHIP	AVG
2018	Tigers West (GCL)	R	0	0	0.00	1	1	0	0	2	0	0	1	4	18.0	0.50	.000
	Lakeland (FSL)	HiA	0	1	4.63	4	4	0	0	12	13	2	2	10	7.7	1.29	.295
Minor League Totals			0	1	3.95	5	5	0	0	14	13	2	3	14	9.2	1.17	.260

2 MATT MANNING, RHP

Born: Jan. 28, 1998. **B-T:** R-R. **HT:** 6-6. **WT:** 190. **Drafted:** HS—Sacramento, 2016 (1st round). **Signed By:** Scott Cerny.

TRACK RECORD: Manning was lauded out of high school in part because of his stuff, but also for his athletic bloodlines. His father, Rich, played two seasons in the NBA, and Matt was a Division I basketball prospect. Manning's 2018 season was delayed two weeks by an oblique injury, but once he got going he masted two Class A levels and climbed to Double-A at age 20.

SCOUTING REPORT: Manning's 6-foot-6 frame gives him excellent extension, which allows his plus 91-95 mph fastball to appear even firmer. His best secondary offering is his low-80s downer curveball, which is a future plus pitch. Manning shows a feel for a changeup that should develop into an average pitch, though it currently lags behind his other secondary offerings. Despite having stabbing action in his arm swing, Manning's athleticism gives him the body control to develop average control, but at times he has struggled to maintain a consistent release point because of the drop in his arm path.

BA GRADE

60 Risk: High

Fastball: 70.
Curve: 60.
CHG: 50. CTL: 50.

THE FUTURE: Tigers personnel applaud Manning's competitiveness. He has to continue to refine the consistency of his delivery while polishing his changeup. His combination of stuff and athleticism gives him the upside of a mid-rotation starter with improved control.

Year	Club (League)	Class	W	L	ERA	G	GS	CG	SV	IP	H	HR	BB	SO	K/9	WHIP	AVG
2016	Tigers West (GCL)	R	0	2	3.99	10	10	0	0	29	27	2	7	46	14.1	1.16	.237
2017	Connecticut (NYP)	SS	2	2	1.89	9	9	0	0	33	27	0	14	36	9.7	1.23	.223
	West Michigan (MWL)	LoA	2	0	5.60	5	5	0	0	18	14	0	11	26	13.2	1.42	.209
2018	West Michigan (MWL)	LoA	3	3	3.40	11	11	0	0	56	47	3	28	76	12.3	1.35	.229
	Lakeland (FSL)	HiA	4	4	2.98	9	9	0	0	51	32	4	19	65	11.4	0.99	.176
	Erie (EL)	AA	0	1	4.22	2	2	0	0	11	11	0	4	13	11.0	1.41	.282
Minor League Totals			11	12	3.36	46	46	0	0	198	158	9	83	262	11.9	1.22	.217

3 ISAAC PAREDES, SS/2B

Born: Feb. 18, 1999. **B-T:** R-R. **HT:** 5-11. **WT:** 225. **Signed:** Mexico, 2015. **Signed By:** Sergio Hernandez/Louie Eljaua (Cubs).

TRACK RECORD: After signing with the Cubs in 2015, Paredes was traded to the Tigers in the July 2017 deal that sent Justin Wilson and Alex Avila to Chicago. He stood out in 2017 as an 18-year-old shortstop who swatted 11 home runs with a low strikeout rate. He added 15 more homers in 2018 as he reached Double-A as a 19-year-old.

SCOUTING REPORT: Paredes' innate knack for putting the barrel on the ball gives him the potential to be a plus hitter. He has a contact-oriented approach with average power. It's a pull-heavy approach and all his power is to his pull side. Equipped with an above-average arm, Paredes is viewed as an average defender at second or third base, who can move around the diamond if necessary. Scouts do not believe he has the range to stick at shortstop. Though he is a below-average runner and already has a stocky frame, his hands and consistency on the defensive end should allow him to stay in the infield.

BA GRADE

55 Risk: High

Hit: 60. Power: 50.
Run: 40. Field: 50.
Arm: 55.

THE FUTURE: Paredes profiles as a first-division regular at second base thanks to his offensive potential. His defensive versatility only adds to his value. He should split 2019 between Double-A Erie and Triple-A Toledo with a chance to make his major league debut in 2020.

Year	Club (League)	Class	AVG	G	AB	R	H	2B	3B	HR	RBI	BB	SO	SB	CS	OBP	SLG
2016	Cubs (AZL)	R	.305	47	167	23	51	14	3	1	26	13	20	4	0	.359	.443
	South Bend (MWL)	LoA	.167	3	12	0	2	0	0	0	0	0	2	0	0	.231	.167
2017	South Bend (MWL)	LoA	.264	92	337	49	89	25	0	7	49	29	54	2	1	.343	.401
	West Michigan (MWL)	LoA	.217	32	115	16	25	3	0	4	21	13	13	0	0	.323	.348
2018	Lakeland (FSL)	HiA	.259	84	301	50	78	19	2	12	48	32	54	1	0	.338	.455
	Erie (EL)	AA	.321	39	131	20	42	9	0	3	22	19	22	1	0	.406	.458
Minor League Totals			.270	297	1063	158	287	70	5	27	166	106	165	8	1	.349	.421

4 FRANKLIN PEREZ, RHP

Born: Dec. 6, 1997. **B-T:** R-R. **HT:** 6-3. **WT:** 197. **Signed:** Venezuela, 2014.
Signed By: Oz Ocampo/Oscar Alvarado (Astros).

TRACK RECORD: Perez was briefly developed as a third baseman at Carlos Guillen's academy in Venezuela, but his arm strength prompted a return to the mound. He ranked as the No. 14 player in the 2014 international class and signed with the Astros for $1 million. He was dealt in 2017 as part of the package that brought ace righthander Justin Verlander to Houston. A knee injury slowed Perez in 2017, but he had more serious injury issues in 2018. He made just seven starts because he missed time with a lat strain and was shut down late in the year with a sore right shoulder.

SCOUTING REPORT: Though his season was derailed by injuries, Perez's feel, control and stuff are promising if he stays healthy. He throws four pitches, including a plus fastball that gets into the mid-90s. He is working with an above-average curveball and a developing slider that could be average or better as well. In addition, Perez has a feel for a plus changeup. He sells the pitch well, and throws it with roughly 10 mph of separation from his fastball. When Perez executes his changeup it shows run and sink away from lefthanded hitters.

THE FUTURE: Perez will need a strong showing in 2019 to prove his health, but if he can get back on track, his stuff is enough project him as future mid-rotation starter thanks to his plus control.

BA GRADE
60 Risk: Extreme
Fastball: 60.
CHG: 60. CB: 55.
SL: 50. CTL: 60.

Year	Club (League)	Class	AVG	G	AB	R	H	2B	3B	HR	RBI	BB	SO	SB	CS	OBP	SLG
2016	Cubs (AZL)	R	.305	47	167	23	51	14	3	1	26	13	20	4	0	.359	.443
	South Bend (MWL)	LoA	.167	3	12	0	2	0	0	0	0	0	2	0	0	.231	.167
2017	South Bend (MWL)	LoA	.264	92	337	49	89	25	0	7	49	29	54	2	1	.343	.401
	West Michigan (MWL)	LoA	.217	32	115	16	25	3	0	4	21	13	13	0	0	.323	.348
2018	Lakeland (FSL)	HiA	.259	84	301	50	78	19	2	12	48	32	54	1	0	.338	.455
	Erie (EL)	AA	.321	39	131	20	42	9	0	3	22	19	22	1	0	.406	.458
Minor League Totals			.270	297	1063	158	287	70	5	27	166	106	165	8	1	.349	.421

5 DAZ CAMERON, OF

Born: Jan. 15, 1997. **B-T:** R-R. **HT:** 6-2. **WT:** 195. **Drafted:** HS—McDonough, Ga., 2015 (1st round supplemental). **Signed By:** Gavin Dickey (Astros).

TRACK RECORD: The son of former all-star outfielder Mike Cameron, Daz was originally drafted by the Astros before being flipped to the Tigers with righthander Franklin Perez and catcher Jake Rogers as part of the package used to acquire Justin Verlander for Houston's run to the World Series. Cameron hit a career-high 14 home runs in 2017, then built on that year by zooming from high Class A Lakeland to Triple-A Toledo in 2018.

SCOUTING REPORT: Cameron is a well-rounded player with no overwhelming tool, but no below-average one either. He unlocked his offensive game with a tweak in his approach. By being more aggressive early in the count he found more pitches on which to do damage. He's an average hitter with average power. Defensively, he's an above-average defender in center field with an above-average arm. He's a plus runner who needs to sharpen his baserunning instincts to become a more efficient basestealer.

THE FUTURE: Cameron could make an appearance in the big leagues at some point in 2019. His ability to play a solid center gives him a path to a future everyday job, while his arm gives him a fallback as a fourth outfielder.

BA GRADE
50 Risk: Medium
Hit: 55. Power: 50.
Run: 60. Field: 55.
Arm: 55.

Year	Club (League)	Class	AVG	G	AB	R	H	2B	3B	HR	RBI	BB	SO	SB	CS	OBP	SLG
2016	Quad Cities (MWL)	LoA	.143	21	77	5	11	2	2	0	6	8	33	4	3	.221	.221
	Tri-City (NYP)	SS	.278	19	79	13	22	3	1	2	14	6	26	8	2	.352	.418
2017	Quad Cities (MWL)	LoA	.271	119	442	78	120	29	8	13	72	45	107	32	12	.350	.462
	West Michigan (MWL)	LoA	.250	3	8	1	2	0	0	0	1	3	4	0	1	.455	.250
2018	Lakeland (FSL)	HiA	.259	58	216	35	56	9	3	3	20	25	69	10	4	.346	.370
	Erie (EL)	AA	.285	53	200	32	57	12	5	5	35	25	53	12	5	.367	.470
	Toledo (IL)	AAA	.211	15	57	8	12	4	1	0	6	2	15	2	2	.246	.316
Minor League Totals			.258	339	1254	206	324	63	23	23	171	139	356	92	39	.341	.400

6 BEAU BURROWS, RHP

Born: Sept. 18, 1996. **B-T:** R-R. **HT:** 6-2. **WT:** 200. **Drafted:** HS—Weatherford, Texas, 2015 (1st round). **Signed By:** Chris Wimmer.

TRACK RECORD: Of the seven prep pitchers drafted in the first round in 2015, two didn't pitch in 2018, a third threw less than 10 innings and a fourth posted a 5.24 ERA in Class A. The durable Burrows has been more of a success story than his peers, as he quickly climbed to Double-A in his second season in pro ball.

SCOUTING REPORT: Everything for Burrows is based off of an effective 92-94 mph fastball that can touch as high as 97. The pitch is more effective when thrown up in the zone for swinging strikes. He backs the pitch up with a pair of breaking balls, which work well in tandem, though neither is a plus pitch on its own. Burrows had more success throwing his low-70s curveball for called strikes, and he has shown the ability bury his mid-80s slider. His fringe-average changeup could develop into an above-average pitch if he could command it better. His delivery, which includes a very high front elbow and works as somewhat of a see-saw, might hinder attempts to improve his fringe-average control.

BA GRADE

50 Risk: Medium

Fastball: 60.
CHG: 55. CB: 50.
SL: 50. CTL: 45

THE FUTURE: Burrows should begin 2019 in Triple-A. The Tigers will try to develop him into a No. 4 starter, but his command issues and secondaries may eventually push him to the bullpen.

Year	Club (League)	Class	W	L	ERA	G	GS	CG	SV	IP	H	HR	BB	SO	K/9	WHIP	AVG
2016	West Michigan (MWL)	LoA	6	4	3.15	21	20	0	0	97	87	2	30	67	6.2	1.21	.240
2017	Lakeland (FSL)	HiA	4	3	1.23	11	11	0	0	59	44	3	11	62	9.5	0.94	.221
	Erie (EL)	AA	6	4	4.72	15	15	1	0	76	79	5	33	75	8.8	1.47	.269
2018	Erie (EL)	AA	10	9	4.10	26	26	0	0	134	126	12	56	127	8.5	1.36	.251
Minor League Totals			27	20	3.38	83	81	1	0	394	354	22	141	364	8.3	1.26	.243

7 PARKER MEADOWS, OF

MIKE JANES /FOUR SEAM IMAGES

Born: Nov. 2, 1999. **B-T:** L-R. **HT:** 6-5. **WT:** 185. **Drafted:** HS—Loganville, Ga., 2018 (2nd round). **Signed By:** Bryson Barber.

TRACK RECORD: Meadows is the younger brother of Rays outfielder Austin Meadows, and both brothers attended Grayson High in Georgia. Austin went ninth overall to the Pirates in 2013. Parker was a third-team high school All-American in 2018, when the Tigers selected him with the first pick in the second round. They spent $2.5 million to keep him from a Clemson commitment. Meadows ranked as the No. 11 prospect in the Rookie-level Gulf Coast League and briefly made it to the college-heavy New York-Penn League in his first summer in pro ball.

SCOUTING REPORT: Meadows has plus raw power and could hit for plus power in games in the future. But scouts have questions about his overall feel to hit, with long arms and a significant hitch in his load, which can be described as something of an arm bar. Even so, Meadows is athletic and a plus runner underway, and while his size might fit better in a corner one day, he

BA GRADE

55 Risk: Extreme

Hit: 45. Power: 60.
Run: 60. Field: 55.
Arm: 60

should be a solid defender in either spot. The profile power and plus arm could make him a right fielder in the future.

THE FUTURE: Meadows' bloodlines give him a feel for the game, and after a strong pro debut in which he showed patience and power, he should move to full-season ball at low Class A West Michigan in 2019.

Year	Club (League)	Class	AVG	G	AB	R	H	2B	3B	HR	RBI	BB	SO	SB	CS	OBP	SLG
2018	Tigers West (GCL)	R	.284	22	74	16	21	2	1	4	8	8	25	3	1	.376	.500
	Connecticut (NYP)	SS	.316	6	19	4	6	1	0	0	2	2	6	0	0	.381	.368
Minor League Totals			.290	28	93	20	27	3	1	4	10	10	31	3	1	.377	.473

8 CHRISTIN STEWART, OF

Born: Dec. 10, 1993. **B-T:** L-R. **HT:** 6-0. **WT:** 205. **Drafted:** Tennessee, 2015 (1st round). **Signed By:** Harold Zonder.

TRACK RECORD: Power has been Stewart's calling card ever since his high school days. His 69 homers over four years at Providence Christian Academy set a Georgia state record. From there, Stewart spent three more years mashing at Tennessee before the Tigers made him the second of their two first-rounders in 2015 and signed him for just shy of $1.8 million.

SCOUTING REPORT: Stewart's plus power remains his carrying tool. He hit 23 home runs at Triple-A Toledo in 2018 to tie for the International League lead. It marked his third straight season with at least 20 homers. The lefthanded-hitting Stewart's home run power is geared strongly to his pull side. His hit tool is just fringe-average, and he has a swing geared to hit balls at the bottom of the zone. But he has the strike-zone awareness to lay off when pitchers work around him, so he posts solid on-base percentages. Stewart will have to continue to crush balls, because his defense in left field and throwing arm, though improved, are well below-average. He has below-average speed as well.

THE FUTURE: Stewart will get at-bats in the big leagues as the Tigers rebuild. He is a hard worker who will look to make the most of his offensive prowess. He will try to prove he's more than a DH.

BA GRADE

45 Risk: Medium

Hit: 45. Power: 60.
Run: 40. Field: 30.
Arm: 30.

Year	Club (League)	Class	AVG	G	AB	R	H	2B	3B	HR	RBI	BB	SO	SB	CS	OBP	SLG
2016	Lakeland (FSL)	HiA	.264	104	356	60	94	22	1	24	68	74	105	3	1	.403	.534
	Erie (EL)	AA	.218	24	87	17	19	2	0	6	19	12	26	0	0	.310	.448
2017	Erie (EL)	AA	.256	136	485	67	124	29	3	28	86	56	138	3	0	.335	.501
2018	Tigers East (GCL)	R	.200	2	5	1	1	0	0	1	1	1	0	0	0	.333	.800
	Tigers West (GCL)	R	.250	1	4	1	1	0	0	1	2	0	0	0	0	.250	1.000
	Toledo (IL)	AAA	.264	122	444	69	117	21	3	23	77	67	108	0	0	.364	.480
	Detroit (AL)	MAJ	.267	17	60	7	16	1	1	2	10	10	13	0	0	.375	.417
Major League Totals			.267	17	60	7	16	1	1	2	10	10	13	0	0	.375	.417
Minor League Totals			.262	460	1637	256	429	87	14	93	297	236	445	11	4	.363	.503

9 WILLI CASTRO, SS

Born: April 24, 1997. **B-T:** B-R. **HT:** 6-1. **WT:** 165. **Signed:** Dominican Republic, 2013. **Signed By:** Ramon Pena/Felix Nivar (Indians).

TRACK RECORD: Castro, who was born in Puerto Rico but raised in the Dominican Republic, became the Indians' top non-Cuban international signee in 2013 when he inked a deal for $825,000. He has been among the youngest players at every stop during his pro career, and he opened 2018 as the fourth-youngest player in the Double-A Eastern League. The Tigers acquired Castro from the Indians as a part of the deal for outfielder Leonys Martin. He finished the year with a cameo at Triple-A Toledo.

SCOUTING REPORT: Switch-hitters can be tricky to project, and that's certainly the case with Castro. For example, at Double-A Akron, he hit all five of his home runs lefthanded, whereas all but one of the four home runs he hit with Double-A Erie came from the right side. Overall, he projects as a below-average hitter with a 5-10 home run pop. He's a solid defender at shortstop who was rated by EL managers as the circuit's best defender at the position. He backs that up with plus arm and above-average speed.

THE FUTURE: With further development and physical maturity, Castro could be a second-division regular. He's likely to spend the bulk of his 2019 at Toledo.

BA GRADE

45 Risk: Medium

Hit: 40. Power: 40.
Run: 55. Field: 55.
Arm: 60.

Year	Club (League)	Class	AVG	G	AB	R	H	2B	3B	HR	RBI	BB	SO	SB	CS	OBP	SLG
2016	Lake County (MWL)	LoA	.259	123	518	68	134	21	8	7	49	19	96	16	11	.286	.371
	Lynchburg (CAR)	HiA	.222	3	9	0	2	0	0	0	0	0	2	0	1	.222	.222
2017	Lynchburg (CAR)	HiA	.291	123	468	69	136	24	3	11	58	28	90	19	9	.337	.425
2018	Akron (EL)	AA	.245	97	371	55	91	20	2	5	39	28	84	13	4	.303	.350
	Erie (EL)	AA	.324	26	105	12	34	9	2	4	13	6	25	4	1	.366	.562
	Toledo (IL)	AAA	.286	5	21	0	6	0	0	0	2	0	5	1	0	.286	.286
Minor League Totals			.267	487	1920	269	512	88	21	30	197	97	366	82	37	.309	.381

10 ALEX FAEDO, RHP

Born: Nov. 12, 1995. **B-T:** R-R. **HT:** 6-5. **WT:** 230. **Drafted:** Florida, 2017 (1st round). **Signed By:** R.J. Burgess.

TRACK RECORD: Surgeries on both knees between Faedo's sophomore and junior seasons at Florida kicked off his draft year with uncertainty. He started slowly in 2017 but finished strong enough to earn Most Outstanding Player honors in the 2017 College World Series as the Gators claimed the national championship. The Tigers selected Faedo 18th overall and signed him for $3.5 million. He made his pro debut at high Class A Lakeland in 2018.

SCOUTING REPORT: The first thing that jumped out about Faedo in 2018 was his missing fastball velocity. He sat 89-92 mph as a pro, down a couple of ticks from the 92-94 he sat in college. The lessened velocity affected all of his pitches. Faedo's average changeup sometimes lacked separation, and his once plus slider dropped a half-grade because of his lack of arm speed. Without the ability to beat hitters with his fastball or command his pitches effectively, Faedo became home run prone. He allowed 15 in just 60 innings with Double-A Erie as a result of poor command that left a lot pitches in the middle of the zone.

THE FUTURE: It's easy to lose sight of the fact that 2018 was Faedo's pro debut. If he can rediscover his previous arm speed, his fastball and slider could still work in a starting role.

BA GRADE
50 Risk: High
Fastball: 55. Slider: 60. CHG: 50. CTL: 50.

Year	Club (League)	Class	W	L	ERA	G	GS	CG	SV	IP	H	HR	BB	SO	K/9	WHIP	AVG
2018	Lakeland (FSL)	HiA	2	4	3.10	12	12	0	0	61	49	3	13	51	7.5	1.02	.217
	Erie (EL)	AA	3	6	4.95	12	12	0	0	60	54	15	22	59	8.9	1.27	.239
Minor League Totals			5	10	4.02	24	24	0	0	121	103	18	35	110	8.2	1.14	.228

11 WENCEEL PEREZ, SS

BA GRADE
50 Risk: High

Born: Oct. 30, 1999. **B-T:** B-R. **HT:** 5-11. **WT:** 170. **Signed:** Dominican Republic, 2016. **Signed By:** Ramon Perez/Carlos Santana.

TRACK RECORD: As an amateur, Perez drew interest for his blend of athleticism and polish at a premium position. He showed a bat that produced plenty of line drives, as well quick-twitch characteristics in the field. The Tigers signed him for $550,000, and watched as he tore up the Dominican Summer League, then zoomed through three levels in 2018 before stopping at low Class A West Michigan.

SCOUTING REPORT: Perez uses quick wrists, solid bat control and a knack for the barrel to produce quality contact from both sides of the plate. Those traits could help his hit tool get to plus with further refinement. The Dominican teenager should be able to build around his plus hit tool with an improved approach as he gets more at-bats. He's a plus runner and works with good hands, quick footwork and enough of a throwing arm to stick at shortstop, providing a tool set that should create a future at a position up the middle.

THE FUTURE: The Tigers like his athleticism, and they think he will be fine at shortstop for now. While he doesn't have the pop to profile at a corner-infield spot, Perez has the skills to be an average big leaguer up the middle. Perez will return to low Class A in 2019, with a possible cameo at high Class A toward the end of the season.

Year	Club (League)	Class	AVG	G	AB	R	H	2B	3B	HR	RBI	BB	SO	SB	CS	OBP	SLG
2017	Tigers (DSL)	R	.314	61	226	31	71	8	1	0	22	27	21	16	6	.387	.358
2018	Tigers West (GCL)	R	.383	20	81	20	31	7	0	2	14	12	14	2	1	.462	.543
	Connecticut (NYP)	SS	.244	21	82	8	20	2	0	1	8	5	12	7	3	.287	.305
	West Michigan (MWL)	LoA	.309	16	68	8	21	3	3	0	9	2	8	4	1	.324	.441
Minor League Totals			.313	118	457	67	143	20	4	3	53	46	55	29	11	.375	.394

12 KODY CLEMENS, 2B

BA GRADE
45 Risk: High

Born: May 15th, 1996. **B-T:** L-R. **HT:** 6-1. **WT:** 170. **Drafted:** Texas, 2018 (3rd round). **Signed By:** Matt Lea.

TRACK RECORD: Clemens, the youngest of seven-time Cy Young Award winner Roger's sons, was drafted by the Astros out of high school but opted to head to college. After Tommy John surgery limited him to DH duties as a sophomore at Texas, Clemens swatted 24 home runs as a junior. The figure was good for second in the NCAA. Even though he was already 22 years old, the Tigers liked the offensive profile and popped him with their third-round pick.

SCOUTING REPORT: Clemens puts the barrel on the ball, and has a plus hit tool with future average power. For a middle infielder, his defensive tools are seen as average across the board and should allow him to stick at second base. While he doesn't possess a plus run tool, he runs the bases well. Known as a leader on the field, Clemens is competitive and has a natural feel for the game.

THE FUTURE: After a solid pro debut, Clemens is likely to return to high Class A before being promoted to the Double-A Erie.

Year	Club (League)	Class	AVG	G	AB	R	H	2B	3B	HR	RBI	BB	SO	SB	CS	OBP	SLG
2018	West Michigan (MWL)	LoA	.302	41	149	18	45	10	2	4	17	21	27	3	1	.387	.477
	Lakeland (FSL)	HiA	.238	11	42	6	10	2	0	1	3	2	12	1	0	.283	.357
Minor League Totals			.288	52	191	24	55	12	2	5	20	23	39	4	1	.365	.450

13 JAKE ROGERS, C

BA GRADE

45 Risk: High

Born: April 18, 1995. **B-T:** R-R. **HT:** 6-1. **WT:** 190. **Drafted:** Tulane, 2016 (3rd round). **Signed By:** Justin Cryer (Astros).

TRACK RECORD: The Astros originally took Rogers in the third round of the 2016 draft before dealing him to the Tigers as part of the package for Justin Verlander. He was lauded as one of the best defensive catchers in his draft class, most notably for a strong, accurate arm that allowed him to throw out nearly 63 percent of attempted basestealers in his junior season at Tulane.

SCOUTING REPORT: Rogers owns a plus arm, with a quick transfer and release, in addition to strong framing skills. There is no doubt he'll stick behind the plate. He threw out 56 percent of attempted basestealers with Double-A Erie in 2018. Rogers studies the game, and receives high praise from his pitching staffs. He's worked to tone down an exaggerated leg kick at the plate, which mitigated his hittability at times. He has solid-average raw power, though his in-game power was helped a bit this season by Erie's cozy dimensions.

THE FUTURE: Rogers is ticketed to spend more time at Double-A to continue developing his hitting. While still has areas to work on, Rogers has the profile behind the dish to help Detroit in the near future.

Year	Club (League)	Class	AVG	G	AB	R	H	2B	3B	HR	RBI	BB	SO	SB	CS	OBP	SLG
2016	Tri-City (NYP)	SS	.253	25	87	11	22	7	1	2	12	13	18	0	2	.369	.425
	Quad Cities (MWL)	LoA	.208	21	72	7	15	3	1	1	4	8	25	1	0	.305	.319
2017	Quad Cities (MWL)	LoA	.255	27	102	17	26	7	1	6	15	9	28	1	0	.336	.520
	Buies Creek (CAR)	HiA	.265	83	313	43	83	18	3	12	55	44	72	13	8	.357	.457
	Lakeland (FSL)	HiA	.143	2	7	0	1	0	0	0	0	1	2	0	0	.250	.143
2018	Erie (EL)	AA	.219	99	352	57	77	15	1	17	56	41	112	7	1	.305	.412
Minor League Totals			.240	257	933	135	224	50	7	38	142	116	257	22	11	.332	.431

14 SERGIO ALCANTARA, SS

BA GRADE

40 Risk: Medium

Born: July 10, 1996. **B-T:** B-R. **HT:** 5-9. **WT:** 168. **Signed:** Dominican Republic, 2012. **Signed By:** Junior Noboa (Diamondbacks).

TRACK RECORD: Alcantara came to Detroit from Arizona as a part of a package of three infielders for J.D Martinez before the August 2017 trade deadline. Alcantara played in 120 games in his first stint in the upper minors with Double-A after spending all of 2017 at high Class A.

SCOUTING REPORT: His profile is clearly defense-first because he is very fluid, athletic and gifted with a 70-grade throwing arm. He is a plus defender who will be an asset on defense at the shortstop position for Detroit. Alcantara's hit tool projects as average and he has a willingness to be patient in the box and draw walks, but his power is well below-average.

THE FUTURE: Alcantara has great defensive value and a solid hit tool, and that combination should bring him to the big leagues in a utility role. He is a trusted defender already, and should find himself playing in the majors within the next two seasons as he continues to get at-bats against advanced pitching.

Year	Club (League)	Class	AVG	G	AB	R	H	2B	3B	HR	RBI	BB	SO	SB	CS	OBP	SLG
2016	Diamondbacks (AZL)	R	.345	7	29	9	10	1	1	0	2	4	2	2	0	.424	.448
	Hillsboro (NWL)	SS	.319	15	47	12	15	2	0	0	8	10	10	4	2	.441	.362
	Kane County (MWL)	LoA	.267	53	180	15	48	6	1	1	16	14	26	3	2	.313	.328
	Visalia (CAL)	HiA	.267	4	15	2	4	1	0	0	0	3	2	0	1	.421	.333
2017	Visalia (CAL)	HiA	.279	86	340	44	95	15	2	3	28	34	57	11	10	.344	.362
	Lakeland (FSL)	HiA	.230	35	126	18	29	4	1	0	7	14	23	4	3	.307	.278
2018	Erie (EL)	AA	.271	120	442	53	120	18	3	1	37	42	95	8	5	.335	.333
Minor League Totals			.257	529	1942	271	500	76	14	7	160	241	376	50	29	.339	.322

15 GREGORY SOTO, LHP

BA GRADE

50 Risk: Extreme

Born: Feb. 11, 1995. **B-T:** L-L. **HT:** 6-1. **WT:** 240. **Drafted:** Dominican Republic, 2012. **Signed By:** Carlos Santana/Ramon Perez.

TRACK RECORD: Soto has long had big league stuff, albeit with little idea of where each of his pitches are going. He's racked up 9.8 strikeouts per nine innings over the course of his six-season career, but has mitigated those whiffs with 5.4 walks per nine innings. Still, the Tigers believe enough in the arm that they added him to their 40-man roster before the 2018 season.

SCOUTING REPORT: Soto works from a three-quarter arm slot and generates an electric fastball that has touched as high as 96 mph and profiles as a plus pitch. Soto's slider sits in the low 80s and is below-average, but shows promise of become an average offering down the line. His changeup lags behind, and he will have to work hard in order for it to get to an average grade. His body and frame are built to accrue innings, which shows in back-to-back seasons of 23 starts in the minors.

THE FUTURE: While Soto needs to develop a better changeup and greatly improve his control in order to start, his fastball and slider are good enough for him to profile as a low-leverage reliever in the relatively near future.

Year	Club (League)	Class	W	L	ERA	G	GS	CG	SV	IP	H	HR	BB	SO	K/9	WHIP	AVG
2016	Connecticut (NYP)	SS	3	2	3.03	15	15	0	0	71	68	1	34	62	7.8	1.43	.256
2017	West Michigan (MWL)	LoA	10	1	2.25	18	18	0	0	96	70	3	54	116	10.9	1.29	.204
	Lakeland (FSL)	HiA	2	1	2.25	5	5	0	0	28	27	1	11	28	9.0	1.36	.267
2018	Lakeland (FSL)	HiA	8	8	4.45	25	23	0	0	113	101	4	70	115	9.1	1.51	.235
Minor League Totals			31	22	3.37	106	89	0	0	436	371	10	261	474	9.8	1.45	.233

16 KYLE FUNKHOUSER, RHP

BA GRADE

45 Risk: High

Born: March 16, 1994. **B-T:** R-R. **HT:** 6-2. **WT:** 220. **Drafted:** Louisville, 2016 (4th round). **Signed By:** Harold Zonder.

TRACK RECORD: After three years at Louisville, Funkhouser gambled on himself. The Dodgers chose him with one of their two first round picks in 2015, but he opted to go back to school for another season. The gambit backfired, and he fell to the fourth round in 2017. Funkhouser dealt with a bout of elbow soreness in 2017, but he came back strong in 2018 before breaking his foot after a promotion to Triple-A.

SCOUTING REPORT: Funkhouser's fastball touches 95 but tends to sit comfortably in the low 90s. His changeup will be average in the future, and his two breaking pitches are of the same grade, though the consistency of both pitches varies from start to start. With average command, he can throw all of his pitches in different counts to give batters a different look. He also gets deception from a compact delivery.

THE FUTURE: As he works to create some consistency with his secondary stuff, Funkhouser will spend more time at Double-A. With a plus fastball and other average offerings, he profiles to fit in as an innings-eater toward the back end of a rotation.

Year	Club (League)	Class	W	L	ERA	G	GS	CG	SV	IP	H	HR	BB	SO	K/9	WHIP	AVG
2016	Connecticut (NYP)	SS	0	2	2.65	13	13	0	0	37	34	0	8	34	8.2	1.13	.246
2017	West Michigan (MWL)	LoA	4	1	3.16	7	7	0	0	31	30	3	13	49	14.1	1.37	.254
	Lakeland (FSL)	HiA	1	1	1.72	5	5	1	0	31	23	1	6	34	9.8	0.93	.205
2018	Erie (EL)	AA	4	5	3.74	17	17	0	0	89	88	10	39	89	9.0	1.43	.266
	Toledo (IL)	AAA	0	2	6.23	2	2	0	0	9	8	0	10	7	7.3	2.08	.258
Minor League Totals			9	11	3.23	44	44	1	0	198	183	14	76	213	9.7	1.31	.251

17 DAWEL LUGO, 2B/3B

BA GRADE

40 Risk: Medium

Born: Dec. 31, 1994. **B-T:** R-R. **HT:** 6-0. **WT:** 190. **Signed:** Dominican Republic, 2011. **Signed By:** Marco Paddy/Hilario Soriano (Blue Jays).

TRACK RECORD: Lugo came to Detroit as one of the pieces in the deal that sent J.D. Martinez to the Diamondbacks in 2017. He made his big league debut in 2018, providing help up the middle for the rebuilding Tigers. While not known for his bat, Lugo hit .269 in 123 games at Triple-A before the promotion. Although he smashed 17 home runs the prior season, Lugo has mostly doubles power.

SCOUTING REPORT: Lugo's hit tool is contact-oriented, as he hits for little power and doesn't draw many walks. Primarily a third baseman, Lugo has been asked to move over to second for the time being. Although he isn't a fast runner, his defense plays as average on the infield. Lugo is gifted with a plus arm, good enough to play on the left or right side of the diamond.

THE FUTURE: Lugo will probably get at-bats at both Triple-A and the big leagues next year as he looks to adjust to the competition. He will also need more defensive repetitions at second base, which will help Detroit see where he best fits on the club. By moving around the infield, Lugo can help his case to become a reliable backup infielder.

Year	Club (League)	Class	AVG	G	AB	R	H	2B	3B	HR	RBI	BB	SO	SB	CS	OBP	SLG
2016	Visalia (CAL)	HiA	.314	79	315	61	99	14	5	13	42	15	41	2	1	.348	.514
	Mobile (SL)	AA	.306	48	173	24	53	9	2	4	20	4	15	1	1	.322	.451
2017	Jackson (SL)	AA	.282	88	341	40	96	21	4	7	43	21	51	1	0	.325	.428
	Erie (EL)	AA	.269	43	175	18	47	6	1	6	22	12	21	2	1	.314	.417
2018	Toledo (IL)	AAA	.269	123	509	56	137	26	3	3	59	9	66	12	4	.283	.350
	Detroit (AL)	MAJ	.213	27	94	10	20	4	1	1	8	7	20	0	0	.267	.309
Major League Totals			.213	27	94	10	20	4	1	1	8	7	20	0	0	.267	.309
Minor League Totals			.275	732	2881	336	792	126	28	50	350	110	418	33	17	.304	.390

18 LOGAN SHORE, RHP

BA GRADE

45 Risk: High

Born: Dec. 28, 1994. **B-T:** R-R. **HT:** 6-2. **WT:** 215. **Drafted:** Florida, 2016 (2nd round). **Signed By:** Trevor Schaffer (Athletics).

TRACK RECORD: Shore moved between high Class A and Double-A a few times in 2018 before being dealt to Detroit as part of the package for righthander Mike Fiers. He logged 17 starts despite dealing with trapezius muscle issues that resulted in a trip to the disabled list.

SCOUTING REPORT: Shore's fastball will get into the low 90s with plus movement, but is seen as an average pitch. His best pitch is his changeup, which he throws with conviction in the upper 70s. The pitch grades as a future plus offering. Shore also features a curveball that sits in the mid-70s and is a clear third pitch. With a solid delivery and clean arm action, the righty shows solid command of his arsenal.

THE FUTURE: After struggling in Double-A, Shore will need to spend more time adapting to better hitters in the upper minors. With a plus changeup, scouts think he can fit in at the back end of a rotation or as an effective member of the bullpen.

Year	Club (League)	Class	W	L	ERA	G	GS	CG	SV	IP	H	HR	BB	SO	K/9	WHIP	AVG
2016	Vermont (NYP)	SS	0	2	2.57	7	7	0	0	21	17	1	7	21	9.0	1.14	.207
2017	Athletics (AZL)	R	0	0	0.00	3	3	0	0	8	2	0	0	13	14.6	0.25	.077
	Stockton (CAL)	HiA	2	5	4.09	17	14	0	1	73	81	5	16	74	9.2	1.33	.277
2018	Stockton (CAL)	HiA	2	0	1.21	4	4	0	0	22	18	0	2	25	10.1	0.90	.220
	Midland (TL)	AA	1	6	5.50	13	13	0	0	69	85	7	19	49	6.4	1.51	.306
Minor League Totals			5	13	3.92	44	41	0	1	193	203	13	44	182	8.5	1.28	.267

19 SANDY BAEZ, RHP

BA GRADE

40 Risk: Medium

Born: Nov. 25, 1993. **B-T:** R-R. **HT:** 6-2. **WT:** 180. **Signed:** Dominican Republic, 2011. **Signed By:** Carlos Santana/Ramon Perez/Miguel Garcia.

TRACK RECORD: Baez, signed on the strength of a projectable frame and a fastball that was bumping into the high 80s as a teenager, has slowly developed into the type of pitcher the Tigers hoped they were getting when they signed him as a 17-year-old. He's moved slowly through the system, but was added to the 40-man roster before the 2018 season and made his major league debut.

SCOUTING REPORT: Baez's fastball is a true 70-grade pitch, sitting in the mid-90s and touching 99. His best secondary pitch is a changeup that shows hints of a future above-average offering because of the confidence and feel with which it is thrown. Baez also throws a slider, but his stiff wrist limits it to a below-average pitch. His frame is quite durable, even though he has a bit of a violent delivery that features a head whack. This hurts his control and causes it to grade out as below-average.

THE FUTURE: Baez is another candidate for Detroit's bullpen in 2019. His plus-plus fastball is a potent weapon, and his changeup gives him a solid, two-pitch combination.

Year	Club (League)	Class	W	L	ERA	G	GS	CG	SV	IP	H	HR	BB	SO	K/9	WHIP	AVG
2016	West Michigan (MWL)	LoA	7	9	3.81	21	21	0	0	113	125	7	28	88	7.0	1.35	.283
2017	Lakeland (FSL)	HiA	6	7	3.86	17	17	0	0	89	88	7	24	92	9.3	1.26	.257
	Erie (EL)	AA	0	1	4.50	2	2	0	0	10	9	3	5	13	11.7	1.40	.237
2018	Erie (EL)	AA	1	9	5.64	33	15	0	1	104	114	19	46	86	7.5	1.54	.284
	Detroit (AL)	MAJ	0	0	5.02	9	0	0	0	14	12	2	9	10	6.3	1.47	.222
Major League Totals			0	0	5.02	9	0	0	0	14	12	2	9	10	6.3	1.47	.222
Minor League Totals			26	36	4.04	123	100	1	2	542	555	44	169	471	7.8	1.34	.267

20 AUSTIN SODDERS, LHP

BA GRADE

45 Risk: High

Born: April 19, 1995. **B-T:** L-L. **HT:** 6-4. **WT:** 210. **Drafted:** UC Riverside, 2016 (7th round). **Signed By:** Steve Pack.

TRACK RECORD: Even before Sodders was born, his family was already making an impact at Baseball America. His father, Mike, was the magazine's first College Player of the Year back in 1981. The younger Sodders relies on pitchability and deception to get his outs, but he spent a large chunk of time in 2018 on the disabled list with a shoulder injury.

SCOUTING REPORT: Sodders' fastball sits in the high 80s and can get into the low 90s. His out pitch is a swing and miss changeup that is a future 55-grade pitch. Sodders' also throws a fringy curveball, but he spins it well enough to be average in the future. His above-average command helps him to get the most out of his arsenal. Sodders throws his glove hand up a bit during his delivery, which adds deception.

THE FUTURE: Despite just eight starts in a return to high Class A Lakeland, Sodders could be in the mix for a spot at Double-A Erie in 2019. He profiles as a back-of-the-rotation starter in the future.

Year	Club (League)	Class	W	L	ERA	G	GS	CG	SV	IP	H	HR	BB	SO	K/9	WHIP	AVG
2016	Connecticut (NYP)	SS	0	3	2.29	13	13	0	0	39	35	2	5	33	7.6	1.02	.230
2017	West Michigan (MWL)	LoA	7	0	1.40	11	11	0	0	64	49	2	13	65	9.1	0.96	.217
	Lakeland (FSL)	HiA	4	5	2.17	12	12	1	0	75	55	0	17	57	6.9	0.96	.203
2018	Lakeland (FSL)	HiA	3	2	4.05	8	8	0	0	47	36	4	8	41	7.9	0.94	.213
Minor League Totals			14	10	2.36	44	44	1	0	225	175	8	43	196	7.8	0.97	.214

21 SPENCER TURNBULL, RHP

BA GRADE

40 Risk: Medium

Born: Sept. 18, 1992. **B-T:** R-R. **HT:** 6-3. **WT:** 215. **Drafted:** Alabama, 2014 (2nd round). **Signed By:** Bryson Barber.

TRACK RECORD: After three solid seasons at Alabama, Turnbull's pro career has been pockmarked by injuries. He missed time with shoulder and elbow issues during the 2016 and 2017 seasons before achieving his largest career workload in terms of starts and innings in 2018.

SCOUTING REPORT: The righthander throws four pitches, highlighted by a fastball that sits 93-94 but can touch as high as 96. Turnbull's best secondary pitch is a low to mid-80s slider. While the pitch can be inconsistent, it shows average upside because of its depth. Both his curveball and changeup are fringe-average offerings. His funky arm action creates a sling-like throwing motion and hampers his control.

THE FUTURE: Turnbull should find himself competing for a bullpen spot in Detroit come 2019.

Year	Club (League)	Class	W	L	ERA	G	GS	CG	SV	IP	H	HR	BB	SO	K/9	WHIP	AVG
2016	Tigers East (GCL)	R	0	0	7.36	2	2	0	0	4	4	2	1	5	12.3	1.36	.267
	Tigers West (GCL)	R	0	1	3.38	4	4	0	0	11	3	0	5	7	5.9	0.75	.091
	Lakeland (FSL)	HiA	1	1	3.00	6	6	0	0	30	24	1	10	27	8.1	1.13	.216
2017	Tigers West (GCL)	R	0	0	4.00	2	2	0	0	9	8	0	2	16	16.0	1.11	.242
	Lakeland (FSL)	HiA	7	3	3.05	15	15	0	0	83	68	3	25	64	7.0	1.13	.230
	Erie (EL)	AA	0	3	6.20	4	4	0	0	20	22	1	8	22	9.7	1.48	.272
2018	Tigers West (GCL)	R	0	0	0.00	1	1	0	0	3	1	0	3	1	1.50	.111
	Lakeland (FSL)	HiA	0	0	0.00	1	1	0	0	5	2	0	0	6	11.6	0.43	.125
	Erie (EL)	AA	4	7	4.47	19	19	1	0	99	92	4	40	105	9.6	1.34	.248
	Toledo (IL)	AAA	1	1	2.03	2	2	0	0	13	8	0	3	19	12.8	0.83	.178
	Detroit (AL)	MAJ	0	2	6.06	4	3	0	0	16	17	1	4	15	8.3	1.29	.262
Major League Totals			0	2	6.06	4	3	0	0	16	17	1	4	15	8.3	1.29	.262
Minor League Totals			24	21	3.59	90	90	2	0	424	371	13	164	403	8.6	1.26	.236

22 BRYAN GARCIA, RHP

BA GRADE

50 Risk: Extreme

Born: April 19, 1995. **B-T:** R-R. **HT:** 6-1. **WT:** 203. **Drafted:** Miami, 2016 (6th round). **Signed By:** Nick Avila.

TRACK RECORD: Garcia had starred as Miami's closer for three seasons when the Tigers popped him with their sixth-round pick in 2016 and put him on the fast track. Garcia zoomed through all four full-season levels in 2017 before having Tommy John surgery that wiped out all of his 2018 season.

SCOUTING REPORT: Garcia's fastball is a plus pitch that gets into the upper 90s. He throws a slider that projects as an above-average pitch with tight shape and good movement. The slider is coupled with a changeup that should be an average pitch with more work. He has average command, which should be enough to be effective in the big leagues.

THE FUTURE: With his maturity and plus stuff, Garcia could make his major league debut late in 2019 with good health, and a solid two-pitch mix could pave the way for a late-inning reliever role.

Year	Club (League)	Class	W	L	ERA	G	GS	CG	SV	IP	H	HR	BB	SO	K/9	WHIP	AVG
2016	Connecticut (NYP)	SS	0	1	1.00	16	0	0	6	18	13	1	3	21	10.5	0.89	.194
	West Michigan (MWL)	LoA	0	1	40.50	1	0	0	0	1	3	0	0	1	13.5	4.50	.600
2017	West Michigan (MWL)	LoA	1	2	3.14	14	0	0	9	14	12	0	4	27	17.0	1.12	.218
	Lakeland (FSL)	HiA	2	0	0.00	7	0	0	0	9	7	0	2	15	15.6	1.04	.233
	Erie (EL)	AA	1	1	0.96	17	0	0	8	19	7	1	8	24	11.6	0.80	.115
	Toledo (IL)	AAA	1	0	4.05	14	0	0	0	13	10	1	8	12	8.1	1.35	.213
2018	Did not play—Injured																
Minor League Totals			5	5	2.20	69	0	0	23	74	52	3	25	100	12.2	1.05	.196

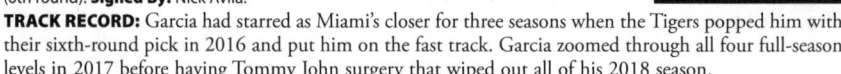

23 MATT HALL, LHP

BA GRADE

40 Risk: Medium

Born: July 23, 1993. **B-T:** L-L. **HT:** 6-0. **WT:** 200. **Drafted:** Missouri State, 2015 (6th round). **Signed By:** Martin Miller.

TRACK RECORD: Since his college days, Hall has been known for his curveball. He used the pitch to whiff 171 batters in 125 innings in his junior year at Missouri State before becoming the Tigers' sixth-round pick in 2015.The pitch also helped him carve up the low minors, including 126 more strikeouts between two Class A levels in his first full pro season.

SCOUTING REPORT: Hall fronts his three-pitch arsenal with a below-average fastball that sits in the high 80s and touches 90. His best pitch is his curveball, which he spins very well and throws in the upper 70s. His changeup is below-average, but has the potential to get to an average pitch with further refinement. He has average control of all his pitches. Detroit personnel point to improved command, especially with the fastball, as a big key for his success in the minors this year.

THE FUTURE: Hall made his major league debut in 2018, and should be in the mix for a spot in the Tigers' bullpen in 2019. Without a step forward with his fastball, Hall's ceiling is a matchup lefty in the pen.

Year	Club (League)	Class	W	L	ERA	G	GS	CG	SV	IP	H	HR	BB	SO	K/9	WHIP	AVG
2016	West Michigan (MWL)	LoA	8	0	1.09	12	12	0	0	66	49	0	21	72	9.8	1.06	.202
	Lakeland (FSL)	HiA	3	2	4.15	12	11	1	0	61	61	6	28	54	8.0	1.47	.264
2017	Lakeland (FSL)	HiA	7	6	2.44	19	18	0	0	103	97	4	38	110	9.6	1.31	.250
	Erie (EL)	AA	1	0	3.09	6	6	0	0	35	30	2	21	39	10.0	1.46	.224
2018	Erie (EL)	AA	5	2	1.58	27	4	0	0	57	33	1	25	76	12.0	1.02	.165
	Toledo (IL)	AAA	4	0	2.67	10	10	0	0	57	46	1	20	59	9.3	1.15	.219
	Detroit (AL)	MAJ	0	0	14.63	5	0	0	0	8	19	1	3	5	5.6	2.75	.452
Major League Totals			0	0	14.63	5	0	0	0	8	19	1	3	5	5.6	2.75	.452
Minor League Totals			28	11	2.48	97	72	1	0	414	349	17	161	444	9.7	1.23	.227

24 JACOB ROBSON, OF

BA GRADE

40 Risk: Medium

Born: Nov. 20, 1994. **B-T:** L-R. **HT:** 5-10. **WT:** 175. **Drafted:** Mississippi State, 2016 (8th round). **Signed By:** Justin Henry.

TRACK RECORD: Robson spent much of 2018 at Double-A before a promotion to Triple-A. He performed well, posting a .295/.376/.440 slash line across the two levels and leading the system with 142 hits and 29 doubles. His 11 home runs were a pleasant surprise in the power department, as his previous high was just three during the 2017 campaign.

SCOUTING REPORT: Robson's tools aren't great, but he does bring a lot of energy and enthusiasm to the table. He is a plus runner who can fit defensively at all three outfield positions with an average throwing arm. His hit tool has the potential to be average, although the power grades out as below-average in spite of his double-digit home run season. Tigers' evaluators love his energetic approach to the game.

THE FUTURE: Robson should expect to spend more time at Triple-A if he does not make the roster out of spring training. He can do a bit of everything for his club, which adds to his versatility. The ability to play all three outfield spots while making solid contact creates a future role of a fourth outfielder moving forward.

Year	Club (League)	Class	AVG	G	AB	R	H	2B	3B	HR	RBI	BB	SO	SB	CS	OBP	SLG
2016	Tigers West (GCL)	R	.267	28	101	16	27	4	2	0	5	16	22	14	4	.368	.347
	Connecticut (NYP)	SS	.329	21	76	14	25	5	1	1	6	15	20	1	2	.440	.461
2017	West Michigan (MWL)	LoA	.329	60	228	38	75	10	1	1	27	31	59	5	9	.408	.395
	Lakeland (FSL)	HiA	.277	58	224	27	62	11	4	2	18	23	59	16	9	.351	.388
2018	Erie (EL)	AA	.286	67	262	46	75	16	3	7	32	39	78	11	4	.382	.450
	Toledo (IL)	AAA	.305	57	220	36	67	13	1	4	15	23	62	7	6	.369	.427
Minor League Totals			.298	291	1111	177	331	59	12	15	103	147	300	54	34	.381	.413

25 DANIEL WOODROW, OF

BA GRADE

40 Risk: Medium

Born: January 26, 1995. **B-T:** L-R. **HT:** 5-10. **WT:** 160. **Drafted:** Creighton, 2016 (12th round). **Signed by:** Ryan Johnson.

TRACK RECORD: Woodrow hit .343 as Creighton's leadoff hitter and starting center fielder as a junior to earn a draft selection in 2016. The undersized speedster has continued to perform in pro ball. He was an All-Star at low Class A in 2017 and Double-A in 2018, and capped his 2018 season with a standout showing in the Arizona Fall League.

SCOUTING REPORT: A scrappy, versatile player with double-plus speed, Woodrow's outfield range fits well in center field as he is able to cover plenty of ground in the gaps. A below average arm will ultimately keep him out of right field long-term. Woodrow's swing does not generate much power, profiling as below-average, but he makes solid contact up the middle from the left side and takes his walks to consistently get on base.

THE FUTURE: Woodrow will head to Triple-A in 2019. His speed and ability to get on-base should prove valuable as a backup outfielder sooner rather than later.

Year	Club (League)	Class	AVG	G	AB	R	H	2B	3B	HR	RBI	BB	SO	SB	CS	OBP	SLG
2016	Tigers West (GCL)	R	.351	18	57	10	20	7	0	0	9	9	12	5	0	.441	.474
	Connecticut (NYP)	SS	.276	36	145	21	40	5	1	0	13	12	32	8	2	.329	.324
2017	West Michigan (MWL)	LoA	.271	116	469	73	127	17	4	0	47	51	93	31	11	.341	.324
2018	Lakeland (FSL)	HiA	.381	5	21	5	8	1	0	0	1	1	5	4	1	.409	.429
	Erie (EL)	AA	.313	92	342	48	107	13	3	3	37	31	71	19	13	.369	.395
Minor League Totals			.292	267	1034	157	302	43	8	3	107	104	213	67	27	.356	.358

26 ANTHONY CASTRO, RHP

BA GRADE
45 Risk: Very High

Born: April 13, 1995. **B-T:** R-R. **HT:** 6-2. **WT:** 180. **Signed:** Venezuela, 2011. **Signed By:** Oscar Garcia/Pedro Chavez.

TRACK RECORD: After signing as a 16-year-old in 2011, Castro's career has been a slow burn. He took five seasons—albeit with a Tommy John surgery included—to reach full-season ball. He reached the upper levels for the first time in 2018 in a three-start shellacking at Double-A Erie at midseason before heading back to high Class A Lakeland.

SCOUTING REPORT: Castro sports a three-pitch mix, fronted by a fastball that works in the mid-90s. The best pitch of the arsenal is his changeup. Castro throws it with good arm action, and it has splitter movement that works down in the zone. His curveball projects as average in the future because it has solid depth and generates some swings and misses. Scouts like Castro's mound presence and his competitive nature on the mound. He isn't a strikeout machine, but moves the ball around effectively to get hitters out.

THE FUTURE: Having three quality pitches should help Castro to adjust to Double-A after his disappointing stint in 2018. Although his stuff might not crack a rotation, the profile should be suited for a long relief role.

Year	Club (League)	Class	W	L	ERA	G	GS	CG	SV	IP	H	HR	BB	SO	K/9	WHIP	AVG
2016	Tigers West (GCL)	R	3	3	4.26	11	10	0	0	51	52	0	16	54	9.6	1.34	.272
2017	West Michigan (MWL)	LoA	10	6	2.49	21	21	1	0	108	91	4	35	95	7.9	1.16	.226
2018	Erie (EL)	AA	0	0	8.10	3	3	0	0	10	8	1	12	4	3.6	2.00	.229
	Lakeland (FSL)	HiA	9	4	2.93	22	20	2	0	117	112	8	43	101	7.8	1.33	.253
Minor League Totals			31	20	3.27	96	90	3	0	454	401	18	183	405	8.0	1.29	.238

27 SAM McMILLAN, C

BA GRADE
45 Risk: Extreme

Born: December 1, 1998. **B-T:** R-R. **HT:** 6-1. **WT:** 195. **Drafted:** HS—Live Oak, Fla., 2017 (5th round). **Signed By:** R.J. Burress.

TRACK RECORD: McMillan was known mostly for his glove as an amateur, and scouts saw little power coming from a frame that lacked much in the way of projection. He earned strong marks for his receiving, and the Tigers liked his upside enough to draft him in the fifth round in 2017 and sign him to a $1 million bonus, which was the highest handed out in his round.

SCOUTING REPORT: While McMillan has a potential plus hit tool, he doesn't show much power at all—he notched just seven extra-base hits in 50 games—and relies mostly on a contact approach and a solid feel for the strike zone. Scouts weren't impressed by his defense this year, noting a league-worst 14 passed balls. His arm is below-average, too, and he threw out just 27 percent of runners with Connecticut. There's plenty of work to be done to get back to his highly touted pre-draft defensive grades.

THE FUTURE: McMillan still has plenty of development remaining, and his profile still gives him a chance to be a backup catcher.

Year	Club (League)	Class	AVG	G	AB	R	H	2B	3B	HR	RBI	BB	SO	SB	CS	OBP	SLG
2017	Tigers West (GCL)	R	.288	37	111	24	32	5	1	3	25	19	17	1	1	.441	.432
2018	Connecticut (NYP)	SS	.158	50	165	16	26	6	1	0	8	25	47	7	2	.312	.206
Minor League Totals			.210	87	276	40	58	11	2	3	33	44	64	8	3	.365	.297

28 BROCK DEATHERAGE, OF

BA GRADE
40 Risk: High

Born: Sept.12th, 1995. **B-T:** L-L. **HT:** 6-1. **WT:** 175 **Drafted:** North Carolina State, 2018 (10th round). **Signed By:** Taylor Black.

TRACK RECORD: Deatherage was excellent over his first two seasons at North Carolina State before hitting a rough patch in his junior year, when he hit just .218. He went back to school for his senior year and showed a power spurt. His 14 home runs in his final season with the Wolfpack exceeded his total for the previous three seasons combined. Drafted in the 10th round and signed for $10,000, he opened his pro career on a high note with three home runs in his first game.

SCOUTING REPORT: The lefty swinger has a hit over power profile, with a future 45 hit tool on the 20-to-80 scouting scale and below-average power. His defense is above-average and he is a plus runner, which should allow him to play in any outfield position. His maturity and natural athleticism allow him to play above the sum of his toolset.

THE FUTURE: He won't be an offensive masher, but his instincts and athleticism could allow him to become a fourth outfielder in the future. The 2019 season should see Deatherage get more at-bats with high Class A Lakeland before he progresses to Double-A.

Year	Club (League)	Class	AVG	G	AB	R	H	2B	3B	HR	RBI	BB	SO	SB	CS	OBP	SLG
2018	Tigers West (GCL)	R	.556	2	9	6	5	0	0	4	7	1	1	0	0	.600	1.889
	West Michigan (MWL)	LoA	.313	46	176	25	55	7	5	2	18	14	50	15	3	.369	.443
	Lakeland (FSL)	HiA	.333	12	45	12	15	1	1	1	5	6	13	4	0	.404	.467
Minor League Totals			.326	60	230	43	75	8	6	7	30	21	64	19	3	.385	.504

29 JASON FOLEY, RHP

Born: Nov. 1, 1995. **B-T:** R-R. **HT:** 6-4. **WT:** 215. **Signed:** Sacred Heart (NDFA). **Signed By:** Jim Bretz

BA GRADE: 45 Risk: Extreme

TRACK RECORD: Struggles at Sacred Heart scuttled Foley's draft chances, but area scout Jim Bretz kept on him during the summer and signed him as an nondrafted free agent. He ranked as one of the organization's hardest throwers and made it to high Class A Lakeland in 2017 before requiring Tommy John surgery that kept him out all of 2018.

SCOUTING REPORT: The profile is highlighted by a 70-grade fastball that can touch triple digits and has good movement. Foley couples the pitch with a future-average slider. It's a harder slider, registering in the mid to upper-80s. His changeup is also high velocity, showing in the high 80s but it's not as reliable as his other offerings at the moment. His control is solid for now, with a future 55-grade in sight in the future.

THE FUTURE: Once Foley rehabs from surgery, he should return to high Class A to continue his progression. His big fastball and solid slider make him a candidate for a late-inning bullpen role.

Year	Club (League)	Class	W	L	ERA	G	GS	CG	SV	IP	H	HR	BB	SO	K/9	WHIP	AVG
2016	Tigers West (GCL)	R	0	0	0.00	1	0	0	1	1	1	0	0	1	9.0	1.00	.250
	Connecticut (NYP)	SS	0	0	4.26	5	0	0	0	6	6	0	7	6	8.5	2.05	.240
2017	West Michigan (MWL)	LoA	3	1	1.55	18	0	0	5	29	20	0	5	36	11.2	0.86	.189
	Lakeland (FSL)	HiA	0	2	6.14	6	0	0	1	7	8	1	2	5	6.1	1.36	.267
2018	Did not play—Injured																
Minor League Totals			3	3	2.68	30	0	0	7	44	35	1	14	48	9.9	1.12	.212

30 WILKEL HERNANDEZ, RHP

Born: April 13, 1999. **B-T:** R-R. **HT:** 6-3. **WT:** 160. **Signed:** Venezuela, 2015. **Signed By:** Marlo Zerpa/Marlon Urdaneta (Angels).

BA GRADE: 45 Risk: Extreme

TRACK RECORD: The Angels signed Hernandez in 2015 based off his projectability and the present mid-80s fastball he was sporting when he was signed. The pitch ticked up shortly after he turned pro, and he turned in an excellent season in 2017 in the Rookie-level Arizona League. He was dealt to the Tigers for Ian Kinsler at the 2017 Winter Meetings.

SCOUTING REPORT: Hernandez has a lively arm that produces fastballs that have touched 96 mph. It's a future 60-grade pitch and pairs well with his curveball, which grades as future-average. His third-best pitch is a changeup, and he doesn't have particularly good control of it at the moment. He has a solid pitcher's body, and there is room for added physicality and further projection with his offerings.

THE FUTURE: With an above-average fastball/curveball combination, Hernandez could eventually find relief work in higher-leverage situations. He will have to improve upon his control, which has the potential to be average. Hernandez will be ticketed for more time in the Midwest League in 2019.

Year	Club (League)	Class	W	L	ERA	G	GS	CG	SV	IP	H	HR	BB	SO	K/9	WHIP	AVG
2016	Angels (DSL)	R	2	0	1.20	5	5	0	0	15	12	0	6	14	8.4	1.20	.231
2017	Angels (AZL)	R	3	1	2.61	11	7	0	0	41	23	1	20	42	9.1	1.04	.161
	Orem (PIO)	R	1	0	3.00	1	0	0	0	3	2	0	2	2	6.0	1.33	.222
2018	Connecticut (NYP)	SS	0	2	7.94	3	3	0	0	6	6	2	4	11	17.5	1.76	.250
	West Michigan (MWL)	LoA	2	5	4.71	10	10	0	0	42	40	4	16	34	7.3	1.33	.250
Minor League Totals			8	8	3.53	30	25	0	0	107	83	7	48	103	8.7	1.22	.214

Houston Astros

BY J.J. COOPER

I t's hard to win one World Series title. It's even tougher to repeat.

Houston's defense of its world title fell two steps short, as they were eliminated by the Red Sox in the ALCS. But overall, it's hard to call 2018 a disappointing season. The Astros' 103 wins were two more than last season and the most in franchise history. Houston's rotation and bullpen were better than the champs, although the lineup suffered through a series of injuries.

Most importantly, looking ahead, the Astros are still positioned to be the class of the AL West. The Astros have a strong core of its lineup under team control for several seasons to come.

Carlos Correa, Alex Bregman and Jose Altuve are all locked up for three seasons or more, and George Springer for two. The club's excellent rotation, however, is more up in the air.

Justin Verlander and Gerrit Cole are both in the final year of their deals in 2019 before hitting free agency. They are one year behind Dallas Keuchel and Charlie Morton, who filed for free agency at the end of the season. Lance McCullers Jr. will miss all of 2019 as he recovers from Tommy John surgery.

Thankfully for the Astros, the team's farm system has five pitching prospects among its top seven prospects, and they all have pitched at Double-A or higher. The Astros have struggled to transition starting pitching prospects to the big league rotation in recent years, and it will be hard to rely on rookies much while battling for another World Series title in 2019. But the Astros are going to have to get production from Forrest Whitley and at least one or two other starting prospects to fill holes over the next couple of seasons.

Off the field, the front office will look much different than the one that led the Astros to the 2017 World Series. Longtime assistant general manager Mike Elias was hired as the Orioles GM, becoming the second Jeff Luhnow lieutenant to get the opportunity to run a team after David Stearns was hired as the Brewers' GM in 2015.

Mike Fast, the director of research and development, opted not to renew his contract and later took a job as special assistant to the GM with the Braves. Sig Mejdal, the team's director of decision sciences, also let his contract run out before joining Elias in Baltimore.

The Astros also lost hitting coach Dave Hudgens to the Blue Jays, assistant hitting coach Jeff Albert to the Cardinals and bullpen coach Doug White to the Angels. All three received promotions in their new roles.

Third baseman Alex Bregman hit 31 homers and 51 doubles in a breakout campaign.

PROJECTED 2022 LINEUP

Catcher	Garrett Stubbs (27)
First Base	Yordan Alvarez (25)
Second Base	Jose Altuve (32)
Third Base	Alex Bregman (28)
Shortstop	Carlos Correa (27)
Left Field	Derek Fisher (28)
Center Field	George Springer (32)
Right Field	Kyle Tucker (25)
Designated Hitter	Seth Beer (25)
No. 1 Starter	Gerrit Cole (31)
No. 2 Starter	Forrest Whitley (24)
No. 3 Starter	Justin Verlander (39)
No. 4 Starter	Josh James (29)
No. 5 Starter	Corbin Martin (26)
Closer	Roberto Osuna (27)

Houston's farm system is starting to show the effects of the later draft picks that come with winning and a series of win-now trades that have helped the big league team during their recent playoff runs. Many of the Astros' trade chips have been surplus talent that didn't fit for them, but it has lessened their prospect depth.

But the Astros have built a player development juggernaut of sorts. Houston consistently makes pitchers better and finds hitters in later rounds. Many of them are not high ceiling enough to fit the Astros' current big league needs, but they provide a seemingly renewable resource of trade chips to help at the deadline.

HOUSTON ASTROS

TOP 2019 ROOKIE: Forrest Whitley, RHP. Kyle Tucker may play more in Houston in 2019, but our bet is that Whitley will make more of an immediate impact when he arrives.
BREAKOUT PROSPECT: Ronnie Dawson, OF. He has worked hard to turn himself into a true center fielder. That defense combined with his power is an interesting combo.
SLEEPER: Jojanse Torres, RHP. He will make his U.S. debut in 2019. He's already shown a 94-99 mph fastball, a promising slider and advanced command and control for his age.

SOURCE OF TOP 30 TALENT			
Homegrown	29	Acquired	1
College	12	Trade	1
High School	4	Rule 5 draft	0
Junior College	3	Independent leagues	0
Nondrafted free agent	0	Free agents/waivers	0
International	10		

LF
Yordan Alvarez (3)
J.J. Matijevic (23)
Alex McKenna (26)

CF
Ronnie Dawson (13)
Myles Straw (15)
Marty Costes

RF
Kyle Tucker (2)
Corey Julks

3B
Abraham Toro (16)
Joe Perez

SS
Freudis Nova (8)
Jonathan Arauz (17)
Jeremy Pena (25)
Deury Carrasco (30)
Miguelangel Sierra

2B
Osvaldo Duarte
Jack Mayfield

1B
Seth Beer (9)

C
Garrett Stubbs (14)
Chuckie Robinson
Cesar Salazar
Jamie Ritchie

LHP

LHSP	LHRP
Framber Valdez (7)	Reymin Guduan (28)
Cionel Perez (12)	Parker Mushinski
	Adam Bleday

RHP

RHSP	RHRP
Forrest Whitley (1)	Dean Deetz (24)
Joshua James (4)	Cristian Javier
Corbin Martin (5)	Akeem Bostick
J.B. Bukauskas (6)	Abdiel Saldana
Bryan Abreu (10)	Jojanse Torres
Jairo Solis (11)	R.J. Freure
Jayson Schroeder (18)	Brandon Bailey
Brandon Bielak (19)	Colin McKee
Tyler Ivey (20)	Mark Moclair
Peter Solomon (21)	Jesus Balaguer
Rogelio Armenteros (22)	Cody Deason
Manny Ramirez (27)	
Brady Rodgers (29)	
Cy Sneed	
Heitor Tokar	

DRAFT ANALYSIS

2018

BEST PURE HITTER: OF/1B Seth Beer (1) was one of the most productive hitters in college baseball over the past three seasons, and he lived up to the billing in his pro debut as well. He has a very advanced approach and draws plenty of walks. He has a chance to be a middle-of-the-order bat with high on-base percentages.

BEST POWER HITTER: Beer has 70 raw power and hit 12 home runs in just 67 games in his pro debut. He has the strength to hit 25-plus home runs in the future. OF Chandler Taylor (10) has 70 raw power as well, although he will have to improve his hitting ability to get it to translate consistently to pro ball. OF Marty Costes (22) doesn't hit the ball in the air as easily as Taylor or Beer, but he matches them in exit velocity.

FASTEST RUNNER: The Astros rarely draft players based on their speed. SS Jeremy Pena (3) is an above-average runner whose speed plays well on the basepaths. OF Austin Dennis (20) also has above-average speed.

BEST DEFENSIVE PLAYER: Pena came into pro ball with a solid defensive reputation, and he showed that with short-season Tri-City. He did commit 10 errors in 36 games as he struggled with fielding errors, but he has the range and hands to remain at the position and develop into at least an above-average defender at short. C Cesar Salazar (7) is an advanced receiver who is an excellent leader behind the plate. His arm is his weakness, but a quick release allows him to make up for it.

BEST ATHLETE: Pena is a twitchy athlete with an excellent first step. He has some impressive strength and speed. OF Alex McKenna (4) isn't as twitchy, but he has a diversified set of athletic tools. He has excellent strength and body control.

BEST FASTBALL: RHP Mark Moclair (12) sat 94-96 mph pretty much every time out, but the quality of his fastball is even better than his velocity as his four-seam fastball has excellent, explosive late life.

TOP DRAFT PICKS OF THE DECADE

Year	Player, Pos.	2018 Org
2009	Jio Mier, SS	Mexican League
2010	Mike Foltynewicz, RHP	Braves
2011	George Springer, OF	Astros
2012	Carlos Correa, SS	Astros
2013	Mark Appel, RHP	Did not play
2014	*Brady Aiken, LHP	Indians
2015	Alex Bregman, SS	Astros
2016	Forrest Whitley, RHP	Astros
2017	J.B. Bukauskas, RHP	Astros
2018	Seth Beer, OF	Astros
* Did not sign		

BEST SECONDARY PITCH: RHP R.J. Freure (6) has a high-spin rate, low-80s curveball with excellent 12-to-6 shape. It's a plus pitch.

BEST PRO DEBUT: Beer hit 12 home runs while slashing .304/.389/.496 in three stops. McKenna hit .311/.394/.512 between short-season and low Class A. RHP Austin Hansen (8) went 2-3, 1.76 with 45 strikeouts in 31 innings.

MOST INTRIGUING BACKGROUND: The Astros drafted Carlos Correa's younger brother 2B J.C. Correa (33) and Alex Bregman's younger brother LHP A.J. Bregman (35). The Astros actually had Alex tell A.J. that the Astros had drafted him.

CLOSEST TO THE MAJORS: Beer finished last year in high Class A and could spend much of 2019 in Double-A in his first full pro season.

BEST LATE-ROUND PICK: RHP J.P. France (14) saw his stuff pick up as a senior at Mississippi State. He could be a useful reliever. Costes was a 25th-round pick of the Astros in 2017 before signing this year as a 20th-round pick. The Astros have long believed in Costes' power-speed combination. RHP Brett Conine (11) has a quality fastball and impressed in his debut with short-season Tri-City.

THE ONE WHO GOT AWAY: The Astros signed everyone they drafted in the top 20 rounds and 30 of their top 32 picks. RHP Brandon Birdsell (39) could develop into a useful starter at Texas A&M.

—J.J. COOPER

2017

In RHPs J.B. Bukauskas (1) and Corbin Martin (2), the Astros landed a pair of premium arms who both reached Double-A in their first full pro season. OF J.J. Matijevic's (2s) 22 home runs in 2018 ranked third in the system.

GRADE: A

2016

RHP Forrest Whitley (1) is the best pitching prospect in the game. OF Ronnie Dawson (2) and 3B Abraham Toro (5) continues to progress and in 2018 reached Double-A. C Jake Rogers was used in the Justin Verlander trade.

GRADE: A

2015

The Astros capatalized on having two top-five picks. 3B Alex Bregman (1) has become a fixture in Houston. OF Kyle Tucker (1) reached Houston and is one of the best prospects in baseball. OF Myles Straw (12) gives the class a third big leaguer.

GRADE: A

1 FORREST WHITLEY, RHP

Born: Sept. 15, 1997. **B-T:** R-R. **Ht:** 6-7. **Wt:** 207.
Drafted: HS—San Antonio, 2016 (1st round).
Signed by: Noel Gonzales-Luna.

After being one of the fastest-moving prep pitchers in recent history in his first full pro season in 2017, Whitley's climb to the majors slowed to a crawl in 2018. A 50-game suspension for testing positive for a performance-enhancing drug held him out until June. Upon returning to Double-A Corpus Christi, he was pulled from an early July start with an oblique injury that forced him to miss the Futures Game. He missed more than a month and then was shut down again in late August with a lat muscle injury. He made an impressive return in the Arizona Fall League (in one outing, he struck out eight of the first nine batters he faced) but his injuries meant he threw fewer than 60 innings all year.

SCOUTING REPORT: It's hard to remember that Whitley once raised concerns with scouts because of his poor conditioning. He slimmed down as a high school senior and continues to be long, lean, athletic and limber. Whitley gets plenty of angle on his fastball thanks to his height and an over-the-top release point. His delivery is relatively clean, but his arm is so fast that his delivery has recoil even though he has a long deceleration into his finish. Whitley's stuff is as good or better than any other minor league pitcher because he has so many quality offerings. He has a chance to be the ultimate rarity—a pitcher with five plus-or-better offerings. It all begins with a 93-97 mph fastball he can run and cut. It has touched 100 mph in shorter outings, but the movement he gets on it makes it a plus-plus pitch. He also throws a plus, 90-92 mph cutter that is a distinctly separate pitch, with enough late movement to shatter bats and sometimes miss them. Whitley uses both a high-spin curveball and high-spin slider, both of which are plus pitches with power and depth, but his best secondary pitch is a plus-plus, 83-85 mph changeup with separation and outstanding late drop. He can throw it either for strikes or as a chase pitch and should be equally effective against righties and lefties.

THE FUTURE: Like any young pitcher, Whitley has to stay healthy, but if he does, he has No. 1 starter potential. He's the best pitching prospect in the minors and some scouts say he is the most promising pitching prospect they have seen.

BILL MITCHELL

BA GRADE	SCOUTING GRADES
70 Risk: High	Fastball: 70. Change: 70. CB: 60. Slider: 60. Cutter: 60. CTL: 55.

Projected future grades on 20-80 scouting scale

TOP PROSPECTS OF THE DECADE

Year	Player, Pos.	2018 Org
2009	Jason Castro, C	Twins
2010	Jason Castro, C	Twins
2011	Jordan Lyles, RHP	Brewers
2012	Jonathan Singleton, 1B/OF	Did not play
2013	Carlos Correa, SS	Astros
2014	Carlos Correa, SS	Astros
2015	Carlos Correa, SS	Astros
2016	A.J. Reed, 1B	Astros
2017	Francis Martes, RHP	Astros
2018	Forrest Whitley, RHP	Astros

BEST TOOLS

Best Pure Hitter	Kyle Tucker
Best Power Hitter	Yordan Alvarez
Fastest Baserunner	Seth Beer
Best Strike-Zone Discipline	Myles Straw
Best Athlete	Ronnie Dawson
Best Fastball	Josh James
Best Curveball	Bryan Abreu
Best Slider	J.B. Bukauskas
Best Changeup	Forrest Whitley
Best Control	Rogelio Armenteros
Best Defensive Catcher	Garrett Stubbs
Best Defensive Infielder	Freudis Nova
Best Infield Arm	Freudis Nova
Best Defensive Outfielder	Myles Straw
Best Outfield Arm	Myles Straw

Year	Club (League)	Class	W	L	ERA	G	GS	CG	SV	IP	H	HR	BB	SO	K/9	WHIP	AVG
2016	Astros (GCL)	R	1	1	7.36	4	2	0	0	7	8	0	3	13	16.0	1.50	.267
	Greeneville (APP)	R	0	1	3.18	4	4	0	0	11	11	0	3	13	10.3	1.24	.244
2017	Quad Cities (MWL)	LoA	2	3	2.91	12	10	0	0	46	42	2	21	67	13.0	1.36	.247
	Buies Creek (CAR)	HiA	3	1	3.16	7	6	0	0	31	28	2	9	50	14.4	1.18	.237
	Corpus Christi (TL)	AA	0	0	1.84	4	2	0	0	15	8	1	4	26	16.0	0.82	.157
2018	Corpus Christi (TL)	AA	0	2	3.76	8	8	0	0	26	15	2	11	34	11.6	0.99	.160
Minor League Totals			6	8	3.28	39	32	0	0	137	112	7	51	203	13.3	1.19	.220

2 KYLE TUCKER, OF

Born: Jan. 17, 1997. **B-T:** L-R. **HT:** 6-4. **WT:** 189. **Drafted:** HS—Tampa, 2015 (1st round). **Signed by:** John Martin.

TRACK RECORD: Nicknamed "Ted" for his resemblance to a young Ted Williams, Tucker even took swings as Williams for a PBS documentary on the Splendid Splinter. With a need in left field, the Astros called Tucker up in early July. But when he went 7-for-55 (.141/.203/.236), the Astros ended the experiment and demoted him at the end of July. He was brought back twice more to play off the bench.

SCOUTING REPORT: Tucker finally found a level that he wasn't ready for when he reached Houston. He had dominated every level of the minors with plus, all-fields power and excellent hand-eye coordination that allows his swing to work. In the big leagues, he proved an easier-than-expected mark for quality breaking balls. Despite his big league hiccup, Tucker projects as a middle-of-the-order bat who can be a plus hitter with plus power. He has already started to slow down, and opposing coaches and scouts were not always impressed with Tucker's effort level, noting that he often jogged down the line. His once-average speed slid to below-average in 2018, though he did steal 20 bases. That limits him in the outfield, but he should be average in either corner. His average arm is playable in right field.

THE FUTURE: Tucker should get another shot to be the Astros' everyday left fielder as a 22-year-old in 2019. He has very little left to prove in Triple-A.

BA GRADE	
60	**Risk:** Medium

Hit: 60. **Power:** 60.
Run: 40. **Field:** 50.
Arm: 50.

Year	Club (League)	Class	AVG	G	AB	R	H	2B	3B	HR	RBI	BB	SO	SB	CS	OBP	SLG
2016	Quad Cities (MWL)	LoA	.276	101	373	43	103	19	5	6	56	40	75	31	9	.348	.402
	Lancaster (CAL)	HiA	.339	16	59	13	20	6	2	3	13	10	6	1	3	.435	.661
2017	Buies Creek (CAR)	HiA	.288	48	177	31	51	12	4	9	43	24	45	12	5	.379	.554
	Corpus Christi (TL)	AA	.265	72	287	39	76	21	1	16	47	22	64	8	4	.325	.512
2018	Fresno (PCL)	AAA	.332	100	407	86	135	27	3	24	93	48	84	20	4	.400	.590
	Houston (AL)	MAJ	.141	28	64	10	9	2	1	0	4	6	13	1	1	.236	.203
Major League Totals			.141	28	64	10	9	2	1	0	4	6	13	1	1	.236	.203
Minor League Totals			.288	400	1535	242	442	97	17	61	285	160	303	90	29	.357	.493

3 YORDAN ALVAREZ, OF/1B

Born: June 27, 1997. **B-T:** L-L. **HT:** 6-5. **WT:** 226. **Signed:** Cuba, 2016. **Signed by:** Ismael Cruz/Mike Tosar (Dodgers).

TRACK RECORD: The Astros acquired Alvarez in the 2016 Josh Fields trade before he had ever played a pro game. In the two seasons since, he has made two Futures Game appearances. Alvarez's biggest issue has been staying healthy. He had wrist injuries each of the past two seasons that have slowed him down, and he has also battled a knee injury.

SCOUTING REPORT: Alvarez is big, strong and surprisingly athletic, though his speed burst is more apparent on the basepaths than in left field, where he is a below-average defender thanks to poor routes and reads. Most scouts say that he fits better at first base, but even there, he'll struggle to unseat the nimble Yuli Gurriel anytime soon. Alvarez is at his best in the batter's box. He has the strength to clear the fence to all parts of the park—nine of his 20 home runs in 2018 were hit between center and left field, eight went to left field or left-center and another three cleared the center field fence. For a tall, long-limbed hitter, Alvarez has excellent plate coverage, in large part because of strike-zone knowledge and an all-fields approach. He has a chance to be an above-average hitter in addition to having plus power, which could lead to 30-homer seasons.

THE FUTURE: Alvarez reached Triple-A before he turned 21, so he's ahead of a normal developmental schedule. Alvarez will return to Triple-A Round Rock, but his combination of power and plate discipline could help Houston at some point in 2019 if injuries arise.

BA GRADE	
60	**Risk:** Medium

Hit: 55. **Power:** 60.
Run: 50. **Field:** 40.
Arm: 45.

Year	Club (League)	Class	AVG	G	AB	R	H	2B	3B	HR	RBI	BB	SO	SB	CS	OBP	SLG
2016	Astros Orange (DSL)	R	.341	16	44	7	15	2	1	1	4	12	7	2	1	.474	.500
2017	Quad Cities (MWL)	LoA	.360	32	111	26	40	6	0	9	33	23	36	2	0	.468	.658
	Buies Creek (CAR)	HiA	.277	58	224	19	62	11	3	3	36	19	41	6	1	.329	.393
2018	Corpus Christi (TL)	AA	.325	43	169	39	55	13	0	12	46	19	45	5	2	.389	.615
	Fresno (PCL)	AAA	.259	45	166	24	43	8	0	8	28	23	47	1	0	.349	.452
Minor League Totals			.301	194	714	115	215	40	4	33	147	96	176	16	4	.381	.507

4 JOSH JAMES, RHP

Born: March 8, 1993. **B-T:** R-R. **HT:** 6-3. **Wt:** 222. **Drafted:** Western Oklahoma JC, 2014 (34th round). **Signed by:** Jim Stevenson.

TRACK RECORD: James didn't strike out a batter an inning in junior college, but Astros scout Jim Stevenson liked his arm. Still an organizational arm after four pro seasons, a sleep apnea diagnosis changed his life. Once James started getting restful sleep, his fastball jumped three grades in 2018, when he ranked fourth in the minors in strikeouts (171) and seventh in opponent average (.191).

SCOUTING REPORT: James pitched at 88-92 mph in 2017 but now sits 95-97 mph and can ramp up to 103 mph, even working as a starter. When he had to learn survival skills with a fringy fastball, he developed a plus changeup. Now that he can blow hitters away with his fastball, his change is a double-plus, 87-90 mph offering with deception. He can drop it off the table or run it away from lefties on the outer half of the plate. The development of James' inconsistent slider will be key to determine just how dominant he can become. He has shown an 87-89 mph Frisbee at times with tilt and power that could be a third plus weapon, but he lacks confidence in the pitch because he tends to hang it. James has fringe-average control but worse command, and his delivery doesn't lend itself to precise control. That will have to improve if he's going to be a successful starter long-term.

THE FUTURE: James will have to prove he can hold the gains he made in 2018, but his stuff is good enough to work as a mid-rotation starter.

BA GRADE

55 **Risk:** Medium

Fastball: 80.
Changeup: 70.
Slider: 50. **CTL:** 45.

Year	Club (League)	Class	W	L	ERA	G	GS	CG	SV	IP	H	HR	BB	SO	K/9	WHIP	AVG
2016	Lancaster (CAL)	HiA	9	5	4.81	23	19	0	1	110	120	11	40	121	9.9	1.45	.273
2017	Corpus Christi (TL)	AA	4	8	4.38	21	11	0	3	76	79	1	32	72	8.5	1.46	.263
2018	Corpus Christi (TL)	AA	0	0	2.49	6	4	0	1	22	17	1	10	38	15.8	1.25	.205
	Fresno (PCL)	AAA	6	4	3.40	17	17	0	0	93	62	8	39	133	12.9	1.09	.187
	Houston (AL)	MAJ	2	0	2.35	6	3	0	0	23	15	3	7	29	11.3	0.96	.183
Major League Totals			2	0	2.35	6	3	0	0	23	15	3	7	29	11.3	0.96	.183
Minor League Totals			27	24	3.61	104	75	0	6	457	415	23	177	498	9.8	1.30	.240

5 CORBIN MARTIN, RHP

Born: Dec. 28, 1995. **B-T:** R-R. **HT:** 6-2. **WT:** 212. **Drafted:** Texas A&M, 2017 (2nd round). **Signed by:** Noel Gonzales-Luna.

TRACK RECORD: As Martin prepared for his junior season at Texas A&M, he was penciled in as the club's closer, hoping to put the wildness that had ruined his sophomore season behind him. He had worked as a reliever in two years with the Aggies and in the Cape Cod League, but A&M moved him to the rotation as a junior. He quickly became the club's ace. As a pro, he's been one of the fastest-moving pitchers from the 2017 draft, reaching Double-A by May and posting a 2.97 ERA in a league where the average ERA was 4.17.

SCOUTING REPORT: It's hard to believe that Martin was ever viewed as a reliever or that he battled control issues. Now, he is a starter with excellent feel for pitching, plenty of polish and a mastery of the details like holding runners and fielding his position. Martin sits 93-95 mph and touches 97 mph. His plus fastball earns those grades for his above-average command and control as much as the pitch's velocity. He locates well to all four corners of the zone. Martin mixes in a slider and curveball. Both earn above-average grades on his best days, with his slider being a little more consistent than his curve. His changeup improved this year from being a below-average to a potentially average pitch.

THE FUTURE: The Astros have pitchers with better stuff and other pitchers who are nearly as refined, but Martin is the best combination of the two. Martin combines stuff and refinement like no other Astros pitching prospect and is a future mid-rotation starter. He will start the 2019 season at Triple-A, but he could work his way into the Astros' big league plans at some point in 2019.

BA GRADE

55 **Risk:** Medium

Fastball: 60.
Slider: 55. **Curve:** 50.
Change: 50. **CTL:** 55.

Year	Club (League)	Class	W	L	ERA	G	GS	CG	SV	IP	H	HR	BB	SO	K/9	WHIP	AVG
2017	Astros (GCL)	R	0	0	0.00	2	1	0	0	5	0	0	1	5	9.0	0.20	.000
	Tri-City (NYP)	SS	0	1	2.60	8	3	0	1	28	20	1	8	38	12.4	1.01	.202
2018	Buies Creek (CAR)	HiA	2	0	0.00	4	3	0	1	19	4	0	7	26	12.3	0.58	.065
	Corpus Christi (TL)	AA	7	2	2.97	21	18	0	0	103	84	7	28	96	8.4	1.09	.221
Minor League Totals			9	3	2.44	35	25	0	2	155	108	8	44	165	9.6	0.98	.194

6 J.B. BUKAUSKAS, RHP

Born: Oct. 11, 1996. **B-T:** R-R. **HT:** 6-0. **WT:** 203. **Drafted:** North Carolina, 2017 (1st round). **Signed by:** Tim Bittner.

TRACK RECORD: Bukauskas' 2018 season was derailed from the start. He was in a spring training car accident, though nothing seemed to be wrong at the time. But Bukauskas started to feel pain when he went to low Class A Quad Cities. Eventually he was diagnosed with a bulging disk in his back and was sidelined for two months.

SCOUTING REPORT: Bukauskas' fastball/slider combo is still his calling card, but the cutter he has developed as a pro has helped give him better survival skills as a starter. Bukauskas' 93-96 mph fastball has gained life as a pro, helping him develop it into a plus pitch. His plus-plus slider has sharp, late tilt that makes it one of the best in the minors. But Bukauskas' slider is mainly an out-of-zone chase pitch, and he struggles to control his fastball. When he's not throwing his fastball for strikes, his cutter gives him another pitch he can locate in the zone. His changeup is a fringe-average pitch that he doesn't seem to throw with much confidence or conviction.

BA GRADE
55 **Risk:** High
Fastball: 60.
Slider: 70. **Cutter:** 50.
Change: 45. **CTL:** 45.

THE FUTURE: Bukauskas' repertoire has invited bullpen projections, but he has shown better-than-expected starter traits as a pro. He's a potential mid-rotation starter who likely will swing from dominating to surviving based on how well he's locating his fastball.

Year	Club (League)	Class	W	L	ERA	G	GS	CG	SV	IP	H	HR	BB	SO	K/9	WHIP	AVG
2017	Astros (GCL)	R	0	0	0.00	1	1	0	0	4	3	0	1	3	6.8	1.00	.231
	Tri-City (NYP)	SS	0	0	4.50	2	2	0	0	6	4	0	4	6	9.0	1.33	.191
2018	Astros (GCL)	R	0	0	10.80	1	1	0	0	2	5	0	0	2	10.8	3.00	.500
	Tri-City (NYP)	SS	0	0	0.00	3	3	0	0	8	8	0	2	9	9.7	1.20	.258
	Quad Cities (MWL)	LoA	1	2	4.20	4	4	0	0	15	15	0	7	21	12.6	1.47	.259
	Buies Creek (CAR)	HiA	3	0	1.61	5	5	0	0	28	13	1	13	31	10.0	0.93	.138
	Corpus Christi (TL)	AA	0	0	0.00	1	1	0	0	6	1	0	2	8	12.0	0.50	.056
Minor League Totals			4	2	2.22	17	17	0	0	69	49	1	29	80	10.4	1.13	.200

7 FRAMBER VALDEZ, LHP

Born: Nov. 19, 1993. **B-T:** L-L. **HT:** 5-11. **WT:** 216. **Signed:** Dominican Republic, 2015. **Signed by:** Oz Ocampo/Tom Shafer/Roman Ocumarez/David Brito.

TRACK RECORD: Valdez didn't sign his first pro contract until he was 21, and teams shied away because of concerns about his elbow. Healthy since signing, he has shot from the Dominican Summer League to the majors in a little over three years.

SCOUTING REPORT: Valdez is largely a two-pitch lefthander. His plus curveball is good enough to allow him to succeed despite a lack of confidence in his below-average changeup. Valdez attacks hitters with two- and four-seam fastballs at 92-95 mph. His two-seamer has good sink down in the zone, but his above-average fastballs are mainly setting up his 78-82 mph curveball. Valdez's curve has plenty of depth, and he can sweep it across the strike zone thanks to his three-quarter arm slot. He can tighten it or loosen it and throw it in or out of the zone. Valdez nibbled against big league righthanders and will need to either improve his changeup or develop a cutter. His delivery is relatively clean and his control is average.

BA GRADE
45 **Risk:** Medium
Fastball: 55.
Curveball: 60.
Change: 40. **CTL:** 50.

THE FUTURE: Valdez's solid work as a starter late in the 2018 season gives him the opportunity to battle for a job in the 2019 rotation.

Year	Club (League)	Class	W	L	ERA	G	GS	CG	SV	IP	H	HR	BB	SO	K/9	WHIP	AVG
2016	Greeneville (APP)	R	1	0	1.69	2	2	0	0	11	7	0	3	15	12.7	0.94	.179
	Tri-City (NYP)	SS	2	1	3.74	5	2	0	0	22	22	0	7	28	11.6	1.34	.259
	Quad Cities (MWL)	LoA	1	3	3.06	6	6	1	0	35	31	0	11	35	8.9	1.19	.244
	Lancaster (CAL)	HiA	0	1	4.76	1	1	0	0	6	8	0	2	1	1.6	1.76	.333
2017	Buies Creek (CAR)	HiA	2	3	2.79	13	9	0	1	61	41	3	29	73	10.7	1.14	.185
	Corpus Christi (TL)	AA	5	5	5.88	12	9	0	0	49	60	4	23	53	9.7	1.69	.306
2018	Corpus Christi (TL)	AA	4	5	4.10	20	13	0	1	94	92	7	29	120	11.4	1.28	.256
	Fresno (PCL)	AAA	2	0	4.15	2	1	0	0	9	8	0	3	9	9.3	1.27	.250
	Houston (AL)	MAJ	4	1	2.19	8	5	0	0	37	22	3	24	34	8.3	1.24	.175
Major League Totals			4	1	2.19	8	5	0	0	37	22	3	24	34	8.3	1.24	.175
Minor League Totals			21	19	3.87	77	43	1	5	323	305	16	124	370	10.3	1.33	.249

8 FREUDIS NOVA, SS

Born: Jan. 12, 2000. **B-T:** R-R. **HT:** 6-1. **WT:** 176. **Signed:** Dominican Republic, 2016. **Signed by:** Oz Campo/Roman Ocumarez/Jose Lima.

TRACK RECORD: Nova was supposed to be the Marlins' big splash on the international market in 2016, but a positive test for a performance-enhancing drug quashed that deal and led to the Astros signing him for less than half of Miami's offer. Nova made his U.S. debut in 2018 as one of the more productive hitters in the Rookie-level Gulf Coast league.

SCOUTING REPORT: Nova showed bat speed, above-average bat-to-ball skills and above-average raw power in the GCL, but he needs plenty of refinement. Right now he has just enough power to get himself into poor habits, and he spent too many at-bats looking for a pitch he could yank down the line, rarely working advantageous counts. He had as many home runs (six) as walks (six). Nova's hand-eye coordination made it work, but he's going to have to improve his selectivity and patience. Defensively, Nova has all the tools to be an above-average shortstop. He's athletic with soft hands and an improved first step, though he's working on his reliability. His plus arm helps him make plays to his back hand, the play that many shortstops struggle to make.

THE FUTURE: Nova has the tools to be a shortstop who can hit enough to be an everyday regular, but he has years of work ahead of him to put it all together. A jump to low Class A Quad Cities would be a big step up in competition level, and it's more likely that Nova will spend one more year in short-season ball.

MIKE JANES/FOUR SEAM IMAGES

BA GRADE

55 Risk: Extreme

Bat: 50. Power: 55.
Run: 60. Field: 55.
Arm: 60.

Year	Club (League)	Class	AVG	G	AB	R	H	2B	3B	HR	RBI	BB	SO	SB	CS	OBP	SLG
2017	Astros Orange (DSL)	R	.247	47	166	30	41	6	0	4	16	15	33	8	3	.342	.355
2018	Astros (GCL)	R	.308	41	146	21	45	3	1	6	28	6	21	9	5	.331	.466
Minor League Totals			.276	88	312	51	86	9	1	10	44	21	54	17	8	.337	.407

9 SETH BEER, OF/1B

Born: Sept. 18, 1996. **B-T:** L-R. **HT:** 6-2. **WT:** 195. **Drafted:** Clemson, 2018 (1st round). **Signed by:** Gavin Dickey.

TRACK RECORD: Beer is the rare player who was never draft-eligible in high school. That's because he enrolled at Clemson six months early, so when his high school class was graduating, Beer was wrapping up an outstanding freshman season in the Atlantic Coast Conference. As a pre-teen, Beer was an elite swimmer. As a 12-year-old, he set a national age group record in the 50-yard backstroke, but he eventually opted to focus on baseball over swimming. So far, it's been a wise choice. Beer finished his college career with 56 home runs and nearly twice as many walks (180) as strikeouts (98).

SCOUTING REPORT: Beer has an excellent batting eye to go with the plus power that gives him the potential to hit 25-30 home runs. He demonstrated that power in his first two pro stops, helping alleviate some of the concerns that revolved around his struggles to hit with a wood bat in summer ball during college. Once he reached high Class A, Beer got too aggressive and chased too many pitches, but he should draw plenty of walks to post high on-base percentages. His batting averages likely won't reflect that, as his average will suffer from bottom-of-the-scale speed. His lefthanded power profile makes shifting on him an easy call, and a second baseman playing in short right field will be able to cut off some hits that otherwise would fall in. What kept Beer from going higher in the draft was his lack of a clear defensive position. He will likely only get slower from here. He is a heavy-footed, well below-average left fielder with a below-average arm and is worse at first base because of poor footwork. The Astros have to hope he can become a below-average defender, but he fits best as a DH.

THE FUTURE: Beer moved quickly in his pro debut and should make it to Double-A in 2019. His bat could be ready for Houston before too long, but unless he shows significant improvement defensively, he'll be the rare young player who tries to break into the majors as a designated hitter. His attributes are similar to long-time Astros minor league slugger A.J. Reed, but the Astros have to hope he can make a bigger MLB impact.

BA GRADE

50 Risk: High

Hit: 45. Power: 70.
Run: 20. Field: 30.
Arm: 40.

Year	Club (League)	Class	AVG	G	AB	R	H	2B	3B	HR	RBI	BB	SO	SB	CS	OBP	SLG
2018	Tri-City (NYP)	SS	.293	11	41	9	12	3	0	4	7	6	10	0	0	.431	.659
	Quad Cities (MWL)	LoA	.348	29	112	15	39	7	0	3	16	15	17	1	0	.443	.491
	Buies Creek (CAR)	HiA	.262	27	107	15	28	4	0	5	19	4	22	0	1	.307	.439
Minor League Totals			.304	67	260	39	79	14	0	12	42	25	49	1	1	.389	.496

10 BRYAN ABREU, RHP

Born: April 22, 1997. **B-T:** R-R. **HT:** 6-1. **WT:** 204. **Signed:** Dominican Republic, 2013. **Signed by:** Oz Ocampo/Marc Russo/Rafael Belen.

TRACK RECORD: The Astros excel at finding low-cost pitchers on the international market. Abreu is another prime example. He sat 84-86 mph before he signed, but he showed an ability to spin a breaking ball. The Astros have watched him fill out and blossom. He jumped to the Midwest League in 2018 and finished with 14.9 strikeouts per nine innings.

SCOUTING REPORT: Abreu is now a broad-shouldered, athletic righthander. He can run his plus, four-seam fastball up to 96 mph and he sits 93-94 mph. He is generally around the zone with his fastball, but his command needs refinement. He falls off the mound to the first base side, which affects his fringe-average control. Abreu's curveball is already the best in the organization. It has 12-to-6 shape, excellent depth and elite rotation at more than 3,000 revolutions per minute. He throws his curve for strikes, and it eludes bats even in the strike zone. Abreu also mixes in a slider and changeup, but both are below-average pitches.

BA GRADE

55 Risk: Extreme

Fastball: 55.
Curve: 70. Slider: 40.
Change: 40. CTL: 45.

THE FUTURE: Abreu's two-pitch combo would move quickly as a reliever, but he has the frame, intelligence and aptitude to start. Added to the 40-man roster, he's ready for high Class A Fayetteville.

Year	Club (League)	Class	W	L	ERA	G	GS	CG	SV	IP	H	HR	BB	SO	K/9	WHIP	AVG
2016	Greeneville (APP)	R	0	1	11.81	3	1	0	0	5	6	0	5	6	10.1	2.06	.286
	Astros (GCL)	R	2	4	3.78	10	3	0	0	33	33	0	15	35	9.5	1.44	.250
2017	Greeneville (APP)	R	1	3	7.98	8	6	0	0	29	29	4	21	40	12.3	1.70	.259
2018	Tri-City (NYP)	SS	2	0	1.13	4	2	0	0	16	11	2	6	22	12.4	1.06	.196
	Quad Cities (MWL)	LoA	4	1	1.64	10	5	0	3	38	22	2	17	68	16.0	1.02	.165
Minor League Totals			11	13	4.32	65	27	0	5	196	154	10	120	242	11.1	1.40	.218

11 JAIRO SOLIS, RHP

BA GRADE

55 Risk: Extreme

Born: Dec. 22, 1999. **B-T:** R-R. **Ht.:** 6-2. **Wt.:** 189. **Signed:** Venezuela, 2016. **Signed by:** Oz Ocampo/Tom Shafer/Roman Ocumarez/Enrique Brito.

TRACK RECORD: Solis got a velocity bump almost immediately after he signed and developed into one of the most refined young arms in Houston's system. Solis was rolling until he left an early August start with an elbow injury, and he ended up needing Tommy John surgery.

SCOUTING REPORT: Solis walked 12 in his first 12 innings, but then settled down to show the polish, stuff and strike-throwing that encourages scouts. Solis sits 93-95 mph and has touched 98 mph with a plus fastball. His above-average, 82-85 mph changeup has developed into a weapon, and he mixes in both a curveball and slider, both of which have at least average potential. Solis' delivery finishes into a somewhat stiff front side, and he did have some outings where he struggled to throw strikes, but scouts believe Solis will be develop at least average control.

THE FUTURE: Solis will spend all of 2019 rehabbing and will not get back into an official game until 2020. If he can make a full recovery, he's one of the highest-ceiling arms in Houston's system.

Year	Club (League)	Class	W	L	ERA	G	GS	CG	SV	IP	H	HR	BB	SO	K/9	WHIP	AVG
2017	Astros Orange (DSL)	R	1	1	2.73	6	4	0	0	26	20	2	8	28	9.6	1.06	.220
	Astros (GCL)	R	1	0	3.00	5	4	0	0	21	19	1	7	24	10.3	1.24	.229
	Greeneville (APP)	R	1	1	1.93	4	2	0	0	14	12	0	6	17	10.9	1.29	.226
2018	Quad Cities (MWL)	LoA	2	5	3.55	13	11	0	0	51	49	1	32	51	9.1	1.60	.259
Minor League Totals			5	7	3.05	28	21	0	0	112	100	4	53	120	9.6	1.37	.240

12 CIONEL PEREZ, LHP

BA GRADE

45 Risk: Medium

Born: May 21, 1996. **B-T:** L-L. **Ht.:** 5-11. **Wt.:** 170. **Signed:** Cuba, 2016. **Signed by:** Charlie Gonzalez/Oz Ocampo.

BACKGROUND: Perez was one of the best young pitchers in Cuba's Serie Nacional as an 18-year-old. The Astros ended up slashing Perez's bonus from $5.15 million to $2 million because of a concern about his elbow. The elbow hasn't been an issue since, and Perez made his major league debut in July.

TRACK RECORD: Although he primarily started in the minors, the skinny Perez fits best as a reliever with the ability to work multiple innings if needed. He attacks hitters with a swing-and-miss, plus-plus fastball that sits 94-96 mph and touches 98 mph, although it sometimes tails off in longer outings. His fastball pairs well with a mid-80s, above-average breaking ball that he manipulates. When he wants to, he can sweep it across the zone early in counts, and he can also throw it with a shorter, harder downward break when he is later in counts or facing a lefthanded. Perez's changeup doesn't do much. It lacks separation or late movement and is a show-me pitch thrown away to righthanded hitters just to set up inside fastballs. Perez had some bouts with wildness, but he generally throws strikes and projects to have average control. **THE FUTURE:** Perez should fit into the big league bullpen. He has the arm and feel to be a high-leverage reliever because of the quality of his fastball.

Year	Club (League)	Class	W	L	ERA	G	GS	CG	SV	IP	H	HR	BB	SO	K/9	WHIP	AVG
2016	Did not play																
2017	Quad Cities (MWL)	LoA	4	3	4.23	12	9	0	2	55	52	2	17	55	8.9	1.25	.254
	Buies Creek (CAR)	HiA	2	1	2.84	5	4	0	0	25	27	1	5	18	6.4	1.26	.276
	Corpus Christi (TL)	AA	0	0	5.54	4	3	0	0	13	15	1	5	10	6.9	1.54	.294
2018	Corpus Christi (TL)	AA	6	1	1.98	16	11	0	1	68	54	3	22	83	10.9	1.11	.213
	Fresno (PCL)	AAA	1	0	3.38	4	0	0	0	5	5	0	6	6	10.1	2.06	.250
	Houston (AL)	MAJ	0	0	3.97	8	0	0	0	11	6	3	7	12	9.5	1.15	.158
Major League Totals			0	0	3.97	8	0	0	0	11	6	3	7	12	9.5	1.15	.158
Minor League Totals			13	5	3.17	41	27	0	3	167	153	7	55	172	9.3	1.24	.244

13 RONNIE DAWSON, OF

BA GRADE
50 Risk: High

Born: May 19, 1995. **B-T:** L-R. **Ht.:** 6-2. **Wt.:** 220. **Drafted:** Ohio State, 2016 (2nd round). **Signed by:** Nick Venuto.

TRACK RECORD: Dawson was both a football and baseball star in high school. He could have played either in college, but he chose baseball and quickly proved it was a wise choice as he became an immediate contributor and eventually the star of the Ohio State lineup. **SCOUTING REPORT:** At Ohio State, Dawson was a left fielder. But given a chance to play center field, Dawson has blossomed. He's only an average runner, but his reads and routes are excellent, allowing him to be an above-average center fielder who earns some plus grades. His arm is fringy. Dawson's swing and approach have changed, and scouts are less enamored. His swing has gotten steeper and more pull-oriented. Dawson has above-average power to do damage, but evaluators are concerned that his current swing will limit his hard contact rate and fringe-average hitting ability unless he tones it down. **THE FUTURE:** Dawson is an interesting collection of tools and skills. As a lefthanded-hitting center fielder with power potential he could develop into an everyday regular, but he still has plenty of offensive refinement ahead. He'll return to Double-A Corpus Christi to start 2019.

Year	Club (League)	Class	AVG	G	AB	R	H	2B	3B	HR	RBI	BB	SO	SB	CS	OBP	SLG
2016	Tri-City (NYP)	SS	.225	70	244	41	55	13	1	7	36	41	66	12	6	.351	.373
2017	Quad Cities (MWL)	LoA	.272	115	434	80	118	23	4	13	60	55	99	17	8	.363	.433
	Buies Creek (CAR)	HiA	.327	13	52	7	17	3	1	0	5	4	9	1	3	.368	.423
2018	Buies Creek (CAR)	HiA	.247	90	332	51	82	18	1	10	49	39	96	29	11	.331	.398
	Corpus Christi (TL)	AA	.289	29	114	18	33	6	1	6	14	6	34	6	3	.341	.518
Minor League Totals			.259	317	1176	197	305	63	8	36	164	145	304	65	31	.350	.418

14 GARRETT STUBBS, C

BA GRADE
45 Risk: Medium

Born: May 26, 1993. **B-T:** L-R. **Ht.:** 5-10. **Wt.:** 175. **Drafted:** Southern California, 2015 (8th round). **Signed by:** Tim Costic.

TRACK RECORD: Stubbs is one of the smallest and skinniest catchers in the game, but he brings a rare athleticism for the position. Stubbs led all Pacific Coast League catchers by throwing out 45 percent of basestealers, and the Astros added him to their 40-man roster after the season. **SCOUTING REPORT:** Stubbs is a better hitter than slugger, and he's athletic enough to play a little bit of everywhere if needed. He runs better than most catchers and has successfully swiped 22 bases since his last caught stealing. Stubbs' low target and athleticism help his ability to block pitches in the dirt, and his receiving is viewed as average. He has an above-average arm and it's accurate. Stubbs uses the entire field when he's locked in at the plate. He's an above-average hitter who could post .300 averages in his best years, although his power is limited to lining balls to the gaps and the sporadic yanked home run. **THE FUTURE:** Stubbs' biggest remaining focus area to be big league ready is to get stronger, which probably relies on him getting a little bigger. His defense and bat are ready if the Astros need a backup.

Year	Club (League)	Class	AVG	G	AB	R	H	2B	3B	HR	RBI	BB	SO	SB	CS	OBP	SLG
2016	Lancaster (CAL)	HiA	.291	55	206	35	60	13	0	6	38	29	37	10	3	.385	.442
	Corpus Christi (TL)	AA	.325	31	120	23	39	9	1	4	16	14	11	5	0	.401	.517
2017	Corpus Christi (TL)	AA	.236	75	263	36	62	13	0	4	25	32	44	8	0	.324	.331
	Fresno (PCL)	AAA	.221	23	77	11	17	5	0	0	12	11	15	3	0	.341	.286
2018	Fresno (PCL)	AAA	.310	84	297	60	92	19	6	4	38	35	53	6	0	.382	.455
Minor League Totals			.278	304	1081	185	301	64	7	18	136	142	165	35	3	.366	.401

15 MYLES STRAW, OF

Born: Oct. 17, 1994. **B-T:** R-R. **Ht.:** 5-10. **Wt.:** 179. **Drafted:** St. John's River (Fla.) JC, 2015 (12th round). **Signed by:** John Martin.

TRACK RECORD: Straw and Rays prospect Nate Lowe formed an exceptional combination at St. John's River (Fla.) JC. As a pro, Straw has stood out for his blazing speed and ability to hit for average. He led the minors in batting in 2016, when he hit .358, and led the minors in 2018 with 70 steals. He earned his first big league promotion in September and a spot on the Astros' Division Series roster as a pinch-runner.
SCOUTING REPORT: Straw's opposite-field approach rarely makes him a threat to hit the ball over an outfielder's head. That approach has worked so far, and he's steadily drawn walks despite lacking the power to frighten pitchers who are behind in counts. Straw handles velocity and doesn't get the bat knocked out of his hands despite his bottom-of-the-scale power, projecting as an above-average hitter. His 70-grade speed helps him beat out infield hits and makes him a threat to steal anytime a base is open. He can play all three outfield spots in part thanks to a plus-plus arm. In center field, he's an above-average defender excellent coming in on balls, but he needs his speed to make up for slower reads on balls over his head.
THE FUTURE: Straw's lack of power limits him, but his speed, arm, defense and bat control give him a shot to be a useful big leaguer. He'll head to spring training with a shot to make the Astros' roster.

Year	Club (League)	Class	AVG	G	AB	R	H	2B	3B	HR	RBI	BB	SO	SB	CS	OBP	SLG
2016	Quad Cities (MWL)	LoA	.374	68	270	40	101	14	6	0	22	29	58	17	10	.432	.470
	Lancaster (CAL)	HiA	.303	19	76	21	23	4	0	1	5	11	17	4	2	.393	.395
2017	Buies Creek (CAR)	HiA	.295	114	437	81	129	17	7	1	41	87	70	36	9	.412	.373
	Corpus Christi (TL)	AA	.239	13	46	9	11	0	0	0	3	7	9	2	0	.340	.239
2018	Corpus Christi (TL)	AA	.327	65	251	47	82	7	3	1	17	35	42	35	6	.414	.390
	Fresno (PCL)	AAA	.257	66	265	48	68	10	3	0	14	38	60	35	3	.349	.317
	Houston (AL)	MAJ	.333	9	9	4	3	0	0	1	1	1	0	2	0	.400	.667
Major League Totals			.333	9	9	4	3	0	0	1	1	1	0	2	0	.400	.667
Minor League Totals			.302	403	1554	293	470	62	22	3	115	236	307	151	39	.394	.376

16 ABRAHAM TORO, 3B

Born: Dec. 20, 1996. **B-T:** B-R. **Ht.:** 6-0. **Wt.:** 190. **Drafted:** Seminole State (Okla.) JC., 2016 (5th round). **Signed by:** Jim Stevenson.

TRACK RECORD: The Astros have long had success finding gems from junior colleges. Toro appears next in line. He earned a bump to Double-A Corpus Christi in early July after emerging as the top hitter at high Class A Buies Creek, and he followed up with a loud performance in the Arizona Fall League.
SCOUTING REPORT: Toro is only a .248 career hitter, but scouts consistently cite him as one of the best hitters in Houston's system. Toro has short legs and his movements and mannerisms appear choppy and unathletic. But watch him over the course of a series or longer and it becomes apparent that he's a better athlete than he looks. Toro has some length to his swing, but he has the bat speed and whip to make it work. He projects to hit 15-20 home runs over a full season and has an average bat as well. There are many more questions defensively. He makes the routine play at third base and has an above-average arm, but his range is limited and he doesn't run well. Houston tried him at catcher in 2017, but that didn't stick.
THE FUTURE: Toro's bat will determine if he becomes an everyday player or an up-and-down player. His defense likely won't cut it as a full-time bench option. He'll start 2019 back at Double-A.

Year	Club (League)	Class	AVG	G	AB	R	H	2B	3B	HR	RBI	BB	SO	SB	CS	OBP	SLG
2016	Greeneville (APP)	R	.254	44	177	20	45	6	3	0	19	10	31	2	1	.301	.322
2017	Tri-City (NYP)	SS	.292	32	106	21	31	8	0	6	16	19	21	1	3	.414	.538
	Quad Cities (MWL)	LoA	.209	37	134	25	28	3	2	9	17	21	30	2	0	.323	.463
2018	Buies Creek (CAR)	HiA	.257	83	296	54	76	20	1	14	56	45	62	5	1	.361	.473
	Corpus Christi (TL)	AA	.230	50	178	16	41	15	2	2	22	17	46	3	3	.317	.371
Minor League Totals			.248	246	891	136	221	52	8	31	130	112	190	13	8	.342	.429

17 JONATHAN ARAUZ, SS

Born: Aug. 3, 1998. **B-T:** L-R. **Ht.:** 6-0. **Wt.:** 173. **Signed:** Panama, 2014. **Signed by:** Norman Anciani (Phillies).

TRACK RECORD: Arauz's career has already been quite eventful. He was traded from the Phillies to the Astros in the Ken Giles trade and introduced himself to his new club inauspiciously by being suspended 50 games after testing positive for methamphetamine. After an excellent first half at low Class A Midwest League, he was the worst hitter in the high Class A Carolina League in the second half of the season.
SCOUTING REPORT: Arauz was viewed as more of a bat-first middle infielder who might be stretched at shortstop when he signed. Now, he's improved his glove but faces questions about how much he'll hit.

At his best, Arauz shows fringe-average power to go with solid ability to manipulate the barrel. Arauz showed little ability to make adjustments from at-bat to at-bat, and when he did make contact, they were defensive swings that did no damage. Defensively, he has improved, showing a better first step and soft hands to go with excellent timing and an average arm. He is an average runner.

THE FUTURE: The Astros opted not to add Arauz to the 40-man roster, taking the risk that Arauz's not-nearly-ready bat would keep teams from picking him in the Rule 5 draft. He needs to return to high Class A to work on putting together better at-bats.

Year	Club (League)	Class	AVG	G	AB	R	H	2B	3B	HR	RBI	BB	SO	SB	CS	OBP	SLG
2016	Greeneville (APP)	R	.249	53	201	26	50	10	1	2	18	19	45	1	3	.323	.338
2017	Quad Cities (MWL)	LoA	.220	36	127	23	28	3	2	0	4	20	18	0	1	.331	.276
	Tri-City (NYP)	SS	.264	33	121	16	32	7	1	1	11	12	29	1	0	.341	.364
2018	Quad Cities (MWL)	LoA	.299	54	204	31	61	11	6	4	29	30	38	7	6	.392	.471
	Buies Creek (CAR)	HiA	.167	71	233	25	39	10	3	4	18	16	36	1	2	.223	.288
Minor League Totals			.240	291	1059	142	254	51	15	13	98	110	195	12	12	.316	.353

18 JAYSON SCHROEDER, RHP

BA GRADE

50 Risk: Extreme

Born: Nov. 14, 1999. **B-T:** R-R. **Ht.:** 6-2. **Wt.:** 195. **Drafted:** HS—Kirkland, Wash., 2018 (2nd round). **Signed by:** Brad Budzinski.

TRACK RECORD: Schroeder was the best prep pitcher in the Northwest in 2018, impressing scouts with his fast arm and advanced feel for three pitches. The Astros signed him for $1.2 million to forgo a Washington commitment. Schroeder didn't pitch much after he signed, but he impressed in short stints.

SCOUTING REPORT: Schroeder showed plenty of velocity and promise as an amateur, but as Astros pitchers often do, he's already throwing harder as a pro. Schroeder sat 93-95 mph and touched 97 mph for the Astros this summer in the Rookie-level Gulf Coast League. His fastball has plenty of life up in the zone, and he's also shown he can sink it. His curveball has also shown plenty of promise as he has an excellent feel for spinning it. While it's not consistent yet, it has the potential to be a plus strikeout pitch as he refines it. His changeup has further to go, but it is also promising.

THE FUTURE: The Astros do an excellent job of taking pitchers and either adding or refining pitches. Schroeder has all the building blocks to be a potential mid-rotation starter.

Year	Club (League)	Class	W	L	ERA	G	GS	CG	SV	IP	H	HR	BB	SO	K/9	WHIP	AVG
2018	Astros (GCL)	R	0	0	1.50	7	5	0	0	18	13	0	9	18	9.0	1.22	.220
Minor League Totals			0	0	1.50	7	5	0	0	18	13	0	9	18	9.0	1.22	.220

19 BRANDON BIELAK, RHP

BA GRADE

45 Risk: High

Born: April 2, 1996. **B-T:** R-R. **Ht.:** 6-2. **Wt.:** 212. **Drafted:** Notre Dame, 2017 (11th round). **Signed by:** Nick Venuto.

TRACK RECORD: After two successful seasons at Notre Dame, Bielak more than doubled his ERA as a junior, posting a 5.55 ERA. He slid to the 11th round because of that, but quickly proved as a pro that he's better than those numbers suggest. His 2.23 ERA was the best in Houston's system in 2018.

SCOUTING REPORT: It's hard for hitters to get comfortable against Bielak because he throws four pitches for strikes and has the confidence to use them in almost any count. His delivery is simple, efficient and repeatable. He challenges hitters down in the zone with a heavy, 91-94 mph fastball. Bielak works comfortably to both sides of the plate. His fastball, curveball, slider and changeup are all potentially average.

THE FUTURE: Bielak has a career 1.91 ERA, but his approach is one that eats up less-experienced hitters. The challenge will get tougher as he heads to Double-A Corpus Christi for an extended look.

Year	Club (League)	Class	W	L	ERA	G	GS	CG	SV	IP	H	HR	BB	SO	K/9	WHIP	AVG
2017	Astros (GCL)	R	1	0	0.00	2	0	0	0	4	3	0	1	5	10.4	0.92	.188
	Tri-City (NYP)	SS	1	1	0.92	8	4	0	1	29	18	0	4	37	11.4	0.75	.171
2018	Buies Creek (CAR)	HiA	5	3	2.10	14	7	0	2	56	44	2	17	74	12.0	1.10	.217
	Corpus Christi (TL)	AA	2	5	2.35	11	10	0	0	61	52	4	22	57	8.4	1.21	.235
Minor League Totals			9	9	1.91	35	21	0	3	151	117	6	44	173	10.3	1.07	.215

20 TYLER IVEY, RHP

BA GRADE

45 Risk: High

Born: May 12, 1996. **B-T:** R-R. **Ht.:** 6-4. **Wt.:** 194. **Drafted:** Grayson (Texas) JC, 2017 (3rd round). **Signed by:** Jim Stevenson.

TRACK RECORD: Ivey was a part of Texas A&M's weekend rotation as a freshman and held that role into the conference schedule. But he eventually moved to the bullpen and opted afterwards to transfer to Grayson (Texas) JC. After a rough debut, Ivey pitched to a 2.97 ERA at the Class A levels in 2018.

SCOUTING REPORT: Ivey is a lanky righthander. His gangliness is magnified by his effortful delivery, which begins with an exaggerated gather. He uses a big leg kick and a high hand break and often finishes with a modest head whack. There's also some length in his takeaway, but his arm is on time and he is consistently around the zone with above-average control. Ivey is always working to get to his breaking balls. His downward-breaking curveball is a plus pitch, and his slider will flash above-average as well. Ivey relies on the breaking balls, but his 89-93 mph fastball could develop into an average pitch as well. It shows some finish when he elevates it. His low-80s changeup is a distant fourth pitch he rarely throws.
THE FUTURE: Ivey has the building blocks to be a back-of-the-rotation starter, especially if he fills out and adds a tick or two to his fastball. He'll compete for a spot in Double-A Corpus Christi's rotation.

Year	Club (League)	Class	W	L	ERA	G	GS	CG	SV	IP	H	HR	BB	SO	K/9	WHIP	AVG
2017	Astros (GCL)	R	0	0	0.00	1	1	0	0	2	1	0	2	3	13.5	1.50	.167
	Tri-City (NYP)	SS	0	3	5.94	11	7	0	0	36	41	2	12	41	10.2	1.46	.281
2018	Quad Cities (MWL)	LoA	1	3	3.46	9	6	0	2	42	36	2	8	53	11.4	1.06	.221
	Buies Creek (CAR)	HiA	3	3	2.69	15	12	1	1	70	50	3	21	82	10.5	1.01	.196
Minor League Totals			4	9	3.65	36	26	1	3	150	128	7	43	179	10.7	1.14	.225

21 PETER SOLOMON, RHP

BA GRADE

45 Risk: High

Born: Aug. 16, 1996. **B-T:** R-R. **Ht.:** 6-4. **Wt.:** 203. **Drafted:** Notre Dame, 2017 (4th round). **Signed by:** Nick Venuto.
TRACK RECORD: Solomon was expected to be the Irish ace for his junior year, but instead he was moved to the bullpen after just four starts. Much like his Notre Dame and Astros teammate Brandon Bielak, the Astros were confident Solomon could be an effective starter, and so far he's rewarded that faith.
SCOUTING REPORT: While he had his biggest success in college as a reliever, Solomon's well-rounded arsenal and approach works well as a starter. He doesn't have a plus pitch yet, but he has an above-average, 92-94 mph fastball that will touch higher in short stints and a 12-to-6 curveball he has a lot of trust in that will flash above-average. He's added a promising cutter as well. His changeup is a below-average pitch that he's yet to show much confidence in. Solomon's delivery is clean and he projects to have average control.
THE FUTURE: The Astros have moved Solomon slower than Bielak, but he has a pretty similar profile with a little firmer stuff. Solomon has a realistic shot of reaching Double-A in 2019.

Year	Club (League)	Class	W	L	ERA	G	GS	CG	SV	IP	H	HR	BB	SO	K/9	WHIP	AVG
2017	Astros (GCL)	R	0	0	0.00	1	1	0	0	1	0	0	0	0	0.0	0.00	.000
2018	Quad Cities (MWL)	LoA	8	1	2.43	19	10	0	0	78	62	2	28	88	10.2	1.16	.218
	Buies Creek (CAR)	HiA	1	0	1.96	5	3	0	0	23	16	0	4	26	10.2	0.87	.195
Minor League Totals			9	1	2.30	25	14	0	0	102	78	2	32	114	10.1	1.08	.211

22 ROGELIO ARMENTEROS, RHP

BA GRADE

40 Risk: Medium

Born: June 30, 1994. **B-T:** R-R. **Ht.:** 6-1. **Wt.:** 229. **Signed:** Cuba, 2014. **Signed by:** Alex Jacobs.
TRACK RECORD: Signed for a modest $40,000 out of Cuba in 2014, Armenteros has proven to be a reliable and durable starter. He handled the picher-destroying Pacific Coast League in 2018, going 8-1, 3.74 for Triple-A Fresno. The Astros rewarded him with a 40-man roster spot after the season.
SCOUTING REPORT: Armenteros carried a little more weight in 2018 and coincidentally or not, he didn't throw as hard as he did in 2017. His fastball, which got to 93-95 mph pretty regularly last year more generally sat 90-92 mph in 2018. It played more as a fringe-average pitch as well, but what Armenteros does is use his fastball to set up an outstanding plus changeup that draws comparisons to Chris Devenski's. The pitch is Armenteros' bread-and-butter in part because his curveball and slider are below-average. The two blend together at times, but neither is sharp enough to be a weapon.
THE FUTURE: Armenteros went to the Dominican Winter League and pitched well. He's ready to be a fill-in starter/long-reliever for the Astros in 2019.

Year	Club (League)	Class	W	L	ERA	G	GS	CG	SV	IP	H	HR	BB	SO	K/9	WHIP	AVG
2016	Quad Cities (MWL)	LoA	0	2	1.93	4	3	0	0	19	12	0	3	20	9.6	0.80	.179
	Lancaster (CAL)	HiA	6	4	4.18	19	16	0	1	90	87	13	37	107	10.7	1.37	.251
	Corpus Christi (TL)	AA	2	0	1.96	3	3	0	0	18	17	1	4	13	6.4	1.15	.262
2017	Corpus Christi (TL)	AA	2	3	1.93	14	10	0	1	65	49	3	19	74	10.2	1.04	.207
	Fresno (PCL)	AAA	8	1	2.16	10	10	0	0	58	42	5	19	72	11.1	1.05	.203
2018	Fresno (PCL)	AAA	8	1	3.74	22	21	1	1	118	106	15	48	134	10.2	1.31	.237
Minor League Totals			29	13	3.18	87	75	1	3	430	366	41	154	481	10.1	1.21	.229

23 J.J. MATIJEVIC, OF

BA GRADE

45 Risk: High

Born: Nov. 14, 1995. **B-T:** L-R. **Ht.:** 6-0. **Wt.:** 203. **Drafted:** Arizona, 2017 (2nd round supplemental). **Signed by:** Mark Ross.

TRACK RECORD: The Astros believe in drafting bats, even if sometimes there are open questions about where the hitter can play passable defense. It was true when they drafted Tyler White, Abraham Toro, Seth Beer and Matijevic. Matijevic was seen as a solid hitter, but scouts saw him as a below-average defender at first base with few other defensive options. So far, that's been an accurate assessment. Matijevic's 22 home runs in 2018 with high Class A Buies Creek were third-most among Astros farmhands, but his defense remains a question.

SCOUTING REPORT: Matijevic has an all-power, all-the-time approach as he looks for balls to hit over the fence. He makes it work with an eye to get pitches to hit, and he did show a better approach as the season wore on. Matijevic has plus power potential, but his sellout approach means it comes with below-average hitting ability. He has to do damage at the plate because Matijevic fits best as a designated hitter. A fringe-average runner, Matijevic's defense in left field is below-average at best and some scouts slap a 30 grade on it. He does have an average, accurate arm.

THE FUTURE: Matijevic will head to Double-A Corpus Christi looking to work on improving his defense. If he can improve to fringe-average, he would be able to make a much better case for a big league job.

Year	Club (League)	Class	AVG	G	AB	R	H	2B	3B	HR	RBI	BB	SO	SB	CS	OBP	SLG
2017	Tri-City (NYP)	SS	.240	53	200	34	48	14	0	6	27	18	60	11	3	.302	.400
	Quad Cities (MWL)	LoA	.125	6	24	2	3	0	0	1	4	1	9	0	1	.192	.250
2018	Quad Cities (MWL)	LoA	.354	13	48	8	17	6	1	3	5	8	10	3	0	.446	.708
	Buies Creek (CAR)	HiA	.266	88	335	58	89	20	3	19	57	36	103	10	13	.335	.513
Minor League Totals			.259	160	607	102	157	40	4	29	93	63	182	24	17	.328	.481

24 DEAN DEETZ, RHP

BA GRADE

45 Risk: High

Born: Nov. 29, 1993. **B-T:** R-R. **Ht.:** 6-1. **Wt.:** 207. **Drafted:** Northeast Oklahoma A&M JC, 2014 (11th round). **Signed by:** Jim Stevenson.

TRACK RECORD: After missing time with Tommy John surgery, Deetz was a teammate of fellow Astros draftee and now A's outfielder Ramon Laureano at Northeastern Oklahoma A&M JC. The Astros added Deetz to their 40-man roster before the 2017 season and kept him there even after he was suspended 80 games for testing positive for a PED. Deetz made his MLB debut as a September callup.

SCOUTING REPORT: Deetz is the epitome of a wild, hard-throwing, power reliever. He attacks hitters with a plus-plus, 94-99 mph fastball and a plus, 85-88 mph slider. Deetz can toy with the break and depth of his slider. When he's trying to finish off a hitter it will dive out of the zone, but he can also tighten it up for a shorter break when he's trying to keep it in the zone. Deetz's control is often as wild as his stuff is impressive. He walked 5.1 batters per nine innings last season, and overall he has firmly below-average control.

THE FUTURE: Scouts see potential for a high-leverage role, but Deetz's control troubles mean he's still a risky bet. The Astros currently have a very deep bullpen, so he's stuck battling for a spot in 2019.

Year	Club (League)	Class	W	L	ERA	G	GS	CG	SV	IP	H	HR	BB	SO	K/9	WHIP	AVG
2016	Lancaster (CAL)	HiA	6	5	4.24	23	16	0	1	93	86	9	45	86	8.3	1.40	.241
	Corpus Christi (TL)	AA	2	0	0.00	2	2	0	0	12	7	0	2	17	12.8	0.75	.175
2017	Corpus Christi (TL)	AA	4	2	1.82	8	6	0	0	40	27	3	9	42	9.5	0.91	.194
	Fresno (PCL)	AAA	3	4	6.40	17	10	0	0	45	46	5	41	55	11.0	1.93	.267
2018	Quad Cities (MWL)	LoA	0	0	3.00	3	1	0	0	3	3	0	5	7	21.0	2.67	.300
	Corpus Christi (TL)	AA	0	0	0.00	3	0	0	0	4	2	0	0	6	14.7	0.55	.154
	Fresno (PCL)	AAA	2	0	0.79	21	0	0	0	34	22	1	18	50	13.2	1.18	.186
	Houston (AL)	MAJ	0	0	5.40	4	0	0	0	3	4	1	1	3	8.1	1.50	.308
Major League Totals			0	0	5.40	4	0	0	0	3	4	1	1	3	8.1	1.50	.308
Minor League Totals			28	18	3.52	104	51	0	1	320	262	20	162	337	9.5	1.33	.222

25 JEREMY PENA, SS

BA GRADE

45 Risk: High

Born: Sept. 27, 1999. **B-T:** R-R. **Ht.:** 6-0. **Wt.:** 197. **Drafted:** Maine, 2018 (3rd round). **Signed by:** Bobby St. Pierre.

TRACK RECORD: Pena grew up around the game as the son of longtime Cardinals second baseman Geronimo Pena. He has a chance to be an even better defender than his father. At Maine, Pena was the team's shortstop from the day he arrived to the day he was drafted in the third round by the Astros. His bat steadily improved in his time with the Black Bears, but even as a junior he was primarily a singles hitter, something that was also true in his pro debut. He walked nearly as much as he struck out but posted an .059 isolated power mark before going down with a leg injury at short-season Tri-City.

SCOUTING REPORT: Pena immediately became one of the best defensive shortstops in Houston's organization. He made 10 errors in 36 games at Tri-City, but he has good hands, smooth actions and an above-average arm. He projects as an above-average defender at shortstop. Pena is also an above-average runner and an adept basestealer. As a hitter, Pena doesn't try to do too much, as he looks to spray hits and work counts. He understands a walk is a useful part of his offensive game, but he's a bottom-of-the-order hitter who doesn't make pitchers sweat because of well below-average power.

THE FUTURE: Pena will jump to low Class A. His glove is an asset, but he'll work to improve at the plate.

Year	Club (League)	Class	AVG	G	AB	R	H	2B	3B	HR	RBI	BB	SO	SB	CS	OBP	SLG
2018	Tri-City (NYP)	SS	.250	36	136	22	34	5	0	1	10	18	19	3	0	.340	.309
Minor League Totals			.250	36	136	22	34	5	0	1	10	18	19	3	0	.340	.309

26 ALEX McKENNA, OF

BA GRADE
45 Risk: High

Born: Sept. 6, 1997. **B-T:** R-R. **Ht.:** 6-2. **Wt.:** 200. **Drafted:** Cal Poly, 2018 (4th round). **Signed by:** Tim Costic.

TRACK RECORD: McKenna has a lengthy track record of being a productive hitter. He hit .347 over his final two seasons at Cal Poly and also showed he could handle a wood bat by hitting .298 in the Cape Cod League in the summer before his junior season. That feel to hit was also apparent in his pro debut.

SCOUTING REPORT: McKenna is the kind of well-rounded player who gets the most out of a solid but unspectacular set of tools. He's strong, athletic and an above-average runner. The Astros will have to help him unlock power that isn't always as apparent in games as it is during batting practice. McKenna has a high handset and a modest load to start his swing with an all-fields contact-oriented approach, but he can show off above-average raw power when he really squares one up. Defensively, McKenna is reliable in all three outfield spots and has a solid-average arm, but his range is a little limited for center field.

THE FUTURE: McKenna is the kind of player who sometimes exceeds expectations. If his power develops, he could be a regular. If not, he has enough athleticism and hitting ability to be a fourth outfielder.

Year	Club (League)	Class	AVG	G	AB	R	H	2B	3B	HR	RBI	BB	SO	SB	CS	OBP	SLG
2018	Tri-City (NYP)	SS	.328	32	116	14	38	7	1	5	21	11	24	6	5	.423	.534
	Quad Cities (MWL)	LoA	.271	12	48	5	13	1	1	2	7	3	16	0	0	.314	.458
Minor League Totals			.311	44	164	19	51	8	2	7	28	14	40	6	5	.394	.512

27 MANNY RAMIREZ, RHP

BA GRADE
50 Risk: Extreme

Born: Nov. 21, 1999. **B-T:** R-R. **Ht.:** 5-11. **Wt.:** 176. **Signed:** Dominican Republic, 2017. **Signed by:** Oz Ocampo/Roman Ocumarez/Leocadio Guevara.

TRACK RECORD: Signed for a modest $50,000, Ramirez has quickly proven to be an astute signing. Pitching in Houston's tandem-starter system, he allowed zero or one run in eight of his 12 outings, but when he struggled, he really struggled, leading to an inflated 4.76 ERA in the Gulf Coast League.

SCOUTING REPORT: Ramirez is undersized without much room to fill out further, but his arm strength is big league-caliber. He already has a plus, 95-97 mph fastball that can blow hitters away. He generates velocity from a compact, fluid motion. His inexperience is much more apparent when he breaks off his curveball. He flashes an ability to spin it, but his control of the breaking ball wavers and he mixes loopy, slow curves with harder, tighter, power breakers. Ramirez's control also has a ways to go, but with his delivery, he has the building blocks to develop at least average control.

THE FUTURE: Ramirez is far from Houston, but he has the foundation and arm of a future power reliever. He'll likely begin the 2019 season in extended spring training.

Year	Club (League)	Class	W	L	ERA	G	GS	CG	SV	IP	H	HR	BB	SO	K/9	WHIP	AVG
2017	Astros Blue (DSL)	R	2	1	3.44	8	1	0	0	18	14	0	12	18	8.8	1.42	.226
2018	Astros (GCL)	R	1	1	4.76	10	5	0	0	34	29	0	15	46	12.2	1.29	.232
	Tri-City (NYP)	SS	0	0	0.00	2	1	0	0	5	1	0	4	9	15.2	0.94	.063
Minor League Totals			3	2	3.90	20	7	0	0	58	44	0	31	73	11.4	1.30	.217

28 REYMIN GUDUAN, LHP

BA GRADE
40 Risk: Medium

Born: March 16, 1992. **B-T:** L-L. **Ht.:** 6-4. **Wt.:** 210. **Signed:** Dominican Republic, 2009. **Signed by:** Felix Francisco/Rafael Belen.

TRACK RECORD: When Guduan signed with the Astros, Ed Wade was still the team's general manager, and Jose Altuve had yet to play a game in full-season ball. It's been a long road from there to here, but Guduan has managed to make 25 appearances for the Astros over the past two seasons.

SCOUTING REPORT: There is no subtlety to Guduan's approach. He attacks hitters with a 95-98 mph plus fastball from the left side. There's not much of a Plan B. He has improved his confidence and feel for his sweepy slider, which is an average pitch, but he struggles to locate both. At this point, it's hard to envision Guduan developing even fringe-average control, as his scouting report (outstanding fastball, below-average control) is the same as when he signed nearly 10 years ago.

THE FUTURE: Guduan's control troubles keep him from filling a high-leverage role, but the quality of his arm will keep giving him chances. He fits best in a more modest relief job.

Year	Club (League)	Class	W	L	ERA	G	GS	CG	SV	IP	H	HR	BB	SO	K/9	WHIP	AVG
2016	Corpus Christi (TL)	AA	1	0	0.69	9	0	0	2	13	7	1	3	19	13.2	0.77	.156
	Fresno (PCL)	AAA	2	3	5.23	34	0	0	0	43	43	2	34	44	9.2	1.79	.256
2017	Fresno (PCL)	AAA	5	7	5.87	39	0	0	1	46	61	4	14	47	9.2	1.63	.316
	Houston (AL)	MAJ	0	0	7.88	22	0	0	0	16	24	1	12	16	9.0	2.25	.338
2018	Fresno (PCL)	AAA	3	3	3.74	43	0	0	2	55	46	5	32	83	13.5	1.41	.217
	Houston (AL)	MAJ	0	0	2.70	3	0	0	0	3	1	1	0	4	10.8	0.30	.091
Major League Totals			0	0	6.98	25	0	0	0	19	25	2	12	20	9.3	1.91	.305
Minor League Totals			20	31	4.80	220	31	0	9	355	363	21	245	438	11.1	1.71	.259

29 BRADY RODGERS, RHP

BA GRADE

40 Risk: Medium

Born: Sept. 17, 1990. **B-T:** R-R. **Ht.:** 6-2. **Wt.:** 210. **Drafted:** Arizona State, 2012 (3rd round). **Signed by:** Mike Brown.

TRACK RECORD: Rodgers will have plenty of reasons to remember May 2. On May 2, 2017 he had Tommy John surgery to repair his right elbow ligament. On May 2, 2018 he became a father for the first time. Rodgers was back at Triple-A Fresno for a third season by July. He had a rough reintroduction, but he did finish strong, allowing only one run in his final 13 innings.

SCOUTING REPORT: Rodgers is a perfectionist because he has to be to survive. All four of his pitches—fastball, curveball, slider and changeup—range from fringe-average to average depending on the day, but when he's on, it all works because he's able to locate them with plus control and above-average command. Rodgers doesn't have a regular swing-and-miss pitch, so he has to move the ball around the strike zone.

THE FUTURE: The Astros kept Rodgers on their 40-man roster throughout his recovery from Tommy John surgery in 2017 and 2018. He's Triple-A rotation depth for the Astros considering the state of their big league rotation, but he could fill a larger role as an up-and-down starter for another team.

Year	Club (League)	Class	W	L	ERA	G	GS	CG	SV	IP	H	HR	BB	SO	K/9	WHIP	AVG
2016	Fresno (PCL)	AAA	12	4	2.86	22	22	2	0	132	129	7	23	116	7.9	1.15	.257
	Houston (AL)	MAJ	0	1	15.12	5	1	0	0	8	15	0	7	3	3.2	2.64	.385
2017	Fresno (PCL)	AAA	2	0	1.10	3	3	0	0	16	14	0	1	11	6.1	0.92	.241
2018	Tri-City (NYP)	SS	0	0	18.00	1	1	0	0	2	3	1	1	3	13.5	2.00	.333
	Buies Creek (CAR)	HiA	0	0	1.50	4	4	0	0	12	12	0	0	7	5.3	1.00	.261
	Fresno (PCL)	AAA	3	3	5.49	8	8	0	0	41	48	4	10	30	6.6	1.41	.289
Major League Totals			0	1	15.12	5	1	0	0	8	15	0	7	3	3.2	2.64	.385
Minor League Totals			50	36	4.07	127	109	2	3	630	684	59	114	510	7.3	1.27	.277

30 DEURY CARRASCO, SS

BA GRADE

50 Risk: Extreme

Born: Sept. 20, 1999. **B-T:** L-R. **Ht.:** 5-9. **Wt.:** 165. **Signed:** Dominican Republic, 2016. **Signed by:** Oz Ocampo/Roman Ocumarez.

TRACK RECORD: One of the top players in the Astros' 2016 international class, Carrasco signed for $480,000. This year, he finished third in the Gulf Coast League in triples (five) and fifth in steals (17).

SCOUTING REPORT: Carrasco is short, but he has the kind of fast-twitch athleticism that scouts love to see in a middle infielder. He's a plus runner who knows how to use his speed. That easy athleticism and body control pays off for him in the dirt as well. He should be able to stick at shortstop as an above-average, relatively sure-handed defender with a plus arm. At the plate, Carrasco's approach fits his skills. He presents a small strike zone and uses that to his advantage as he draws walks and sprays the ball around. He has very little power, but he can produce pesky at-bats.

THE FUTURE: Carrasco will have to keep getting stronger to prove he can be more than a useful utility-man, but he has a nice combination of skills and tools as a base to build on over the next several years.

Year	Club (League)	Class	AVG	G	AB	R	H	2B	3B	HR	RBI	BB	SO	SB	CS	OBP	SLG
2017	Astros Orange (DSL)	R	.266	64	207	44	55	9	1	0	17	50	48	32	14	.407	.319
2018	Astros (GCL)	R	.242	38	120	17	29	3	5	1	8	16	34	17	6	.336	.375
	Tri-City (NYP)	SS	.250	7	24	3	6	2	0	0	2	1	10	0	1	.280	.333
Minor League Totals			.256	109	351	64	90	14	6	1	27	67	92	49	21	.376	.339

Kansas City Royals

BY BILL MITCHELL

The 2018 season was most definitely a rebuilding year for the Kansas City Royals, and it showed as the big league club finished dead last in the American League Central division with a 58-104 record. First baseman Eric Hosmer left as a free agent prior to the season and veterans Mike Moustakas, Kelvin Herrera, Jon Jay and Lucas Duda were traded to contenders during the second half of the year. There wasn't a lot of other veteran depth to deal with left-handed starter Danny Duffy suffering through a down year and outfielder Alex Gordon continuing his free fall with his third straight subpar season.

For an organization in rebuild mode, it was promising that three of the more surprising performances at the big league level came from young players. The most significant jump forward came from talented, 23-year-old shortstop Raul A. Mondesi, whose bat finally lived up to its potential with the switch-hitter smacking 14 home runs and posting an impressive .804 OPS. Rule 5 pick Brad Keller turned out to be one of the team's best pitchers, with the 23-year-old right-hander starting 20 games after beginning the year in the bullpen and finishing with a solid 9-6 record, 3.08 ERA. First baseman Ryan O'Hearn homered in his first big league game on July 31 en route to finishing with 12 long balls and a .950 OPS.

The organization's most significant accomplishment came in the June draft, when they turned a wealth of extra picks into a rotation full of Division I college arms and a trio of athletic outfielders. Five of those picks taken in the top three rounds—pitchers Brady Singer, Jackson Kowar, Daniel Lynch and Kris Bubic, and outfielder Kyle Isbel—now rank among the organization's top ten prospects. The 104-loss season slots the Royals for the second overall pick in 2019, giving them the chance to add a premier talent next summer.

Only two of the Royals seven minor league affiliates posted winning records in 2018, with low Class A Lexington capturing the South Atlantic League championship, but it was a good year from a development standpoint. Outfield prospect Seuly Matias hit home runs by the bunches during the early part of the Sally League season, with a league-leading 31 homers through July before the native Dominican's year ended prematurely in mid-August due to a freak injury when he suffered a deep cut to his thumb on the cargo door of the team bus. 18-year-old Yefri Del Rosario took a big jump forward in his first season with the

Ryan O'Hearn mashed 12 home runs in 44 games during a rookie-year power surge.

PROJECTED 2022 LINEUP

Catcher	M.J. Melendez (23)
First Base	Nick Pratto (23)
Second Base	Nicky Lopez (27)
Third Base	Whit Merrifield (33)
Shortstop	Adalberto Mondesi (26)
Left Field	Kyle Isbel (25)
Center Field	Khalil Lee (24)
Right Field	Seuly Matias (23)
Designated Hitter	Ryan O'Hearn (28)
No. 1 Starter	Brady Singer (25)
No. 2 Starter	Danny Duffy (33)
No. 3 Starter	Daniel Lynch (25)
No. 4 Starter	Jackson Kowar (25)
No. 5 Starter	Brad Keller (26)
Closer	Josh Staumont (28)

organization after the Braves were forced to release the right-handed pitcher as part of the penalties incurred for multiple violations in the international marketplace.

The only major front office change came when former minor league pitcher Alec Zumwalt replaced Ronnie Richardson as farm director. Zumwalt is now in charge of a much-improved farm system with the likelihood that it will get stronger while the big league team continues to rebuild. With a major league depth chart that sure doesn't look pretty the short-term outlook in Kansas City isn't promising, but the patience of the team's supporters should be rewarded in time.

KANSAS CITY ROYALS

TOP 2019 ROOKIE: Nicky Lopez, SS. He has moved quickly through the system and should get his shot as part of the new youth movement. **BREAKOUT PROSPECT:** Yefri Del Rosario, RHP. The former Braves farmhand increased his fastball velocity and finished strong in his first full season. **SLEEPER:** Nathan Eaton, 3B. The VMI product played all over the field in his pro debut at Idaho Falls and profiles as a super utility type.

SOURCE OF TOP 30 TALENT			
Homegrown	26	Acquired	4
College	13	Trade	3
Junior college	2	Rule 5 draft	1
High school	5	Independent league	0
Nondrafted free agent	0	Free agent/waivers	0
International	6		

LF
Brewer Hicklen (20)
Jackson Lueck

CF
Khalil Lee (2)
Kyle Isbel (9)
Blake Perkins (26)
Michael Gigliotti (27)
Eric Cole
Donnie Dewees

RF
Seuly Matias (8)
Kort Peterson (29)
Juan Carlos Negret
Elier Hernandez

3B
Kelvin Gutierrez (12)
Emmanuel Rivera (22)
Nathan Eaton

SS
Nicky Lopez (5)
Cristian Perez
Jeison Guzman
Humberto Arteaga

2B
Gabriel Cancel
Erick Mejia
Jose Marquez

1B
Nick Pratto (7)
Frank Schwindel

C
MJ Melendez (6)
Meibrys Viloria (14)
Cam Gallagher
Sebastian Rivero
Michael Emodi
Chase Vallot

LHP

LHSP	LHRP
Daniel Lynch (3)	Richard Lovelady (17)
Kris Bubic (10)	Gabe Speier
Austin Cox (16)	Holden Capps
Rylan Kaufman (25)	Austin Lambright
Foster Griffin (30)	
Daniel Tillo	
Marcelo Martinez	

RHP

RHSP	RHRP
Brady Singer (1)	Josh Staumont (24)
Jackson Kowar (4)	Chris Ellis
Yefri Del Rosario (11)	Yunior Marte
Sam McWilliams (13)	Jake Newberry
Scott Blewett (15)	Andres Machado
Carlos Hernandez (18)	Walker Sheller
Yohanse Morel (19)	
Gerson Garabito (21)	
Zach Haake (23)	
Arnaldo Hernandez (28)	
Trevor Oaks	
Jonathan Bowlan	
Janser Lara	
Charlie Neuweiler	
Scott Barlow	

DRAFT ANALYSIS

2018

BEST PURE HITTER: 2B Kyle Isbel (3) hit .322/.390/.504 at Nevada-Las Vegas before getting off to a hot start in his pro debut, with a .326/.389/.504 line in Rookie ball and low Class-A. Isbel is at least an above-average hitter.

BEST POWER HITTER: OF Eric Cole (4) increased his power output during his junior season at Arkansas and that uptick seemed to translate to wood bats, with seven home runs and a .229 isolated slugging in the Pioneer League.

FASTEST RUNNER: OF Kevon Jackson (8) was a track star at his Queen Creek High in Arizona. He's at least a 70-grade runner and some scouts have gone as far as putting an 80 on his wheels.

BEST DEFENSIVE PLAYER: Isbel is athletic enough to be a plus defensive second baseman, and he also has previous experience in center field.

BEST ATHLETE: C Nathan Eaton (21) moves surprisingly well for a catcher and has used his legs to great effect on the bases. Eaton swiped 46 bags during his two seasons with Virginia Military Institute at an 85 percent success rate, and went 19-for-24 in the Pioneer League.

BEST FASTBALL: RHP Zach Haake (6) has reached the upper 90s and has a 70-grade fastball. Both RHP Jonathan Bowlan (2) and RHP Jackson Kowar (1) have fastballs that get into the mid-90s. However, LHP Daniel Lynch (1) began seeing increased velocity late in the season and was up to 97 mph in low Class-A Lexington.

BEST SECONDARY PITCH: Kowar gets a nod here for aclearly plus changeup, while Kansas City's first overall selection, RHP Brady Singer (1) has a devastating slider that's also a plus offering. LHP Kris Bubic (1s) has a plus changeup from the left side while LHP Austin Cox (5) has an above-average slider and curveball. Take your pick.

TOP DRAFT PICKS OF THE DECADE

Year	Player, Pos.	2018 Org
2009	Aaron Crow, RHP	Mexican League
2010	Christian Colon, SS	Mets
2011	Bubba Starling, OF	Royals
2012	Kyle Zimmer, RHP	Royals
2013	Hunter Dozier, SS	Royals
2014	Brandon Finnegan, LHP	Reds
2015	Ashe Russell, RHP	Did not play
2016	A.J. Puckett, RHP (2nd round)	White Sox
2017	Nick Pratto, 1B	Royals
2018	Brady Singer, RHP	Royals

BEST PRO DEBUT: It's hard to not go with Lynch here, as his increased stuff raised his future ceiling significantly, with the results to back it up. He threw 51.1 innings combined between the Appalachian and South Atlantic Leagues, with a combined 1.58 ERA, 10.7 K/9 and 1.4 BB/9.

MOST INTRIGUING BACKGROUND: Cox was an under-the-radar product out of a small Georgia college, but he ranked near the top of the country in strikeouts (124). RHP Christian Cosby (14) didn't move to the mound until last season, but he has a 6-foot-5, 215-pound frame and some scouts think he'll be in the triple digits with his fastball.

CLOSEST TO THE MAJORS: Singer, Kowar and Lynch could all move quickly through the minor league system as polished collegiate arms.

BEST LATE-ROUND PICK: LHP Rylan Kaufman (12) signed for the highest Day 3 bonus of any player in the 2018 draft, signing for $722,500. Kaufman rewarded the Royals' confidence by posting a 3.86 ERA with a 10.3 K/9 and 2.6 BB/9.

THE ONE WHO GOT AWAY: C Adam Hackenberg (39) has big tools with plus raw power and 70-grade arm strength, but will head to Clemson.

—CARLOS COLLAZO

2017

The Royals went heavy on upside in 2017 and the early returns on 1B Nick Pratto (1) and C M.J. Melendez (2) have been good. OF Brewer Hicklen (7) looks to be the best of the rest, but Pratto and Melendez give the class a solid foundation.
GRADE: B

2016

OF Khalil Lee (3) has become the top hitter in the system and has reached the upper levels. SS Nicky Lopez (5) reached Triple-A and has proven dependable. Top-pick RHP A.J. Puckett (2) was in 2017 traded to Chicago for Melky Cabrera.
GRADE: D

2015

The class was topped by prep RHPs Ashe Russell (1) and Nolan Watson (1). Russell hasn't pitched since 2016, while Watson has struggled mightily as a pro. RHP Josh Staumont (2) has premium stuff, but is still trying to harness it.
GRADE: F

1 BRADY SINGER, RHP

Born: Aug. 4, 1996. **B-T:** R-R. **HT:** 6-5. **WT:** 210.
Drafted: Florida, 2018 (1st round).
Signed by: Jim Buckley.

Singer was another in the long line of highly-acclaimed starting pitchers coming out of the University of Florida. But the righthander's pedigree goes further back then his time in Gainesville. He was a Blue Jays second-round pick out of high school who opted not to sign. The decision to skip pro ball the first time around turned out to be a wise choice by Singer. He was a key member of the Gators' rotation as a sophomore and junior and was the Baseball America College Player of the Year in 2018. Coming into the season, Singer was seen as a potential top-five pick for the 2018 draft. He slid to the 18th pick, but his $4.25 million bonus was nearly $1 million above the slot for that pick and was the 11th richest bonus in the first round. After pitching deep into the College World Series, Singer waited until three days before the deadline to sign. Because of Singer's heavy college workload in addition to a minor hamstring problem after reporting to the Royals' complex this summer, he has yet to make his official pro debut. He did pitch in instructional league.

SCOUTING REPORT: The Royals were thrilled to get a near major league-ready pitcher that far into the draft. They see Singer as a starter with a durable body and competitive makeup. He flashes two plus pitches—a fastball and slider—delivered from a lower arm slot. That arm slot concerned some scouts, and they said they felt it limited his ability to consistently throw his changeup. While still a bit rusty during instructional league, Singer looked the part. His fastball sat 91-94 mph, which was close to his college velocity, with good movement down in the zone. His lower arm slot helps him get plenty of run on his fastball. He has good feel for his sharp slider, which comes in around 83 mph. He didn't have to use a changeup much in college and the pitch still is inconsistent for him. Singer has yet to become comfortable throwing it frequently, but it has potential to give him another above-average offspeed weapon. His control grades as above-average.

THE FUTURE: Singer will likely start his career in a loaded high Class A Wilmington rotation in 2019. His advanced control and competitiveness give him a chance to be a mid-rotation starter. With his big-game experience and arsenal, Singer will move quickly through the system and could reach Double-A before the end of his first pro season.

BILL MITCHELL

BA GRADE	SCOUTING GRADES
60 Risk: V. High	Fastball: 60. Slider: 60. Changeup: 50. Control: 55.

Projected future grades on 20-80 scouting scale

TOP PROSPECTS OF THE DECADE

Year	Player, Pos.	2018 Org
2009	Mike Moustakas, 3B	Brewers
2010	Mike Montgomery, LHP	Cubs
2011	Eric Hosmer, 1B	Padres
2012	Mike Montgomery, LHP	Cubs
2013	Kyle Zimmer, RHP	Royals
2014	Kyle Zimmer, RHP	Royals
2015	Adalberto Mondesi	Royals
2016	Adalberto Mondesi	Royals
2017	Josh Staumont, RHP	Royals
2018	Nick Pratto, 1B	Royals

BEST TOOLS

Best Hitter for Average	Nicky Lopez
Best Power Hitter	Seuly Matias
Best Strike-Zone Discipline	Nicky Lopez
Fastest Baserunner	Tyler James
Best Athlete	Khalil Lee
Best Fastball	Josh Staumont
Best Curveball	Yefri Del Rosario
Best Slider	Brady Singer
Best Changeup	Jackson Kowar
Best Control	Daniel Lynch
Best Defensive Catcher	Sebastian Rivero
Best Defensive Infielder	Nicky Lopez
Best Infield Arm	Kelvin Gutierrez
Best Defensive Outfielder	Bubba Starling
Best Outfield Arm	Seuly Matias

Year	Club (League)	Class	W	L	ERA	G	GS	CG	SV	IP	H	HR	BB	SO	K/9	WHIP	AVG
2018	Did not play																

2 KHALIL LEE, OF

Born: June 26, 1998. **B-T:** L-L. **HT:** 5-10. **WT:** 192. **Drafted:** HS—Oakton, Va., 2016 (3rd round). **Signed by:** Jim Farr.

TRACK RECORD: Lee continued on the fast track through the Royals' system, making it to Double-A three days after his 20th birthday. The athletic outfielder took big strides forward in 2018, especially in cutting his strikeout rate from 32 percent in his first full season to 25 percent. He was one of the most productive players in the Carolina League before his midseason promotion to Double-A. He also improved his walk rate from 12 to 14 percent. He missed the last month of 2018 to back soreness but made up for lost time with an assignment to the Arizona Fall League.

SCOUTING REPORT: The key to Lee's improvement at the plate resulted from cutting down on his swing with two strikes and using the whole field more often. The larger ballparks in the Carolina League helped to suppress his home run total, which dropped from 17 in 2017 to six in 2018. But Lee projects to hit for more power as he matures. He shows easy plus raw power in batting practice and scouts believe he has good feel to hit and keeps his hands back and works deep counts. While not a burner, Lee is a smart baserunner and has the above-average speed, athleticism and arm to stay in center field.

THE FUTURE: Lee will return to Double-A Northwest Arkansas to start the 2019 season. In a system with a number of high-ceiling prospects in the lower levels of the minors, Lee stands out because he's not that far away from the big leagues. Lee should be starting in Kansas City by the end of 2020.

BA GRADE

50 Risk: Medium

Hit: 55. Power: 55.
Run: 55. Field: 60.
Arm: 60.

Year	Club (League)	Class	AVG	G	AB	R	H	2B	3B	HR	RBI	BB	SO	SB	CS	OBP	SLG
2016	Royals (AZL)	R	.269	49	182	43	49	9	6	6	29	33	57	8	4	.396	.484
2017	Lexington (SAL)	LoA	.237	121	451	71	107	24	6	17	61	65	171	20	18	.344	.430
2018	Wilmington (CAR)	HiA	.270	71	244	42	66	13	4	4	41	48	75	14	3	.402	.406
	NW Arkansas (TL)	AA	.245	29	102	15	25	5	0	2	10	11	28	2	2	.330	.353
Minor League Totals			.252	270	979	171	247	51	16	29	141	157	331	44	27	.368	.426

3 DANIEL LYNCH, LHP

Born: Nov. 17, 1996. **B-T:** L-L. **HT:** 6-6. **WT:** 190. **Drafted:** Virginia, 2018 (1st round). **Signed by:** Jim Farr.

TRACK RECORD: Lynch shot up draft boards late in the spring of 2018 when he showed improved stuff and control in late-season outings, including an excellent Atlantic Coast Conference tournament start in front of many Royals front office officials. Based on an outstanding pro debut between Rookie-level Burlington and low Class A Lexington, Lynch has solidified the belief that his improvement is sustainable.

SCOUTING REPORT: After sitting 88-92 mph for much for his college career, Lynch's velocity bumped up to 93-95 late in his college career. It got even better when he got on the mound as a pro. He continued to sit 93-95 and started touching 97. He commands his plus fastball to both sides of the plate and is able to front-door his two-seamer back over the plate against righthanded hitters. Lynch throws two 83-85 mph breaking balls, and he varies the shape between the two. Both pitches have sharp downward bite and generate swings and misses, with his wipeout slider being the better of the two. His 85 mph changeup flashes above-average potential but is currently his most inconsistent pitch. It's a good pitch when he sells it, but he too often tries to guide it. Lynch has embraced his new power-oriented approach as he has embraced attack hitters with his new-found power.

THE FUTURE: Lynch will move up to high Class A Wilmington in 2019, along with fellow first-rounders Brady Singer and Jackson Kowar, forming three-fifths of the Blue Rocks rotation. Lynch's rapid improvement gives him a shot of becoming one of the better lefthanded pitching prospects in the minors, but he needs to prove he can sustain his late-season 2018 form over a full season.

BA GRADE

55 Risk: High

Fastball: 60.
Slider: 60. Curve: 50.
Change: 60. CTL: 60.

Year	Club (League)	Class	W	L	ERA	G	GS	CG	SV	IP	H	HR	BB	SO	K/9	WHIP	AVG
2018	Burlington (APP)	R	0	0	1.59	3	3	0	0	11	9	0	2	14	11.1	0.97	.209
	Lexington (SAL)	LoA	5	1	1.58	9	9	0	0	40	35	1	6	47	10.6	1.03	.243
Minor League Totals			5	1	1.58	12	12	0	0	51	44	1	8	61	10.7	1.01	.235

4 JACKSON KOWAR, RHP

Born: Oct. 4, 1996. **B-T:** R-R. **HT:** 6-5. **WT:** 180. **Drafted:** Florida, 2018 (1st round). **Signed by:** Jim Buckley.

TRACK RECORD: Royals scouts obviously liked what they saw from the University of Florida pitching staff in 2018 because they used their top two draft picks to grab the Gators' top two starters. They took Brady Singer at No. 18 and Kowar at No. 33. Like Singer, Kowar had a very storied Gators career. Kowar finished with the third-best winning percentage (.803) in Florida history. His final outing in the College World Series saw him strikeout 13 in 6.2 shutout innings.

SCOUTING REPORT: Like Singer, Kowar already sports a pair of plus pitches. His wipeout plus-plus changeup is already regarded as the best in the organization. He has easy velocity, and his fastball touched 97 mph in his pro debut. He delivers his pitches with a clean arm action, and he should be able to improve his velocity as he adds strength to his tall, lean frame. Kowar generates fastball arm speed and screwball action on his 85-87 mph changeup, which has plenty of fading life. His breaking ball got slurvy at Florida before he settled into a mid-to-upper-70s curveball that projects to be an average pitch as he gets more consistency with it. That will be a key development focus for him as a pro because he's long struggled to find a breaking ball he is comfortable using regularly. Kowar pitches with a free-and-easy delivery, though he can get in trouble when he gets too quick with his delivery and leaves pitches up in the zone.

THE FUTURE: Kowar will continue to pair with Singer as they advance to the big leagues. They will start the season together at high Class A Wilmington.

BA GRADE
55 Risk: High
Fastball: 60.
Curveball: 50.
Change: 70. **CTL:** 50.

Year	Club (League)	Class	W	L	ERA	G	GS	CG	SV	IP	H	HR	BB	SO	K/9	WHIP	AVG
2018	Lexington (SAL)	LoA	0	1	3.42	9	9	0	0	26	19	2	12	22	7.5	1.18	.200
Minor League Totals			0	1	3.42	9	9	0	0	26	19	2	12	22	7.5	1.18	.200

5 NICKY LOPEZ, SS/2B

Born: March 13, 1995. **B-T:** L-R. **HT:** 5-11. **WT:** 175. **Drafted:** Creighton, 2016 (5th round). **Signed by:** Matt Price.

TRACK RECORD: Lopez was a three-year starter at Creighton. As a Blue Jay he steadily improved, showing a solid glove and a sparkplug mentality as a hitter. The Royals were enamored with his approach and said they believed he was among the best college shortstops in the 2016 draft class, even though 11 college shortstops were drafted before him. Three years later, he's living up to those expectations. The overachieving Lopez continued to impress in 2018 by advancing to Triple-A midway through his second full professional season. He has walked more than he has struck out and posted a .371 on-base percentage in his pro career.

SCOUTING REPORT: Lopez is a smart and instinctive ballplayer who consistently plays above his solid but unspectacular tools. While he needs to keep adding strength to his slight frame, he has good barrel control and understands the strike zone. He works counts and knows how to take his walks. He's an above-average hitter with excellent on-base skills, even if he likely never will hit more than 10 home runs. While his range at either shortstop or second base is no better than average, he gets his body in the right position to make plays, and his average arm is enough because of an excellent internal clock. Lopez is extremely reliable—he made only five errors in 2018 and made zero errors in 32 games at second base. He's a plus runner with good instincts on the bases.

THE FUTURE: With Whit Merrifield and Adalberto Mondesi set in the Royals' middle infield, Lopez will get additional seasoning at Triple-A. While not yet on the 40-man roster, he likely will make his big league debut in 2019. He is at least an option as utility infielder, but he has potential to be an everyday second baseman if the opportunity arises.

BA GRADE
45 Risk: Medium
Hit: 55. **Power:** 40.
Run: 60. **Field:** 55.
Arm: 55.

Year	Club (League)	Class	AVG	G	AB	R	H	2B	3B	HR	RBI	BB	SO	SB	CS	OBP	SLG
2016	Burlington (APP)	R	.281	62	231	54	65	6	5	6	29	35	30	24	4	.393	.429
2017	Wilmington (CAR)	HiA	.295	70	285	42	84	12	7	2	27	36	23	14	8	.376	.407
	NW Arkansas (TL)	AA	.259	59	232	26	60	6	1	0	11	16	29	7	4	.312	.293
2018	NW Arkansas (TL)	AA	.331	73	281	42	93	8	5	2	27	33	23	9	4	.397	.416
	Omaha (PCL)	AAA	.278	57	223	33	62	6	2	7	26	27	29	6	2	.364	.417
Minor League Totals			.291	321	1252	197	364	38	20	17	120	147	134	60	22	.371	.394

6 MJ MELENDEZ, C

Born: Nov. 28, 1998. **B-T:** L-R. **HT:** 6-1. **WT:** 185. **Drafted:** HS—Palmetto Bay, Fla., 2017 (2nd round). **Signed by:** Alex Mesa.

TRACK RECORD: The son of Florida International head coach Mervyl Melendez, M.J. showed good aptitude at the plate and advanced skills behind it. Melendez shared catching duties at low Class A Lexington with Sebastian Rivero for the South Atlantic League champs. Both Melendez and Rivero earned spots in the SAL all-star game. Melendez's 19 home runs were fifth-most in the South Atlantic League and he finished second in the league with 54 extra-base hits. Amazingly for a catcher, he also finished third in the league with nine triples.

BA GRADE
50 Risk: High
Hit: 50. **Power:** 60.
Run: 50. **Field:** 60.
Arm: 60.

SCOUTING REPORT: Melendez makes hard contact at the plate with a level swing and good hand-eye coordination that gives him power to all fields. Plus, he shows the aptitude to adjust during at-bats. Despite hitting .251, Melendez projects as an average hitter. He sells out for power at times, as evidenced by his 30 percent strikeout rate in 2018, but he gets to his plus power. Melendez is an average runner who runs much better than the average catcher. Behind the plate, he needs to continue working on the mechanics of his setup and receiving, but he works well with pitchers. He is bilingual and calls a good game. His plus arm helped him tie for the Sally league lead by throwing out 42 percent of basestealers.

THE FUTURE: Young catchers don't typically hit like Melendez did in 2018. He projects as a first-division regular with a power bat behind the plate. He'll move on to high Class A Wilmington in 2019 where his power will likely be sapped by his home park. He needs to continue to improve his contact rate, but he has a ceiling few minor league catchers can match.

Year	Club (League)	Class	AVG	G	AB	R	H	2B	3B	HR	RBI	BB	SO	SB	CS	OBP	SLG
2017	Royals (AZL)	R	.262	47	168	25	44	8	3	4	30	26	60	4	2	.374	.417
2018	Lexington (SAL)	LoA	.251	111	419	52	105	26	9	19	73	43	143	4	6	.322	.492
Minor League Totals			.254	158	587	77	149	34	12	23	103	69	203	8	8	.337	.470

7 NICK PRATTO, 1B

Born: Oct. 6, 1998. **B-T:** L-L. **HT:** 6-1. **WT:** 195. **Drafted:** HS—Huntington Beach, Calif., 2017 (1st). **Signed by:** Rich Amaral.

TRACK RECORD: Pratto was the Royals' first-round pick in 2017 after an illustrious high school career in Southern California and with multiple Team USA clubs. He was also an effective pitcher in high school, but scouts were unanimous that his pro future was as a hitter. Pratto got off to a slow start in 2018 but finished strong by compiling a 1.106 OPS in his final 32 games and followed that with a .333/.474/.600 batting line in the South Atlantic League playoffs. He also was named the MVP of the league's all-star game.

BA GRADE
50 Risk: High
Hit: 60. **Power:** 50.
Run: 45. **Field:** 55.
Arm: 55.

SCOUTING REPORT: Pratto's late-season improvement at the plate came after he shortened his swing and got more aggressive. Before that, he struggled to handle premium velocity, but his adjustments helped him fix that issue. His 28 percent strikeout rate was surprisingly high for a hitter with his advanced approach and batting eye—most scouts have seen him as a hit-first first baseman with developing power. While scouts question whether he'll develop the plus home run power desired from a first baseman, he has the potential to be a plus hitter who needs to figure out how to tap into his plus raw power. A fringe-average runner, Pratto is a heady baserunner. He's an above-average defender with good footwork, good hands and instincts.

THE FUTURE: Pratto's strong finish helped allay some concerns about his bat. He'll have to continue to develop more power, but he has the potential to be an everyday first baseman with a plus bat and at least average power.

Year	Club (League)	Class	AVG	G	AB	R	H	2B	3B	HR	RBI	BB	SO	SB	CS	OBP	SLG
2017	Royals (AZL)	R	.247	52	198	25	49	15	3	4	34	24	58	10	4	.330	.414
2018	Lexington (SAL)	LoA	.280	127	485	79	136	33	2	14	62	45	150	22	5	.343	.443
Minor League Totals			.271	179	683	104	185	48	5	18	96	69	208	32	9	.339	.435

8 SEULY MATIAS, OF

Born: Sept. 4, 1998. **B-T:** R-R. **HT:** 6-3. **WT:** 204. **Signed:** Dominican Republic, 2015. **Signed by:** Fausto Morel.

TRACK RECORD: Matias had a chance to break the South Atlantic League record for home runs, which was set by Russell Branyan with 40 in 1996. But a freak accident when he caught his thumb in the cargo door of the team bus caused him to miss the last month of the season. Even so, Matias finished with 31 homers as well as an impressive opposite-field shot in the Futures Game.

SCOUTING REPORT: Despite projecting to be a below-average hitter, Matias has plenty of impact potential thanks to his plus-plus power and impressive set of tools. Matias is looking to drive the ball at every opportunity—all but one of his home runs was hit to left or center field. He made progress at the plate in his first full season, showing an ability to make adjustments, especially in the second half when he toned down his aggressiveness against breaking balls. Matias will need to cut down his strikeout rate from a lofty 35 percent, but his overall improvements indicate that he will improve his contact rate when he gains better control of his aggressive nature at the plate. Matias has prototype right field tools as an average defender with a plus-plus arm and above-average speed underway.

BA GRADE
55 Risk: Extreme
Hit: 40. Power: 70.
Run: 50. Field: 55.
Arm: 70.

THE FUTURE: Matias has a lofty ceiling but also carries more risk than any other Royals Top 10 Prospect. Few players with strikeout rates like Matias figure out how to make enough contact to get to their power at the major league level, but those who do can be impact players. He will jump to high Class A Wilmington in 2019.

Year	Club (League)	Class	AVG	G	AB	R	H	2B	3B	HR	RBI	BB	SO	SB	CS	OBP	SLG
2016	Royals (DSL)	R	.125	7	24	2	3	1	0	0	2	2	13	0	0	.222	.167
	Royals (AZL)	R	.250	46	172	32	43	11	2	8	29	22	73	2	4	.348	.477
2017	Burlington (APP)	R	.243	57	222	27	54	13	3	7	36	16	72	2	1	.297	.423
2018	Lexington (SAL)	LoA	.231	94	338	62	78	13	1	31	63	24	131	6	0	.303	.550
Minor League Totals			.235	204	756	123	178	38	6	46	130	64	289	10	5	.309	.484

9 KYLE ISBEL, OF

Born: March 3, 1997. **B-T:** L-R. **HT:** 5-11. **WT:** 183. **Drafted:** Nevada-Las Vegas, 2018 (3rd round). **Signed by:** Kenny Munoz.

TRACK RECORD: Isbel went from a productive hitter to a middle-of-the-lineup masher as a junior at UNLV thanks to a big increase in his power—he hit 14 home runs as a junior after hitting seven in his first two seasons combined. Isbel's increased power came with increased selectivity at the plate that boosted his on-base percentage. That boosted Isbel up draft boards in 2018. The Royals grabbed the lefthanded hitter in the third round. He quickly showed he was too advanced for Rookie-level Idaho Falls in his pro debut and advanced to low Class A Lexington where he helped the Legends win the South Atlantic League title.

SCOUTING REPORT: Isbel profiles as a top-of-the-order bat with very good plate discipline. He's better suited to get on-base and run around the bases than to drive people in. He projects as an above-average hitter who uses a compact swing to shoot balls to the gaps. He's more of a doubles hitter for now

BA GRADE
50 Risk: High
Hit: 55. Power: 45.
Run: 60. Field: 60.
Arm: 55

but has above-average raw power and should park 10-15 home runs over the fence eventually. He's also an aggressive baserunner with plus speed. Isbel is still relatively new to the outfield, having entered college as a second baseman, and his inexperience shows at times with some of the routes he takes. He should be able to stay in center field with his first-step quickness and an above-average arm.

THE FUTURE: Isbel's advanced baseball instincts, raw tools and hard-nosed style of play should allow him to jump to what should be a stacked high Class A Wilmington club next year.

Year	Club (League)	Class	AVG	G	AB	R	H	2B	3B	HR	RBI	BB	SO	SB	CS	OBP	SLG
2018	Idaho Falls (PIO)	R	.381	25	105	27	40	10	1	4	18	14	17	12	3	.454	.610
	Lexington (SAL)	LoA	.289	39	159	30	46	12	1	3	14	12	43	12	3	.345	.434
Minor League Totals			.326	64	264	57	86	22	2	7	32	26	60	24	6	.389	.504

10 KRIS BUBIC, LHP

Born: Aug. 19, 1997. **B-T:** L-L. **HT:** 6-3. **WT:** 220. **Drafted:** Stanford, 2018 (1st round supplemental). **Signed by:** Josh Hallgren

TRACK RECORD: Bubic capped his three-year career at Stanford with an outstanding junior season in which he went 8-1, 2.62. The Royals continued their run on college arms with the extra draft picks they had accumulated, selecting Bubic in the supplemental first round with the 40th overall pick.

SCOUTING REPORT: Bubic profiles as a back-of-the-rotation innings-burner with a high floor and less ceiling than his fellow Royals first-rounders. His 90-94 mph fastball has good run and sink. It's a pitch that he can cut to his glove side and sink to his arm side. The gem of Bubic's arsenal is his plus changeup with late sink. His mid-to-high 70s curveball has medium depth and 12-to-6 movement. It projects as an average pitch. Bubic gets some deception from his low-effort delivery, which features a pause in the back that creates timing issues for opposing hitters.

THE FUTURE: The Royals added a plethora of high-profile college pitchers to their system via the 2018 draft. That could create a logjam at the lower levels of the system in 2019. Bubic's most likely landing spot out of spring training will be low Class A Lexington.

BILL MITCHELL

BA GRADE

50 Risk: High

Fastball: 55.
Curveball: 50.
Change: 60. CTL: 55.

Year	Club (League)	Class	W	L	ERA	G	GS	CG	SV	IP	H	HR	BB	SO	K/9	WHIP	AVG
2018	Idaho Falls (PIO)	R	2	3	4.03	10	10	0	0	38	38	2	19	53	12.6	1.50	.253
Minor League Totals			2	3	4.03	10	10	0	0	38	38	2	19	53	12.6	1.50	.253

11 YEFRI DEL ROSARIO, RHP

BA GRADE

50 Risk: High

Born: Sept. 23, 1999. **B-T:** R-R. **Ht.:** 6-2. **Wt.:** 180. **Signed:** Dominican Republic, 2016. **Signed by:** Jonathan Cruz (Braves).

TRACK RECORD: Del Rosario had originally signed with the Braves in 2016 for $1 million, but he was declared a free agent in 2017 as part of Major League Baseball's sanctions against Atlanta for circumvention of international signing rules. The Royals signed him for $665,000. The Braves' loss is the Royals' gain as Del Rosario's stock rose in parallel with an uptick in his fastball velocity.

SCOUTING REPORT: Del Rosario was named the organization's pitcher of the month for August, when he posted a 5-0, 0.75 mark. He commands his 92-95 mph fastball with late life to both sides of the plate and is adept at pitching inside to hitters. His 79-80 mph curveball flashes as a plus pitch with good shape, and he gets swings and misses on it, but he misses up in the zone when he doesn't throw it from the same slot as his fastball. Del Rosario commands his 88-89 mph changeup, but it's too firm. His delivery is unique and gets a little funky, providing deception, but he gets in trouble when he throws across his body.

THE FUTURE: Del Rosario will move up to high Class A Wilmington in 2019 as part of a prospect-packed rotation. The odds that he remains a starting pitcher have increased.

Year	Club (League)	Class	W	L	ERA	G	GS	CG	SV	IP	H	HR	BB	SO	K/9	WHIP	AVG
2017	Braves (DSL)	R	0	0	1.80	2	2	0	0	5	1	0	4	7	12.6	1.00	.067
	Braves (GCL)	R	1	1	3.90	11	6	0	0	32	37	1	10	29	8.1	1.45	.285
2018	Lexington (SAL)	LoA	6	5	3.19	15	15	0	0	79	69	10	29	72	8.2	1.24	.227
Minor League Totals			7	6	3.33	28	23	0	0	116	107	11	43	108	8.4	1.29	.238

12 KELVIN GUTIERREZ, 3B

BA GRADE

45 Risk: Medium

Born: Aug. 28, 1994. **B-T:** R-R. **Ht.:** 6-3. **Wt.:** 215. **Signed:** Dominican Republic, 2013. **Signed by:** Modesto Ulloa (Nationals).

TRACK RECORD: The best-known of the three prospects acquired from the Nationals for Kelvin Herrera in June 2018, Gutierrez played all of 2018 in Double-A after seeing time in the Arizona Fall League the year before. His results at the plate with the two teams were practically identical, combining for a .275/.329/.400 slash line and a career-high 11 home runs.

SCOUTING REPORT: Gutierrez has consistently shown the defensive skills to play third base at the big league level, but he's yet to prove he has the power needed for the position. He has a relatively simple inside-out, line-drive swing with quick hands at the plate, routinely producing hard contact to all fields. The Royals' hitting coaches had him adjust his swing to reduce the length, allowing him to get to pitches sooner. There's quickness in Gutierrez's bat, with power to right-center field and the ability to barrel good velocity. Defensively, Gutierrez is an above-average defender thanks to soft hands and good first-step quickness. His arm grades as plus-plus. He got a few games at shortstop this year just as a look to increase

his versatility. Gutierrez has fringe-average speed but used his instincts to steal 20 bases in 24 attempts.
THE FUTURE: Gutierrez will move to Triple-A. If the power emerges, he could be a regular, but otherwise, there are few big league roster spots for backup third basemen.

Year	Club (League)	Class	AVG	G	AB	R	H	2B	3B	HR	RBI	BB	SO	SB	CS	OBP	SLG
2016	Auburn (NYP)	SS	.323	9	31	5	10	3	0	0	6	3	5	4	0	.371	.419
	Hagerstown (SAL)	LoA	.300	96	377	58	113	19	6	3	48	29	65	19	7	.349	.406
	Potomac (CAR)	HiA	.237	10	38	7	9	1	0	1	2	3	5	2	2	.326	.342
2017	Potomac (CAR)	HiA	.288	58	222	34	64	10	6	2	16	19	59	3	0	.347	.414
	Nationals (GCL)	R	.212	10	33	6	7	3	1	0	1	4	7	2	0	.297	.364
2018	Harrisburg (EL)	AA	.274	58	230	36	63	6	3	5	26	16	62	10	1	.321	.391
	NW Arkansas (TL)	AA	.277	65	242	29	67	8	3	6	40	20	46	10	3	.337	.409
Minor League Totals			.284	481	1812	268	514	90	25	18	217	156	366	65	21	.344	.391

13 SAM MCWILLIAMS, RHP

BA GRADE

45 Risk: High

Born: Sept. 4, 1995. **B-T:** R-R. **Ht.:** 6-7. **Wt.:** 190. **Drafted:** HS—Hendersonville, Tenn., 2014 (8th round). **Signed by:** Nate Dion (Phillies).

TRACK RECORD: McWilliams' combination of promise and inconsistency has been part of the reason he's been traded twice—teams can dream on his potential, but also worry about whether he'll ever reach it. McWilliams was considered one of the highest-ceiling pitchers in the Rule 5 draft and the Royals quickly made him the No. 2 pick in that draft.
SCOUTING REPORT: The 6-foot-7 McWilliams is still refining his delivery and trying to find consistency. He's toned down the tempo of his delivery as a pro, and now always pitches from the stretch with a simple leg lift and gather. At his best, his 91-95 mph plus fastball and slider can be a devastating one-two pairing as his slider will flash above-average to plus at its best. But he mixes sharp sliders with some spinners that don't do a lot. And while he can elevate the fastball for swings and misses out of the zone, he's not nearly as consistent with his fastball location when he tries to locate to his armside. His changeup is still a fringy pitch, but he continues to work on it to make it a viable third offering.
THE FUTURE: McWilliams' below-average control is his biggest hurdle. He has potential to be a back-of-the-rotation starter eventually, but he's not ready to do that. As a Rule 5 pick, he will more likely fit as a power arm in the bullpen, where he can focus on his fastball and slider and air it out.

Year	Club (League)	Class	W	L	ERA	G	GS	CG	SV	IP	H	HR	BB	SO	K/9	WHIP	AVG
2016	Kane County (MWL)	LoA	3	6	3.98	15	15	0	0	75	86	4	18	43	5.2	1.39	.292
2017	Kane County (MWL)	LoA	11	6	2.84	25	25	0	0	133	112	5	31	98	6.6	1.08	.231
2018	Visalia (CAL)	HiA	1	1	2.10	5	5	0	0	26	20	1	6	32	11.2	1.01	.215
	Charlotte, FL (FSL)	HiA	0	1	3.86	3	3	0	0	12	13	0	3	7	5.4	1.37	.277
	Montgomery (SL)	AA	6	7	5.02	19	15	0	0	100	111	13	40	94	8.4	1.50	.282
Minor League Totals			23	26	3.77	83	75	0	0	403	399	25	109	305	6.8	1.26	.260

14 MEIBRYS VILORIA, C

BA GRADE

45 Risk: High

Born: Feb. 2, 1997. **B-T:** L-R. **Ht.:** 5-11. **Wt.:** 220. **Signed:** Colombia, 2013. **Signed by:** Rafael Miranda.

TRACK RECORD: With the big league team needing an extra catcher after the trade of Drew Butera, Viloria was called up to the majors and played in 10 games in September.
SCOUTING REPORT: A defense-first backstop, Viloria has a plus arm with a quick release, throwing out 41 percent of would-be base stealers in 2018, consistent with his totals in previous seasons. He's bilingual and knows how to call games behind the plate. Offensively, Viloria has a good feel for hitting with good hands and solid bat speed. He has above-average raw power, but is more of a gap-to-gap, line-drive hitter because his swing is naturally geared to using all fields. Improving his walk rate from six percent in 2017 to 10 percent in 2018 is a positive sign. He is a tough kid who plays the game with passion.
THE FUTURE: Noted for his strong makeup and good catch-and-throw skills, Viloria profiles best as a backup catcher with good leadership skills and at least average grades on many of his tools. With more development in his bat, he could be at least a part-time starter. Although his ceiling may not be very high, his advanced catch-and-throw skills make a big league future fairly certain.

Year	Club (League)	Class	AVG	G	AB	R	H	2B	3B	HR	RBI	BB	SO	SB	CS	OBP	SLG
2016	Idaho Falls (PIO)	R	.376	58	226	54	85	28	3	6	55	20	36	1	1	.436	.606
2017	Lexington (SAL)	LoA	.259	101	363	42	94	25	0	8	52	25	79	4	3	.313	.394
2018	Wilmington (CAR)	HiA	.260	100	358	34	93	16	1	6	44	40	75	2	1	.342	.360
	Kansas City (AL)	MAJ	.259	10	27	4	7	2	0	0	4	1	9	0	0	.286	.333
Major League Totals			.259	10	27	4	7	2	0	0	4	1	9	0	0	.286	.333
Minor League Totals			.283	350	1248	170	353	79	5	23	192	126	241	8	6	.355	.409

15 SCOTT BLEWETT, RHP

BA GRADE
45 Risk: High

Born: April 10, 1996. **B-T:** R-R. **Ht.:** 6-6. **Wt.:** 210. **Drafted:** HS—Baldwinsville, N.Y., 2014 (2nd round). **Signed by:** Bobby Gandolfo.

TRACK RECORD: Blewett's climb through the Royals' system has been a slow simmer. After three seasons in Class A, Blewett made it to Double-A in 2018 with mixed results. It seemed to click late in the season when he went 3-0, 2.59 over his final six starts. He continued that surge in the Arizona Fall League.

SCOUTING REPORT: With a tall, strong frame, Blewett certainly passes the eye test. He possesses above-average command of his 92-96 mph fastball, which comes from a powerful, high three-quarter delivery that he is still working on repeating. His average curveball with solid three-quarter break has gotten better and flashes plus, but it will occasionally flatten out and roll. He gets good action on his changeup, which flashes as an average pitch, but at 84-86 mph it is still a touch too firm.

THE FUTURE: After his strong finish in Double-A and impressive stint in the Arizona Fall League, Blewett should be ready for the challenge of pitching in the hitter-friendly Triple-A Pacific Coast League.

Year	Club (League)	Class	W	L	ERA	G	GS	CG	SV	IP	H	HR	BB	SO	K/9	WHIP	AVG
2016	Lexington (SAL)	LoA	8	11	4.31	25	25	2	0	129	138	10	51	121	8.4	1.46	.275
2017	Wilmington (CAR)	HiA	7	10	4.07	27	27	1	0	153	153	16	52	129	7.6	1.34	.262
2018	NW Arkansas (TL)	AA	8	6	4.79	26	25	1	0	148	164	12	49	100	6.1	1.44	.282
Minor League Totals			27	34	4.54	104	102	4	0	540	570	47	191	439	7.3	1.41	.272

16 AUSTIN COX, LHP

BA GRADE
45 Risk: High

Born: March 28, 1997. **B-T:** L-L. **Ht.:** 6-4. **Wt.:** 185. **Drafted:** Mercer, 2018 (5th round). **Signed by:** Jim Buckley.

TRACK RECORD: Drafted in the fifth round and signed for $447,500, Cox had an impressive pro debut in 2018. His pure stuff at Mercer was generally better than his results, with opponents hitting .284 despite him striking out 12.7 hitters per nine innings, which ranked in the top 10 among all Division I pitchers.

SCOUTING REPORT: The source of Cox's issues in college was a quick delivery that he didn't always repeat. The Royals worked to get him to slow his delivery down, as well as learn how to pitch to the edges of the strike zone while keeping the ball out of the middle of the plate. Cox has an elite ability to miss bats, using an above-average fastball in the mid-90s with average or better movement and two good breaking balls that could be considered plus pitches in the future. Rounding out his pitch mix is an above-average changeup, while his control projects to be fringe-average.

THE FUTURE: Cox could be either a starter or a multi-inning reliever. He should make it to full-season ball at low Class A Lexington.

Year	Club (League)	Class	W	L	ERA	G	GS	CG	SV	IP	H	HR	BB	SO	K/9	WHIP	AVG
2018	Burlington (APP)	R	1	1	3.78	9	9	0	0	33	29	1	15	51	13.8	1.32	.228
Minor League Totals			1	1	3.78	9	9	0	0	33	29	1	15	51	13.8	1.32	.228

17 RICHARD LOVELADY, LHP

BA GRADE
40 Risk: Medium

Born: July 7, 1995. **B-T:** L-L. **Ht.:** 6-0. **Wt.:** 175. **Drafted:** Kennesaw State, 2016 (10th round). **Signed by:** Sean Gibbs.

TRACK RECORD: Lovelady continued his rapid progress, spending all year in Triple-A in only his second full pro season.

SCOUTING REPORT: With some funk in his delivery, Lovelady gives hitters uncomfortable at-bats. His 91-95 mph fastball with solid-average life was slightly down in terms of velocity this year, but it did not reduce his effectiveness as the life and movement of the pitch was still there. His fastball has hard tailing action with sink, and he locates it to both sides, but the biggest factor is the elite extension he gets from his drive off the mound. Lovelady's go-to offspeed offering is his 83-87 mph slider, a plus pitch that gets swings and misses. His fringe-average changeup is used infrequently.

THE FUTURE: With his pure stuff and ability to get righthanded hitters out, Lovelady can function as more than just a lefty specialist. He should make it to Kansas City in 2019.

Year	Club (League)	Class	W	L	ERA	G	GS	CG	SV	IP	H	HR	BB	SO	K/9	WHIP	AVG
2016	Royals (AZL)	R	2	0	1.74	8	0	0	3	10	4	0	2	14	12.2	0.58	.111
	Idaho Falls (PIO)	R	0	1	1.84	13	0	0	6	15	10	0	7	16	9.8	1.16	.200
2017	Wilmington (CAR)	HiA	1	0	1.08	21	0	0	7	33	18	0	4	41	11.1	0.66	.154
	NW Arkansas (TL)	AA	3	2	2.16	21	0	0	3	33	28	1	13	36	9.7	1.23	.228
2018	Omaha (PCL)	AAA	3	3	2.47	46	0	0	9	73	53	3	21	71	8.8	1.01	.204
Minor League Totals			9	6	2.02	109	0	0	28	165	113	4	47	178	9.7	0.97	.193

18 CARLOS HERNANDEZ, RHP

BA GRADE
45 Risk: High

Born: March 11, 1997. **B-T:** R-R. **Ht.:** 6-4. **Wt.:** 200. **Signed:** Venezuela, 2016. **Signed by:** Richard Castro/Joelvis Gonzalez.

TRACK RECORD: Hernandez is the classic late bloomer, not signing with the Royals until he was 19 for $15,000 in 2016. His first full season with low Class A Lexington was interrupted twice, once early in the season when he returned home to Venezuela for a family emergency and then again when he was shut down for the last month of the season due to minor soreness.

SCOUTING REPORT: Hernandez overpowers hitters with a 93-95 mph fastball that touches 97 mph with late life. His 80-82 mph, power curveball has the potential to be a plus pitch, and he's effective at selling his 80-84 mph, split-grip changeup, especially to lefthanded hitters. Hernandez throws all three pitches for strikes, and both secondary offerings have the potential to be plus pitches. There's still room for improvement with his delivery, as he gets late with his arm and misses up in the strike zone.

THE FUTURE: Hernandez needs to smooth out his delivery and further refine his impressive arsenal. Some scouts view him as a future reliever with the potential to be a power arm in the back of a bullpen. He will battle to fit in a stacked starting rotation at high Class A Wilmington.

Year	Club (League)	Class	W	L	ERA	G	GS	CG	SV	IP	H	HR	BB	SO	K/9	WHIP	AVG
2017	Burlington (APP)	R	1	4	5.49	12	11	0	0	62	64	6	27	62	9.0	1.46	.266
2018	Lexington (SAL)	LoA	6	5	3.29	15	15	0	0	79	71	7	23	82	9.3	1.18	.236
Minor League Totals			7	9	4.26	27	26	0	0	142	135	13	50	144	9.1	1.31	.249

19 YOHANSE MOREL, RHP

BA GRADE
50 Risk: Extreme

Born: August 23, 2000. **B-T:** R-R. **Ht.:** 6-0. **Wt.:** 170. **Signed:** Dominican Republic, 2017. **Signed by:** Moises de la Mota/Johnny DiPuglia (Nationals).

TRACK RECORD: Morel had barely started his career in the Nationals' organization, pitching just one game in the Dominican Summer League before being one of three prospects acquired by the Royals in exchange for major league reliever Kelvin Herrera in June 2018. He immediately headed west to make his Royals debut in the Rookie-level Arizona League, pitching most of the summer at age 17.

SCOUTING REPORT: Morel is not physically big, coincidentally drawing comparisons to Herrera at the same age because of the way his arm works and the potential for added velocity. He's a fierce competitor on the mound, delivering his pitches with an athletic, loose power arm. Morel's 90-93 mph fastball, which touches 95 mph, has late life and the chance to play up, but it gets flat at times resulting in hard contact. His slurvy breaking ball—a hard pitch with bigger shape—flashed plus at times but projects as more of an average pitch. Morel's changeup was an above-average pitch in the AZL but then flashed plus potential during instructional league. He improved his command in the fall by better repeating the finish and delivery of his pitches. Morel shows a good aptitude to learn.

THE FUTURE: Most scouts in the Arizona League projected Morel as a future reliever because he commanded his pitches better in shorter bursts, but he has the arsenal to be a starting pitcher with plenty of developmental years ahead. He'll need another year of short-season ball in 2019.

Year	Club (League)	Class	W	L	ERA	G	GS	CG	SV	IP	H	HR	BB	SO	K/9	WHIP	AVG
2018	Nationals (DSL)	R	0	0	8.10	1	1	0	0	3	6	0	1	5	13.5	2.10	.375
	Royals (AZL)	R	1	2	3.71	12	7	0	0	44	40	1	16	47	9.7	1.28	.240
Minor League Totals			1	2	4.02	13	8	0	0	47	46	1	17	52	10.0	1.34	.251

20 BREWER HICKLEN, OF

BA GRADE
45 Risk: High

Born: Feb. 9, 1996. **B-T:** R-R. **Ht.:** 6-2. **Wt.:** 208. **Drafted:** Alabama-Birmingham, 2017 (7th round). **Signed by:** Nick Hamilton.

TRACK RECORD: Hicklen was a two-sport athlete at Alabama-Birmingham, doubling as a wide receiver until the school dropped its football program in 2015. Drafted in the seventh round in 2017, Hicklen signed for $337,500. He was slowed by injuries in his first pro season, but had a solid 2018 that was split between low Class A Lexington and high Class A Wilmington. He was especially effective in Lexington, leading the team in batting average, on-base percentage and slugging percentage.

SCOUTING REPORT: Pure strength and raw power are Hicklen's most noticeable attributes. He's not real loose athletically, with the athleticism coming from his strength. While he has above-average to plus raw power, Hicklen projects to hit for average more than power. He was good plate coverage and lays off secondary pitches out of the strike zone, but he has a tendency to chase fastballs up in the zone. As expected from a former wide receiver, Hicklen is a plus runner underway but closer to above-average out of the box. He's an average fielder with fringe-average range. While his arm is no more than fringe-average, he gets rid of balls quickly to make up for any shortage in arm strength. Hicklen is a vocal leader on the field, constantly inspiring his teammates.

THE FUTURE: A potential power-speed threat, Hicklen is viewed by some scouts as a fourth outfielder. A future role as a starting outfielder isn't out of the question, however, especially as he continues to develop his baseball skills to go along with his raw athleticism. He'll head back to Wilmington in 2019.

Year	Club (League)	Class	AVG	G	AB	R	H	2B	3B	HR	RBI	BB	SO	SB	CS	OBP	SLG
2017	Royals (AZL)	R	.348	19	69	19	24	3	3	3	13	9	24	13	3	.439	.609
	Idaho Falls (PIO)	R	.299	20	87	19	26	8	2	1	10	9	22	3	1	.384	.471
2018	Wilmington (CAR)	HiA	.211	22	71	11	15	4	0	1	3	4	26	6	0	.263	.310
	Lexington (SAL)	LoA	.307	82	306	59	94	18	3	17	65	24	98	29	6	.378	.552
Minor League Totals			.298	143	533	108	159	33	8	22	91	46	170	51	10	.373	.514

21 GERSON GARABITO, RHP

Born: Aug. 19, 1995. **B-T:** R-R. **Ht.:** 6-0. **Wt.:** 202. **Signed:** Dominican Republic, 2012. **Signed by:** Edis Perez.

BA GRADE
45 Risk: High

TRACK RECORD: It's been a slow climb through the Royals' system for Garabito. He first pitched in the Dominican Summer League in 2013, but while he's had to repeat levels at times, the Dominican native flashes enough stuff.

SCOUTING REPORT: Garabito pitches up in the strike zone with his fastball, moving it around enough and throwing it to both sides of the plate to get away with the location. His fastball gets up to 95-96 mph, with his comfort zone more in the 91-92 mph range. He's got a big curveball that he throws in any count with good depth and action. Garabito's changeup is still a work in progress and was a below-average pitch early in the season before flashing above-average potential later in the year. His athleticism gives him a loose, fluid delivery with some length in his arm action, and he has a sturdy build with a strong lower half.

THE FUTURE: Garabito was not added to the 40-man roster to keep him out of the Rule 5 draft and he went unpicked. He'll head to Double-A to begin 2019. He's likely more of a future bullpen arm using his fastball-curveball combination.

Year	Club (League)	Class	W	L	ERA	G	GS	CG	SV	IP	H	HR	BB	SO	K/9	WHIP	AVG
2016	Lexington (SAL)	LoA	2	11	4.80	18	18	0	0	81	78	9	35	61	6.8	1.40	.256
2017	Royals (AZL)	R	0	0	6.00	2	2	0	0	3	4	1	1	2	6.0	1.67	.333
	Lexington (SAL)	LoA	4	5	2.81	15	15	0	0	77	52	8	19	72	8.4	0.92	.191
2018	Wilmington (CAR)	HiA	8	6	3.16	26	26	1	0	142	117	12	73	116	7.3	1.33	.226
Minor League Totals			20	25	3.32	100	87	1	0	436	350	33	191	371	7.7	1.24	.221

22 EMMANUEL RIVERA, 3B

Born: June 29, 1996. **B-T:** R-R. **Ht.:** 6-2. **Wt.:** 195. **Drafted:** Interamerican (P.R.) JC, 2015 (19th round). **Signed by:** Johnny Ramos.

BA GRADE
45 Risk: High

TRACK RECORD: Rivera put up another strong year at high Class A Wilmington in 2018, posting a .280/.333/.427 slash line despite missing time to an oblique injury. He's made steady progress in the Royals' system, with his breakout coming in 2017 at low Class A Lexington. While he's not a high-profile prospect, Rivera plays with a low-key demeanor and needs to be watched over a longer period of time to appreciate his value.

SCOUTING REPORT: At the plate, Rivera is a consistent gap-to-gap hitter who puts together good at-bats and finds ways to put balls in play. He has yet to show much in-game power, with only 18 home runs in his two full seasons combined, but he shows average raw power in batting practice. He may get more over-the-fence power as he advances and gets more loft in his swing, but that's not his game as he wants to hit for a high average and move runners. Defensively, Rivera has the range and hands to handle third base. He has a plus arm but doesn't always show it off because he tries to make everything look easy. A below-average runner who doesn't steal a lot of bases, Rivera is smart and knows how to run bases.

THE FUTURE: Rivera should be ready to move to Double-A in 2019, which will be a good test. The biggest question remaining will be to see if he can develop at least a touch more power to better profile at third base.

Year	Club (League)	Class	AVG	G	AB	R	H	2B	3B	HR	RBI	BB	SO	SB	CS	OBP	SLG
2016	Burlington (APP)	R	.249	58	217	25	54	13	4	2	27	21	44	7	3	.317	.373
2017	Lexington (SAL)	LoA	.310	122	464	60	144	27	5	12	72	31	87	8	10	.364	.468
2018	Royals (AZL)	R	.192	7	26	4	5	0	1	0	2	1	6	0	0	.222	.269
	Wilmington (CAR)	HiA	.280	99	375	45	105	25	6	6	61	29	59	3	2	.333	.427
Minor League Totals			.274	324	1197	147	328	70	16	20	176	105	228	27	19	.338	.409

23 ZACH HAAKE, RHP

Born: Oct. 8, 1996. **B-T:** R-R. **Ht.:** 6-4. **Wt.:** 186. **Drafted:** Kentucky, 2018 (6th round). **Signed by:** Mike Farrell.

BA GRADE
45 Risk: High

TRACK RECORD: Haake made a circuitous journey through the college ranks, spending one year each at Arkansas State, John A Logan (Ill.) JC, and finally at Kentucky where he split his Wildcats season between the bullpen and the rotation. The Royals continued loading their 2018 draft class with a smorgasbord of college pitchers by taking Haake in the sixth round, despite an ugly 8.37 ERA in his final college season.
SCOUTING REPORT: Haake's difficulties at Kentucky stemmed from moving back and forth between the rotation and the bullpen, as he didn't have the endurance to succeed the second time through a lineup. The first item of business when reporting to the Royals' complex was to start a throwing program to build up his endurance. He also worked on his delivery in order to stay on line and repeat his delivery and his finish more often. Haake's fastball sits 93-98 mph, pitching most often at 95-96 mph in instructional league, but it comes in fairly straight. His 85-86 mph changeup is a below-average offering but showed improvement in the fall, while his average, 84-87 mph slider is still a work in progress that could become above-average in the future. With a tall, slender frame, Haake has plenty of room to get stronger.
TRACK RECORD: Haake's three-pitch mix in college indicates a future in the starting rotation, but Haake's track record could indicate a bullpen role is more likely, unless the Royals' conditioning program pays off. Haake will most likely begin 2019 with low Class A Lexington.

Year	Club (League)	Class	W	L	ERA	G	GS	CG	SV	IP	H	HR	BB	SO	K/9	WHIP	AVG
2018	Royals (AZL)	R	0	0	1.86	5	4	0	0	10	7	1	2	10	9.3	0.93	.200
	Idaho Falls (PIO)	R	0	0	1.59	2	2	0	0	6	2	0	2	4	6.4	0.71	.111
Minor League Totals			0	0	1.76	7	6	0	0	15	9	1	4	14	8.2	0.85	.170

24 JOSH STAUMONT, RHP

Born: Dec. 21, 1993. **B-T:** R-R. **Ht.:** 6-3. **Wt.:** 200. **Drafted:** Azusa Pacific (Calif.), 2015 (2nd round). **Signed by:** Colin Gonzalez.

BA GRADE
45 Risk: Extreme

TRACK RECORD: Staumont has long struggled to improve his command and control. He continues to frustrate, with his electric stuff playing down because of his lack of control, although he slightly lowered his walk rate from 7.8 walks per nine innings in 2017 to 7.0 walks per nine in 2018. Staumont spent the entire 2018 season in Triple-A, pitching mostly out of the bullpen. The Royals worked him in relief, primarily to simplify things and have him pitch out of the stretch.
SCOUTING REPORT: Staumont continually entices with an electric, 91-97 mph fastball that touches 100 mph. The ball jumps out his hand, regularly recording a high spin rate. The biggest issue is that Staumont's control is a 20 on the scouting scale. Staumont attacked hitters better in 2018. He struggles to land his fringe-average, 76-80 mph curveball, but it can be a plus offering with swing-and-miss potential on the rare ocassions when he does command it. His 82-84 mph changeup is a firm, below-average pitch.
THE FUTURE: Staumont could be a high-leverage reliever using just his four-seam fastball and curveball if his control improves. If not, it's hard to envision him being able to contribute in a big league bullpen.

Year	Club (League)	Class	W	L	ERA	G	GS	CG	SV	IP	H	HR	BB	SO	K/9	WHIP	AVG
2016	Wilmington (CAR)	HiA	2	10	5.05	18	15	0	0	73	62	3	67	94	11.6	1.77	.230
	NW Arkansas (TL)	AA	2	1	3.04	11	11	0	0	50	42	2	37	73	13.1	1.57	.232
2017	Omaha (PCL)	AAA	3	8	6.28	16	15	0	0	76	64	14	63	93	11.0	1.67	.227
	NW Arkansas (TL)	AA	3	4	4.44	10	10	0	0	49	42	2	34	45	8.3	1.56	.244
2018	Omaha (PCL)	AAA	2	5	3.51	41	5	0	1	74	59	4	52	103	12.5	1.49	.217
Minor League Totals			15	29	4.35	114	60	0	2	362	290	25	285	466	11.6	1.59	.221

25 RYLAN KAUFMAN, LHP

Born: June 23, 1999. **B-T:** L-L. **Ht.:** 6-4. **Wt.:** 190. **Drafted:** San Jacinto (Texas) JC, 2018 (12th round). **Signed by:** Sean Gallagher.

BA GRADE
45 Risk: Extreme

TRACK RECORD: The Royals' 12th-round pick, Kaufman signed for $722,500—a higher signing bonus than all but their first four picks in 2018. Kaufman posted a 7-1, 2.18 record for a San Jacinto (Texas) JC team that advanced to the Junior College World Series.
SCOUTING REPORT: Kaufman's most notable strength is his extremely high spin-rate breaking ball—a slurvy pitch that comes through with curveball shape at 73-76 mph. His fastball ranges from 87-93 mph, but the velocity should jump as he adds strength to his tall, lean body. Kaufman's changeup has good action at 83-84 mph, routinely drawing swings and misses. He uses a free and easy delivery with a sneaky arm action that hides the ball well from hitters. The Royals also like Kaufman's baseball savvy and intelligence, rooming him with the more experienced Brady Singer during instructional league.

THE FUTURE: Kaufman pitched at two levels in 2018, making very brief appearances in both the Rookie-level Arizona and Pioneer leagues. He may be held back in extended spring training to better manage his innings, but he could get to low Class A Lexington at some point in 2019.

Year	Club (League)	Class	W	L	ERA	G	GS	CG	SV	IP	H	HR	BB	SO	K/9	WHIP	AVG
2018	Royals (AZL)	R	0	1	9.00	2	2	0	0	2	4	0	1	1	4.5	2.50	.400
	Idaho Falls (PIO)	R	0	0	1.80	2	2	0	0	5	2	0	1	7	12.6	0.60	.111
Minor League Totals			0	1	3.86	4	4	0	0	7	6	0	2	8	10.3	1.14	.214

26 BLAKE PERKINS, OF

BA GRADE

40 Risk: High

Born: Sept. 10, 1996. **B-T:** S-R. **Ht.:** 6-1. **Wt.:** 165. **Drafted:** HS—Buckeye, Ariz. (2nd round). **Signed by:** Mitch Sokol (Nationals).

TRACK RECORD: After being drafted by the Nationals in the second round and signing for $800,000 in 2015, Perkins was traded to the Royals in exchange for Kelvin Herrera in June 2018.

SCOUTING REPORT: Drawing multiple comparisons to major league outfielder Jon Jay, Perkins best fits the profile of a fourth outfielder if he can make a significant improvement at the plate. He's a glove-first player, a plus defender in center field with mature instincts, excellent routs and an above-average arm. He controls the strike zone well, as evidenced by his 15 percent walk rate, but his 22 percent strikeout rate indicates that he needs to make more contact in order to take advantage of his above-average speed. He has no power. He also needs to improve his instincts on the bases.

THE FUTURE: Perkins will move to Double-A in 2019. He has to hit more to be a viable major leaguer.

Year	Club (League)	Class	AVG	G	AB	R	H	2B	3B	HR	RBI	BB	SO	SB	CS	OBP	SLG
2016	Auburn (NYP)	SS	.233	56	210	31	49	5	1	1	16	25	39	10	3	.318	.281
	Hagerstown (SAL)	LoA	.200	7	25	4	5	0	0	0	2	5	6	0	1	.333	.200
2017	Hagerstown (SAL)	LoA	.255	129	482	105	123	27	4	8	48	72	118	31	8	.354	.378
2018	Potomac (CAR)	HiA	.234	65	252	39	59	11	0	1	21	42	67	12	5	.344	.290
	Wilmington (CAR)	HiA	.240	64	233	48	56	11	1	2	18	50	67	17	4	.381	.322
Minor League Totals			.239	370	1368	248	327	59	8	13	117	207	333	74	26	.341	.322

27 MICHAEL GIGLIOTTI, OF

BA GRADE

40 Risk: High

Born: Feb. 14, 1996. **B-T:** L-L. **Ht.:** 6-1. **Wt.:** 180. **Drafted:** Lipscomb, 2017 (4th round). **Signed by:** Nick Hamilton.

TRACK RECORD: The Royals' fourth-round pick out of Lipscomb in 2017, Gigliotti had a solid debut season, ut his second pro season ended early when he tore his ACL after only six games.

SCOUTING REPORT: Gigliotti profiles as a top-of-the-order hitter with elite plate discipline, using his advanced knowledge of the strike zone to work counts and focus on making contact. He has a strong frame and quick hands with an efficient bat path. His below-average power is balanced by the plus-plus speed he showed prior to his knee injury. Gigliotti gets good jumps and reads on fly balls, and his average arm is enough for center field.

THE FUTURE: Assuming he's back to full strength in 2019, Gigliotti should move to high Class A Wilmington. That determination won't be made until he's back in action during spring training, however.

Year	Club (League)	Class	AVG	G	AB	R	H	2B	3B	HR	RBI	BB	SO	SB	CS	OBP	SLG
2017	Burlington (APP)	R	.329	42	155	30	51	8	3	3	30	32	21	15	5	.442	.477
	Lexington (SAL)	LoA	.302	22	86	14	26	5	1	1	8	8	20	7	5	.378	.419
2018	Lexington (SAL)	LoA	.235	6	17	3	4	1	0	1	2	6	5	1	0	.435	.471
Minor League Totals			.314	70	258	47	81	14	4	5	40	46	46	23	10	.421	.457

28 ARNALDO HERNANDEZ, RHP

BA GRADE

40 Risk: High

Born: Feb. 9, 1996. **B-T:** R-R. **Ht.:** 6-0. **Wt.:** 175. **Signed:** Venezuela, 2012. **Signed by:** Alberto Garcia/Richard Castro/Orlando Estevez.

TRACK RECORD: After signing out of Venezuela as a 16-year-old in 2012, Hernandez has long been considered more of an organizational depth piece than prospect. He jumped onto the prospect radar by moving across three levels in 2018, however, finishing the year with 10 strong outings in the Triple-A Pacific Coast League.

SCOUTING REPORT: Hernandez is an effective strike-thrower. He moves the ball up, down, in and out, all while changing speeds. A strong competitor, it's Hernandez's feel for pitching that separates him. He uses both his four-seam and two-seam fastball, with his four-seamer sitting 90-94 mph while his two-seamer comes in a tick slower with arm-side run. His best pitch is a changeup with sink that flashes as a plus offering, and he also has an average 79-82 mph curveball with depth.

THE FUTURE: Hernandez was added to the Royals' 40-man roster this offseason to keep him out of the Rule 5 draft. He'll head to Spring Training with a chance to make the big league team in some capacity.

Year	Club (League)	Class	W	L	ERA	G	GS	CG	SV	IP	H	HR	BB	SO	K/9	WHIP	AVG
2016	Idaho Falls (PIO)	R	5	2	5.86	14	14	0	0	71	99	7	18	63	8.0	1.66	.334
2017	Lexington (SAL)	LoA	2	1	3.63	15	5	1	1	57	63	9	8	58	9.2	1.25	.278
	Omaha (PCL)	AAA	1	0	1.74	2	2	0	0	10	9	0	4	6	5.2	1.26	.231
2018	Wilmington (CAR)	HiA	6	4	4.22	14	12	1	0	64	77	3	19	53	7.5	1.50	.301
	NW Arkansas (TL)	AA	1	0	4.41	3	3	0	0	16	20	1	6	16	8.8	1.59	.323
	Omaha (PCL)	AAA	5	1	3.55	10	9	2	0	58	45	8	19	36	5.6	1.10	.210
Minor League Totals			29	13	3.85	82	61	4	2	376	404	33	89	330	7.9	1.31	.275

29 KORT PETERSON, OF

BA GRADE

40 Risk: High

Born: April 29, 1994. **B-T:** L-R. **Ht.:** 6-1. **Wt.:** 195. **Drafted:** UCLA, 2016 (23rd round). **Signed by:** Rich Amaral.

TRACK RECORD: While Peterson's performance in college and in summer wood bat leagues didn't stand out, his raw tools got him drafted out of UCLA in the 23rd round in 2016. At 24 years old, it might be easy to dismiss Peterson as too old to be regarded as a prospect. But he's performed well at every level. He made it to Double-A Arkansas midway through 2018 after starting the year with high Class A Wilmington, recording career bests in home runs (15), RBIs (60) and stolen bases (11).

SCOUTING REPORT: Peterson is lauded for his plus makeup as well as being a student of the game and level-headed. He has good feel for the barrel and a nice, smooth swing that is quiet at the plate. His raw power grades as plus-plus, and while he combined to hit 15 home runs in 112 games at two levels in 2018, there should be more in-game power coming. There's still too much swing and miss in his game. Peterson steals bases more on instincts than with his average speed, and he was successful on 11 of 15 attempts in 2018. He's played mostly right field in his pro career. His slightly above-average arm is enough for the position and it plays up because he knows when to go after runners and throw behind them.

THE FUTURE: Peterson is slated to go back to Double-A in 2019. He could be a backup outfielder.

Year	Club (League)	Class	AVG	G	AB	R	H	2B	3B	HR	RBI	BB	SO	SB	CS	OBP	SLG
2016	Burlington (APP)	R	.347	49	176	39	61	12	4	5	35	17	38	7	2	.437	.545
2017	Lexington (SAL)	LoA	.290	52	193	24	56	12	2	1	19	17	54	5	3	.374	.389
	Wilmington (CAR)	HiA	.333	11	39	7	13	3	2	1	1	2	11	0	0	.366	.590
2018	Wilmington (CAR)	HiA	.292	62	219	34	64	17	2	8	33	17	59	5	1	.365	.498
	NW Arkansas (TL)	AA	.229	50	166	24	38	8	3	7	27	12	61	6	3	.301	.440
Minor League Totals			.293	224	793	128	232	52	13	22	115	65	220	23	9	.371	.474

30 FOSTER GRIFFIN, LHP

BA GRADE

40 Risk: High

Born: July 27, 1995. **B-T:** R-L. **Ht.:** 6-3. **Wt.:** 200. **Drafted:** HS—Orlando, 2014 (1st round). **Signed by:** Jim Buckley.

TRACK RECORD: One of two first-round picks by the Royals in 2014, Griffin had a breakout year in 2017, regaining his prospect luster with an uptick in fastball velocity and a more aggressive attitude on the mound. He wasn't the same pitcher when he returned to Double-A Arkansas in 2018, however, nibbling too much.

SCOUTING REPORT: Griffin has good aptitude on the mound to go with his adequate three-pitch mix. He normally throws his 89-92 mph fastball with average command, but his velocity would often drop during rough periods. Griffin has both a two-seam and four-seam fastball, getting tail from the former and cut with the latter. His best pitch is a changeup, an average offering. Earlier in the season, he used his changeup infrequently against lefthanded hitters but started going to the pitch more often later in the season. Griffin rounds out his arsenal with an average, 11-to-5 curveball.

THE FUTURE: Griffin will be challenged with an assignment to Triple-A Omaha, where he'll have to continue his aggressiveness on the mound. He projects best as an up-and-down starting pitcher because of his lack of a plus pitch and his struggles to miss bats. The Royals left him unprotected in the Rule 5 draft and he went unpicked.

Year	Club (League)	Class	W	L	ERA	G	GS	CG	SV	IP	H	HR	BB	SO	K/9	WHIP	AVG
2016	Lexington (SAL)	LoA	1	4	3.38	7	7	0	0	37	35	3	9	29	7.0	1.18	.243
	Wilmington (CAR)	HiA	5	10	6.23	20	20	0	0	95	130	9	43	76	7.2	1.81	.330
2017	Wilmington (CAR)	HiA	4	2	2.86	10	10	0	0	57	43	2	20	60	9.5	1.11	.210
	NW Arkansas (TL)	AA	11	5	3.61	18	18	0	0	105	108	11	34	81	7.0	1.36	.271
2018	NW Arkansas (TL)	AA	10	12	5.13	28	26	0	0	153	197	20	40	117	6.9	1.55	.315
Minor League Totals			35	41	4.66	116	114	0	0	577	655	55	193	453	7.1	1.47	.287

Los Angeles Angels

BY MIKE DIGIOVANNA

You see it in the lean, muscular physique and dynamic toolset of Jo Adell, the arm speed and electric stuff of Griffin Canning, the plate discipline and elite bat-to-ball skills of Luis Rengifo and the blazing foot speed and vertical leap of Jordyn Adams.

The farm system has received a much-needed injection of athleticism under general manager Billy Eppler and scouting director Matt Swanson, whose targeting of high-risk, high-reward prospects could pay dividends for a big league club that hasn't won a playoff game since 2009.

Eppler, who is entering his fourth season with the Angels, and Swanson, entering his third, have gravitated toward high-end athletes because they believe they adjust quicker and move through the system more rapidly than more polished prospects with lower ceilings.

The Angels used their four first-round picks from 2011-2016 (they forfeited 2012 and 2013 first-round picks for signing Albert Pujols and Josh Hamilton) on college players who were more big league ready than most high schoolers but who had limited upside.

C.J. Cron (2011) has averaged 18 homers for six big league seasons but strikes out too much to be a perennial all-star. Lefthander Sean Newcomb (2014) reached the big leagues with Atlanta in 2017 but is more middle-of-the-rotation starter than ace.

Top picks Taylor Ward (2015) and Matt Thaiss (2016) switched positions after being drafted as catchers. Thaiss went to first base and Ward to third. Ward reached the big leagues last summer, but neither he nor Thaiss projects as an all-star.

Swanson used his first pick as scouting director in 2017 on Adell, a prep star who reached Double-A Mobile as a 19-year-old last summer and is being touted as a potential franchise player.

Swanson chose the UCLA standout with his second pick in 2017. The righthander jumped three levels in 2018 and is poised to crack the Angels' rotation in 2019.

The Angels used their top two picks in 2018 on high schoolers with extremely raw tools and high ceilings—Adams and shortstop Jeremiah Jackson.

Eppler and Swanson have tried to standardize the mindset of scouts and the language they use so they understand exactly what they're looking for. They want players who will get bigger, faster and stronger. They want raw materials that can be molded, shaped and developed by minor league coaches and instructors.

They're more interested in projectable power than current power, how hard a pitcher could

Shohei Ohtani showed superstar potential on the mound and in the batter's box in 2018.

PROJECTED 2022 LINEUP

Catcher	Jack Kruger (27)
First Base	Matt Thaiss (27)
Second Base	Jahmai Jones (24)
Third Base	Taylor Ward (28)
Shortstop	Andrelton Simmons (32)
Left Field	Jo Adell (23)
Center Field	Mike Trout (30)
Right Field	Brandon Marsh (24)
Designated Hitter	Justin Upton (34)
No. 1 Starter	Shohei Ohtani (27)
No. 2 Starter	Tyler Skaggs (30)
No. 3 Starter	Griffin Canning (26)
No. 4 Starter	Jose Suarez (24)
No. 5 Starter	Jaime Barria (25)
Closer	Keynan Middleton (28)

throw in three or four years, not now.

The approach is bearing fruit. A system that was among baseball's worst earlier this decade has moved to the middle of the pack and could soon supplement a big league roster that features the game's best player in Mike Trout, the most intriguing player in Shohei Ohtani and a great shortstop in Andrelton Simmons.

The addition of a premier starter and reliever, better overall health and a boost from within could transform the Angels, under new manager Brad Ausmus, into the kind of contender that might convince Trout to sign an extension before his six-year contract expires after 2020.

LOS ANGELES ANGELS

TOP 2019 ROOKIE: Griffin Canning, RHP. His workload will probably be limited, giving him a better chance to impact the rotation in the second half.

BREAKOUT PROSPECT: Jeremiah Jackson, SS. He could rocket through the system thanks to his athleticism, aptitude, wiry strength and the way the ball jumps off his bat.

SLEEPER: Brett Hanewich, RHP. A 2017 ninth-round pick out of Stanford, Hanewich features a 100 mph fastball that he used to strike out the side in November's Arizona Fall League all-star game.

SOURCE OF TOP 30 TALENT			
Homegrown	22	Acquired	8
College	9	Trades	6
Junior college	0	Rule 5 draft	0
High school	8	Independent leagues	0
International	5	Free agents/waivers	2
Nondrafted free agents	0		

LF
Brennon Lund (30)
Orlando Martinez

CF

Jo Adell (1)
Brandon Marsh (3)
Jordyn Adams (7)
D'Shawn Knowles (13)
Trent Deveaux (22)
Jose Reyes
Bo Way

RF

Michael Hermosillo (18)
Brandon Sandoval

3B
Kevin Maitan (21)
Jose Rojas (28)
Zach Houchins

SS
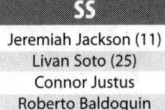
Jeremiah Jackson (11)
Livan Soto (25)
Connor Justus
Roberto Baldoquin

2B

Jahmai Jones (5)
Luis Rengifo (6)
Leonardo Rivas
Franklin Torres

1B
Matt Thaiss (8)
Jared Walsh (14)
David MacKinnon

C
Jack Kruger (17)
Jose Briceno (26)
Keinner Pina
Marlin Marcano

LHP

LHSP	LHRP
Jose Suarez (4)	Williams Jerez (23)
Patrick Sandoval (1)	Adrian Almeida
	Conor Lillis-White

RHP

RHSP	RHRP
Griffin Canning (2)	Ty Buttrey (9)
Jose Soriano (10)	Jake Jewell (27)
Chris Rodriguez (15)	Brett Hanewich
Stiward Aquino (16)	Jeremy Rhoades
Luis Madero (19)	Zac Ryan
Jeremy Beasley (20)	Robinson Pina
Aaron Hernandez (24)	Isaac Mattson
John Swanda (29)	
Jesus Castillo	
Joe Gatto	
Kyle Bradish	
Luis Pena	
Simon Mathews	
Oliver Ortega	
Matt Ball	

DRAFT ANALYSIS

2018

BEST PURE HITTER: The Angels drafted prep hitters with their first two picks before selecting pitchers with their next 11 picks and 16 of their next 18. So, both OF Jordyn Adams (1) and SS Jeremiah Jackson (2) stand out in the class for their hittability with Jackson holding the edge on Adams in that department. Jackson has some swing and miss in his game, but when his timing is down, he has good feel at the plate.

BEST POWER HITTER: Jackson also has at least plus raw power that he's already unlocking in games, hitting seven home runs in 43 games this summer. Some scouts also gave Adams plus raw power. Fastest Runner: OF Datren Bray (19) is a true top-of-the-scale runner who is still raw as a player. Adams may have that kind of speed now, but he'll probably end up with closer to 70-grade speed as he physically matures.

BEST DEFENSIVE PLAYER: Adams and Bray both profile as plus defenders in center field thanks to their speed. Both need to refine their defense, but the tools are there to be high-end defenders.

BEST ATHLETE: Adams signed with North Carolina to play both football and baseball and has elite athleticism. He was slated to play wide receiver and those tools stand out on the diamond.

BEST FASTBALL: RHP Aaron Hernandez (3) this spring ran his fastball up to 98 mph for Texas A&M-Corpus Christi. RHP Kyle Bradish (4) in short stints throws his fastball in the mid 90s with cutting action, leading to plenty of swings and misses.

BEST SECONDARY PITCH: Both Bradish and RHP Andrew Wantz (7) have breaking balls that grade out as plus. Bradish's is a deep, 12-to-6 curveball, while Wantz throws a slider that helped him strike out 47 of the 99 batters he faced in pro ball.

BEST PRO DEBUT: Wantz impressed out of the bullpen as a senior sign, averaging more than 18

TOP DRAFT PICKS OF THE DECADE

Year	Player, Pos.	2018 Org
2009	Randal Grichuk, OF	Blue Jays
2010	Cam Bedrosian, RHP	Angels
2011	C.J. Cron, 1B	Rays
2012	R.J. Alvarez, RHP (3rd round)	Rangers
2013	Hunter Green, LHP (2nd round)	Did not play
2014	Sean Newcomb, LHP	Braves
2015	Taylor Ward, C	Angels
2016	Matt Thaiss, C	Angels
2017	Jo Adell, OF	Angels
2018	Jordyn Adams, OF	Angels

strikeouts per nine innings. Adams was off to a solid start to the summer and was promoted to the Pioneer League before an injury cut his season short.

MOST INTRIGUING BACKGROUND: If it weren't for Adams, RHP William English (5) would clearly be the best athlete in the Angels' draft class. He was the first inner-city Detroit player drafted since 1988, has two-way talent on the diamond and played basketball in high school.

CLOSEST TO THE MAJORS: Wantz and RHP Austin Warren (6) both pitched well over the summer and, as relievers, figure to move quickly in the minor leagues. Both have fastballs that reach 95 mph and mix in good sliders.

BEST LATE-ROUND PICK: RHP Connor Van Scyoc (11) offers plenty of projection on the mound that is typical of a northern prep pitcher. RHP Luis Alvarado (17) was a two-way player at Nebraska but his future is on the mound, where he has a big arm and will be developed as a starter.

THE ONE WHO GOT AWAY: RHP Isaiah Campbell (24) this spring was inconsistent as he worked his way back from an injury that cost him his sophomore season. But he has an ideal pitcher's frame and big stuff. He'll return to Arkansas to front its rotation as a redshirt junior.

—TEDDY CAHILL

2017

This class delivered the Angels' top two prospects. OF Jo Adell (1) exploded in his first full professional season, reaching Double-A as a 19-year-old. RHP Griffin Canning (2) made his pro debut and quickly reached Triple-A.

GRADE: A

2016

It's been a mixed bag so far. 1B Matt Thaiss (1) is nearing Anaheim, though his impact remains to be seen. OF Brandon Marsh (2) is a premier athlete still finding consistency. RHP Chris Rodriguez (4) has upside but has dealt with injuries.

GRADE: C

2015

C Taylor Ward (1) and 2B David Fletcher (6) made their big league debuts in 2018. 2B Jahmai Jones (2) underwent a position change and reached Double-A. The Angels should get at least one regular from the class, though the jury is still out.

GRADE: C

1 JO ADELL, OF

Born: April 8, 1999. **B-T:** R-R. **Ht:** 6-3. **Wt:** 208.
Drafted: HS—Louisville, 2017 (1st round).
Signed by: John Burden.

The 10th overall pick in 2017, Adell dominated two Rookie-level leagues after signing for just under $4.4 million, then spent less than two months at low Class A Burlington in 2018 before being promoted twice during the season. He joined high Class A Inland Empire on May 20 and Double-A Mobile on July 31, making an impressive jump for a 19-year-old one year removed from high school. Adell was the only Angels prospect in the 2018 Futures Game, and he doubled and scored the winning run despite being one of the game's youngest players. His meteoric rise through the system was slowed by a jammed right thumb that sidelined him for a week in early August and led to some struggles at Double-A, but that hardly dampened the Angels' excitement.
SCOUTING REPORT: The broad-shouldered, muscular Adell is a dynamic athlete with high-end power, excellent bat speed, plus speed and a plus arm. His quick hands allow him to get to high pitches, and there is a maturity and a purpose to his preparation and approach. He uses the whole field, adjusts quickly and stays balanced in his swing. One area Adell can improve is his pitch recognition and plate discipline—he had 111 strikeouts and 32 walks in 441 plate appearances in 2018. He destroys fastballs but needs to avoid chasing breaking balls below the zone. Adell's plus speed makes him an asset on the basepaths and in center field. He's still working on getting better jumps and running more efficient routes in center field, but he has the youth and athleticism to stick there. His speed may not translate into high stolen base figures as he matures physically and adds muscle but speed should still be a big part of his game. Adell is highly mature for his age, with both an exceptional work ethic and a congenial personality.
THE FUTURE: Scouting director Matt Swanson described Adell as "a potential franchise player," the night the Angels drafted him. After two pro seasons, Adell has lived up to that both with his play and his personality. He is the most highly touted Angels prospect since Mike Trout, and the two will likely soon play together in the Angels' outfield. Adell is slated to start 2019 back at Double-A and should move to Triple-A quickly, putting him one injury away from Anaheim.

DONN PARRIS/FOUR SEAM IMAGES

BA GRADE	SCOUTING GRADES
70 Risk: High	Hit: 60. Power: 70. Run: 60. Field: 55. Arm: 60.

Projected future grades on 20-80 scouting scale

TOP PROSPECTS OF THE DECADE

Year	Player, Pos.	2018 Org
2009	Nick Adenhart, RHP	Deceased
2010	Hank Conger, C	Mexican League
2011	Mike Trout, OF	Angels
2012	Mike Trout, OF	Angels
2013	Kaleb Cowart, 3B	Angels
2014	Taylor Lindsey, 2B	Did not play
2015	Andrew Heaney, LHP	Angels
2016	Taylor Ward, C	Angels
2017	Jahmai Jones, OF	Angels
2018	Shohei Ohtani, RHP/DH	Angels

BEST TOOLS

Best Hitter for Average	Luis Rengifo
Best Power Hitter	Jo Adell
Best Strike-Zone Discipline	Luis Rengifo
Fastest Baserunner	Jordyn Adams
Best Athlete	Jo Adell
Best Fastball	Brett Hanewich
Best Curveball	Stiward Aquino
Best Slider	Griffin Canning
Best Changeup	Jose Suarez
Best Control	Luis Madero
Best Defensive Catcher	Keinner Pina
Best Defensive Infielder	Livan Soto
Best Infield Arm	Kevin Maitan
Best Defensive Outfielder	Brandon Marsh
Best Outfield Arm	Brandon Marsh

Year	Club (League)	Class	AVG	G	AB	R	H	2B	3B	HR	RBI	BB	SO	SB	CS	OBP	SLG
2017	Angels (AZL)	R	.288	31	118	18	34	6	6	4	21	10	32	5	0	.351	.542
	Orem (PIO)	R	.376	18	85	25	32	5	2	1	9	4	17	3	2	.411	.518
2018	Burlington (MWL)	LoA	.326	25	95	23	31	7	1	6	29	11	26	4	1	.398	.611
	Inland Empire (CAL)	HiA	.290	57	238	46	69	19	3	12	42	15	63	9	2	.345	.546
	Mobile (SL)	AA	.238	17	63	14	15	6	0	2	6	6	22	2	0	.324	.429
Minor League Totals			.302	148	599	126	181	43	12	25	107	46	160	23	5	.362	.539

2 GRIFFIN CANNING, RHP

Born: May 11, 1996. **B-T:** R-R. **Ht:** 6-1. **Wt:** 170. **Signed:** UCLA, 2017 (2nd round) Signed by: Ben Diggins.

TRACK RECORD: The Angels slow-played Canning in 2017, keeping him in Arizona to work on strength and conditioning after he threw 119 innings over 17 starts as UCLA junior. He took the mound as a pro in 2018 and skyrocketed, rising three levels from high Class A to Triple-A.

SCOUTING REPORT: Limber and athletic, wiry and strong, Canning generates tremendous arm speed and torque out of his thin frame. His four-pitch mix includes a four-seam fastball that now averages 94-95 mph and touches 98, up from 90-94 in college. He has two above-average secondary pitches, an 85-87 mph slider that runs down and away from righthanded batters and an 80-82 curveball with 11-to-5 shape. His changeup is rarely used but flashes average and is improving. Canning has a mental edge to rival his stuff. He is fearless on the mound and seems to dial up his velocity and command in big spots.

THE FUTURE: Canning shook off reports of "potential issues" in a predraft MRI by showing durability under a 113-inning workload. His size and stuff draw frequent comparisons with fellow UCLA product and Indians righthander Trevor Bauer. He is on track to reach the big leagues in 2019 and settle in as a mid-rotation starter.

BA GRADE

55 Risk: Medium

Fastabll: 60.
Curve: 60. **Slider:** 50.
Change: 45. **CTL:** 50.

Year	Club (League)	Class	W	L	ERA	G	GS	CG	SV	IP	H	HR	BB	SO	K/9	WHIP	AVG
2017	Did not play—Injured																
2018	Inland Empire (CAL)	HiA	0	0	0.00	2	2	0	0	9	4	0	3	12	12.5	0.81	.133
	Mobile (SL)	AA	1	0	1.97	10	10	0	0	46	27	2	19	49	9.7	1.01	.170
	Salt Lake (PCL)	AAA	3	3	5.49	13	13	0	0	59	68	6	22	64	9.8	1.53	.294
Minor League Totals			4	3	3.65	25	25	0	0	113	99	8	44	125	9.9	1.26	.236

3 BRANDON MARSH, OF

Born: Dec. 18, 1997. **B-T:** L-R. **Ht:** 6-4. **Wt:** 210. **Drafted:** HS—Buford, Ga., 2016 (2nd round). **Signed by:** Todd Hogan.

TRACK RECORD: Marsh signed for $1.073 million as a second-rounder in 2016 and appears fully recovered from a stress reaction in his back that briefly didn't require surgery but sidelined him. After flashing five-tool potential as one of the best players in the Pioneer League in 2017, he played a full season between low Class A Burlington and high Class A Inland Empire in 2018 and tantalized with his promise of power, speed and center field defense.

SCOUTING REPORT: A standout wide receiver in high school, Marsh is arguably the best athlete in the Angels' system. Scouts love his defensive instincts, plus speed, route-running and his strong, accurate arm. He is the best pure center fielder in the system—even better than Jo Adell—and his arm can change games. Marsh is more raw at the plate. He shows above-average raw power and recognizes pitches, but he doesn't always swing with intent and his strikeout totals are consistently high. At times his swing can look mechanical, even a little stiff. When he does connect, Marsh drives the ball to the gaps, and the way the ball comes off his bat leads scouts to project more power.

THE FUTURE: Marsh has the speed and instincts to excel defensively in any outfield spot. He'll try to make the necessary offensive adjustments at Double-A in 2019.

BA GRADE

55 Risk: High

Hit: 50. **Power:** 50.
Run: 60. **Field:** 60.
Arm: 60.

Year	Club (League)	Class	AVG	G	AB	R	H	2B	3B	HR	RBI	BB	SO	SB	CS	OBP	SLG
2016	Did not play—Injured																
2017	Orem (PIO)	R	.350	39	177	47	62	13	5	4	44	9	35	10	2	.396	.548
2018	Burlington (MWL)	LoA	.295	34	132	26	39	12	1	3	24	21	40	4	0	.390	.470
	Inland Empire (CAL)	HiA	.256	93	371	59	95	15	6	7	46	52	118	10	4	.348	.385
Minor League Totals			.288	166	680	132	196	40	12	14	114	82	193	24	6	.368	.444

4 JOSE SUAREZ, LHP

Born: Jan. 3, 1998. **B-T:** L-L. **Ht:** 5-10. **Wt:** 170. **Signed:** Venezuela, 2014.
Signed by: Carlos Ramirez/Mauro Zerpa/Lebi Ochoa.
TRACK RECORD: Suarez has such an advanced feel for pitching and knack for missing bats that he jumped from high Class A to Triple-A within the first two months of 2018 at age 20. Originally signed for $300,000 as a 16-year-old, Suarez improved his strikeout rate from 10.7 batters per nine innings in 2016 to 11.8 in 2017. He maintained a high rate (10.9) in 2018 despite spending most of the season at Triple-A.
SCOUTING REPORT: Suarez is slightly plump and hardly imposing, but his stuff is real. His fastball averages 92 mph and touches 95 with a late arm-side movement. His best pitch is a plus 81 mph changeup he throws with deception and sinking action, and his mid-70s curveball is an above-average swing-and-miss pitch when he lands it, though he's still learning to command it. Suarez works fast with an easy, repeatable high-three quarters delivery with good direction to the plate that yields above-average control.

BA GRADE
50 Risk: Medium
Fastball: 50.
Curve: 50.
Change: 60. CTL: 55.

THE FUTURE: Suarez is advanced for his age and proved durable under a 117-inning workload as a 20-year-old. He has put himself in consideration for the Angels' rotation in 2019 and will enter spring training with the chance to show he deserves a shot.

Year	Club (League)	Class	W	L	ERA	G	GS	CG	SV	IP	H	HR	BB	SO	K/9	WHIP	AVG
2016	Angels (AZL)	R	1	3	5.36	11	5	0	0	40	48	1	13	46	10.3	1.51	.296
	Orem (PIO)	R	0	1	0.00	1	1	0	0	4	6	0	1	7	14.5	1.62	.300
2017	Angels (AZL)	R	1	0	1.93	3	3	0	0	14	10	1	4	19	12.2	1.00	.208
	Burlington (MWL)	LoA	5	1	3.62	12	12	0	0	55	49	7	18	71	11.7	1.23	.243
2018	Inland Empire (CAL)	HiA	0	1	2.00	2	2	0	0	9	6	0	1	18	18.0	0.78	.182
	Mobile (SL)	AA	2	1	3.03	7	7	0	0	30	34	0	8	51	15.5	1.42	.286
	Salt Lake (PCL)	AAA	1	4	4.48	17	17	0	0	78	81	5	35	73	8.4	1.48	.268
Minor League Totals			13	14	3.68	68	60	0	0	303	305	14	92	331	9.8	1.31	.262

5 JAHMAI JONES, 2B

Born: Aug. 4, 1997. **B-T:** R-R. **Ht:** 6-0. **Wt:** 215. **Drafted:** HS—Norcross, Ga., 2015 (2nd round). **Signed by:** Todd Hogan.
TRACK RECORD: Jones reported to his first big league camp in 2018 as an outfielder but was moved to second base in March, a challenging transition that led to a drop-off at the plate. Jones' OPS dropped nearly 75 points from 2017 to 2018 as he focused on learning his new position, but he still made it up to Double-A.
SCOUTING REPORT: Despite Jones' 2018 struggles, evaluators still see strong offensive tools. He has plus bat speed, average power and a good feel for the strike zone. He is thick and strong, and the ball jumps off his bat to all fields. His plus speed makes him a basestealing threat, and he can turn on the jets to log doubles and triples. Defensively, Jones remains a work in progress at second base. He sat back on grounders and let the ball play him early in 2018 but learned to be more aggressive with his first step, which improved his range and helped him get better hops and angles. Jones struggles with the short,

BA GRADE
50 Risk: High
Hit: 50. Power: 45.
Run: 60. Field: 45.
Arm: 50.

softer throw from the hole and still needs polish turning the pivot on double plays.
THE FUTURE: Jones has a chance to be to be playable at second base in the words of one evaluator. The hope is his offense ticks back up in 2019 as he gets more comfortable playing his new position.

Year	Club (League)	Class	AVG	G	AB	R	H	2B	3B	HR	RBI	BB	SO	SB	CS	OBP	SLG
2016	Orem (PIO)	R	.321	48	196	49	63	12	3	3	20	21	29	19	6	.404	.459
	Burlington (MWL)	LoA	.242	16	62	8	15	1	0	1	10	5	13	1	0	.294	.306
2017	Burlington (MWL)	LoA	.272	86	346	54	94	18	4	9	30	32	63	18	7	.338	.425
	Inland Empire (CAL)	HiA	.302	41	172	32	52	11	3	5	17	13	43	9	6	.368	.488
2018	Inland Empire (CAL)	HiA	.235	75	298	47	70	10	5	8	35	43	63	13	3	.338	.383
	Mobile (SL)	AA	.245	48	184	33	45	10	4	2	20	24	51	11	1	.335	.375
Minor League Totals			.267	354	1418	251	378	68	21	30	152	155	295	87	30	.348	.408

6 LUIS RENGIFO, SS/2B

Born: Feb. 26, 1997. **B-T:** B-R. **Ht:** 5-10. **Wt:** 165. **Signed:** Venezuela, 2014.
Signed by: Tim Kissner/Emilio Carrasquel/Illich Salazar (Mariners).

TRACK RECORD: Rengifo signed with the Mariners for $360,000 out of Venezuela in 2014 and was traded to the Rays in 2017. Just before 2018 spring training, the Angels acquired Rengifo from Tampa Bay for C.J. Cron. Rengifo surprised even the Angels with a breakout 2018. He jumped three levels from high Class A to Triple-A, showing superb plate discipline and bat-to-ball skills. Overall he hit .299 with 41 steals and as many walks as strikeouts (75), causing one front office official to liken Rengifo to "finding gold."

SCOUTING REPORT: Rengifo is a strong and athletic switch-hitter with a compact swing and a line-drive approach. He stays in the strike zone and doesn't chase, allowing him to find good pitches to drive on a line. He doesn't elevate for home runs but has extra-base power and is getting stronger. Rengifo steals bags more with his superb instincts than his average speed, though he finds another gear underway. A natural shortstop who is still improving at second base, Rengifo is an average defender with an average arm up the middle.

BA GRADE
45 Risk: Medium
Hit: 50. **Power:** 40.
Run: 55. **Field:** 50.
Arm: 50.

THE FUTURE: Rengifo is in position to reach the majors in 2019. Most see him as a future utility infielder, but he does all the little things to potentially be more than that.

Year	Club (League)	Class	AVG	G	AB	R	H	2B	3B	HR	RBI	BB	SO	SB	CS	OBP	SLG
2016	Mariners (AZL)	R	.239	34	109	16	26	7	2	1	9	13	31	22	3	.325	.367
2017	Clinton (MWL)	LoA	.250	102	400	65	100	24	4	11	44	33	80	29	14	.318	.413
	Bowling Green (MWL)	LoA	.250	23	96	14	24	3	1	1	8	8	17	5	3	.308	.333
2018	Inland Empire (CAL)	HiA	.323	41	161	36	52	11	3	2	16	27	22	22	8	.426	.466
	Mobile (SL)	AA	.305	40	151	37	46	10	5	2	21	23	22	13	2	.420	.477
	Salt Lake (PCL)	AAA	.274	46	190	36	52	9	5	3	27	25	31	6	6	.358	.421
Minor League Totals			.270	410	1551	292	418	85	28	23	180	190	270	127	49	.358	.405

7 JORDYN ADAMS, OF

Born: Oct. 18, 1999. **B-T:** R-R. **Ht:** 6-2. **Wt:** 180. **Drafted:** HS—Cary, N.C., 2018 (1st round). **Signed by:** Chris McAlphin.

BILL MITCHELL

TRACK RECORD: A standout outfielder and wide receiver in high school, Adams was committed to play both baseball and football in college at North Carolina, where his father was the defensive line coach for the football team. Instead, the Angels drafted him 17th overall and signed him for an over-slot $4.1 million bonus to turn pro. Adams' first season after signing was cut short by a broken jaw, but he still advanced to Rookie-level Orem.

SCOUTING REPORT: Adams boasts tantalizing athleticism but is raw in baseball skills because of his two-sport background. At 6-foot-2, 180 pounds, he is a wiry strong with excellent bat speed and is a plus-plus runner. He has a chance to be an impact defender in center field as he hones his instincts, and he began showing plus power late in his senior season. The main question with Adams is how much he'll hit. Adams' bat progressed rapidly between his junior and senior years of high school, but his track record as even an average hitter is short.

BA GRADE
55 Risk: Extreme
Hit: 50. **Power:** 45.
Run: 70. **Field:** 55.
Arm: 45.

THE FUTURE: How quickly Adams rises through the system will depend on his hitting development. He has the speed to be a leadoff man or the projectable power to grow into a middle-of-the-order bat, depending on what he emphasizes. He'll get his first taste of full-season ball with low Class A Burlington in 2019.

Year	Club (League)	Class	AVG	G	AB	R	H	2B	3B	HR	RBI	BB	SO	SB	CS	OBP	SLG
2018	Angels (AZL)	R	.243	20	70	8	17	2	2	0	5	10	23	5	2	.354	.329
	Orem (PIO)	R	.314	9	35	5	11	4	1	0	8	4	7	0	1	.375	.486
Minor League Totals			.267	29	105	13	28	6	3	0	13	14	30	5	3	.361	.381

8 MATT THAISS, 1B

Born: May 6, 1995. **B-T:** L-R. **Ht:** 6-0. **Wt:** 195. **Drafted:** Virginia, 2016 (1st round). **Signed by:** Nick Gorneault.

TRACK RECORD: Thaiss, a converted catcher who signed for $2.15 million as the 16th overall pick in 2016, made some subtle adjustments in his stance, hips and swing path in 2018 in an effort to eliminate a bat tip and elevate the ball more. The results were tangible. Thaiss hit 16 homers with a .467 slugging percentage in 125 games across Double-A and Triple-A, up from nine homers and a .385 slugging percentage in 2017.

SCOUTING REPORT: Despite a lower walk rate with his power spike, Thaiss still has the best plate discipline in the system. He has a unique ability to control the strike zone and spoil tough pitches, often extending at-bats. He pounces on mistakes and drives the ball up the middle and to his pull side. Thaiss has made huge strides defensively at first base after looking rigid and uncomfortable in his first instructional league. He may never be a Gold Glover, but his range, hands, ability to pick balls in the dirt and turn the 3-1 play have improved to make him an average defender.

THE FUTURE: Thaiss is finally beginning to show the kind of power that warranted a switch to first base, though he projects more as a contributor than a star. He's in line to make his big league debut in 2019.

BA GRADE
45 **Risk:** Medium
Hit: 55. **Power:** 45.
Run: 30. **Field:** 55.
Arm: 45.

Year	Club (League)	Class	AVG	G	AB	R	H	2B	3B	HR	RBI	BB	SO	SB	CS	OBP	SLG
2016	Orem (PIO)	R	.338	15	65	16	22	7	1	2	12	4	4	2	4	.394	.569
	Burlington (MWL)	LoA	.276	52	199	24	55	12	3	4	31	22	28	1	0	.351	.427
2017	Inland Empire (CAL)	HiA	.265	84	336	46	89	13	4	8	48	40	59	4	3	.353	.399
	Mobile (SL)	AA	.292	49	178	29	52	14	0	1	25	37	50	4	3	.412	.388
2018	Mobile (SL)	AA	.287	40	157	24	45	10	2	6	25	16	35	2	1	.352	.490
	Salt Lake (PCL)	AAA	.277	85	368	54	102	24	6	10	51	28	68	6	3	.328	.457
Minor League Totals			.280	325	1303	193	365	80	16	31	192	147	244	19	14	.357	.437

9 TY BUTTREY, RHP

Born: March 31, 1993. **B-T:** L-R. **Ht:** 6-6. **Wt:** 230. **Drafted:** HS—Charlotte, 2012 (4th round). **Signed by:** Quincy Boyd (Red Sox).

TRACK RECORD: Buttrey was one of two relief prospects the Angels acquired from the Red Sox for second baseman Ian Kinsler on July 30, and the big righthander reached the big leagues for the first time on Aug. 16 after seven seasons in the minors. Within three weeks, Buttrey was closing games for the Angels and touching 100 mph.

SCOUTING REPORT: The physically imposing, 6-foot-6 Buttrey comes down at hitters with power stuff from a high three-quarters arm slot. His fastball averages 96 mph and touches 100, and he mixes in a sharp swing-and-miss slider in the low 80s and a mid-80s changeup. His fastball tends to straighten out and become more hittable when elevated, but he's been able to generate ground balls with his changeup, which he throws with good arm speed and at times looks like a splitter. Control problems forced Buttrey to move from the rotation to the bullpen in the minors, but he's figured out his delivery in relief and shows average control.

THE FUTURE: Buttrey will open 2019 in the Angels' bullpen. He has a chance to stake his claim as their closer of the future.

BA GRADE
45 **Risk:** Medium
Fastball: 70.
Slider: 55.
Change: 50. **CTL:** 45.

Year	Club (League)	Class	W	L	ERA	G	GS	CG	SV	IP	H	HR	BB	SO	K/9	WHIP	AVG
2016	Portland (EL)	AA	1	9	4.44	33	9	0	0	79	80	6	46	52	5.9	1.59	.261
2017	Pawtucket (IL)	AAA	1	1	7.64	10	0	0	0	18	21	2	10	18	9.2	1.75	.296
	Portland (EL)	AA	1	4	3.72	30	0	0	4	46	39	1	23	56	11.0	1.35	.234
2018	Pawtucket (IL)	AAA	1	1	2.25	32	0	0	1	44	36	4	14	64	13.1	1.14	.216
	Angels (AZL)	R	0	0	0.00	1	1	0	0	1	0	0	0	3	27.0	0.00	.000
	Salt Lake (PCL)	AAA	0	1	2.25	4	0	0	0	4	2	0	1	7	15.8	0.75	.143
	Los Angeles (AL)	MAJ	0	1	3.31	16	0	0	4	16	15	0	5	20	11.0	1.22	.238
Major League Totals			0	1	3.31	16	0	0	4	16	15	0	5	20	11.0	1.22	.238
Minor League Totals			17	34	3.95	168	66	0	5	458	443	25	196	399	7.8	1.40	.254

10 JOSE SORIANO, RHP

Born: Oct. 20, 1998. **B-T:** R-R. **HT:** 6-3. **Wt:** 168. **Signed:** Dominican Republic, 2016. **Signed by:** Domingo Garcia/Alfredo Ulloa.

TRACK RECORD: The Angels signed Soriano for just $70,000 in 2016 and quickly watched him grow into one of their top pitching prospects. After starring at the Rookie levels, Soriano began 2018 in extended spring training before reporting to low Class A Burlington in June, where he held opponents to a .217 average and one homer in 14 starts. He also struggled with his control, recording 35 walks and 42 strikeouts in 46.1 innings.

SCOUTING REPORT: As Soriano adds strength to his wiry frame and more consistency to his delivery, there is still room for projection on a fastball that sits 94-96 mph. Though the pitch doesn't have a ton of movement, it has late life and induces a fair amount of ground balls. Soriano has always flashed a plus low-80s curveball, and he is developing a mid-80s changeup he grew more confident in last season. Soriano grew about three inches after signing and is still figuring out his newly long limbs. As he adds muscle and strength, he should improve the timing and mechanics of his delivery.

THE FUTURE: Soriano has a chance to grow into a hard-throwing starter as he matures. He'll move to high Class A Inland Empire in 2019.

	BA GRADE	
50	**Risk:** High	

Fastball: 70.
Curve: 50.
Change: 45. **CTL:** 45.

Year	Club (League)	Class	W	L	ERA	G	GS	CG	SV	IP	H	HR	BB	SO	K/9	WHIP	AVG
2016	Angels (DSL)	R	3	5	1.58	14	14	0	0	57	37	2	30	45	7.1	1.18	.187
2017	Angels (AZL)	R	2	2	2.94	12	10	0	0	49	43	2	14	37	6.8	1.16	.234
	Orem (PIO)	R	0	0	2.70	1	1	0	0	3	4	0	4	2	5.4	2.40	.308
2018	Burlington (MWL)	LoA	1	6	4.47	14	14	0	0	46	34	1	35	42	8.2	1.49	.217
Minor League Totals			6	13	2.89	41	39	0	0	156	118	5	83	126	7.3	1.29	.214

11 JEREMIAH JACKSON, SS

	BA GRADE	
55	**Risk:** Extreme	

Born: March 26, 2000. **B-T:** R-R. **Ht.:** 6-0. **Wt.:** 165. **Drafted:** HS—Mobile, Ala., 2018 (2nd round). **Signed by:** J.T. Zink.

TRACK RECORD: Jackson established himself as the top prep prosect in Alabama for the 2018 draft and signed with the Angels for $1.194 million. He performed so well in a 21-game stint in the Rookie-level Arizona League after signing that he was promoted to Orem as one of youngest players in the Pioneer League. Jackson looked a little overmatched at that level, but still posted an .805 OPS with 27 extra-base hits in 43 games in his pro debut.

SCOUTING REPORT: Jackson is an offensive-oriented middle infielder with a strong, athletic frame, easy, loose hands and plus bat speed, a combination that gives him eye-popping power for his size. He's still lanky, but he has a chance for 20-plus home runs as he matures physically. The Angels changed his swing pre-pitch, trying to get him lower in his stance so he can improve his bat path and barrel up the ball more consistently, with the hope he can be an average hitter. He is an above-average runner. Jackson's range and arm strength are good enough to stick at shortstop, but his low three-quarters arm slot causes some of his throws to sail. He also needs to improve his footwork.

THE FUTURE: Jackson's combination of athleticism, instincts and aptitude excites the Angels. Whether he sticks at short or moves to second base, he has the bat to profile at both. He'll begin his first full season at low Class A Burlington in 2019.

Year	Club (League)	Class	AVG	G	AB	R	H	2B	3B	HR	RBI	BB	SO	SB	CS	OBP	SLG
2018	Angels (AZL)	R	.317	21	82	13	26	4	2	5	14	7	25	6	1	.374	.598
	Orem (PIO)	R	.198	22	91	13	18	6	3	2	9	8	34	4	1	.260	.396
Minor League Totals			.254	43	173	26	44	10	5	7	23	15	59	10	2	.314	.491

12 PATRICK SANDOVAL, LHP

	BA GRADE	
50	**Risk:** High	

Born: Oct. 18, 1996. **B-T:** L-L. **Ht.:** 6-3. **Wt.:** 190. **Drafted:** HS—Mission Viejo, Calif., 2015 (11th round). **Signed by:** Brad Budzinksi (Astros).

TRACK RECORD: Sandoval jumped on the national radar with a 42-inning scoreless streak at the Class A levels last summer, and the Angels acquired him for catcher Martin Maldonado in July. Sandoval finished the year eighth in the minors with a 2.06 ERA.

SCOUTING REPORT: Sandoval's fastball ranges from 88-94 mph and he can dial it up and down as needed. He has good feel for an average mid-70s curve and low 80s slider, but his signature pitch is a plus 80-mph changeup he throws with great arm speed. Sandoval's high-effort, up-tempo delivery, which matches his energetic makeup, needs a little polish, but he still has average control.

THE FUTURE: With four pitches and polish, Sandoval projects as a back-of-the-rotation starter and could also be a good multi-inning reliever. He will likely start 2019 back at Double-A and could be in Triple-A by the All-Star break.

Year	Club (League)	Class	W	L	ERA	G	GS	CG	SV	IP	H	HR	BB	SO	K/9	WHIP	AVG
2016	Greeneville (APP)	R	2	3	5.30	13	8	0	0	53	53	4	25	51	8.7	1.48	.266
2017	Buies Creek (CAR)	HiA	0	1	10.13	1	0	0	0	3	4	0	1	2	6.8	1.88	.333
	Tri-City (NYP)	SS	1	1	3.79	4	4	0	0	19	19	0	6	28	13.3	1.32	.257
	Quad Cities (MWL)	LoA	2	2	3.83	9	7	0	1	40	38	1	16	48	10.8	1.35	.244
2018	Quad Cities (MWL)	LoA	7	1	2.49	14	10	0	1	65	58	4	11	71	9.8	1.06	.231
	Buies Creek (CAR)	HiA	2	0	2.74	5	3	0	1	23	12	1	4	26	10.2	0.70	.156
	Inland Empire (CAL)	HiA	1	0	0.00	3	3	0	0	15	6	0	6	21	12.9	0.82	.118
	Mobile (SL)	AA	1	0	1.37	4	4	0	0	20	12	0	8	27	12.4	1.02	.174
Minor League Totals			16	11	3.46	59	45	0	3	250	224	11	81	285	10.3	1.22	.235

13 D'SHAWN KNOWLES, OF

BA GRADE

55 Risk: Extreme

Born: Jan. 16, 2001. **B-T:** B-R. **Ht.:** 6-0. **Wt.:** 165. **Signed:** Bahamas, 2017. **Signed by:** Carlos Gomez.

TRACK RECORD: Knowles made huge strides in 2018 and was one of the organization's biggest risers. A solid stint in the Arizona League earned Knowles a promotion to the Rookie-level Pioneer League, where the 17-year-old was one of the top hitters in the league (.949 OPS) in the 28 games he was there.

SCOUTING REPORT: Knowles was so raw in 2017 that the Angels had to teach him how to take a professional batting practice. His bat-to-ball skills improved dramatically in 2018, when he learned how to square the ball up consistently. Knowles has plus speed, a solid arm and plus defensive instincts in center field. He has a clean, compact, quiet swing from both sides of the plate with gap-to-gap power. His power should increase as he gets bigger and stronger, but Knowles projects more as a leadoff-type with his speed and contact skills. A fearless, hard-nosed approach in the field and at the plate has served Knowles well.

THE FUTURE: If Knowles improves as rapidly in the next two years as he did in 2018, he could develop into a high-end prospect. He'll see full-season ball as an 18-year-old in 2019.

Year	Club (League)	Class	AVG	G	AB	R	H	2B	3B	HR	RBI	BB	SO	SB	CS	OBP	SLG
2018	Angels (AZL)	R	.301	30	113	19	34	4	1	1	14	15	27	7	4	.385	.381
	Orem (PIO)	R	.321	28	109	27	35	9	2	4	15	13	38	2	3	.398	.550
Minor League Totals			.311	58	222	46	69	13	3	5	29	28	65	9	7	.391	.464

14 JARED WALSH, 1B/OF

BA GRADE

45 Risk: Medium

Born: July 30, 1993. **B-T:** L-L. **Ht.:** 6-1. **Wt.:** 210. **Drafted:** Georgia, 2015 (39th round). **Signed by:** Todd Hogan.

TRACK RECORD: Walsh played both ways in college at Georgia but was drafted by the Angels strictly as a position player. He transformed in 2018 into to a dangerous slugger. He rose from high Class A all the way to Triple-A, finishing tied for the system lead in doubles (34) and home runs (29). The Angels also began experimenting with him on the mound, and the lefthander posted a 1.59 ERA in eight appearances.

SCOUTING REPORT: Walsh leveled out the uppercut in his swing and produced a more consistent bat path through the zone, adjustments that transformed him into one of the organization's best power-hitting prospects. Walsh now turns around good velocity with plus lefthanded power to all fields. Walsh still swings at pitches he shouldn't and projects as an average hitter at best, but that's enough with his power. Defensively, Walsh is a smooth defender with plus hands and instincts, a strong arm and excellent footwork around the bag at first base. He's a below-average runner and still raw in the outfield.

THE FUTURE: Walsh gives the Angels something they need as a lefthanded-power bat, and his ability to mop up on the mound at the end of blowouts gives him another edge. He'll start 2019 back in Triple-A and has a chance to make his big league debut during the season.

Year	Club (League)	Class	AVG	G	AB	R	H	2B	3B	HR	RBI	BB	SO	SB	CS	OBP	SLG
2016	Burlington (MWL)	LoA	.290	109	393	55	114	30	1	7	36	31	81	2	0	.344	.425
2017	Mobile (SL)	AA	.232	20	69	7	16	3	0	3	9	3	29	1	0	.274	.406
	Inland Empire (CAL)	HiA	.331	70	275	43	91	29	1	8	52	26	72	1	0	.395	.531
2018	Inland Empire (CAL)	HiA	.275	40	149	28	41	8	1	13	36	24	50	0	1	.365	.604
	Mobile (SL)	AA	.289	41	149	26	43	13	0	8	26	21	48	1	0	.382	.537
	Salt Lake (PCL)	AAA	.270	47	178	32	48	13	0	8	37	16	56	0	0	.333	.478
Minor League Totals			.294	360	1333	211	392	108	7	49	225	133	355	5	1	.360	.496

15 CHRIS RODRIGUEZ, RHP

BA GRADE

50 Risk: Extreme

Born: July 20, 1998. **B-T:** R-R. **Ht.:** 6-2. **Wt.:** 185. **Drafted:** HS—Miami, 2016 (4th round). **Signed by:** Ralph Reyes.

TRACK RECORD: Rodriguez flashed tantalizing stuff at low Class A Burlington in 2017, but a stress reaction in his lower back suffered in spring training ultimately confined him to the Angels' Arizona training complex all of last season. In the end, the Angels decided it would be best for Rodriguez to focus on his rehabilitation instead of pitching for an affiliate.

SCOUTING REPORT: Rodriguez has power stuff and a varied arsenal. He has a lively four-seam fastball that averages 95 mph, a sinking two-seam fastball that runs in to righthanded hitters, a changeup with screwball-like fading action at 83-86 mph, a big 80-mph overhand curve and a firm 86-mph slider with a distinctly different break than his curve. He throws all his pitches for strikes, although he can catch to much of the plate and be hittable.

THE FUTURE: A year without pitching competitively stunted Rodriguez's growth, but the Angels still remain high on him because of his vast repertoire and competitiveness. Rodriguez is still only 20, and if he pitches in full-season ball in 2019, he will remain on a solid developmental track.

Year	Club (League)	Class	W	L	ERA	G	GS	CG	SV	IP	H	HR	BB	SO	K/9	WHIP	AVG
2016	Angels (AZL)	R	0	0	1.59	7	5	0	0	11	6	0	3	17	13.5	0.79	.154
2017	Orem (PIO)	R	4	1	6.40	8	8	0	0	32	35	1	7	32	8.9	1.30	.271
	Burlington (MWL)	LoA	1	2	5.84	6	6	0	0	25	32	1	7	24	8.8	1.58	.314
Minor League Totals			5	3	5.40	21	19	0	0	68	73	2	17	73	9.6	1.32	.270

16 STIWARD AQUINO, RHP

BA GRADE

50 Risk: Extreme

Born: June 20, 1999. **B-T:** R-R. **Ht.:** 6-6. **Wt.:** 215. **Signed:** Dominican Republic, 2016. **Signed by:** Domingo Garcia/Frankie Thon.

TRACK RECORD: Aquino, who signed for $100,000 as a 17-year-old in 2016, had Tommy John surgery last February and did not pitch in 2018, but he attacked his rehabilitation and nutrition programs with such vigor that he added 25-30 pounds to his lanky frame. Armed with exciting stuff to begin with, Aquino now stands 6-foot-6, 215-pounds with a frame one Angles official likened to a wide receiver.

SCOUTING REPORT: Aquino's fastball sat at 93-95 mph and touched 96 mph in the Dominican Summer League in 2017, the last time he saw game action, and has a chance to be more now that he's added weight and strength. He complements his heater with a low-80s power curve that has a real downer action. Before suffering his elbow injury, Aquino worked on a changeup that is now a functional third pitch. Aquino is extremely coordinated for his size and has a clean, simple, repeatable delivery.

THE FUTURE: Aquino is not expected to pitch until sometime around the All-Star break, and the Angels will closely monitor his innings and pitch counts as he rebuilds arm strength. Aquino has the potential to be the best of the Angels' collection of young Latin American arms.

Year	Club (League)	Class	W	L	ERA	G	GS	CG	SV	IP	H	HR	BB	SO	K/9	WHIP	AVG
2017	Angels (DSL)	R	0	2	4.56	7	4	0	0	24	25	1	9	29	11.0	1.44	.272
	Angels (AZL)	R	1	0	1.59	2	0	0	0	6	5	0	4	2	3.2	1.59	.250
2018	Did not play—Injured																
Minor League Totals			1	2	3.99	9	4	0	0	29	30	1	13	31	9.5	1.47	.268

17 JACK KRUGER, C

BA GRADE

45 Risk: High

Born: Oct. 26, 1994. **B-T:** R-R. **Ht.:** 6-1. **Wt.:** 185. **Drafted:** Mississippi State, 2016 (20th round). **Signed by:** J.T. Zink.

TRACK RECORD: Kruger bounced around during his college career before finishing at Mississippi State, hwere he won the 2016 Southeastern Conference title. Kruger was invited to big league spring training after his first full season and took off in 2018, and finishing tied for second in the system in batting (.299)

SCOUTING REPORT: Kruger has all the intangibles you want in a catcher, with an advanced understanding of the game and a good rapport with his pitchers. He's very athletic, is a good receiver and he blocks pitches well. The one caveat is his below-average arm strength. Kruger is a relatively accurate thrower, but he needs to improve his quickness, transfer, release and overall strength. Offensively, Kruger has good bat-to-ball skills and a good awareness of the strike zone. He has an advanced plan at the plate and drives the ball up the middle and to the gaps with authority. He's an above-average runner.

THE FUTURE: The ability to hit and call a good game can expedite a catcher's journey to a big league team, but unless Kruger can throw well enough to keep runners honest, he's going to have a hard time cracking an everyday role. He'll try to improve his arm at Triple-A in 2019.

Year	Club (League)	Class	AVG	G	AB	R	H	2B	3B	HR	RBI	BB	SO	SB	CS	OBP	SLG
2016	Angels (AZL)	R	.154	3	13	3	2	0	0	0	0	1	3	0	0	.267	.154
	Orem (PIO)	R	.330	27	103	14	34	7	1	0	14	6	11	6	1	.366	.417
2017	Burlington (MWL)	LoA	.232	69	267	34	62	13	2	4	23	21	54	2	1	.296	.341
	Inland Empire (CAL)	HiA	.255	35	137	21	35	4	1	1	16	18	26	0	0	.338	.321
2018	Inland Empire (CAL)	HiA	.294	56	221	25	65	12	0	3	16	27	46	11	3	.378	.389
	Mobile (SL)	AA	.305	41	174	25	53	10	1	4	24	4	31	2	2	.328	.443
Minor League Totals			.274	231	915	122	251	46	5	12	93	77	171	21	7	.336	.375

18 MICHAEL HERMOSILLO, OF

BA GRADE

40 Risk: Medium

Born: Jan. 17, 1995. **B-T:** R-R. **Ht.:** 5-11. **Wt.:** 190. **Drafted:** HS—Ottawa, Ill. 2013 (28th round). **Signed by:** Joel Murrie.

TRACK RECORD: A gradual four-year rise through the system culminated with Hermosillo's first big league callup last May, but he looked uncomfortable in four stints with the Angels. He still showed exciting athleticism and improved power at Triple-A, with 12 homers in 68 games, but he was unable to barrel up the ball consistently and swung at too many pitches outside the strike zone in the majors.

SCOUTING REPORT: The Angels remain high on Hermosillo's athletic ability. A former high school football standout who was committed to Illinois as a running back/defensive back, Hermosillo has explosive speed, a strong arm and good instincts in center field. He has also improved as a base-stealing threat. He made solid contact and showed good plate discipline in his first three minor league seasons, but his strikeout-to-walk ratio dipped as he faced better pitching. Hermosillo added some power in 2018, but his swing has some length to it and some holes that might prevent him from playing every day in the big leagues

THE FUTURE:. Hermosillo's ability to play all three outfield spots, makes him a safe bet to be part of the outfield rotation in 2019. Whether he can make enough contact will determine if he ever starts.

Year	Club (League)	Class	AVG	G	AB	R	H	2B	3B	HR	RBI	BB	SO	SB	CS	OBP	SLG
2016	Burlington (MWL)	LoA	.326	37	138	22	45	8	1	2	22	18	22	4	3	.411	.442
	Inland Empire (CAL)	HiA	.309	40	149	36	46	7	4	4	17	16	30	6	7	.393	.490
2017	Inland Empire (CAL)	HiA	.321	13	53	5	17	6	0	0	2	9	15	5	2	.438	.434
	Mobile (SL)	AA	.248	77	278	40	69	13	2	4	26	40	73	21	9	.361	.353
	Salt Lake (PCL)	AAA	.287	30	115	20	33	6	1	5	16	7	28	9	2	.341	.487
2018	Salt Lake (PCL)	AAA	.267	68	273	43	73	14	4	12	46	30	87	10	5	.357	.480
	Los Angeles (AL)	MAJ	.211	31	57	7	12	4	0	1	1	3	17	0	1	.274	.333
Major League Totals			.211	31	57	7	12	4	0	1	1	3	17	0	1	.274	.333
Minor League Totals			.268	423	1514	247	405	74	16	30	177	201	365	90	48	.366	.397

19 LUIS MADERO, RHP

BA GRADE

45 Risk: High

Born: April 15, 1997. **B-T:** R-R. **Ht.:** 6-3 **Wt.:** 185. **Signed:** Venezuela, 2015. **Signed by:** Marlin Urdaneta/Andres Garcia (Diamondbacks).

TRACK RECORD: Madero trained with former D-backs scout Miguel Nava as an amateur in Venezuela and signed with Arizona when he was 16. He never got out of short-season ball in four seasons with the D-backs, and they traded him to the Angels for David Hernandez in 2017. In his first full season in the Angels system, Madero jumped from low Class A to high Class A.

SCOUTING REPORT: Madero worked hard in the weight room to add muscle before last season and the results could be seen in his fastball, which reached 94-95 mph toward the end of 2018 after topping out at 91 mph in 2017. He can throw his breaking ball, which is a more side-to-side slurve than curveball, and his swing-and-miss changeup, which has nice fading action, in any count. He has a smooth, repeatable delivery and takes a big stride off the mound, creating good extension. Madero is polished for his age and has good command. The Angels love his work ethic and are encouraged by the strides he made last year.

THE FUTURE: Madero's increased velocity now makes him a viable starting pitching prospect. He may see Double-A in 2019.

Year	Club (League)	Class	W	L	ERA	G	GS	CG	SV	IP	H	HR	BB	SO	K/9	WHIP	AVG
2016	Missoula (PIO)	R	0	2	11.07	5	5	0	0	20	32	3	15	9	4.0	2.31	.364
	Diamondbacks (AZL)	R	3	2	3.61	6	6	0	0	42	46	2	15	34	7.2	1.44	.275
2017	Missoula (PIO)	R	3	1	3.99	5	5	0	0	29	29	3	6	28	8.6	1.19	.261
	Hillsboro (NWL)	SS	1	1	8.24	4	4	0	0	20	28	2	5	17	7.8	1.68	.337
	Burlington (MWL)	LoA	1	2	7.76	6	6	0	0	27	42	3	9	18	6.1	1.91	.362
2018	Burlington (MWL)	LoA	2	7	4.26	14	14	0	0	61	69	5	15	49	7.2	1.37	.283
	Inland Empire (CAL)	HiA	2	1	2.44	9	9	0	0	44	41	3	12	46	9.3	1.20	.246
Minor League Totals			23	25	4.21	78	64	0	0	365	373	21	113	323	8.0	1.33	.264

20 JEREMY BEASLEY, RHP

BA GRADE

45 Risk: High

Born: Nov. 20, 1995. **B-T:** R-R. **Ht.:** 6-3. **Wt.:** 215. **Drafted:** Clemson, 2017 (30th round). **Signed by:** Chris McAlpin.

TRACK RECORD: Beasley had a rocky junior season after transferring to Clemson from junior college. He fell to the Angels in the 30th round of the 2017 draft. In his first full season as a pro Beasley returned to form, reaching Double-A and leading the Angels' system with a 2.66 ERA.

SCOUTING REPORT: Beasley has the mentality and mound demeanor of a bulldog, often grunting and snarling his way through appearances, and he's developing the stuff to match. His fastball sits at 92 mph and touches 95-96 mph. His real weapon is a sharp 83-84 mph splitter that draws comparison's to some of the best splitters in the majors, and he backs it up with decent slider. Beasley's high-tempo delivery and general arm action has a more reliever look to it, but he holds his stuff and throws strikes with above-average control.

THE FUTURE: Beasley has been compared to Matt Shoemaker with his fastball-splitter combination and has come to be regarded as a huge sleeper in the Angels system. Even if he stalls as a starter, he attacks hitters with the gusto necessary to be a solid reliever.

Year	Club (League)	Class	W	L	ERA	G	GS	CG	SV	IP	H	HR	BB	SO	K/9	WHIP	AVG
2017	Angels (AZL)	R	1	0	3.18	4	0	0	0	6	3	0	0	6	9.5	0.53	.150
	Orem (PIO)	R	2	1	3.12	13	0	0	1	26	21	3	12	31	10.7	1.27	.219
2018	Burlington (MWL)	LoA	0	2	2.35	6	5	0	0	23	16	0	7	19	7.4	1.00	.198
	Inland Empire (CAL)	HiA	3	2	3.05	9	6	0	1	44	48	4	11	48	9.7	1.33	.281
	Mobile (SL)	AA	3	3	2.44	10	7	0	0	44	32	3	14	37	7.5	1.04	.206
Minor League Totals			9	8	2.76	42	18	0	2	143	120	10	44	141	8.9	1.14	.229

21 KEVIN MAITAN, SS/3B

BA GRADE

50 Risk: Extreme

Born: Feb. 12, 2000. **B-T:** S-R. **Ht.:** 6-2. **Wt.:** 190. **Signed:** Venezuela, 2016. **Signed by:** Gordon Blakely/Mike Silvestri/Rolando Petit (Braves).

TRACK RECORD: Maitan's stock has fallen dramatically since the Braves signed him as a 16-year-old, with concerns about his work ethic, poor recognition of secondary pitches, inability to make consistent contact and overall defense to blame. The Angels in Dec. 2017 gave him an additional $2.2 million after he was declared a free agent due to the Braves international bonus scandal. In his first season with his new organization, he committed 18 errors in 21 games at shortstop and 14 errors in 40 games at third base, with his occasionally out-of-whack footwork leading to fielding miscues and inaccurate throws.

SCOUTING REPORT: Maitan is big-bodied with bad weight, but he's still strong for his age. His thick lower half provides a foundation for plus raw power, and he showed the ability to adjust his offensive approach to get to it. He chased a lot of pitches outside the strike zone early in the season, but lowered his chase rate significantly as the year went on. The switch-hitting Maitan has a righthanded swing is quick, powerful and direct to the ball, but his lefthanded swing is too long with less bat speed. Maitan no longer has any chance to play shortstop with his size and below-average instincts, but his strong arm and solid hands give him a chance to be an average third baseman in time.

THE FUTURE: Maitan's end-of-season improvements give reason for hope, but he needs to get in better shape and has a long way to go. He may see low Class A Burlington in 2019.

Year	Club (League)	Class	AVG	G	AB	R	H	2B	3B	HR	RBI	BB	SO	SB	CS	OBP	SLG
2017	Braves (GCL)	R	.314	9	35	5	11	3	0	0	3	2	10	1	0	.351	.400
	Danville (APP)	R	.220	33	127	10	28	5	1	2	15	9	39	1	0	.273	.323
2018	Orem (PIO)	R	.248	63	262	42	65	13	1	8	26	19	66	1	2	.306	.397
Minor League Totals			.245	105	424	57	104	21	2	10	44	30	115	3	2	.300	.375

22 TRENT DEVEAUX, OF

BA GRADE

50 Risk: Extreme

Born: May 4, 2000. **B-T:** R-R. **Ht.:** 6-2. **Wt.:** 175. **Signed:** Bahamas, 2017. **Signed by:** Carlos Gomez.

TRACK RECORD: Deveaux represented the Angels' return to the international market when he signed for $1.2 million out of the Bahamas in 2017. His first season wasn't particularly productive as he made constant adjustments. The Angels moved him from shortstop to the outfield, and offensively he switched into three or four different stances and was unable to find any semblance of a rhythm at the plate.

SCOUTING REPORT: Deveaux, a former sprinter in the Bahamas, is an elite athlete and runner. He has been clocked at 6.2 seconds in the 60-yard dash, an 80-grade time. He's still learning to steal bases but has little trouble scoring from first on balls hit to the gaps. Deveaux has the makings of a premier defender in center field, with a solid arm, plus range and plus instincts. The biggest question is his bat. He hunted fastballs early and struggled with offspeed pitches in his debut, but he seemed to find a little more rhythm to his swing in the final two weeks. The Angels sent Deveaux to the Dominican instructional league for a month of work after the season, hoping he would find a comfortable setup and swing that will allow him to recognize pitches better, keep the bat in the zone longer and make more consistent contact.

THE FUTURE: It was a rough first season, but the Angels still love Deveaux's athleticism and the way the ball comes off his bat. He'll start 2019 in extended spring training.

Year	Club (League)	Class	AVG	G	AB	R	H	2B	3B	HR	RBI	BB	SO	SB	CS	OBP	SLG
2018	Angels (AZL)	R	.199	44	166	20	33	5	0	1	11	24	68	7	4	.309	.247
Minor League Totals			.199	44	166	20	33	5	0	1	11	24	68	7	4	.309	.247

23 WILLIAMS JEREZ, LHP

BA GRADE
40 Risk: Medium

Born: May 16, 1992. **B-T:** L-L. **Ht.:** 6-4. **Wt.:** 200. **Drafted:** HS—Brooklyn, 2011 (2nd round). **Signed by:** Ray Fagnant (Red Sox).

TRACK RECORD: Falling out of playoff contention in 2018 allowed the Angels to get a lengthy look at Jerez, part of the trade that sent Ian Kinsler to Boston. A converted outfielder who is now five years into his pitching career, Jerez showed flashes of the potential that could lead to a matchup reliever role.

SCOUTING REPORT: Jerez has a heavy four-seam fastball that averaged 95 mph in the big leagues and touches 98 and a sharp slider that averaged 88 mph from the left side. He also has a split-finger fastball that has been effective against righthanders. To take the next step, he must continue to drive his pitches down in the zone consistently and hone his mechanics so his delivery doesn't get out of sync.

THE FUTURE: Jerez has been dominant at Triple-A, and he has the stuff to pitch in a big league bullpen. Whether he fixes his delivery to throw more strikes will determine how much he pitches there in 2019.

Year	Club (League)	Class	W	L	ERA	G	GS	CG	SV	IP	H	HR	BB	SO	K/9	WHIP	AVG
2016	Portland (EL)	AA	1	6	4.71	40	0	0	0	65	70	6	30	65	9.0	1.54	.282
2017	Portland (EL)	AA	2	0	3.33	29	0	0	4	51	50	3	17	47	8.2	1.31	.258
	Pawtucket (IL)	AAA	0	2	3.75	9	0	0	0	12	9	3	6	10	7.5	1.25	.209
2018	Pawtucket (IL)	AAA	2	1	3.63	34	0	0	5	52	48	6	24	69	11.9	1.38	.241
	Salt Lake (PCL)	AAA	0	1	17.18	4	0	0	1	4	8	0	2	5	12.3	2.73	.421
	Los Angeles (AL)	MAJ	0	0	6.00	17	0	0	0	15	17	3	8	15	9.0	1.67	.270
Major League Totals			0	0	6.00	17	0	0	0	15	17	3	8	15	9.0	1.67	.270
Minor League Totals			14	15	3.58	171	0	0	15	307	306	23	121	322	9.4	1.39	.260

24 AARON HERNANDEZ, RHP

BA GRADE
45 Risk: High

Born: Dec. 2, 1996. **B-T:** R-R. **Ht.:** 6-1. **Wt.:** 175. **Drafted:** Texas A&M-Corpus Christi, 2018 (3rd round). **Signed by:** Rudy Vasquez.

TRACK RECORD: Hernandez missed the 2017 season at Texas A&M Corpus-Christi for academic reasons but bounced back to have a strong 2018 season. Hernandez was one of 12 pitchers the Angels drafted and held back from pitching after signing, an approach influenced by the wave of pitching injuries that has plagued the organization over the past three years.

SCOUTING REPORT: Hernandez has a lively sinking fastball that sits around 92 mph and can run up to 95-96. He pitches across his body, helping to hide the ball from opposing hitters. Hernandez's main secondary is an 80-83 mph slider he has tightened up and throws for strikes, and he has flashed an above-average changeup as well. His up-tempo delivery and quick arm speed seem to match his fiery demeanor on the mound, although some see those traits and think he is best suited in the bullpen long-term.

THE FUTURE:. Hernandez spent last summer improving his strength and durability. He should reach low Class A Burlington and perhaps high Class A Inland Empire in 2019.

Year	Club (League)	Class	AVG	G	AB	R	H	2B	3B	HR	RBI	BB	SO	SB	CS	OBP	SLG
2018	Did not play																

25 LIVAN SOTO, SS/2B

BA GRADE
50 Risk: Extreme

Born: June 22, 2000. **B-T:** L-R. **Ht.:** 6-2. **Wt.:** 160. **Signed:** Venezuela, 2016. **Signed by:** Rolando Petit (Braves).

TRACK RECORD: The Angels signed Soto, one of the 12 Braves prospects declared free agents by MLB as punishment for the team violating international signing rules, in 2017. Soto is undersized and he has little power potential, but he quickly established himself as one of the best defensive infielders in the system.

SCOUTING REPORT: Soto has exceptional hand-eye coordination, good bat-to-ball skills and has shown a potential to hit for average. He changed his swing last season, but his flatter path to the ball wasn't as natural and generated no power. Plate discipline is a strength—he had as many walks as strikeouts in 2017. Soto's defensive instincts, along with his fast-twitch actions, good first step, quick hands and transfer, play at shortstop, but his arm is just average.

THE FUTURE: The Angels won't know what they have in Soto until he matures physically. Most scouts believe he might profile better as a second baseman, but some believe he can stick at shortstop because of his ability to compensate for his arm with good positioning, footwork and body control. He has a chance to see full-season ball in 2019.

Year	Club (League)	Class	AVG	G	AB	R	H	2B	3B	HR	RBI	BB	SO	SB	CS	OBP	SLG
2017	Braves (GCL)	R	.225	47	173	24	39	5	0	0	14	27	26	7	3	.332	.254
2018	Orem (PIO)	R	.291	44	172	31	50	10	0	0	11	24	24	9	3	.385	.349
Minor League Totals			.258	91	345	55	89	15	0	0	25	51	50	16	6	.358	.301

26 JOSE BRICENO, C

BA GRADE

40 Risk: Medium

Born: Sept. 19, 1992. **B-T:** R-R. **Ht.:** 6-1. **Wt.:** 210. **Signed:** Venezuela, 2009. **Signed by:** Francisco Cartaya/Ronaldo Fernandez (Rockies).

TRACK RECORD: Signed by the Rockies in 2009 and traded to the Braves for David Hale in Jan. 2015, Briceno joined Andrelton Simmons in the trade to the Angels in Nov. 2015. After quietly ascending as one of the top defensive catchers in the Angels system, Briceno made his big league debut in 2018.

SCOUTING REPORT: Briceno's defense is his calling card. He presents a strong target, is a willing blocker and shuts down running games. He has above-average arm strength with above-average accuracy, an efficient transfer and clean footwork. The result was 44 percent of attempted basestealers thrown out in his major league debut, compared to the average of 28 percent. Briceno packs impressive raw power to all fields and enough contact ability to get to it. He's a fringe-average hitter who doesn't walk much, but his power plays.

THE FUTURE: Briceno has all the traits of a defensive-oriented backup who plays in the majors for a long time. He's ready to serve in that role for the Angels in 2019.

Year	Club (League)	Class	AVG	G	AB	R	H	2B	3B	HR	RBI	BB	SO	SB	CS	OBP	SLG
2016	Inland Empire (CAL)	HiA	.240	33	125	10	30	6	0	1	11	9	28	1	1	.285	.312
	Arkansas (TL)	AA	.225	62	227	25	51	12	2	3	21	11	42	2	2	.259	.335
	Salt Lake (PCL)	AAA	.300	3	10	2	3	1	0	0	3	2	1	0	0	.417	.400
2017	Mobile (SL)	AA	.194	92	351	34	68	12	2	9	41	23	73	7	2	.242	.316
	Salt Lake (PCL)	AAA	.200	3	10	1	2	0	0	0	0	0	1	1	0	.200	.200
2018	Salt Lake (PCL)	AAA	.277	29	112	22	31	5	0	8	25	4	22	3	0	.297	.536
	Los Angeles (AL)	MAJ	.239	46	117	12	28	2	0	5	10	8	35	0	1	.299	.385
Major League Totals			.239	46	117	12	28	2	0	5	10	8	35	0	1	.299	.385
Minor League Totals			.241	562	2039	251	492	111	6	49	249	129	378	54	19	.291	.374

27 JAKE JEWELL, RHP

BA GRADE

40 Risk: Medium

Born: May 16, 1993. **B-T:** R-R. **Ht.:** 6-3. **Wt.:** 200. **Drafted:** Northeastern Oklahoma A&M JC, 2014 (5th round). **Signed by:** Drew Chadd.

TRACK RECORD: Jewell's climb through the minors appeared to have a happy ending when he earned his first callup last June. But in his third appearance, he suffered a fractured right fibula covering home on a wild pitch in Fenway Park and had season-ending surgery.

SCOUTING REPORT: Jewell's stuff played up and he developed more of an attacking mentality after he moved from the rotation to the bullpen last season. He combines a four-seam fastball that touches 97 mph and has a natural cut with a two-seam fastball he throws in the low-90s. He mostly works those two pitches, and occasionally mixes in an average 86-89 mph slider and a fringy changeup. Jewell struggles with a wandering arm slot and as a result has below-average control, but it's less of an issue in relief.

THE FUTURE: Jewell is expected to be ready for the start of spring training. It's possible he could find his way to the back of a bullpen if he throws more strikes, but he projects more as a middle or long reliever.

Year	Club (League)	Class	W	L	ERA	G	GS	CG	SV	IP	H	HR	BB	SO	K/9	WHIP	AVG
2016	Inland Empire (CAL)	HiA	2	15	6.31	28	27	0	0	137	191	10	65	104	6.8	1.87	.334
2017	Inland Empire (CAL)	HiA	0	1	2.25	3	3	0	0	16	11	1	3	15	8.4	0.88	.183
	Mobile (SL)	AA	7	8	4.84	24	23	1	0	125	136	14	41	81	5.8	1.42	.284
2018	Mobile (SL)	AA	1	0	2.08	7	0	0	2	13	15	1	2	11	7.6	1.31	.313
	Salt Lake (PCL)	AAA	2	4	3.60	19	0	0	3	25	23	2	17	24	8.6	1.60	.240
	Los Angeles (AL)	MAJ	0	1	9.00	3	0	0	0	2	2	0	1	1	4.5	1.50	.250
Major League Totals			0	1	9.00	3	0	0	0	2	2	0	1	1	4.5	1.50	.250
Minor League Totals			19	38	4.91	124	77	1	7	470	531	37	175	380	7.3	1.50	.289

28 JOSE ROJAS, 3B/1B

Born: Feb. 24, 1993. **B-T:** L-R. **Ht.:** 6-0. **Wt.:** 200. **Drafted:** Vanguard (Calif.), 2016 (36th round). **Signed by:** Ben Diggins.

BA GRADE
40 Risk: Medium

TRACK RECORD: Rojas has been the best of them and a Cinderella story. He was a California League All-Star in his first full season as a pro, then in 2017 hit .304 in Double-A and ascended to Triple-A.
SCOUTING REPORT: Rojas takes an advanced approach that produces some of the highest quality at-bats in the Angels system on a consistent basis. He has the ability to keep his barrel through the zone for line-drive contact or drop the head on pitches low and inside for long home runs to right. Rojas' best position at third base but he has enough athleticism to stand in at second base as needed.
THE FUTURE: Rojas doesn't have anything that will make him a starter in the big leagues, but as a lefthanded hitter who has multi-positional versatility, he may be able to carve out a reserve role.

Year	Club (League)	Class	AVG	G	AB	R	H	2B	3B	HR	RBI	BB	SO	SB	CS	OBP	SLG
2016	Orem (PIO)	R	.308	59	221	45	68	15	3	5	31	22	29	9	4	.372	.471
2017	Inland Empire (CAL)	HiA	.319	79	317	44	101	20	5	7	50	17	64	4	8	.355	.479
	Mobile (SL)	AA	.227	44	172	16	39	9	1	4	20	6	35	0	1	.259	.360
2018	Mobile (SL)	AA	.304	84	312	57	95	21	3	17	65	36	75	9	4	.381	.554
	Salt Lake (PCL)	AAA	.217	19	69	10	15	3	0	0	6	2	13	1	0	.233	.261
Minor League Totals			.291	285	1091	172	318	68	12	33	172	83	216	23	17	.344	.467

29 JOHN SWANDA, RHP

Born: March 18, 1999. **B-T:** R-R. **Ht.:** 6-2. **Wt.:** 185. **Drafted:** HS—Des Moines, 2017 (4th round). **Signed by:** Joel Murrie.

BA GRADE
50 Risk: Extreme

TRACK RECORD: Swanda played mostly shortstop in high school and didn't pitch much until about a month before the 2017 draft, but he is beginning to show why the Angels went well over slot to sign him as a pitcher. After he was arrested in the offseason for operating a vehicle under the influence and possession of a fake I.D., Swanda had what the Angels considered a productive 10 starts at Rookie-level Orem.
SCOUTING REPORT: Swanda's delivery is clean with a good, loose arm action and no glaring mechanical flaws. He throws a fastball between 89-92 mph and has good feel for a changeup and a slurve-like curve that. As a former infielder, he fields his position well. Swanda should gain more fastball velocity with physical maturity and strength and improve as he gains more seasoning on the mound.
THE FUTURE: The Angels are encouraged by the direction he is heading. He should be able to increase his workload at low Class A Burlington in 2019.

Year	Club (League)	Class	W	L	ERA	G	GS	CG	SV	IP	H	HR	BB	SO	K/9	WHIP	AVG
2017	Angels (AZL)	R	1	2	9.31	7	1	0	0	10	13	1	6	6	5.6	1.97	.333
2018	Orem (PIO)	R	0	4	4.50	10	10	0	0	30	37	4	7	26	7.8	1.47	.291
Minor League Totals			1	6	5.67	17	11	0	0	40	50	5	13	32	7.3	1.59	.301

30 BRENNON LUND, OF

Born: Nov. 27, 1994. **B-T:** L-R. **Ht.:** 5-10. **Wt.:** 185. **Drafted:** Brigham Young, 2016 (11th round). **Signed by:** Chad Hermansen.

BA GRADE
40 Risk: High

TRACK RECORD: Lund spent the entire 2018 season at Double-A Mobile, where he showed a little more power to the pull side, decent plate discipline and improved overall defense, especially in center field.
SCOUTING REPORT: Though he is a prototypical leadoff hitter with good hands and a good feel for the strike zone, Lund is athletic and strong for his size, which could portend more power. He's an above-average runner with a slightly below-average arm. The Angels worked with Lund defensively on pre-pitch preparation, positioning and thinking about plays before they happen. Lund got better jumps, his route efficiency improved, and he seemed much more aware of his surroundings in the outfield.
THE FUTURE: Lund could reach the big leagues if he adds some pop, minimizes his tendency to chase pitches and improves defensively in center field, but it will probably be as a reserve. He'll move to Triple-A in 2019 and is in position to see Anaheim at some point during the season.

Year	Club (League)	Class	AVG	G	AB	R	H	2B	3B	HR	RBI	BB	SO	SB	CS	OBP	SLG
2016	Orem (PIO)	R	.397	18	73	15	29	3	0	2	11	7	11	7	2	.463	.521
	Burlington (MWL)	LoA	.271	45	181	19	49	9	2	1	19	12	33	8	1	.316	.359
2017	Burlington (MWL)	LoA	.306	46	173	25	53	7	4	2	18	24	26	14	3	.400	.428
	Inland Empire (CAL)	HiA	.321	46	196	26	63	11	0	3	23	16	41	5	4	.385	.423
	Mobile (SL)	AA	.287	29	122	17	35	3	0	1	6	3	33	1	2	.310	.336
2018	Mobile (SL)	AA	.264	100	401	63	106	20	6	8	59	43	102	21	5	.343	.404
Minor League Totals			.292	284	1146	165	335	53	12	17	136	105	246	56	17	.359	.404

Los Angeles Dodgers

BY KYLE GLASER

The Dodgers remain the class of the National League West, as well as the NL as a whole. Climbing that final step is proving difficult.

The Dodgers won their sixth straight NL West title and reached the World Series for the second straight year in 2018. But once again they fell short of the elusive championship, losing to the Red Sox in five games.

Whereas in 2017 making the World Series was a grand accomplishment, expectations have now changed.

Falling from 104 wins in 2017 to 92 wins in 2018, and going from losing the World Series in seven games to losing it in five, feels like regression, and the fanbase's patience is wearing thin.

The Dodgers have now gone 30 years since their last World Series title, the franchise's longest championship drought since relocating to Los Angeles in 1958.

The good news is the Dodgers are in position to maintain their place as one of the NL's best for years to come. Whereas many teams age out by the time they've won six straight division titles, the Dodgers still boast a cavalcade of young stars with their best years ahead of them. Back-to-back Rookies of the Year Corey Seager and Cody Bellinger remain franchise cornerstones in their early 20s, although how Seager returns from his season-ending Tommy John surgery remains to be seen. Walker Buehler's rise gave the Dodgers a third straight year with a rookie sensation, as well as an heir apparent to Clayton Kershaw at the front of their rotation. Max Muncy followed Chris Taylor as the Dodgers' out-of-nowhere superstar, and both remain in their 20s. Joc Pederson, Kike Hernandez and Yasiel Puig remain comfortably under 30 as well. Julio Urias' return to health was a critical development, and he still will be just 22 on Opening Day.

The Dodgers shipped out a dozen prospects to acquire Manny Machado, Brian Dozier, David Freese, Ryan Madson and Dylan Floro during the year, but they had system depth to withstand out. A particularly productive 2016 draft yielded six of the Dodgers current top 10 prospects, and catcher Keibert Ruiz headlines a bevy of intriguing international signees.

And now the Dodgers have more ammunition to further add to their system. After spending nearly $90 million—including overage taxes—on their 2015 international class, the Dodgers were unable to sign anyone internationally for more than $300,000 in either 2016 or 2017. Those restrictions are now over, and free of the penalty the Dodgers signed the top Dominican prospect in

Max Muncy went from minor league free agent afterthought to 35-home run slugger.

PROJECTED 2022 LINEUP

Catcher	Keibert Ruiz (23)
First Base	Max Muncy (31)
Second Base	Gavin Lux (24)
Third Base	Will Smith (27)
Shortstop	Corey Seager (28)
Left Field	Joc Pederson (30)
Center Field	Cody Bellinger (26)
Right Field	Alex Verdugo (26)
No. 1 Starter	Clayton Kershaw (34)
No. 2 Starter	Walker Buehler (27)
No. 3 Starter	Julio Urias (25)
No. 4 Starter	Dustin May (24)
No. 5 Starter	Ross Stripling (32)
Closer	Dennis Santana (26)

the 2018 class in catcher Diego Cartaya.

With a core of both stars and complementary players still in their 20s and a well-rounded farm system below them, the Dodgers' reign atop the NL West is not in danger of ending anytime soon.

But winning the NL West, or the National League for that matter, is no longer a satisfactory result. Championships are the expectation in Los Angeles, particularly for a team with the payroll and star power the Dodgers possess.

The talent is there for the Dodgers to climb that final step, both next year and for years after. The only question now is if they can actually take it, and finally bring the Commissioner's Trophy back to Chavez Ravine.

DEPTH CHART

LOS ANGELES DODGERS

TOP 2019 ROOKIE: Dennis Santana, RHP. After an injury-shortened major league debut, the hard-throwing righthander is capable of boosting the Dodgers' rotation or bullpen as needed.
BREAKOUT PROSPECT: Zach Willeman, RHP. The big righthander returned from Tommy John surgery touching 100 mph while flashing two plus breaking balls.
SLEEPER: Deacon Liput, SS/2B. The 10th-round pick made a quick impression with his advanced batting skill and ability to play both middle infield positions.

SOURCE OF TOP 30 TALENT

Homegrown	30	Acquired	0
College	12	Trade	0
Junior college	1	Rule 5 draft	0
High school	6	Independent league	0
Nondrafted free agent	0	Free agent/waivers	0
International	11		

LF
Logan Landon
Zach Reks

CF
Jeren Kendall (16)
Brayan Morales
Tim Locastro

RF
Alex Verdugo (2)
DJ Peters (10)
Carlos Rincon (27)
Cody Thomas (30)

3B
Cristian Santana (13)
Miguel Vargas (19)
Matt Beaty (23)

SS
Gavin Lux (3)
Omar Estevez (24)
Jacob Amaya (28)
Ronny Brito
Errol Robinson

2B
Deacon Liput
Zach McKinstry
Devin Mann

1B
Edwin Rios (12)
Jared Walker

C
Keibert Ruiz (1)
Will Smith (5)
Diego Cartaya (11)
Connor Wong (15)
Kyle Farmer

LHP

LHSP	LHRP
Robinson Ortiz (21)	Caleb Ferguson (6)
John Rooney (25)	Bryan Warzek
Ben Holmes	Logan Salow
	Leo Crawford

RHP

RHSP	RHRP
Dustin May (4)	Yadier Alvarez (14)
Dennis Santana (7)	Josh Sborz (22)
Tony Gonsolin (8)	Jordan Sheffield
Mitchell White (9)	Stetson Allie
Michael Grove (17)	Andre Scrubb
Gerardo Carrillo (18)	Nolan Long
Zach Willeman (20)	Marshall Kasowski
Edwin Uceta (26)	Yaisel Sierra
Braydon Fisher (29)	Parker Curry
Andrew Sopko	Melvin Jimenez
Isaac Anderson	Shea Spitzbarth
Morgan Cooper	
Max Gamboa	

DRAFT ANALYSIS

2018

BEST PURE HITTER: 2B Devin Mann (5) takes a high-contact approach with a short, compact load and clean, flat swing that sprays the ball around to all fields. He hit .303 at Louisville and was the only position player the Dodgers drafted in their first six picks. Mann is plenty physical at 6-foot-3, 180 pounds, and the Dodgers think they can make some adjustments to help him tap into power.

BEST POWER HITTER: OF Niko Hulsizer (18) hit 44 home runs in three years at Morehead State and won the 2017 College Home Run Derby with 49 longballs at cavernous T.D. Ameritrade Park in Omaha. His toned body packs plus-plus raw power to all fields. 1B Meaux Landry (22) isn't far behind in terms of raw power.

FASTEST RUNNER: OF Aldrich De Jongh (17) is a legitimate 80 runner who gets to top speed quickly with twitchy quickness and an explosive first step.

BEST DEFENSIVE PLAYER: OF James Outman (7) is an all-around defensive standout with plus speed that reaches plus-plus underway, superb athletic instincts and a plus arm. He's exceptional in the corners and has a chance to plus defensively in center field.

BEST ATHLETE: Outman was an all-section middle linebacker in high school and routinely displays that same physical athleticism on the diamond.

BEST FASTBALL: RHP Michael Grove (2) was up to 96 mph with good carry through the upper third of the strike zone before Tommy John surgery wiped out his junior season at West Virginia. The Dodgers suspect he may throw even harder once he fully recovers.

BEST SECONDARY PITCH: LHP Bryan Warzek (6) has an 11-to-5, high-spin curveball that draws above-average grades. It plays up with deception out of his lower arm slot and a slight pause in his delivery. RHP Braydon Fisher (4) throws a mid-80s slider with three-quarters tilt and short break that flashes plus, but he doesn't yet have the physi-

TOP DRAFT PICKS OF THE DECADE

Year	Player, Pos.	2018 Org
2009	Aaron Miller, LHP (1st round supp)	Did not play
2010	Zach Lee, RHP	Rays
2011	Chris Reed, LHP	Atlantic League
2012	Corey Seager, 3B	Dodgers
2013	Chris Anderson, RHP	Did not play
2014	Grant Holmes, RHP	Athletics
2015	Walker Buehler, RHP	Dodgers
2016	Gavin Lux, SS	Dodgers
2017	Jeren Kendall, OF	Dodgers
2018	*J.T. Ginn, RHP	—

* Did not sign

cal strength to repeat it.

BEST PRO DEBUT: 2B/SS Deacon Liput (10) jumped straight to low Class A Great Lakes and hit .280/.322/.446 as the Loons leadoff hitter while ably playing both shortstop and second base. He further impressed with his leadership skills.

MOST INTRIGUING BACKGROUND: OF Jeremiah Vison (36) is 5-foot-4, 145 pounds. The tiny Golden West (Calif.) JC product is a plus-plus runner and a plus defender in center field.

CLOSEST TO THE MAJORS: LHP John Rooney (3) is a polished lefthander up to 94 mph with two average secondaries and one of the best pickoff moves evaluators can remember. He projects to move fast as a lefty with command and weapons.

BEST LATE-ROUND PICK: LHP Austin Drury (34) pitches aggressively with fastball up to 92 mph and an average curveball. He fell in the draft due to control issues as a starter at North Florida but moved to relief after signing and logged a 1.21 ERA with 28 strikeouts and six walks in 29.2 innings.

THE ONE WHO GOT AWAY: RHP J.T. Ginn (1) didn't sign as the 30th overall pick and went to Mississippi State. He should be one of the Bulldogs' top starters right away with a fastball up to 99 mph and a plus breaking ball. He will be a draft-eligible sophomore in 2020.

—KYLE GLASER

2017

A high strikeout rate has hampered OF Jeren Kendall (1) so far as a pro, but his upside remains significant. C Connor Wong (3) had a solid first full pro season. RHP Zach Pop (7) and Rylan Bannon (8) were used in the Manny Machado trade.

GRADE: C

2016

This class has produced impressive volume and upside. SS Gavin Lux (1) was named the team's minor leaguer of the year. He, C Will Smith (1), RHP Dustin May (3) and OF DJ Peters (4) have reached the upper levels of the system.

GRADE: A

2015

RHP Walker Buehler (1) finished third in NL Rookie of the Year voting and established himself as one of the Dodgers' top starters. OF Willie Calhoun (4), used in the Yu Darvish trade, is also a big leaguer, though still working to find a role in Texas.

GRADE: A

1 KEIBERT RUIZ, C

Born: July 20, 1998. **B-T:** B-R. **HT:** 6-0. **WT:** 200.
Signed: Venezuela, 2014.
Signed by: Francisco Cartaya/Pedro Avila.

JOHN WILLIAMSON

Ruiz mainly attracted teams with his defense as an amateur in Venezuela, training at the academy run by former major league shortstop Carlos Guillen. Almost immediately after signing with the Dodgers, Ruiz began holding his own against older players. At age 17 he moved to the Rookie-level Pioneer League and hit .354 as the league's youngest player. At 18 he jumped to full-season ball and hit .316 with an .813 OPS between low Class A and high Class A. And in his age-19 season, as the rare teenaged catcher in the upper levels, Ruiz had the lowest strikeout rate of any hitter in Double-A, hit a career-high with 12 home runs and ably handled Tulsa's high-octane pitching staff.

SCOUTING REPORT: Ruiz originally intrigued with his defense, but as he's progressed his offense stands out first and foremost. He is a gifted switch-hitter with excellent timing, bat speed and loose wrists that enable him to manipulate the barrel to all parts of the zone, giving him excellent plate coverage against all types of pitches. He has an aggressive approach and doesn't walk much, but he stays within the strike zone and rarely swings and misses. Ruiz puts together good at-bats from both sides of the plate, but he has faster hand speed and more natural lift in his lefthanded swing. Ruiz has progressively added strength and increased his home run total every season, now projecting for double-digit homers to go with a plus bat. Ruiz's defense lags behind his offense but is still advanced for his age and constantly improving. He shows good timing blocking balls, is an above-average—if sometimes inconsistent—receiver and has developed a knack for backpicking runners. He has an average, accurate arm that occasionally gets slowed down by footwork and transfer issues, but he made strides to clean those up and improved his caught stealing rate to a career-best 26 percent in 2018. Ruiz also became more confident handling a staff, from presenting gameplans to pitchers to knowing when to take mound visits.

THE FUTURE: Ruiz's success on both sides of the ball as a teenager in Double-A made him the top catching prospect in baseball for many evaluators. His potential as a switch-hitting, middle-of-the-order catcher has him positioned to be next in the long line of Dodgers great homegrown backstops.

BA GRADE	SCOUTING GRADES
60 Risk: High	Hit: 60. Power: 45. Run: 40. Field: 55. Arm: 50.

Projected future grades on 20-80 scouting scale.

TOP PROSPECTS OF THE DECADE

Year	Player, Pos.	2018 Org
2009	Andrew Lambo, OF	Did not play
2010	Dee Gordon, SS	Mariners
2011	Dee Gordon, SS	Mariners
2012	Zach Lee, RHP	Rays
2013	Hyun-Jin Ryu, LHP	Dodgers
2014	Joc Pederson, OF	Dodgers
2015	Corey Seager, SS	Dodgers
2016	Corey Seager, SS	Dodgers
2017	Cody Bellinger, 1B	Dodgers
2018	Walker Buehler, RHP	Dodgers

BEST TOOLS

Best Hitter for Average	Alex Verdugo
Best Power Hitter	D.J. Peters
Best Strike-Zone Discipline	Alex Verdugo
Fastest Baserunner	Brayan Morales
Best Athlete	Jeren Kendall
Best Fastball	Dustin May
Best Curveball	Tony Gonsolin
Best Slider	Mitchell White
Best Changeup	Tony Gonsolin
Best Control	Dustin May
Best Defensive Catcher	Will Smith
Best Defensive Infielder	Jacob Amaya
Best Infield Arm	Cristian Santana
Best Defensive Outfielder	Jeren Kendall
Best Outfield Arm	Alex Verdugo

Year	Club (League)	Class	AVG	G	AB	R	H	2B	3B	HR	RBI	BB	SO	SB	CS	OBP	SLG
2016	Dodgers (AZL)	R	.485	8	33	5	16	4	1	0	15	3	4	0	0	.513	.667
	Ogden (PIO)	R	.354	48	189	28	67	18	2	2	33	12	23	0	0	.393	.503
2017	Great Lakes (MWL)	LoA	.317	63	227	34	72	16	1	2	24	18	30	0	0	.372	.423
	R. Cucamonga (CAL)	HiA	.315	38	149	24	47	7	1	6	27	7	23	0	0	.344	.497
2018	Tulsa (TL)	AA	.268	101	377	44	101	14	0	12	47	26	33	0	1	.328	.401
Minor League Totals			.309	302	1125	149	348	67	6	23	165	74	128	4	3	.357	.441

2 ALEX VERDUGO, OF

Born: May 15, 1996. **B-T:** L-L. **HT:** 6-0. **WT:** 205. **Drafted:** HS—Tucson, 2014 (2nd round). **Signed by:** Dustin Yount.

TRACK RECORD: Verudgo rose quickly after the Dodgers drafted him 62nd overall in 2014 and signed him for $914,600. He represented Mexico in the World Baseball Classic at age 20, reached the majors by 21 and had a chance for a larger role in his age-22 season last year, but the Dodgers' outfield glut forced him back to Triple-A. Verdugo finished fifth in the Pacific Coast League with a .329 average, and hit .260 over three callups with the Dodgers.

SCOUTING REPORT: Verdugo is the purest hitter in the Dodgers system with a simple, balanced swing. He generates hard line drives to all fields and is extremely patient, recording nearly as many walks (86) as strikeouts (97) over the last two years. Verdugo's average home run power is mostly to his pull side, but he can drive the ball hard the other way too. Verdugo stays dialed in at the plate, but an indifferent attitude affects the rest of his game. He has average speed and gets good jumps in right field when he's focused, but he often isn't and lets balls drop that shouldn't. His slow motor also shows up on the bases, frustrating teammates and coaches alike.

BA GRADE
55 Risk: Medium
Hit: 60. **Power:** 50.
Run: 50. **Field:** 50.
Arm: 60

THE FUTURE: Verdugo has the potential to be high-average, moderate power outfielder like Nick Markakis, but only if he improves his effort. He'll try to secure regular at-bats with the Dodgers in 2019.

Year	Club (League)	Class	AVG	G	AB	R	H	2B	3B	HR	RBI	BB	SO	SB	CS	OBP	SLG
2016	Tulsa (TL)	AA	.273	126	477	58	130	23	1	13	63	44	67	2	6	.336	.407
2017	Oklahoma City (PCL)	AAA	.314	117	433	67	136	27	4	6	62	52	50	9	3	.389	.436
	Los Angeles (NL)	MAJ	.174	15	23	1	4	0	0	1	1	2	4	0	1	.240	.304
2018	Oklahoma City (PCL)	AAA	.329	91	343	44	113	19	0	10	44	34	47	8	5	.391	.472
	Los Angeles (NL)	MAJ	.260	37	77	11	20	6	0	1	4	8	14	0	0	.329	.377
Major League Totals			.240	52	100	12	24	6	0	2	5	10	18	0	1	.309	.360
Minor League Totals			.309	512	1955	270	605	116	12	41	271	171	247	44	16	.367	.444

3 GAVIN LUX, SS/2B

Born: Nov. 23, 1997. **B-T:** L-R. **HT:** 6-2. **WT:** 190. **Drafted:** HS—Kenosha, Wis., 2016 (1st round). **Signed by:** Trey Magnuson.

TRACK RECORD: When the Dodgers drafted Lux 20th overall in 2016, he was a skinny teenager with athleticism and instincts—his uncle Augie Schmidt was the No. 2 pick in 1982—but was short on physicality. After a middling first full season, Lux bulked up and broke out in 2018. Bigger, stronger and faster, Lux led all full-season minor league shortstops in batting average and slugging percentage as he surged from high Class A to Double-A, winning Dodgers minor league player of the year.

SCOUTING REPORT: Lux caught up to velocity and recognized pitches even when he struggled, and his added strength with a swing adjustment unlocked an above-average hitter with growing power. Lux has a rhythmic, athletic setup that allows him to fire his barrel through the zone, and his path adjustment to get on plane resulted in significantly more hard contact in the air. Lux mostly pulls the ball on a line, but can elevate for home runs to tease average power. Lux stayed limber as he got stronger and remains an above-average runner with plus baserunning instincts. He has the range, hands, athleticism and above-average arm strength for shortstop, but accuracy issues have him largely projected to second base

ZACHARY LACEY/FOUR SEAM IMAGES

BA GRADE
55 Risk: High
Hit: 55. **Power:** 50.
Run: 55. **Field:** 55.
Arm: 55

THE FUTURE: Lux has the bat to profile at either middle infield position, likely as a No. 2-type hitter with a lot of doubles. He'll see Triple-A Oklahoma City in 2018.

Year	Club (League)	Class	AVG	G	AB	R	H	2B	3B	HR	RBI	BB	SO	SB	CS	OBP	SLG
2016	Dodgers (AZL)	R	.281	48	192	34	54	10	5	0	18	25	43	1	0	.365	.385
	Ogden (PIO)	R	.387	8	31	7	12	3	0	0	3	3	8	1	0	.441	.484
2017	Great Lakes (MWL)	LoA	.244	111	434	68	106	14	8	7	39	56	88	27	10	.331	.362
2018	R. Cucamonga (CAL)	HiA	.324	88	358	64	116	23	7	11	48	43	68	11	7	.396	.520
	Tulsa (TL)	AA	.324	28	105	21	34	4	1	4	9	14	20	2	2	.408	.495
Minor League Totals			.288	283	1120	194	322	54	21	22	117	141	227	42	19	.368	.432

4 DUSTIN MAY, RHP

Born: Sept. 6, 1997. **B-T:** R-R. **HT:** 6-6. **WT:** 180. **Drafted:** HS—Justin, Texas, 2016 (3rd round). **Signed by:** Josh Herzenberg.

TRACK RECORD: A string-bean skinny high schooler with bushy red hair, May sat in the low 90s when the Dodgers drafted him in the third round in 2016 and signed him for $997,500. After two years of growth and patience, May's fastball velocity jumped from 89-92 mph to 93-96 mph in 2018 and sent him skyrocketing. He cruised through high Class A up to Double-A as a 20-year-old, capping his season with a win in the clinching game of the Texas League championship series.

SCOUTING REPORT: May's ability to command his fastball and pitch downhill made his heater a weapon even at lower velocities. Now with his velocity bump, it's a true plus pitch with power sink. May used his fastball about 55 percent of the time early in the season, but after bumping that usage to around 70 percent in mid-June, he took off. May's power curveball and cutter each flash above-average but aren't consistent because they're relatively new to his arsenal. His low 80s power curve replaced his slider, and his cutter became his go-to pitch for lefties after his firm, below-average changeup stalled. May is the rare long-limbed pitcher with plus control, pounding the zone and limiting his walks at every level.

THE FUTURE: May has size, velocity, control and performance all on his side. If he improves his secondaries, he can be a mid-rotation starter or better.

BA GRADE

55 Risk: High

Fastball: 60.
Curve: 55. Cutter: 50.
Change: 40. CTL: 60

Year	Club (League)	Class	W	L	ERA	G	GS	CG	SV	IP	H	HR	BB	SO	K/9	WHIP	AVG
2016	Dodgers (AZL)	R	0	1	3.86	10	6	0	1	30	37	0	4	34	10.1	1.35	.291
2017	Great Lakes (MWL)	LoA	9	6	3.88	23	23	0	0	123	121	8	26	113	8.3	1.20	.250
	R. Cucamonga (CAL)	HiA	0	0	0.82	2	1	0	0	11	6	0	1	15	12.3	0.64	.150
2018	R. Cucamonga (CAL)	HiA	7	3	3.29	17	17	0	0	98	91	9	17	94	8.6	1.10	.241
	Tulsa (TL)	AA	2	2	3.67	6	6	0	0	34	27	0	12	28	7.3	1.14	.209
Minor League Totals			18	12	3.55	58	53	0	1	297	282	17	60	284	8.6	1.15	.243

5 WILL SMITH, C/3B

Born: March 28, 1995. **B-T:** R-R. **HT:** 6-0. **WT:** 195. **Drafted:** Louisville, 2016 (1st round). **Signed by:** Marty Lamb.

TRACK RECORD: An infielder by trade, Smith impressed with his ability to catch Kyle Funkhouser, Zack Burdi and other triple-digit flamethrowers at Louisville and signed with the Dodgers for $1,772,500 as the 32nd overall pick in 2016. He immediately showed the same impressive catching ability as a pro, guiding Walker Buehler, Yadier Alvarez, Dennis Santana and other high-octane arms through the Dodgers system. Despite missing a month with a deep thumb bone bruise, Smith hit a career-high 20 home runs between Double-A and Triple-A in 2018, all while splitting his time between catcher (49 games) and third base (43) so fellow catching prospect Keibert Ruiz could also get reps behind the plate.

SCOUTING REPORT: Smith's best asset is his athleticism. He has quick feet, soft hands and an above-average arm he can get to from multiple angles, making him a plus defensive catcher and above-average defender at third base. Smith was a contact hitter in college, but the Dodgers reworked his swing to generate more loft. An adjustment to get ready a tick earlier revealed above-average power in 2018, although his uphill swing yields more swings and misses than expected given his solid bat speed, hands, direction and approach and drains his ability to hit for average.

THE FUTURE: The Dodgers brought Smith to Los Angeles at the end of 2018 to observe how big leaguer catchers prepare. His ML debut is on the horizon in 2019.

BA GRADE

50 Risk: Medium

Hit: 45. Power: 55.
Run: 55. Field: 60.
Arm: 55.

Year	Club (League)	Class	AVG	G	AB	R	H	2B	3B	HR	RBI	BB	SO	SB	CS	OBP	SLG
2016	Ogden (PIO)	R	.321	7	28	4	9	0	0	1	5	4	1	0	0	.394	.429
	Great Lakes (MWL)	LoA	.256	23	82	12	21	1	0	1	7	11	18	2	1	.371	.305
	R. Cucamonga (CAL)	HiA	.216	25	97	13	21	4	0	2	12	14	31	1	0	.330	.320
2017	R. Cucamonga (CAL)	HiA	.232	72	250	38	58	15	3	11	43	37	71	6	2	.355	.448
	Tulsa (TL)	AA	.000	1	1	0	0	0	0	0	0	0	1	1	0	.667	.000
2018	Tulsa (TL)	AA	.264	73	265	48	70	14	0	19	53	36	75	4	0	.358	.532
	Oklahoma City (PCL)	AAA	.138	25	87	9	12	4	0	1	6	7	37	1	0	.206	.218
Minor League Totals			.236	226	810	124	191	38	3	35	126	109	234	15	3	.342	.420

6 CALEB FERGUSON, LHP

Born: July 2, 1996. **B-T:** L-L. **HT:** 6-3. **WT:** 215. **Drafted:** HS—West Jefferson, Ohio, 2014 (38th round). **Signed by:** Marty Lamb.

TRACK RECORD: Ferguson had Tommy John surgery his senior year of high school, but the Dodgers gave him $100,000 to sign as a 38th-rounder even with the injury. After rehab and three years of careful workload management, the Dodgers turned Ferguson loose in 2017, and he went out and won the California League ERA title. He followed with 10 dominant starts at Double-A and Triple-A to open 2018 and reached the majors in June.

SCOUTING REPORT: Previously able to touch 94 mph only in his first inning before dropping to 89-92, Ferguson improved his nutrition and fitness in 2018 and better sustained his velocity. With a slimmer and stronger body, his fastball is now sits 93-95 mph and touches 97 in relief, and he holds it over multiple innings. His main secondary is an above-average upper 70s curveball with 12-to-6 bite that he controls better than his fastball. Ferguson's fringy changeup is raw and rarely used, but his fastball-curveball is combo potent enough he still had reverse-splits, posting better numbers against righties (.661 OPS) than lefties (.733).

THE FUTURE: Ferguson has already shown himself to be a relief in the majors. Depending on the Dodgers' needs and if he's given the chance to develop his third pitch, he could still grow into a rotation piece.

BA GRADE
45 Risk: Low
Fastball: 60.
Curveball: 55.
Change: 45. CTL: 50

Year	Club (League)	Class	W	L	ERA	G	GS	CG	SV	IP	H	HR	BB	SO	K/9	WHIP	AVG
2016	Dodgers (AZL)	R	1	0	1.50	2	0	0	0	6	4	0	0	11	16.5	0.67	.167
	Ogden (PIO)	R	1	0	0.90	2	2	0	0	10	4	0	2	11	9.9	0.60	.114
	Great Lakes (MWL)	LoA	1	4	2.68	10	10	0	0	50	49	3	3	41	7.3	1.03	.255
2017	R. Cucamonga (CAL)	HiA	9	4	2.87	25	24	0	0	122	113	6	55	140	10.3	1.37	.246
2018	Tulsa (TL)	AA	3	0	1.38	8	8	0	0	39	31	2	10	40	9.2	1.05	.217
	Oklahoma City (PCL)	AAA	0	0	2.25	2	2	0	0	8	6	0	7	12	13.5	1.63	.194
	Los Angeles (NL)	MAJ	7	2	3.49	29	3	0	2	49	43	8	12	59	10.8	1.12	.230
Major League Totals			7	2	3.49	29	3	0	2	49	43	8	12	59	10.8	1.12	.230
Minor League Totals			15	11	2.80	63	50	0	1	250	224	11	98	271	9.7	1.29	.238

7 DENNIS SANTANA, RHP

Born: April 12, 1996. **B-T:** R-R. **HT:** 6-2. **WT:** 160. **Signed:** Dominican Republic, 2012. **Signed by:** Bob Engle/Patrick Guerrero/Elvio Jimenez.

TRACK RECORD: Santana, whose basketball-loving father named him after Dennis Rodman, signed with the Dodgers as a shortstop for $170,000 but converted to pitching after his first season. The lanky righthander took to pitching quickly, earning all-star honors in the Midwest League in 2016 and California League in 2017 before shooting through Double-A and Triple-A up to the majors in 2018. Santana earned the win his major league debut on June 1 and was set to make his first start on June 7, but was scratched with a strained rotator cuff and missed the rest of the season.

SCOUTING REPORT: The long-limbed Santana whips his arm around his body out of a low slot to create a potent combination of deception, velocity and movement. His fastball sits 93-95 mph and touches 97 with significant sink and run, handcuffing righthanded batters and occasionally busting his catcher's thumb. It's a plus offering, but its premium movement also makes the pitch difficult to command. Santana's above-average 82-85 mph slider is effective against righties but runs into the barrel against lefties, so the continued improvement of his 85-87 mph changeup will be key. It flashes average and Santana is confident throwing it.

THE FUTURE: Santana's has the stuff and track record to start, but his arm slot and resulting suspect command have most evaluators preferring him in the bullpen, where he has closer upside.

BA GRADE
50 Risk: Medium
Fastball: 60.
Slider: 55.
Change: 50. CTL: 50.

Year	Club (League)	Class	W	L	ERA	G	GS	CG	SV	IP	H	HR	BB	SO	K/9	WHIP	AVG
2016	Great Lakes (MWL)	LoA	5	9	3.07	25	14	0	0	111	84	2	56	124	10.0	1.26	.209
2017	R. Cucamonga (CAL)	HiA	5	6	3.57	17	14	0	0	86	87	5	22	92	9.7	1.27	.262
	Tulsa (TL)	AA	3	1	5.51	7	7	0	0	33	32	2	23	37	10.2	1.68	.256
2018	Tulsa (TL)	AA	0	2	2.56	8	8	0	0	39	26	3	14	51	11.9	1.03	.183
	Oklahoma City (PCL)	AAA	1	1	2.45	2	2	0	0	11	10	0	2	14	11.5	1.09	.238
	Los Angeles (NL)	MAJ	1	0	12.27	1	0	0	0	4	6	0	1	4	9.8	1.91	.375
Major League Totals			1	0	12.27	1	0	0	0	4	6	0	1	4	9.8	1.91	.375
Minor League Totals			18	25	3.59	92	57	1	4	361	306	17	170	408	10.2	1.32	.226

8 TONY GONSOLIN, RHP

Born: May 14, 1994. **B-T:** R-R. **HT:** 6-2. **WT:** 180. **Drafted:** St. Mary's, 2016 (9th round). **Signed by:** Tom Kunis.

TRACK RECORD: Gonsolin played both ways at St. Mary's as the Gaels starting right fielder and top reliever/spot starter. The Dodgers, intrigued by his fastball up to 95 mph, drafted Gonsolin in the ninth round in 2016 and signed him for $2,500 with the idea his velocity would jump if he focused solely on pitching. That hunch proved correct. Gonsolin sat in the low 90s when he signed, humped up to the mid-90s midway through his first full season and was touching 99 mph by the end of the year. He asked the Dodgers for the chance to start in 2018 and took advantage when they granted his request, leading the system in ERA (2.60) and strikeouts (155) as he rose to Double-A.

SCOUTING REPORT: Gonsolin flashes three above-average or better pitches as a starter, though not always at the same time. His fastball sits 94-96 mph with ride and he holds that velocity into the late innings. His 78-81 mph curveball with big depth was voted the best breaking pitch in the California League, and his diving 85-88 mph split-change increasingly became a favored option. He also flashes an average upper-80s short slider. Gonsolin mixes well and throws all his pitches for strikes, although his command is a bit scattered. He remains a dangerous hitter owing to his two-way past.

THE FUTURE: Gonsolin's four-pitch mix has him firmly in the Dodgers rotation plans. He'll see Triple-A in 2019.

BA GRADE

50 Risk: High

Fastball: 60.
Cuve: 55. Slider: 50.
Change: 55. CTL: 50

Year	Club (League)	Class	W	L	ERA	G	GS	CG	SV	IP	H	HR	BB	SO	K/9	WHIP	AVG
2016	Ogden (PIO)	R	1	0	2.60	10	0	0	2	17	12	1	5	15	7.8	0.98	.200
	Great Lakes (MWL)	LoA	0	2	5.27	9	0	0	2	14	17	0	3	10	6.6	1.46	.309
2017	Great Lakes (MWL)	LoA	0	1	3.38	3	0	0	1	8	8	2	0	12	13.5	1.00	.242
	R. Cucamonga (CAL)	HiA	7	5	3.92	39	0	0	5	62	61	5	18	73	10.6	1.27	.254
2018	R. Cucamonga (CAL)	HiA	4	2	2.69	17	17	0	0	84	72	5	26	106	11.4	1.17	.227
	Tulsa (TL)	AA	6	0	2.44	9	9	0	0	44	32	3	16	49	9.9	1.08	.203
Minor League Totals			18	10	3.14	87	26	0	10	229	202	16	68	265	10.4	1.18	.234

9 MITCHELL WHITE, RHP

Born: Dec. 28, 1994. **B-T:** R-R. **HT:** 6-4. **WT:** 207. **Drafted:** Santa Clara, 2016 (2nd round). **Signed by:** Tom Kunis.

TRACK RECORD: White's career has been a frustrating tale of success interrupted by injury. He had Tommy John surgery right before college but recovered to emerge as Santa Clara's ace as redshirt sophomore and be drafted 65th overall. In his first full season he posted a 2.93 ERA while advancing to Double-A but also missed six weeks with a broken toe. In 2018 he missed the first month of the season due to general soreness and struggled to find a rhythm most of the year before finishing with a 3.00 ERA over his final eight starts.

SCOUTING REPORT: White has plus stuff at his best but is woefully inconsistent. Sometimes he'll work 94-97 mph, others he'll be 90-93, and most often he's 92-95. White has a fluid arm action but crosses his body and loses his direction to the plate, resulting in his stuff playing down and an inability to locate to his armside. Tulsa pitching coach Dave Borkowski made late-season tweaks to liven White's backside, yielding some improvement. White's short, tight upper 80s slider is his most consistent pitch and shows plus at its best. His 12-to-6 curveball flashes above-average and his changeup average, but neither are consistent.

THE FUTURE: White looks like a potential frontline starter at his best but struggles to sustain it. Maintaining his health and refined delivery will be key in 2019.

BA GRADE

55 Risk: Very High

Fastball: 55.
Curve: 50. Slider: 60.
Change: 45. CTL: 50

Year	Club (League)	Class	W	L	ERA	G	GS	CG	SV	IP	H	HR	BB	SO	K/9	WHIP	AVG
2016	Dodgers (AZL)	R	0	0	0.00	2	2	0	0	4	3	0	0	8	18.0	0.75	.200
	Great Lakes (MWL)	LoA	0	0	0.00	8	4	0	0	16	3	0	6	20	11.3	0.56	.058
	R. Cucamonga (CAL)	HiA	1	0	0.00	1	0	0	0	2	1	0	0	2	9.0	0.50	.167
2017	R. Cucamonga (CAL)	HiA	2	1	3.72	9	9	0	0	39	26	0	16	49	11.4	1.09	.187
	Dodgers (AZL)	R	0	0	0.00	3	3	0	0	7	2	0	2	8	10.3	0.57	.091
	Tulsa (TL)	AA	1	1	2.57	7	7	0	0	28	17	2	13	31	10.0	1.07	.168
2018	Tulsa (TL)	AA	6	7	4.53	22	22	0	0	105	114	12	34	88	7.5	1.41	.273
Minor League Totals			10	9	3.45	52	47	0	0	201	166	14	71	206	9.2	1.18	.220

10 DJ PETERS, OF

Born: Dec. 12, 1995. **B-T:** R-R. **HT:** 6-6. **WT:** 225. **Drafted:** Western
Nevada JC, 2016 (4th round). **Signed by:** Tom Kunis.

BA GRADE

50 Risk: High

Hit: 40. Power: 60.
Run: 50. Field: 50.
Arm: 55.

TRACK RECORD: Muscular and massive at 6-foot-6, 225 pounds, Peters set
Western Nevada JC's single-season home run record in 2016 and signed with
the Dodgers for $247,500 as a fourth-round pick. Playing for the organization
he grew up rooting for in L.A. suburb Glendora, Peters led the Pioneer League
in total bases in his pro debut, won California League MVP his first full season
and led the Double-A Texas League with 29 home runs in 2018, although that
came with league-high 192 strikeouts.
SCOUTING REPORT: Peters' carrying tool is his enormous raw power, which
some scouts grade an 80. With a chiseled core and long limbs, Peters creates
prodigious leverage and demolishes anything left over the plate, frequently
clearing 400 feet to all fields. Peters long arms leave him vulnerable to velocity inside however, and he led both the California (189) and Texas leagues in
strikeouts despite good strike-zone discipline because he swings and misses in
the zone so much. Peters is tremendously athletic for his size and actually a serviceable center fielder with
average speed and long strides that allow him to cover enough ground. His above-average arm strength
helps him profile in right, although accuracy is an issue.
THE FUTURE: Peters' strikeout rate is alarming, but the hope is he can get to his power enough to make
an impact. He'll move to Triple-A in 2019.

Year	Club (League)	Class	AVG	G	AB	R	H	2B	3B	HR	RBI	BB	SO	SB	CS	OBP	SLG
2016	Ogden (PIO)	R	.351	66	262	63	92	24	3	13	48	35	66	5	3	.437	.615
2017	R. Cucamonga (CAL)	HiA	.276	132	504	91	139	29	5	27	82	64	189	3	3	.372	.514
2018	Tulsa (TL)	AA	.236	132	491	79	116	23	3	29	60	45	192	1	2	.320	.473
Minor League Totals			.276	330	1257	233	347	76	11	69	190	144	447	9	8	.366	.519

11 DIEGO CARTAYA, C

BA GRADE

55 Risk: Extreme

Born: Sept. 7, 2001. **B-T:** R-R. **HT:** 6-2. **WT:** 199. **Signed:** Venezuela, 2018.
Signed by: Luis Marquez/Roman Barinas/Cliff Nuiter/Jean Castro.
TRACK RECORD: Cartaya ranked as the No. 3 prospect in the 2018 international class after a decorated
amateur career, headlined by representing Venezuela at international tournaments since he was 10.The
Dodgers locked onto Cartaya early and signed him for $2.5 million on the first day of the signing period.
SCOUTING REPORT: The 17-year-old Cartaya is beyond his years in terms of his baseball IQ and feel
for the game. He is a polished hitter with a short, quick swing that drives the ball to all fields and has a
sharp understanding of the strike zone. He recognizes pitches, rarely chases and overall has the traits of a
potential plus hitter with a high on-base percentage. His power is mostly to the gaps now, but he could
grow into average home run pop with physical maturity. Defensively, Cartaya is a smooth, athletic receiver
with a plus arm and quick exchange, and he shows solid flexibility and agility in blocking balls.
THE FUTURE: Cartaya shows all the promising traits of a well-rounded catcher, but the journey for teen-
age catchers is long and rife with potential pratfalls. He'll get his first taste of pro ball in 2018.

Year	Club (League)	Class	AVG	G	AB	R	H	2B	3B	HR	RBI	BB	SO	SB	CS	OBP	SLG
2018	Did not play—Signed 2019 contract																

12 EDWIN RIOS, 1B/3B

BA GRADE

45 Risk: Medium

Born: April 21, 1994. **B-T:** L-R. **HT:** 6-3. **WT:** 220. **Drafted:** Florida
International, 2015 (6th round). **Signed by:** Adrian Casanova.
TRACK RECORD: Rios finished second in the nation with 18 home runs his junior year at Florida
International and the Dodgers drafted him in the sixth round. He's raked ever since entering pro ball,
piecing together a career .302/.351/.528 line with 64 homers in just under three seasons' worth of games.
Rios was in line for his major league debut in 2018, but a strained oblique and subsequent hamstring
injury limited him to 88 games at Triple-A.
SCOUTING REPORT: Rios is a 6-foot-3, 220-pound lefthanded masher with plus power generated by fast
hands and excellent timing. He gets to his home run power both to the opposite field and to his pull side,
and hits both righties (.309 in 2018) and lefties (.291). Rios rarely walks and his swing can get a little
long, but he has hit for average at every level. Rios focused on improving his defense in 2018 and became
average at first base and playable at third base, as well surprisingly decent in left field. He's a below-average

runner but has good short-area quickness and reaction times. His above-average arm plays best in the infield with a quick release.

THE FUTURE: With Max Muncy and Cody Bellinger at first base, Rios is going to have to continue improving his defense at third base and left field to get into the Dodgers lineup. Otherwise, his bat makes him an interesting trade candidate.

Year	Club (League)	Class	AVG	G	AB	R	H	2B	3B	HR	RBI	BB	SO	SB	CS	OBP	SLG
2016	Great Lakes (MWL)	LoA	.252	33	119	17	30	8	1	6	13	8	44	3	1	.305	.487
	R. Cucamonga (CAL)	HiA	.367	42	177	37	65	11	1	16	46	8	35	0	0	.394	.712
	Tulsa (TL)	AA	.254	33	122	14	31	7	0	5	17	8	31	0	0	.304	.434
2017	Tulsa (TL)	AA	.317	77	306	47	97	21	0	15	62	17	69	1	1	.358	.533
	Oklahoma City (PCL)	AAA	.296	51	169	23	50	13	0	9	29	18	42	0	1	.368	.533
2018	Oklahoma City (PCL)	AAA	.304	88	309	45	94	25	0	10	55	23	110	0	1	.355	.482
Minor League Totals			.302	346	1277	192	386	92	2	64	235	89	361	4	5	.351	.528

13 CRISTIAN SANTANA, 3B

BA GRADE

50 Risk: High

Born: Feb. 24, 1997. **B-T:** R-R. **HT:** 6-2. **WT:** 175. **Signed:** Dominican Republic, 2014. **Signed by:** Bob Engle/Patrick Guerrero/Franklin Taveras.

TRACK RECORD: Santana signed for $50,000 in 2013 and largely stayed under the radar until a breakout 2017. Facing skepticism he could repeat it, Santana went to high Class A Rancho Cucamonga in 2018 and finished tied for the California League lead in home runs (24), led the league in RBIs (109) and was named postseason MVP after batting .308 with a 1.154 OPS to lead the Quakes to the California League championship.

SCOUTING REPORT: Santana is a physical, explosive hitter who punishes fastballs. His physicality and bat speed to produce plus power to all fields, sending balls over scoreboards in left field and out over deep gaps in right-center. Santana crushes the hard stuff, but he is very aggressive and extremely poor at recognizing breaking balls, fishing below the zone and swinging and missing wildly. Santana's is a plus defender who makes incredible reaction plays at third base, although his mobility on the move needs to improve. His plus-plus arm is the best in the Dodgers system.

THE FUTURE: Santana's power, defense and ability to hit a fastball give him the solid foundation of an everyday player. Whether he improves his breaking ball recognition will determine if he gets there.

Year	Club (League)	Class	AVG	G	AB	R	H	2B	3B	HR	RBI	BB	SO	SB	CS	OBP	SLG
2016	Dodgers (AZL)	R	.256	42	172	26	44	6	2	8	24	5	46	0	1	.278	.453
2017	Ogden (PIO)	R	.537	10	41	18	22	2	1	5	16	6	6	0	0	.583	1.000
	Great Lakes (MWL)	LoA	.322	44	174	18	56	9	0	5	25	5	42	0	1	.339	.460
2018	R. Cucamonga (CAL)	HiA	.274	131	548	75	150	23	0	24	109	20	143	2	2	.302	.447
Minor League Totals			.280	324	1270	174	356	60	4	45	203	58	301	7	12	.313	.440

14 YADIER ALVAREZ, RHP

BA GRADE

50 Risk: Extreme

Born: Dec. 28, 1994. **B-T:** R-R. **HT:** 6-3. **WT:** 175. **Signed:** Cuba, 2015. **Signed by:** Miguel Tosar/Bob Engle/Patrick Guerrero.

TRACK RECORD: The Dodger stunned the industry when they signed Alvarez for $16 million in 2015 despite the fact he failed to make Cuba's junior national team because he was so wild. After teasing progress in his 2016 debut, Alvarez fell back into his wild ways in 2017 and melted down at Double-A Tulsa in 2018. He missed the first three months with a groin strain, had nearly as many walks (43) as strikeouts (52) in 48.1 innings after he returned, and reportedly left the team briefly in September after a disagreement with management, although the Dodgers dispute the details of that account.

SCOUTING REPORT: Alvarez's flaws are tolerated because he tantalizes with an easy 95-99 mph fastball. He generates plus arm speed and is hard to pick up, helping his fastball play despite the fact it's often left over the plate. Both his upper 80s slider and 12-to-6 curveball flash above-average-to-plus, but he has no control of either of them. Alvarez's control is well below-average and results in frequent non-competitive pitches, although a move to the stretch full-time late in the year yielded improvement.

THE FUTURE: Alvarez flashes moments of a power fastball and two plus breaking balls, and that's what evaluators hold onto. He'll try to show he's improved and matured in 2019.

Year	Club (League)	Class	W	L	ERA	G	GS	CG	SV	IP	H	HR	BB	SO	K/9	WHIP	AVG
2016	Dodgers (AZL)	R	1	1	1.80	5	5	0	0	20	9	0	10	26	11.7	0.95	.127
	Great Lakes (MWL)	LoA	3	2	2.29	9	9	0	0	39	31	1	11	55	12.6	1.07	.214
2017	R. Cucamonga (CAL)	HiA	2	4	5.31	14	11	0	1	59	61	3	25	61	9.3	1.45	.263
	Tulsa (TL)	AA	2	2	3.55	7	7	0	0	33	29	1	25	36	9.8	1.64	.234
2018	Dodgers (AZL)	R	0	0	1.29	2	2	0	0	7	5	0	1	10	12.9	0.86	.208
	Tulsa (TL)	AA	1	2	4.66	17	8	0	1	48	37	2	43	52	9.7	1.66	.211
Minor League Totals			9	11	3.83	54	42	0	2	207	172	7	115	240	10.4	1.39	.223

15 CONNOR WONG, C

Born: May 9, 1996. **B-T:** R-R. **HT:** 6-1. **WT:** 181. **Drafted:** Houston, 2017 (3rd round). **Signed by:** Clint Bowers.

BA GRADE
45 Risk: High

TRACK RECORD: Wong is the latest of the infielders-turned-catchers the Dodgers love, following Kyle Farmer, Austin Barnes and Will Smith. Wong played shortstop his freshman year at Houston before moving to catcher and hit at both spots, leading the Dodgers to draft him in the third round in 2017. Wong made a strong impression in his first full season, finishing in the top 10 in the California League in home runs (19) and OPS (.831) while providing a steady presence behind the plate to lead high Class A Rancho Cucamonga to the championship.

SCOUTING REPORT: Wong is slight physically but makes up for it with his athleticism and preparation. He is a studious observer who absorbs copious amounts of data on hitters to help his pitchers. On the field, Wong is an above-average athlete who receives and throws well with an average arm. His lack of experience catching shows in blocking sometimes, particularly to his right. As a hitter, Wong is aggressive and jumps on first-pitch fastballs, but he struggled after pitchers adjusted and started him with breaking balls, resulting in a 32 percent strikeout rate. He has the average power to drive home runs out to left field when he connects.

THE FUTURE: Wong's athleticism and intangibles have evaluators liking him as a potential backup catcher. He'll try to show he's more at Double-A Tulsa in 2019.

Year	Club (League)	Class	AVG	G	AB	R	H	2B	3B	HR	RBI	BB	SO	SB	CS	OBP	SLG
2017	Dodgers (AZL)	R	.000	1	1	0	0	0	0	0	0	0	1	0	0	.000	.000
	Great Lakes (MWL)	LoA	.278	27	97	19	27	6	0	5	18	7	26	1	1	.336	.495
2018	R. Cucamonga (CAL)	HiA	.269	102	383	64	103	20	2	19	60	38	138	6	2	.350	.480
Minor League Totals			.270	130	481	83	130	26	2	24	78	45	165	7	3	.347	.482

16 JEREN KENDALL, OF

Born: Feb. 4, 1996. **B-T:** L-R. **HT:** 6-0. **WT:** 190. **Drafted:** Vanderbilt, 2017 (1st round). **Signed by:** Marty Lamb.

BA GRADE
45 Risk: High

TRACK RECORD: Kendall looked like a potential top-10 pick after starring for U.S. Collegiate National Team in 2016, drawing comparisons to Kenny Lofton. A concerning amount of swings and misses the following spring at Vanderbilt dropped him to 24th overall. Kendall continued to show premier athleticism his first full season with high Class A Rancho Cucamonga, but also a distressing amount of whiffs. He hit just .215/.300/.356 with a 32 percent strikeout rate, tied for third-worst in the California League.

SCOUTING REPORT: Kendall is one of the most dynamic athletes in baseball. He's a plus-plus runner who gets to top speed quickly, is a Gold Glove-caliber center fielder who runs pristine routes, and has a plus, accurate arm that yielded 11 assists. He even flashes plus raw power out of his sneaky strong frame. Kendall's problem is he has yet to find a workable setup at the plate, resulting in a terrifying number of late, non-competitive swings. With an upright, inanimate stance, Kendall doesn't catch up to velocity and freezes on breaking balls. He draws walks and is a dangerous basestealer when he gets on, but pitchers who throw strikes neutralize him. For the second straight year the Dodgers spent instructional league tinkering with Kendall's setup, aiming to get him in a better position to hit.

THE FUTURE: Kendall's big tools give him upside, but his hitting has to improve significantly to even be a backup. He'll try to make the needed adjustments in 2019.

Year	Club (League)	Class	AVG	G	AB	R	H	2B	3B	HR	RBI	BB	SO	SB	CS	OBP	SLG
2017	Ogden (PIO)	R	.455	5	22	5	10	1	1	1	7	0	3	4	0	.455	.727
	Great Lakes (MWL)	LoA	.221	35	140	21	31	5	7	2	18	13	42	5	8	.290	.400
2018	R. Cucamonga (CAL)	HiA	.215	114	438	68	94	20	3	12	42	52	158	37	14	.300	.356
Minor League Totals			.225	154	600	94	135	26	11	15	67	65	203	46	22	.303	.380

17 MICHAEL GROVE, RHP

Born: Dec. 18, 1996. **B-T:** R-R. **HT:** 6-3. **WT:** 200. **Drafted:** West Virginia, 2018 (2nd round). **Signed by:** Jonah Rosenthal.

BA GRADE
50 Risk: Extreme

TRACK RECORD: Grove was shaping up as a possible future first-rounder his sophomore year at West Virginia, but he blew out his elbow in his ninth start and had Tommy John surgery, causing him to miss the rest of 2017 and all of 2018. The Dodgers saw enough when Grove was healthy to believe in him and drafted him in the second round, No. 68 overall.

SCOUTING REPORT: Grove enticed before his injury as a superb athlete with two potential plus pitches. He has pristine pitchers body at 6-foot-3, 200 pounds and is athletic and explosive in his delivery. When healthy, Grove's fastball sat an easy 93-96 mph with excellent carry through the upper third of the strike zone. His 85-86 mph power slider with vertical drop tunneled well off his fastball, giving him a second plus offering. Grove rarely threw a changeup in college, so the Dodgers put him in a changeup development camp to try different grips and see what works.

THE FUTURE: Grove's stuff wasn't quite back yet in instructs, but he is expected to be ready by Opening Day. If everything comes back, he has mid-rotation potential.

Year	Club (League)	Class	W	L	ERA	G	GS	CG	SV	IP	H	HR	BB	SO	K/9	WHIP	AVG
2018	Did not play—Injured																

18 GERARDO CARRILLO, RHP

BA GRADE
50 Risk: Extreme

Born: Sept. 3, 1998. **B-T:** R-R. **HT:** 6-0. **WT:** 154. **Signed:** Mexico, 2016.
Signed by: Mike Brito/Roman Barinas/Juvenal Soto.

TRACK RECORD: Carrillo signed with the Dodgers for $75,000 in 2016 after training with the Mexican League's Tijuana Toros and intriguing with his quick right arm. After a strong showing in the DSL in 2017, Carrillo made his U.S. debut in 2018 and was promoted out of the Rookie-Level Arizona League after just four appearances. He handled the aggressive promotion beautifully, turning in a 1.65 ERA over nine starts at low Class A Great Lakes.

SCOUTING REPORT: Carrillo is nicknamed "The Assassin" for two reasons. First, he is meticulously poised and unflappable, mowing down his opponents with precision. And second, his stuff is deadly. Carrillo is all of 6 feet, 154 pounds, but he sits 90-94 mph and touches 97 with heavy sink at the bottom of the strike zone. His changeup is an above-average pitch that overwhelmed lower level hitters, and he teases an average curveball. Carrillo repeats his clean delivery to throw all his pitches for strikes, keeping hitters guessing and drawing uncomfortable swings. He wore down at the end of the year and was sitting 87-90 by his final start, but he had the guile to battle through. Though he only struck out 6.8 batters-per-nine in the Midwest League, he limited opponents to a .192 average.

THE FUTURE: Carrillo's stuff excites, but he has yet to throw more than 60 innings in a season and his small frame yields durability questions. He'll try to show he can hold up at high Class A Rancho Cucamonga in 2019.

Year	Club (League)	Class	W	L	ERA	G	GS	CG	SV	IP	H	HR	BB	SO	K/9	WHIP	AVG
2017	Dodgers2 (DSL)	R	5	2	2.79	14	10	0	0	48	44	1	14	32	6.0	1.20	.237
2018	Dodgers (AZL)	R	2	0	0.82	4	1	0	1	11	6	0	2	13	10.6	0.73	.154
	Great Lakes (MWL)	LoA	2	1	1.65	9	9	0	0	49	35	3	15	37	6.8	1.02	.200
Minor League Totals			9	3	2.08	27	20	0	1	108	85	4	31	82	6.8	1.07	.213

19 MIGUEL VARGAS, 3B

BA GRADE
50 Risk: Extreme

Born: Nov. 17, 1999. **B-T:** R-R. **HT:** 6-3. **WT:** 198. **Signed:** Cuba, 2017.
Signed by: Roman Barinas/Mike Tosar.

TRACK RECORD: Vargas is the son of Cuban baseball legend Lazaro Vargas, an infielder who played 22 years in Cuba's Serie Nacional and won two Olympic gold medals with the country's national team. After the younger Vargas starred for Cuba in the 2014 15U World Cup in Mexico and 2015 18U World Cup in Japan, father and son left the island together in Nov. 2015. Nearly two years later, in Sept. 2017, the Dodgers signed Miguel Vargas for $300,000.

SCOUTING REPORT: Vargas had a reputation as one of Cuba's top youth hitters and lived up to it in his pro debut, batting .400/.464/.592 at the Rookie levels before finishing the year at low Class A Great Lakes. Strong and physical at 6-foot-3, 198 pounds, Vargas combines an advanced approach, supreme hand-eye coordination and plus raw power. He has an inside-out swing that primarily sends drives for doubles into the right-center gap, but once he learns to pull the ball evaluators expect his home run numbers to spike. Defensively, Vargas has quick hands and an above-average arm at third base, but his slow-twitch body has most evaluators projecting him to first.

THE FUTURE: Vargas will have to mash to rise as a likely first baseman, but he has the offensive tools to do it. He'll start 2019 back at Great Lakes.

Year	Club (League)	Class	AVG	G	AB	R	H	2B	3B	HR	RBI	BB	SO	SB	CS	OBP	SLG
2018	Dodgers (AZL)	R	.419	8	31	6	13	3	1	0	2	5	3	1	0	.514	.581
	Ogden (PIO)	R	.394	22	94	25	37	11	1	2	22	8	13	6	1	.447	.596
	Great Lakes (MWL)	LoA	.213	23	75	4	16	1	1	0	6	10	20	0	0	.307	.253
Minor League Totals			.330	53	200	35	66	15	3	2	30	23	36	7	1	.404	.465

20 ZACH WILLEMAN, RHP

Born: March 27, 1996. **B-T:** R-R. **HT:** 6-2. **WT:** 175. **Drafted:** Kent State, 2017 (19th round). **Signed by:** Marty Lamb

TRACK RECORD: Willeman spent two years as Kent State's closer before moving to the rotation as a junior in 2017. He pitched well as a starter and had late draft helium, but he had Tommy John surgery a week before the draft and fell. The Dodgers snagged him in the 19th round and signed him for $125,000. Willeman sat 90-95 before surgery, but after nearly 14 months of rehab with the Dodgers he returned in late July comfortably sitting 94-96 mph and touching 99.

SCOUTING REPORT: Willeman is a broad, physical power pitcher with premier stuff. His fastball velocity stands out, and he impresses even more with two power breaking balls that flashed plus. His hard slider checked in 91-92 mph and his hammer power curveball clocked 83-84. Willeman's control was a little off, but not beyond what was expected from someone who hadn't pitched in a year. His head stays still in his delivery and he reaches top velocity with little effort, enough to project average control.

THE FUTURE: Willeman threw only 19.1 innings, so his durability remains an open question. With a premium fastball and two potential plus secondaries, his upside is enormous if he can stay healthy.

Year	Club (League)	Class	W	L	ERA	G	GS	CG	SV	IP	H	HR	BB	SO	K/9	WHIP	AVG
2017	Did not play—Injured																
2018	Dodgers (AZL)	R	1	0	0.84	5	0	0	0	11	2	0	7	14	11.8	0.84	.065
	Great Lakes (MWL)	LoA	2	0	2.16	3	1	0	0	8	10	0	1	10	10.8	1.32	.333
Minor League Totals			3	0	1.42	8	1	0	0	19	12	0	8	24	11.4	1.05	.197

21 ROBINSON ORTIZ, LHP

Born: Jan, 4, 2000. **B-T:** L-L. **HT:** 6-0. **WT:** 180. **Signed:** Dominican Republic, 2017. **Signed by:** Luis Marquez/Roman Barinas/Laiky Uribe.

TRACK RECORD: Ortiz was little known as an international amateur and didn't sign for nearly a year after becoming eligible, landing with the Dodgers for $60,000 in June 2017. After impressing in the DSL after signing, Ortiz made his U.S. debut in 2018.

SCOUTING REPORT: Ortiz is a strong, mature-bodied lefthander with the smooth delivery to log innings. His above-average fastball sits 92-94 mph and plays up with gloveside life. He shows feel to spin a tick above average breaking ball, although it's presently a little slurvy, and his excellent hand speed portends an above-average changeup. Ortiz commands all of his offerings and shows an advanced feel to pitch. He's also an eager learner with makeup conducive to improving. Ortiz's frame doesn't leave much more room for growth, but the Dodgers are confident he'll get stronger and add velocity.

THE FUTURE: The Dodgers internally liken Ortiz to Caleb Ferguson with his mature body, competitiveness and feel for three pitches. He'll move to full-season ball with low Class A Great Lakes in 2019.

Year	Club (League)	Class	W	L	ERA	G	GS	CG	SV	IP	H	HR	BB	SO	K/9	WHIP	AVG
2017	Dodgers (DSL)	R	2	2	3.13	11	11	0	0	37	33	0	5	35	8.4	1.02	.229
2018	Dodgers (AZL)	R	2	2	4.18	11	9	0	0	32	27	2	12	42	11.7	1.21	.231
Minor League Totals			4	4	3.62	22	20	0	0	70	60	2	17	77	9.9	1.11	.230

22 JOSH SBORZ, RHP

Born: Dec. 17, 1993. **B-T:** R-R. **HT:** 6-3. **WT:** 225. **Drafted:** Virginia, 2015 (2nd round supplemental). **Signed by:** Clair Rieson.

TRACK RECORD: Sborz won Most Outstanding Player at the 2015 College World Series as Virginia's relief ace. The Dodgers drafted him in the second round that summer and tried to develop him as a starter, but Sborz returned to relief in 2018 and moved to the doorstep of the majors. After some initial bumps at Triple-A, he held opponents scoreless in 12 of his final 15 appearances and didn't allow a hit in three playoff outings.

SCOUTING REPORT: Sborz sat in the low 90s as a starter but ticked up in relief. His fastball sits 94-95 mph out of the bullpen and frequently gets to 96-97. Sborz comes straight over the top and powers his fastball downhill to both corners, although it occasionally sails on him. Sborz's vertical upper 80s slider is a plus pitch at its best, but his command of it inconsistent. When it's on, he looks the part of a late-inning reliever with two plus pitches and a competitive streak. Sborz is capable of pitching back-to-back days and can go multiple innings if needed.

THE FUTURE: Sborz's move to relief fits squarely with the Dodgers bullpen needs. He was added to the 40-man roster after the season and will likely make his ML debut in 2019.

Year	Club (League)	Class	W	L	ERA	G	GS	CG	SV	IP	H	HR	BB	SO	K/9	WHIP	AVG
2016	R. Cucamonga (CAL)	HiA	8	4	2.66	20	19	0	0	108	82	8	30	108	9.0	1.03	.207
	Tulsa (TL)	AA	0	1	3.78	10	0	0	1	17	17	2	6	17	9.2	1.38	.258
2017	Tulsa (TL)	AA	8	8	3.86	24	24	0	0	117	106	8	56	81	6.2	1.39	.243
2018	Tulsa (TL)	AA	3	1	2.76	13	0	0	6	16	11	1	5	24	13.2	0.98	.193
	Oklahoma City (PCL)	AAA	1	1	4.38	33	0	0	0	37	38	0	15	47	11.4	1.43	.266
Minor League Totals			20	17	3.35	113	46	0	9	317	273	22	121	302	8.6	1.24	.230

23 MATT BEATY, 3B/1B

BA GRADE
40 Risk: Medium

Born: April 28, 1993. **B-T:** L-R. **HT:** 6-0. **WT:** 210. **Drafted:** Belmont, 2015 (12th round). **Signed by:** Marty Lamb.

TRACK RECORD: Beaty finished in the top five in Belmont history in hits, RBIs and walks and was drafted by the Dodgers in the 12th round in 2015. He starred from the outset, making the California League all-star team in his first full season and winning Texas League player of the year in his second. An intercostal strain followed by a torn UCL in his thumb limited him to just 31 games at Triple-A Oklahoma City.

SCOUTING REPORT: Beaty lacks huge tools but has always hit, batting .309/.366/.445 in his pro career. He has innate feel for the barrel, takes an advanced, patient approach and makes quick adjustments. He is a line-drive hitter who uses the whole field, and he can elevate to his pull side for home runs. He rarely strikes out and wears pitchers down with consistent, competitive at-bats. Beaty is solid-average at both third and first base with an average arm, and he saw time at second base and left field in 2018 to enhance his versatility. He plays hard with a grinder mentality, endearing him to teammates and evaluators alike.

THE FUTURE: Beaty's ML debut is on the horizon in 2019. He'll break in as a bench player and has a chance to become more.

Year	Club (League)	Class	AVG	G	AB	R	H	2B	3B	HR	RBI	BB	SO	SB	CS	OBP	SLG
2016	R. Cucamonga (CAL)	HiA	.297	124	489	66	145	30	0	11	88	40	74	6	1	.352	.425
2017	Tulsa (TL)	AA	.326	116	438	61	143	31	1	15	69	35	54	3	3	.378	.505
2018	Dodgers (AZL)	R	.375	3	8	0	3	0	0	0	2	0	0	0	0	.375	.375
	Oklahoma City (PCL)	AAA	.277	31	101	13	28	10	0	1	12	12	17	0	0	.378	.406
Minor League Totals			.309	342	1307	180	404	79	3	31	199	110	176	13	7	.366	.445

24 OMAR ESTEVEZ, SS

BA GRADE
45 Risk: High

Born: Feb. 25, 1998. **B-T:** R-R. **HT:** 5-10. **WT:** 168. **Signed:** Cuba, 2015. **Signed by:** Roman Barinas/Mike Tosar.

TRACK RECORD: The Dodgers gave Estevez $6 million during their 2015 Cuban signing spree that included Yadier Alvarez and Yusniel Diaz. After looking like a poor investment for two years, Estevez overhauled his approach, swing and preparation and turned into a different player in 2018. On the back of scorching second half, Estevez led the California League in runs (87) and doubles (43).

SCOUTING REPORT: Estevez chased everything and pulled off the ball for two seasons before changing it up. He began doing weighted ball hitting drills to help him stay through the baseball, and once that clicked, it opened up the big part of the field and the doubles came in spades. With increased confidence and success came improved pitch selection as well, with Estevez overall showing the potential to be an average hitter with gap power. Estevez's tools are lacking beyond his bat. He has decent hands but is a below-average runner with a thick lower half who will have to move off shortstop. His arm is fringy.

THE FUTURE: Estevez's long-term defensive home will be second base, and only if he hits. He'll try to maintain his improvements at Double-A Tulsa in 2019.

Year	Club (League)	Class	AVG	G	AB	R	H	2B	3B	HR	RBI	BB	SO	SB	CS	OBP	SLG
2016	Great Lakes (MWL)	LoA	.255	122	471	46	120	32	2	9	61	26	121	3	6	.298	.389
2017	R. Cucamonga (CAL)	HiA	.256	120	457	56	117	24	3	4	47	33	97	2	2	.309	.348
2018	R. Cucamonga (CAL)	HiA	.278	128	515	87	143	43	2	15	84	45	138	3	1	.336	.456
Minor League Totals			.263	370	1443	189	380	99	7	28	192	104	356	8	9	.315	.400

25 JOHN ROONEY, LHP

BA GRADE
45 Risk: High

Born: Jan. 28, 1997. **B-T:** L-L. **HT:** 6-5. **WT:** 235. **Drafted:** Hofstra, 2018 (3rd round). **Signed by:** Paul Murphy.

TRACK RECORD: After posting ERAs above 5.00 his first two years at Hofstra, Rooney stood out in the summer of 2017 in the Cape Cod League and then had an All-American junior season. Rooney finished second in the nation with a 1.23 ERA, set the program record for strikeouts (108) and innings pitched (95). The Dodgers drafted him in the third round, No. 104 overall, and signed him for $563,240.

SCOUTING REPORT: An imposing 6-foot-5, 235 pounds, Rooney cleaned up his previously husky body and improved his stuff and control as a result. His fastball sits in the low 90s and ramps up to 94 mph with ride, and Rooney commands it in all four quadrants of the strike zone. He mixes in an above-average mid-80s slider and his changeup began showing average. He mixes all his pitches and keeps traffic off the bases with an elite pickoff move. After signing, he picked off 10 runners in eight games.

THE FUTURE: Rooney's track record is short, but the Dodgers believe he'll move fast as a lefthanded strikethrower with three pitches. He'll head to high Class A Rancho Cucamonga in 2019.

Year	Club (League)	Class	W	L	ERA	G	GS	CG	SV	IP	H	HR	BB	SO	K/9	WHIP	AVG
2018	Dodgers (AZL)	R	0	0	0.00	2	2	0	0	5	2	0	1	7	12.6	0.60	.143
	Great Lakes (MWL)	LoA	0	0	2.40	6	6	0	0	15	12	0	7	14	8.4	1.27	.240
Minor League Totals			0	0	1.80	8	8	0	0	20	14	0	8	21	9.5	1.10	.219

26 EDWIN UCETA, RHP

BA GRADE
45 Risk: High

Born: Jan. 1, 1998. **B-T:** R-R. **HT:** 6-0. **WT:** 155. **Signed:** Dominican Republic, 2016. **Signed by:** Luis Marquez/Matt Doppelt.

TRACK RECORD: The Dodgers have had success signing older international pitchers at a discount in recent years, with Uceta a prime example. Signed for just $10,000 as an 18-year-old out of the Dominican Republic, Uceta helped pitch Rookie-level Ogden to the Pioneer League championship in his first season. In his second, he ranked seventh in the Midwest League in ERA (3.25) before a promotion to high Class A Rancho Cucamonga.

SCOUTING REPORT: Uceta is still growing into his slight frame, giving him some projection on his three-pitch mix. His fastball sits 90-92 mph and touches 94, and he backs it up with a sweeping slider that starts in the righthanded batter's box and ends up on the outside corner. He mostly relies on his fastball and slider, but his changeup flashes average and has shown better in the past. Uceta has average control and sometimes spends a little too much time in the strike zone, resulting in high home runs allowed totals.

THE FUTURE: Uceta's stuff is a tick light at present, so a lot depends on him filling out and adding velocity. He'll start back at Rancho Cucamonga in 2019.

Year	Club (League)	Class	W	L	ERA	G	GS	CG	SV	IP	H	HR	BB	SO	K/9	WHIP	AVG
2016	Dodgers2 (DSL)	R	0	1	1.20	5	2	0	0	15	11	0	1	11	6.6	0.80	.193
	Dodgers (DSL)	R	2	0	2.20	6	1	0	0	16	9	1	2	17	9.4	0.67	.158
2017	Ogden (PIO)	R	2	3	6.59	14	14	0	0	56	63	8	14	62	10.0	1.38	.278
2018	Great Lakes (MWL)	LoA	5	6	3.25	20	20	0	0	100	91	9	27	103	9.3	1.18	.241
	R. Cucamonga (CAL)	HiA	0	0	6.97	5	5	0	0	21	17	7	12	28	12.2	1.40	.224
Minor League Totals			9	10	4.29	50	42	0	0	208	191	25	56	221	9.6	1.19	.240

27 CARLOS RINCON, OF

BA GRADE
45 Risk: Very High

Born: Oct. 14, 1997. **B-T:** R-R. **HT:** 6-3. **WT:** 190. **Signed:** Dominican Republic, 2015. **Signed by:** Patrick Guerrero/Manelik Pimentel.

TRACK RECORD: The Dodger signed Rincon for $325,000 as part of their massive 42-player, $90-million international signing class in 2015. A physical outfielder who struggled to translate his big power from batting practice into games as an amateur, Rincon labored to hit as a pro until moving to high Class A Rancho Cucamonga at the end of 2018, when he went off for 15 home runs in 29 games.

SCOUTING REPORT: Rincon is an extremely competitive, aggressive player, and that aggressiveness got the best of him early in his career. Under the calming influence of Rancho Cucamonga manager Drew Saylor, Rincon learned to dial it back and threw himself into the advance scouting process. Better prepared and more relaxed, Santana began hunting fastballs and putting his easy plus raw power into play. Rincon remains aggressive and prone to strikeouts, but he's moving in the right direction. Santana is a well below average runner and well below average defender in both corner outfield spots. He reads fly balls better in right field and has an average arm.

THE FUTURE: Rincon's future is tied squarely to his bat. He'll try to carry his late-season outburst over into in 2019.

Year	Club (League)	Class	AVG	G	AB	R	H	2B	3B	HR	RBI	BB	SO	SB	CS	OBP	SLG
2016	Dodgers (DSL)	R	.364	26	77	19	28	5	2	6	26	15	23	8	2	.458	.714
	Dodgers (AZL)	R	.301	26	103	13	31	6	3	7	23	2	30	0	2	.314	.621
2017	Great Lakes (MWL)	LoA	.198	87	334	41	66	13	1	18	48	32	143	6	1	.270	.404
	Ogden (PIO)	R	.275	14	51	8	14	4	0	3	13	1	16	0	0	.288	.529
2018	Great Lakes (MWL)	LoA	.226	81	288	28	65	13	2	7	33	41	91	5	1	.331	.358
	R. Cucamonga (CAL)	HiA	.327	29	110	36	36	9	0	15	35	16	31	0	1	.427	.818
Minor League Totals			.249	263	963	145	240	50	8	56	178	107	334	19	7	.330	.492

28 JACOB AMAYA, SS

BA GRADE

45 Risk: Extreme

Born: Sept. 3, 1998. **B-T:** R-R. **HT:** 6-0. **WT:** 180. **Drafted:** HS—West Covina, Calif., 2017 (11th round). **Signed by:** Bobby Darwin.

TRACK RECORD: Amaya's grandfather Frank Amaya played four seasons as a shortstop in the Brooklyn Dodgers organization beginning in 1955. The younger Amaya raised his draft profile with a star showing at the 2017 National High School Invitational as a senior and the Dodgers drafted him in the 11th round.
SCOUTING REPORT: Amaya lacks huge tools but keeps getting on base and playing plus defense everywhere he goes. He has the plate discipline and pitch recognition of a leadoff hitter, and his growing strength is gradually producing harder contact. Amaya's swing is more suited for doubles than home runs, but as he picks out the right pitches to drive evaluators can envision double-digit home runs to go with an average bat. Amaya's advanced instincts at shortstop have him in the right in position to make seemingly every play. He is an average runner who gets excellent jumps and reads off the bat, and he has an above-average arm with a good internal clock.
THE FUTURE: Amaya's advanced offensive approach and impressive shortstop defense have the Dodgers high on him. He'll spend 2019 at the class A levels.

Year	Club (League)	Class	AVG	G	AB	R	H	2B	3B	HR	RBI	BB	SO	SB	CS	OBP	SLG
2017	Dodgers (AZL)	R	.254	34	118	17	30	4	1	2	14	19	25	4	2	.364	.356
2018	Ogden (PIO)	R	.346	32	127	44	44	9	3	3	24	27	29	11	4	.465	.535
	Great Lakes (MWL)	LoA	.265	27	98	13	26	1	0	1	5	20	18	3	3	.390	.306
Minor League Totals			.292	93	343	71	100	14	4	6	43	66	72	18	9	.409	.408

29 BRAYDON FISHER, RHP

BA GRADE

45 Risk: Extreme

Born: July 26, 2000. **B-T:** R-R. **HT:** 6-4. **WT:** 180. **Drafted:** HS—League City, Texas, 2018 (4th round). **Signed by:** Clint Bowers.

TRACK RECORD: Fisher rose late in the 2018 draft after his fastball jumped from the upper 80s in summer showcases to 92-95 mph the spring of his senior year. The Dodgers made him the first-player ever drafted from Clear Falls High in League City, Texas, when they picked him in the fourth round.
SCOUTING REPORT: Fisher is all projection as a super skinny teenager. He can run his fastball up to 95 mph but can't hold it and sits 90-92 overall. He is a plus athlete with a clean arm action. Fisher's main secondary is a tilted slider with short, horizontal break in the low 80s that flashes plus. He also shows feel for an average changeup with fade and armside movement. Fisher walked nine in 22 innings after signing, but evaluators consider that as a small sample size blip and project above-average control.
THE FUTURE: Fisher has years of strength gains ahead and is firmly a long-term project. He's likely to begin 2019 in extended spring training.

Year	Club (League)	Class	W	L	ERA	G	GS	CG	SV	IP	H	HR	BB	SO	K/9	WHIP	AVG
2018	Dodgers (AZL)	R	1	2	2.05	11	9	0	0	22	21	2	9	19	7.8	1.36	.259
Minor League Totals			1	2	2.05	11	9	0	0	22	21	2	9	19	7.8	1.36	.259

30 CODY THOMAS, OF

BA GRADE

40 Risk: High

Born: Oct. 8, 1994. **B-T:** L-R. **HT:** 6-4. **WT:** 211. **Drafted:** Oklahoma, 2016 (13th round). **Signed by:** Josh Herzenberg.

TRACK RECORD: Thomas began his college career at Oklahoma as a football/baseball player and focused on football before settling on baseball and impressing enough to be drafted him in the 13th round. After understandably struggling in his first taste of pro ball given his lack of game experience, Thomas jumped to high Class A Rancho Cucamonga in 2018 and led the California League in total bases (248).
SCOUTING REPORT: Thomas is extremely physical and athletic in his 6-foot-4, 211-pound frame. He has plus raw power from the left side and gets to it with his pure strength, and he moves well enough to play all three outfield positions with average speed and an average arm. Thomas' hitting ability lags behind, with a rigid stiffness that prevents him from adjusting mid-swing if he's not on time.
THE FUTURE: Thomas' lefthanded power and ability to play all three outfield intrigue. He's still improving as a baseball player and may have another leap in him.

Year	Club (League)	Class	AVG	G	AB	R	H	2B	3B	HR	RBI	BB	SO	SB	CS	OBP	SLG
2016	Dodgers (AZL)	R	.500	7	22	10	11	1	1	3	6	3	3	1	0	.571	1.045
	Ogden (PIO)	R	.276	52	210	41	58	9	3	16	44	18	84	9	3	.360	.576
2017	Great Lakes (MWL)	LoA	.222	121	460	59	102	18	4	20	65	43	150	6	7	.293	.409
2018	R. Cucamonga (CAL)	HiA	.285	127	499	82	142	35	7	19	87	48	163	5	2	.355	.497
Minor League Totals			.263	307	1191	192	313	63	15	58	202	112	400	21	12	.337	.487

Miami Marlins

BY KEGAN LOWE

A new era of Marlins baseball was ushered in this past season, even as the results remained strikingly similar to the last decade-plus. After trading away outfielders Giancarlo Stanton (Yankees), Christian Yelich (Brewers) and Marcell Ozuna (Cardinals), as well as second baseman Dee Gordon (Mariners), the Marlins finished Year 1 of their latest rebuild with an NL-worst 63-98 record.

It was the franchise's ninth consecutive losing season, dating back to 2010 when the then-Florida Marlins finished 87-75. The 2018 season also marked the 15th straight season in which the Marlins failed to qualify for the playoffs, the longest active postseason drought in the National League.

Brian Anderson hit 34 doubles and recorded a .357 on-base percentage as a rookie.

After an offseason filled with trading away major league-level talent in exchange for minor league prospects, the Marlins expectedly finished last among MLB teams in total attendance (811,104). Miami was the only major league franchise to not have at least one million fans attend their home games in 2018, and the franchise's attendance fell nearly 50 percent from the previous season.

Yet, despite all of the obvious negatives surrounding the major league team in 2018, there were some newfound reasons for optimism. For starters, the Marlins played 26 rookies in 2018, with none performing better than Brian Anderson. A 2014 third-round pick, Anderson finished fourth in the National League Rookie of the Year voting. The 25-year-old led Miami in on-base percentage (.357), runs (87) and doubles (34), and he showed the versatility needed to handle either third base or right field on a full-time basis moving forward.

Things didn't move quite as smoothly for outfielder Lewis Brinson, who came to Miami in the deal that sent Christian Yelich to the Brewers and entered 2018 as the Marlins' No. 1 prospect. Brinson, who began the year as Miami's leadoff hitter and everyday center fielder, hit just .199/.240/.338 with 11 home runs and 120 strikeouts in 109 games. It was a disappointing rookie season for the 24-year-old native of Fort Lauderdale, Fla., but Brinson was just one of the many young and talented prospects who have entered the organization over the past 18 months.

In fact, nine of the Marlins' current Top 10 Prospects were acquired by Miami since the new ownership group, led by venture capitalist Bruce Sherman and former Yankees shortstop Derek Jeter, took over for former Marlins owner Jeffery Loria in late 2017. Six of the Marlins' current Top 10 Prospects came over in the Stanton, Yelich, Ozuna and Gordon trades, while the organiza-

PROJECTED 2022 LINEUP

Catcher	Will Banfield (22)
First Base	Connor Scott (22)
Second Base	Isan Diaz (26)
Third Base	Brian Anderson (29)
Shortstop	Jose Devers (22)
Left Field	Monte Harrison (26)
Center Field	Victor Victor Mesa (25)
Right Field	Lewis Brinson (28)
No. 1 Starter	Sandy Alcantara (26)
No. 2 Starter	Jose Ureña (30)
No. 3 Starter	Jorge Guzman (26)
No. 4 Starter	Nick Neidert (25)
No. 5 Starter	Trevor Rogers (24)
Closer	Edward Cabrera (24)

tion's new No. 1 prospect, Victor Victor Mesa, was the No. 1 international free agent in the 2018-19 class. The Marlins were able to sign the 22-year-old Mesa, and his 17-year-old brother Victor Mesa Jr., for a combined $6.25 million in October 2018, showcasing even more desire to rebuild the organization with young, controllable players.

In all, the Marlins ended the 2017 season with arguably the worst farm system in all of baseball. Fast forward less than 18 months later and the Marlins have significantly upgraded their minor league talent. However, it's still not considered among the top 20 systems in baseball—a mark they haven't achieved since 2014.

MIAMI MARLINS

TOP 2019 ROOKIE: Sandy Alcantara, RHP. After making six big league starts in 2018, he should be a full-time member of the rotation in 2019.
BREAKOUT PROSPECT: Jordan Holloway, RHP. Following a full recovery from Tommy John surgery, the 22-year-old will showcase some of the best pure stuff of any pitcher in the system.
SLEEPER: Harold Ramirez, OF. A minor league free agent signed by the Marlins in December 2018, the 24-year-old is a career .301/.355/.413 hitter with above-average power. After receiving an invite to spring traing, he could see time in Miami in 2019.

SOURCE OF TOP 30 TALENT			
Homegrown	17	Acquired	13
College	4	Trades	12
Junior college	2	Rule 5 draft	1
High school	8	Independent leagues	0
Nondrafted free agents	0	Free agents/waivers	0
International	3		

LF
Brian Miller (13)
Tristan Pompey (16)
Austin Dean (25)
Davis Bradshaw (27)

CF
Victor Victor Mesa (1)
Connor Scott (5)
Thomas Jones
Brayan Hernandez
Milton Smith

RF
Monte Harrison (3)
Victor Mesa Jr. (30)
Isaac Galloway
Harold Ramirez
John Norwood
Isael Soto

3B
James Nelson (19)
Marcos Rivera
Julio Machado

SS
Jose Devers (10)
Osiris Johnson (14)
Joe Dunand (21)
Christopher Torres (26)
Ynmanol Marinez
Dalvy Rosario

2B
Isan Diaz (8)
Bryson Brigman (24)
Riley Mahan (28)
Justin Twine

1B
Peter O'Brien
Garrett Cooper
Eric Jagielo

C
Will Banfield (9)
Chad Wallach
Roy Morales
Nick Fortes
Cameron Barstad
Keegan Fish

LHP

LHSP	LHRP
Trevor Rogers (11)	Jose Quijada
Braxton Garrett (12)	Jeff Kinley
McKenzie Mills	Dylan Lee
Daniel Castano	
Sean Guenther	
Brett Lilek	
Dakota Bennett	

RHP

RHSP	RHRP
Sandy Alcantara (2)	Riley Ferrell (22)
Nick Neidert (4)	Brett Graves
Jorge Guzman (6)	Ben Meyer
Edward Cabrera (7)	Tyler Kinley
Jordan Holloway (15)	Kyle Keller
Jordan Yamamoto (17)	Tommy Eveld
Zac Gallen (18)	
Robert Dugger (20)	
Jeff Brigham (23)	
Matt Givin (29)	
Merandy Gonzalez	
Cody Poteet	
Brady Puckett	
Taylor Braley	
Chris Vallimont	

DRAFT ANALYSIS

2018

BEST PURE HITTER: OF Davis Bradshaw (11) hit .376/.453/.484 with seven extra-base hits and 13 stolen bases in the Gulf Coast League and was then promoted to short-season Batavia, where he hit .324/.368/.352. The lefthanded hitter has plus-plus speed and an advanced approach at the plate.
BEST POWER HITTER: SS Osiris Johnson (2) has quick hands and plus bat speed, leading scouts to project plus power in the future.
FASTEST RUNNER: Bradshaw stole 20 bases in 25 attempts during his pro debut. OF Milton Smith (22) also has plus-plus speed, and he recorded seven stolen bases in 10 attempts in the Gulf Coast League. Both use their excellent speed in the outfield, where they feature above-average range.
BEST DEFENSIVE PLAYER: Considered by many evaluators to be the best defensive catcher in last year's draft, C Will Banfield (2s) has a plus arm, with some scouts even labeling it a future plus-plus arm behind the plate. Banfield threw out nearly 39 percent of potential basestealers in his pro debut.
BEST ATHLETE: OF Connor Scott (1) was considered one of the most athletic players in the 2018 draft. At 6-foot-4 and 180 pounds, Scott is at least a plus runner, with some considering him a current plus-plus runner, and he also possess a plus arm.
BEST FASTBALL: RHP Chris Vallimont's (5) fastball touches 98 mph and sits in the mid-90s. He needs to improve his control, as he walked 23 batters in 29 innings in the New York-Penn League, but his fastball remains one of his strongest assets.
BEST SECONDARY PITCH: RHP Cason Sherrod's (7) main out-pitch is his slider, with features sharp bite and good tilt from a low three-quarter slot.
BEST PRO DEBUT: In a combined 48 games at low Class A Greensboro and high Class A Jupiter, OF Tristan Pompey (3) hit .302/.413/.407 with 12 extra-base hits and nine stolen bases.

TOP DRAFT PICKS OF THE DECADE

Year	Player, Pos	2018 Org
2009	Chad James, LHP	Did not play
2010	Christian Yelich, OF	Brewers
2011	Jose Fernandez, RHP	Deceased
2012	Andrew Heaney, LHP	Angels
2013	Colin Moran, 3B	Pirates
2014	Tyler Kolek, RHP	Marlins
2015	Josh Naylor, 1B	Padres
2016	Braxton Garrett, LHP	Marlins
2017	Trevor Rogers, LHP	Marlins
2018	Connor Scott, OF	Marlins

MOST INTRIGUING BACKGROUND: The second cousin of 2007 NL MVP Jimmy Rollins, Johnson's father Marcel played in the minors with the Mets and Braves. Johnson has worked with Rollins on improving his defense at shortstop.
CLOSEST TO THE MAJORS: The younger brother of Blue Jays outfield prospect Dalton Pompey, the switch-hitting Tristan led all SEC hitters with a .410 batting average in conference games in 2017, and he has the college pedigree typical of players who are able to track through the minors quickly.
BEST LATE-ROUND PICK: Listed at 5-foot-8 and 175 pounds, LHP Zach Wolf (18) isn't physically imposing on the mound, but he proved to have excellent stuff in his pro debut. The University of Seattle product works with a low-90s fastball that regularly hits 94 mph and a potential swing-and-miss curveball with solid bite and 11-to-5 break.
THE ONE WHO GOT AWAY: The Marlins signed 29 of their first 30 picks, with the exception of RHP Zach Greene (15), who chose to return to South Alabama for his senior season. The Marlins took a late chance on LHP Garrett McDaniels (30), who ranked No. 203 on the BA 500 but will honor his commitment to Coastal Carolina.

—KEGAN LOWE

2017

LHP Trevor Rogers (1) in 2018 made his professional debut and showed both his promise and how far he still has to go. OF Brian Miller (1s) and SS Joe Dunand (2) both reached Double-A Jacksonville, but scuffled in the Southern League.
GRADE: C

2016

LHP Braxton Garrett (1) missed the 2018 season as he recovered from Tommy John surgery. RHP Michael King (12) took off after being traded to the Yankees, reaching Triple-A. 3B James Nelson (15) has been a solid late-round find.
GRADE: C

2015

RHP Ben Meyer (29) gave the class a big leaguer, but its most impactful players are now in the Padres' system. 1B Josh Naylor (1) had a solid year in Double-A and RHP Chris Paddack (8) impressed as he returned from Tommy John surgery.
GRADE: B

1 VICTOR VICTOR MESA, OF

Born: July 20, 1996. **B-T:** R-R. **Ht.:** 5-9. **Wt:** 163.
Signed: Cuba, 2018. **Signed by:** Fernando Seguignol.

The son of Victor Mesa, who was one of the top Cuban baseball players of the 1980s and '90s, Victor Victor Mesa was the No. 1 international free agent in 2018. The Marlins signed him and his 17-year-old brother Victor Mesa Jr. in October. Victor Victor signed for $5.25 million, which was the largest bonus in the 2018-19 international free agent class. The 22-year-old outfielder has been playing in Cuba's top professional league, Serie Nacional, since he was 16. While playing against much older competition, Mesa produced a .275/.334/.378 slash line with 10 home runs and 74 stolen bases in more than 300 career games, and he also went 3-for-7 with a pair of doubles in the 2017 World Baseball Classic. After leaving Cuba in May to train and establish residency in the Dominican Republic, the Mesa brothers were declared free agents by Major League Baseball in September before signing with the Marlins one month later.
SCOUTING REPORT: A premium athlete, Mesa is already considered a plus defender in center field, with some scouts grading both his arm and his speed as 70 tools. Mesa uses his speed well in the outfield, with a quick first step and strong route-running ability helping extend his range, while his arm routinely prevents baserunners from taking an extra base. Offensively, Mesa profiles best as a top-of-the-order hitter, most likely settling in as a No. 2 hitter. As a 20-year-old in Cuba, he hit .354/.399/.539 with seven home runs and 40 stolen bases, showcasing a potential plus hit tool. Mesa has shown quick bat speed, above-average barrel control and a solid approach at the plate in the past. With an inside-out swing, Mesa's power is probably no more than fringe-average, but some believers think he could grow into above-average power as he continues to mature. Mesa has been hampered by injuries throughout his career, and a desire to work with U.S. medical staffs and use major league facilities to stay healthy helped convince him to leave Cuba.
THE FUTURE: Mesa has a chance to be a cornerstone of the Marlins' ongoing rebuild thanks to his plus glove and ability to hit for average and steal bases near the top of the lineup. He will probably open 2019 at high Class A Jupiter, where he would be in close proximity to Victor Jr., who will likely begin at extended spring training. If Mesa's transition goes smoothly, he could make his major league debut by the end of 2020.

MATT ROBERTS/GETTY IMAGES

BA GRADE	SCOUTING GRADES
60 Risk: High	Hit: 55. Power: 45. Speed: 70. Field: 60. Arm: 70.

Projected future grades on 20-80 scouting scale.

TOP PROSPECTS OF THE DECADE

Year	Player, Pos	2018 Org
2009	Cameron Maybin, OF	Mariners
2010	Giancarlo Stanton, OF	Yankees
2011	Matt Dominguez, 3B	Japan
2012	Christian Yelich, OF	Brewers
2013	Jose Fernandez, RHP	Deceased
2014	Andrew Heaney, LHP	Angels
2015	Tyler Kolek, RHP	Marlins
2016	Tyler Kolek, RHP	Marlins
2017	Braxton Garrett, LHP	Marlins
2018	Sandy Alcantara, RHP	Marlins

BEST TOOLS

Best Hitter for Average	Brian Miller
Best Power Hitter	Sean Reynolds
Best Strike-Zone Discipline	Isan Diaz
Fastest Baserunner	Brian Miller
Best Athlete	Monte Harrison
Best Fastball	Jorge Guzman
Best Curveball	Jordan Holloway
Best Slider	Nick Neidert
Best Changeup	Jordan Yamamoto
Best Control	Nick Neidert
Best Defensive Catcher	Will Banfield
Best Defensive Infielder	Jose Devers
Best Infield Arm	Marcos Rivera
Best Defensive Outfielder	Monte Harrison
Best Outfield Arm	Isael Soto

Year	Club (League)	Class	AVG	G	AB	R	H	2B	3B	HR	RBI	BB	SO	SB	CS	OBP	SLG
2016	Matanzas (CNS)	CUB	.354	70	254	55	90	14	6	7	44	17	19	40	10	.399	.539
2017	Industriales (CNS)	CUB	.237	21	76	19	18	5	0	0	9	12	9	6	3	.341	.303
2018	Did not play—Signed 2019 contract																
Cuban League Totals			.275	312	1036	171	285	43	17	10	132	76	143	74	26	.334	.378

2 SANDY ALCANTARA, RHP

Born: Sept. 7, 1995. **B-T:** R-R. **Ht.:** 6-4. **Wt.:** 170. **Signed:** Dominican Republic, 2013. **Signed by:** Rodney Jimenez (Cardinals).

TRACK RECORD: The top prospect the Marlins received by trading Marcell Ozuna to the Cardinals in December 2017, Alcantara had a solid first season with his new club. The righthander got his first taste of Triple-A in 2018 before making six starts for Miami.

SCOUTING REPORT: Alcantara is armed with a plus-plus fastball, which previously topped out at 102 mph. In 2018, he threw more 92-95 mph two-seam fastballs, though he is still capable of using his upper-90s four-seamer when needed. Alcantara's issue is getting his fastball over the plate for strike one, and his fringe-average control has hampered his development. A tall, lanky right-hander, Alcantara walked more than three batters per nine innings in 2018, and that number increased to more than six walks per nine in his limited, 34-inning sample in the big leagues. All three of his secondary offerings have above-average to plus potential, though Alcantara relied more heavily on his mid-to-upper 80s slider against righthanders, while backing off using his low-80s curveball as much. His upper-80s changeup provides another potential swing-and-miss pitch, most notably against lefthanders.

BA GRADE
50 Risk: Medium
Fastball: 70.
Curve: 50. SL: 50.
Change: 50. CTL: 45.

THE FUTURE: Alcantara has the pure stuff of a frontline starter, but his control will decide his fate. After ending 2018 in the Marlins' rotation, the 23-year-old should compete for a spot in the Opening Day rotation in 2019.

Year	Club (League)	Class	W	L	ERA	G	GS	CG	SV	IP	H	HR	BB	SO	K/9	WHIP	AVG
2016	Peoria (MWL)	LoA	5	7	4.08	17	17	0	0	90	78	4	45	119	11.9	1.36	.228
	Palm Beach (FSL)	HiA	0	4	3.62	6	6	1	0	32	25	0	14	34	9.5	1.21	.216
2017	Springfield, MO (TL)	AA	7	5	4.31	25	22	0	0	125	125	13	54	106	7.6	1.43	.262
	St. Louis (NL)	MAJ	0	0	4.32	8	0	0	0	8	9	2	6	10	10.8	1.80	.273
2018	Jupiter (FSL)	HiA	0	0	3.97	3	3	0	0	11	10	0	5	8	6.4	1.32	.238
	New Orleans (PCL)	AAA	6	3	3.89	19	19	0	0	116	107	10	38	88	6.8	1.25	.246
	Miami (NL)	MAJ	2	3	3.44	6	6	0	0	34	25	3	23	30	7.9	1.41	.214
Major League Totals			2	3	3.61	14	6	0	0	42	34	5	29	40	8.5	1.49	.227
Minor League Totals			23	32	3.94	94	90	2	0	496	460	31	195	461	8.4	1.32	.245

3 MONTE HARRISON, OF

Born: Aug. 10, 1995. **B-T:** R-R. **Ht.:** 6-3. **Wt.:** 220. **Drafted:** HS—Lee's Summit, Mo., 2014 (2nd round). **Signed by:** Drew Harrison (Brewers).

TRACK RECORD: After a breakout 2017 in which he hit 21 home runs and stole 27 bases with the Brewers' high Class A affiliate, Harrison was acquired by the Marlins for eventual National League MVP Christian Yelich in January. Harrison took a step back while getting his first taste of Double-A in 2018, though he continued showing off the power-speed combination that makes him such an enticing prospect despite his swing-and-miss issues.

SCOUTING REPORT: Perhaps the best pure athlete in the Marlins' system, Harrison has excellent bat speed and plus raw power. When he makes contact, he consistently hits the ball as hard as any Marlins prospect. Harrison has recently toned down his high leg kick and replaced it with a simpler toe tap he now uses as a timing mechanism. With fewer moving parts in his swing, Harrison is aiming to cut down his strikeout rate (37 percent in Double-A) without sacrificing too much power. Harrison started using the muted toe tap

BA GRADE
55 Risk: Extreme
Hit: 45. Power: 60.
Run: 60. Field: 60.
Arm: 60.

in the Arizona Fall League, where he hit .288/.374/.342 with three extra-base hits and 20 strikeouts in 73 at-bats. Defensively, Harrison has the range to play an above-average center field, though his plus arm strength would also play in right field.

THE FUTURE: Harrison may possess the highest upside of any position player in the Marlins' system, and he'll continue to work on making more consistent contact at Triple-A New Orleans in 2019.

Year	Club (League)	Class	AVG	G	AB	R	H	2B	3B	HR	RBI	BB	SO	SB	CS	OBP	SLG
2016	Brewers (AZL)	R	.211	5	19	4	4	1	1	0	1	4	4	0	0	.375	.368
	Wisconsin (MWL)	LoA	.221	75	267	34	59	11	1	6	37	20	97	8	3	.294	.337
2017	Wisconsin (MWL)	LoA	.265	63	223	32	59	12	1	11	32	29	70	10	3	.359	.475
	Carolina (CAR)	HiA	.278	59	230	41	64	16	1	10	35	14	69	16	1	.341	.487
2018	Jacksonville (SL)	AA	.240	136	521	85	125	20	3	19	48	44	215	28	9	.316	.399
Minor League Totals			.242	462	1699	271	411	77	13	52	197	170	603	114	24	.331	.394

4 NICK NEIDERT, RHP

Born: Nov. 20, 1996. **B-T:** R-R. **Ht.:** 6-1. **Wt.:** 180. **Drafted:** HS—Suwanee, Ga., 2015 (2nd round). **Signed by:** Dustin Evans (Mariners).

TRACK RECORD: The Mariners' top draft pick in 2015, Neidert was one of three prospects traded to the Marlins in December 2017 for Dee Gordon and international bonus pool money. After being honored as the California League pitcher of the year in 2017, Neidert was even better as a 21-year-old in Double-A and was named the Marlins' minor league pitcher of the year with a stellar season in 2018.

SCOUTING REPORT: Listed at 6-foot-1, 180 pounds, Neidert isn't overpowering, though his fastball regularly sits between 91-93 mph. He locates his fastball well to both sides of the plate and uses a plus changeup to prohibit hitters from sitting on his fastball. Neidert's low-80s breaking ball doesn't grade out much better than average, but he isn't afraid to throw it in any count. All three of Neidert's pitches play up because of his plus control and ability to keep hitters off-balance.

BA GRADE

50 Risk: High

Fastball: 55.
Slider: 50.
Change: 60. **CTL:** 60.

THE FUTURE: Neidert may not have the upside to match other pitching prospects in the Marlins' system, such as fellow righthanders Sandy Alcantara, Jorge Guzman or Edward Cabrera, but he is the safest bet to maximize his potential. Neidert will begin 2019 in Triple-A New Orleans, with a late-season callup to Miami possible, if not likely.

Year	Club (League)	Class	W	L	ERA	G	GS	CG	SV	IP	H	HR	BB	SO	K/9	WHIP	AVG
2016	Clinton (MWL)	LoA	7	3	2.57	19	19	0	0	91	75	7	13	69	6.8	0.97	.225
2017	Modesto (CAL)	HiA	10	3	2.76	19	19	0	0	104	95	7	17	109	9.4	1.07	.244
	Arkansas (TL)	AA	1	3	6.56	6	6	0	0	23	33	4	5	13	5.0	1.63	.324
2018	Jacksonville (SL)	AA	12	7	3.24	26	26	0	0	153	142	17	31	154	9.1	1.13	.250
Minor League Totals			30	18	3.01	81	81	0	0	407	370	36	75	368	8.1	1.09	.244

5 CONNOR SCOTT, OF

Born: Oct. 8, 1999. **B-T:** L-L. **Ht.:** 6-4. **Wt.:** 180. **Drafted:** HS—Tampa, 2018 (1st round). **Signed by:** Donavan O'Dowd.

TRACK RECORD: Drafted 13th overall in 2018, Scott signed with the Marlins for just north of $4 million, the largest draft bonus the organization has ever given a position player. A second-team high school All American, Scott attended Tampa's Plant High, the same school as current Astros outfield prospect Kyle Tucker, with whom Scott is often compared.

SCOUTING REPORT: Though he has an unusual gait, Scott is at least a plus runner, which helps him on the bases and in the outfield. He played exclusively center field in his pro debut, where he showed acceptable range, but he could move to a corner as he continues to fill out his 6-foot-4 frame. Scott has plus arm strength and he routinely threw in the low 90s as a high school pitcher. The 19-year-old fills out his five-tool potential with power that could develop as plus and solid feel to hit. His bat clearly—and expectedly—lagged behind his defense when the Marlins aggressively pushed him to low Class A Greensboro.

MIKE JANES/FOUR SEAM IMAGES

BA GRADE

55 Risk: Extreme

Hit: 50. Power: 55.
Run: 60. Field: 55.
Arm: 60.

THE FUTURE: The Marlins sent Scott to the South Atlantic League with the intent of preparing him for that same level in 2019. With the Marlins moving affiliates from Greensboro, N.C., to Clinton, Iowa, Scott should expect to play a full season in the low Class A Midwest League, where Miami will hope to see the five-tool outfielder that made Scott such a highly touted draft pick.

Year	Club (League)	Class	AVG	G	AB	R	H	2B	3B	HR	RBI	BB	SO	SB	CS	OBP	SLG
2018	Marlins (GCL)	R	.223	27	103	15	23	1	4	0	8	14	29	8	5	.319	.311
	Greensboro (SAL)	LoA	.211	23	76	4	16	2	0	1	5	10	27	1	3	.295	.276
Minor League Totals			.218	50	179	19	39	3	4	1	13	24	56	9	8	.309	.296

6 JORGE GUZMAN, RHP

Born: Jan. 28, 1996. **B-T:** R-R. **Ht.:** 6-2. **Wt.:** 182. **Signed:** Dominican Republic, 2014. **Signed by:** Oz Ocampo/Ramon Ocumarez/Francis Mojica (Astros).

TRACK RECORD: After signing with the Astros out of the Dominican Republic in 2014, Guzman was traded to the Yankees in November 2016 as part of the Brian McCann deal. Less than 13 months later, he was one of three players, along with minor league shortstop Jose Devers and major league second baseman Starlin Castro, traded to the Marlins for 2017 National League MVP Giancarlo Stanton.

SCOUTING REPORT: Guzman is one of the hardest-throwing starters in the minors, with his elite fastball consistently sitting in the upper 90s with a peak velocity of 103 mph. His control took a step back in 2018, however, with his walk rate going from 2.4 per nine innings in 2017 to 6.0 per nine in 2018. Guzman's changeup shows plus potential, but he needs to continue refining his slider to become an above-average offering. Improved control and continued development of his slider will go a long way for Guzman. He's hard to square up, but there are scouts who believe his future is in the bullpen.

BA GRADE
50 Risk: High
Fastball: 80.
Slider: 50.
Change: 55. CTL: 45.

THE FUTURE: Guzman challenges fellow righthander Sandy Alcantara for best pure stuff in the Marlins' system, and if everything clicks he could become a future frontline starter. After skipping the low Class A level entirely once he joined the Marlins' organization, he will likely begin 2019 with Double-A Jacksonville, where improving his control and reducing his walk rate will prove vital.

Year	Club (League)	Class	W	L	ERA	G	GS	CG	SV	IP	H	HR	BB	SO	K/9	WHIP	AVG
2016	Astros (GCL)	R	1	1	3.12	7	4	0	0	17	4	0	10	25	13.0	0.81	.071
	Greeneville (APP)	R	2	3	4.76	6	4	0	0	23	25	1	7	29	11.5	1.41	.272
2017	Staten Island (NYP)	SS	5	3	2.30	13	13	1	0	67	51	4	18	88	11.9	1.04	.212
2018	Jupiter (FSL)	HiA	0	9	4.03	21	21	0	0	96	84	7	64	101	9.5	1.54	.239
Minor League Totals			11	20	3.80	64	54	1	0	258	227	14	129	272	9.5	1.38	.234

7 EDWARD CABRERA, RHP

Born: April 13, 1998. **B-T:** R-R. **Ht.:** 6-4. **Wt.:** 175. **Signed:** Dominican Republic, 2015. **Signed by:** Albert Gonzalez/Sandy Nin/Domingo Ortega.

TRACK RECORD: Cabrera signed for $100,000 out of the Dominican Republic in 2015, which is so far proving to be a steal for the Marlins. After spending time in the Rookie-level Gulf Coast League in 2016 and pitching at short-season Batavia in 2017, Cabrera got his first taste of full-season ball in the low Class A South Atlantic League in 2018.

SCOUTING REPORT: Cabrera is similar to fellow Marlins righthanders Sandy Alcantara and Jorge Guzman in that he showcases a high-velocity fastball that has cleared the 100 mph mark. Standing at a lean 6-foot-4, Cabrera's plus fastball most regularly sits in the mid-90s as a starter with good, late life in the zone. He has a potential plus breaking ball and is working on a changeup that flashes plus at times but remains inconsistent. Like Guzman, Cabrera still needs to work on controlling his high-powered arsenal. His walk rate increased to roughly 3.8 walks per nine innings in 2018.

BA GRADE
50 Risk: High
Fastball: 70.
Slider: 55.
Change: 50. CTL: 50.

THE FUTURE: After spending the entirety of his age-20 season in low Class A, Cabrera will move to high Class A Jupiter in 2019. His ceiling is no lower than that of a mid-rotation starter, though he, like Guzman, could conceivably end up as a late-inning, power reliever.

Year	Club (League)	Class	W	L	ERA	G	GS	CG	SV	IP	H	HR	BB	SO	K/9	WHIP	AVG
2016	Marlins (GCL)	R	2	6	4.21	11	7	0	0	47	54	1	10	28	5.4	1.36	.289
2017	Batavia (NYP)	SS	1	3	5.30	13	6	0	0	36	42	1	8	32	8.1	1.40	.286
2018	Greensboro (SAL)	LoA	4	8	4.22	22	22	1	0	100	105	11	42	93	8.3	1.47	.270
Minor League Totals			7	17	4.43	46	35	1	0	183	201	13	60	153	7.5	1.43	.278

8 ISAN DIAZ, 2B

Born: May 27, 1996. **B-T:** L-R. **Ht.:** 5-10. **Wt.:** 185. **Drafted:** HS—Springfield, Mass., 2014 (2nd round supplemental). **Signed by:** Mike Serbalik (D-backs).

TRACK RECORD: Yet another trade acquisition by the Marlins, Diaz joined outfielders Lewis Brinson and Monte Harrison, as well as righthander Jordan Yamamoto, in the deal that sent Christian Yelich to the Brewers. A stocky, 5-foot-10 second baseman, Diaz was drafted out of his Massachusetts high school by the D-backs in 2014 before being traded to the Brewers in a five-player deal that sent shortstop Jean Segura to Arizona in 2016.

SCOUTING REPORT: Diaz has the profile of an offensive second baseman, with plus raw power that he continues to tap into in games. He has hit at least 13 home runs in each of the last four seasons, with one evaluator theorizing that he could have a Rougned Odor-type impact in the majors. Diaz is at least an average hitter with a willingness to hit the ball the other way, and his strikeout (26 percent) and walk rates (13 percent) have remained relatively consistent. Diaz is an above-average second baseman who has worked to improve his footwork around the bag. He is a good athlete with at least average speed, and he stole a career-high 14 bases in 2018 while at Double-A Jacksonville and Triple-A New Orleans.

THE FUTURE: Diaz will likely return to New Orleans to start 2019 but could take over Miami's everyday second base role by the end of the season.

BA GRADE

50 Risk: High

Hit: 50. Power: 55.
Run: 50. Field: 55.
Arm: 50.

Year	Club (League)	Class	AVG	G	AB	R	H	2B	3B	HR	RBI	BB	SO	SB	CS	OBP	SLG
2016	Wisconsin (MWL)	LoA	.264	135	507	71	134	34	5	20	75	72	148	11	8	.358	.469
2017	Carolina (CAR)	HiA	.222	110	383	59	85	20	0	13	54	62	121	9	3	.334	.376
2018	Jacksonville (SL)	AA	.245	83	294	44	72	19	1	10	42	53	95	10	3	.365	.418
	New Orleans (PCL)	AAA	.204	36	137	19	28	4	4	3	14	15	45	4	0	.281	.358
Minor League Totals			.254	481	1775	273	451	109	21	62	257	261	530	52	26	.353	.444

9 WILL BANFIELD, C

MIKE JANES/FOUR SEAM IMAGES

Born: Nov. 18, 1999. **B-T:** R-R. **Ht.:** 6-0. **Wt.:** 200. **Drafted:** HS—Snellville, Ga., 2018 (2nd round). **Signed by:** Christian Castorri.

TRACK RECORD: The 69th overall pick in 2018, Banfield signed with the Marlins for $1.8 million, well above the slot value of $894,600 and the club's second-largest draft bonus in 2018. A Vanderbilt commit, Banfield was widely considered the draft's best defensive catcher among high school backstops.

SCOUTING REPORT: It all starts with defense with Banfield, who has the potential to be a plus defensive catcher and already possesses a plus arm. He is nimble behind the plate, with the lateral quickness and soft hands needed to become an above-average receiver. Banfield has plus raw power and hit three home runs in 48 at-bats as an 18-year-old in the low Class A South Atlantic League. Like many highly drafted preps, Banfield's bat will decide his future. He has shown above-average bat speed, helping him tap into his pull-side power, but there were some swing-and-miss concerns with Banfield going into the draft that he will have to answer.

BA GRADE

50 Risk: Extreme

Hit: 45. Power: 50.
Run: 40. Field: 60.
Arm: 70.

THE FUTURE: Like first-rounder Connor Scott, Banfield was aggressively pushed to low Class A Greensboro for the final month of 2018 to prepare him for that level in 2019. He will likely spend most, if not all, of 2019 with newly affiliated Clinton of the Midwest League, where he'll look to improve his hit tool to combine with his plus defensive potential.

Year	Club (League)	Class	AVG	G	AB	R	H	2B	3B	HR	RBI	BB	SO	SB	CS	OBP	SLG
2018	Marlins (GCL)	R	.256	24	82	7	21	8	1	0	14	7	28	0	1	.330	.378
	Greensboro (SAL)	LoA	.208	15	48	5	10	0	0	3	4	4	15	0	0	.269	.396
Minor League Totals			.238	39	130	12	31	8	1	3	18	11	43	0	1	.308	.385

10 JOSE DEVERS, SS

Born: Dec. 7, 1999. **B-T:** L-R. **Ht.:** 6-0. **Wt.:** 155. **Signed:** Dominican Republic, 2016. **Signed by:** Juan Rosario (Yankees).

TRACK RECORD: The cousin of Red Sox third baseman Rafael Devers, Jose signed with the Yankees out of the Dominican Republic for $250,000 in 2016. He was then traded to the Marlins in December 2017, along with major leaguer Starlin Castro and fellow top-10 prospect Jorge Guzman, for Giancarlo Stanton, allowing Miami's ownership to clear $265 million of the then-$295 million left on Stanton's contract.

SCOUTING REPORT: A slightly built, glove-first shortstop, Devers is a much different prospect than his cousin. Lauded for his instincts, he stands out for his athleticism, footwork and soft hands at shortstop, all of which allow his average arm to play up from the left side of the infield. Devers' glove is clearly ahead of his lefthanded bat, but he has a contact-oriented swing and plus speed that allowed him to hold his own against older competition at two Class A stops despite his current lack of strength. Devers' power will likely never be more than fringe-average, but his plus defense and feel to hit should carry him up the ranks as a defense-first shortstop with the potential of an everyday regular.

THE FUTURE: Devers played the majority of his age-18 season in the low Class A South Atlantic League, though he received a promotion to high Class A Jupiter in August. He played in just two games in the Florida State League because of a minor injury, but he's fully healthy now and should spend most of 2019 with the Hammerheads.

BA GRADE	
50	Risk: Extreme

Hit: 50. **Power:** 40.
Run: 60. **Field:** 60.
Arm: 50.

Year	Club (League)	Class	AVG	G	AB	R	H	2B	3B	HR	RBI	BB	SO	SB	CS	OBP	SLG
2017	Yankees1 (DSL)	R	.239	11	46	4	11	2	1	0	7	0	16	1	0	.255	.326
	Yankees1 (GCL)	R	.246	42	138	17	34	7	2	1	9	18	21	15	3	.359	.348
2018	Greensboro (SAL)	LoA	.273	85	337	46	92	12	4	0	24	15	49	13	6	.313	.332
	Jupiter (FSL)	HiA	.250	2	8	1	2	0	0	0	2	1	0	0	0	.333	.250
Minor League Totals			.263	140	529	68	139	21	7	1	42	34	86	29	9	.322	.335

11 TREVOR ROGERS, LHP

BA GRADE	
50	Risk: Extreme

Born: Nov. 13, 1997. **B-T:** L-L. **Ht.:** 6-6. **Wt.:** 185. **Drafted:** HS—Carlsbad, N.M., 2017 (1st round). **Signed by:** Scott Stanley.

TRACK RECORD: The cousin of former Marlins outfielder Cody Ross, Rogers was drafted with the 13th overall pick in 2017. After signing for $3.4 million, Rogers did not pitch in 2017, with the Marlins citing general fatigue after a long senior season for Carlsbad (N.M.) High. The 6-foot-6 lefthander made his pro debut in May 2018, eventually making 17 starts and completing 72.2 innings for low Class A Greensboro in his first season.

SCOUTING REPORT: Rogers has a smooth, fluid delivery that produces a seemingly effortless mid-90s fastball, routinely touching 96 mph with above-average command. Perhaps expected after a nearly year-long layoff from pitching competitively, Rogers' secondary stuff was wildly inconsistent in 2018. Neither his changeup nor slider graded out better than average, although both pitches flashed above-average potential. Rogers often struggled to land his offspeed pitches in the zone, allowing hitters to sit on his fastball and leading to Rogers' .295 opponent average. He struck out 10.53 batters per nine innings, however, showcasing the swing-and-miss potential he still possesses when his stuff is working.

THE FUTURE: With a full season under his belt, Rogers should be more prepared for high Class A Jupiter in 2019. Continued development of his slider and changeup will be vital for Rogers to reach his potential as a mid-rotation starter.

Year	Club (League)	Class	W	L	ERA	G	GS	CG	SV	IP	H	HR	BB	SO	K/9	WHIP	AVG
2018	Greensboro (SAL)	LoA	2	7	5.82	17	17	0	0	73	86	4	27	85	10.5	1.56	.295
Minor League Totals			2	7	5.82	17	17	0	0	73	86	4	27	85	10.5	1.56	.295

12 BRAXTON GARRETT, LHP

BA GRADE	
50	Risk: Extreme

Born: Aug. 5, 1997. **B-T:** L-L. **Ht.:** 6-3. **Wt.:** 190. **Drafted:** HS—Florence, Ala., 2016 (1st round). **Signed by:** Mark Willoughby.

TRACK RECORD: Since being drafted by the Marlins with the No. 7 overall pick and signing for an above-slot $4,195,900 bonus in 2016, Garrett has completed just 15.1 professional innings in more than two and a half years. After not pitching professionally in his draft year, the Alabama native made just four starts for low Class A Greensboro in 2017 before having Tommy John surgery that June.

SCOUTING REPORT: The highest-drafted prep pitcher out of Alabama since righthander Rick James (No. 6, Cubs) in 1965, Garrett's true, north-to-south curveball was considered one of the best offspeed offerings in the 2016 draft. In addition to his potentially plus curveball, Garrett has a low-90s fastball that was reportedly in the 92-93 mph range in the Marlins' fall instructional league once he returned to the mound post-surgery. Known for having at least above-average command coming into the 2016 draft, Garrett also has a third-pitch changeup that's shown late fading life in the past.

THE FUTURE: Garrett should enter spring training with limited restrictions in 2019 as he looks to make his first professional appearance since May 2017. At 21 years old but with scant professional experience, Garrett could begin the season at low Class A Clinton before making his way to high Class A Jupiter.

Year	Club (League)	Class	W	L	ERA	G	GS	CG	SV	IP	H	HR	BB	SO	K/9	WHIP	AVG
2017	Greensboro (SAL)	LoA	1	0	2.93	4	4	0	0	15	13	3	6	16	9.4	1.24	.220
2018	Did not play—Injured																
Minor League Totals			1	0	2.93	4	4	0	0	15	13	3	6	16	9.4	1.24	.220

13 BRIAN MILLER, OF

BA GRADE

45 Risk: High

Born: Aug. 20, 1995. **B-T:** L-R. **Ht.:** 6-1. **Wt.:** 186. **Drafted:** North Carolina, 2017 (1st round supplemental). **Signed by:** Blake Newsome.

TRACK RECORD: Originally recruited as a preferred walk-on at North Carolina, Miller excelled in three years with the Tar Heels before the Marlins drafted him with the 36th overall pick in 2017. The 6-foot-1, 186-pound outfielder split his first full season of pro ball between high Class A Jupiter and Double-A Jacksonville, and then he ended the year with a stint in the Arizona Fall League.

SCOUTING REPORT: Considered by many to be a 70-grade runner, Miller led all Marlins minor leaguers with 40 stolen bases in 2018. His speed is also an asset in the outfield, where he has the potential to be an average center fielder with an average arm. Miller has hit just one home run in 185 minor league games, and he'll likely never have much more than fringe-average power. His line-drive swing, advanced contact skills and speed give him a chance to be a plus hitter, however, and he's a career .304 hitter with a strikeout rate below 13 percent in the minors.

THE FUTURE: After excelling in Class A, Miller struggled in his first taste of Double-A (.632 OPS) and didn't fare much better in the AFL (.641 OPS). He will likely head back to Double-A to begin 2019. Miller's lack of power limits his ceiling as an everyday regular, but his speed, hit tool and ability to fill in at all three outfield positions give him the safe landing spot of a fourth outfielder.

Year	Club (League)	Class	AVG	G	AB	R	H	2B	3B	HR	RBI	BB	SO	SB	CS	OBP	SLG
2017	Greensboro (SAL)	LoA	.322	57	233	42	75	17	1	1	28	23	35	21	6	.384	.416
2018	Jupiter (FSL)	HiA	.324	62	256	28	83	13	3	0	29	14	27	19	6	.358	.398
	Jacksonville (SL)	AA	.267	66	262	29	70	8	2	0	14	18	39	21	7	.319	.313
Minor League Totals			.304	185	751	99	228	38	6	1	71	55	101	61	19	.353	.374

14 OSIRIS JOHNSON, SS

BA GRADE

50 Risk: Extreme

Born: Oct. 18, 2000. **B-T:** R-R. **Ht.:** 6-0. **Wt.:** 181. **Drafted:** HS—Alameda, Calif. (2nd round). **Signed by:** John Hughes.

TRACK RECORD: The second cousin of 2007 NL MVP Jimmy Rollins and son of former minor leaguer Marcel Johnson, Osiris Johnson was the Marlins' second-round pick in 2018. One of the youngest players in his draft class, Johnson signed for $1.35 million instead of heading to Cal State Fullerton.

SCOUTING REPORT: Only 18 years old, Johnson is known for his quick-twitch athleticism and loud, albeit raw, tools. Johnson previously split time between shortstop and center field, but after working intensely on his arm action and footwork at shortstop with Rollins throughout high school, Johnson—and the Marlins—are committed to him sticking on the dirt. He has quick hands and at least an average arm to go along with plus speed, giving him a chance to be an above-average defender in the future. Despite being listed at just 6 feet and 181 pounds, Johnson has plus raw power and even shows a propensity to drive the ball the other way and into the right-center field gap. There were some swing-and-miss concerns with Johnson heading into the draft, and it will be his currently average hit tool that will decide his fate as an everyday shortstop in the future.

THE FUTURE: Johnson finished 2018 in low Class A and will head back to that level in 2019, where he'll continue to be one of the youngest players in the league.

Year	Club (League)	Class	AVG	G	AB	R	H	2B	3B	HR	RBI	BB	SO	SB	CS	OBP	SLG
2018	Marlins (GCL)	R	.301	25	103	12	31	8	2	1	13	4	19	7	2	.333	.447
	Greensboro (SAL)	LoA	.188	23	85	4	16	3	0	2	6	1	34	0	2	.205	.294
Minor League Totals			.250	48	188	16	47	11	2	3	19	5	53	7	4	.276	.378

15 JORDAN HOLLOWAY, RHP

BA GRADE

50 Risk: Extreme

Born: June 13, 1996. **B-T:** R-R. **Ht.:** 6-4. **Wt.:** 190. **Drafted:** HS—Arvada, Colo., 2014 (20th round). **Signed by:** Scott Stanley.

TRACK RECORD: A 20th-round pick in 2014 who signed for an above-slot $400,000, Holloway never pitched above low Class A and had Tommy John surgery in June 2017. He recovered in time to make five appearances in 2018, throwing 7.2 scoreless innings in the Gulf Coast and New York-Penn leagues.

SCOUTING REPORT: Holloway has always had electric stuff, headlined by an upper-90s fastball that has touched 98 mph as recently as the instructional league in 2018. At 6-foot-4, he gets solid downhill angle on his fastball, which gets on hitters quickly, and he can snap off a potentially plus curveball. His changeup still needs refinement to become an above-average pitch, but it's his lack of innings and previous fringe-average control that are his biggest hurdles. Although it was an extremely small sample, it was encouraging to see Holloway walk zero hitters in 7.2 innings in 2018.

THE FUTURE: The Marlins decided to put Holloway on the 40-man roster this offseason and protect him from the Rule 5 draft. He has fully recovered from Tommy John surgery, and the 22-year-old should begin 2019 in high Class A Jupiter with the chance to move quickly as a high-risk, high-reward starting pitcher.

Year	Club (League)	Class	W	L	ERA	G	GS	CG	SV	IP	H	HR	BB	SO	K/9	WHIP	AVG
2016	Greensboro (SAL)	LoA	2	4	6.16	8	8	0	0	31	31	8	15	24	7.0	1.50	.261
	Batavia (NYP)	SS	0	3	6.23	5	5	0	0	17	21	0	13	17	8.8	1.96	.280
2017	Greensboro (SAL)	LoA	1	2	5.22	11	11	0	0	50	41	10	24	50	9.0	1.26	.220
2018	Marlins (GCL)	R	0	0	0.00	3	3	0	0	3	4	0	0	5	16.9	1.50	.286
	Batavia (NYP)	SS	0	0	0.00	2	2	0	0	5	0	0	0	4	7.2	0.00	.000
Minor League Totals			9	19	4.73	55	51	0	0	209	203	18	100	152	6.5	1.45	.252

16 TRISTAN POMPEY, OF

BA GRADE

45 Risk: High

Born: March 23, 1997. **B-T:** B-R. **Ht.:** 6-4. **Wt.:** 200. **Drafted:** Kentucky, 2018 (3rd round). **Signed by:** Alex Smith.

TRACK RECORD: The younger brother of Blue Jays outfield prospect Dalton Pompey, Tristan was a college standout at Kentucky, where he was a career .321/.426/.521 hitter with 24 home runs and 21 stolen bases in 165 games. The Marlins drafted Pompey in the third round and signed him for $645,000 in 2018.

SCOUTING REPORT: Listed at 6-foot-4 and 200 pounds, Pompey is a corner outfielder who slots best in left field because of his average foot speed and below-average arm. With that defensive profile, it'll be Pompey's bat that carries him, and he should continue to hit for more power as he adds strength. Pompey's track record of hitting in the Southeastern Conference gives some scouts the belief that he'll be an above-average hitter with above-average power in the future, although he was seen as a divisive prospect entering the draft because there will be so much pressure on his bat to perform.

THE FUTURE: Pompey advanced to high Class A in 2018, performing well at each of his stops in the minors. Pompey will likely begin 2018 back at high Class A Jupiter, although his middle-of-the-order offensive production could carry him to Double-A Jacksonville by mid-season.

Year	Club (League)	Class	AVG	G	AB	R	H	2B	3B	HR	RBI	BB	SO	SB	CS	OBP	SLG
2018	Marlins (GCL)	R	.250	4	12	1	3	0	0	0	1	3	4	1	1	.400	.250
	Greensboro (SAL)	LoA	.314	24	86	12	27	4	0	2	9	16	22	5	3	.422	.430
	Jupiter (FSL)	HiA	.291	24	86	13	25	5	0	1	13	13	21	4	1	.396	.384
Minor League Totals			.299	52	184	26	55	9	0	3	23	32	47	10	5	.408	.397

17 JORDAN YAMAMOTO, RHP

BA GRADE

45 Risk: High

Born: May 11, 1996. **B-T:** R-R. **Ht.:** 6-0. **Wt.:** 185. **Drafted:** HS—Honolulu, 2014 (12th round). **Signed by:** (Brewers).

TRACK RECORD: A 12th-round pick by the Brewers in 2014, Yamamoto was one of four prospects traded to the Marlins in January as part of the Christian Yelich trade. Yamamoto dealt with minor injuries in his first year with the Marlins, but he finished the season strong in the Arizona Fall League.

SCOUTING REPORT: Yamamoto isn't overpowering, sitting mostly 89-93 mph with his fastball, but all of his stuff tends to play up because of his above-average to plus control. His late-breaking, downer curveball is his best secondary offering, flashing plus at times but consistently grading as an above-average pitch. Yamamoto has feel for a changeup, giving him three average-or-better pitches.

THE FUTURE: Despite being an undersized righthander, Yamamoto has performed well at each of his previous stops and was added to the Marlins' 40-man roster this offseason. He's made only three starts in Double-A, so he's likely to begin 2019 back in Jacksonville before a possible in-season promotion to Triple-A New Orleans. He has the potential of a mid-rotation starter.

Year	Club (League)	Class	W	L	ERA	G	GS	CG	SV	IP	H	HR	BB	SO	K/9	WHIP	AVG
2016	Wisconsin (MWL)	LoA	7	8	3.82	27	18	0	0	134	130	6	31	152	10.2	1.20	.252
2017	Carolina (CAR)	HiA	9	4	2.51	22	18	2	1	111	91	8	30	113	9.2	1.09	.223
2018	Jupiter (FSL)	HiA	4	1	1.55	7	7	0	0	41	26	0	8	47	10.4	0.84	.182
	Marlins (GCL)	R	1	0	2.45	3	3	0	0	11	5	1	2	15	12.3	0.64	.135
	Jacksonville (SL)	AA	1	0	2.12	3	3	0	0	17	12	1	4	23	12.2	0.94	.190
Minor League Totals			23	20	3.78	86	63	2	2	398	385	31	110	431	9.8	1.24	.253

18 ZAC GALLEN, RHP

BA GRADE

40 Risk: Medium

Born: Aug. 3, 1995. **B-T:** R-R. **Ht.:** 6-2. **Wt.:** 191. **Drafted:** North Carolina, 2016 (3rd round). **Signed by:** Charles Peterson (Cardinals).

TRACK RECORD: A constant member of North Carolina's starting rotation during his three collegiate years, Gallen was drafted by the Cardinals in the third round in 2016. A year and a half later, the New Jersey native was traded to the Marlins as part of the deal that sent Marcell Ozuna to St. Louis.

SCOUTING REPORT: Gallen is known more for his control than pure stuff, although his upper-80s cutter has become an above-average pitch that he can throw in any count. He stays in the low 90s with his fastball, touching 94 mph, and he changes speeds effectively with both a changeup and curveball. All of Gallen's offerings are average-or-better pitches, and even though his walk rate ticked up to a career-worst 3.24 walks per nine innings this season, his above-average control helps all of his pitches play up.

THE FUTURE: Gallen spent all of 2018 in Triple-A, and he has now thrown more than 150 innings at the minors' highest level. He should be ready for the majors sometime in 2019, even if the Marlins' crowded starting rotation keeps him in Triple-A to start the year. Gallen has the potential of a No. 4 starter, and his collegiate and minor league track record suggests he is a safe bet to reach that ceiling in the near future.

Year	Club (League)	Class	W	L	ERA	G	GS	CG	SV	IP	H	HR	BB	SO	K/9	WHIP	AVG
2016	Cardinals (GCL)	R	0	0	1.86	6	3	0	1	10	7	0	0	15	14.0	0.72	.194
2017	Palm Beach (FSL)	HiA	5	2	1.62	9	9	1	0	56	44	1	10	56	9.1	0.97	.215
	Springfield, MO (TL)	AA	4	5	3.79	13	13	0	0	71	76	8	19	42	5.3	1.33	.270
	Memphis (PCL)	AAA	1	1	3.48	4	4	0	0	21	18	2	6	23	10.0	1.16	.237
2018	New Orleans (PCL)	AAA	8	9	3.65	25	25	0	0	133	148	14	48	136	9.2	1.47	.281
Minor League Totals			18	17	3.22	57	54	1	1	291	293	25	83	272	8.4	1.29	.260

19 JAMES NELSON, 3B

BA GRADE

45 Risk: High

Born: Oct. 18, 1997. **B-T:** R-R. **Ht.:** 6-2. **Wt.:** 180. **Drafted:** Cisco (Texas) JC, 2016 (15th round). **Signed by:** Ryan Wardinsky.

TRACK RECORD: An 18th-round pick by the Red Sox out of high school, Nelson instead attended Cisco (Texas) JC for one year before the Marlins signed him for $75,000 as a 15th-round pick in 2016. Nelson had a breakout season at low Class A Greensboro in 2017, winning the organization's minor league player of the year award before dealing with nagging injuries with high Class A Jupiter in 2018.

SCOUTING REPORT: Nelson has always shown excellent bat speed and the ability to keep his barrel in the zone for an extended period of time, but his strikeout rate increased to a career-worst 26.1 percent in 2018. Most of his struggles can be attributed to a still-evolving approach at the plate, which could use some additional maturation. Nelson has above-average power that should continue to improve as he fills out his 6-foot-2 frame. He's an above-average runner underway, and shows good range at third base as a former high school shortstop, but he will likely never be much of a stolen base threat. Defensively, Nelson has all the tools necessary, including an above-average arm, to be an above-average third baseman.

THE FUTURE: The Marlins still view Nelson as an everyday third baseman, although he'll return to high Class A Jupiter in 2019 to prove that he's fully recovered from knee and hamstring injuries.

Year	Club (League)	Class	AVG	G	AB	R	H	2B	3B	HR	RBI	BB	SO	SB	CS	OBP	SLG
2016	Marlins (GCL)	R	.284	43	162	26	46	10	0	1	24	14	30	7	3	.344	.364
2017	Greensboro (SAL)	LoA	.309	102	395	41	122	31	3	7	59	26	106	6	2	.354	.456
2018	Jupiter (FSL)	HiA	.211	62	232	27	49	10	0	2	28	13	66	1	0	.262	.280
Minor League Totals			.275	207	789	94	217	51	3	10	111	53	202	14	5	.325	.385

20 ROBERT DUGGER, RHP

BA GRADE

45 Risk: High

Born: July 3, 1995. **B-T:** R-R. **Ht.:** 6-2. **Wt.:** 180. **Drafted:** Texas Tech, 2016 (18th round). **Signed by:** Taylor Terrasas (Mariners).

TRACK RECORD: A reliever during his collegiate days, Dugger was the Mariners' 18th-round pick in 2016. Midway through 2017, Dugger moved to the starting rotation and his prospect status spiked, leading the Marlins to ask for the 6-foot-2 righthander in the trade that sent Dee Gordon to Seattle.

SCOUTING REPORT: Dugger attacks hitters with both a four-seam and two-seam fastball, with the two-seamer usually sitting 92-93 mph with sink while his four-seamer is straighter but comes across in the mid-90s. Dugger also has a trio of offspeed pitches, including a low- to mid-80s slider that has become his main out-pitch against righthanders. Dugger's changeup and upper-70s curveball keep hitters off-balance and gives him five average-or-better pitches. Dugger's has at least average control of his entire arsenal.

THE FUTURE: Dugger has been a consistent performer since transitioning to the starting rotation, and he should get his first taste of Triple-A New Orleans in 2019. Dugger is one of several Marlins righthanded pitching prospects with a chance to become a mid- to back-of-the-rotation starter in the big leagues soon.

Year	Club (League)	Class	W	L	ERA	G	GS	CG	SV	IP	H	HR	BB	SO	K/9	WHIP	AVG
2016	Mariners (AZL)	R	0	0	1.04	4	0	0	2	9	6	0	1	9	9.3	0.81	.188
	Tacoma (PCL)	AAA	0	0	6.75	2	0	0	0	4	5	0	4	9.0	1.25	.294
	Everett (NWL)	SS	2	1	5.47	6	6	0	0	26	25	5	10	25	8.5	1.33	.250
2017	Clinton (MWL)	LoA	4	1	2.00	22	9	1	2	72	55	4	16	69	8.6	0.99	.206
	Modesto (CAL)	HiA	2	5	3.94	9	9	0	0	46	49	4	16	47	9.3	1.42	.272
2018	Jupiter (FSL)	HiA	3	1	2.40	7	7	0	0	41	40	2	7	34	7.4	1.14	.253
	Jacksonville (SL)	AA	7	6	3.79	18	18	3	0	109	100	13	36	107	8.8	1.24	.245
Minor League Totals			18	14	3.31	68	49	4	4	307	280	28	86	295	8.6	1.19	.241

21 JOE DUNAND, SS

BA GRADE

45 Risk: High

Born: Sept. 20, 1995. **B-T:** R-R. **Ht.:** 6-2. **Wt.:** 205. **Drafted:** North Carolina State, 2017 (2nd round). **Signed by:** Blake Newsome.

TRACK RECORD: The nephew of Alex Rodriguez, Dunand was a three-year starter at North Carolina State, where he played third base as a freshman and then took over as the starting shortstop for his final two years. He was the Marlins' second-round pick in 2017, signing for $1.2 million.

SCOUTING REPORT: At 6-foot-2 and 205 pounds with a strong lower half, Dunand isn't a prototypical shortstop, although the Marlins are sticking with him in the middle for now. He has the arm strength, footwork and power profile to transition seamlessly to third base, if needed, although he's been at least an average defender at shortstop so far. Dunand's bat took a step back as he was challenged in 2018. He struggled to make contact in Double-A, striking out in nearly 30 percent of his plate appearances, but he was still able to tap into his potentially plus power. Dunand is a fringe-average runner.

THE FUTURE: Regardless of whether Dunand ends up as an average defensive shortstop or an above-average defensive third baseman, it will be his bat that decides his future. He'll head back to Double-A in 2019 looking to make more contact and reach base more often.

Year	Club (League)	Class	AVG	G	AB	R	H	2B	3B	HR	RBI	BB	SO	SB	CS	OBP	SLG
2017	Marlins (GCL)	R	.375	5	16	4	6	3	0	1	3	3	4	0	0	.476	.750
	Jupiter (FSL)	HiA	.364	3	11	1	4	2	0	0	1	2	4	0	1	.462	.545
2018	Jupiter (FSL)	HiA	.263	66	243	39	64	8	1	7	42	20	54	2	0	.326	.391
	Jacksonville (SL)	AA	.212	61	217	25	46	13	0	7	28	16	71	0	1	.276	.369
Minor League Totals			.246	135	487	69	120	26	1	15	74	41	133	2	2	.313	.396

22 RILEY FERRELL, RHP

BA GRADE

45 Risk: High

Born: Oct. 18, 1993. **B-T:** R-R. **Ht.:** 6-2. **Wt.:** 233. **Drafted:** Texas Christian, 2015 (3rd round). **Signed by:** Jim Stevenson (Astros).

TRACK RECORD: Ferrell looked like a potentially fast-moving reliever when the Astros drafted the Texas Christian closer. But Ferrell's track to the majors was temporarily derailed by shoulder surgery to alleviate an aneurysm. He returned to the mound in 2017, but control troubles, which troubled him in college, popped back up in 2018. The Marlins snagged Ferrell with the fourth pick in the 2018 Rule 5 draft.

SCOUTING REPORT: Ferrell's 94-97 mph fastball is a little straight, but it has enough velocity to be a plus pitch. Ferrell's slider hasn't developed into the plus pitch that looked possible in college, but it's an average pitch. To be an effective big league reliever, Ferrell's going to have to improve his below-average control. He stays direct to the plate and his arm works well, but he loses the strike zone for batters at a time.

THE FUTURE: Now with the Marlins, Ferrell should make his major league debut at some point in 2019. Ferrell's ceiling is as a setup man if he can throw strikes more consistently.

Year	Club (League)	Class	W	L	ERA	G	GS	CG	SV	IP	H	HR	BB	SO	K/9	WHIP	AVG
2016	Lancaster (CAL)	HiA	0	1	1.80	8	0	0	4	10	9	1	2	14	12.6	1.10	.237
2017	Buies Creek (CAR)	HiA	0	0	0.00	2	0	0	2	2	0	0	0	5	22.5	0.00	.000
	Corpus Christi (TL)	AA	2	2	3.81	36	0	0	4	52	51	2	14	55	9.5	1.25	.263
2018	Corpus Christi (TL)	AA	2	2	1.90	21	0	0	7	24	14	1	18	33	12.5	1.35	.171
	Fresno (PCL)	AAA	2	1	6.75	22	0	0	2	28	34	4	16	34	10.9	1.79	.296
Minor League Totals			6	6	3.54	101	0	0	20	132	118	8	63	158	10.7	1.37	.240

23 JEFF BRIGHAM, RHP

Born: Feb. 16, 1992. **B-T:** R-R. **Ht.:** 6-0. **Wt.:** 200. **Drafted:** Washington, 2014 (4th round). **Signed by:** Henry Jones (Dodgers).

TRACK RECORD: After missing his junior season at Washington while recovering from Tommy John surgery, Brigham was drafted in the fourth round by the Dodgers in 2014. He was traded to the Marlins in July 2015, but has struggled with injuries throughout his career and finally made it to the majors in 2018.
SCOUTING REPORT: Brigham missed two months in 2018 with an oblique injury, but when healthy he shows a mid-90s fastball and a plus, low-80s slider. Brigham's stuff backed up once he got to the majors, but this was likely a byproduct of overthrowing. Brigham will have to show improved control if he wants to stick in the majors, and his fringy, mid-80s changeup will have to be more consistent to remain a starter.
THE FUTURE: Brigham will enter spring training with a chance to earn a big league roster spot, although he could start the year refining his control at Triple-A New Orleans.

Year	Club (League)	Class	W	L	ERA	G	GS	CG	SV	IP	H	HR	BB	SO	K/9	WHIP	AVG
2016	Jupiter (FSL)	HiA	7	8	4.04	27	23	0	1	123	115	6	47	112	8.2	1.32	.246
2017	Jupiter (FSL)	HiA	4	2	2.90	11	11	0	0	59	49	2	20	53	8.1	1.17	.226
2018	Marlins (GCL)	R	1	0	0.00	1	1	0	0	5	2	0	0	5	9.0	0.40	.118
	Jacksonville (SL)	AA	4	1	1.18	7	7	0	0	38	27	1	9	41	9.7	0.95	.211
	New Orleans (PCL)	AAA	5	2	3.44	9	9	0	0	52	53	7	13	48	8.3	1.26	.266
	Miami (NL)	MAJ	0	4	6.06	4	4	0	0	16	16	2	13	12	6.6	1.78	.271
Major League Totals			0	4	6.06	4	4	0	0	16	16	2	13	12	6.6	1.78	.271
Minor League Totals			29	23	3.55	91	80	0	1	418	393	26	152	389	8.4	1.30	.251

24 BRYSON BRIGMAN, SS/2B

Born: June 19, 1995. **B-T:** R-R. **Ht.:** 5-11. **Wt.:** 180. **Drafted:** San Diego, 2016 (3rd round) Signed by: Gary Patchett (Mariners).

TRACK RECORD: Brigman was a draft-eligible sophomore when the Mariners selected him with their 2016 third-round pick. The Marlins acquired him in the deal that sent Cameron Maybin to Seattle.
SCOUTING REPORT: Considered one of the top all-around college shortstops in the 2016 draft, Brigman fits more of a utility profile at the next level. Defensively, Brigman is an average shortstop, although his average arm fits better at second base. He has the soft hands and quick feet needed to be a capable defender at either position, and he is an above-average runner. It's been long thought that Brigman's fringe-average hit tool would limit him to a backup role, but he showed signs of improvement in 2018. His power will likely never grade out as more than average.
THE FUTURE: After an assignment to the Arizona Fall League, Brigman will return to Double-A Jacksonville in 2019. His lack of any one carrying tool will likely force him to a utility role in the majors.

Year	Club (League)	Class	AVG	G	AB	R	H	2B	3B	HR	RBI	BB	SO	SB	CS	OBP	SLG
2016	Everett (NWL)	SS	.260	68	265	51	69	6	1	0	19	41	43	17	12	.369	.291
2017	Clinton (MWL)	LoA	.235	120	463	55	109	14	4	2	36	44	74	16	8	.306	.296
2018	Modesto (CAL)	HiA	.304	98	381	47	116	13	7	2	38	37	58	15	6	.373	.391
	Jupiter (FSL)	HiA	.338	17	71	9	24	4	0	0	5	3	13	4	0	.368	.394
	Jacksonville (SL)	AA	.310	12	42	1	13	2	0	1	6	2	6	2	0	.348	.429
Minor League Totals			.271	315	1222	163	331	39	12	5	104	127	194	54	26	.346	.335

25 AUSTIN DEAN, OF

Born: Oct. 14, 1993. **B-T:** R-R. **Ht.:** 6-1. **Wt.:** 190. **Drafted:** HS—Spring, Texas, 2012 (4th round). **Signed by:** Ryan Wardinsky.

TRACK RECORD: The Marlins drafted Dean, a Texas high school infielder, with their fourth-round pick in 2012 and then watched his slow ascent through the minors finally pay off with his major league debut this past August. After advancing one level per year until 2016, Dean stalled in Double-A for two years and opened 2018 there, as well. A hot start pushed him to Triple-A, where he played 87 games before spending the final month and a half of the major league season in Miami.
SCOUTING REPORT: Typically limited to left field because of his fringe-average foot speed and average arm strength, Dean has improved enough defensively to the point that he should be considered an average defensive left fielder for now. After two stagnant years in Double-A, Dean had a breakout season in 2018, showcasing a mature approach and consistent contact at both Double-A and Triple-A. Dean has the strength and bat speed to produce plus raw power, and he hit a career-high 16 home runs in 2018.
THE FUTURE: Dean will enter spring training with a chance to earn the Marlins' everyday left field job. If he doesn't win the competition, he could continue serving as a bench bat for the Marlins.

Year	Club (League)	Class	AVG	G	AB	R	H	2B	3B	HR	RBI	BB	SO	SB	CS	OBP	SLG
2016	Jacksonville (SL)	AA	.238	130	480	60	114	23	5	11	67	48	110	1	2	.307	.375
2017	Marlins (GCL)	R	.412	4	17	3	7	2	0	1	7	0	2	0	0	.412	.706
	Jacksonville (SL)	AA	.282	61	234	29	66	14	4	4	30	14	46	3	1	.323	.427
2018	Jacksonville (SL)	AA	.420	22	81	13	34	8	1	3	14	6	7	0	0	.466	.654
	New Orleans (PCL)	AAA	.326	87	316	58	103	12	4	9	54	33	49	2	2	.397	.475
	Miami (NL)	MAJ	.221	34	113	16	25	4	0	4	14	7	22	1	0	.279	.363
Major League Totals			.221	34	113	16	25	4	0	4	14	7	22	1	0	.279	.363
Minor League Totals			.280	649	2431	344	681	135	27	47	319	223	449	30	23	.343	.416

26 CHRISTOPHER TORRES, SS/2B

BA GRADE

45 Risk: High

Born: Feb. 6, 1998. **B-T:** B-R. **Ht.:** 5-11. **Wt.:** 170. **Signed:** Dominican Republic, 2014. **Signed by:** Tim Kissner/Eddy Toledo/Kevin Dominguez (Mariners).

TRACK RECORD: Torres signed with the Mariners in 2014 for $375,000 and then had strong debuts in both the Dominican Summer and Arizona leagues. He was traded to the Marlins in the deal that sent Dee Gordon to Seattle, but he dealt with a recurring ankle injury that limited him to just 39 games in 2018.
SCOUTING REPORT: A switch-hitter, Torres displays more impact from the left side of the plate. He hit .302/.445/.395 in 111 plate appearances against righthanders in 2018, compared to just .129/.206/.226 in 34 trips against lefties. Torres, who considered ditching his righthanded swing in the past, shows a simpler, more pure swing from the left side, and he has the chance to be an above-average switch-hitter if he could get his righthanded swing to match. Torres is a plus runner but will likely never have more than fringe-average power, although he has quick hands that generates solid bat speed. Defensively, Torres has a plus arm and enough range to play shortstop, but the Marlins are working on getting him familiar with second base in order to expand his defensive versatility and get more playing time, when healthy.
THE FUTURE: With Jose Devers slated to be the everyday shortstop at high Class A Jupiter, and Osiris Johnson handling that same role at low Class A Clinton, Torres will take on more of a utility role in 2019. Shoulder and ankle injuries have limited Torres during the past two seasons, so he'll have to prove he can stay healthy and produce before he gets buried on the Marlins' depth chart.

Year	Club (League)	Class	AVG	G	AB	R	H	2B	3B	HR	RBI	BB	SO	SB	CS	OBP	SLG
2016	Mariners (AZL)	R	.257	44	167	31	43	9	4	0	17	19	44	12	4	.337	.359
2017	Mariners (AZL)	R	.222	4	9	1	2	0	2	0	1	3	5	1	0	.417	.667
	Everett (NWL)	SS	.238	48	193	44	46	8	6	6	22	36	64	13	3	.324	.435
2018	Marlins (GCL)	R	.000	2	6	1	0	0	0	0	0	1	1	0	0	.143	.000
	Batavia (NYP)	SS	.348	7	23	6	8	1	1	1	4	4	5	0	1	.429	.609
	Greensboro (SAL)	LoA	.250	30	88	20	22	0	1	1	6	21	30	3	1	.394	.307
Minor League Totals			.250	199	701	143	175	26	17	10	80	124	205	49	18	.364	.378

27 DAVIS BRADSHAW, OF

BA GRADE

45 Risk: High

Born: April 25, 1998. **B-T:** L-R. **Ht.:** 6-3. **Wt.:** 175. **Drafted:** Meridian (Miss.) JC, 2018 (11th round). **Signed by:** Mark Willoughby.

TRACK RECORD: Originally a 35th-round pick of the Brewers in 2017, Bradshaw chose not to sign and instead went to Meridian (Miss.) JC for one year. After slashing .422/.523/.718 with more walks (29) than strikeouts (23) in his one season at Meridian, Bradshaw was drafted by the Marlins in the 11th round and signed for $125,000 in 2018.
SCOUTING REPORT: Bradshaw is a plus-plus runner, and his speed allowed him to play all three outfield spots and steal 20 bases in 25 attempts during his 46-game pro debut. Defensively, he's probably best suited for center field in the future, given his speed, average arm strength, and lack of a true power profile, although his versatility gives him the floor of a fourth outfielder. A lefthanded hitter, Bradshaw has a short, compact swing and made consistent contact in 2018, striking out in less than 15 percent of his plate appearances. Bradshaw's power is the least developed of his five tools, and he will need to continue to fill out his 6-foot-3 frame in order to reach average power in the future.
THE FUTURE: Bradshaw should begin 2019 in low Class A Clinton, where he'll share an outfield with Marlins' 2018 first-round pick Connor Scott. Even if Scott's presence pushes Bradshaw to left field, it'll be his plus-plus speed and potential above-average hit tool that keeps him on the prospect radar, despite a current lack of power.

Year	Club (League)	Class	AVG	G	AB	R	H	2B	3B	HR	RBI	BB	SO	SB	CS	OBP	SLG
2018	Marlins (GCL)	R	.376	27	93	18	35	4	3	0	13	10	13	15	1	.453	.484
	Batavia (NYP)	SS	.324	19	71	7	23	2	0	0	6	2	14	5	4	.368	.352
Minor League Totals			.354	46	164	25	58	6	3	0	19	12	27	20	5	.418	.427

28 RILEY MAHAN, 2B

BA GRADE **45** Risk: High

Born: Dec. 31, 1995. **B-T:** L-R. **Ht.:** 6-3. **Wt.:** 185. **Drafted:** Kentucky, 2017 (3rd round). **Signed by:** Alex Smith.

TRACK RECORD: A 40th-round pick of the Giants in 2014, Mahan went to Kentucky, where he was one of the most productive college hitters in the 2017 draft. The Marlins drafted Mahan in the third round.

SCOUTING REPORT: Praised for his hitting ability coming into the 2017 draft, Mahan has struggled with strikeouts in pro ball. Spending the entirety of his age-22 season at high Class A Jupiter, Mahan struck out in 27.5 percent of his plate appearances and posted a .638 OPS with only three home runs. A naturally aggressive hitter, Mahan got stuck chasing too many pitches this past season, and his walk rate was just barely north of five percent. Mahan has above-average raw power, but it's yet to translate into pro ball. Defensively, Mahan is an average second baseman, and some scouts think he would be better suited in left field. He's an above-average runner with an above-average arm, so he should be able to hold his own in the outfield, although the Marlins are so far pleased with his play at second base, where his bat profiles best.

THE FUTURE: Despite a lackluster season in high Class A, the 23-year-old Mahan should move to Double-A Jacksonville. He'll need to make more contact and rekindle some of the offensive production he was known for in college in order to regain his status as a potential everyday regular for the Marlins.

Year	Club (League)	Class	AVG	G	AB	R	H	2B	3B	HR	RBI	BB	SO	SB	CS	OBP	SLG
2017	Greensboro (SAL)	LoA	.259	6	27	4	7	1	0	1	4	0	7	0	0	.259	.407
2018	Jupiter (FSL)	HiA	.250	110	424	38	106	23	3	3	40	24	127	7	2	.298	.340
Minor League Totals			.251	116	451	42	113	24	3	4	44	24	134	7	2	.296	.344

29 MATT GIVIN, RHP

BA GRADE **50** Risk: Extreme

Born: June 17, 1999. **B-T:** R-R. **Ht.:** 6-3. **Wt.:** 180. **Drafted:** HS—Lone Tree, Colo., 2017 (20th round). **Signed by:** Scott Stanley.

TRACK RECORD: Coming out of his Colorado high school, Givin was committed to Xavier. The Marlins had other ideas, as they drafted Givin in the 20th round in 2017 and signed him for a well over-slot bonus of $458,000. Givin had Tommy John surgery in April and missed the entire 2018 season.

SCOUTING REPORT: Listed at a slim, 6-foot-3 and 180 pounds, Givin, like most Colorado prep pitchers, was considered raw and had a relatively short track record coming into the draft. His fastball sits in the low 90s and should continue to add velocity as he physically matures, while his fading changeup is his go-to offspeed offering. Givin also has a low-80s curveball, and both offspeed pitches could project as above-average in the future. The Marlins are most impressed with Givin's control, which flashes above-average.

THE FUTURE: After having Tommy John surgery, Givin, who will turn 20 in June, is expected to be sidelined until mid-2019. He could head to the New York-Penn League if his rehab goes well.

Year	Club (League)	Class	W	L	ERA	G	GS	CG	SV	IP	H	HR	BB	SO	K/9	WHIP	AVG
2017	Marlins (GCL)	R	0	0	0.39	7	7	0	0	23	16	0	6	19	7.3	0.94	.198
2018	Did not play—Injured																
Minor League Totals			0	0	0.39	7	7	0	0	23	16	0	6	19	7.3	0.94	.198

30 VICTOR MESA JR., OF

BA GRADE **50** Risk: Extreme

Born: Sept. 8, 2001. **B-T:** L-R. **Ht.:** 5-11. **Wt.:** 175. **Signed:** Cuba, 2018. **Signed by:** Fernando Seguignol.

TRACK RECORD: Mesa Jr. is the younger brother of the Marlins' No. 1 prospect Victor Victor Mesa and signed with the club for $1 million in October. In 2018, Mesa Jr. hit .440/.560/.667 with 24 walks and 15 strikeouts in 125 plate appearances in Cuba's 18U league. He led the league in batting average, on-base and slugging percentage, and finished second in the league with 15 stolen bases.

SCOUTING REPORT: A one-time switch-hitter, Mesa has decided to hit solely lefthanded and struck out just 24 times in 405 plate appearances over the last three years in Cuba's 15U and 18U national leagues. In addition to his contact ability, Mesa has a chance for above-average power. Defensively, Mesa split time between left field and first base last year in Cuba's 18U national league, but he was only playing first base while nursing a sore arm. Mesa is expected to spend time at all three outfield positions in extended spring training, and he could be an above-average corner outfielder with above-average speed and arm strength.

THE FUTURE: Mesa will open 2019 in extended spring training, where he should be close to his older brother, who is expected to start the year at high Class A Jupiter.

Year	Club (League)	Class	W	L	ERA	G	GS	CG	SV	IP	H	HR	BB	SO	K/9	WHIP	AVG
2018	Did not play—Signed 2019 contract																

Milwaukee Brewers

BY TOM HAUDRICOURT

When contemplating future moves, team decision-makers almost always get their cue from the performance on the field. Accordingly, when the 2017 Brewers pushed their rebuilding process forward to the point of missing a wild card berth by only one game, owner Mark Attanasio and general manager David Stearns decided to hit the accelerator.

On Jan. 25, 2018, the Brewers stunned the baseball world by trading for Marlins outfielder Christian Yelich and signing free agent outfielder Lorenzo Cain. Just like that, the team was in "go for it" mode in 2018.

Stearns showed he would use his restocked farm system as currency to make moves, sending top prospects Lewis Brinson, Monte Harrison and Isan Diaz to the Marlins for Yelich. When it came time to add veterans for the stretch run, other top prospects such as Luis Ortiz, Brett Phillips and Kodi Medeiros were dealt.

It soon became evident that the rebuild was over far sooner than anyone expected. The Brewers stripped down their roster in 2015-16, trading veterans for prospects, but Stearns also acquired big league talent to keep things moving in the right direction.

Five games behind the Cubs on Labor Day, the Brewers went on a late surge, forced Game 163 and took the National League Central crown from Chicago. Next came a three-game sweep of Colorado in the Division Series. The Brewers then pushed Los Angeles to seven games in the NL Championship Series, falling just short of their first World Series appearance since 1982.

Manager Craig Counsell, who masterfully used a deep, talented bullpen, continued to grow into one of the top managers in the game, and the Brewers appeared well-stocked for years to come. Though some prospects were dealt away, Stearns and Co. introduced numerous young players who showed they were ready to contribute, including righthanders Corbin Burnes, Brandon Woodruff and Freddy Peralta, all of whom played important roles in the Brewers forging the NL's best record.

With few long-term contracts tying up finances and all of their key players still under control, the Brewers believe they are in an excellent position. Top prospect Keston Hiura, a hitting prodigy who should be their second baseman in the near future, is on the horizon.

The Brewers also saw huge leaps in the farm system from center fielder Corey Ray and righthander Zach Brown, named the organization's hitter and pitcher of the year, respectively. Management's commitment continues to be to build as much

Freddy Peralta was one of the Brewers' young pitchers who shined on the big stage in 2018.

PROJECTED 2022 LINEUP

Catcher	Jacob Nottingham (27)
First Base	Jesus Aguilar (32)
Second Base	Keston Hiura (25)
Third Base	Travis Shaw (32)
Shortstop	Orlando Arcia (27)
Left Field	Lorenzo Cain (36)
Center Field	Corey Ray (27)
Right Field	Christian Yelich (30)
No. 1 Starter	Corbin Burnes (27)
No. 2 Starter	Brandon Woodruff (29)
No. 3 Starter	Jimmy Nelson (33)
No. 4 Starter	Freddy Peralta (26)
No. 5 Starter	Zach Davies (29)
Closer	Josh Hader (28)

from within as possible while adding proven big leaguers when the opportunities arise, as evidenced by the Cain and Yelich moves.

Milwaukee continues to push the envelope in the area of analytics, crunching numbers harder than the IRS to make personnel moves and come up with game plans. The Brewers also inserted a revolving door at the back end of their big league roster, effectively shuffling pitchers back and forth from the minors to keep fresh arms available.

The Brewers made full use of every asset and bit of data to be the best team they could with limited finances and revenues. They succeeded much sooner than anyone expected, and they are primed for more successful seasons.

MILWAUKEE BREWERS

TOP 2019 ROOKIE: Corbin Burnes, RHP. After a sensational big league debut as a reliever in 2018, he is projected to return to the rotation.
BREAKOUT PROSPECT: Braden Webb, RHP. He started putting it together in 2018 and the talent obviously is there.
SLEEPER: Tyrone Taylor, OF. He re-established himself as a prospect in 2018, getting added to 40-man roster.

SOURCE OF TOP 30 TALENT			
Homegrown	24	Acquired	6
College	6	Trade	6
Junior college	2	Rule 5 draft	0
High school	12	Independent league	0
Nondrafted free agent	0	Free agent/waivers	0
International	4		

LF
Troy Stokes Jr. (15)
Trent Grisham (27)
Tyrone Taylor

CF
Corey Ray (3)
Joe Gray (9)
Carlos Rodriguez (19)
Eduarqui Fernandez (21)
Larry Ernesto (24)
Je'Von Ward (25)
Jesus Lujano

RF
Tristen Lutz (8)
Micah Bello (23)
Cooper Hummel

3B
Lucas Erceg (5)
Weston Wilson
Dallas Carroll

SS
Brice Turang (4)
Mauricio Dubon (6)
Eduardo Garcia (28)
Luis Aviles

2B
Keston Hiura (1)
Jake Hager
Devon Hairston
Tucker Neuhaus

1B
Jake Gatewood (12)
Chad McClanahan (30)
Ronnie Gideon

C
Jacob Nottingham (10)
Payton Henry (11)
Mario Feliciano (22)
Max McDowell

LHP

LHSP	LHRP
Aaron Ashby (16)	Quintin Torres-Costa
Cameron Roegner	Daniel Brown
Nathan Kirby	Brad Kuntz
Blake Lillis	

RHP

RHSP	RHRP
Corbin Burnes (2)	Cody Ponce (26)
Zack Brown (7)	Tristan Archer
Braden Webb (13)	Nate Griep
Trey Supak (14)	Jon Olczak
Caden Lemons (17)	Danny Reynolds
Adrian Houser (18)	
Marcos Diplan (20)	
Carlos Herrera (29)	
Bubba Derby	
Aaron Wilkerson	
Conor Harber	
Thomas Jankins	
Alec Bettinger	
Bowden Francis	
Devin Williams	

DRAFT ANALYSIS

2018

BEST PURE HITTER: SS Brice Turang (1) has an advanced approach at the plate with above-average pitch recognition and terrific feel for the strike zone. He brings plus bat-to-ball skills to the table as well and has no issues going to the opposite field with pitches on the outer half.

BEST POWER: C David Fry (7) was a senior sign out of Northwestern State who signed for $10,000, but the Brewers love his aggressive swing. Fry hit .315/.406/.563 with 12 home runs and 15 doubles in 61 Pioneer League games.

FASTEST RUNNER: SS Korry Howell (12) is a plus-plus runner who's occasionally turned in sub 4.0-second times from home-to-first. Currently a shortstop, Howell's speed would translate nicely to the outfield if he winds up moving in the future.

BEST DEFENSIVE PLAYER: Turang has smooth actions at shortstop with an innate feel for the position, taking excellent routes and adjusting well on tough hops. Turang has plus arm strength that he'll use when necessary. OF Joe Gray (2) flashes plus defense in center field, with plus arm strength.

BEST ATHLETE: Gray has loads of raw athleticism and strength, but isn't a pure burner of a runner. OF Micah Bello (2s) is an above-average runner with good body control who played football and helped Hilo (Hawaii) High to a state title.

BEST FASTBALL: RHP Drew Rasmussen (6) could have the best fastball if he comes back from his second Tommy John surgery. When healthy, Rasmussen was up to 98 mph. LHP Aaron Ashby (4) takes this category if Rasmussen doesn't return to form, with a deceptive, 92-95 mph fastball.

BEST SECONDARY PITCH: Ashby's curveball fueled him to 156 strikeouts in just 74.2 innings this spring, but the Brewers actually prefer a power slider that has impressive depth and two-plane break. Both of his secondaries are above-average.

TOP DRAFT PICKS OF THE DECADE

Year	Player, Pos	2018 Org
2009	Eric Arnett, RHP	Did not play
2010	*Dylan Covey, RHP	White Sox
2011	Taylor Jungmann, RHP	Japan
2012	Clint Coulter, C	Brewers
2013	Devin Williams, RHP (2nd round)	Brewers
2014	Kodi Medeiros, LHP	White Sox
2015	Trent Grisham, OF	Brewers
2016	Corey Ray, OF	Brewers
2017	Keston Hiura, 2B	Brewers
2018	Brice Turang, SS	Brewers

*Did not sign

BEST PRO DEBUT: Andrews struck out 41 percent of the batters he faced and pushed his way to low Class A Wisconsin after signing for $75,000 out of Long Beach State. He posted a 2.18 ERA across two levels and 33 innings, with 54 strikeouts and just seven walks, showing a true out-pitch in his changeup.

MOST INTRIGUING BACKGROUND: Ashby's uncle Andy pitched in the majors for 14 years, posting a 4.12 ERA with the Phillies, Rockies, Padres, Braves and Dodgers from 1991-2004.

CLOSEST TO THE MAJORS: Rasmussen could move quickly if he returns to health, while Ashby could move quickly with some minor adjustments.

BEST LATE-ROUND PICK: RHP Reese Olson (13) threw a lot of strikes in the Atlanta-area this spring and developed a reputation of an advanced feel arm, but he impressed the Brewers with his pure stuff, touching 94 mph with his fastball.

THE ONE WHO GOT AWAY: OF Elijah Cabell (14) shares a lot of similar traits with Gray, and has huge power potential. But after not signing in the 14th round, he will attend Florida State, where he could earn early playing time as a freshman.

— CARLOS COLLAZO

2017

2B Keston Hiura (1) has lived up to his reputation as a hitter and has become the team's top prospect. Prep picks OF Tristen Lutz (1s) and RHP Caden Lemons (2) need more time but have shown solid raw tools at the outset of their pro careers.

GRADE: B

2016

RHP Corbin Burnes (4) shot through the minors and in 2018 established himself in the Brewers' bullpen. OF Corey Ray (1) bounced back from a tough first full pro season and RHP Zack Brown (5) took a step forward in Double-A.

GRADE: A

2015

RHP Eric Hanhold (6) gave this class a big leaguer when he debuted in September for the Mets. OF Trent Grisham (1) and RHP Cody Ponce (2) had lackluster leasons in Double-A but still have a chance to reach Milwaukee.

GRADE: F

1 KESTON HIURA, 2B

Born: Aug. 2, 1996. **B-T:** R-R. **Ht:** 5-11. **Wt:** 190.
Drafted: UC Irvine, 2017 (1st). **Signed by:** Wynn Pelzer.

The Brewers considered Hiura the top college hitter in the 2017 draft and did not hesitate to take him with the ninth overall pick, despite a problematic elbow that relegated him to DH as a junior at UC Irvine. He signed for a below-slot $4 million and was assigned to the Rookie-level Arizona League to undergo a throwing program. The Brewers' confidence in Hiura's offensive ability has already been rewarded. He soared from high Class A to Double-A in his first full season and earned a Futures Game selection in 2018. Hiura's elbow also held up and allowed him to play second base regularly starting in June, easing fears that he might need Tommy John surgery. To work further on his defense, he was assigned to the Arizona Fall League, where he continued to open eyes with his offensive prowess. Including an impressive stint at big league camp in 2018, Hiura has exuded confidence in his ability to hit, and it's easy to see why. The Brewers have not had a hitter with this kind of upside since Ryan Braun, the fifth overall pick in 2005.

SCOUTING REPORT: Hiura has a compact, powerful stroke with tremendous bat speed and the hand-eye coordination to barrel pitches consistently. With so few moving parts in his swing, he should be able to avoid long droughts. Though not a power hitter per se, he has explosive hands and enough pop to project to be above-average in that department, with an approach of hitting to all fields. Hiura projects to hit for a high average with good power for the position. Though not a threat to steal bases, he is an average runner and shows good instincts and awareness on the basepaths and has shown the ability to take a bag when opponents aren't paying attention. Hiura merely will have to hold his own in the field, where he has shown improvement since turning pro, with decent footwork and range. His calling card is his bat, and it's a good one.

THE FUTURE: It's up to the Brewers to decide whether to push Hiura to Triple-A to begin 2019, or with an in-season promotion. One thing is certain: Hiura will be the Brewers' starting second baseman and middle-of-the-order hitter sometime in the near future. Teams already have tried to pry Hiura away in trade proposals, but the Brewers have no intention of trading a young hitter with this kind of potential.

JOE ROBBINS/GETTY IMAGES

BA GRADE	SCOUTING GRADES
60 Risk: Medium	Hit: 60. Power: 55. Run: 50. Field: 50. Arm: 45.

Projected future grades on 20-80 scouting scale.

TOP PROSPECTS OF THE DECADE

Year	Player, Pos	2018 Org
2009	Alcides Escobar, SS	Royals
2010	Alcides Escobar, SS	Royals
2011	Jake Odorizzi, RHP	Twins
2012	Wily Peralta, RHP	Royals
2013	Wily Peralta, RHP	Royals
2014	Jimmy Nelson, RHP	Brewers
2015	Tyrone Taylor, OF	Brewers
2016	Orlando Arcia, SS	Brewers
2017	Lewis Brinson, OF	Marlins
2018	Lewis Brinson, OF	Marlins

BEST TOOLS

Best Hitter for Average	Keston Hiura
Best Power Hitter	Corey Ray
Best Strike-Zone Discipline	Trent Grisham
Fastest Baserunner	Corey Ray
Best Athlete	Corey Ray
Best Fastball	Braden Webb
Best Curveball	Zack Brown
Best Slider	Marcos Diplan
Best Changeup	Trey Supak
Best Control	Christian Taugner
Best Defensive Catcher	Payton Henry
Best Defensive Infielder	Brice Turang
Best Infield Arm	Lucas Erceg
Best Defensive Outfielder	Troy Stokes Jr.
Best Outfield Arm	Joe Gray

Year	Club (League)	Class	AVG	G	AB	R	H	2B	3B	HR	RBI	BB	SO	SB	CS	OBP	SLG
2017	Brewers (AZL)	R	.435	15	62	18	27	3	5	4	18	6	13	0	2	.500	.839
	Wisconsin (MWL)	LoA	.333	27	105	14	35	11	2	0	15	7	24	2	0	.374	.476
2018	Carolina (CAR)	HiA	.320	50	206	38	66	16	3	7	23	14	47	4	6	.382	.529
	Biloxi (SL)	AA	.272	73	279	36	76	18	2	6	20	22	56	11	5	.339	.416
Minor League Totals			.313	165	652	106	204	48	12	17	76	49	140	17	13	.374	.502

2 CORBIN BURNES, RHP

Born: Oct. 22, 1994. **B-T:** R-R. **HT:** 6-3. **WT:** 205. **Drafted:** St. Mary's, 2016 (4th round). **Signed by:** Joe Graham.

TRACK RECORD: Burnes began the season in the Triple-A Colorado Springs rotation but moved to relief with the Brewers wanting to see if he could help them during their second-half playoff push. He performed so well that he was quickly transitioned to high-leverage situations and pitched critical innings in the NL Championship Series. Despite that success, the plan is for Burnes to return to starting in 2019.

SCOUTING REPORT: Burnes has the four-pitch repertoire of a starter and pounds the strike zone with all of those pitches, keeping hitters on the defensive. With a quick arm action, he throws his fastball in the 93-95 mph range with natural movement, doing a good job of keeping it down in the strike zone. He relied more on his above-average mid-80s slider in 2018, which was death on righthanded hitters when he put it where he wanted. Burnes mixes in an upper-80s split-changeup and upper-70s curveball, both average, that give opponents more pitches to process. He maintains his stuff deep into starts with plus control and can be a groundball machine when he keeps his fastball low in the zone. The Brewers love the way Burnes competes and shows great mound presence even under stress.

THE FUTURE: Burnes will audition for the big league rotation in 2019. His confidence and conviction in his pitches is apparent, and the Brewers think he is a star in the making.

BA GRADE
55 Risk: Low
Fastball: 60.
Slider: 55. Curve: 50.
Change: 50. CTL: 60.

Year	Club (League)	Class	W	L	ERA	G	GS	CG	SV	IP	H	HR	BB	SO	K/9	WHIP	AVG
2016	Brewers (AZL)	R	0	0	1.29	3	1	0	0	7	3	0	2	10	12.9	0.71	.125
	Wisconsin (MWL)	LoA	3	0	2.20	9	5	0	0	29	20	1	16	31	9.7	1.26	.200
2017	Carolina (CAR)	HiA	5	0	1.05	10	10	0	0	60	37	1	16	56	8.4	0.88	.181
	Biloxi (SL)	AA	3	3	2.10	16	16	1	0	86	66	2	20	84	8.8	1.00	.212
2018	Colorado Springs (PCL)	AAA	3	4	5.15	19	13	0	0	79	83	7	31	81	9.3	1.45	.275
	Milwaukee (NL)	MAJ	7	0	2.61	30	0	0	1	38	27	4	11	35	8.3	1.00	.199
Major League Totals			7	0	2.61	30	0	0	1	38	27	4	11	35	8.3	1.00	.199
Minor League Totals			14	7	2.77	57	45	1	0	260	209	11	85	262	9.1	1.13	.222

3 COREY RAY, OF

Born: Sept. 22, 1994. **B-T:** L-L. **HT:** 5-11. **WT:** 185. **Drafted:** Louisville, 2016 (1st round). **Signed by:** Jeff Simpson.

TRACK RECORD: No prospect in the Brewers' system had more to prove than Ray, the fifth overall pick in 2016 who signed for a franchise-record $4.125 million. He suffered a knee injury in instructional league in 2016 that required minor surgery, then he got totally out of whack in 2017 with his hitting mechanics. He regrouped in 2018 at Double-A Biloxi, rediscovering his power stroke and performing so well he won Southern League MVP.

SCOUTING REPORT: With his swing back in order, Ray displayed tremendous bat speed and power with plenty of hard contact. He still has considerable work to do in pitch recognition and plate discipline after striking out 176 times. Strikeouts likely will remain a part of Ray's game due to his aggressiveness and long swing, but it's a fair trade-off for the all-fields power he generates. Ray's plus speed makes him a threat to steal any time he reaches base, and it also allows him to chase down balls in center field, where he is above-average with an average arm.

THE FUTURE: Now that his confidence is back, Ray should continue to improve as a hitter. He'll head to Triple-A San Antonio in 2019 and fits t he swing-and-miss, power-packed profile being played at the top level these days.

BA GRADE
55 Risk: High
Hit: 45. Power: 55.
Run: 60. Field: 55.
Arm: 50.

Year	Club (League)	Class	AVG	G	AB	R	H	2B	3B	HR	RBI	BB	SO	SB	CS	OBP	SLG
2016	Brevard County (FSL)	HiA	.247	57	231	24	57	13	2	5	17	20	54	9	5	.307	.385
	Wisconsin (MWL)	LoA	.083	3	12	2	1	0	0	0	0	0	3	4	1	.313	.083
2017	Carolina (CAR)	HiA	.241	112	449	56	108	30	4	7	48	48	156	24	10	.313	.372
2018	Biloxi (SL)	AA	.239	135	532	86	127	32	7	27	74	60	176	37	7	.323	.477
Minor League Totals			.239	307	1224	168	293	75	13	39	139	131	390	71	23	.317	.417

4 BRICE TURANG, SS

Born: Nov. 21, 1999. **B-T:** L-R. **HT:** 6-1. **WT:** 165. **Drafted:** HS—Corona, Calif., 2018 (1st round). **Signed by:** Wynn Pelzer.

TRACK RECORD: Turang put together a pristine amateur track record, starting all four years at Santiago High in Southern California's top division and starring for USA Baseball's 18U National Team in both 2016 and 2017. He was frequently mentioned as the possible No. 1 pick leading up to the 2018 draft and put together a solid senior year, but he fell short of sky-high expectations and fell victim to so-called prospect fatigue and slid to the Brewers at No. 21 overall. He signed for $3,411,100 at the deadline and passed up an opportunity to play at Louisiana State.

SCOUTING REPORT: Turang ranked among the more polished prep players as an advanced hitter with solid plate discipline and a gift for putting the ball in play to all fields. He takes a smooth, lefthanded stroke that covers the entire plate and lines the ball hard from line to line. His calling card is his speed, a plus tool that makes him a difference-maker on the bases and also a shortstop who covers vast expanses up the middle. Turang flashes sure hands and good footwork and a strong enough arm to remain at shortstop. The biggest knocks against him are his slight build, fringy strength and limited power potential. Turang is the son of former big league outfielder Brian Turang, and is a baseball gym rat who knows how to survive and play the game.

THE FUTURE: Turang has a chip on his shoulder after sliding down the draft. After batting .283 with a .396 on-base percentage at the Rookie levels, low Class A Wisconsin is next.

BA GRADE

55 Risk: Extreme

Hit: 55. **Power:** 40.
Run: 60. **Field:** 55.
Arm: 50.

Year	Club (League)	Class	AVG	G	AB	R	H	2B	3B	HR	RBI	BB	SO	SB	CS	OBP	SLG
2018	Brewers (AZL)	R	.319	13	47	11	15	2	0	0	7	9	6	8	1	.421	.362
	Helena (PIO)	R	.268	29	112	26	30	4	1	1	11	22	28	6	1	.385	.348
Minor League Totals			.283	42	159	37	45	6	1	1	18	31	34	14	2	.396	.352

5 ZACK BROWN, RHP

Born: Dec. 15, 1994. **B-T:** R-R. **HT:** 6-1. **WT:** 180. **Drafted:** Kentucky, 2016 (5th round). **Signed by:** Jeff Simpson.

TRACK RECORD: Brown fell in the 2016 draft after a miserable 2-11, 6.08 junior year at Kentucky, but the Brewers stayed with him and signed him for just over $400,000 in the fifth round. After conquering the Class A levels in 2017, he broke out with Double-A Biloxi in 2018, going 9-1, 2.44 and winning Southern League pitcher of the year.

SCOUTING REPORT: Brown has made huge strides commanding his three-pitch mix, allowing him to produce his best results as a pro and maintain his stuff deep into games. He throws his fastball in the 92-95 mph range and hits both corners of the plate while also using a two-seamer to induce a ton of ground balls. Brown began using his curveball more as a pro and it has been his best pitch at times, growing to plus and keeping hitters off his hard stuff. He also developed a better feel for an average changeup, which also made his fastball play more. In short, Brown became a pitcher rather than a thrower, and the Brewers love the way he competes and attacks the zone.

THE FUTURE: Brown is firmly on the Brewers' radar after winning the Brewers' minor league pitcher of the year award. He will open 2019 at Triple-A as a starter and could make his major league debut as a reliever, much like Josh Hader and Corbin Burnes.

BA GRADE

50 Risk: High

Fastball: 55.
Curveball: 60.
Change: 50. **CTL:** 50.

Year	Club (League)	Class	W	L	ERA	G	GS	CG	SV	IP	H	HR	BB	SO	K/9	WHIP	AVG
2016	Helena (PIO)	R	0	2	13.50	3	2	0	0	5	11	0	5	5	8.4	3.00	.423
	Wisconsin (MWL)	LoA	1	2	3.00	9	4	0	1	33	29	3	5	29	7.9	1.03	.221
2017	Wisconsin (MWL)	LoA	4	5	3.39	18	13	0	0	85	78	7	34	84	8.9	1.32	.249
	Carolina (CAR)	HiA	3	0	2.16	4	4	0	0	25	24	1	2	23	8.3	1.04	.250
2018	Brewers (AZL)	R	0	0	0.00	1	1	0	0	2	3	0	1	3	13.5	2.00	.333
	Biloxi (SL)	AA	9	1	2.44	22	21	1	0	126	95	8	36	116	8.3	1.04	.207
Minor League Totals			17	10	2.97	57	45	1	1	276	240	19	83	260	8.5	1.17	.232

6 MAURICIO DUBON, SS/2B

Born: July 19, 1994. **B-T:** R-R. **HT:** 6-0. **WT:** 175. **Drafted:** HS—Sacramento, 2013 (26th round). **Signed by:** Demond Smith (Red Sox).

TRACK RECORD: Acquired from the Red Sox with Travis Shaw in the Tyler Thornburg trade in December 2016, Dubon got off to a brilliant start in 2018 at Triple-A Colorado Springs, including a 23-game hit streak. Then, trying to escape a rundown in a game against Oklahoma City, he suffered a torn anterior cruciate ligament in his left knee, ending his season after just one month. **SCOUTING REPORT:** Dubon is a good athlete with sharp instincts in all areas of the game. He has superb bat-to-ball skills at the plate and solid bat speed, allowing him to generate consistent line-drive contact. He seldom walks but doesn't strike out much, and he projects to at least an average hitter who will hit enough to make up for little home run power. Dubon is a natural shortstop but also is comfortable at second base, with the hands, range and arm to play either side of the bag. He has above-average speed and is very aggressive on the bases, making him a constant threat to steal. He plays with a high energy and enthusiasm, showing an obvious love for the game, and he demonstrates both leadership skills and maturity on and off the field.

THE FUTURE: Dubon is expected to be recovered by Opening Day. A return to Triple-A is likely, with his major league debut on target as long his knee holds up.

BA GRADE

45 Risk: Medium

Hit: 55. **Power:** 40.
Run: 55. **Field:** 55.
Arm: 55.

Year	Club (League)	Class	AVG	G	AB	R	H	2B	3B	HR	RBI	BB	SO	SB	CS	OBP	SLG
2016	Salem (CAR)	HiA	.306	62	235	53	72	11	3	0	29	33	25	24	4	.387	.379
	Portland (EL)	AA	.339	62	251	48	85	20	6	6	40	11	36	6	3	.371	.538
2017	Biloxi (SL)	AA	.272	71	268	34	73	14	0	2	24	25	42	31	9	.334	.347
	Colorado Springs (PCL)	AAA	.272	58	224	40	61	15	0	6	33	14	34	7	6	.320	.420
2018	Colorado Springs (PCL)	AAA	.343	27	108	18	37	9	2	4	18	2	19	6	3	.348	.574
Minor League Totals			.299	486	1868	311	559	101	15	26	229	136	266	117	42	.348	.411

7 TRISTEN LUTZ, OF

Born: Aug. 22, 1998. **B-T:** R-R. **HT:** 6-3. **WT:** 210. **Drafted:** HS—Arlington, Texas, 2017 (1st round supplemental). **Signed by:** K.J. Hendricks.

TRACK RECORD: The Brewers paid Lutz more than $2.3 million as the 34th overall pick in 2017, going nearly $370,000 above slot value to lure him away from Texas. The native Texan got off to a slow start in the cold weather of the Midwest League but stayed strong mentally. As the Brewers expected, Lutz heated up with the weather, posted an .814 OPS from May 15 onward at low Class A Wisconsin.

SCOUTING REPORT: Lutz's biggest upside is considered to be his budding above-average power, but he also is an impressive athlete with the tools to succeed. His power comes from bat speed and sheer strength, which will only play better as he gains experience and collects more at-bats. The Brewers do not think Lutz will be an all-or-nothing hitter because he recognizes pitches well for his age and is willing to use the whole field. He runs the bases well as an average runner with advanced instincts and shows better range in center field than might be expected. His future almost certainly is in right field because of his above-average, accurate arm.

THE FUTURE: Lutz's power potential, athleticism and maturity gives him a solid foundation the Brewers are high on. He'll move to high Class A Carolina as a 20-year-old in 2019.

BA GRADE

50 Risk: High

Hit: 50. **Power:** 55.
Run: 50. **Field:** 50.
Arm: 55.

Year	Club (League)	Class	AVG	G	AB	R	H	2B	3B	HR	RBI	BB	SO	SB	CS	OBP	SLG
2017	Helena (PIO)	R	.333	24	93	23	31	1	1	6	16	12	21	2	4	.432	.559
	Brewers (AZL)	R	.279	16	68	12	19	4	3	3	11	4	21	1	0	.347	.559
2018	Wisconsin (MWL)	LoA	.245	119	444	63	109	33	3	13	63	46	139	9	3	.321	.421
Minor League Totals			.263	159	605	98	159	38	7	22	90	62	181	12	7	.342	.458

8 LUCAS ERCEG, 3B

Born: May 1, 1995. **B-T:** L-R. **HT:** 6-3. **WT:** 200. **Drafted:** Menlo (Calif.), 2016 (2nd round). **Signed by:** Joe Graham.

TRACK RECORD: Some thought Erceg would breeze through the Brewers' system as an advanced college hitter, but his progress has been slowed by health issues. Already dealing with a bulging disc in his lower back, Erceg was hit in the head with a pitch in April 2018 at Double-A Biloxi and struggled for several weeks to get going at the plate. He improved in the second half, but his overall numbers were still down from previous seasons.

SCOUTING REPORT: Erceg has several tools that excite the Brewers, topped by his raw power. He can hit balls out of sight, showing tremendous pull power when pitchers miss their spots. As with most power hitters, he has swing and miss in his game and can get overly aggressive, taking big hacks at suspect pitches and limiting his walk rate and ability to get on base. A good athlete, Erceg has a strong arm but needs to slow down and not rush his throws. He committed a Southern League-leading 23 errors in 2018. He normally has good footwork around the bag and also runs the bases alertly with average speed.

THE FUTURE: The tools and work ethic are there for Erceg to be successful, but he must stay healthy and improve his plate discipline to reach the majors. He should see Triple-A San Antonio in 2019.

BA GRADE	
50	**Risk:** High

Hit: 45. Power: 55.
Run: 50. Field: 55.
Arm: 60.

Year	Club (League)	Class	AVG	G	AB	R	H	2B	3B	HR	RBI	BB	SO	SB	CS	OBP	SLG
2016	Helena (PIO)	R	.400	26	105	17	42	8	1	2	22	8	16	8	1	.452	.552
	Wisconsin (MWL)	LoA	.281	42	167	17	47	9	3	7	29	12	38	1	3	.328	.497
2017	Carolina (CAR)	HiA	.256	127	496	66	127	33	1	15	81	35	95	2	3	.307	.417
	Colorado Springs (PCL)	AAA	.400	3	10	2	4	2	0	0	2	1	1	0	0	.455	.600
2018	Biloxi (SL)	AA	.248	123	463	52	115	21	1	13	51	37	82	3	1	.306	.382
Minor League Totals			.270	321	1241	154	335	73	6	37	185	93	232	14	8	.323	.428

9 JOE GRAY, OF

Born: March 12, 2000. **B-T:** R-R. **HT:** 6-1. **WT:** 195. **Drafted:** HS—Hattiesburg, Miss., 2018 (2nd round). **Signed by:** Scott Nichols.

TRACK RECORD: Much like first-round pick Brice Turang, Gray was on high school prospect watch lists since before he could drive. And much like Turang, Gray plateaued a bit and dropped further in the 2018 draft than originally expected. Thus the Brewers were excited to get a player with his athleticism in the second round for a $1.1 million price tag. to forgo a Mississippi commitment. Gray hit .182 in the Rookie-level Arizona League but showed a good eye and got on base enough to make a positive impression.

SCOUTING REPORT: Gray gets scouts' attention with his plus raw power and tremendous arm strength, his two biggest tools. He also runs well enough to play center field, though he may move to right field as he matures and gets bigger. What remains to be seen is if Gray will make enough consistent contact to take advantage of his power and above-average speed on the bases. During his showcase days, Gray often tweaked his batting stance and needs to find a consistent setup that works.

THE FUTURE: The Brewers believe a young player with raw tools like Gray can develop into an impact player. He will play the entire 2019 season at age 19, so he has plenty of time to prove them right.

BILL MITCHELL

BA GRADE	
55	**Risk:** Extreme

Hit: 45. Power: 60.
Run: 55. Field: 55.
Arm: 60.

Year	Club (League)	Class	AVG	G	AB	R	H	2B	3B	HR	RBI	BB	SO	SB	CS	OBP	SLG
2018	Brewers (AZL)	R	.182	24	77	14	14	5	0	2	9	18	25	6	0	.347	.325
Minor League Totals			.182	24	77	14	14	5	0	2	9	18	25	6	0	.347	.325

10 JACOB NOTTINGHAM, C

Born: April 3, 1995. **B-T:** R-R. **HT:** 6-3. **WT:** 230. **Drafted:** HS—Redlands, Calif., 2013 (6th round). **Signed by:** Brad Budzinski (Astros).

TRACK RECORD: Ever since the Brewers acquired Nottingham in the trade that sent Khris Davis to Oakland in February 2016, there have been questions whether he could put his physical gifts together offensively and defensively. After middling results in two seasons at Double-A, Nottingham made huge strides at Triple-A in 2018 and was rewarded with his first big league callup. A couple of injuries, including a chip fracture in his right wrist suffered on a foul tip, limited him to 50 games, the only downside to his season.

SCOUTING REPORT: Nottingham's 6-foot-3, 230-pound size helps him produce big power but hinders his quickness and agility behind the plate. He has worked hard to improve his game-calling and blocking, now showing enough to get the job done at an average level to go with his above-average arm. Nottingham's mammoth raw power has yet to yield big home run totals because he's still too aggressive with too many strikeouts. He has moved in the right direction by reducing his strikeout rate and improving his on-base percentage each year.

THE FUTURE: Nottingham's biggest improvements have come on the defensive side, the key for any catching prospect. He now projects as a power-hitting backup at least and is still young enough to emerge as more.

BA GRADE
45 Risk: Medium

Hit: 40. Power: 50.
Run: 30. Field: 50.
Arm: 55.

Year	Club (League)	Class	AVG	G	AB	R	H	2B	3B	HR	RBI	BB	SO	SB	CS	OBP	SLG
2016	Biloxi (SL)	AA	.234	112	415	46	97	14	0	11	37	29	138	9	2	.295	.347
2017	Biloxi (SL)	AA	.209	101	325	37	68	21	2	9	48	37	87	7	3	.326	.369
2018	Colorado Springs (PCL)	AAA	.281	50	178	33	50	10	2	10	36	14	59	2	1	.347	.528
	Milwaukee (NL)	MAJ	.200	9	20	2	4	1	0	0	0	4	8	0	0	.333	.250
Major League Totals			.200	9	20	2	4	1	0	0	0	4	8	0	0	.333	.250
Minor League Totals			.257	474	1703	237	438	98	9	53	251	152	475	27	12	.333	.419

11 TREY SUPAK, RHP

BA GRADE
45 Risk: Medium

Born: May 31, 1996. **B-T:** R-R. **Ht.:** 6-5. **Wt.:** 235. **Drafted:** HS—La Grange, Texas, 2014 (2nd round supplemental). **Signed by:** Trevor Haley (Pirates).

TRACK RECORD: The more you see Supak, the more you like him. Originally acquired from the Pirates with Keon Broxton for Jason Rogers in December 2015, Supark was so impressive last season in his first nine starts at high Class A Carolina that the Brewers bumped him up to Double-A Biloxi, where he became one of the most consistent performers on a strong staff.

SCOUTING REPORT: Supak has picked up velocity in recent seasons and now regularly works in the 93-95 mph range, taking advantage of his 6-foot-5 height to add good downhill plane. Supak's curveball has become an above-average pitch, and he has shown good aptitude in improving his changeup to average as well. By improving command of his pitches, his strikeout totals have remained strong while his walk rate has improved. In particular, the Brewers love the way Supak competes and makes big pitches when needed.

THE FUTURE: As he continues to work on his delivery and smoothing out his mechanics, Supak projects to be a reliable, durable starter with a four-pitch mix. He'll move to Triple-A Colorado Springs in 2019.

Year	Club (League)	Class	W	L	ERA	G	GS	CG	SV	IP	H	HR	BB	SO	K/9	WHIP	AVG
2016	Helena (PIO)	R	1	1	1.29	4	2	0	0	14	10	0	1	11	7.1	0.79	.200
	Wisconsin (MWL)	LoA	2	3	3.86	11	6	0	1	44	48	3	17	40	8.1	1.47	.274
2017	Wisconsin (MWL)	LoA	2	2	1.76	8	7	0	0	41	21	1	10	53	11.6	0.76	.156
	Carolina (CAR)	HiA	3	4	4.60	15	11	0	1	72	65	12	28	57	7.1	1.29	.241
2018	Carolina (CAR)	HiA	2	1	1.76	9	9	0	0	51	39	2	16	48	8.5	1.04	.208
	Biloxi (SL)	AA	6	6	2.91	16	16	0	0	87	74	4	28	75	7.8	1.18	.232
Minor League Totals			18	22	3.43	79	65	0	2	362	317	28	116	328	8.2	1.20	.238

12 PAYTON HENRY, C

BA GRADE
45 Risk: High

Born: June 24, 1997. **B-T:** R-R. **HT:** 6-2. **WT:** 225. **Drafted:** HS—Pleasant Grove, Utah, 2016 (6th round). **Signed by:** Jeff Scholzen.

TRACK RECORD: Following two years in Rookie-ball after signing for $550,600 as a sixth-round pick in 2016, Henry moved to full-season ball in 2018 and played the entire season as low Class A Wisconsin's No. 1 catcher. Though his .234 batting average and overall numbers weren't impressive, the Brewers loved his take-charge approach behind the plate, high energy level and leadership skills he displayed.

SCOUTING REPORT: Henry has physical strength that plays on both sides of the ball. He has above-average raw power that should continue to develop, although he still has some swing and miss to his game as well as a tendency to try to pull the ball too often. Henry manages the strike zone decently well, drawing enough walks to assure a fine on-base percentage. Behind the plate, Payton is a solid defender with above-average arm strength that helps him control the run game. He threw out 35 percent of attempted base stealers in 2018 while showing sub-1.95 second pop times, an above-average to plus arm.

THE FUTURE: Henry's intangibles and defense behind the plate give him a strong foundation to work from, as does his budding power. He'll try to take the next steps as an overall hitter at high Class A Carolina in 2019.

Year	Club (League)	Class	AVG	G	AB	R	H	2B	3B	HR	RBI	BB	SO	SB	CS	OBP	SLG
2016	Brewers (AZL)	R	.256	24	82	15	21	7	0	0	17	6	19	0	1	.333	.341
2017	Helena (PIO)	R	.242	55	207	38	50	17	1	7	33	30	69	1	0	.344	.435
2018	Wisconsin (MWL)	LoA	.234	98	337	44	79	15	2	10	41	38	124	7	5	.327	.380
Minor League Totals			.240	177	626	97	150	39	3	17	91	74	212	8	6	.334	.393

13 JAKE GATEWOOD, 1B

BA GRADE

45 Risk: High

Born: Sept. 25, 1995. **B-T:** R-R. **Ht:** 6-6. **Wt.:** 215. **Drafted:** HS—Clovis, Calif., 2014 (1st round supplemental). **Signed by:** Dan Huston.

TRACK RECORD: Long considered a boom-or-bust prospect because of his immense power and swing-and-miss tendencies, Gatewood was in the midst of his best season at Double-A Biloxi before he suffered a torn ACL in his left knee in July 2018 while running to first base. It was particularly unfortunate because Gatewood had already set career highs with 19 home runs and .767 OPS in 94 games.

SCOUTING REPORT: With great leverage and extension out of his physical, 6-foot-6 frame, Gatewood has big power to all fields and can hit the ball a long way. He is aggressive and doesn't draw many walks, but sharper vision thanks to new contact lenses has helped improve his plate discipline and pitch recognition. Drafted as a shortstop, Gatewood initially moved to third base and now is considered an athletic first baseman who has learned his way around the bag.

THE FUTURE: Gatewood's knee injury came at an unfortunate time in his development. He won't be ready for spring training and will hope to get out to an affiliate by the summer.

Year	Club (League)	Class	AVG	G	AB	R	H	2B	3B	HR	RBI	BB	SO	SB	CS	OBP	SLG
2016	Wisconsin (MWL)	LoA	.240	126	496	70	119	33	0	14	64	18	141	3	2	.268	.391
2017	Carolina (CAR)	HiA	.269	111	420	66	113	36	1	11	53	43	132	7	5	.340	.438
	Biloxi (SL)	AA	.239	23	92	9	22	4	2	4	9	8	29	3	0	.300	.457
2018	Biloxi (SL)	AA	.244	94	352	45	86	19	1	19	59	28	114	2	0	.302	.466
Minor League Totals			.244	513	1953	263	477	126	6	61	274	142	620	30	20	.297	.409

14 BRADEN WEBB, RHP

BA GRADE

45 Risk: High

Born: April 25, 1995. **B-T:** R-R. **Ht.:** 6-3. **Wt.:** 200. **Drafted:** South Carolina, 2016 (3rd round). **Signed by:** Steve Smith.

TRACK RECORD: Webb was projected to be a high pick out of Owasso (Okla.) High in 2014 after throwing consecutive no-hitters to start his senior season, but he injured his elbow in his third start and had Tommy John surgery. He spent one year rehabbing and one year pitching at South Carolina before the Brewers drafted him in the third round in 2016 and signed him for $700,000. After a fine pro debut at low Class A Wisconsin, Webb moved up two levels to Double-A in 2018.

SCOUTING REPORT: Webb's stuff is progressively coming back. His fastball sits 91-93 mph and can reach 96 mph, and he gives batters a different look with a mid-80s two-seamer. Webb's big out pitch is a 12-to-6 curveball that buckles knees in the mid- to upper 70s, but there's also days it's below-average and loopy at 72-74 mph. He has worked to improve his mid-80s changeup. Webb's command of all three pitches has improved, but there is still work to be done.

THE FUTURE: Webb will start 2019 back at Double-A Biloxi. He gets a little better every year, a trend the Brewers hope will continue enough to make him a back-end starter.

Year	Club (League)	Class	W	L	ERA	G	GS	CG	SV	IP	H	HR	BB	SO	K/9	WHIP	AVG
2017	Wisconsin (MWL)	LoA	6	7	4.36	22	13	1	3	87	72	8	39	90	9.3	1.28	.222
2018	Carolina (CAR)	HiA	5	8	4.20	21	21	0	0	101	89	9	56	104	9.3	1.44	.239
	Biloxi (SL)	AA	1	0	1.80	4	3	0	0	20	13	0	10	24	10.8	1.15	.186
Minor League Totals			12	15	4.04	47	37	1	3	207	174	17	105	218	9.5	1.35	.227

15 TROY STOKES JR., OF

BA GRADE

45 Risk: High

Born: Feb. 2, 1996. **B-T:** R-R. **Ht.:** 5-9. **Wt.:** 200. **Drafted:** HS—Baltimore, 2014 (4th round). **Signed by:** Dan Nellum.

TRACK RECORD: Ever since the Brewers drafted Stokes in the fourth round in 2014 and signed him for $400,000 to forgo a Maryland commitment, his calling card has been his outfield defense. Stokes won the minor league Gold Glove award for left field at Double-A Biloxi in 2018, and he added some sock with 19 homers followed by a strong offensive showing in the Venezuelan Winter League.

SCOUTING REPORT: Stokes' above-average speed already was a big part of his game, and his growing power gives him two coveted tools. At 5-9, 200 pounds, Stokes has a strong, compact frame with a short, compact swing that sends balls out to left field with average power. That tendency to pull leaves a lot of swing and miss in his game, however, as evidenced by his 147 strikeouts and .233 batting average. Still, Stokes' overall approach at the plate is solid, resulting in walks and an acceptable on-base rate. His speed plays well both on the basepaths and in the outfield, but a below-average arm limits him to left field.

THE FUTURE: Stokes' blend of power and speed, in combination with great defensive skills, gives him a chance to keep rising. He will open 2019 at Triple-A San Antonio.

Year	Club (League)	Class	AVG	G	AB	R	H	2B	3B	HR	RBI	BB	SO	SB	CS	OBP	SLG
2016	Wisconsin (MWL)	LoA	.268	86	314	50	84	20	4	4	29	36	62	20	4	.358	.395
2017	Carolina (CAR)	HiA	.248	100	363	60	90	19	5	14	56	47	77	21	9	.342	.444
	Biloxi (SL)	AA	.252	35	135	19	34	9	0	6	18	16	34	9	3	.333	.452
2018	Biloxi (SL)	AA	.233	129	467	74	109	23	6	19	58	65	147	19	2	.343	.430
Minor League Totals			.252	459	1677	283	423	93	18	48	206	221	417	114	27	.353	.415

16 AARON ASHBY, LHP

BA GRADE

45 Risk: High

Born: May 24, 1998. **B-T:** R-L. **Ht.:** 6-1. **Wt.:** 170. **Drafted:** Crowder (Mo.) JC, 2018 (4th round). **Signed by:** Drew Anderson.

TRACK RECORD: Ashby is the nephew of 14-year big league pitcher and fellow Crowder (Mo.) JC alum Andy Ashby. He led all Division I junior college pitchers with 156 strikeouts in 2018, an average of 18.8 strikeouts per nine innings. The Brewers drafted him in the fourth round and signed him for an above-slot $520,000 to forgo a Tennessee commitment. Ashby moved quickly after signing, making seven starts at low Class A Wisconsin and posting a 2.17 ERA.

SCOUTING REPORT: Ashby's fastball velocity has crept from the upper 80s in college to 91-93 mph as a professional, with room for more growth. Ashby's best pitch is a plus, sharp-breaking curveball he can spin harder to morph into a slider, giving him two breaking balls to confuse hitters. Few young hitters are adept at hitting breaking balls of his quality, leading to a total of 66 strikeouts in 57.2 innings in his pro debut. Ashby has a funky delivery that gives him great deception but also hampers his strike-throwing at times. He doesn't throw his changeup much, and it remains to be seen how his stuff will play against advanced hitters as he moves up the ladder.

THE FUTURE: Ashby gets a lot of strikeouts by getting hitters to chase his breaking stuff, and at the very least projects to a situational lefty in the majors. The Brewers think with maturity and more work on his changeup, he can remain in a starting role.

Year	Club (League)	Class	W	L	ERA	G	GS	CG	SV	IP	H	HR	BB	SO	K/9	WHIP	AVG
2018	Helena (PIO)	R	1	2	6.20	6	3	0	1	20	18	3	8	19	8.4	1.28	.234
	Wisconsin (MWL)	LoA	1	1	2.17	7	7	0	0	37	40	1	9	47	11.3	1.31	.274
Minor League Totals			2	3	3.59	13	10	0	1	58	58	4	17	66	10.3	1.30	.260

17 CADEN LEMONS, RHP

BA GRADE

50 Risk: Extreme

Born: Dec. 2, 1998. **B-T:** R-R. **Ht.:** 6-6. **Wt.:** 175. **Drafted:** HS—Vestavia Hills, Ala., 2017 (2nd round). **Signed by:** Scott Nichols.

TRACK RECORD: The 6-foot-6 Lemons showed signs of growing into his body as a high school senior and signed with the Brewers for $1.45 million as the 46th overall pick in 2017. He remained in Rookie-ball his entire first season and showed he remains a work in progress with many rough edges to be smoothed. He posted a 5.97 ERA in 10 outings at the rookie levels, allowing more than one hit per inning.

SCOUTING REPORT: Lemons is a long-term project whose progress will come as he fills out his tall, lanky frame and gets stronger physically. Pitching from a three-quarter arm slot, Lemons gets good movement on his low-90s fastball but also struggles to repeat his delivery, leading to below-average control. He mixes in two breaking balls—a low-80s slider that flashes average and a fringy curveball—and dabbles with a changeup as well. In addition to lacking the coordination to repeat his delivery, Lemons' arm speed is also not yet where it needs to be, further hampering his stuff.

THE FUTURE: It's going to take time to put everything together, but the Brewers think a 6-foot-6 pitcher with the potential to throw four pitches is worth the time and effort to develop. Lemons will get his first look at full-season ball in 2019 at low Class A Wisconsin.

Year	Club (League)	Class	W	L	ERA	G	GS	CG	SV	IP	H	HR	BB	SO	K/9	WHIP	AVG
2017	Brewers (AZL)	R	0	1	6.75	3	3	0	0	3	2	1	0	1	3.4	0.75	.200
2018	Brewers (AZL)	R	0	0	1.38	5	4	0	0	13	7	0	5	11	7.6	0.92	.149
	Helena (PIO)	R	1	2	6.27	5	5	0	0	19	26	2	9	17	8.2	1.88	.321
Minor League Totals			1	3	4.46	13	12	0	0	34	35	3	14	29	7.6	1.43	.254

18 ADRIAN HOUSER, RHP

Born: Feb. 2, 1993. **B-T:** R-R. **Ht.:** 6-3. **Wt.:** 230. **Drafted:** HS—Locust Grove, Okla., 2011 (2nd round). **Signed by:** Jim Stevenson (Astros).

BA GRADE
40 Risk: Medium

TRACK RECORD: Houser has been a prospect for a while as a second-round pick of the Astros in 2011. After coming to Milwaukee in the Carlos Gomez trade in July 2015, his career was sidetracked by Tommy John surgery that wiped out most of 2016 and 2017, but in 2018 he climbed back up through Double-A and Triple-A and made seven relief appearances with the Brewers. He became a fixture of sports talk radio when, on June 18 against the Phillies, he vomited twice on the mound.
SCOUTING REPORT: Pitching in short relief bursts in the majors, Houser threw his fastball in the 95-97 mph range with good sinking action that produced a lot of groundouts. A big, physical workhorse, Houser throws a powerful curveball in the low 80s with his changeup serving as a third pitch that continues to need work. He has worked hard since his injury to repeat his delivery and pitch to contact. To give him innings and allow him to work on all of his pitches, the Brewers continued to use Houser in a starting role in the minors.
THE FUTURE: The Brewers will continue to develop Houser as a starter, but his future in the majors will likely be in the bullpen as a multi-inning reliever with a power fastball and curveball.

Year	Club (League)	Class	W	L	ERA	G	GS	CG	SV	IP	H	HR	BB	SO	K/9	WHIP	AVG
2016	Biloxi (SL)	AA	3	7	5.25	13	13	0	0	70	76	5	22	56	7.2	1.39	.279
2017	Brewers (AZL)	R	0	1	1.04	6	6	0	0	9	4	1	4	16	16.6	0.92	.129
	Wisconsin (MWL)	LoA	1	0	1.00	3	2	0	0	9	5	0	0	11	11.0	0.56	.156
2018	Biloxi (SL)	AA	0	1	4.73	8	8	0	0	27	30	3	7	30	10.1	1.39	.286
	Milwaukee (NL)	MAJ	0	0	3.29	7	0	0	0	14	13	0	7	8	5.3	1.46	.255
	Colorado Springs (PCL)	AAA	2	3	5.19	13	13	0	0	52	66	6	18	37	6.4	1.62	.314
Major League Totals			0	0	3.29	7	0	0	0	14	13	0	7	8	5.3	1.46	.255
Minor League Totals			23	35	4.33	131	110	0	0	551	559	36	187	490	8.0	1.35	.264

19 CARLOS RODRIGUEZ, OF

Born: Dec. 7, 2000. **B-T:** L-L. **Ht.:** 5-10. **Wt.:** 150. **Signed:** Venezuela, 2017. **Signed by:** Jose Rodriguez.

BA GRADE
50 Risk: Extreme

TRACK RECORD: Rodriguez caught the attention of scouts while playing in national and international tournaments in Venezuela, showing an advanced feel for hitting not often seen at that age with a fluid, graceful swing. He became considered one of the top outfield prospects in the 2017-18 international signing period, and the Brewers nabbed him with a $1.355 million signing bonus. Rodriguez made his pro debut in the Dominican Summer League and was so advanced finished stateside in the Rookie-level Arizona League, batting .325 between the two levels.
SCOUTING REPORT: Rodriguez is small in stature at 5-foot-10, 150 pounds, but is highly athletic with tools to be a plus hitter. He also has the plus speed to make an impact on the bases and be an above-average defender in center field. Rodriguez projects to have a strong enough arm to remain in center, where he will have more impact. He has not shown much pop but stings the ball to all fields, hitting line drives with solid bat speed. The Brewers expect his trend of high batting averages will continue as he moves up the ladder.
THE FUTURE: Rodriguez will play the entire 2019 season at age 18 and has yet to physically mature, so he still has a long way to go. A return to the AZL is likely.

Year	Club (League)	Class	AVG	G	AB	R	H	2B	3B	HR	RBI	BB	SO	SB	CS	OBP	SLG
2018	Brewers (DSL)	R	.323	56	217	38	70	13	1	2	32	7	19	12	8	.358	.419
	Brewers (AZL)	R	.350	5	20	4	7	0	0	0	1	2	1	2	1	.409	.350
Minor League Totals			.325	61	237	42	77	13	1	2	33	9	20	14	9	.363	.414

20 MARCOS DIPLAN, RHP

BA GRADE

45 Risk: High

Born: Sept. 18, 1996. **B-T:** R-R. **Ht.:** 6-0. **Wt.:** 175. **Signed:** Dominican Republic, 2013. **Signed by:** Willie Espinal/Mike Daly (Rangers).

TRACK RECORD: A former top prospect who has stagnated, Diplan returned to high Class A for the third straight year in 2018 and finally held his own for a half-season before getting a bump to Double-A Biloxi. Though he finished strong with a 10-strikeout game in the Southern League playoffs, his longstanding control issues remained a real issue with 74 walks in 118 total innings.

SCOUTING REPORT: When he does command his pitches, Diplan has an electric arm with a fastball in the low to mid-90s, a plus slider and a decent feel for his changeup. His control issues are caused by inconsistent mechanics, with Diplan struggling to repeat his delivery. He has been one of the younger pitchers at each level of the organization and has matured physically along the way, creating different challenges as his body changes.

THE FUTURE: Diplan will be 22 all of next year and has has time to get squared away, but he needs to start throwing more strikes to advance to the major leagues. The Brewers will continue to develop Diplan as a starting pitcher. If strike-throwing remains a challenge, he will soon switch to relief.

Year	Club (League)	Class	W	L	ERA	G	GS	CG	SV	IP	H	HR	BB	SO	K/9	WHIP	AVG
2016	Wisconsin (MWL)	LoA	6	2	1.80	17	11	0	1	70	49	3	32	89	11.4	1.16	.191
	Brevard County (FSL)	HiA	1	2	4.98	10	6	1	0	43	47	4	18	40	8.3	1.50	.276
2017	Carolina (CAR)	HiA	7	8	5.23	26	22	0	0	126	126	11	71	119	8.5	1.57	.266
2018	Carolina (CAR)	HiA	3	2	3.52	13	13	0	0	61	58	3	38	60	8.8	1.57	.261
	Biloxi (SL)	AA	2	6	4.58	12	11	0	0	57	58	6	36	57	9.0	1.65	.266
Minor League Totals			28	24	3.74	104	83	1	3	472	417	33	252	476	9.1	1.42	.241

21 EDUARQI FERNANDEZ, OF

BA GRADE

50 Risk: Extreme

Born: Nov. 20, 2001. **B-T:** R-R. **Ht.:** 6-2. **Wt.:** 176. **Signed:** Dominican Republic, 2018. **Signed by:** Julio de la Cruz.

TRACK RECORD: The Brewers have tried to stockpile as many young, middle-of-the-field players they can find, thinking that is the true currency of baseball. So it was not surprising when they went after Fernandez in the 2018-19 international period, signing him for $1.1 million.

SCOUTING REPORT: Though obviously still quite young, Fernandez profiles as a center fielder with good offensive and defensive tools and a makeup that scouts noticed. Fernandez is aggressive at the plate, driving the ball to all fields with a good bat path that projects to have power as he matures physically. If he fills out to the point of no longer fitting in center, he could slide to a corner outfield spot with enough projected power to play there. Speed is a big part of Fernandez's game—he was clocked consistently at 6.4 seconds in the 60-yard-dash, which is elite speed—and he also has an above-average arm. Fernandez shows an advanced knowledge of the proper routes to take in the outfield and generally shows good instincts for his age in all areas of the game.

THE FUTURE: Fernandez will make his pro debut in 2019. He may be advanced enough to jump to the Rookie-level Arizona League before the year is out.

Year	Club (League)	Class	AVG	G	AB	R	H	2B	3B	HR	RBI	BB	SO	SB	CS	OBP	SLG
2018	Did not play—Signed 2019 contract																

22 MARIO FELICIANO, C

BA GRADE

45 Risk: Very High

Born: Nov. 29, 1998. **B-T:** R-R. **Ht.:** 6-1. **Wt.:** 195. **Drafted:** HS—Florida, P.R., 2016 (2nd round supplemental). **Signed by:** Charlie Sullivan.

TRACK RECORD: Feliciano has moved slowly since the Brewers signed him for $800,000 as the 75th overall pick in 2016, in large part due to injury. He missed the first two months of 2018 with an arm injury and played in just 42 games for high Class A Carolina. The Brewers sent him to the Arizona Fall League to get more at-bats, but he reported right shoulder discomfort and had arthroscopic surgery at the beginning of November.

SCOUTING REPORT: When healthy, Feliciano projects as an offensive player. He has a smooth swing with good barrel-to-ball ability that generates hard contact to all fields. He has shown a natural feel for hitting at a young age and should hit for average with health and experience. Feliciano has shown some power, but it has not translated to many home runs. As he gets stronger and learns better pitch recognition, his power is expected to play more into the double-digit home run range. For a catcher, Feliciano is a good athlete who runs respectably, and that athleticism helps him behind the plate, where he moves well and displays an above-average arm.

THE FUTURE: Feliciano's physical tools are there, but he needs to stay on the field and accumulate more games behind the plate to work things out. He is expected to be ready for spring training.

Year	Club (League)	Class	AVG	G	AB	R	H	2B	3B	HR	RBI	BB	SO	SB	CS	OBP	SLG
2016	Brewers (AZL)	R	.265	29	117	16	31	5	3	0	16	7	19	2	2	.307	.359
2017	Wisconsin (MWL)	LoA	.251	104	402	47	101	16	4	4	36	34	72	10	2	.320	.331
2018	Brewers (AZL)	R	.286	4	14	0	4	1	0	0	2	2	3	0	1	.375	.357
	Carolina (CAR)	HiA	.205	42	146	20	30	7	1	3	12	13	59	2	0	.282	.329
Minor League Totals			.244	179	679	83	166	29	6	7	66	56	153	14	5	.311	.336

23 MICAH BELLO, OF

BA GRADE

45 Risk: Extreme

Born: July 21, 2000. **B-T:** R-R. **Ht.:** 5-11. **Wt.:** 165. **Drafted:** HS—Hilo, Hawaii, 2018 (2nd round supplemental). **Signed by:** Josh Belovsky.

TRACK RECORD: The Brewers have been one of the most active teams in mining Hawaii for talent, namely drafting Kodi Medeiros, Jordan Yamamoto and Quintin Torres-Costa in recent years. They grabbed undisputed top talent on the island again in 2018, selecting Bello with the 73rd overall pick and signing him for $550,000 to pass up a St. Mary's scholarship.

SCOUTING REPORT: Bello has a long track record of performing well offensively, both in high school and in high school showcases on the mainland, and he is the highest-drafted position player from Hawaii since 2013. He uses a small leg kick and good bat speed to produce solid contact and line drives to all fields. He has solid-average speed that makes him a threat to steal bases and also plays well in the outfield. With a plus arm, he has the tools to be an above-average defender, although he's more likely to shift to a corner.

THE FUTURE: Bello has a chance to be a top-of-the-order table-setter with some extra-base potential as he matures physically. Bello debuted in the Rookie-level Arizona League and probably will be moved up a notch to the Pioneer League next summer.

Year	Club (League)	Class	AVG	G	AB	R	H	2B	3B	HR	RBI	BB	SO	SB	CS	OBP	SLG
2018	Brewers (AZL)	R	.240	39	154	25	37	4	3	1	15	18	41	10	1	.324	.325
Minor League Totals			.240	39	154	25	37	4	3	1	15	18	41	10	1	.324	.325

24 LARRY ERNESTO, OF

BA GRADE

45 Risk: Extreme

Born: Sept. 12, 2000. **B-T:** S-R. **Ht.:** 6-2. **Wt.:** 175. **Signed:** Dominican Republic, 2017. **Signed by:** Rodalfo Rosario.

TRACK RECORD: The Brewers quickly zeroed in on the athletic Ernesto during the 2017-18 international signing period and agreed to sign him for a $1.8 million bonus. The switch-hitter showed a good approach at the plate, especially for his age, sending line drives to all fields. He spent most of the 2018 season in the Dominican Summer League, where he struggled to make contact at times because of over-aggressiveness at the plate.

SCOUTING REPORT: The switch-hitting Ernesto has the tools to hit if he improves his approach. He is a better hitter from the left side of plate, but the Brewers think he will become a factor from both sides and eventually develop more power as he matures physically. He has above-average speed that plays well in center field and on the bases. Ernesto shows good instincts in center but needs to work on improving his routes and angles on drives in the gaps. His arm strength is above-average and should improve with physical maturity.

THE FUTURE: The Brewers see the tools for Ernesto to develop into an all-around performer on both sides of the ball. Improving his strength and approach will be key for him to get there.

Year	Club (League)	Class	AVG	G	AB	R	H	2B	3B	HR	RBI	BB	SO	SB	CS	OBP	SLG
2018	Brewers (DSL)	R	.236	53	203	38	48	13	2	5	20	14	68	9	4	.294	.394
	Brewers (AZL)	R	.350	5	20	4	7	2	0	0	2	1	6	0	1	.364	.450
Minor League Totals			.247	58	223	42	55	15	2	5	22	15	74	9	5	.300	.399

25 JE'VON WARD, OF

BA GRADE

45 Risk: Extreme

Born: Oct. 25, 1999. **B-T:** L-R. **Ht.:** 6-5. **Wt.:** 190. **Drafted:** HS—Cypress, Calif., 2017 (12th round). **Signed by:** Wynn Pelzer.

TRACK RECORD: Ward drew uneven reviews his senior year of high school, but the Brewers gambled on the tools they saw in the 2017 Boras Classic and the fact he was just 17 at the time. They paid him $475,000 as a 12th-rounder, nearly four times the recommended slot amount, to forgo a scholarship to Southern California. Ward made his pro debut in the Rookie-level Arizona League and looked raw, but he moved up one notch to Rookie-level Helena in 2018 and flourished offensively as his tools came together.

SCOUTING REPORT: Ward is the son of former Notre Dame wide receiver Reggie Ward and the nephew

of former Pro Bowl NFL safety Mark Carrier. With those bloodlines, his best attribute is his above-average speed and long strides. That speed gives Ward an advantage breaking out of the left side of the batter's box and also makes him a threat to steal bases. It also allows him to cover the gaps well in center field, although his instincts need work. The Brewers think Ward also has untapped, average power potential that will come forth as he gets more experience and learns how to unleash it in games. For now, he has a compact lefthanded swing that made more contact as the year went on and his strike-zone awareness improved.
THE FUTURE: The Brewers think there is upside to be developed in a still very young player with Ward. With further skill development, he may move to low Class A Wisconsin in 2019.

Year	Club (League)	Class	AVG	G	AB	R	H	2B	3B	HR	RBI	BB	SO	SB	CS	OBP	SLG
2017	Brewers (AZL)	R	.276	32	123	15	34	6	0	0	15	9	39	2	7	.326	.325
2018	Helena (PIO)	R	.307	64	238	40	73	13	2	2	21	32	57	13	5	.391	.403
Minor League Totals			.296	96	361	55	107	19	2	2	36	41	96	15	12	.370	.377

26 CODY PONCE, RHP

BA GRADE
40 Risk: High

Born: April 25, 1994. **B-T:** R-R. **Ht.:** 6-6. **Wt.:** 240. **Drafted:** Cal Poly Pomona, 2015 (2nd round). **Signed by:** Josh Belovsky.
TRACK RECORD: Ponce's track has been up and down since the Brewers drafted him in the second round in 2015 and signed him for just over $1.1 million. After a forearm strain derailed his progress in 2016, he bounced back with a strong 2017 and reached Double-A by the end of the year. But he returned to Biloxi in 2018 and the sailing wasn't nearly as smooth, prompting a switch from a starting to relieving.
SCOUTING REPORT: Ponce has dialed back what once was an upper-90s fastball to achieve better command and now sits 90-93 mph and will touch 95 mph. He pairs his fastball with an average, upper-80s cutter he uses to attack lefthanded hitters. His curveball sometimes is his second-best pitch, and he can throw it more as a "slurve" when needed. Ponce often throws his below-average changeup too firmly, but that pitch won't be as important if he remains a reliever. He throws all of his pitches for strikes and uses his physical size to his advantage, throwing the ball on a downward plane to induce groundball outs, although nothing he throws is plus.
THE FUTURE: It has become evident that Ponce's future at the top level is probably as a reliever, where he can reach back for more with his fastball and focus on pitching in shorter bursts.

Year	Club (League)	Class	W	L	ERA	G	GS	CG	SV	IP	H	HR	BB	SO	K/9	WHIP	AVG
2016	Brevard County (FSL)	HiA	2	8	5.25	17	17	0	0	72	84	6	17	69	8.6	1.40	.285
2017	Carolina (CAR)	HiA	8	8	3.38	22	22	1	0	120	130	14	25	94	7.1	1.29	.274
	Biloxi (SL)	AA	2	1	1.53	3	3	0	0	18	10	0	5	9	4.6	0.85	.175
2018	Biloxi (SL)	AA	7	6	4.36	29	11	0	0	95	88	10	34	88	8.3	1.28	.244
Minor League Totals			21	24	3.77	85	62	1	3	356	359	31	90	300	7.6	1.26	.260

27 TRENT GRISHAM, OF

BA GRADE
40 Risk: High

Born: Nov. 1, 1996. **B-T:** L-L. **Ht.:** 6-0. **Wt.:** 210. **Drafted:** HS—North Richland Hills, Texas, 2015 (1st round). **Signed by:** K.J. Hendricks.
TRACK RECORD: Grisham, who used to go by the last name Clark, was considered one of the best prep hitters in the country when the Brewers drafted him in the first round in 2015, but he's never lived up to that as a pro. He put together a second straight uninspiring season in 2018, this time at Double-A Biloxi after the Brewers tried to challenge him.
SCOUTING REPORT: Grisham still is trying to find a consistent stroke at the plate. He has a good eye, drawing enough walks each season to produce a respectable OBP (.356 in 2018) but has shown little power while compiling low batting averages every season. Grisham often is too passive at the plate, taking good pitches and falling behind in the count, leading to too many strikeouts for a hitter of his supposed caliber. When he does choose to swing, he hits enough line drives to make you wonder if power eventually will come, but he also takes an alarming number of noncompetitive swings where he pulls off the ball. Grisham continues to play all three outfield positions, with his average speed and below-average arm fitting best in left field.
THE FUTURE: Grisham is still young enough to hope he will turn it around, but it's time for a big season that befits a first-round pick.

Year	Club (League)	Class	AVG	G	AB	R	H	2B	3B	HR	RBI	BB	SO	SB	CS	OBP	SLG
2016	Wisconsin (MWL)	LoA	.231	59	221	27	51	15	2	2	24	37	68	5	10	.346	.344
2017	Carolina (CAR)	HiA	.224	133	456	78	102	21	6	8	45	98	140	37	5	.361	.349
2018	Biloxi (SL)	AA	.233	107	335	45	78	10	2	7	31	63	87	11	3	.356	.337
Minor League Totals			.242	354	1219	189	295	53	16	19	121	237	339	78	26	.367	.358

28 EDUARDO GARCIA, SS

Born: July 10, 2002. **B-T:** R-R. **Ht.:** 6-2. **Wt.:** 160. **Signed:** Venezuela, 2018.
Signed by: Reinaldo Hidalgo.

BA GRADE
45 Risk: Extreme

TRACK RECORD: Garcia had not yet turned 16 when the international signing period began in 2018, so the Brewers had to wait a week or so to make his signing official. They were so impressed with his tools and growth potential that they gave him a $1.1 million bonus out of Venezuela.

SCOUTING REPORT: Garcia caught the eye of scouts with strong showings in showcase events in the Dominican Republic and Colombia, quickly establishing himself as one of the top defenders available on the international market. It's impossible at his age and weight to project Garcia as having power, but his hitting mechanics already are advanced enough to think he'll at least sting line drives into the gaps. He is expected to be an average runner and already shows the hands and range you want at shortstop with a plus arm. His defense projects to be ahead of his offense, although he's so young a lot can change.

THE FUTURE: Garcia will be a fascinating project to watch develop in the coming years. He will get his first experience as a pro in the Dominican Summer League in 2019.

Year	Club (League)	Class	AVG	G	AB	R	H	2B	3B	HR	RBI	BB	SO	SB	CS	OBP	SLG
2018	Did not play—Signed 2019 contract																

29 CARLOS HERRERA, RHP

Born: Oct. 26, 1997. **B-T:** R-R. **Ht.:** 6-2. **Wt.:** 160. **Signed:** Dominican Republic, 2014. **Signed by:** Eddy Toledo/Scott Hunter (Mariners).

BA GRADE
40 Risk: High

TRACK RECORD: Originally acquired from the Mariners with Freddy Peralta for Adam Lind in December 2015, Herrera progressed up to low Class A Wisconsin in 2017 but spun his wheels at the same level in 2018, largely due to control issues. In 85.2 innings, when piggybacking as a starter/reliever, he issued 48 walks, uncorked 17 wild pitches and hit 10 batters.

SCOUTING REPORT: Herrera has added strength since being acquired and has more physical maturity ahead. For now, he throws his fastball consistently in the low 90s and spins a solid curveball that projects above-average. His below-average changeup is still developing.

THE FUTURE: The Brewers still believe Herrera has considerable upside and the stuff to advance through the system. He merely needs to learn how to repeat his delivery and throw strikes. He may get a shot high Class A Carolina in 2019.

Year	Club (League)	Class	W	L	ERA	G	GS	CG	SV	IP	H	HR	BB	SO	K/9	WHIP	AVG
2016	Brewers (AZL)	R	3	6	4.50	14	6	0	0	50	52	4	12	49	8.8	1.28	.271
2017	Helena (PIO)	R	2	0	4.29	4	4	0	0	21	16	5	5	26	11.1	1.00	.219
	Wisconsin (MWL)	LoA	3	2	3.79	9	5	1	0	38	24	4	17	26	6.2	1.08	.181
2018	Wisconsin (MWL)	LoA	3	6	5.46	28	10	0	1	86	95	5	48	60	6.3	1.67	.292
Minor League Totals			15	16	4.33	69	39	1	2	275	255	22	95	234	7.7	1.27	.250

30 CHAD McCLANAHAN, 1B/3B

Born: Dec. 22, 1997. **B-T:** L-R. **Ht.:** 6-5. **Wt.:** 200. **Drafted:** HS—Phoenix, 2016 (11th round). **Signed by:** Jeff Scholzen.

BA GRADE
45 Risk: Extreme

TRACK RECORD: It is fair to say McClanahan has been somewhat slow to fulfill the promise the Brewers saw when they selected him in the 11th round in 2016 but gave him $1.2 million, second-round money. He finally gained some traction last season in his second time around with Rookie-level Helena, getting on base more and flashing more power.

SCOUTING REPORT: McClanahan and intrigues with his power. The plus raw power potential he has flashed at times but has been slow to develop in game action, however. McClanahan has shown good strike-zone judgment and a feel for the proper swing path that serves him best, but he still has some swing and miss in his game. As he continues gain experience, the Brewers believe he'll hit for power more consistently. He has seen some action in the corner outfield, but he is likely destined for first base.

THE FUTURE: McLanahan will get another crack at full-season ball in 2019. He needs to start translating his power into games to keep moving up.

Year	Club (League)	Class	AVG	G	AB	R	H	2B	3B	HR	RBI	BB	SO	SB	CS	OBP	SLG
2016	Brewers (AZL)	R	.208	35	144	22	30	7	1	3	14	11	45	1	2	.277	.333
2017	Helena (PIO)	R	.234	63	235	33	55	8	1	3	30	39	78	5	5	.339	.315
2018	Helena (PIO)	R	.301	49	183	30	55	14	3	8	35	24	55	3	4	.382	.541
	Wisconsin (MWL)	LoA	.171	21	76	8	13	2	0	1	8	6	33	0	0	.261	.237
Minor League Totals			.240	168	638	93	153	31	5	15	87	80	211	9	11	.329	.375

Minnesota Twins

BY MIKE BERARDINO

As it turned out, loading up on last-minute free agents didn't work out for the Twins in 2018.

Minnesota flopped under the weight of a franchise-record $128 million payroll, prompting a midsummer sell-off of mostly prospective free agents. The team then fired manager Paul Molitor with two years and $3.25 million left on his contract. That dismissal came less than a calendar year after Molitor, a Hall of Fame player and St. Paul, Minn., native, was voted American League Manager of the Year for leading the Twins to their first postseason in seven years.

Rocco Baldelli became the Twins' first outside managerial hire since Ray Miller in the mid-1980s. At 37, the hope is the erstwhile Woonsocket Rocket will relate better to a young roster and get the best out of players still struggling to find a foothold.

Another hometown hero departed with the retirement of first baseman Joe Mauer, who reached the end of an eight-year, $184 million contract and could be Cooperstown-bound. C.J. Cron was claimed on waivers to help fill the void following a 30-homer season with the Rays.

Thus continued the Twins' clear commitment to a complete overhaul of their baseball operations under the front-office duo of chief baseball officer Derek Falvey and general manager Thad Levine.

At season's end, the Twins didn't just push Molitor and the bulk of his coaching staff out the door. They also made multiple changes in their support staff and minor league coaching hierarchy.

Young pitchers Kohl Stewart and Stephen Gonsalves, products of the 2013 draft, finally reached the majors after starting the year in Double-A, but neither experienced much success on his maiden voyage. Righthander Fernando Romero debuted with better results in his 11-start audition, but former first-rounders Nick Gordon and Tyler Jay lost ground.

Among the remaining rookies, outfielder Jake Cave, acquired from the Yankees in the spring, reliever Gabriel Moya and catchers Mitch Garver and Williams Astudillo enjoyed successful debuts. However, potential franchise players Byron Buxton and Miguel Sano continued to struggle with injuries and ineffectiveness, to the point where both were demoted to the minors during the year.

Picking 20th in the draft—the second under scouting director Sean Johnson—the Twins took Oregon State corner outfielder Trevor Larnach, signed him for 18 percent under slot and were immediately pleased to see him crushing baseballs at multiple levels of pro ball. The club lacked its

Fernando Romero shined brilliantly at times during an up-and-down 2018 rookie season.

HANNAH FOSLIEN/GETTY IMAGES

PROJECTED 2022 LINEUP

Catcher	Ryan Jeffers (25)
First Base	Brent Rooker (27)
Second Base	Jorge Polanco (28)
Third Base	Jose Miranda (22)
Shortstop	Royce Lewis (23)
Left Field	Eddie Rosario (30)
Center Field	Byron Buxton (28)
Right Field	Alex Kirilloff (24)
Designated Hitter	Trevor Larnach (25)
No. 1 Starter	Jose Berrios (28)
No. 2 Starter	Brusdar Graterol (23)
No. 3 Starter	Fernando Romero (27)
No. 4 Starter	Jhoan Duran (24)
No. 5 Starter	Blayne Enlow (23)
Closer	Trevor May (32)

supplemental second-round pick (74th overall) after trading it to the Padres in the Phil Hughes salary dump and its third-rounder (95th overall) after the March signing of free agent Lance Lynn to a one-year deal. Still, the Twins struck gold with the second-round selection of UNC Wilmington catcher Ryan Jeffers.

On the international front, Fred Guerrero's group nabbed 16-year-old Venezuelan outfielder Misael Urbina with a signing bonus of $2.75 million.

The good news exclusively came in the minor leagues for the Twins in 2018. To get back on track in 2019, disappointing young players like Buxton and Sano will have to click.

MINNESOTA TWINS

TOP 2019 ROOKIE: Lewis Thorpe, LHP. The hard-throwing Aussie is finally healthy and can contribute both as a starter and in relief.
BREAKOUT PROSPECT: Jordan Balazovic, RHP. The wiry Canadian started to put it all together in 2018.
SLEEPER: Jovani Moran, LHP. The fresh arm could vault forward behind new slider and a plus changeup.

SOURCE OF TOP 30 TALENT			
Homegrown	23	Acquired	7
College	10	Trade	6
Junior college	0	Rule 5 draft	0
High school	8	Independent league	0
Nondrafted free agent	0	Free agent/waivers	1
International	5		

LF
Akil Baddoo (19)
LaMonte Wade (21)
Luke Raley (24)
Jacob Pearson

CF
Misael Urbina (12)
Aaron Whitefield (28)
Gabriel Maciel (29)
Gilberto Celestino (30)
Zack Granite
Tanner English

RF
Alex Kirilloff (2)
Trevor Larnach (5)
Jaylin Davis

3B
Jose Miranda (13)
Andrew Bechtold
Brian Schales

SS
Royce Lewis (1)
Wander Javier (4)
Ricky De La Torre

2B
Yunior Severino (10)
Luis Arraez (11)
Nick Gordon (15)
Michael Helman (27)
Travis Blankenhorn

1B
Brent Rooker (6)
Lewin Diaz

C
Ryan Jeffers (9)
Ben Rortvedt (22)
Willians Astudillo
Caleb Hamilton
Brian Navaretto

LHP

LHSP	LHRP
Lewis Thorpe (17)	Andrew Vasquez
Stephen Gonsalves (18)	Alex Robinson
Jovani Moran	Tyler Jay
Lachlan Wells	Devin Smeltzer

RHP

RHSP	RHRP
Brusdar Graterol (3)	John Curtiss (26)
Jhoan Duran (7)	Chase De Jong
Blayne Enlow (8)	Cody Stashak
Griffin Jax (14)	Jake Reed
Jorge Alcala (16)	Tom Hackimer
Jordan Balazovic (20)	Hector Lujan
Zack Littell (23)	
Landon Leach (25)	
Kohl Stewart	
Josh Winder	
Luis Rijo	
Dakota Chalmers	

DRAFT ANALYSIS

2018

BEST PURE HITTER: OF Trevor Larnach (1) has hit everywhere he's gone in his career—from Oregon State to the Cape Cod League to pro ball. He is a patient hitter and does a good job of barreling up balls.

BEST POWER: Larnach has plus power that he finally tapped into in 2018 after hitting five home runs in 139 games in his first two years of college between Oregon State and the Cape. Catchers Ryan Jeffers (2) and Chris Williams (8) also have plus raw power.

FASTEST RUNNER: OF DaShawn Keirsey (4) is a plus runner, and he uses that speed well in the outfield. His speed has come all the way back after he broke and dislocated his hip as a sophomore in a collision with the outfield wall.

BEST DEFENSIVE PLAYER: Keirsey can fly around the outfield and profiles well in center field. Beyond his speed, he also has a strong arm.

BEST ATHLETE: Keirsey stands out for his loud raw tools and athleticism. With his speed, power and arm strength, he has the ability to impact the game in several ways.

BEST FASTBALL: RHP Josh Winder (7) this spring mostly pitched 88-92 mph but has already seen his velocity tick up since signing. He made some adjustments and now throws his fastball 90-94 mph, touching 96 mph, with improved life on the pitch.

BEST SECONDARY PITCH: RHP Cole Sands (5) has turned his changeup into a strong offering that gives him a weapon against lefthanded hitters. Winder's curveball is also an above-average secondary pitch.

BEST PRO DEBUT: The Twins surprised some by taking Jeffers in the second round, but this summer he did his best to show why they did so. He crushed Appalachian League pitching and was promoted to low Class A Cedar Rapids and finished the summer with 17 doubles and seven home runs in 64 games.

TOP DRAFT PICKS OF THE DECADE

Year	Player, Pos.	2018 Org
2009	Kyle Gibson, RHP	Twins
2010	Alex Wimmers, RHP	Atlantic League
2011	Levi Michael, SS	Mets
2012	Byron Buxton, OF	Twins
2013	Kohl Stewart, RHP	Twins
2014	Nick Gordon, SS	Twins
2015	Tyler Jay, LHP	Twins
2016	Alex Kirilloff ,OF	Twins
2017	Royce Lewis, SS	Twins
2018	Trevor Larnach, OF	Twins

MOST INTRIGUING BACKGROUND: OF Joe Garry (9) went from largely unknown to a ninth-round pick during his senior year. He last fall put himself on the radar with a strong performance in Jupiter and carried that into the spring, where his well-above average speed and athleticism stood out. He was coached in his youth league by former big leaguer Matt Lawton.

CLOSEST TO THE MAJORS: Larnach this summer reached low Class A Cedar Rapids and is advanced enough to make quick work of the minor leagues. Jeffers' debut suggests he could move quickly as well, but he may be slowed because he needs time to develop behind the plate.

BEST LATE-ROUND PICK: 2B Michael Helman (11) has plus speed and last season showed good feel for hitting at Texas A&M. 3B Michael Davis (24) got his pro career off to a strong start and hit nine home runs at Cedar Rapids. He may convert to catching where he would profile better, especially thanks to his well-above average arm strength.

THE ONE WHO GOT AWAY: RHP Seth Halvorsen (30) this spring was the best prep player in Minnesota, but the Twins weren't able to keep him close to home. Halvorsen instead opted to head to Missouri, where he has a chance to be a two-way player for the Tigers and is expected to quickly make an impact.

—TEDDY CAHILL

2017

SS Royce Lewis (1) has so far lived up to expectations as the first overall pick. OF Brent Rooker (1s) was tested at Double-A but still hit 22 homers. Prep RHPs Landon Leach (2) and Blayne Enlow (3) continue to show promise.

GRADE: A

2016

OF Alex Kiriloff (1) bounced back in a big way after missing 2017 due to injury, showing off his big tools. RHP Griffin Jax (3) is starting to move quickly with his military commitment deferred and 2B/3B Jose Miranda (2s) started to blossom.

GRADE: B

2015

LHP Andrew Vasquez (32) made his MLB debut and OF LaMonte Wade (9) may be next. But that might be it. LHP Tyler Jay (1) went unpicked in the Rule 5 draft and prep 3Bs Travis Blankenhorn (3) and Trey Cabbage (4) have struggled.

GRADE: F

1 ROYCE LEWIS, SS

Born: June 5, 1999. **B-T:** R-R. **Ht:** 6-2. **Wt:** 188.
Drafted: HS—San Juan Capistrano, Calif., 2017
(1st round). **Signed by:** John Leavitt.

Picking No. 1 overall in 2017 for just the third time in club history, the Twins passed on advanced college pitchers Brendan McKay (Louisville) and Kyle Wright (Vanderbilt) as well as elite high school arms Hunter Greene and MacKenzie Gore. Instead they ignored predraft concerns about Lewis' hit tool and opted for him after falling in love with his five-tool potential, outstanding makeup and franchise-level charisma. Lewis accepted a club-record draft bonus of $6.725 million that was nearly a full million below slot value. He shined in his full-season debut by ranking as the No. 1 prospect in both the Midwest and Florida State leagues.

SCOUTING REPORT: Lewis endured a pair of lengthy hitting slumps in 2018, one apiece in each league. He also learned how to fight his way out of bad habits that may have come from trying to play through patellar tendinitis in his left knee. With a high waist and wide shoulders, Lewis shows high-end athleticism and the ability to make quick, natural adjustments. The Twins got him to calm down his leg kick with two strikes, but they had no issues with his early-count aggressiveness. Lewis has learned to turn on inside pitches but still struggles at times with soft stuff away. Instinctive and smart, he shows advanced plate discipline and drastically cut his flyball rate after earning a July promotion to the bigger ballparks of the FSL. He still managed to help lead high Class A Fort Myers to a league title while flashing plus speed and a basestealer's mentality. After seeing time at third base and center field at JSerra Catholic High, he has worked extensively on his footwork, range and throwing mechanics at shortstop with minor league infield coordinator Sam Perlozzo. Rival scouts still see a funkiness to Lewis' throwing motion, which includes a higher-than-normal release point, but his arm strength and accuracy have improved. His hands are soft, his reactions are good and he goes back well on pop-ups.

THE FUTURE: Lewis figures to return to Fort Myers in 2019. Industry debate will continue about his ability to stay at shortstop, but he will be given every opportunity to play himself off the position as he climbs the ranks. While Alex Kirilloff has narrowed the gap considerably, Lewis still merits the mantle of No. 1 prospect.

DENNIS HUBBARD/FOUR SEAM IMAGES

BA GRADE	SCOUTING GRADES
65 Risk: High	Hit: 70. Power: 55. Run: 60. Field: 60. Arm: 55.

Projected future grades on 20-80 scouting scale

TOP PROSPECTS OF THE DECADE

Year	Player, Pos.	2018 Org
2009	Aaron Hicks, OF	Yankees
2010	Aaron Hicks, OF	Yankees
2011	Kyle Gibson, RHP	Twins
2012	Miguel Sano ,3B/SS	Twins
2013	Miguel Sano, 3B	Twins
2014	Byron Buxton, OF	Twins
2015	Byron Buxton, OF	Twins
2016	Byron Buxton, OF	Twins
2017	Nick Gordon, SS	Twins
2018	Royce Lewis, SS	Twins

BEST TOOLS

Best Hitter for Average	Alex Kirilloff
Best Power Hitter	Brent Rooker
Best Strike-Zone Discipline	Alex Kirilloff
Fastest Baserunner	Royce Lewis
Best Athlete	Royce Lewis
Best Fastball	Brusdar Graterol
Best Curveball	Blayne Enlow
Best Slider	Brusdar Graterol
Best Changeup	Stephen Gonsalves
Best Control	Griffin Jax
Best Defensive Catcher	Ben Rortvedt
Best Defensive Infielder	Royce Lewis
Best Infield Arm	Andrew Bechtold
Best Defensive Outfielder	Aaron Whitefield
Best Outfield Arm	Tanner English

Year	Club (League)	Class	AVG	G	AB	R	H	2B	3B	HR	RBI	BB	SO	SB	CS	OBP	SLG
2017	Twins (GCL)	R	.271	36	133	38	36	6	2	3	17	19	17	15	2	.390	.414
	Cedar Rapids (MWL)	LoA	.296	18	71	16	21	2	1	1	10	6	16	3	1	.363	.394
2018	Cedar Rapids (MWL)	LoA	.315	75	295	50	93	23	0	9	53	24	49	22	4	.368	.485
	Fort Myers (FSL)	HiA	.255	46	188	33	48	6	3	5	21	19	35	6	4	.327	.399
Minor League Totals			.288	175	687	137	198	37	6	18	101	68	117	46	11	.361	.438

2 ALEX KIRILLOFF, OF

Born: Nov. 9, 1997. **B-T:** L-L. **Ht:** 6-2. **Wt:** 195. **Drafted:** HS—Pittsburgh, 2016 (1st round). **Signed by:** Jay Weitzel.

TRACK RECORD: It's hard to imagine a better return season after Tommy John surgery than the one Kirilloff enjoyed in 2018. Inflammation in his throwing elbow ultimately led to season-ending surgery in March 2017, but he used that time to pack on 20 pounds of muscle.

SCOUTING REPORT: It didn't take Kirilloff long to outgrow Max Kepler comparisons and head straight for Christian Yelich territory. He shows a consistently smooth lefthanded swing with excellent balance, strong wrists and quick hands. He could stand to walk more but doesn't chase much and shows outstanding barrel awareness. He drives the ball to center and left-center field with ease and authority. His hit tool and power potential are both plus if not double-plus. When pitchers started pounding Kirilloff up-and-in more after his promotion to high Class A Fort Myers in late June, he made adjustments and started turning on more inside mistakes. An average runner who moves well for his size, he has improved his reads and routes and should be able to stay in right field, though his arm, which is a tick below-average might be better suited for left.

BA GRADE

60 Risk: High

Hit: 70. Power: 55.
Run: 50. Field: 50.
Arm: 45

THE FUTURE: Kirilloff should head to Double-A Pensacola in 2019. He should be pushing for a big league look by midseason 2020 at the latest.

Year	Club (League)	Class	AVG	G	AB	R	H	2B	3B	HR	RBI	BB	SO	SB	CS	OBP	SLG
2016	Elizabethton (APP)	R	.306	55	216	33	66	9	1	7	33	11	32	0	1	.341	.454
2017	Did not play—Injured																
2018	Cedar Rapids (MWL)	LoA	.333	65	252	36	84	20	5	13	56	24	47	1	1	.391	.607
	Fort Myers (FSL)	HiA	.362	65	260	39	94	24	2	7	45	14	39	3	2	.393	.550
Minor League Totals			.335	185	728	108	244	53	8	27	134	49	118	4	4	.377	.541

3 BRUSDAR GRATEROL, RHP

Born: Aug. 26, 1998. **B-T:** R-R. **Ht:** 6-1. **Wt:** 180. **Signed:** Venezuela, 2014. **Signed by:** Jose Leon.

TRACK RECORD: Graterol has gained 60 pounds since he signed, and he used his rehab period from Tommy John surgery to get stronger. After a 40-inning taste of the new Graterol in 2017, he built on those gains at two levels in 2018, helping pitch Class A Fort Myers to a Florida State League title.

SCOUTING REPORT: Before his surgery, Graterol sat 87-88 mph with his fastball but showed a clean delivery. Since his return, he pitches at 96-100 mph and touches 101 while throwing exclusively two-seamers. With his renewed commitment to conditioning, especially to his strong legs and hindquarters, Graterol can maintain that 80-grade fastball into the later innings. His tight, late-breaking slider shows plus-plus potential at 87-90 mph, and at times it is almost unhittable. His average curveball tends to get loopy at 82-84 mph, and his power changeup can be too firm despite heavy sink. Graterol studies video of All-Star righty Jose Berrios and patterns his approach after him, on and off the mound.

BA GRADE

60 Risk: High

Fastball: 70.
Slider: 60. Curve: 50.
Change: 40. CTL: 55

THE FUTURE: Graterol, who has an endearing sense of humor and has worked hard to improve his English, could return to Fort Myers to open 2019. He projects as a potential rotation-topping ace.

Year	Club (League)	Class	W	L	ERA	G	GS	CG	SV	IP	H	HR	BB	SO	K/9	WHIP	AVG
2016	Did not play—Injured																
2017	Twins (GCL)	R	2	0	1.40	5	2	0	0	19	10	1	4	21	9.8	0.72	.152
	Elizabethton (APP)	R	2	1	3.92	5	5	0	0	21	16	1	9	24	10.5	1.21	.213
2018	Cedar Rapids (MWL)	LoA	3	2	2.18	8	8	0	0	41	30	3	9	51	11.1	0.94	.195
	Fort Myers (FSL)	HiA	5	2	3.12	11	11	0	0	61	59	0	19	56	8.3	1.29	.261
Minor League Totals			12	6	2.71	33	30	0	0	153	127	5	42	169	9.9	1.10	.225

4 WANDER JAVIER, SS

Born: Dec. 29, 1998. **B-T:** R-R. **Ht:** 6-1. **Wt:** 165. **Signed:** Dominican Republic, 2015. **Signed by:** Fred Guerrero.

TRACK RECORD: A torn labrum in Javier's non-throwing shoulder required surgery in May, costing him all of the 2018 season. Signed for $4 million in July 2015 as the No. 9 international prospect, he still holds the Twins' bonus record for a foreign amateur. Hamstring issues plagued Javier in his first pro summer in 2016, but he shined at Rookie-level Elizabethton in 2017.

SCOUTING REPORT: A plus runner with plus athleticism, Javier shows plus range, a plus arm and a true shortstop's profile. He has worked hard to improve his English and his body, which was wiry and bit gangly when he signed. Javier junked a big leg kick in favor of a simpler setup and swing that now features quiet hands and a small lift of his front foot. He was able to take part in batting practice in time for fall hitter's minicamp, where he again showed good barrel awareness, an inside-out swing and the ability to hit the ball with authority into the opposite gap.

THE FUTURE: Look for the Twins to take things slowly with Javier, who figures to open 2019 at extended spring training. Once the weather warms up at low Class A Cedar Rapids, he should get a chance to test himself and pile up some much-needed game reps.

BA GRADE
60 Risk: Extreme
Hit: 60. Power: 50.
Run: 55. Field: 55.
Arm: 60.

Year	Club (League)	Class	AVG	G	AB	R	H	2B	3B	HR	RBI	BB	SO	SB	CS	OBP	SLG
2016	Twins (DSL)	R	.308	9	26	7	8	3	0	2	6	4	5	0	0	.400	.654
2017	Elizabethton (APP)	R	.299	41	157	34	47	13	1	4	22	19	49	4	3	.383	.471
2018	Did not play—Injured																
Minor League Totals			.301	50	183	41	55	16	1	6	28	23	54	4	3	.386	.497

5 TREVOR LARNACH, OF

Born: Feb. 26, 1997. **B-T:** L-R. **Ht:** 6-4. **Wt:** 210. **Drafted:** Oregon State, 2018 (1st round). **Signed by:** Kyle Blackwell.

TRACK RECORD: After hitting just three homers as an Oregon State sophomore, Larnach remade his swing to create better angle and higher exit velocity. The late-blooming Larnach completed his transformation with a game-winning, two-run homer to complete a miracle comeback in Game 2 of the College World Series against Arkansas. He became the first college outfielder the Twins had taken in the first round since 1969.

SCOUTING REPORT: Larnach taught himself to hit with power to center and left-center field while maintaining high-end plate coverage. He closed out his first pro summer with a strong showing at low Class A Cedar Rapids, where he showcased strong plate discipline skills, including a strong swinging-strike rate, walk rate and strikeout rate—especially for a hitter with power. Defensively, Larnach grades as a shade below-average in right field. His arm is fringe-average, and his speed, routes and jumps are average at best. His defense won't impede his ability to impact the major leagues with his potent lefthanded bat.

THE FUTURE: Larnach worked extensively with hitting coordinator Rick Eckstein on elevating the ball to his pull side. He could open 2019 at high Class A Fort Myers

BA GRADE
55 Risk: High
Hit: 50. Power: 60.
Run: 40. Field: 45.
Arm: 45.

Year	Club (League)	Class	AVG	G	AB	R	H	2B	3B	HR	RBI	BB	SO	SB	CS	OBP	SLG
2018	Elizabethton (APP)	R	.311	18	61	10	19	5	0	2	16	10	11	2	0	.413	.492
	Cedar Rapids (MWL)	LoA	.297	24	91	17	27	8	1	3	10	11	17	1	0	.373	.505
Minor League Totals			.303	42	152	27	46	13	1	5	26	21	28	3	0	.390	.500

6 BRENT ROOKER, OF/1B

Born: Nov. 1, 1994. **B-T:** R-R. **Ht:** 6-3. **Wt:** 215. **Drafted:** Mississippi State, 2017 (1st round supplemental). **Signed by:** Derrick Dunbar.

TRACK RECORD: Rooker improved his stock greatly by returning to Mississippi State after nearly accepting a modest 38th-round bonus from the Twins in 2016. A year later, the Memphis-area product went 35th overall and received the full slot figure of $1.935 million after posting the second-highest exit velocity in college baseball.

SCOUTING REPORT: Rooker slowed down a bit after an eye-popping pro debut. Pushed to Double-A Chattanooga to start 2018, he found his low-ball swing tested with hard stuff above the belt. Too often, Rooker struggled with pitch recognition by chasing high fastballs and power breaking balls out of the zone. His strikeout rate crept up to 26.4 percent, while he still managed to walk 9.9 percent of the time. Hopes have faded for converting Rooker into a full-time left fielder, a la Josh Willingham, mainly due to Rooker's below-average arm and poor reads. Even at first base, the ball gets on him in a hurry. He is a smart baserunner with good instincts despite below-average speed.

THE FUTURE: A high ankle sprain led the Twins to pull Rooker from the Arizona Fall League. He is expected to return to Double-A to open 2019.

BA GRADE

55 Risk: High

Hit: 45. **Power:** 60.
Run: 40. **Field:** 40.
Arm: 40

Year	Club (League)	Class	AVG	G	AB	R	H	2B	3B	HR	RBI	BB	SO	SB	CS	OBP	SLG
2017	Elizabethton (APP)	R	.282	22	85	19	24	5	0	7	17	11	21	2	2	.364	.588
	Fort Myers (FSL)	HiA	.280	40	143	23	40	6	0	11	35	16	47	0	0	.364	.552
2018	Chattanooga (SL)	AA	.254	130	503	72	128	32	4	22	79	56	150	6	1	.333	.465
Minor League Totals			.263	192	731	114	192	43	4	40	131	83	218	8	3	.343	.497

7 JHOAN DURAN, RHP

Born: Jan. 8, 1998. **B-T:** R-R. **Ht:** 6-5. **Wt:** 175. **Signed:** Dominican Republic, 2014. **Signed by:** Jose Ortiz/Junior Noboa (Diamondbacks).

TRACK RECORD: The key piece in a three-player package received from the D-backs for Eduardo Escobar at the July 2018 trade deadline, Duran was only throwing in the upper 80s when he signed for $65,000 a month before his 17th birthday. Just two years later, he was touching 98 mph.

SCOUTING REPORT: Even at 6-foot-5, 215 pounds, Duran still has plenty of projection remaining on his strong, durable frame. He sits 96-98 mph with his four-seam fastball but relies more on a 93-94 mph "splinker," which he throws with his fingers spread, generating tremendous late movement. Duran still needs to tighten his slider, which he struggles to command, and his changeup is a work in progress. But he has a clean arm and repeats his smooth delivery out of a high three-quarter arm slot. Duran's swinging-strike and groundball rates were both above-average for the low Class A Midwest League. Quiet and coachable, he is married with a young child.

THE FUTURE: After dominating at times in 2018, Duran should soon be ready for the challenge of the Florida State League. He could end up as a mid-rotation starter with a fallback option as a back-end bullpen arm.

BA GRADE

55 Risk: High

Fastball: 70.
Split: 60. **Slider:** 45.
Curve: 40. **CTL:** 45.

Year	Club (League)	Class	W	L	ERA	G	GS	CG	SV	IP	H	HR	BB	SO	K/9	WHIP	AVG
2016	Diamondbacks (AZL)	R	1	2	5.85	4	4	0	0	20	24	1	5	13	5.9	1.45	.312
	Missoula (PIO)	R	0	1	3.55	3	3	0	0	13	14	1	5	9	6.4	1.50	.250
2017	Diamondbacks (AZL)	R	0	2	7.15	3	3	0	0	11	19	0	4	13	10.3	2.03	.352
	Hillsboro (NWL)	SS	6	3	4.24	11	11	0	0	51	44	5	17	36	6.4	1.20	.228
2018	Kane County (MWL)	LoA	5	4	4.73	15	15	0	0	65	69	6	28	71	9.9	1.50	.268
	Cedar Rapids (MWL)	LoA	2	1	2.00	6	6	0	0	36	19	2	10	44	11.0	0.81	.154
Minor League Totals			18	14	4.03	54	54	0	0	259	251	16	91	230	8.0	1.32	.252

8 BLAYNE ENLOW, RHP

Born: March 21, 1999. **B-T:** R-R. **Ht:** 6-4. **Wt:** 200. **Drafted:** HS—St. Amant, La., 2017 (3rd round). **Signed by:** Greg Rusner.

TRACK RECORD: Signed away from an Louisiana State commitment for $2 million, nearly triple the slot value of $755,500, Enlow caught the Twins' eye pitching for Team USA's 18U team. That came after a harrowing car accident entering his sophomore year in which he suffered a broken ankle and pelvis and spent eight weeks in a wheelchair. Doctors warned him he might never reach his prior potential, but Enlow built himself back up from an atrophied 130 pounds. His 2018 season was disrupted by a back strain and a sprained left ankle.

BA GRADE

50 Risk: High

Fastball: 60.
Curve: 60. **Slider:** 50.
Change: 50. **CTL:** 55.

SCOUTING REPORT: Enlow pitches at 89-92 mph and touches 95 mph from a high three-quarter arm slot. He projects to add even more velocity as he fills out, but his best weapon remains an above-average 78-82 mph sharp downer curveball. He also features a hard 84-85 mph slider and a fringy changeup that projects as future average with sink and fade. Enlow still needs work on controlling the running game and must keep the game from speeding up on him at times. His 6.8 strikeouts per nine innings and his swinging-strike rate were both below the low Class A Midwest League average. Some felt he was around the plate almost too much.

THE FUTURE: Despite some command issues at Cedar Rapids, Enlow still has a mid-rotation ceiling. He should reach high Class A Fort Myers by midseason.

Year	Club (League)	Class	W	L	ERA	G	GS	CG	SV	IP	H	HR	BB	SO	K/9	WHIP	AVG
2017	Twins (GCL)	R	3	0	1.33	6	1	0	0	20	10	1	4	19	8.4	0.69	.141
2018	Cedar Rapids (MWL)	LoA	3	5	3.26	20	17	0	1	94	94	4	35	71	6.8	1.37	.263
Minor League Totals			6	5	2.91	26	18	0	1	114	104	5	39	90	7.1	1.25	.242

9 RYAN JEFFERS, C

Born: June 3, 1997. **B-T:** R-R. **Ht:** 6-4. **Wt:** 228. **Drafted:** UNC Wilmington, 2018 (2nd round). **Signed by:** Matt Williams.

TRACK RECORD: Drafted 59th overall and signed for a below-slot figure of $800,000, Jeffers wasted little time making the Twins look smart for snatching him from a deep group of draft-eligible catchers. A standout catcher at UNC Wilmington, where he helped the Seahawks reached the NCAA Tournament, he came out mashing at Rookie-level Elizabethton and quickly earned a promotion to the Midwest League.

SCOUTING REPORT: Two semesters shy of completing his physics degree, Jeffers has a natural curiosity that plays well with the pitchers he must handle and the coaches who work with him. Catching coordinator Tanner Swanson helped him build on the natural feel he showed in college for pitch framing. Jeffers has enough arm strength, but his blocking and footwork are below-average. A Buster Posey fan growing up in North Carolina, he is determined to stay behind the plate. When Jeffers did cool off with the bat, it was because

BA GRADE

50 Risk: High

Hit: 50. **Power:** 55.
Run: 40. **Field:** 40.
Arm: 55.

he was trying to let the ball get too deep in the zone. He quickly made the adjustment and resumed raking with a smooth, natural stroke that generates easy power.

THE FUTURE: The Twins are committed to keeping Jeffers behind the plate, so he could return to low Class A Cedar Rapids. Rival scouts are skeptical about his glove—he doesn't profile at other positions because of his body type and actions—but love his bat.

Year	Club (League)	Class	AVG	G	AB	R	H	2B	3B	HR	RBI	BB	SO	SB	CS	OBP	SLG
2018	Elizabethton (APP)	R	.422	28	102	29	43	7	0	3	16	20	16	0	1	.543	.578
	Cedar Rapids (MWL)	LoA	.288	36	139	19	40	10	0	4	17	14	30	0	0	.361	.446
Minor League Totals			.344	64	241	48	83	17	0	7	33	34	46	0	1	.444	.502

10 YUNIOR SEVERINO, 2B

Born: Oct. 3, 1999. **B-T:** B-R. **Ht:** 6-1. **Wt:** 189. **Signed:** Dominican Republic, 2016. **Signed by:** Jonathan Cruz (Braves).

TRACK RECORD: Severino landed in the Twins' lap in late 2017 after their pursuit of Kevin Maitan fell short. The Twins paid Severino $2.5 million after the former Braves prospect was declared a free agent because of the team's rules violations. A huge fan of Robinson Cano, Severino has shown little interest in returning to short or trying third base since moving to second with the Braves.

SCOUTING REPORT: Blessed with strong wrists and forearms, Severino generates tremendous bat speed that suggests power potential in the 20-25 homer range. A switch-hitter, he grades out as a future plus hitter with plus raw power. His arm is above-average but his range and footwork must improve. His below-average speed limits his range, but his reads off the bat have improved and his hands are good enough to stay up the middle.

THE FUTURE: If he doesn't open 2019 in the low Class A Midwest League, Severino should get there once the spring thaw arrives.

	BA GRADE	
55	Risk:	Extreme

Hit: 55. **Power:** 55.
Run: 45. **Field:** 45.
Arm: 50

Year	Club (League)	Class	AVG	G	AB	R	H	2B	3B	HR	RBI	BB	SO	SB	CS	OBP	SLG
2017	Braves (DSL)	R	.189	10	37	6	7	2	1	0	2	8	6	0	0	.348	.297
	Braves (GCL)	R	.286	48	189	27	54	17	2	3	27	16	61	0	1	.345	.444
2018	Elizabethton (APP)	R	.263	49	198	32	52	8	0	8	28	17	52	0	1	.321	.424
Minor League Totals			.267	107	424	65	113	27	3	11	57	41	119	0	2	.334	.422

11 LUIS ARRAEZ, 2B

	BA GRADE	
50	Risk:	High

Born: April 9, 1997. **B-T:** L-R. **HT:** 5-10. **WT:** 184. **Signed:** Venezuela, 2013. **Signed by:** Jose Leon.

TRACK RECORD: Added to the 40-man roster for the first time in November, Arraez made a successful return in 2018 from a torn anterior cruciate ligament in his right knee.

SCOUTING REPORT: Signed out of Venezuela seven months after his 16th birthday for just $40,000, Arraez has packed on 30 pounds since signing. Blessed with outstanding hand-eye coordination, Arraez hit his way out of the Florida State League and continued to impress in his first taste of the Southern League. Drawing comparisons to Carlos Baerga with more pull-side power, Arraez is still learning to handle hard stuff on the inner third. At worst he's a hit-tool fiend with the ability to spray the ball to all fields. Defensively, Arraez is athletic with feet that work well around the bag. His arm is average at best while his speed is below-average, but he shows soft hands, constant energy and leadership skills. Despite the questions about his arm, some believe he could handle third.

THE FUTURE: Arraez figures to open 2019 in Double-A, where he'll aim to hit over .300 once again.

Year	Club (League)	Class	AVG	G	AB	R	H	2B	3B	HR	RBI	BB	SO	SB	CS	OBP	SLG
2016	Cedar Rapids (MWL)	LoA	.347	114	475	67	165	31	3	3	66	31	51	3	3	.386	.444
2017	Fort Myers (FSL)	HiA	.385	3	13	1	5	0	1	0	1	0	0	0	0	.385	.538
2018	Fort Myers (FSL)	HiA	.320	60	228	27	73	14	3	1	20	19	28	2	3	.373	.421
	Chattanooga (SL)	AA	.298	48	178	25	53	6	0	2	16	13	16	2	0	.345	.365
Minor League Totals			.329	313	1216	166	400	72	8	6	137	98	114	25	19	.381	.416

12 MISAEL URBINA, OF

	BA GRADE	
55	Risk:	Extreme

Born: April 26, 2002. **B-T:** R-R. **HT:** 5-11. **WT:** 170. **Signed:** Venezuela, 2018. **Signed by:** Fred Guerrero.

TRACK RECORD: Urbina was one of the top Venezuelan prospects in 2018, with the Twins making him the prize signing of their international class when the 2018-19 signing period opened on July 2. He had ranked as the No. 10 prospect in the international class.

SCOUTING REPORT: While several other highly-regarded 2018 international prospects face questions about their future positions, Urbina projects to stick at a premium position in center field. An athletic, high-intensity player, Urbina works diligently at his defense and it shows. He was one of the best defensive outfielder in the 2018 class, maximizing his plus speed by getting good jumps off the bat and taking sharp routes with good closing speed. His arm is a fringe-average tool. The split among Urbina with scouts was on the offensive side. He has good bat speed and puts a surprising charge into the ball during games, with occasional pull shots over the fence in batting practice. Scouts highest on Urbina saw him hit well in games and liked his compact swing, though others didn't see that type of performance and saw risk with his swing path.

THE FUTURE: Urbina is many years away from the big leagues, but he has a chance to develop into an everyday center fielder.

Year	Club (League)	Class	AVG	G	AB	R	H	2B	3B	HR	RBI	BB	SO	SB	CS	OBP	SLG
2018	Did not play—Signed 2019 contract																

13 JOSE MIRANDA, 2B/3B

BA GRADE 50 Risk: High

Born: June 29, 1998. **B-T:** R-R. **HT:** 6-2. **WT:** 180. **Drafted:** HS—Guaynabo, P.R., 2016 (2nd round supplemental). **Signed by:** Freddie Thon.

TRACK RECORD: The second Puerto Rican player taken in his draft class and signed for $775,000, Miranda improved his conditioning and his defense in 2018. His range, actions and footwork flashed above-average at second base and his above-average arm remains plenty strong enough to handle third base, where he again split time.

SCOUTING REPORT: At the plate he continued to show excellent barrel awareness with the chance for plus power as he continues to hone his strike-zone discipline. Overshadowed in the first half by Royce Lewis and Alex Kirilloff, Miranda blossomed after their promotions and later joined them at high Class A Fort Myers for the title push. For much of July some felt he was the best hitter in the Midwest League. Miranda has good balance at the plate with quiet hands and the ability to drive the ball to all fields. An average runner with a projectable frame who could yet outgrow second base, Miranda swung and missed just 11 percent of the time but could stand to walk more.

THE FUTURE: Miranda figures to open 2019 at Fort Myers, where he will play both second and third.

Year	Club (League)	Class	AVG	G	AB	R	H	2B	3B	HR	RBI	BB	SO	SB	CS	OBP	SLG
2016	Twins (GCL)	R	.227	55	185	14	42	7	1	1	20	19	36	4	5	.308	.292
2017	Elizabethton (APP)	R	.283	54	223	43	63	8	2	11	43	16	24	2	3	.340	.484
2018	Cedar Rapids (MWL)	LoA	.277	104	401	52	111	22	1	13	72	26	51	0	1	.326	.434
	Fort Myers (FSL)	HiA	.216	27	102	9	22	5	0	3	10	5	11	0	2	.292	.353
Minor League Totals			.261	240	911	118	238	42	4	28	145	66	122	6	11	.322	.408

14 GRIFFIN JAX, RHP

BA GRADE 50 Risk: High

Born: Nov. 22, 1994. **B-T:** R-R. **HT:** 6-2. **WT:** 195. **Drafted:** Air Force, 2016 (3rd round). **Signed by:** Ted Williams.

TRACK RECORD: The son of former NFL linebacker Garth Jax, the younger Jax stood out on the pitcher's mound instead at Air Force. The Twins took him in the third round in 2016, signing him for $645,600, but soon saw the Department of Defense bring back the traditional restrictions on pro sports participation for graduates of service academies. That change held through Jax's first two pro summers as he was limited to just 40 total innings. The rules changed again, this team to his benefit, with the return of baseball as an Olympic medal sport for 2020. Jax took full advantage of the increased development time, piling up 109 combined innings via the Florida State and Arizona Fall leagues.

SCOUTING REPORT: Exhibiting excellent command with a loose, quick arm and a low-stress delivery, Jax spots his 90-93 mph fastball to all four quadrants. He must be pinpoint as his stuff lacks late action, but his touch and feel are advanced considering his limited mound time. Jax has a big-breaking slider that projects as a plus offering and a good feel for his change, which some evaluators feel will be his best pitch. With plus makeup, athleticism and an aggressive approach, he could still add some muscle to a lean build.

THE FUTURE: Entering his age-24 season already, Jax figures to start at Double-A Pensacola. He could move quickly now that he's able to defer his military commitment.

Year	Club (League)	Class	W	L	ERA	G	GS	CG	SV	IP	H	HR	BB	SO	K/9	WHIP	AVG
2016	Elizabethton (APP)	R	0	1	4.15	4	0	0	0	9	15	2	1	8	8.3	1.85	.385
2017	Elizabethton (APP)	R	0	1	3.86	1	1	0	0	5	6	1	0	7	13.5	1.29	.300
	Cedar Rapids (MWL)	LoA	2	1	2.39	4	4	0	0	26	19	1	7	13	4.4	0.99	.200
2018	Fort Myers (FSL)	HiA	3	4	3.70	15	14	0	0	88	93	3	15	66	6.8	1.23	.274
Minor League Totals			5	7	3.46	24	19	0	0	127	133	7	23	94	6.6	1.23	.269

15 NICK GORDON, SS/2B

BA GRADE 45 Risk: Medium

Born: Oct. 24, 1995. **B-T:** L-R. **HT:** 6-0. **WT:** 170. **Drafted:** HS—Orlando, 2014 (1st round). **Signed by:** Brett Dowdy.

TRACK RECORD: Outstanding bloodlines have long been a selling point for the son of former all-star pitcher Tom "Flash" Gordon and the younger half-brother of the Mariners' Dee Gordon. Drafted fifth overall in 2014 out of an Orlando-area high school, the Florida State signee received a $3.851 million signing bonus from the Twins. Gordon reached the All-Star Futures Game in 2017 after a star turn in

Arizona the prior fall. However, he stumbled in his first extended look at Triple-A last season, losing confidence in the field and seeing his gap power disappear after tearing up the Double-A Southern League.
SCOUTING REPORT: Never a burner like Dee, Gordon at his best is an instinctive runner who shows advanced barrel awareness, solid plate discipline and a line-drive swing. Too many careless mistakes in the field along with questions about his range and throwing accuracy have knocked down his value. Gordon's lean, almost-scrawny frame raises doubts about his ability to be more than a utility type.
THE FUTURE: Gordon figures to open 2019 back at Rochester, where he should get more chances to play additional positions besides the keystone spots.

Year	Club (League)	Class	AVG	G	AB	R	H	2B	3B	HR	RBI	BB	SO	SB	CS	OBP	SLG
2016	Fort Myers (FSL)	HiA	.291	116	461	56	134	23	6	3	52	23	87	19	13	.335	.386
2017	Chattanooga (SL)	AA	.270	122	519	80	140	29	8	9	66	53	134	13	7	.341	.408
2018	Chattanooga (SL)	AA	.333	42	162	22	54	10	3	5	20	11	27	7	2	.381	.525
	Rochester (IL)	AAA	.212	99	382	40	81	13	4	2	29	23	82	13	3	.262	.283
Minor League Totals			.273	556	2240	323	611	104	32	21	253	160	463	88	40	.328	.376

16 JORGE ALCALA, RHP

BA GRADE
50 Risk: High

Born: July 28, 1995. **B-T:** R-R. **HT:** 6-3. **WT:** 180. **Signed:** Dominican Republic, 2014. **Signed by:** Oz Ocampo/Roman Ocumarez/Leocadio Guevara (Astros).
TRACK RECORD: Acquired from the Astros along with center fielder Gilberto Celestino in the Ryan Pressly trade last July, Alcala suffered a neck strain in his final outing before the deal and was never fully healthy in his brief Twins debut.
SCOUTING REPORT: Signed as a late-blooming 18-year-old, Alcala has seen his fastball velocity jump from 90-92 as a teen to as high as 102 mph, although he pitches at 92-98 mph with late explosion. His electric arm works well with excellent arm speed, but he sometimes gets out of sync with his twitchy delivery. His changeup is solid-average and he throws two distinct breaking balls, including an 88-90 mph slider that sometimes flattens out and a curve that flashes plus but often lacks precision.
THE FUTURE: Worst case, Alcala could land in the back of the bullpen, but the plan is to keep developing him as a starter with mid-rotation projection. He has yet to reach 110 innings in a season and won't be Rule 5 eligible until December 2019, so starting him back at Double-A would make sense.

Year	Club (League)	Class	W	L	ERA	G	GS	CG	SV	IP	H	HR	BB	SO	K/9	WHIP	AVG
2016	Astros (GCL)	R	1	1	1.21	6	3	0	1	22	14	0	6	35	14.1	0.90	.175
	Greeneville (APP)	R	2	1	1.80	6	4	0	0	20	12	0	8	20	9.0	1.00	.174
	Tri-City (NYP)	SS	0	1	5.27	3	3	0	0	14	20	1	4	15	9.9	1.76	.345
2017	Quad Cities (MWL)	LoA	2	0	2.03	6	4	0	0	31	16	3	12	35	10.2	0.90	.155
	Buies Creek (CAR)	HiA	5	6	3.45	16	14	1	0	78	55	7	33	60	6.9	1.12	.200
2018	Buies Creek (CAR)	HiA	1	4	3.03	10	7	0	2	39	25	2	18	45	10.5	1.11	.182
	Corpus Christi (TL)	AA	2	3	3.54	9	5	0	1	41	36	1	17	37	8.2	1.30	.243
	Chattanooga (SL)	AA	0	4	5.85	5	4	0	0	20	23	4	14	22	9.9	1.85	.280
Minor League Totals			15	20	3.18	73	46	1	5	297	228	18	131	289	8.8	1.21	.213

17 LEWIS THORPE, LHP

BA GRADE
50 Risk: High

Born: Nov. 23, 1995. **B-T:** R-L. **HT:** 6-1. **WT:** 200. **Signed:** Australia, 2012. **Signed by:** Howard Norsetter.
TRACK RECORD: Thorpe got his career fully rolling after missing two full seasons in the wake of Tommy John surgery in April 2015 and a bout of mononucleosis in 2016. Back on the mound, he reached Futures Game in 2018 and later Triple-A Rochester as well. Signed for $500,000, the richest Australian bonus in the 2012-13 international class, Thorpe added two inches and 35 pounds in his first two pro seasons.
SCOUTING REPORT: Thorpe's fastball sits at 89-92 mph and touches 94, but it plays up due to angle and carry with some deception. His cutter/slider is 85-87 mph, allowing him to chew up lefties when he's on. He continues to improve his changeup and he also has a 12-to-6 curve.
THE FUTURE: Once considered a potential mid-rotation starter, Thorpe has been knocked down a couple of pegs to a fourth-starter projection. To get there, he must figure out how to pitch backwards more often.

Year	Club (League)	Class	W	L	ERA	G	GS	CG	SV	IP	H	HR	BB	SO	K/9	WHIP	AVG
2016	Did not play—Injured																
2017	Chattanooga (SL)	AA	1	0	6.00	1	1	0	0	6	5	2	2	7	10.5	1.17	.217
	Fort Myers (FSL)	HiA	3	4	2.69	16	15	0	0	77	62	3	31	84	9.8	1.21	.226
2018	Chattanooga (SL)	AA	8	4	3.58	22	21	0	0	108	105	13	30	131	10.9	1.25	.251
	Rochester (IL)	AAA	0	3	3.32	4	4	0	0	22	20	3	6	26	10.8	1.20	.244
Minor League Totals			19	14	3.18	71	65	0	0	328	286	30	111	392	10.7	1.21	.234

18 STEPHEN GONSALVES, LHP

Born: July 8, 1994 **B-T:** L-L. **HT:** 6-5. **WT:** 213. **Drafted:** HS—San Diego, 2013 (4th round). **Signed by:** John Leavitt.

BA GRADE

45 Risk: Medium

TRACK RECORD: After top-seven ERA finishes in the minors in the 2015-16 seasons, Gonsalves battled through shoulder strains at the Arizona Fall League and early in the 2017 season. The loss of a couple of ticks off his already-modest fastball led to some delivery tweaks that ultimately led to command issues last season, both before and after his big league debut.

SCOUTING REPORT: Long-levered with generally good mound presence and a three-quarters arm slot, Gonsalves pitches in the high 80s now with an above-average changeup and two average breaking balls. His 1-to-6 curveball has flashed above-average in the past. The fastball used to touch 94 mph with glove-side run, but it's ticked down though Gonsalves has shown the moxie to pitch through it.

THE FUTURE: Gonsalves should get another crack at the back of the rotation in 2019.

Year	Club (League)	Class	W	L	ERA	G	GS	CG	SV	IP	H	HR	BB	SO	K/9	WHIP	AVG
2016	Fort Myers (FSL)	HiA	5	4	2.33	11	11	1	0	66	43	2	20	66	9.0	0.96	.188
	Chattanooga (SL)	AA	8	1	1.82	13	13	1	0	74	43	1	37	89	10.8	1.08	.171
2017	Chattanooga (SL)	AA	8	3	2.68	15	15	0	0	87	67	7	23	96	9.9	1.03	.207
	Rochester (IL)	AAA	1	2	5.56	5	4	0	0	23	27	4	8	22	8.7	1.54	.294
2018	Chattanooga (SL)	AA	3	0	1.77	4	4	0	0	20	11	2	10	25	11.1	1.03	.167
	Rochester (IL)	AAA	9	3	2.96	19	18	0	0	100	65	6	55	95	8.5	1.20	.187
	Minnesota (AL)	MAJ	2	2	6.57	7	4	0	0	25	28	2	22	16	5.8	2.03	.283
Major League Totals			2	2	6.57	7	4	0	0	25	28	2	22	16	5.8	2.03	.283
Minor League Totals			53	20	2.46	113	108	3	0	599	423	28	238	634	9.5	1.10	.199

19 AKIL BADDOO, OF

Born: Aug. 16, 1998. **B-T:** L-L. **HT:** 6-1. **WT:** 209. **Drafted:** HS—Conyers, Ga., 2016 (2nd round supplemental). **Signed by:** Jack Powell.

BA GRADE

50 Risk: High

TRACK RECORD: A compensation pick after the Twins failed to sign Kentucky righthander Kyle Cody, Baddoo accepted a $750,000 bonus to spurn those same Wildcats.

SCOUTING REPORT: After growing two inches and adding 25 pounds of muscle, Baddoo surged up the prospect charts in his first full season, when he walked more than he struck out. Last year started slowly, however, as he was bothered by hamstring issues during the first half, but the above-average runner (sub 4.1 seconds to first) still shows potential to be a high-end basestealer. His route-running improved in center, but his below-average arm and funky throwing motion eventually figure to push him to left. A high-energy spark plug who is popular with teammates, Baddoo showed more ability to drive the ball at Cedar Rapids but still has some swing-and-miss, though he pushed his walk rate to 14.3 percent.

THE FUTURE: Baddoo figures to open 2019 at high Class A Fort Myers, where he'll look to hit more.

Year	Club (League)	Class	AVG	G	AB	R	H	2B	3B	HR	RBI	BB	SO	SB	CS	OBP	SLG
2016	Twins (GCL)	R	.178	38	107	15	19	0	2	2	15	18	36	8	1	.299	.271
2017	Twins (GCL)	R	.267	20	75	18	20	4	3	1	10	9	13	4	0	.360	.440
	Elizabethton (APP)	R	.357	33	126	39	45	15	2	3	19	27	19	5	4	.478	.579
2018	Cedar Rapids (MWL)	LoA	.243	113	437	83	106	22	11	11	40	74	124	24	5	.351	.419
Minor League Totals			.255	204	745	155	190	41	18	17	84	128	192	41	10	.367	.427

20 JORDAN BALAZOVIC, RHP

Born: Sept. 17, 1998. **B-T:** R-R. **HT:** 6-4. **WT:** 175. **Drafted:** HS—Mississauga, Ont., 2016 (5th round). **Signed by:** Walt Burrows.

BA GRADE

50 Risk: High

TRACK RECORD: Snatched two rounds after Griffin Jax in the 2016 draft, Balazovic signed for $515,000 and needed a couple of years to make the transition to pro ball.

SCOUTING REPORT: Balazovic visits both sides of the plate at 91-95 mph and touches 97. He is learning to work up in the zone effectively as well. He found a new grip for his hard slider, which can be hit and miss, but flashes above-average when it's on. His changeup projects as an average pitch, giving him more than enough weapons to post a nine-inning strikeout rate of 11.4 with a 13.4-percent swinging-strike rate in the Midwest League. Competitive with a repeatable delivery, Balazovic has improved his work habits as he's gained maturity though some still question his makeup. Those off-field improvements enabled him to move past a disappointing 2017 in the Gulf Coast League, where he walked 4.5 batters per nine.

THE FUTURE: Balazovic should open the year in Fort Myers and projects as a mid-rotation starter at best.

Year	Club (League)	Class	W	L	ERA	G	GS	CG	SV	IP	H	HR	BB	SO	K/9	WHIP	AVG
2016	Twins (GCL)	R	2	1	1.97	8	6	0	1	32	26	0	5	16	4.5	0.97	.217
2017	Twins (GCL)	R	1	3	4.91	10	3	0	0	40	47	5	20	29	6.5	1.66	.298
2018	Cedar Rapids (MWL)	LoA	7	3	3.94	12	11	0	0	62	54	5	18	78	11.4	1.17	.233
Minor League Totals			10	7	3.76	30	20	0	1	134	127	10	43	123	8.3	1.27	.249

21 LAMONTE WADE, OF

BA GRADE

50 Risk: High

Born: Jan. 1, 1994. **B-T:** L-L. **HT:** 6-1. **WT:** 189. **Drafted:** Maryland, 2015 (9th round). **Signed by:** John Wilson.

TRACK RECORD: A ninth-round steal after a broken hamate bone marred his junior season at Maryland, Wade signed for $163,800 after slugging the Terps past top-ranked UCLA in an NCAA regional.

SCOUTING REPORT: Wade saw his strikeout rate climb in his first crack at Triple-A last season, but his plate discipline has been a consistent strength as he's risen through the system and even back to his college days. Wade has a line drive swing with some pull-side power, but he doesn't project to add much more. With a sturdy frame and above-average speed, Wade has overcome a fringe-average arm well enough to play some center field. He projects as a solid fourth outfielder who profiles best on the corners. He is also an instinctive baserunner with a career success rate of 78.7 percent as a basestealer.

THE FUTURE: Look for Wade to head back to Triple-A to start 2019 and push for a big league debut.

Year	Club (League)	Class	AVG	G	AB	R	H	2B	3B	HR	RBI	BB	SO	SB	CS	OBP	SLG
2016	Cedar Rapids (MWL)	LoA	.280	56	207	32	58	6	3	4	27	44	27	5	3	.410	.396
	Fort Myers (FSL)	HiA	.318	32	110	17	35	8	1	4	24	10	17	1	1	.386	.518
2017	Chattanooga (SL)	AA	.292	117	424	74	124	22	3	7	67	76	71	9	2	.397	.408
2018	Chattanooga (SL)	AA	.298	46	171	30	51	2	1	7	27	26	20	5	2	.393	.444
	Rochester (IL)	AAA	.229	74	253	24	58	9	3	4	21	38	54	5	1	.337	.336
Minor League Totals			.284	393	1410	214	400	55	16	35	211	241	225	37	10	.391	.420

22 BEN RORTVEDT, C

BA GRADE

45 Risk: High

Born: Sept. 25, 1997. **B-T:** L-R. **HT:** 5-10. **WT:** 190. **Drafted:** HS—Verona, Wis., 2016 (2nd round). **Signed by:** Mark Wilson.

TRACK RECORD: Signed away from an Arkansas commitment for $900,000, Rortvedt is a rare Wisconsin prep product taken in the first three rounds who looked better in his second stint in the Midwest League.

SCOUTING REPORT: Fiery and competitive, he shows a plus arm and continues to polish his footwork, blocking and game-calling. Most importantly, after some initial resistance, he worked on his pitch framing with minor league catching coordinator Tanner Swanson. A below-average runner with a wiry, compact frame, Rortvedt shows tremendous flexibility and is more than athletic enough for the position. At the plate, however, he has struggled to decide what type of hitter he wants to be. While his default mode tends to be spraying line drives with a short, quick swing, the Twins' development staff wants to see him sacrifice some contact to get to more of his pull-side power. He handled a promotion to high Class A Fort Myers, helping the Miracle to a Florida State League championship.

THE FUTURE: Defense will get Rortvedt to the majors, but he'll need to hit to stay there long-term.

Year	Club (League)	Class	AVG	G	AB	R	H	2B	3B	HR	RBI	BB	SO	SB	CS	OBP	SLG
2016	Twins (GCL)	R	.203	20	59	3	12	3	0	0	3	5	8	0	0	.277	.254
	Elizabethton (APP)	R	.250	13	40	2	10	0	0	0	7	5	2	0	0	.348	.250
2017	Cedar Rapids (MWL)	LoA	.224	88	304	33	68	16	0	4	30	22	60	1	0	.284	.316
2018	Cedar Rapids (MWL)	LoA	.276	39	145	14	40	9	2	1	16	10	35	1	0	.325	.386
	Fort Myers (FSL)	HiA	.250	51	172	20	43	7	1	4	27	21	29	0	0	.337	.372
Minor League Totals			.240	211	720	72	173	35	3	9	83	63	134	2	0	.308	.335

23 ZACK LITTELL, RHP

BA GRADE

40 Risk: Medium

Born: Oct. 5, 1995. **B-T:** R-R. **HT:** 6-3. **WT:** 200. **Drafted:** HS—Mebane, N.C., 2013 (11th round). **Signed by:** Devitt Moore (Mariners).

TRACK RECORD: A late-blooming prospect traded twice before turning 22, Littell has come a long way since the Mariners signed him out of a small North Carolina high school. Acquired from the Yankees in the Jaime Garcia deal in July 2017, Littell continues to defy doubters and made his ML debut in 2018.

SCOUTING REPORT: A Duke signee out of high school, Littell has improved his conditioning and command while showing plus pitchability to go with his durable frame. He can work his 91-94 mph fastball up in the zone due to a high spin rate, and his curveball has good bite and depth with the chance to be a plus pitch. His changeup should be at least average with swing-and-miss moments. Littell is highly coachable with a repeatable delivery and was among the best adapters to the opener expirement the Twins tried.

THE FUTURE: After mixed results in three separate big league stints, Littell should get another chance to win a spot in the back of the rotation.

Year	Club (League)	Class	W	L	ERA	G	GS	CG	SV	IP	H	HR	BB	SO	K/9	WHIP	AVG
2016	Clinton (MWL)	LoA	5	5	2.76	16	16	2	0	98	94	5	21	95	8.8	1.18	.258
	Bakersfield (CAL)	HiA	8	1	2.51	12	11	0	0	68	64	3	13	61·	8.1	1.13	.246
2017	Tampa (FSL)	HiA	9	1	1.64	13	11	2	0	71	64	4	15	57	7.2	1.11	.251
	Trenton (EL)	AA	5	0	2.05	7	7	0	0	44	37	3	8	52	10.6	1.02	.224
	Chattanooga (SL)	AA	5	0	2.81	7	7	0	0	42	33	1	18	33	7.1	1.22	.223
2018	Chattanooga (SL)	AA	0	3	5.87	5	5	0	0	23	28	3	7	32	12.5	1.52	.308
Rochester (IL)		AAA	6	6	3.57	19	15	0	0	106	100	5	40	98	8.3	1.32	.248
	Minnesota (AL)	MAJ	0	2	6.20	8	2	0	0	20	25	3	11	14	6.2	1.77	.298
Major League Totals			0	2	6.20	8	2	0	0	20	25	3	11	14	6.2	1.77	.298
Minor League Totals			46	33	3.32	122	112	4	1	667	653	33	175	603	8.1	1.24	.258

24 LUKE RALEY, OF/1B

BA GRADE

45 Risk: High

Born: Sept. 19, 1994. **B-T:** L-R. **HT:** 6-3. **WT:** 220. **Drafted:** Lake Erie (Ohio), 2016 (7th round). **Signed by:** Marty Lamb (Dodgers).

TRACK RECORD: While the Twins probably waited too long to trade Brian Dozier, they at least salvaged a potential impact bat in the self-made Raley. Compared by some to a lefty-swinging version of Brent Rooker, Raley signed for $147,500 as the Dodgers' seventh-round pick in 2016.

SCOUTING REPORT: Raley is a physical presence who is still growing into his projectable frame and is more athletic than he appears. He is at least average in left field, where his accurate arm flashes above-average and his jumps and routes are solid. Raley shows the ability to get the ball in the air and drive it to all fields with 70-grade raw power but his plate discipline needs to improve. An average runner, Raley has seen time at all three outfield spots and he's ahead of Rooker as a defender at first base as well.

THE FUTURE: A strained left shoulder limited Raley to just 14 at-bats in the Arizona Fall League, but he figures to open 2019 at Triple-A Rochester with a chance to make his big league debut.

Year	Club (League)	Class	AVG	G	AB	R	H	2B	3B	HR	RBI	BB	SO	SB	CS	OBP	SLG
2016	Dodgers (AZL)	R	.625	5	16	4	10	1	0	1	2	2	2	0	0	.684	.875
	Ogden (PIO)	R	.417	5	24	6	10	2	2	1	5	1	1	0	0	.440	.792
	Great Lakes (MWL)	LoA	.245	56	200	24	49	11	4	2	17	15	47	4	4	.319	.370
2017	R. Cucamonga (CAL)	HiA	.295	123	478	102	141	21	11	14	62	43	124	9	1	.375	.473
2018	Tulsa (TL)	AA	.275	93	386	65	106	17	5	17	53	24	105	3	0	.345	.477
	Chattanooga (SL)	AA	.276	27	98	15	27	2	3	3	16	12	32	1	0	.371	.449
Minor League Totals			.285	309	1202	216	343	54	25	38	155	97	311	17	5	.361	.467

25 LANDON LEACH, RHP

BA GRADE

50 Risk: Extreme

Born: July 12, 1999. **B-T:** R-R. **HT:** 6-4. **WT:** 205. **Drafted:** HS—Ajax, Ont., 2017 (2nd round). **Signed by:** Walt Burrows.

TRACK RECORD: Nagging shoulder issues limited Leach to just seven Gulf Coast League outings in his first full pro season, but he used the downtime to work on his body. Already blessed with a pitcher's frame, the converted catcher now deadlifts 500 pounds and could take a big step forward in 2019, when he won't turn 20 until mid-July.

SCOUTING REPORT: The first Canadian player taken in the 2017 draft, Leach landed on the Twins' radar that spring on a Florida tour with the Canadian Junior National Team. He grew two inches and added 25 pounds of good weight in the months before the draft. Signed under slot for $1.4 million, Leach pitches at 90-94 mph and has touched 97. His sharp-breaking 84-86 mph slider has plus potential, his 78-80 mph curve is average and he has a good feel for his changeup at 79-81 mph. Fluent in French with a serious personality, Leach's hockey background shows through in his mound presence and high-end competitiveness. He repeats his delivery well and knows how to use his height to work downhill, which helped produced a 23.7 percent swinging-strike rate last season.

THE FUTURE: Leach should get his first taste of the Midwest League in 2019, where the early-season cold weather shouldn't bother him a bit.

Year	Club (League)	Class	W	L	ERA	G	GS	CG	SV	IP	H	HR	BB	SO	K/9	WHIP	AVG
2017	Twins (GCL)	R	2	0	3.38	5	2	0	0	13	11	0	6	10	6.8	1.28	.220
2018	Twins (GCL)	R	0	1	2.18	7	6	0	0	21	16	1	10	16	7.0	1.26	.216
Minor League Totals			2	1	2.65	12	8	0	0	34	27	1	16	26	6.9	1.26	.218

26 JOHN CURTISS, RHP

BA GRADE
45 Risk: High

Born: April 5, 1993. **B-T:** R-R. **HT:** 6-4. **WT:** 210. **Drafted:** Texas, 2014 (6th round). **Signed by:** Marty Esposito

TRACK RECORD: Signed for $266,900 as a sixth-rounder in 2014, Curtiss overcame UCL and thoracic-outlet syndrome surgeries in an eight-month span as the Texas closer. An academic All-America and aspiring country singer-songwriter who graduated in three years with an English degree, Curtiss endured a tough 2015 that included a concussion and elbow pain that cost him two months. He overcame it all to make his ML debut in 2017 and return in 2018, though he hasn't had success at the level.

SCOUTING REPORT: Curtiss' fastball tops out at 98 mph and sits at 94-96 mph, but it's his tight mid-80s slider that serves as his two-strike weapon. On the down side, his groundball rate dipped to 39 percent at Triple-A, where his nine-inning walk rate jumped over 5 and his ERA was 5.22 combined in June and July. He struggles to hold runners and his emotions have gotten the best of him at times in the majors, but he's smart enough to figure things out.

THE FUTURE: Command and confidence appear to be the only things holding Curtiss back from a permanent spot near the back end of the Twins' bullpen. He should get another shot at proving he belongs in 2019 after brief looks the last two years went poorly. The stuff is certainly there.

Year	Club (League)	Class	W	L	ERA	G	GS	CG	SV	IP	H	HR	BB	SO	K/9	WHIP	AVG
2016	Cedar Rapids (MWL)	LoA	0	0	0.00	6	0	0	2	8	2	0	2	17	19.1	0.50	.077
	Fort Myers (FSL)	HiA	0	2	3.06	38	0	0	3	53	42	0	23	68	11.5	1.23	.220
2017	Chattanooga (SL)	AA	2	0	0.72	21	0	0	13	25	12	0	12	35	12.6	0.96	.140
	Rochester (IL)	AAA	0	0	1.85	18	0	0	6	24	11	0	10	33	12.2	0.86	.131
	Minnesota (AL)	MAJ	0	0	8.31	9	0	0	0	9	9	2	2	10	10.4	1.27	.257
2018	Rochester (IL)	AAA	2	4	2.77	38	1	0	10	55	41	3	31	61	9.9	1.30	.200
	Minnesota (AL)	MAJ	0	1	5.68	8	0	0	0	6	8	0	4	7	9.9	1.89	.308
Major League Totals			0	1	7.20	17	0	0	0	15	17	2	6	17	10.2	1.53	.279
Minor League Totals			10	10	2.94	151	14	0	36	251	210	14	99	306	11.0	1.23	.225

27 MICHAEL HELMAN, 2B

BA GRADE
45 Risk: High

Born: May 23, 1996. **B-T:** R-R. **HT:** 6-0. **WT:** 190. **Drafted:** Texas A&M, 2018 (11th round). **Signed by:** Greg Runser.

TRACK RECORD: An undersized catcher growing up in Lincoln, Neb., Helman didn't receive a single Division I offer out of high school. Moved to second base soon after arriving at Hutchinson (Kan.) Community College, the late bloomer hit .487 with 17 homers and 30 stolen bases as a sophomore to earn his way to Texas A&M.

SCOUTING REPORT: After signing with the Twins for $220,000 as an 11th-rounder, Helman enjoyed a scorching first pro summer. Some see another Brian Dozier in Helman, who is a few inches taller than the former Twins second baseman. Helman could walk more but the Twins love his contact rate and barrel awareness. He shows more gap power than one would expect from his appearance. Helman thought the Rockies might take him as high as Round 3, but sliding out of the first 10 rounds just gave him more fuel for the long climb ahead. A fringe-average runner with an average arm, Helman would add power as he adds muscle. He lacks positional flexibility but some believe he could handle third if needed.

THE FUTURE: Humble with strong makeup, Helman should open 2019 at high Class A Fort Myers.

Year	Club (League)	Class	AVG	G	AB	R	H	2B	3B	HR	RBI	BB	SO	SB	CS	OBP	SLG
2018	Elizabethton (APP)	R	.375	12	40	8	15	0	1	2	7	3	4	6	1	.435	.575
	Cedar Rapids (MWL)	LoA	.355	27	107	20	38	6	1	2	15	6	14	4	5	.398	.486
Minor League Totals			.361	39	147	28	53	6	2	4	22	9	18	10	6	.409	.510

28 AARON WHITEFIELD, OF

BA GRADE
45 Risk: High

Born: Sept. 2, 1996. **B-T:** R-R. **HT:** 6-4. **WT:** 200. **Signed:** Australia, 2015. **Signed by:** Howard Norsetter.

TRACK RECORD: Despite a broken hamate bone that cost him two months last season, Whitefield remains one of the more intriguing prospects in the system. Signed out of Australia for $70,000 late in the 2014-15 international signing period, Whitefield is the product of professional softball-playing parents and focused on softball into his mid-teens.

SCOUTING REPORT: A true center fielder who rates as the best defensive outfielder in the system, the sturdy Aussie roams both gaps with plus range. Although his arm is just average, he is an above-average runner who has clocked sub-4.0 times to first from the right side. Still somewhat raw due to his background, Whitefield hit just .163 in his first 32 games after returning from the hamate injury before stabilizing in August. Intense, coachable and able to make adjustments quickly, his raw power remains and that should carry over into games more once he improves his contact rate (23.5 percent strikeout rate in 2018). **THE FUTURE:** Whitefield was a top performer at the Twins' fall minicamp and was expected to recoup some of his lost at-bats while playing for Team Australia at the Pan Am Games qualifier as well as in the Australian League. Whitefield figures to open 2019 back in the Florida State League.

Year	Club (League)	Class	AVG	G	AB	R	H	2B	3B	HR	RBI	BB	SO	SB	CS	OBP	SLG
2016	Twins (GCL)	R	.298	51	191	30	57	7	0	2	17	19	47	31	9	.370	.366
2017	Cedar Rapids (MWL)	LoA	.262	116	413	66	108	18	6	11	57	31	118	32	9	.318	.414
2018	Twins (GCL)	R	.250	5	16	2	4	1	0	0	2	4	4	0	0	.400	.313
	Fort Myers (FSL)	HiA	.211	65	213	33	45	7	0	2	10	17	56	20	7	.272	.272
Minor League Totals			.255	244	851	132	217	33	6	15	87	73	229	84	25	.319	.361

29 GABRIEL MACIEL, OF

BA GRADE
45 Risk: High

Born: Jan. 10, 1999. **B-T:** B-R. **HT:** 5-10. **WT:** 170. **Signed:** Brazil, 2015.
Signed by: Kelvin Kondo/Mack Hayashi (Diamondbacks).
TRACK RECORD: When the Twins traded popular utility infielder Eduardo Escobar to the Diamondbacks amid a breakout season, they came away with a top-10 arm in Jhoan Duran and a switch-hitting center fielder in Maciel. Originally signed in October 2015 out of Brazil for $90,000, Maciel is from Londrina, a city with a strong Japanese influence and thus baseball tradition. Maciel made his name at the 18U World Cup in Japan and was signed a month later.
SCOUTING REPORT: Blessed with first-step quickness and considered an above-average runner, Maciel has been successful on just 58 percent of his stolen-base attempts the past two seasons. He isn't the defender Akil Baddoo is in center but has a solid-average arm and good instincts. At the plate he lacks thump, especially from the left side, but puts the ball in play and uses the whole field.
THE FUTURE: Some question his bat speed and wonder how much higher his ceiling really is, but Maciel's athleticism is enough to buy him time to develop. It also helps that Maciel, who figures to open at high Class A Fort Myers, doesn't have to be added to the 40-man roster until November 2020.

Year	Club (League)	Class	AVG	G	AB	R	H	2B	3B	HR	RBI	BB	SO	SB	CS	OBP	SLG
2016	Diamondbacks (AZL)	R	.289	37	149	28	43	3	0	0	10	12	22	11	4	.341	.309
	Missoula (PIO)	R	.266	23	79	15	21	2	0	0	4	5	19	11	1	.318	.291
2017	Missoula (PIO)	R	.323	52	217	40	70	14	1	3	25	24	34	9	8	.389	.438
2018	Kane County (MWL)	LoA	.287	68	279	44	80	10	0	1	16	30	50	14	5	.362	.333
	Cedar Rapids (MWL)	LoA	.263	30	118	16	31	4	2	2	7	5	21	2	5	.302	.381
Minor League Totals			.291	210	842	143	245	33	3	6	62	76	146	47	23	.353	.359

30 GILBERTO CELESTINO, OF

BA GRADE
45 Risk: Very High

Born: Feb. 13, 1999. **B-T:** R-L. **HT:** 6-0. **WT:** 170. **Signed:** Dominican Republic, 2015. **Signed by:** Oz Ocampo/Roman Ocumarez (Astros).
TRACK RECORD: Scouted by then-Rangers assistant general manager Thad Levine as a 15-year-old in the Dominican Republic, Celestino and the executive met up again after Levine's current team acquired him from the Astros in the Ryan Pressly deal.
SCOUTING REPORT: A well-rounded player with solid-average tools across the board and a chance to be a plus defender, Celestino is the classic "whole is greater than the sum of its parts" prospect. At fall minicamp, former Twins hitting coordinator Rick Eckstein changed Celestino's awkward bat grip, which had been cutting off his swing and limiting his exit velocity. Celestino doesn't have as high of a ceiling as Gabriel Maciel, another center fielder acquired the same day from Arizona in the Eduardo Escobar trade, but he's an instinctive defender who shows excellent reads and routes to go with an above-average arm. His speed is just average and he projects as an average hitter with average power if the changes take hold. He was voted the top prospect in the New York-Penn League but struggled in the conversion to the Appalachian League after the trade.
THE FUTURE: Coachable with fast-improving English skills and a fairly high floor, Celestino figures to open 2019 in the Midwest League.

Year	Club (League)	Class	AVG	G	AB	R	H	2B	3B	HR	RBI	BB	SO	SB	CS	OBP	SLG
2016	Astros Orange (DSL)	R	.279	38	136	22	38	9	3	2	17	25	23	9	2	.388	.434
	Astros (GCL)	R	.200	18	55	7	11	3	1	0	2	8	16	6	1	.308	.291
2017	Greeneville (APP)	R	.268	59	235	38	63	10	2	4	24	22	59	10	2	.331	.379
2018	Corpus Christi (TL)	AA	.000	3	8	0	0	0	0	0	0	0	5	0	0	.000	.000
	Tri-City (NYP)	SS	.323	34	127	18	41	8	0	4	21	10	25	14	0	.387	.480
	Elizabethton (APP)	R	.266	27	109	13	29	4	1	1	13	6	16	8	2	.308	.349
Minor League Totals			.272	179	670	98	182	34	7	11	77	71	144	47	7	.345	.393

New York Mets

BY MATT EDDY

The 2018 Mets played like a playoff team for four months and like the worst team in baseball in the other two. The silver lining for the club was that its .549 winning percentage in July, August and September coincided with key major league player development.

Outfielder Michael Conforto compiled an .849 OPS in the final three months of 2018. In that same span, 22-year-old shortstop Amed Rosario made more contact and hit the ball with more authority. Rookie second baseman Jeff McNeil hit .329 and was a revelation following his late-July callup. Outfielder Brandon Nimmo finished with a .411 on-base percentage in his final 70 games.

On the mound, righthander Zack Wheeler went 11-4, 2.06 in his final 15 starts, finally looking healthy after 2015 Tommy John surgery.

Wheeler teamed with ace Jacob deGrom—who won the National League Cy Young Award with a 1.70 ERA that was the sixth lowest in the past 50 seasons—and Noah Syndergaard and Steven Matz to give the Mets a playoff-caliber rotation.

Despite a strong rotation, the Mets fell short in several other key areas, such as the bullpen, team defense, power production and OBP.

Into that reality stepped Brodie Van Wagenen, a former agent whom the Mets hired as general manager in October. Sandy Alderson had stepped down as GM in late June amid health concerns after an eight-year run. Before taking the helm, Van Wagenen had served as co-head of the baseball division at CAA, where he represented deGrom, Syndergaard and Yoenis Cespedes, among others.

Van Wagenen assumed control of a Mets roster stocked with both high-upside players and critical flaws, but his organization's farm system brimmed with the most talent it had seen since 2015, when Conforto, Matz, Nimmo, Rosario and Syndergaard all were prospects.

Van Wagenen and the Mets decided to leverage that minor league talent in trades to improve the major league team for 2019 and 2020, the final two years before deGrom can leave as a free agent. Wheeler has one season left under club control, and Syndergaard has three, making the next few seasons mission critical for the franchise.

The new GM's first major transaction brought 36-year-old second baseman Robinson Cano and 25-year-old all-star closer Edwin Diaz from the Mariners in a deal centered around the Mets' No. 4 and 5 prospects, outfielder Jarred Kelenic and righthander Justin Dunn. The Mets had drafted Kelenic sixth overall in 2018 out of high school.

The Mets assumed five years and $100 million of Cano's contract, but in the deal also cleared the

Drafted in 2011, outfielder Brandon Nimmo showed plus power and patience in 2018.

PROJECTED 2022 LINEUP

Catcher	Kevin Plawecki (31)
First Base	Peter Alonso (27)
Second Base	Andres Gimenez (23)
Third Base	Robinson Cano (39)
Shortstop	Amed Rosario (26)
Left Field	Jeff McNeil (30)
Center Field	Brandon Nimmo (29)
Right Field	Michael Conforto (29)
No. 1 Starter	Jacob deGrom (34)
No. 2 Starter	Noah Syndergaard (29)
No. 3 Starter	Zack Wheeler (32)
No. 4 Starter	Steven Matz (31)
No. 5 Starter	Anthony Kay (27)
Closer	Edwin Diaz (28)

nearly $37 million owed Jay Bruce and Anthony Swarzak. The Mets used some of those savings to sign 29-year-old reliever Jeurys Familia and 31-year-old catcher Wilson Ramos on the free agent market. Center field and bullpen depth remained areas of need in mid-December.

While international director Chris Becerra jumped ship to join the Red Sox after the season, Van Wagenen moved quickly to staff his front office. He hired assistant general managers Allard Baird to oversee scouting and player development and Adam Guttridge to head the analytics department. The Mets followed by hiring Jared Banner as farm director. Both Baird and Banner worked for the World Series-champion Red Sox in 2018.

ANDY LEWIS/GETTY IMAGES

NEW YORK METS

TOP 2019 ROOKIE: Peter Alonso, 1B. A rookie season of .250 with 25 home runs and a high walk rate is in play for the big league-ready slugger with power and discipline.

BREAKOUT PROSPECT: Desmond Lindsay, OF. The Mets have been waiting on Lindsay seemingly forever, but a swing tweak has him positioned to tap into his power in 2019.

SLEEPER: Kevin Smith, LHP. The 2018 seventh-rounder out of Georgia toyed with same-side batters in his pro debut (2-for-24) with a low arm slot, deceptive motion and big-breaking slider.

SOURCE OF TOP 30 TALENT			
Homegrown	24	Acquired	6
College	9	Trade	6
Junior college	0	Rule 5 draft	0
High school	8	Independent league	0
Nondrafted free agent	0	Free agent/waivers	0
International	7		

LF
Matt Winaker
Adrian Hernandez
Quinn Brodey

CF
Desmond Lindsay (11)
Ross Adolph (18)
Ranfy Adon

RF
Freddy Valdez
Luis Medina
Stanley Consuegra
Zach Rheams

3B
Mark Vientos (4)
Will Toffey (19)
William Lugo (29)
David Thompson
Michael Paez

SS
Andres Gimenez (1)
Ronny Mauricio (3)
Luis Guillorme (14)
Sebastian Espino
Manny Rodriguez
L.A. Woodard

2B
Shervyen Newton (7)
Luis Santana (13)
Gavin Cecchini (15)
Carlos Cortes (22)
Luis Carpio
Gregory Guerrero

1B
Peter Alonso (2)
Jeremy Vasquez

C
Francisco Alvarez (12)
Tomas Nido (16)
Patrick Mazeika
Ali Sanchez
Nick Meyer
Juan Uriarte

LHP

LHSP
Anthony Kay (5)
David Peterson (6)
Thomas Szapucki (10)

LHRP
Daniel Zamora (24)
Kevin Smith

RHP

RHSP
Simeon Woods-Richardson (8)
Franklyn Kilome (9)
Jordan Humphreys (17)
Adam Hill (21)
Chris Viall (26)
Tony Dibrell (27)
Junior Santos (28)
Tylor Megill (30)
Jose Butto
Christian James
David Marcano

RHRP
Eric Hanhold (20)
Ryder Ryan (23)
Drew Smith (25)
Ryley Gilliam
Kyle Dowdy
Bryce Montes de Oca
Bobby Wahl
Tyler Bashlor
Matt Blackham
Corey Taylor
Tim Peterson

DRAFT ANALYSIS

2018

BEST PURE HITTER: OF Jarred Kelenic (1) hit .413 in a 12-game tune-up in the Rookie-level Gulf Coast League before advancing to Rookie-level Kingsport. He endured a 4-for-50 stretch early in the Appalachian League but recovered to hit .330/.378/.524 in 24 games from Aug. 3 to the end of the season. Kelenic turned 19 in July and was old for his class, but he has extensive wood-bat experience, having played Wisconsin high school ball with wood and having starring for Team USA.

BEST POWER HITTER: OF Zach Rheams (27) launched 17 home runs as a Texas Tech senior, then advanced quickly to low Class A Columbia, where he hit eight homers in 45 games. He posted elite exit velocities in pro ball that rival system-mate Peter Alonso.

FASTEST RUNNER: SS L.A. Woodard (16) is an 80 runner on the 20-80 scouting scale who swiped 23 bases as a Middle Tennessee State junior and eight more in his pro debut.

BEST DEFENSIVE PLAYER: The Mets believe Kelenic is a center fielder with plus range and plus arm strength. C Nick Meyer (6) is a Team USA vet who called his own game at Cal Poly and records consistent sub-2.0 second pop times on throws to second base. SS Manny Rodriguez (10) made highlight-reel plays at short-season Brooklyn and owns a plus-plus arm.

BEST ATHLETE: Kelenic embodies the Mets' focus on acquiring up-the-middle athletes.

BEST FASTBALL: RHP Bryce Montes de Oca (9) touched 100 mph at Missouri but didn't pitch after signing because of a hip injury. RHP Simeon Woods-Richardson (2) topped out at 97 mph and averaged 93 in a pair of Rookie-ball assignments. The Mets haven't drafted a premium prep arm like him since taking Michael Fulmer in 2011.

BEST SECONDARY PITCH: RHP Ryley Gilliam (5) walked 5.2 batters per nine innings as a Clemson junior and continued to hand out free passes in pro ball, but his 12-to-6 curveball with tight rotation helped him strike out 16.1 per nine at short-season Brooklyn. He commands his 78-82 mph, high-spin breaking ball well.

BEST PRO DEBUT: OF Ross Adolph (12) hit .276/.348/.509 at short-season Brooklyn and ranked third in the New York-Penn League with an .857 OPS. The lefthanded hitter from Toledo claimed MVP honors at the league's all-star game, and his home park at Brooklyn might have obfuscated his power. He homered seven times on the road but hit zero at home.

MOST INTRIGUING BACKGROUND: Cal State Fullerton RHP Tommy Wilson (19) is the son of actor Thomas F. Wilson, who portrayed Biff Tannen in the "Back To The Future" films.

CLOSEST TO THE MAJORS: As a reliever who sits 94-96 mph and misses bats with a plus breaking pitch, Gilliam could move quickly.

BEST LATE-ROUND PICK: The distinction goes to Adolph, Rheams or 22nd-round SS Jaylen Palmer, who played high school ball not far from Citi Field in Flushing, N.Y. He's a strong athlete who hit .310 in the Rookie-level Gulf Coast League while playing shortstop and third base.

THE ONE WHO GOT AWAY: OF Jake Mangum (32) opted to return to Mississippi State. The center fielder was drafted as a sophomore, so he's given up little negotiating power by returning to school.

—MATT EDDY

TOP DRAFT PICKS OF THE DECADE

Year	Player, Pos	2018 Org
2009	Steven Matz, LHP (2nd round)	Mets
2010	Matt Harvey, RHP	Reds
2011	Brandon Nimmo, OF	Mets
2012	Gavin Cecchini, SS	Mets
2013	Dominic Smith, 1B	Mets
2014	Michael Conforto, OF	Mets
2015	Desmond Lindsay, OF (2nd round)	Mets
2016	Justin Dunn, RHP	Mets
2017	David Peterson, LHP	Mets
2018	Jarred Kelenic, OF	Mets

2017

The Mets went college heavy at the top of this draft but the early returns weren't impressive for that group. Prep 3B Mark Vientos (2) is the class' standout so far, while LHP David Peterson (1) had a mised first full professional season.

GRADE: C

2016

1B Peter Alonso (2) hit 36 home runs, nearly powering his way to New York. RHP Justin Dunn (1) was a part of the package sent to Seattle for Robinson Cano and Edwin Diaz. LHP Anthony Kay (1) made a solid return from injury.

GRADE: B

2015

OF Desmond Lindsay (2), LHP Thomas Szapucki (5) and RHP Jordan Humphreys (18) have all been hampered by injuries. OF Kevin Kaczmarski (9) and LHP P.J. Conlon (13) both reached the big leagues, but neither provides significant value.

GRADE: C

1 ANDRES GIMENEZ, SS

Born: Sept. 4, 1998. **B-T:** L-R. **Ht.:** 5-11. **Wt.:** 161.
Signed: Venezuela, 2015.
Signed by: Robert Espejo/Hector Rincones.

When international scouting director Chris Becerra left the Mets to join the Red Sox after the 2018 season, he left the organization stocked with high-upside shortstops. Gimenez succeeded Amed Rosario as the system's No. 1 prospect, and Ronny Mauricio has a chance to succeed Gimenez in a year or two. Gimenez ranked as the No. 2 prospect in the 2015 international signing class and three years later had reached Double-A Binghamton as a teenager. He accelerated his timetable in 2018 by taming the pitcher-friendly high Class A Florida State League and moving to the Eastern League in late July. All told, Gimenez set career highs with six home runs, 29 doubles and 38 stolen bases. Scouts regarded him as one of the top talents in both the Florida State and Eastern leagues, and at the Futures Game he struck a 106.5 mph ground ball—albeit for a double play—that was hit harder than all but five other fair balls at the exhibition.

SCOUTING REPORT: Gimenez is proof positive that looks can be deceiving. His lean physique, baby face and smaller stature belie a quick-twitch athlete with well-rounded skills, a high baseball IQ and leadership qualities. Elite contact ability and a quick, loose lefthanded swing give him above-average—and possibly plus—hitting potential. A discerning batting eye will keep his walk rate and on-base percentage high. While Gimenez shows merely gap power now, he generates impressive torque with his hips, and as his body matures he will hit for average home run totals. He is an average runner who reads pitchers well and uses his knowledge of game situations to steal bases. Scouts project Gimenez as a plus defender at shortstop with a plus, accurate arm. A quick first step, sure hands and quick exchange from glove to hand make him a reliable defender. Intense focus and a strong work ethic tie the whole package together on both sides of the ball.

THE FUTURE: Gimenez has the ceiling of first-division shortstop, but the presence of Rosario in New York might push him to second base, a position he played sporadically until starting there the majority of the time in the 2018 Arizona Fall League. Gimenez should reach Triple-A Syracuse in 2019 and could receive a late-season callup with an eye toward regular big league work in 2020.

MIKE JANES/FOUR SEAM IMAGES

BA GRADE	SCOUTING GRADES		
55	**Risk:** Medium	Hit: 50. Power: 50. Run: 50. Field: 60. Arm: 60.	

Projected future grades on 20-80 scouting scale

TOP PROSPECTS OF THE DECADE

Year	Player, Pos	2018 Org
2009	Fernando Martinez, OF	Did not play
2010	Jenrry Mejia, RHP	Mets
2011	Jenrry Mejia, RHP	Mets
2012	Zack Wheeler, RHP	Mets
2013	Zack Wheeler, RHP	Mets
2014	Noah Syndergaard, RHP	Mets
2015	Noah Syndergaard, RHP	Mets
2016	Steven Matz, LHP	Mets
2017	Amed Rosario, SS	Mets
2018	Andres Gimenez, SS	Mets

BEST TOOLS

Best Hitter for Average	Andres Gimenez
Best Power Hitter	Peter Alonso
Best Strike-Zone Discipline	Jeremy Vasquez
Fastest Baserunner	Ranfy Adon
Best Athlete	Ronny Mauricio
Best Fastball	Eric Hanhold
Best Curveball	Ryley Gilliam
Best Slider	David Peterson
Best Changeup	Anthony Kay
Best Control	David Peterson
Best Defensive Catcher	Ali Sanchez
Best Defensive Infielder	Luis Guillorme
Best Infield Arm	Andres Gimenez
Best Defensive Outfielder	Ross Adolph
Best Outfield Arm	Stanley Consuegra

Year	Club (League)	Class	AVG	G	AB	R	H	2B	3B	HR	RBI	BB	SO	SB	CS	OBP	SLG
2016	Mets2 (DSL)	R	.360	31	114	24	41	10	4	1	17	21	13	7	1	.461	.544
	Mets1 (DSL)	R	.340	31	100	28	34	10	0	2	21	25	9	6	7	.478	.500
2017	Columbia (SAL)	LoA	.265	92	347	50	92	9	4	4	31	28	61	14	8	.346	.349
2018	St. Lucie (FSL)	HiA	.282	85	308	43	87	20	4	6	30	22	70	28	11	.348	.432
	Binghamton (EL)	AA	.277	37	137	19	38	9	1	0	16	9	22	10	3	.344	.358
Minor League Totals			.290	276	1006	164	292	58	13	13	115	105	175	65	30	.375	.413

2 PETER ALONSO, 1B

Born: Dec. 7, 1994. **B-T:** R-R. **Ht.:** 6-3. **Wt.:** 245. **Drafted:** Florida, 2016 (2nd round). **Signed by:** Jon Updike.

TRACK RECORD: Alonso led the minors with 36 home runs and 119 RBIs in a 2018 season split between Double-A Binghamton and Triple-A Las Vegas, but his signature moments stand out more than raw totals. At the Futures Game he clobbered a homer that sailed over the left-field foul pole at 113.6 mph, an uncharted exit velocity for a ball hit so high. Then in the Arizona Fall League he turned around a 103 mph fastball from Blue Jays prospect Nate Pearson for a homer to center field. No major leaguer has homered on a pitch that fast in four years of Statcast data.

SCOUTING REPORT: Alonso is a polarizing prospect for scouts because his strengths and weaknesses are so pronounced. He makes the ball disappear in a hurry when he catches it with 70-grade raw power and elite exit velocities. Alonso's disciplined plate approach helps him draw walks and wait for pitches to slug, but more advanced pitchers have had success inducing him to expand his zone against breaking pitches. Despite being a bottom-of-the-scale runner, he should hit for a decent average because he hits the ball so hard. Defense is Alonso's bugaboo and has become his developmental focal point. Hard hands and limited mobility at first base turn some routine plays into adventures, but he scoops throws from infielders well. He must keep working to become even adequate defensively.

THE FUTURE: Alonso is an American League player in a National League organization. Alonso's bat should create significantly more runs than his glove allows, and he will be big league ready early in 2019.

BA GRADE

55 Risk: Medium

Hit: 45. Power: 70.
Run: 20. Field: 40.
Arm: 40.

Year	Club (League)	Class	AVG	G	AB	R	H	2B	3B	HR	RBI	BB	SO	SB	CS	OBP	SLG
2016	Brooklyn (NYP)	SS	.321	30	109	20	35	12	1	5	21	11	22	0	1	.382	.587
2017	St. Lucie (FSL)	HiA	.286	82	308	45	88	23	0	16	58	25	64	3	4	.361	.516
	Binghamton (EL)	AA	.311	11	45	7	14	4	1	2	5	2	7	0	0	.340	.578
2018	Binghamton (EL)	AA	.317	64	218	42	69	12	0	15	52	42	49	0	2	.441	.578
	Las Vegas (PCL)	AAA	.260	67	258	50	67	19	1	21	67	33	78	0	1	.355	.585
Minor League Totals			.291	254	938	164	273	70	3	59	203	113	220	3	8	.381	.561

3 RONNY MAURICIO, SS

Born: April 4, 2001. **B-T:** B-R. **Ht.:** 6-4. **Wt.:** 166. **Signed:** Dominican Republic, 2017. **Signed by:** Marciano Alvarez/Gerardo Cabrera.

TRACK RECORD: The switch-hitting Mauricio wore down while showcasing for teams, but the Mets stuck with him and signed him for $2.1 million in 2017, when he ranked as the No. 3 prospect in his international signing class. He made his pro debut in the Rookie-level Gulf Coast League in 2018 and shined as the circuit's No. 2 prospect. He hit .322/.333/.510 before fading in August and then received a cameo in the Appalachian League.

SCOUTING REPORT: Mauricio is uncommonly developed—physically and at the plate—for a player who played all season at 17. He grew two inches to 6-foot-4 after signing and filled out his once-skinny frame to profile as a future impact hitter. Mauricio has all the attributes to develop a plus bat with plus power. Both his hand speed and bat speed stand out on the Mets' internal metrics, and his timing and barrel frequency are impressive. Long limbs could make him susceptible to hard stuff up and in, and his aggressive approach could cut into his on-base ability. Mauricio has below-average speed out of the batter's box but he accelerates underway with long, gliding strides. His plus athleticism and 70-grade arm suit him at shortstop, where he compensates for average range with smooth actions and quick reads.

THE FUTURE: Mauricio could jump to low Class A Columbia in 2019, along with the other high-end prospects from a loaded Rookie-level Kingsport team. His ability on both sides of the ball should make him a first-division regular, if not shortstop then at third base.

BA GRADE

60 Risk: Extreme

Hit: 60. Power: 60.
Run: 40. Field: 50.
Arm: 70.

Year	Club (League)	Class	AVG	G	AB	R	H	2B	3B	HR	RBI	BB	SO	SB	CS	OBP	SLG
2018	Mets (GCL)	R	.279	49	197	26	55	13	3	3	31	10	31	1	6	.307	.421
	Kingsport (APP)	R	.233	8	30	6	7	3	0	0	4	3	9	1	0	.286	.333
Minor League Totals			.273	57	227	32	62	16	3	3	35	13	40	2	6	.304	.410

4 MARK VIENTOS, 3B

Born: Dec. 11, 1999. **B-T:** R-R. **Ht.:** 6-4. **Wt.:** 185. **Drafted:** HS—Plantation, Fla., 2017 (2nd round). **Signed by:** Cesar Aranguren.

TRACK RECORD: The youngest player in the 2017 draft, Vientos has spent two seasons in Rookie ball, but the time has not been spent idly. The high school shortstop shifted to third base in 2018 at Rookie-level Kingsport, while physical maturation has helped him develop his offensive game. Vientos ranked fourth in the Appalachian League with 11 home runs and third with 52 RBIs while drawing 37 walks against 43 strikeouts.

SCOUTING REPORT: Vientos hits the ball hard consistently thanks to hand speed and bat speed that rank among the best in the system. His projectable frame should equate to further strength gains and power production. Vientos started slowly in the Appy League, hitting .230 through his first 25 games, which underscores how his timing at the plate can be disrupted. Because of this he might not be more than a fringe hitter, but his disciplined approach will prop up his on-base percentage. As any fielder new to third base, Vientos needs reps at third base to learn the footwork and associated angles at the hot corner, but his plus arm fits the prototype.

BA GRADE

55 Risk: Very High

Hit: 45. Power: 60.
Run: 30. Field: 50.
Arm: 60.

THE FUTURE: Power production will be key to Vientos' future, and in that regard his early career has been a success. He profiles as a second-division regular or better as he embarks on full-season ball at low Class A Columbia in 2019.

Year	Club (League)	Class	AVG	G	AB	R	H	2B	3B	HR	RBI	BB	SO	SB	CS	OBP	SLG
2017	Mets (GCL)	R	.259	47	174	22	45	12	0	4	24	14	42	0	2	.316	.397
	Kingsport (APP)	R	.294	4	17	1	5	2	0	0	2	1	4	0	0	.333	.412
2018	Kingsport (APP)	R	.287	60	223	32	64	12	0	11	52	37	43	1	0	.389	.489
Minor League Totals			.275	111	414	55	114	26	0	15	78	52	89	1	2	.357	.447

5 ANTHONY KAY, LHP

Born: March 21, 1995. **B-T:** L-L. **Ht.:** 6-0. **Wt.:** 218. **Drafted:** Connecticut, 2016 (1st round). **Signed by:** Michael Pesce.

TRACK RECORD: The 31st overall pick in 2016, Kay had Tommy John surgery after signing and missed the entirety of his first two pro seasons. He made up for lost time in 2018 by pitching at two Class A levels, striking out a batter per inning as he regained feel he lost after his layoff.

SCOUTING REPORT: Kay returned to the hill in 2018 as a different pitcher than he was in college. More a fastball/changeup lefty at Connecticut, he emerged in pro ball with a vicious, top-to-bottom 80 mph curveball that he locates to both sides of the plate. His peak curveball approached 3,000 revolutions per minute, while his average spin rate ranked inside the top 10 percent in the minors. Kay tops out at 96 mph and sits 92-94 with an above-average, high-spin fastball that plays at the top of the zone in conjunction with his curve and mid-80s changeup at the bottom of the zone. His change flashes above-average potential and sinking action. Kay pitches with a bulldog demeanor and wants to strike out opponents.

BA GRADE

50 Risk: High

Fastball: 60.
Curveball: 60.
CHG: 55. CTL: 50.

THE FUTURE: Kay has mid-rotation potential if he can refine his curveball into a swing-and-miss pitch and improve his overall command. He will be ready for Double-A at some point in 2019 with a possible big league ETA of 2020.

Year	Club (League)	Class	W	L	ERA	G	GS	CG	SV	IP	H	HR	BB	SO	K/9	WHIP	AVG
2016	Did not play—Injured																
2017	Did not play—Injured																
2018	Columbia (SAL)	LoA	4	4	4.54	13	13	0	0	69	73	6	22	78	10.1	1.37	.275
	St. Lucie (FSL)	HiA	3	7	3.88	10	10	0	0	53	51	1	27	45	7.6	1.46	.262
Minor League Totals			7	11	4.26	23	23	0	0	123	124	7	49	123	9.0	1.41	.270

6 DAVID PETERSON, LHP

Born: Sept. 3, 1995. **B-T:** L-L. **Ht.:** 6-6. **Wt.:** 240. **Drafted:** Oregon, 2017 (1st round). **Signed by:** Jim Reeves.

TRACK RECORD: Peterson shined as an Oregon junior in 2017 and went to the Mets 20th overall. His pro workload has been interrupted by an ingrown toenail in his debut and then a tweaked knee at the outset of 2018. He struck out 8.1 per nine innings at two Class A levels in his full-season debut, but more notable was his contact management. He allowed just two home runs in 22 starts to go with a groundball rate of nearly 65 percent that ranked third in the minors among minor league starters with at least 100 innings.

SCOUTING REPORT: Peterson is a physical, 6-foot-6 lefthander with ample starter traits if not necessarily a huge ceiling. His fastball sits 89-91 mph and tops out 93 but looks a few ticks faster to batters because his elite extension boosts his effective velocity. His fastball runs to his arm side. Peterson's best pitch is a slurvy, swing-and-miss slider at 78-81 mph that he commands as a chase pitch against lefthanders, a back-foot equalizer against righthanders and as a get-me-over pitch for called strikes. The unique angles he creates from his height and three-quarters arm slot help him leverage the ball down in the strike zone and limit hard contact. Peterson shows some feel for a fringy changeup that he will need to refine to work away from the barrels of righthanders.

THE FUTURE: Peterson has the best control and best slider in the system, with both grading as plus for some scouts. He and will rely on those attributes to prop up the rest of an arsenal befitting of a No. 4 starter.

BA GRADE

50 Risk: High

Fastball: 55. Slider: 60. CHG: 50. CTL: 60.

Year	Club (League)	Class	W	L	ERA	G	GS	CG	SV	IP	H	HR	BB	SO	K/9	WHIP	AVG
2017	Brooklyn (NYP)	SS	0	0	2.45	3	3	0	0	4	4	0	1	6	14.7	1.36	.267
2018	Columbia (SAL)	LoA	1	4	1.82	9	9	0	0	59	46	1	11	57	8.6	0.96	.214
	St. Lucie (FSL)	HiA	6	6	4.33	13	13	0	0	69	74	1	19	58	7.6	1.35	.273
Minor League Totals			7	10	3.14	25	25	0	0	132	124	2	31	121	8.3	1.18	.248

7 SHERVYEN NEWTON, SS

Born: April 24, 1999. **B-T:** B-R. **Ht.:** 6-4. **Wt.:** 180. **Signed:** Curacao, 2015. **Signed by:** Sendly Reina/Hector Rincones/Harold Herrera/Chris Becerra.

TRACK RECORD: Born in the Netherlands, Newton trained in Curacao at the same facility as Jonathan Schoop and Jurickson Profar. The Mets signed him for just $50,000 as part of the same 2015 signing class that also included system No. 1 prospect Andres Gimenez. Newton didn't make his U.S. debut until 2018, when he thrived at Rookie-level Kingsport. He led the Appalachian League with 16 doubles and ranked second with 46 walks and 50 runs.

SCOUTING REPORT: Newton is a tall, athletic middle infielder with wicked bat speed and room to fill out and add power. He's a switch-hitter who can drive the ball deep to his pull side while batting lefthanded with quick hands he uses to keep his bat on plane through the hitting zone. Some scouts see potential 70-grade power down the line as his 6-foot-4 frame matures. Newton works deep counts and collects lots of walks and strikeouts, which will depress his average but boost his on-base percentage. He is a below-average runner who some scouts project to third base or possibly even an outfield corner. The Mets think Newton has the range, hands and plus arm to stay on the dirt, possibly at second base.

THE FUTURE: Newton speaks multiple languages and translates for teammates, and that maturity will serve him as he advances to low Class A Columbia in 2019. His bat could be special if he keeps developing.

BA GRADE

55 Risk: Extreme

Hit: 45. Power: 60. Run: 40. Field: 45. Arm: 60.

Year	Club (League)	Class	AVG	G	AB	R	H	2B	3B	HR	RBI	BB	SO	SB	CS	OBP	SLG
2016	Mets2 (DSL)	R	.169	35	118	18	20	5	1	0	5	22	32	0	5	.347	.229
2017	Mets2 (DSL)	R	.311	66	241	51	75	11	9	1	31	50	57	10	4	.433	.444
2018	Kingsport (APP)	R	.280	56	207	50	58	16	2	5	41	46	84	4	0	.408	.449
Minor League Totals			.270	157	566	119	153	32	12	6	77	118	173	14	9	.405	.401

8 SIMEON WOODS-RICHARDSON, RHP

Born: Sept. 27, 2000. **B-T:** R-R. **Ht.:** 6-3. **Wt.:** 210. **Drafted:** HS—Sugar Land, Texas, 2018 (2nd round). **Signed by:** Ray Corbett.

TRACK RECORD: One of the youngest players in the 2018 draft class, Woods-Richardson wowed scouts at showcase events and then gained velocity as a high school senior. The Mets nabbed him at No. 48 overall as the 12th prep pitcher drafted. He made an abbreviated debut at two levels of Rookie ball and put up a 26-to-4 strikeout-to-walk ratio. He didn't turn 18 until a month after his season ended.

SCOUTING REPORT: Tall, athletic and broad shouldered, Woods-Richardson is a prototype fireballing Texas high school pitching prospect. What sets him apart is his fiery, almost angry, mound demeanor and "now" stuff. He topped out at 97 mph and sat 93 from an overhand arm slot. His fastball plays up thanks to a high spin rate and plus extension. Woods-Richardson has advanced feel for a plus 12-to-6 curveball with tight break that sits in the mid-to-high 70s. He also uses a fringe mid-80s changeup that shows promising fade and average potential.

BA GRADE
55 Risk: Extreme
Fastball: 60.
Curve: 60.
CHG: 50. CTL: 50.

THE FUTURE: Woods-Richardson clearly has the raw stuff to impact games in the big leagues—if he can navigate the long, perilous journey high school pitchers face in pro ball. An assignment to short-season Brooklyn is probable for 2019.

Year	Club (League)	Class	W	L	ERA	G	GS	CG	SV	IP	H	HR	BB	SO	K/9	WHIP	AVG
2018	Mets (GCL)	R	1	0	0.00	5	2	0	1	11	9	0	4	15	11.9	1.15	.209
	Kingsport (APP)	R	0	0	4.50	2	2	0	0	6	6	1	0	11	16.5	1.00	.250
Minor League Totals			1	0	1.56	7	4	0	1	17	15	1	4	26	13.5	1.10	.224

9 FRANKLYN KILOME, RHP

Born: June 25, 1995. **B-T:** R-R. **Ht.:** 6-6. **Wt.:** 175. **Signed:** Dominican Republic, 2013. **Signed by:** Koby Perez (Phillies).

TRACK RECORD: Signed by the Phillies for just $40,000 a few months shy of his 18th birthday, Kilome developed into one of the system's best pitching prospects as he added weight to his tall, skinny frame and tweaked his mechanics. Philadelphia traded him to Mets at the 2018 trade deadline for Asdrubal Cabrera. Kilome turned in three quality starts in seven tries for Double-A Binghamton after the trade but had Tommy John surgery in October and will miss all of 2019.

SCOUTING REPORT: Kilome's work ethic and track record for durability—he had never missed a start or bullpen session for the Phillies—attracted the Mets, so his injury was surprising. He embodies the pitcher type the Mets have sought to acquire in recent seasons. Kilome is a 6-foot-6, power-oriented righthander with a 93-95 mph fastball that peaks at 97 mph and plays up thanks to a high spin rate and plus extension in his delivery. His curveball is a

BA GRADE
50 Risk: Very High
Fastball: 60.
CB: 60. SL: 45.
CHG: 45. CTL: 45.

power spinner in the mid-to-high 70s that plays as plus. Kilome rounds out his arsenal with a fringy slider and changeup. His entire four-pitch arsenal is undermined by fringe-average control and high walk rates.

THE FUTURE: If he doesn't improve his fastball command, Kilome has the raw stuff to dominate out of the bullpen. He should assume a rotation role when he returns to the mound in 2020 and could be ready for Triple-A in short order.

Year	Club (League)	Class	W	L	ERA	G	GS	CG	SV	IP	H	HR	BB	SO	K/9	WHIP	AVG
2016	Lakewood (SAL)	LoA	5	8	3.85	23	23	0	0	115	113	6	50	130	10.2	1.42	.259
2017	Clearwater (FSL)	HiA	6	4	2.59	19	19	0	0	97	96	5	37	83	7.7	1.37	.265
	Reading (EL)	AA	1	3	3.64	5	5	0	0	30	25	2	15	20	6.1	1.35	.238
2018	Reading (EL)	AA	4	6	4.24	19	19	0	0	102	96	7	51	83	7.3	1.44	.257
	Binghamton (EL)	AA	0	3	4.03	7	7	0	0	38	31	3	10	42	9.9	1.08	.223
Minor League Totals			22	27	3.55	95	92	0	0	471	438	26	195	419	8.0	1.34	.251

10 THOMAS SZAPUCKI, LHP

Born: June 12, 1996. **B-T:** R-L. **Ht.:** 6-2. **Wt.:** 181. **Drafted:** HS—Palm Beach Gardens, Fla., 2015 (5th round). **Signed by:** Cesar Aranguren.

TRACK RECORD: Szapucki struck out nearly 15 batters per nine innings in a pair of short-season assignments in 2016, but a pair of injuries compromised his 2017 encore. First he dealt with a shoulder impingement at low Class A Columbia that forced him out of action in April in May, then he had Tommy John surgery in July that knocked him out for the entire 2018 season.

SCOUTING REPORT: Szapucki threw two electrifying pitches when healthy and had obvious major league impact potential. His stabbing arm action has been described by scouts as being more typical of a reliever, but he repeats his low three-quarters arm slot and generates power and high spin on his fastball and breaking ball. Szapucki sits 93 mph and bumps 96 with electric life out of his lower arm slot. His high-spin curveball reaches home plate at 76-80 mph with sweeping, two-plane break. Below-average feel for his changeup and below-average control headline his to-do list.

BA GRADE
55 Risk: Extreme
Fastball: 60.
Curveball: 60.
CHG: 40. CTL: 45.

THE FUTURE: Health permitting, Szapucki is a near lock to pitch in the big leagues. On the high end of his forecast, he could be a potential No. 3 starter or high-leverage reliever. But first he must navigate a complete minor league season, which he will attempt to do in 2019.

Year	Club (League)	Class	W	L	ERA	G	GS	CG	SV	IP	H	HR	BB	SO	K/9	WHIP	AVG
2016	Kingsport (APP)	R	2	1	0.62	5	5	0	0	29	16	2	9	47	14.6	0.86	.157
	Brooklyn (NYP)	SS	2	2	2.35	4	4	0	0	23	10	0	11	39	15.3	0.91	.130
2017	Columbia (SAL)	LoA	1	2	2.79	6	6	0	0	29	24	0	10	27	8.4	1.17	.231
2018	Did not play—Injured																
Minor League Totals			5	5	2.27	18	15	0	0	83	55	2	30	116	12.5	1.02	.187

11 DESMOND LINDSAY, OF

BA GRADE
50 Risk: Very High

Born: Jan. 15, 1997. **B-T:** R-R. **Ht.:** 6-0. **Wt.:** 200. **Drafted:** HS—Sarasota, Fla., 2015 (2nd round). **Signed by:** Cesar Aranguren.

TRACK RECORD: The Mets' top pick in 2015, Lindsay has not produced offensively since reaching full-season ball in 2017. Injuries have cut into his playing time—he hit the disabled list in 2018 with a flare-up in his elbow that required nerve transposition surgery the year before—but even when healthy Lindsay hasn't resembled the hitter from early in his pro career. Something seemed to click during an assignment to the Arizona Fall League, even though he received sporadic play as a member of the taxi squad.

SCOUTING REPORT: Lindsay matched his home run total from the regular season (three) in just eight AFL games as he emphasized a new swing that allowed him to contact the ball out front. That enabled him to hit the ball in the air for power thanks to his above-average exit velocities. Lindsay had been letting the ball travel too deep and was hitting too many ground balls, but if his new approach sticks, the Mets are willing to accept a few strikeouts for more power. He has always worked deep counts and draws walks at a high rate. Lindsay is a plus runner who has developed into an above-average center fielder as a pro after playing third base in high school. His arm is average and enough for center or left.

THE FUTURE: Lindsay is one of the strongest and most athletic players in the Mets' system, but things just haven't clicked for him at the plate. Perhaps swing tweaks and an AFL confidence boost will do the trick in 2019, when he should be able to reach Double-A even if he has to repeat high Class A St. Lucie first.

Year	Club (League)	Class	AVG	G	AB	R	H	2B	3B	HR	RBI	BB	SO	SB	CS	OBP	SLG
2016	Mets (GCL)	R	.364	5	11	3	4	1	0	0	0	5	5	0	0	.563	.455
	Brooklyn (NYP)	SS	.297	32	111	18	33	5	0	4	17	20	26	3	1	.418	.450
2017	Columbia (SAL)	LoA	.220	65	214	40	47	10	1	8	30	33	77	4	2	.327	.388
2018	Mets (GCL)	R	.300	6	20	4	6	2	0	0	3	3	7	2	0	.400	.400
	St. Lucie (FSL)	HiA	.218	84	294	27	64	11	5	3	30	37	89	7	7	.310	.320
Minor League Totals			.241	227	764	105	184	36	8	16	93	116	244	19	13	.346	.372

12 FRANCISCO ALVAREZ, C

BA GRADE
55 Risk: Extreme

Born: Nov. 19, 2001. **B-T:** R-R. **Ht.:** 5-11. **Wt.:** 190. **Signed:** Venezuela, 2018. **Signed by:** Andres Nunez/Ismael Perez.

TRACK RECORD: Alvarez's family owned a construction business in Venezuela, and Francisco took part in the family trade by handling 90-pound bags of concrete at age 10. That work ethic and raw strength serve him as a catcher, a position he took up at a young age. Alvarez's tools marked him as the No. 9 prospect in the 2018 international signing class, and the Mets signed him on July 2 when he was 16.

SCOUTING REPORT: Alvarez has such large hands, wide forearms and intense grip strength that team-mates have taken to nicknaming him "The Thing" from the Fantastic Four comic books. He is an intense competitor with the quick-twitch actions and toughness to become an everyday catcher. Alvarez hits for power in games with a short, explosive stroke, and he can drive the ball straightaway and to right field with above-average power. He has the barrel control, bath path and plate discipline to hit for a solid average. Alvarez's defensive ability and arm grade as above-average, though he needs to improve his lateral agility. He runs deceptively well despite his position and stocky frame.

THE FUTURE: Alvarez faces a long trek to the big leagues, but he could be worth the wait. With a chance for an above-average bat and above-average defense to go with a grinding, win-at-all-costs mentality, he has first-division potential behind the plate.

Year	Club (League)	Class	AVG	G	AB	R	H	2B	3B	HR	RBI	BB	SO	SB	CS	OBP	SLG
2018	Did not play—Signed 2019 contract																

13 LUIS SANTANA, 2B

BA GRADE
50 Risk: Very High

Born: July 20, 1999. **B-T:** R-R. **Ht.:** 5-8. **Wt.:** 175. **Signed:** Dominican Republic, 2016. **Signed by:** Daurys Nin.

TRACK RECORD: The Mets' international scouting department took the unusual step of signing Santana for $200,000 based on only one look. His bat looked that convincing. Signed just shy of his 17th birth-day, Santana spent two years in the Dominican Summer League before embarking on an assignment to Rookie-level Kingsport in 2018. He hit .348 to rank fifth in the Appalachian League while placing third with a .446 on-base percentage.

SCOUTING REPORT: Santana may be 5-foot-8, but he trained in both baseball and boxing in the Dominican Republic and plays with his hair on fire. His bat-to-balls skills, fearlessness and hitting rhythm give him a ceiling of a plus hitter. Scouts marvel at his ability to be in good hitting position and on time to rifle the ball to all fields. He won't reach big home run totals, but his gap power and high contract rate will keep defenses honest. Santana is an average runner who doesn't steal many bases. He is a reliable defender at second base with average range and an average arm.

THE FUTURE: Santana plays with flair and if anything will need to keep his energy focused to reach his ceiling. After an eye-opening U.S. debut, he is firmly on the organization's prospect radar as he eyes an assignment to low Class A Columbia in 2019.

Year	Club (League)	Class	AVG	G	AB	R	H	2B	3B	HR	RBI	BB	SO	SB	CS	OBP	SLG
2016	Mets1 (DSL)	R	.375	3	8	1	3	0	0	0	1	0	1	0	1	.444	.375
	Mets2 (DSL)	R	.284	19	67	2	19	4	2	0	10	3	6	0	1	.342	.403
2017	Mets2 (DSL)	R	.325	65	237	47	77	12	8	3	52	34	22	16	4	.430	.481
2018	Kingsport (APP)	R	.348	53	204	34	71	13	0	4	35	27	23	8	3	.446	.471
Minor League Totals			.329	140	516	84	170	29	10	7	98	64	52	24	9	.426	.465

14 LUIS GUILLORME, SS/2B

BA GRADE
40 Risk: Low

Born: Sept. 27, 1994. **B-T:** L-R. **Ht.:** 5-10. **Wt.:** 195. **Drafted:** HS—Coral Springs, Fla., 2013 (10th round). **Signed by:** Mike Silvestri.

TRACK RECORD: Guillorme has started at least 50 games at shortstop for each Mets affiliate from Rookie-level Kingsport up to Triple-A Las Vegas. He completed his six-year trek to the big leagues in 2018, when he spent much of May and June in the big leagues filling in for the injured Todd Frazier. Guillorme played second base and third base in New York but not shortstop.

SCOUTING REPORT: Guillorme is the best defensive infielder in the system, with quick reflexes and sure hands that make him reliable at second, third or short. He doesn't have classic range at shortstop or a can-non for an arm, but he is above-average in both regards. Guillorme is a rare sight in today's power-oriented game. The lefthanded hitter sprays the ball around and in particular likes to wear out the opposite field. Scouts who like him see a future plus hitter because of this trait and also his patient yet high-contact plate approach. He has virtually no power and isn't much of a runner or stolen base threat.

THE FUTURE: Without power or speed, Guillorme will have to be a consistent .300 hitter to avoid being relegated to a utility infield or possibly even up-and-down role.

Year	Club (League)	Class	AVG	G	AB	R	H	2B	3B	HR	RBI	BB	SO	SB	CS	OBP	SLG
2016	St. Lucie (FSL)	HiA	.263	123	441	47	116	16	2	1	46	43	63	4	2	.332	.315
2017	Binghamton (EL)	AA	.283	128	481	70	136	20	0	1	43	72	55	4	3	.376	.331
2018	New York (NL)	MAJ	.209	35	67	4	14	2	0	0	5	7	3	1	0	.284	.239
	Las Vegas (PCL)	AAA	.304	69	247	41	75	15	2	3	33	30	39	2	1	.380	.417
Major League Totals			.209	35	67	4	14	2	0	0	5	7	3	1	0	.284	.239
Minor League Totals			.287	543	2021	287	580	81	4	5	205	234	272	40	22	.363	.338

15 GAVIN CECCHINI, 2B/SS

Born: Dec. 22, 1993. **B-T:** R-R. **Ht.:** 6-2. **Wt.:** 200. **Drafted:** HS—Lake Charles, La., 2012 (1st round). **Signed by:** Tommy Jackson.

BA GRADE
45 Risk: Medium

TRACK RECORD: Cecchini entered 2018 with a lot to prove after a lackluster 2017 he spent repeating the Triple-A Pacific Coast League. At spring training he popped two home runs in seven games before being sent to minor league camp. Cecchini kept hitting at Las Vegas through May 9, but that's when he was hit by a pitch in his right foot and sustained a bruise that cost him the rest of the season.
SCOUTING REPORT: Cecchini has grown noticeably stronger since the Mets drafted him 12th overall in 2012. He improved his swing plane and softened his front-foot landing in 2018, and the early results were tangible in terms of a higher flyball rate and enhanced power production. Cecchini retained a high contact rate with the swing change and could approach fringe-average power to go with a solid-average hit tool. A fringe-average runner, he is a capable second baseman with above-average range but he is stretched at shortstop by sketchy throwing accuracy.
THE FUTURE: Positional flexibility could be key to Cecchini's future with the Mets, especially after 2018 rookie Jeff McNeil made such a rousing debut at second base. He could begin his fourth straight season at Triple-A in 2018, with his bat determining if and when he is called to New York.

Year	Club (League)	Class	AVG	G	AB	R	H	2B	3B	HR	RBI	BB	SO	SB	CS	OBP	SLG
2016	Las Vegas (PCL)	AAA	.325	117	446	71	145	27	2	8	55	48	55	4	1	.390	.448
	New York (NL)	MAJ	.333	4	6	2	2	2	0	0	2	0	2	0	0	.429	.667
2017	Las Vegas (PCL)	AAA	.267	110	453	68	121	27	3	6	39	40	61	5	4	.329	.380
	New York (NL)	MAJ	.208	32	77	4	16	2	0	1	7	4	19	0	1	.256	.273
2018	Las Vegas (PCL)	AAA	.294	30	109	14	32	11	1	2	9	7	15	1	1	.342	.468
	St. Lucie (FSL)	HiA	.500	1	4	1	2	0	0	0	0	0	0	0	0	.500	.500
Major League Totals			.217	36	83	6	18	4	0	1	9	4	21	0	1	.270	.301
Minor League Totals			.284	602	2306	338	654	135	17	32	246	226	342	30	21	.348	.399

16 TOMAS NIDO, C

Born: April 12, 1994. **B-T:** R-R. **Ht.:** 6-0. **Wt.:** 210. **Drafted:** HS—Maitland, Fla., 2012 (8th round). **Signed by:** Mike Silvestri.

BA GRADE
40 Risk: Low

TRACK RECORD: Nido opened 2018 back at Double-A Binghamton after spending the entire 2017 season there—but that didn't last long. The Mets called him up in April when catchers Travis d'Arnaud and Kevin Plawecki both went on the disabled list. Nido didn't do much with the opportunity, hitting .158 with one extra-base hit through the end of May before being demoted. He returned to New York at the end of August.
SCOUTING REPORT: If Nido fashions a big league career, it will be on the strength of his defensive skill. He has above-average all-around ability behind the plate. He blocks and receives well but draws the strongest raves for his ability to frame strikes for his pitchers. He records consistent plus pop times on throws to second base and has a plus arm. At the plate, Nido has shown strong bat-to-ball skills in the minors, but major league pitchers have enticed him to expand his zone and chase breaking balls in the dirt, leading to predictably poor results. He has some power to his pull side but isn't a significant home run threat.
THE FUTURE: Nido will play all of 2019 at age 25 and still has time on his side, because catchers tend to develop later. He should get plenty of reps at Triple-A Syracuse.

Year	Club (League)	Class	AVG	G	AB	R	H	2B	3B	HR	RBI	BB	SO	SB	CS	OBP	SLG
2016	St. Lucie (FSL)	HiA	.320	90	344	38	110	23	2	7	46	19	42	0	1	.357	.459
2017	Binghamton (EL)	AA	.232	102	367	41	85	19	1	8	60	30	63	0	0	.287	.354
	New York (NL)	MAJ	.300	5	10	0	3	1	0	0	3	0	2	0	0	.300	.400
2018	Las Vegas (PCL)	AAA	.235	6	17	3	4	2	0	0	1	2	2	0	0	.316	.353
	Binghamton (EL)	AA	.278	57	212	23	59	18	1	5	30	7	36	0	0	.302	.443
	New York (NL)	MAJ	.167	34	84	10	14	3	0	1	9	4	27	0	0	.200	.238
Major League Totals			.181	39	94	10	17	4	0	1	12	4	29	0	0	.210	.255
Minor League Totals			.263	470	1688	182	444	94	7	30	224	100	314	4	5	.304	.380

17 JORDAN HUMPHREYS, RHP

Born: June 11, 1996. **B-T:** R-R. **Ht.:** 6-2. **Wt.:** 223. **Drafted:** HS—Crystal River, Fla., 2015 (18th round). **Signed by:** Jon Updike.

BA GRADE
50 Risk: Very High

TRACK RECORD: Tommy John surgery cost Humphreys nearly half of 2017 and all of 2018, but he is poised to resume his climb up the Mets' organizational depth chart in 2019. Prior to his August 2017 surgery, Humphreys had breezed through low Class A Columbia, going 10-1, 1.42 in 11 starts to reach high Class A St. Lucie.

SCOUTING REPORT: Control was a major asset for Humphreys prior to his elbow injury. If he makes a full recovery, his strike-throwing ability could be a separator. He paints both sides of the plate with a low-90s fastball that bumps 94 mph, while showing precocious fastball command for a young pitcher. Humphreys has grown into his 6-foot-2 frame since turning pro out of the Florida high school ranks, and all his stuff has ticked up. His above-average, high-spin, high-70s curveball changes eye levels and allows him to work north with his fastball and south with his breaking ball. He still must develop feel for his changeup to round out his arsenal and profile as a No. 4 starter.

THE FUTURE: Humphreys could move quickly if he regains the form he showed in 2017 and could reach Double-A by the end of 2019. That would be a boon to a Mets system thin in upper-level starting pitchers.

Year	Club (League)	Class	W	L	ERA	G	GS	CG	SV	IP	H	HR	BB	SO	K/9	WHIP	AVG
2016	Kingsport (APP)	R	3	5	3.76	12	12	0	0	69	65	3	15	76	9.9	1.15	.247
	Brooklyn (NYP)	SS	0	1	1.50	1	1	0	0	6	7	0	1	9	13.5	1.33	.292
2017	Columbia (SAL)	LoA	10	1	1.42	11	11	2	0	70	41	2	9	80	10.3	0.72	.168
	St. Lucie (FSL)	HiA	0	0	4.09	2	2	0	0	11	17	1	3	3	2.5	1.82	.340
2018	Did not play—Injured																
Minor League Totals			13	7	2.58	33	26	2	2	168	142	6	29	175	9.4	1.02	.226

18 ROSS ADOLPH, OF

BA GRADE
45 Risk: High

Born: Dec. 17, 1996. **B-T:** L-R. **Ht.:** 6-1. **Wt.:** 203. **Drafted:** Toledo, 2018 (12th round). **Signed by:** Chris Hervey.

TRACK RECORD: Adolph tied a Toledo school record with 15 home runs as a junior in 2018, when the Mets made him a 12th-round pick. He played above his draft status in his pro debut by ranking third in the short-season New York-Penn League in slugging (.509) and OPS (.857).

SCOUTING REPORT: Adolph showed a discerning eye in college and began unlocking power as he put in time in the weight room. He hit all seven of his home runs in his pro debut on the road, away from Brooklyn, a notoriously tough park for lefthanded power. He led the NYPL with 13 triples, an indicator of his plus speed and ability to drive the ball to the gaps. Adolph is the system's best defensive outfielder thanks to all-out abandon, plus athleticism and above-average range in center field. He uses his speed to steal bases effectively

THE FUTURE: The Mets were excited by what they saw from Adolph in his pro debut. If he can develop an average bat with average power, he could have a long career as an extra outfielder or possible starter. He's ready for full-season ball in 2019.

Year	Club (League)	Class	AVG	G	AB	R	H	2B	3B	HR	RBI	BB	SO	SB	CS	OBP	SLG
2018	Brooklyn (NYP)	SS	.276	61	232	47	64	9	12	7	35	21	52	14	3	.348	.509
Minor League Totals			.276	61	232	47	64	9	12	7	35	21	52	14	3	.348	.509

19 WILL TOFFEY, 3B

BA GRADE
45 Risk: High

Born: Dec. 31, 1994. **B-T:** L-R. **Ht.:** 6-2. **Wt.:** 205. **Drafted:** Vanderbilt, 2017 (4th round). **Signed by:** Dillon Tung (Athletics).

TRACK RECORD: Drafted out of high school and then as an eligible Vanderbilt sophomore in 2016, Toffey didn't sign until after his junior year in 2017, when the Athletics drafted him in the fourth round. Oakland traded him to the Mets a year later, along with reliever Bobby Wahl and $1 million in international bonus pool money, for closer Jeurys Familia. Toffey was 23 during his 2018 full-season debut, so in light of his age, the Mets promoted him to Double-A Binghamton after acquiring him.

SCOUTING REPORT: Toffey recorded a career-best .179 isolated slugging percentage at Double-A after the trade but faces questions about his power potential. The Mets hope offseason shoulder surgery will free up his swing to get to his solid-average raw power. Toffey has an outstanding batting approach that helped him run a 16 percent walk rate in 2018 and a .375 on-base percentage in pro ball. His ability to work counts and wait for his pitch should help him access his power. He makes consistent hard, line-drive contact that equates to an average hit tool with gap power. Toffey profiles at third base with above-average range and arm strength.

THE FUTURE: Toffey's lefthanded bat sets him apart at third base, and if he can get to more power, he could develop into a second-division regular with strong on-base skills. He should reach Triple-A in 2019.

Year	Club (League)	Class	AVG	G	AB	R	H	2B	3B	HR	RBI	BB	SO	SB	CS	OBP	SLG
2017	Vermont (NYP)	SS	.263	57	209	38	55	11	2	1	22	38	45	2	2	.377	.349
2018	Stockton (CAL)	HiA	.244	48	164	17	40	8	0	5	32	29	49	0	0	.357	.384
	Binghamton (EL)	AA	.254	41	134	23	34	12	0	4	19	30	36	2	0	.394	.433
Minor League Totals			.254	146	507	78	129	31	2	10	73	97	130	4	2	.375	.383

20 ERIC HANHOLD, RHP

BA GRADE

40 Risk: Medium

Born: Nov. 1, 1993. **B-T:** R-R. **Ht.:** 6-5. **Wt.:** 220. **Drafted:** Florida, 2015 (6th round). **Signed by:** John Shelby III (Brewers).

TRACK RECORD: The Brewers drafted Hanhold, who worked primarily as a reliever at Florida, in the sixth round in 2015 and intended to develop him as a starter because of his 6-foot-5 frame, repertoire and track record working in the rotation in premium college summer leagues. Milwaukee abandoned the idea in 2017, the same year they traded him to the Mets in an August waiver trade for Neil Walker.

SCOUTING REPORT: Everything Hanhold throws is hard. After pitching in the low 90s early in his pro career, his four-seam fastball velocity bumped up to 94-97 mph in 2018 and tickled triple digits. He wasn't able to throw his fastball by big league hitters in a small sample, and even in the minors he tended to be too hittable. Hanhold's plus-plus 88-90 mph slider could be an equalizer. It has devastating late break and wipeout potential in and out of the strike zone. He also throws a changeup occasionally.

THE FUTURE: Hanhold made his major league debut as a September callup in 2018 but appeared in just three games before a left oblique strain ended his season. He should see plenty of big league work in 2019 as an up-and-down reliever who has a chance to pitch himself into higher leverage work.

Year	Club (League)	Class	W	L	ERA	G	GS	CG	SV	IP	H	HR	BB	SO	K/9	WHIP	AVG
2016	Brevard County (FSL)	HiA	2	12	4.81	19	19	1	0	101	120	12	33	64	5.7	1.51	.300
2017	Carolina (CAR)	HiA	8	3	3.94	30	3	0	2	64	71	3	21	60	8.4	1.44	.286
2018	Binghamton (EL)	AA	3	1	2.84	17	0	0	8	25	21	1	9	32	11.4	1.18	.223
	Mets (GCL)	R	0	0	0.00	1	0	0	0	1	0	0	0	3	27.0	0.00	.000
	Brooklyn (NYP)	SS	0	0	0.00	3	1	0	0	4	1	0	0	2	4.5	0.25	.077
	Las Vegas (PCL)	AAA	2	2	7.11	14	0	0	0	19	25	1	7	20	9.5	1.68	.333
	New York (NL)	MAJ	0	0	7.71	3	0	0	0	2	4	0	1	2	7.7	2.14	.364
Major League Totals			0	0	7.71	3	0	0	0	2	4	0	1	2	7.7	2.14	.364
Minor League Totals			15	23	4.85	95	31	1	10	251	289	19	78	204	7.3	1.46	.294

21 ADAM HILL, RHP

BA GRADE

45 Risk: High

Born: March 24, 1997. **B-T:** R-R. **Ht.:** 6-6. **Wt.:** 185. **Drafted:** South Carolina, 2018 (4th round). **Signed by:** Daniel Coles.

TRACK RECORD: Hill looked like a first-round pick early in 2018 before losing feel for the strike zone. . The Mets snagged him in the fourth round and assigned him to short-season Brooklyn, where he struck out 15.3 batters per nine innings while averaging about 30 pitches per appearance.

SCOUTING REPORT: Hill's arm action reminds scouting director Marc Tramuta of former Mets starter John Maine, whom he scouted and signed for the Orioles in 2002. At 6-foot-6, Hill is two inches taller than Maine but throws with a similar low three-quarters arm slot and misses bats up in the zone despite modest fastball velocity. Hill pitched at 91-92 mph in his pro debut but hit 96 as a college junior. He gets swings and misses above the barrel with the riding life on his fastball. Hill's above-average curveball registers at 79-84 mph with good break. He can shape the pitch to sweep across the zone or throw it with tighter break for swings and misses. He must continue to refine a below-average changeup.

THE FUTURE: Hill can pitch effectively in short bursts using only his fastball, but to profile as a starter he must develop consistency of his secondary pitches and sharpen his control.

Year	Club (League)	Class	W	L	ERA	G	GS	CG	SV	IP	H	HR	BB	SO	K/9	WHIP	AVG
2018	Brooklyn (NYP)	SS	1	1	2.35	9	0	0	0	15	16	1	7	26	15.3	1.50	.262
Minor League Totals			1	1	2.35	9	0	0	0	15	16	1	7	26	15.3	1.50	.262

22 CARLOS CORTES, 2B

BA GRADE

45 Risk: High

Born: June 30, 1997. **B-T:** L-B. **Ht.:** 5-7. **Wt.:** 197. **Drafted:** South Carolina, 2018 (3rd round). **Signed by:** Daniel Coles.

TRACK RECORD: Mets scouts were convinced of Cortes' hitting potential despite his stocky, 5-foot-7 frame and no true defensive home. He signed for $1 million and received one of just three seven-figure bonuses in the third round of the 2018 draft. Cortes is fully ambidextrous. He throws lefthanded while playing outfield and righty at second base, the only position he played during his pro debut.

SCOUTING REPORT: Cortes may be short, but he's no slap hitter. He has a powerful, disciplined hitting approach that enabled him to rank top 10 in the Southeastern Conference in home runs (15) and walks (43). Cortes has the above-average raw power for double-digit home runs and the low swing-and-miss rate to hit for a decent average. He plays a workmanlike second base but doesn't stand out for his range, and his fringe-average arm is short for the left side of the infield. He is a below-average runner.

THE FUTURE: Cortes' body type has led scouts to speculate that he would fit at catcher. The Mets haven't worked him out behind the plate and for now are committed to developing him at second base.

Year	Club (League)	Class	AVG	G	AB	R	H	2B	3B	HR	RBI	BB	SO	SB	CS	OBP	SLG
2018	Brooklyn (NYP)	SS	.264	47	178	26	47	5	2	4	24	17	34	1	0	.338	.382
Minor League Totals			.264	47	178	26	47	5	2	4	24	17	34	1	0	.338	.382

23 RYDER RYAN, RHP

BA GRADE
45 Risk: High

Born: May 11, 1995. **B-T:** R-R. **Ht.:** 6-2. **Wt.:** 205. **Drafted:** North Carolina, 2016 (30th round). **Signed by:** Bob Mayer (Indians).

TRACK RECORD: Ryan showed promise as a hitter in high school, but when he hit 96 mph off the mound as a senior, he became a draft prospect as a pitcher. He played third base sparingly for two years at North Carolina before leaving the team. He made only one pitching appearance at UNC. Regardless, the Indians drafted Ryan as a pitcher in 2016 and signed him for $100,000 as a 30th-round pick. Cleveland traded him to the Mets a year later in an August waiver trade for Jay Bruce.

SCOUTING REPORT: Because he was relatively new to pitching, Ryan moved slowly in his first full season of 2017, which he spent as a reliever at low Class A. As he wore down, he ran up a 6.27 ERA and .304 opponent average in his final 25 appearances. Ryan showed more stamina in 2018 by reaching Double-A Binghamton at the end of May. He throws a pair of high-spin pitches and shows good feel for the strike zone. His fastball sits 94-96 mph and has touched 98 from a low three-quarters arm slot. The pitch misses bats up in the zone with riding life and plus spin. His slider has improved in pro ball and flashes above-average potential with 81-85 mph velocity, tight spin and depth. Ryan throws a changeup occasionally.

THE FUTURE: The Mets have toyed with the idea of moving Ryan to the rotation or at the very least using him as a multi-inning reliever. He is on track for a big league debut in late 2019 or 2020.

Year	Club (League)	Class	W	L	ERA	G	GS	CG	SV	IP	H	HR	BB	SO	K/9	WHIP	AVG
2016	Indians (AZL)	R	0	1	3.86	15	0	0	1	19	21	1	9	24	11.6	1.61	.284
2017	Lake County (MWL)	LoA	3	4	4.79	33	0	0	6	41	44	4	17	49	10.7	1.48	.267
	Columbia (SAL)	LoA	0	0	2.08	8	0	0	0	13	6	1	5	13	9.0	0.85	.133
2018	St. Lucie (FSL)	HiA	1	0	1.77	16	0	0	2	20	14	0	5	23	10.2	0.93	.200
	Binghamton (EL)	AA	3	3	4.13	26	0	0	3	33	27	5	10	36	9.9	1.13	.223
Minor League Totals			7	8	3.71	98	0	0	12	126	112	11	46	145	10.4	1.25	.236

24 DANIEL ZAMORA, LHP

BA GRADE
40 Risk: Medium

Born: April 15, 1993. **B-T:** L-L. **Ht.:** 6-3. **Wt.:** 195. **Drafted:** Stony Brook, 2015 (40th round). **Signed by:** Steve Skrinar (Pirates).

TRACK RECORD: The Pirates drafted Zamora out of Stony Book in the 40th round in 2015, eight picks before the Angels made the final pick of the draft. A starter in college, he worked exclusively as a reliever in the Pirates' system before Pittsburgh traded him to the Mets prior to the 2018 season for Josh Smoker. Zamora pitched well enough at Double-A Binghamton in 2018 to earn an August callup.

SCOUTING REPORT: Zamora is effectively a one-pitch pitcher who threw his 76-80 mph slider nearly 80 percent of the time in a big league debut spanning 16 appearances and nine innings. No other reliever threw a slider (or curveball) more frequently than Zamora. It's a plus pitch with elite spin and significant vertical drop delivered from a near sidearm arm slot. His slider generates swings and misses from batters on both sides of the plate. He throws a fringe 88-90 mph fastball mostly to keep batters off his slider.

THE FUTURE: Zamora is the heir apparent to Jerry Blevins as the Mets' matchup lefthander, a role he is ready to assume in 2019.

Year	Club (League)	Class	W	L	ERA	G	GS	CG	SV	IP	H	HR	BB	SO	K/9	WHIP	AVG
2016	West Virginia (SAL)	LoA	3	2	3.46	21	0	0	1	39	32	2	15	45	10.4	1.21	.219
2017	Bradenton (FSL)	HiA	2	4	1.86	37	0	0	9	53	48	2	17	61	10.3	1.22	.237
	Altoona (EL)	AA	0	0	0.00	2	0	0	0	3	2	0	2	6	0.0	1.33	.200
2018	Binghamton (EL)	AA	1	1	3.67	39	1	0	2	49	36	3	15	65	11.9	1.04	.191
	New York (NL)	MAJ	1	0	3.00	16	0	0	0	9	6	1	3	16	16.0	1.00	.194
Major League Totals			1	0	3.00	16	0	0	0	9	6	1	3	16	16.0	1.00	.194
Minor League Totals			7	7	2.84	113	1	0	14	165	139	8	53	198	10.8	1.17	.223

25 DREW SMITH, RHP

BA GRADE
40 Risk: Medium

Born: Sept. 24, 1993. **B-T:** R-R. **Ht.:** 6-2. **Wt.:** 190. **Drafted:** Dallas Baptist, 2015 (3rd round). **Signed by:** Chris Wimmer (Tigers).

TRACK RECORD: The Mets acquired seven minor league relievers in a series of 2017 trades, and Smith was one of four to reach the big leagues in 2018. He was also the most effective, recording a 3.54 ERA in 27 appearances. The Mets acquired him when they traded Lucas Duda to the Rays near the trade deadline. **SCOUTING REPORT:** Smith sat 95-97 mph with an average velocity of 96 and peak velocity near 99 in the big leagues. That made him one of the top 40 hardest-throwing major league relievers in 2018. His curveball keeps the same company in terms of spin rate. It's a 78-82 mph breaking pitch with tight, top-to-bottom rotation. But despite impressive raw inputs, Smith needs to tighten command of his primary weapons for them to truly play as plus. He also throws a fringe changeup that surprises batters. **THE FUTURE:** Smith has the raw weaponry to dominate, but unless he takes another step forward at age 25 in 2019, he probably fits best in a medium-leverage relief role.

Year	Club (League)	Class	W	L	ERA	G	GS	CG	SV	IP	H	HR	BB	SO	K/9	WHIP	AVG
2016	West Michigan (MWL)	LoA	1	2	2.96	35	0	0	4	49	34	0	23	62	11.5	1.17	.205
2017	Lakeland (FSL)	HiA	1	0	0.77	7	0	0	0	12	4	0	4	12	9.3	0.69	.108
	Durham (IL)	AAA	0	0	0.00	1	0	0	0	1	1	0	0	0	0.0	1.00	.333
	Charlotte, FL (FSL)	HiA	0	2	2.20	20	0	0	7	29	26	1	5	28	8.8	1.08	.239
	Montgomery (SL)	AA	0	0	0.00	3	0	0	0	4	1	0	0	0	0.0	0.27	.091
	Binghamton (EL)	AA	3	2	1.80	11	0	0	0	15	8	1	5	17	10.2	0.87	.151
2018	Binghamton (EL)	AA	0	0	2.08	2	0	0	1	4	2	0	1	6	12.5	0.69	.143
	Las Vegas (PCL)	AAA	5	1	2.76	23	1	0	2	33	26	3	12	30	8.3	1.16	.226
	New York (NL)	MAJ	1	1	3.54	27	0	0	0	28	34	2	6	18	5.8	1.43	.309
Major League Totals			1	1	3.54	27	0	0	0	28	34	2	6	18	5.8	1.43	.309
Minor League Totals			13	7	1.99	115	1	0	16	177	119	5	55	193	9.8	0.98	.193

26 CHRIS VIALL, RHP

BA GRADE

45 Risk: High

Born: Sept. 28, 1995. **B-T:** R-R. **Ht.:** 6-9. **Wt.:** 253. **Drafted:** Stanford, 2016 (6th round). **Signed by:** Tyler Holmes.

TRACK RECORD: A college pitcher with a 4.80 ERA and walk rate of 6.5 per nine innings in three years of Pacific-12 Conference play might not seem worthy of a sixth-round pick. But most college pitchers aren't Viall, a 6-foot-9, 250-pound Stanford righthander with a high-90s fastball. **SCOUTING REPORT:** Viall had ulnar transposition surgery that delayed the start to his 2017 season and a shoulder strain and triceps injury in 2018 that limited him to 15 starts at low Class A Columbia. He sported one of the highest swinging-strike rates in the SAL in 2018 with a 91-95 mph fastball that touches 99 and plays up thanks to the incredible extension in his delivery. His low-to-mid-80s slider is an above-average weapon he still needs to command and show batters he can throw for strikes. A below-average changeup rounds out his arsenal. Like most ultra-tall pitchers, Viall struggles to coordinate the long levers in his delivery and sync them to repeat his foot strike and arm slot. His control suffers as a result. **THE FUTURE:** Because of his fastball-heavy approach and dubious control, Viall probably fits best in the bullpen. But for 2019 he needs innings, which he will accrue in the high Class A St. Lucie rotation.

Year	Club (League)	Class	W	L	ERA	G	GS	CG	SV	IP	H	HR	BB	SO	K/9	WHIP	AVG
2016	Kingsport (APP)	R	0	2	6.75	9	6	0	0	20	18	2	17	27	12.2	1.75	.228
2017	Brooklyn (NYP)	SS	0	3	3.42	9	5	0	0	26	17	2	14	31	10.6	1.18	.187
2018	Columbia (SAL)	LoA	3	7	4.75	15	15	0	0	66	61	8	41	94	12.8	1.54	.244
Minor League Totals			3	12	4.79	33	26	0	0	113	96	12	72	152	12.1	1.49	.229

27 TONY DIBRELL, RHP

BA GRADE

45 Risk: High

Born: Nov. 8, 1995. **B-T:** R-R. **Ht.:** 6-3. **Wt.:** 190. **Drafted:** Kennesaw State, 2017 (4th round). **Signed by:** Tommy Jackson.

TRACK RECORD: Drawn to Dibrell's athleticism, projectable frame and quick arm, the Mets drafted him in the fourth round in 2017. He advanced to low Class A Columbia in 2018 and tied for the South Atlantic League with 147 strikeouts in 131 innings. **SCOUTING REPORT:** Dibrell pitches at 90-91 mph but has reached 95 on occasion, while the extension in his delivery increases his effective velocity. His above-average fastball is true, so he has to be precise, but scouts who like him project him to add a tick or two to his average fastball velocity. Dibrell throws a slider and changeup that flash above-average potential. His change is the better of the two, and he uses it to rack up swings and misses in both advantage and disadvantage counts. His slurvy breaking ball doesn't feature much power or spin but its big break catches hitters off balance. **THE FUTURE:** Dibrell has to throw more strikes to reach his ceiling of No. 5 starter or swingman, but he has the potential for three above-average pitches and thus has "overachiever" written all over him.

Year	Club (League)	Class	W	L	ERA	G	GS	CG	SV	IP	H	HR	BB	SO	K/9	WHIP	AVG
2017	Brooklyn (NYP)	SS	1	1	5.03	12	0	0	0	20	19	4	8	28	12.8	1.37	.253
2018	Columbia (SAL)	LoA	7	6	3.50	23	23	1	0	131	112	10	54	147	10.1	1.27	.228
Minor League Totals			8	7	3.70	35	23	1	0	151	131	14	62	175	10.5	1.28	.231

28 JUNIOR SANTOS, RHP

BA GRADE
50 Risk: Extreme

Born: Aug. 16, 2001. **B-T:** R-R. **Ht.:** 6-8. **Wt.:** 218. **Signed:** Dominican Republic, 2017. **Signed by:** Anderson Taveras/Gerardo Cabrera.

TRACK RECORD: The Mets don't typically invest heavily in 16-year-old international pitchers, but they made an exception for Santos, who they viewed as the steal of the 2017 international signing class when they inked him in September of that year for $275,000. He pitched effectively in the Dominican Summer League in 2018 as a 16-year-old in his pro debut.

SCOUTING REPORT: Santos was 6-foot-6 when he signed but quickly grew another two inches. Despite his height, he shows the plus body control and athleticism to throw consistent strikes. He pitched at 93-95 mph for much of 2018 before wearing down late and pitching more at 91-93, albeit with plus extension and spin. He muscled up to 97 mph in side sessions and could sit in the mid-90s consistently when he matures. Santos needs to improve the power and break on his high-70s slider by keeping his fingers on top of the ball as he delivers it. The pitch features promising spin and movement. He also throws a promising mid-80s changeup with two-seam fastball action.

THE FUTURE: Santos is driven to improve and has outstanding makeup, making him one of the most intriguing pitching prospects at the lower levels of the system.

Year	Club (League)	Class	W	L	ERA	G	GS	CG	SV	IP	H	HR	BB	SO	K/9	WHIP	AVG
2018	Mets1 (DSL)	R	1	1	2.80	11	10	0	0	45	35	1	6	36	7.2	0.91	.219
	Mets (GCL)	R	0	0	0.00	3	0	0	0	5	4	0	0	3	5.4	0.80	.222
Minor League Totals			1	1	2.52	14	10	0	0	50	39	1	6	39	7.0	0.90	.219

29 WILLIAM LUGO, 3B

BA GRADE
50 Risk: Extreme

Born: Jan. 2, 2002. **B-T:** R-R. **Ht.:** 6-3. **Wt.:** 215. **Signed:** Dominican Republic, 2018. **Signed by:** Fernando Encarnacion/Gerardo Cabrera.

TRACK RECORD: The Mets committed more than 80 percent of their nearly $5 million bonus pool to two players—Venezuelan catcher Francisco Alvarez and Dominican outfielder Freddy Valdez—on the first day of the 2018 international signing period. Then New York added an additional $1 million in pool money when they traded Jeurys Familia to the Athletics on July 21, granting the international scouting department the funds to sign Dominican third baseman William Lugo for $475,000 on Aug. 23.

SCOUTING REPORT: Lugo puts an aggressive, confident swing on pitches in the zone and lays off borderline pitches, hitting lasers all over the field. His well-developed 6-foot-3 body gives him present plus power potential with a chance to add more. Despite a 215-pound frame that will only continue adding weight, Lugo is agile enough to stay on the infield, possibly at third base, where he has average upside as a defender. His below-average speed and body type could make first base a possibility in a few years.

THE FUTURE: Lugo's hitting aptitude gives him a shot to bypass the Dominican Summer League and earn a roster spot in a U.S. Rookie league.

Year	Club (League)	Class	AVG	G	AB	R	H	2B	3B	HR	RBI	BB	SO	SB	CS	OBP	SLG
2018	Did not play—Signed 2019 contract																

30 TYLOR MEGILL, RHP

BA GRADE
50 Risk: Extreme

Born: July 28, 1995. **B-T:** R-R. **Ht.:** 6-7. **Wt.:** 230. **Drafted:** Arizona, 2018 (8th round). **Signed by:** Brian Reid.

TRACK RECORD: Megill worked as a reliever in his junior and senior seasons at Arizona, and the Mets inked him for $50,000 as an eighth-round senior sign in 2018. He made two starts among his 10 appearances for short-season Brooklyn in his pro debut, and the Mets plan to develop him as a starter.

SCOUTING REPORT: While his résumé may be short, Megill checks a lot of boxes the Mets look for when scouting amateur pitchers. He generates extension in his delivery thanks to a 6-foot-8 frame and imparts a high spin rate on his pitches. Megill ranged from 92-96 mph in 2018 and shows starter traits with a relatively clean delivery and feel for three pitches. His power mid-80s slider flashes plus potential but tends to flatten out. He hasn't had a chance to develop his below-average changeup while working shorter outings the past two seasons.

THE FUTURE: Megill will work as a starter in pro ball if for no other reason that to sharpen his fastball and slider for a potential future bullpen role. He heads to low Class A Columbia in 2019.

Year	Club (League)	Class	W	L	ERA	G	GS	CG	SV	IP	H	HR	BB	SO	K/9	WHIP	AVG
2018	Brooklyn (NYP)	SS	1	2	3.21	10	2	0	0	28	18	2	14	36	11.6	1.14	.180
Minor League Totals			1	2	3.21	10	2	0	0	28	18	2	14	36	11.6	1.14	.180

New York Yankees

BY JOSH NORRIS

PAUL BERESWILL/GETTY IMAGES

Gleyber Torres looks like a fixture on the Yankees' infield after a terrific rookie year.

After a 2017 season that saw them finish a game from the World Series, it seemed like things were aligning nicely for the Yankees to be a dominant force in 2018. Those feelings escalated when the team swung a trade with the Marlins that placed reigning NL MVP Giancarlo Stanton in the middle of a lineup that already contained rising sluggers Aaron Judge and Gary Sanchez.

The lineup was also given a boost by a pair of young and talented infielders that included second baseman Gleyber Torres and third baseman Miguel Andujar. Torres, the prize in the 2016 trade of Aroldis Chapman to the Cubs, hit 24 home  runs and looked like a cornerstone piece of the team's future. Andujar was similarly spectacular, clubbing 47 doubles, 27 homers and finishing second to Angels sensation Shohei Ohtani for the AL Rookie of the Year award.

Add that to a rotation fronted by burgeoning ace Luis Severino and a bullpen stocked with a glut of high-velocity arms, and it was easy to understand why things seemed rosy in the Bronx.

For much of the first half of the season, things were going as planned. Judge and Stanton were fearsome, Severino was in the thick of the Cy Young race and the Yankees were neck and neck with white-hot Boston for the division title. The clubs were tied on July 1, but a rough patch shortly there after put New York 4.5 games off the pace heading into the all-star break.

General manager Brian Cashman reached into his farm system to acquire reliever Zach Britton and starters Lance Lynn and J.A. Happ, but the momentum of those moves was muted on July 26 by Judge's broken wrist. The injury kept him out until the middle of September, by which point the Red Sox had clinched the division and relegated the Yankees to the Wild Card game.

The Yankees walloped the A's to move on to the division series, but were summarily trounced by the Red Sox in the Division Series. The four-game beatdown included a 16-1 whooping that by the end had backup catcher Austin Romine surrendering a home run that sealed a cycle for Boston utilityman Brock Holt. The Red Sox dominated the rest of the way, and by the end of the month were celebrating their fourth World Series since 2004.

Torres and Andujar were the farm system's obvious bright spots, but the rest of the system was inconsistent at best. Top prospect Estevan Florial suffered a broken wrist that stunted what was slated to be a pivotal season. Righthanders Albert Abreu, Chance Adams and Luis Medina all dealt with injuries, inconsistency or both. Two

PROJECTED 2022 LINEUP

Catcher	Gary Sanchez (29)
First Base	Luke Voit (31)
Second Base	Gleyber Torres (25)
Third Base	Miguel Andujar (27)
Shortstop	Didi Gregorius (32)
Left Field	Clint Frazier (27)
Center Field	Aaron Hicks (32)
Right Field	Aaron Judge (30)
Designated Hitter	Giancarlo Stanton (32)
No. 1 Starter	Luis Severino (28)
No. 2 Starter	Masahiro Tanaka (33)
No. 3 Starter	James Paxton (33)
No. 4 Starter	Jonathan Loaisiga (27)
No. 5 Starter	Jordan Montgomery (29)
Closer	Aroldis Chapman (34)

of the system's less-heralded arms, Deivi Garcia and Roansy Contreras, moved quickly up the ladder, and outfielders Everson Pereira and Antonio Cabello began scratching the surface of their enviable potential.

The Yankees kicked off their offseason in typically grandiose fashion by dealing a trio of prospects, fronted by top arm Justus Sheffield, for Mariners lefthander James Paxton. With the team under the luxury tax threshold, a stated goal of ownership over the last few years, the Yankees were expected to spend big over the rest of the offseason to bolster their young corps and keep up with Boston at the top of the division. The ultimate goal, of course, is World Series No. 28.

NEW YORK YANKEES

TOP 2019 ROOKIE: Jonathan Loaisiga, RHP. If healthy, he could figure prominently in the rotation.

BREAKOUT PROSPECT: Yoendrys Gomez, RHP. His projectability and present stuff make for an intriguing combination.

SLEEPER: Roberto Chirinos, SS: An excellent defender already, Chirinos held his own in the Gulf Coast League as a 17-year-old.

SOURCE OF TOP 30 TALENT			
Homegrown	27	Acquired	3
College	5	Trade	2
Junior college	2	Rule 5 draft	0
High school	2	Independent league	0
Nondrafted free agent	0	Free agent/waivers	1
International	18		

LF
Canaan Smith

CF

Estevan Florial (1)
Everson Pereira (3)
Antonio Cabello (8)
Raimfer Salinas (27)
Kevin Alcantara (29)
Ryder Green

RF
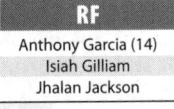
Anthony Garcia (14)
Isiah Gilliam
Jhalan Jackson

3B
Dermis Garcia
Oswaldo Cabrera
Andres Chaparro

SS
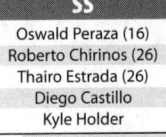
Oswald Peraza (16)
Roberto Chirinos (26)
Thairo Estrada (26)
Diego Castillo
Kyle Holder

2B

Tyler Wade
Hoy Park

1B
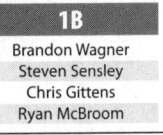
Brandon Wagner
Steven Sensley
Chris Gittens
Ryan McBroom

C
Anthony Seigler (4)
Jason Lopez (20)
Antonio Gomez (28)
Josh Breaux (30)

LHP

LHSP	LHRP
Dalton Lehnen	Stephen Tarpley
Josh Maciejewski	J.P. Sears
Nestor Cortes	Reiver Sanmartin

RHP

RHSP	RHRP
Jonathan Loaisiga (2)	Joe Harvey
Michael King (5)	Ben Heller
Deivi Garcia (6)	J.P. Feyereisen
Roansy Contreras (7)	Glenn Otto
Albert Abreu (9)	Cale Coshow
Matt Sauer (10)	Jefry Valdez
Luis Medina (11)	
Clarke Schmidt (12)	
Chance Adams (13)	
Osiel Rodriguez (15)	
Garrett Whitlock (17)	
Nick Nelson (18)	
Trevor Stephan (19)	
Juan Then (21)	
Frank German (22)	
Domingo Acevedo (23)	
Yoendrys Gomez (24)	
Luis Gil (25)	
Freicer Perez	
Tanner Myatt	
Rony Garcia	
Adonis Rosa	

DRAFT ANALYSIS

2018

BEST PURE HITTER: Switch-hitting catcher Anthony Seigler (1) showed the ability as an amateur to make plenty of contact from both sides of the plate while handling both velocity and offspeed stuff with equal aplomb. He also showed excellent plate discipline in a truncated first pro season, with more walks (14) than strikeouts (12) over 24 games.

BEST POWER HITTER: Although he didn't hit a home run in his pro debut, catcher Josh Breaux (2) displayed plus-plus raw power as an amateur while at McLennan (Texas) JC. The Yankees believe he'll start to show that thump next year.

FASTEST RUNNER: Troy OF Brandon Lockridge (5) produced sub-4.0 second times to first from the right side, which would make him an 80-grade runner on the 20-to-80 scouting scale. Lockridge stole 25 bases in 28 tries at Troy in 2018. He stole only three bases in five attempts in his pro debut.

BEST DEFENSIVE PLAYER: Seigler's ability to receive quality, high-velocity arms and throw out runners with a plus-plus throwing arm stands out.

BEST ATHLETE: Isaiah Pasteur (13) showed speed that was neck-and-neck with Lockridge, as well as other attributes that the Yankees' performance science team looks for in their players.

BEST FASTBALL: North Florida RHP Frank German (4) was up to 98 mph with his fastball as a pro after sitting 92-94 mph during a dominating junior season. German posted a 1.58 ERA for North Florida with the 11th best strikeout-to-walk ratio in Division I. He carried that success into pro ball, where he had a 12.2 K/9 and 1.8 BB/9 in 30 innings. Florence-Darlington (S.C.) Tech RHP Tanner Myatt (11) has touched 99 mph.

BEST SECONDARY PITCH: North Carolina RHP Rodney Hutchison (6) made his slider harder and tighter before turning pro, and the results were evident with 31 strikeouts in 32 innings with

TOP DRAFT PICKS OF THE DECADE

Year	Player, Pos.	2018 Org
2009	Slade Heathcott, OF	Atlantic League
2010	Cito Culver, SS	Marlins
2011	Dante Bichette Jr., 3B (1st round supp.)	Amer. Assoc.
2012	Ty Hensley, RHP	Frontier League
2013	Eric Jagielo, 3B	Marlins
2014	Jacob Lindgren, LHP (2nd round)	Braves
2015	James Kaprielian, RHP	Athletics
2016	Blake Rutherford, OF	White Sox
2017	Clarke Schmidt, RHP	Yankees
2018	Anthony Seigler, C	Yankees

short-season Staten Island.

BEST PRO DEBUT: Although his time on the field was lessened by nagging hamstring injuries and a concussion, making it to Rookie-level Pulaski and handling high-velocity arms like Albert Abreu in the instructional league was impressive for Seigler. He hit .269/.379/.342 between the two stops. German was impressive in his pair of stops as well.

MOST INTRIGUING BACKGROUND: In addition to being a switch-hitter, Seigler also pitched with both arms as a high schooler. He sat in the upper 80s from both sides and touched as high as 92 mph from the right side.

CLOSEST TO THE MAJORS: German or Hutchison fit here, with Hutchison's path likely quicker as a reliever with a major college pedigree

BEST LATE-ROUND PICK: Myatt's fastball-slider combination and improving control made him a nice snag in the 11th round.

THE ONE WHO GOT AWAY: The Yankees signed every player they drafted in the top 30 rounds, so they didn't miss on much. C Patrick Winkel (31) is an intriguing catcher defensively who will play for Connecticut. RHP Landon Marceaux (37) was one of the most polished pitchers in the high school class. He'll pitch for Louisiana State.

—JOSH NORRIS

2017

The early returns have been limited for this class. RHP Clarke Schmidt (1) returned to action in 2018 after undergoing Tommy John surgery and the Yankees have taken it slow with RHP Matt Sauer (2). RHP Garrett Whitlock (18) has been a strong late-round pick and reached Double-A Trenton in his professional debut.

GRADE: C

2016

The Yankees have mined this class extensively for trade chips. OF Blake Rutherford (1), 2B Nick Solak (2), OF Dom Thompson-Williams (5) and RHP Taylor Widener (12) have been used to acquire Brandon Drury, Todd Frazier, James Paxton and David Robertson. RHP Nick Nelson (4) is left to carry the class' flag in New York.

GRADE: C

2015

RHP James Kaprielian (1) helped the Yankees acquire Sonny Gray but he hasn't pitched since 2016 due to Tommy John surgery. The class has produced three big leaguers in RHPs Chance Adams (5) and Cody Carroll (22) and LHP Josh Rogers (11). Adams projects to provide the most impact of the trio.

GRADE: C

1 ESTEVAN FLORIAL, OF

Born: Nov. 25, 1997. **B-T:** L-L. **Ht.:** 6-1. **Wt.:** 207.
Signed: Haiti, 2015. **Signed by:** Esteban Castillo.

The Yankees wanted to sign Florial well before they did, but an identification issue scuttled their plans. Once the details got sorted out and Florial had served a suspension, New York inked him for $300,000 and watched as he rose through the ranks to near the top of a very deep system. After a breakout season at the lower levels in 2017 that vaulted him to the top of the Yankees' ranking and made him a top trade target, Florial endured what essentially was a lost season in 2018. He broke the hamate bone in his right wrist, which sidelined him for two months at high Class A Tampa. In all, Florial was limited to just 84 games. He made up for lost time in the Arizona Fall League, though his numbers suggested a player still struggling to regain his timing and pitch recognition.

SCOUTING REPORT: Florial remains a tantalizing but risky combination of outstanding tools and limited refinement. He generates above-average power thanks to quick hands and above-average bat speed. He can drive the ball to left field and center nearly as easily as he yanks it over a right-field fence, but he needs to make solid contact more consistently. Florial is relatively patient and is not prone to chase, but his bat has a long path to the strike zone thanks to high handset he uses to start his swing. Evaluators noticed improved angles and routes in center field. He's also got a plus throwing arm that would help him profile in right field if that becomes necessary. Florial is a plus runner who is faster than that once he gets going, though he needs to refine his instincts on the basepaths to become a bigger threat to steal. Evaluators inside and outside the organization also point to outstanding makeup that they believe will help him turn his tools into skills.

THE FUTURE: Florial is likely to head back to the Florida State League to try to reclaim his 2017 magic. A strong first half should get him to Double-A Trenton. His future will depend on the development of his offense. If he can make more consistent contact and start turning his raw power into home runs, then he'll go a long way toward reaching his ceiling as a center fielder with all-star potential. If not, his defense will allow him to at least serve as a fourth outfielder.

MIKE JANES/FOUR SEAM IMAGES

BA GRADE	SCOUTING GRADES
55 Risk: High	Hit: 55. Power: 55. Run: 60. Field: 60. Arm: 60.

Projected future grades on 20-80 scouting scale.

TOP PROSPECTS OF THE DECADE

Year	Player, Pos.	2018 Org
2009	Austin Jackson, OF	Indians
2010	Jesus Montero, C	Mexican League
2011	Jesus Montero, C	Mexican League
2012	Jesus Montero, C	Mexican League
2013	Mason Williams, OF	Reds
2014	Gary Sanchez, C	Yankees
2015	Luis Severino, RHP	Yankees
2016	Jorge Mateo, SS	Athletics
2017	Gleyber Torres, SS	Yankees
2018	Gleyber Torres, SS	Yankees

BEST TOOLS

Best Hitter for Average	Antonio Cabello
Best Power Hitter	Anthony Garcia
Best Strike-Zone Discipline	Brandon Wagner
Fastest Baserunner	Estevan Florial
Best Athlete	Estevan Florial
Best Fastball	Luis Medina
Best Curveball	Luis Medina
Best Slider	Albert Abreu
Best Changeup	Domingo Acevedo
Best Control	Michael King
Best Defensive Catcher	Anthony Seigler
Best Defensive Infielder	Diego Castillo
Best Infield Arm	Roberto Chirinos
Best Defensive Outfielder	Estevan Florial
Best Outfield Arm	Estevan Florial

Year	Club (League)	Class	AVG	G	AB	R	H	2B	3B	HR	RBI	BB	SO	SB	CS	OBP	SLG
2016	Tampa (FSL)	HiA	.125	2	8	0	1	0	0	0	0	0	2	0	0	.125	.125
	Pulaski (APP)	R	.225	60	236	36	53	10	1	7	25	28	78	10	2	.315	.364
	Charleston, SC (SAL)	LoA	.300	5	20	4	6	0	1	1	5	2	5	0	0	.348	.550
2017	Charleston, SC (SAL)	LoA	.297	91	344	64	102	21	5	11	43	41	124	17	7	.373	.483
	Tampa (FSL)	HiA	.303	19	76	13	23	2	2	2	14	9	24	6	1	.368	.461
2018	Yankees2 (GCL)	R	.429	4	14	5	6	0	0	1	3	2	3	2	0	.500	.643
	Yankees1 (GCL)	R	.647	5	17	5	11	3	1	2	5	2	2	3	0	.684	1.294
	Tampa (FSL)	HiA	.255	75	294	45	75	16	3	3	27	44	87	11	10	.354	.361
Minor League Totals			.281	318	1233	223	347	63	21	34	175	158	386	64	25	.365	.449

2 JONATHAN LOAISIGA, RHP

Born: Nov. 2, 1994. **B-T:** R-R. **Ht.:** 5-11. **Wt.:** 165. **Signed:** Nicaragua, 2012.
Signed by: Sandy Moreno (Giants).

TRACK RECORD: Loaisiga is one of the better gems unearthed by the Yankees' pro scouting staff. The Giants released Loaisiga after shoulder injuries sidelined him for two seasons. The Yankees liked what they saw in a tryout camp, but soon after they signed him he needed Tommy John surgery. The Yankees were rewarded with a pitcher with electric stuff. He made his big league debut in 2018 but also missed a month with a sore shoulder.

SCOUTING REPORT: Loaisiga missed enough time with injuries throughout his career that he needed to be added to the 40-man roster after the 2017 season even though he had barely pitched in full-season ball. But he jumped from Class A to the major leagues in just two months thanks to three pitches that grade as above-average or better. He throws a plus fastball that sits 95-96 mph and touches 98, though it is straight enough that it doesn't miss a lot of bats. His fastball sets up a hard changeup that grades as plus. His mid-80s curveball is more of an above-average offering, but on his best days, it is a plus pitch that gets swings and misses. Nothing in Loaisiga's delivery precludes him from throwing strikes.

THE FUTURE: Loaisiga could be a mid-rotation starter if he can stay healthy, but that's a big concern.

BA GRADE
55 Risk: High
Fastball: 60.
Slider: 60.
CHG: 55. CTL: 50.

Year	Club (League)	Class	W	L	ERA	G	GS	CG	SV	IP	H	HR	BB	SO	K/9	WHIP	AVG
2016	Charleston, SC (SAL)	LoA	0	0	7.71	1	1	0	0	2	2	1	1	2	7.7	1.29	.222
2017	Yankees2 (GCL)	R	0	0	0.00	1	1	0	0	2	0	0	0	0	0.0	0.00	.000
	Yankees1 (GCL)	R	0	1	2.63	6	6	0	0	14	10	1	2	15	9.9	0.88	.196
	Staten Island (NYP)	SS	1	0	0.53	4	4	0	0	17	7	0	1	18	9.5	0.47	.121
2018	Tampa (FSL)	HiA	3	0	1.35	4	4	0	0	20	19	0	1	26	11.7	1.00	.244
	Yankees2 (GCL)	R	0	0	0.00	1	1	0	0	2	1	0	1	1	5.4	1.20	.167
	Trenton (EL)	AA	3	1	3.93	9	9	0	0	34	37	6	6	40	10.5	1.25	.278
	New York (AL)	MAJ	2	0	5.11	9	4	0	0	25	26	3	12	33	12.0	1.54	.271
Major League Totals			2	0	5.11	9	4	0	0	25	26	3	12	33	12.0	1.54	.271
Minor League Totals			15	3	2.59	39	39	0	0	160	136	12	28	142	8.0	1.03	.230

3 EVERSON PEREIRA, OF

Born: April 10, 2001. **B-T:** R-R. **Ht.:** 5-10. **Wt.:** 191. **Signed:** Venezuela, 2017.
Signed by: Roney Calderon.

TRACK RECORD: The Yankees completed their 2017 international class by signing outfielders Raimfer Salinas and Antonio Cabello, but their biggest signing since July 2 was Pereira, who got $1.5 million. He's bulked up significantly since signing, and now stands at a sturdy 190 pounds. Salinas, Cabello and Pereira are all working toward futures in center field, so to help find playing time Pereira was pushed to Rookie-level Pulaski for his pro debut just two months after he turned 17.

SCOUTING REPORT: As an amateur, Pereira was lauded for his all-around blend of skills, and scouts saw the same against more advanced competition. He doesn't have any 70- or 80-grade tools, but some scouts were confident enough to put future plus grades on his hit, run and raw power already. They also saw a defender in center field with plus range and instincts with an average throwing arm. Those things were especially impressive on the surface, but even moreso because they were coming from someone so young.

THE FUTURE: It wouldn't be surprising to see the Yankees continue to be aggressive with Pereira and move him to low Class A Charleston to begin the year with the possibility of him moving back to short-season Staten Island in June if needed. He's a long way off, but he has a chance to be an impact player in the big leagues.

BA GRADE
60 Risk: Extreme
Hit: 60. Power: 60.
Run: 60. Field: 55.
Arm: 50.

Year	Club (League)	Class	AVG	G	AB	R	H	2B	3B	HR	RBI	BB	SO	SB	CS	OBP	SLG
2018	Pulaski (APP)	R	.263	41	167	21	44	8	2	3	26	15	60	3	2	.322	.389
Minor League Totals			.263	41	167	21	44	8	2	3	26	15	60	3	2	.322	.389

4 ANTHONY SEIGLER, C

Born: June 20, 1999. **B-T:** B-B. **Ht.:** 5-10. **Wt.:** 188. **Drafted:** HS—Cartersville, Ga., 2018 (1st round). **Signed by:** Darryl Monroe.

TRACK RECORD: Seigler earned high marks on the amateur circuit for his unique blend of skills. Not only is he an accomplished switch-hitter, but he made waves on the mound as a switch-pitcher also. The Yankees aren't going to put him on the mound, but he's still an intriguing prospect as a catcher and he drew the starting nod at the position during the 18U World Cup. He also showed strong makeup in pro ball, going so far as to request a Spanish-speaking roommate so he could work on learning the language.

SCOUTING REPORT: Seigler brings a smooth, compact swing from both sides of the plate that should help make him at least an average hitter as he develops. He's not likely to produce big-time home run power, but he has shown the ability to drive the ball out of the park from the right side. Realistically, he's going to be more of a gap-to-gap hitter with plenty of doubles. Behind the plate, Seigler is at least a plus defender and could become even better as he matures. He's got a near-elite arm that has produced pop times of better than 1.9 seconds both as an amateur and a pro. He shows trust in his arm by aggressively back-picking runners at first base.

THE FUTURE: Seigler's first test in pro ball was abbreviated by injuries to his hamstrings and a late-season concussion, but he returned in time to see action at instructional league. He could start 2019 in low Class A.

BA GRADE

60 Risk: Extreme

HIT: 50. PWR: 45.
RUN: 45. FLD: 65.
ARM: 70.

Year	Club (League)	Class	AVG	G	AB	R	H	2B	3B	HR	RBI	BB	SO	SB	CS	OBP	SLG
2018	Yankees2 (GCL)	R	.333	12	36	7	12	2	0	1	4	6	7	0	0	.429	.472
	Pulaski (APP)	R	.209	12	43	4	9	1	0	0	5	8	5	0	0	.340	.233
Minor League Totals			.266	24	79	11	21	3	0	1	9	14	12	0	0	.379	.342

5 MICHAEL KING, RHP

Born: May 25, 1994. **B-T:** R-R. **Ht.:** 6-3. **Wt.:** 210. **Drafted:** Boston College, 2016 (12th round). **Signed by:** Steve Payne (Marlins).

TRACK RECORD: The Yankees picked up King in a seemingly minor trade that sent the Marlins Caleb Smith and Garrett Cooper. He ended up as the Yankees' most productive minor league pitcher in 2018, advancing from high Class A Tampa to Triple-A with little resistance along the way.

SCOUTING REPORT: Many pitchers in the Yankees' system have a higher upside than King, but he is one of the safest bets for a big league career, even if it's most likely as a back-of-the-rotation starter. While none of King's pitches is truly a knockout, his plus command amplifies his entire arsenal. He throws a pair of fastballs—a two-seamer and a cutter, the latter of which was added in Triple-A. The cutter is thrown in the high 80s, while the two-seamer averaged 92 mph. His two-seamer is his money pitch, and it has above-average action. He's particularly adept at starting the two-seamer at the hip of lefthanded hitters and bringing it back over the inside corner for a strike. He backs up his fastballs with a changeup that is near plus and an average slider, though his command helps each pitch play up.

THE FUTURE: King will probably head back to Triple-A Scranton/Wilkes-Barre to begin 2019 as he prepares for an in-season callup.

BA GRADE

50 Risk: Medium

FB: 55. SL: 50.
CH: 50.
CTRL: 60.

Year	Club (League)	Class	W	L	ERA	G	GS	CG	SV	IP	H	HR	BB	SO	K/9	WHIP	AVG
2016	Marlins (GCL)	R	1	1	10.80	4	0	0	0	5	11	0	2	3	5.4	2.60	.440
	Batavia (NYP)	SS	2	2	3.38	10	1	0	1	21	22	0	6	15	6.3	1.31	.278
	Greensboro (SAL)	LoA	0	0	0.00	1	0	0	0	4	4	0	1	2	4.2	1.15	.235
2017	Greensboro (SAL)	LoA	11	9	3.14	26	25	2	0	149	141	14	21	106	6.4	1.09	.252
2018	Tampa (FSL)	HiA	1	3	1.79	7	7	0	0	40	33	1	10	45	10.0	1.07	.219
	Trenton (EL)	AA	6	2	2.09	12	11	1	0	82	65	4	13	76	8.3	0.95	.220
	Scranton/W-B (IL)	AAA	4	0	1.15	6	6	1	0	39	20	3	6	31	7.2	0.67	.147
Minor League Totals			25	17	2.59	66	50	4	1	341	296	22	59	278	7.3	1.04	.234

6 DEIVI GARCIA, RHP

Born: May 19, 1999. **B-T:** R-R. **Ht.:** 5-10. **Wt.:** 167. **Signed:** Dominican Republic, 2015. **Signed by:** Miguel Benitez.

TRACK RECORD: After signing a huge international class in 2014, the Yankees began 2015 in the international penalty box, meaning they could not sign any player for more than $300,000. Despite the limitations, that signing class has already produced three intriguing prospects, including outfielder Estevan Florial, righthander Luis Medina and Garcia, who ranked among the system's biggest risers in 2018.

SCOUTING REPORT: The biggest knock on Garcia is his size and high-effort delivery, which many scouts believe will eventually force a move to the bullpen. His stuff, however, has been dominant. He struck out 12.8 hitters per nine innings across three levels in 2018. He uses a three-pitch mix that starts with a low-90s fastball that topped out around 95 mph from a whip-quick arm. The gem of his arsenal is his power curveball. The pitch shows downer break and has an elite spin rate of better than 3,000 revolutions per minute. He needs to shorten the break on the pitch, but the spin and bite are enough to get plenty of swings and misses. The Yankees believe his changeup has developed to the point that it is nearing the quality of his curveball.

THE FUTURE: Garcia likely will return to high Class A Tampa after making five starts there in 2018.

BA GRADE
55 Risk: High
FB: 55. CB: 60. CH: 45. CTRL: 60.

Year	Club (League)	Class	W	L	ERA	G	GS	CG	SV	IP	H	HR	BB	SO	K/9	WHIP	AVG
2016	Yankees2 (DSL)	R	1	5	2.61	12	12	0	0	48	23	1	32	61	11.4	1.14	.149
2017	Yankees1 (DSL)	R	1	1	1.17	3	3	0	0	15	10	1	2	18	10.6	0.78	.196
	Yankees2 (GCL)	R	3	0	3.24	4	2	0	0	17	9	3	4	24	13.0	0.78	.155
	Pulaski (APP)	R	2	1	4.50	6	5	0	0	28	23	3	13	43	13.8	1.29	.232
2018	Charleston, SC (SAL)	LoA	2	4	3.76	8	8	0	0	41	31	5	10	63	13.9	1.01	.205
	Tampa (FSL)	HiA	2	0	1.27	6	6	0	0	28	19	0	8	35	11.1	0.95	.192
	Trenton (EL)	AA	1	0	0.00	1	1	0	0	5	0	0	2	7	12.6	0.40	.000
Minor League Totals			12	11	2.81	40	37	0	0	182	115	13	71	251	12.4	1.02	.183

7 ROANSY CONTRERAS, RHP

Born: Nov. 7, 1999. **B-T:** R-R. **Ht.:** 6-0. **Wt.:** 197. **Signed:** Dominican Republic, 2016. **Signed by:** Juan Rosario.

TRACK RECORD: The Yankees were in the international penalty phase in 2016, meaning they could not sign any player for more than $300,000. Even so, their scouts found Contreras and signed him for $250,000. He trained with Basilio Vizcaino, otherwise known as Cachaza, who trained current Yankees Gary Sanchez and Miguel Andujar. The Yankees liked Contreras for his smooth arm action and relatively easy delivery, which at the time produced 88-91 fastballs.

SCOUTING REPORT: After a first pro season split between the Dominican Summer League and the Rookie-level Gulf Coast League, Contreras moved to the short-season New York-Penn League halfway through 2018. With Staten Island, he showed the makings of a solid three-pitch mix headed by a fastball in the 91-94 mph range with hints of 96. The pitch featured running life to both sides of the plate. His best secondary pitch was a 78-81 mph downer curveball that was inconsistent but had the potential to be above-average once he gained the feel necessary to spin it more consistently. His third pitch is a mid-80s changeup with average sinking action when he keeps it down in the zone. There's still projectability left in his body, which scouts believe could be the difference between a back-end starter or a mid-rotation piece.

THE FUTURE: Contreras so thoroughly dominated at Staten Island that he moved up to low Class A Charleston toward the end of the season. He'll likely return there in 2019.

BA GRADE
50 Risk: High
FB: 60. CB: 55. CH: 50. CTRL: 50.

Year	Club (League)	Class	W	L	ERA	G	GS	CG	SV	IP	H	HR	BB	SO	K/9	WHIP	AVG
2017	Yankees1 (DSL)	R	0	3	3.68	6	6	0	0	22	25	2	5	17	7.0	1.36	.278
	Yankees1 (GCL)	R	4	1	4.26	8	5	0	0	32	35	2	12	17	4.8	1.48	.276
2018	Staten Island (NYP)	SS	0	0	1.26	5	5	0	0	29	15	1	9	32	10.0	0.84	.158
	Charleston, SC (SAL)	LoA	0	2	3.38	7	7	0	0	35	29	4	12	28	7.3	1.18	.225
Minor League Totals			4	6	3.15	26	23	0	0	117	104	9	38	94	7.2	1.21	.236

8 ANTONIO CABELLO, OF

Born: Nov. 1, 2000. **B-T:** R-R. **Ht.:** 5-10. **Wt.:** 160. **Signed:** Venezuela, 2017.
Signed by: Darwin Bracho.

TRACK RECORD: The Yankees spent a good chunk of the 2017 offseason acquiring international bonus pool space in their effort to sign Japanese two-way talent Shohei Ohtani. Once Ohtani eliminated them, however, they spread that money around to acquire other targets, including Cabello and outfielder Raimfer Salinas. The pair signed with the Yankees just before Christmas, meaning neither player even had the benefit of an instructional league before embarking on their first pro seasons.
SCOUTING REPORT: Cabello was advanced enough in extended spring training that the Yankees moved him quickly out of the Dominican Summer League to the Rookie-level Gulf Coast League. To earn that boost, Cabello displayed a diverse blend of skills, showing plus speed and the potential for a plus bat with plus power and plus defense in center field. He also shows an advanced ability to hit the ball hard, with exit velocities as high as 106 mph already. His throwing arm is already at least average. Cabello was a catcher as an amateur, meaning his outfield defense will be the toughest tool to gauge.
THE FUTURE: Cabello dislocated his non-throwing shoulder late in the season and needed surgery, which cost him a chance to participate in instructional league. He has a chance to be a true impact bat in the middle of the order.

BA GRADE
55 Risk: Extreme
HIT: 60. PWR: 60.
FLD: 60. SPD: 60.
ARM: 50.

CLIFF WELCH

Year	Club (League)	Class	AVG	G	AB	R	H	2B	3B	HR	RBI	BB	SO	SB	CS	OBP	SLG
2018	Yankees (DSL)	R	.227	6	22	5	5	0	1	0	1	6	6	5	1	.433	.318
	Yankees2 (GCL)	R	.321	40	137	21	44	9	4	5	20	21	34	5	5	.426	.555
Minor League Totals			.308	46	159	26	49	9	5	5	21	27	40	10	6	.427	.522

9 ALBERT ABREU, RHP

Born: Sept. 26, 1995. **B-T:** R-R. **Ht.:** 6-2. **Wt.:** 213. **Signed:** Dominican Republic, 2013. **Signed by:** Oz Ocampo/Rafael Belen/Francis Mojica (Astros).

TRACK RECORD: Abreu was part of package the Yankees received from the Astros for Brian McCann after the 2016 season. The other player, Jorge Guzman, was dealt to the Marlins in the deal that made Giancarlo Stanton a Yankee. Abreu opened eyes in his first season in the organization, but he dealt with injuries and ineffectiveness in 2018. It all began with an appendectomy toward the end of spring training and elbow inflammation at midseason.
SCOUTING REPORT: In terms of stuff, Abreu still shows the big, upper-90s fastball that the Yankees sought when they acquired him from Houston. The pitch has late life and is particularly effective when thrown up in the zone. He backs up his fastball with a power curveball in the mid-80s and a changeup that each project as at least above-average, if not plus, offerings. He also throws a slider, but he leans heavily on his three main pitches. While Abreu's pure stuff is tantalizing, his command is fringy at best. He struggles to repeat his delivery at times, and will get strikeout-happy and try to overthrow. The Yankees also would like to see him pitch inside more effectively to both righthanders and lefthanders.
THE FUTURE: Abreu was limited to just 73 innings, making 2018 a bit of a lost year. He still has huge upside and will likely return to high Class A Tampa.

BA GRADE
50 Risk: High
FB: 70. CB: 60.
CH: 55.
CTRL: 45.

Year	Club (League)	Class	W	L	ERA	G	GS	CG	SV	IP	H	HR	BB	SO	K/9	WHIP	AVG
2016	Quad Cities (MWL)	LoA	2	8	3.50	21	14	0	4	90	62	5	49	104	10.4	1.23	.193
	Lancaster (CAL)	HiA	1	0	5.40	3	2	0	0	12	12	2	9	11	8.5	1.80	.267
2017	Charleston, SC (SAL)	LoA	1	0	1.84	3	2	0	0	15	9	1	3	22	13.5	0.82	.180
	Yankees1 (GCL)	R	0	0	2.08	2	2	0	0	4	3	0	0	8	16.6	0.69	.177
	Tampa (FSL)	HiA	1	3	4.19	9	9	0	0	34	33	2	15	31	8.1	1.40	.252
2018	Yankees1 (GCL)	R	0	1	18.00	1	1	0	0	2	4	0	0	2	9.0	2.00	.400
	Yankees2 (GCL)	R	0	2	27.00	2	2	0	0	3	10	0	2	3	9.0	4.00	.476
	Tampa (FSL)	HiA	4	3	4.16	13	13	0	0	63	54	9	29	65	9.3	1.32	.229
	Trenton (EL)	AA	0	0	0.00	1	1	0	0	5	0	0	1	4	7.2	0.20	.000
Minor League Totals			14	22	3.63	82	67	1	5	342	270	22	158	355	9.3	1.25	.214

10 MATT SAUER, RHP

Born: Jan. 21, 1999. **B-T:** R-R. **Ht.:** 6-4. **Wt.:** 195. **Drafted:** HS—Santa Maria, Calif., 2017 (2nd round). **Signed by:** Bobby Dejardin.

TRACK RECORD: Sauer dedicated himself to a workout plan between his junior and senior years of high school and experienced a jump in velocity as a result, peaking at 97 mph. In turn, his draft stock improved and the Yankees popped him with their second-round pick and signed him just under $2.5 million, nearly double the recommended slot. He spent his first season as a pro in limited action at the Rookie-level Gulf Coast League before moving to short-season Staten Island.

BA GRADE

50 Risk: High

FB: 55. CH: 50.
CB: 50.
CTL: 45.

SCOUTING REPORT: Sauer shows the potential for three average or better pitches out of a physical, durable frame. He starts his arsenal with a low-90s fastball at 90-94 mph with natural cutting life and occasional sink generated by a three-quarters arm slot. He backs up the fastball with a curveball in the mid-80s and a changeup in the 83-88 mph range that flash average. His curveball is inconsistent with both its power and depth, but it is ahead of his changeup at this point. His changeup comes in firm at times but shows sinking action at its best. To unlock his potential, Sauer needs to better his fringe-average control by improving the consistency of his delivery and direction toward home plate.

THE FUTURE: Sauer is likely to move up to low Class A Charleston in 2019, his first test of full-season ball. He has the potential to be a back-end starter if his offspeed pitches and control continue to develop.

Year	Club (League)	Class	W	L	ERA	G	GS	CG	SV	IP	H	HR	BB	SO	K/9	WHIP	AVG
2017	Yankees2 (GCL)	R	0	2	5.40	6	6	0	0	12	13	0	8	12	9.3	1.80	.271
2018	Staten Island (NYP)	SS	3	6	3.90	13	13	0	0	67	60	3	18	45	6.0	1.16	.236
Minor League Totals			3	8	4.12	19	19	0	0	79	73	3	26	57	6.5	1.26	.242

11 LUIS MEDINA, RHP

BA GRADE

55 Risk: Extreme

Born: May 3, 1999. **B-T:** R-R. **Ht.:** 6-3. **Wt.:** 195. **Signed:** Dominican Republic, 2015. **Signed by:** Juan Rosario.

TRACK RECORD: The Yankees signed Medina out of the Dominican Republic for $280,000 as a 16-year-old, when he was already showcasing a fastball that touched triple-digits. He skipped over the Rookie-level Gulf Coast League and made his stateside debut in Rookie-level Pulaski in 2017 and returned there in 2018. He's already shown some of the best pure stuff in the system, but has coupled it with some of the worst control.

SCOUTING REPORT: Medina's calling card is still his top-shelf fastball, which continues to eclipse 100 mph. At his best, Medina threw the pitch with excellent angle and sinking action. He doesn't throw nearly enough strikes with his fastball, however, walking hitters en masse and giving up hits when he leaves it over the fat part of the plate. Medina backs up the fastball with a plus, downer curveball and a changeup that is still in its early stages but shows plus future potential. Medina's delivery leaves a lot to be desired. He's stiff out front and loses his release point, which has led to well below-average command and control. There are also questions surrounding his mental toughness.

THE FUTURE: Medina will pitch all of season at 20 years old, so he has got time to iron out his delivery and harness his tremendous arsenal. If he can't hack it as a starter, he still has a chance to be a dynamic reliever.

Year	Club (League)	Class	W	L	ERA	G	GS	CG	SV	IP	H	HR	BB	SO	K/9	WHIP	AVG
2016	Yankees1 (DSL)	R	0	0	1.93	3	3	0	0	5	2	0	4	4	7.7	1.29	.143
2017	Yankees1 (DSL)	R	1	1	5.74	4	3	0	0	16	17	0	10	17	9.8	1.72	.270
	Pulaski (APP)	R	1	1	5.09	6	6	0	0	23	14	1	14	22	8.6	1.22	.171
2018	Pulaski (APP)	R	1	3	6.25	12	12	0	0	36	32	3	46	47	11.8	2.17	.239
Minor League Totals			3	5	5.56	25	24	0	0	79	65	4	74	90	10.2	1.75	.222

12 CLARKE SCHMIDT, RHP

BA GRADE

50 Risk: High

Born: Feb. 20, 1996. **B-T:** R-R. **Ht.:** 6-1. **Wt.:** 200. **Drafted:** South Carolina, 2017 (1st round). **Signed by:** Billy Godwin.

TRACK RECORD: After two successful seasons at South Carolina, Schmidt's draft year was cut short by Tommy John surgery. Even so, the Yankees liked what they'd seen and selected Schmidt with the 16th overall pick and signed him to a below-slot bonus of $2,184,300. He made his pro debut in 2018 at the Rookie-level Gulf Coast League before making two starts with short-season Staten Island.

SCOUTING REPORT: Schmidt pitched sparsely this season, but when he got on the mound he showed a plus fastball in the mid-90s that touched 97 mph. He paired the pitch with a plus slider as well as a seldom-thrown changeup. As with most undersized righthanders, there are questions about whether Schmidt's stature and his high-effort delivery will lead to a relief role long-term. That's a long way away, however, and his future will become clearer once he makes his full-season debit
THE FUTURE: After a cautious first taste of pro ball, Schmidt should have the reins taken off in 2019.

Year	Club (League)	Class	W	L	ERA	G	GS	CG	SV	IP	H	HR	BB	SO	K/9	WHIP	AVG
2017	Did not play—Injured																
2018	Yankees2 (GCL)	R	0	0	1.23	3	3	0	0	7	4	0	2	8	9.8	0.82	.167
	Yankees1 (GCL)	R	0	2	7.04	3	2	0	0	8	8	1	2	12	14.1	1.30	.267
	Staten Island (NYP)	SS	0	1	1.08	2	2	0	0	8	4	0	2	10	10.8	0.72	.143
Minor League Totals			0	3	3.09	8	7	0	0	23	16	1	6	30	11.6	0.94	.195

13 CHANCE ADAMS, RHP

BA GRADE
50 Risk: High

Born: May 13, 1996. **B-T:** R-R. **Ht.:** 6-0. **Wt.:** 215. **Drafted:** Dallas Baptist, 2015 (5th round). **Signed by:** Mike Leuzinger.

TRACK RECORD: Adams pitched as a reliever at Dallas Baptist, but the Yankees drafted him with an eye toward the rotation and moved him there in his first full. He was excellent over his first two full seasons but had surgery to remove bone chips from his right elbow before the 2018 season, and his stuff stepped backward as a result. Adams still made his big league debut during the season.
SCOUTING REPORT: The most concerning part of Adams' season was the decline of his fastball post-surgery. In past years, the pitch sat in the mid-90s. Now, it's more of a low-90s offering with flecks of 95-96. The pitch registered a slightly above-average spin rate of 2,326 rpms in the big leagues. His most effective offspeed pitch is still his slider, a low-80s offering with sharp, late snap. His curveball and changeup haven't progressed quite as far as projected, and there are times when Adams seems reluctant to throw them. Both are fringe-average pitches.
THE FUTURE: Although Adams was transitioned into the bullpen down the stretch in the big leagues, the Yankees will give him another chance at a starter and hope his velocity returns. He'll start 2019 back at Triple-A Scranton/Wilkes-Barre.

Year	Club (League)	Class	W	L	ERA	G	GS	CG	SV	IP	H	HR	BB	SO	K/9	WHIP	AVG
2016	Tampa (FSL)	HiA	5	0	2.65	12	12	0	0	58	41	4	15	73	11.4	0.97	.196
	Trenton (EL)	AA	8	1	2.07	13	12	0	0	70	35	5	24	71	9.2	0.85	.145
2017	Trenton (EL)	AA	4	0	1.03	6	6	0	0	35	23	2	15	32	8.2	1.09	.183
	Scranton/W-B (IL)	AAA	11	5	2.89	21	21	0	0	115	81	9	43	103	8.0	1.08	.197
2018	Scranton/W-B (IL)	AAA	4	5	4.78	27	23	2	0	113	101	16	58	113	9.0	1.41	.236
	New York (AL)	MAJ	0	1	7.04	3	1	0	0	8	8	3	4	4	4.7	1.57	.267
Major League Totals			0	1	7.04	3	1	0	0	8	8	3	4	4	4.7	1.57	.267
Minor League Totals			35	12	2.98	93	74	2	0	426	305	36	164	437	9.2	1.10	.197

14 ANTHONY GARCIA, OF

BA GRADE
55 Risk: Extreme

Born: Sept. 5, 2000. **B-T:** S-R. **Ht.:** 6-6. **Wt.:** 234. **Signed:** Dominican Republic, 2017. **Signed by:** Jose Sabino.

TRACK RECORD: Garcia stuck out for his size, speed and power as an amateur and signed with the Yankees for $500,000 out of the Dominican Republic in 2017. He showed enough in extended spring training to skip the Dominican Summer League and make his professional debut in the Rookie-level Gulf Coast League as a 17-year-old. His 10 home runs led the league, and his .513 slugging percentage was fifth.
SCOUTING REPORT: Garcia's signature asset is his double-plus raw power from both sides of the plate. His home runs were storied around the GCL, and he hit multiple balls over the Yankees' player development complex, which sits beyond the right-field wall. With that power, however, came a strikeout rate of nearly 40 percent. That figure was backed up by a walk rate of 11.9 percent. Garcia is an above-average runner, down a tick from his amateur days, but is a little quicker underway. He bounced back and forth between left and right field, where he was a bit crude while adjusting to a body that just underwent a massive growth spurt. An average arm lets him profile at either spot.
THE FUTURE: Garcia finished the year at Rookie-level Pulaski, and he's likely to return to the level after a few months in extended spring training. He's a boom-or-bust prospect with an extremely high ceiling.

Year	Club (League)	Class	AVG	G	AB	R	H	2B	3B	HR	RBI	BB	SO	SB	CS	OBP	SLG
2018	Yankees (DSL)	R	.125	4	16	3	2	1	1	0	4	3	8	0	0	.263	.313
	Yankees2 (GCL)	R	.244	44	156	18	38	6	3	10	20	18	73	3	0	.320	.513
	Pulaski (APP)	R	.095	5	21	4	2	1	0	0	0	2	7	0	0	.174	.143
Minor League Totals			.218	53	193	25	42	8	4	10	24	23	88	3	0	.300	.456

15 OSIEL RODRIGUEZ, RHP

BA GRADE

55 Risk: Extreme

Born: Nov. 22, 2001. **B-T:** R-R. **Ht.:** 6-2. **Wt.:** 210. **Signed:** Cuba, 2018.
Signed by: Jose Sabino/Edgar Mateo/Rudy Gomez.

TRACK RECORD: Rodriguez ranked as the No. 1 pitching prospect in the 2018 international class and earned that rep by sporting a 0.39 ERA with 127 strikeouts in 69 innings in Cuba's national 15-and-under league. The Yankees signed Rodriguez for $600,000 in August after securing extra bonus-pool money in trades with the White Sox and Cardinals.

SCOUTING REPORT: After throwing in the high 80s as a 14-year-old, Rodriguez experienced spurts in both size and velocity. He now throws his heater in the low-to-mid 90s with peaks at 97 mph. He couples the pitch with a curveball in the mid-70s that he can both sweep across the strike zone or throw with more depth. He also has feel for a changeup, which the Yankees feel could be plus with repetition. Rodriguez throws from multiple angles now, but the Yankees are trying to help him find consistent mechanics.

THE FUTURE: Rodriguez stayed in the Dominican Republic for the instructional league, but the Yankees have been aggressive with their talented teenagers of late. A career-opening assignment to the Rookie-level Gulf Coast League in 2019 isn't out of the question.

Year	Club (League)	Class	W	L	ERA	G	GS	CG	SV	IP	H	HR	BB	SO	K/9	WHIP	AVG
2018	Did not play—Signed 2019 contract																

16 OSWALD PERAZA, SS

BA GRADE

55 Risk: Extreme

Born: June 15, 2000. **B-T:** R-R. **Ht.:** 6-0. **Wt.:** 180. **Signed:** Venezuela, 2016. **Signed by:** Roney Calderon/Jose Gavidia.

TRACK RECORD: The Yankees signed Peraza for $175,000 as part of a 2016 international class that also included Roansy Contreras and the since-traded Jose Devers. Pezara attracted with a solid blend of tools across the board, as well as a frame that would allow him to add more strength without sacrificing the flexibility and athleticism necessary to play shortstop. He made it to the Rookie-level Gulf Coast League in his pro debut before moving to Rookie-level Pulaski in 2018.

SCOUTING REPORT: The most appealing part of Peraza's game is his bat. Evaluators see at least an average future hitter with average raw power, with some seeing future plus in both departments. His in-game power is limited now because of his size and lack of present strength, though his plus bat speed and sound stroke could lead to more power in time. Defensively, Peraza shows outstanding instincts at shortstop, which helps mitigate his somewhat limited range. He's an average runner and shows smooth actions and a solid internal clock. He's got an average arm but needs to clean up his mechanics to improve his accuracy.

THE FUTURE: Scouts are split on Peraza's ability to stick at shortstop, but he's young enough to improve as he moves up the ladder. That journey should continue at low Class A Charleston in 2019.

Year	Club (League)	Class	AVG	G	AB	R	H	2B	3B	HR	RBI	BB	SO	SB	CS	OBP	SLG
2017	Yankees1 (DSL)	R	.361	10	36	10	13	3	2	0	10	7	2	1	0	.467	.556
	Yankees2 (GCL)	R	.266	48	184	34	49	10	1	0	24	16	36	12	2	.363	.332
2018	Pulaski (APP)	R	.250	36	140	25	35	3	2	1	11	14	41	8	1	.333	.321
Minor League Totals			.269	94	360	69	97	16	5	1	45	37	79	21	3	.363	.350

17 GARRETT WHITLOCK, RHP

BA GRADE

50 Risk: High

Born: June 11, 1996. **B-T:** R-R. **Ht.:** 6-5. **Wt.:** 190. **Drafted:** Alabama-Birmingham, 2017 (18th round). **Signed by:** Mike Wagner.

TRACK RECORD: Whitlock was a draft-eligible sophomore at Alabama-Birmingham and got off to a hot start in his second season with the Blazers before a bout of food poisoning and a back strain scuttled the second half of the year. Still, his stuff and an impressive turn in the Cape Cod League convinced the Yankees to take a flyer on him in the 18th round and sign him for $247,500, almost double the recommended slot amount.

SCOUTING REPORT: Whitlock is a true sinker-slider pitcher. He starts his repertoire with a low-90s two-seamer that peaked at 95 mph in 2018. The pitch plays up thanks to nearly seven feet of his extension in his delivery, a figure well above-average. The action on the pitch also helped him coax a 1.71 groundout-to-airout ratio, the second-best in the organization behind only Nick Green. Whitlock couples his sinker with a slurvy, potentially average slider that shows occasional plus depth in the 79-82 mph range. He's been able to land it for strikes and use to get swings and misses as well. His changeup, thrown in the same velocity band as his breaking ball, is his clear third pitch. He's shown feel for it but needs to develop it further. His delivery is a little bit rigid, which gives evaluators some pause when projecting his potential role.

THE FUTURE: Whitlock has the ceiling of an innings-eating back-end starter, with a solid fallback option of a setup reliever. He'll return to Double-A Trenton in 2019.

Year	Club (League)	Class	W	L	ERA	G	GS	CG	SV	IP	H	HR	BB	SO	K/9	WHIP	AVG
2017	Yankees2 (GCL)	R	0	0	1.04	3	3	0	0	9	4	0	0	14	14.5	0.46	.138
	Pulaski (APP)	R	1	0	7.94	2	0	0	0	6	10	1	0	8	12.7	1.76	.400
2018	Charleston, SC (SAL)	LoA	2	2	1.13	7	7	0	0	40	23	1	7	44	9.9	0.75	.168
	Trenton (EL)	AA	1	0	0.84	2	1	0	0	11	10	0	7	4	3.4	1.59	.263
Tampa (FSL)		HiA	5	3	2.44	14	13	1	0	70	60	2	27	74	9.5	1.24	.231
Minor League Totals			9	5	2.07	28	24	1	0	135	107	4	41	144	9.6	1.10	.219

18 NICK NELSON, RHP

BA GRADE
50 Risk: High

Born: Dec. 5, 1995. **B-T:** R-R. **Ht.:** 6-2. **Wt.:** 203. **Drafted:** Gulf Coast State (Fla.) JC, 2016 (4th round). **Signed by:** Mike Wagner.

TRACK RECORD: Nelson was a two-way player in college, but scouts were more intrigued by what he could do on the mound. His first two seasons as a pro were fair before a breakout 2018. His 144 strikeouts across three levels ranked second in the system behind only Michael King. His command was lacking, however, as he walked nearly five batters per nine innings.

SCOUTING REPORT: Nelson works with a power arsenal fronted by fastball that averaged 95 mph, touched as high as 98 and showed solid carry through the zone. He holds his velocity throughout his starts. Nelson buttresses the fastball with a sharp-biting, downer curveball in the 78-80 mph range as well as an 87-90 mph changeup that lags behind his other offerings. His command issues are particularly vexing to evaluators, who see a simple, clean delivery. He shows a mild tendency toward nibbling which, if alleviated, could help him cut down his walks.

THE FUTURE: Nelson could find himself as back-end starter if he irons out his command and sharpens his changeup. If not, his fastball and curveball may be enough for him to carve out a bullpen role.

Year	Club (League)	Class	W	L	ERA	G	GS	CG	SV	IP	H	HR	BB	SO	K/9	WHIP	AVG
2016	Pulaski (APP)	R	0	3	3.38	10	10	0	0	21	14	0	22	19	8.0	1.69	.200
2017	Charleston, SC (SAL)	LoA	3	12	4.56	22	22	0	0	101	103	5	50	110	9.8	1.52	.270
2018	Charleston, SC (SAL)	LoA	1	1	3.65	5	5	0	0	25	18	1	7	35	12.8	1.01	.198
	Tampa (FSL)	HiA	7	5	3.36	18	17	0	0	88	69	1	47	99	10.1	1.31	.214
	Trenton (EL)	AA	0	0	5.19	3	3	0	0	9	10	1	9	10	10.4	2.19	.278
Minor League Totals			11	21	3.95	58	57	0	0	244	214	8	135	273	10.1	1.43	.237

19 TREVOR STEPHAN, RHP

BA GRADE
45 Risk: High

Born: Nov. 25, 1995. **B-T:** R-R. **Ht.:** 6-5. **Wt.:** 225. **Drafted:** Arkansas, 2017 (3rd round). **Signed by:** Matt Ranson.

TRACK RECORD: After beginning his college career as a reliever at Hill (Texas) JC, Stephan transferred to Arkansas and pitched in the rotation as a junior. His stuff ticked up with the Razorbacks, which led the Yankees to draft him with their third-round selection and sign him for $797.500. He began his first pro season at high Class A Tampa in 2018 before jumping to Double-A Trenton in late May.

SCOUTING REPORT: Stephan pitches primarily with a fastball and a slider, and worked hard in 2018 to improve his changeup. His fastball, which sits in the low-to-mid 90s, shows the type of riding life through the zone that the Yankees covet. He backs that pitch up with an above-average, sweeping slider that he uses to get strikeouts. His changeup needs more repetition, but the organization believes it can be solid-average with improvement. He delivers from a funky, low-slot delivery that adds deception. Stephan worked with pitching coordinator Scott Aldred this year to change his release point and help him stay on top of the baseball throughout his delivery.

THE FUTURE: There's still a split camp about whether Stephan's ultimate future is in the bullpen or as a starter. He'll continue try to stay in the rotation back at Double-A Trenton in 2019.

Year	Club (League)	Class	W	L	ERA	G	GS	CG	SV	IP	H	HR	BB	SO	K/9	WHIP	AVG
2017	Yankees1 (GCL)	R	0	0	0.00	1	1	0	0	2	0	0	0	1	4.5	0.00	.000
	Staten Island (NYP)	SS	1	1	1.39	10	9	0	0	32	20	0	6	43	12.0	0.80	.177
2018	Tampa (FSL)	HiA	3	1	1.98	7	7	1	0	41	23	5	9	49	10.8	0.78	.160
	Trenton (EL)	AA	3	8	4.54	17	17	0	0	83	80	5	29	91	9.8	1.31	.253
Minor League Totals			7	10	3.18	35	34	1	0	159	123	10	44	184	10.4	1.05	.212

20 JASON LOPEZ, C

BA GRADE
45 Risk: High

Born: March 16, 1998. **B-T:** R-R. **Ht.:** 5-10. **Wt.:** 190. **Signed:** Venezuela, 2014. **Signed by:** Alan Atacho/Ricardo Finol.

TRACK RECORD: Lopez was part of the Yankees' ballyhooed 2014 international spending spree, though his signing was far less heralded than other high-dollar acquisitions. He showcased as a third baseman at Carlos Guillen's academy in Venezuela, but the Yankees wanted to see him at catcher. The player obliged, the team liked what it saw and signed him for $100,000.

SCOUTING REPORT: Lopez stands out more for his defense than his offense at this point, but he's no pushover at the plate. He has enough raw power to launch impressive home runs in batting practice. The in-game power started to peek through in 2018, when he hit eight home runs in 302 at-bats after hitting just one home run each of his previous three seasons. He doesn't walk much, but he shows solid bat to balls skills and limits his strikeouts. Lopez future plus arm and a quick release behind the plate, and he threw out 35 percent of basestealers between both Class A levels. He still needs to improve his game-calling and his blocking, as shown by his 17 passed balls.

THE FUTURE: Lopez ended the year with high Class A Tampa and is likely to return there in 2019. He has the future of second-division regular or a solid backup.

Year	Club (League)	Class	AVG	G	AB	R	H	2B	3B	HR	RBI	BB	SO	SB	CS	OBP	SLG
2016	Yankees2 (GCL)	R	.192	11	26	2	5	1	0	1	7	1	8	1	0	.267	.346
2017	Yankees1 (DSL)	R	.100	6	20	3	2	1	0	0	2	4	4	0	1	.280	.150
	Staten Island (NYP)	SS	.240	49	150	21	36	6	1	1	10	24	36	2	0	.345	.313
2018	Charleston, SC (SAL)	LoA	.285	72	256	35	73	19	0	8	30	15	57	7	3	.330	.453
	Tampa (FSL)	HiA	.196	13	46	6	9	3	1	0	5	2	11	0	0	.220	.304
Minor League Totals			.248	193	644	98	160	36	2	11	73	68	144	21	8	.323	.362

21 JUAN THEN, RHP

BA GRADE

50 Risk: Extreme

Born: Feb. 7, 2000. **B-T:** R-R. **Ht.:** 6-0. **Wt.:** 178. **Signed:** Dominican Republic, 2016. **Signed by:** Eddy Toledo (Mariners).

TRACK RECORD: The Mariners liked Then's quick arm and projectable frame and signed him out of the Dominican Republic for $77,000 in 2016 before flipping him, along with lefty J.P. Sears, to the Yankees for reliever Nick Rumbelow. He made his Yankees debut in 2018, posting a 2.70 ERA in 11 starts in the Rookie-level Gulf Coast League.

SCOUTING REPORT: Then boasts a three-pitch mix that starts with a low-90s fastball that touches 95 mph. The pitch features running and riding action out of an overhand slot. He backs up his fastball with a 78-82 mph curveball with hard, downward snap. The pitch is inconsistent but projects plus with repetition and development. He also throws a mid-80s change that shows hard sinking action and could be average in the future. There are some concerns about his somewhat straight fastball, which is exacerbated by his lack of size and little remaining projectability.

THE FUTURE: Then has a chance to stick in the rotation as his arsenal develops, but the bullpen is also a possibility. He should pitch at one of the Yankees' two short-season affiliates in 2019.

Year	Club (League)	Class	W	L	ERA	G	GS	CG	SV	IP	H	HR	BB	SO	K/9	WHIP	AVG
2017	Mariners (DSL)	R	2	2	2.64	13	13	0	0	61	50	3	15	56	8.2	1.06	.220
2018	Yankees1 (GCL)	R	0	3	2.70	11	11	0	0	50	38	2	11	42	7.6	0.98	.210
Minor League Totals			2	5	2.67	24	24	0	0	111	88	5	26	98	7.9	1.02	.216

22 FRANK GERMAN, RHP

BA GRADE

45 Risk: High

Born: Sept. 22, 1997. **B-T:** R-R. **Ht.:** 6-2. **Wt.:** 195. **Drafted:** North Florida, 2018 (4th round). **Signed by:** Ronnie Merrill.

TRACK RECORD: After a freshman season split between the rotation and the bullpen, German spent the next two years at North Florida as a stalwart starter. He was excellent as a sophomore before turning it up a notch in his junior year, when he went 8-3 with a 1.58 ERA that ranked fifth in Division I. The Yankees jumped on him in the fourth round and signed him for $347,500.

SCOUTING REPORT: German's calling card is his high-end fastball. His fastball sat in the low-to-mid 90s and touched as high as 98 with short-season Staten Island, with hard, lateral movement to both sides of the plate. His secondary pitches need some work, but his main offspeed weapon is a slurvy slider in the low 80s. The pitch needs to be tightened, but scouts see the potential for an above-average offering as German continues to develop. His changeup is his third offering and in the very early stages of development. He slows his arm noticeably when he throws it, and also changes his arm slot.

THE FUTURE: After spending his pro debut beating up on inferior competition in the short-season Staten Island, German will get his first real challenge in full-season ball in 2019.

Year	Club (League)	Class	W	L	ERA	G	GS	CG	SV	IP	H	HR	BB	SO	K/9	WHIP	AVG
2018	Yankees2 (GCL)	R	0	0	0.00	1	1	0	0	2	0	0	0	3	13.5	0.00	.000
	Staten Island (NYP)	SS	1	3	2.22	10	4	0	1	28	22	0	6	38	12.1	0.99	.206
Minor League Totals			1	3	2.08	11	5	0	1	30	22	0	6	41	12.2	0.92	.195

23 DOMINGO ACEVEDO, RHP

BA GRADE
45 Risk: High

Born: March 6, 1994. **B-T:** R-R. **Ht.:** 6-6. **Wt.:** 242. **Drafted:** Dominican Republic, 2012. **Signed by:** Esteban Castillo.

TRACK RECORD: Acevedo signed for $7,500 as a projectable 18-year-old and has spent the bulk of his career tantalizing with his potential but stagnating because of injuries. Acevedo has eclipsed 100 innings just once in six seasons despite being a starter, and has only two appearances at Triple-A. He was limited to just 69.1 innings in 2018 because of a variety of injuries, the latest of which kept him from an appearance in the Arizona Fall League.

SCOUTING REPORT: Acevedo starts his arsenal with a big fastball that can sit in the mid 90s and peaks at 98 mph. A severe blister issue that curtailed the early portion of his season also meant he needed time to rebuild his velocity. His mid-80s slider grades well in analytic circles because of its high swing-and-miss rate, but garners lower rankings from scouts because it's highly inconsistent. Acevedo's upper-80s changeup, historically regarded as the better of his two offspeeds, still projects plus and features power sink away from lefthanders. He still needs to improve his command, which has been hindered by a longer arm action. He must also prove he can stay healthy.

THE FUTURE: After a long stay in Double-A Trenton, Acevedo is likely to move to Triple-A Scranton/Wilkes-Barre in 2019. He fits either in the back of a rotation or the middle of a bullpen.

Year	Club (League)	Class	W	L	ERA	G	GS	CG	SV	IP	H	HR	BB	SO	K/9	WHIP	AVG
2016	Charleston, SC (SAL)	LoA	3	1	1.90	8	8	0	0	43	34	1	7	48	10.1	0.96	.221
	Tampa (FSL)	HiA	2	3	3.22	10	10	1	0	50	49	3	15	54	9.7	1.27	.261
2017	Tampa (FSL)	HiA	0	4	4.57	7	7	0	0	41	49	5	9	52	11.3	1.40	.290
	Scranton/W-B (IL)	AAA	1	1	4.38	2	2	0	0	12	12	0	8	8	5.8	1.62	.255
	Trenton (EL)	AA	5	1	2.38	14	14	1	0	79	65	8	17	82	9.3	1.03	.223
2018	Staten Island (NYP)	SS	0	0	3.86	2	2	0	0	5	5	0	1	3	5.8	1.29	.294
	Trenton (EL)	AA	3	3	2.92	14	10	0	0	65	51	3	20	52	7.2	1.10	.217
Minor League Totals			18	16	2.85	85	80	2	0	401	362	22	110	417	9.4	1.18	.240

24 YOENDRYS GOMEZ, RHP

BA GRADE
50 Risk: Extreme

Born: Oct. 5, 1999. **B-T:** R-R. **Ht.:** 6-4. **Wt.:** 174. **Signed:** Venezuela, 2016. **Signed by:** Alan Atacho.

TRACK RECORD: The Yankees signed Gomez out of Venezuela for $50,000 in 2016 on the strength of a lanky, projectable frame and a fastball that touched 92 mph. He put together a nondescript first pro campaign in the Dominican Summer League before moving stateside in 2018 and pitching primarily with the Rookie-level Gulf Coast League. He struck out 10 hitters per nine innings there.

SCOUTING REPORT: Gomez has grown into more velocity as his body has matured. His fastball now sits in the low 90s and touches as high as 96 mph. It fastball plays up thanks to excellent extension out of his high three-quarters delivery. He backs up his heater with a 75-78 mph curveball with late snap out of the zone and a mid-80s changeup with moderate fade. Each has a chance to be at least average with more repetition and mechanical consistency. Gomez flashes a clean delivery and consistent arm action, portending average control even though his walk rate was a touch high in his debut.

THE FUTURE: Gomez has the upside of a No. 3 or 4 starter but has a long way to go. He'll head to Rookie-level Pulaski in 2019 to continue working toward that ceiling.

Year	Club (League)	Class	W	L	ERA	G	GS	CG	SV	IP	H	HR	BB	SO	K/9	WHIP	AVG
2017	Yankees1 (DSL)	R	0	3	4.78	10	8	0	0	32	36	2	12	32	9.0	1.50	.288
	Yankees2 (GCL)	R	0	0	12.00	1	1	0	0	3	5	0	6	1	3.0	3.67	.417
2018	Yankees (DSL)	R	1	0	1.00	2	2	0	0	9	2	0	7	7	7.0	1.00	.080
	Yankees1 (GCL)	R	3	1	2.33	10	9	0	0	39	27	1	15	43	10.0	1.09	.194
Minor League Totals			4	4	3.48	23	20	0	0	83	70	3	40	83	9.0	1.33	.233

25 LUIS GIL, RHP

BA GRADE
50 Risk: Extreme

Born: June 3, 1998. **B-T:** R-R. **Ht.:** 6-4. **Wt.:** 194. **Signed:** Dominican Republic, 2014. **Signed by:** Luis Lajara (Twins).

TRACK RECORD: Gil signed with the Twins as a 16-year-old in 2014 and was dealt to the Yankees before the 2018 season in a one-for-one deal for outfielder Jake Cave. The Yankees skipped Gil over the Rookie-level Gulf Coast League in favor of starting his stateside career in the Rookie-level Appalachian League.

SCOUTING REPORT: The first thing that jumps out about Gil is his fastball. The pitch already sits in the mid-to-upper 90s and touches triple-digits. At its best, the pitch shows explosive riding life up and in to lefthanders. He pairs his heater primarily with a curveball in the 79-84 mph range that shows variable break. It is most effective when it shows more depth than sweep. With more consistency, the pitch could project as above-average. He also throws a firm, low-90s changeup in its nascent stages. Wiry and long-levered, Gil tends to lose the zone when his delivery gets out of sync, the reason behind an ugly 6.3 walk rate in 2018.

THE FUTURE: Gil will head to low Class A Charleston in 2019 to keep sharpening his arsenal and command.

Year	Club (League)	Class	W	L	ERA	G	GS	CG	SV	IP	H	HR	BB	SO	K/9	WHIP	AVG
2016	Did not play—Injured																
2017	Twins (DSL)	R	0	2	2.59	14	14	0	0	42	31	2	20	49	10.6	1.22	.205
2018	Pulaski (APP)	R	2	1	1.37	10	10	0	0	39	21	1	25	58	13.3	1.17	.154
	Staten Island (NYP)	SS	0	2	5.40	2	2	0	0	7	11	1	6	10	13.5	2.55	.344
Minor League Totals			3	7	2.76	42	26	0	2	111	78	6	77	141	11.4	1.40	.196

26 THAIRO ESTRADA, SS

Born: Feb. 22, 1996. **B-T:** R-R. **Ht.:** 5-9. **Wt.:** 185. **Signed:** Venezuela, 2012. **Signed by:** Alan Atacho/Ricardo Finol.

BA GRADE
45 Risk: High

TRACK RECORD: Things looked rosy for Estrada after a breakout year at Double-A Trenton in 2017 followed by a strong stint in the Arizona Fall League. That progress came to a tragic halt when he was shot in the right hip during an attempted robbery in his native Venezuela during the offseason. The first surgery to remove the bullet in Venezuela was botched, and the bullet remained in his body the entire season until finally being removed in the U.S. in November.

SCOUTING REPORT: Before his injuries, Estrada showed a potential average bat with a glove and arm that each projected as plus. His bat was geared for gap-to-gap line drives with a flat path that produced a lot of contact, although it limited his already-scant power potential. Estrada showed quick hands, a strong arm and steady instincts in the field. He's an above-average runner but needs to sharpen his baserunning.

THE FUTURE: Even with a full six-week stint in the Arizona Fall League, 2018 was a lost season. He'll try to regain his health and prospect shine back at Triple-A in 2019.

Year	Club (League)	Class	AVG	G	AB	R	H	2B	3B	HR	RBI	BB	SO	SB	CS	OBP	SLG
2016	Charleston, SC (SAL)	LoA	.286	35	140	11	40	3	1	5	19	8	21	11	3	.324	.429
	Tampa (FSL)	HiA	.292	83	315	52	92	15	1	3	30	29	46	7	5	.355	.375
2017	Trenton (EL)	AA	.301	122	495	72	149	19	4	6	48	34	56	8	11	.353	.392
2018	Tampa (FSL)	HiA	.222	10	45	4	10	2	0	0	5	0	9	0	0	.234	.267
	Scranton/W-B (IL)	AAA	.152	8	33	1	5	1	0	0	3	0	8	0	0	.176	.182
Minor League Totals			.283	394	1532	218	433	71	11	18	151	113	211	49	28	.340	.379

27 RAIMFER SALINAS, OF

Born: Dec. 31, 2000. **B-T:** R-R. **Ht.:** 6-0. **Wt.:** 175. **Signed:** Venezuela, 2017. **Signed by:** Darwin Bracho.

BA GRADE
50 Risk: Extreme

TRACK RECORD: After Shohei Ohtani signed with the Angels, the Yankees, who had accumulated extra bonus-pool money in the hopes of signing the Japanese two-way star, shifted some of that money to Salinas. The outfielder possessed one of the best all-around skill sets available in the 2017 international class, and ranked No. 10 among that year's July 2 prospects.

SCOUTING REPORT: Salinas shows excellent balance at the plate, with an all-fields approach and fringe-average power now that has the potential to develop further as he matures. He didn't get to show off those tools in 2018 because of a swollen knee and a ligament injury to his ring finger that limited him to just 11 games, though he did make his stateside debut as a 17-year-old. When healthy, he shows double-plus speed, a strong throwing arm and the ability to glide to balls in center field.

THE FUTURE: After a lost 2018 season, Salinas will likely return to the Rookie-level Gulf Coast League in 2019.

Year	Club (League)	Class	AVG	G	AB	R	H	2B	3B	HR	RBI	BB	SO	SB	CS	OBP	SLG
2018	Yankees (DSL)	R	.095	6	21	4	2	1	0	0	2	5	5	4	2	.321	.143
	Yankees2 (GCL)	R	.125	5	16	0	2	0	0	0	0	2	5	0	1	.300	.125
Minor League Totals			.108	11	37	4	4	1	0	0	2	7	10	4	3	.312	.135

28 ANTONIO GOMEZ, C

Born: Nov. 13, 2001. **B-T:** R-R. **Ht.:** 6-2. **Wt.:** 205. **Signed:** Venezuela, 2018. **Signed by:** Edgar Mateo/Raul Gonzalez.

BA GRADE
50 Risk: Extreme

TRACK RECORD: Gomez ranked No. 14 among the 2018 July 2 class, and signed with the Yankees on the strength of phenomenal defense and burgeoning offensive abilities shown at international showcases.

SCOUTING REPORT: Gomez's strongest tool is his throwing arm, which ranks as a 70 on the 20-to-80 scouting scale. That arm was on display at at February 2018 showcase, when he threw out four runners, including one from his knees, with a pop times as low as 1.83 seconds. He's got quick feet as well, but could stand to improve his receiving. Offensively, Gomez's bat-to-ball skills improved as he matured, and his power slowly grew. That trend could continue as he learns to incorporate his lower half into his swing more often.

THE FUTURE: The Yankees have been aggressive with their most talented international prospects recently, and Gomez could join one of the team's two clubs in the Rookie-level Gulf Coast League come June.

Year	Club (League)	Class	W	L	ERA	G	GS	CG	SV	IP	H	HR	BB	SO	K/9	WHIP	AVG
2018	Did not play—Signed 2019 contract																

29 KEVIN ALCANTARA, OF

BA GRADE

50 Risk: Extreme

Born: July 12, 2002. **B-T:** R-R. **Ht.:** 6-5. **Wt.:** 175. **Signed:** Dominican Republic, 2018. **Signed by:** Edgar Mateo/Juan Piron.

TRACK RECORD: Alcantara ranked No. 15 among the 2018 July 2 class, one spot behind fellow Yankees prospect Antonio Gomez. The Yankees signed five from that group, including Alcantara for a bonus of $1 million. Scouting Report: There are some questions about Alcantara's hit tool because of his long levers, and will require adjustments as he matures. Still, evaluators have seen him perform well in games, allowing them to believe that he can improve. He already shows pull-side power, but gets in trouble when he tries to sell out to get to it too often. He's a graceful runner with the long strides suggested by someone of his frame, which will help him stick in center field. He's got an above-average arm as well, and has been known to diligently use batting practice as a time to refine his reads and jumps. His arm should play well enough if he gets too big for center field, and some evaluators have compared him to big league outfield Dexter Fowler.

THE FUTURE: If he shows well in extended spring training, Alcantara could come stateside as a 17-year-old, which the Yankees have shown the willingness to do in recent years. He also could stay back in the Dominican Summer League as well.

Year	Club (League)	Class	AVG	G	AB	R	H	2B	3B	HR	RBI	BB	SO	SB	CS	OBP	SLG
2018	Did not play—Signed 2019 contract																

30 JOSH BREAUX, C

BA GRADE

45 Risk: Very High

Born: Oct. 7, 1997. **B-T:** R-R. **Ht.:** 6-1. **Wt.:** 224. **Drafted:** McLennan (Texas) JC, 2018 (2nd round). **Signed by:** Mike Leuzinger.

TRACK RECORD: Breaux pitched and caught during his two seasons at McLennan (Texas) JC. He drew significant interest as a pitcher at because of his mid- to upper-90s fastball, but the Yankees drafted him in the second round as a catcher after he swatted 37 home runs in two seasons.

SCOUTING REPORT: As a catcher only, the Yankees bought into Breaux's high-end power. He produced some of the highest exit velocities in the system after signing. In order to take advantage of how hard he hits the ball, the Yankees want to introduce more loft to Breaux's swing after he hit nearly 89 percent grounders and infield flies in the New York-Penn League. Breaux has double-plus arm strength behind the plate, as expected because of his pitching velocity, but he threw out just 2 of 22 basestealers because of a slow-twitch body. He's an average blocker, although that's less true in two-strike counts.

THE FUTURE: Breaux needs to clean up his receiving and hitting ability and will likely move to low Class A Charleston in 2019. He's got the profile of a backup catcher with power, though pitching will always provide him with an intriguing alternate path.

Year	Club (League)	Class	AVG	G	AB	R	H	2B	3B	HR	RBI	BB	SO	SB	CS	OBP	SLG
2018	Yankees1 (GCL)	R	.125	3	8	0	1	0	0	0	0	1	1	0	0	.222	.125
	Staten Island (NYP)	SS	.280	27	100	6	28	9	0	0	13	3	20	0	0	.295	.370
Minor League Totals			.269	30	108	6	29	9	0	0	13	4	21	0	0	.289	.352

Oakland Athletics

BY MATT EDDY

The Athletics entered the 2018 season with the lowest payroll in baseball and ended it in the American League Wild Card Game. Along the way, Oakland won 97 games and put a scare into the eventual division-champion Astros by tying them for the top spot in the AL West on Aug. 18.

The Athletics' season ended with a 7-2 loss in Yankee Stadium, but a period of regular playoff contention could be just beginning. Oakland's lean payroll—just six players are projected to earn $5 million or more in 2019—is a testament to the organization's recent success in the draft and typical skill at evaluating pro acquisitions in trades.

The club's top two returning position players for 2019 are both draft picks. Third baseman Matt Chapman (2014 first round) and first baseman Matt Olson (2012 supplemental first) won Gold Gloves in 2018 while combining to produce 12.5 wins above replacement. Chad Pinder, a 2013 draft pick, started multiple games at six positions and supplied power, especially against lefthanders.

These examples are notable for an organization that saw little return from drafting college position players Jemile Weeks, Grant Green and Michael Choice with mid-first-round picks from 2008-10.

Trades for DH Khris Davis, closer Blake Treinen, shortstop Marcus Semien, lefthander Sean Manaea and 2018 rookie outfielder Ramon Laureano are shaping up to be significant wins for the organization, though the specter of the Josh Donaldson trade with the Blue Jays lingers.

Donaldson won an MVP award in 2015, his first season in Toronto, while 23-year-old second baseman Franklin Barreto, the headliner headed to Oakland, has not yet hit his stride in cups of coffee in 2017 and 2018. Barreto has, however, demonstrated an extreme flyball approach while slugging .482 in two seasons at Triple-A Nashville.

In recent years, the A's have emphasized signing premium athletes on the amateur market. That was most apparent in the 2018 draft, when they selected Oklahoma two-sport star Kyler Murray with the No. 9 overall pick. As part of a $4.6 million bonus agreement with Murray, the A's permitted him to play quarterback at OU in 2018 before reporting to spring training in 2019.

The fact that Murray played so well that he won the Heisman Trophy complicates his situation. He is more of a prototype prospect in baseball as a power-speed outfielder, though his contract does not explicitly forbid him from pursuing pro football if an NFL team drafts him high in April.

In 2016, the A's blew past their internation-

Power reliever Lou Trivino was an 11th-round pick from Division II Slippery Rock in 2013.

PROJECTED 2022 LINEUP

Catcher	Sean Murphy (27)
First Base	Matt Olson (28)
Second Base	Franklin Barreto (26)
Third Base	Matt Chapman (29)
Shortstop	Jorge Mateo (27)
Left Field	Ramon Laureano (27)
Center Field	Kyler Murray (24)
Right Field	Austin Beck (23)
Designated Hitter	Stephen Piscotty (31)
No. 1 Starter	Jesus Luzardo (24)
No. 2 Starter	A.J. Puk (27)
No. 3 Starter	Sean Manaea (30)
No. 4 Starter	Grant Holmes (26)
No. 5 Starter	Jharel Cotton (30)
Closer	Lou Trivino (30)

al bonus pool to sign Cuban outfielder Lazaro Armenteros and Dominican second baseman Marcos Brito. As a result, Oakland faced signing restrictions in both 2017 and 2018, so it instead traded portions of its international budget to help acquire prospects Dustin Fowler, Jorge Mateo and James Kaprielian in 2017 and relievers Jeurys Familia and Shawn Kelley in 2018. In the latter season, the club buttressed a dominant bullpen led by Treinen and rookie Lou Trivino, an 11th-round pick out of Division II Slippery Rock in 2013.

After the 2018 season, the A's extended the contracts of executive vice president of baseball operations Billy Beane, general manager David Forst and AL Manager of the Year Bob Melvin.

DEPTH CHART

OAKLAND ATHLETICS

TOP 2019 ROOKIE: Jesus Luzardo, LHP. The top prospect lefthander in the minors finished at Triple-A and will assume a rotation spot at some point in 2019.

BREAKOUT PROSPECT: Greg Deichmann, OF. A hamate injury scuttled his full-season debut in 2018, but he has rare power and a plan at the plate.

SLEEPER: Lawrence Butler, OF. The 2018 sixth-rounder out of an Atlanta high school showed big power in instructional league and has a bead on an assignment to low Class A in 2019.

SOURCE OF TOP 30 TALENT			
Homegrown	**23**	**Acquired**	**7**
College	16	Trade	7
Junior college	0	Rule 5 draft	0
High school	2	Independent league	0
Nondrafted free agent	0	Free agent/waivers	0
International	5		

LF
Lazaro Armenteros (6)
Tyler Ramirez (24)
Dairon Blanco (29)
Lawrence Butler
Luke Persico

CF
Kyler Murray (4)
Austin Beck (5)
Jameson Hannah (7)
Skye Bolt (20)
Luis Barrera (21)
Kevin Richards

RF
Greg Deichmann (11)
Rafael Rincones

3B
Sheldon Neuse (10)
Jordan Diaz (28)

SS
Jorge Mateo (9)
Jeremy Eierman (12)
Kevin Merrell (22)
Nick Allen (23)
Alexander Campos
Yerdel Vargas

2B
Eli White (8)
Marcos Brito (17)
Nate Mondou
Nick Ward

1B
Alfonso Rivas (18)

C
Sean Murphy (3)
Jonah Heim (30)
Santis Sanchez
Cesarre Astorri

LHP

LHSP	LHRP
Jesus Luzardo (1)	Dalton Sawyer
A.J. Puk (2)	
Hogan Harris	

RHP

RHSP	RHRP
James Kaprielian (13)	J.B. Wendelken (26)
Grant Holmes (14)	Miguel Romero
Parker Dunshee (15)	Carlos Ramirez
Brian Howard (16)	Sam Sheehan
Daulton Jefferies (19)	Calvin Coker
Gus Varland (25)	
Brady Feigl (27)	
Chase Cohen	
Matt Milburn	
Wyatt Marks	
James Naile	
Rafael Kelly	
Ismael Aquino	

DRAFT ANALYSIS

2018

BEST PURE HITTER: 1B Alfonso Rivas (4) hit .285/.397/.383 in 61 games for short-season Vermont. He ranked fourth in the New York-Penn League in walks and on-base percentage. The A's love the lefthanded-hitting Rivas' approach and barrel frequency, and they think he has room to develop physically and find more power.

BEST POWER: SS Jeremy Eierman (2s) dropped 23 home runs as a Missouri State sophomore but followed with zero homers for Team USA and then just 10 as a MSU junior. He found his power stroke at short-season Vermont by clubbing eight homers to rank fifth in the New York-Penn League, and the A's love his bat speed and plus power potential as a middle infielder. Oakland snagged physical 6-foot-4 OF Lawrence Butler (6) from the Atlanta high school ranks, and he impressed A's field staff in the Rookie-level Arizona League with his big lefthanded power and desire to learn.

FASTEST RUNNER: Drafted ninth overall, Oklahoma OF Kyler Murray (1) turns in 70 run times on the 20-80 scouting scale to first base, but that's only because he doesn't get out of the batter's box well. He is an 80 runner underway.

BEST DEFENSIVE PLAYER: Murray has a chance to be a premium defender in center field.

BEST ATHLETE: What Murray can do on the diamond is truly astonishing given that, prior to 2018, he had focused on football since he was a high school senior. He posts high exit velocities, he runs and he defends.

BEST FASTBALL: Georgia Southern RHP Chase Cohen (9) topped out at 97 mph in short outings in the New York-Penn League. His delivery features a slight hesitation in his leg lift, and the A's feel he has the repertoire to start.

BEST SECONDARY PITCH: Mississippi RHP Brady Feigl (5) ranges from 90-93 mph as a starter and throws a power curveball in the low 80s.

TOP DRAFT PICKS OF THE DECADE

Year	Player, Pos	2018 Org
2009	Grant Green, SS	Mexican Lge
2010	Michael Choice, OF	Mexican Lge
2011	Sonny Gray, RHP	Yankees
2012	Addison Russell, SS	Cubs
2013	Billy McKinney, OF	Blue Jays
2014	Matt Chapman, 3B	Athletics
2015	Richie Martin, SS	Athletics
2016	A.J. Puk, LHP	Athletics
2017	Austin Beck, OF	Athletics
2018	Kyler Murray, OF	Athletics

BEST PRO DEBUT: RHP Gus Varland (14) pitched at Division II Concordia (Minn.) and flies under the radar—but maybe not for long. He ran his fastball up to the mid-90s and showed an intriguing breaking ball in a pro debut he finished with five starts for low Class A Beloit. At three stops he recorded a 0.95 ERA in 38 innings with 50 strikeouts and eight walks.

MOST INTRIGUING BACKGROUND: Murray is the greatest two-sport athlete since Russell Wilson (2010 draft) or perhaps Jeff Samardzija (2006). Wilson ultimately chose football, though he signed for just $200,000 as a fourth-round pick. Murray signed for $4.66 million.

CLOSEST TO THE MAJORS: Feigl could jump on the fast track if he moves to the bullpen.

BEST LATE-ROUND PICK: Varland is the obvious pick as a 14th-rounder from a D-II program, but the A's are excited to see what they have in switch-hitting Vanderbilt OF Alonzo Jones (25). Coming out of high school, Jones was perhaps the fastest player in the 2015 draft, but injuries and poor production plagued him at Vandy.

THE ONE WHO GOT AWAY: The Athletics signed 36 of the 41 players they drafted and they didn't miss out on any of their main draft targets.

—MATT EDDY

2017

The A's bet on upside and it will take time to see the true returns. OF Austin Beck (1) was raw in his full-season debut. OF Greg Deichmann (2) was limited by injury. 3B Will Toffey (4) was a part of the trade for Jeurys Familia and reached Double-A.

GRADE: B

2016

LHP A.J. Puk (1) missed 2018 due to Tommy John surgery but still is one of the best pitching prospects in the game. C Sean Murphy (3) reached Triple-A and INF Eli White (11) took a step forward in Double-A.

GRADE: A

2015

This class has stumbled badly in pro ball and now has a lot riding on SS Richie Martin (1), who was picked first overall in the Rule 5 Draft by the Orioles. OF Skyle Bolt (4) and RHP James Naile (20) have advanced to the upper levels of the minors.

GRADE: D

1 JESUS LUZARDO, LHP

Born: Sept. 30, 1997. **B-T:** L-L. **HT:** 6-1. **WT:** 205.
Drafted: HS—Parkland, Fla., 2016 (3rd round).
Signed by: Alex Morales (Nationals).

Born in Peru to Venezuelan parents, Luzardo will become the first Peruvian-born major leaguer when he debuts. The quality of his stuff ensures that he will be remembered as more than the answer to a trivia question. Luzardo moved with his family to Florida when he was 1 and went on to attend Stoneman Douglas High. He was sidelined for much of his senior season after having Tommy John surgery in March but still ranked as the No. 50 prospect for the 2016 draft. The Nationals selected him in the third round. When Luzardo returned to the mound in 2017, he made just three appearances in the Rookie-level Gulf Coast League before Washington traded him and two others to the Athletics in a deal for relievers Sean Doolittle and Ryan Madson. Luzardo emerged as one of the top pitching prospects in baseball in 2018, when he earned an Opening Day assignment to high Class A Stockton, despite having just 12 appearances in short-season ball, then quickly advanced to Double-A Midland and spent August at Triple-A Nashville.
SCOUTING REPORT: Few pitching prospects combine feel for three plus or better pitches with plus control like Luzardo. He dots both sides of the plate at 92-93 mph and tops out at 97 when he smells a strikeout. His plus fastball is true but features late hop and appears to jump at batters thanks to a high spin rate. Luzardo's mid-80s changeup is one of the best in the minors, and he isn't afraid to throw the 70-grade pitch to same-side batters or throw it twice in a row. The pitch fades and dives dramatically to his arm side, away from the barrel of righthanded hitters. Luzardo has made progress with his low-80s curveball since turning pro, to the point it usually plays above-average and flashes plus. He can land his 1-to-7 downer breaking ball for strikes or alter its shape as needed. A cohesive delivery helps Luzardo control his pitches and gives him a chance to develop plus command to go with a repertoire that missed bats at an elite rate in the minors in 2018.
THE FUTURE: The A's expect Luzardo to factor in their big league rotation at some point in 2019. He has No. 2 starter potential based on his pitch quality, polished command and confident, competitive mound presence.

COURTESY MIDLAND ROCK HOUNDS

BA GRADE	SCOUTING GRADES
70 Risk: High	Fastball: 60. Changeup: 70. Curveball: 60. Control: 60.

Projected future grades on 20-80 scouting scale

TOP PROSPECTS OF THE DECADE

Year	Player, Pos	2018 Org
2009	Brett Anderson, LHP	Athletics
2010	Chris Carter, OF	Twins
2011	Grant Green, SS	Mexican League
2012	Jarrod Parker, RHP	Did not play
2013	Addison Russell, SS	Cubs
2014	Addison Russell, SS	Cubs
2015	Daniel Robertson, SS	Rays
2016	Franklin Barreto, SS	Athletics
2017	Franklin Barreto, SS	Athletics
2018	A.J. Puk, LHP	Athletics

BEST TOOLS

Best Hitter for Average	Eli White
Best Power Hitter	Greg Deichmann
Best Strike-Zone Discipline	Alfonso Rivas
Fastest Baserunner	Dairon Blanco
Best Athlete	Jorge Mateo
Best Fastball	Jesus Luzardo
Best Curveball	Jesus Luzardo
Best Slider	Miguel Romero
Best Changeup	Boomer Biegalski
Best Control	Matt Milburn
Best Defensive Catcher	Sean Murphy
Best Defensive Infielder	Nick Allen
Best Infield Arm	Jorge Mateo
Best Defensive Outfielder	Skye Bolt
Best Outfield Arm	Austin Beck

Year	Club (League)	Class	W	L	ERA	G	GS	CG	SV	IP	H	HR	BB	SO	K/9	WHIP	AVG
2016	Did not play—Injured																
2017	Nationals (GCL)	R	1	0	1.32	3	3	0	0	14	14	1	0	15	9.9	1.02	.259
	Athletics (AZL)	R	0	1	1.54	4	3	0	0	12	9	0	1	13	10.0	0.86	.205
	Vermont (NYP)	SS	1	0	2.00	5	5	0	0	18	12	1	4	20	10.0	0.89	.188
2018	Stockton (CAL)	HiA	2	1	1.23	3	3	0	0	15	6	0	5	25	15.3	0.75	.120
	Midland (TL)	AA	7	3	2.29	16	16	0	0	79	58	5	18	86	9.8	0.97	.204
	Nashville (PCL)	AAA	1	1	7.31	4	4	0	0	16	25	2	7	18	10.1	2.00	.362
Minor League Totals			12	6	2.53	35	34	0	0	153	124	9	35	177	10.4	1.04	.219

2 A.J. PUK, LHP

Born: April 25, 1995. **B-T:** L-L. **HT:** 6-7. **WT:** 200. **Drafted:** Florida, 2016 (1st round). **Signed by:** Trevor Schaffer.

TRACK RECORD: The Athletics pounced on Puk—the No. 1 prospect on the BA draft board in 2016—when the Florida lefthander fell to No. 6. Wild in college, he streamlined his delivery in 2017 and led all minor league starters with 13.2 strikeouts per nine innings while advancing to Double-A Midland. Puk pitched well at big league camp in 2018 but tore his ulnar collateral ligament and had Tommy John surgery in April.

SCOUTING REPORT: Puk opened spring training with 10 scoreless innings and would have factored in the 2018 rotation had he not injured his elbow and missed the year. He touched 99 mph in Cactus League games and sat in the mid-90s with a double-plus fastball that batters struggle to square up. He has surrendered just three home runs in 158 pro innings because of the extreme downhill plane, incredible extension and unique angle he creates from his 6-foot-7 frame. Puk throws a vicious mid-80s slider with lateral movement that draws plus-plus grades from some scouts. He has gained confidence with his changeup since turning pro and sells the pitch with improved arm action and deception to the point where it flashes fringe-average. He should be able to develop average major league control.

THE FUTURE: Puk generates swings and misses with all three of his pitches and profiles as a No. 2 starter, assuming he makes a full recovery from surgery. He and Jesus Luzardo could team to give Oakland a lethal one-two punch at the top of its rotation.

BA GRADE

70 Risk: Extreme

Fastball: 70.
Slider: 70.
CHG: 45. CTL: 50.

Year	Club (League)	Class	W	L	ERA	G	GS	CG	SV	IP	H	HR	BB	SO	K/9	WHIP	AVG
2016	Vermont (NYP)	SS	0	4	3.03	10	10	0	0	33	23	0	12	40	11.0	1.07	.185
2017	Stockton (CAL)	HiA	4	5	3.69	14	11	0	0	61	44	1	23	98	14.5	1.10	.196
	Midland (TL)	AA	2	5	4.36	13	13	0	0	64	64	2	25	86	12.1	1.39	.256
Minor League Totals			6	14	3.82	37	34	0	0	158	131	3	60	224	12.8	1.21	.219

3 SEAN MURPHY, C

Born: Oct. 10, 1994. **B-T:** R-R. **HT:** 6-3. **WT:** 215. **Drafted:** Wright State, 2016 (3rd round). **Signed by:** Rich Sparks.

TRACK RECORD: Murphy slipped to the Athletics in the third round in 2016 in part because he broke the hamate bone in his left wrist as a Wright State junior. He broke the hamate in his *other* hand in 2018, costing him a chance to play in the Futures Game and interrupting what had been a standout campaign at Double-A Midland.

SCOUTING REPORT: Murphy is an exceptional defensive catcher who should hit enough to avoid being relegated to the bottom of the lineup. A high school growth spurt pushed him to 6-foot-3, but he retains the agility of a smaller man and the accompanying chip on his shoulder. Murphy shows at least plus raw power in batting practice and has the bat speed and strength to hit home runs, though he hasn't completely synced his swing in games to the satisfaction of all scouts. He has hit for average in the minors thanks to above-average plate discipline and plate coverage and an all-fields approach. Baserunners don't often test Murphy, whose double-plus arm and consistent sub-2 second pop times draw consistent praise. All he needs is improved throwing accuracy. He blocks and receives well but like most young catchers must add nuance to his game-calling and pitch presentation.

THE FUTURE: Murphy returned to action at the tail end of 2018 and then added offseason reps in the Dominican League. He will catch every day at Triple-A Las Vegas in 2019 until the A's call him up to begin what should be a lengthy career as a first-division catcher.

BA GRADE

55 Risk: High

Hit: 45. Power: 55.
Run: 30. Field: 60.
Arm: 70.

Year	Club (League)	Class	AVG	G	AB	R	H	2B	3B	HR	RBI	BB	SO	SB	CS	OBP	SLG
2016	Athletics (AZL)	R	.000	1	3	1	0	0	0	0	0	0	0	0	0	.000	.000
	Vermont (NYP)	SS	.237	22	76	10	18	1	0	2	7	9	12	1	0	.318	.329
2017	Stockton (CAL)	HiA	.297	45	165	22	49	11	0	9	26	11	33	0	0	.343	.527
	Midland (TL)	AA	.209	53	191	25	40	7	0	4	22	21	34	0	0	.288	.309
2018	Athletics (AZL)	R	.200	2	5	1	1	1	0	0	0	0	1	0	0	.200	.400
	Midland (TL)	AA	.288	68	257	51	74	26	2	8	43	23	47	3	0	.358	.498
	Nashville (PCL)	AAA	.250	3	8	2	2	0	0	0	0	3	2	0	0	.500	.250
Minor League Totals			.261	194	705	112	184	46	2	23	98	67	129	4	0	.331	.430

4 KYLER MURRAY, OF

Born: Aug. 7, 1997. **B-T:** R-R. **HT:** 5-11. **WT:** 195. **Drafted:** Oklahoma, 2018 (1st round). **Signed by:** Chris Reilly.

TRACK RECORD: Murray vexed scouts in 2018 because he had major league potential in both baseball and football—with no clear indication which sport he preferred. The Athletics thought his upside in baseball outweighed the downside of losing him to the NFL, so they selected him ninth overall and signed him for a near-slot bonus of $4.66 million. The deal allowed Murray to play quarterback for Oklahoma in 2018, when he won the Heisman Trophy and led the Sooners to the college football playoff.

SCOUTING REPORT: Despite not playing baseball regularly since he was a high school junior, Murray showed remarkable ability on the diamond as a redshirt sophomore in 2018. More surprising was that it came on the heels of a lackluster 2017, both in Big 12 Conference and Cape Cod League play. He hit for power, recorded high-end exit velocities and showed surprising fluidity in center field. He is a premium athlete who could be a standout defensive center fielder with an at least average arm. He appeared to pace himself in college by not cutting loose on throws or on the bases, and scouts believe he has more in the tank, with a chance for plus power, plus speed and a plus glove.

THE FUTURE: Murray has not participated in baseball activities since signing but committed to attending Oakland's minicamp in February as he prepares for his first spring training and what could be his first pro season in 2019. But because he has one year of college eligibility left on the gridiron, and because he could be drafted by an NFL team in April, the book is not entirely closed on football.

BA GRADE: 60 Risk: Extreme. Hit: 50. Power: 60. Run: 60. Field: 60. Arm: 50.

COURTESY OKLAHOMA

Year	Club (League)	Class	AVG	G	AB	R	H	2B	3B	HR	RBI	BB	SO	SB	CS	OBP	SLG
2018	Did not play																

5 AUSTIN BECK, OF

Born: Nov. 21, 1998. **B-T:** R-R. **HT:** 6-1. **WT:** 200. **Drafted:** HS—Lexington, N.C., 2017 (1st round). **Signed by:** Neil Avent.

TRACK RECORD: A torn anterior cruciate ligament in his left knee cost Beck time on the showcase circuit as a rising high school senior, but it didn't cost him in the draft. The Athletics drafted him sixth overall in 2017 as the first prep bat off the board. Because he had less track record with wood bats, Beck struggled at the outset of his pro career before finding his footing, but he led the low Class A Midwest League with 146 hits in 2018, his full-season debut.

SCOUTING REPORT: With a more sound hitting approach and a bit more discipline, Beck could develop into a plus hitter with a strong defensive profile. A tendency to chase up in the zone, put early-count pitches in play and pop the ball up on the infield restricted his hit tool at Beloit, but still he hit .296 as a 19-year-old in a pitcher's league. Beck shows above-average power in batting practice but hasn't accessed it in games because his swing emphasizes line drives rather than loft. Strength and bat speed won't be a barrier to unlocking his power. Beck is a plus runner who can go get the ball in center field with plus range and plus athleticism. He keeps runners honest with a plus arm.

THE FUTURE: If Beck shows power, he could develop into an impact center fielder, but early in his pro career he is viewed by some scouts as a future second-division starter or extra outfielder. He can begin to alter perceptions with a big year in the high Class A California League in 2019.

BA GRADE: 50 Risk: High. Hit: 60. Power: 40. Run: 60. Field: 60. Arm: 60.

Year	Club (League)	Class	AVG	G	AB	R	H	2B	3B	HR	RBI	BB	SO	SB	CS	OBP	SLG
2017	Athletics (AZL)	R	.211	41	152	23	32	7	4	2	28	17	51	7	1	.293	.349
2018	Beloit (MWL)	LoA	.296	123	493	58	146	29	4	2	60	30	117	8	6	.335	.383
Minor League Totals			.276	164	645	81	178	36	8	4	88	47	168	15	7	.325	.375

6 LAZARO ARMENTEROS, OF

Born: May 22, 1999. **B-T:** R-R. **HT:** 6-0. **WT:** 182. **Signed:** Cuba, 2016. **Signed by:** Raul Gomez.

TRACK RECORD: The Athletics were smitten by Armenteros when they scouted him at the 15U World Cup in 2015. They signed the 17-year-old Cuban outfielder a year later for $3 million, even knowing it would trigger penalties that would diminish their ability to sign international free agents during the 2017 and 2018 periods. Armenteros spent his first full season at low Class A Beloit in 2018, missing April while in extended spring training and most of June with a left quad strain.

SCOUTING REPORT: Armenteros' double-plus raw power, selective batting eye and major league body attracted attention in the Midwest League. The A's expect his game power to improve as he learns to stop chasing breaking balls and continues to adapt to U.S. culture. He could develop plus power and an average hit tool thanks to an all-fields hitting approach and knack for hard contact. Armenteros runs well for his size and has strong baserunning instincts, but he is limited to left field by a below-average arm and a body type that projects to slow down as he matures.

THE FUTURE: Armenteros must get to his power regularly to profile as a major league left fielder. He can begin addressing that at high Class A Stockton in 2019.

BA GRADE
50 Risk: High
Hit: 40. Power: 60.
Run: 50. Field: 50.
Arm: 40.

Year	Club (League)	Class	AVG	G	AB	R	H	2B	3B	HR	RBI	BB	SO	SB	CS	OBP	SLG
2017	Athletics (DSL)	R	.167	6	18	6	3	0	0	0	1	3	9	2	2	.385	.167
	Athletics (AZL)	R	.288	41	156	24	45	9	4	4	22	16	48	10	1	.376	.474
2018	Beloit (MWL)	LoA	.277	79	292	43	81	8	2	8	39	36	115	8	6	.374	.401
Minor League Totals			.277	126	466	73	129	17	6	12	62	55	172	20	9	.375	.416

7 JAMESON HANNAH, OF

Born: Aug. 10, 1997. **B-T:** L-L. **HT:** 5-9. **WT:** 185. **Drafted:** Dallas Baptist, 2018 (2nd round). **Signed by:** Chris Reilly.

TRACK RECORD: Hannah parlayed a career year as a Dallas Baptist junior into a second-round selection by the Athletics in 2018. Reliever Vic Black is the only DBU player ever to be drafted higher—by one pick. Hannah hit the ground running at short-season Vermont before being sidelined with a left foot sprain that limited him to just 23 games. He continued to rehab in instructional league, appearing in games only near the end.

SCOUTING REPORT: Hannah packs surprising pull-side punch into a 5-foot-9 frame but is best known for a sweet lefthanded swing paired with plus athleticism and double-plus speed. Scouts express confidence in his ability to hit for average because of his quick, fluid, compact stroke that lives in the hitting zone. Hannah drives the ball to both gaps and keeps infielders honest by dropping down occasional bunts. He is a plus runner out of the box and a 70 underway who is an expert baserunner with an elite success rate on stolen bases. Hannah profiles as a plus center fielder who reads angles well but has an unremarkable arm.

THE FUTURE: Hannah's attributes give him a high floor and make him a probable big leaguer, if only as an extra or semi-regular outfielder. But if he realizes his offensive potential, he can advance quickly and impact games as a table-setter.

BA GRADE
50 Risk: High
Hit: 60. Power: 40.
Run: 70. Field: 60.
Arm: 40.

Year	Club (League)	Class	AVG	G	AB	R	H	2B	3B	HR	RBI	BB	SO	SB	CS	OBP	SLG
2018	Vermont (NYP)	SS	.279	23	86	14	24	4	1	1	10	9	24	6	0	.347	.384
Minor League Totals			.279	23	86	14	24	4	1	1	10	9	24	6	0	.347	.384

8 ELI WHITE, 2B/SS

Born: June 26, 1994. **B-T:** R-R. **HT:** 6-2. **WT:** 175. **Drafted:** Clemson, 2016 (11th round). **Signed by:** Neil Avent.

TRACK RECORD: Drafted in the late rounds out of both high school and as an eligible sophomore, White returned to Clemson for his junior year in 2016 but hit just .272 with limited power. Intrigued by White's athleticism, the Athletics selected him in the 11th round. He climbed to Double-A Midland in 2018 and began turning tools into skills. He led the Texas League in hits (154), on-base percentage (.388) and runs (81), while ranking second in average (.306), third in walks (62) and fifth in doubles (30).

SCOUTING REPORT: White stands as the best pure hitter in Oakland's system and was regarded as the best defensive second baseman in the TL. Plus speed enables him to steal bases and also dabble in center field. The biggest player development challenges facing White are learning to pull the ball and improving his launch angle to hit more home runs. Even if he doesn't, his strong plate discipline and loose swing produce power to the right-center field gap, while an all-fields approach gives him a plus hit tool. A shortstop in college, White tends to be error-prone at the position and profiles best at second base with the requisite range, arm and actions.

BA GRADE
50 Risk: High
Hit: 60. Power: 40.
Run: 60. Field: 60.
Arm: 50.

THE FUTURE: White shares some similarities with Chris Taylor as an athletic college shortstop who runs but isn't quite reliable enough to play shortstop every day. Like Taylor, White looks at home playing second base, third base or outfield, and his bat will determine his ultimate big league role.

Year	Club (League)	Class	AVG	G	AB	R	H	2B	3B	HR	RBI	BB	SO	SB	CS	OBP	SLG
2016	Athletics (AZL)	R	.000	1	3	0	0	0	0	0	0	0	0	0	0	.000	.000
	Vermont (NYP)	SS	.279	64	233	31	65	11	1	2	25	26	65	12	3	.348	.361
2017	Stockton (CAL)	HiA	.270	115	448	71	121	32	6	4	36	41	121	12	5	.342	.395
2018	Midland (TL)	AA	.306	130	504	81	154	30	8	9	55	62	116	18	9	.388	.450
Minor League Totals			.286	310	1188	183	340	73	15	15	116	129	302	42	17	.362	.411

9 JORGE MATEO, SS

Born: June 23, 1995. **B-T:** R-R. **HT:** 6-0. **WT:** 190. **Signed:** Dominican Republic, 2012. **Signed by:** Juan Rosario (Yankees).

TRACK RECORD: Mateo ranked as the Yankees' No. 1 prospect in 2016 and then checked in at No. 3 for the Athletics in 2018 after joining the organization, along with Dustin Fowler and James Kaprielian, in the Sonny Gray trade. After a big season at Double-A in 2017, Mateo appeared close to big league ready. Instead he scuffled through a miserable 2018 season at Triple-A Nashville in which nothing went right.

SCOUTING REPORT: Mateo draws plus grades for his glove, double-plus grades for his arm and some 80 grades for his speed, but he came up short where it counts most—his bat—in the Pacific Coast League. He hit .230 because of poor plate discipline, too many swinging strikes and too many lazy fly balls for a batter with below-average power and a low walk rate. If Mateo can improve his launch angle and swing at more strikes, he has the bat speed and exit velocity to succeed. Even as an elite runner, Mateo stole just 25 bases in Triple-A, calling into question his basestealing instincts. Plus range and quickness gives him a chance to excel at shortstop if he curtail his error rate by improving his throwing accuracy.

BA GRADE
50 Risk: High
Hit: 45. Power: 40.
Run: 80. Field: 60.
Arm: 70.

THE FUTURE: Barring an offensive breakthrough, Mateo's clearest path to Oakland will be as a glove-first shortstop or utility player. He has pro experience at second base and center field that could come into play down the line.

Year	Club (League)	Class	AVG	G	AB	R	H	2B	3B	HR	RBI	BB	SO	SB	CS	OBP	SLG
2016	Tampa (FSL)	HiA	.254	113	464	65	118	16	9	8	47	33	108	36	15	.306	.379
2017	Tampa (FSL)	HiA	.240	69	275	39	66	16	8	4	11	16	79	28	3	.288	.400
	Trenton (EL)	AA	.300	30	120	26	36	9	3	4	26	15	32	11	7	.381	.525
	Midland (TL)	AA	.292	30	137	25	40	5	7	4	20	9	33	13	3	.333	.518
2018	Nashville (PCL)	AAA	.230	131	470	50	108	17	16	3	45	29	139	25	10	.280	.353
Minor League Totals			.261	583	2286	350	597	102	62	33	224	198	569	259	67	.324	.403

10 SHELDON NEUSE, 3B

Born: Dec. 10, 1994. **B-T:** R-R. **HT:** 6-0. **WT:** 195. **Drafted:** Oklahoma, 2016 (2nd round). **Signed by:** Ed Gustafson (Nationals).

TRACK RECORD: Neuse led the Big 12 Conference in slugging in 2016, when the Nationals made him a second-round pick. He advanced slowly in pro ball at first—until the Athletics acquired him in the 2017 deal that sent relievers Sean Doolittle and Ryan Madson to Washington. Neuse rapidly advanced to high Class A and then Double-A after the trade. A strong showing in the 2017 Arizona Fall League and then at big league camp set the stage for Neuse to open 2018 at Triple-A Nashville.

SCOUTING REPORT: Neuse lost all his momentum in the first half of the Pacific Coast League season, when he hit .224 with a 37 percent strikeout rate. He chased too many pitches and generally looked overmatched by the rapid ascension. Neuse reclaimed his season by hitting .321 in the second half with a 24 percent strikeout rate, indicating grit and mental toughness to overcome adversity. He drives the ball to the gaps but doesn't loft the ball well enough to produce big home run totals. He is a well below-average runner with heavy feet, but he is more than capable at third base, where his range is average and his arm plus. He touched 95 mph off the mound as a college closer.

THE FUTURE: The A's have third base locked down with Matt Chapman, necessitating either a position switch or a new organization for Neuse, who has seen time at shortstop and second base in pro ball.

BA GRADE
45 Risk: Medium
Hit: 50. Power: 40. Run: 30. Field: 50. Arm: 60.

Year	Club (League)	Class	AVG	G	AB	R	H	2B	3B	HR	RBI	BB	SO	SB	CS	OBP	SLG
2016	Auburn (NYP)	SS	.230	36	126	16	29	5	3	1	11	13	26	2	2	.305	.341
2017	Hagerstown (SAL)	LoA	.291	77	292	40	85	19	3	9	51	25	66	12	5	.349	.469
	Stockton (CAL)	HiA	.386	22	83	21	32	3	0	7	22	9	25	2	0	.457	.675
	Midland (TL)	AA	.373	18	67	9	25	4	0	0	6	6	21	0	0	.427	.433
2018	Nashville (PCL)	AAA	.263	135	499	48	131	26	3	5	55	32	172	4	1	.304	.357
Minor League Totals			.283	288	1067	134	302	57	9	22	145	85	310	20	8	.337	.415

11 GREG DEICHMANN, OF

BA GRADE
50 Risk: High

Born: May 31, 1995. **B-T:** L-R. **HT:** 6-2. **WT:** 190. **Drafted:** Louisiana State, 2017 (2nd round). **Signed by:** Kelcey Mucker.

TRACK RECORD: The Athletics drafted Deichmann in the second round in 2017 following a powerful year in the Southeastern Conference. He then showed everything scouts could want to see from a corner bat in his pro debut at short-season Vermont. Deichmann played so well in 2018 spring training that the A's repeatedly brought him to big league camp. Everything fell apart after that in a lost 2018 season.

SCOUTING REPORT: Deichmann dealt with right wrist issues all season that inhibited his swing. An early-season strain gave way to a fractured hamate that wasn't resolved until September surgery. Despite his lost time and offensive downturn, Deichmann still produced above-average power at high Class A Stockton and projects to deliver much more in the future. High-end exit velocities and double-plus raw power should translate to 20-25 homers annually, while a compact swing and knowledge of the strike zone should make him a near-average hitter. Deichmann has a classic right field profile with average range, a strong arm and surprising athleticism.

THE FUTURE: A return to health in 2019 should restore the luster to Deichmann's prospect status. If things go according to plan, he should spend ample time in Double-A.

Year	Club (League)	Class	AVG	G	AB	R	H	2B	3B	HR	RBI	BB	SO	SB	CS	OBP	SLG
2017	Vermont (NYP)	SS	.274	46	164	31	45	10	4	8	30	28	40	4	1	.385	.530
2018	Athletics (AZL)	R	.289	11	38	9	11	2	2	1	7	5	8	0	0	.372	.526
	Stockton (CAL)	HiA	.199	47	166	18	33	14	0	6	21	17	63	0	1	.276	.392
Minor League Totals			.242	104	368	58	89	26	6	15	58	50	111	4	2	.336	.467

12 JEREMY EIERMAN, SS

BA GRADE
50 Risk: High

Born: Sept. 10, 1996. **B-T:** R-R. **HT:** 6-1. **WT:** 205. **Drafted:** Missouri State, 2018 (2nd round supplemental). **Signed by:** Al Skorupa.

TRACK RECORD: Eierman cranked 23 home runs as a Missouri State sophomore in 2017 to rank fifth in Division I. For an encore he hit just .287 with 10 homers, on the heels of a poor showing with Team USA. That didn't deter the Athletics, who were intrigued by Eierman's power, speed and defensive chops when they selected him with the first pick of the supplemental second round, making him the third college shortstop drafted in 2018.

SCOUTING REPORT: Eierman nearly totaled his junior home run output with short-season Vermont, hitting eight in 62 games to rank fifth in the New York-Penn League. He shows plus bat speed and records big exit velocities that produce plus raw power, but critics point to a stiff swing that creates holes for pitchers to exploit. Poor pitch recognition in his debut manifested in a high strikeout total and a low batting average. The A's helped him tweak his hand position and improve the rhythm in his swing at instructional league. Eierman has the raw tools to stick at shortstop, with average range and a plus, accurate arm, but some scouts project him to third base based on his stocky body type. He is an average runner out of the batter's box but plus underway and is a heady baserunner who steals bases occasionally.

THE FUTURE: Eierman is a well-rounded shortstop who has demonstrated power, speed and a sound glove in the past. His future role depends on how his hit tool and pitch selection develop.

Year	Club (League)	Class	AVG	G	AB	R	H	2B	3B	HR	RBI	BB	SO	SB	CS	OBP	SLG
2018	Vermont (NYP)	SS	.235	62	247	36	58	8	2	8	26	13	70	10	4	.283	.381
Minor League Totals			.235	62	247	36	58	8	2	8	26	13	70	10	4	.283	.381

13 JAMES KAPRIELIAN, RHP

BA GRADE

50 Risk: Very High

Born: March 2, 1994. **B-T:** R-R. **HT:** 6-4. **WT:** 200. **Drafted:** UCLA, 2015 (1st round). **Signed by:** Bobby DeJardin (Yankees).

TRACK RECORD: Drafted 16th overall by the Yankees in 2015, Kaprielian shined in his pro debut and then again for three starts in 2016 before a strained flexor tendon shut him down. The condition of his elbow didn't improve in 2017, and he had Tommy John surgery in April of that year. His rehab stretched well into 2018 and was interrupted by a July shoulder injury that kept him off the field for a second straight season. While Kaprielian was on the disabled list in 2017, the Yankees traded him and two other players to the Athletics for Sonny Gray.

SCOUTING REPORT: Kaprielian returned to the mound at the tail end of instructional league in 2018, but after missing nearly three entire seasons he understandably looked rusty. During his lengthy rehab he lowered his arm slot slightly to ease stress on arm. Kaprielian when last healthy sat in the mid 90s and peaked at 97 mph while showing feel for spin. His slider and curveball both flashed plus, and his changeup showed average potential with sinking action, giving him a potential four-pitch repertoire. He draws praise for his competitive makeup but not his high-stress delivery.

THE FUTURE: At his peak Kaprielian showed a double-plus fastball with two plus breaking pitches, but after a three-year layoff—and just 29 pro innings to his name—it's impossible to forecast what's in store for 2019.

Year	Club (League)	Class	W	L	ERA	G	GS	CG	SV	IP	H	HR	BB	SO	K/9	WHIP	AVG
2016	Tampa (FSL)	HiA	2	1	1.50	3	3	0	0	18	8	1	3	22	11.0	0.61	.136
2017	Did not play—Injured																
2018	Did not play—Injured																
Minor League Totals			2	2	2.45	8	6	0	0	29	18	1	7	36	11.0	0.85	.176

14 GRANT HOLMES, RHP

BA GRADE

50 Risk: Very High

Born: March 22, 1996. **B-T:** L-R. **HT:** 6-1. **WT:** 215. **Drafted:** HS—Conway, S.C., 2014 (1st round). **Signed by:** Lon Joyce (Dodgers).

TRACK RECORD: The Dodgers drafted Holmes 22nd overall in 2014 and developed him up to high Class A in 2016 before trading him with two other pitching prospects to the Athletics for Rich Hill and Josh Reddick. Holmes gathered momentum at Double-A Midland in 2017, when he led the Texas League with 150 strikeouts and addressed his platoon-split issue with lefthanded batters. A rotator cuff injury cost him all but two starts in 2018, however, and clouded his outlook for 2019.

SCOUTING REPORT: Holmes returned to the mound in 2018 to make one start for high Class A Stockton in the California League playoffs. The A's brought him to instructional league to ready for an assignment to the Arizona Fall League, but that plan was scuttled when he had a setback after one appearance. Holmes' high-spin fastball plays at 92-94 mph up in the zone and peaks at 96. His power curveball draws consistent plus grades from scouts, and the cutter he developed in 2017 shows promise and average potential. He never has shown much feel for a changeup. Below-average control and imprecise fastball command have long hinted at a future in the bullpen.

THE FUTURE: Holmes showed no durability concerns prior to his 2018 shoulder injury, so he could continue to develop as a starter when he returns. Now that Holmes is a member of the 40-man roster, he could be in line for spot starts in 2019 if he is healthy and effective.

Year	Club (League)	Class	W	L	ERA	G	GS	CG	SV	IP	H	HR	BB	SO	K/9	WHIP	AVG
2016	R. Cucamonga (CAL)	HiA	8	4	4.02	20	18	0	1	105	103	6	43	100	8.5	1.39	.254
	Stockton (CAL)	HiA	3	3	6.91	6	5	0	0	29	44	4	10	24	7.5	1.88	.355
2017	Midland (TL)	AA	11	12	4.49	29	24	0	0	148	149	15	61	150	9.1	1.42	.262
2018	Stockton (CAL)	HiA	0	0	4.50	2	2	0	0	6	4	1	2	8	12.0	1.00	.174
Minor League Totals			30	26	4.13	92	83	0	1	440	425	35	183	457	9.3	1.38	.254

15 PARKER DUNSHEE, RHP

BA GRADE

45 Risk: High

Born: Feb. 12, 1995. **B-T:** R-R. **HT:** 6-1. **WT:** 205. **Drafted:** Wake Forest, 2017 (7th round). **Signed by:** Neil Avent.

TRACK RECORD: Following a four-year college career at Wake Forest, Dunshee tossed 38.1 scoreless innings at short-season Vermont in his pro debut. He continued to limit runs in 2018, when he ranked 15th in the minors with a 2.33 ERA while spending half the season at Double-A Midland.

SCOUTING REPORT: Dunshee placed eighth in the minors with 163 strikeouts, but he doesn't have a power pitcher's physique or repertoire. He pitches at 87-90 mph and bumps 92 while dotting the black on both sides of the plate. Sometimes he cuts his average fastball to his glove side to get in on lefthanded batters to avoid platoon-split damage. He elevates his fastball as well as any pitcher in the system with late hop on the pitch. Dunshee relies on commanding his fastball and cutter but throws a well-rounded arsenal of average pitches that includes a roundhouse curveball he can drop for strikes, a slider he can manipulate as either short or sweeping and a developing changeup he sells with arm speed.

THE FUTURE: The A's believe they found a seventh-round gem in Dunshee, who has the pitchability to reach the majors in a swingman role. His big league ETA is late 2019 or 2020.

Year	Club (League)	Class	W	L	ERA	G	GS	CG	SV	IP	H	HR	BB	SO	K/9	WHIP	AVG
2017	Athletics (AZL)	R	0	0	13.50	1	0	0	0	2	5	1	0	3	13.5	2.50	.455
	Vermont (NYP)	SS	1	0	0.00	12	9	0	0	38	15	0	8	45	10.6	0.60	.119
2018	Stockton (CAL)	HiA	6	2	2.70	12	10	0	0	70	61	7	17	82	10.5	1.11	.238
	Midland (TL)	AA	7	4	2.01	12	12	0	0	81	59	5	14	81	9.0	0.90	.205
Minor League Totals			14	6	1.98	37	31	0	0	191	140	13	39	211	9.9	0.94	.206

16 BRIAN HOWARD, RHP

BA GRADE

45 Risk: High

Born: April 25, 1995. **B-T:** R-R. **HT:** 6-9. **WT:** 185. **Drafted:** Texas Christian, 2017 (8th round). **Signed by:** Chris Reilly.

TRACK RECORD: Howard used his 6-foot-9 height to his advantage in four years at Texas Christian—he struck out a batter per inning and recorded a 1.11 WHIP—before signing with the Athletics as an eighth-round senior in 2017. He advanced to Double-A Midland for the second half of 2018 and ranked among the organization's leaders for ERA (2.91) and strikeouts (140).

SCOUTING REPORT: Howard mixes four average pitches and throws strikes, which has been too much for minor league hitters to handle. He generates plus plane and angle on his 89-92 mph two-seam fastball that sits 91 and peaks at 93. He changes eye levels and upsets opponents' timing with a slow 12-to-6 curveball in the low 70s that is his swing-and-miss weapon. He pairs his curve with a sweepy slider in the high 70s. Howard's above-average mid-80s cutter was a go-to pitch in college and he still uses it to good effect to his glove side. His average changeup shows fade and separation. He could add velocity if he fills out his ultra-lean frame.

THE FUTURE: Howard's repertoire allows him to operate at various velocity registers, while his control forces batters to be ready for any pitch in any count. He might not have a plus pitch in his repertoire, but his extreme height and pitching style share similarities with Doug Fister. He will be a candidate to pick up major league starts as a No. 5 type.

Year	Club (League)	Class	W	L	ERA	G	GS	CG	SV	IP	H	HR	BB	SO	K/9	WHIP	AVG
2017	Vermont (NYP)	SS	2	1	1.15	11	6	0	1	31	22	0	1	29	8.3	0.73	.200
2018	Stockton (CAL)	HiA	7	3	2.38	12	11	0	0	72	53	9	14	77	9.6	0.93	.201
	Midland (TL)	AA	4	4	3.48	12	12	0	0	67	65	7	23	63	8.4	1.31	.249
Minor League Totals			13	8	2.58	35	29	0	1	171	140	16	38	169	8.9	1.04	.220

17 MARCOS BRITO, 2B

BA GRADE

50 Risk: Extreme

Born: March 6, 2000. **B-T:** B-R. **HT:** 6-0. **WT:** 165. **Signed:** Dominican Republic, 2016. **Signed by:** Diego Bordas.

TRACK RECORD: The Athletics shot past their international bonus pool allotment with their 2016 signing class, which was headlined by Cubans Lazaro Armenteros and Norge Ruiz. Brito signed for $1.1 million as part of Oakland's spending spree and has spent his brief pro career as one of the youngest players in his leagues. He was one of seven 18-year-old regular position players in the short-season New York-Penn League in 2018, and his youth showed with a .241/.325/.288 batting line.

SCOUTING REPORT: A wiry switch-hitter, Brito has readily apparent feel for the strike zone and for the barrel. He probably won't ever develop more than average power, but he can handle the bat and is disciplined enough to take borderline pitches for balls. The ball comes off his bat better from the left side, and his all-fields approach gives him a shot to hit for average with gap power. Brito is an athletic middle infielder and plus runner who looks sharp at second base with plus range and an above-average arm. He recorded the most assists (134) and turned the most double plays (29) among NYPL second basemen.

THE FUTURE: Brito has several development years ahead of him, but his high-energy style and high skill level at such a young age indicate his major league potential. If he doesn't stick as a regular second baseman, his speed, defensive fluidity and switch-hitting bat would be interesting in a utility role.

Year	Club (League)	Class	AVG	G	AB	R	H	2B	3B	HR	RBI	BB	SO	SB	CS	OBP	SLG
2017	Athletics (DSL)	R	.178	14	45	3	8	1	0	0	8	13	8	5	0	.339	.200
	Athletics (AZL)	R	.234	44	171	30	40	4	2	1	17	21	42	4	1	.320	.298
2018	Vermont (NYP)	SS	.241	54	212	29	51	5	1	1	20	27	50	7	6	.325	.288
Minor League Totals			.231	112	428	62	99	10	3	2	45	61	100	16	7	.325	.283

18 DAULTON JEFFERIES, RHP

BA GRADE
50 Risk: Extreme

Born: Aug. 2, 1995. **B-T:** L-R. **HT:** 6-0. **WT:** 180. **Drafted:** California, 2016 (1st round supplemental). **Signed by:** Jermaine Clark.

TRACK RECORD: Dating back to his college days at California, Jefferies has typically been either effective or injured. A shoulder injury as a junior in 2016 cost him mound time but not standing in the draft—the Athletics took him 37th overall. Jefferies hasn't returned to game action since having Tommy John surgery in April 2017, essentially missing two complete seasons and logging just 20 pro innings in three years.

SCOUTING REPORT: Teams overlooked Jefferies' 6-foot stature in the draft because of his high-level athleticism and track record with Team USA, and had he stayed healthy as a junior he could have been one of the top college pitchers selected. That athleticism helps him find the strike zone with three pitches. His quick arm produced 90-92 mph fastballs with a peak velocity of 96 mph when he was healthy. Jefferies' changeup bottoms out as it nears the plate, and opponents look foolish swinging at his arm speed. It can be a 70-grade pitch. His slider grades as below-average with more horizontal break than vertical. Control is a strong suit for Jefferies, but he used his rehab time to further improve his direction to the plate.

THE FUTURE: Jefferies and James Kaprielian, former Pacific-12 Conference rivals, both had Tommy John around the same time and have spent 2017 and 2018 rehabbing together. They could both see time at Double-A Midland in 2019—health permitting.

Year	Club (League)	Class	W	L	ERA	G	GS	CG	SV	IP	H	HR	BB	SO	K/9	WHIP	AVG
2016	Athletics (AZL)	R	0	0	2.38	5	5	0	0	11	11	0	2	17	13.5	1.15	.262
2017	Stockton (CAL)	HiA	0	0	2.57	2	1	0	0	7	7	0	1	6	7.7	1.14	.241
2018	Athletics (AZL)	R	0	0	0.00	1	1	0	0	2	1	0	0	5	22.5	0.50	.143
Minor League Totals			0	0	2.21	8	7	0	0	20	19	0	3	28	12.4	1.08	.244

19 ALFONSO RIVAS, 1B

BA GRADE
50 Risk: Extreme

Born: Sept. 13, 1996. **B-T:** L-L. **HT:** 6-0. **WT:** 180. **Drafted:** Arizona, 2018 (4th round). **Signed by:** Scott Cousins.

TRACK RECORD: Rivas showcased strong plate discipline and hit .326 in three years at Arizona before the Athletics drafted him in the fourth round in 2018. In his pro debut he ranked fourth in the short-season New York-Penn League in walks (36) and on-base percentage (.397).

SCOUTING REPORT: Rivas homered only once in his pro debut and topped out at seven in a season in college, so hitting for power is the biggest question he faces as a pro. The A's are optimistic he can develop 15-homer power with 30-plus doubles based on his smooth lefthanded swing and advanced strike-zone knowledge. A below-average runner, Rivas would be stretched in left field, but that won't be necessary if his bat develops. That's because he is a sharp defensive first baseman with good hands and plus potential.

THE FUTURE: The A's express confidence in Rivas reaching his ceiling as a plus hitter with roughly average power. If everything comes together, he could move quickly.

Year	Club (League)	Class	AVG	G	AB	R	H	2B	3B	HR	RBI	BB	SO	SB	CS	OBP	SLG
2018	Vermont (NYP)	SS	.285	61	214	33	61	16	1	1	28	36	44	7	4	.397	.383
Minor League Totals			.285	61	214	33	61	16	1	1	28	36	44	7	4	.397	.383

20 SKYE BOLT, OF

BA GRADE

45 Risk: High

Born: Jan. 15, 1994. **B-T:** B-R. **HT:** 6-3. **WT:** 190. **Drafted:** North Carolina, 2015 (4th round). **Signed by:** Neil Avent.

TRACK RECORD: Projection more than production got Bolt drafted in the fourth round in 2015 after a spotty career at North Carolina. Three years in pro ball had produced much the same result until Bolt began turning tools into skills in 2018 at high Class A Stockton and then Double-A Midland. He hit 19 home runs and stole 19 bases before showing continued power and speed in the Arizona Fall League.
SCOUTING REPORT: Bolt built his reputation as an amateur in part because of his prototypical frame and hints of five-tool ability, even as scouts questioned his instincts for the game. A switch-hitter with a line-drive swing, Bolt reduced his strikeout rate in 2018 and hit with more authority, particularly batting lefthanded. The increased power is crucial for a player with a fringe-average hit tool, albeit with strong plate discipline. Bolt is the best athlete in the system and also its best defensive outfielder. He is a plus center fielder with a strong, accurate arm. He is an above-average runner but not a prolific basestealer.
THE FUTURE: If Bolt can build on his 2018 success as he returns to the Texas League in 2019, then he could become a useful outfield piece in the big leagues.

Year	Club (League)	Class	AVG	G	AB	R	H	2B	3B	HR	RBI	BB	SO	SB	CS	OBP	SLG
2016	Beloit (MWL)	LoA	.231	101	342	34	79	20	2	5	37	42	88	10	5	.318	.345
2017	Stockton (CAL)	HiA	.243	114	432	76	105	24	7	15	66	53	134	9	8	.327	.435
2018	Stockton (CAL)	HiA	.266	46	169	28	45	8	4	9	32	31	47	9	3	.382	.521
	Midland (TL)	AA	.256	78	285	41	73	18	3	10	37	27	75	10	1	.325	.446
Minor League Totals			.245	391	1409	205	345	80	18	43	191	177	388	40	18	.331	.419

21 LUIS BARRERA, OF

BA GRADE

45 Risk: High

Born: Nov. 15, 1995. **B-T:** L-L. **HT:** 6-0. **WT:** 180. **Signed:** Dominican Republic, 2012. **Signed by:** Raymond Abreu.

TRACK RECORD: The Athletics signed Barrera for $450,000 in 2012. At the time, he was a slender 16-year-old who required two years in the Dominican Summer League before he was ready for the Rookie-level Arizona League in 2015. He has steadily climbed the ladder ever since and began to earn acclaim in 2018, when he hit .297 with 23 stolen bases and finished the season at Double-A Midland.
SCOUTING REPORT: Barrera has matured physically in recent seasons but hasn't strayed from his roots. He is a line-drive hitter who runs well and applies his plus speed in center field and on the bases, where he is a strong baserunner. He is selective enough to make pitchers throw him strikes. Barrera shows hints of power in batting practice but a low launch angle translates to well below-average power in games. As he has grown stronger, he is finding the gaps more frequently, aided by his double-plus speed. Barrera reads the ball off the bat in center field and always seems to get a good jump. He has an average arm.
THE FUTURE: As a lefthanded-hitting center fielder with speed—but without a projected impact bat—Barrera's future role will depend a lot on just how well his speed and defense play.

Year	Club (League)	Class	AVG	G	AB	R	H	2B	3B	HR	RBI	BB	SO	SB	CS	OBP	SLG
2016	Vermont (NYP)	SS	.321	41	159	26	51	10	0	2	18	16	29	5	2	.379	.421
	Beloit (MWL)	LoA	.286	19	70	8	20	4	2	1	4	4	17	3	1	.320	.443
2017	Beloit (MWL)	LoA	.277	73	278	41	77	13	7	3	22	16	61	13	7	.320	.406
	Stockton (CAL)	HiA	.228	35	114	15	26	2	0	4	16	8	25	3	1	.276	.351
2018	Stockton (CAL)	HiA	.284	88	313	51	89	18	7	3	46	32	63	10	4	.354	.415
	Midland (TL)	AA	.328	36	131	24	43	8	4	0	18	9	18	13	3	.378	.450
Minor League Totals			.273	384	1352	199	369	63	26	17	159	120	273	53	21	.334	.396

22 KEVIN MERRELL, SS

BA GRADE

45 Risk: High

Born: Dec. 14, 1995. **B-T:** L-R. **HT:** 6-1. **WT:** 180. **Drafted:** South Florida, 2017 (1st round supplemental). **Signed by:** Trevor Schaffer.

TRACK RECORD: Merrell's 80-grade speed has played as advertised in pro ball, but he didn't get to show it off as much as he would have liked at high Class A Stockton in 2018. That's because he missed most of the second half with a second-degree sprain of his left elbow and then had a concussion scare while rehabbing in Arizona. Merrell didn't hit much when healthy. He dealt with nagging injuries and batted just .267 with 13 extra-base hits and five steals in 62 games in the California League.
SCOUTING REPORT: Merrell hit .384 as a South Florida junior and then .320 in his pro debut at short-season Vermont, and scouts who like him give him a future average hit tool and below-average power. Reaching his ceiling will require Merrell to improve his plate discipline and his bat path so that he can hit to the middle of the field rather than pulling everything. He tends to put a lot of topspin on the ball because of his hand position at contact, hampering his ability to drive the ball. Merrell collects his share

of infield hits, though his basestealing aggressiveness and technique need work. He played left field and second base in college but has made strides at shortstop in pro ball to project as average. He has improved his footwork and aggressiveness to the ball, while his arm grades as above-average.

THE FUTURE: Merrell is something of a throwback player, and if he hits he could develop into a big league table-setter, perhaps in a multi-positional role that would include center field and middle infield.

Year	Club (League)	Class	AVG	G	AB	R	H	2B	3B	HR	RBI	BB	SO	SB	CS	OBP	SLG
2017	Vermont (NYP)	SS	.320	31	125	27	40	5	1	2	9	9	22	10	3	.362	.424
2018	Stockton (CAL)	HiA	.267	62	270	38	72	10	3	0	24	15	66	5	4	.308	.326
	Athletics (AZL)	R	.600	4	10	3	6	0	2	0	1	1	1	2	1	.636	1.000
	Vermont (NYP)	SS	.500	5	16	4	8	0	1	0	0	3	3	0	0	.579	.625
Minor League Totals			.299	102	421	72	126	15	7	2	34	28	92	17	8	.344	.382

23 NICK ALLEN, SS

BA GRADE

45 Risk: High

Born: Oct. 8, 1998. **B-T:** R-R. **HT:** 5-9. **WT:** 155. **Drafted:** HS—San Diego, 2017 (3rd round). **Signed by:** Anthony Aloisi.

TRACK RECORD: Were he a few inches taller than his listed 5-foot-9, Allen probably would have been a first-round pick in 2017 based on his defensive prowess. Instead he fell to the Athletics in the third round but still signed for $2 million, which is back-of-the-first-round money. Allen has been pushed aggressively in pro ball and spent his first full season at low Class A Beloit. He didn't hit much but did lead Midwest League shortstops in assists (315) and fielding percentage (.965).

SCOUTING REPORT: Allen is a plus defender with a preternatural feel for taking the right angle to the ball. His above-average arm is enhanced by a quick release and pinpoint accuracy to the degree that he rarely makes throwing errors. He turns in plus run times to first base and is a quality baserunner who swiped 24 bags in the MWL. Allen has hit .242 with one home run in his first two pro seasons, though his fortune improved late in 2018 with Beloit. He hit .330/.368/.423 in his final 24 games. As an amateur, Allen could drive the ball with aluminum bats but hasn't had the same success with wood. The A's worked with him in instructional league to improve his strike-zone awareness, hunt his pitch and not hit so many balls in the air for lazy fly outs.

THE FUTURE: Allen has work to do to develop an average major league bat, but he has good hand-eye coordination, takes competitive at-bats and could grow into more power as he physically matures.

Year	Club (League)	Class	AVG	G	AB	R	H	2B	3B	HR	RBI	BB	SO	SB	CS	OBP	SLG
2017	Athletics (AZL)	R	.254	35	138	26	35	3	2	1	14	13	28	7	3	.322	.326
2018	Beloit (MWL)	LoA	.239	121	460	51	110	17	6	0	34	34	85	24	8	.301	.302
Minor League Totals			.242	156	598	77	145	20	8	1	48	47	113	31	11	.306	.308

24 TYLER RAMIREZ, OF

BA GRADE

45 Risk: High

Born: Feb. 21, 1995. **B-T:** L-L. **HT:** 5-9. **WT:** 185. **Drafted:** North Carolina, 2016 (7th round). **Signed by:** Neil Avent.

TRACK RECORD: Ramirez hit .301 in three years at North Carolina and has showcased his sweet lefthanded swing in the Athletics' system since turning pro. In a full season at Double-A Midland in 2018 he ranked second in the Texas League in doubles (35), third in walks (62) and fifth in on-base percentage (.370). He also placed third in strikeouts (148), indicating that contact rate is his biggest area for improvement.

SCOUTING REPORT: The A's view Ramirez as a potential David DeJesus type of player based on his lefthanded bat, on-base-oriented approach and physical stature. Ramirez has plus potential as a hitter based on his short, direct swing path and ability to drive the ball line to line. His below-average power won't produce many home runs, but his sneaky solid-average speed allows him to leg out doubles and triples. Ramirez is patient and will wait for his pitch, and he hangs in against lefthanders. An instinctive defender in left field, he can hold his own in center with average range and an average, accurate arm.

THE FUTURE: Ramirez is ready for Triple-A, but as a corner player without big power, he faces an uphill climb to a regular big league role. In the right situation, his OBP skills could make him attractive as a table-setter.

Year	Club (League)	Class	AVG	G	AB	R	H	2B	3B	HR	RBI	BB	SO	SB	CS	OBP	SLG
2016	Athletics (AZL)	R	.286	8	28	5	8	3	2	0	8	1	10	1	0	.310	.536
	Vermont (NYP)	SS	.220	48	150	22	33	8	1	2	15	19	39	5	0	.324	.327
2017	Stockton (CAL)	HiA	.301	76	279	51	84	12	2	7	39	45	80	5	2	.399	.434
	Midland (TL)	AA	.308	58	208	29	64	11	1	4	24	28	53	3	3	.395	.428
2018	Midland (TL)	AA	.287	134	512	73	147	35	4	10	79	62	148	5	4	.370	.430
Minor League Totals			.285	324	1177	180	336	69	10	23	165	155	330	19	9	.374	.420

25 GUS VARLAND, RHP

BA GRADE
45 Risk: High

Born: Nov. 6, 1996. **B-T:** L-R. **HT:** 6-1. **WT:** 205. **Drafted:** Concordia-St. Paul (Minn.), 2018 (14th round). **Signed by:** Derek Lee.

TRACK RECORD: Varland sliced through Division II competition as a junior, drawing notice from upper Midwest scouts with a 1.04 ERA and 11.8 strikeouts per nine innings. He pitched his way to low Class A Beloit in his pro debut and recorded an 0.95 ERA with 50 strikeouts and eight walks in 38 innings.

SCOUTING REPORT: Varland's stuff is better than his draft round would indicate. He pitched at 93 mph in his debut and maxed out near 96 and backed it up with crisp breaking stuff and an aggressive pitching style. His fastball features explosive life up in the zone thanks to a high spin rate. His slider has above-average potential and nice tilt in the mid-80s, while his fringe curveball gives him the element of surprise in the high 70s. Varland went to instructional league to develop his changeup and found a grip he likes.

THE FUTURE: Varland was the breakout star of Oakland's 2018 draft and could reach Double-A by the end of his first full season. Without a knockout pitch, he profiles more as a swingman starter or reliever.

Year	Club (League)	Class	W	L	ERA	G	GS	CG	SV	IP	H	HR	BB	SO	K/9	WHIP	AVG
2018	Athletics (AZL)	R	0	0	0.00	1	1	0	0	1	1	0	1	0	0.0	2.00	.333
	Vermont (NYP)	SS	0	1	1.02	7	5	0	0	18	14	0	4	22	11.2	1.02	.215
	Beloit (MWL)	LoA	0	0	0.93	5	5	0	0	19	8	1	3	28	13.0	0.57	.123
Minor League Totals			0	1	0.95	13	11	0	0	38	23	1	8	50	11.8	0.82	.173

26 J.B. WENDELKEN, RHP

BA GRADE
40 Risk: Medium

Born: March 24, 1993. **B-T:** R-R. **HT:** 6-0. **WT:** 220. **Drafted:** Middle Georgia JC, 2012 (13th round). **Signed by:** Tim Hyers (Red Sox).

TRACK RECORD: Drafted by the Red Sox in 2012, Wendelken has been around long enough to be traded for two players who are now out of baseball: Jake Peavy and Brett Lawrie. Wendelken made his big league debut with Oakland in 2016, got hammered and then had Tommy John surgery that fall.

SCOUTING REPORT: The key to Wendelken's comeback was reworking his delivery and arm swing with minor league pitching coordinator Gil Patterson and rehab pitching coordinator Craig Lefferts. As a result, Wendelken added a tick of velocity and rounded out his arsenal. He topped out at 98 mph and averaged 95 in the big leagues and backed up his fastball with a plus breaking ball and now-usable change-up. His fastball gets swings and misses in the zone and his curveball induces chases in and out of the zone.

THE FUTURE: In his return to Oakland, Wendelken allowed one run in 17 innings and recorded an 0.78 WHIP, hinting at his potential to pitch high-leverage relief innings in 2019.

Year	Club (League)	Class	W	L	ERA	G	GS	CG	SV	IP	H	HR	BB	SO	K/9	WHIP	AVG
2016	Nashville (PCL)	AAA	1	4	4.11	39	0	0	5	46	48	5	26	65	12.7	1.61	.259
	Oakland (AL)	MAJ	0	0	9.95	8	0	0	0	13	18	3	9	12	8.5	2.13	.327
2017	Did not play—Injured																
2018	Midland (TL)	AA	0	1	3.38	11	0	0	3	13	11	3	10	23	15.5	1.58	.220
	Nashville (PCL)	AAA	1	1	2.80	22	1	0	3	35	29	2	10	52	13.2	1.10	.223
	Oakland (AL)	MAJ	0	0	0.54	13	0	0	0	17	8	1	5	14	7.6	0.78	.140
Major League Totals			0	0	4.60	21	0	0	0	29	26	4	14	26	8.0	1.36	.232
Minor League Totals			19	20	3.96	187	28	1	30	400	409	36	126	444	10.0	1.34	.261

27 BRADY FEIGL, RHP

BA GRADE
45 Risk: High

Born: Nov. 27, 1995. **B-T:** R-R. **HT:** 6-5. **WT:** 230. **Drafted:** Mississippi, 2018 (5th round). **Signed by:** Kelcey Mucker.

TRACK RECORD: Drafted late in 2017, Feigl returned to Mississippi as a redshirt junior in 2018 and spent his first full college season in the rotation. He missed bats while taking every turn, and that trend continued in a pro debut in which he struck out 34 in 26 innings.

SCOUTING REPORT: The Athletics like the angle on Feigl's fastball, which ranges from 90-93 mph and scraped 94 in pro ball. The 6-foot-5 righty generates late movement that makes him hard for opponents to barrel. Feigl's power curveball in the low 80s is his go-to out pitch and works in concert with his fastball. Deception in his delivery adds to his overall effectiveness. Feigl throws a changeup but it's a third pitch.

THE FUTURE: With extensive bullpen time in college, Feigl could jump on a fast track if he assumes that role as a pro. For now, he will continue developing as a starter in 2019.

Year	Club (League)	Class	W	L	ERA	G	GS	CG	SV	IP	H	HR	BB	SO	K/9	WHIP	AVG
2018	Vermont (NYP)	SS	1	1	1.35	8	5	0	0	20	6	0	7	27	12.2	0.65	.091
	Beloit (MWL)	LoA	0	1	3.00	3	3	0	0	6	5	1	1	7	10.5	1.00	.217
Minor League Totals			1	2	1.73	11	8	0	0	26	11	1	8	34	11.8	0.73	.124

28 JORDAN DIAZ, 3B

Born: Aug. 13, 2000. **B-T:** R-R. **HT:** 5-10. **WT:** 175. **Signed:** Colombia, 2016.
Signed by: Jose Quintero.

TRACK RECORD: The Athletics signed Diaz for $275,000 out of Colombia on the strength of his bat. In the Rookie-level Arizona League in 2018, he showcased quality bat-to-ball skills and strike-zone awareness by hitting .277 with a .371 on-base percentage with nearly as many walks (19) as strikeouts (22).

SCOUTING REPORT: Diaz draws attention for his short righthanded swing and line-drive approach with gap power. He hits to all fields and frequently barrels balls for resounding hits. Scouts are mixed on Diaz's power potential because his 5-foot-10 frame is quickly maxing out and offers little in the way of projection. Diaz throws well at third base and has good hands, but his actions can be stiff at times.

THE FUTURE: Diaz does many things well in the batter's box, and his bat could carry him up the ladder.

Year	Club (League)	Class	AVG	G	AB	R	H	2B	3B	HR	RBI	BB	SO	SB	CS	OBP	SLG
2017	Athletics (AZL)	R	.185	8	27	2	5	0	0	0	2	0	4	1	0	.179	.185
	Athletics (DSL)	R	.255	42	137	14	35	7	0	0	18	6	22	2	0	.295	.307
2018	Athletics (AZL)	R	.277	48	159	23	44	11	2	1	25	19	22	0	2	.371	.390
Minor League Totals			.260	98	323	39	84	18	2	1	45	25	48	3	2	.325	.337

29 DAIRON BLANCO, OF

Born: April 26, 1993. **B-T:** R-R. **HT:** 6-0. **WT:** 170. **Signed:** Cuba, 2017.
Signed by: Raymond Abreu.

TRACK RECORD: Blanco was regarded as Cuba's fastest player when he defected to the Dominican Republic. He came to terms with the Athletics in December 2017. Because of a two-year layoff from game action, Blanco began his U.S. career at high Class A Stockton in 2018 even though he turned 25 in April.

SCOUTING REPORT: Blanco started slowly in the California League but redeemed his season. He hit .323/.360/.462 in his final 48 games with Stockton, appearing on track for a promotion to Double-A before a left hamate injury sidelined him for the season on July 4. He had surgery in August. Blanco is a top-of-the-scale runner who steals bases aggressively and efficiently. He will never have more than fringe power because he doesn't pull the ball well, but he has strength and an all-fields hitting approach, which could equate to a plus hit tool. He has plus range and below-average arm to excel in left field.

THE FUTURE: Blanco must keep developing his bat to profile as a major leaguer, but even in the absence of more power he could fill an extra outfielder role. Double-A is the next test.

Year	Club (League)	Class	AVG	G	AB	R	H	2B	3B	HR	RBI	BB	SO	SB	CS	OBP	SLG
2016	Did not play																
2017	Did not play																
2018	Stockton (CAL)	HiA	.291	82	313	39	91	13	10	1	37	25	66	22	2	.342	.406
Minor League Totals			.291	82	313	39	91	13	10	1	37	25	66	22	2	.342	.406

30 JONAH HEIM, C

Born: June 27, 1995. **B-T:** B-R. **HT:** 6-4. **WT:** 225. **Drafted:** HS—Amherst, N.Y., 2013 (4th round). **Signed by:** Kirk Fredriksson (Orioles).

TRACK RECORD: Heim reached Double-A in the second half of 2018. While he scuffled in the Texas League, it marked key progress for the switch-hitting catcher drafted by the Orioles in the fourth round in 2013 out of a suburban Buffalo high school. Baltimore traded Heim to the Rays for Steve Pearce in 2016, then Tampa Bay traded him to the Athletics for Joey Wendle after the 2017 season.

SCOUTING REPORT: In his first season in the Oakland system, Heim threw out 33 percent of basestealers with average arm strength but above-average pop times. He receives and blocks well with an ease of operation behind the plate and feel for calling a game. Heim makes steady contact and works the middle of the field. He has the raw power for double-digit home runs with a leveraged, strength-oriented swing.

THE FUTURE: Scouts who like Heim see him developing into a second-division catcher or backup.

Year	Club (League)	Class	AVG	G	AB	R	H	2B	3B	HR	RBI	BB	SO	SB	CS	OBP	SLG
2016	Frederick (CAR)	HiA	.216	88	291	30	63	14	1	7	30	33	51	2	0	.300	.344
	Charlotte, FL (FSL)	HiA	.222	14	45	4	10	1	0	1	3	2	11	0	0	.255	.311
2017	Bowling Green (MWL)	LoA	.268	77	291	45	78	17	1	9	53	27	57	0	1	.327	.426
	Charlotte, FL (FSL)	HiA	.218	16	55	3	12	3	0	0	8	3	17	1	0	.262	.273
2018	Stockton (CAL)	HiA	.292	80	312	41	91	21	1	7	49	29	60	3	1	.353	.433
	Midland (TL)	AA	.182	39	137	16	25	4	0	1	11	10	22	0	0	.238	.234
Minor League Totals			.239	432	1515	172	362	85	4	27	183	129	281	10	3	.300	.354

Philadelphia Phillies

BY BEN BADLER

After beating Arizona on Aug. 7, the Phillies were 64-49 and holding a 1.5 game lead over the Braves for first place in the National League East. By the end of August, the Phillies dropped to second place, and after going 8-20 in September, the Phillies finished 80-82, which was good for a sixth straight season under .500.

In 2019, that should change. The rebuild in Philadelphia isn't over, but it would be a major disappointment if the Phillies did not reach the playoffs this season.

The upgrades have already begun. The Phillies traded shortstop J.P. Crawford—their No. 1 prospect the previous four seasons—to Seattle to get Jean Segura, who has hit a combined .308/.353/.449 the last three seasons and averaged 4.3 WAR per season, according to Baseball-Reference.com. The Phillies included Carlos Santana in that trade, allowing them to shift Rhys Hoskins back to his natural position at first base, while also adding veteran outfielder Andrew McCutchen as a free agent.

Those additions should help a team that ranked 22nd in baseball in runs scored in 2018. The lineup won't get much help from the farm system this year, but some of the biggest offensive boosts could come through the development of homegrown players in their mid-20s like Nick Williams, Scott Kingery, Jorge Alfaro and Maikel Franco.

The farm system should provide more support for the pitching staff. The strength of Philadelphia's minor league system is its pitching.

The best prospect is Sixto Sanchez, an electric righthander who missed most of 2018 due to injury but has the upside to be a No. 1 starter. Sanchez and No. 4 prospect, righthander Adonis Medina, should both start in Double-A, giving them an opportunity to help later in 2019. Righthander Enyel de los Santos and lefthanders JoJo Romero and Ranger Suarez should all get major league starts in 2019 to bolster the back of the big league team's rotation.

The depth of pitching the Phillies have accumulated sticks out. The team's Latin American scouts signed Sanchez, Medina and Suarez each for under $100,000, just as they did with Mauricio Llovera and Edgar Garcia. Their pitching finds haven't been limited to Latin America. Righthander Spencer Howard, their second-round pick in 2017, saw his stuff and stock increase in the second half and is a breakout candidate for 2019. Lefthanders Will Stewart, Kyle Dohy and Zach Warren all look like promising picks after the 10th round.

The Phillies are lighter in prospects who project to open 2019 at the upper levels. Some of that is

Rookie catcher Jorge Alfaro showed off a strong arm and nice power for a backstop.

RICH SCHULTZ/GETTY IMAGES

PROJECTED 2022 LINEUP

Catcher	Jorge Alfaro (29)
First Base	Rhys Hoskins (29)
Second Base	Scott Kingery (28)
Third Base	Alec Bohm (25)
Shortstop	Jean Segura (32)
Left Field	Adam Haseley (26)
Center Field	Odubel Herrera (30)
Right Field	Nick Williams (28)
No. 1 Starter	Aaron Nola (29)
No. 2 Starter	Sixto Sanchez (23)
No. 3 Starter	Jake Arrieta (36)
No. 4 Starter	Adonis Medina (25)
No. 5 Starter	Vince Velasquez (30)
Closer	Seranthony Dominguez (27)

the recent wave of hitters the Phillies graduated from the farm system, but the disappointments of 2015 and 2016 first-rounders Cornelius Randolph and Mickey Moniak, who went No. 1 overall, has also hurt. The Phillies hope to reverse that trend with third baseman Alec Bohm, the No. 3 overall pick in 2018.

Shortstop Luis Garcia is further away, but the team's No. 3 prospect could be the best in the organization within the next couple of seasons. Signed for $2.5 million from the Dominican Republic in 2017, Garcia earned stellar reviews both for his hitting ability (he won the Rookie-level Gulf Coast League batting title as a 17-year-old) and plus defensive potential.

PHILADELPHIA PHILLIES

TOP 2019 ROOKIE: Enyel de los Santos, RHP. He, JoJo Romero and Ranger Suarez could all help the Phillies' rotation in 2019.

BREAKOUT PROSPECT: Logan O'Hoppe, C. A 23rd-round pick in 2018, he has quickly garnered attention as a player on the rise after playing well all-around in his pro debut.

SLEEPER: Fernando Ortega, RHP. At 6-foot-4, 160 pounds, he has an extremely skinny build with room to grow a fastball that already touches 93 mph at 17 and feel for his secondaries after signing out of the Dominican Republic in 2018.

SOURCE OF TOP 30 TALENT			
Homegrown	29	Acquired	1
College	11	Trade	1
Junior college	1	Rule 5 draft	0
High school	3	Independent league	0
Nondrafted free agent	0	Free agent/waivers	0
International	14		

LF
Adam Haseley (5)
Cornelius Randolph
Ben Pelletier

CF
Mickey Moniak (12)
Simon Muzziotti

RF
Austin Listi (20)
Jhailyn Ortiz (24)
Matt Vierling (29)
Jose Pujols
Dylan Cozens

3B
Alec Bohm (2)
Jake Holmes

SS
Luis Garcia (3)
Arquimedes Gamboa (28)
Jonathan Guzman
Alexeis Azuaje
Nick Maton

2B
Daniel Brito (23)
Nicolas Torres (26)

1B
Darick Hall

C
Logan O'Hoppe (14)
Rodolfo Duran (22)
Rafael Marchan (25)
Deivi Grullon
Abrahan Gutierrez

LHP

LHSP	LHRP
JoJo Romero (6)	Kyle Dohy (17)
Ranger Suarez (9)	Zach Warren (19)
Will Stewart (11)	
Cole Irvin (21)	
Kyle Young	
David Parkinson	
Manuel Silva	
Joalbert Angulo	
Jhordany Mezquita	

RHP

RHSP	RHRP
Sixto Sanchez (1)	Edgar Garcia (18)
Adonis Medina (4)	Connor Brogdon
Enyel de los Santos (7)	Addison Russ
Spencer Howard (8)	
Francisco Morales (10)	
Colton Eastman (13)	
Mauricio Llovera (15)	
Starlyn Castillo (16)	
Connor Seabold (27)	
James McArthur (30)	
Ramon Rosso	
Dominic Pipkin	
Fernando Ortega	
Drew Anderson	
Victor Santos	
Tom Eshelman	
Kevin Gowdy	

DRAFT ANALYSIS

2018

BEST PURE HITTER: The Phillies added one of the best hitters in college baseball, 3B Alec Bohm (1) with the No. 3 overall pick. Despite a slow start to his pro career, Bohm has an impressive track record of hitting at Wichita State and in the Cape Cod League. OF Matt Vierling (5) has shown impressive feel for hitting out of Notre Dame.

BEST POWER HITTER: At 6-foot-5, Bohm has the strength, leverage and bat speed to generate plus power, with improved plate discipline in 2018 that helped him tap into that power with even more frequency. Vierling sticks out with above-average raw power, while 3B Matt Kroon (18) and OF Luke Miller (22) both have big power too.

FASTEST RUNNER: OF Corbin Williams (24) is an 80 runner on the 20-80 scouting scale, blazing the 60-yard dash in 6.25 seconds.

BEST DEFENSIVE PLAYER: The Phillies may have found a steal in C Logan O'Hoppe (23), who had a big debut offensively in the GCL and is also a solid-average receiver with a plus arm.

BEST ATHLETE: While he's not a super quick-twitch athlete with burner speed, SS Logan Simmons (6) has good body control at shortstop.

BEST FASTBALL: RHP Dominic Pipkin (9) is the hardest thrower in the Phillies' draft, running his fastball to 96 mph. RHP James McArthur (12) has a heavy fastball that's reached 95-96 mph, and RHP Tyler McKay (16) has a plus fastball as well.

BEST SECONDARY PITCH: RHP Colton Eastman (4) flashes a plus changeup that some scouts feel is his best pitch, but the Phillies think it's his plus curveball that's a separator with late, biting action. McArthur (12) also flashes an above-average curve.

BEST PRO DEBUT: The Phillies quickly and aggressively pushed Vierling to low Class A Lakewood, where he thrived, batting .293/.342/.473 in 50 games.

MOST INTRIGUING BACKGROUND: Kroon's father Marc pitched in Nippon Professional Baseball in Japan. Marc led the NPB's Central League with 41 saves in 2008 and threw 101 mph.

CLOSEST TO THE MAJORS: There's a strong track record of advanced college hitters drafted in the top 5-7 picks racing their way to the big leagues. Bohm fits that exact mold and could make an impact in the Philadelphia's lineup by 2020.

BEST LATE-ROUND PICK: The Phillies may have gotten a late-round gem from a Long Island high school in O'Hoppe. He projects to stick behind the plate and the early returns offensively have been exciting after he batted .367/.411/.532 in 34 games in the Rookie-level Gulf Coast League.

THE ONE WHO GOT AWAY: The Phillies used their second-to-last pick on C Matt Nelson (39), who is going to Florida State. He has a chance to be an above-average receiver with a strong arm.

—BEN BADLER

TOP DRAFT PICKS OF THE DECADE

Year	Player, Pos	2018 Org
2009	Kelly Dugan, OF (2nd round)	Did not play
2010	Jesse Biddle, LHP	Braves
2011	Larry Greene, OF (1st round supp)	Did not play
2012	Shane Watson, RHP (1st round supp)	Atlantic Lge
2013	J.P. Crawford, SS	Phillies
2014	Aaron Nola, RHP	Phillies
2015	Cornelius Randolph, SS	Phillies
2016	Mickey Moniak, OF	Phillies
2017	Adam Haseley, OF	Phillies
2018	Alec Bohm, 3B	Phillies

2017

OF Adam Haseley (1) and RHP Spencer Howard (2) both got off to slow starts but rebounded, and Haseley reached Double-A. LHPs Zach Warren (14) and Kyle Dohy (16) look to be good late-round finds.

GRADE: B

2016

OF Mickey Moniak (1) was the draft's top overall pick and hasn't lived up to the expectations. RHP Kevin Gowdy (2) has been sidelined by injury. LHP JoJo Romero (4) put together a solid year in Double-A.

GRADE: D

2015

2B Scott Kingery (2) signed a long-term contract before being promoted in 2018 to the big leagues but struggled as a rookie. LHP Will Stewart (20) had a breakout season as a 20-year-old in the South Atlantic League.

GRADE: C

1 SIXTO SANCHEZ, RHP

Born: July 29, 1998. **B-T:** R-R. **Ht.:** 6-0. **Wt.:** 210. **Signed:**
Dominican Republic, 2015. **Signed by:** Carlos Salas.

At a tryout for a Cuban catcher, the Phillies were instead drawn to Sanchez, an eligible 16-year-old converted catcher who had quick, easy arm action and a fastball that reached the low 90s. They signed him shortly after that for $35,000. Sanchez spent his first year getting acclimated in the Dominican Summer League, then had a breakthrough in 2016 in the Rookie-level Gulf Coast League, where he led the league with an 0.50 ERA while running his fastball up to 98 mph. Sanchez became one of the game's elite pitching prospects in 2017, reaching high Class A Clearwater just after his 19th birthday and touching 100 mph. In 2018, Sanchez showed electric stuff but made just eight starts before being shut down for the year with right elbow inflammation. The Phillies had hoped Sanchez would pitch in the Arizona Fall League, but a sore collarbone prevented him from playing there.
SCOUTING REPORT: Few pitching prospects in the minors can match Sanchez's blend of premium stuff, control and easy, athletic delivery. His fastball explodes on hitters, parking in the mid-90s and regularly touching 100 mph. Unlike many other young flamethrowers, Sanchez doesn't have any issues throwing his fastball over the plate, as he's an advanced strike-thrower who and he projects to have plus or better control. While the injury cut Sanchez's 2018 season short, he still showed exciting progress by turning his slider into a wipeout pitch with two-plane tilt that misses bats against both lefties and righties. That's in addition to his changeup, which flashes plus with good sink and running action. If Sanchez can maintain the progress he showed with his slider before getting injured, his strikeout rate could spike as he mixes that in and gains a better understanding of how to sequence hitters. He is a good athlete who fields his position well and generates his velocity without much effort to his mechanics.
THE FUTURE: The 95 innings Sanchez threw in 2017 were a career high, so he still has to prove his durability. But if he shows he can handle a starter's workload, he could develop into a true frontline starter along the lines of the Yankees' Luis Severino. He's advanced enough to go to Double-A Reading in 2019 with a chance to get to Philadelphia by the end of the season.

MIKE JANES/FOUR SEAM

BA GRADE	SCOUTING GRADES
65 Risk: High	Fastball: 70. Slider: 60. Changeup: 60. Control: 70.

Projected future grades on 20-80 scouting scale.

TOP PROSPECTS OF THE DECADE

Year	Player, Pos	2018 Org
2009	Domonic Brown, OF	Mexican Lge
2010	Domonic Brown, OF	Mexican Lge
2011	Domonic Brown, OF	Mexican Lge
2012	Trevor May, RHP	Twins
2013	Jesse Biddle, LHP	Braves
2014	Maikel Franco, 3B	Phillies
2015	J.P. Crawford, SS	Phillies
2016	J.P. Crawford, SS	Phillies
2017	J.P. Crawford, SS	Phillies
2018	J.P. Crawford, SS	Phillies

BEST TOOLS

Best Hitter for Average	Alec Bohm
Best Power Hitter	Dylan Cozens
Best Strike-Zone Discipline	Alec Bohm
Fastest Baserunner	Corbin Williams
Best Athlete	Alexeis Azuaje
Best Fastball	Sixto Sanchez
Best Curveball	Colton Eastman
Best Slider	Adonis Medina
Best Changeup	Sixto Sanchez
Best Control	Cole Irvin
Best Defensive Catcher	Rodolfo Duran
Best Defensive Infielder	Luis Garica
Best Infield Arm	Luis Garica
Best Defensive Outfielder	Simon Muzziotti
Best Outfield Arm	Jose Pujols

Year	Club (League)	Class	W	L	ERA	G	GS	CG	SV	IP	H	HR	BB	SO	K/9	WHIP	AVG
2016	Phillies (GCL)	R	5	0	0.50	11	11	0	0	54	33	0	8	44	7.3	0.76	.181
2017	Lakewood (SAL)	LoA	5	3	2.41	13	13	1	0	67	46	1	9	64	8.6	0.82	.191
	Clearwater (FSL)	HiA	0	4	4.55	5	5	1	0	28	27	1	9	20	6.5	1.30	.252
2018	Clearwater (FSL)	HiA	4	3	2.51	8	8	1	0	47	39	1	11	45	8.7	1.07	.224
Minor League Totals			15	12	2.48	48	39	3	0	221	177	3	43	191	7.8	0.99	.217

2 ALEC BOHM, 3B

Born: Aug. 3, 1996. **B-T:** R-R. **Ht.:** 6-5. **Wt.:** 235. **Drafted:** Wichita State, 2018 (1st round). **Signed by:** Justin Munson.

TRACK RECORD: After ranking second in the Cape Cod League in batting average (.351) in the summer of 2017, Bohm batted .339/.436/.625 with more walks (39) and extra-base hits (31) than strikeouts (28) for Wichita State his junior year. The Phillies drafted him with the third overall pick and signed him for $5.85 million.

SCOUTING REPORT: One of the top hitters in college baseball in 2018, Bohm has an encouraging combination of raw power and pure hitting ability for a big man. At 6-foot-5, he is a strong, physical hitter with fast bat speed and leverage in his swing to generate plus raw power. Bohm has a big strike zone to cover and he manages it well with a keen eye for balls and strikes that improved over the course of his college years. He approaches his at-bats with a smart plan and the ability to make adjustments, despite a soft offensive debut in pro ball. Bohm has a chance to stick at third base, where he has a solid-average arm, but he's a below-average runner whose lack of first-step quickness inhibits his range, so there's some risk he might end up at first base.

BA GRADE	
60	**Risk:** High

Hit: 60. **Power:** 60.
Fastball: 40. **Field:** 40.
Arm: 55.

THE FUTURE: The Phillies sent 2017 first-rounder Adam Haseley to high Class A Clearwater for his first full season, with Bohm likely to follow that same path. If Bohm can stay at third base, he has the offensive upside to be a plus everyday regular at the position.

Year	Club (League)	Class	AVG	G	AB	R	H	2B	3B	HR	RBI	BB	SO	SB	CS	OBP	SLG
2018	Phillies East (GCL)	R	.222	4	9	0	2	0	0	0	2	0	4	0	0	.200	.222
	Phillies (GCL)	R	.391	7	23	8	9	1	1	0	3	2	0	2	0	.481	.522
	Williamsport (NYP)	SS	.224	29	107	9	24	5	1	0	12	10	19	1	0	.314	.290
Minor League Totals			.252	40	139	17	35	6	2	0	17	12	23	3	0	.335	.324

3 LUIS GARCIA, SS

Born: Oct. 1, 2000. **B-T:** B-R. **Ht.:** 5-11. **Wt.:** 170. **Signed:** Dominican Republic, 2017. **Signed by:** Carlos Salas.

TRACK RECORD: Garcia was one of the top players in a stacked 2017 class of international prospects, with the Phillies signing him for $2.5 million. The Phillies aggressively pushed Garcia to the Rookie-level Gulf Coast League to make his pro debut, and he won the batting title by hitting .369 and ranked third in on-base percentage.

SCOUTING REPORT: As an amateur, Garcia earned widespread praise from scouts for his defense. He's a smooth defender who is light on his feet with soft hands and a plus arm. Garcia has the ability to make the flashy, acrobatic plays, but he separates himself from most young shortstops because of his calm, collected poise and smart decision-making, which is why he committed just five errors in 43 games. When Garcia signed, scouts were split on whether he would fit better at the top or bottom of a lineup, but he looked excellent at the plate in the GCL, showing signs of a potential future .300 hitter with

BA GRADE	
60	**Risk:** Very High

Hit: 60. **Power:** 40.
Fastball: 55. **Field:** 60.
Arm: 60.

strong on-base skills. A solid-average runner, Garcia tracks pitches well and controls the strike zone, setting up from both sides with a calm, quiet approach and a short stroke to shoot line drives to all fields with doubles power.

THE FUTURE: Garcia is still at least a few years away, but he could soon become the Phillies' top prospect as a potential plus hitter with plus defense at a premium position. He will be one of the youngest players in the low Class A South Atlantic League in 2019.

Year	Club (League)	Class	AVG	G	AB	R	H	2B	3B	HR	RBI	BB	SO	SB	CS	OBP	SLG
2018	Phillies West (GCL)	R	.369	43	168	33	62	11	3	1	32	15	21	12	8	.433	.488
Minor League Totals			.369	43	168	33	62	11	3	1	32	15	21	12	8	.433	.488

4 ADONIS MEDINA, RHP

Born: Dec. 18, 1996. **B-T:** R-R. **Ht.:** 6-1. **Wt.:** 185. **Signed:** Dominican Republic, 2014. **Signed by:** Koby Perez/Carlos Salas.

TRACK RECORD: Signed out of the Dominican Republic for $70,000 at 17, Medina had a handful of meltdown outings during the 2018 season that caused his ERA to swell but still flashed electric stuff and ranked third in the high Class A Florida League with 123 strikeouts.

SCOUTING REPORT: Medina has three pitches that grade out or at least flash plus. He throws a plus fastball that sits at 92-96 mph with late movement and can scrape 97. Medina generates good extension out front, which helps his fastball get on hitters faster than they expect. His slider has made huge strides over the last two seasons, to the point where it's now plus—a nasty swing-and-miss pitch with two-plane depth to both righthanded hitters or when he throws it to the back foot of lefties. His changeup is another pitch that flashes plus, thought it's not consistent yet. Medina is an athletic strike-thrower, though he needs to tighten his command and improve his pitch sequencing, both of which led to trouble despite his stuff last year.

BA GRADE
55 Risk: High
Fastball: 60.
Slider: 60.
Change: 60. Control: 55.

THE FUTURE: Medina has the athleticism and delivery that point to a pitcher who should be able to make command improvements. If he can do that, he can be a mid-rotation starter, with Double-A Reading up next.

Year	Club (League)	Class	W	L	ERA	G	GS	CG	SV	IP	H	HR	BB	SO	K/9	WHIP	AVG
2016	Williamsport (NYP)	SS	5	3	2.92	13	13	0	0	65	47	5	24	34	4.7	1.10	.203
2017	Lakewood (SAL)	LoA	4	9	3.01	22	22	0	0	120	103	7	39	133	10.0	1.19	.227
2018	Clearwater (FSL)	HiA	10	4	4.12	22	21	1	0	111	103	11	36	123	9.9	1.25	.245
Minor League Totals			24	21	3.21	78	66	1	1	367	317	24	115	347	8.5	1.18	.231

5 ADAM HASELEY, OF

Born: April 12, 1996. **B-T:** L-L. **Ht.:** 6-1. **Wt.:** 195. **Drafted:** Virginia, 2017 (1st round). **Signed by:** Paul Murphy.

TRACK RECORD: Haseley was a two-way player at Virginia and one of the best hitters in the country when the Phillies drafted him No. 8 overall in 2017. After signing that summer and in the first half of 2018, Haseley had yet to perform above a modest level, but in the second half he turned things around and finished strong with Double-A Reading.

SCOUTING REPORT: Haseley has a knack for barreling balls, striking out in just 14 percent of his plate appearances in 2018. However, he had to adjust in pro ball to better velocity, especially up and in on his hands. Haseley has a direct, inside-out swing with an approach geared toward using the middle of the field and going the opposite way. During the season he adjusted his stance to get more upright in an attempt to create better leverage. If he can learn to create a more out-front contact point on pitches he can drive, that could help him tap more into his average raw power, though Haseley will probably always

BA GRADE
50 Risk: High
Hit: 55. Power: 50.
Run: 55. Field: 50.
Arm: 50.

have more of a hit-over-power profile. He is a slightly above-average runner with an average arm, which might be enough for him to handle center field, though he might move around all three outfield spots, which would put added pressure on his power coming around if he spends more time on the corners.

THE FUTURE: Haseley has some tweener outfielder risk, but if either his pure hitting ability can carry him or he can develop more game power, he has the potential to develop into an average regular. He will open 2019 back in Double-A, with a chance to reach the majors either by the end of the season or 2020.

Year	Club (League)	Class	AVG	G	AB	R	H	2B	3B	HR	RBI	BB	SO	SB	CS	OBP	SLG
2017	Phillies (GCL)	R	.583	3	12	3	7	1	1	0	4	2	3	1	1	.643	.833
	Williamsport (NYP)	SS	.270	37	137	18	37	9	0	2	18	14	28	5	3	.350	.380
	Lakewood (SAL)	LoA	.258	18	66	15	17	3	1	1	6	6	13	0	1	.315	.379
2018	Clearwater (FSL)	HiA	.300	79	330	54	99	13	5	5	38	19	54	7	3	.343	.415
	Reading (EL)	AA	.316	39	136	23	43	4	0	6	17	16	19	0	1	.403	.478
Minor League Totals			.298	176	681	113	203	30	7	14	83	57	117	13	9	.360	.424

6 JOJO ROMERO, LHP

Born: Sept. 9, 1996. **B-T:** L-L. **Ht.:** 6-0. **Wt.:** 190. **Drafted:** Yavapai (Ariz.) JC, 2016 (4th round). **Signed by:** Brad Holland.

TRACK RECORD: Coming off a strong first full season in 2017, Romero opened 2018 with a 7.18 ERA in his first five starts. After that, he posted a 2.69 ERA with an 83-to-30 strikeout-to-walk ratio in 80.1 innings before a strained oblique in July shut him down for the year.

SCOUTING REPORT: Romero has a diverse pitch mix, and early in 2018, he was throwing them all at hitters and trying to get them to chase. That approach didn't work for Romero, however, because he often fell behind in the count and batters were able to do damage against him. After a rough start, he altered his approach by attacking hitters more with his power sinker and changeup. As his fastball command improved, so did the results. Romero mixes four- and two-seam fastballs from the low 90s up to 96 mph. He's at his best when he's attacking with his sinker and changeup—which flashes above-average—to mess with the timing of hitters. Romero has an average curveball and sprinkles in a slider and cutter as well. He's an athletic pitcher with quick feet to help him control the running game.

BA GRADE

50 Risk: Medium

Fastball: 55.
Change: 60. Curve: 50.
Slider: 45. CTL: 55

THE FUTURE: With three average to plus pitches and good control from the left side, Romero projects as a potential No. 3 or 4 starter. He should head to Triple-A Lehigh Valley for 2019 with a chance to help the big league rotation after the all-star break.

Year	Club (League)	Class	W	L	ERA	G	GS	CG	SV	IP	H	HR	BB	SO	K/9	WHIP	AVG
2016	Williamsport (NYP)	SS	2	2	2.56	10	10	1	0	46	44	2	11	31	6.1	1.20	.256
2017	Lakewood (SAL)	LoA	5	1	2.11	13	13	1	0	77	61	2	21	79	9.3	1.07	.223
	Clearwater (FSL)	HiA	5	2	2.24	10	10	0	0	52	43	2	15	49	8.4	1.11	.223
2018	Reading (EL)	AA	7	6	3.80	18	18	0	0	107	97	13	41	100	8.4	1.29	.241
Minor League Totals			19	11	2.85	51	51	2	0	281	245	19	88	259	8.3	1.18	.235

7 ENYEL DE LOS SANTOS, RHP

Born: Dec. 25, 1995. **B-T:** R-R. **Ht.:** 6-3. **Wt.:** 200. **Signed:** Dominican Republic, 2014. **Signed by:** Eddy Toledo/Domingo Toribio (Mariners).

TRACK RECORD: De los Santos signed with the Mariners for $15,000 out of the Dominican Republic in 2014, went to the Padres after the 2015 season in the Joaquin Benoit trade, then arrived in the Phillies organization in December 2017 when they traded Freddy Galvis to San Diego. De los Santos proved steady and reliable throughout his 2018 time in Triple-A Lehigh Valley, then made his major league debut in July, with most of his big league outings coming as a reliever.

SCOUTING REPORT: De los Santos is a durable power arm who has thrown 145-plus innings each of the last two seasons. His best pitch is his fastball, which mostly ranges from 92-97 mph and has topped at 98. De los Santos relies heavily on his fastball and keeps hitters off balance with a solid-average changeup at 85-89 mph. It's not a true out pitch, but it can miss bats, induce weak contact and help him against lefties, who had a nearly identical OPS

BA GRADE

45 Risk: Low

Fastball: 60.
Curveball: 40.
Change: 55. CTL: 50.

against him as righties. The biggest risk with de los Santos is his lack of a reliable breaking ball, because his curve is below-average.

THE FUTURE: De los Santos has the durability to start if he can develop a better breaking pitch, which could make him an innings-eating starter at the back of a rotation. If not, he could find success as a two-pitch reliever.

Year	Club (League)	Class	W	L	ERA	G	GS	CG	SV	IP	H	HR	BB	SO	K/9	WHIP	AVG
2016	Fort Wayne (MWL)	LoA	3	2	2.91	11	7	0	0	53	38	2	14	45	7.7	0.99	.199
	Lake Elsinore (CAL)	HiA	5	3	4.35	15	15	0	0	68	70	11	24	52	6.8	1.38	.267
2017	San Antonio (TL)	AA	10	6	3.78	26	24	0	0	150	131	12	48	138	8.3	1.19	.237
2018	Lehigh Valley (IL)	AAA	10	5	2.63	22	22	1	0	127	104	12	43	110	7.8	1.16	.226
	Philadelphia (NL)	MAJ	1	0	4.74	7	2	0	0	19	19	2	8	15	7.1	1.42	.271
Major League Totals			1	0	4.74	7	2	0	0	19	19	2	8	15	7.1	1.42	.271
Minor League Totals			34	16	3.40	87	81	1	0	460	404	40	147	416	8.1	1.20	.238

8 SPENCER HOWARD, RHP

Born: July 28, 1996. **B-T:** R-R. **Ht.:** 6-3. **Wt.:** 205. **Drafted:** Cal Poly, 2017 (2nd round). **Signed by:** Shane Bowers.

TRACK RECORD: After a strong April in 2018, it was a bit puzzling when Howard finished June with a 5.06 ERA at low Class A Lakewood, particularly for a second-round pick out of college in the low Class A South Atlantic League with high-end stuff. From July on, Howard dominated, posting a 2.36 ERA with 71 strikeouts and 20 walks in 53.1 innings in his final 10 regular season starts. He capped off his season with a complete-game no-hitter in the playoffs.

SCOUTING REPORT: Howard has some of the best pure stuff in the organization, with a fastball that improved in the second half of 2018. Sitting in the low-to-mid-90s early in the season, Howard by the end of the year was parking in the mid-90s and reached 100 mph in the playoffs. His fastball has late life that helps him get swings and misses in the zone and when he elevates. Howard added more power to both his fastball and his slider, a deep-breaking putaway pitch that grades out as plus. He throws a curveball and a changeup that both are average pitches at times. Howard will need to throw more strikes to reach his potential, especially as he faces more advanced hitters.

THE FUTURE: There's a wide range of outcomes for Howard, who could become a No. 2 or 3 starter if he harnesses his control. If not, he has the stuff to pitch high-leverage relief innings.

BA GRADE
55 Risk: Very High
Fastball: 70.
Slider: 60. Curve: 50.
Change: 50. CTL: 45

Year	Club (League)	Class	W	L	ERA	G	GS	CG	SV	IP	H	HR	BB	SO	K/9	WHIP	AVG
2017	Williamsport (NYP)	SS	1	1	4.45	9	9	0	0	28	22	0	18	40	12.7	1.41	.214
2018	Lakewood (SAL)	LoA	9	8	3.78	23	23	1	0	112	101	6	40	147	11.8	1.26	.240
Minor League Totals			10	9	3.91	32	32	1	0	140	123	6	58	187	12.0	1.29	.235

9 RANGER SUAREZ, LHP

Born: Aug. 26, 1995. **B-T:** L-L. **Ht.:** 6-1. **Wt.:** 190. **Signed:** Venezuela, 2012. **Signed by:** Jesus Mendez.

TRACK RECORD: Suarez was a longshot, pitchability lefty when the Phillies signed him out of Venezuela for $25,000. Over the years, he has added more power to complement his savvy and become a legitimate prospect. He split 2018 between Double-A Reading and Triple-A Lehigh Valley and made his big league debut.

SCOUTING REPORT: In 2017, Suarez adjusted his lower-half mechanics to stay into his back leg more, which helped his velocity jump to sit in the low 90s and reach as high as 95 mph. He maintained that velocity throughout the 2018 season, and hides the ball well in his delivery, adding deception that helps his stuff play up. The secondary pitch Suarez leans on most is his mid-80s changeup, a solid-average offering. His slider isn't consistent but when it's on, it can be an average pitch. Suarez doesn't have one wipeout pitch, but he's a smart pitcher who mixes and matches both his stuff and his location. He's a good athlete who fields his position well and has quick feet to control the running game.

THE FUTURE: Suarez projects as a back-end starter and should compete for a spot in Philadelphia's rotation to open the season, though there's a chance he could begin the year back in Triple-A.

BA GRADE
45 Risk: Medium
Fastball: 50.
Changeup: 55.
Slider: 50. CTL: 55.

Year	Club (League)	Class	W	L	ERA	G	GS	CG	SV	IP	H	HR	BB	SO	K/9	WHIP	AVG
2016	Williamsport (NYP)	SS	6	4	2.81	13	13	2	0	74	61	4	24	53	6.5	1.15	.223
2017	Lakewood (SAL)	LoA	6	2	1.59	14	14	1	0	85	52	4	24	90	9.5	0.89	.177
	Clearwater (FSL)	HiA	2	4	3.82	8	8	0	0	38	43	1	11	38	9.1	1.43	.293
2018	Reading (EL)	AA	4	3	2.76	12	12	1	0	75	64	2	20	54	6.5	1.12	.235
	Lehigh Valley (IL)	AAA	2	0	2.74	9	9	0	0	49	48	2	15	31	5.7	1.28	.257
	Philadelphia (NL)	MAJ	1	1	5.40	4	3	0	0	15	21	3	6	11	6.6	1.80	.339
Major League Totals			1	1	5.40	4	3	0	0	15	21	3	6	11	6.6	1.80	.339
Minor League Totals			28	17	2.27	87	75	4	3	451	370	17	102	381	7.6	1.05	.223

10 FRANCISCO MORALES, RHP

Born: Oct. 27, 1999. **B-T:** R-R. **Ht.:** 6-5. **Wt.:** 220. **Signed:** Venezuela, 2016. **Signed by:** Jesus Mendez.

TRACK RECORD: The Phillies signed Morales out of Venezuela for $720,000 when he was one of the top international pitching prospects in the 2016 class. After a promising pro debut in 2017 in the Rookie-level Gulf Coast League, Morales went to a college-heavy short-season New York-Penn League as an 18-year-old and struggled, though the raw stuff he showed still impressed.

BA GRADE

55 **Risk:** Extreme

Fastball: 60.
Slider: 60.
Change: 50. **CTL:** 50.

SCOUTING REPORT: Morales showed exciting flashes in 2018, including a pair of double-digit strikeout games and an overall strikeout rate of 10.9 per nine innings, though his lack of command got him into trouble against older hitters. He generates downhill plane on his plus fastball, which ranges from 92-96 mph and might have a little more room for growth. He gets good extension out front, helping his fastball play up. His plus slider is a finishing pitch that helped him pile up strikeouts. Morales has shown feel for a changeup when he uses it, though that pitch remains a work in progress. His struggles in 2018 mostly stemmed from his command escaping him, leading to too many walks and unfavorable counts. Morales is a young, long-limbed pitcher who still is learning to sync everything and repeat his mechanics and release point consistently so he can throw more frequent strikes.

THE FUTURE: With better command, Morales has the potential to develop into a mid-rotation starter, though that projection comes with significant risk. He will make his full season debut at low Class A Lakewood in 2019.

Year	Club (League)	Class	W	L	ERA	G	GS	CG	SV	IP	H	HR	BB	SO	K/9	WHIP	AVG
2017	Phillies (GCL)	R	3	2	3.05	10	9	0	0	41	34	1	20	44	9.6	1.31	.225
2018	Williamsport (NYP)	SS	4	5	5.27	13	13	0	0	56	54	6	33	68	10.9	1.54	.244
Minor League Totals			7	7	4.33	23	22	0	0	98	88	7	53	112	10.3	1.44	.237

11 WILL STEWART, LHP

BA GRADE

45 **Risk:** High

Born: July 14, 1997. **B-T:** L-L. **Ht.:** 6-2. **Wt.:** 175. **Drafted:** HS—Hazel Green, Ala., 2015 (20th round). **Signed by:** Mike Stauffer.

TRACK RECORD: The Phillies have popped a variety of intriguing players in the later rounds of their recent drafts, including Stewart, a 20th-round pick in 2015 who signed for $100,000. Stewart made his full-season debut in 2018 and was extremely efficient with his pitches, walking just 1.7 batters per nine innings and ranking second in the league with a 2.06 ERA.

SCOUTING REPORT: Stewart has success by throwing strikes, getting groundballs and disrupting hitters' timing with his changeup and location. Stewart operates off an 89-93 mph fastball. He touched 95 mph, becoming another example of a Phillies prospect who was able to better use his legs and synchronize his body to squeeze out a little extra velocity. Strong and athletic, Stewart repeats his delivery with plus control, spotting his fastball well to both sides of the plate and getting a lot of grounders. Stewart's slider is below-average, but he's able to keep lefties and righties off balance with an above-average changeup.

THE FUTURE: Stewart needs to improve his breaking ball, but if he does he could develop along the lines of Ranger Suarez and fit as a back-end starter. He's scheduled to start 2019 in high Class A Clearwater.

Year	Club (League)	Class	W	L	ERA	G	GS	CG	SV	IP	H	HR	BB	SO	K/9	WHIP	AVG
2016	Phillies (GCL)	R	2	3	4.06	11	7	0	0	44	34	1	19	35	7.1	1.20	.217
2017	Williamsport (NYP)	SS	4	2	4.18	13	13	0	0	60	64	3	25	58	8.7	1.48	.267
2018	Lakewood (SAL)	LoA	8	1	2.06	20	20	2	0	114	90	5	21	90	7.1	0.98	.218
Minor League Totals			15	6	3.20	56	40	2	0	239	206	12	80	203	7.6	1.20	.232

12 MICKEY MONIAK, OF

BA GRADE

45 **Risk:** High

Born: May 13, 1998. **B-T:** L-R. **Ht.:** 6-2. **Wt.:** 185. **Drafted:** HS—Carlsbad, Calif., 2016 (1st round). **Signed by:** Mike Garcia.

TRACK RECORD: Moniak won Baseball America's High School Player of the Year award in 2016. The Phillies drafted Moniak that year with the No. 1 overall pick, but his stock has been on a decline since then. Moniak struggled in his first full season in 2017 and did so again last year, though he did rebound in the second half, batting .297/.347/.470 in 53 games from July through the end of the season.

SCOUTING REPORT: When the Phillies drafted Moniak, they considered him the best hitter in the country, a potential middle-of-the-order hitter who could play Gold Glove defense in center field. Moniak still has a smooth, sound lefthanded swing, but his pure hitting ability isn't as advanced as initially expected. Moniak can barrel fastballs, but he struggles with pitch recognition and has to take a more selective hitting approach. Moniak's final two months provided the most encouraging signs for his future since he turned pro, with better plate discipline during that time. Moniak hit the ball harder in the second half, and has the potential to hit 10-15 home runs. An average runner with an above-average arm, Moniak played better defense in 2018, and grades out as a fringe-average fielder.

THE FUTURE: While a lot of clubs have Moniak as a future fourth outfielder, his finish to the 2018 season offers some hope he could still develop into an everyday player.

Year	Club (League)	Class	AVG	G	AB	R	H	2B	3B	HR	RBI	BB	SO	SB	CS	OBP	SLG
2016	Phillies (GCL)	R	.284	46	176	27	50	11	4	1	28	11	35	10	4	.340	.409
2017	Lakewood (SAL)	LoA	.236	123	466	53	110	22	6	5	44	28	109	11	7	.284	.341
2018	Clearwater (FSL)	HiA	.270	114	433	50	117	28	3	5	55	22	100	6	5	.304	.383
Minor League Totals			.258	283	1075	130	277	61	13	11	127	61	244	27	16	.301	.369

13 COLTON EASTMAN, RHP

BA GRADE 45 Risk: High

Born: Aug. 22, 1996. **B-T:** R-R. **Ht.:** 6-3. **Wt.:** 185. **Drafted:** Cal State Fullerton, 2018 (4th round). **Signed by:** Demerius Pittman.

TRACK RECORD: The Phillies have a taste for polished Cal State Fullerton starters. They traded for Tom Eshelman after the 2015 season, drafted Connor Seabold in 2017, then in 2018 drafted Eastman, who signed for $522,900 as a fourth-rounder after spending three years in Fullerton's starting rotation.

SCOUTING REPORT: Like Eshelman and Seabold, Eastman's fastball is light by modern standards, but he separates himself from the others with swing-and-miss offspeed pitches. Eastman sits at 88-91 mph and touches 93, locating his fastball well with potentially above-average control. Ask scouts what Eastman's best secondary pitch is and it depends on the day they saw him, but both his curveball and changeup can miss barrels. His changeup has lively action and earns plus grades at times, while his curveball was inconsistent his junior year, but at its best it flashed above-average with a high spin rate and late bite.

THE FUTURE: The Phillies have shown a flair for squeezing extra velocity out of their pitching prospects, which would make Eastman more dangerous. Even with his current fastball and ability to manipulate his secondary stuff, Eastman could develop into a back-end starter with a chance to move quickly.

Year	Club (League)	Class	W	L	ERA	G	GS	CG	SV	IP	H	HR	BB	SO	K/9	WHIP	AVG
2018	Williamsport (NYP)	SS	0	2	3.00	8	8	0	0	18	18	1	7	23	11.5	1.39	.269
Minor League Totals			0	2	3.00	8	8	0	0	18	18	1	7	23	11.5	1.39	.269

14 LOGAN O'HOPPE, C

BA GRADE 50 Risk: Extreme

Born: Feb. 2, 2000. **B-T:** R-R. **Ht.:** 6-2. **Wt.:** 185. **Drafted:** HS—West Islip, N.Y., 2018 (23rd round). **Signed by:** Alex Agostino/Tom Downing.

TRACK RECORD: The Phillies have scouted Long Island high schools heavily, drafting lefthanders Nick Fanti and Kyle Young and rigthhander Ben Brown with late-round picks in recent years. The latest is O'Hoppe, a catcher from a Long Island high school who could be the best of the group. O'Hoppe signed for $215,000 as a 23rd-round pick, then shined on both sides of the ball in the Gulf Coast League.

SCOUTING REPORT: O'Hoppe is an advanced defender for his age. He has soft hands and receives the ball well, showing good agility and flexibility behind the plate. He also has a plus arm, erasing 33 percent of basestealers in the GCL. Known for his defensive ability as an amateur, O'Hoppe also hit well in his pro debut. He's an aggressive hitter with a knack for the barrel. His swing is geared for loft, though his power is mostly to the gaps right now, with a chance for 10-15 home runs as he continues to add strength.

THE FUTURE: O'Hoppe has quickly emerged as one of the most promising sleepers in the organization, with a chance for a breakthrough year if he can keep it up next season in low Class A Lakewood.

Year	Club (League)	Class	AVG	G	AB	R	H	2B	3B	HR	RBI	BB	SO	SB	CS	OBP	SLG
2018	Phillies West (GCL)	R	.367	34	109	19	40	10	1	2	21	10	28	2	1	.411	.532
Minor League Totals			.367	34	109	19	40	10	1	2	21	10	28	2	1	.411	.532

15 MAURICIO LLOVERA, RHP

BA GRADE 45 Risk: High

Born: April 17, 1996. **B-T:** R-R. **Ht.:** 5-11. **Wt.:** 200. **Signed:** Venezuela, 2014. **Signed by:** Carlos Salas.

TRACK RECORD: Llovera was an 18-year-old in Venezuela when the Phillies signed him for $7,500. He developed into a power arm, moving to the bullpen to open 2017 with low Class A Lakewood, but shifted back to the rotation midway through the year and stayed in that role in 2018 with high Class A Clearwater.

SCOUTING REPORT: Llovera generates big velocity from a smaller, stocky build with excellent arm speed, sitting in 93-97 mph with the ability to crank it up to 99 mph. His changeup improved in 2018, flashing as an average pitch when he maintains his arm speed, though it comes in firm off his fastball in the upper 80s. His slider also flashes average when he stays on top of the ball. Llovera's mechanics have a good dose of effort to them and his command is still shaky, so there's still a high probability he ends up in the bullpen.

THE FUTURE: The Phillies will keep developing Llovera as a starter, with a chance he could fit into the back of a rotation, but he could be a late-inning reliever with a chance to reach Philadelphia in 2019. He's ticketed for Double-A Reading.

Year	Club (League)	Class	W	L	ERA	G	GS	CG	SV	IP	H	HR	BB	SO	K/9	WHIP	AVG
2016	Phillies (GCL)	R	7	1	1.87	11	10	0	0	53	39	0	12	56	9.5	0.96	.205
2017	Lakewood (SAL)	LoA	2	4	3.35	30	10	0	0	86	81	2	33	94	9.8	1.33	.250
2018	Clearwater (FSL)	HiA	8	7	3.72	23	22	1	0	121	100	14	34	137	10.2	1.11	.221
Minor League Totals			19	16	3.22	75	52	1	0	307	256	17	96	330	9.7	1.15	.225

16 STARLYN CASTILLO, RHP

BA GRADE
50 Risk: Extreme

Born: Feb. 24, 2002. **B-T:** R-R. **Ht.:** 5-11. **Wt.:** 210. **Signed:** Dominican Republic, 2018. **Signed by:** Carlos Salas/Franklin Felida.

BACKGROUND: Castillo ranked as the top 2018 pitching prospect in the Dominican Republic, with the Phillies signing him for a $1.6 million bonus.

SCOUTING REPORT: Typically, top 16-year-old pitching prospects from Latin America have lean, athletic frames with high-end physical projection. Castillo, however, is built like a linebacker with a wide back and strong legs on a physically mature body. Castillo's advanced physicality helps him generate outstanding velocity for his age, ranging from 91-97 mph. Castillo's fastball alone helped him overpower amateur hitters and he complements that with a power breaking ball and a solid changeup at times. His secondary pitches are inconsistent, as is his control, with Castillo going through stretches where he's a solid strike-thrower, and others where his ability to find the zone escapes him, with his front side flying open.

THE FUTURE: Castillo is a young power arm still working on touch and feel, but his stuff is advanced for his age. He could make his pro debut next year in the Rookie-level Gulf Coast League.

Year	Club (League)	Class	W	L	ERA	G	GS	CG	SV	IP	H	HR	BB	SO	K/9	WHIP	AVG
2018	Did not play—Injured																

17 KYLE DOHY, LHP

BA GRADE
45 Risk: High

Born: Sept. 17, 1996. **B-T:** L-L. **Ht.:** 6-2. **Wt.:** 188. **Drafted:** Cal Poly Pomona, 2017 (16th round). **Signed by:** Demerius Pittman.

TRACK RECORD: Dohy entered 2017 as one of the top Division II prospects in the country, but he struggled badly with his control, dropping him to the Phillies in the 16th round. After walking a batter per inning in his pro debut, Dohy didn't look like a fast-track pitcher, but he climbed three levels in 2018, finishing the year in Double-A Reading's bullpen.

SCOUTING REPORT: After getting his legs more into his delivery, Dohy has grown his fastball from the low-90s to sitting more low-to-mid 90s with a peak of 97 mph in short bursts as a reliever. He gets whiffs on his fastball up in the zone and on both of his secondary pitches, leading him to strike out an incredible 41 percent of batters faced last year. One is a plus slider that's devastating against lefties, breaking sharp and late with two-plane depth. His changeup can also induce whiffs, flashing above-average. Dohy is a good athlete who threw more strikes in 2018, though he struggled again with his control once he reached Double-A.

THE FUTURE: Dohy has a starter's repertoire, but he has found a role that clicks for him in relief. He's a potential multi-inning reliever who could pitch in high-leverage situations, with a chance to reach the big leagues by the end of the 2019 season.

Year	Club (League)	Class	W	L	ERA	G	GS	CG	SV	IP	H	HR	BB	SO	K/9	WHIP	AVG
2017	Williamsport (NYP)	SS	2	1	3.60	13	0	0	0	20	12	0	20	22	9.9	1.60	.182
2018	Lakewood (SAL)	LoA	3	3	0.80	24	0	0	7	34	16	1	17	63	16.8	0.98	.144
	Clearwater (FSL)	HiA	2	1	1.64	7	0	0	2	11	5	1	3	18	14.7	0.73	.135
	Reading (EL)	AA	2	5	5.56	18	0	0	1	23	13	3	22	30	11.9	1.54	.169
Minor League Totals			9	10	2.78	62	0	0	10	87	46	5	62	133	13.7	1.24	.158

18 EDGAR GARCIA, RHP

BA GRADE

40 Risk: Medium

Born: Oct. 4, 1996. **B-T:** R-R. **Ht.:** 6-1. **Wt.:** 200. **Signed:** Dominican Republic, 2014. **Signed by:** Carlos Salas.

TRACK RECORD: The Phillies signed Garcia for $30,000 out of the Dominican Republic when he was 17. While Garcia started 15 games in 2017 after opening the year in the bullpen, he was strictly a reliever last season for Double-A Reading and Triple-A Lehigh Valley, with his 10.3 K/9 at Reading the highest strikeout rate at any level of his career.

SCOUTING REPORT: Garcia has solid-average control of a fastball that grew as the season went on, sitting at 90-92 mph early and getting to 92-95 mph by the end of the year. He can scrape 96 mph, with his fastball producing lively armside run and sink. Garcia's best pitch, however, is his plus slider—a swing-and-miss weapon to both righties and lefties with hard downward action. Garcia has a show-me changeup in his repertoire, but he leans on his fastball and slider, sometimes throwing more sliders than fastballs.

THE FUTURE: Garcia could open the year back in Triple-A, but if he's pitching well he should make his major league debut in 2019. His fastball/sldier mix should allow him to become an effective middle reliever.

Year	Club (League)	Class	W	L	ERA	G	GS	CG	SV	IP	H	HR	BB	SO	K/9	WHIP	AVG
2016	Lakewood (SAL)	LoA	4	1	2.80	27	4	0	2	61	59	6	15	59	8.7	1.21	.249
2017	Clearwater (FSL)	HiA	3	4	4.47	27	15	0	0	89	95	10	31	89	9.0	1.42	.271
2018	Reading (EL)	AA	7	2	3.32	47	0	0	8	60	45	6	25	68	10.3	1.17	.204
	Lehigh Valley (IL)	AAA	0	1	7.71	5	0	0	0	5	4	2	2	4	7.7	1.29	.235
Minor League Totals			17	10	3.54	130	22	0	14	272	250	25	87	273	9.0	1.24	.239

19 ZACH WARREN, LHP

BA GRADE

45 Risk: High

Born: June 9, 1996. **B-T:** L-L. **Ht.:** 6-5. **Wt.:** 200. **Drafted:** Tennessee, 2017 (14th round). **Signed by:** Timi Moni.

TRACK RECORD: Warren played for USA Baseball's Collegiate National Team in the summer of 2016, but during his junior year at Tennessee in 2017 he posted a 6.31 ERA and a 34-29 K-BB mark in 51 innings, dropping him to the Phillies in the 14th round. With low Class A Lakewood for his first full season in 2018, Warren looked totally different, striking out 44 percent of the batters he faced coming out of the BlueClaws' bullpen.

SCOUTING REPORT: Warren has a tall, physically imposing frame, but at Tennessee he had trouble syncing up his long levers in his delivery, leading to scattered command and a high ERA. While his control is still below-average, he made significant strides synchronizing his mechanics and his fastball jumped multiple grades. In college, Warren typically worked in the upper 80s, but in 2018 he was sitting at 93-96 mph. He added more power and sharpness to his breaking pitch, a plus curveball that he can crank up to the low 80s, with tight, spiking action to dive underneath the barrels of hitters.

THE FUTURE: Warren looks like another quality late-round find by the Phillies. With a prolific ability to miss bats, Warren could develop into a high-leverage reliever, with high Class A Clearwater his next step.

Year	Club (League)	Class	W	L	ERA	G	GS	CG	SV	IP	H	HR	BB	SO	K/9	WHIP	AVG
2017	Williamsport (NYP)	SS	0	3	3.00	16	0	0	0	33	29	0	15	40	10.9	1.33	.236
2018	Lakewood (SAL)	LoA	3	2	1.91	39	0	0	15	57	33	2	28	100	15.9	1.08	.172
Minor League Totals			3	5	2.31	55	0	0	15	90	62	2	43	140	14.1	1.17	.197

20 AUSTIN LISTI, OF/1B

BA GRADE

45 Risk: High

Born: Nov. 5, 1993. **B-T:** R-R. **Ht.:** 6-0. **Wt.:** 218. **Drafted:** Dallas Baptist, 2017 (17th round). **Signed by:** Brian Kohlscheen.

TRACK RECORD: Listi produced a monster senior season for Dallas Baptist, batting .336/.454/.735 with 24 home runs in 63 games, breaking the DBU record with 53 career home runs. Drafted as a 23-year-old, late-round senior sign, Listi kept raking in his first full season with the Phillies, winning the Paul Owens award as the organization's top minor league hitter before finishing the year in the Arizona Fall League.

SCOUTING REPORT: At 24, Listi was old for his levels last season, though that's because he stayed in college for four seasons and missed the 2015 campaign when he entered SEAL training in preparation for the Navy, though he didn't enlist and returned to baseball in 2016. It's been an unconventional path for Listi, but he has hit and hit for power through Double-A. Listi has quick hands and there is some stiffness to his stroke, but he doesn't swing and miss much, making consistent contact with a good plan at the plate. Listi has above-average raw power and he gets to it in games with a swing geared to lift the ball and a pull-minded approach. A well-below-average runner, Listi mostly split time between first base, left field and DH, with an average arm that allowed him to play some right field as well.

THE FUTURE: Listi will be 25 in 2019, with a chance to open the year in Triple-A Lehigh Valley. There's some risk he could follow the career path of former Phillies prospect Darin Ruf, but Listi he has shown enough hitting ability to go with his power that he could squeeze out a better career.

Year	Club (League)	Class	AVG	G	AB	R	H	2B	3B	HR	RBI	BB	SO	SB	CS	OBP	SLG
2017	Williamsport (NYP)	SS	.293	22	75	14	22	5	0	3	17	8	16	3	0	.372	.480
	Lakewood (SAL)	LoA	.242	31	120	16	29	7	2	4	11	4	30	0	0	.276	.433
2018	Clearwater (FSL)	HiA	.344	58	209	37	72	16	1	9	45	34	42	0	0	.453	.560
	Reading (EL)	AA	.281	65	217	26	61	9	0	9	39	28	52	0	0	.372	.447
Minor League Totals			.296	176	621	93	184	37	3	25	112	74	140	3	0	.383	.486

21 COLE IRVIN, LHP

BA GRADE

40 Risk: High

Born: Jan. 31, 1994. **B-T:** L-L. **Ht.:** 6-4. **Wt.:** 190. **Drafted:** Oregon, 2016 (5th round). **Signed by:** Hilton Richardson.

TRACK RECORD: Irvin was a first-team All-Freshman pitcher at Oregon in 2013, then missed the entire 2014 season with Tommy John surgery. He has moved quickly since the Phillies drafted him in 2016, winning the Triple-A International League Pitcher of the Year award in 2018.

SCOUTING REPORT: Irvin squeezes the most out of his ability as a thoroughly prepared student of the game. That's important for Irvin because his stuff doesn't allow him much margin for error. He's an athletic pitcher who commands his fastball well, pitching in the upper-80s to low-90s with good movement. His best secondary pitch is an average changeup that he has the confidence to throw whether he's ahead or behind in the count. He throws a curveball and slider that are both fringe-average pitches. Irvin has posted modest strikeout rates in his career, relying more on his ability to change speeds and locate to have success. Despite having TJ in college, Irvin has thrown 150-plus innings in both 2017 and 2018.

THE FUTURE: Irvin might have enough stuff to stick around as a starter in the back of a rotation, though there's risk he could be more of an up-and-down guy.

Year	Club (League)	Class	W	L	ERA	G	GS	CG	SV	IP	H	HR	BB	SO	K/9	WHIP	AVG
2016	Williamsport (NYP)	SS	5	1	1.97	10	7	0	0	46	36	2	8	37	7.3	0.96	.209
2017	Clearwater (FSL)	HiA	4	6	2.55	12	11	0	0	67	68	2	14	52	7.0	1.22	.265
	Reading (EL)	AA	5	3	4.06	13	13	0	0	84	72	12	24	66	7.0	1.14	.228
2018	Lehigh Valley (IL)	AAA	14	4	2.57	26	25	1	0	161	135	11	35	131	7.3	1.05	.227
Minor League Totals			28	14	2.84	61	56	1	0	358	311	27	81	286	7.2	1.09	.232

22 RODOLFO DURAN, C

BA GRADE

45 Risk: Very High

Born: Feb. 19, 1998. **B-T:** R-R. **Ht.:** 5-9. **Wt.:** 185. **Signed:** Dominican Republic, 2014. **Signed by:** Carlos Salas.

TRACK RECORD: The Phillies signed Duran for $75,000 after the 2014 season, with Duran spending the next three years in the organization's short-season affiliates. His first taste of full-season baseball came in 2018, when Duran posted big power numbers and impressed with his defense for low Class A Lakewood.

SCOUTING REPORT: Duran has the skills to develop into an average to plus defensive catcher. With a plus arm and quick transfer, Duran produces pop times in the low-1.9s, which helped him throw out 48 percent of runners in 2017 and 42 percent in 2018. Duran is flexible behind the plate, but his throwing is more advanced than his blocking, as he still lets too many balls sneak past him. Solid-average raw power is his offensive carrying tool, with strong wrists and forearms helping Duran post a .235 isolated power in 2018. Duran doesn't swing and miss excessively, but he needs to improve his breaking ball recognition and would benefit from a more selective approach, with a pull-heavy mentality that leaves him vulnerable on the outer third and hampers his on-base percentage.

THE FUTURE: Duran has the offensive ability to develop into a power-hitting catcher along the lines of Wilin Rosario, though with the tools to be a better defender. He's headed to high Class A Clearwater in 2019.

Year	Club (League)	Class	AVG	G	AB	R	H	2B	3B	HR	RBI	BB	SO	SB	CS	OBP	SLG
2016	Williamsport (NYP)	SS	.222	2	9	1	2	0	0	0	0	0	1	0	0	.222	.222
	Phillies (GCL)	R	.315	32	73	14	23	2	1	3	14	4	14	1	1	.346	.493
2017	Williamsport (NYP)	SS	.252	48	159	14	40	9	3	0	6	8	36	0	1	.298	.346
2018	Lakewood (SAL)	LoA	.260	88	311	44	81	17	1	18	46	20	75	1	1	.304	.495
Minor League Totals			.254	206	633	84	161	31	6	21	76	35	143	3	5	.296	.422

23 DANIEL BRITO, 2B

Born: Jan. 13, 1998. **B-T:** L-R. **Ht.:** 6-1. **Wt.:** 180. **Signed:** Venezuela, 2014.
Signed by: Carlos Salas.

BA GRADE	
45	Risk: Very High

TRACK RECORD: Signed for $650,000 as a 16-year-old in Venezuela, Brito repeated low Class A Lakewood in 2018 and struggled his first two months. His numbers ticked up in June, with Brito batting .278/.337/.361 over his final 47 games before an early August promotion to high Class A Clearwater.

SCOUTING REPORT: Brito and shortstop Arquimedes Gamboa formed a promising but vexing middle infield in Clearwater, with both showing flashes of raw talent that has yet to translate into offensive performance. Brito has the components to be a good hitter with a fairly loose, sound swing and good bat control. However, he can get too aggressive and pull-happy, leaving him vulnerable on the outer third, and when Brito struggles, he has a habit of pressing, causing his troubles to compound. Where Brito did make progress is on defense. An average runner with an average arm, Brito improved his first-step reads off the bat and improved his range, grading out as a plus fielder with good hands at second base.

THE FUTURE: Brito has a chance to develop into an everyday second baseman, but there's still considerable risk until his performance ticks up for more than a short burst. He will open 2019 back in Clearwater.

Year	Club (League)	Class	AVG	G	AB	R	H	2B	3B	HR	RBI	BB	SO	SB	CS	OBP	SLG
2016	Phillies (GCL)	R	.284	47	190	35	54	10	5	2	25	21	27	7	2	.355	.421
2017	Lakewood (SAL)	LoA	.239	112	447	54	107	15	1	6	32	33	95	12	9	.298	.318
2018	Lakewood (SAL)	LoA	.252	92	329	33	83	13	2	4	31	27	64	15	6	.309	.340
	Clearwater (FSL)	HiA	.250	27	92	8	23	5	2	0	7	6	19	1	1	.300	.348
Minor League Totals			.255	338	1270	163	324	53	13	12	114	122	227	43	27	.325	.346

24 JHAILYN ORTIZ, OF

Born: Nov. 18, 1998. **B-T:** R-R. **Ht.:** 6-3. **Wt.:** 240. **Signed:** Dominican Republic, 2015. **Signed by:** Sal Agostinelli.

BA GRADE	
45	Risk: Very High

TRACK RECORD: The Phillies made a big bet on Ortiz in 2015, signing the 16-year-old outfielder for $4.01 million, a franchise record for an international amateur signing. Ortiz had big power and a shaky hit tool, but he was trending up after the 2017 season when he mashed in short-season Williamsport. But in his full-season debut with low Class A Lakewood in 2019, Ortiz fell flat, dinging his stock significantly.

SCOUTING REPORT: Ortiz's best tool is his raw power. He's a strong, enormous teenager with plus-plus power that shows up in BP or when he gets a fastball that crosses through his swing path. Ortiz has the upside to hit 30-plus home runs in a season, but he has a long way to go as a hitter. He struggled to recognize breaking pitches last season, often looking lost with his timing and balance, leading to an alarming 33 percent strikeout rate. Ortiz looks like a first baseman and he might end up there. He's a well below-average runner with limited range, although his arm is a plus tool.

THE FUTURE: Ortiz's 2018 season raised a lot of red flags, but he will still just be 20 next season.

Year	Club (League)	Class	AVG	G	AB	R	H	2B	3B	HR	RBI	BB	SO	SB	CS	OBP	SLG
2016	Phillies (GCL)	R	.231	47	173	29	40	9	1	8	27	17	53	8	2	.325	.434
2017	Williamsport (NYP)	SS	.302	47	159	27	48	15	1	8	30	18	47	5	1	.401	.560
2018	Lakewood (SAL)	LoA	.225	110	405	51	91	18	2	13	47	35	148	2	2	.297	.375
Minor League Totals			.243	204	737	107	179	42	4	29	104	70	248	15	5	.327	.429

25 RAFAEL MARCHAN, C

Born: Feb .25, 1999. **B-T:** B-R. **Ht.:** 5-9. **Wt.:** 180. **Signed:** Venezuela, 2015. **Signed by:** Jesus Mendez.

BA GRADE	
45	Risk: Very High

TRACK RECORD: Marchan played shortstop and was the top offensive performer on Venezuela's U-15 World Cup team in 2014, but his stocky build and lack of range didn't fit at shortstop, so he moved behind the plate and signed with the Phillies for $200,000. Marchan didn't do much when he got to the U.S. in 2017, but hit well as a 19-year-old in the short-season New York-Penn League in 2018.

SCOUTING REPORT: Marchan's best attribute is his knack for putting the ball in play. His swing is short and flat, staying through the hitting zone a long time. He has a contact-oriented approach, striking out in just nine percent of his plate appearances last season while spreading line drives around to all fields. Marchan is mostly a singles hitter—he has yet to homer in 125 career games—and while he can shoot a ball into the alleys, he doesn't project to crack double-digit home runs. Marchan conquered throwing issues from earlier in his career and improved his arm strength to become an above-average tool. There are still some questions about whether Marchan will stick behind the plate, as he will need to improve his ability to block pitches in the dirt.

THE FUTURE: Marchan's hitting ability could carry him as an offensive-minded catcher, though he will need to get stronger to do more damage on contact. Low Class A Lakewood is up next.

Year	Club (League)	Class	AVG	G	AB	R	H	2B	3B	HR	RBI	BB	SO	SB	CS	OBP	SLG
2016	Phillies2 (DSL)	R	.333	44	171	23	57	7	1	0	34	16	14	6	0	.380	.386
2017	Phillies (GCL)	R	.238	30	84	10	20	5	0	0	10	4	8	1	0	.290	.298
2018	Williamsport (NYP)	SS	.301	51	196	28	59	8	2	0	12	11	18	9	6	.343	.362
Minor League Totals			.302	125	451	61	136	20	3	0	56	31	40	16	6	.347	.359

26 NICOLAS TORRES, 2B

BA GRADE

45 Risk: Extreme

Born: Sept. 23, 1999. **B-T:** R-R. **Ht.:** 5-10. **Wt.:** 160. **Signed:** Venezuela, 2016. **Signed by:** Jesus Mendez.

TRACK RECORD: Despite limited stature, Torres stood out enough as an amateur in Venezuela for the Phillies to sign him for $665,000 when he was 16. After making his debut in the Dominican Summer League in 2017, Torres continued to show a promising combination of hitting and athleticism in the Rookie-level Gulf Coast League last year.

SCOUTING REPORT: Torres' two main tools are his hitting ability and his speed. He was hitting .375/.398/.513 through July, and while his numbers dipped in the final month of the season, Torres batted over .300 for the second straight year. There are some unconventional aspects to Torres' swing, but he makes consistent contact and did a better job of hitting to all fields in 2018 after getting pull-happy the previous year. He has minimal power and doesn't look like he will hit mroe than 6-10 home runs per year. Torres is a plus runner with the athleticism and defensive actions to stick in the middle infield, but he has a below-average arm, so the Phillies have developed him at second base, where he could be an average or better defender.

THE FUTURE: Torres will have to get stronger to drive the ball with more impact, but his bat and ability to stick in the middle of the diamond make him an intriguing sleeper for the organization.

Year	Club (League)	Class	AVG	G	AB	R	H	2B	3B	HR	RBI	BB	SO	SB	CS	OBP	SLG
2017	Phillies White (DSL)	R	.333	69	240	40	80	13	4	0	28	11	31	11	7	.383	.421
2018	Phillies East (GCL)	R	.302	39	139	19	42	8	1	1	19	8	27	7	1	.340	.396
Minor League Totals			.322	108	379	59	122	21	5	1	47	19	58	18	8	.368	.412

27 CONNOR SEABOLD, RHP

BA GRADE

40 Risk: High

Born: Jan. 24, 1996. **B-T:** R-R. **Ht.:** 6-3. **Wt.:** 196. **Drafted:** Cal State Fullerton, 2017 (3rd round). **Signed by:** Demerius Pittman.

TRACK RECORD: Seabold was a three-year starter at Fullerton, where he dissected hitters with pinpoint command. Signed for $525,000 as a third-round pick in 2017, Seabold moved through two levels in his first full season, reaching Double-A Reading at the end of June.

SCOUTING REPORT: As a junior at Fullerton, Seabold mostly sat 87-88 mph and touched 92 mph. He was up a bit from there in 2018, getting as high as 94, with excellent ability to locate his fastball. His control is a potential 70 on the 20-80 scale. There might not be any more velocity coming for Seabold, so getting more out of his offspeed stuff will be key for him. He doesn't have a true out pitch right now, though his changeup is an average offering and his most advanced secondary weapon. His slurvy curveball is a fringe-average pitch.

THE FUTURE: Seabold could have enough in his arsenal to become a back-end starter, though there's risk his stuff might top out beneath that level. If he pitches well in 2019, he's a candidate to make his major league debut by the end of the year, though 2020 seems more likely.

Year	Club (League)	Class	W	L	ERA	G	GS	CG	SV	IP	H	HR	BB	SO	K/9	WHIP	AVG
2017	Williamsport (NYP)	SS	2	0	0.90	5	0	0	0	10	5	0	2	13	11.7	0.70	.143
2018	Clearwater (FSL)	HiA	4	4	3.77	12	12	1	0	72	57	6	14	68	8.5	0.99	.213
	Reading (EL)	AA	1	4	4.91	11	11	0	0	59	55	10	19	64	9.8	1.26	.241
Minor League Totals			7	8	4.04	28	23	1	0	140	117	16	35	145	9.3	1.08	.221

28 ARQUIMEDES GAMBOA, SS

BA GRADE

45 Risk: Extreme

Born: Sept. 23, 1997. **B-T:** B-R. **Ht.:** 6-0. **Wt.:** 185. **Drafted:** Venezuela, 2014. **Signed by:** Carlos Salas.

TRACK RECORD: Gamboa was a high-profile international prospect when he was 16, signing out of Venezuela for $900,000. He struggled the next two seasons, but showed signs that things were starting to click for him at the end of the 2017 season. He didn't carry that success over into 2018, however,

struggling in the high Class A Florida State League and then after the season in the Arizona Fall League.
SCOUTING REPORT: Gamboa has been a frustrating prospect, exhibiting promising tools and athleticism with glimpses of being able to put things together at the plate, but never in more than short bursts. Gamboa is an athletic shortstop with a plus arm. He's an above-average runner who reacts well off the bat and has solid range for the position. While Gamboa has the tools to stick at shortstop, he needs to show more at the plate. The Phillies have pushed him aggressively and Gamboa doesn't strike out excessively, but he's a pull-heavy hitter who rolls over a lot of grounders to the right side. He's a switch-hitter whose swing is better from the left side, though he didn't hit well from either side in 2018. Gamboa has gap power, with a chance to grow into 8-12 home runs.
THE FUTURE: The Phillies have promoted Gamboa one level each season, but he probably needs to repeat the FSL in 2019.

Year	Club (League)	Class	AVG	G	AB	R	H	2B	3B	HR	RBI	BB	SO	SB	CS	OBP	SLG
2016	Williamsport (NYP)	SS	.200	35	130	15	26	6	0	2	15	9	28	5	1	.254	.292
2017	Lakewood (SAL)	LoA	.261	79	307	44	80	12	3	6	29	33	52	8	0	.328	.378
2018	Clearwater (FSL)	HiA	.214	114	434	49	93	14	4	2	37	53	111	6	4	.304	.279
Minor League Totals			.221	278	1061	131	235	39	10	10	97	110	241	27	7	.296	.305

29 MATT VIERLING, OF

BA GRADE

40 Risk: Very High

Born: Sept. 16, 1996. **B-T:** R-R. **Ht.:** 6-3. **Wt.:** 205. **Drafted:** Notre Dame, 2018 (5th round). **Signed by:** Justin Morgenstern.

TRACK RECORD: An unsigned 30th-round pick of the Cardinals out of high school in 2015, Vierling hit well at Notre Dame, though he struggled to make contact with wood bats in the summer of 2017 in the Cape Cod League. After the Phillies drafted Vierling in the fifth round in 2018, he signed for $380,000 and helped ease those wood bat concerns by hitting well in low Class A Lakewood.
SCOUTING REPORT: Vierling has slightly above-average raw power with lift in his swing. Scouts who followed Vierling as an amateur had concerns about his pure hitting ability moving up at higher levels, but he helped ease some of those concerns with how well he hit in full-season ball after signing. Vierling is athletic and moves around well in the outfield for his size, playing some center field but fitting best in a corner. He also spent time pitching at Notre Dame, running his fastball into the low 90s, and it translates to a plus arm in the outfield.
THE FUTURE: If Vierling can carry over his initial pro success in 2019, he could move quickly.

Year	Club (League)	Class	AVG	G	AB	R	H	2B	3B	HR	RBI	BB	SO	SB	CS	OBP	SLG
2018	Williamsport (NYP)	SS	.420	12	50	8	21	3	1	1	6	3	2	2	1	.453	.580
	Lakewood (SAL)	LoA	.293	50	184	24	54	15	0	6	25	10	38	5	5	.342	.473
Minor League Totals			.321	62	234	32	75	18	1	7	31	13	40	7	6	.365	.496

30 JAMES McARTHUR, RHP

BA GRADE

45 Risk: Extreme

Born: Dec. 11, 1996. **B-T:** R-R. **Ht.:** 6-7. **Wt.:** 230. **Drafted:** Mississippi, 2018 (12th round). **Signed by:** Mike Stauffer.

TRACK RECORD: McArthur was a three-year starter at Mississippi, but there was never a year where everything clicked for him. He never posted an ERA under 4.00, including a junior season with a 4.48 ERA and a 58-38 K-BB mark in 66 innings. The Phillies liked his combination of size and stuff, signing McArthur for $215,000 as a 12th-round pick in 2018, and he showed encouraging signs with strong performance in his pro debut.
SCOUTING REPORT: McArthur has an extra-large, 6-foot-7 frame, sitting in the 92-94 mph range and touching 96 with good extension that helps his fastball get on hitters quickly. His breaking ball flashes above-average with sharp, late biting action when it's on, though it's still inconsistent. He also throws a changeup that's a below-average pitch. Like a lot of extremely tall pitchers, McArthur struggled to control his delivery, leading to troubles with his command and control in college, although he was a solid-strike thrower in a small sample size with short-season Williamsport.
THE FUTURE: It might take some time for everything to click for McArthur, but there are some signs of him being another quality late-round pick for the Phillies. He's scheduled for low Class A Lakewood in 2019.

Year	Club (League)	Class	W	L	ERA	G	GS	CG	SV	IP	H	HR	BB	SO	K/9	WHIP	AVG
2018	Phillies West (GCL)	R	0	0	0.00	1	0	0	0	1	1	0	0	2	18.0	1.00	.250
	Williamsport (NYP)	SS	2	0	0.64	8	5	0	0	28	15	0	10	31	9.8	0.88	.158
	Lakewood (SAL)	LoA	0	0	0.00	1	1	0	0	4	0	0	1	2	4.5	0.25	.000
Minor League Totals			2	0	0.54	10	6	0	0	33	16	0	11	35	9.5	0.81	.145

Pittsburgh Pirates

BY DUSTIN DOPIRAK

For decades, Pirates ownership has been chided for being cheap, and for years, its front office has drawn criticism from fans for not making bold moves at the trade deadline. The Pirates made some important late-season moves during their three straight trips to the postseason from 2013 to 2015, then mostly sold at the deadline in 2016 and 2017, and they had been loath to part with top prospects.

Late in 2018, however, the Pirates made moves that flew in the face of their traditional philosophy and could alter the course of the organization for years to come. It remains to be seen whether the alteration will be for better or worse.

The Pirates acquired starter Chris Archer and reliever Keone Kela—both among the most sought after arms on the trade market—but they paid a heavy price to acquire both. The Pirates gave the Rays Austin Meadows and Tyler Glasnow, both of who were considered jewels of the Pittsburgh farm system before being called up to the big leagues, then added 2017 first-round righthander Shane Baz as a player to be named. Drafted out of high school from Texas, Baz was still in the embryonic stage of his development, but signs suggested he had a top-of-the-rotation arm and he was the No. 2 rated prospect in the Pirates' system at the time. Kela was less expensive, but the Pirates still had to give up a Top 10 Prospect in hard-throwing lefthander Taylor Hearn.

The payoff was not immediate. The Pirates finished 82-79 to post their fourth winning season since 1992, but they faded from playoff contention by September. Archer finished strong with a 2.70 ERA in September, but his 6.45 ERA in August was a big part of the reason the Pirates fell out of the race in the first place.

Archer is, however, potentially under contract for three more seasons because of options in 2020 and 2021. He, Jameson Taillon, Trevor Williams and Joe Musgrove give the Pirates a talented core for their rotation, and No. 1 prospect Mitch Keller is in Triple-A and could join the rotation by the end of 2019. If those five perform, it might not matter much that the Pirates are low on top-line starting pitchers behind them in the system. But if they don't, the Pirates could be hamstrung in that department for years.

Trading away Meadows was also seismic for the organization. With him, the Pirates had four potential top-to-middle-of-the-order bats, counting also Starling Marte, Corey Dickerson and Gregory Polanco. Without him, and with Polanco sidelined with a shoulder injury for the early part

Homegrown ace Jameson Taillon logged a career high 32 starts and 191 innings.

PROJECTED 2022 LINEUP

Catcher	Elias Diaz (31)
First Base	Josh Bell (29)
Second Base	Kevin Kramer (28)
Third Base	Ke'Bryan Hayes (25)
Shortstop	Cole Tucker (25)
Left Field	Gregory Polanco (30)
Center Field	Travis Swaggerty (24)
Right Field	Oneil Cruz (24)
No. 1 Starter	Jameson Taillon (30)
No. 2 Starter	Mitch Keller (26)
No. 3 Starter	Joe Musgrove (29)
No. 4 Starter	Trevor Williams (30)
No. 5 Starter	Steven Brault (30)
Closer	Felipe Vasquez (30)

of 2019, there will be a hole in the outfield. The Pirates will have to make due with sub-optimal options.

The Pirates do, however, have talent coming up in the infield, and they could elevate shortstop Kevin Newman and second baseman Kevin Kramer to the majors with the loss of free agents Josh Harrison and Jody Mercer. Third baseman Ke'Bryan Hayes won a minor league Gold Glove for the second straight season and might not be far from the big leagues either.

But for the organization as a whole, the 2018 season will ultimately be defined by what they had to give up. The Pirates still have a young core, but the prospect depth has thinned.

PITTSBURGH PIRATES

TOP 2019 ROOKIE: Kevin Newman, SS. With Jordy Mercer gone, Newman will get every opportunity win the job at shortstop.

BREAKOUT PROSPECT: Jonah Davis, OF. He caught fire in his junior year in California and kept raking in the Appalachian League. Another big year could fast track him.

SLEEPER: Rodolfo Castro, 2B. The 19-year old Dominican hit 12 home runs at low Class A West Virginia and seems to have found his defensive home after switching from shortstop

SOURCE OF TOP 30 TALENT			
Homegrown	26	Acquired	4
College	10	Trade	4
Junior college	0	Rule 5 draft	0
High school	11	Independent league	0
Nondrafted free agent	0	Free agent/waivers	0
International	5		

LF
Bryan Reynolds (8)
Jonah Davis (24)
Logan Hill
Jordan George
Casey Hughston

CF
Travis Swaggerty (3)
Jason Martin (10)
Lolo Sanchez (12)
Jared Oliva (19)
Sergio Campaña (20)

RF
Calvin Mitchell (9)
Conner Uselton (25)
Bligh Madris

3B
Ke'Bryan Hayes (2)
Hunter Owen
Dylan Busby

SS
Oneil Cruz (4)
Kevin Newman (6)
Cole Tucker (7)
Ji-Hwan Bae (18)
Stephen Alemais (26)
Adrian Valerio

2B
Kevin Kramer (5)
Pablo Reyes (23)
Alfredo Reyes
Rodolfo Castro

1B
Will Craig (16)
Mason Martin
Erich Weiss
Albert Baur

C
Deon Stafford (22)
Jacob Stallings
Jin-De Hang
Jason Delay
Christian Kelley

LHP	
LHSP	**LHRP**
Brandon Waddell	Blake Weimer
Braeden Ogle	
Domingo Robles	
Cam Vieaux	

RHP	
RHSP	**RHRP**
Mitch Keller (1)	Nick Burdi
Luis Escobar (12)	Alex McRae
Steven Jennings (13)	Yeudy Garcia
Braxton Ashcraft (14)	Tanner Anderson
Clay Holmes (17)	Beau Sulser
Tahnaj Thomas (15)	Angel German
Cody Bolton (21)	
J.T. Brubaker (27)	
Gage Hinsz (28)	
Dario Argazal (29)	
Santiago Florez (30)	
Travis MacGregor	
Tyler Eppler	
Scooter Hightower	

DRAFT ANALYSIS

2018

BEST PURE HITTER: OF Travis Swaggerty (1) improved himself each year at South Alabama, and the Pirates rewarded him by taking him with the No. 10 overall pick. While Swaggerty has five impressive tools, he's got a great approach at the plate—he walked 54 times to 38 strikeouts in as a junior—and at least an average hit tool.

BEST POWER HITTER: OF Jonah Davis (15) has plus raw power that he finally started tapping into as a junior with California, hitting a career-high 14 home runs. The returns in pro ball are strong, as Davis hit 12 home runs, six triples and 15 doubles in the Appalachian League, with the fifth-best slugging percentage in the league (.612).

FASTEST RUNNER: Swaggerty is a 60-grade runner who swiped 48 bags in college before going 9-for-12 in the New York Penn League. OF Daniel Amaral (14) is also a 60-grade runner.

BEST DEFENSIVE PLAYER: SS Connor Kaiser (3) was lauded for his reliable defense at shortstop throughout college, as a sure-handed, steady glove lacking elite range but equipped with above-average arm strength. C Grant Koch (5) steadily improved himself behind the plate at Arkansas, and has an accurate arm with a solid transfer and footwork. Swaggerty profiles as a plus defender in center field with his speed and above-average arm.

BEST ATHLETE: Swaggerty might be the obvious answer here as the five-tool center fielder with an obvious plus run tool, but Ashcraft was an elite high school football player who set many records as a wide receiver with Robinson (Texas) High.

BEST FASTBALL: RHP Logan Stoelke (9) has an above-average fastball that's been up to 95 mph. Stoelke had a solid pro debut, posting a 1.59 ERA across two leagues, with a 13.9 K/9—all for a $50,000 signing bonus.

BEST SECONDARY PITCH: There are a number of candidates here between RHP Aaron Shortridge's (4) solid changeup, or a slider from RHP Braxton Ashcraft (2) or RHP Conner Loeprich (20).

TOP DRAFT PICKS OF THE DECADE

Year	Player, Pos	2018 Org
2009	Tony Sanchez, C	Rangers
2010	Jameson Taillon, RHP	Pirates
2011	Gerrit Cole, RHP	Astros
2012	*Mark Appel, RHP	Did not play
2013	Austin Meadows, OF	Rays
2014	Cole Tucker, SS	Pirates
2015	Kevin Newman, SS	Pirates
2016	Will Craig, 3B	Pirates
2017	Shane Baz, RHP	Rays
2018	Travis Swaggerty, OF	Pirates

* Did not sign

BEST PRO DEBUT: It's hard to argue with the .306/.398/.612 line and extra-base hitting that Davis managed in the Appy League, but 18-year-old OF Jack Herman (30) hitting .340/.435/.489 with just one fewer walk than strikeout in the Gulf Coast League is a loud pro debut as well.

MOST INTRIGUING BACKGROUND: Amaral's father Rich was a 10-year major leaguer and played at least 95 innings at every position outside of catcher and pitcher. He finished fifth in the 1993 AL Rookie of the Year voting.

CLOSEST TO THE MAJORS: Swaggerty is a college performer with plus defense at a premium position and an advanced hit tool.

BEST LATE-ROUND PICK: Davis and Herman are both solid options, though RHP Michael Burrows (11) is also a name to keep an eye on after ranking as the No. 5 prospect out of the state of Connecticut and signing for $500,000.

THE ONE WHO GOT AWAY: RHP Gunnar Hoglund (1s) had one of the best spring seasons of any prep player in the class and made a jump forward with his stuff while also possessing arguably the best command of any high school pitcher. Some scouts projected future 60 command on him. He'll head to Mississippi ,where he should provide an instant impact in the rotation.

— CARLOS COLLAZO

2017

RHP Shane Baz (1) has excited and was a key piece of the trade for Chris Archer. OF Calvin Mitchell (2) had a strong full-season debut. Fellow prep picks RHP Steven Jennings (2) and OF Conner Uselton (2s) were limited by injuries.

GRADE: B

2016

1B Will Craig (1) and SS Stephen Alemais (3) are the only two players from this class to make the book. While neither has lived up to expectations, they both reached Double-A and have shown some intriguing tools.

GRADE: D

2015

Five players from this class have reached the big leagues, including the Pirates' first pick - SS Kevin Newman (1) - and their last - LHP Daniel Zamora (40). 3B Ke'Bryan Hayes (1) isn't in that group yet but could be the best of the class.

GRADE: B

1 MITCH KELLER, RHP

Born: April 4, 1996. **B-T:** R-R. **HT:** 6-3. **WT:** 195.
Drafted: HS—Cedar Rapids, Iowa, 2014 (2nd round).
Signed by: Matt Bimeal.

BRAD KRAUSE/FOUR SEAM

Keller's velocity spiked about 10 mph between his junior and senior years of high school, and the mid-90s fastball he displayed at showcase events instantly made him a major prospect. A second-round pick, he was committed to North Carolina but was lured into pro ball by the Pirates' $1 million bonus offer. He made the high Class A Florida State League all-star team in 2017 before being promoted to Double-A Altoona in August of that year. He began 2018 with the Curve and was promoted to Triple-A Indianapolis after allowing just four runs in five starts from May 31-June 25. He also drew the start for the U.S. in the Futures Game. Keller wasn't as consistent at Triple-A, giving up eight runs in 2.2 innings in his first start and finishing the season with a 4.82 ERA.

SCOUTING REPORT: Keller's fastball and curveball are the best in the Pirates' system. He has put muscle on a rangy frame and sits 94-96 mph without a lot of exertion. When he rears back, he can reach 99 mph. He can locate to all four quadrants with late life, tilt and armside run. His plus curveball takes an 11-to-5 shape with hard downward bite. He's struggled for years to perfect his changeup. It doesn't have the velocity differential that the Pirates were hoping for, but it does have enough sink to it that it works as an average groundball pitch. Part of Keller's struggles in 2018 came because of mechanical problems on the backside of his delivery that led to his pitches coming out of his hand flat. He focused on eliminating those problems late in the season but still had the worst season of his career in terms of command. He walked a career-high 55 batters, and Triple-A batters hit .280 off him, evidence that he was missing too much in the middle of the plate.

THE FUTURE: Keller will begin the 2019 season in Indianapolis and have to prove he can consistently dominate before the Pirates consider calling him up to the majors. His long-term future is as a top-to-middle of the rotation arm, most likely as a No. 2 or 3 starter, and the Pirates will likely want to see him make a big league start in September if not sooner. Keller's development is vital to the Pirates success in upcoming years.

BA GRADE / SCOUTING GRADES

60 Risk: Medium

Fastball: 70. Curveball: 60.
Change: 50. Control: 60.

Projected future grades on 20-80 scouting scale.

TOP PROSPECTS OF THE DECADE

Year	Player, Pos	2018 Org
2009	Pedro Alvarez, 3B	Orioles
2010	Pedro Alvarez, 3B	Orioles
2011	Jameson Taillon, RHP	Pirates
2012	Gerrit Cole, RHP	Astros
2013	Gerrit Cole, RHP	Astros
2014	Gregory Polanco, OF	Pirates
2015	Tyler Glasnow, RHP	Rays
2016	Tyler Glasnow, RHP	Rays
2017	Austin Meadows, OF	Rays
2018	Mitch Keller, RHP	Pirates

BEST TOOLS

Best Hitter for Average	Bryan Reynolds
Best Power Hitter	Oneil Cruz
Best Strike-Zone Discipline	Ke'Bryan Hayes
Fastest Baserunner	Cole Tucker
Best Athlete	Cole Tucker
Best Fastball	Mitch Keller
Best Curveball	Mitch Keller
Best Slider	Luis Escobar
Best Changeup	Brandon Waddell
Best Control	Steven Jennings
Best Defensive Catcher	Deon Stafford
Best Defensive Infielder	Ke'Bryan Hayes
Best Infield Arm	Oneil Cruz
Best Defensive Outfielder	Jared Oliva
Best Outfield Arm	Bryan Reynolds

Year	Club (League)	Class	W	L	ERA	G	GS	CG	SV	IP	H	HR	BB	SO	K/9	WHIP	AVG
2016	West Virginia (SAL)	LoA	8	5	2.46	23	23	0	0	124	96	4	18	131	9.5	0.92	.211
	Bradenton (FSL)	HiA	1	0	0.00	1	1	0	0	6	5	0	1	7	10.5	1.00	.227
2017	West Virginia (NYP)	SS	0	0	0.00	2	2	0	0	4	2	0	1	7	15.8	0.75	.143
	Bradenton (FSL)	HiA	6	3	3.14	15	15	0	0	77	57	5	20	64	7.4	1.00	.207
	Altoona (EL)	AA	2	2	3.12	6	6	0	0	35	25	2	11	45	11.7	1.04	.197
2018	Altoona (EL)	AA	9	2	2.72	14	14	0	0	86	64	7	32	76	8.0	1.12	.208
	Bradenton (FSL)	HiA	0	0	2.25	1	1	0	0	4	7	0	1	2	4.5	2.00	.389
	Indianapolis (IL)	AAA	3	2	4.82	10	10	0	0	52	59	3	22	57	9.8	1.55	.280
Minor League Totals			29	17	3.02	87	86	0	0	436	359	22	135	443	9.2	1.13	.224

2 KE'BRYAN HAYES, 3B

Born: Jan. 28, 1997. **B-T:** R-R. **HT:** 6-1. **WT:** 210. **Drafted:** HS—Tomball, Texas, 2015 (1st round). **Signed by:** Tyler Stohr.

TRACK RECORD: Hayes, the son of 14-year big league third baseman Charlie Hayes, has been arguably the most consistent position player in the Pirates' system the last two seasons. After missing most of 2016 with a cracked rib, he was an all-star at high Class A Bradenton in 2017 and at Double-A Altoona in 2018.

SCOUTING REPORT: Hayes has excellent hands and a slow heartbeat at third base, which makes him one of the best gloves in the minors. He isn't fazed by big swings or scorched grounders, and he has an excellent feel for how to read angles off the bat. He has a plus arm and makes steady, accurate throws with plenty of backspin carry across the diamond. Hayes has a short, compact swing with excellent plate discipline. Even through his home run figures are still modest—the seven he hit in 2018 were a career high—he's getting more carry into the gaps. He finished with 45 extra-base hits in 2018, with 31 doubles nearly doubling his previous career high. He isn't a blazer, but he did steal 27 bases in 2017 and 12 in 2018. The Pirates want him to add weight and strength, which could slow him down a tick.

BA GRADE
55 Risk: Medium
Hit: 55. **Power:** 45.
Run: 55. **Field:** 70.
Arm: 60.

THE FUTURE: Hayes will head to Triple-A Indianapolis and isn't far from being Pittsburgh's third baseman.

Year	Club (League)	Class	AVG	G	AB	R	H	2B	3B	HR	RBI	BB	SO	SB	CS	OBP	SLG
2016	West Virginia (SAL)	LoA	.263	65	247	27	65	12	1	6	37	16	51	6	5	.319	.393
	Pirates (GCL)	R	.400	2	5	0	2	1	0	0	0	1	1	0	0	.500	.600
2017	Bradenton (FSL)	HiA	.278	108	421	66	117	16	7	2	43	41	76	27	5	.345	.363
2018	Altoona (EL)	AA	.293	117	437	64	128	31	7	7	47	57	84	12	5	.375	.444
Minor League Totals			.285	348	1295	189	369	65	16	15	147	143	243	53	17	.360	.395

3 ONEIL CRUZ, SS

Born: Oct. 4, 1998. **B-T:** L-R. **HT:** 6-6. **WT:** 175. **Signed:** Dominican Republic, 2015. **Signed by:** Patrick Guerrero/Franklin Taveras/Bob Engle (Dodgers).

TRACK RECORD: When the Dodgers signed Cruz, he was already tall and strong. But he has grown another two inches since signing. The Pirates were thrilled to acquire him in the 2017 trade that sent reliever Tony Watson to the Dodgers. In 2018, Cruz showed he could harness his potential by hitting .286/.343/.488 at low Class A West Virginia.

SCOUTING REPORT: Cruz made massive improvements in his return to low Class A. He slashed his strikeout rate to 22.6 percent while getting to his power more regularly, largely because he showed a much better concept of what pitch he was looking for and cut down on chases out of the zone. His height and long levers mean he has a big strike zone, but Cruz has near top-of-the-scale raw power to go with excellent athleticism. He has a plus-plus arm and surprising speed. There has never been a 6-foot-6 major league shortstop, and Cruz likely won't change that, but he showed improvement in his ability to chop his feet and get down to grounders. He projects as an above-average defender at third base or right field with 20 homer-20 steal potential.

BA GRADE
60 Risk: Extreme
Hit: 50. **Power:** 60.
Run: 55. **Field:** 50.
Arm: 60.

THE FUTURE: Cruz is ready for high Class A Bradenton. He's a risky prospect, but one with all-star potential.

Year	Club (League)	Class	AVG	G	AB	R	H	2B	3B	HR	RBI	BB	SO	SB	CS	OBP	SLG
2016	Dodgers (DSL)	R	.294	55	187	28	55	18	5	0	23	22	44	11	5	.367	.444
2017	Great Lakes (MWL)	LoA	.240	89	342	51	82	9	1	8	36	28	110	8	7	.293	.342
	West Virginia (SAL)	LoA	.218	16	55	9	12	2	1	2	8	8	22	0	0	.317	.400
2018	West Virginia (SAL)	LoA	.286	103	402	66	115	25	7	14	59	34	100	11	5	.343	.488
Minor League Totals			.268	263	986	154	264	54	14	24	126	92	276	30	17	.329	.424

4 TRAVIS SWAGGERTY, OF

Born: Aug. 19, 1997. **B-T:** L-L. **HT:** 5-11. **WT:** 180. **Drafted:** South Alabama, 2018 (1st round). **Signed by:** Darren Mazeroski.

TRACK RECORD: Swaggerty went undrafted after earning all-state honors at Denham Springs High in Louisiana. He initially went to South Alabama as a two-way player but focused on the outfield and put on muscle to add power to his athleticism. He hit 27 home runs and stole 48 bases at South Alabama. He got a little power-hungry as a junior as he struggled more at the plate, but the Pirates still believed in his bat, picking him 10th overall in 2018.

SCOUTING REPORT: Swaggerty is a well-rounded player with potentially no below-average tool if he can improve his hitting. At his best, he shows patience and a short, controlled swing with power thanks to buggy whip in his swing. His quest for power has gotten him into bad habits at times. Swaggerty should stay in center field as an above-average defender. He has plus speed to get to balls in the gap and the above-average arm strength to make throws from center even when he's off balance.

THE FUTURE: The Pirates generally take their time moving players up the ladder, so it wouldn't be a surprise to see Swaggerty head to low Class A Greensboro to start the 2019 season, but he shouldn't finish there as an experienced college star.

BA GRADE

55 Risk: High

Hit: 55. Power: 50.
Run: 60. Field: 55.
Arm: 55.

Year	Club (League)	Class	AVG	G	AB	R	H	2B	3B	HR	RBI	BB	SO	SB	CS	OBP	SLG
2018	West Virginia (NYP)	SS	.288	36	139	22	40	9	1	4	15	15	40	9	3	.365	.453
	West Virginia (SAL)	LoA	.129	16	62	6	8	1	1	1	5	7	18	0	0	.225	.226
Minor League Totals			.239	52	201	28	48	10	2	5	20	22	58	9	3	.322	.383

5 KEVIN KRAMER, 2B

Born: Oct. 3, 1993. **B-T:** L-R. **HT:** 6-0. **WT:** 200. **Drafted:** UCLA, 2015 (2nd round). **Signed by:** Rick Allen.

TRACK RECORD: In Kramer's first two years in the Pirates' system, he developed a reputation as a reliable singles and doubles hitter. After hitting 29 doubles in 2016, he began focusing on hitting more fly balls in a 2017 season shortened by a fractured hand. That switch paid off at Triple-A Indianapolis in 2018 as he reached career highs in both home runs (15) and doubles (35). That earned him a September callup, where he registered five hits but also struck out 20 times in 37 at-bats.

SCOUTING REPORT: Kramer allowed his swing to get bigger with a little more of an uppercut so he could take advantage of added muscle and power. He has accepted more strikeouts and sacrificed what was an above-average hit tool to have average power potential. It's a concession that should pay off for a bat-first second baseman. Defensively, Kramer has good hands but fringy range at second base. His fringe-average arm also limited him in stints at shortstop and third base.

FUTURE: The Pirates would like to keep Kramer in Indianapolis for more seasoning when the season starts. He's on the 40-man roster and should see plenty of big league time in 2019.

BA GRADE

50 Risk: Medium

Hit: 55. Power: 50.
Run: 50. Field: 50.
Arm: 45.

Year	Club (League)	Class	AVG	G	AB	R	H	2B	3B	HR	RBI	BB	SO	SB	CS	OBP	SLG
2016	Bradenton (FSL)	HiA	.277	118	444	56	123	29	2	4	57	48	63	3	9	.352	.378
2017	Altoona (EL)	AA	.297	53	202	31	60	17	3	6	27	17	50	7	2	.380	.500
	Pirates (GCL)	R	.000	1	2	0	0	0	0	0	1	0	1	0	0	.000	.000
	West Virginia (NYP)	SS	.231	3	13	1	3	0	0	0	2	0	2	1	0	.286	.231
2018	Indianapolis (IL)	AAA	.311	129	476	73	148	35	3	15	59	38	127	13	5	.365	.492
	Pittsburgh (NL)	MAJ	.135	21	37	5	5	0	0	0	4	2	20	0	0	.175	.135
Major League Totals			.135	21	37	5	5	0	0	0	4	2	20	0	0	.175	.135
Minor League Totals			.293	362	1364	204	400	90	12	25	166	133	279	36	20	.363	.432

6 COLE TUCKER, SS

Born: July 3, 1996. **B-T:** B-R. **HT:** 6-3. **WT:** 185. **Drafted:** HS—Phoenix, 2014 (1st round). **Signed by:** Mike Steele.

TRACK RECORD: The Pirates coaxed Tucker out of a commitment to Arizona by taking him in the first round in 2014. Labrum surgery ended his 2015 season and cost him time in 2016. In 2017 he suffered a thumb injury and a hand fracture but had his best pro season, stealing 47 bases and slugging .408 combined at high Class A Bradenton and Double-A Altoona. He struggled early in 2018 but a solid July got him back on track. He finished with 33 extra-base hits and 35 stolen bases, then played well in the Arizona Fall League.

SCOUTING REPORT: Tucker has a wiry frame with long levers, and with that much body to control, he can get out of sync at times. He was off balance in the batter's box for most of 2018 and didn't seem to even out until the end of the season. Still, he has some gap-to-gap power, and his plus speed with long strides makes him a constant threat to steal bases. Defensively, he's a fluid athlete with above-average range and an above-average arm, making him a prototype shortstop.

THE FUTURE: Tucker will begin 2019 at Triple-A Indianapolis. He should compete with Kevin Newman to be the Pirates' everyday shortstop in 2020 or shortly thereafter.

BA GRADE
50 Risk: High

Hit: 45. Power: 40.
Run: 60. Field: 55.
Arm: 55.

Year	Club (League)	Class	AVG	G	AB	R	H	2B	3B	HR	RBI	BB	SO	SB	CS	OBP	SLG
2016	West Virginia (SAL)	LoA	.262	15	61	9	16	4	2	1	2	4	9	1	1	.308	.443
	Bradenton (FSL)	HiA	.238	65	269	36	64	12	1	1	25	29	62	5	6	.312	.301
2017	Bradenton (FSL)	HiA	.282	68	277	46	78	15	6	4	32	34	70	37	12	.361	.422
	Altoona (EL)	AA	.257	42	167	25	43	4	5	2	18	21	31	11	3	.349	.377
2018	Altoona (EL)	AA	.259	133	517	77	134	21	7	5	44	55	104	35	12	.333	.356
Minor League Totals			.266	444	1771	278	471	75	26	17	159	185	363	127	45	.337	.366

7 KEVIN NEWMAN, SS

Born: Aug. 4, 1993. **B-T:** R-R. **HT:** 6-1. **WT:** 180. **Drafted:** Arizona, 2015 (1st round). **Signed by:** Derrick Van Dusen.

TRACK RECORD: Newman twice won the Cape Cod League batting title and hit .370 as a junior at Arizona. He has maintained that hit-first, zero-power reputation as a professional. He has slumped whenever he has tried to produce more power, but he stayed inside himself at Triple-A Indianapolis at 2018, hitting .302 with a career-high 30 doubles. That led to his first big league callup, though he hit .209 in 31 games in the majors.

SCOUTING REPORT: The Pirates and Newman have accepted that he isn't going to be a power hitter, and it hasn't worked to try to turn him into one. He has excellent plate coverage and a level, compact swing, so he hits line-drive singles without a lot of lift. The hope is that he can do that well enough at the major league level to hit at the top of the order. Defensively, he's sure-handed with improving if not spectacular range, and he's becoming more fluid as an athlete. He projects as an above-average defender with an average arm.

THE FUTURE: Newman's time to be the Pirates' everyday shortstop has come. How he performs in 2019 will decide whether he can maintain the spot when Cole Tucker is ready to make the leap.

BA GRADE
45 Risk: Medium

Hit: 55. Power: 30.
Run: 50. Field: 55.
Arm: 50.

Year	Club (League)	Class	AVG	G	AB	R	H	2B	3B	HR	RBI	BB	SO	SB	CS	OBP	SLG
2016	Bradenton (FSL)	HiA	.366	41	164	24	60	10	1	3	24	17	12	4	1	.428	.494
	Altoona (EL)	AA	.288	61	233	41	67	11	2	2	28	26	24	6	3	.361	.378
2017	Altoona (EL)	AA	.259	82	343	42	89	18	2	4	30	22	40	4	2	.310	.359
	Indianapolis (IL)	AAA	.283	40	166	23	47	11	2	0	11	7	22	7	1	.314	.373
2018	Indianapolis (IL)	AAA	.302	109	437	74	132	30	2	4	35	31	50	28	11	.350	.407
	Pittsburgh (NL)	MAJ	.209	31	91	7	19	2	0	0	6	4	23	0	1	.247	.231
Major League Totals			.209	31	91	7	19	2	0	0	6	4	23	0	1	.247	.231
Minor League Totals			.288	394	1600	243	461	94	11	15	145	122	178	62	20	.343	.389

8 CALVIN MITCHELL, OF

Born: March 8, 1999. **B-T:** L-L. **HT:** 6-0. **WT:** 190. **Drafted:** HS—San Diego, 2017 (2nd round). **Signed by:** Brian Tracy.

TRACK RECORD: Mitchell fell into the Pirates' lap in the 2017 draft thanks to a rough start to his senior high school season that dropped him just enough to make him a second-round pick. After a modest debut in the Rookie-level Gulf Coast League, Mitchell showed off his power at low Class A West Virginia in 2018.

SCOUTING REPORT: Mitchell has an advanced and polished hitting approach for a young hitter. Scouts are very confident that he will be a plus hitter. He has a smooth, quick swing, and he can sit back and get the barrel on outside pitches to drive them out the opposite way. His approach is advanced for a 19-year-old, and he has a good feel for the strike zone and what pitches he wants to hit. His speed, however, is below-average, and his defensive abilities are far behind his offensive abilities. He profiles as a corner outfielder whose fringy arm strength makes him most likely a left fielder. The Pirates consider him a vocal leader of the 2017 draft class, and he will be carrying the banner for it heading into his second full professional season.

THE FUTURE: Mitchell will have to hit to rise, but has the tools to do so. He will open 2019 at high Class A Bradenton.

BA GRADE
50 Risk: High
Hit: 50. Power: 55.
Run: 45. Field: 40.
Arm: 45.

Year	Club (League)	Class	AVG	G	AB	R	H	2B	3B	HR	RBI	BB	SO	SB	CS	OBP	SLG
2017	Pirates (GCL)	R	.245	43	159	17	39	11	0	2	20	24	35	2	3	.351	.352
2018	West Virginia (SAL)	LoA	.280	119	443	55	124	29	3	10	65	41	109	4	5	.344	.427
Minor League Totals			.271	162	602	72	163	40	3	12	85	65	144	6	8	.346	.407

9 BRYAN REYNOLDS, OF

Born: Jan. 27, 1995. **B-T:** B-R. **HT:** 6-3. **WT:** 205. **Drafted:** Vanderbilt, 2016 (2nd round). **Signed by:** Jeff Wood (Giants).

TRACK RECORD: Reynolds has a long-standing track record as a singles and doubles hitter. He posted a career .329 average at Vanderbilt, hit .346 in the Cape Cod League, and he has yet to hit under .300 at any pro stop. The Pirates acquired him in the Andrew McCutchen trade before the 2018 season. Even after breaking his hamate bone in April, he hit .342 in August to finish at .302 for the year.

SCOUTING REPORT: Reynolds swing is compact and level, and he has a good feel for the zone, but he doesn't have a lot of lift in his swing and frequently puts the ball on the ground. He has good speed and he can hit to all fields from both sides of the plate, but his extra-base hit numbers are low. He finished 2018 with 28, including just seven home runs. Reynolds helps himself out with a solid defensive profile. He has above-average speed and makes decisive reads in the outfield. He runs efficient routes and has a strong and accurate enough arm to play any outfield position. He is solid enough to play center field as a fill-in but his range would be stretched if asked to play there every day.

THE FUTURE: Reynolds will likely begin 2019 at Triple-A Indianapolis. His lack of home run power might consign him to a fourth outfielder role.

BA GRADE
45 Risk: Medium
Hit: 55. Power: 45.
Run: 55. Field: 50.
Arm: 45.

Year	Club (League)	Class	AVG	G	AB	R	H	2B	3B	HR	RBI	BB	SO	SB	CS	OBP	SLG
2016	Salem-Keizer (NWL)	SS	.312	40	154	28	48	12	1	5	30	11	41	2	0	.368	.500
	Augusta (SAL)	LoA	.317	16	63	11	20	5	0	1	8	3	20	1	0	.348	.444
2017	San Jose (CAL)	HiA	.312	121	491	72	153	26	9	10	63	37	106	5	3	.364	.462
2018	Altoona (EL)	AA	.302	88	331	56	100	18	3	7	46	43	73	4	4	.381	.438
Minor League Totals			.309	265	1039	167	321	61	13	23	147	94	240	12	7	.369	.459

10 JASON MARTIN, OF

Born: Sept. 5, 1995. **B-T:** L-R. **HT:** 5-10. **WT:** 185. **Drafted:** HS—Orange, Calif., 2013 (8th round). **Signed by:** Brad Budzinski (Astros).

TRACK RECORD: Martin had a track record of hitting in five seasons in the Astros' system, but he was both unprotected and undrafted in the Rule 5 draft after the 2017 season. The Pirates acquired him as part of the trade that sent Gerrit Cole to Houston. Martin had one of the most impressive first halves of any position player in the system, hitting .325/.392/.522 with nine home runs at Double-A Altoona. He struggled after a promotion to Triple-A Indianapolis, however, finishing with more strikeouts (52) than hits (45).

SCOUTING REPORT: Martin has whip in his swing and average power he generates from his lower half, but he also has a significant leg kick, which can leave him vulnerable against breaking balls. His hands work well at the plate, which gives him a chance to be a .270-.280 hitter. He's an above-average runner who has posted double-digit stolen bases in every season of his career. He has enough to have the range to play center field on occasion and be an above-average left fielder. His arm is his one below-average tool.

BA GRADE

45 Risk: Medium

Hit: 50. Power: 50.
Run: 55. Field: 55.
Arm: 40.

THE FUTURE: Martin was added to the 40-man roster in November. He should be battling Reynolds for a backup outfield role in Pittsburgh before long.

Year	Club (League)	Class	AVG	G	AB	R	H	2B	3B	HR	RBI	BB	SO	SB	CS	OBP	SLG
2016	Lancaster (CAL)	HiA	.270	110	400	74	108	22	7	23	75	55	108	20	12	.357	.533
2017	Buies Creek (CAR)	HiA	.287	46	174	34	50	11	2	7	29	20	42	9	5	.354	.494
	Corpus Christi (TL)	AA	.273	79	300	38	82	24	3	11	37	19	82	7	6	.319	.483
2018	Altoona (EL)	AA	.325	68	255	49	83	13	5	9	34	28	61	7	8	.392	.522
	Indianapolis (IL)	AAA	.211	59	213	20	45	5	3	4	21	17	52	5	4	.270	.319
Minor League Totals			.270	580	2162	354	583	109	38	63	293	246	493	86	66	.343	.443

11 LUIS ESCOBAR, RHP

BA GRADE

50 Risk: High

Born: May 30, 1996. **B-T:** R-R. **HT:** 6-2. **WT:** 210. **Signed:** Colombia, 2013. **Signed by:** Rene Gayo/Orlando Covo.

TRACK RECORD: Escobar signed for $150,000 when he was a 17-year-old, 155-pound third baseman, but he showed enough strength in his arm that the Pirates decided he had a much brighter future standing on the mound. They brought him along slowly and he didn't pitch a full minor league season until 2017 when he struck out 168 batters in 131.2 innings at low Class A West Virginia. He was added to the 40-man roster before the 2018 season. His stats weren't as impressive in 2018, but good enough to move from high Class A Bradenton to Double-A Altoona and he did hold Double-A hitters to a .227 average.

SCOUTING REPORT: Escobar is still evolving into a pitcher. He has the velocity swing that generally sits in the 93-95 mile per hour range but can hit 97 when he rears back. It has ride up in the zone, and plays well off a sharp 12-6 curveball. He's developing good feel for a changeup as well. However, he still struggles with fastball command, and he's walked 119 batters in the last two seasons, including 21 in 35.2 innings in Altoona.

THE FUTURE: Escobar stuff still makes him one of the best pitching prospects in the Pirates system, but he won't advance past Double-A until he shows a better handle of it.

Year	Club (League)	Class	W	L	ERA	G	GS	CG	SV	IP	H	HR	BB	SO	K/9	WHIP	AVG
2016	West Virginia (NYP)	SS	6	5	2.93	15	12	0	0	68	50	4	28	61	8.1	1.15	.208
2017	West Virginia (SAL)	LoA	10	7	3.83	26	25	1	0	132	97	9	60	168	11.5	1.19	.200
2018	Bradenton (FSL)	HiA	7	6	3.98	17	16	0	0	93	76	9	38	85	8.3	1.23	.224
	Altoona (EL)	AA	4	0	4.54	7	7	0	0	36	30	4	21	25	6.3	1.43	.227
Minor League Totals			31	23	3.90	91	86	1	0	430	339	29	195	415	8.7	1.24	.216

12 LOLO SANCHEZ, OF

BA GRADE

50 Risk: Very High

Born: April 23, 1999. **B-T:** R-R. **HT:** 5-11. **WT:** 168. **Signed:** Dominican Republic, 2015. **Signed by:** Rene Gayo

TRACK RECORD: The Pirates invested $450,000 in Sanchez when they signed him in 2015. He turned 19 in 2018 during his first full season of pro baseball, but he has shown impressive maturity so far. In the Gulf Coast League in 2017, he recorded more walks (21) than strikeouts (19), stole 14 bases and slashed .284/.359/.417. He had a harder time in the South Atlantic League with low Class A West Virginia in 2018, but still kept his strikeout rate low and his stolen base figure high, finishing fourth in the league with 30 steals.

SCOUTING REPORT: Sanchez's speed will always be a weapon, and his fringe-average hit tool could evolve as he learns how to better handle quality breaking balls. Sanchez can get the barrel on the ball, but the Pirates aren't expecting to see consistent home run power–he has well below-average power. In fact, Sanchez would be better served to try to hit for less power. Right now, he's too pull oriented for a table-setter. He's a plus defender in center field with plus speed. He takes efficient routes and has a better than average arm, especially for his size.

THE FUTURE: Sanchez will most likely begin 2019 at high Class A Bradenton. With his lack of power, he's going to hit a lot better to have any shot to be an MLB regular or even a solid backup.

Year	Club (League)	Class	AVG	G	AB	R	H	2B	3B	HR	RBI	BB	SO	SB	CS	OBP	SLG
2016	Pirates (DSL)	R	.235	45	153	19	36	4	1	0	10	24	18	4	8	.359	.275
2017	Pirates (GCL)	R	.284	51	204	42	58	11	2	4	20	21	19	14	7	.359	.417
2018	West Virginia (SAL)	LoA	.243	114	378	57	92	18	1	4	34	41	72	30	13	.322	.328
Minor League Totals			.253	210	735	118	186	33	4	8	64	86	109	48	28	.340	.341

13 STEVEN JENNINGS, RHP

BA GRADE
50 Risk: Extreme

Born: Nov. 13, 1998. **B-T:** R-R. **HT:** 6-2. **WT:** 175. **Drafted:** HS—Smithville, Tenn., 2017 (2nd round). **Signed by:** Jerry Jordan.

TRACK RECORD: Jennings, who was a star quarterback as well as a pitcher at Smithville, Tenn.'s DeKalb County High, posted a 0.52 ERA with 99 strikeouts in 51.2 innings as a senior. He signed for $1.9 million, passing up on a commitment to Mississippi. He spent his first two professional summers in rookie level ball thanks in part that a fractured rib that held him back at the start of 2018.

SCOUTING REPORT: Jennings has shown decent velocity, excellent control and good feel for several pitches. His fastball sits between 89-92 mph, but it has armside run, he can move it around, and he will probably be able to add velocity to it as he gains strength. He has a tight slider with late life that is currently his best secondary pitch, but he also has feel for a curveball and a change up, and he can throw all four of his pitches for strikes.

THE FUTRE: Spring training will be important for Jennings, but a good showing could get him a shot at low-A Greensboro.

Year	Club (League)	Class	W	L	ERA	G	GS	CG	SV	IP	H	HR	BB	SO	K/9	WHIP	AVG
2017	Pirates (GCL)	R	0	2	4.10	10	10	0	0	26	31	2	10	13	4.4	1.56	.282
2018	Bristol (APP)	R	3	4	4.82	13	13	0	0	65	68	5	27	53	7.3	1.45	.260
Minor League Totals			3	6	4.61	23	23	0	0	92	99	7	37	66	6.5	1.48	.266

14 BRAXTON ASHCRAFT, RHP

BA GRADE
50 Risk: Extreme

Born: Oct. 5, 1999. **B-T:** L-R. **HT:** 6-5. **WT:** 195. **Drafted:** HS—Waco, Texas, 2018 (2nd round). **Signed by:** Phil Huttmann.

TRACK RECORD: Ashcraft's long levers and athleticism made him a star wide receiver in football-mad Texas, and he caught 37 touchdown passes as a high school junior. He focused on baseball as a senior, though, and struck out 103 batters in 70.1 innings while also hitting .391. He had a scholarship offer to Baylor, his hometown school, but the Pirates lured him away with a $1.825 million bonus. He was a late sign and made just five starts in the Rookie-level Gulf Coast League.

SCOUTING REPORT: The Pirates are fans of tall, athletic righthanders who can pitch with downhill angle—and Ashcraft fits that bill. His fastball sat in the 80s for much of the spring, but he let loose more in the summer and topped out at 94, sitting around 92 with some arm-side run. He also has an off-speed slider with some drop to it and feel for a change-up that sits in the low-80s.

THE FUTURE: Ashcraft will almost certainly begin in extended spring training and begin 2019 at either the Rookie-level Bristol or short-season West Virginia. His progress may take some time, but he could develop into a rotation staple.

Year	Club (League)	Class	W	L	ERA	G	GS	CG	SV	IP	H	HR	BB	SO	K/9	WHIP	AVG
2018	Pirates (GCL)	R	0	1	4.58	5	5	0	0	18	16	2	5	12	6.1	1.19	.242
Minor League Totals			0	1	4.58	5	5	0	0	18	16	2	5	12	6.1	1.19	.242

15 TAHNAJ THOMAS, RHP

BA GRADE
50 Risk: Extreme

Born: June 16, 1999. **B-T:** R-R. **Ht.:** 6-4. **Wt.:** 190. **Signed:** Bahamas, 2016. **Signed by:** Koby Perez (Indians).

TRACK RECORD: When the Indians signed Thomas, he was a 6-foot-4 Bahamian shortstop who wanted to stay in the dirt. But Cleveland was convinced that his arm was special. After multiple conversations he agreed to sign with the Indians for $200,000 as a pitcher. So far, it's been shown to be a wise move. He missed the start of the Arizona League season with a visa issue, but by the Arizona League he was in fine form again. The Pirates acquired him in November in the trade that sent Jordan Luplow and Max Moroff to Cleveland.

SCOUTING REPORT: Thomas is on a slow track because he is still very new to pitching, but he has the makings of a durable mid-rotation starter if it all comes together as he has size and athleticism to go with promising stuff. He sits 92-96 mph with a potentially plus fastball. After working with a slurvy slider in 2017, Thomas sharpened it into a tighter pitch with better slider shape in 2018. Thomas delivery is effortful and he needs to improve his below-average control.

THE FUTURE: Thomas is still figuring out what he's doing on the mound, but he's made impressive strides in velocity, durability and feel for pitching in the past two seasons. It's unlikely he'll be ready for a full-season assignment.

Year	Club (League)	Class	W	L	ERA	G	GS	CG	SV	IP	H	HR	BB	SO	K/9	WHIP	AVG
2017	Indians (DSL)	R	0	2	3.38	3	3	0	0	5	3	0	8	5	8.4	2.06	.167
	Indians (AZL)	R	0	3	6.00	13	10	0	0	33	35	4	25	29	7.9	1.82	.282
2018	Indians 1 (AZL)	R	0	0	4.58	8	6	0	0	20	13	2	10	27	12.4	1.17	.188
Minor League Totals			0	5	5.28	24	19	0	0	58	51	6	43	61	9.5	1.62	.242

16 WILL CRAIG, 1B

BA GRADE

45 Risk: High

Born: Nov. 16, 1994. **B-T:** R-R. **HT:** 6-3. **WT:** 212. **Drafted:** Wake Forest, 2016 (1st round). **Signed by:** Jerry Jordan.

TRACK RECORD: Craig was an All-American at Wake Forest and considered one of the best power hitters in the nation when the Pirates took him in 2016. He hit 37 home runs and slugged .623 in three years there. It took a while, but that power finally showed up at the professional level for Craig in 2018.

SCOUTING REPORT: After hitting a combined eight home runs at short-season West Virginia in 2016 and high Class A Bradenton in 2017, Craig took more of an all-or-nothing approach in 2018 with Double-A Altoona. His average (.248) and on-base percentage (.321) hit career lows, his walks dipped and his strikeouts hit a career high, but the power numbers also showed up as he started getting the ball into the air more often. He hit 20 homers and 30 doubles, drove in 102 runs and slugged .448. The Pirates hope to see a little more of a balance between the hit tool and the power tool in 2019, because they were just as enamored with his .347 average at Wake Forest as the home runs. He's yet to show he can have an average hit tool with average power at the same time. However, the power figures provided a needed boost of confidence. Defensively, the former third baseman has settled in at first, and the Pirates are pleased with his footwork and ability to pick up bounced throws.

THE FUTURE: Josh Bell likely blocks Craig from getting a shot to be a starter in Pittsburgh any time soon, but he will have a good chance to begin 2019 at Triple-A Indianapolis. He needs to show he can hit for average and power if he has a hope of being a big league regular.

Year	Club (League)	Class	AVG	G	AB	R	H	2B	3B	HR	RBI	BB	SO	SB	CS	OBP	SLG
2016	West Virginia (NYP)	SS	.280	63	218	28	61	12	0	2	23	41	37	2	0	.412	.362
2017	Bradenton (FSL)	HiA	.271	123	458	59	124	26	1	6	61	62	106	1	3	.373	.371
2018	Altoona (EL)	AA	.248	132	480	73	119	30	3	20	102	42	128	6	3	.321	.448
Minor League Totals			.263	318	1156	160	304	68	4	28	186	145	271	9	6	.360	.401

17 CLAY HOLMES, RHP

BA GRADE

40 Risk: Medium

Born: March 27, 1993. **B-T:** R-R. **HT:** 6-5. **WT:** 230. **Drafted:** HS—Slocomb, Ala., 2011 (9th round). **Signed by:** Darren Mazeroski.

TRACK RECORD: Seven years after earning the highest signing bonus ever given to a ninth-round pick—$1.2 million—Holmes finally broke into the big leagues in 2018. Holmes' career track was disrupted in 2014 because of Tommy John surgery, which cost him all of that season and most of 2015. He worked his way back with average performances at Double-A Altoona in 2016 and Triple-A Indianapolis in 2017, and he made his debut in April with the Pirates in need of long relief help.

SCOUTING REPORT: Holmes had one strong start with the Pirates but was largely overmatched. He walked 23 batters in 26.1 innings and posted a 6.84 ERA. His heavy sinker averages 94 mph and gives him an outstanding groundball rate. But when he's behind in counts, it's not good enough to throw by hitters. He has a looping fringe-average curveball and a sharp above-average slider/cutter, but he struggles with well below-average control and command, especially when he's trying to paint the corners. He struck out 100 batters in 95.1 innings at Triple-A in 2018, but his strikeout rates are usually modest.

THE FUTURE: Holmes' sinker and velocity will probably mean another year of spot starts, long relief and trips back and forth from Pittsburgh to Indianapolis.

Year	Club (League)	Class	W	L	ERA	G	GS	CG	SV	IP	H	HR	BB	SO	K/9	WHIP	AVG
2016	Altoona (EL)	AA	10	9	4.22	26	26	0	0	136	138	10	64	101	6.7	1.48	.272
2017	Indianapolis (IL)	AAA	10	5	3.36	25	24	0	0	113	96	4	59	99	7.9	1.38	.238
2018	Bradenton (FSL)	HiA	0	0	1.50	1	1	0	0	6	4	0	0	8	12.0	0.67	.190
	Indianapolis (IL)	AAA	8	3	3.40	22	16	1	0	95	94	4	40	100	9.4	1.41	.260
	Pittsburgh (NL)	MAJ	1	3	6.84	11	4	0	0	26	30	2	23	21	7.2	2.01	.291
Major League Totals			1	3	6.84	11	4	0	0	26	30	2	23	21	7.2	2.01	.291
Minor League Totals			39	28	3.54	122	114	1	0	565	504	26	269	458	7.3	1.37	.244

18 JI-HWAN BAE, SS

BA GRADE

45 Risk: High

Born: July 26, 1999. **B-T:** L-R. **Ht.:** 6-1. **Wt.:** 170. **Signed:** Korea, 2018. **Signed by:** Fu Chun Chiang.

TRACK RECORD: Bae is one of many former Braves signees who found themselves looking for a new team after MLB slapped sanctions on Atlanta for violating rules in regards to international signings. In Bae's case, his 2017 contract with Atlanta was never officially approved. But because he'd spurned the Korean Baseball Organization draft for Atlanta, he was ineligible to sign with a KBO team. He signed with Pittsburgh for $1.2 million in March, but immediately ran into trouble when he was found guilty of assaulting his ex-girlfriend. He returned to Korea to deal with the charge, which resulted in a fine, but was back for the Gulf Coast League schedule.

SCOUTING REPORT: Bae profiles as a light-hitting shortstop with a solid glove. His setup begins with high hands and a coiled load. His swing then spins him towards first-base with the kind of jail-break swing that is popular in Asian baseball. It helps him take advantage of his plus speed, but it also ensures that he rarely drives the ball. His approach is all about making contact. Defensively he should be able to stay at shortstop.

THE FUTURE: Bae's hitting ability and defense gives him a path to the majors leagues, but without changes in his approach, it's hard to see him being more than a useful utility hitter.

Year	Club (League)	Class	AVG	G	AB	R	H	2B	3B	HR	RBI	BB	SO	SB	CS	OBP	SLG
2018	Pirates (GCL)	R	.271	35	129	24	35	6	2	0	13	15	16	10	4	.362	.349
Minor League Totals			.271	35	129	24	35	6	2	0	13	15	16	10	4	.362	.349

19 JARED OLIVA, OF

BA GRADE

45 Risk: High

Born: November 27, 1995. **B-T:** R-R. **HT:** 6-3. **WT:** 185. **Drafted:** Arizona, 2017 (7th round). **Signed by:** Derrick Van Dusen.

TRACK RECORD: Oliva went to Arizona as a walk-on after spending a significant amount of his career at Valencia High in California as a reserve. However, he started on a College World Series team as a redshirt sophomore and slashed .321/.385/.498 as a junior to catch the Pirates' eye.

SCOUTING REPORT: A strong spring training in 2018 earned him a spot at high Class A Bradenton, and he caught fire at the plate in the first half, hitting a combined .326 in the months of May and June with nine home runs and 29 RBIs. His production cooled off in July and August, but he still led the Florida State League in runs scored with 75 and finished second in stolen bases with 33. He has long limbs but good bat control and can tighten up his swing when he needs to. He has plus speed and a better than average arm and takes efficient routes to the ball, so the Pirates think he fits in center field for the long term. They also like his makeup and consider him to be a clubhouse leader in the long term.

THE FUTURE: Oliva will most likely start next season at Double-A Altoona, following in Bryan Reynolds and Jason Martin's footsteps as a likely fourth outfielder who aspires to do more.

Year	Club (League)	Class	AVG	G	AB	R	H	2B	3B	HR	RBI	BB	SO	SB	CS	OBP	SLG
2017	West Virginia (NYP)	SS	.266	56	222	30	59	10	7	0	17	17	57	15	4	.327	.374
2018	Bradenton (FSL)	HiA	.275	108	396	75	109	24	4	9	47	40	91	33	8	.354	.424
Minor League Totals			.272	164	618	105	168	34	11	9	64	57	148	48	12	.344	.406

20 SERGIO CAMPAÑA, OF

BA GRADE

50 Risk: Extreme

Born: March 29, 2002. **B-T:** R-R. **HT:** 6-1. **WT:** 165. **Signed:** Dominican Republic, 2018. **Signed by:** Victor Santana.

TRACK RECORD: Campaña is the younger brother of Marino Campaña, a 21-year-old corner outfielder with the Red Sox who spent the 2018 season with low Class A Greenville. Campaña hit well at the COPABE U-15 Pan American Championships in Colombia, where he batted .364 (8-for-22) with two home runs, three walks and two strikeouts. The Pirates signed him for $500,000.

SCOUTING REPORT: Campaña has a prototype build for center field, with a lean, athletic frame and room to add considerable strength. He has quick-burst actions, gliding around center field with plus speed and a good gait, though his arm is below-average. Campaña's twitchiness shows in his fast hands and bat speed, with a compact stroke and gap power that could become average or better with physical maturity. Campaña has certain attributes that suggest he should be a good hitter, though his offensive performance went on a bit of a roller coaster as an amateur, mixing productive at-bats with a lot of strikeouts at times.

THE FUTURE: With a chance to hit and stay at a premium position, Campaña is one of the organization's most intriguing sleepers at the lower levels. He will likely debut in the Dominican Summer League.

Year	Club (League)	Class	AVG	G	AB	R	H	2B	3B	HR	RBI	BB	SO	SB	CS	OBP	SLG
Did not play																	

21 CODY BOLTON, RHP

BA GRADE

50 Risk: High

Born: June 19, 1998. **B-T:** R-R. **HT:** 6-3. **WT:** 185. **Drafted:** HS—Tracy, Calif., 2017 (6th round). **Signed by:** Mike Sansoe.

TRACK RECORD: Bolton dominated at Tracy High, going 24-6, 1.42 and 201 strikeouts against 65 walks in three years as a starter. The Pirates took him in the sixth round in 2017, and like most of their high school starters, he spent his first summer in the Rookie-level Gulf Coast League and his first spring in extended spring training. However, he performed so well there that the Pirates moved him past short-season ball and directly to low Class A West Virginia in late May.

SCOUTING REPORT: In his first three West Virginia starts, Bolton pitched 15.1 scoreless innings, striking out 19 batters and walking just four. His fastball is a plus pitch. He can hit 95 mph with it and get swings and misses at both the top and the bottom of the zone. He can go up in the zone with ride and down in the zone with sink and armside run. He also has good command of a tight slider and a changeup up that sits in the low 80s.

THE FUTURE: Bolton has made just nine starts in low Class A, so he likely will return there in 2019. He should reach high Class A Bradenton at some point.

Year	Club (League)	Class	W	L	ERA	G	GS	CG	SV	IP	H	HR	BB	SO	K/9	WHIP	AVG
2017	Pirates (GCL)	R	0	2	3.16	9	9	0	0	26	23	1	8	22	7.7	1.21	.240
2018	West Virginia (SAL)	LoA	3	3	3.65	9	9	0	0	44	43	6	7	45	9.1	1.13	.253
Minor League Totals			3	5	3.47	18	18	0	0	70	66	7	15	67	8.6	1.16	.248

22 DEON STAFFORD, C

BA GRADE

50 Risk: High

Born: March 17, 1996. **B-T:** R-R. **HT:** 5-11. **WT:** 211. **Drafted:** St. Joseph's, 2017 (5th round). **Signed by:** Dan Radcliff.

TRACK RECORD: Stafford is one of the most decorated players in the history of St. Joseph's, earning All-Atlantic 10 Conference honors three straight seasons and setting school single-season records for hits (85) and home runs (18) in 2016.

SCOUTING REPORT: Stafford advanced to low Class A West Virginia in 2018, and he is the most promising catcher in the system. Behind the plate, he's grown in his ability to understand pitch sequencing and call a game, and he has the charisma of a captain. He had throwing issues early in the season, but his pop times have improved. At the plate, he has good bat speed and feel for the barrel and has shown power to all fields with 16 home runs and a .428 slugging percentage in his first two seasons. He struck out 99 times in 2018, but has generally shown good plate discipline and understanding of the zone.

THER FUTURE: Stafford will most likely start 2019 in high Class A Bradenton.

Year	Club (League)	Class	AVG	G	AB	R	H	2B	3B	HR	RBI	BB	SO	SB	CS	OBP	SLG
2017	West Virginia (NYP)	SS	.280	45	182	22	51	11	1	4	28	15	53	3	1	.332	.418
2018	West Virginia (SAL)	LoA	.253	94	344	60	87	19	5	11	49	28	99	0	3	.316	.433
Minor League Totals			.262	139	526	82	138	30	6	15	77	43	152	3	4	.321	.428

23 PABLO REYES, 3B/OF

BA GRADE

40 Risk: Medium

Born: Sept. 5, 1993. **B-T:** R-R. **HT:** 5-8. **WT:** 170. **Signed:** Dominican Republic, 2012. **Signed by:** Victor Santana.

TRACK RECORD: Reyes signed for $90,000 out of the Dominican Republic in 2012, when the Pirates expected him to be an everyday shortstop. He hasn't made more than 36 appearances in a season at short since his first summer in the Dominican Summer League, but he has since been molded into a Josh Harrison-style super utility player.

SCOUTING REPORT: The Pirates called Reyes up in September and in just 18 games, he played second base, third base, left field and right field. He also got extensive work in center field as a minor leaguer. All of Reyes' tools are average or just slightly above, but the total package might get him on the roster in 2019. He had by far the most successful September of the late-season call-ups, slashing .293/.349/.483 with three home runs in 18 games. He's never hit below .265 in a full minor league season, he's finished with double-digit home runs three times, and he registered 115 minor-league stolen bases. His arm isn't great, but it plays at second or third.

THE FUTURE: Unlike Harrison, Reyes might never win an everyday starting job, but he could be a valuable member of the bench, especially early in 2019 with Gregory Polanco expected to miss time with a shoulder injury.

Year	Club (League)	Class	AVG	G	AB	R	H	2B	3B	HR	RBI	BB	SO	SB	CS	OBP	SLG
2016	Bradenton (FSL)	HiA	.265	89	306	41	81	20	1	5	45	37	47	13	8	.341	.386
2017	Altoona (EL)	AA	.274	115	420	62	115	21	3	10	50	51	70	21	14	.356	.410
2018	Altoona (EL)	AA	.244	12	45	3	11	3	0	0	5	4	5	3	0	.306	.311
	Indianapolis (IL)	AAA	.289	110	356	52	103	20	4	8	36	28	71	13	7	.341	.435
	Pittsburgh (NL)	MAJ	.293	18	58	9	17	2	0	3	7	5	11	0	1	.349	.483
Major League Totals			.293	18	58	9	17	2	0	3	7	5	11	0	1	.349	.483
Minor League Totals			.277	591	2062	309	571	123	15	41	263	236	320	115	55	.352	.411

24 JONAH DAVIS, OF

BA GRADE
50 Risk: Extreme

Born: July 2, 1997. **B-T:** L-R. **HT:** 5-10. **WT:** 181. **Drafted:** California, 2018 (15th round). **Signed by:** Mike Sansoe

TRACK RECORD: Davis, the son of a jazz pianist and an opera singer, won a starting job in his sophomore year at California and then broke out as a junior, hitting .321/.406/.606 with 14 home runs and 58 RBIs to earn first-team all-Pacific-12 Conference honors. He was just as productive in his pro debut.

SCOUTING REPORT: Davis' strikeout rate is high—in a combined 105 professional and college games in 2018, he struck out 134 times—but he showed above-average power to all fields. His stance is upright, but he has good plate coverage and gets his bat through the zone quickly. He has above-average speed and a playable arm. He likely eventually will end up in a corner outfield spot.

THE FUTURE: Davis is expected to open next season at low Class A Greensboro. He has to keep hitting to prove he can be more than a solid org player, but so far he's off to a great start.

Year	Club (League)	Class	AVG	G	AB	R	H	2B	3B	HR	RBI	BB	SO	SB	CS	OBP	SLG
2018	Bristol (APP)	R	.306	51	206	46	63	15	6	12	34	27	59	6	5	.398	.612
Minor League Totals			.306	51	206	46	63	15	6	12	34	27	59	6	5	.398	.612

25 CONNER USELTON, OF

BA GRADE
50 Risk: Extreme

Born: May 20, 1998. **B-T:** R-R. **HT:** 6-3. **WT:** 185. **Drafted:** HS—Moore, Okla., 2017 (2nd round supplemental). **Signed by:** Phil Hutmann.

TRACK RECORD: Uselton, a former high school quarterback, was given a $900,000 signing bonus out of Southmoore High thanks to a combination of raw athleticism and power. So far as a professional, he hasn't had a lot of opportunity to display either, as he's raised questions about his conditioning and has struggled when he has gotten on the field.

SCOUTING REPORT: Uselton blew out his hamstring in just his second game as a professional in 2017 in the Rookie-level Gulf Coast League. He wasn't well conditioned when he arrived for spring training, and 2018 was an uphill battle throughout. He finished with just three extra-base hits, none of them home runs, in 43 games with Rookie-level Bristol, a very disappointing result for as right fielder with plus power potential. Uselton has a lot of work to do to project as a below-average hitter. He still has a long ways to go with his swing mechanics, which include a significant amount of wasted motion, but the Pirates at least saw some impact and bat speed return towards the end of the season.

THE FUTURE: They hope he will have turned the corner by spring training and that 2019 will not be as much of a wasted season as 2018 was.

Year	Club (League)	Class	AVG	G	AB	R	H	2B	3B	HR	RBI	BB	SO	SB	CS	OBP	SLG
2017	Pirates (GCL)	R	.429	2	7	0	3	1	0	0	1	0	1	0	0	.429	.571
2018	Bristol (APP)	R	.225	43	160	15	36	2	1	0	14	12	31	0	2	.280	.250
Minor League Totals			.234	45	167	15	39	3	1	0	15	12	32	0	2	.286	.263

26 STEPHEN ALEMAIS, 2B/SS

BA GRADE

45 Risk: High

Born: April 12, 1995. **B-T:** R-R. **HT:** 6-0. **WT:** 190. **Drafted:** Tulane, 2016 (3rd round). **Signed by:** Wayne Mathis.

TRACK RECORD: Alemais, a native of the Bronx, was considered one of the best players in the history of Tulane. A first-team All-American Athletic Conference pick as a junior, he was celebrated for his spectacular plays at shortstop. He's a fluid athlete with outstanding range to both his right and his left, and a strong enough arm to play the position.

SCOUTING REPORT: With Cole Tucker manning shortstop at Double-A Altoona in 2018, Alemais spent most of the year playing second base. He was steady there as well, so that adds versatility to his list of tools as he makes his way up the ladder. Alemais has very little power, but he's a good bat handler and can occasionally drive the gaps for doubles. He doesn't strike out much, draws walks, and has better than average speed with 36 stolen bases in the past three seasons. Alemais can capably play second or short, which is a requirement for a major league utility infielder.

THE FUTURE: Whether he starts 2019 in Altoona or Triple-A Indianapolis will likely determined by how the major league infield shakes out, but his defense should get him on a major league bench by 2020.

Year	Club (League)	Class	AVG	G	AB	R	H	2B	3B	HR	RBI	BB	SO	SB	CS	OBP	SLG
2016	West Virginia (NYP)	SS	.263	39	156	23	41	5	0	1	18	5	18	9	3	.297	.314
	West Virginia (SAL)	LoA	.189	11	37	2	7	1	1	0	2	2	11	1	3	.244	.270
2017	West Virginia (SAL)	LoA	.217	29	120	14	26	5	2	3	11	6	32	5	3	.266	.367
	Pirates (GCL)	R	.259	8	27	6	7	3	0	0	2	4	5	0	0	.355	.370
	Bradenton (FSL)	HiA	.317	30	101	10	32	6	0	1	20	14	14	5	2	.393	.406
2018	Altoona (EL)	AA	.279	120	402	56	112	16	4	1	34	44	69	16	9	.346	.346
Minor League Totals			.267	237	843	111	225	36	7	6	87	75	149	36	20	.328	.348

27 J.T. BRUBAKER, RHP

BA GRADE

40 Risk: Medium

Born: Nov. 17, 1993. **B-T:** R-R. **HT:** 6-4. **WT:** 175. **Drafted:** Akron, 2015 (6th round). **Signed by:** Trevor Haley.

TRACK RECORD: Brubaker had unspectacular numbers at Akron, posting a 3.63 ERA and 72 strikeouts in 89.1 innings as a junior, but the Pirates liked his rangy frame and signed him for below slot money. He was more dominant in the New York-Penn League than he ever was in college, however, posting a 0.94 WHIP and 49 strikeouts against 12 walks in his pro debut.

SCOUTING REPORT: Brubaker found it more difficult to retire high Class A and Double-A hitters in 2016 and 2017, but he was dominant in his first six starts at Double-A in 2018. He moved up to Triple-A Indianapolis and was the Pirates' most reliable starter there with a 3.10 ERA. The biggest improvement for Brubaker was execution with his fastball. With long limbs, his above-average fastball can touch 96 mph without over-exerting himself, but he was too often missing in the middle of the plate. He was more consistent in dotting the corners in 2018, which produced more strikeouts and soften the contact some. He also throws an average slider in the upper 80s with a sharp downward break, an average curveball and a fringe-average firm change up that isn't much slower than the fastball but that can produce ground balls.

THE FUTURE: Brubaker will likely still be in the Triple-A rotation to start 2019 but could get a major league look if he continues to perform. The Pirates added him to their 40-man roster during the offseason.

Year	Club (League)	Class	W	L	ERA	G	GS	CG	SV	IP	H	HR	BB	SO	K/9	WHIP	AVG
2015	West Virginia (NYP)	SS	6	4	2.82	15	15	0	0	73	57	3	12	49	6.0	0.94	.216
2016	West Virginia (SAL)	LoA	4	5	3.48	12	12	0	0	62	56	9	24	77	11.2	1.29	.241
	Bradenton (FSL)	HiA	2	6	5.32	14	14	1	0	68	77	6	22	43	5.7	1.46	.289
2017	Altoona (EL)	AA	7	6	4.44	26	24	0	0	130	150	9	45	109	7.6	1.50	.291
2018	Altoona (EL)	AA	2	2	1.80	6	6	0	0	35	29	1	8	35	9.0	1.06	.218
	Indianapolis (IL)	AAA	8	4	3.10	22	22	0	0	119	121	7	36	96	7.3	1.32	.268
Minor League Totals			29	27	3.68	95	93	1	0	487	490	35	147	409	7.6	1.31	.263

28 GAGE HINSZ, RHP

BA GRADE

45 Risk: Extreme

Born: April 20, 1996. **B-T:** R-R. **HT:** 6-4. **WT:** 210. **Drafted:** HS—Billings, Mont., 2014 (11th round). **Signed by:** Max Kwan.

TRACK RECORD: Hinsz's 2018 season was ended thanks to the terrifying news that his aortic valve had narrowed to the point that he needed open-heart surgery. He missed the entire 2018 season as a result but was back on the mound in the fall for instructional league in the Dominican Republic.

SCOUTING REPORT: In the fall, Hinsz was once again showing signs of being the player the Pirates drafted and convinced to pass on a scholarship to Oregon State. He has a fastball that touches 96 mph with sink and a hard-diving curveball as well as a changeup. His problem so far in the minor leagues has been leaving too many pitches up in the zone. Florida State Leaguers hit .296 against him at high Class A Bradenton in 2017.

THE FUTURE: Just getting back on the field is good news for Hinsz. It's possible that Hinsz will have to repeat the FSL in 2019 and prove he can get such hitters out before the Pirates are willing to move him up to Double-A Altoona.

Year	Club (League)	Class	W	L	ERA	G	GS	CG	SV	IP	H	HR	BB	SO	K/9	WHIP	AVG
2014	Pirates (GCL)	R	0	0	3.38	3	2	0	0	8	8	0	4	7	7.9	1.50	.267
2015	Bristol (APP)	R	3	4	3.79	10	9	0	0	38	37	1	23	24	5.7	1.58	.252
2016	West Virginia (SAL)	LoA	6	8	3.66	17	17	0	0	93	93	8	25	67	6.5	1.26	.266
2017	Bradenton (FSL)	HiA	5	5	5.61	20	19	0	0	95	112	9	31	52	4.9	1.51	.296
2018	Did not play—Injured																
Minor League Totals			14	17	4.46	50	47	0	0	234	250	18	83	150	5.8	1.42	.276

29 DARIO ARGAZAL, RHP

BA GRADE

45 Risk: Extreme

Born: Dec. 28, 1994. **B-T:** R-R. **HT:** 6-3. **WT:** 216. **Signed:** Panama, 2012.
Signed by: Rene Gayo.

TRACK RECORD: Argazal has risen steadily through the Pirates' minor league ranks thanks to his ability to get ground outs and avoid walking batters. He has walked just 76 batters in 519.2 innings and has never issued more than 18 walks in a season.

SCOUTING REPORT: Argazal was on track for his best season as a professional in 2018, throwing six no-hit innings in the season opener with Double-A Altoona and posting a 1.30 ERA and 0.82 WHIP as of May 13. However, a shoulder injury cost him two months, and he ended the season by allowing 10 runs, including five home runs, in three innings in his final start. He has an fringe-average fastball with down-hill plane that sits between 90-92 mph, a fringe-average changeup that matches it and an average slider he can use for swings and misses. The Pirates want to see more confidence in his stuff, and believe there is more velocity in his arm than he has shown. Argazal's plus control is vital to his success.

THE FUTURE: Argazal might need to open at Altoona in 2019 to prove himself before he can move up to Indianapolis.

Year	Club (League)	Class	W	L	ERA	G	GS	CG	SV	IP	H	HR	BB	SO	K/9	WHIP	AVG
2016	West Virginia (SAL)	LoA	8	12	4.20	27	27	0	0	150	173	18	18	88	5.3	1.27	.294
2017	Bradenton (FSL)	HiA	14	13	2.91	14	13	0	0	80	73	4	10	63	7.1	1.03	.243
	Altoona (EL)	AA	0	1	4.50	1	1	0	0	4	3	0	2	2	4.5	1.25	.231
2018	Bradenton (FSL)	HiA	0	0	0.00	2	2	0	0	8	3	0	0	4	4.5	0.38	.120
	Altoona (EL)	AA	5	6	3.99	15	14	0	0	86	91	9	13	52	5.5	1.21	.275
Minor League Totals			33	31	3.48	98	95	0	0	520	536	39	76	320	5.5	1.18	.267

30 SANTIAGO FLOREZ, RHP

BA GRADE

45 Risk: Extreme

Born: May 9, 2000. **B-T:** R-R. **HT:** 6-5. **WT:** 222. **Signed:** Colombia, 2017.
Signed by: Orlando Covo.

TRACK RECORD: Florez is a long way from being a major league pitcher, but he can already light up the radar gun like one. He was well into extended spring training in 2018 before he turned 18, but the Pirates have already seen him hit 95 mph with his fastball.

SCOUTING REPORT: Florenz doesn't have man strength yet, but he has a large frame, and the more he grows the more he can add to his velocity. He doesn't have a fully-developed pitch arsenal yet, but he does have some feel to spin a breaking ball. Control is an issue, as Florez has walked nearly as many batters (61) as he has struck out (65), but opponents aren't squaring him up. He has allowed just two home runs in 96 2/3 innings between the Dominican Summer League and Gulf Coast League and teams are hitting just .225 against him.

THE FUTURE: The Pirates will take time with Florenz, especially early as he transitions to American culture, but his velocity could portend something special in the long run.

Year	Club (League)	Class	W	L	ERA	G	GS	CG	SV	IP	H	HR	BB	SO	K/9	WHIP	AVG
2017	Pirates (DSL)	R	2	5	4.56	14	14	0	0	53	43	2	38	30	5.1	1.52	.222
2018	Pirates (GCL)	R	5	2	4.15	10	10	0	0	43	37	0	23	35	7.3	1.38	.230
Minor League Totals			7	7	4.38	24	24	0	0	97	80	2	61	65	6.1	1.46	.225

St. Louis Cardinals

BY KYLE GLASER

For so many years, the Cardinals were a beacon of stability in Major League Baseball, immune to the chaos of firings and player spats and postseason droughts that afflicted other franchises.

In 2018, after years of springing leaks, the dam keeping that reputation intact ruptured.

The Cardinals missed the postseason for the third straight season, the first time St. Louis has gone three consecutive years without October baseball since 1997-99. Manager Mike Matheny was fired on July 13, the first time the Cardinals fired a manager in-season since 1995. President of baseball operations John Mozeliak told a radio station he "couldn't defend" the energy level of high-priced but underperforming outfielder Dexter Fowler, leading to a week of media drama generally reserved for New York or Boston. A report detailing closer Bud Norris' "merciless riding" of rookie reliever Jordan Hicks emerged soon after, furthering the perception of a club in disarray.

Somehow, despite it all, the Cardinals managed to go 88-74 and remain in the playoff race until the season's final week. Third base coach Mike Shildt took over as manager after Matheny's firing and guided the club to a 41-28 record, shedding the interim label and earning the permanent job.

Veterans Matt Carpenter and Yadier Molina remain high-performing mainstays, and a cadre of kids helped keep the Cardinals afloat. Rookies Harrison Bader, Tyler O'Neill and Yairo Munoz all played an integral part stabilizing the Cardinals offensively and defensively. More impressive was the pitching, where Jack Flaherty emerged as the Cardinals' top starter, Hicks became the hardest-throwing reliever in baseball and rookies Austin Gomber, Dakota Hudson and Daniel Poncedeleon arrived midseason to stabilize the staff in the midst of injuries and an on-the-fly July bullpen rebuild.

The successful transition of the young players was important, because the Cardinals' long-established core is aging. Molina is 36. Carpenter is 33. Adam Wainwright is 37. Contributors Jose Martinez, Jedd Gyorko and Miles Mikolas are all 30. While Michael Wacha and Paul DeJong and remain in their 20s, the Cardinals need more if they are to regain their perennial-contender status of years past, and they're hoping a fruitful farm can provide that.

That help may arrive soon. The Cardinals' top three prospects already have big league time and 11 of their top 15 have seen Triple-A. The Cardinals have shed a lot of talent in recent years via trade—Stephen Piscotty, Tommy Pham, Mike Leake, Luke Voit, Randal Grichuk and Aledmys Diaz in the last two years alone—and the hope is the afore-

Rookie Jack Flaherty finished with a 3.34 ERA and led the Cardinals with 182 strikeouts.

MITCHELL LAYTON/GETTY IMAGES

PROJECTED 2022 LINEUP

Catcher	Andrew Knizner (27)
First Base	Paul Goldschmidt (34)
Second Base	Yairo Muñoz (27)
Third Base	Nolan Gorman (22)
Shortstop	Paul DeJong (28)
Left Field	Elehuris Montero (23)
Center Field	Harrison Bader (28)
Right Field	Tyler O'Neill (27)
No. 1 Starter	Carlos Martinez (30)
No. 2 Starter	Alex Reyes (27)
No. 3 Starter	Jack Flaherty (26)
No. 4 Starter	Miles Mikolas (33)
No. 5 Starter	Dakota Hudson (27)
Closer	Jordan Hicks (25))

mentioned youngsters can seize the opportunities created by their departures.

To help give those youngsters time, the Cardinals made one of the biggest moves of the offseason in acquiring Paul Goldschmidt from the D-backs. Though Goldschmidt is only signed through 2019, he significantly aids the Cardinals' primary goal of winning now.

Molina, Carpenter and Wainwright's contracts will all be expired after 2020. Wacha and Marcell Ozuna will hit free agency by then.

The Cardinals and their fanbase would love nothing more than one last run with their decorated core, and in the process return St. Louis to its pedestal as one of baseball's most stable franchises.

ST. LOUIS CARDINALS

TOP 2019 ROOKIE: Alex Reyes, RHP. He is better than ever with improved control and a fourth pitch, but his health remains a concern.
BREAKOUT PROSPECT: Tommy Edman, SS/2B. With a clean swing, elite basestealing ability and the versatility to play all over the infield, he should carve out a role in the majors soon.
SLEEPER: Jesus Cruz, RHP. The unflappable Mexican righthander sits 94-96 mph as a starter with an 85-87 mph power slider, and those should tick up even more if he moves to the bullpen, as expected.

SOURCE OF TOP 30 TALENT			
Homegrown	21	Acquired	9
College	8	Trade	9
Junior college	0	Rule 5 draft	0
High school	3	Independent league	0
Nondrafted free agent	0	Free agent/waivers	0
International	10		

LF
Randy Arozarena (17)

CF
Lane Thomas (7)
Conner Capel (26)
Scott Hurst (27)
Jonatan Machado

RF
Tyler O'Neill (2)
Dylan Carlson (10)
Justin Williams (14)
Adolis Garcia (15)
Jhon Torres (19)
Victor Garcia

3B
Nolan Gorman (4)
Elehuris Montero (5)
Malcom Nunez (9)
Evan Mendoza

SS
Tommy Edman (12)
Edmundo Sosa (22)
Edwin Figuera
Delvin Perez
Mateo Gil

2B
Max Schrock (25)
Ramon Urias

1B
Luken Baker (23)
Leandro Cedeno (28)
John Nogowski
Rangel Ravelo

C
Andrew Knizner (8)
Ivan Herrera (21)
Dennis Ortega
Jeremy Martinez

LHP

LHSP	LHRP
Genesis Cabrera (6)	Ryan Sherriff
Austin Warner (30)	Evan Sisk
Steven Gingery	Jacob Patterson
Evan Kruczynski	

RHP

RHSP	RHRP
Alex Reyes (1)	Griffin Roberts (18)
Dakota Hudson (3)	Seth Elledge (24)
Ryan Helsley (11)	Giovanny Gallegos (29)
Daniel Poncedeleon (13)	Connor Jones
Jake Woodford (16)	Derian Gonzalez
Johan Oviedo (20)	Junior Fernandez
Chris Ellis	Jesus Cruz
Alvaro Seijas	Roel Ramirez
Casey Meisner	Will Latcham
Jake Walsh	Mike O'Reilly
Alex Fagalde	
Anthony Shew	

DRAFT ANALYSIS

2018

BEST PURE HITTER: 1B Luken Baker (2) is known as a masher because of his 265-pound size, but he has a patient approach, recognizes pitches and consistently finds the barrel to grade as a solid-average or better hitter.

BEST POWER HITTER: 3B Nolan Gorman (1) shows plus-plus power in games and hits it out to all fields, with the potential to grow into 80-grade power at maturity. Baker generates plus power with his sheer strength, and 1B Kevin Woodall (10) generates tremendous leverage from his 6-foot-7, 245-pound frame.

FASTEST RUNNER: 2B Brandon Riley (14) is an above-average runner and the fastest in a Cardinals draft class short on speed.

BEST DEFENSIVE PLAYER: SS Mateo Gil (3) shows impressive maturity and confidence at shortstop for a teenager to go with soft hands and an above-average arm.

BEST ATHLETE: Gil has impressive body awareness and showed a promising baseline from which to get stronger, faster and more explosive as he reaches physical maturity.

BEST FASTBALL: RHP Griffin Roberts (1s) was up to 97 mph after signing with natural running life out of his low, three-quarter arm slot.

BEST SECONDARY PITCH: Roberts' slider was considered the best in the draft class and consistently showed plus in his pro debut. LHP Steven Gingery (4) had a borderline plus-plus changeup prior to Tommy John surgery and will try to showcase it again when he returns.

BEST PRO DEBUT: Gorman hit 17 home runs in 63 games while becoming just the seventh prep first-rounder to reach low Class A in his draft year this decade. OF Justin Toerner (28) hit .312 with a .410 on-base percentage and 11 stolen bases as he raced through three levels up to high Class A Palm Beach.

TOP DRAFT PICKS OF THE DECADE

Year	Player, Pos	2018 Org
2009	Shelby Miller, RHP	D-backs
2010	Zack Cox, 3B	Did not play
2011	Kolten Wong, 2B	Cardinals
2012	Michael Wacha, RHP	Cardinals
2013	Marco Gonzales, LHP	Mariners
2014	Luke Weaver, RHP	Cardinals
2015	Nick Plummer, OF	Cardinals
2016	Delvin Perez, SS	Cardinals
2017	Scott Hurst, OF (3rd round)	Cardinals
2018	Nolan Gorman, 3B	Cardinals

MOST INTRIGUING BACKGROUND: RHP Francisco Justo (12) barely played his senior year of high school because he had to get a job to support his family after his father broke his ankle and couldn't work. Justo moved from New York to the Dominican Republic for six months to train after graduating, returned and landed a spot at Monroe (N.Y.) JC. Gil is the son of former Rangers and Angels utilityman Benji Gil, C Benito Santiago Jr. (34) is the son of the longtime catcher and 2B Cole Kreuter (36) is the son of former MLB catcher Chad Kreuter. RHP Parker Kelly (20) is the younger brother of Cardinals catching prospect Carson Kelly.

CLOSEST TO THE MAJORS: Roberts' 94-97 mph fastball and plus slider have him primed to move quickly if he shifts to the bullpen.

BEST LATE-ROUND PICK: Toerner has hit everywhere he's been and shows above-average speed, solid-average defense in center field and enough arm strength for all three outfield spots.

THE ONE WHO GOT AWAY: SS Alerick Soularie (29) hit .402 with 10 home runs and flashed tantalizing athleticism at San Jacinto (Texas) JC, but he ended up honoring his commitment to Tennessee.

— KYLE GLASER

2017

The Cardinals didn't have a pick in the first two rounds, leaving OF Scot Hurst (3) as their top selection. He's the only player from the class to appear in the handbook, though OF Chase Pinder (7), LHP Evan Kruczynski, 3B Evan Mendoza (11) and RHP Will Latcham (17) all reached Double-A in their first full pro season.

GRADE: F

2016

Two of the Cardinals' three first round picks have found early success, as OF Dylan Carlson played well in the Florida State League as a 19-year-old and RHP Dakota Hudson reached the big leagues. SS Delvin Perez (1), however, has struggled. SS Tommy Edman (6) and C Andrew Knizner (7) have provided solid value.

GRADE: B

2015

The Cardinals have gotten a strong trio of big leaguers from this class in OF Harrison Bader (3), RHP Jordan Hicks (3s) and INF Paul DeJong (4). After DeJong was the NL Rookie of the Year runner up in 2017, Bader finished sixth in the voting in 2018. Hicks has established himself as a bullpen regular for the Cardinals.

GRADE: A

1 ALEX REYES, RHP

Born: Aug. 29, 1994. **B-T:** R-R. **Ht.:** 6-3. **Wt.:** 175.
Signed: Dominican Republic, 2012.
Signed by: Rodney Jimenez/Angel Ovalles.

Reyes has flashed elite stuff since signing with the Cardinals for $950,000 out of the Dominican Republic in 2012, but staying on the mound has been a persistent problem. He missed a month in 2015 with shoulder soreness, served a 50-game suspension in 2016 after testing positive for marijuana and missed the entire 2017 season after having Tommy John surgery. His return in 2018 was cut short too. After a yearlong recovery from TJ and four minor league rehab starts, Reyes returned the majors with a start in Milwaukee on May 30 but was removed after just four innings as his velocity cratered. Tests revealed a torn tendon in his lat muscle in the right side of his back, and on June 6 he had his second straight season-ending surgery.

SCOUTING REPORT: Even with an alarming health record, Reyes remains one of baseball's top pitching prospects. His top-of-the-scale fastball sits 95-97 mph in starts and has been clocked as high as 102 mph in relief. He elevates his heater for swings and misses and blows it by hitters even when he misses his spot. While Reyes' fastball command is imperfect, he improved his body and delivery during his Tommy John rehab to stay more compact and on line to the plate. Reyes' most notable secondary is a plus-plus curveball in the 78-80 mph range with hard 12-to-6 bite, but he struggles to consistently locate it, especially to his arm side. To give him a more consistent breaking ball, Reyes added a short slider when he reached the majors in 2016 and has progressively upped its velocity to 86-88 mph. While his curveball draws higher grades from evaluators because of its break and movement, he commands his above-average slider better. Reyes also boasts a plus changeup, a sinking 88-90 mph offering that generates swings and misses. He has struggled to control his high-octane arsenal, but his improved fitness and tighter delivery led to vastly improved strike-throwing.

THE FUTURE: Reyes still has all the attributes of a front-of-the-rotation starter. His health record, however, remains a huge red flag. Reyes is expected to be fully recovered in time for spring training.

LAWRENCE ILES/GETTY IMAGES

BA GRADE	SCOUTING GRADES
70 Risk: Extreme	Fastball: 80. Curveball: 70. Slider: 55. Change: 60. CTL: 50.

Projected future grades on 20-80 scouting scale.

TOP PROSPECTS OF THE DECADE

Year	Player, Pos	2018 Org
2009	Colby Rasmus, OF	Orioles
2010	Shelby Miller, RHP	D-backs
2011	Shelby Miller, RHP	D-backs
2012	Shelby Miller, RHP	D-backs
2013	Oscar Taveras, OF	Deceased
2014	Oscar Taveras, OF	Deceased
2015	Marco Gonzales, LHP	Mariners
2016	Alex Reyes, RHP	Cardinals
2017	Alex Reyes, RHP	Cardinals
2018	Alex Reyes, RHP	Cardinals

BEST TOOLS

Best Hitter for Average	Elehuris Montero
Best Power Hitter	Tyler O'Neill
Best Strike-Zone Discipline	John Nogowski
Fastest Baserunner	Tyler O'Neill
Best Athlete	Adolis Garcia
Best Fastball	Alex Reyes
Best Curveball	Alex Reyes
Best Slider	Dakota Hudson
Best Changeup	Steven Gingery
Best Control	Alex Fagalde
Best Defensive Catcher	Dennis Ortega
Best Defensive Infielder	Edwin Figuera
Best Infield Arm	Elehuris Montero
Best Defensive Outfielder	Lane Thomas
Best Outfield Arm	Adolis Garcia

Year	Club (League)	Class	W	L	ERA	G	GS	CG	SV	IP	H	HR	BB	SO	K/9	WHIP	AVG
2016	Memphis (PCL)	AAA	2	3	4.96	14	14	0	0	65	63	6	32	93	12.8	1.45	.252
	St. Louis (NL)	MAJ	4	1	1.57	12	5	0	1	46	33	1	23	52	10.2	1.22	.201
2017	Did not play--Injured																
2018	Palm Beach (FSL)	HiA	0	0	0.00	1	1	0	0	3	4	0	1	6	16.2	1.50	.286
	Peoria (MWL)	LoA	1	0	0.00	1	1	0	0	5	1	0	2	12	21.6	0.60	.063
	Springfield (TL)	AA	1	0	0.00	1	1	0	0	8	1	0	3	13	15.3	0.52	.045
	Memphis (PCL)	AAA	1	0	0.00	1	1	0	0	7	1	0	1	13	16.7	0.29	.048
	St. Louis (NL)	MAJ	0	0	0.00	1	1	0	0	4	3	0	2	2	4.5	1.25	.250
Major League Totals			4	1	1.44	13	6	0	1	50	36	1	25	54	9.7	1.22	.205
Minor League Totals			23	21	3.27	73	73	1	0	357	276	14	177	493	12.4	1.27	.213

2 TYLER O'NEILL, OF

Born: June 22, 1995. **B-T:** R-R. **Ht.:** 5-11. **Wt.:** 210. **Drafted:** HS—Maple Ridge, B.C., 2013 (3rd round). **Signed by:** Wayne Norton (Mariners).

TRACK RECORD: The son of a Canadian bodybuilder, O'Neill established himself as a premier power prospect with 75 home runs in two and a half seasons before the Mariners traded him to the Cardinals for Marco Gonzales at the 2017 trade deadline. O'Neill kept crushing with 38 home runs in 101 games at Triple-A Memphis in 2018. He added nine more in 61 games during his big league debut with the Cardinals.

SCOUTING REPORT: A walking ball of muscle, O'Neill swings hard and often. With lightning bat speed and tremendous strength, he sends jaw-dropping home runs out to all fields, and he has leveled out his swing a bit to make more contact and get to his power more. O'Neill does serious damage when he connects, but his uphill swing results in an alarming amount of swings and misses in the strike zone, particularly against spin. Though he improved his strikeout and walk rates in Triple-A, his strikeout rate spiked to 40 percent in the majors. O'Neill, who does offer defensive value, showed himself to be a nearly plus-plus runner in the outfield despite his bulk, as well as a plus defender in both corners with an above-average arm.

THE FUTURE: O'Neill has the power to lead the league in home runs someday, but he needs to get his strikeouts under control. He's successfully adjusted before and will try to again in 2019. He'll return to the majors in 2019.

BA GRADE

55 Risk: Medium

Hit: 45. **Power:** 70.
Run: 60. **Field:** 60.
Arm: 55.

Year	Club (League)	Class	AVG	G	AB	R	H	2B	3B	HR	RBI	BB	SO	SB	CS	OBP	SLG
2016	Jackson (SL)	AA	.293	130	492	68	144	26	4	24	102	62	150	12	2	.374	.508
2017	Tacoma (PCL)	AAA	.244	93	349	54	85	21	2	19	56	44	108	9	2	.328	.479
	Memphis (PCL)	AAA	.253	37	146	23	37	5	1	12	39	10	43	5	0	.304	.548
2018	Memphis (PCL)	AAA	.311	64	238	61	74	9	2	26	63	29	68	3	1	.385	.693
	St. Louis (NL)	MAJ	.254	61	130	29	33	5	0	9	23	7	57	2	0	.303	.500
Major League Totals			.254	61	130	29	33	5	0	9	23	7	57	2	0	.303	.500
Minor League Totals			.273	519	1963	319	535	98	14	127	402	207	618	52	14	.346	.531

3 DAKOTA HUDSON, RHP

Born: Sept. 15, 1994. **B-T:** R-R. **Ht.:** 6-5. **Wt.:** 215. **Drafted:** Mississippi State, 2016 (1st round). **Signed by:** Clint Brown.

TRACK RECORD: With each passing year, Hudson adds another accolade. In 2016, he won a Southeastern Conference championship as Mississippi State's ace and was drafted 34th overall in 2016. In 2017, he won the Texas League's pitcher of the year award, and in 2018 he was named the Pacific Coast League pitcher of the year. He earned his first big league callup in 2018, joining the Cardinals during their July bullpen rebuild and emerged as the Cardinals' seventh-inning man down the stretch.

SCOUTING REPORT: The physical, 6-foot-5 Hudson is a groundball pitcher extraordinaire with a power arsenal both starting and in relief. With his biting, 94-97 mph sinker and sharp, 89-92 mph slider, Hudson allowed only one home run in 129 innings in 2018 and averaged more than two groundball outs for every air out. Both his sinker and slider are plus pitches, and he has an average, mid-80s changeup at his disposal against lefties. Hudson draws weak contact but doesn't consistently attack the zone, resulting in a high walk rate (3.3 BB/9) and low strikeout rate (6.5 K/9) for his career. The Cardinals chalk it up to confidence and think it can be fixed, but outside evaluators question Hudson's "pie-thrower" arm action and see fringy command at best.

THE FUTURE: Hudson has the durability, pedigree and stuff to start if he can tweak his command. If not, he profiles well in late relief.

BA GRADE

55 Risk: Medium

Fastball: 60.
Slider: 60.
Change: 60. **CTL:** 45.

Year	Club (League)	Class	W	L	ERA	G	GS	CG	SV	IP	H	HR	BB	SO	K/9	WHIP	AVG
2016	Cardinals (GCL)	R	1	0	0.00	4	1	0	0	4	4	0	0	9	20.3	1.00	.235
	Palm Beach (FSL)	HiA	1	1	0.96	8	0	0	3	9	6	0	7	10	9.6	1.39	.188
2017	Springfield (TL)	AA	9	4	2.53	18	18	1	0	114	111	5	34	77	6.1	1.27	.255
	Memphis (PCL)	AAA	1	1	4.42	7	7	0	0	39	36	2	15	19	4.4	1.32	.252
2018	Memphis (PCL)	AAA	13	3	2.50	19	19	0	0	112	107	1	38	87	7.0	1.30	.254
	St. Louis (NL)	MAJ	4	1	2.63	26	0	0	0	27	19	0	18	19	6.3	1.35	.196
Major League Totals			4	1	2.63	26	0	0	0	27	19	0	18	19	6.3	1.35	.196
Minor League Totals			25	9	2.69	56	45	1	3	278	264	8	94	202	6.5	1.29	.251

4 NOLAN GORMAN, 3B

Born: May 10, 2000. **B-T:** L-R. **HT:** 6-3. **WT:** 210. **Drafted:** HS—Phoenix, 2018 (1st round). **Signed by:** Mauricio Rubio.

TRACK RECORD: Gorman emerged early as the top power prospect in the 2018 draft. He won the high school home run derby during All-Star weekend at Marlins Park in 2017 and then won the Under Armour All-America home run derby at Wrigley Field a few weeks later. He continued to crush his senior year, headlined by a 400-plus foot shot in the Arizona 6A state playoffs. The Cardinals drafted Gorman 19th overall and signed him for $3,231,700 to forgo an Arizona commitment. He immediately delivered on his power promise, hitting 17 homers in his first 63 games while reaching low Class A Peoria.
SCOUTING REPORT: Gorman is as strong as any player his age. He displays easy, plus-plus power against mid-90s velocity, making balls disappear to right field. Gorman doesn't see lefthanders well and breaking balls give him trouble, but he adjusts quickly, shows power to all fields and makes enough contact to project for a .250-.260 average with 30-plus home runs per season. Gorman is a touch stiff at third base, leaving evaluators split whether he will stick there. His range plays up with a quick first step and reactions, but he'll have to maintain his body and agility to be an average defender. His arm strength is above-average, though a questionable arm action hurts his accuracy.
THE FUTURE: Gorman has the bat to be future middle-of-the-order mainstay regardless of position. He finished his debut at low Class A Peoria and will start back there in 2019.

BA GRADE
60 Risk: Very High
Hit: 50. Power: 70.
Run: 40. Field: 50.
Arm: 55.

Year	Club (League)	Class	AVG	G	AB	R	H	2B	3B	HR	RBI	BB	SO	SB	CS	OBP	SLG
2018	Johnson City (APP)	R	.350	38	143	41	50	10	1	11	28	24	37	1	3	.443	.664
	Peoria (MWL)	LoA	.202	25	94	8	19	3	0	6	16	10	39	0	2	.280	.426
Minor League Totals			.291	63	237	49	69	13	1	17	44	34	76	1	5	.380	.570

5 ELEHURIS MONTERO, 3B

Born: Aug. 17, 1998. **B-T:** R-R. **HT:** 6-3. **WT:** 195. **Signed:** Dominican Republic, 2014. **Signed by:** Angel Ovalles.

TRACK RECORD: The Cardinals signed Montero for $300,000 out of the Dominican Republic shortly after he turned 16 in 2014. They have pushed him quickly since, and he's responded every time. After playing in the Dominican Summer League at 16 and making his U.S. debut at age 18, Montero made his full-season debut in 2018 and won low Class A Midwest League MVP honors. He led the MWL in average (.322), slugging percentage (.504) and OPS (.910) at Peoria before a late-season late promotion to high Class A Palm Beach.
SCOUTING REPORT: Montero is a physical, strong-bodied hitter whose bat has a chance to be "special" in one evaluator's words. He possesses supreme hand-eye coordination, drives the ball to all fields with plus raw power and has enough bat speed to overcome his holes. He makes quick in-game adjustments and got better at understanding pitchers' plans as the year went on. Montero is still learning to pull the ball, and once he does evaluators project him for 25-30 home runs while maintaining a steady average. Montero has average hands and a plus arm at third base, but his big frame limits his mobility and overall he is fringe-average defender. He particularly needs to improve his footwork, rhythm and coordination in order to maintain his accuracy on his throws.
THE FUTURE: Whether Montero stays at third base or moves to first or the outfield, he has the bat to make an impact. He'll begin 2019 at high Class A Palm Beach.

BA GRADE
55 Risk: High
Hit: 60. Power: 55.
Run: 45. Field: 45.
Arm: 60.

Year	Club (League)	Class	AVG	G	AB	R	H	2B	3B	HR	RBI	BB	SO	SB	CS	OBP	SLG
2015	Cardinals (DSL)	R	.252	57	230	31	58	9	1	3	30	26	56	0	1	.328	.339
2016	Cardinals (DSL)	R	.260	61	227	41	59	14	2	1	26	28	51	2	1	.349	.352
2017	Cardinals (GCL)	R	.277	52	173	30	48	16	1	5	36	22	33	0	2	.370	.468
2018	Peoria (MWL)	LoA	.322	103	382	68	123	28	3	15	69	33	81	2	0	.381	.529
	Palm Beach (FSL)	HiA	.286	24	98	13	28	9	0	1	13	5	22	1	0	.330	.408
Minor League Totals			.285	297	1110	183	316	76	7	25	174	114	243	5	4	.357	.433

6 GENESIS CABRERA, LHP

Born: Oct. 10, 1996. **B-T:** L-L. **HT:** 6-1. **WT:** 210. **Signed:** Dominican Republic, 2013. **Signed by:** Carlos Batista/Danny Santana (Rays).

TRACK RECORD: Cabrera signed with the Rays for $34,000 in 2013 and quickly surpassed his peers who signed for more. He skipped over the Gulf Coast League at 18 and reached Double-A by age 20 while touching 97 mph with his fastball. The Cardinals, facing an organizational need for lefthanders with velocity, acquired Cabrera alongside Justin Williams and Roel Ramirez in exchange for outfielder Tommy Pham at the 2018 trade deadline.

SCOUTING REPORT: Cabrera is an athletic lefty with power stuff but below-average control due to a violent delivery. His plus-plus fastball sits 94-96 mph, touching 98 mph, and he holds his velocity deep into starts. His short, upper-80s slider has above-average potential, and his third pitch is a firm, upper-80s changeup with solid depth and late fade that plays well off his fastball. He also has a curveball he shows feel to spin, though it's inconsistent because he cuts it off. Because of his delivery, Cabrera struggles to repeat his arm slot and locate consistently, especially with his secondary pitches. He also gets too cocky at times, resulting in poor pitch selection and overthrowing.

MATT TUREK/SPRINGFIELD CARDINALS

BA GRADE

50 Risk: High

Fastball: 70.
Slider: 55. Curve: 45.
Change: 50. CTL: 40.

THE FUTURE: Cabrera reminds many of Pirates closer Felipe Vasquez with his power stuff but questionable control from the left side. The Cardinals plan to keep Cabrera as a starting pitcher at Tripe-A Memphis, but they won't hesitate to call him up in relief, if needed.

Year	Club (League)	Class	W	L	ERA	G	GS	CG	SV	IP	H	HR	BB	SO	K/9	WHIP	AVG
2016	Bowling Green (MWL)	LoA	11	5	3.88	23	22	2	0	116	110	9	48	96	7.4	1.36	.255
2017	Charlotte (FSL)	HiA	4	5	2.84	13	12	0	0	70	45	3	25	60	7.8	1.00	.185
	Montgomery (SL)	AA	5	4	3.62	12	12	0	0	65	75	6	27	51	7.1	1.58	.292
2018	Montgomery (SL)	AA	7	6	4.12	21	20	0	0	114	90	11	57	124	9.8	1.29	.218
	Springfield (TL)	AA	1	3	4.74	5	5	0	0	25	24	3	13	21	7.7	1.50	.255
	Memphis (PCL)	AAA	0	0	0.00	1	0	0	0	2	0	0	1	3	13.5	0.50	.000
Minor League Totals			30	24	3.65	94	74	2	0	437	380	32	178	400	8.2	1.28	.236

7 LANE THOMAS, OF

Born: Aug. 23, 1995. **B-T:** R-R. **HT:** 6-1. **WT:** 210. **Drafted:** HS—Knoxville, 2014 (5th round). **Signed by:** Nate Murrie (Blue Jays).

TRACK RECORD: Thomas signed with the Blue Jays for $750,000 as a fifth-round pick in 2014 but stalled at the lower levels of in Toronto's system. Needing money for an international class headlined by Eric Pardinho, the Blue Jays sent Thomas to the Cardinals for $500,000 in bonus pool space on the first day of the 2017 international signing period. Thomas suffered a broken wrist in 2016 and a broken foot in 2017, but full health in 2018 led to a breakout year. He led the Cardinals' system with 27 home runs—he'd hit 18 in the previous four seasons combined—as he advanced from Double-A to Triple-A, adding 17 steals and posting an .823 OPS.

SCOUTING REPORT: Thomas combines solid tools with a natural feel for the game. Strong and athletic in his 6-foot-1, 210-pound frame, he takes consistent, competitive at-bats and drives home runs out on a line with a sound swing. Thomas has some plate coverage issues and will swing and miss, but he works counts and makes hard contact when he connects. Defensively, he's an above-average center fielder with plus instincts. He positions himself well, gets good jumps and is a plus runner underway, nabbing anything hit in his zone. His above-average arm is another weapon.

SCOTT ROVAK/ST. LOUIS CARDINALS

BA GRADE

45 Risk: Medium

Hit: 45. Power: 55.
Run: 60. Field: 55.
Arm: 55.

THE FUTURE: The Cardinals envision Thomas as a sort of Harrison Bader-lite, albeit with more power. He is in line to make his major league debut in 2019.

Year	Club (League)	Class	AVG	G	AB	R	H	2B	3B	HR	RBI	BB	SO	SB	CS	OBP	SLG
2016	Blue Jays (GCL)	R	.429	6	21	8	9	5	0	1	4	2	6	2	1	.478	.810
	Lansing (MWL)	LoA	.216	81	282	50	61	14	1	7	27	45	107	17	5	.330	.348
2017	Dunedin (FSL)	HiA	.252	73	274	34	69	12	6	4	38	27	84	8	7	.319	.383
	Palm Beach (FSL)	HiA	.257	9	35	5	9	0	1	0	3	3	10	2	2	.308	.314
2018	Springfield (TL)	AA	.260	100	384	63	100	16	4	21	67	43	101	13	9	.337	.487
	Memphis (PCL)	AAA	.275	32	131	21	36	7	2	6	21	7	33	4	1	.321	.496
Minor League Totals			.250	405	1527	233	381	81	18	45	214	165	434	61	32	.325	.415

8 ANDREW KNIZNER, C

Born: Feb. 3, 1995. **B-T:** R-R. **Ht.:** 6-1. **Wt.:** 200. **Drafted:** North Carolina State, 2016 (7th round). **Signed by:** Charles Peterson.

TRACK RECORD: Knizner played third base his freshman year at North Carolina State before moving to catcher as a sophomore. His offense scuffled with the position change, causing him to slip to the seventh round of the 2016 draft. Knizner signed for just $185,300 but rebounded quickly in pro ball. He hit .302 while reaching Double-A in his first full season and hit .313 with Triple-A Memphis in 2018, when he was also selected to the Futures Game.

SCOUTING REPORT: Knizner is an offensive catcher with all the tools to hit. He turns around good velocity with a quick bat, recognizes offspeed pitches and uses the whole field. His swing is more geared for line drives to the gaps, but he can turn on inside fastballs and drive them out to left field for home runs. Knizner is aggressive and doesn't walk much, but he doesn't strike out either with good hand-eye coordination and natural timing. While Knizner's is a consensus above-average hitter, his defensive reviews are more mixed. His arm ranges from fringy to average, and his blocking, hands and footwork are still a bit rough. He's a smart leader who calls a good game and works hard behind the plate, showing all the intangibles to catch.

THE FUTURE: Knizner has improved defensively, but he still has work to do. He'll try to take the next step at Triple-A Memphis in 2019.

BA GRADE
45 Risk: Medium
Hit: 55. Power: 45.
Run: 30. Field: 45.
Arm: 50.

Year	Club (League)	Class	AVG	G	AB	R	H	2B	3B	HR	RBI	BB	SO	SB	CS	OBP	SLG
2016	Johnson City (APP)	R	.319	53	185	35	59	12	1	6	42	21	21	0	0	.423	.492
2017	Peoria (MWL)	LoA	.279	44	179	18	50	10	1	8	29	9	22	1	1	.325	.480
	Springfield (TL)	AA	.324	51	182	27	59	13	0	4	22	14	27	0	1	.371	.462
2018	Springfield (TL)	AA	.313	77	281	39	88	13	0	7	41	23	40	0	1	.365	.434
	Memphis (PCL)	AAA	.315	17	54	3	17	5	0	0	4	4	8	0	0	.383	.407
Minor League Totals			.310	242	881	122	273	53	2	25	138	71	118	1	3	.373	.460

9 MALCOM NUNEZ, 3B

Born: March 9, 2001. **B-T:** R-R. **HT:** 5-11. **WT:** 205. **Signed:** Cuba, 2018. **Signed by:** Alix Martinez/Angel Ovalles.

TRACK RECORD: A standout slugger in Cuba's youth national leagues, Nunez hit a tournament-best .667 (18-for-27) at the 2016 15U World Cup in Japan to lead Cuba to the gold medal and solidify himself as a top international prospect. The Cardinals couldn't sign any international free agents for more than $300,000 in 2018, and they didn't think that would be enough to sign Nunez, but rotating agents and unclear signability chased away some of their competition. The Cardinals stayed on Nunez, and once his price came down they inked him for $300,000. He promptly went out and won the Dominican Summer League triple crown, batting .415 with 13 homers and 59 RBIs in 44 games as an age-appropriate 17-year-old.

SCOUTING REPORT: Nunez is a strong, thick-bodied teenager who is more masher than pure hitter. His physically mature tool set contains plus power, plus arm strength and plenty of bat speed, and he has a sound idea of the strike zone. He especially punishes anything on the outer half of the plate, where he can get his arms extended. Nunez is deceptively athletic in his heavy, 5-foot-11, 205-pound frame, but he's still a below-average runner and fringy defender at third base, with the possibility for worse if he doesn't maintain his physique.

THE FUTURE: Nunez will move to the U.S. in 2019, and his bat is prodigious enough he could see time in low Class A Peoria. His ceiling is high, but he's many years away and will have to watch his fitness.

BA GRADE
55 Risk: Extreme
Hit: 55. Power: 60.
Run: 30. Field: 45.
Arm: 60.

Year	Club (League)	Class	AVG	G	AB	R	H	2B	3B	HR	RBI	BB	SO	SB	CS	OBP	SLG
2018	Cardinals Blue (DSL)	R	.415	44	164	44	68	16	2	13	59	26	29	3	0	.497	.774
Minor League Totals			.415	44	164	44	68	16	2	13	59	26	29	3	0	.497	.774

10 DYLAN CARLSON, OF

Born: Oct. 23, 1998. **B-T:** B-L. **Ht.:** 6-3. **Wt.:** 195. **Drafted:** HS—Elk Grove, Calif., 2016 (1st round). **Signed by:** Zach Mortimer.

TRACK RECORD: Jeff Carlson built a prep baseball powerhouse in 29 years as the coach of Elk Grove (Calif.) High, producing big leaguers David Hernandez, J.D. Davis and Rowdy Tellez. Carlson's son Dylan became the program's highest player drafted when the Cardinals picked him 33rd overall in 2016, and he signed for $1.35 million.

SCOUTING REPORT: Carlson has yet to post big numbers, but he's been steady as one of the youngest players at every level he's played. At age 19 in 2018, Carlson posted a .731 OPS in the Florida State League that was 40 points higher than the average. The switch-hitter has a better swing from the right side and is loopier from the left, but he manages the strike zone from both sides and shows bat speed, hand-eye coordination and average power. Carlson is an above-average right fielder who flashes a plus arm, and he can handle center field in a pinch. He's a smart, steady player who stays on an even keel.

BA GRADE
50 Risk: High
Hit: 50. **Power:** 50.
Run: 50. **Field:** 55.
Arm: 55.

THE FUTURE: Carlson's on-base skills and growing power fit in an outfield corner, especially if he can refine his lefthanded swing. He'll head to Double-A Springfield as a 20-year-old in 2019.

Year	Club (League)	Class	AVG	G	AB	R	H	2B	3B	HR	RBI	BB	SO	SB	CS	OBP	SLG
2016	Cardinals (GCL)	R	.251	50	183	30	46	13	3	3	22	16	52	4	2	.313	.404
2017	Peoria (MWL)	LoA	.240	115	383	63	92	18	1	7	42	52	116	6	6	.342	.347
2018	Peoria (MWL)	LoA	.234	13	47	5	11	3	0	2	9	10	10	2	0	.368	.426
	Palm Beach (FSL)	HiA	.247	99	376	63	93	19	3	9	53	52	78	6	3	.345	.386
Minor League Totals			.245	277	989	161	242	53	7	21	126	130	256	18	11	.340	.376

11 RYAN HELSLEY, RHP

BA GRADE
50 Risk: High

Born: July 18, 1994. **B-T:** R-R. **Ht.:** 6-1. **Wt.:** 195. **Drafted:** Northeastern State (Okla.), 2015 (5th round). **Signed by:** Aaron Looper

TRACK RECORD: The Cardinals made Helsley one of the few active Cherokee Nation members ever drafted when they picked him in the fifth round out of Division II Northeastern State in 2015. Helsley shot up the minors with a 27-9, 2.58 career record and was in position for his MLB debut in 2018, but he was shut down with shoulder fatigue at Triple-A on June 10 and made only one appearance the rest of the year.

SCOUTING REPORT: Though a tad undersized at 6-foot-1, Helsley is a pure power pitcher with a strong frame and thick, sturdy legs. His fastball sits 94-95 mph and touches 98 mph, and he uses his heater liberally with an aggressive, strike-throwing mentality. Helsley backs his fastball up with an 80-81 mph power curveball with hard, late drop that draws average-or-better grades, and his upper-80s cutter is another hard offering that projects above-average to plus. His 84-86 mph changeup is his "soft" offering, and is fringe-average but usable. Helsley struggles at times to harness all his power, resulting in inconsistent command and fringe-average control. He struck out 10.5 batters per nine innings in 2018, but also walked 4.1 per nine.

THE FUTURE: Helsley has the stuff to start, but with control concerns and now a shoulder issue, the Cardinals prefer him as a reliever. Barring an injury setback, he should make his big league debut in 2019.

Year	Club (League)	Class	W	L	ERA	G	GS	CG	SV	IP	H	HR	BB	SO	K/9	WHIP	AVG
2016	Peoria (MWL)	LoA	10	2	1.61	17	17	0	0	95	77	3	19	109	10.3	1.01	.216
2017	Palm Beach (FSL)	HiA	8	2	2.69	17	16	1	0	94	72	3	30	91	8.7	1.09	.213
	Springfield (TL)	AA	3	1	2.67	6	6	0	0	34	25	4	15	41	11.0	1.19	.200
	Memphis (PCL)	AAA	0	0	3.60	1	1	0	0	5	7	0	3	5	9.0	2.00	.350
2018	Springfield (TL)	AA	3	2	4.39	7	7	1	0	41	30	5	20	44	9.7	1.22	.203
	Memphis (PCL)	AAA	2	1	3.71	5	5	0	0	27	18	2	9	34	11.5	1.01	.188
	Cardinals (GCL)	R	0	0	0.00	1	1	0	0	3	1	0	3	4	13.5	1.50	.111
Minor League Totals			27	9	2.58	65	62	2	0	338	263	18	118	363	9.7	1.13	.212

12 TOMMY EDMAN, SS/2B

BA GRADE
45 Risk: Medium

Born: May 9, 1995. **B-T:** S-R. **Ht.:** 5-10. **Wt.:** 180. **Signed:** Stanford, 2016 (6th round). **Signed by:** Zach Mortimer.

TRACK RECORD: Edman has consistently outperformed initial impressions since his days as Stanford's No. 3 hitter at all of 5-foot-10, 180 pounds. A sixth-round pick in 2016, Edman climbed three levels to Double-A his first full season and ascended to Triple-A in his second, batting .301 with 30 steals and finishing as the starting second baseman and leadoff hitter on Memphis' Triple-A championship team.

SCOUTING REPORT: Edman's bat speed is modest, but the switch-hitter takes a disciplined approach, recognizes pitches and has a level swing that stays in the zone for a long time. He's not much of a home run threat, but he picks out the right pitches to drive for extra-bases. Edman's above-average speed plays up with his superb instincts. He makes all the plays at both shortstop and second base with good positioning and soft hands, and his fringe-average arm plays up with an advanced internal clock.

THE FUTURE: The Cardinals envision Edman filling the utility infield role of Greg Garcia and Daniel Descalso before him. Edman has more tools than both of them, however, and may ascend to more.

Year	Club (League)	Class	AVG	G	AB	R	H	2B	3B	HR	RBI	BB	SO	SB	CS	OBP	SLG
2016	State College (NYP)	SS	.286	66	255	61	73	14	5	4	33	48	29	19	3	.400	.427
2017	Peoria (MWL)	LoA	.284	38	155	24	44	8	5	2	18	15	19	8	2	.347	.439
	Palm Beach (FSL)	HiA	.257	18	70	7	18	2	1	1	11	7	18	0	1	.338	.357
	Springfield (TL)	AA	.247	63	219	20	54	12	2	2	26	16	34	5	2	.298	.347
2018	Springfield (TL)	AA	.299	109	452	71	135	23	3	6	36	35	76	27	5	.350	.403
	Memphis (PCL)	AAA	.318	17	66	13	21	0	1	1	5	8	11	3	0	.382	.394
Minor League Totals			.283	311	1217	196	345	59	17	16	129	129	187	62	13	.353	.399

13 DANIEL PONCEDELEON, RHP

BA GRADE

45 Risk: Medium

Born: Jan 16, 1992. **B-T:** R-R. **HT:** 6-4. **WT:** 185. **Drafted:** Embry-Riddle (Fla.), 2014 (9th round). **Signed by:** Charlie Gonzalez.

TRACK RECORD: A senior sign in 2014, Poncedeleon's career nearly ended in 2017, when he took a comebacker off his right temple, fracturing his skull and requiring emergency surgery to stop the bleeding in his brain. After months of inactivity followed by rehab, and with a permanent dent in his head, Poncedeleon amazingly returned in time for 2018 spring training. On July 23, just over 14 months after the comebacker nearly killed him, Poncedeleon fired seven no-hit innings against the Reds in his big league debut.

SCOUTING REPORT: More than just an inspiring story, Poncedeleon has real stuff. He starts his arsenal with an above-average, sinking fastball that sits 93-94 mph and touches 96 mph. He has an average 83-85 mph changeup he uses against lefties and an average 89-92 mph cutter for righties, along with a mid-70s curveball he'll mix in. Poncedeleon is throwing a tick harder since his return, and his strikeout rate (9.8 per nine innings) jumped to a career-high in 2018, but so did his walk rate (4.4 per nine).

THE FUTURE: Poncedelon excelled as a long reliever/spot starter in 2018, his expected long-term role.

Year	Club (League)	Class	W	L	ERA	G	GS	CG	SV	IP	H	HR	BB	SO	K/9	WHIP	AVG
2016	Springfield (TL)	AA	9	8	3.52	27	27	1	0	151	128	10	56	122	7.3	1.22	.231
2017	Memphis (PCL)	AAA	2	0	2.17	6	6	0	0	29	20	2	13	25	7.8	1.14	.196
2018	Memphis (PCL)	AAA	9	4	2.24	19	18	1	0	96	69	4	50	110	10.3	1.24	.197
	St. Louis (NL)	MAJ	0	2	2.73	11	4	0	1	33	24	2	13	31	8.5	1.12	.205
Major League Totals			0	2	2.73	11	4	0	1	33	24	2	13	31	8.5	1.12	.205
Minor League Totals			34	17	2.66	84	80	3	0	440	356	21	163	396	8.1	1.18	.221

14 JUSTIN WILLIAMS, OF

BA GRADE

45 Risk: Medium

Born: Aug. 20, 1995. **B-T:** L-R. **HT:** 6-2. **WT:** 215. **Drafted:** HS—Houma, La., 2013 (2nd round). **Signed by:** Rusty Pendergrass (Diamondbacks).

TRACK RECORD: A second-round pick by the D-backs in 2013, Williams was traded him to the Rays in the Jeremy Hellickson deal in 2014. Williams made his major league debut with a one-game stint in Tampa Bay on July 21, 2018 before the Rays traded him to the Cardinals for Tommy Pham 10 days later.

SCOUTING REPORT: Williams' mix of athleticism and power intrigue, but he's still very raw. He takes defensive, segmented swings, and the Cardinals see him as a swing-change candidate. He flashes plus raw power, and the hope is a swing change can unlock that in games. Williams' jumps and instincts come and go in right field, but he works hard and has the plus arm for the position. He's a fringe-average runner so he's mostly limited to the corners, although he can cover center in a pinch.

THE FUTURE: The Cardinals feel they got a fourth outfielder at worst with Williams' lefthanded power and ability to move around the outfield. If he can successfully implement a swing change, he may be more.

Year	Club (League)	Class	AVG	G	AB	R	H	2B	3B	HR	RBI	BB	SO	SB	CS	OBP	SLG
2016	Charlotte, FL (FSL)	HiA	.330	51	194	23	64	11	0	4	31	6	26	0	1	.350	.448
	Montgomery (SL)	AA	.250	39	148	20	37	7	2	6	28	5	30	0	1	.277	.446
2017	Montgomery (SL)	AA	.301	96	366	53	110	21	3	14	72	37	69	6	2	.364	.489
2018	Tampa Bay (AL)	MAJ	.000	1	1	0	0	0	0	0	0	0	0	0	0	.000	.000
	Durham (IL)	AAA	.258	94	356	41	92	18	0	8	46	25	81	4	3	.313	.376
	Memphis (PCL)	AAA	.217	21	69	8	15	3	0	3	11	5	17	0	1	.276	.391
Major League Totals			.000	1	1	0	0	0	0	0	0	0	0	0	0	.000	.000
Minor League Totals			.296	548	2102	275	623	120	12	47	319	127	424	17	13	.340	.432

15 ADOLIS GARCIA, OF

Born: March 2, 1993. **B-T:** R-R. **Ht.:** 6-1. **Wt.:** 180. **Signed:** Cuba, 2017.
Signed by: Matt Slater/Moises Rodriguez.

TRACK RECORD: Garcia played five seasons in Cuba's Serie Nacional and won the league's MVP award in 2016. The Cardinals gave him $2.5 million after he defected, capping a push to sign talent from the island nation. A tooled-up athlete with an uber-aggressive approach, Garcia spent just under two seasons in the upper minors tailoring his game before the Cardinals called him for his big league debut on Aug. 8.
SCOUTING REPORT: Few position players in the Cardinals' system can match Garcia's tools. He has plus raw power, is a plus runner, has a cannon arm from right field that is a borderline 80 tool and is a plus defender in right field. What hampers Garcia is a poor approach. He's a wild swinger with little plate discipline, resulting in gobs of strikeouts. He has stretches where he puts an approach together, waits for a fastball and stays behind the ball, but he has yet to show he can maintain it for any extended period of time.
THE FUTURE: Garcia's speed, defense and power have already gotten him to the big leagues. Whether he can even mildly improve his approach will determine if he becomes more than a reserve.

Year	Club (League)	Class	AVG	G	AB	R	H	2B	3B	HR	RBI	BB	SO	SB	CS	OBP	SLG
2016	Yomiuri (CL)	JPN	.000	4	7	0	0	0	0	0	0	0	3	0	0	.000	.000
2017	Springfield (TL)	AA	.285	84	309	43	88	23	0	12	55	26	77	12	8	.339	.476
	Memphis (PCL)	AAA	.301	40	136	21	41	11	2	3	10	7	31	3	1	.342	.478
2018	Memphis (PCL)	AAA	.256	112	406	62	104	25	4	22	71	14	99	10	3	.281	.500
	St. Louis (NL)	MAJ	.118	21	17	3	2	1	0	0	1	0	7	0	0	.118	.176
Major League Totals			.118	21	17	3	2	1	0	0	1	0	7	0	0	.118	.176
Minor League Totals			.274	236	851	126	233	59	6	37	136	47	207	25	12	.313	.488

16 JAKE WOODFORD, RHP

Born: Oct. 28, 1996. **B-T:** R-R. **Ht.:** 6-4. **Wt.:** 210. **Drafted:** HS—Tampa, 2015 (1st round supplemental). **Signed by:** Mike Dibiase.

TRACK RECORD: Woodford served as the ace of Tampa's Plant High in 2015 while BA High School Player of the Year Kyle Tucker anchored the lineup. Tucker went fifth overall to the Astros in the draft and Woodford went 39th to the Cardinals. Woodford moved from Double-A to Triple-A as a 21-year-old in 2018 and finished second in the Cardinals' organization in innings pitched (145).
SCOUTING REPORT: Woodford's fastball sits 93 mph and touches 96 mph. It's above-average velocity, but Woodford is still learning how to use his heater effectively. He shies away from pitching inside and doesn't demonstrate much confidence in his fastball, resulting in a lot of deep counts and a rising walk rate. Woodford's best secondary is an average cutter with good velocity, but he falls in love with it too much. He has an average changeup and breaking ball, but he doesn't use either pitch regularly enough.
THE FUTURE: Woodford is young and durable, and the hope is he'll learn to use his arsenal better with time and experience. He'll start back at Triple-A in 2019.

Year	Club (League)	Class	W	L	ERA	G	GS	CG	SV	IP	H	HR	BB	SO	K/9	WHIP	AVG
2016	Peoria (MWL)	LoA	5	5	3.31	21	21	0	0	109	104	7	37	82	6.8	1.30	.254
2017	Palm Beach (FSL)	HiA	7	6	3.10	23	21	0	0	119	128	7	39	72	5.4	1.40	.280
2018	Springfield (TL)	AA	3	8	5.22	16	16	0	0	81	94	13	35	56	6.2	1.59	.290
	Memphis (PCL)	AAA	5	5	4.50	12	12	0	0	64	64	5	27	45	6.3	1.42	.261
Minor League Totals			21	24	3.77	80	75	0	1	399	416	33	145	276	6.2	1.41	.271

17 RANDY AROZARENA, OF

Born: Feb. 28, 1995 **B-T:** R-R. **Ht.:** 5-11. **Wt.:** 170. **Signed:** Cuba, 2016.
Signed by: Ramon Garcia.

TRACK RECORD: The Cardinals signed Arozarena for $1.25 million in 2016, banking on his record as a speedy catalyst in Cuba's Serie Nacional and international competition. After reaching Double-A in his first year in the U.S. in 2017, Arozarena made the Futures Game and reached Triple-A in 2018.
SCOUTING REPORT: Arozarena is a plus runner who plays fast and hard, sometimes to his detriment. At his best, Arozarena shoots balls gap-to-gap, lays down bunts and takes his walks to get on base. As he neared the majors at Triple-A, however, Arozarena veered from playing hard into playing reckless. He showed a propensity for wild swings, poor pitch selection and running when he shouldn't. Arozarena has the ingredients to hit with quick-twitch athleticism, bat speed and surprising pop, but his lack of adjustments create hesitation about how much he'll actually produce. Arozarena can handle center field but others in the system are better, so he primarily projects to left field with his average arm.
THE FUTURE: Arozarena has tools, but he has to improve his approach and decision-making. He'll be 24 on Opening Day and needs to show progress soon.

Year	Club (League)	Class	AVG	G	AB	R	H	2B	3B	HR	RBI	BB	SO	SB	CS	OBP	SLG
2016	Tijuana (MEX)	AAA	.100	5	20	3	2	1	0	0	0	2	3	0	0	.182	.150
2017	Palm Beach (FSL)	HiA	.275	70	265	38	73	22	3	8	40	13	53	10	4	.333	.472
	Springfield (TL)	AA	.252	51	163	34	41	10	1	3	9	27	34	8	3	.366	.380
2018	Springfield (TL)	AA	.396	24	91	22	36	5	0	7	21	6	25	9	3	.455	.681
	Memphis (PCL)	AAA	.232	89	267	42	62	16	0	5	28	28	59	17	5	.328	.348
Minor League Totals			.266	239	806	139	214	54	4	23	98	76	174	44	15	.348	.428

18 GRIFFIN ROBERTS, RHP

BA GRADE
50 Risk: High

Born: June 13, 1996. **B-T:** R-R. **HT:** 6-3. **WT:** 205. **Drafted:** Wake Forest, 2018 (1st round supplemental). **Signed by:** T.C. Calhoun.

TRACK RECORD: Roberts pitched out of the bullpen his first two seasons at Wake Forest before moving to the starting rotation as a junior. He began the transition in the Cape Cod League and pitched to a 1.96 ERA while earning all-star honors, and followed up in the spring by leading the Atlantic Coast Conference with 130 strikeouts in just 96.2 innings. The Cardinals drafted Roberts 43rd overall in 2018.

SCOUTING REPORT: Roberts starts his arsenal with an above-average fastball in the low to mid-90s that plays up with running life. His real weapon is a slider that was one of the best breaking balls in the 2018 draft class. It's a plus pitch with exceptional movement and depth, and it locks up both lefthanded and righthanded hitters while drawing swings and misses both in and out of the zone. He flashes an average changeup with fade for his third pitch. Roberts has some reliever risk to him with a high-effort delivery and low, three-quarter arm slot that borders on sidearm. Control issues in his history further lead many to believe he'll be best off pitching out of the bullpen.

THE FUTURE: The Cardinals will start Roberts for now, knowing his fastball/slider combination will play well in relief as a fallback. He will likely begin his first full season at high Class A Palm Beach, but not until he serves a 50-game suspension after twice testing positive for cannabis.

Year	Club (League)	Class	W	L	ERA	G	GS	CG	SV	IP	H	HR	BB	SO	K/9	WHIP	AVG
2018	Cardinals (GCL)	R	0	1	6.23	7	2	0	1	9	6	0	4	11	11.4	1.15	.194
	Palm Beach (FSL)	HiA	0	0	0.00	1	0	0	0	1	0	0	0	2	18.0	0.00	.000
Minor League Totals			0	1	5.59	8	2	0	1	10	6	0	4	13	12.1	1.03	.176

19 JHON TORRES, OF

BA GRADE
55 Risk: Extreme

Born: March 29, 2000. **B-T:** R-R. **HT:** 6-4. **WT:** 199. **Signed:** Colombia, 2016. **Signed by:** Domingo Toribio/Felix Nivar/Koby Perez (Indians).

TRACK RECORD: The Cardinals took note of Torres playing for Colombia's 15U national team at the Pan-American Championships in Mexico in 2015, but had limited interest in the very tall, very skinny, very raw outfielder. Torres signed with the Indians for $150,000 a year later and suddenly filled out, becoming bigger, stronger and faster. He made his U.S. debut in 2018 and quickly became a favorite of scouts in the Arizona League, and the Cardinals acquired him alongisde outfielder Conner Capel in exchange of Oscar Mercado in July.

SCOUTING REPORT: The 6-foot-4, 199-pound Torres has blossomed into a prototypical power-hitting right fielder. He is patient with a mature approach, and when he gets his pitch he unloads with plus raw power to all fields. Torres is more slugger than hitter, but he has the feel for the barrel to make his power play and projects to hit for a solid average. Torres is a decent athlete for his size as an average runner who is light on his feet and gets good jumps. His biggest weapon is his arm, a 70-grade hose from right field.

THE FUTURE: Torres projects to a corner, so there will always be pressure on his bat. He's handled it so far and will aim to continue at low Class A Peoria in 2019.

Year	Club (League)	Class	AVG	G	AB	R	H	2B	3B	HR	RBI	BB	SO	SB	CS	OBP	SLG
2017	Indians (DSL)	R	.255	54	184	25	47	7	3	5	35	28	41	4	4	.363	.408
2018	Indians 2 (AZL)	R	.273	27	99	16	27	3	0	4	16	11	24	3	0	.351	.424
	Cardinals (GCL)	R	.397	17	63	11	25	6	0	4	14	8	13	1	1	.493	.683
Minor League Totals			.286	98	346	52	99	16	3	13	65	47	78	8	5	.383	.462

20 JOHAN OVIEDO, RHP

BA GRADE
50 Risk: Very High

Born: March 2, 1998. **B-T:** R-R. **Ht.:** 6-6. **Wt.:** 210. **Signed:** Cuba, 2016. **Signed by:** Angel Ovalles.

TRACK RECORD: Oviedo signed with the Cardinals for $1.9 million in 2016. After three years in short-season ball, Oviedo made the jump to low Class A Peoria in 2018 and had a learning year. He went 2-6, 5.02 in the first half but adjusted to go 8-4, 3.06 in the second half.

SCOUTING REPORT: Physically huge at 6-foot-6, 210 pounds, Oviedo is a mix of big stuff and poor control often seen in young, long-limbed starters. Oviedo takes time to warm up, often pitching in the low 90s in the early innings before jumping to 93-96 mph in the middle innings. His curveball flashes plus, but he's very inconsistent and will throw multiple poor ones before snapping off a plus one. He's more consistent with his above-average, potentially plus changeup. Oviedo's three above-average or better pitches led him to 118 strikeouts in the Midwest League, but he also led the league with 78 walks.

THE FUTURE: Like many tall pitchers, Oviedo will take time to develop control. His size and stuff intrigue enough for evaluators to consider him a potential back-end starter.

Year	Club (League)	Class	W	L	ERA	G	GS	CG	SV	IP	H	HR	BB	SO	K/9	WHIP	AVG
2016	Cardinals (DSL)	R	0	1	1.66	7	7	0	0	22	19	0	6	29	12.0	1.15	.238
2017	Johnson City (APP)	R	2	1	4.88	6	6	0	0	28	22	0	18	31	10.1	1.45	.220
	State College (NYP)	SS	2	2	4.56	8	8	0	0	47	53	3	18	39	7.4	1.50	.285
2018	Peoria (MWL)	LoA	10	10	4.22	25	23	0	1	122	108	6	79	118	8.7	1.54	.238
Minor League Totals			14	14	4.12	46	44	0	1	218	202	9	121	217	8.9	1.48	.246

21 IVAN HERRERA, C

BA GRADE

50 Risk: Extreme

Born: June 1, 2000. **B-T:** R-R. **Ht.:** 6-0. **Wt.:** 180. **Signed:** Panama, 2016.
Signed by: Damaso Espino.

TRACK RECORD: Herrera signed for $200,000 out of Panama in 2016. He hit .335 in the Dominican Summer League in his pro debut, and in 2018 he hit .348/.423/.500 in the Gulf Coast League.

SCOUTING REPORT: Herrera is an offensive catcher with one of the purest swings in the system. He has a quick, compact stroke that is direct to the ball, and his efficient swing path helps him both turn around velocity and square up breaking pitches. His power is mostly to the gaps with his flat-line drive stroke, but evaluators expect him to grow into 10-15 home runs as he fills out physically. Herrera is built to catch with a broad back, thick legs and a blue-collar mindset, but his skills are behind. He has fringe-average arm strength and his overall game awareness is lacking, particularly in controlling the run game. His blocking and receiving were problematic, resulting in seven passed balls in 20 games.

THE FUTURE: Herrera has work to do behind the plate, but the Cardinals are optimistic he'll get there.

Year	Club (League)	Class	AVG	G	AB	R	H	2B	3B	HR	RBI	BB	SO	SB	CS	OBP	SLG
2017	Cardinals (DSL)	R	.335	49	170	21	57	15	0	1	27	18	36	2	2	.425	.441
2018	Cardinals (GCL)	R	.348	28	112	23	39	6	4	1	25	11	20	1	1	.423	.500
	Springfield (TL)	AA	.000	2	4	0	0	0	0	0	0	0	2	0	0	.200	.000
Minor League Totals			.336	79	286	44	96	21	4	2	52	29	58	3	3	.421	.458

22 EDMUNDO SOSA, SS

BA GRADE

40 Risk: Medium

Born: March 6, 1996. **B-T:** R-R. **Ht.:** 5-11. **Wt.:** 170. **Signed:** Panama, 2012.
Signed by: Arquimedes Nieto.

TRACK RECORD: Sosa signed for $425,000 out of Panama in 2012 as a headliner in a loaded Cardinals international class that included Alex Reyes and Magneuris Sierra. A series of injuries, including left wrist tendinitis in 2016 and a broken hamate bone in 2017, delayed his progress, but he stayed healthy in 2018 and moved quickly, jumping from Double-A to Triple-A and earning his first major league callup.

SCOUTING REPORT: Sosa has defensive tools that help him profile up the middle. He's an above-average defender at shortstop with sneaky speed and above-average hands, and his above-average arm makes all the throws. While Sosa's instincts are subpar, he began positioning himself better at Triple-A and started getting to more balls without having to range as far, a positive and much-needed development. He also improved his effort and focus, which had lacked in the past. Sosa made an adjustment to use his hands more in his swing and surprised with 30 doubles and 13 home runs. He doesn't make enough contact or walk enough to project as more than a fringe-average hitter, but the newfound power helps his cause.

THE FUTURE: Sosa projects as a glove-first utility infielder, but his offense and defense are trending up.

Year	Club (League)	Class	AVG	G	AB	R	H	2B	3B	HR	RBI	BB	SO	SB	CS	OBP	SLG
2016	Peoria (MWL)	LoA	.268	88	351	42	94	13	1	3	30	19	71	5	4	.307	.336
	Palm Beach (FSL)	HiA	.294	9	34	3	10	0	2	0	4	1	8	0	0	.314	.412
2017	Springfield (TL)	AA	.000	1	4	0	0	0	0	0	0	1	0	0	0	.200	.000
	Cardinals (GCL)	R	.364	6	22	7	8	1	0	1	2	1	2	0	0	.391	.545
	Palm Beach (FSL)	HiA	.285	51	193	25	55	10	1	0	14	12	34	3	0	.329	.347
2018	Springfield (TL)	AA	.276	67	261	34	72	17	1	7	32	9	52	1	2	.308	.429
	Memphis (PCL)	AAA	.262	56	191	31	50	13	0	5	27	13	42	5	2	.321	.408
	St. Louis (NL)	MAJ	.000	3	2	1	0	0	0	0	0	1	1	0	0	.333	.000
Major League Totals			.000	3	2	1	0	0	0	0	0	1	1	0	0	.333	.000
Minor League Totals			.281	429	1637	242	460	78	17	27	175	112	293	35	20	.334	.399

23 LUKEN BAKER, 1B

Born: March 10, 2017. **B-T:** R-R. **HT:** 6-4. **WT:** 265. **Drafted:** Texas Christian, 2018 (2nd round supplemental). **Signed by:** Tom Lipari.

BA GRADE

45 Risk: High

TRACK RECORD: Baker became a folk hero at Texas Christian as a 265-pound, two-way freshman who led the Horned Frogs to the College World Series in 2016. The big-bodied Texan gave up pitching as a sophomore to focus on hitting and altogether batted .347 with 28 home runs and 129 RBIs over three collegiate seasons. The Cardinals drafted Baker in the supplemental second round in 2018.

SCOUTING REPORT: Baker has plus raw power and doesn't have to swing hard to get to it, allowing him the bat control to be regarded as an average-or-better hitter. Baker can hit, but he's a tough fit defensively. He mostly DH'd in college and is a below-average first baseman with limited range, although he catches what he gets to and picks balls out of the dirt fine. He doesn't move well enough to play anywhere else and has a concerning injury history, including elbow surgery in 2017 and a broken left fibula as junior.

THE FUTURE: Baker is going to have to hit, and his bat will be tested at high Class A Palm Beach in 2019.

Year	Club (League)	Class	AVG	G	AB	R	H	2B	3B	HR	RBI	BB	SO	SB	CS	OBP	SLG
2018	Cardinals (GCL)	R	.500	8	24	10	12	2	0	1	7	3	4	0	0	.536	.708
	Peoria (MWL)	LoA	.288	37	139	16	40	9	0	3	15	16	31	0	0	.359	.417
Minor League Totals			.319	45	163	26	52	11	0	4	22	19	35	0	0	.386	.460

24 SETH ELLEDGE, RHP

Born: May 20, 1996. **B-T:** R-R. **HT:** 6-3. **WT:** 230. **Drafted:** Dallas Baptist, 2017 (4th round). **Signed by:** Ty Bowman (Mariners).

BA GRADE

45 Risk: High

TRACK RECORD: Elledge's 26 career saves at Dallas Baptist set a school record before the Mariners drafted him in the fourth round in 2017. Thirteen months later, the Mariners traded Elledge to the Cardinals.

SCOUTING REPORT: Elledge is a classic, big-bodied reliever with a fastball and slider. He pitches exclusively from the stretch and has a little bit of a cross-body delivery, adding a tick of deception to his already potent stuff. Elledge's fastball sits 93-94 mph and plays up with late life and carry, and he backs it up with an 83-84 mph slider that flashes average with sharp vertical break. Elledge has a lot of effort in his delivery and loses his command and control, particularly on his fastball.

THE FUTURE: Elledge has a chance to be a middle-to-late inning reliever if he can tighten his fastball command and overall control. He should begin 2019 back at Double-A.

Year	Club (League)	Class	W	L	ERA	G	GS	CG	SV	IP	H	HR	BB	SO	K/9	WHIP	AVG
2017	Everett (NWL)	SS	0	0	4.50	4	0	0	0	4	2	0	2	7	15.8	1.00	.154
	Clinton (MWL)	LoA	3	0	3.00	15	0	0	5	21	14	1	6	35	15.0	0.95	.182
2018	Modesto (CAL)	HiA	5	1	1.17	31	0	0	9	38	18	1	15	54	12.7	0.86	.140
	Springfield (TL)	AA	3	1	4.32	13	0	0	4	17	13	3	6	20	10.8	1.14	.220
Minor League Totals			11	2	2.48	63	0	0	18	80	47	5	29	116	13.1	0.95	.169

25 MAX SCHROCK, 2B

Born: Oct. 12, 1994. **B-T:** L-R. **HT:** 5-8. **WT:** 180. **Drafted:** South Carolina, 2015 (13th round). **Signed by:** Paul Faulk (Nationals).

BA GRADE

40 Risk: Medium

TRACK RECORD: Schrock was drafted by the Nationals and traded to the A's before coming to St. Louis in the Stephen Piscotty deal. The 2016 minor league hits leader, Schrock suffered an oblique injury on the first day of camp and appeared in only two spring training games, then reported to Triple-A Memphis.

SCOUTING REPORT: The 5-foot-8 Schrock long played above his tools with a short stroke, good hand-eye coordination and an ability to battle and spoil pitches. Facing the best stuff he's seen at Triple-A, however, Schrock's pitch selection regressed and he started pressing. While he rarely struck out, he also rarely walked and mostly hit the ball weakly on the ground. When right, he hammered strikes gap-to-gap, but those instances became fewer and fewer as he expanded for the zone. Defensively, Schrock is average at second base and playable at third with an average arm. He's an average runner who ticks up underway.

THE FUTURE: Schrock has to prove he can hit upper-level pitching. He'll try again at Triple-A in 2019.

Year	Club (League)	Class	AVG	G	AB	R	H	2B	3B	HR	RBI	BB	SO	SB	CS	OBP	SLG
2016	Hagerstown (SAL)	LoA	.326	67	270	46	88	20	2	4	39	22	20	15	3	.381	.459
	Potomac (CAR)	HiA	.341	54	232	30	79	11	0	5	29	9	22	7	2	.373	.453
	Stockton (CAL)	HiA	.111	2	9	0	1	0	0	0	0	0	0	0	0	.111	.111
	Midland (TL)	AA	.391	6	23	3	9	1	0	0	3	0	0	0	1	.375	.435
2017	Midland (TL)	AA	.324	106	417	55	135	20	1	6	44	35	42	4	2	.382	.420
2018	Memphis (PCL)	AAA	.249	114	417	41	104	22	0	4	42	24	36	10	5	.296	.331
Minor League Totals			.305	395	1540	206	469	84	7	21	171	103	136	38	14	.353	.409

26 CONNER CAPEL, OF

Born: May 19, 1997. **B-T:** L-L. **HT:** 6-1. **WT:** 185. **Drafted:** HS—Katy, Texas, 2016 (5th round). **Signed by:** Kyle Van Hook (Indians).

TRACK RECORD: Capel, whose father Mike pitched three seasons in the majors, was the Indians' fifth-round pick in 2016. He made the Carolina League all-star team as an Indians prospect in the summer of 2018, and a just over a month later the Cardinals acquired him and Jhon Torres for Oscar Mercado.

SCOUTING REPORT: Capel intrigues as a center fielder with above-average raw power and above-average speed, although he hasn't made it all click. Capel has worked to clean up his lefthanded swing and cut down on his strikeouts, but overall he's a fringe-average hitter who is neutralized by lefthanders. After hitting 22 home runs and posting a .482 slugging percentage in the Midwest League, Capel slipped to seven home runs with a .376 slugging percentage in 2018. It's important Capel finds his power because he could project as a corner outfielder long-term with average defense. His above-average arm is an asset.

THE FUTURE: Capel is going to have to hit to be a big leaguer, even in a reserve role. He'll try to make the necessary offensive strides at Double-A Springfield in 2019.

Year	Club (League)	Class	AVG	G	AB	R	H	2B	3B	HR	RBI	BB	SO	SB	CS	OBP	SLG
2016	Indians (AZL)	R	.210	35	138	22	29	5	3	0	13	11	20	10	3	.270	.290
2017	Lake County (MWL)	LoA	.249	119	438	73	109	22	7	22	61	43	107	15	10	.319	.482
2018	Lynchburg (CAR)	HiA	.261	89	322	47	84	17	3	6	44	49	72	15	10	.355	.388
	Palm Beach (FSL)	HiA	.248	29	117	11	29	6	1	1	19	7	30	0	1	.296	.342
Minor League Totals			.247	272	1015	153	251	50	14	29	137	110	229	40	24	.322	.410

27 SCOTT HURST, OF

Born: March 25, 1996. **B-T:** L-R. **Ht.:** 5-10. **Wt.:** 175. **Drafted:** Cal State Fullerton, 2017 (3rd round). **Signed by:** Brock Ungricht.

TRACK RECORD: Hurst battled a back injury his first two seasons at Cal State Fullerton but broke out as a junior, hitting .328 to lead the Titans to the College World Series. The Cardinals, stripped of their first- and second-round draft picks in 2017 as the penalty for former scouting director Chris Correa's hacking of the Astros' internal database, made Hurst their first pick when they drafted him in the third round.

SCOUTING REPORT: Hurst is a solid, undersized athlete who does everything well. He's an above-average runner who plays an average center field with clean reads and routes, he flashes an above-average arm and he's a solid-average contact hitter. Hurst has a good understanding of the strike zone and drives the ball with a short, compact swing. He doesn't have much power and occasionally gets beat by velocity, but he takes advantage of hittable pitches and finished with a .312/.389/.447 slash line at the Class A levels.

THE FUTURE: Hurst will have to stick in center with his lack of power. He has a chance to do that as a lefthanded-hitting bench option.

Year	Club (League)	Class	AVG	G	AB	R	H	2B	3B	HR	RBI	BB	SO	SB	CS	OBP	SLG
2017	State College (NYP)	SS	.282	55	213	36	60	11	6	3	21	22	58	6	4	.354	.432
2018	Peoria (MWL)	LoA	.295	49	190	28	56	11	1	3	25	19	41	7	4	.361	.411
	Cardinals (GCL)	R	.400	5	15	5	6	3	0	0	2	5	2	2	0	.550	.600
	Palm Beach (FSL)	HiA	.354	14	48	10	17	6	0	1	9	8	10	1	0	.439	.542
Minor League Totals			.298	123	466	79	139	31	7	7	57	54	111	16	8	.373	.440

28 LEANDRO CEDENO, 1B/OF

Born: Aug. 22, 1998. **B-T:** R-R. **HT:** 6-2. **WT:** 195. **Signed:** Venezuela, 2014. **Signed by:** Estuar Ruiz.

TRACK RECORD: The Cardinals signed Cedeno as a catcher out of Venezuela in 2014 but knew he wasn't going to stick behind the plate. They loved his bat and massive raw power, and he's delivered. Cedeno finished second in the Appalachian League in hits (75), home runs (14) and total bases (132) and third in OPS (1.011) in 2018, showing 400-plus foot home run power that had opposing managers buzzing.

SCOUTING REPORT: Cedeno turns heads with his nearly top-of-the-scale power. He hit one homer over Johnson City's 24-foot wall in center field 420 feet away, something no one in the league can recall ever happening. Cedeno generates his power with a short, compact swing, and he has an advanced plan for someone his age in waiting for a ball he can crush. He has hitter's instincts, and the sound off his bat is different than anyone else's. Cedeno has to hit because he doesn't offer much else. He has a thick body and doesn't move well, limiting him to first base long-term.

THE FUTURE: Cedeno will have to continue mashing to rise. He has a chance to convert skeptics at low Class A Peoria in 2019.

Year	Club (League)	Class	AVG	G	AB	R	H	2B	3B	HR	RBI	BB	SO	SB	CS	OBP	SLG
2016	Cardinals (DSL)	R	.290	47	193	32	56	15	4	4	30	12	42	0	0	.332	.472
2017	Cardinals (GCL)	R	.351	9	37	8	13	4	0	4	12	1	7	0	0	.359	.784
2018	Johnson City (APP)	R	.336	59	223	47	75	13	1	14	47	22	69	2	1	.419	.592
Minor League Totals			.303	142	545	100	165	36	6	24	99	44	133	2	1	.365	.523

29 GIOVANNY GALLEGOS, RHP

BA GRADE

40 Risk: Medium

Born: Aug. 14, 1991. **B-T:** R-R. **Ht.:** 6-2. **Wt.:** 210. **Signed:** Mexico, 2011
Signed by: Lee Stigman (Yankees).

TRACK RECORD: Gallegos signed with the Yankees out of Mexico in 2011 and reached the majors six years later, pitching out of the Yankees' bullpen in both 2017 and 2018. The Cardinals acquired Gallegos and fellow reliever Chasen Shreve from the Yankees at the July 2018 trade deadline.

SCOUTING REPORT: Gallegos comes after hitters with a 94-96 mph fastball that plays plus with downhill angle and tailing action. He pairs his heater with an plus, 83-85 mph power curveball that sometimes looks like as a slider because he manipulates the shape and spin of the pitch. He also has a below-average changeup he'll mix in against lefties. A former starter, Gallegos is capable of going multiple innings. He pounds the strike zone—sometimes too much as he leaves pitches over the plate that get hit.

THE FUTURE: Gallegos will have a shot to win a spot in the Cardinals' bullpen in spring training. He's already 27, so the time is now to stake his claim.

Year	Club (League)	Class	W	L	ERA	G	GS	CG	SV	IP	H	HR	BB	SO	K/9	WHIP	AVG
2016	Trenton (EL)	AA	2	1	1.09	17	0	0	2	33	20	1	7	53	14.5	0.82	.171
	Scranton/W-B (IL)	AAA	5	1	1.40	25	0	0	2	45	28	4	10	53	10.6	0.84	.178
2017	Scranton/W-B (IL)	AAA	4	2	2.08	28	0	0	5	43	28	4	11	69	14.3	0.90	.180
	New York (AL)	MAJ	0	0	4.87	16	0	0	0	20	21	3	5	22	9.7	1.28	.263
2018	New York (AL)	MAJ	0	0	4.50	4	0	0	1	10	10	2	3	10	9.0	1.30	.278
	Scranton/W-B (IL)	AAA	2	1	3.90	17	0	0	2	28	24	1	7	41	13.3	1.12	.231
	Memphis (PCL)	AAA	0	0	0.54	13	0	0	1	17	7	0	3	16	8.6	0.60	.130
	St. Louis (NL)	MAJ	0	0	0.00	2	0	0	0	1	1	0	0	2	13.5	0.75	.200
Major League Totals			0	1	4.55	22	0	0	1	32	32	5	8	34	9.7	1.26	.264
Minor League Totals			23	20	2.79	192	26	0	18	410	347	30	82	452	9.9	1.05	.227

30 AUSTIN WARNER, LHP

BA GRADE

40 Risk: Medium

Born: June 27, 1994. **B-T:** L-L. **HT:** 5-11. **WT:** 185. **Signed:** Frontier League, 2017. **Signed by:** Jim Foster.

TRACK RECORD: Warner went undrafted after four years at Division II Bellarmine (Ky.) and pitched parts of two seasons with River City in the independent Frontier League before the Cardinals signed him midway through 2017. Meant to be organizational filler, Warner instead shot up three levels to Triple-A in his first full season.

SCOUTING REPORT: Warner is an undersized lefthander who competes with an outstanding mound presence. His fastball sits 91-94 mph on his best days and 88-92 mph on others, but no matter his velocity he attacks the strike zone and seizes the tempo to put hitters on the defensive. He holds his stuff deep into his starts and seems to find another gear in pressure situations. Warner's main secondary is an average curveball with depth, and he mixes in a changeup that flashes average. Warner gets too much of the plate sometimes and doesn't have much deception, so he proved more hittable once he got to Triple-A. He still managed to limit runs by stepping up in big spots.

THE FUTURE: Warner's stuff is a little short to project more than a swingman or lefty reliever in the majors, but with his competitive edge and ability to pitch, he may get there in 2019.

Year	Club (League)	Class	W	L	ERA	G	GS	CG	SV	IP	H	HR	BB	SO	K/9	WHIP	AVG
2016	River City (FRN)	IND	4	1	4.42	10	6	0	0	39	42	6	14	42	9.8	1.45	--
2017	Palm Beach (FSL)	HiA	1	0	0.00	1	0	0	0	3	2	0	1	3	9.0	1.00	.200
	Cardinals (GCL)	R	1	0	0.77	3	2	0	0	12	9	0	0	19	14.7	0.77	.209
	Peoria (MWL)	LoA	2	4	3.00	9	9	0	0	48	43	4	14	51	9.6	1.19	.236
2018	Palm Beach (FSL)	HiA	3	3	3.41	12	12	1	0	74	78	1	13	77	9.4	1.23	.274
	Springfield (TL)	AA	2	3	5.34	6	6	0	0	32	28	3	19	25	7.0	1.47	.231
	Memphis (PCL)	AAA	1	2	4.33	7	7	0	0	35	56	7	11	23	5.9	1.90	.371
Minor League Totals			10	12	3.57	38	36	1	0	204	216	15	58	198	8.7	1.34	.273

San Diego Padres

BY KYLE GLASER

For the first time since A.J. Preller took over as the Padres' general manager in August 2014, the clock is starting to tick.

The Padres have eight straight losing seasons entering 2019, second-longest behind only the Marlins. After years of repeated promises about the farm system coming to the rescue, the youngsters haven't been nearly enough to elevate the Padres out of baseball's bottom tier. What was supposed to be a step forward in 2018 instead turned into a giant step back, with a 66-96 record that was the worst of the Padres eight-season losing skid.

Preller's biggest moves—signing James Shields, acquiring and extending Wil Myers, signing Eric Hosmer to the largest contract in franchise history—have largely flopped, and the constant trading of anyone remotely good for more prospects has soured all but the clubs' hardcore fans. The Padres finished 11th in the National League in attendance in 2018, their lowest showing since 2014.

The Padres long-promised nirvana borne of a rebuild needs to start bearing fruit in the form of wins in 2019. In that sense, there have been some promising developments toward that goal. Joey Lucchesi and Eric Lauer held their own as rookies in the starting rotation, while the continued development of Hunter Renfroe and emergence of Franmil Reyes gives the Padres two homegrown power hitters to pencil into the middle of their lineup. But for all the players who took steps forward, the offensive shortcomings of expected cornerstones Manny Margot and Austin Hedges have to be reversed, as do the downward trends of Hosmer and Myers, for the Padres to even dream of a winning record, let alone playoff contention.

The first wave of the rebuild largely arrived the last two years, and now the second wave is ready to ascend. Luis Urias and Francisco Mejia made their Padres debuts last fall and are ready for larger roles. Chris Paddack, Logan Allen, Cal Quantrill are in position to reinforce a rotation in dire need of help, while the expected return of Dinelson Lamet from injury should be a boon as well. And of course, anointed franchise savior Fernando Tatis Jr. is on the doorstep after starring at Double-A.

That top-level prospect talent is enviable. Combined with incredible depth that is the result of three consecutive Top-10 draft picks, countless veteran-for-prospect trades and $80 million spent internationally in 2016-17, the Padres boast the No. 1 farm system in baseball.

But a farm system is ultimately only as good as the big leaguers it produces, and this management group's track record of turning top prospects into

Franmil Reyes supplied big power with 16 homers as a surprise rookie contributor.

PROJECTED 2022 LINEUP

Catcher	Francisco Mejia (26)
First Base	Eric Hosmer (32)
Second Base	Luis Urias (25)
Third Base	Hudson Potts (23)
Shortstop	Fernando Tatis Jr. (23)
Left Field	Hunter Renfroe (30)
Center Field	Manuel Margot (27)
Right Field	Franmil Reyes (24)
No. 1 Starter	MacKenzie Gore (23)
No. 2 Starter	Adrian Morejon (23)
No. 3 Starter	Chris Paddack (26)
No. 4 Starter	Luis Patino (22)
No. 5 Starter	Joey Lucchesi (29)
Closer	Andres Muñoz (23)

impact big leaguers is decidedly mixed.

In part because they recognize the need to start showing measurable progress, the Padres spent the offseason discussing trades for headline players like Noah Syndergaard and marquee free agent signings like Manny Machado.

Preller and his staff have been given a long leash by managing partner Peter Seidler, but frustration is mounting.

As 2019 opens, Padres management knows the club has to start turning upward, and the top prospects have to show they can actually develop into effective big leaguers.

If they don't, the pressure is only going to turn up more.

SAN DIEGO PADRES

TOP 2019 ROOKIE: Luis Urias, 2B. He will open the season as the Padres' second baseman and gives them a much-needed on-base threat.
BREAKOUT PROSPECT: Tirso Ornelas, OF. The physical lefthanded hitter should only tap into his big power more as he matures. He's in position for a big year in the California League.
SLEEPER: Blake Hunt, C. Hunt's arm strength and feel to hit keep improving, key developments to go with his impressive mix of power, physicality and athleticism.

SOURCE OF TOP 30 TALENT			
Homegrown	22	Acquired	8
College	6	Trade	8
Junior college	0	Rule 5 draft	0
High school	7	Independent league	0
Nondrafted free agent	0	Free agent/waivers	0
International	9		

LF
Robbie Podorsky
Jack Suwinski

CF
Jeisson Rosario (22)
Buddy Reed (25)
Edward Olivares
Michael Gettys
Grant Little

RF
Tirso Ornelas (20)
Jorge Ona

3B
Hudson Potts (15)
Owen Miller (23)
Ty France (28)
Jason Vosler

SS
Fernando Tatis Jr. (1)
Xavier Edwards (21)
Gabriel Arias (30)
Javier Guerra
Justin Lopez

2B
Luis Urias (3)
Esteury Ruiz (26)
Tucupita Marcano (27)
Esteban Quiroz
Eguy Rosario

1B
Josh Naylor (9)
Brad Zunica

C
Francisco Mejia (4)
Austin Allen (16)
Luis Campusano (19)
Blake Hunt
Luis Torrens

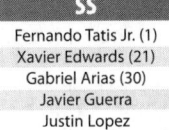
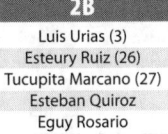

LHP

LHSP	LHRP
MacKenzie Gore (2)	Brad Wieck
Adrian Morejon (5)	Nick Margevicius
Logan Allen (8)	Kyle McGrath
Ryan Weathers (13)	Jerry Keel
Osvaldo Hernandez	Travis Radke
Tom Cosgrove	
Manuel Partida	

RHP

RHSP	RHRP
Chris Paddack (6)	Andres Munoz (17)
Luis Patino (7)	Trey Wingenter (24)
Cal Quantrill (10)	Gerardo Reyes
Michel Baez (11)	Ronald Bolanos
Anderson Espinoza (12)	David Bednar
Jacob Nix (14)	Dauris Valdez
Reggie Lawson (18)	Dylan Coleman
Pedro Avila (29)	
Brett Kennedy	
Jesse Scholtens	
Emmanuel Ramirez	
Mason Thompson	
Frank Lopez	

DRAFT ANALYSIS

2018

BEST PURE HITTER: SS/2B Xavier Edwards (2) shows the ingredients of a potential plus hitter with a simple, repeatable swing, exceptional hand-eye coordination and an advanced approach driven by a beyond-his-years maturity. The switch-hitter batted lefthanded almost exclusively after signing due to a wrist injury but should return to switch-hitting in 2019.

BEST POWER HITTER: 3B/2B Sean Guilbe (12) combines bat speed with impressive natural strength to produce plus raw power, if not more. He has a "do damage" mentality and looks to impact the ball with every swing, resulting in loud contact when he connects but also lots of strikeouts.

FASTEST RUNNER: Edwards is a 70-grade runner who plays at that speed in the field and on the bases. OF Juwuan Harris (7) might beat Edwards in a 60-yard dash, but he's faster underway than off initial burst and plays a tick slower than Edwards in games.

BEST DEFENSIVE PLAYER: Edwards possess strong instincts and exceptional short-area quickness playing up the middle. He's a plus defender at second base and shows the range, footwork and actions for shortstop, though his fringe-average arm is likely to push him to second long-term.

BEST ATHLETE: Harris starred in both baseball and football at Rutgers. In addition to being the Scarlet Knights' starting center fielder for three seasons, Harris was a Big Ten all-freshman selection at wide receiver before converting to safety as a sophomore and tying for the team lead in interceptions.

BEST FASTBALL: RHP Dylan Coleman (4) sits 94 mph as a starter, 96 mph as a reliever and has touched 99 mph. He adds run and sink to his fastball when he gets on top of it, although he's not quite consistent with that yet.

BEST SECONDARY PITCH: LHP Ryan Weathers (1) has a potential plus changeup with heavy sink and fade that he locates to both sides of the plate. He plays it off his two-seam fastball especially well. LHP Alexuan Vega (6) flashes a plus curveball when

TOP DRAFT PICKS OF THE DECADE

Year	Player, Pos.	2018 Org
2009	Donavan Tate, OF	Did not play
2010	*Karsten Whitson, RHP	Did not play
2011	Cory Spangenberg, 2B	Padres
2012	Max Fried, LHP	Braves
2013	Hunter Renfroe, OF	Padres
2014	Trea Turner, SS	Nationals
2015	Austin Smith, RHP (2nd round)	Padres
2016	Cal Quantrill, RHP	Padres
2017	MacKenzie Gore, LHP	Padres
2018	Ryan Weathers, LHP	Padres

* Did not sign

he hits his release point. At it's best, his hook is a 1-to-7 power offering with depth and size.

BEST PRO DEBUT: SS Owen Miller (3) tallied 100 hits in 75 games after signing to produce a .336/.386/.460 slash line between short-season Tri-City and low Class A Fort Wayne. He was promoted to Double-A San Antonio for the Texas League playoffs and added nine more hits in eight postseason games.

MOST INTRIGUING BACKGROUND: Harris was one of the top two-sport athletes available in the 2018 draft. OF Dwanya Williams-Sutton (5) went out for soccer for the first time since he was seven as a high school senior and scored 24 goals to earn all-state honors in North Carolina.

CLOSEST TO THE MAJORS: Miller already reached Double-A at the end of his first season. His mix of an advanced offensive game and defensive versatility around the infield gives him a chance to reach San Diego within the year.

BEST LATE-ROUND PICK: RHP Nick Thwaits (15) didn't stand out at summer showcases prior to his senior year but saw his stuff jump in the spring, sitting 89-94 mph with feel to spin a breaking ball and feel for a changeup.

THE ONE WHO GOT AWAY: 3B Jake Plastiak (28) intrigued as a 6-foot-3, 200-pound switch-hitting third baseman who showed feel to hit and flashes of power, but he chose to honor his commitment to Wichita State rather than sign.

— KYLE GLASER

2017

LHP MacKenzie Gore (1) was limited by blisters, leaving this somewhat incomplete. But he and C Luis Campusano (2) have shown significant upside at the outset of their professional careers.

GRADE: B

2016

LHPs Eric Lauer (1) and Joey Lucchesi (4) quickly got to the big leagues and joined the rotation. RHP Cal Quantrill (1) should soon join them and 3B Hudson Potts (1) stands out for his impressive tools.

GRADE: B

2015

Despite not having a first-round pick and RHP Austin Smith (2) struggling, the Padres have gotten five big leaguers out of this draft. RHP Jacob Nix (3) and C Austin Allen (4) have the most upside of the class.

GRADE: C

1 FERNANDO TATIS JR., SS

Born: Jan. 2, 1999. **B-T:** R-R. **Ht.:** 6-3. **Wt.:** 185.
Signed: Dominican Republic, 2015.
Signed by: Miguel Peguero (White Sox)

BILL MITCHELL

ernando Tatis had a quality decade-long career, but his son Fernando Jr. projects to be even better. The younger Tatis was lightly regarded as an international amateur in the Dominican Republic and wasn't even invited to MLB's international showcase when he was 16. The White Sox went against the consensus and signed him for $700,000. Shortly after signing, Tatis grew two inches and filled out, developing newfound leverage and power. The Padres scouted Tatis heavily and, before he ever played a pro game, acquired him and righthander Erik Johnson from the White Sox for James Shields in June 2016 and blossomed into one of baseball's top prospects. A unique blend of power, speed and athleticism, Tatis was on pace for another 20-20 season in 2018, but he suffered a broken left thumb on a headfirst slide in late July and had season-ending surgery. **SCOUTING REPORT:** Strong and lithe in his long, athletic physique, Tatis has a chance to be a rare everyday shortstop who is a true power-speed threat. Tatis has a loose, rhythmic swing with a lot of moving parts that sometimes get out of whack but when everything is in sync, he is an offensive force. Tatis tracks pitches deep and powers his barrel through the zone, driving the ball with excellent extension and leverage. Balls explode off his bat from gap-to-gap, and he shows off his plus-plus raw power with towering pullside home runs. Tatis has bouts of over-aggressiveness that lead to elevated strikeout totals, but he generally self-corrects. An above-average hitter with plus power and possibly more, Tatis enhances his offensive game with his speed. While he previously stole bags with average speed and advanced instincts, he improved his body composition and is now a plus runner who reaches plus-plus underway. That improved fitness also led to quicker reactions and more range at shortstop, silencing concerns about him moving off the position. With plus-plus arm strength, reliable hands and now wide lateral range, Tatis could be an above-average or plus defender at short. **THE FUTURE:** Tatis has the talent to be a perennial all-star shortstop and the personality to be the face of the Padres franchise. He'll begin 2019 at Triple-A El Paso and has a chance to make his ML debut at 20 years old.

BA GRADE	SCOUTING GRADES
70 Risk: Medium	**Hit:** 55. **Power:** 60. **Run:** 60. **Field:** 60. **Arm:** 70.

Projected future grades on 20-80 scouting scale.

TOP PROSPECTS OF THE DECADE

Year	Player, Pos.	2018 Org
2009	Kyle Blanks, 1B	Did not play
2010	Donavan Tate, OF	Did not play
2011	Casey Kelly, RHP	Giants
2012	Anthony Rizzo, 1B	Cubs
2013	Casey Kelly, RHP	Giants
2014	Austin Hedges, C	Padres
2015	Matt Wisler, RHP	Reds
2016	Javier Guerra, SS	Padres
2017	Anderson Espinoza, RHP	Padres
2018	Fernando Tatis Jr., SS	Padres

BEST TOOLS

Best Hitter for Average	Luis Urias
Best Power Hitter	Fernando Tatis Jr.
Best Strike-Zone Discipline	Luis Urias
Fastest Baserunner	Buddy Reed
Best Athlete	Jeisson Rosario
Best Fastball	Andres Muñoz
Best Curveball	Adrian Morejon
Best Slider	Luis Patino
Best Changeup	Chris Paddack
Best Control	Chris Paddack
Best Defensive Catcher	Luis Campusano
Best Defensive Infielder	Gabriel Arias
Best Infield Arm	Javier Guerra
Best Defensive Outfielder	Buddy Reed
Best Outfield Arm	Michael Gettys

Year	Club (League)	Class	AVG	G	AB	R	H	2B	3B	HR	RBI	BB	SO	SB	CS	OBP	SLG
2016	Padres (AZL)	R	.273	43	176	35	48	13	1	4	20	10	44	14	2	.312	.426
	Tri-City (NWL)	SS	.273	12	44	4	12	4	2	0	5	3	13	1	1	.306	.455
2017	Fort Wayne (MWL)	LoA	.281	117	431	78	121	26	7	21	69	75	124	29	15	.390	.520
	San Antonio (TL)	AA	.255	14	55	6	14	1	0	1	6	2	17	3	0	.281	.327
2018	San Antonio (TL)	AA	.286	88	353	77	101	22	4	16	43	33	109	16	5	.355	.507
Minor League Totals			.280	274	1059	200	296	66	14	42	143	123	307	63	23	.358	.487

2 MACKENZIE GORE, LHP

Born: Feb. 24, 1999. **B-T:** L-L. **Ht.:** 6-3. **Wt.:** 191. **Drafted:** HS—Whiteville, N.C., 2017 (1st round). **Signed by:** Nick Brannon.

TRACK RECORD: Gore allowed just 16 earned runs in four years at Whiteville (N.C.) High and won BA's High School Player of the Year award in 2017. The Padres drafted him third overall and signed him for $6.7 million, the largest draft bonus in franchise history. Gore received rave reviews in his first spring training, but blister issues sent him to the disabled list twice at low Class A Fort Wayne and led to an underwhelming 2018 season. After Gore's blisters returned a third time, the Padres shut him down in late August.

SCOUTING REPORT: When healthy, Gore checks every box as a lean, premium athlete with a loose arm, sky-high leg kick and four pitches that flash plus. His fastball sits 93-94 mph, touches 96, and gets on hitters quickly with his long extension. Gore's blisters sapped the command of his heater, but they most seriously affected his breaking balls. At their best his curveball sits 77-80 mph with sharp 1-to-7 snap and his slider works 84-86 mph with tight, late break, but his inability to grip them resulted in both playing down to average with inconsistent velocity and location. His upper 80s changeup is his fourth pitch but still shows plus with sink at the bottom of the zone.

THE FUTURE: Gore's recurring blisters are troubling and prevent him from pitching his best. He'll try to show he's past them in 2019.

BA GRADE

65 Risk: Very High

Fastball: 60.
Curve: 60. Slider: 55.
Change: 60. CTL: 60

Year	Club (League)	Class	W	L	ERA	G	GS	CG	SV	IP	H	HR	BB	SO	K/9	WHIP	AVG
2017	Padres (AZL)	R	0	1	1.27	7	7	0	0	21	14	0	7	34	14.3	0.98	.184
2018	Fort Wayne (MWL)	LoA	2	5	4.45	16	16	0	0	61	61	5	18	74	11.0	1.30	.260
Minor League Totals			2	6	3.62	23	23	0	0	82	75	5	25	108	11.9	1.22	.241

3 LUIS URIAS, 2B

Born: June 3, 1997. **B-T:** R-R. **Ht.:** 5-9. **Wt.:** 185. **Signed:** Mexico, 2013 **Signed by:** Chad MacDonald/Robert Rowley.

TRACK RECORD: The Padres purchased Urias' rights from Mexico City for $100,000 when he was 16 in a deal facilitated by club owner Alfredo Harp Helu, a minority stakeholder in the Padres. Urias wasted no time validating the deal. He won the California League batting title and MVP award as a 19 year old, represented Mexico in the World Baseball Classic and led the Texas League in on-base percentage in his age-20 season. Last year Urias hit a team-best .298 at Triple-A El Paso, started the Futures Game, and made his major league debut at 21.

SCOUTING REPORT: Urias has the gifts of a potential .300 hitter. Short but mighty, the 5-foot-9 Urias takes advantage of his compact strike zone with a quick, level swing that produces hard line drives to all fields. He has an elite eye and rarely chases, forcing pitchers to come to him and punishing hittable pitches when they do. Urias' build and swing aren't conducive to home runs, but with his quick bat he can square up a fastball and drive it out when he finds a ball where he wants it. Defensively, Urias is an above-average second baseman with sure hands, clean footwork and an impressive vertical leap to go with an above-average arm. He can fill in as an average shortstop, although his range there is stretched.

THE FUTURE: Urias' pure stroke and elite eye give him a chance to contend for batting titles at his peak. He'll be the Padres everyday second baseman in 2019.

BA GRADE

55 Risk: Medium

Hit: 70. Power: 40.
Run: 45. Field: 55.
Arm: 55.

Year	Club (League)	Class	AVG	G	AB	R	H	2B	3B	HR	RBI	BB	SO	SB	CS	OBP	SLG
2016	El Paso (PCL)	AAA	.444	3	9	6	4	0	0	1	3	5	1	1	0	.667	.778
	Lake Elsinore (CAL)	HiA	.330	120	466	71	154	26	5	5	52	40	36	7	13	.397	.440
2017	San Antonio (TL)	AA	.296	118	442	77	131	20	4	3	38	64	65	7	5	.398	.380
2018	El Paso (PCL)	AAA	.296	120	450	83	133	30	7	8	45	67	109	2	1	.398	.447
	San Diego (NL)	MAJ	.208	12	48	5	10	1	0	2	5	3	10	1	0	.264	.354
Major League Totals			.208	12	48	5	10	1	0	2	5	3	10	1	0	.264	.354
Minor League Totals			.306	467	1756	301	538	87	18	17	169	220	244	35	38	.397	.405

4 FRANCISCO MEJIA, C/OF

Born: Oct. 27, 1995. **B-T:** B-R. **HT:** 5-10. **WT:** 180. **Signed:** Dominican Republic, 2012. **Signed by:** Ramon Pena (Indians).

TRACK RECORD: Signed by the Indians for $350,000, Mejia rose to prominence in 2016 when he engineered a 50-game hit streak at the Class A levels, the longest in the modern era of the minor leagues. In desperate need of bullpen help, the Indians traded Mejia to the Padres for Brad Hand and Adam Cimber at the 2018 trade deadline. Mejia made his first Padres start on Sept. 6 at Cincinnati and homered in his first two at-bats.

SCOUTING REPORT: The switch-hitting Mejia possesses elite-hand eye coordination that allows him to project as a plus hitter. He squares balls up in all parts of the strike zone and sometimes even outside of it, producing hard contact gap-to-gap. Mejia gets to his double-digit home run power more righthanded than left, but his premium bat speed makes him a threat from both sides. Mejia's issue is he swings at absolutely everything. His ultra aggressiveness led to an 29 strikeout rate and weak contact against pitcher's pitches, an unsustainable approach he'll need to corral. Mejia has a bazaooka for a right arm and the athleticism to be a solid-average catcher, but he often lacks focus, resulting in numerous passed balls. In part because of his lack of reliability, the Indians experimented with Mejia at third base and left field.

THE FUTURE: Mejia will start in a timeshare with Austin Hedges behind the plate. Whether he eventually supplants Hedges will depend on how much his plate discipline and defensive focus improve.

BA GRADE
60 Risk: High
Hit: 60. Power: 45.
Run: 40. Field: 50.
Arm: 80.

Year	Club (League)	Class	AVG	G	AB	R	H	2B	3B	HR	RBI	BB	SO	SB	CS	OBP	SLG
2016	Lake County (MWL)	LoA	.347	60	239	41	83	17	3	7	51	15	39	1	0	.384	.531
	Lynchburg (CAR)	HiA	.333	42	168	22	56	12	1	4	29	13	24	1	2	.380	.488
2017	Akron (EL)	AA	.297	92	347	52	103	21	2	14	52	24	53	7	2	.346	.490
	Cleveland (AL)	MAJ	.154	11	13	1	2	0	0	0	1	1	3	0	0	.214	.154
2018	Cleveland (AL)	MAJ	.000	1	2	0	0	0	0	0	0	0	2	0	0	.500	.000
	Columbus (IL)	AAA	.279	79	305	32	85	22	1	7	45	18	58	0	0	.328	.426
	El Paso (PCL)	AAA	.328	31	122	22	40	8	1	7	23	7	25	0	0	.364	.582
	San Diego (NL)	MAJ	.185	20	54	6	10	2	0	3	8	3	19	0	0	.241	.389
Major League Totals			.174	32	69	7	12	2	0	3	9	6	22	0	0	.250	.333
Minor League Totals			.293	509	1925	262	564	119	13	54	313	138	342	18	10	.347	.452

5 ADRIAN MOREJON, LHP

Born: Feb. 27, 1999. **B-T:** L-L. **Ht.:** 6-1. **Wt.:** 210. **Signed:** Cuba, 2016. **Signed by:** David Post/Trevor Schumm/Felix Feliz.

TRACK RECORD: Morejon pitched Cuba to the gold medal at the 2014 15-and-under World Cup in Mexico City, winning MVP with a complete-game victory over the United States. Two years later, the Padres signed Morejon for $11 million the day after MLB declared him a free agent. Morejon embarked on his first full season in 2018 with high Class A Lake Elsinore and earned plaudits as the California League's No. 1 pitching prospect, arm soreness limited him to just two starts after the all-star break.

SCOUTING REPORT: As expected when he signed, Morejon has grown into his frame and added significant velocity. Now a sturdy 6-foot-1, 210 pounds, Morejon sits 93-96 mph on his fastball and touches 98 with impressive ease. At one point he had trouble commanding his high-spin curveball, but in mid-May he found the right arm stroke and release point and began breaking it off as a second plus pitch, drawing chases below the zone. His traditional changeup with fade flashes plus and is better than his knuckle-change, but both are weapons. Morejon's control is his weak point, leaving his fastball up and losing his curveball feel on occasion.

THE FUTURE: Morejon draws comparisons to Carlos Rodon as a big-bodied lefty with potent stuff. Like Rodon, Morejon has struggled to stay healthy. He'll try to reach 70 innings for the first time in 2019.

BA GRADE
60 Risk: High
Fastball: 70.
Curve: 60.
Change: 55. CTL: 50.

Year	Club (League)	Class	W	L	ERA	G	GS	CG	SV	IP	H	HR	BB	SO	K/9	WHIP	AVG
2016	Did not play																
2017	Tri-City (NWL)	SS	2	2	3.57	7	7	0	0	35	37	2	3	35	8.9	1.13	.266
	Fort Wayne (MWL)	LoA	1	2	4.23	6	6	0	0	28	28	2	13	23	7.5	1.48	.264
2018	Padres 1 (AZL)	R	0	1	6.75	1	1	0	0	3	5	0	0	4	13.5	1.88	.385
	Lake Elsinore (CAL)	HiA	4	4	3.30	13	13	0	0	63	54	6	24	70	10.1	1.24	.233
Minor League Totals			7	9	3.65	27	27	0	0	128	124	10	40	132	9.3	1.28	.253

6 CHRIS PADDACK, RHP

Born: Jan. 8, 1996. **B-T:** R-R. **Ht.:** 6-4. **Wt.:** 195. **Drafted:** HS—Cedar Park,
Texas, 2015 (8th round). **Signed by:** Ryan Wardinsky (Marlins).

BA GRADE

60 Risk: High

Fastball: 60.
Curve: 40.
Change: 70. CTL: 70.

TRACK RECORD: The Padres' 2016 summer sell-off kicked into high gear when they traded Fernando Rodney to the Marlins for Paddack in June. Paddack succumbed to Tommy John surgery three starts into his Padres career and missed the next 22 months, but he returned with a vengeance in 2018. The big Texan delivered a 2.10 ERA between high Class A Lake Elsinore and Double-A San Antonio, with a jaw-dropping 120 strikeouts and eight walks in 90 innings.

SCOUTING REPORT: Paddack earned the nickname "The Executioner" at Lake Elsinore for his ruthless precision in eliminating opponents. He sits 91-94 mph and reaches 97 on his lively fastball with carry, dialing it up and down with pristine command in all four quadrants of the strike zone. He pairs his plus fastball with an 82-84 mph changeup that is one of the best in the minors. He sells it with identical arm speed before it falls off the table with late depth at the bottom of the strike zone, getting both swings and misses and called strikes on both sides of the plate. Paddack's fastball, changeup and control are all plus or better, but his loopy 72-76 mph curveball is firmly below-average. He uses it less than 10 percent of the time, knowing it's extremely hittable the few times it lands in the strike zone.

THE FUTURE: The list of successful big league righthanders without a breaking ball is a short one. Paddack will debut in 2019 and try to show he's an exception.

Year	Club (League)	Class	W	L	ERA	G	GS	CG	SV	IP	H	HR	BB	SO	K/9	WHIP	AVG
2016	Greensboro (SAL)	LoA	2	0	0.95	6	6	0	0	28	9	2	2	48	15.2	0.39	.098
	Fort Wayne (MWL)	LoA	0	0	0.64	3	3	0	0	14	11	0	3	23	14.8	1.00	.212
2017	Did not play—Injured																
2018	Lake Elsinore (CAL)	HiA	4	1	2.24	10	10	0	0	52	43	3	4	83	14.3	0.90	.223
	San Antonio (TL)	AA	3	2	1.91	7	7	1	0	38	23	1	4	37	8.8	0.72	.177
Minor League Totals			13	6	1.82	37	33	1	0	178	123	7	20	230	11.7	0.80	.193

7 LUIS PATINO, RHP

Born: Oct. 26, 1999. **B-T:** R-R. **HT:** 6-0. **WT:** 192. **Signed:** Colombia, 2016.
Signed by: Andres Cabadias/Chris Kemp.

TRACK RECORD: Patino weighed 150 pounds and sat 84-87 mph during a bullpen session at a Colombian showcase in 2016, but Padres international director Chris Kemp liked the converted shortstop's loose arm and athleticism and signed him for $130,000 on July 2. Patino filled out and made rapid velocity gains even faster than imagined. Up to 192 pounds and throwing in the mid-90s, Patino made his full-season debut in 2018 with low Class A Fort Wayne and became the talk of the Midwest League. He posted a 2.16 ERA in 17 starts, touching 99 mph as an 18-year-old.

BA GRADE

60 Risk: Very High

Fastball: 60.
Slider: 60. Curve: 55.
Change: 55. CTL: 55

SCOUTING REPORT: Patino is slightly undersized, but his stuff is huge. Loose and athletic with a chest-high leg kick, Patino sits 94-95 mph on his explosive fastball and touches 98-99. His 84-87 mph hard slider is the best in the organization, giving him two plus, power pitches he deploys aggressively. Patino is a plus athlete who repeats his delivery and alters his leg kick to further disrupt hitters timing, all while keeping above-average control of his power stuff. Patino is still finding feel for his softer offerings. His 78-80 mph curveball flashes plus but is inconsistent, and the unreliability of his mid-80s changeup led lefties to torch him for a .345/.421/.457 line.

THE FUTURE: Patino's arm and athleticism excite, but there's a long way to go. He was shut down after 83.1 innings and needs to prove his durability, and he still has to find a pitch for lefties.

Year	Club (League)	Class	W	L	ERA	G	GS	CG	SV	IP	H	HR	BB	SO	K/9	WHIP	AVG
2017	Padres (DSL)	R	2	1	1.69	4	4	0	0	16	11	0	2	15	8.4	0.81	.193
	Padres (AZL)	R	2	1	2.48	9	8	0	0	40	32	2	16	43	9.7	1.20	.213
2018	Fort Wayne (MWL)	LoA	6	3	2.16	17	17	0	0	83	65	1	24	98	10.6	1.07	.220
Minor League Totals			10	5	2.20	30	29	0	0	139	108	3	42	156	10.1	1.08	.215

8 LOGAN ALLEN, LHP

Born: May 23, 1997. **B-T:** L-L. **Ht.:** 6-3. **Wt.:** 200. **Drafted:** HS—Bradenton, Fla., 2015 (8th round). **Signed by:** Stephen Hargett (Red Sox).

TRACK RECORD: The Padres targeted Allen in the 2015 draft and got him in a trade five months later, acquiring him from the Red Sox as one of four prospects for Craig Kimbrel. After a slow burn his first two seasons with the Padres, Allen catapulted in 2018. He logged a 2.54 ERA between Double-A and Triple-A as a 21-year-old, winning Texas League pitcher of the year and leading the system in wins (14) and strikeouts (154).

SCOUTING REPORT: Though not as flashy as others, the steady Allen is more accomplished than any pitcher in the Padres system. All four of his pitches are competitive major league offerings, and he possesses a warrior mentality with an advanced feel for attacking hitters. Allen comes right at opponents with a 90-93 mph fastball, commanding it to both sides of the plate. His changeup is a plus pitch that dives late for swings and misses over the top. Allen's third pitch is an average slider that has some cut action, and when it's not working he can flip in an effective curveball. Allen throws everything for strikes and became more durable as he improved his pitch efficiency, completing six innings in 16 of 19 starts in 2018.

THE FUTURE: Allen's four-pitch mix and durability have him set to log innings at the back of a rotation at the very least. His ML debut should come in 2019.

BA GRADE

50 Risk: Medium

Fastball: 50.
Change: 60. Curve: 50.
Slider: 50. CTL: 50

Year	Club (League)	Class	W	L	ERA	G	GS	CG	SV	IP	H	HR	BB	SO	K/9	WHIP	AVG
2016	Padres (AZL)	R	0	0	3.00	3	3	0	0	6	5	0	1	8	12.0	1.00	.217
	Tri-City (NWL)	SS	0	1	7.71	1	1	0	0	2	4	0	1	4	15.4	2.14	.364
	Fort Wayne (MWL)	LoA	3	4	3.33	15	11	0	0	54	48	2	22	47	7.8	1.30	.242
2017	Fort Wayne (MWL)	LoA	5	4	2.11	13	13	0	0	68	49	1	26	85	11.2	1.10	.201
	Lake Elsinore (CAL)	HiA	2	5	3.97	11	10	0	0	57	60	2	18	57	9.1	1.38	.272
2018	San Antonio (TL)	AA	10	6	2.75	20	19	0	0	121	89	7	38	125	9.3	1.05	.205
	El Paso (PCL)	AAA	4	0	1.63	5	5	0	0	28	21	4	13	26	8.5	1.23	.206
Minor League Totals			24	20	2.75	76	70	0	0	360	294	16	120	378	9.4	1.15	.222

9 JOSH NAYLOR, 1B/OF

Born: June 22, 1997. **B-T:** L-L. **Ht.:** 5-11. **Wt.:** 250. **Drafted:** HS—Mississauga, Ont. (1st round). **Signed by:** Steve Payne (Marlins).

TRACK RECORD: Naylor became the highest-drafted Canadian position player ever when the Marlins took him 12th overall in 2015. One year later, they traded him to the Padres in the deal for Andrew Cashner. After teasing with uncanny hand-eye coordination and huge raw power, Naylor turned his tools into production in 2018. He set career-highs in batting average (.297), home runs (17), RBIs (74) and OPS (.830) at Double-A San Antonio, overcoming challenging hitting conditions.

SCOUTING REPORT: Naylor has heavyset frame at 5-foot-11, 250 pounds with a protruding belly, but he crushes baseballs. Naylor uses his powerful legs and thick trunk to generate huge torque and bat speed, turning around elite velocity with thunderous collisions on contact. While Naylor always had strong strike-zone discipline, he began picking out better pitches to drive in 2018 and saw career-highs in every power category while maintaining nearly as many walks (63) as strikeouts (69). Evaluators see a potential plus hitter with plus power, but no one is sure where Naylor will play. He's decent at his natural first base, but with Eric Hosmer there, the Padres began playing Naylor in left field in 2018. While Naylor is sneaky athletic with short-area quickness and surprising speed, he's still a below-average defender learning to play under control.

THE FUTURE: Naylor spent the offseason doing intense beach workouts in California. Like Kyle Schwarber, Naylor will have to slim down to make left field work.

BA GRADE

50 Risk: Medium

Hit: 55. Power: 55.
Run: 45. Field: 40.
Arm: 55.

Year	Club (League)	Class	AVG	G	AB	R	H	2B	3B	HR	RBI	BB	SO	SB	CS	OBP	SLG
2016	Greensboro (SAL)	LoA	.269	89	342	42	92	24	2	9	54	22	62	10	3	.317	.430
	Lake Elsinore (CAL)	HiA	.252	33	139	17	35	5	0	3	21	3	22	1	1	.264	.353
2017	Lake Elsinore (CAL)	HiA	.297	72	283	41	84	16	2	8	45	27	48	7	1	.361	.452
	San Antonio (TL)	AA	.250	42	156	18	39	9	0	2	19	16	36	2	1	.320	.346
2018	San Antonio (TL)	AA	.297	128	501	72	149	22	1	17	74	64	69	5	5	.383	.447
Minor League Totals			.284	389	1519	198	431	80	6	40	229	136	248	26	11	.346	.423

10 CAL QUANTRILL

Born: Feb. 10, 1995. **B-T:** L-R. **Ht.:** 6-3. **Wt.:** 208. **Drafted:** Stanford, 2016 (1st round). **Signed by:** Sam Ray.

TRACK RECORD: Quantrill starred on Canada's junior national teams and looked like a future No. 1 overall pick his freshman year at Stanford, but he had Tommy John surgery three starts into his sophomore year and missed all of his junior year too. The Padres still took him seventh overall in 2016 and gave him a full slot bonus of just under $4 million. Quantrill built back up over three pro seasons and logged 148 innings in 2018, overcoming a rocky stint at Double-A to finish strong in Triple-A.

SCOUTING REPORT: Quantrill, the son of former All-Star reliever Paul, flashes plus stuff but has yet to find consistency post-surgery. At his best Quantrill sits 93-95 with downhill angle on his fastball, a plus changeup and a slider that has improved to average and become a swing-and-miss pitch. Other times he'll work in the low 90s with decreased changeup feel and poor command, surrendering hits en masse. Quantrill is fiercely competitive and sometimes gets frustrated with himself, affecting his ability to execute. His main issue has been locating inside, with lefties in particular punishing him for a .305/.376/.468 line in 2018.

THE FUTURE: Quantrill still flashes mid-rotation potential with three quality pitches. Improving his command, composure and consistency will be key before his major league debut in 2019.

BA GRADE

55 Risk: High

Fastball: 60.
Change: 60.
Slider: 50. **CTL:** 50.

Year	Club (League)	Class	W	L	ERA	G	GS	CG	SV	IP	H	HR	BB	SO	K/9	WHIP	AVG
2016	Padres (AZL)	R	0	2	5.27	5	5	0	0	14	12	0	2	16	10.5	1.02	.231
	Tri-City (NWL)	SS	0	2	1.93	5	5	0	0	19	15	0	2	28	13.5	0.91	.205
	Fort Wayne (MWL)	LoA	0	1	17.36	2	2	0	0	5	12	1	4	2	3.9	3.43	.522
2017	Lake Elsinore (CAL)	HiA	6	5	3.67	14	14	0	0	74	78	5	24	76	9.3	1.38	.273
	San Antonio (TL)	AA	1	5	4.04	8	8	0	0	42	52	5	16	34	7.2	1.61	.296
2018	San Antonio (TL)	AA	6	5	5.15	22	22	0	0	117	135	12	38	101	7.8	1.48	.288
	El Paso (PCL)	AAA	3	1	3.48	6	6	0	0	31	39	4	5	22	6.4	1.42	.300
Minor League Totals			16	21	4.46	62	62	0	0	301	343	27	91	279	8.3	1.44	.284

11 MICHEL BAEZ, RHP

BA GRADE

55 Risk: High

Born: Jan. 21, 1996. **B-T:** R-R. **Ht.:** 6-8. **Wt.:** 220. **Signed:** Cuba, 2016. **Signed by:** Trevor Schumm/Jake Koenig.

TRACK RECORD: Baez briefly played professionally in Cuba's Serie Nacional and signed with the Padres for $3 million in Dec. 2016. He thrilled in his U.S. debut in 2017 but took a step back in 2018.

SCOUTING REPORT: Baez is physically huge at 6-foot-8, 220 pounds. Previously an advantage, his size became a hindrance in 2018 as he struggled to repeat his delivery or stay on line to the plate with any consistency. With inconsistent direction, mechanics and arm speed, Baez's fastball ranged anywhere from 90-98 mph, though it was more regularly in the 94-mph range. He struggles to locate to his gloveside, but he can elevate for swings and misses. Baez's lack of direction hurts the consistency of his 82-86 mph slider and 73-77 mph curveball, which are both pitches that have flashed above-average but often play below that. While neither of his breaking balls have become regular weapons, he does have better command of an above-average 85-86 changeup. Back issues have delayed Baez's start two years in a row.

THE FUTURE: Baez still flashes solid stuff, but not often enough to confidently project a starter anymore.

Year	Club (League)	Class	W	L	ERA	G	GS	CG	SV	IP	H	HR	BB	SO	K/9	WHIP	AVG
2016	Did not play																
2017	Padres (AZL)	R	1	0	3.60	1	1	0	0	5	2	1	2	7	12.6	0.80	.133
	Fort Wayne (MWL)	LoA	6	2	2.45	10	10	0	0	59	41	8	8	82	12.6	0.84	.192
2018	Lake Elsinore (CAL)	HiA	4	7	2.91	17	17	0	0	87	73	5	33	92	9.6	1.22	.229
	San Antonio (TL)	AA	0	3	7.36	4	4	0	0	18	22	4	12	21	10.3	1.85	.301
Minor League Totals			11	12	3.25	32	32	0	0	169	138	18	55	202	10.8	1.14	.222

12 ANDERSON ESPINOZA, RHP

BA GRADE

60 Risk: Extreme

Born: March 9, 1998. **B-T:** R-R. **Ht.:** 6-0. **Wt.:** 160. **Signed:** Venezuela, 2014. **Signed by:** Eddie Romero/Manny Padron (Red Sox).

TRACK RECORD: Espinoza ranked as the top pitching prospect in the 2014 international class and signed with the Red Sox for $1.8 million. The Padres acquired him for Drew Pomeranz at the 2016 All-Star break Espinoza missed all of 2017 and 2018 with forearm soreness followed by Tommy John surgery.

SCOUTING REPORT: Prior to surgery, Espinoza teased as an electric righthander in the mold of the late

Yordano Ventura. Espinoza has an athletic delivery and a lightning-quick arm, firing 95-98 fastballs with late tail to both sides of the plate. His mid-80s changeup gives him another plus or better pitch, and his upper 70s curveball with 11-to-5 shape was rapidly improving and flashing plus as well. But after two seasons away and multiple missed recovery targets—Espinoza did not pitch in instructional league as had been planned—whether that stuff still exists is an open question.

THE FUTURE: Espinoza began to throw bullpens around Thanksgiving, giving the Padres cautious optimism that he will return to games in 2019. He will be rolled out slowly and targeted for 90 innings.

Year	Club (League)	Class	W	L	ERA	G	GS	CG	SV	IP	H	HR	BB	SO	K/9	WHIP	AVG
2016	Greenville (SAL)	LoA	5	8	4.38	17	17	0	0	76	77	2	27	72	8.5	1.37	.269
	Fort Wayne (MWL)	LoA	1	3	4.73	8	7	0	0	32	38	1	8	28	7.8	1.42	.290
2017	Did not play—Injured																
2018	Did not play—Injured																
Minor League Totals			6	13	3.35	40	39	0	0	167	156	3	49	165	8.9	1.23	.248

13 RYAN WEATHERS, LHP

BA GRADE

60 Risk: Extreme

Born: Dec. 17, 1999. **B-T:** L-L. **HT:** 6-1. **WT:** 200. **Drafted:** HS—Loretto, Tenn., 2018 (1st round). **Signed by:** Tyler Stubblefield.

TRACK RECORD: Weathers is the son of 19-year big league pitcher David Weathers, and he led Loretto (Tenn.) HS to its first state championship in basketball as a senior. When he held 90s velocity into the ninth inning of the Tennessee Class A state championship baseball game, the Padres decided he was their man. They drafted Weathers seventh overall and signed him for $5,226,500 to pass up Vanderbilt. Weathers moved quickly, making three starts at low Class A just three months out of high school.

SCOUTING REPORT: Weathers impresses more with his poise and feel than any one offering. He pitches inside with a 90-94 mph four-seam fastball and outside with a 90-93 mph two-seamer, mixing them equally and working both sides of the plate. His mid-70s curveball lands for strikes as an average to above-average pitch, and his changeup flashes plus with heavy fade and mirrors his two-seamer. Weathers works quickly, throws strikes with above-average control and stays poised when things don't go his way, showing impressive maturity for a teen.

THE FUTURE: The Padres think Weathers has the intangibles to move fast despite being a high school pick. He'll see high Class A Lake Elsinore in 2019.

Year	Club (League)	Class	W	L	ERA	G	GS	CG	SV	IP	H	HR	BB	SO	K/9	WHIP	AVG
2018	Padres (AZL)	R	0	2	3.86	4	4	0	0	9	8	2	3	9	8.7	1.18	.211
	Fort Wayne (MWL)	LoA	0	1	3.00	3	3	0	0	9	11	0	1	9	9.0	1.33	.282
Minor League Totals			0	3	3.44	7	7	0	0	18	19	2	4	18	8.8	1.25	.247

14 JACOB NIX, RHP

BA GRADE

45 Risk: Medium

Born: Jan. 9, 1996. **B-T:** R-R. **Ht.:** 6-4. **Wt.:** 220. **Drafted:** HS—Bradenton, Fla., 2015 (3rd round). **Signed by:** Chris Kelly.

TRACK RECORD: The Astros drafted Nix in the fifth round out of Los Alamitos (Calif.) High in 2014, but their failure to sign Brady Aiken cost them the bonus pool money necessary to sign Nix. Nix spent a year at postgrad IMG Academy before the Padres drafted him in the third round. A groin strain delayed Nix's start, and he missed two additional weeks with an infected abscess on his rear. But Nix pitched well when healthy at Triple-A and made his major league debut Aug. 10.

SCOUTING REPORT: Nix has yet to pitch more than 100 innings in any season, but he's been effective when healthy. Big and physical at 6-foot-4, 220 pounds, Nix throws three pitches for strikes: a 93-95 mph fastball, a 76-78 mph curveball that flashes plus but is inconsistent and an average low 80s changeup. Nix throws strikes, but he lacks deception and none of his offerings are swing-and-miss pitches, so he relies on balls in play being turned into outs. His command wavers, leading to a volatile mix of strong outings with clunkers when he catches too much of the plate.

THE FUTURE: Nix's three pitch-mix and physicality are that of a solid starter.

Year	Club (League)	Class	W	L	ERA	G	GS	CG	SV	IP	H	HR	BB	SO	K/9	WHIP	AVG
2016	Fort Wayne (MWL)	LoA	3	7	3.93	25	25	0	0	105	115	5	20	90	7.7	1.28	.280
2017	Lake Elsinore (CAL)	HiA	4	3	4.32	11	10	1	0	67	78	5	10	51	6.9	1.32	.297
	San Antonio (TL)	AA	1	2	5.53	6	6	0	0	28	32	0	9	22	7.2	1.48	.281
2018	San Antonio (TL)	AA	2	3	2.05	9	9	0	0	53	39	3	9	41	7.0	0.91	.211
	El Paso (PCL)	AAA	1	0	0.00	1	1	0	0	6	5	0	0	3	4.5	0.83	.250
	San Diego (NL)	MAJ	2	5	7.02	9	9	0	0	42	52	8	13	21	4.5	1.54	.304
Major League Totals			2	5	7.02	9	9	0	0	42	52	8	13	21	4.5	1.54	.304
Minor League Totals			11	17	3.85	59	54	1	0	278	292	14	55	226	7.3	1.25	.272

15 HUDSON POTTS, 3B

BA GRADE	
50	Risk: High

Born: Oct. 28, 1998. **B-T:** R-R. **Ht.:** 6-3. **Wt.:** 205. **Drafted:** HS—Southlake, Texas, 2016 (1st round). **Signed by:** Matt Schaffner.

TRACK RECORD: The Padres drafted Potts 24th overall in 2016 and signed him for an under-slot $1 million signing bonus. He made the discount look good with 39 homers in his first two full seasons, including a 2018 in which he led the high Class A California League in doubles (35) and total bases (202) before being promoted to Double-A as a 19-year-old.

SCOUTING REPORT: Potts is a teenager but is built like a man with a physical, well-proportioned body that allows him to produce plus power. Potts hits velocity and uses the whole field well, turning on pitches in the middle of the zone and inside for home runs to left and driving fastballs on the outer half to right for doubles. Potts knows the strike zone and rarely chases, but he swings and misses inside the zone troublingly often. His contact percentage in the zone was 77 percent in 2018, shy of the ML average 85 percent, and makes him a projected below-average hitter. A converted shortstop, Potts made great strides defensively in his second year playing third base, showing smooth hands and an above-average arm.

THE FUTURE: Potts draws comparisons to Trevor Plouffe as a potential low-average, solid-power third baseman who starts in his best years. He'll be just 20 at Double-A in 2019 and has time to outperform that projection.

Year	Club (League)	Class	AVG	G	AB	R	H	2B	3B	HR	RBI	BB	SO	SB	CS	OBP	SLG
2016	Padres (AZL)	R	.295	43	183	35	54	12	2	1	21	9	34	8	4	.333	.399
	Tri-City (NWL)	SS	.233	16	60	7	14	0	1	0	6	9	13	2	1	.352	.267
2017	Fort Wayne (MWL)	LoA	.253	125	491	67	124	23	4	20	69	23	140	0	1	.293	.438
2018	Lake Elsinore (CAL)	HiA	.281	106	406	66	114	35	1	17	58	37	112	3	1	.350	.498
	San Antonio (TL)	AA	.154	22	78	5	12	0	0	2	5	10	33	1	0	.258	.231
Minor League Totals			.261	312	1218	180	318	70	8	40	159	88	332	14	7	.319	.430

16 AUSTIN ALLEN, C

BA GRADE	
45	Risk: Medium

Born: Jan. 16, 1994. **B-T:** L-R. **Ht.:** 6-2. **Wt.:** 220. **Drafted:** Florida Tech, 2015 (4th round). **Signed by:** Willie Bosque.

TRACK RECORD: Allen's bat made him the top Division II player drafted in 2015. He hit better than .280 with 22 home runs for the second straight season in 2018, this time at offense-stifling Double-A San Antonio, and had the most home runs of any catcher in the minor leagues. As important, Allen got leaner and lighter—to a career-low 220 pounds— which allowed him to get out of the crouch quicker and increase his caught-stealing rate from 21 percent to 36 percent.

SCOUTING REPORT: Allen is country strong and gets to his plus lefthanded power regularly in games. He frequently sends balls 400-plus feet out to right field, and can power out the occasional opposite-field homer as well. While he's always been a good fastball hitter, Allen has fine-tuned his eye and started to recognize offspeed pitches better in 2018, proving he can hit upper-level pitching and showing himself to be an above-average hitter. Allen's weight loss made him a bit more mobile defensively behind the plate, but he's still not especially athletic or flexible and is serviceable at best at catcher. He started 19 games at first base at San Antonio, his first extended exposure to the position.

THE FUTURE: The Padres envision Allen providing impact power as a platoon catcher/first baseman. He was placed on the 40-man roster and may make his ML debut in 2019.

Year	Club (League)	Class	AVG	G	AB	R	H	2B	3B	HR	RBI	BB	SO	SB	CS	OBP	SLG
2016	Fort Wayne (MWL)	LoA	.320	109	409	52	131	22	0	7	61	29	69	0	0	.364	.425
	San Antonio (TL)	AA	.273	3	11	1	3	0	0	1	1	0	0	0	0	.273	.545
2017	Lake Elsinore (CAL)	HiA	.283	121	463	71	131	31	1	22	81	44	109	0	1	.353	.497
2018	San Antonio (TL)	AA	.290	119	451	59	131	31	0	22	56	37	97	0	3	.351	.506
Minor League Totals			.290	405	1530	206	443	94	2	54	233	131	313	1	6	.350	.459

17 ANDRES MUNOZ, RHP

BA GRADE	
55	Risk: Extreme

Born: Jan. 16, 1999. **B-T:** R-R. **Ht.:** 6-2. **Wt.:** 165. **Signed:** Mexico, 2015 **Signed by:** Trevor Schumm.

TRACK RECORD: The Padres made Munoz their top international signing in 2015 for $700,000. A quick-armed teenager who sat 88-92 mph when he signed at age 16, Munoz jumped up to 95 mph at 17, began touching 100 at 18 and then established himself as one of the hardest-throwing pitchers in the sport by 19. A platelet-rich plasma injection delayed Munoz's start, but he went out to Double-A in June and saved seven games in eight tries, averaging nearly 100 mph on his fastball and frequently reaching 103.

SCOUTING REPORT: Munoz's fastball leaves batters quivering and scouts salivating. It is a true 80-grade pitch with elite velocity and riding life, getting swings and misses even when hitters know it's coming.

Munoz expertly climbs the ladder with his fastball, and gets whiffs from both lefties and righties. Munoz's secondary pitch is a mid-80s slider that flashes average but is inconsistent, though it plays up with batters geared up for his fastball. Munoz's velocity is exciting, but health and below-average control are not. **THE FUTURE:** Munoz has closer potential, but he has to stay healthy and tighten his control. If he does, his major league debut could come in 2019 at age 20.

Year	Club (League)	Class	W	L	ERA	G	GS	CG	SV	IP	H	HR	BB	SO	K/9	WHIP	AVG
2016	Padres (AZL)	R	1	1	5.49	16	1	0	0	20	16	1	16	26	11.9	1.63	.213
2017	Tri-City (NWL)	SS	3	0	3.80	21	0	0	1	24	15	2	16	35	13.3	1.31	.177
	Fort Wayne (MWL)	LoA	0	0	3.86	3	0	0	0	2	2	0	2	3	11.6	1.71	.222
2018	Tri-City (NWL)	SS	0	0	0.00	5	0	0	0	6	0	0	2	9	14.3	0.35	.000
	San Antonio (TL)	AA	2	1	0.95	20	0	0	7	19	11	0	11	19	9.0	1.16	.175
Minor League Totals			6	2	3.20	65	1	0	8	70	44	3	47	92	11.8	1.29	.177

18 REGGIE LAWSON, RHP

Born: Aug. 2, 1997. **B-T:** R-R. **Ht.:** 6-4. **Wt.:** 205. **Drafted:** HS—Victorville, Calif., 2016 (2nd round supplemental). **Signed by:** Jeff Stevens.

TRACK RECORD: Lawson closed out Team USA's gold-medal victory over Japan at the 2015 18U World Cup in dominant fashion to generate first-round buzz, but an oblique strain limited him to just six starts during his senior year of high school and dropped him down into the supplemental second round. The Padres picked Lawson 71st overall and signed him for $1.9 million. Lawson battled inconsistent stuff and control his first two years before breaking out for his best season in 2018. **SCOUTING REPORT:** Previously raw and lanky, Lawson bulked up to add strength and coordination and saw his stuff tick up. Now a physical, muscular 6-foot-4, Lawson works 93-96 mph on his fastball and holds his velocity. He pounds the zone to both sides of the plate at his best, and he made mechanical improvements to leave his heater up less frequently. Lawson began throwing his changeup more in 2018 and flashed a plus offering with sink in the mid-80s, although it's still inconsistent. His below-average curveball lacked power, so rather than continue attempting to hone that, he learned a slider in instructs and introduced it as a swing-and-miss pitch at 83-84 mph in the On Deck Classic. **THE FUTURE:** Lawson flashes rotation upside and keeps trending up. He'll move to Double-A in 2019 where he will attempt to improve his strikethrowing.

Year	Club (League)	Class	W	L	ERA	G	GS	CG	SV	IP	H	HR	BB	SO	K/9	WHIP	AVG
2016	Padres (AZL)	R	0	0	8.31	5	3	0	0	9	12	0	3	7	7.3	1.73	.316
2017	Fort Wayne (MWL)	LoA	4	6	5.30	17	17	0	0	73	65	8	35	89	11.0	1.37	.236
2018	Lake Elsinore (CAL)	HiA	8	5	4.69	24	22	0	0	117	130	11	51	117	9.0	1.55	.280
Minor League Totals			12	11	5.07	46	42	0	0	199	207	19	89	213	9.6	1.49	.266

19 LUIS CAMPUSANO, C

Born: Sept. 29, 1998. **B-T:** R-R. **Ht.:** 6-0. **Wt.:** 213. **Drafted:** HS—Augusta, Ga., 2017 (2nd round). **Signed by:** Tyler Stubblefield.

TRACK RECORD: The Padres made Campusano the first catcher selected in the 2017 draft when they took him 39th overall. He went out to low Class A Fort Wayne and made the Midwest League all-star game in a promising start to his first full season, but a foul tip off his mask resulted in a season-ending concussion in late July, his second concussion in as many years. **SCOUTING REPORT:** Campusano's defense is ahead of his offense, but he's well-rounded and capable at both. He projects to be above-average to plus defender behind the plate, with advanced natural instincts and feel for managing a game. Campusano receives quietly, is a solid blocker and has plus arm strength he likes to show off, sometimes throwing runners out from his knees. Campusano's swing is a brute strength swing that results in a lot of hard hit ground balls, and the Padres believe double-digit home runs will come as he learns to elevate. He shows a feel for contact and doesn't strike out much, a promising foundation to be an average hitter or better. Campusano's talent is evident, but his standoffish attitude towards media, management and even teammates perturbs many. **THE FUTURE:** Campusano has the skills to be an everyday catcher, but his concussions are concerning and his makeup needs to improve. He'll move to high Class A Lake Elsinore in 2019.

Year	Club (League)	Class	AVG	G	AB	R	H	2B	3B	HR	RBI	BB	SO	SB	CS	OBP	SLG
2017	Padres (AZL)	R	.278	24	90	3	25	4	0	1	13	6	14	0	1	.327	.356
	Padres (AZL)	R	.250	13	44	5	11	0	0	3	12	9	11	0	1	.377	.455
2018	Fort Wayne (MWL)	LoA	.288	70	260	26	75	11	0	3	40	19	43	0	1	.345	.365
Minor League Totals			.282	107	394	34	111	15	0	7	65	34	68	0	3	.345	.373

20 TIRSO ORNELAS, OF

BA GRADE

50 Risk: High

Born: March 11, 2000. **B-T:** L-L. **HT:** 6-3. **WT:** 200. **Signed:** Mexico, 2016.
Signed by: Chris Kemp/Bill McLaughlin.

TRACK RECORD: The Padres continued their relationship with the Mexican League's Mexico City franchise by purchasing Ornelas' rights for $1.5 million in 2016. He immediately opened eyes when he arrived at the Padres' complex and continued to impress as the second-youngest player on Opening Day in the Midwest League in 2018. Physical and patient, Ornelas showed an advanced approach and growing power before a bone bruise in his right hand ended his season in late July.

SCOUTING REPORT: At times Ornelas looks like the best hitting prospect in the Padres system. Physically imposing at 6-foot-3, 200 pounds with big power from the left side, Ornelas takes a steady approach, sees the ball well and takes his walks while limiting his strikeouts. Ornelas' swing is powerful and pretty, but he's still young and fine-tuning it. He'll be too steep in his entry into the zone at times, resulting in weak popups to left. When he's right, he powers balls out to right field and teases 25-plus home run potential. Ornelas has improved to an average runner and catches what he gets to in right field, but he will have to watch his size to avoid a move to first base.

THE FUTURE: Ornelas' bat is going to be his carrying card. Staying healthy and getting his swing more consistent are the goals for 2019.

Year	Club (League)	Class	AVG	G	AB	R	H	2B	3B	HR	RBI	BB	SO	SB	CS	OBP	SLG
2017	Padres (AZL)	R	.276	53	196	46	54	11	3	3	26	40	61	0	0	.399	.408
2018	Fort Wayne (MWL)	LoA	.252	86	309	45	78	13	3	8	40	40	68	5	1	.341	.392
Minor League Totals			.261	139	505	91	132	24	6	11	66	80	129	5	1	.364	.398

21 XAVIER EDWARDS, SS

BA GRADE

55 Risk: Extreme

Born: Aug. 9, 1999. **B-T:** B-R. **HT:** 5-10. **WT:** 155. **Drafted:** HS—Coconut Creek, Fla., 2018 (1st round supplemental). **Signed by:** Brian Cruz.

TRACK RECORD: Scouts considered Edwards arguably the most skilled player in the 2018 draft class, but he fell out of the first round because he's listed at 5-foot-10, 155 pounds and is really closer to 5-7. The Padres didn't expect Edwards to still be available at pick No. 38 and were ecstatic when he was, quickly selecting him and signing him for $1.3 million to forgo a Vanderbilt commitment. Edwards lived up early to his pre-draft raves, batting .346/.453/.409 with 22 steals in 45 games after signing while advancing to short-season Tri-City.

SCOUTING REPORT: Edwards fits the bill of an old-school leadoff hitter. A quick, twitchy athlete, Edwards has an advanced eye and quick, simple stroke from both sides that sprays the ball to all fields on a line. He rarely strikes out and is happy to take a walk. Once Edwards gets on base, he is a base-stealing terror with his plus-plus speed and advanced feel for baserunning and the game in general. Edwards' quickness and advanced feel translate to the middle infield, where he is a plus defender at shortstop with slick hands and range. His fringe-average arm is his one drawback and may eventually force him to second base.

THE FUTURE: Edwards' advanced skills and feel have thus far rendered his size irrelevant. He'll aim to continue that in full-season ball in 2019.

Year	Club (League)	Class	AVG	G	AB	R	H	2B	3B	HR	RBI	BB	SO	SB	CS	OBP	SLG
2018	Padres 1 (AZL)	R	.384	21	73	19	28	4	1	0	11	13	10	12	1	.471	.466
	Tri-City (NWL)	SS	.314	24	86	21	27	4	0	0	5	18	15	10	0	.438	.360
Minor League Totals			.346	45	159	40	55	8	1	0	16	31	25	22	1	.453	.409

22 JEISSON ROSARIO, OF

BA GRADE

50 Risk: High

Born: Oct. 22, 1999. **B-T:** L-L. **Ht.:** 6-1. **Wt.:** 191. **Signed:** Dominican Republic, 2016. **Signed by:** Felix Feliz/Ysrael Rojas/Alvin Duran.

TRACK RECORD: Rosario ranked as one of the top players in the 2016 international class and signed with the Padres for $1.85 million out of the Dominican Republic. Rosario made his full-season debut in 2018 and shined as low Class A Fort Wayne's leadoff hitter and center fielder).

SCOUTING REPORT: Rosario is a uniquely gifted athlete who can throw with both arms and run down almost any ball in center field. He is a plus runner with excellent closing speed, a true plus defensive center fielder with an average arm that keeps baserunners honest. Rosario has excellent plate discipline and bat to ball skills, although he's mostly a slap hitter to the opposite field and doesn't project to hit for much power. Rosario previously would get overly frustrated at times, but he matured and had no such issues in 2018.

THE FUTURE: Rosario has the tools to hit at the top or bottom of an order while playing a strong center field, but needs to add strength. He'll move to high Class A Lake Elsinore in 2019.

Year	Club (League)	Class	AVG	G	AB	R	H	2B	3B	HR	RBI	BB	SO	SB	CS	OBP	SLG
2017	Padres (AZL)	R	.299	52	187	31	56	10	0	1	24	33	36	8	6	.404	.369
2018	Fort Wayne (MWL)	LoA	.271	117	436	79	118	17	5	3	34	66	108	18	12	.368	.353
Minor League Totals			.279	169	623	110	174	27	5	4	58	99	144	26	18	.379	.358

23 OWEN MILLER, SS/3B

BA GRADE

50 Risk: High

Born: Nov. 15, 1996. **B-T:** R-R. **HT:** 6-0. **WT:** 190. **Drafted:** Illinois State, 2018 (3rd round). **Signed by:** Troy Hoerner.

TRACK RECORD: Miller hit .345 over three years as Illinois State's starting shortstop and was drafted in the third round by the Padres, signing for $500,000. Known as an advanced hitter and reliable defender, Miller shot up the minors faster than anyone else in the 2018 draft.

SCOUTING REPORT: Miller has always hit and projects to continue to hit. He stays balanced, has a simple, repeatable swing, controls the strike-zone and consistently finds the barrel, driving balls on a line with his considerable upper-body strength. Miller has a flatter stroke more geared for line drives to the gaps, but his approach, strength and bat-to-ball skills are enough to project 10-15 home runs as he matures to go with a .270 or better average. Miller is a sneaky good athlete with above-average speed. He has reliable hands and solid lateral range at shortstop, although his fringy arm strength may force a move.

THE FUTURE: Scouts who covered both Miller and Paul DeJong at Illinois State think Miller was the better hitter, and he has an actual shortstop pedigree, with a 2019 ML debut not out of the question.

Year	Club (League)	Class	AVG	G	AB	R	H	2B	3B	HR	RBI	BB	SO	SB	CS	OBP	SLG
2018	Tri-City (NWL)	SS	.335	49	191	22	64	8	3	2	20	15	24	4	4	.395	.440
	Fort Wayne (MWL)	LoA	.336	26	107	18	36	11	0	2	13	4	17	0	0	.368	.495
Minor League Totals			.336	75	298	40	100	19	3	4	33	19	41	4	4	.386	.460

24 TREY WINGENTER, RHP

BA GRADE

45 Risk: Medium

Born: April 15, 1994. **B-T:** R-R. **Ht.:** 6-7. **Wt.:** 200. **Drafted:** Auburn, 2015 (17th round). **Signed by:** Steve Moritz.

TRACK RECORD: The 6-foot-7 Wingenter sat 88-92 mph in high school when he was drafted in the 38th round by the Mariners, bumped up to 92-94 in college at Auburn and shot up even more after the Padres drafted him and moved him to the bullpen. He touched 100 mph for the first time at Double-A San Antonio in 2017 and reached the big leagues in 2018.

SCOUTING REPORT: The massive Wingenter has the stuff of a late-inning dynamo. His fastball sits 97-98 and touches 100 while coming downhill at hitters from his towering release point. Wingenter's heater is difficult to touch when he spots it, but his long limbs detract from his control and lead to walks and occasional mistake pitches. Wingenter controls his mid-80s slider better than his fastball, making it an above-average pitch with power and depth.

THE FUTURE: Wingenter's size and stuff make him a late-relief option immediately and a potential closer if he can improve his control. He'll open 2019 in the Padres bullpen.

Year	Club (League)	Class	W	L	ERA	G	GS	CG	SV	IP	H	HR	BB	SO	K/9	WHIP	AVG
2016	Fort Wayne (MWL)	LoA	1	0	0.82	8	0	0	4	11	6	0	2	14	11.5	0.73	.162
	San Antonio (TL)	AA	0	0	0.00	1	0	0	1	3	0	0	1	5	15.0	0.33	.000
	Lake Elsinore (CAL)	HiA	2	1	2.03	30	0	0	4	44	36	0	17	46	9.3	1.20	.229
2017	San Antonio (TL)	AA	2	1	2.45	49	0	0	20	48	33	6	19	64	12.1	1.09	.193
2018	El Paso (PCL)	AAA	3	3	3.45	40	0	0	4	44	29	4	24	53	10.8	1.20	.186
	San Diego (NL)	MAJ	0	0	3.79	22	0	0	0	19	13	3	11	27	12.8	1.26	.191
Major League Totals			0	0	3.79	22	0	0	0	19	13	3	11	27	12.8	1.26	.191
Minor League Totals			9	7	2.98	140	0	0	33	169	128	10	70	198	10.5	1.17	.210

25 BUDDY REED, OF

BA GRADE

50 Risk: High

Born: April 27, 1995. **B-T:** B-R. **HT:** 6-4. **WT:** 210. **Drafted:** Florida, 2016 (2nd round). **Signed by:** Chris Kelly.

TRACK RECORD: Reed was drafted in the 35th round out of high school by the Rangers and started all three years in Florida's outfield. The Padres drafted Reed in the second round in 2016 and signed him for $1.075 million. Reed struggled to hit in college and his first two pro seasons, but he overhauled his stance and broke out in 2018. After getting into a low crouch and choking up to emphasize contact, Reed hit .324 at high Class A Lake Elsinore, made the Futures Game and hit .333 in the Arizona Fall League.

SCOUTING REPORT: Reed is an electrifying athlete capable of changing a game in a variety of ways. He's a plus-plus runner who stole 51 bases despite raw instincts, is a Gold Glove-caliber defender in center field and his arm is a cannon. But even with his revamped offensive setup, evaluators are skeptical Reed will hit. The switch-hitter struggles to catch up to good velocity and doesn't recognize breaking pitches, and he has a huge hole on the inner half that was exploited in Double-A.

THE FUTURE: Reed's tools are huge, but few believe he'll hit enough to be more than a backup.

Year	Club (League)	Class	AVG	G	AB	R	H	2B	3B	HR	RBI	BB	SO	SB	CS	OBP	SLG
2016	Tri-City (NWL)	SS	.254	51	205	31	52	9	4	0	13	22	53	15	5	.326	.337
2017	Fort Wayne (MWL)	LoA	.234	88	316	48	74	17	8	6	35	23	97	12	8	.290	.396
2018	Lake Elsinore (CAL)	HiA	.324	79	315	54	102	21	7	12	47	24	84	33	7	.371	.549
	San Antonio (TL)	AA	.179	43	179	21	32	7	0	1	15	12	63	18	3	.227	.235
Minor League Totals			.256	261	1015	154	260	54	19	19	110	81	297	78	23	.311	.403

26 ESTEURY RUIZ, 2B

BA GRADE

55 Risk: Extreme

Born: Feb. 15, 1999. **B-T:** R-R. **Ht.:** 6-0. **Wt.:** 169. **Signed:** Dominican Republic, 2015. **Signed by:** Edys de Oleo (Royals).

TRACK RECORD: Ruiz signed with the Royals for $100,000 in 2015 and got the Padres attention two years later in the Rookie-level Arizona League. Ruiz followed up with 12 home runs and 49 stolen bases at low Class A Fort Wayne in 2018, but that came with a concerning 29 percent strikeout rate.

SCOUTING REPORT: Ruiz physically resembles Alfonso Soriano with his crouched stance, long body and whippy swing, but he's not that level of player. Ruiz is a plus runner and smart basestealer, and he showed above-average power at times. Ruiz's shortcoming is he is overly aggressive, swinging through fastballs up and breaking balls down. He doesn't adjust his approach with two strikes and his swing is long, preventing from projecting as more than a fringe-average hitter. Ruiz has the athleticism to play second base, but his hard hands and poor throwing accuracy portend a move to the outfield.

THE FUTURE: Ruiz's power-speed combo is exciting, but he has to improve his approach.

Year	Club (League)	Class	AVG	G	AB	R	H	2B	3B	HR	RBI	BB	SO	SB	CS	OBP	SLG
2016	Royals (DSL)	R	.313	56	217	44	68	18	5	5	26	19	35	13	10	.378	.512
2017	Royals (AZL)	R	.419	21	86	22	36	10	6	3	23	4	20	9	0	.440	.779
	Padres (AZL)	R	.300	31	120	23	36	10	4	1	16	9	34	17	6	.364	.475
2018	Fort Wayne (MWL)	LoA	.253	117	439	63	111	20	5	12	53	38	141	49	11	.324	.403
Minor League Totals			.291	225	862	152	251	58	20	21	118	70	230	88	27	.354	.478

27 TUCUPITA MARCANO, 2B/SS

BA GRADE

55 Risk: Extreme

Born: Sept. 16, 1999. **B-T:** L-R. **HT:** 6-0. **WT:** 165. **Signed:** Venezuela, 2016. **Signed by:** Antonio Alejos/Yfrain Linares.

TRACK RECORD: Raul Marcano hailed from Tucupita, Venezuela and was one of the country's biggest baseball stars in the 1990s. He had a son in 1999 and named him after his hometown. Tucupita Marcano became quite the prospect of his own and signed with the Padres for $320,000 in 2016.

SCOUTING REPORT: Marcano is a wiry 6 feet, 165 pounds with a compact lefthanded swing that produces tons of contact. He keeps his hands in near his belly and his barrel remains in the zone an incredibly long time, allowing him to stay on balls and drive them wherever they're pitched. Marcano draws more walks than strikeouts with an advanced approach, is an adept bunter and hits velocity from line-to-line, projecting as a potential plus hitter. Marcano's body and swing don't allow for much power projection, although he's strong in his frame. Marcano is a plus runner and a fundamentally sound defender in the middle infield, although his inconsistent arm ranges from below-average to above-average and makes him a better fit at second base than shortstop.

THE FUTURE: Marcano has a good foundation, but will need to strength to impact the ball at higher levels. He'll start 2019 at low Class A Fort Wayne.

Year	Club (League)	Class	AVG	G	AB	R	H	2B	3B	HR	RBI	BB	SO	SB	CS	OBP	SLG
2017	Padres (DSL)	R	.206	49	170	17	35	4	2	0	15	34	15	10	3	.337	.253
2018	Padres (AZL)	R	.395	35	124	33	49	4	1	0	17	26	10	10	7	.497	.444
	Tri-City (NWL)	SS	.314	17	70	12	22	1	2	1	9	4	6	5	0	.355	.429
Minor League Totals			.291	101	364	62	106	9	5	1	41	64	31	25	10	.396	.352

28 TY FRANCE, 3B

BA GRADE

45 Risk: Medium

Born: July 13, 1994. **B-T:** L-R. **HT:** 6-0. **WT:** 205. **Drafted:** San Diego State, 2015 (34th round). **Signed by:** Josh Emmerick.

TRACK RECORD: France hit .336 with a .905 OPS in three years at San Diego State, twice earning All-America honors, but an injury his junior year led to a draft-day slide. The Padres snagged France in the

34th round and signed him for $100,000. Using his draft-day fall as motivation, France has continued to mash as a pro. He led the Padres system in total bases (236), runs (84) and RBIs (96) and tied for the lead in home runs (22) while moving from Double-A to Triple-A in 2018.

SCOUTING REPORT: France's best attribute is his feel to hit. He handles velocity, has excellent barrel awareness and uses the whole field. He lines his base hits into right-center and pulls balls to left for his home runs, jumping from five homers in 2017 to 22 last year after making setup and swing adjustments. He's especially clutch in high-leverage situations. France enhances his on-base ability with a unique gift for getting hit-by-pitches. He's been hit 72 times in three full seasons. France is just an average athlete who is a fringy defender at third base, but he's playable and can flip over to first base as needed.

THE FUTURE: France is often compared to Ty Wigginton, another late-round pick with San Diego ties who hit his way to the majors. France's big league debut is on the horizon in 2019.

Year	Club (League)	Class	AVG	G	AB	R	H	2B	3B	HR	RBI	BB	SO	SB	CS	OBP	SLG
2016	Fort Wayne (MWL)	LoA	.237	68	219	35	52	8	0	5	35	44	49	3	3	.400	.342
	Lake Elsinore (CAL)	HiA	.304	60	224	39	68	16	0	9	38	15	47	3	4	.373	.496
2017	Lake Elsinore (CAL)	HiA	.288	30	111	10	32	4	2	0	19	7	16	1	0	.389	.360
	San Antonio (TL)	AA	.275	97	363	42	100	20	1	5	39	22	68	1	0	.341	.377
2018	San Antonio (TL)	AA	.263	112	415	66	109	22	2	17	77	33	70	3	4	.349	.448
	El Paso (PCL)	AAA	.287	25	94	18	27	8	0	5	19	13	19	0	0	.382	.532
Minor League Totals			.275	458	1661	246	457	98	5	42	263	177	319	15	13	.374	.416

29 PEDRO AVILA, RHP

BA GRADE
45 Risk: High

Born: Jan. 14, 1997. **B-T:** R-R. **Ht.:** 5-11. **Wt.:** 190. **Signed:** Venezuela, 2014. **Signed by:** German Robles (Nationals).

TRACK RECORD: Avila signed with the Nationals for $50,000 in 2014 and was traded to the Padres for Derek Norris two years later. After leading Padres minor leaguers in strikeouts in 2017, Avila finished second in the high Class A California League with 142 strikeouts in 2018.

SCOUTING REPORT: Avila is undersized but throws three quality pitches for strikes. His fastball sits 91-93 mph and touches 95, and his above-average 74-77 mph curveball is one of the top breaking balls in the system. His 82-85 mph changeup also improved to above-average, deceiving hitters out of the hand with similar arm speed before dropping late. Avila falls in love with his secondaries too much at times and loses his command in the zone, but those are fixable with maturity. Avila is a bit chubby, but he's a good athlete who repeats his delivery and keeps the ball around the strike zone, although his command can be scattered.

THE FUTURE: Avila projects as a fifth starter or swingman for most evaluators. He'll move to Double-A Amarillo in 2019.

Year	Club (League)	Class	W	L	ERA	G	GS	CG	SV	IP	H	HR	BB	SO	K/9	WHIP	AVG
2016	Hagerstown (SAL)	LoA	7	7	3.48	20	20	0	0	93	86	10	38	92	8.9	1.33	.249
2017	Lake Elsinore (CAL)	HiA	1	4	4.98	10	9	0	0	43	50	2	18	53	11.0	1.57	.284
	Fort Wayne (MWL)	LoA	7	1	3.05	14	14	0	0	86	74	3	15	117	12.3	1.04	.231
2018	Lake Elsinore (CAL)	HiA	7	9	4.27	24	20	0	1	131	136	8	54	142	9.8	1.45	.270
Minor League Totals			29	24	3.59	82	76	0	1	416	393	24	143	496	10.7	1.29	.249

30 GABRIEL ARIAS, SS

BA GRADE
50 Risk: Extreme

Born: Feb. 27, 2000. **B-T:** R-R. **Ht.:** 6-1. **Wt.:** 201. **Signed:** Venezuela, 2016. **Signed by:** Luis Prieto/Yfrain Linares/Trevor Schumm

TRACK RECORD: The Padres signed Arias for $1.9 million out of Venezuela in 2016 and moved him quickly, sending him to low Class A Fort Wayne and the Australian Winter League when he was just 17. Arias returned to Fort Wayne in 2018 expecting big things, but longstanding issues with his swing resulted in a disappointing .240/.302/.352 slash line with a 30 percent strikeout rate.

SCOUTING REPORT: Arias entices with his tools and an alluring body. He projects as a plus defensive shortstop who moves smoothly in all directions and has a plus-plus arm. He shows flashes of plus power and can get it to all fields, but he's never been a natural hitter and falls into bad swing habits. He starts with a bat wrap and gets around the ball, and he rarely gets his hands through the zone on time. He hasn't shown the ability to adjust his approach, repeating the same mistakes over and over again.

THE FUTURE: Arias' defense and hints of power keep evaluators interested, but there is a lot to fix offensively. He'll still be just 19 years old in 2019 and has time.

Year	Club (League)	Class	AVG	G	AB	R	H	2B	3B	HR	RBI	BB	SO	SB	CS	OBP	SLG
2017	Padres (AZL)	R	.275	37	153	18	42	6	3	0	13	10	51	4	6	.329	.353
	Fort Wayne (MWL)	LoA	.242	16	62	8	15	1	0	0	4	2	16	1	0	.266	.258
2018	Fort Wayne (MWL)	LoA	.240	124	455	54	109	27	3	6	55	41	149	3	3	.302	.352
Minor League Totals			.248	177	670	80	166	34	6	6	72	53	216	8	9	.305	.343

San Francisco Giants

BY KEGAN LOWE

After a disappointing 2017 season, the Giants' front office went all-in on adding even more veteran talent to a roster that was already one of the oldest in baseball. Under the direction of then-general manager Bobby Evans, who has since been fired and replaced, San Francisco traded for 31-year-old outfielder Andrew McCutchen and 32-year-old third baseman Evan Longoria, while also signing veteran outfielder Austin Jackson and lefthanded reliever Tony Watson.

Instead of the win-now moves paying off in the short-term, the Giants found themselves three games under .500 by mid-August and decided to trade McCutchen to the Yankees for a pair of prospects on Aug. 31. After sending the 2013 National League MVP to the East Coast, the Giants lost 11 straight games from Sept. 1-12 and ended the season with a 73-89 record, nearly 20 games out of a playoff position.

Armed with one of the two oldest lineups in baseball alongside the Mariners, the Giants finished 29th in the majors in runs per game (3.72), home runs (133) and OPS (.667). The Giants' pitching staff was close to league average, but it wasn't enough to mask one of the worst offenses in baseball.

As a result, 2018 marked the second straight losing season for the Giants, who hadn't experienced consecutive sub-.500 seasons since undergoing four straight losing seasons from 2005-08. And it was the first time the Giants failed to qualify for the postseason in an "even year" since finishing fourth in the NL West with a 72-90 record in 2008.

The results weren't much better down on the farm, either. Only the Angels (.430) and Reds (.453) had a worse organizational winning percentage than the Giants, whose domestic minor league teams combined for a .457 mark. The Giants also joined the Angels, Marlins and Orioles as the only organizations to have zero minor league affiliates qualify for the playoffs.

The organization-wide disappointment led to a change at the top, as the aforementioned Evans was fired during the final week of the regular season. Nearly two months later, the Giants hired former Dodgers general manager Farhan Zaidi as the franchise's new president of baseball operations. A respected baseball mind, Zaidi helped oversee the Dodgers' ongoing success, which includes six straight NL West division championships and back-to-back NL pennants in 2017 and 2018.

With the highest payroll in baseball in 2018, Zaidi takes over a franchise that isn't afraid to

Rookie Andrew Suarez wound up making 29 starts for the Giants even with a 4.49 ERA.

PROJECTED 2022 LINEUP

Catcher	Joey Bart (25)
First Base	Buster Posey (35)
Second Base	Joe Panik (31)
Third Base	Evan Longoria (36)
Shortstop	Brandon Crawford (35)
Left Field	Chris Shaw (28)
Center Field	Steven Duggar (28)
Right Field	Heliot Ramos (22)
No. 1 Starter	Madison Bumgarner (32)
No. 2 Starter	Logan Webb (25)
No. 3 Starter	Shaun Anderson (27)
No. 4 Starter	Andrew Suarez (29)
No. 5 Starter	Sean Hjelle (24)
Closer	Melvin Adon (28)

spend money to see on-field results. He also adopts a farm system that has recently added an influx of high-end talent despite its overall lack of prospect depth. The Giants drafted former Georgia Tech catcher Joey Bart with the No. 2 overall pick in 2018 and then signed shortstop Marco Luciano, who was the No. 2 international free agent in the 2018 class, for $2.6 million last July.

San Francisco also has the 10th overall pick in the 2019 draft, which should add another impact player capable of ranking among the organization's top-five prospects to the system. Add it all up, and Zaidi should oversee a relatively quick turnaround in San Francisco, helping restore a franchise that has grown accustomed to winning.

DEPTH CHART

SAN FRANCISCO GIANTS

TOP 2019 ROOKIE: Shaun Anderson, RHP. The 24-year-old could use more seasoning in Triple-A, but he has the stuff to make an impact in the back of the Giants' rotation in 2019.
BREAKOUT PROSPECT: Juan De Paula, RHP. The skinny 21-year-old has all the makings of a mid-rotation starter and will receive some much-needed full-season experience in 2019.

SOURCE OF TOP 30 TALENT			
Homegrown	26	Acquired	4
College	12	Trades	4
Junior college	1	Rule 5 draft	0
High school	5	Independent leagues	0
Nondrafted free agents	0	Free agents/waivers	0
International	8		

SLEEPER: Manuel Geraldo, SS. Armed with the best infield arm in the system, the 22-year-old has the potential to be a plus defensive shortstop and shown signs of an improved hit tool and developing power.

LF	CF	RF
Chris Shaw (11)	Heliot Ramos (3)	Sandro Fabian (26)
Heath Quinn (15)	Alexander Canario (8)	Mike Gerber
Dylan Davis	Jairo Pomares (14)	Aaron Bond
Diego Rincones	Drew Ferguson	Luis Matos
Ismael Munguia	Bryce Johnson	Bryan Hernandez
	Richgelon Juliana	
	P.J. Hilson	
	Malique Ziegler	
	Jose Layer	

3B	SS	2B	1B
Luis Toribio (9)	Marco Luciano (3)	Ryan Howard (24)	Gio Brusa
Jacob Gonzalez (27)	Abiatal Avelino (23)	Jalen Miller (30)	Jonah Arenado
Ryder Jones	Manuel Geraldo	C.J. Hinojosa	Francisco Tostado
Sean Roby	Edison Mora		John Riley
David Villar			

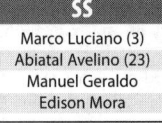

C
Joey Bart (1)
Aramis Garcia (16)
Ricardo Genoves
Matt Winn
Tanner Murphy
Jeffry Parra

LHP		RHP	
LHSP	**LHRP**	**RHSP**	**RHRP**
Seth Corry (20)	Travis Bergen	Shaun Anderson (4)	Melvin Adon (12)
Garrett Williams (21)	Josh Osich	Sean Hjelle (5)	Ray Black (17)
Conner Menez (25)	Sam Moll	Logan Webb (6)	Camilo Doval (19)
Juan Sanchez		Gregory Santos (7)	Sam Coonrod (22)
John Gavin		Jake Wong (10)	Sam Wolff
Joey Marciano		Juan De Paula (13)	Tyler Rogers
Mac Marshall		Jose Marte (18)	Chase Johnson
		Tyler Beede (28)	Dillon McNamara
		Blake Rivera (29)	Dan Slania
		Keaton Winn	Rodolfo Martinez
		Garrett Cave	Pat Ruotolo
		Jordan Johnson	Nolan Riggs
		Aaron Phillips	Frank Rubio
		Raffi Vizcaino	Peter Lannoo
		Solomon Bates	John Russell
		Ben Madison	

DRAFT ANALYSIS

2018

BEST PURE HITTER: C Joey Bart (1) was considered one of the best pure hitters in the draft, regardless of position. In his pro debut, Bart hit .298/.369/.613 in the short-season Northwest League, where he was the league's No. 1 prospect. Bart has a sizable leg kick in his load, but he showcases an easy swing and exceptional barrel control.
BEST POWER HITTER: Bart has plus raw power to all fields and hit 13 home runs in 45 games in the Northwest League. Bart has the power to project as a middle-of-the-order mainstay, and scouts were impressed with his ability to impact the baseball without completely selling out for power.
FASTEST RUNNER: OF P.J. Hilson (6) was considered one of the speedier center fielders in the draft, with scouts consistently putting 70 grades on his speed coming out of his Arkansas high school.
BEST DEFENSIVE PLAYER: The best offensive player in the Giants' 2018 draft class is also the best defensive player, as Bart displays a plus arm and proved to have excellent game-calling ability as a college catcher. Evaluators complimented Bart's footwork and effort behind the plate in his debut, noting his fearlessness when blocking pitches.
BEST ATHLETE: A 70-grade runner with above-average range in center field, Hilson also touched 93 mph off the mound in high school. If he would have made it to Alabama, there's a real chance Hilson would have been developed as a two-way player.
BEST FASTBALL: RHP Jake Wong (3) routinely sits in the low to mid 90s, and he topped out at 97 mph in the Cape Cod League last summer. Scouts described Wong as possessing a "heavy" fastball, and the 6-foot-2, 215-pound righthander pounds the zone with his heater, walking less than two batters per nine innings in his pro debut.
BEST SECONDARY PITCH: Standing 6-foot-11, RHP Sean Hjelle (2) can give hitters problems with an above-average, low-80s curveball with plenty of power and depth. Wong has a sharp slider, while RHP Ben Madison's (9) above-average slider helped him lead all NAIA pitchers with 16 strikeouts per nine innings last spring at Central Baptist (Ark.).

TOP DRAFT PICKS OF THE DECADE

Year	Player, Pos.	2018 Org
2009	Zack Wheeler, RHP	Mets
2010	Gary Brown, OF	Did not play
2011	Joe Panik, SS	Giants
2012	Chris Stratton, RHP	Giants
2013	Christian Arroyo, SS	Rays
2014	Tyler Beede, RHP	Giants
2015	Phil Bickford, RHP	Brewers
2016	Bryan Reynolds, OF (2nd round)	Pirates
2017	Heliot Ramos, OF	Giants
2018	Joey Bart, C	Giants

BEST PRO DEBUT: Bart had one of the best pro debuts of any first-round pick in 2018. Combined with his six-game stop in the Arizona League, Bart hit .294/.364/.588 with 13 home runs and 40 RBIs in his first 51 games as a professional, all while playing excellent defense behind the plate.
MOST INTRIGUING BACKGROUND: The son of the 1987 AL MVP, OF George Bell Jr. (13) is a 20-year-old out of Connors State (Okla.) JC. Bell Jr.'s father, also an outfielder, enjoyed a 12-year major league career and was a three-time all-star.
CLOSEST TO THE MAJORS: Bart will forever be compared to Buster Posey. And if Posey's career arc is any indication, then Bart could be on the fast track. Posey played in 172 minor league games and made his ML debut less than 16 months after being drafted. It wouldn't be a surprise to see Bart in San Francisco by the end of 2020.
BEST LATE-ROUND PICK: LHP Jacob Lopez (26) impressed in the Arizona League. In nine appearances (four starts) for the AZL Giants Orange, Lopez had a 1.42 ERA and 34 strikeouts in 25.1 innings. Opponents hit just .202 off Lopez, who boasted a 0.95 WHIP.
THE ONE WHO GOT AWAY: OF Ryan Olenek (17) was the first Giants draftee not to sign, instead returning to Mississippi for his senior season. The 6-foot-5, 180-pound Olenek was a first-team All-SEC selection and hit .350 with 18 doubles and three home runs as a junior.

—KEGAN LOWE

2017

OF Heliot Ramos (1) needs more refinement but had a solid first full professional season. Fellow prep picks 3B Jacob Gonzalez (2) and LHP Seth Corry (3) also are progressing. RHP Jason Bahr (5) was dealt to Texas.

GRADE: C

2016

The Giants mined this class for their moves before the 2018 season. OF Bryan Reynolds (2) was a part of the Andrew McCutchen trade and LHP Matt Krook (4) and RHP Stephen Woods (8) were used in the Evan Longoria deal.

GRADE: C

2015

Three members of the class in 2018 made their big league debuts. LHP Andrew Suarez (2) established himself in the rotation and OF Steven Duggar (6) impressed before an injury ended his season early. OF Chris Shaw (1) is also in the mix.

GRADE: B

1 JOEY BART, C

Born: Dec. 15, 1996. **B-T:** R-R. **Ht.:** 6-3. **Wt.:** 220.
Drafted: Georgia Tech, 2018 (1st round).
Signed by: Luke Murton.

Coming out of Buford (Ga.) High in 2015, Bart ranked No. 183 on the BA 500 but fell to the Rays in the 27th round in large part due to his strong commitment to Georgia Tech. In Atlanta, Bart was following in the footsteps of former major league backstops Jason Varitek and Matt Wieters, who also attended Georgia Tech. A career .321/.407/.544 hitter for the Yellow Jackets, Bart led the Atlantic Coast Conference in hitting (.359) as a junior in 2018, when he was named ACC player of the year, ACC defensive player of the year and was selected as a first-team All-American. Bart became the highest MLB draft pick in Georgia Tech history when the Giants selected him with the No. 2 overall pick and subsequently signed him for $7.025 million—the largest signing bonus for a position player in draft history.

SCOUTING REPORT: Bart is the Giants' clear No. 1 prospect, and he has the chance to impact the game in a myriad of ways. At the plate, Bart projects for plus, all-fields power. Scouts were impressed with Bart's ability to tap into his raw power without completely selling out in games, and he hit 13 home runs and 14 doubles in just 45 games in the short-season Northwest League. With Bart's track record of hitting in the ACC, and then his successful, albeit brief, pro debut, evaluators feel confident grading his hit tool as at least above-average, with the potential to become a plus hitter. Defensively, Bart has a plus arm, and it grades out even better for its accuracy than it does pure arm strength, of which there is plenty. He routinely records sub 2.0-second pop times, and the Georgia native was lauded by scouts throughout his collegiate career for calling his own games behind the plate. Bart has just fringe-average speed, but he showed the athleticism and lateral quickness needed to be considered an above-average receiver with the ability to routinely block tough pitches in the dirt.

THE FUTURE: Bart will likely start his first full season of pro ball in high Class A San Jose. Bart will forever be compared to Buster Posey, the catcher the Giants drafted the last time the organization had a top-five pick. Even if the Giants decide to move Bart along slower than Posey, it wouldn't be a surprise to see Bart in San Francisco by the end of the 2020 season. If all goes well in San Jose at the beginning of 2019, Bart could be promoted to Double-A Richmond by midseason.

BILL MITCHELL

BA GRADE	SCOUTING GRADES
60 Risk: High	Hit: 50. Power: 60. Run: 40. Field: 60. Arm: 60.

Projected future grades on 20-80 scouting scale.

TOP PROSPECTS OF THE DECADE

Year	Player, Pos.	2018 Org
2009	Madison Bumgarner, LHP	Giants
2010	Buster Posey, C	Giants
2011	Brandon Belt, 1B	Giants
2012	Gary Brown, OF	Did not play
2013	Kyle Crick, RHP	Pirates
2014	Kyle Crick, RHP	Pirates
2015	Andrew Susac, C	Orioles
2016	Christian Arroyo, SS	Rays
2017	Tyler Beede, RHP	Giants
2018	Heliot Ramos, OF	Giants

BEST TOOLS

Best Hitter for Average	Luis Toribio
Best Power Hitter	Chris Shaw
Best Strike-Zone Discipline	Luis Toribio
Fastest Baserunner	P.J. Hilson
Best Athlete	P.J. Hilson
Best Fastball	Melvin Adon
Best Curveball	Logan Webb
Best Slider	Gregory Santos
Best Changeup	Shaun Anderson
Best Control	Sean Hjelle
Best Defensive Catcher	Joey Bart
Best Defensive Infielder	Manuel Geraldo
Best Infield Arm	Manuel Geraldo
Best Defensive Outfielder	Richgelon Juliana
Best Outfield Arm	P.J. Hilson

Year	Club (League)	Class	AVG	G	AB	R	H	2B	3B	HR	RBI	BB	SO	SB	CS	OBP	SLG
2018	Giants Orange (AZL)	R	.261	6	23	3	6	1	1	0	1	1	7	0	0	.320	.391
	Salem-Keizer (NWL)	SS	.298	45	181	35	54	14	2	13	39	12	40	2	1	.369	.613
Minor League Totals			.294	51	204	38	60	15	3	13	40	13	47	2	1	.364	.588

2 MARCO LUCIANO, SS

Born: Sept. 10, 2001. **B-T:** R-R. **Ht.:** 6-2. **Wt.:** 178. **Signed:** Dominican Republic, 2018. **Signed by:** Jonathan Bautista.

TRACK RECORD: Luciano was ranked as the No. 2 international prospect in the 2018 class, trailing only the Marlins' current No. 1 prospect Victor Victor Mesa. Luciano signed for $2.6 million, which was the Giants' largest international signing bonus since spending $6 million to sign Lucius Fox in 2015.
SCOUTING REPORT: A plus athlete with tremendous offensive upside, Luciano will begin his pro career as a shortstop, although there are some who believe he will eventually outgrow the position. If that's the case, Luciano has the hands to play third base, but also the athleticism to play either center or right field. For now, the 17-year-old is a plus runner with an above-average arm who will get every chance to stick at shortstop. Luciano has strong hands and quick bat speed, leading scouts to project plus power to all fields as a potential above-average hitter. There were some swing-and-miss concerns with Luciano early in the scouting process, but he has a strong sense for the strike zone and a compact swing.
THE FUTURE: Luciano will likely stay back in extended spring training before making his stateside debut in the Rookie-level Arizona League later in 2019. There is a chance he could play in the Dominican Summer League, but the preference, as of now, seems to be having Luciano go ahead and get accumulated in the U.S. as an advanced 17-year-old international prospect.

BILL MITCHELL

BA GRADE

60 Risk: Extreme

HIT: 50. **POW:** 60.
SPD: 60. **FLD:** 50.
ARM: 55.

Year	Club (League)	Class	AVG	G	AB	R	H	2B	3B	HR	RBI	BB	SO	SB	CS	OBP	SLG
2018	Did not play—Signed 2019 contract																

3 HELIOT RAMOS, OF

Born: Sept. 7, 1999. **B-T:** R-R. **Ht.:** 6-2. **Wt.:** 185. **Drafted:** HS—Guaynabo, P.R., 2017 (1st round). **Signed by:** Junior Roman.

TRACK RECORD: The younger brother of Henry Ramos, a Dodgers minor leaguer who played with Triple-A Oklahoma City in 2018, and Hector Ramos, a forward on the Puerto Rican national soccer team, Heliot is another exceptional athlete in the Ramos family. The No. 19 pick in 2017, Ramos signed with the Giants for just north of $3.1 million.
SCOUTING REPORT: Exclusively a center fielder in his pro career, there are some who feel Ramos will be best suited for right field in the future as he continues to fill out his 6-foot-2 frame. Regardless, the Giants have been pleased with what they've seen from Ramos as an at least average center fielder and feel he'll be an above-average right fielder, at worst, in AT&T Park, which plays big in right field. Ramos is helped by his current plus speed, although his thick lower half leads many to believe he'll slow down as he matures, and his above-average arm plays at either position. Ramos' power profiles in right field as well, with the potential to become a middle-of-the-order bat with 25-plus home run potential. Ramos' hit tool is the biggest question. He has a short swing and can drive the ball to all fields, but he'll likely never draw many walks and he struck out more than 25 percent of the time in low Class A. He's naturally an aggressive hitter, and he usually makes loud contact when he connects.
THE FUTURE: Ramos has the chance to be a dangerous power-speed threat in the middle of the Giants' lineup if he continues to refine all of his exciting tools. He'll advance to high Class A San Jose in 2019.

BA GRADE

55 Risk: Very High

HIT: 45. **POW:** 55.
SPD: 60. **FLD:** 55.
ARM: 55.

Year	Club (League)	Class	AVG	G	AB	R	H	2B	3B	HR	RBI	BB	SO	SB	CS	OBP	SLG
2017	Giants (AZL)	R	.348	35	138	33	48	11	6	6	27	10	48	10	2	.404	.645
2018	Augusta (SAL)	LoA	.245	124	485	61	119	24	8	11	52	35	136	8	7	.313	.396
Minor League Totals			**.268**	**159**	**623**	**94**	**167**	**35**	**14**	**17**	**79**	**45**	**184**	**18**	**9**	**.333**	**.451**

4 SHAUN ANDERSON, RHP

Born: Oct. 29, 1994. **B-T:** R-R. **Ht.:** 6-4. **Wt.:** 225. **Drafted:** Florida, 2016 (3rd round). **Signed by:** Stephen Hargett (Red Sox).

TRACK RECORD: A third-round pick out of Florida by the Red Sox in 2016, Anderson was acquired by the Giants, alongside fellow righthander Gregory Santos, in the July 2017 trade that sent third baseman Eduardo Nunez to Boston. An extremely effective reliever at Florida, Anderson has been almost exclusively a starter with both the Red Sox and Giants, and he has the frame, pitch mix and durability to stick as a starter in the majors.

SCOUTING REPORT: Anderson has four average-or-better pitches with above-average control that helps all of his offerings play up. He attacks hitters with a 92-94 mph fastball that can touch 96 mph, and his best offspeed pitch is an upper-80s slider. Anderson also uses an average changeup and curveball that are effective because of his ability to throw strikes with all four of his pitches in nearly any count. Evaluators praise Anderson for his ability to maneuver through a lineup multiple times, regularly keeping hitters guessing and off-balance with a strong baseball acumen.

BA GRADE	
50	Risk: High
FB: 55. SL: 55.	
CB: 50. CHG: 50.	
CTL: 55.	

THE FUTURE: Anderson is knocking on the door of the majors. He spent the final three months of 2018 in Triple-A Sacramento with middling success, but he could be promoted to San Francisco by mid-2019. He projects best as a No. 3 or No. 4 starter.

Year	Club (League)	Class	W	L	ERA	G	GS	CG	SV	IP	H	HR	BB	SO	K/9	WHIP	AVG
2016	Lowell (NYP)	SS	0	0	30.38	2	2	0	0	3	12	1	0	4	13.5	4.50	.571
2017	Greenville (SAL)	LoA	3	0	2.33	7	7	0	0	39	30	1	11	37	8.6	1.06	.216
	Salem (CAR)	HiA	3	3	3.99	11	11	0	0	59	53	6	18	48	7.4	1.21	.236
	San Jose (CAL)	HiA	3	3	3.51	6	5	0	0	26	19	1	4	22	7.7	0.90	.198
2018	Richmond (EL)	AA	6	5	3.45	17	16	0	0	94	93	9	22	93	8.9	1.22	.256
	Sacramento (PCL)	AAA	2	2	4.18	8	8	0	0	47	48	5	11	34	6.5	1.25	.261
Minor League Totals			17	13	3.81	51	49	0	0	267	255	23	66	238	8.0	1.20	.248

5 SEAN HJELLE, RHP

Born: May 7, 1997. **B-T:** R-R. **Ht.:** 6-11. **Wt.:** 225. **Drafted:** Kentucky, 2018 (2nd round). **Signed by:** Kevin Christman.

TRACK RECORD: Line one with Hjelle is his immense height, standing at a legitimate 6-foot-11. As a freshman at Kentucky, Hjelle served as the team's closer before transitioning to the Friday starter's role fo his sophomore and junior seasons. Hjelle was the Southeastern Conference pitcher of the year in 2017, and he was drafted by the Giants in the second round in 2018. He signed for $1.5 million.

SCOUTING REPORT: Hjelle is similar to fellow Giants prospect Shaun Anderson in that he finds success with multiple average-or-better pitches, despite not having a true out pitch. Hjelle has a tick more life on his fastball than Anderson, regularly working in the 92-95 mph range with arm-side run. Hjelle's low-80s curveball has effective 12-to-6 shape that can elicit swings and misses, and his changeup could be an above-average pitch. The lanky righthander obviously has plenty of room to add weight to his 6-foot-11

BA GRADE	
50	Risk: High
FB: 55. CB: 55.	
CHG: 50.	
CTL: 55.	

frame, which could help squeeze out even more fastball velocity. All of Hjelle's pitches play up because of his above-average control, and his track record suggests he's a durable starter who has had major success at every level he's pitched.

THE FUTURE: Hjelle will likely begin 2019 in the starting rotation for high Class A San Jose, which should be the most prospect-heavy team in the Giants' system. Assuming good health, Hjelle's ceiling is that of a No. 3 starter, and his floor should not fall below a solid No. 5 starter.

Year	Club (League)	Class	W	L	ERA	G	GS	CG	SV	IP	H	HR	BB	SO	K/9	WHIP	AVG
2018	Salem-Keizer (NWL)	SS	0	0	5.06	12	12	0	0	21	24	4	4	22	9.3	1.31	.273
Minor League Totals			0	0	5.06	12	12	0	0	21	24	4	4	22	9.3	1.31	.273

6 LOGAN WEBB, RHP

Born: Nov. 18, 1996. **B-T:** R-R. **Ht.:** 6-2. **Wt.:** 220. **Drafted:** HS—Rocklin, Calif., 2014 (4th round). **Signed by:** Keith Snider.

TRACK RECORD: A high school quarterback in Rocklin, Calif., Webb burst onto the baseball scouting scene during his senior year before the Giants drafted him in the fourth round in 2014. Webb agreed to an over-slot, $600,000 bonus, signing him away from his commitment to Cal Poly. After making it to low Class A in 2016, Webb blew out his elbow early in the season and needed Tommy John surgery. He returned in June 2017 and completed a career-high 104 innings in 2018, advancing as high as Double-A Richmond.

SCOUTING REPORT: Webb has two plus pitches, headlined by a mid- to upper-90s fastball that routinely touches 98 mph. His fastball is described as being heavy, while his low-80s breaking ball has wipeout, swing-and-miss potential with a slurvy shape. The righthander is still working on a third-pitch changeup, but it's well behind his fastball and breaking ball. It often comes across too firm, not creating enough separation from his heater. Webb's control is still raw ever since returning from his surgery and shouldn't currently be considered better than average. He walked roughly four batters per nine innings in 2018, although the Giants were focused on limiting his innings, so he was likely airing it out in short stints more than he will in the future.

BA GRADE	
50	Risk: High

FB: 60. SL: 60.
CHG: 45.
CTL: 45.

THE FUTURE: Webb will return to Double-A, where he'll headline Richmond's rotation in 2019. He has more upside than fellow righthanders Shaun Anderson or Sean Hjelle, but he also has significant reliever risk until he further refines his changeup and control.

Year	Club (League)	Class	W	L	ERA	G	GS	CG	SV	IP	H	HR	BB	SO	K/9	WHIP	AVG
2016	Augusta (SAL)	LoA	2	3	6.21	9	9	0	0	42	54	7	12	30	6.4	1.57	.303
2017	Salem-Keizer (NWL)	SS	2	0	2.89	15	0	0	0	28	26	1	7	31	10.0	1.18	.241
2018	San Jose (CAL)	HiA	1	3	1.82	21	20	0	0	74	54	2	36	74	9.0	1.22	.207
	Richmond (EL)	AA	1	2	3.82	6	6	0	0	31	30	4	11	26	7.6	1.34	.254
Minor League Totals			9	14	3.77	68	50	0	0	239	243	16	85	206	7.8	1.37	.264

7 GREGORY SANTOS, RHP

Born: Aug. 28, 1999. **B-T:** R-R. **Ht.:** 6-2. **Wt.:** 190. **Signed:** Dominican Republic, 2015. **Signed by:** Eddie Romero/Manny Nanita (Red Sox).

TRACK RECORD: Santos originally signed with the Red Sox for $275,000 in 2015. He was acquired by the Giants in July 2017, when the Red Sox traded Santos and righthander Shaun Anderson in exchange for third baseman Eduardo Nunez. After pitching in the Dominican Summer League in 2016 and 2017, Santos spent 2018 in the short-season Northwest League, where he made 12 starts. Santos missed time late in 2018 after he was struck in the head by a 105 mph line drive off the bat of Blue Jays' prospect Griffin Conine. He was taken off the field in an ambulance, but returned to the mound just 18 days later and made two additional starts before the season ended.

SK VOLCANOES

BA GRADE	
55	Risk: Extreme

FB: 60. SL: 60.
CHG: 40.
CTL: 50.

SCOUTING REPORT: Still only 19 years old, Santos may have the highest upside of any pitcher currently in the system. Regarded as a big, strong, athlete, Santos has a heavy, mid-90s fastball that he keeps down in the zone with good angle, regularly touching 98 mph. Despite his youth, Santos does an excellent job of holding his velocity, and his fastball is complemented by a plus, upper-80s slider with good tilt. Santos still needs to develop his changeup. It's a below-average pitch right now that only flashes average. He has solid mechanics, does a good job of keeping himself in-line when going toward the plate, and as a result has average control.

THE FUTURE: Santos should be ready for his first taste of full-season ball at low Class A Augusta in 2019. Although he has the upside of a No. 2 starter, there is also some reliever risk with Santos, who likely remains at least three years away from the majors.

Year	Club (League)	Class	W	L	ERA	G	GS	CG	SV	IP	H	HR	BB	SO	K/9	WHIP	AVG
2016	Red Sox2 (DSL)	R	3	3	4.17	16	10	0	1	41	40	1	26	25	5.5	1.61	.258
2017	Red Sox (DSL)	R	2	0	0.89	8	8	0	0	30	22	0	15	24	7.1	1.22	.206
	Giants (DSL)	R	1	0	1.93	4	4	0	0	19	21	2	5	17	8.2	1.39	.273
2018	Salem-Keizer (NWL)	SS	2	5	4.53	12	12	0	0	50	64	3	15	46	8.3	1.59	.311
Minor League Totals			8	8	3.29	40	34	0	1	140	147	6	61	112	7.2	1.49	.270

8 ALEXANDER CANARIO, OF

Born: May 7, 2000. **B-T:** R-R. **Ht.:** 6-1. **Wt.:** 165. **Signed:** Dominican Republic, 2016. **Signed by:** Ruddy Moreta.

TRACK RECORD: The Giants signed Canario for just $60,000 in 2016, which may turn out to be one of the franchise's better investments in recent memory. After spending 2017 in the Dominican Summer League, Canario made his stateside debut in the Rookie-level Arizona League in 2018. He got off to a slow start in the AZL, but caught fire in July, when he posted a 1.030 OPS and hit four of his six home runs.

SCOUTING REPORT: Helped by his above-average speed and arm strength, Canario has the chance to be an above-average defender in center field. There are some who project him to move to right field, where his arm and power would profile well, but the Giants have liked what they've seen from Canario in center field. He has above-average or even plus range, although he is still raw when it comes to route running and defensive instincts. The 18-year-old Canario has above-average raw power and should grow into more. After show-ing an advanced feel for the strike zone in the DSL, Canario's strikeout rate jumped from 14.6 percent in 2017 to nearly 25 percent in the AZL. His swing gets long when he tries to sell out for more power, but overall he has an advanced approach at the plate and increased his walk rate to 13 percent in 2018.

THE FUTURE: The next step for Canario is the short-season Northwest League. He'll need to improve his consistency, but the Giants are confident he has the raw tools necessary to be an impact center fielder with above-average power and speed if he can iron out his current kinks.

ZACHARY LUCY/FOUR SEAM

BA GRADE

55 Risk: Extreme

HIT: 45. POW: 55.
SPD: 55. FLD: 55.
ARM: 55.

Year	Club (League)	Class	AVG	G	AB	R	H	2B	3B	HR	RBI	BB	SO	SB	CS	OBP	SLG
2017	Giants (DSL)	R	.294	66	235	42	69	17	4	5	45	33	40	18	10	.391	.464
2018	Giants Black (AZL)	R	.250	45	176	36	44	5	2	6	19	27	51	8	5	.357	.403
Minor League Totals			.275	111	411	78	113	22	6	11	64	60	91	26	15	.376	.438

9 LUIS TORIBIO, 3B

Born: Sept. 28, 2000. **B-T:** L-R. **Ht.:** 6-1. **Wt.:** 165. **Signed:** Dominican Republic, 2017. **Signed by:** Ruddy Moreta.

TRACK RECORD: Just a few months too young to be a member of the 2016 international free agent class, Toribio had to wait until July 2017 to sign with the Giants for $300,000. Toribio was one of several $300,000 signings the Giants made in 2017, although early indications are Toribio's bonus may be money well spent. The 6-foot-1 lefthanded hitter spent last season in the Dominican Summer League, where he led his team in hits (58), doubles (13), home runs (10) and total bases (103).

SCOUTING REPORT: Toribio is an offense-first third baseman who draws comparisons to current Red Sox third baseman Rafael Devers. He's an above-average hitter with an approach at the plate that is mature well beyond his years. Toribio's walk rate was nearly 19 percent in the DSL, and while some-times that can be an indictment of the pitching in the minors' lowest level, evaluators said Toribio's feel for the strike zone is truly advanced. He has good loft in his swing with plus raw power that he taps into regularly, as evidenced by his .209 isolated slugging percentage in 2018. The struggle for Toribio will come defensively, as he's a below-average runner with fringe-average range at third base. His arm is average and plays well at third base, but he committed a team-worst 19 errors in the DSL and needs continued work at the position.

STACY JO GRANT

BA GRADE

55 Risk: Extreme

HIT: 55. POW: 60.
SPD: 40. FLD: 40.
ARM: 50.

THE FUTURE: Toribio should keep climbing the ladder with a stop in the Rookie-level Arizona League in 2019. Improving his third base defense will be the biggest key for Toribio to reach his potential, as he has middle-of-the-order offensive skills.

Year	Club (League)	Class	AVG	G	AB	R	H	2B	3B	HR	RBI	BB	SO	SB	CS	OBP	SLG
2018	Giants (DSL)	R	.270	64	215	44	58	13	1	10	39	51	62	4	1	.423	.479
Minor League Totals			.270	64	215	44	58	13	1	10	39	51	62	4	1	.423	.479

10 JAKE WONG, RHP

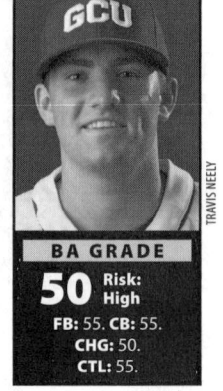

TRAVIS NEELY

Born: Sept. 3, 1996. **B-T:** R-R. **Ht.:** 6-2. **Wt.:** 215. **Drafted:** Grand Canyon, 2018 (3rd round). **Signed by:** Chuck Hensley.

TRACK RECORD: Wong significantly raised his stock over the past two seasons, serving as Grand Canyon's ace and pitching well in the Cape Cod League before the Giants drafted him in the third round in 2018. After signing for $850,000, the 6-foot-2 righthander made his pro debut in the short-season Northwest League, where he impressed in 11 starts.

SCOUTING REPORT: Wong features a heavy fastball that touches 97 mph, but more regularly sits 92-96 mph. Scouts commented that Wong's fastball has above-average life, helping the pitch play up. His curveball is at least above-average with solid 11-to-5 shape, while his changeup earns future 50s from scouts. Evaluators were impressed with Wong's ability to attack hitters, and he showed above-average control while averaging one strikeout per inning.

THE FUTURE: The highest drafted player out of Grand Canyon in 25 years, Wong will move to full-season ball in 2019. Even if he starts the season at low Class A Augusta, a promotion to high Class A is possible. Wong has the ceiling of a mid-rotation starter.

BA GRADE

50 Risk: High

FB: 55. **CB:** 55.
CHG: 50.
CTL: 55.

Year	Club (League)	Class	W	L	ERA	G	GS	CG	SV	IP	H	HR	BB	SO	K/9	WHIP	AVG
2018	Salem-Keizer (NWL)	SS	0	2	2.30	11	11	0	0	27	28	1	6	27	8.9	1.24	.259
Minor League Totals			0	2	2.30	11	11	0	0	27	28	1	6	27	8.9	1.24	.259

11 CHRIS SHAW, OF

BA GRADE

50 Risk: High

Born: Oct. 20, 1993. **B-T:** L-R. **Ht.:** 6-3. **Wt.:** 226. **Drafted:** Boston College, 2015 (1st round). **Signed by:** Mark O'Sullivan.

TRACK RECORD: A first-rounder out of Boston College in 2015, Shaw signed with the Giants for $1.4 million in large part due to his plus lefthanded power. After hitting 81 home runs in 404 minor league games, Shaw made his major league debut on Aug. 31.

SCOUTING REPORT: Shaw has plus, all-fields power and has the potential to hit 25-plus home runs in a full major league season. However, Shaw struggled with swing-and-miss issues in Triple-A, and those problems were exacerbated in a very brief appearance in the big leagues. Shaw's strikeout rate was above 34 percent in Triple-A and jumped to 37.1 percent in the majors, a direct byproduct of being too aggressive and chasing too many pitches. Shaw's bat will have to carry him, however, as he's an fringe-average defensive left fielder, at best, with limited range and an average arm.

THE FUTURE: Shaw will compete for an Opening Day roster spot with the Giants in 2019, although he'll have to prove he can hit and make contact more regularly to carve out an everyday role. Starting in Triple-A isn't out of the question, although his plus power could make him a valuable platoon option.

Year	Club (League)	Class	AVG	G	AB	R	H	2B	3B	HR	RBI	BB	SO	SB	CS	OBP	SLG
2016	San Jose (CAL)	HiA	.285	72	270	47	77	22	0	16	55	28	70	0	0	.357	.544
	Richmond (EL)	AA	.246	60	232	26	57	16	4	5	30	20	55	0	0	.309	.414
2017	Richmond (EL)	AA	.293	37	133	16	39	9	0	6	28	18	26	0	0	.383	.496
	Sacramento (PCL)	AAA	.289	88	336	42	97	25	1	18	50	20	106	0	0	.328	.530
2018	Sacramento (PCL)	AAA	.259	101	394	55	102	21	2	24	65	21	144	0	0	.308	.505
	San Francisco (NL)	MAJ	.185	22	54	2	10	2	0	1	7	7	23	1	0	.274	.278
Major League Totals			.185	22	54	2	10	2	0	1	7	7	23	1	0	.274	.278
Minor League Totals			.274	404	1543	208	423	104	7	81	258	126	442	0	0	.334	.508

12 MELVIN ADON, RHP

BA GRADE

50 Risk: High

Born: June 9, 1994. **B-T:** R-R. **Ht.:** 6-3. **Wt.:** 195. **Signed:** Dominican Republic, 2015. **Signed by:** Pablo Peguero/Felix Peguero/Jesus Stephens.

TRACK RECORD: Considered a late-bloomer, Adon signed with the Giants as a 20-year-old out of the Dominican Republic in 2015. Adon was used as a starter in his first four years in the Giants' system, but exclusively came out of the bullpen in a successful stint in the 2018 Arizona Fall League. The Giants liked what they saw, added him to the 40-man roster this offseason and his future now resides in the bullpen.

SCOUTING REPORT: Adon has a plus fastball that touched 102 mph in the AFL. His fastball is straight and doesn't feature a ton of life, but there's no denying its premium velocity is among the best in the game. His second pitch is an above-average power slider that flashes plus and works well off his fastball. Below-average control is a concern for Adon, who walked nearly four batters per nine innings in 2018. His control out of the bullpen in the AFL was better, however, as he walked just three batters in 21 innings.

THE FUTURE: Although high Class A San Jose is the highest level Adon has pitched at in the minors, he should move quickly now that he is expected to be a full-time reliever. Adon could see time in the back of the Giants' bullpen in 2019.

Year	Club (League)	Class	W	L	ERA	G	GS	CG	SV	IP	H	HR	BB	SO	K/9	WHIP	AVG
2016	Salem-Keizer (NWL)	SS	5	5	5.48	14	14	0	0	67	85	3	34	55	7.4	1.77	.317
2017	Augusta (SAL)	LoA	3	11	4.35	23	19	0	0	99	110	5	35	89	8.1	1.46	.277
2018	San Jose (CAL)	HiA	2	5	4.87	16	15	0	0	78	82	6	34	71	8.2	1.49	.278
	Giants Orange (AZL)	R	0	1	7.71	2	0	0	0	5	9	0	3	8	15.4	2.57	.409
Minor League Totals			14	22	4.36	69	62	0	0	318	343	16	127	277	7.8	1.48	.277

13 JUAN DE PAULA, RHP

BA GRADE

50 Risk: Very High

Born: Sept. 22, 1997. **B-T:** R-R. **Ht.:** 6-3. **Wt.:** 165. **Signed:** Dominican Republic, 2014. **Signed by:** Eddy Toledo/Tim Kissner (Mariners).

TRACK RECORD: A $175,000 signing out of the Dominican Republic by the Mariners in 2014, De Paula has been traded twice in his career. He was acquired by the Giants in the August 2018 deal that sent Andrew McCutchen to the Yankees. After spending the majority of the last two seasons in the short-season New-York Penn League, the 21-year-old De Paula made only one start in the Giants organization in 2018, striking out nine and walking one in five innings with low Class A Augusta before the season ended.

SCOUTING REPORT: A skinny, 6-foot-3 righthander with plenty of room to add weight to his frame, De Paula has a plus fastball that sits in the mid-90s and touches 98 mph with above-average life. He has feel for both a changeup and curveball, although both pitches are currently below-average offerings with the chance to become average or above-average pitches in the future. De Paula's secondary pitches and overall control lack consistency at the moment, but that's widely to be expected from a 21-year-old with only one, late-season start in full-season ball.

THE FUTURE: De Paula has the three-pitch mix of a mid-rotation starter. He's raw and needs to improve his fringe-average control, but he'll receive much-needed experience at low Class A Augusta in 2019.

Year	Club (League)	Class	W	L	ERA	G	GS	CG	SV	IP	H	HR	BB	SO	K/9	WHIP	AVG
2016	Mariners (AZL)	R	1	2	3.07	11	7	0	0	41	41	2	11	53	11.6	1.27	.253

14 JAIRO POMARES, OF

BA GRADE

50 Risk: Extreme

Born: Aug. 4, 2000. **B-T:** L-R. **Ht.:** 6-1. **Wt.:** 185. **Signed:** Cuba, 2018. **Signed by:** Jonathan Bautista/Gabriel Elias.

TRACK RECORD: Pomares joined shortstop Marco Luciano as the Giants' top international signings in 2018. The 17-year-old outfielder out of Cuba was ranked as the No. 11 international prospect and signed for just under $1 million. Pomares played in Cuba's 15U national league in 2015, when he ranked sixth in the league in batting average by hitting .383/.447/.533 with 16 walks and just six strikeouts.

SCOUTING REPORT: Pomares has a fluid, compact stroke resulting in a high contact rate from the left side. He has a mature approach at the plate for only being 18 years old, and he has above-average raw power for his age. Pomares is an above-average runner and has the chance to stick in center field, although that could change depending on how he physically matures. He played mostly left field while in Cuba in 2015, but he has an average arm that should play at all three outfield positions.

THE FUTURE: Pomares will likely start his Giants career in the Dominican Summer League.

Year	Club (League)	Class	AVG	G	AB	R	H	2B	3B	HR	RBI	BB	SO	SB	CS	OBP	SLG
2018	Did not play—Signed 2019 contract																

15 HEATH QUINN, OF

BA GRADE

45 Risk: High

Born: June 7, 1995. **B-T:** R-R. **Ht.:** 6-3. **Wt.:** 220. **Drafted:** Samford, 2016 (3rd round). **Signed by:** Jeff Wood.

TRACK RECORD: Quinn was one of the top power hitters coming out of college in 2016. The Giants drafted him out of Samford with their third-round pick, signing the righthanded hitter for $625,900. Quinn skipped low Class A and went straight to high Class A San Jose in his first full year, but he struggled with injuries was forced to repeat the level in 2018. He performed much better in his second go-round.

SCOUTING REPORT: Quinn is a typical, run-producing corner outfielder, projecting best as a plus left fielder with an above-average arm in San Francisco's expansive AT&T Park. Quinn has above-average power, but he's most likely an average hitter with a propensity for strikeouts. The strikeouts are mostly a result of a swing that can get long, as he shows good command of the strike zone with a career walk rate near 10 percent. Quinn is an average runner, but he should never be much of a stolen base threat.

THE FUTURE: After skipping low Class A but spending two years at high Class A, Quinn is right on track. He'll begin 2019 at Double-A Richmond.

Year	Club (League)	Class	AVG	G	AB	R	H	2B	3B	HR	RBI	BB	SO	SB	CS	OBP	SLG
2016	Giants (AZL)	R	.600	2	5	4	3	1	0	0	0	2	1	0	0	.778	.800
	Salem-Keizer (NWL)	SS	.337	54	205	37	69	19	1	9	34	26	50	3	0	.423	.571
	San Jose (CAL)	HiA	.353	4	17	2	6	1	0	0	0	2	7	0	0	.421	.412
2017	San Jose (CAL)	HiA	.228	75	272	24	62	9	0	10	29	20	86	0	0	.290	.371
2018	San Jose (CAL)	HiA	.300	96	357	53	107	24	0	14	51	42	98	4	1	.376	.485
Minor League Totals			.289	231	856	120	247	54	1	33	114	92	242	7	1	.366	.470

16 ARAMIS GARCIA, C

BA GRADE
45 Risk: High

Born: Jan. 12, 1993. **B-T:** R-R. **Ht.:** 6-2. **Wt.:** 220. **Drafted:** Florida International, 2014 (2nd round). **Signed by:** Jose Alou.

TRACK RECORD: The Giants' second-round pick in 2014 out of Florida International, Garcia made his major league debut on Aug. 31. He performed well with the Giants in a brief look, although he had subpar numbers in his first full year at Triple-A before receiving his first big league callup.

SCOUTING REPORT: Considered an average to above-average defensive catcher with a plus arm behind the plate, Garcia's future role in the majors rests heavily on his bat. He has plus raw power that should play above-average in games in the major leagues, but his hit tool has never been considered better than average. Garcia struck out nearly 30 percent of the time in Triple-A in 2018, and that rate jumped to nearly 50 percent in limited major league at-bats. Garcia has never shown much patience at the plate, and he has a rather lengthy swing.

THE FUTURE: Between Buster Posey and Joey Bart, Garcia seems destined for a long-term backup role in San Francisco. With the weakness at the catcher's position across baseball, however, Garcia could be one of the best 30 big league catchers as soon as 2019, especially if his hit tool takes any slight step forward.

Year	Club (League)	Class	AVG	G	AB	R	H	2B	3B	HR	RBI	BB	SO	SB	CS	OBP	SLG
2016	Giants (AZL)	R	.227	6	22	1	5	1	0	0	4	0	1	0	0	.217	.273
	San Jose (CAL)	HiA	.257	41	144	20	37	6	0	2	20	14	42	1	0	.323	.340
2017	San Jose (CAL)	HiA	.272	81	324	43	88	20	1	17	65	15	73	0	0	.314	.497
	Richmond (EL)	AA	.282	22	78	11	22	12	0	0	8	9	21	0	0	.360	.436
2018	Richmond (EL)	AA	.233	80	301	36	70	14	1	11	33	20	76	0	1	.287	.395
	Sacramento (PCL)	AAA	.237	10	38	5	9	1	0	0	4	2	12	0	0	.268	.263
	San Francisco (NL)	MAJ	.286	19	63	8	18	1	0	4	9	2	31	0	0	.308	.492
Major League Totals			.286	19	63	8	18	1	0	4	9	2	31	0	0	.308	.492
Minor League Totals			.255	371	1403	179	358	79	3	47	215	114	349	2	2	.316	.416

17 RAY BLACK, RHP

BA GRADE
45 Risk: High

Born: June 26, 1990. **B-T:** R-R. **Ht.:** 6-5. **Wt.:** 225. **Drafted:** Pittsburgh, 2011 (7th round). **Signed by:** John DiCarlo.

TRACK RECORD: Black has dealt with a bevy of injuries throughout his career, dating back to his high school days and impacting his throwing shoulder, pitching elbow, knees, back and more. The injuries have led Black to consider quitting baseball numerous times, but he had a career year in 2018 and finally made it to the big leagues more than seven years after being the Giants' seventh-round pick in 2011.

SCOUTING REPORT: When healthy, Black has one of the best arms in baseball. He has a heavy, plus-plus fastball that sits 97-102 mph and a pair of above-average breaking balls in a mid-80s slider and low-80s curveball. Black has fringe-average control and is a reliever all the way because of durability issues, but his offspeed pitches play up because hitters focus so heavily on his premium velocity. Because of injuries, Black hadn't completed more than 35.1 innings in a season since high school. The 28-year-old was much healthier in 2018 and made 62 appearances between Double-A, Triple-A and the majors.

THE FUTURE: Black has the ceiling of an elite setup man or closer in the majors, if he can stay healthy. That's a big if for Black, who needs to continue working on controlling his explosive arsenal in order to get the most out of his premium three-pitch mix.

Year	Club (League)	Class	W	L	ERA	G	GS	CG	SV	IP	H	HR	BB	SO	K/9	WHIP	AVG
2016	Richmond (EL)	AA	1	4	4.88	35	0	0	6	31	17	1	32	53	15.2	1.56	.159
2017	Giants (AZL)	R	0	0	3.86	3	0	0	0	2	2	0	3	7	27.0	2.14	.222
2018	Richmond (EL)	AA	0	0	0.90	10	0	0	4	10	4	0	4	20	18.0	0.80	.118
	Sacramento (PCL)	AAA	3	0	3.16	26	0	0	1	26	15	2	8	46	16.1	0.90	.167
	San Francisco (NL)	MAJ	2	2	6.17	26	0	0	0	23	17	4	10	33	12.7	1.16	.207
Major League Totals			2	2	6.17	26	0	0	0	23	17	4	10	33	12.7	1.16	.207
Minor League Totals			8	8	3.47	131	5	0	12	130	68	6	88	248	17.2	1.20	.152

18 JOSE MARTE, RHP

BA GRADE

45 Risk: High

Born: June 14, 1996. **B-T:** R-R. **Ht.:** 6-3. **Wt.:** 180. **Signed:** Dominican Republic, 2015. **Signed by:** Ruddy Moreta.

TRACK RECORD: An international signing in July 2015, Marte made his full-season debut in low Class A Augusta and completed a career-high 118.2 innings. The 22-year-old is still raw with room to fill out his 6-foot-3, 180-pound frame, but he joins fellow righthanders Melvin Adon and Camilo Doval as Giants class of 2015 international signings who have a chance to make an impact in San Francisco.

SCOUTING REPORT: Marte throws a heavy fastball, although it remains inconsistent in terms of velocity. He can throw anywhere from 90-98 mph with his heater, averaging 94-95 mph, but it consistently plays as a plus pitch when he keeps it down in the zone. Marte's offspeed is still a work in progress, as both his slider and changeup are current below-average pitches with the chance to be average offerings in the future. Marte improved his control in 2018, but it still currently grades out as average, at best.

THE FUTURE: Marte is rather raw with his approach on the mound, and there are questions as to whether he'll remain as a starter. For now, he'll head to high Class A San Jose as a starting pitcher, but both his offspeed pitches and control need to improve if he wants to stay in the rotation.

Year	Club (League)	Class	W	L	ERA	G	GS	CG	SV	IP	H	HR	BB	SO	K/9	WHIP	AVG
2016	Giants (DSL)	R	1	1	1.89	5	5	0	0	19	12	0	10	18	8.5	1.16	.182
2017	Salem-Keizer (NWL)	SS	2	5	5.33	14	14	0	0	54	61	2	34	42	7.0	1.76	.281
	Giants (AZL)	R	0	0	0.00	1	0	0	0	1	0	0	0	2	18.0	0.00	.000
2018	Augusta (SAL)	LoA	7	7	4.70	25	25	0	0	119	127	10	50	112	8.5	1.49	.275
Minor League Totals			10	13	4.58	45	44	0	0	193	200	12	94	174	8.1	1.53	.268

19 CAMILO DOVAL, RHP

BA GRADE

45 Risk: High

Born: July 4, 1997. **B-T:** R-R. **Ht.:** 6-2. **Wt.:** 185. **Signed:** Dominican Republic, 2015. **Signed by:** Gabriel Arias.

TRACK RECORD: An international signing by the Giants in 2015, Doval made his stateside debut in 2017 in the Rookie-level Arizona League, where he posted the league's second-best strikeout rate (14.2 strikeouts per nine). In Doval's full-season debut in 2018, he allowed seven earned runs in his first 0.2 innings, but then settled down and allowed only 11 earned runs over his final 52.1 innings (1.89 ERA).

SCOUTING REPORT: Doval is a pure reliever, but his fastball sits 93-99 mph, usually averaging 95 mph with movement. He's able to cut and sink his fastball, although sometimes that's happenstance because of his explosive and rather violent delivery. Doval's hard slider has a chance to be a plus pitch in the future, and it's especially lethal against righthanders, who hit just .137 off of him in 2018. Doval lacks a third pitch, which helped lefties hit .280 against him in low Class A. Doval struck out more than 13.2 batters per nine innings in 2018, but his current below-average control led to him walk 4.58 hitters per nine.

THE FUTURE: Doval will jump to high Class A San Jose in 2019, armed with two plus pitches.

Year	Club (League)	Class	W	L	ERA	G	GS	CG	SV	IP	H	HR	BB	SO	K/9	WHIP	AVG
2016	Giants (DSL)	R	2	0	1.83	12	0	0	1	20	10	0	10	20	9.2	1.02	.159
2017	Giants (AZL)	R	1	2	3.90	17	0	0	1	32	23	0	13	51	14.2	1.11	.197
2018	Augusta (SAL)	LoA	0	3	3.06	44	0	0	11	53	40	2	27	78	13.2	1.26	.205
Minor League Totals			3	5	3.09	73	0	0	13	105	73	2	50	149	12.8	1.17	.198

20 SETH CORRY, LHP

BA GRADE

45 Risk: High

Born: Nov. 3, 1998. **B-T:** L-L. **Ht.:** 6-2. **Wt.:** 195. **Drafted:** HS—Highland, Utah, 2017 (3rd round). **Signed by:** Chuck Hensley.

TRACK RECORD: Corry had one of the best fastball-curveball combinations of any high school pitcher in the 2017 draft, but fell to the third round because of control issues. So far, Corry has lived up to his pre-draft expectations, showcasing two above-average pitches while walking nearly six batters per nine innings.

SCOUTING REPORT: Corry has an above-average fastball from the left side, sitting 90-94 mph with life. His curveball is also an above-average pitch, with 12-to-6 break and the chance to be a plus pitch. Corry's third-pitch changeup is wildly inconsistent, drawing below-average to above-average grades from scouts depending on the day. A lot of Corry's inconsistency, including the issues with his current below-average control, stem from an effortful delivery that has a lot of moving parts and a violent finish.

THE FUTURE: Corry has the potential of a mid-rotation starter if he can find consistency with his change-up and improve his control. The Giants will send Corry to low Class A Augusta as a starter in 2019, but he could always transition into an effective two-pitch lefthander out of the bullpen.

Year	Club (League)	Class	W	L	ERA	G	GS	CG	SV	IP	H	HR	BB	SO	K/9	WHIP	AVG
2017	Giants (AZL)	R	0	2	5.55	13	10	0	0	24	14	1	22	21	7.8	1.48	.163
2018	Giants Orange (AZL)	R	3	1	2.61	9	9	0	0	38	38	1	17	42	9.9	1.45	.260
	Salem-Keizer (NWL)	SS	1	2	5.49	5	5	0	0	20	14	1	15	17	7.8	1.47	.200
Minor League Totals			4	5	4.17	27	24	0	0	82	66	3	54	80	8.8	1.46	.219

21 GARRETT WILLIAMS, LHP

BA GRADE

45 Risk: High

Born: Sept. 15, 1994. **B-T:** L-L. **Ht.:** 6-1. **Wt.:** 205. **Drafted:** Oklahoma State, 2016 (7th round). **Signed by:** Daniel Murray.

TRACK RECORD: A hard-throwing righthander out of Oklahoma State, Williams was the Giants' seventh-round pick in 2016. Following a breakout first full season in 2017, Williams struggled mightily in 2018. After cracking a nail on his throwing hand late in spring training, Williams never fully recovered and walked nearly seven batters per nine innings while recording a 6.06 ERA in the Double-A Eastern League. **SCOUTING REPORT:** Pitching from a low, three-quarter arm slot, Williams' 90-94 mph fastball jumps on hitters as it nears the plate. He struggled with fastball command in 2018, which put him behind in the count often. His hard, low-80s power curveball is his best offspeed pitch, grading out above-average, but his third-pitch changeup is currently below-average. The key for Williams will be finding the strike zone. His control has long been below-average dating back to his days at Oklahoma State, and after improving in that area in 2017, Williams took a step back this past season. **THE FUTURE:** Williams will be a starter at Double-A Richmond in 2019, but he has serious reliever risk. He'll need to throw more strikes and refine his changeup to reach his ceiling of a mid-rotation starter.

Year	Club (League)	Class	W	L	ERA	G	GS	CG	SV	IP	H	HR	BB	SO	K/9	WHIP	AVG
2016	Giants (AZL)	R	1	0	2.57	3	1	0	0	7	4	0	3	5	6.4	1.00	.174
	Salem-Keizer (NWL)	SS	1	2	5.68	7	7	0	0	25	28	1	14	22	7.8	1.66	.275
2017	Augusta (SAL)	LoA	4	3	2.25	12	11	0	0	64	59	0	25	58	8.2	1.31	.234
	San Jose (CAL)	HiA	2	2	2.45	6	5	0	0	33	28	3	10	38	10.4	1.15	.221
2018	Richmond (EL)	AA	3	9	6.06	33	15	0	1	82	96	6	61	73	8.0	1.92	.294
Minor League Totals			11	16	4.18	61	39	0	1	211	215	10	113	196	8.4	1.55	.259

22 SAM COONROD, RHP

BA GRADE

45 Risk: High

Born: Sept. 22, 1992. **B-T:** R-R. **Ht.:** 6-2. **Wt.:** 190. **Drafted:** Southern Illinois, 2014 (5th round). **Signed by:** James Gabella.

TRACK RECORD: After showing tantalizing stuff as a three-year starter at Southern Illinois, Coonrod was the Giants' fifth-round pick in 2014. He pitched well until reaching Double-A in 2017, when he struggled and then needed Tommy John surgery late in the season. Coonrod returned less than 12 months later, making 10 combined appearances in the Arizona League and high Class A California League in 2018. **SCOUTING REPORT:** After working as a starter throughout college and the first four years of his pro career, the Giants decided to move Coonrod to the bullpen post-Tommy John. Described as having a reliever's mentality, Coonrod attacks hitters with an above-average, low- to mid-90s fastball and an above-average, mid- to upper-80s slider. With only average control and a high-effort delivery, Coonrod's two-pitch mix works best in shorter stints, and he's proven equally adept at getting both right and lefthanders out. **THE FUTURE:** Coonrod has been added to the Giants' 40-man roster, but he'll likely begin 2019 in the bullpen for Triple-A Sacramento. Coonrod has the ceiling of a setup man, but the much more likely scenario is a middle-relief, seventh inning-type role.

Year	Club (League)	Class	W	L	ERA	G	GS	CG	SV	IP	H	HR	BB	SO	K/9	WHIP	AVG
2016	San Jose (CAL)	HiA	5	3	1.98	11	11	0	0	64	46	3	22	42	5.9	1.07	.204
	Richmond (EL)	AA	4	3	3.03	13	13	0	0	77	59	7	38	52	6.1	1.25	.214
2017	Richmond (EL)	AA	4	11	4.69	24	18	0	0	104	96	7	42	94	8.2	1.33	.249
2018	Giants Black (AZL)	R	0	0	5.06	4	2	0	0	5	6	0	1	10	16.9	1.31	.261
	San Jose (CAL)	HiA	0	0	5.68	6	0	0	0	6	5	0	2	13	18.5	1.11	.200
Minor League Totals			21	22	3.46	96	71	0	0	396	347	20	145	350	8.0	1.24	.236

23 ABIATAL AVELINO, SS/2B

BA GRADE

40 Risk: Medium

Born: Feb. 14, 1995. **B-T:** R-R. **Ht.:** 5-11. **Wt.:** 195. **Signed:** Dominican Republic, 2011. **Signed by:** Jose Sabino (Yankees).

TRACK RECORD: Avelino signed with the Yankees for $300,000 in 2011, but the long-time New York prospect was traded to the Giants alongside righthander Juan De Paula in the August 2018 deal that sent Andrew McCutchen to the Yankees. Avelino made his major league debut shortly after, appearing in six September games for the Giants.

SCOUTING REPORT: Avelino is an average defensive shortstop with above-average arm strength and average range. He's long been considered a future utility infielder in the major leagues because of his below-average power and fringe-average hit tool, but he did show improved power with 15 home runs in 2018. Avelino is an above-average runner and could be an above-average defender at second base, but he's a career .270 hitter who lacks the typical power production teams are seeking from everyday regulars
THE FUTURE: Likely to begin the season with Triple-A Sacramento, Avelino will enter spring training with the chance to make the Giants' roster as a backup infielder in 2019.

Year	Club (League)	Class	AVG	G	AB	R	H	2B	3B	HR	RBI	BB	SO	SB	CS	OBP	SLG
2016	Tampa (FSL)	HiA	.266	93	357	54	95	17	2	6	34	29	63	20	13	.325	.375
	Trenton (EL)	AA	.244	33	127	15	31	11	0	0	14	10	19	1	2	.307	.331
2017	Tampa (FSL)	HiA	.219	9	32	1	7	1	0	0	2	2	5	4	0	.265	.250
	Scranton/W-B (IL)	AAA	.213	20	61	5	13	1	1	0	6	5	10	3	1	.284	.262
	Trenton (EL)	AA	.270	69	230	35	62	12	4	3	28	14	33	4	0	.315	.396
2018	Trenton (EL)	AA	.337	49	190	32	64	7	2	10	28	18	37	15	4	.392	.553
	Scranton/W-B (IL)	AAA	.252	74	274	33	69	6	6	5	38	14	61	10	2	.291	.372
	Sacramento (PCL)	AAA	.154	3	13	2	2	0	0	0	1	0	3	2	0	.154	.154
	San Francisco (NL)	MAJ	.273	6	11	1	3	0	0	0	0	0	3	0	0	.273	.273
Major League Totals			.273	6	11	1	3	0	0	0	0	0	3	0	0	.273	.273
Minor League Totals			.270	642	2443	386	659	113	24	31	241	195	409	172	51	.330	.374

24 RYAN HOWARD, SS

BA GRADE
40 Risk: Medium

Born: July 25, 1994. **B-T:** R-R. **Ht.:** 6-2. **Wt.:** 195. **Drafted:** Missouri, 2016 (5th round). **Signed by:** Daniel Murray.
TRACK RECORD: A starting college shortstop in the Southeastern Conference, Howard was drafted in the 31st round as a draft-eligible sophomore in 2015 but chose to return to Missouri for his junior season. One year later, he raised his stock enough for the Giants to draft him with a fifth-round pick.
SCOUTING REPORT: Much like fellow Giants' infielder Abiatal Avelino, Howard is capable defender whose below-average power likely pushes him into a utility role in the future. Howard is an average hitter—he's improved his walk rate and decreased his strikeout rate over the past two seasons—but unlike Avelino, Howard isn't capable of playing an everyday shortstop in the majors. A below-average runner with limited range, Howard is an above-average second or third baseman with an average arm.
THE FUTURE: Howard is slated for Triple-A Sacramento in 2019. He's behind Avelino in the race to be the Giants' next utility infielder, but most evaluators believe Howard will be in the big leagues soon.

Year	Club (League)	Class	AVG	G	AB	R	H	2B	3B	HR	RBI	BB	SO	SB	CS	OBP	SLG
2016	Giants (AZL)	R	.250	2	8	1	2	0	0	0	0	2	0	0	0	.400	.250
	Salem-Keizer (NWL)	SS	.272	59	224	33	61	10	0	4	31	13	24	2	2	.313	.371
2017	San Jose (CAL)	HiA	.306	127	526	59	161	21	0	9	50	23	81	7	2	.342	.397
2018	Richmond (EL)	AA	.273	117	422	44	115	32	4	4	50	39	55	9	5	.336	.396
Minor League Totals			.287	305	1180	137	339	63	4	17	131	77	160	18	9	.335	.391

25 CONNER MENEZ, LHP

BA GRADE
45 Risk: High

Born: May, 29, 1995. **B-T:** L-L. **Ht.:** 6-3. **Wt.:** 205. **Signed:** The Master's (Calif.), 2016 (14th round). **Signed by:** Chuck Fick.
TRACK RECORD: The Giants' 14th-round pick in 2016, Menez had a career-best year in 2018. The majority of his work came for Double-A Richmond, where he struck out 92 batters in 74 innings.
SCOUTING REPORT: Menez throws from a low, three-quarter arm slot with an above-average fastball that sits 90-95 mph. He gets excellent extension from the mound, allowing his fastball to get on hitters faster than the radar readings may suggest. Menez has a true four-pitch mix with a curveball, slider and changeup, although none consistently grades out better than average. His slider can flash plus at times with good tilt. Menez showed below-average control in 2018, walking more than four batters per nine innings.
THE FUTURE: Although the Giants have stuck with Menez as a starter, he may be best suited for a relief role in the future. He's scheduled for Triple-A Sacramento in 2019.

Year	Club (League)	Class	W	L	ERA	G	GS	CG	SV	IP	H	HR	BB	SO	K/9	WHIP	AVG
2016	Giants (AZL)	R	2	0	2.57	8	2	0	0	21	15	0	4	26	11.1	0.90	.190
	Salem-Keizer (NWL)	SS	0	1	7.20	1	1	0	0	5	5	0	1	4	7.2	1.20	.278
	San Jose (CAL)	HiA	2	0	4.94	6	5	0	0	27	29	4	11	20	6.6	1.46	.266
2017	San Jose (CAL)	HiA	7	7	4.41	23	22	0	0	114	127	5	50	99	7.8	1.55	.282
2018	Sacramento (PCL)	AAA	1	1	3.27	2	2	0	0	11	6	0	5	9	7.4	1.00	.162
	San Jose (CAL)	HiA	2	5	4.83	11	11	0	0	50	48	2	21	70	12.5	1.37	.250
	Richmond (EL)	AA	6	4	4.38	15	15	0	0	74	73	1	34	92	11.2	1.45	.261
Minor League Totals			20	18	4.40	66	58	0	0	303	303	12	126	320	9.5	1.42	.260

26 SANDRO FABIAN, OF

BA GRADE

45 Risk: Very High

Born: March 6, 1998. **B-T:** R-R. **Ht.:** 6-1. **Wt.:** 180. **Signed:** Dominican Republic, 2014. **Signed by:** Pablo Peguero/Felix Peguero/Jonathan Bautista.

TRACK RECORD: A $500,000 signing out of the Dominican Republic in 2014, Fabian, 20, was one of the youngest players in the high Class A California League in 2018. The Giants have aggressively pushed Fabian ever since he joined the organization, but this past season the athletic outfielder struggled mightily.
SCOUTING REPORT: Fabian projects best as a plus defensive right fielder with a plus, accurate arm. His power has improved over the last couple of seasons, and he hit 10 home runs despite being mostly overmatched in the California League. His power should settle in as average in the future. The biggest concern with Fabian this season was his overly aggressive approach that resulted in a career-worst 24 percent strikeout rate. Fabian has shown below-average plate discipline in the past and has never drawn many walks, and those weaknesses were exposed when he was challenged in high Class A. With a more mature approach, Fabian could be an average hitter with time. He's an average runner who has never stolen more than five bases in a season.
THE FUTURE: Fabian will return to the California League in 2019. He'll need to make more contact to reach his ceiling of a plus defensive right fielder with a hit-over-power profile.

Year	Club (League)	Class	AVG	G	AB	R	H	2B	3B	HR	RBI	BB	SO	SB	CS	OBP	SLG
2016	Giants (AZL)	R	.340	42	159	30	54	13	5	2	35	7	28	3	1	.364	.522
2017	Augusta (SAL)	LoA	.277	122	480	51	133	30	0	11	61	10	88	5	4	.297	.408
2018	San Jose (CAL)	HiA	.200	112	406	47	81	19	1	10	35	26	107	1	2	.260	.325
Minor League Totals			.259	341	1287	175	333	72	8	26	168	58	270	11	7	.304	.388

27 JACOB GONZALEZ, 3B

BA GRADE

45 Risk: Very High

Born: June 26, 1998. **B-T:** R-R. **Ht.:** 6-3. **Wt.:** 190. **Drafted:** HS—Scottsdale, Ariz., 2017 (2nd round). **Signed by:** Chuck Hensley.

TRACK RECORD: The son of five-time All-Star Luis Gonzalez, Jacob was well-known in the baseball community before the Giants drafted him with the 58th overall pick in 2017. After a strong pro debut in the Arizona League in 2017, Gonzalez skipped short-season ball and spent his first full season with low Class A Augusta. The jump proved challenging, as he struggled to get on base and tap into his plus raw power.
SCOUTING REPORT: Gonzalez was playing OK for Augusta during the first half of the season before posting an OPS just barely over .450 in August and September. The 6-foot-3 righthanded hitter struggled to get the ball in the air and as a result hit into way too many groundouts. Gonzalez is just an average third baseman with limited range. He has above-average arm strength, but the accuracy isn't consistent, so the Giants are banking on his bat improving. Gonzalez has plus raw power and is a bigger and more physical hitter than his father, who hit more than 350 career home runs in the majors.
THE FUTURE: Gonzalez is yet another Giants prospect who should be slated for high Class A San Jose in 2019, joining the likes of Joey Bart, Heliot Ramos and others. That's no guarantee, however, as his late-season slump could push him back to low Class A Augusta, where he was largely overmatched.

Year	Club (League)	Class	AVG	G	AB	R	H	2B	3B	HR	RBI	BB	SO	SB	CS	OBP	SLG
2017	Giants (AZL)	R	.339	46	168	23	57	15	1	1	21	16	23	0	1	.418	.458
2018	Augusta (SAL)	LoA	.227	122	459	54	104	20	2	8	45	31	107	7	5	.296	.331
Minor League Totals			.257	168	627	77	161	35	3	9	66	47	130	7	6	.330	.365

28 TYLER BEEDE, RHP

BA GRADE

45 Risk: Very High

Born: May 23, 1993. **B-T:** R-R. **Ht.:** 6-3. **Wt.:** 210. **Drafted:** Vanderbilt, 2014 (1st round). **Signed by:** Andrew Jefferson.

TRACK RECORD: A standout, three-year performer at Vanderbilt, Beede was the Giants' first-round pick in 2014. He seemed poised to grab a spot in San Francisco's rotation in 2017, but disappointed in his first taste of Triple-A. Beede struggled through his first two major league starts in April, and his numbers worsened when he was sent back to Triple-A before moving to the bullpen for the last three months of 2018.
SCOUTING REPORT: Beede is at a crossroads in his career, with questions as to whether he is a starter or reliever. Out of the bullpen, Beede shows flashes of plus stuff with a fastball up to 97 mph. His three off-speed offerings—a cutter, curveball and changeup—lack consistency and vary in grades depending on the appearance, but his hard breaking ball and late-fading changeup flash above-average potential most often. While his pitch mix suggests Beede could remain a starter, his below-average control hurts those chances. Beede, who has struggled with his control since his time at Vanderbilt, walked more than six batters per nine innings in 2018. He has a career 5.81 ERA in 190.2 combined innings at Triple-A and in the majors.

THE FUTURE: The Giants don't seem fully committed to moving Beede to the bullpen quite yet, and he could get one last chance as a starter in Triple-A. If he remains ineffective early in 2019, Beede could make it back to San Francisco as a reliever. His stuff should play up in shorter stints, but he'll only be effective if he stays around the strike zone with more regularity than he has in the past.

Year	Club (League)	Class	W	L	ERA	G	GS	CG	SV	IP	H	HR	BB	SO	K/9	WHIP	AVG
2016	Richmond (EL)	AA	8	7	2.81	24	24	1	0	147	136	9	53	135	8.2	1.28	.248
2017	Sacramento (PCL)	AAA	6	7	4.79	19	19	0	0	109	121	14	39	83	6.9	1.47	.282
2018	San Jose (CAL)	HiA	0	0	1.80	1	1	0	0	5	1	0	3	4	7.2	0.80	.067
	San Francisco (NL)	MAJ	0	1	8.22	2	2	0	0	8	9	0	8	9	10.6	2.22	.290
	Giants Orange (AZL)	R	0	0	0.00	1	0	0	0	1	0	0	0	2	18.0	0.00	.000
	Sacramento (PCL)	AAA	4	9	7.05	33	10	0	0	74	82	10	56	75	9.1	1.86	.288
Major League Totals			0	1	8.22	2	2	0	0	8	9	0	8	9	10.6	2.22	.290
Minor League Totals			23	34	4.21	106	82	1	0	476	469	39	202	403	7.6	1.41	.260

29 BLAKE RIVERA, RHP

BA GRADE

45 Risk: Very High

Born: Jan. 9, 1998. **B-T:** R-R. **Ht.:** 6-4. **Wt.:** 225. **Drafted:** Wallace State (Ala.) JC, 2018 (4th round). **Signed by:** Jeff Wood.

TRACK RECORD: After his freshman season at Wallace State (Ala.) JC, Rivera was drafted by the Giants in the 32nd round in 2017. Instead of signing, he chose to return to Wallace State for his sophomore season, when he posted a 10-0, 1.75 record with 98 strikeouts in 67 innings. The Giants were so impressed they selected Rivera again, this time making him their fourth-round pick a year later. Rivera draws the unfair comparison to current major league closer Craig Kimbrel, who also returned to Wallace State for his sophomore season and went from a 33rd-rounder in 2007 to a third-round pick in 2008.

SCOUTING REPORT: Rivera made eight starts in nine appearances in his pro debut, although there are split opinions over whether Rivera will be a starter or reliever in the future. Rivera has an above-average, 93-96 mph fastball and a power curveball that has the chance to be a plus, swing-and-miss pitch. His curveball remains inconsistent, however, and his control was below-average in his brief pro debut. Because of these flaws, it seems Rivera will eventually be best used in a high-leverage relief role, where his strikeout potential with two above-average or better pitches will excel.

THE FUTURE: Rivera will begin 2019 in low Class A Augusta's starting rotation. Depending on his results, Rivera could eventually transition into a fast-rising, late-inning reliever.

Year	Club (League)	Class	W	L	ERA	G	GS	CG	SV	IP	H	HR	BB	SO	K/9	WHIP	AVG
2018	Salem-Keizer (NWL)	SS	0	0	6.16	9	8	0	0	19	20	2	11	14	6.6	1.63	.263
Minor League Totals			0	0	6.16	9	8	0	0	19	20	2	11	14	6.6	1.63	.263

30 JALEN MILLER, 2B

BA GRADE

40 Risk: High

Born: Dec. 19, 1996. **B-T:** R-R. **Ht.:** 5-11. **Wt.:** 190. **Drafted:** HS—Sandy Springs, Ga., 2015 (3rd round). **Signed by:** Andrew Jefferson.

TRACK REPORT: A third-round pick out of Sandy Springs, Ga., Miller was considered one of the best all-around high school shortstops in the 2015 draft. Miller has played mostly second base since joining the Giants' organization, however. He struggled during his first three years but was much improved while playing for high Class A San Jose in 2018.

SCOUTING REPORT: After aggressively pushing Miller in his first two full seasons in the minors, the Giants allowed Miller to repeat high Class A in 2018, when he was still just 21 years old. The move paid off, as Miller got on-base at a higher clip and showed improved power with the ability to impact the baseball more often. Miller will never draw many walks, and he still chases too many pitches outside of the strike zone, but he has the potential to be an average hitter with fringe-average power. Defensively, Miller is an above-average second baseman with the ability to play shortstop in a backup role. He has a fringe-average arm, but he's a plus runner and shows solid range in the field with the ability to steal bases, as well.

THE FUTURE: Lauded for his makeup and work ethic, Miller will be tested at Double-A Richmond in 2019. If he's able to produce like he did in 2018, then there's still hope he could be an everyday second baseman in the majors. If he struggles to hit the more advanced pitching, then Miller's future could come as backup or utility infielder.

Year	Club (League)	Class	AVG	G	AB	R	H	2B	3B	HR	RBI	BB	SO	SB	CS	OBP	SLG
2016	Augusta (SAL)	LoA	.223	112	457	65	102	20	5	5	44	26	107	11	5	.271	.322
2017	San Jose (CAL)	HiA	.227	117	431	61	98	25	4	6	44	31	100	6	4	.283	.346
2018	San Jose (CAL)	HiA	.276	123	511	73	141	35	2	14	62	27	121	11	4	.321	.434
Minor League Totals			.241	396	1573	227	379	85	12	25	163	101	370	39	15	.293	.358

Seattle Mariners

BY BILL MITCHELL

The story of the 2018 Mariners can be summarized with one line, just like in many of their recent seasons—they were good, but just not good enough.

For the first half of 2018 it looked like all the preseason and in-season moves made by general manager Jerry Dipoto were paying off. They had one of the best records (53-31) in the American League just past the midway point. The Mariners won 19 of 28 games in June and were not far behind the Astros for first place in the AL West. But the wheels fell off in the second half when the offense disappeared. Seattle went 36-43 for the last three months and finished 89-73.

Thus the longest playoff drought in baseball continued. The Mariners haven't reached the postseason since winning 116 games in 2001.

Despite a subpar year from Felix Hernandez, Seattle's pitching staff carried the team. James Paxton put up another strong year, and the Mariners received surprising performances from Marco Gonzales and journeyman Wade Leblanc. The bullpen was especially strong, with closer Edwin Diaz recording a major league best 57 saves.

The loss of Robinson Cano to a PED suspension for half the season hurt the offense, though the in-season acquisition of Denard Span and the versatility of Dee Gordon helped lessen the blow. Ageless slugger Nelson Cruz continued to pace the offense, receiving help from all-star outfielder Mitch Haniger, but down seasons from third baseman Kyle Seager and first baseman Ryon Healy were too much to overcome.

While helping to reinforce the big league team, the frequent trades made by Dipoto continued to weaken an already barren farm system. Thus the Mariners received no meaningful contributions from rookies in 2018.

In light of the club's poor finish and with Cruz headed for free agency—not to mention the apparent strength of the division-rival Astros, Athletics and Angels—the Mariners shifted their focus from trying to win in 2019 to trying to win in the future. Dipoto kick-started the rebuild by consummating five trades before the Winter Meetings.

As the Mariners re-imagined their roster, they focused on near major league-ready talent. Dipoto's rapid succession of trades sent catcher Mike Zunino to the Rays, Paxton to the Yankees, Cano and Diaz to the Mets and shortstop Jean Segura to the Phillies.

In addition to reducing the Mariners' projected 2019 payroll by more than $35 million, the flurry of trades netted Seattle seven Top 30 Prospects, including No. 1 Justus Sheffield, No. 2 Jarred

The Mariners' trade of ace James Paxon helped kick off the club's major offseason rebuild.

STEPHEN BRASHEAR/GETTY IMAGES

PROJECTED 2022 LINEUP

Catcher	Omar Narvaez (30)
First Base	Evan White (26)
Second Base	Dee Gordon (34)
Third Base	Kyle Seager (34)
Shortstop	J.P. Crawford (27)
Left Field	Jarred Kelenic (22)
Center Field	Mallex Smith (29)
Right Field	Mitch Haniger (31)
Designated Hitter	Kyle Lewis (26)
No. 1 Starter	Justus Sheffield (26)
No. 2 Starter	Justin Dunn (26)
No. 3 Starter	Logan Gilbert (25)
No. 4 Starter	Marco Gonzales (30)
No. 5 Starter	Erik Swanson (28)
Closer	Wyatt Mills (27)

Kelenic and No. 5 Justin Dunn. The Mariners also acquired 25-year-old center fielder Mallex Smith and 24-year-old shortstop J.P. Crawford, who entered 2018 as the No. 16 prospect in baseball before exhausting his rookie eligibility.

Those additions bolstered a system that was steadily improving. First baseman Evan White made swing adjustments to add more power. Outfielder Kyle Lewis continued to make progress in his return from a serious knee injury suffered in his 2016 pro debut. Touted international signees Julio Rodriguez and Noelvi Marte showed plenty of promise in their pro debuts, while a strong 2018 draft, headed by Stetson righthander Logan Gilbert, brought in more talent.

DEPTH CHART

SEATTLE MARINERS

TOP 2019 ROOKIE: Justus Sheffield, LHP. He got a taste of the big leagues with the Yankees in 2018 and is certain to get plenty of time with the Mariners in 2019.

BREAKOUT PROSPECT: Wyatt Mills, RHP. He struggled in his first attempt at Double-A late in 2018 but saw his fastball velocity bump up in the fall.

SOURCE OF TOP 30 TALENT			
Homegrown	18	Acquired	12
College	12	Trade	12
Junior college	0	Rule 5 draft	0
High school	2	Independent league	0
Nondrafted free agent	0	Free agent/waivers	0
International	4		

SLEEPER: Keegan McGovern, OF. The Georgia product mashed in his pro debut spent mostly in low Class A and could continue to boost his stock with a strong season at high Class A Modesto.

LF
Keegan McGovern
Eric Filia

CF
Jarred Kelenic (2)
Josh Stowers (9)
Braden Bishop (12)
Jake Fraley (14)
Dom Thompson-Williams (17)
Luis Liberato
Ian Miller

RF
Julio Rodriguez (4)
Kyle Lewis (7)
Nick Zammarelli

3B
Joe Rizzo (22)
Dylan Moore

SS
Noelvi Marte (8)
Juan Querecuto (19)
Cesar Izturis Jr.

2B
Donnie Walton (26)
Joseph Rosa
Chris Mariscal

1B
Evan White (3)
Dan Vogelbach (16)
Joey Curletta (21)

C
Cal Raleigh (10)
Jake Anchia
Joe DeCarlo

LHP	
LHSP	**LHRP**
Justus Sheffield (1)	Matt Tenuta
Brayan Perez (20)	Spencer Herrmann
Anthony Misiewicz (25)	Rigo Beltran Jr.
Ricardo Sanchez	
Holden Laws	
Jorge Benitez	
Max Roberts	
Oliver Jaskie	

RHP	
RHSP	**RHRP**
Justin Dunn (4)	Matt Festa (15)
Logan Gilbert (6)	Wyatt Mills (18)
Erik Swanson (11)	Nolan Hoffman (23)
Sam Carlson (13)	Joey Gerber (24)
Max Povse (30)	Art Warren (27)
Damon Casetta-Stubbs	Gerson Bautista (28)
Darren McCaughan	David McKay (29)
Ljay Newsome	Brandon Brennan
Tyler Suellentrop	Ruben Alaniz
	Matt Walker
	JT Salter
	Joey O'Brien

DRAFT ANALYSIS

2018

BEST PURE HITTER: OF Josh Stowers (2) and C Cal Raleigh (3) are both above-average hitters with solid plate discipline. Both this spring walked more than they struck out and impressed this summer.

BEST POWER HITTER: C Jake Anchia (7) broke the career home run record at Nova Southeastern (Fla.), J.D. Martinez's alma mater, and his well above-average raw power may already rank as the best in the Mariners' system. Stowers and Raleigh both also provide solid power, and Raleigh hit eight home runs in just 38 games with short-season Everett.

FASTEST RUNNER: Stowers has plus speed and ranks among the fastest players in the Mariners' system. He makes that speed play on the bases and he stole 20 bases in 58 games with Everett in 2018.

BEST DEFENSIVE PLAYER: SS Ryan Ogren (12) developed a strong defensive reputation at Elon and has the pure tools to stick at shortstop, if he hits enough to be a regular.

BEST FASTBALL: RHP Logan Gilbert (1) last summer in the Cape Cod League ran his fastball up to 97 mph and gets elite extension with his loose, simple delivery, helping his stuff play up. He this spring was more typically throwing in the low 90s, but he also likely pitched with mononucleosis for much of the spring before it was diagnosed after the draft.

BEST SECONDARY: RHP Joey Gerber (8) gets plus grades on his slider that plays well out of the bullpen. Gilbert this spring led the nation with 163 strikeouts in 112.1 innings in part thanks to his breaking ball.

BEST PRO DEBUT: OF Keegan McGovern (9) earned All-America honors as a senior with Georgia in 2018 and then carried that momentum into pro ball. The Mariners challenged him with an assignment to low Class A Clinton, and he hit .268/.351/.523 with 15 home runs.

BEST ATHLETE: McGovern, who was also a football standout in high school, and Stowers both impress with their athleticism. OF Charlie

TOP DRAFT PICKS OF THE DECADE

Year	Player, Pos.	2018 Org
2009	Dustin Ackley, OF	Angels
2010	Taijuan Walker, RHP (1st round supp)	D-backs
2011	Danny Hultzen, LHP	Cubs
2012	Mike Zunino, C	Mariners
2013	D.J. Peterson, 3B	Reds
2014	Alex Jackson, OF	Braves
2015	Nick Neidert, RHP (2nd round)	Marlins
2016	Kyle Lewis, OF	Mariners
2017	Evan White, 1B	Mariners
2018	Logan Gilbert, RHP	Mariners

McConnell (13) also played hockey in high school and is a plus runner.

MOST INTRIGUING BACKGROUND: RHP Joey O'Brien (6) is the son of a Marine and was born in Japan. in 2017, he moved to the U.S. to pitch at JC of Southern Nevada, where he was a standout two-way player. His brother, Richard, was selected in the NPB draft in 2017.

CLOSEST TO THE MAJORS: Though Gilbert has yet to make his professional debut due to his illness, it would not come as a surprise if he is the first player from this class to reach the major leagues. McGovern's fast professional start has also put him on an accelerated track.

BEST LATE-ROUND PICK: Though the Mariners loaded up on college players (32 of the 34 players they signed went to two- or four-year colleges in 2018), they also landed a couple intriguing prep players. RHP Damon Casetta-Stubbs (11) and LHP Holden Laws (16) fit a similar profile as projectable pitchers who already have good strike-throwing ability.

THE ONE WHO GOT AWAY: The Mariners signed their first 34 picks before the streak ended with RHP Will Gambino (35). Gambino and LHP Justin Wrobleski (36) are both athletic, promising pitchers with fastballs that reach the mid-90s already. Gambino is now at Kentucky, while Wrobleski has two-way potential at Clemson.

—**TEDDY CAHILL**

2017

1B Evan White (1) has become the system's top home-grown prospect. RHP Sam Carlson (2) missed 2018 after having Tommy John surgery. College RHPs Wyatt Mills (3) and Seth Elledge (4) are sprinting through the minors.

GRADE: C

2016

OF Kyle Lewis (1) has struggled to stay healthy in pro ball, but did reach Double-A in 2018, while RHP Matt Festa (7) made his big league debut. RHP Robert Dugger (18), traded to Miami, has shown promise at Double-A.

GRADE: C

2015

RHP Nick Neidert (2) was in 2017 traded as part of the Dee Gordon deal and had a solid year in Double-A. RHP Andrew Moore (2s) reached the big leagues in 2017 but didn't return in 2018 and was traded to the Rays.

GRADE: D

1 JUSTUS SHEFFIELD, LHP

Born: May 13, 1996. **B-T:** L-L. **HT:** 6-0. **WT:** 200.
Drafted: HS—Tullahoma, Tenn., 2014 (1st round).
Signed by: Chuck Bartlett (Indians).

Sheffield ranked as the Yankees' top prospect heading into the 2018 offseason before being the key acquisition in the trade to the Mariners for ace James Paxton. Sheffield signed with the Indians out of high school as a first-round pick and was traded to the Yankees with Clint Frazier in 2016 to help the Indians acquire reliever Andrew Miller. Sheffield missed time in 2017 with an oblique issue and missed one start in 2018 with tightness in his left shoulder. The Yankees moved him to the bullpen in August to prepare him for a bullpen role in New York in September. He struggled to throw strikes in three late-season outings in New York.

SCOUTING REPORT: Sheffield is a starter who attacks hitters like a late-inning reliever. Everything he throws is hard and he shows little finesse. He attacks hitters with an effort-filled delivery. A generation ago, that would likely lead to a move to the bullpen, but today Sheffield will get to prove that his all-out approach can work for five to six innings per start. After much debate, the Yankees sent Sheffield back to Double-A Trenton to begin the 2018 season so he could continue to sharpen the command of his mid-90s fastball. He worked to add two-plane break to his mid-80s slider. He was successful at times in this regard, with the pitch showing more depth in particular during his stint in the big leagues. Now, he'll need to work to repeat the mechanics that allowed him to make this alteration. His 87-89 mph changeup had been too firm for the Yankees' taste, and they wanted to see him figure out a grip that would allow him to get more separation between it and his fastball. The Yankees said that in spurts he showed the ability to dial back his offspeed pitches, but sometimes, especially when he moved to the bullpen, adrenaline took over and he reverted back to throwing everything as hard as possible. Expect to see better results now that his major league debut is behind him.

THE FUTURE: Sheffield will likely return to Triple-A in 2019, but this time across the country in Tacoma. He should be making big league starts for the Mariners at some point in 2019.

MIKE JANES/FOUR SEAM

BA GRADE	SCOUTING GRADES
60 Risk: Medium	Fastball: 60. Changeup: 55. Slider: 55. Control: 50.

Projected future grades on 20-80 scouting scale.

TOP PROSPECTS OF THE DECADE

Year	Player, Pos	2018 Org
2009	Greg Halman, OF	Deceased
2010	Dustin Ackley, OF	Angels
2011	Dustin Ackley, 2B	Angels
2012	Taijuan Walker, RHP	D-backs
2013	Mike Zunino, C	Mariners
2014	Taijuan Walker, RHP	D-backs
2015	Alex Jackson, OF	Braves
2016	Alex Jackson, OF	Braves
2017	Kyle Lewis, OF	Mariners
2018	Kyle Lewis, OF	Mariners

BEST TOOLS

Best Hitter for Average	Jarred Kelenic
Best Power Hitter	Joey Curletta
Best Strike-Zone Discipline	Eric Filia
Fastest Baserunner	Ian Miller
Best Athlete	Kyle Lewis
Best Fastball	Gerson Bautista
Best Curveball	Anthony Misiewicz
Best Slider	Justus Sheffield
Best Changeup	Oliver Jaskie
Best Control	Darren McCaughan
Best Defensive Catcher	Cal Raleigh
Best Defensive Infielder	Evan White
Best Infield Arm	Juan Querecuto
Best Defensive Outfielder	Braden Bishop
Best Outfield Arm	Julio Rodriguez

Year	Club (League)	Class	W	L	ERA	G	GS	CG	SV	IP	H	HR	BB	SO	K/9	WHIP	AVG
2016	Lynchburg (CAR)	HiA	7	5	3.59	19	19	0	0	95	91	6	40	93	8.8	1.37	.252
	Tampa (FSL)	HiA	3	1	1.73	5	5	0	0	26	14	0	10	27	9.3	0.92	.157
	Trenton (EL)	AA	0	0	0.00	1	1	0	0	4	2	0	3	9	20.3	1.25	.125
2017	Yankees2 (GCL)	R	0	1	1.93	2	2	0	0	5	4	0	1	6	11.6	1.07	.235
	Trenton (EL)	AA	7	6	3.18	17	17	1	0	93	94	14	33	82	7.9	1.36	.258
2018	Trenton (EL)	AA	1	2	2.25	5	5	0	0	28	16	1	14	39	12.5	1.07	.163
	Scranton/W-B (IL)	AAA	6	4	2.56	20	15	0	0	88	66	3	36	84	8.6	1.16	.204
	New York (AL)	MAJ	0	0	10.13	3	0	0	0	3	4	1	3	0	0.0	2.63	.364
Major League Totals			0	0	10.13	3	0	0	0	3	4	1	3	0	0.0	2.63	.364
Minor League Totals			36	24	3.08	103	94	1	0	488	446	32	184	507	9.4	1.29	.239

2 JARRED KELENIC, OF

Born: July 16, 1999. **B-T:** L-L. **HT:** 6-1. **WT:** 196. **Drafted:** HS—Waukesha, Wis., 2018 (1st). **Signed by:** Chris Hervey (Mets).

TRACK RECORD: Kelenic won a pair of gold medals for USA Baseball's 18U National Team, then graduated early from his Wisconsin high school to train for the 2018 draft. His pedigree and dedication paid off when the Mets drafted him sixth overall as the first prep player off the board and signed him for a franchise-record $4.5 million bonus. After one summer in the Mets organization, Kelenic was the jewel of the prospect haul for the Mariners in the trade that sent Robinson Cano and Edwin Diaz to New York.

SCOUTING REPORT: Kelenic immediately became the Mariners' best position prospect after the trade and could develop into a center fielder with five average or better tools. He has a long track record with wood bats and a simple, quick lefthanded swing honed by countless hours in the batting cage. His feel for the barrel gives him a plus hit tool, while his strong batting eye makes him an on-base threat who will bat toward the top of a lineup. Kelenic's raw power is at least plus and as he tweaks his approach and launch angle he should get to above-average pop in games. Projected as an average runner, his raw speed might be a bit short of the center field prototype, but he has the instincts to stick there as a solid-average defender. An above-average arm could make him a plus defender on a corner

THE FUTURE: Kelenic turned 19 in July after the draft and was old for his high school class, but that should help ease his transition to low Class A West Virginia in 2019.

BA GRADE

60 Risk: Very High

Hit: 60. Power: 55. Run: 50. Field: 50. Arm: 55.

ROBERT GURGANUS/FOUR SEAM

Year	Club (League)	Class	AVG	G	AB	R	H	2B	3B	HR	RBI	BB	SO	SB	CS	OBP	SLG
2018	Mets (GCL)	R	.413	12	46	9	19	2	2	1	9	4	11	4	0	.451	.609
	Kingsport (APP)	R	.253	44	174	33	44	8	4	5	33	22	39	11	1	.350	.431
Minor League Totals			.286	56	220	42	63	10	6	6	42	26	50	15	1	.371	.468

3 EVAN WHITE, 1B

Born: April 26, 1996. **B-T:** R-L. **HT:** 6-3. **WT:** 205. **Drafted:** Kentucky, 2017 (1st round). **Signed by:** Jackson Laumann.

TRACK RECORD: White comes by his athleticism naturally. Both his father and grandfather played in the minor leagues, and his parents were both college basketball players. Undrafted out of his Ohio high school, he earned second team All-America honors as a Kentucky junior in 2017. A career .356 hitter for the Wildcats, he also played with USA Baseball's Collegiate National Team in the summer before his junior year. The 17th overall pick in 2017, White began his pro career at short-season Everett, though his season was curtailed by a quad injury. He got in a full season in 2018, mostly at high Class A Modesto followed by six weeks in the Arizona Fall League.

SCOUTING REPORT: White's footwork around the first base bag is so graceful that his movements there have been called ballet-like. He earns plus-plus grades for his defense. He has very good instincts and soft hands. A plus hitter with advanced skills and a plan at the plate, White is a hit-over-power type who uses all fields and makes hard contact. Questions have been raised as to whether he will hit for enough power to profile as a starting first baseman, though his above-average raw power and good exit velocities hint at a chance to exceed his average power projections. White started answering doubts about his power in the second half of 2018 by lowering his hands, keeping his bat in the hitting zone longer and staying through the ball. The results showed when he hit five of his 11 Cal League home runs in August. He has a good swing and finds the barrel a lot, and he studies opposing pitchers' tendencies.

THE FUTURE: While he doesn't have the same power profile, White has been compared with the Dodgers' Cody Bellinger as a first baseman who could also play center field. First base is a position of need for the Mariners, so White could advance quickly. He'll advance to Double-A Arkansas in 2019 and could see time at Triple-A.

BA GRADE

55 Risk: High

Hit: 55. Power: 50. Run: 60. Field: 70. Arm: 55.

JOSE CARLOS MAGANA

Year	Club (League)	Class	AVG	G	AB	R	H	2B	3B	HR	RBI	BB	SO	SB	CS	OBP	SLG
2017	Everett (NWL)	SS	.277	14	47	6	13	1	1	3	12	6	6	1	1	.345	.532
2018	Tacoma (PCL)	AAA	.222	4	18	0	4	2	0	0	0	0	5	0	0	.222	.333
	Modesto (CAL)	HiA	.303	120	476	72	144	27	7	11	66	52	103	4	3	.375	.458
Minor League Totals			.298	138	541	78	161	30	8	14	78	58	114	5	4	.368	.460

4 JULIO RODRIGUEZ, OF

BILL MITCHELL

Born: Dec. 29, 2000. **B-T:** R-R. **HT:** 6-3. **WT:** 180. **Signed:** Dominican Republic, 2017. **Signed by:** Eddy Toledo/Tim Kissner

TRACK RECORD: Rodriguez dominated the Dominican Summer League just one year after signing with the Mariners for $1.75 million. Named the team MVP after posting a .929 OPS, Rodriguez's season ended in mid-August when he injured a foot attempting to steal a base, but he was able to participate in the Mariners' fall development programs.

SCOUTING REPORT: A smart hitter for his age with very good control of the zone and the ability make adjustments at the plate, Rodriguez's loudest tool is his plus-plus raw power, which already ranks among the best in the organization. His rhythmic righthanded swing gives him a solid bat path through the zone. While only an average runner, he runs the bases well. Rodriguez should develop solid instincts and routes in right field, where he should be at least an average defender. He gained enough arm strength since signing that his arm now earns a 70 grade.

BA GRADE
60 Risk: Extreme
Hit: 55. **Power:** 60.
Run: 45. **Field:** 50.
Arm: 70.

THE FUTURE: Rodriguez has as much upside as any prospect in the Mariners' organization. His advanced baseball acumen and tool set may allow him to start his U.S. career at short-season Everett or perhaps even low Class A West Virginia. It would not be a surprise to see Rodriguez at the top of the Mariners' prospect list heading into 2020.

Year	Club (League)	Class	AVG	G	AB	R	H	2B	3B	HR	RBI	BB	SO	SB	CS	OBP	SLG
2018	Mariners (DSL)	R	.315	59	219	50	69	13	9	5	36	30	40	10	0	.404	.525
Minor League Totals			.315	59	219	50	69	13	9	5	36	30	40	10	0	.404	.525

5 JUSTIN DUNN, RHP

Born: Sept. 22, 1995. **B-T:** R-R. **HT:** 6-2. **WT:** 185. **Drafted:** Boston College, 2016 (1st). **Signed by:** Michael Pesce (Mets).

TRACK RECORD: Dunn spent most of his time in college in the bullpen, and then scuffled in his full-season debut in the high Class A Florida State League. But after he made 24 starts while taming the FSL and reaching Double-A in 2018, his future appears firmly planted in the rotation. Based on that development, the Mariners acquired Dunn in December as one of the top prospects in the deal that sent Robinson Cano and Edwin Diaz to the Mets.

SCOUTING REPORT: Dunn evolved from thrower to pitcher in 2018 by working his fastball to both sides of the plate and up and down in the zone at 93-95 mph from an effortless delivery. He can sink his fastball for early-count groundball outs or throw it with riding life up in the zone for swinging strikes. Dunn's slider is his go-to secondary weapon, and it flashes plus with two-plane break to neutralize righthanded hitters. He committed to throwing his changeup in 2018 and made huge strides. The mid-80s pitch fades to his

BA GRADE
55 Risk: High
Fastball: 60.
Slider: 60.
Change: 50. **CTL:** 50.

arm side and bottoms out as it approaches the plate, erasing the ugly platoon split he had in 2017. His athletic motion allows him to throw first-pitch strikes and grants him access to future average control.

THE FUTURE: Dunn is positioned to assume any role the Mariners need in the second half of 2019, be it multi-inning reliever or spot starter. Long term he has the profile of a No. 3 or 4 starter.

Year	Club (League)	Class	W	L	ERA	G	GS	CG	SV	IP	H	HR	BB	SO	K/9	WHIP	AVG
2016	Brooklyn (NYP)	SS	1	1	1.50	11	8	0	0	30	25	1	10	35	10.5	1.17	.227
2017	St. Lucie (FSL)	HiA	5	6	5.00	20	16	0	0	95	101	5	48	75	7.1	1.56	.273
2018	St. Lucie (FSL)	HiA	2	3	2.36	9	9	0	0	46	43	2	15	51	10.1	1.27	.243
	Binghamton (EL)	AA	6	5	4.22	15	15	0	0	90	85	7	37	105	10.5	1.36	.258
Minor League Totals			14	15	3.87	55	48	0	0	261	254	15	110	266	9.2	1.40	.258

6 LOGAN GILBERT, RHP

Born: May 5, 1997. **B-T:** R-R. **HT:** 6-6. **WT:** 225. **Drafted:** Stetson, 2018 (1st round). **Signed by:** Rob Mummau.

TRACK RECORD: Gilbert excelled at Stetson by going 23-3, 2.48 with 11.2 strikeouts per nine innings in three seasons. After signing for $3,883,800 he spent most of the summer recovering from a bout of mononucleosis and toe surgery and did not pitch professionally.

SCOUTING REPORT: Gilbert profiles as a workhorse with a heavy power fastball with life and downward action. After pitching in the mid-90s during the 2017 Cape Cod League, his heater was more regularly in the low 90s as a college junior. But even with the diminished velocity, his fastball projects to be an above-average thanks to excellent extension in his delivery and late life on the pitch. Both of his breaking balls—a spike-curveball and a hard slider—were no better than average pitches to outside observers. The Mariners see the potential for both breaking balls to be plus, especially his curveball with two-plane action and depth. Rounding out Gilbert's arsenal is a potentially average mid-80s changeup with fade. His athleticism allows him to repeat a free-and-easy, high three-quarters arm slot.

THE FUTURE: Gilbert should be advanced enough to jump straight to full-season ball to start his pro career in 2019, but staying behind in extended spring training to manage his innings in his first season is also a possibility.

BA GRADE

55 Risk: High

Fastball: 60.
Curve: 55. Slider: 50.
Change: 50. CTL: 55.

Year	Club (League)	Class	W	L	ERA	G	GS	CG	SV	IP	H	HR	BB	SO	K/9	WHIP	AVG
2018	Did not play																

7 KYLE LEWIS, OF

Born: July 14, 1995. **B-T:** R-R. **HT:** 6-4. **WT:** 210. **Drafted:** Mercer, 2016 (1st round). **Signed by:** John Wiedenbauer.

TRACK RECORD: Lewis tore the anterior cruciate ligament in his right knee in a home plate collision in his 2016 pro debut. He has been working his way back from that injury ever since. Lewis' 2018 season got a late start when he was held back in extended spring training until May to strengthen his knee. After an appearance in the California League all-star game, Lewis moved up to Double-A Arkansas for the remainder of 2018.

SCOUTING REPORT: At the plate Lewis is balanced and short to the ball, with loose hands and the ability to adjust to fastballs in the zone, but he sometimes looks like he's trying to make up for lost time in every at-bat. He struggled to make consistent contact after the move to Double-A and has yet to show the plus-plus raw power he had in college and his pro debut. He is a fringe-average runner because of his knee injuries. Lewis is still capable of making highlight-reel plays in the outfield, with his average speed underway and solid instincts being the strong points. His lack of first-step quickness will likely push him to right field. He has an above-average arm.

THE FUTURE: Barring any further issues with his knee, Lewis should be ready for a full workload in 2019, likely heading back to Double-A to start the year.

BA GRADE

55 Risk: Very High

Hit: 50. Power: 60.
Run: 45. Field: 55.
Arm: 55.

Year	Club (League)	Class	AVG	G	AB	R	H	2B	3B	HR	RBI	BB	SO	SB	CS	OBP	SLG
2016	Everett (NWL)	SS	.299	30	117	26	35	8	5	3	26	16	22	3	0	.385	.530
2017	Mariners (AZL)	R	.263	11	38	9	10	2	1	1	7	4	14	1	0	.348	.447
	Modesto (CAL)	HiA	.255	38	149	20	38	4	0	6	24	15	38	2	1	.323	.403
2018	Modesto (CAL)	HiA	.260	49	196	21	51	18	0	5	32	11	55	0	0	.303	.429
	Arkansas (TL)	AA	.220	37	132	18	29	8	0	4	20	17	32	1	0	.309	.371
Minor League Totals			.258	165	632	94	163	40	6	19	109	63	161	7	1	.328	.430

8 NOELVI MARTE, SS

BILL MITCHELL

Born: Oct. 16, 2001. **B-T:** R-R **HT:** 6-0. **WT:** 187. **Signed:** Dominican Republic, 2018. **Signed by:** Eddy Toledo/Tim Kissner.

TRACK RECORD: Marte was one of top infield prospects in the 2018 international signing class, with the Mariners signing the Dominican Republic native for $1.55 million. While he has yet to make his pro debut, Marte participated in programs at the Mariners' complex in Peoria, Ariz., in the fall.

SCOUTING REPORT: Marte was more than just a player groomed to stand out in showcases. He also showed the ability to perform in game situations. He has intriguing power-speed potential, with an advanced approach at the plate, good strike-zone awareness and plenty of raw power from a compact stroke with whippy bat speed. While he's got a strong build, Marte is light on his feet. He's a plus-plus runner, a tick better than he was when he signed because of added strength. He's got plenty of work to do to be able to stay at shortstop, including improving his footwork and arm accuracy. Marte's future position will likely be determined by how much he grows as the body matures.

BA GRADE
55 Risk: Extreme
Hit: 55. Power: 55.
Run: 60. Field: 50.
Arm: 55.

THE FUTURE: Like Julio Rodriguez before him, Marte will begin his pro career in the Dominican Summer League in 2019 and may spend the whole summer there before making his U.S. debut in 2020.

Year	Club (League)	Class	AVG	G	AB	R	H	2B	3B	HR	RBI	BB	SO	SB	CS	OBP	SLG
2018	Did not play—Signed 2019 contract																

9 JOSH STOWERS, OF

Born: Feb. 25, 1997. **B-T:** R-R. **HT:** 6-1. **WT:** 200. **Drafted:** Louisville, 2018 (2nd round). **Signed by:** Jackson Laumann.

TRACK RECORD: Stowers was one of the top hitters for the storied Louisville program in his final two college seasons. He compiled a .929 OPS in his sophomore year with the Cardinals followed by an even better 1.036 as a junior. The Mariners grabbed Stowers with a second-round pick in 2018, and he began his pro career at short-season Everett. He ranked second in the Northwest League with 37 walks and fourth with 20 stolen bases.

SCOUTING REPORT: The biggest question Stowers faces is whether he can stay in center field, because he needs to improve his reads and jumps. His thicker frame, which draws comparisons with former big leaguer Marlon Byrd, is not a prototypical center fielder's body, but his plus speed is enough for the position if he makes the rest of the necessary improvements. Otherwise, a below-average arm would limit him to left field. Stowers' bat will likely carry him. He has a plus hit tool, and his sharp batting eye is expected to help him

BA GRADE
50 Risk: High
Hit: 50. Power: 50.
Run: 60. Field: 50.
Arm: 45.

at higher levels when pitchers are around the zone more. With average power, Stowers projects to be able to hit 15-20 home runs per year.

THE FUTURE: Stowers will get his first taste of full-season ball after spring training with a likely assignment to low Class A West Virginia in 2019.

Year	Club (League)	Class	AVG	G	AB	R	H	2B	3B	HR	RBI	BB	SO	SB	CS	OBP	SLG
2018	Everett (NWL)	SS	.260	58	200	32	52	15	0	5	28	37	57	20	4	.380	.410
Minor League Totals			.260	58	200	32	52	15	0	5	28	37	57	20	4	.380	.410

10 CAL RALEIGH, C

Born: Nov. 26, 1996. **B-T:** B-R. **HT:** 6-3. **WT:** 215. **Drafted:** Florida State, 2018 (3rd round). **Signed by:** Rob Mummau.

TRACK RECORD: The switch-hitting Raleigh was a three-year starter at Florida State. He hit much better as a junior, compiling a team-leading 1.030 OPS with 13 home runs to make up for a lackluster sophomore season. While Raleigh faced plenty of questions about his ability to hit with wood bats, the Mariners drafted him in the third round in 2018, attracted to his potential power bat and catcher profile.

SCOUTING REPORT: Raleigh's carrying tool is his above-average raw power from both sides of the plate. He manages the strike zone well with a swing that is similar from both sides. The Mariners were pleasantly surprised with Raleigh's defense in his pro debut at short-season Everett, with the above-average arm and blocking techniques indicating he has a chance to be an above-average defender. He also scored well in the organization's pitch-framing metrics. Raleigh was praised for his work ethic. The son of a one-time college coach, Raleigh has been around the game all his life, and it shows in his baseball IQ.

THE FUTURE: Raleigh will head to low Class A West Virginia with much of the rest of the Mariners' 2018 draft class. He already is the system's best catcher.

BA GRADE
50 Risk: High
Hit: 50. **Power:** 50.
Run: 30. **Field:** 50.
Arm: 50.

Year	Club (League)	Class	AVG	G	AB	R	H	2B	3B	HR	RBI	BB	SO	SB	CS	OBP	SLG
2018	Everett (NWL)	SS	.288	38	146	25	42	10	1	8	29	18	29	1	1	.367	.534
Minor League Totals			.288	38	146	25	42	10	1	8	29	18	29	1	1	.367	.534

11 ERIK SWANSON, RHP

BA GRADE
45 Risk: Medium

Born: Sept. 4, 1993. **B-T:** R-R. **HT:** 6-3. **WT:** 235. **Drafted:** Iowa Western JC, 2014 (8th round). **Signed by:** Dustin Smith (Rangers).

TRACK RECORD: The Mariners acquired Swanson from the Yankees as one of three prospects exchanged for James Paxton. Originally drafted by the Rangers, Swanson transferred from Wabash (Ill.) JC to Iowa Western JC in 2014 and showed enough there to get drafted in the eighth round. He went all the way to Triple-A Round Rock with Texas in 2015 before being dealt to the Yankees for Carlos Beltran at the 2016 trade deadline. After beginning 2018 at high Class A Tampa, he finished the year by starting Game 1 of the International League playoffs for Triple-A Scranton/Wilkes-Barre.

SCOUTING REPORT: Swanson throws a high-spin fastball with extraordinary riding action and carry through the zone at 91-93 mph while touching a tick higher. He couples the pitch with a mid-80s slider and a low-80s changeup. Both secondary pitches project as average offerings with a little bit more refinement. A big reason for his improvement in 2018 was an uptick in fastball command, particularly when throwing the pitch up in the zone. Some scouts are concerned that he won't be able to get the ball to his glove side as often as necessary because of his delivery. His only real hiccup came in the form of an oblique strain that cost him a chunk of time at midseason.

THE FUTURE: Swanson will go to spring training with a chance to crack the Mariners' rotation, and he projects as a No. 5 starter. Additional Triple-A seasoning is the most likely Opening Day assignment.

Year	Club (League)	Class	W	L	ERA	G	GS	CG	SV	IP	H	HR	BB	SO	K/9	WHIP	AVG
2016	Hickory (SAL)	LoA	6	4	3.43	19	15	0	1	81	77	4	25	78	8.6	1.25	.248
	Charleston, SC (SAL)	LoA	0	1	3.60	5	2	0	0	15	14	0	5	15	9.0	1.27	.246
2017	Tampa (FSL)	HiA	7	3	3.95	20	20	0	0	100	115	10	14	84	7.5	1.29	.291
2018	Trenton (EL)	AA	5	0	0.42	8	7	0	0	43	22	0	15	55	11.6	0.87	.155
	Staten Island (NYP)	SS	0	0	4.05	2	2	0	0	7	8	0	0	6	8.1	1.20	.308
	Scranton/W-B (IL)	AAA	3	2	3.86	14	13	0	0	72	63	0	14	78	9.7	1.06	.230
Minor League Totals			23	12	3.35	93	59	1	2	357	328	25	87	354	8.9	1.16	.245

12 BRADEN BISHOP, OF

BA GRADE
45 Risk: Medium

Born: Aug. 22, 1993. **B-T:** R-R. **HT:** 6-1. **WT:** 190. **Drafted:** Washington, 2015 (3rd round). **Signed by:** Jeff Sakamoto.

TRACK RECORD: Bishop was athletic enough in high school that he could have played college football as a wide receiver, but he instead chose to stick to baseball at Washington. He continues to receive acclaim for his 4MOM foundation that raises money for Alzheimer's disease in support of his mother. Bishop was progressing well during the first half of 2018 at Double-A Arkansas. Unfortunately, his season ended early when he suffered a broken hand after being hit by a pitch.

SCOUTING REPORT: Bishop added strength and lowered his hands. That allowed him to get more power into his swing, which has helped him drive the baseball more frequently, giving him a chance to hit double-digit home runs while still being an average hitter. Early in the 2018 season, he was struggling to improve his launch angle, but it all came together for him by midseason when he hit .379/.443/.544 in June. Any offense that Bishop provides will come in addition to what he brings to the field and basepaths, because he is a plus runner and plus-plus defender in center field.

THE FUTURE: The Mariners added Bishop to the 40-man roster in November in his first year of eligibility. He will head to Triple-A Tacoma and could reach Seattle in 2019.

Year	Club (League)	Class	AVG	G	AB	R	H	2B	3B	HR	RBI	BB	SO	SB	CS	OBP	SLG
2016	Clinton (MWL)	LoA	.290	63	248	38	72	5	1	1	21	25	48	6	1	.363	.331
	Bakersfield (CAL)	HiA	.247	41	166	19	41	6	0	2	22	11	39	2	0	.300	.319
2017	Modesto (CAL)	HiA	.296	88	355	71	105	25	3	2	32	45	65	16	5	.385	.400
	Arkansas (TL)	AA	.336	31	125	18	42	9	1	1	11	15	15	6	1	.417	.448
2018	Arkansas (TL)	AA	.284	84	345	70	98	20	0	8	33	37	68	5	2	.361	.412
Minor League Totals			.294	363	1458	250	428	73	6	16	141	138	268	48	12	.366	.385

13 SAM CARLSON, RHP

BA GRADE

50 Risk: Extreme

Born: Dec. 3, 1998. **B-T:** R-R. **HT:** 6-4. **WT:** 195. **Drafted:** HS—Burnsville, Minn., 2017 (2nd round). **Signed by:** Ben Collman.

TRACK RECORD: Carlson had a strong commitment to Florida before the Mariners signed him for an over-slot $2 million in the second round of the 2017 draft. After two short but impressive appearances in Rookie ball in 2017, Carlson was shut down with some minor soreness that did not look to be a long-term issue. Elbow and forearm tenderness kept him off the mound at 2018 spring training, but he began throwing bullpen sessions in early summer before it was determined that he needed Tommy John surgery in July.

SCOUTING REPORT: Carlson has a prototype pitcher's frame with room to add strength. Prior to the injury, he threw a heavy fastball with late action and natural sink up to 96 mph. His above-average mid-80s slider has late action and tilt, complemented by a changeup that flashes plus. With a loose, quick arm, Carlson uses a delivery that is easy and free-flowing.

THE FUTURE: The Mariners hope that Carlson can be throwing bullpens again by late July and are targeting 2020 for a return to game action. He'll still be just 21, but the Mariners will need to speed his development at that point because he will be in his fourth pro season before he receives significant pro mound experience.

Year	Club (League)	Class	W	L	ERA	G	GS	CG	SV	IP	H	HR	BB	SO	K/9	WHIP	AVG
2017	Mariners (AZL)	R	0	0	3.00	2	2	0	0	3	4	0	0	3	9.0	1.33	.364
2018	Did not play—Injured																
Minor League Totals			0	0	3.00	2	2	0	0	3	4	0	0	3	9.0	1.33	.364

14 JAKE FRALEY, OF

BA GRADE

45 Risk: High

Born: May 25, 1995. **B-T:** L-L. **HT:** 6-0. **WT:** 195. **Drafted:** Louisiana State, 2016 (2nd round supplemental). **Signed by:** Rickey Drexler (Rays).

TRACK RECORD: The Mariners acquired Fraley in the trade that sent Mike Zunino to the Rays for Mallex Smith. Fraley missed most of 2017 with a knee injury and then the early part of 2018 with a foot injury after spending the offseason in the Australian Baseball League. Healthy for the second half of 2018, he hit .347/.415/.547 at high Class A Charlotte.

SCOUTING REPORT: Fraley has a good approach at the plate with above-average bat speed and a simple, balanced swing, but his 2018 numbers overstate his impact potential. He has a track record for putting the bat on the ball and drawing walks. While he hits righthanders better, Fraley has shown that he holds his own against southpaws. His below-average power results in more doubles to the gap than balls over the fence. His best tool is his plus speed, allowing him to stay in center field, but he needs to develop better instincts on the bases. Above-average range and a fringe-average arm are enough for all three outfield positions, and his most likely big league role will be as a versatile backup outfielder.

THE FUTURE: Fraley will have to prove that he can stay on the field after battling injuries. The Mariners will move him quickly to try to make up for lost time. His most likely role is as a fourth outfielder.

Year	Club (League)	Class	AVG	G	AB	R	H	2B	3B	HR	RBI	BB	SO	SB	CS	OBP	SLG
2016	Hudson Valley (NYP)	SS	.238	55	206	34	49	9	7	1	18	26	34	33	9	.339	.364
2017	Charlotte, FL (FSL)	HiA	.170	26	94	6	16	3	1	1	12	7	24	1	3	.238	.255
	Rays (GCL)	R	.467	4	15	6	7	3	0	1	2	2	3	1	1	.529	.867
2018	Charlotte, FL (FSL)	HiA	.347	66	225	39	78	19	7	4	41	26	44	11	8	.415	.547
Minor League Totals			.278	151	540	85	150	34	15	7	73	61	105	48	21	.359	.435

15 MATT FESTA, RHP

BA GRADE

40 Risk: Medium

Born: March 11, 1993. **B-T:** R-R. **Ht.:** 6-2. **Wt.:** 195. **Drafted:** East Stroudsburg (Pa.), 2016 (7th round). **Signed by:** Ross Vecchio.

TRACK RECORD: Signed for $5,000 after being drafted in the seventh round out of Division II East Stroudsburg, Festa turned out to be first Mariners 2016 draft pick to reach the big leagues. He made eight relief appearances for Seattle in 2018, capping off a rapid ascent. Festa's 2018 season was delayed by a hip flexor issue, but he proved to be effective at Double-A Arkansas.

SCOUTING REPORT: While he has a more diverse mix than most relievers, Festa is at his best when using his 92-94 mph fastball in conjunction with his plus slider. The latter is a harder pitch with glove-side cut that typically sits around 87 mph, and he uses it often as a strikeout pitch against righthanders. He also uses a sinker, most notably against lefthanders, and mixes in a changeup and 12-to-6 curveball in the low 80s, albeit less frequently than the rest of his repertoire. Festa's above-average control is the difference-maker for him. He delivers his pitches with a loose, high three-quarter arm slot that he repeats.

THE FUTURE: After getting a taste of the big leagues in 2018, Festa will go to spring training with a chance to break camp in the Mariners' bullpen. He doesn't have the velocity to profile as a closer but should be effective in high-leverage situations.

Year	Club (League)	Class	W	L	ERA	G	GS	CG	SV	IP	H	HR	BB	SO	K/9	WHIP	AVG
2016	Everett (NWL)	SS	6	2	3.73	14	8	0	0	60	60	3	14	58	8.7	1.23	.259
2017	Modesto (CAL)	HiA	4	2	3.23	42	1	0	6	70	61	7	19	99	12.8	1.15	.229
2018	Arkansas (TL)	AA	5	2	2.76	44	0	0	20	49	50	6	12	67	12.3	1.27	.263
	Seattle (AL)	MAJ	0	0	2.16	8	1	0	0	8	13	0	2	4	4.3	1.80	.351
Major League Totals			0	0	2.16	8	1	0	0	8	13	0	2	4	4.3	1.80	.351
Minor League Totals			15	6	3.27	100	9	0	26	179	171	16	45	224	11.3	1.21	.248

16 DAN VOGELBACH, 1B/DH

BA GRADE

40 Risk: Medium

Born: Dec. 17, 1992. **B-T:** L-R. **Ht.:** 6-0. **Wt.:** 250. **Drafted:** HS—Fort Myers, Fla., 2011 (2nd round). **Signed by:** Lukas McKnight (Cubs).

TRACK RECORD: Vogelbach's productive 2018 spring training, when he hit over .400 with seven home runs, earned him a spot on the Mariners' Opening Day roster, but a slow start had him back at Triple-A Tacoma before the end of April. He returned to Seattle for other short stints, but inconsistent playing time resulted in subpar production. Vogelbach put up good numbers at Triple-A Tacoma, hitting .290/.434/.595 with 20 home runs and more walks than strikeouts in 294 at-bats.

SCOUTING REPORT: There are many who still believe Vogelbach will hit if given the opportunity, but it will likely need to be as a DH. At the plate, he has a good approach, strong hands and an ability to use all fields with plus raw power. He tapped into his raw power in games more often in 2018, with his 24 combined home runs between Triple-A and the major league marking a career high. Vogelbach is a well below-average defender at first base and a bottom-of-the-scale runner.

THE FUTURE: Vogelbach's improvement at Triple-A was a positive sign. With the Mariners moving into rebuild mode and free agent DH Nelson Cruz unlikely to return, Vogelbach could get another shot at that role in at least a platoon capacity in 2019.

Year	Club (League)	Class	AVG	G	AB	R	H	2B	3B	HR	RBI	BB	SO	SB	CS	OBP	SLG
2016	Iowa (PCL)	AAA	.318	89	305	53	97	18	2	16	64	55	67	0	0	.425	.548
	Tacoma (PCL)	AAA	.240	44	154	26	37	7	0	7	32	42	34	0	0	.404	.422
	Seattle (AL)	MAJ	.083	8	12	0	1	0	0	0	0	1	6	0	0	.154	.083
2017	Tacoma (PCL)	AAA	.290	125	459	65	133	25	0	17	83	76	98	3	1	.388	.455
	Seattle (AL)	MAJ	.214	16	28	0	6	1	0	0	2	3	9	0	0	.290	.250
2018	Tacoma (PCL)	AAA	.290	84	297	54	86	16	0	20	60	77	59	0	1	.434	.545
	Seattle (AL)	MAJ	.207	37	87	9	18	2	0	4	13	13	26	0	0	.324	.368
Major League Totals			.197	61	127	9	25	3	0	4	15	17	41	0	0	.301	.315
Minor League Totals			.287	753	2714	425	779	159	7	120	498	489	550	15	12	.395	.483

17 DOM THOMPSON-WILLIAMS, OF

BA GRADE

45 Risk: High

Born: April 21, 1995. **B-T:** L-L. **Ht.:** 6-0. **Wt.:** 190. **Drafted:** South Carolina, 2016 (5th round). **Signed by:** Billy Godwin (Yankees).

TRACK RECORD: Thompson-Williams' third pro season was his best to date, prompting the Mariners to acquire him as part of a three-prospect return from the Yankees in the James Paxton trade. He was originally drafted by the Yankees in the fifth round in 2016 after his lone season at South Carolina, having played two previous years at Iowa Western JC. Thompson-Williams spent most of 2018 at high Class A Tampa and hit .299/.356/.517 with 22 home runs and 20 stolen bases. He was one of only six minor league players to reach the 20-20 mark in 2018, despite missing a month to a hamstring injury.

SCOUTING REPORT: Thompson-Williams, who will turn 24 early in 2019, may be an example of a raw athlete breaking out later in his career. He has explosive, quick-twitch athleticism, combined with sneaky power to all fields, and has at least average raw power with a chance for more to come. An above-average defender with an average arm, Thompson-Williams can stay in center field but can also handle all three positions in a fourth outfielder role. His run times in 2018 were inconsistent, perhaps due to his hamstring problems, but he's at least an average runner out of the box and a tick better in the field.

THE FUTURE: After a strong season in the Florida State League, Thompson-Williams will head to Double-A Arkansas in 2019 and could see Triple-A by midseason.

Year	Club (League)	Class	AVG	G	AB	R	H	2B	3B	HR	RBI	BB	SO	SB	CS	OBP	SLG
2016	Staten Island (NYP)	SS	.246	56	195	30	48	8	1	3	16	28	43	15	5	.348	.344
2017	Staten Island (NYP)	SS	.277	41	141	17	39	7	0	3	22	18	30	7	6	.366	.390
	Charleston, SC (SAL)	LoA	.188	23	80	6	15	2	0	0	6	9	15	2	2	.270	.213
2018	Charleston, SC (SAL)	LoA	.378	10	37	7	14	1	0	5	9	2	7	3	2	.425	.811
	Tampa (FSL)	HiA	.290	90	331	56	96	16	4	17	65	31	95	17	7	.356	.517
Minor League Totals			.270	220	784	116	212	34	5	28	118	88	190	44	22	.350	.434

18 WYATT MILLS, RHP

BA GRADE

45 Risk: High

Born: Jan. 25, 1995. **B-T:** R-R. **Ht.:** 6-3. **Wt.:** 175. **Drafted:** Gonzaga, 2017 (3rd round). **Signed by:** Alex Ross/Jeff Sakamoto.

TRACK RECORD: Mills pitched exclusively out of the bullpen in four years at Gonzaga, where he recorded a 1.79 ERA with 12 saves as a senior. Drafted in the third round in 2017 with the intention of moving through the Mariners' system quickly, Mills made it to Double-A Arkansas by the end of his first full season and then spent time in the Arizona Fall League.

SCOUTING REPORT: Pitching from a sidearm slot, Mills gives hitters a different look, with his pitches appearing to come out of his hip. It's a funky, deceptive delivery, but he repeats it well. Mills' typical 88-92 mph fastball has both sink and armside movement, and he showed increased velocity in the AFL, when he sat 94-95 mph. His average 81-84 mph slider has two-plane movement and can be a swing-and-miss pitch, but it currently doesn't have enough tilt and needs to thrown in the zone more often against more advanced hitters. Mills throws his 80-83 mph changeup for strikes, using it more often against lefthanded batters, but he's predominately a fastball/slider reliever.

THE FUTURE: After a successful stint in AFL, Mills should be ready to give Double-A another shot in 2019 and will likely make it to Triple-A before long. He could be pitching in high-leverage situations if he maintains the increased velocity and improves his slider.

Year	Club (League)	Class	W	L	ERA	G	GS	CG	SV	IP	H	HR	BB	SO	K/9	WHIP	AVG
2017	Everett (NWL)	SS	0	1	2.57	7	0	0	2	7	3	0	3	11	14.1	0.86	.120
	Clinton (MWL)	LoA	0	1	1.35	11	0	0	4	13	5	0	6	18	12.2	0.83	.111
2018	Modesto (CAL)	HiA	6	0	1.91	35	0	0	11	42	29	1	9	49	10.4	0.90	.193
	Arkansas (TL)	AA	0	2	10.13	9	0	0	0	11	18	0	4	10	8.4	2.06	.367
Minor League Totals			6	4	3.07	62	0	0	17	73	55	1	22	88	10.8	1.05	.204

19 JUAN QUERECUTO, SS

BA GRADE

50 Risk: Extreme

Born: Sept. 21, 2000. **B-T:** R-R. **Ht.:** 6-2. **Wt.:** 175. **Signed:** Venezuela, 2017. **Signed by:** Emilio Carrasquel/Tim Kissner.

TRACK RECORD: Signed by the Mariners in 2017 for $1.225 million, Querecuto spent 2018 playing shortstop in the Dominican Summer League. His high baseball IQ comes naturally because his father Juan played in the Blue Jays' farm system and his brother Juniel played in the Diamondbacks' organization in 2018 after reaching the big leagues with the Rays in 2016.

SCOUTING REPORT: Querecuto is known for his skills more than his tools. He consistently does the little things well with a knack of regularly being in the right spot at the right time. He made strides at the plate in 2018 by better controlling the barrel and using all fields. With good strike-zone awareness, Querecuto is more of a contact, gap-to-gap hitter with current below-average power. He spent the fall at the Mariners' complex in Arizona improving his strength, so there may be more power to come as he physically matures. A below-average runner, Querecuto compensates with instincts and positioning at shortstop, and his plus-plus arm already ranks as the best infield arm in the Mariners' system.

THE FUTURE: Querecuto will make his U.S. debut in the Rookie-level Arizona League in 2019.

Year	Club (League)	Class	AVG	G	AB	R	H	2B	3B	HR	RBI	BB	SO	SB	CS	OBP	SLG
2018	Mariners (DSL)	R	.243	64	243	37	59	8	2	3	29	25	54	3	6	.331	.329
Minor League Totals			.243	64	243	37	59	8	2	3	29	25	54	3	6	.331	.329

20 BRAYAN PEREZ, LHP

Born: Sept. 5, 2000. **B-T:** L-L. **Ht.:** 6-0. **Wt.:** 170. **Signed:** Venezuela, 2017.
Signed by: Tim Kissner.

BA GRADE
50 Risk: Extreme

TRACK RECORD: The Mariners' 2017 international signing class is beginning to look more interesting, which should add intrigue to the organization's Rookie-level Arizona League affiliate in 2019. Perez, a pitchability Venezuelan lefthander who signed for $350,000, projects as the best pitcher from that signing class. He had an impressive debut in the Dominican Summer League, when he struck out 58 batters in 53 innings while walking just 11.

SCOUTING REPORT: Perez is already known for his advanced feel to pitch. He throws an 85-91 mph fastball with deception, and he is projected to add velocity with added strength and maturity. He throws a slurvy 73-77 mph breaking ball that can look like either a slider or curveball depending on how he adds or subtracts velocity. Regardless, it's his best out pitch and could be a plus offering with further refinement. Perez's changeup is still a work in progress, but he delivers all his pitches from a smooth, easy delivery and a low three-quarters slot.

THE FUTURE: Perez will begin 2019 at the Mariners' complex in Peoria, Ariz., before joining the AZL team.

Year	Club (League)	Class	W	L	ERA	G	GS	CG	SV	IP	H	HR	BB	SO	K/9	WHIP	AVG
2018	Mariners (DSL)	R	1	3	3.57	15	10	0	0	53	50	1	11	58	9.8	1.15	.248
Minor League Totals			1	3	3.57	15	10	0	0	53	50	1	11	58	9.8	1.15	.248

21 JOEY CURLETTA, 1B

Born: March 8, 1994. **B-T:** R-R. **Ht.:** 6-4. **Wt.:** 245. **Drafted:** HS—Phoenix, 2012 (6th round). **Signed by:** Dustin Yount (Dodgers).

BA GRADE
40 Risk: Medium

TRACK RECORD: Curletta was known for his impressive plus raw power but not much else during the first six years of his pro career—five of which were spent with the Dodgers before being traded to the Phillies and then the Mariners in March 2017. Something clicked for Curletta at Double-A Arkansas in 2018, when led the Texas League in both OPS (.865) and walks (81). The improved approach resulted in Curletta being named Texas League MVP and the Mariners' minor league hitter of the year. It also earned him a 40-man roster spot in the offseason. Otherwise he would have been a minor league free agent.

SCOUTING REPORT: Curletta got his body in better shape, became a smarter hitter and improved his two-strike approach in 2018. He used a quieter setup at the plate and got more loft in his swing, allowing him to hit home runs on more than just mistake pitches. Curletta has easy plus-plus raw power from the right side. His strikeout rate didn't improve much from 2017, but he increased his walk rate from 11.7 percent in high Class A to 14.6 percent in Double-A. An outfielder through the early part of his career with a strong arm that made switching to the mound a possibility, Curletta has strictly played first base the last two years. He's a below-average defender at first base and a below-average runner, but he has recently made strides by getting his body in better condition.

THE FUTURE: Curletta draws some comparisons with fellow Mariners' prospect Dan Vogelbach as a bat-first player. Curletta's likely assignment will be Triple-A Tacoma.

Year	Club (League)	Class	AVG	G	AB	R	H	2B	3B	HR	RBI	BB	SO	SB	CS	OBP	SLG
2016	R. Cucamonga (CAL)	HiA	.267	77	270	40	72	13	5	13	54	27	87	0	2	.338	.496
	Tulsa (TL)	AA	.206	29	97	7	20	4	0	4	13	10	37	0	0	.280	.371
2017	Modesto (CAL)	HiA	.256	121	454	72	116	37	1	15	68	62	136	13	1	.343	.441
2018	Arkansas (TL)	AA	.282	129	465	70	131	24	0	23	94	81	130	1	1	.383	.482
Minor League Totals			.264	698	2520	342	665	160	8	78	402	294	702	32	19	.342	.427

22 JOE RIZZO, 3B

Born: March 31, 1998. **B-T:** L-R. **Ht.:** 5-9. **Wt.:** 194. **Drafted:** HS—Vienna, Va., 2016 (2nd round). **Signed by:** Ross Vecchio.

BA GRADE
40 Risk: High

TRACK RECORD: Drafted out of a Virginia high school in the second round in 2016, Rizzo took a step back in 2018. He hit .241/.303/.321 for high Class A Modesto in the hitter-friendly California League. Rizzo also didn't do much to answer questions about whether he could handle third base.

SCOUTING REPORT: Despite not showing a lot of impact with his bat in 2018, Rizzo still has believers who think he can develop into a serviceable hitter. He's still learning to make adjustments, possesses solid bat-to-ball skills and has outstanding makeup. He shows good raw power, but it has yet to show up in games. The biggest question is where Rizzo fits on the field because he is not very skilled defensively. His tick above-average arm is enough for third base, but he struggles with range to both his right and left. At 5-foot-9, Rizzo is too short for first base, and his below-average speed limits his chances at other positions.

THE FUTURE: Rizzo will return to Modesto in 2019, when he'll be 21 and more age-appropriate for the Cal League. It'll be a key year for Rizzo, who needs to show growth in both his bat and glove.

Year	Club (League)	Class	AVG	G	AB	R	H	2B	3B	HR	RBI	BB	SO	SB	CS	OBP	SLG
2016	Mariners (AZL)	R	.291	39	148	21	43	7	1	2	21	17	36	2	1	.355	.392
2017	Clinton (MWL)	LoA	.254	110	410	47	104	17	0	7	50	63	113	3	1	.354	.346
	Modesto (CAL)	HiA	.200	5	20	1	4	0	1	0	1	1	8	0	0	.238	.300
2018	Modesto (CAL)	HiA	.241	123	461	46	111	21	2	4	55	40	108	6	1	.303	.321
Minor League Totals			.252	277	1039	115	262	45	4	13	127	121	265	11	3	.330	.341

23 NOLAN HOFFMAN, RHP

BA GRADE

45 Risk: Very High

Born: Aug. 9, 1997. **B-T:** R-R. **Ht.:** 6-4. **Wt.:** 190. **Drafted:** Texas A&M, 2018 (5th round). **Signed by:** Austin Wates.

TRACK RECORD: After spending two seasons at Hutchinson (Kan.) JC, Hutchinson went to Texas A&M. He posted a 1.24 ERA in 32 relief appearances in 2018, then signed for $300,000 after being drafted by the Mariners in the fifth round. He started his pro career with six short appearances in the Rookie-level Arizona League. In July, Hoffman was promoted to short-season Everett, where he posted a 2.45 ERA.

SCOUTING REPORT: Hoffman could be considered the next version of fellow Mariners righthander Wyatt Mills, because he delivers pitches from a low arm slot. Hoffman pitches from an even lower slot than Mills, using submarine depth while drawing comparisons with major league reliever Darren O'Day. His upper-80s to low-90s fastball is an average pitch that comes across the plate heavy with late, plus sink. His fastball plays up because he locates it to both sides of the plate, while his fringe-average slider has whip and three-quarter tilt. He has below-average stuff now with plus movement and projected plus command.

THE FUTURE: Like Mills, Hoffman has enough stuff, command and deception to move quickly. If he doesn't skip a level and start the 2019 season at high Class A Modesto, then he should get there before the end of the year. An uptick in velocity and improvement in his breaking ball would help solidify his projection as a solid middle reliever.

Year	Club (League)	Class	W	L	ERA	G	GS	CG	SV	IP	H	HR	BB	SO	K/9	WHIP	AVG
2018	Mariners (AZL)	R	1	0	1.35	6	0	0	0	7	3	0	1	7	9.5	0.60	.136
	Everett (NWL)	SS	1	3	2.45	15	0	0	4	18	17	0	7	16	7.9	1.31	.254
Minor League Totals			2	3	2.16	21	0	0	4	25	20	0	8	23	8.3	1.12	.225

24 JOEY GERBER, RHP

BA GRADE

45 Risk: Very High

Born: May 3, 1997. **B-T:** R-R. **Ht.:** 6-4. **Wt.:** 215. **Drafted:** Illinois, 2018 (8th round). **Signed by:** Ben Collman.

TRACK RECORD: A pure reliever with an aggressive delivery, Gerber was a closer at Illinois and averaged just over 12 strikeouts per nine innings during his three years in college. Drafted by the Mariners in the eighth round in 2018, Gerber pitched well at both short-season Everett and at low Class A Clinton in his pro debut, combining for a 2.10 ERA and 15 strikeouts per nine innings.

SCOUTING REPORT: The 6-foot-4 Gerber is an imposing figure on the mound who comes right at hitters with premium velocity. He has what's been called violent velocity—a plus fastball that he throws for strikes from 92-96 mph with movement, life and sink. His fringe-average slider flashed above-average potential, but he needs to make it sharper more consistently. He had a decent changeup in college but rarely used it. Gerber uses a herky-jerky delivery with effort, but he stays online with a quick tempo to keep hitters from getting comfortable in the box.

THE FUTURE: After dominating hitters in low Class A, look for Gerber to start 2019 at high Class A Modesto.

Year	Club (League)	Class	W	L	ERA	G	GS	CG	SV	IP	H	HR	BB	SO	K/9	WHIP	AVG
2018	Everett (NWL)	SS	1	0	1.93	13	0	0	6	14	9	0	6	21	13.5	1.07	.188
	Clinton (MWL)	LoA	0	0	2.31	9	0	0	2	12	9	0	5	22	17.0	1.20	.220
Minor League Totals			1	0	2.10	22	0	0	8	26	18	0	11	43	15.1	1.13	.202

25 ANTHONY MISIEWICZ, LHP

BA GRADE

40 Risk: High

Born: Nov. 1, 1994. **B-T:** R-L. **Ht.:** 6-1. **Wt.:** 190. **Drafted:** Michigan State, 2015 (18th round). **Signed by:** Jay Catalano.

TRACK RECORD: Used mostly as a reliever in college, Misiewicz has worked primarily in the rotation since turning pro. Traded to the Rays in August 2017, he was reacquired by the Mariners four months later via trade. Misiewicz struggled at Double-A in 2018 but got back on track in the Arizona Fall League.

SCOUTING REPORT: Misiewicz is a gritty, strike-throwing competitor with a four-pitch mix who gets by with finesse more than pure stuff. His fringe-average fastball sits 88-92 mph with some tail, and his 79-81 mph above-average curveball has late angle and sharp, downward action. His 86-88 mph slider is more of a cutter that he throws for strikes. Misiewicz also mixes in a low-80s changeup that showed improvement in the AFL. He repeats his high three-quarters arm slot well, but it doesn't provide a lot of deception.

THE FUTURE: Misiewicz doesn't have a record of pitching deep into his starts, and he is generally more effective in shorter stints, marking him as a likely relief candidate.

Year	Club (League)	Class	W	L	ERA	G	GS	CG	SV	IP	H	HR	BB	SO	K/9	WHIP	AVG
2016	Bakersfield (CAL)	HiA	7	10	4.79	29	29	1	0	158	166	21	47	115	6.6	1.35	.272
2017	Modesto (CAL)	HiA	5	2	4.96	16	16	0	0	78	82	6	27	85	9.8	1.40	.265
	Arkansas (TL)	AA	3	3	4.35	7	7	0	0	41	40	4	11	32	7.0	1.23	.270
	Montgomery (SL)	AA	3	1	3.49	5	5	1	0	28	26	3	5	24	7.6	1.09	.239
2018	Mariners (AZL)	R	0	0	0.00	2	2	0	0	5	2	0	0	4	7.2	0.40	.118
	Arkansas (TL)	AA	3	12	5.51	21	21	0	0	98	133	14	29	91	8.4	1.65	.319
Minor League Totals			24	30	4.53	94	87	2	0	455	479	49	129	391	7.7	1.34	.271

26 DONNIE WALTON, 2B/SS

BA GRADE
40 Risk: High

Born: May 25, 1994. **B-T:** L-R. **Ht.:** 5-10. **Wt.:** 184. **Drafted:** Oklahoma State, 2016 (5th round). **Signed by:** Ty Bowman.

TRACK RECORD: A four-year starter at Oklahoma State and the son of a coach, Walton is selfless and plays hard. He hit well at high Class A Modesto in 2018 before scuffling at Double-A.

SCOUTING REPORT: Walton is fundamentally strong and has an uncanny ability to slow the game down, with a reputation for pushing his teammates to work harder by example. He has a good approach at the plate and does the little things well, including bunting, advancing runners and taking the extra base. Despite below-average speed, Walton steals bases and is a strong baserunner because of his advanced instincts. He's a capable defender at all infield positions with a tick above-average arm.

THE FUTURE: Walton is future utility infielder with a high likelihood of reaching that ceiling.

Year	Club (League)	Class	AVG	G	AB	R	H	2B	3B	HR	RBI	BB	SO	SB	CS	OBP	SLG
2016	Everett (NWL)	SS	.281	43	178	43	50	8	1	5	23	22	24	6	0	.361	.421
2017	Mariners (AZL)	R	.313	5	16	2	5	0	0	2	5	1	0	2	0	.353	.688
	Modesto (CAL)	HiA	.269	67	242	37	65	16	1	2	24	27	49	6	6	.349	.368
2018	Modesto (CAL)	HiA	.309	57	217	35	67	12	3	3	19	30	37	8	3	.402	.433
	Arkansas (TL)	AA	.236	62	208	22	49	14	1	1	22	21	34	3	1	.325	.327
Minor League Totals			.274	234	861	139	236	50	6	13	93	101	144	25	10	.359	.391

27 ART WARREN, RHP

BA GRADE
40 Risk: High

Born: March 23, 1993. **B-T:** R-R. **Ht.:** 6-3. **Wt.:** 230. **Drafted:** Ashland (Ohio), 2015 (23rd round). **Signed by:** Jay Catalano/Devitt Moore.

TRACK RECORD: Warren struggled with a shoulder issue and worked just 15.2 innings at Double-A Arkansas in 2018, his second full year as a reliever.

SCOUTING REPORT: When healthy, Warren uses a four-seam fastball that sits 92-97 mph and touches 99 with extension and late life up in the zone. The velocity and movement on his fastball helps the pitch compensate for his below-average command. Warren also uses an overhand 12-to-6 curveball that sits 80-84 mph with depth and hard finish. He also has a hard low-90s slider and a below-average changeup in the mid-to-upper 80s that is also a little too firm.

THE FUTURE: Warren will be 26 on Opening Day, but he could get to the big leagues at some point in 2019 if he's healthy and able to maintain his stuff.

Year	Club (League)	Class	W	L	ERA	G	GS	CG	SV	IP	H	HR	BB	SO	K/9	WHIP	AVG
2016	Clinton (MWL)	LoA	9	1	2.19	14	14	0	0	74	71	1	18	55	6.7	1.20	.253
	Bakersfield (CAL)	HiA	2	1	5.15	13	6	0	0	37	42	1	28	38	9.3	1.91	.284
2017	Modesto (CAL)	HiA	3	1	3.06	43	0	0	8	65	58	5	25	67	9.3	1.28	.247
2018	Arkansas (TL)	AA	2	1	1.72	14	0	0	2	16	10	0	14	22	12.6	1.53	.185
Minor League Totals			16	5	3.05	90	20	0	10	198	188	7	88	192	8.7	1.39	.253

28 GERSON BAUTISTA

BA GRADE
40 Risk: High

Born: May 31, 1995. **B-T:** R-R. **HT:** 6-3. **WT:** 195. **Signed:** Dominican Republic, 2013. **Signed by:** Manny Nanita (Red Sox).

TRACK RECORD: Bautista has been traded twice since signing with the Red Sox at 17, first to the Mets in the 2017 Addison Reed deal and then to the Mariners in the Robinson Cano/Edwin Diaz deal in

December 2018. After pitching mostly at Triple-A Las Vegas in 2018, with a few big league appearances mixed in, Bautista finished the year with a promising stint in the Arizona Fall League.

SCOUTING REPORT: Bautista's top pitch is his blazing four-seam fastball that averages 98 mph and touches triple digits. His heater comes out of a high-effort delivery with a long arm action. His mid-80s slider has two-plane action, but he struggles to command the pitch, especially to his glove side. He infrequently throws a low-90s split-changeup that can get swings-and-misses. While Bautista's 2018 numbers were inflated by poor luck on balls in play, the consistency of his offerings remains an issue.

THE FUTURE: Bautista flashes high-leverage stuff but is held back by the poor command. He tantalized in small samples in the AFL but resembles an up-and-down middle reliever with a raw power arm.

Year	Club (League)	Class	W	L	ERA	G	GS	CG	SV	IP	H	HR	BB	SO	K/9	WHIP	AVG
2016	Lowell (NYP)	SS	0	0	0.87	8	0	0	5	10	5	0	2	13	11.3	0.68	.143
	Greenville (SAL)	LoA	1	4	3.24	15	0	0	1	25	20	3	11	23	8.3	1.24	.213
2017	Salem (CAR)	HiA	3	2	5.16	27	0	0	4	45	54	2	28	53	10.5	1.81	.292
	St. Lucie (FSL)	HiA	0	1	1.26	10	0	0	5	14	10	0	3	20	12.6	0.91	.204
2018	Binghamton (EL)	AA	1	0	4.82	6	0	0	0	9	12	0	0	15	14.5	1.29	.316
	New York (NL)	MAJ	0	1	12.46	5	0	0	0	4	8	2	5	3	6.2	3.00	.444
	Las Vegas (PCL)	AAA	1	5	5.22	31	0	0	3	40	54	3	18	54	12.3	1.82	.314
Major League Totals			0	1	12.46	5	0	0	0	4	8	2	5	3	6.2	3.00	.444
Minor League Totals			13	12	3.12	122	23	0	18	257	228	10	110	251	8.8	1.32	.235

29 DAVID McKAY, RHP

BA GRADE 40 Risk: High

Born: March 31, 1995. **B-T:** R-R. **Ht.:** 6-3. **Wt.:** 205. **Drafted:** Florida Atlantic, 2016 (14th round). **Signed by:** Alex Mesa (Royals).

TRACK RECORD: The Mariners purchased McKay from the Royals during 2018 spring training to provide organizational depth. He provided much more than that by reaching Double-A Arkansas and then earning a spot in the Arizona Fall League all-star showcase.

SCOUTING REPORT: McKay profiles as a reliever, with his slightly above-average 92-95 mph fastball possessing both tail and a heavy sinking action. The gem of his arsenal is an 84-87 mph slider that projects to be a plus pitch with good depth. The key to his improvement was dropping his arm angle to a more comfortable three-quarters slot, allowing him to control the strike zone better.

THE FUTURE: McKay is targeted for Triple-A Tacoma in 2019 and has a middle reliever ceiling.

Year	Club (League)	Class	W	L	ERA	G	GS	CG	SV	IP	H	HR	BB	SO	K/9	WHIP	AVG
2016	Burlington (APP)	R	3	3	2.64	12	5	0	0	44	38	3	15	41	8.3	1.20	.233
2017	Lexington (SAL)	LoA	0	0	13.03	6	0	0	0	10	19	4	5	11	10.2	2.48	.404
	Idaho Falls (PIO)	R	6	5	6.49	14	14	0	0	79	104	13	18	68	7.7	1.54	.313
2018	Tacoma (PCL)	AAA	0	0	0.00	1	0	0	0	1	0	0	0	0	0.0	0.00	.000
	Modesto (CAL)	HiA	1	1	3.52	6	0	0	0	8	11	0	1	14	16.4	1.57	.324
	Arkansas (TL)	AA	5	1	2.49	35	0	0	1	51	36	3	21	71	12.6	1.13	.199
Minor League Totals			15	10	4.73	74	19	0	1	192	208	23	60	205	9.6	1.39	.274

30 MAX POVSE, RHP

BA GRADE 40 Risk: High

Born: Aug. 23, 1993. **B-T:** R-R. **Ht.:** 6-8. **Wt.:** 185. **Drafted:** UNC Greensboro, 2014 (3rd round). **Signed by:** Billy Best (Braves).

TRACK RECORD: Povse entered 2018 with a chance to pitch innings for the big league team, but instead he took a big step backward. A poor performance with Triple-A Tacoma resulted in the 6-foot-8 right-hander being demoted to Double-A.

SCOUTING REPORT: Povse had gotten stronger and more coordinated in 2017 to help keep his long levers in sync, but he still has work to do. His fastball sits 93-95 mph with downward angle. His secondary offerings include an upper-70s curveball that he struggles to land and a firm upper-80s changeup. His height gives his delivery some deception but also causes issues with his release point.

THE FUTURE: Povse needs to conquer Triple-A before getting another shot in Seattle.

Year	Club (League)	Class	W	L	ERA	G	GS	CG	SV	IP	H	HR	BB	SO	K/9	WHIP	AVG
2016	Carolina (CAR)	HiA	5	5	3.71	15	15	0	0	87	89	5	17	91	9.4	1.21	.262
	Mississippi (SL)	AA	4	1	2.93	11	11	0	0	71	61	4	12	48	6.1	1.03	.236
2017	Arkansas (TL)	AA	3	2	3.46	9	8	0	0	39	34	1	14	32	7.4	1.23	.235
	Seattle (AL)	MAJ	0	0	7.36	3	0	0	0	4	9	1	1	2	4.9	2.73	.450
	Tacoma (PCL)	AAA	1	4	7.39	13	5	0	0	32	41	3	12	29	8.2	1.67	.315
2018	Tacoma (PCL)	AAA	1	6	8.84	8	8	0	0	37	40	6	28	45	11.0	1.85	.280
	Arkansas (TL)	AA	4	3	3.41	10	10	0	0	61	62	2	19	60	8.9	1.34	.266
Major League Totals			0	0	7.36	3	0	0	0	4	9	1	1	2	4.9	2.73	.450
Minor League Totals			27	28	4.25	95	85	0	0	451	443	24	136	402	8.0	1.28	.257

Tampa Bay Rays

BY J.J. COOPER

Thanks to the opener, a never-ending stream of versatile infielders and a deep bullpen, the Rays surprised almost everyone in 2018 by winning 90 games.

They also finished 18 games out of first place and seven games out of a playoff spot. Welcome to the American League East, where being good sometimes isn't nearly good enough.

The 2018 season was the Rays' first winning record in six seasons, but it should be the start of a winning trend. This Rays group is built to succeed for several years to come. But it's also fair to wonder if that will be enough in a division where the Red Sox and Yankees aren't going anywhere.

The Rays had the fourth youngest lineup and the fourth youngest pitching staff in the majors in 2018. This is a team on the rise that also has one of the best farm systems in baseball.

Top prospect Wander Franco is a couple of years away from making an impact, but the Rays should have a steady stream of solid contributors arriving in 2019 and 2020.

What the Rays are doing should be nearly impossible. They have once again built a competitive team under spending constraints that make other lower-revenue franchises look like free spenders.

The Rays are not only young, they have a roster that's almost entirely cost controlled. The Rays managed to succeed in 2018 during a season in which they were getting younger. Rookie shortstop Willy Adames, first baseman Jake Bauers, second baseman/outfielder Brandon Lowe and utilityman Joey Wendle all worked their way into the lineup. The pitching staff got quality innings from rookies Ryan Yarbrough, Diego Castillo, Tyler Glasnow and Ryne Stanek. All together, 23 different rookies played for the Rays last season.

The Rays kept getting younger when they traded away Chris Archer to the Pirates at last year's July trade deadline. In that trade, the Rays acquired Glasnow, a long-time Pirates pitching prospect. They quickly managed to turn him into a productive starter. With Austin Meadows also penciled into the Rays' 2019 lineup, the club managed to pick up two potential long-term regulars for Archer, plus righthander Shane Baz, the club's No. 11 prospect.

With such a young team, the Rays should have financial flexibility. The biggest decisions Tampa Bay will have to make is to decide which prospects to filter in over the next two years.

The pitching staff should be able to add Brent Honeywell and Brendan McKay to the rotation in late in 2019 or early in 2020. Jesus Sanchez

Rookie shortstop Willy Adames started slowly but hit .321/.399/.460 in his final 55 games.

PROJECTED 2022 LINEUP

Catcher	Ronaldo Hernandez (24)
First Base	Nate Lowe (26)
Second Base	Brandon Lowe (27)
Third Base	Wander Franco (21)
Shortstop	Willy Adames (26)
Left Field	Austin Meadows (27)
Center Field	Vidal Brujan (24)
Right Field	Jesus Sanchez (24)
Designated Hitter	Yandy Diaz (30)
No. 1 Starter	Blake Snell (29)
No. 2 Starter	Brent Honeywell (27)
No. 3 Starter	Brendan McKay (26)
No. 4 Starter	Tyler Glasnow (28)
No. 5 Starter	Ryan Yarbrough (30)
Closer	Shane McClanahan (25)

and Nate Lowe could reach Tampa Bay on similar timetables.

With three first-round picks in the 2018 draft, the Rays brought in another significant talent infusion, led by lefthander Matthew Liberatore. The club has done a better job of drafting in recent years, but the biggest improvement on the farm has been an international department that has begun to produce a steady stream of excellent prospects.

Between a young big league team and a deep farm system, the Rays are in the best shape they've been organizationally in several years. Now they'll have to see if that's enough in a division with two perennial powers.

DEPTH CHART

TAMPA BAY RAYS

TOP 2019 ROOKIE: Brandon Lowe, 2B/OF. He has plenty of power, but a crowded Rays depth chart will make it tough to get 400 at-bats.
BREAKOUT PROSPECT: Nick Schnell, OF. With his feel for hitting and athleticism, he has a chance to be one of the best hitters in the Midwest League in 2019.
SLEEPER: Jelfry Marte, SS. Marte could be the next in a productive line of Rays international signees thanks to his excellent, quick-twitch athleticism, plus speed and solid defense at shortstop.

SOURCE OF TOP 30 TALENT			
Homegrown	22	Acquired	8
College	10	Trade	8
Junior College	1	Rule 5 draft	0
High School	6	Independent league	0
Nondrafted free agent	0	Free agent/waivers	0
International	5		

LF
Moises Gomez (10)
Jordan Qsar

CF
Josh Lowe (17)
Andrew Velazquez (19)
Tanner Dodson (16)
Ryan Boldt
Garrett Whitley
Grant Witherspoon

RF
Jesus Sanchez (6)
Nick Schnell (15)

3B
Osmy Gregorio
Adrian Rondon

SS
Wander Franco (1)
Taylor Walls (22)
Lucius Fox (23)
Jelfry Marte
Ford Proctor

2B
Vidal Brujan (7)
Brandon Lowe (8)
Nick Solak (13)
Tyler Frank (24)
Kean Wong
Tristan Gray

1B
Nate Lowe (9)
Brendan McKay (3)
Joe McCarthy (25)

C
Ronaldo Hernandez (4)
Nick Ciuffo
Michael Perez
Chris Betts
David Rodriguez
Michael Berglund

LHP

LHSP	LHRP
Brendan McKay (3)	Colin Poche (20)
Matthew Liberatore (5)	Matt Krook (30)
Shane McClanahan (12)	Nick Sprengel
Brock Burke (14)	
Anthony Banda (21)	
Resly Linares	
Luis Moncada	
Josh Fleming	
Steffon Moore	

RHP

RHSP	RHRP
Brent Honeywell (2)	Tanner Dodson (16)
Shane Baz (11)	Ian Gibaut (18)
Austin Franklin (26)	Jamie Schultz
David Mercado (27)	Miguel Lara
Drew Strotman (28)	Tommy Romero
Jose De Leon (29)	Simon Rosenblum-Larson
Tobias Myers	Justin Marsden
Taj Bradley	
Jose Mujica	
Miller Hogan	
Justin Montgomery	

DRAFT ANALYSIS

2018

BEST PURE HITTER: OF Nick Schnell (1) was one of the most productive hitters in the country during the spring. He has loose, strong hands and well above-average bat speed. SS Tyler Frank (2) may not hit the averages that Schnell will produce, but his excellent understanding of the strike zone and his patience allows him to make plenty of contact and post excellent on-base percentages.
BEST POWER HITTER: OF Grant Witherspoon (4) hit 12 home runs at Tulane and another five at Rookie-level Pulaski. He has above-average power as does OF Jordan Qsar (25). Qsar found his power with 13 home runs in his senior season at Pepperdine and another 14 in 211 at-bats as a pro.
FASTEST RUNNER: OF Beau Brundage (33) and SS K.V. Edwards (36) are both plus-plus runners, although both have work to do on stealing bases. Brundage was thrown out in eight of 12 attempts at Portland this spring, while Edwards was 9-of-17 on steals with Cowley County (Kan.) JC.
BEST DEFENSIVE PLAYER: Frank will be able to stay up the middle, but SS Ford Proctor (3) has a better shot to stay at shortstop. Proctor's above-average arm and excellent hands help him make up for limited range. C Michael Berglund (8) is a solid receiver with an average arm.
BEST ATHLETE: Schnell has excellent baseball athleticism thanks to his size, strength and quick first step. OF/RHP Tanner Dodson's (2s) loose athleticism helps him be able to both be an effective pitcher and a useful outfielder.
BEST FASTBALL: LHP Shane McClanahan's (1) fastball has touched 100 mph and has excellent riding life. Dodson's 92-95 mph sinker touches 98 mph and is hard to lift. LHP Nick Sprengel (15) can touch 96 mph, and he showed improved control and consistency in his pro debut.
BEST SECONDARY PITCH: Dodson's slider has the look of a late-inning weapon. It's hard (it can bump the low 90s at times), and he can bury it when needed. LHP Matthew Liberatore (1) has a plus changeup that flashes better than that.

TOP DRAFT PICKS OF THE DECADE

Year	Player, Pos.	2018 Org
2009	*LeVon Washington, 2B	Did not play
2010	Justin O'Conner, C	American Assoication
2011	Taylor Guerrieri, RHP	Blue Jays
2012	Richie Shaffer, 3B	Brewers
2013	Nick Ciuffo, C	Rays
2014	Casey Gillaspie, 1B	White Sox
2015	Garrett Whitley, OF	Rays
2016	Josh Lowe, 3B	Rays
2017	Brendan McKay, LHP/1B	Rays
2018	Matthew Liberatore, LHP	Rays
* Did not sign

BEST PRO DEBUT: Dodson went 1-0, 1.44 with one strikeout per inning. He also hit .277/.344/.369 as a center fielder. RHP Simon Rosenblum-Larson (19) is a low-slot righthander who went 1-3, 1.16 with 14.4 K/9.
MOST INTRIGUING BACKGROUND: The Rays are committed to letting Dodson both hit and pitch, much like they have let 2017 first-round pick Brendan McKay do both. Dodson's ability to play a solid outfield and also serve as a potential high-leverage reliever gives him a solid shot of doing both in the big leagues.
CLOSEST TO THE MAJORS: Dodson's two-way status may slow him, but his fastball-slider combo could make him a reliever who would move very quickly if he focused on pitching. McClanahan could also be a fast-moving reliever, but the Rays will take a slow-and-steady approach.
BEST LATE-ROUND PICK: Rosenblum-Larson could make it to the majors as a matchup reliever. LHP Steffon Moore (26) impressed in the Appalachian League. Qsar hit .289/.422/.573 with 14 home runs in his pro debut.
THE ONE WHO GOT AWAY: The Rays signed every player they drafted in the top 20 rounds. RHP Eric Cerantola (30) is an ex-hockey player who should be effective for Mississippi State thanks to a low-90s fastball and 12-to-6 curveball.

—J.J. COOPER

2017

LHP/1B Brendan McKay (1) was slowed by an oblique injury but he's still progressing as a two-way player. RHPs David Mercado (2) and Drew Strotman (4) still have upside but aren't as advanced.
GRADE: B

2016

Brothers OF Josh Lowe (1) and 1B Nate Lowe (13) highlight this class. Nate is closing in on Tampa and Josh stands out for his tools. OF Jake Fraley (2s) was traded in the Mike Zunino deal.
GRADE: C

2015

2B/OF Brandon Lowe (3) impressed in the big leagues after debuting in August. RHP Ian Gibaut (11) should soon join him in Tampa and OF Joe McCarthy (5) has promise, but has struggled with injuries.
GRADE: C

1 WANDER FRANCO, SS

Born: March 1, 2001. **B-T:** B-R. **Ht.:** 5-10. **Wt.:** 170.
Signed: Dominican Republic, 2017.
Signed by: Danny Santana.

Franco models his game after that of his Bani neighbor Jose Ramirez. Scouts who watch Franco play see many similarities. Like Ramirez, Franco is also a switch-hitter with a similar approach. But unlike Ramirez, who has emerged as a star, Franco was the No. 1 prospect in the 2017 international signing class who signed for $2.8 million. The Rays aggressively pushed him, and he responded by being the best hitter in the Appalachian League as a 17-year-old. Some scouts believed he could have jumped straight to high Class A with few issues. His dominance at the plate reminded many of what Vladimir Guerrero Jr. did in the Appy League in 2016, but Franco was actually more productive than Guerrero at the same age.

SCOUTING REPORT: Franco is already one of the best hitters in the minors, even if he's half a decade younger than many other top prospects. He can hit just about any fastball with a short swing from either side of the plate and excellent bat speed. He stays balanced and keeps his head nearly still while generating outstanding bat speed. Unlike many prodigies blessed with amazing wrists and special hand-eye coordination, Franco already recognizes spin and refuses to chase sliders and changeups. Franco has the ability to hit just about anything and everything, but he pairs that with advanced plate discipline. He will get over-aggressive with fastballs out of the zone, but he drives them. In the upper levels of the minors, he will have to learn to tone down his eagerness to swing at fastballs, but that's one of the few blemishes he has as a hitter. Franco projects as a future .300 or better hitter with the ability to hit 25-30 home runs. Scouts differ more on how much power Franco will develop, but most are confident projecting plus or even 70-grade power. Defensively, he has body control but lacks elite twitch. His instincts, above-average arm and hands give him a shot to be an average or even above-average shortstop, and he could be a plus defender at second base or third base.

THE FUTURE: The Rays are an organization that typically moves prospects slowly, but Franco will likely force a speed-up. He will likely begin the season at low Class A Bowling Green, but he likely won't end the season there. Multiple scouts from other organizations said they feel comfortable projecting he will be a perennial all-star as an elite hitter who can play up the middle defensively.

TONY FARLOW

BA GRADE	SCOUTING GRADES
75 Risk: V. High	**Hit:** 70. **Power:** 70. **Run:** 50. **Field:** 55. **Arm:** 55.

Projected future grades on 20-80 scouting scale

TOP PROSPECTS OF THE DECADE

Year	Player, Pos.	2018 Org
2009	David Price, LHP	Red Sox
2010	Desmond Jennings, OF	Mexican Legaue
2011	Jeremy Hellickson, RHP	Nationals
2012	Matt Moore, LHP	Rangers
2013	Wil Myers, OF	Padres
2014	Jake Odorizzi, RHP	Twins
2015	Willy Adames, SS	Rays
2016	Blake Snell, LHP	Rays
2017	Willy Adames, SS	Rays
2018	Brent Honeywell, RHP	Rays

BEST TOOLS

Best Hitter for Average	Wander Franco
Best Power Hitter	Jesus Sanchez
Best Strike-Zone Discipline	Wander Franco
Fastest Baserunner	Vidal Brujan
Best Athlete	Josh Lowe
Best Fastball	Shane McClanahan
Best Curveball	Matthew Liberatore
Best Slider	Shane Baz
Best Changeup	Brent Honeywell
Best Control	Brendan McKay
Best Defensive Catcher	Nick Ciuffo
Best Defensive Infielder	Lucius Fox
Best Infield Arm	Jermaine Palacios
Best Defensive Outfielder	Josh Lowe
Best Outfield Arm	Tanner Dodson

Year	Club (League)	Class	AVG	G	AB	R	H	2B	3B	HR	RBI	BB	SO	SB	CS	OBP	SLG
2018	Princeton (APP)	R	.351	61	242	46	85	10	7	11	57	27	19	4	3	.418	.587
Minor League Totals			.351	61	242	46	85	10	7	11	57	27	19	4	3	.418	.587

2 BRENT HONEYWELL, RHP

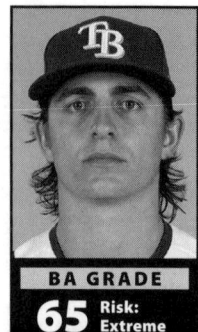

Born: March 31, 1995. **B-T:** R-R. **Ht.:** 6-2. **Wt.:** 180. **Drafted:** Walters State (Tenn.) JC, 2014 (2nd round supplemental). **Signed by:** Brian Hickman.

TRACK RECORD: Honeywell felt his elbow ligament pop while throwing batting practice early in spring training. An MRI confirmed what Honeywell already knew, and he had Tommy John surgery that will lead to a late start to his 2019 season.

SCOUTING REPORT: Prior to his surgery, Honeywell was ready to get outs in the big leagues. He has a five-pitch mix, with all his pitches showing average or better potential. He had little trouble mixing in two breaking balls, a changeup and a screwball while blowing hitters away with a 93-95 mph fastball that touched 99 mph. Honeywell's plus fastball sets up a plus changeup he uses to both baffle hitters and induce them to chase out of the strike zone. But he's just as comfortable getting ahead with an average curveball that sets up an above-average, mid-80s slider with the power and late break to be a swing-and-miss offering. He could stand to use his 70-grade screwball more often. Honeywell has improved the consistency of his release point to the point where he has above-average control.

BA GRADE
65 Risk: Extreme
Fastball: 60. **CHG:** 60.
Screwball: 70.
SL: 55. **CB:** 55. **CTL:** 55.

THE FUTURE: If his stuff returns to form, Honeywell has all the pieces to be a No. 2 starter. He will likely be ready to join the Rays by June or July.

Year	Club (League)	Class	W	L	ERA	G	GS	CG	SV	IP	H	HR	BB	SO	K/9	WHIP	AVG
·2016	Charlotte, FL (FSL)	HiA	4	1	2.41	10	10	0	0	56	43	5	11	64	10.3	0.96	.211
	Montgomery (SL)	AA	3	2	2.28	10	10	0	0	59	51	4	14	53	8.0	1.10	.231
2017	Montgomery (SL)	AA	1	1	2.08	2	2	0	0	13	4	1	4	20	13.8	0.62	.100
	Durham (IL)	AAA	12	8	3.64	24	24	0	0	124	130	11	31	152	11.1	1.30	.268
2018	Did not play—Injured																
Minor League Totals			31	19	2.88	79	78	1	0	416	357	27	93	458	9.9	1.08	.230

3 BRENDAN McKAY, LHP/1B

Born: Dec. 18, 1995. **B-T:** L-L. **Ht.:** 6-2. **Wt.:** 212. **Drafted:** Louisville, 2017 (1st round). **Signed by:** James Bonnici.

TRACK RECORD: The 2017 Baseball America College Player of the Year was a three-time first-team All-America selection while starring both at the plate and on the mound. McKay had few hiccups as a pitcher in 2018 aside from a month-long absence with a strained oblique.

SCOUTING REPORT: McKay is a better prospect as a pitcher than a hitter, and he has all the traits of a future No. 3 starter. He has plus control, a varied array of pitches and the aptitude to manipulate all of them. The cutter he learned during his junior year at Louisville has become a plus pitch. He varies its shape to where it looks like a bat-missing slider at times. His plus fastball has also picked up a little velocity. He sat 92-94 mph and touched higher, but it's his ability to spot his heater, especially to his glove side, that makes him effective. He locates his average curveball and changeup. As a hitter, McKay has excel-

BA GRADE
60 Risk: High
Fastball: 60. **Cut:** 60.
Curveball: 50.
Change: 50. **CTL:** 60.

lent pitch recognition and strike-zone awareness, but he tilts into passivity. He tends to take early-count strikes. He has plus raw power but hit just six home runs in 56 games while batting .214/.368/.359.

THE FUTURE: McKay is ready for Double-A as a pitcher. That will test him as a hitter, but the Rays see no reason to force him to focus on solely pitching just yet.

Year	Club (League)	Class	W	L	ERA	G	GS	CG	SV	IP	H	HR	BB	SO	K/9	WHIP	AVG
2017	Hudson Valley (NYP)	SS	1	0	1.80	6	6	0	0	20	10	3	5	21	9.5	0.75	.149
2018	Bowling Green (MWL)	LoA	2	0	1.09	6	6	0	0	25	8	1	2	40	14.6	0.41	.096
	Rays (GCL)	R	0	0	1.50	2	2	0	0	6	2	0	1	9	13.5	0.50	.095
	Charlotte, FL (FSL)	HiA	3	2	3.21	11	9	0	0	48	45	2	11	54	10.2	1.17	.256
Minor League Totals			6	2	2.29	25	23	0	0	98	65	6	19	124	11.3	0.85	.187

Year	Club (League)	Class	AVG	G	AB	R	H	2B	3B	HR	RBI	BB	SO	SB	CS	OBP	SLG
2017	Hudson Valley (NYP)	SS	.232	36	125	16	29	4	1	4	22	21	33	2	0	.349	.376
2018	Bowling Green (MWL)	LoA	.254	21	63	12	16	2	0	1	16	28	13	0	0	.484	.333
	Rays (GCL)	R	.000	3	10	1	0	0	0	0	0	2	0	1	0	.083	.000
	Charlotte, FL (FSL)	HiA	.210	32	119	19	25	6	1	5	21	16	38	0	0	.317	.403
Minor League Totals			.221	92	317	48	70	12	2	10	61	65	85	2	0	.361	.366

4 RONALDO HERNANDEZ, C

Born: Nov. 11, 1997. **B-T:** R-R. **Ht.:** 6-1. **Wt.:** 190. **Signed:** Colombia, 2014.
Signed by: Angel Contreras.

TRACK RECORD: The last time the Rays had a homegrown catcher serve as their starter was Toby Hall in 2007. The Rays passed on drafting Buster Posey the following year and haven't produced a regular at the position since. Hernandez could change that. An infielder as an amateur whom the Rays converted to catching, Hernandez ranked second in the Midwest League with 21 home runs and second in the minors among catchers (behind the Padres Austin Allen).

BA GRADE
60 Risk: Very High
Hit: 45. Power: 60.
Run: 30. Field: 45.
Arm: 70.

SCOUTING REPORT: Hernandez has some of the best power potential in the Rays system with legitimate 20-plus homer potential. His swing varies from short with no-load to longer and leveraged depending on the situation. Hernandez will have to stay on top of his conditioning because his body is already mature, and he's taller and heavier than his listed weight. He is doing yoga to try to help maintain his flexibility. Hernandez has shown steady improvement with his English-language skills, and he carries himself as a confident leader. A below-average receiver, he needs to improve his blocking ability and soften his hands as he receives and frames. He has a 70 arm that can shut down running games.

THE FUTURE: If Hernandez continues to put in the work defensively, he has potential to be the rare everyday catcher who is an offensive asset. Much like the rest of his Bowling Green teammates, he's ready for high Class A Charlotte, where he should be among the league's best prospects.

Year	Club (League)	Class	AVG	G	AB	R	H	2B	3B	HR	RBI	BB	SO	SB	CS	OBP	SLG
2016	Rays (DSL)	R	.340	54	206	34	70	12	0	6	35	20	12	3	5	.406	.485
2017	Princeton (APP)	R	.332	54	223	42	74	22	1	5	40	16	39	2	2	.382	.507
2018	Bowling Green (MWL)LoA	.284	109	405	68	115	20	1	21	79	31	69	10	4	.339	.494
Minor League Totals			.306	230	878	147	269	54	3	32	158	70	126	15	11	.364	.484

5 MATTHEW LIBERATORE, LHP

Born: Nov. 6, 1999. **B-T:** L-L. **HT:** 6-5. **WT:** 200. **Drafted:** HS—Glendale, Ariz., 2018 (1st round). **Signed by:** David Hamblett.

TRACK RECORD: Liberatore started the gold medal game for USA Baseball's 18U World Cup champs and was seen as a possible top-five pick heading into the spring of 2018. After impressing early in the season he slid down draft boards when his fastball backed up late in his senior year and his control wasn't as sharp. Still, no one expected to see him fall to the 16th pick, where the Rays pounced. Scouts who saw him as a pro wondered why he fell so far, as he immediately went back to dominating hitters. In August, he posted a 0.79 ERA with only 13 hits and eight walks in 22.2 innings while he struck out 27.

BA GRADE
60 Risk: Extreme
Fastball: 60.
Curveball: 60.
Change: 60. CTL: 55.

SCOUTING REPORT: Liberatore lacks the near top-of-the-scale fastball of many prep first-round pitchers, but he has an above-average fastball with excellent extension, the ability to spin a breaking ball, competitiveness, a long, projectable frame and a clean delivery. Liberatore sits 92-93 mph and touches 95, but it's his plus curveball and changeup that can overwhelm hitters. His changeup is quite advanced for a high school draftee because it has excellent deception, and he has the conviction to throw it in a variety of counts. There are scouts who believe he will add a little more velocity as he matures and fills out, but his current stuff is good enough to succeed even without a jump.

THE FUTURE: Liberatore has the look of a mid-rotation starter, and if he adds strength and velocity, he could end up being a potential front-of-the-rotation stalwart. The Rays move prep pitchers slowly, so an assignment to short-season Hudson Valley would be a sign of confidence in him.

Year	Club (League)	Class	W	L	ERA	G	GS	CG	SV	IP	H	HR	BB	SO	K/9	WHIP	AVG
2018	Rays (GCL)	R	1	2	0.98	8	8	0	0	28	16	0	11	32	10.4	0.98	.170
	Princeton (APP)	R	1	0	3.60	1	1	0	0	5	5	0	2	5	9.0	1.40	.294
Minor League Totals			2	2	1.38	9	9	0	0	33	21	0	13	37	10.2	1.04	.189

6 JESUS SANCHEZ, OF

Born: Oct. 7, 1997. **B-T:** L-R. **Ht.:** 6-2. **Wt.:** 190. **Signed:** Dominican Republic, 2014. **Signed by:** Danny Santana.

TRACK RECORD: The Rays went into the penalty box with a massive 2014 international signing class. Despite whiffing on their biggest signing, Adrian Rondon, the class has proven to be an outstanding influx of talent with Ronaldo Hernandez, Diego Castillo and Resly Linares. But the most productive of those signees has been Sanchez, who has hit better than .300 at every stop until a late-season struggle at Double-A Montgomery.

SCOUTING REPORT: Sanchez has elite bat speed and excellent hand-eye coordination, which gives him a path to being an above-average hitter with 25-plus home run power. He can drive balls in or out of the zone, which is an asset and weakness, because he swings and connects with pitches he should take. Sanchez's barrel control keeps him from striking out too much. Unlike many young lefthanded hitters, he has little trouble hitting lefthanders. He consistently posts some of the best exit velocities in the Rays' system. Sanchez has an odd gait, but he consistently turns in plus run times and is an impressive athlete. Defensively, he should be at least average in right field with an average arm.

BA GRADE

55 Risk: High

Hit: 55. Power: 60.
Run: 55. Field: 50.
Arm: 50.

THE FUTURE: Sanchez will return to Montgomery in 2019. He profiles as an athletic everyday right fielder one whose swing and body type offers reminders of the late Cardinals outfielder Oscar Taveras.

Year	Club (League)	Class	AVG	G	AB	R	H	2B	3B	HR	RBI	BB	SO	SB	CS	OBP	SLG
2016	Rays (GCL)	R	.323	42	164	25	53	6	8	4	31	6	31	1	5	.341	.530
	Princeton (APP)	R	.347	14	49	8	17	4	0	3	8	3	12	1	0	.385	.612
2017	Bowling Green (MWL)	LoA	.305	117	475	81	145	29	4	15	82	32	91	7	2	.348	.478
2018	Charlotte, FL (FSL)	HiA	.301	90	359	56	108	24	2	10	64	15	71	6	3	.331	.462
	Montgomery (SL)	AA	.214	27	98	14	21	8	0	1	11	11	21	1	1	.300	.327
Minor League Totals			.306	351	1384	220	424	84	21	37	241	87	258	24	12	.347	.478

7 VIDAL BRUJAN, 2B

Born: Feb. 9, 1998. **B-T:** B-R. **Ht.:** 5-9. **Wt.:** 155. **Signed:** Dominican Republic, 2014. **Signed by:** Danny Santana.

TRACK RECORD: Brujan signed for just $15,000 as one of the lower-profile signings in a loaded Rays' 2014 international class. Ever since he's been one of the best players for every team he's played on. He served as Bowling Green's spark plug before performing even better with high Class A Charlotte.

SCOUTING REPORT: Brujan is a 70 runner who finished second in the minors with 55 stolen bases. He's also an average defensive second baseman who has the first-step burst and an above-average arm that leads some scouts to wonder if he could handle shortstop in a pinch. Others believe he could be a plus defender in center field. His internal clock needs to improve. While Brujan has only gap power and doesn't project to hit more than 5-10 home runs per season, his line-drive swing gives him a chance to hit .300 with high on-base percentages because he works counts and doesn't chase. His righthanded swing looks nearly identical to his lefthanded stroke, but the consistency of his at-bats and power in his swing are better from the left side.

BA GRADE

55 Risk: High

Hit: 60. Power: 30.
Run: 70. Field: 55.
Arm: 55.

THE FUTURE: The Rays are stacked with promising second basemen, but Brujan's combination of athleticism and on-base skills is hard to ignore. He will play in the big leagues because of his athleticism, but he has a chance to be much more than just a role player. The Rays love positional versatility among their players. While Brujan has focused on second base so far, he has the athleticism and speed to become a much more versatile defender in upcoming years.

Year	Club (League)	Class	AVG	G	AB	R	H	2B	3B	HR	RBI	BB	SO	SB	CS	OBP	SLG
2016	Rays (GCL)	R	.282	49	202	41	57	12	5	1	8	14	15	8	5	.344	.406
	Hudson Valley (NYP)	SS	.000	2	8	1	0	0	0	0	0	1	1	2	0	.111	.000
2017	Hudson Valley (NYP)	SS	.285	67	260	51	74	15	5	3	20	34	36	16	8	.378	.415
2018	Bowling Green (MWL)	LoA	.313	95	377	86	118	18	5	5	41	48	53	43	15	.395	.427
	Charlotte, FL (FSL)	HiA	.347	27	98	26	34	7	2	4	12	15	15	12	4	.434	.582
Minor League Totals			.300	300	1171	253	351	61	21	15	101	150	136	103	44	.387	.426

8 BRANDON LOWE, 2B/OF

Born: July 6, 1994. **B-T:** L-R. **Ht.:** 5-10. **Wt.:** 175. **Drafted:** Maryland, 2015 (3rd round). **Signed by:** Lou Wieben.

TRACK RECORD: Lowe (whose name rhymes with "now") has fulfilled area scout Lou Wieben's conviction that he was one of the best hitters in the 2015 draft. He suffered a torn anterior cruciate ligament in his knee in 2013 and broke his right fibula in 2015, but he has hit ever since getting healthy. Lowe was the Florida State League MVP in 2017 and was even better in his encore, reaching the big leagues in August.

SCOUTING REPORT: Lowe is a bat-first second baseman, but he has worked to become an average defender while becoming playable in left and right field, where his above-average speed helps. His fringe-average arm limits him at second, but he has improved his ability to turn the double play and can make the throw from short right field on shifts. Offensively, Lowe gets to plus raw power thanks to a swing with leverage. That leads scouts to believe he'll hit for above-average power with an average hit tool. His hands work well, allow-ing him to handle quality fastballs, and he puts together competitive at-bats against same-side pitchers.

THE FUTURE: The Rays have emphasized developing second basemen who can hit. Lowe should earn at-bats with the Rays in the outfield and at second base.

BA GRADE	
50	**Risk:** Medium
Hit: 50. **Power:** 55.	
Run: 55. **Field:** 50.	
Arm: 45.	

Year	Club (League)	Class	AVG	G	AB	R	H	2B	3B	HR	RBI	BB	SO	SB	CS	OBP	SLG
2016	Bowling Green (MWL)	LoA	.248	107	379	67	94	15	3	5	42	60	77	6	3	.357	.343
2017	Charlotte, FL (FSL)	HiA	.311	90	315	62	98	34	3	9	46	47	65	6	3	.403	.524
	Montgomery (SL)	AA	.253	24	95	8	24	5	1	2	12	2	26	1	1	.270	.389
2018	Montgomery (SL)	AA	.291	54	199	37	58	17	1	8	41	35	55	8	2	.400	.508
	Durham (IL)	AAA	.304	46	181	36	55	14	0	14	35	22	47	0	1	.380	.613
	Tampa Bay (AL)	MAJ	.233	43	129	16	30	6	2	6	25	16	38	2	1	.324	.450
Major League Totals			.233	43	129	16	30	6	2	6	25	16	38	2	1	.324	.450
Minor League Totals			.281	321	1169	210	329	85	8	38	176	166	270	21	10	.374	.465

9 NATE LOWE, 1B

Born: July 7, 1995. **B-T:** L-R. **Ht.:** 6-4. **Wt.:** 235. **Drafted:** Mississippi State, 2016 (13th round). **Signed by:** Rickey Drexler.

TRACK RECORD: Once viewed as an organizational player, Lowe transformed himself into a prospect in 2018 after getting into better shape and improving his flexibility in the offseason. He played at three different colleges (Mercer, St. John's River (Fla.) JC and Mississippi State) before joining the Rays as a 13th-round pick in 2016, the same year in which Tampa Bay drafted his brother Josh in the first round. He became the rare Rays prospect to play at three levels in the same season.

SCOUTING REPORT: Lowe's improved conditioning wasn't his only tweak. He simplified and shortened a long swing that had always left him vulnerable to fastballs. Pitchers soon learned that fastballs that used to tie him up turned into home runs. Lowe had always had good pitch recognition, and he had long been able to hit breaking balls and changeups. Getting more pull-oriented and looser at the plate paid off when he squared up more balls. Lowe has plus power to go with an average hit tool. He has to hit as a first baseman who doesn't run well and is a below-average defender.

THE FUTURE: Lowe has one season on his résumé in which he has produced, but scouts say that his newfound power and improved swing are no flukes. His plus power is alluring and now that Jake Bauers is traded, his path to a major league role is clearer.

BA GRADE	
55	**Risk:** High
Hit: 50. **Power:** 60.	
Run: 30. **Field:** 50.	
Arm: 40.	

Year	Club (League)	Class	AVG	G	AB	R	H	2B	3B	HR	RBI	BB	SO	SB	CS	OBP	SLG
2016	Hudson Valley (NYP)	SS	.300	67	247	26	74	18	2	4	40	30	39	1	0	.382	.437
2017	Bowling Green (MWL)	LoA	.293	63	229	34	67	13	0	5	35	36	53	0	1	.387	.415
	Charlotte, FL (FSL)	HiA	.249	52	173	21	43	10	1	2	24	28	53	1	1	.355	.353
2018	Charlotte, FL (FSL)	HiA	.356	51	194	39	69	15	0	10	44	25	33	0	0	.432	.588
	Montgomery (SL)	AA	.340	51	188	36	64	11	0	13	42	35	30	1	1	.444	.606
	Durham (IL)	AAA	.260	28	100	18	26	6	1	4	16	8	27	0	0	.327	.460
Minor League Totals			.303	312	1131	174	343	73	4	38	201	162	235	3	3	.393	.476

10 MOISES GOMEZ, OF

Born: Aug. 27, 1998. **B-T:** R-R. **Ht.:** 5-11. **Wt.:** 195. **Signed:** Venezuela, 2015. **Signed by:** Juan Castillo/Ronnie Blanco.

BACKGROUND: The Rays found a bargain in Gomez, who quickly emerged as the best player in the Venezuelan Summer League in 2015. He led the low Class A Midwest League with 60 extra-base hits and 34 doubles.

SCOUTING REPORT: Many evaluators compare Gomez with Marcell Ozuna because they have similar builds and a similar swing path. Gomez has plus power thanks to plenty of strength in his hands and wrists. He has the over-aggressiveness that is often a problem for young hitters. He doesn't recognize breaking balls out of the hand yet and chases pitches in the dirt too often. But Gomez has the hand-eye coordination to develop into an average hitter. He is an above-average runner, but he likely will slow to average as his body matures. Defensively, Gomez should develop into an average corner outfielder with an average arm. He has a good first step and can run, but he looks lost at times.

THE FUTURE: Gomez could be an above-average regular if he improves his pitch recognition. He will head to high Class A Charlotte in 2019.

BA GRADE

55 Risk: High

Hit: 50. Power: 60.
Run: 50. Field: 50.
Arm: 50.

Year	Club (League)	Class	AVG	G	AB	R	H	2B	3B	HR	RBI	BB	SO	SB	CS	OBP	SLG
2016	Rays (GCL)	R	.220	47	168	20	37	9	3	1	10	12	37	4	3	.273	.327
2017	Princeton (APP)	R	.275	53	211	37	58	11	0	5	28	13	52	10	1	.328	.398
2018	Bowling Green (MWL)	LoA	.280	122	471	67	132	34	7	19	82	34	137	4	3	.328	.503
Minor League Totals			.276	269	1030	162	284	64	12	31	154	82	254	27	11	.331	.451

11 SHANE BAZ, RHP

BA GRADE

60 Risk: Extreme

Born: June 17, 1999. **B-T:** R-R. **Ht.:** 6-3. **Wt.:** 190. **Drafted:** HS—Tomball, Texas, 2017 (1st round). **Signed by:** Wayne Mathis (Pirates).

TRACK RECORD: Baz was viewed as one of the best arms in the 2017 draft class, but he never got to pitch in full-season ball with his original team as Pittsburgh sent him to the Rays as the player to be named in last July's Chris Archer trade.

SCOUTING REPORT: Baz is many innings and many years away from his ceiling. He struggles to sync up his lower half with his arm, and his arm often ends up trying to make up for inconsistencies in how he drives off the mound, which leads to timing issues in his delivery. He also gets too rotational at times and ends up spinning off the mound. He currently has near bottom-of-the-scale control. But Baz has one of the fastest arms in the minors. He can touch 99 mph with his fastball (it sits 92-95 mph) and unleashes high-80s sliders. Both could end up being plus-plus pitches eventually, but he struggles to land his slider and potentially above-average curve right now. His fastball has some natural cut and he mixes in a changeup as well. Nothing is consistent yet, but Baz's arm works well and his delivery is promising.

THE FUTURE: Baz could end up being a fire-breathing Noah Syndergaard-esque ace, but he needs to improve his control by three or four grades to reach that potential. A more likely landing spot is as a closer.

Year	Club (League)	Class	W	L	ERA	G	GS	CG	SV	IP	H	HR	BB	SO	K/9	WHIP	AVG
2017	Pirates (GCL)	R	0	3	3.80	10	10	0	0	24	26	2	14	19	7.2	1.69	.289
2018	Bristol (APP)	R	4	3	3.97	10	10	0	0	45	45	2	23	54	10.7	1.50	.250
	Princeton (APP)	R	0	2	7.71	2	2	0	0	7	11	1	6	5	6.4	2.43	.367
Minor League Totals			4	8	4.26	22	22	0	0	76	82	5	43	78	9.2	1.64	.273

12 SHANE McCLANAHAN, LHP

BA GRADE

55 Risk: Very High

Born: April 28, 1997. **B-T:** L-L. **Ht.:** 6-1. **Wt.:** 188. **Drafted:** South Florida, 2018 (1st round). **Signed by:** Brett Foley.

BACKGROUND: A potential top 10 pick, McClanahan ended up sliding almost out of the first round when he failed to allay scouts' concerns about his ability to remain a starter. Tommy John surgery that sidelined him in 2016 and fastball command and control that wavered significantly from game to game left many teams convinced he'll end up as a power reliever. McClanahan finished second in Division I with 14.5 strikeouts per nine innings and struck out 54 percent of all batters he faced in his pro debut.

SCOUTING REPORT: While McClanahan's delivery is effortful, he can reach 100 mph although he generally sits 93-95. It's rare velocity and has life in the strike zone. McClanahan does struggle to stay in sync. He'll need to rectify that to improve his below-average control. The Rays would like to work on figuring out how to add a little more separation with his 88-90 mph changeup, but he showed confidence in it at South Florida. McClanahan's slider gives him a shot to have three above-average or better pitches down the road. He does a good job of making it look like a fastball, but it's too inconsistent.

THE FUTURE: McClanahan will work on developing his stamina and consistency as a starter at low Class A Bowling Green. He most likely will end up as a potentially dominating closer or setup man.

Year	Club (League)	Class	W	L	ERA	G	GS	CG	SV	IP	H	HR	BB	SO	K/9	WHIP	AVG
2018	Rays (GCL)	R	0	0	0.00	2	2	0	0	3	1	0	0	6	18.0	0.33	.100
	Princeton (APP)	R	0	0	0.00	2	2	0	0	4	2	0	1	7	15.8	0.75	.154
Minor League Totals			0	0	0.00	4	4	0	0	7	3	0	1	13	16.7	0.57	.130

13 NICK SOLAK, 2B

BA GRADE
45 Risk: Medium

Born: Jan. 11, 1995. **B-T:** R-R. **Ht.:** 5-10. **Wt.:** 180. **Drafted:** Louisville, 2016 (2nd round). **Signed by:** Mike Gibbons (Yankees).

TRACK RECORD: Solak has long been a productive hitter. The Yankees shipped him to the Rays just before spring training in 2018 in the deal that saw Brandon Drury head to New York.

SCOUTING REPORT: Solak has always hit and he'll continue to hit. He's a plus hitter with a short, simple swing that has always worked for him. He consistently puts together competitive at-bats that are annoying for a pitcher and he draws enough walks to post lofty on-base percentages. And he has developed average power to punish pitchers' mistakes even though his swing isn't geared for power. What the Rays haven't figured out yet is where Solak can play. He's a below-average defender at second base. He's reliable when he gets to a ball (he made just two errors all season) but he has below-average feet and range and struggles to turn double plays. The Rays tried him in the outfield (which he also played at Louisville). His plus speed is an asset, but he's fringy there as well. Solak's average arm is adequate wherever he plays.

THE FUTURE: Observers believe Solak is a more consistent hitter than teammate Brandon Lowe, but Lowe has more power, is a better defender at second and has already reached Tampa Bay, so Solak's path to everyday at-bats with the Rays is murky. He's ready for Triple-A.

Year	Club (League)	Class	AVG	G	AB	R	H	2B	3B	HR	RBI	BB	SO	SB	CS	OBP	SLG
2016	Staten Island (NYP)	SS	.321	64	240	48	77	13	1	3	25	30	39	8	0	.412	.421
2017	Tampa (FSL)	HiA	.301	100	346	56	104	17	4	10	44	53	76	13	4	.397	.460
	Trenton (EL)	AA	.286	30	119	16	34	9	1	2	9	10	24	1	1	.344	.429
2018	Montgomery (SL)	AA	.282	126	478	91	135	17	3	19	76	68	112	21	6	.384	.450
Minor League Totals			.296	320	1183	211	350	56	9	34	154	161	251	43	11	.390	.445

14 BROCK BURKE, LHP

BA GRADE
50 Risk: High

Born: Aug. 4, 1996. **B-T:** L-L. **Ht.:** 6-4. **Wt.:** 200. **Drafted:** HS—Evergreen, Colo., 2014 (3rd round). **Signed by:** Ryan Henderson.

TRACK RECORD: When the Rays drafted Burke, they were spending nearly $1 million to get a pitcher with a lot of work to do. Burke rarely bumped above 90 mph and his control was shaky. The Rays put him on a weighted ball program and watched him grow into a stronger pitcher with much-improved control.

SCOUTING REPORT: Burke grew into an impressive, well-rounded starting pitcher, mixing four pitches. While no pitch is plus, Burke's fastball and changeup are both above-average and both breaking balls are at least fringe-average. Burke now sits 92-94 mph and touches 97 (up a tick from 2017). The fastball helps set up an above-average low-80s changeup that has plenty of separation, some deception and some late fade. There are scouts who believe Burke should pick the slider or the curve and focus on refining one breaking ball. At its best the slider is a 2-to-7 breaker with late tilt, but it and his loopier curveball often blend together. Burke has shown average control and command.

THE FUTURE: Burke was added to the 40-man roster after the season. He'll likely begin 2019 back in Montgomery, but should reach Triple-A Durham in 2019. He projects as a No. 4 starter.

Year	Club (League)	Class	W	L	ERA	G	GS	CG	SV	IP	H	HR	BB	SO	K/9	WHIP	AVG
2016	Hudson Valley (NYP)	SS	3	3	3.39	13	13	0	0	61	53	1	29	61	9.0	1.34	.235
2017	Bowling Green (MWL)	LoA	6	0	1.10	10	10	0	0	57	37	0	20	59	9.3	0.99	.181
	Charlotte, FL (FSL)	HiA	5	6	4.64	13	13	0	0	66	75	6	16	49	6.7	1.38	.291
2018	Charlotte, FL (FSL)	HiA	3	5	3.84	16	13	0	0	82	85	4	30	87	9.5	1.40	.263
	Montgomery (SL)	AA	6	1	1.95	9	9	0	0	55	39	2	14	71	11.5	0.96	.193
Minor League Totals			27	20	3.41	80	74	0	0	388	359	17	132	374	8.7	1.27	.244

15 NICK SCHNELL, OF

BA GRADE
55 Risk: Extreme

Born: March 27, 2000. **B-T:** L-R. **Ht.:** 6-3. **Wt.:** 180. **Drafted:** HS—Indianapolis, 2018 (1st round). **Signed by:** James Bonnici.

TRACK RECORD: Coming out of the summer showcase season in 2017, Schnell was seen as a promising outfielder who was likely to make it to Louisville. Schnell gained close to 20 pounds for his senior season and changed that narrative. He hit .535 with 15 home runs as he proved to teams he was a first-round pick. Schnell didn't show that power in the Gulf Coast League, but he did control the strike zone.

SCOUTING REPORT: Schnell has a loose, handsy swing that allows him to drive the ball to all fields. For as much power as he showed during his high school season, he's more likely to end up as a plus hitter with average power rather than a future mid-order masher, although his above-average bat speed does give him a chance to exceed that power projection. A hit-over-power profile should work because he's a solid athlete. Schnell is currently an above-average runner. If he can retain that speed, he could stay in center field, but most likely he'll end up as an above-average defender in a corner with an above-average arm.

THE FUTURE: Schnell has enough polish to handle a jump to low Class A Bowling Green. If he improves half as much in 2019 as he did in 2018, he should be one of the better hitters in the Midwest League.

Year	Club (League)	Class	AVG	G	AB	R	H	2B	3B	HR	RBI	BB	SO	SB	CS	OBP	SLG
2018	Rays (GCL)	R	.239	19	67	8	16	4	1	1	4	14	23	2	6	.378	.373
Minor League Totals			.239	19	67	8	16	4	1	1	4	14	23	2	6	.378	.373

16 TANNER DODSON, RHP/OF

BA GRADE
50 Risk: High

Born: May 9, 1997. **B-T:** B-R. **Ht.:** 6-1. **Wt.:** 160. **Drafted:** California, 2018 (2nd round supplemental). **Signed by:** Alan Hull.

TRACK RECORD: Dodson's father Bo was a first baseman/outfielder who was a third-round pick (63rd overall) of the Brewers in 1989. Tanner went eight picks later in his draft, but was a supplemental second round pick because there are more teams picking now.

SCOUTING REPORT: Dodson is following in Brendan McKay's footsteps as a two-way player for the Rays and like McKay, Dodson is seen as a better prospect on the mound than in the outfield. Dodson dominated New York-Penn League hitters with a 95-98 mph fastball with power and sink and a hard 88-90 mph slider. The slider is a little more erratic than the fastball, but both are pitches that can miss bats and both have potential to be plus-plus pitches. Righthanders hit .104/.200/.104 against him. His stuff sometimes does tail off in his second and third innings of work. Dodson is above-average defensively in center fielder and an above-average runner with a plus arm. He has little power, but he puts the bat on the ball from both sides of the plate.

THE FUTURE: If he were only an outfielder, Dodson wouldn't be seen as a significant prospect, but his defense and base-running provide extra value on top of his potential to be a late-inning reliever.

Year	Club (League)	Class	W	L	ERA	G	GS	CG	SV	IP	H	HR	BB	SO	K/9	WHIP	AVG
2018	Hudson Valley (NYP)	SS	1	0	1.44	9	0	0	1	25	12	0	5	25	9.0	0.68	.143
Minor League Totals			1	0	1.44	9	0	0	1	25	12	0	5	25	9.0	0.68	.143

Year	Club (League)	Class	AVG	G	AB	R	H	2B	3B	HR	RBI	BB	SO	SB	CS	OBP	SLG
2018	Hudson Valley (NYP)	SS	.273	49	198	30	54	7	3	2	19	20	34	8	3	.344	.369
Minor League Totals			.273	49	198	30	54	7	3	2	19	20	34	8	3	.344	.369

17 JOSH LOWE, OF

BA GRADE
50 Risk: High

Born: Feb. 2, 1998. **B-T:** L-R. **Ht.:** 6-4. **Wt.:** 205. **Drafted:** HS—Marietta, Ga., 2016 (1st round). **Signed by:** Milt Hill.

TRACK RECORD: The 13th pick in the 2016 draft, Lowe saw his older brother Nate emerge as a significant prospect with a breakout 2018 season that included a trip to the Futures Game. Josh's season wasn't as enjoyable. He showed up stronger, but it didn't pay off in on-field results.

SCOUTING REPORT: If Lowe can be an average hitter, his other tools will ensure he's an impact big leaguer. He's a plus runner and a plus defender in center field with an above-average arm. Lowe also has long shown plus raw power. But there's reason to worry about Lowe's ability to hit. The Rays worked to get Lowe to hit the ball in the air more often and he did, but it didn't pay off in extra-base hits. Lowe's season statistically was worse than 2017, but there are reasons for hope. He struck out less and walked more and he's shown steady improvement in picking out hittable pitches. But he's failing to square up hittable pitches in the zone. Some scouts believe he got too uphill in his swing, and his swing can get long.

THE FUTURE: Lowe is one of the most physically gifted players in the team's system. He still could be an impact everyday regular if it all comes together, but he has considerable work to do at the plate.

Year	Club (League)	Class	AVG	G	AB	R	H	2B	3B	HR	RBI	BB	SO	SB	CS	OBP	SLG
2016	Rays (GCL)	R	.258	28	93	14	24	6	1	2	15	20	27	1	1	.386	.409
	Princeton (APP)	R	.238	26	80	11	19	0	2	3	11	17	32	1	1	.360	.400
2017	Bowling Green (MWL)	LoA	.268	118	456	60	122	26	2	8	55	42	144	22	8	.326	.386
2018	Charlotte, FL (FSL)	HiA	.238	105	399	62	95	25	3	6	47	47	117	18	6	.322	.361
Minor League Totals			.253	277	1028	147	260	57	8	19	128	126	320	42	16	.333	.379

18 IAN GIBAUT, RHP

BA GRADE

45 Risk: Medium

Born: Nov. 11, 1993. **B-T:** R-R. **Ht.:** 6-3. **Wt.:** 235. **Drafted:** Tulane, 2015 (11th round). **Signed by:** Rickey Drexler.

TRACK RECORD: Much as Diego Castillo did in 2017, Gibaut readied himself for a big league role by serving as Durham's closer. It's a role he also held at Tulane and he's been quite good at it, in part because he's always been effective against both lefthanders and righthanders.

SCOUTING REPORT: Gibaut's foundation as a pitcher has always been a big fastball. He sits 95-99 mph, although the fastball earns some 60 grades rather than the 70 its velocity would indicate because it can be a little straight. Gibault then mixes in a hard 89-91 mph slider with short but sharp tilt. It doesn't earn better grades because Gibaut hasn't proven he can consistently throw it for strikes, so hitters can learn to lay off of it. He has a fringy changeup. Gibault's control has always been fringe-average at best.

THE FUTURE: Gibaut was added to the 40-man roster in November and is ready to help the big league bullpen. He doesn't have closer-type stuff, but he should be a valuable, durable seventh-inning option.

Year	Club (League)	Class	W	L	ERA	G	GS	CG	SV	IP	H	HR	BB	SO	K/9	WHIP	AVG
2016	Bowling Green (MWL)	LoA	1	0	0.93	7	0	0	1	10	6	0	1	18	16.8	0.72	.171
	Charlotte, FL (FSL)	HiA	1	2	2.85	27	0	0	3	47	45	2	19	45	8.6	1.35	.253
2017	Charlotte, FL (FSL)	HiA	1	0	2.16	5	0	0	2	8	5	0	1	14	15.1	0.72	.172
	Montgomery (SL)	AA	6	1	2.22	43	0	0	10	53	33	6	26	63	10.8	1.12	.174
2018	Durham (IL)	AAA	4	3	2.09	48	0	0	14	56	35	3	21	75	12.1	1.00	.181
Minor League Totals			16	7	2.25	142	0	0	31	204	147	13	76	253	11.2	1.09	.201

19 ANDREW VELAZQUEZ, SS/OF

BA GRADE

45 Risk: Medium

Born: July 14, 1994. **B-T:** B-R. **Ht.:** 5-10. **Wt.:** 160. **Drafted:** HS—Bronx, N.Y., 2012 (7th round). **Signed by:** Todd Donovan (Diamondbacks).

TRACK RECORD: Acquired by the Rays in a deal that sent Jeremy Hellickson to the D-backs. Velazquez's prospect status had waned since as scouts didn't believe his bat or glove were strong enough to be an everyday shortstop. But he began playing outfield in 2018, and his versatility got him to the majors.

SCOUTING REPORT: Velazquez has gone full circle as a player. He was an outfielder for most of his high school career before moving to shortstop. Now moving to center field has kick-started his career because he quickly established himself as an exceptional defender there. While Velazquez is an average defender at shortstop, he's at least a plus defender in center and there are scouts who say he's plus-plus. He's also a plus runner who uses that speed well on the basepaths. And he's a contact hitter from both sides of the plate. He projects to have below-average power with a contact-oriented approach.

THE FUTURE: Velazquez's value is in his versatility. He doesn't hit enough to be a regular at any one spot, but his ability to play an excellent center field, second, shortstop or third base makes him a useful utility-man. He'll compete for a big league spot in spring training.

Year	Club (League)	Class	AVG	G	AB	R	H	2B	3B	HR	RBI	BB	SO	SB	CS	OBP	SLG
2016	Charlotte, FL (FSL)	HiA	.262	75	286	31	75	6	2	1	14	21	71	11	6	.313	.308
2017	Montgomery (SL)	AA	.232	108	375	49	87	17	4	9	37	30	112	18	9	.294	.371
2018	Montgomery (SL)	AA	.229	8	35	5	8	2	1	2	4	1	11	2	0	.250	.514
	Durham (IL)	AAA	.258	117	423	63	109	16	6	12	41	34	124	29	5	.317	.409
	Tampa Bay (AL)	MAJ	.300	13	10	3	3	1	0	0	0	1	3	1	0	.417	.400
Major League Totals			.300	13	10	3	3	1	0	0	0	1	3	1	0	.417	.400
Minor League Totals			.266	601	2263	338	603	86	41	34	204	209	619	144	46	.331	.386

20 COLIN POCHE, LHP

BA GRADE

40 Risk: Low

Born: Jan. 17, 1994. **B-T:** L-L. **Ht.:** 6-3. **Wt.:** 185. **Drafted:** Dallas Baptist, 2016 (14th round). **Signed by:** J.R. Salinas (Diamondbacks).

TRACK RECORD: Poche blew out his elbow as a sophomore at Arkansas, decided to transfer while he rehabbed and then became Dallas Baptist's ace as a redshirt junior. His lack of velocity (he sat 85-89 mph) meant he lasted until the 14th round despite a solid record of college success. After a dominating 2017 season, Poche was announced on May 1, 2018 as a player to be named in the three-team deal that sent Steven Souza Jr. to Arizona and Brandon Drury to New York.

SCOUTING REPORT: Poche still fails to light up radar guns, but that hasn't prevented him from being the most dominating reliever in the minors the past two seasons. Poche's 0.82 ERA last year was easily the best in full season baseball for anyone with 50 or more innings and he struck out more than half of the batters he faced in June. Poche's dominance comes from a stealth fastball that generally sits 90-92 mph but generates swings and misses like it's 102 mph. Poche's delivery is short in the back and he gets excellent extension. The pitch plays much better than its velocity or even its spin rate would indicate. Some scouts

grade Poche's heater as an above-average pitch because it plays up. Others slap a plus grade on it because of how hitters struggle with it. He did wear down a little as the season wore on and he has no above-average second pitch—his curveball is average but he can manipulate its shape. Poche has average control.
THE FUTURE: What you see isn't what you get with Poche, but it's about time to see if his invisi-ball will play as well in the majors.

Year	Club (League)	Class	W	L	ERA	G	GS	CG	SV	IP	H	HR	BB	SO	K/9	WHIP	AVG
2016	Hillsboro (NWL)	SS	1	2	3.19	21	4	0	0	31	20	2	17	36	10.5	1.19	.194
2017	Kane County (MWL)	LoA	2	0	1.09	13	0	0	1	25	16	0	6	44	16.1	0.89	.186
	Visalia (CAL)	HiA	1	1	1.40	18	0	0	2	26	14	0	13	37	13.0	1.05	.163
2018	Jackson (SL)	AA	0	0	0.00	9	0	0	1	11	3	0	2	23	18.8	0.45	.086
	Montgomery (SL)	AA	1	0	0.00	3	0	0	0	5	1	0	0	9	16.2	0.20	.067
	Durham (IL)	AAA	5	0	1.08	28	2	0	1	50	29	2	17	78	14.0	0.92	.172
Minor League Totals			10	3	1.47	92	6	0	5	147	83	4	55	227	13.9	0.94	.168

21 ANTHONY BANDA, LHP

BA GRADE

50 Risk: Very High

Born: Aug. 10, 1993. **B-T:** L-L. **Ht.:** 6-2. **Wt.:** 190. **Drafted:** San Jacinto (Texas) JC, 2012 (10th round). **Signed by:** Brian Sankey (Brewers).

TRACK RECORD: When the Brewers drafted Banda in 2012, he was a projectable lefty with a fringe-average fastball. He's transformed himself into a power pitcher. He was sent to the Rays in Feb. 2018 in the three-team deal that sent Steven Souza Jr. to the D-backs. He made three starts with the Rays in May before going down with an elbow injury that required Tommy John surgery.
SCOUTING REPORT: Banda is a fast worker with a high-tempo delivery that sometimes can lead to him getting a little out of sync. He attacks hitters with a 93-96 mph four-seam plus fastball with enough giddyup and life to generate swings and misses up in the zone. He relies heavily on the fastball, but his high-80s changeup has potential to be an average pitch as well thanks to solid deception and occasional late sink. Banda will mix in a fringy slurvy 81-84 mph slider primarily against lefthanded hitters. At times in the minors it's shown some bite, but he's rarely shown the confidence in it in the majors. He also has toyed with a slower get-over curveball. Banda is generally around the zone with fringe-average control.
THE FUTURE: Banda's surgery will likely sideline him until 2020, but if he can make a full recovery, he has the kind of quality fastball that's a perfect foundation of a mid-rotation starter or a setup man. He'll be working on rehabbing his injury throughout 2019.

Year	Club (League)	Class	W	L	ERA	G	GS	CG	SV	IP	H	HR	BB	SO	K/9	WHIP	AVG
2016	Mobile (SL)	AA	6	2	2.12	13	13	0	0	76	70	4	28	84	9.9	1.28	.241
	Reno (PCL)	AAA	4	4	3.67	13	13	0	0	74	73	6	27	68	8.3	1.36	.257
2017	Reno (PCL)	AAA	8	7	5.39	22	22	0	0	122	125	15	51	116	8.6	1.44	.266
	Arizona (NL)	MAJ	2	3	5.96	8	4	0	0	26	26	1	10	25	8.8	1.40	.255
2018	Tampa Bay (AL)	MAJ	1	0	3.68	3	1	0	0	15	12	1	3	10	6.1	1.02	.235
	Durham (IL)	AAA	4	3	3.64	8	8	0	0	42	43	3	18	49	10.5	1.45	.272
Major League Totals			3	3	5.13	11	5	0	0	40	38	2	13	35	7.8	1.26	.248
Minor League Totals			44	37	3.81	138	121	1	2	687	695	52	257	674	8.8	1.39	.263

22 TAYLOR WALLS, SS

BA GRADE

45 Risk: High

Born: July 10, 1996. **B-T:** B-R. **Ht.:** 5-10. **Wt.:** 180. **Drafted:** Florida State, 2017 (3rd round). **Signed by:** Brett Foley.

TRACK RECORD: After an excellent sophomore season that earned All-America honors, Walls slumped as a junior. After he was drafted by the Rays, Walls finished his Florida State career with a flourish, setting a school record by reaching base safely in 14 consecutive plate appearances.
SCOUTING REPORT: What impresses scouts about Walls is he's a well-rounded athlete with no real plus tool, but a lot of 50s on his scouting report. He's a reliable defender who steadily makes the routine play, although he lacks plus range. He's an average defender at short who should be fine at second base, even though he has only played shortstop as a pro. He can flash an above-average arm. Walls is an above-average hitter with below-average power. He is an above-average runner who stole 31 bases in 2018.
THE FUTURE: Walls profiles as a second-division shortstop or more likely as the kind of versatile, multi-position semi-regular the Rays love to develop. He heads to high Class A Charlotte knowing Wander Franco will soon be nipping at his heels.

Year	Club (League)	Class	AVG	G	AB	R	H	2B	3B	HR	RBI	BB	SO	SB	CS	OBP	SLG
2017	Hudson Valley (NYP)	SS	.213	46	164	22	35	9	0	1	21	29	53	5	4	.330	.287
2018	Bowling Green (MWL)	LoA	.304	120	467	87	142	28	6	6	57	66	80	31	12	.393	.428
Minor League Totals			.281	166	631	109	177	37	6	7	78	95	133	36	16	.376	.391

23 LUCIUS FOX, SS

BA GRADE	
45	Risk: High

Born: July 2, 1997. **B-T:** B-R. **Ht.:** 6-1. **Wt.:** 175. **Signed:** Bahamas, 2015.
Signed by: Jose Alou/Joe Salermo (Giants).

TRACK RECORD: Fox signed with the Giants for $6 million out of the Bahamas, but looked overmatched in 2016 in Augusta. The Rays believed he was better than he showed in his pro debut and acquired him in the Matt Moore trade. The Rays have slowed his development pace and he responded with a promising season. He finished fifth in Florida State League with a .371 on-base percentage.

SCOUTING REPORT: Fox is one of the best athletes the Rays have with quick-twitch athleticism to go with plus-plus speed. He's got work to do on improving his reliability defensively, and he sometimes sits back on balls he should attack, but he has the tools to be an above-average defender at shortstop with an above-average arm. Fox has developed his strike-zone awareness and has a contact-oriented approach. He's better from the right side, but has started to pull the ball more regularly as a lefthanded hitter. Fox projects as an average hitter with well-below-average power, which means his glove is going to have to be excellent.

THE FUTURE: Fox's lack of power will likely limit him to being a useful big league backup as a switch-hitting shortstop with contact skills and a solid glove at shortstop and second base. But he could also prove to be a second-division regular who bats at the bottom of the lineup.

Year	Club (League)	Class	AVG	G	AB	R	H	2B	3B	HR	RBI	BB	SO	SB	CS	OBP	SLG
2016	Augusta (SAL)	LoA	.207	75	285	46	59	6	4	2	16	37	76	25	7	.305	.277
2017	Bowling Green (MWL)	LoA	.275	77	302	45	83	13	3	2	27	33	80	27	10	.359	.358
	Charlotte, FL (FSL)	HiA	.235	30	115	19	27	3	0	1	12	12	33	3	3	.321	.287
2018	Charlotte, FL (FSL)	HiA	.282	89	351	54	99	17	1	2	30	42	79	23	7	.371	.353
	Montgomery (SL)	AA	.221	27	104	14	23	3	1	1	9	8	20	6	2	.284	.298
Minor League Totals			**.252**	**298**	**1157**	**178**	**291**	**42**	**9**	**8**	**94**	**132**	**288**	**84**	**29**	**.339**	**.324**

24 TYLER FRANK, SS

BA GRADE	
45	Risk: High

Born: Jan. 15, 1997. **B-T:** R-R. **Ht.:** 6-0. **Wt.:** 185. **Drafted:** Florida Atlantic, 2018 (2nd round). **Signed by:** Victor Rodriguez.

TRACK RECORD: When the Owls needed a fill-in catcher in 2016, Frank volunteered even though he hadn't played the position since he was a little kid. He also handled a move to third base and left field with USA Baseball's College National Team with no issues. But his main position has been shortstop.

SCOUTING REPORT: Frank gets the most out of a well-rounded set of average tools. At the plate, Frank doesn't try to do too much, as his patience and strike zone awareness pay off in a contact-oriented approach. He led the New York-Penn League in on-base percentage in his debut. His knack for putting barrel on ball earns future above-average hit grades from scouts. Frank has fringe-average power potential. Defensively, he's reliable but a little limited at shortstop by his average range and average arm. He profiles better at second or third. He's a fringe-average runner.

THE FUTURE: Frank fits the team's profile of drafting productive college middle infielders who can hit. The Rays have already worked on having him play everywhere around the infield, which will become more important in 2019 as he jumps to full season ball. He'll have to compete for time at shortstop with either Taylor Walls or Wander Franco.

Year	Club (League)	Class	AVG	G	AB	R	H	2B	3B	HR	RBI	BB	SO	SB	CS	OBP	SLG
2018	Hudson Valley (NYP)	SS	.288	51	177	37	51	14	1	2	22	33	28	3	3	.425	.412
Minor League Totals			**.288**	**51**	**177**	**37**	**51**	**14**	**1**	**2**	**22**	**33**	**28**	**3**	**3**	**.425**	**.412**

25 JOE McCARTHY, OF/1B

BA GRADE	
45	Risk: High

Born: Feb. 23, 1994. **B-T:** L-L. **Ht.:** 6-3. **Wt.:** 220. **Drafted:** Virginia, 2015 (5th round). **Signed by:** Lou Wieben.

TRACK RECORD: McCarthy was an extremely productive hitter at Virginia, but he fell in the 2015 draft because of a back injury that ruined his junior season. As a pro, he's shown the same on-base ability and feel for hitting, but he's also continued to battle back problems. He missed nearly three months with a back injury and then saw his Arizona Fall League season end early because of a broken hand.

SCOUTING REPORT: McCarthy is an average hitter, but he posts excellent on-base percentages because of his ability to control the strike zone and draw walks. McCarthy's bat speed is only average, but he works counts well. There's more concern about his power potential. McCarthy has never hit 10 home runs in a pro season, but the hope is with big league baseball he can find 12-15 home runs if he gets 500 big league at-bats. His back injuries have cost him some speed–he's now a below-average runner–and have limited his defense. He takes excellent routes, but he's range-limited by his footspeed. He's also played first base.

THE FUTURE: The Rays added McCarthy to their 40-man roster in November. His long history of back injuries is a significant concern, but he's been a productive hitter capable of posting .350-plus on-base percentages with sporadic power. He's ready for a callup whenever the Rays need a useful corner bat.

Year	Club (League)	Class	AVG	G	AB	R	H	2B	3B	HR	RBI	BB	SO	SB	CS	OBP	SLG
2016	Bowling Green (MWL)	LoA	.288	43	153	31	44	12	0	3	29	33	30	11	2	.425	.425
	Charlotte, FL (FSL)	HiA	.283	61	198	20	56	9	3	5	31	28	38	8	3	.376	.434
2017	Montgomery (SL)	AA	.284	127	454	76	129	31	8	7	56	90	94	20	5	.409	.434
2018	Rays (GCL)	R	.100	3	10	0	1	0	0	0	1	1	5	0	0	.167	.100
	Charlotte, FL (FSL)	HiA	.000	3	10	0	0	0	0	0	1	3	4	1	0	.231	.000
	Durham (IL)	AAA	.269	47	160	31	43	13	1	8	25	25	43	3	1	.377	.513
Minor League Totals			.277	333	1169	182	324	72	14	23	164	198	237	61	14	.390	.422

26 AUSTIN FRANKLIN, RHP

BA GRADE
50 Risk: Extreme

Born: Oct. 2, 1997. **B-T:** R-R. **Ht.:** 6-3. **Wt.:** 215. **Drafted:** HS—Paxton, Fla., 2016 (3rd round). **Signed by:** Brett Foley.

TRACK RECORD: The Rays loved Franklin's projectability and ceiling when they picked him in the 2016 draft. They put him on their typical development path as he spent his first full season in short-season ball. He was putting together a solid season in the Midwest League when he instead became another statistic in a rough year for Rays pitchers. Franklin blew out his elbow in mid-July.

SCOUTING REPORT: Before Franklin went down, he was showing all the makings of a solid back-of-the-rotation starter with an excellent pitcher's frame and three solid-average pitches. His 92-94 mph fastball, 11-to-5 curveball and changeup all generally sit around average, although he'd flash a plus curveball a few times in most outings and at his best his changeup will flash above-average too. His smooth delivery should allow him to eventually improve his below-average control into average control going forward.

THE FUTURE: Franklin's Tommy John surgery will likely sideline him for all of 2019. When he gets back on the mound in games that count in 2020, he could jump directly to high Class A.

Year	Club (League)	Class	W	L	ERA	G	GS	CG	SV	IP	H	HR	BB	SO	K/9	WHIP	AVG
2016	Rays (GCL)	R	1	2	2.70	11	9	0	1	43	30	0	16	40	8.3	1.06	.192
2017	Hudson Valley (NYP)	SS	4	2	2.21	13	13	0	0	69	51	4	31	71	9.2	1.18	.207
2018	Bowling Green (MWL)	LoA	6	5	3.62	16	15	0	0	82	77	6	31	65	7.1	1.32	.247
Minor League Totals			11	9	2.91	40	37	0	1	195	158	10	78	176	8.1	1.21	.221

27 DAVID MERCADO, RHP

BA GRADE
50 Risk: Extreme

Born: April 15, 1999. **B-T:** R-R. **Ht.:** 6-4. **Wt.:** 160. **Drafted:** HS—San Diego, 2017 (2nd round). **Signed by:** Jaime Jones.

TRACK RECORD: Mercado, who was known as Michael Mercado when drafted but has since asked to be called David, was one of Stanford's top signees in its 2017 recruiting class. The Rays, however, picked him 40th overall and paid him which made for an easier decision to go pro.

SCOUTING REPORT: Mercado has yet to grow into his 6-foot-4 frame and his arm can be a little late catching up to his lower half. But he has solid present stuff with a 91-94 mph fastball that shows solid sink. Mercado doesn't have much life when he leaves the fastball up. Mercado's curveball gets slurvy and slow at times, but he'll tighten it up into a sharper 77-78 mph pitch that dives across the strike zone with 2-to-8 movement. His low-80s changeup shows promise to be an above-average pitch although he lacks consistency. His hard cutter plays well off the fastball and could develop into an above-average pitch.

THE FUTURE: Mercado is nowhere close to being a finished product, but the Rays slow-and-steady development plan for pitchers will avoid throwing him too far over his head. The hope is that he can gain weight and strength that will pay off in firmer stuff. He already shows average control.

Year	Club (League)	Class	W	L	ERA	G	GS	CG	SV	IP	H	HR	BB	SO	K/9	WHIP	AVG
2017	Rays (GCL)	R	0	0	1.69	8	8	0	0	21	21	1	4	14	5.9	1.17	.256
2018	Hudson Valley (NYP)	SS	1	2	5.22	11	11	0	0	50	55	6	16	38	6.8	1.42	.274
Minor League Totals			1	2	4.16	19	19	0	0	71	76	7	20	52	6.6	1.35	.269

28 DREW STROTMAN, RHP

BA GRADE
50 Risk: Extreme

Born: Sept. 3, 1996. **B-T:** R-R. **Ht.:** 6-3. **Wt.:** 195. **Drafted:** St. Mary's 2017 (4th round). **Signed by:** Alan Hull.

TRACK RECORD: St. Mary's moved Strotman to the starting rotation and saw him blow up as a prospect thanks to an excellent 14-strikeout start against Santa Clara right before the draft. The Rays have continued to develop him as a starter, a transition that was going well until Strotman had to leave a mid-May start with an elbow injury. He became yet another Rays pitcher to undergo Tommy John surgery.

SCOUTING REPORT: Before he went down with his elbow injury, Strotman was mixing together four solid-average pitches. His 93-95 mph fastball and hard slider are the two pitches that have the best chance to be above-average, but Strotman's success has come from mixing up his pitch selection. He also throws a potentially average changeup and curve. The former reliever now projects to have average control.

THE FUTURE: The timing of Strotman's surgery would put his recovery timetable right on track to have him ready to go as the 2019 minor league season ends. That makes it likely that instead he'll get two full offseasons of recovery time before he returns to the mound in 2020.

Year	Club (League)	Class	W	L	ERA	G	GS	CG	SV	IP	H	HR	BB	SO	K/9	WHIP	AVG
2017	Hudson Valley (NYP)	SS	2	3	1.78	11	7	0	0	51	29	0	9	42	7.5	0.75	.168
2018	Bowling Green (MWL)	LoA	3	0	3.52	9	9	0	0	46	40	0	18	43	8.4	1.26	.241
Minor League Totals			5	3	2.61	20	16	0	0	97	69	0	27	85	7.9	0.99	.204

29 JOSE DE LEON, RHP

BA GRADE

50 Risk: Extreme

Born: Aug. 7, 1992. **B-T:** R-R. **Ht.:** 6-2. **Wt.:** 190. **Drafted:** Southern, 2013 (24th round). **Signed by:** Matthew Paul (Dodgers).

TRACK RECORD: It's fair to wonder if De Leon will ever return to the form he showed in 2015 and 2016 when he was one of the best starting pitching prospects in baseball. The Rays have never really seen that version of De Leon since he was acquired in 2017 for Logan Forsythe. He missed time with a flexor strain and a lat strain in 2017 and missed all of 2018 because of Tommy John surgery in March.

SCOUTING REPORT: The Rays have to hope that De Leon's absolute lack of stuff in 2017 was a precursor of the elbow injury that wiped out his 2018 season. With the Dodgers, De Leon had a 90-94 mph above-average fastball with late life, a plus changeup and an average slider. With the Rays, he was sometimes trying to survive without even one average pitch as his fastball backed up to 86-89 mph.

THE FUTURE: The Rays decided to keep De Leon on the 40-man roster, which is an indication that they believe there's still a chance he can be a big league starter. De Leon's timetable should have him back on the mound pitching in games by midseason.

Year	Club (League)	Class	W	L	ERA	G	GS	CG	SV	IP	H	HR	BB	SO	K/9	WHIP	AVG
2016	Oklahoma City (PCL)	AAA	7	1	2.61	16	16	0	0	86	61	9	20	111	11.6	0.94	.194
	Los Angeles (NL)	MAJ	2	0	6.35	4	4	0	0	17	19	5	7	15	7.9	1.53	.288
2017	Tampa Bay (AL)	MAJ	1	0	10.13	1	0	0	0	3	4	1	3	2	6.8	2.63	.333
	Durham (IL)	AAA	0	2	6.75	3	3	0	0	12	14	1	6	14	10.5	1.67	.292
	Rays (GCL)	R	1	0	0.75	3	2	0	0	12	4	1	1	12	9.0	0.42	.103
	Charlotte, FL (FSL)	HiA	1	0	1.88	4	3	0	0	14	11	0	9	18	11.3	1.40	.216
2018	Did not play—Injured																
Major League Totals			3	0	6.86	5	4	0	0	20	23	6	10	17	7.8	1.68	.295
Minor League Totals			25	15	3.32	77	72	1	0	369	302	32	115	490	12.0	1.13	.220

30 MATT KROOK, LHP

BA GRADE

50 Risk: Extreme

Born: Oct. 21, 1994. **B-T:** L-L. **Ht.:** 6-4. **Wt.:** 195. **Drafted:** Oregon, 2016 (4th round). **Signed by:** Larry Casian (Giants).

TRACK RECORD: A supplemental first-round pick of the Marlins out of high school, Krook didn't sign after the Marlins lowered their offer because they worried about the results of his physical He did end up blowing out his elbow at Oregon and struggled with his control when he returned. Those control troubles have carried over to pro ball, but the Rays took a chance on his potential and acquired him in the Evan Longoria trade. They almost immediately moved him to the bullpen.

SCOUTING REPORT: It's highly possible that Krook will never put it all together, but scouts and coaches rave about his fastball movement because his sinker has movement that draws comparisons to Zach Britton. Now Britton threw his sinker at 95-96 at his best, while Krook's fastball sits anywhere from 90-96, so the comparisons aren't perfect, but it's a bat misser. Krook's slider has also shown plus potential, but it's his sinker that is the key to future success. At its best, his changeup is an above-average pitch too. Krook's delivery is very long in the back and he spikes too many pitches in the dirt. If Krook can throw strikes consistently, he has closer-caliber stuff. He misses enough bats that if he could develop just fringe-average control he could be effective, but right now his control is closer to the bottom of the scale.

THE FUTURE: Krook has long tantalized with potential. He's still only 24 and he's ready for Triple-A, so there's still time for him to improve his control enough to be a useful setup man.

Year	Club (League)	Class	W	L	ERA	G	GS	CG	SV	IP	H	HR	BB	SO	K/9	WHIP	AVG
2016	Giants (AZL)	R	0	1	1.59	2	1	0	0	6	6	0	2	2	3.2	1.41	.261
	Salem-Keizer (NWL)	SS	1	3	6.17	11	10	0	0	35	35	2	33	39	10.0	1.94	.263
2017	San Jose (CAL)	HiA	4	9	5.12	25	17	0	0	91	75	4	66	105	10.3	1.54	.217
2018	Montgomery (SL)	AA	4	2	4.26	37	6	0	0	74	57	3	50	95	11.6	1.45	.218
Minor League Totals			9	15	4.89	75	34	0	0	206	173	9	151	241	10.5	1.57	.227

Texas Rangers

BY BEN BADLER

Heading into the 2007 season, the Rangers had the No. 28 farm system in baseball.

One year later, general manager Jon Daniels added Elvis Andrus, Neftali Feliz and Matt Harrison in a trade for Mark Teixeira, Chris Davis had a breakout season and the team's Latin American scouting was starting to take off. By 2008, the Rangers jumped from the No. 28 farm system to No. 4, fueling a run of five playoff teams in seven years from 2010-16.

Today, the Rangers' farm system isn't as dire as it was in 2007, but they are going to need another major renovation, because the path for Texas to return to the playoffs isn't clear.

The Rangers finished 67-95, last in the American League West. Their .414 winning percentage tied the 2014 team for the organization's worst mark in the last 30 years.

More troubling than the losing is that there are not many signs of an imminent turnaround.

Rougned Odor rebounded from a down year in 2017. Joey Gallo put together a second season with 40-plus home runs. Otherwise, there weren't many positive signs for the future on the 2018 Rangers. Outfielder Nomar Mazara was still 23 but hasn't had his breakthrough season yet, while outfielder Willie Calhoun, the team's No. 1 prospect entering the season, scuffled in Triple-A to start the year and struggled when he was called up.

Beyond Calhoun, the Rangers simply did not get much help from their farm system in 2018. That trend may continue in 2019. Among the Rangers' top 30 prospects, just one player has played at Double-A or above.

The best stocked position for Rangers prospects is center field, bolstered by the $2.8 million signing of Cuban outfielder Julio Pablo Martinez in March. They also have Leody Taveras, a plus defender and still a talented prospect, but one whose stock fell in 2018 with a modest offensive showing, mitigated some by the Rangers pushing him to the high Class A Carolina League at 19. Bubba Thompson, who spent the year one level behind Taveras in low Class A Hickory, is the most exciting athlete in the system. The earliest any of them would help in Texas is 2020, and they probably will need more time than that.

Things are a little different on the pitching side, where righthander Jonathan Hernandez and lefthanders Taylor Hearn and Joe Palumbo all have Double-A experience. Their No. 1 overall prospect is righthander Hans Crouse, whose electric stuff gives him the upside to pitch at the front of a rotation, but with four full-season levels to go

Willie Calhoun had another productive year in the minors but failed to hit in the majors.

PROJECTED 2022 LINEUP

Catcher	Isiah Kiner-Falefa (27)
First Base	Ronald Guzman (27)
Second Base	Rougned Odor (28)
Third Base	Anderson Tejeda (24)
Shortstop	Elvis Andrus (33)
Left Field	Joey Gallo (28)
Center Field	Julio Pablo Martinez (26)
Right Field	Nomar Mazara (27)
Designated Hitter	Willie Calhoun (27)
No. 1 Starter	Hans Crouse (23)
No. 2 Starter	Cole Ragans (22)
No. 3 Starter	Jonathan Hernandez (25)
No. 4 Starter	Taylor Hearn (27)
No. 5 Starter	Joe Palumbo (27)
Closer	C.D. Pelham (27)

before making the jump to the major leagues, that potential comes with significant risk. Crouse leads a promising group of young starting pitching at the lower levels.

While the Padres, White Sox and Blue Jays are all bad teams too, they also have top farm systems with impact players on the cusp of breaking into the majors. After missing the playoffs in 2017 and 2018, the Rangers have little hopes of competing in 2019, and it would take a major overhaul to get back in 2020.

The Rangers can return to the postseason, but with at least three and possibly four straight years without playoff baseball, the franchise is at is most painful point in a decade.

TEXAS RANGERS

TOP 2019 ROOKIE: Taylor Hearn, LHP. With the Rangers thin on pitching at the upper levels, Hearn should have plenty of opportunities to get to the big leagues in 2019.

BREAKOUT PROSPECT: Osleivis Basabe, SS. He stood out for high quick-twitch athleticism as an amateur, but he boosted his stock with a strong year at the plate in the DSL in 2018.

SLEEPER: Frainyer Chavez, SS. A 22nd-round pick in 2018, Chavez hit well in his pro debut in the Rookie-level Arizona League and was even more impressive defensively.

SOURCE OF TOP 30 TALENT			
Homegrown	27	Acquired	3
College	2	Trade	3
Junior college	2	Rule 5 draft	0
High school	13	Independent league	0
Nondrafted free agent	0	Free agent/waivers	0
International	10		

LF
Miguel Aparicio

CF
Julio Pablo Martinez (2)
Leody Taveras (3)
Bubba Thompson (9)
Pedro Gonzalez

RF
Scott Heineman (26)

3B
Diosbel Arias (27)
Sherten Apostel
Andy Ibanez
Charles LeBlanc
Brendon Davis
Yanio Perez

SS
Anderson Tejeda (5)
Osleivis Basabe (12)
Jonathan Ornelas (15)
Chris Seise (17)
Frainyer Chavez
Jayce Easley
Ryan Dorow

2B
Keyber Rodriguez (29)
Yonny Hernandez

1B
Tyreque Reed (21)
Curtis Terry

C
Randy Florentino (19)
David Garcia (22)
Jose Rodriguez (23)
Sam Huff (28)
Heriberto Hernandez
Jose Trevino
Yohel Pozo

LHP

LHSP	LHRP
Taylor Hearn (7)	C.D. Pelham (13)
Joe Palumbo (8)	Jeffrey Springs
Cole Ragans (11)	Yohander Mendez
John King	Brett Martin

RHP

RHSP	RHRP
Hans Crouse (1)	DeMarcus Evans (16)
Cole Winn (4)	Kye Cody (24)
Jonathan Hernandez (6)	Emmanuel Clase (25)
Mason Englert (10)	Alex Speas (30)
Owen White (14)	Joe Barlow
Tyler Phillips (18)	Michael Matuella
A.J. Alexy (20)	
Jordan Romano	
Yerry Rodriguez	
Ronny Henriquez	
Emerson Martinez	
Jason Bahr	
Edgar Arredondo	
Reid Anderson	

DRAFT ANALYSIS

2018

BEST PURE HITTER: In a pitching-heavy draft (seven of the team's top 10 picks were pitchers), SS Jonathan Ornelas (3) stood out for his innate barrel awareness. While it's not a classic, pure swing, Ornelas has an advanced approach and bat-to-ball skills.

BEST POWER HITTER: The Rangers didn't draft a 70 raw power-type slugger this year. Ornelas makes consistent hard contact, with the strength projection and bat speed to grow into more power.

FASTEST RUNNER: SS Jayce Easley (5) is a plus runner who stole 22 bases in 26 attempts over 42 games in the Rookie-level Arizona League.

BEST DEFENSIVE PLAYER: Frainyer Chavez (22) showed a good internal clock, quickness and arm strength from shortstop.

BEST ATHLETE: In high school, RHP Owen White (2) played basketball and was the quarterback on the football team. He's a bouncy athlete whose athleticism shows on the mound with the way he fields his position.

BEST FASTBALL: The Rangers used their top pick on RHP Cole Winn (1), who was up to 96 mph leading up to the draft. Winn didn't pitch in any official games after signing as the Rangers wanted to carefully the workloads of their draft picks, but at instructional league he was pumping 93-96 mph. RHP Cole Uvila (40) is a 24-year-old reliever who sits in the mid-90s.

BEST SECONDARY PITCH: Winn's curveball is a plus pitch. It has sharp, 12-to-6 break with good depth that should give him a swing-and-miss out pitch to pile up strikeouts.

BEST PRO DEBUT: Three of the organization's top four draft picks were high school pitchers—Winn, White and RHP Mason Englert (4)—who the Rangers didn't let throw a pitch after signing. Ornelas, their third-round pick, had an auspicious debut, batting .302/.389/.459 in 48 games in the Rookie-level Arizona League.

MOST INTRIGUING BACKGROUND: Born and raised in Venezuela, Chavez was granted religious asylum by the U.S. with his parents, brother and sister in 2014. He went to Little Elm (Tex.) High, a 45-minute drive from Globe Life Park, before going to Midland (Tex.) JC. The Rangers also drafted C Xavier Valentin (19), the son of Javier Valentin, who spent 10 seasons in the majors with the Reds, Twins and Devil Rays.

CLOSEST TO THE MAJORS: The top of the Rangers' draft was high school-heavy. RHP Tim Brennan (7) posted an 84-5 K-BB mark with St. Joseph's, leading Division 1 baseball in strikeout-to-walk ratio. His pure stuff is fringy but his ability to locate should help him progress quickly.

BEST LATE-ROUND PICK: Chavez was a pleasant surprise in the 22nd round, sticking out for his defense and performing well at the plate in his pro debut. RHP Billy Layne (11), who the Rangers originally drafted out of high school three years ago but went to Seton Hall before the Rangers got him again, has a starter's delivery, a low-90s fastball and feel for both a curveball and changeup. Uvila is a wild card with a big fastball in the 40th round.

THE ONE WHO GOT AWAY: Jonathan Edwards (16) is a 6-foot-6 RHP out of Eagle's Landing High in McDonough, Ga., who the Rangers tried to sign but he instead chose Kennesaw State. This fall, Edwards has been up to 97 mph. The Rangers took late-round fliers on RHPs Owen Sharts (32) and Austin Becker (37), ranked No. 162 and No. 65 on the BA 500, respectively, but figured both would head to college.

— BA STAFF

TOP DRAFT PICKS OF THE DECADE

Year	Player, Pos.	2018 Org
2009	*Matt Purke, LHP	Mets
2010	Kellin Deglan, C	Yankees
2011	Kevin Matthews, LHP	Frontier League
2012	Lewis Brinson, OF	Marlins
2013	Chi Chi Gonzalez, RHP	Rangers
2014	Luis Ortiz, RHP	Orioles
2015	Dillon Tate, RHP	Orioles
2016	Cole Ragans, LHP	Rangers
2017	Bubba Thompson, OF	Rangers
2018	Cole Winn, RHP	Rangers
* Did not sign		

2017

RHP Hans Crouse (2) has ascended to become the system's top prospect after an exciting first full pro season. OF Bubba Thompson (1) is still raw but has exciting upside, while SS Chris Seise (1) lost his 2018 season to injury..

GRADE: B

2016

LHP Cole Ragans (1) and RHPs Alex Speas (2) and Kyle Cody (6), the three players with the most upside in this class, were all in 2018 derailed by Tommy John surgery. C Sam Huff (7) has flashed exciting tools but is still raw.

GRADE: D

2015

LHPs Jeffrey Springs (30) and C.D. Pelham (33) in 2018 made their big league debuts and Pelham figures to become a bullpen mainstay in Texas. RHP Dillon Tate (1) was again traded, this time to Baltimore as a part of a package for Zach Britton.

GRADE: C

1 HANS CROUSE, RHP

Born: Sept. 15, 1998. **B-T:** L-R. **HT:** 6-4. **WT:** 185.
Drafted: HS—Dana Point, Calif., 2017 (2nd round).
Signed by: Steve Flores.

BILL MITCHELL

P itching for USA Baseball's 18U national team as a high school senior in 2016, Crouse fired seven scoreless innings with 11 strikeouts in Team USA's gold-medal game victory against Cuba in the COPABE Pan American Championship in Mexico. It was the beginning of a dominant senior campaign for Crouse, whom the Rangers drafted in the second round of the 2017 draft . Soon after signing, Crouse quickly looked more like a first-round pick when he reported to the Rookie-level Arizona League and picked apart hitters. The Rangers handle their high school pitching prospects with extreme caution, so Crouse opened 2018 with short-season Spokane. A cut on his thumb sidetracked his first outing, but Crouse quickly showed why he has the most upside of any pitcher in the organization, highlighted by a July 13 outing with 12 strikeouts and only one hit allowed in seven scoreless innings. By August the Rangers promoted him to low Class A Hickory.

SCOUTING REPORT: Crouse is a power pitcher who can overwhelm hitters with an electric fastball that sits in the mid-90s. It ranges mostly from 92-97 mph and has reached 99. His fastball combines excellent velocity with a high-end spin rate, giving him the ability to throw frequent strikes and dominate all quadrants of the strike zone. He generates empty swings when he elevates. Crouse's slider also flashes plus, coming out of his hand on the same plane as his fastball before breaking late to dive underneath barrels. He has flashed a good changeup at times, but right now it's still a tick below-average pitch that he hasn't needed to throw much, so using and improving that offering will be a focal point for his development. Crouse has traditional stuff for an elite pitching prospect, but his delivery is atypical. He'll mix in the occasional shimmy and wiggle, a la Johnny Cueto, leading to a high-effort, herky-jerky motion that finishes with a head whack. That gives some scouts concerns about Crouse's future command and whether his fiery, high-energy style might fit better in relief, though others think he should be fine as long as he can maintain his body control despite the effort.

THE FUTURE: Crouse is likely to return to Hickory to open 2019. He has several levels to climb, but he has the raw stuff to develop into a frontline starter.

BA GRADE	SCOUTING GRADES
60 Risk: V. High	Fastball: 70. Slider: 60. Changeup: 50. Control: 55.

Projected future grades on 20-80 scouting scale.

TOP PROSPECTS OF THE DECADE

Year	Player, Pos.	2018 Org
2009	Neftali Feliz, RHP	D-backs
2010	Neftali Feliz, RHP	D-backs
2011	Martin Perez, LHP	Rangers
2012	Jurickson Profar, SS	Rangers
2013	Jurickson Profar, SS/2B	Rangers
2014	Rougned Odor, 2B	Rangers
2015	Joey Gallo, 3B	Rangers
2016	Joey Gallo, 3B	Rangers
2017	Leody Taveras ,OF	Rangers
2018	Willie Calhoun, OF	Rangers

BEST TOOLS

Best Hitter for Average	Julio Pablo Martinez
Best Power Hitter	Sam Huff
Best Strike-Zone Discipline	Yonny Hernandez
Fastest Baserunner	Bubba Thompson
Best Athlete	Bubba Thompson
Best Fastball	Hans Crouse
Best Curveball	Cole Winn
Best Slider	Alex Speas
Best Changeup	Tyler Phillips
Best Control	Tyler Phillips
Best Defensive Catcher	Jose Trevino
Best Defensive Infielder	Anderson Tejeda
Best Infield Arm	Anderson Tejeda
Best Defensive Outfielder	Leody Taveras
Best Outfield Arm	Leody Taveras

Year	Club (League)	Class	W	L	ERA	G	GS	CG	SV	IP	H	HR	BB	SO	K/9	WHIP	AVG
2017	Rangers (AZL)	R	0	0	0.45	10	6	0	0	20	7	1	7	30	13.5	0.70	.109
2018	Spokane (NWL)	SS	5	1	2.37	8	8	0	0	38	25	2	11	47	11.1	0.95	.179
	Hickory (SAL)	LoA	0	2	2.70	5	5	0	0	17	18	1	8	15	8.1	1.56	.273
Minor League Totals			5	3	1.93	23	19	0	0	75	50	4	26	92	11.1	1.02	.185

2 JULIO PABLO MARTINEZ, OF

Born: March 21, 1996. **B-T:** L-L. **HT:** 5-9. **WT:** 175. **Signed:** Cuba, 2018. **Signed by:** Willy Espinal/Jose Fernandez.

TRACK RECORD: Martinez excelled in Cuba's junior national leagues as a teenager, then progressed to Cuba's top league, batting .333/.469/.498 in 264 plate appearances in his final season in Serie Nacional. After leaving Cuba, he signed with the Rangers in March 2018 for $2.8 million. The Rangers brought him along slowly to get him acclimated to a new country and professional baseball, so he spent most of 2018 at short-season Spokane, but he performed well after the season when they sent him to the Arizona Fall League.

SCOUTING REPORT: Martinez didn't play any competitive baseball for a while, so early in the season he was just getting his timing back. When he's at his best, he blends power and speed at a premium position. He has a smaller build, but his strong wrists help generate plenty of bat speed and a tick above-average raw power to knock the ball over the fence from left-center over to his pull side. He handles pitches down in the zone well, though with his bat path there is some swing-and-miss, especially in the upper half. Martinez is a plus runner with an average arm in center field. His outfield play improved as the season went on and he got back to game speed, and he projects to stick at the position as at least an average defender.

THE FUTURE: Now that he's had an acclimation period, Martinez could take off in 2019. He might start 2019 at one of the Rangers' Class A levels, though the club also has to figure out where to assign fellow center fielders Leody Taveras and Bubba Thompson.

BA GRADE
55 Risk: High
Hit: 55. Power: 55.
Run: 60. Field: 50.
Arm: 50

Year	Club (League)	Class	AVG	G	AB	R	H	2B	3B	HR	RBI	BB	SO	SB	CS	OBP	SLG
2016	Cuban Team (C-A)	IND	.231	19	78	10	18	3	0	1	9	9	16	4	2	.307	.308
2017	Trois-Rivieres (C-A)	IND	.297	57	236	48	70	11	2	7	21	17	56	20	4	.345	.449
2018	Rangers1 (DSL)	R	.409	7	22	10	9	1	1	1	3	9	7	2	3	.606	.682
	Spokane (NWL)	SS	.252	60	234	49	59	9	5	8	21	34	69	11	6	.351	.436
Minor League Totals			.266	67	256	59	68	10	6	9	24	43	76	13	9	.378	.457

3 LEODY TAVERAS, OF

Born: Sept. 8 1998. **B-T:** B-R. **HT:** 6-1. **WT:** 190. **Signed:** Dominican Republic, 2015. **Signed by:** Willy Espinal/Gil Kim/Thad Levine.

TRACK RECORD: Taveras ranked as one of the premium prospects in a stacked 2015 international class, signing that year on July 2 for $2.1 million. The Rangers have pushed Taveras aggressively, so while he didn't do much damage at the plate in 2018, at 19 he was also one of the youngest players in high Class A.

SCOUTING REPORT: A cousin of former major leaguer Willy Taveras, Leody is another speedy center fielder who shines in the field. Taveras reads the ball well off the bat with a quick first step to get to his plus speed, gliding around the outfield with excellent range. He backs it up with a plus arm and projects as a plus defender, with some scouts saying he's plus-plus. While Taveras' defense still drew praise, there was growing skepticism among scouts about his future hitting ability. He is a patient hitter with good bat-to-ball skills, but the contact he made often lacked any impact. Some of that comes down to pitch selection and learning to hunt his pitch swinging at pitches he can do damage with rather than simply making light contact. Getting stronger will be crucial for Taveras, both to drive the ball with more force and to maintain better swing position from both sides of the plate.

THE FUTURE: A repeat of 2018 would drop Taveras' stock considerably, so 2019 will be key for him to show that he's enough of an offensive threat to hit toward the top of the lineup. He is a good candidate to return to the Carolina League, though the Rangers will have to manage fellow center fielders Julio Pablo Martinez and Bubba Thompson as well.

BA GRADE
55 Risk: Very High
Hit: 50. Power: 45.
Run: 60. Field: 60.
Arm: 60.

Year	Club (League)	Class	AVG	G	AB	R	H	2B	3B	HR	RBI	BB	SO	SB	CS	OBP	SLG
2016	Rangers2 (DSL)	R	.385	11	39	6	15	2	2	0	9	6	5	4	3	.467	.538
	Rangers (AZL)	R	.278	33	144	22	40	6	3	1	15	11	24	11	4	.329	.382
	Spokane (NWL)	SS	.228	29	123	14	28	6	1	0	9	8	26	3	1	.271	.293
2017	Hickory (SAL)	LoA	.249	134	522	73	130	20	7	8	50	47	92	20	6	.312	.360
2018	Down East (CAR)	HiA	.246	132	521	65	128	16	7	5	48	51	96	19	11	.312	.332
Minor League Totals			.253	339	1349	180	341	50	20	14	131	123	243	57	25	.315	.351

4 COLE WINN, RHP

Born: Nov. 25, 1999. **B-T:** R-R. **HT:** 6-2. **WT:** 190. **Drafted:** HS—Orange, Calif., 2018 (1st round). **Signed by:** Steve Flores.

TRACK RECORD: Winn transferred from Colorado to Orange (Calif.) Lutheran High as a high school senior to play in one of the country's top high school baseball conferences. He dominated to earn the BA High School Player of the Year honors. The Rangers drafted him No. 10 overall in 2018 and signed him for $3.15 million. The Rangers shut down their top prep pitching picks after signing, so Winn threw only briefly during instructional league.

SCOUTING REPORT: Winn has a promising combination of stuff and polish for a high school draft pick. He has an easy, compact and repeatable delivery, which helps him locate his 92-96 mph fastball well to both sides of the plate. Winn's out pitch is his mid-70s curveball, and while he had trouble landing it for strikes at instructs, it's a plus pitch with sharp 12-to-6 break that can change eye levels and miss bats. He introduced a slider as well with average potential to his repertoire. While his changeup hasn't been a focal point, it shows good sink when he does throw it.

THE FUTURE: Winn is advanced for a high school pitching prospect, but The Rangers have been conservative when assigning young pitchers, so Winn could follow Hans Crouse's path and start in extended spring training in 2019 before reporting to short-season Spokane in June. He could develop into a mid-rotation or better starter.

BILL MITCHELL

BA GRADE	
60	Risk: **Extreme**

Fastball: 60.
Curve: 60. **Slider:** 50.
Change: 50. **CTL:** 60.

Year	Club (League)	Class	W	L	ERA	G	GS	CG	SV	IP	H	HR	BB	SO	K/9	WHIP	AVG
2018	Did not play																

5 ANDERSON TEJEDA, SS

Born: May 1, 1998. **B-T:** L-R. **HT:** 5-11. **WT:** 185. **Signed:** Dominican Republic, 2014. **Signed by:** Rodolfo Rosario/Roberto Aquino.

TRACK RECORD: Signed for $100,000 in 2014, Tejeda has flashed big tools with spurts of performance to match. In 2018, he took a big leap forward both offensively and defensively at high Class A Down East.

SCOUTING REPORT: Coming into 2018, Tejeda once faced questions on whether he would stick at shortstop, but the Rangers emphasized developing his first-step quickness and footwork, both of which made major progress in 2018, with Tejeda now projecting to remain a shortstop. He showed better reactions off the bat and cut down on his throwing errors with a better understanding of how to use his feet, which kept his throws more online. That helped him take advantage of his 70-grade arm one of the game's best infield arms, which grades as at least a 70 tool. Tejeda's offensive profile is one the Rangers have experience with: big power and a lot of strikeouts as he works to develop a better plan. He has plus raw power to go deep to all fields, giving him 25-plus home run potential, but he also had a 27 percent strikeout rate. Tejeda's bat control, strike-zone discipline and understanding of how opposing pitchers are trying to attack him will all have to improve against upper-level pitching. He also had large platoon splits and will have to hit better against lefties.

THE FUTURE: Some scouts now prefer Tejeda to Leody Taveras because he has more power to do damage on contact, while Taveras has better bat control and strike-zone discipline. Tejeda will start 2019 in Double-A and could develop into a power-hitting regular at shortstop.

BA GRADE	
55	Risk: **Very High**

Hit: 45. **Power:** 60.
Run: 50. **Field:** 55.
Arm: 70.

Year	Club (League)	Class	AVG	G	AB	R	H	2B	3B	HR	RBI	BB	SO	SB	CS	OBP	SLG
2016	Rangers1 (DSL)	R	.262	11	42	9	11	2	3	1	7	5	4	5	0	.340	.524
	Rangers (AZL)	R	.293	32	133	22	39	12	6	1	21	8	36	1	0	.331	.496
	Spokane (NWL)	SS	.277	23	94	15	26	0	1	8	19	5	33	1	0	.313	.553
2017	Hickory (SAL)	LoA	.247	115	401	68	99	24	9	8	53	36	132	10	7	.309	.411
2018	Down East (CAR)	HiA	.259	121	467	76	121	17	5	19	74	49	142	11	4	.331	.439
Minor League Totals			.268	357	1342	226	360	74	30	41	214	128	396	37	18	.334	.460

6 JONATHAN HERNANDEZ, RHP

Born: July 6, 1996. **B-T:** R-R. **HT:** 6-2. **WT:** 185. **Signed:** Dominican Republic, 2013. **Signed by:** Willy Espinal/Mike Daly.

TRACK RECORD: Hernandez opened 2018 by picking apart high Class A Carolina League hitters, prompting the Rangers to promote him to Double-A Frisco in June. He had a difficult time adjusting to the new level, posting a 7.14 ERA in his first eight starts. His results were better in August, when Hernandez settled in with a 1.14 ERA over his final four starts.

SCOUTING REPORT: Hernandez pitches off a lively fastball that sits at 93-96 mph and tops out at 99. The pitch has good armside run and plays up because of its high spin rate and his ability to get extension out front. Hernandez's improved slider was a separator for him to start the season. It flashed as a plus pitch with good tilt and helped him get a lot of swinging strikes down and away. At times his changeup flashes average with good fade, though that's still an inconsistent pitch. He flips over an occasional show-me curveball. Hernandez ran into trouble when his fastball command (especially to his glove side) and sometimes just ability to find the strike zone deserted him, leading to too many walks and hitters sitting in advantageous counts.

THE FUTURE: Hernandez has a history of taking time to adjust to a new level, so tightening his fastball command will be key for him against better hitters. If he does, he could develop into a mid-rotation starter with a chance to pitch in Texas by the end of the 2019 season.

BA GRADE
50 Risk: Medium
Fastball: 70.
Slider: 60. **Change:** 50.
Curve: 45. **CTL:** 55.

Year	Club (League)	Class	W	L	ERA	G	GS	CG	SV	IP	H	HR	BB	SO	K/9	WHIP	AVG
2016	Hickory (SAL)	LoA	10	9	4.56	24	22	1	0	116	110	14	49	85	6.6	1.37	.252
2017	Hickory (SAL)	LoA	2	5	4.86	9	9	0	0	46	55	5	13	46	8.9	1.47	.306
	Down East (CAR)	HiA	3	6	3.44	14	13	0	0	65	66	2	31	64	8.8	1.48	.271
2018	Down East (CAR)	HiA	4	2	2.20	10	10	0	0	57	37	6	17	77	12.1	0.94	.184
	Frisco (TL)	AA	4	4	4.92	12	12	0	0	64	58	6	36	57	8.0	1.47	.247
Minor League Totals			32	30	3.55	107	97	1	0	515	471	41	197	457	8.0	1.30	.244

7 TAYLOR HEARN, LHP

Born: Aug. 30, 1994. **B-T:** L-L. **HT:** 6-5. **WT:** 210. **Drafted:** Oklahoma Baptist, 2015 (5th round). **Signed by:** Ed Gustafson (Nationals).

TRACK RECORD: The Nationals drafted Hearn in 2015, then traded him and Felipe Rivero to Pittsburgh one year later for Mark Melancon. Hearn spent two years with the Pirates, who traded him to the Rangers in July 2018 in the Keone Kela deal.

SCOUTING REPORT: Hearn pitches off a fastball that can overpower hitters. It sits in the mid-90s and reaches 98 mph. His premium velocity from the left side is particularly uncomfortable for opponents because of his angle and long arms that create good extension out front, with the ability to get swings and misses up in the zone. After the 2017 season, Hearn went to the Arizona Fall League, where he changed the grip on his slider. It's still inconsistent, but it now flashes above-average. He has a solid changeup, too, that at times is an average offering. Hearn can pile up strikeouts—he had 9.8 per nine innings in 2018—but improving his command and pitch sequencing are focal points for his development.

BA GRADE
50 Risk: Medium
Fastball: 70.
Slider: 55.
Change: 50. **CTL:** 50.

THE FUTURE: If Hearn can tighten his fastball command and refine his pitchability, he has the makings of a mid-rotation starter. If not, he has the stuff to pitch high-leverage relief innings. He's ticketed for the Triple-A Nashville rotation to open 2019.

Year	Club (League)	Class	AVG	G	AB	R	H	2B	3B	HR	RBI	BB	SO	SB	CS	OBP	SLG
2016	Pirates (DSL)	R	.205	48	171	24	35	7	1	1	9	24	61	1	1	.308	.275
2017	Pirates (DSL)	R	.258	61	198	43	51	12	4	9	48	56	49	4	5	.422	.495
2018	Bristol (APP)	R	.259	41	139	28	36	7	0	7	26	32	42	3	1	.406	.460
	Spokane (NWL)	SS	.351	12	37	7	13	1	0	1	10	9	8	0	1	.469	.459
Minor League Totals			.248	162	545	102	135	27	5	18	93	121	160	8	8	.388	.415

8 JOE PALUMBO, LHP

Born: Oct. 26, 1994. **B-T:** L-L. **HT:** 6-1. **WT:** 190. **Drafted:** HS—West Islip, N.Y., 2013 (30th round). **Signed by:** Takeshi Sakurayama.

TRACK RECORD: Palumbo didn't do much to distinguish himself as a 30th-round pick in his first three seasons with the Rangers, but he had a breakout season in 2016 to emerge as a legitimate prospect. After three starts in 2017, however, Palumbo went down for the year with Tommy John surgery. He returned in June 2018 and by the end of the season looked like same pitcher he was before TJ.

SCOUTING REPORT: As the season progressed, so did Palumbo's fastball. It started at 90-92 mph early in the season and ramped up to touch 95 with more frequency later in the year. Palumbo throws frequent strikes with his fastball and it gets on hitters faster than they anticipate with his short arm stroke and cross-body delivery adding deception. His curveball was erratic in early outings coming back from surgery, but by the end of the year it was a more reliable, swing-and-miss offering that graded as plus. Palumbo has shown good feel for a changeup that has the potential to be an average pitch as well, although coming back from surgery he went with a fastball-heavy approach.

BA GRADE

50 Risk: High

Fastball: 55.
Curve: 60.
Change: 50. **CTL:** 55.

THE FUTURE: Likely ticketed for Double-A to open 2019, Palumbo could make his major league debut by the end of the season. If he proves to be durable enough to handle a starter's role, he has a chance to develop into a No. 3 or 4 starter.

Year	Club (League)	Class	W	L	ERA	G	GS	CG	SV	IP	H	HR	BB	SO	K/9	WHIP	AVG
2016	Hickory (SAL)	LoA	7	5	2.24	33	7	0	8	96	71	5	36	122	11.4	1.11	.202
2017	Down East (CAR)	HiA	1	0	0.66	3	3	0	0	14	4	0	4	22	14.5	0.59	.087
2018	Rangers (AZL)	R	0	0	4.00	3	3	0	0	9	5	1	1	15	15.0	0.67	.161
	Down East (CAR)	HiA	1	4	2.67	6	6	0	0	27	24	3	6	34	11.3	1.11	.226
	Frisco (TL)	AA	1	0	1.93	2	2	0	0	9	6	0	3	10	9.6	0.96	.182
Minor League Totals			18	17	2.64	87	37	0	8	276	215	12	104	317	10.3	1.15	.210

9 BUBBA THOMPSON, OF

Born: June 9, 1998. **B-T:** R-R. **HT:** 6-2. **WT:** 185. **Drafted:** HS—Mobile, Ala., 2017 (1st round). **Signed by:** Brian Morrison.

TRACK RECORD: Thompson was an all-state quarterback who had offers to play Division I football, but he opted to sign with the Rangers for $2.1 million as the No. 26 overall pick in 2017. Thompson was old for his high school class—he turned 19 right before the draft—and has shown promising physical upside and considerable risk as a pro.

SCOUTING REPORT: Thompson fits a familiar profile for Rangers draft picks as an explosive athlete with loud tools and raw baseball skills. His best tool is his plus-plus speed, which makes him a threat to steal 30 bases and is an asset for him in center field. His defense is unrefined—his first-step reads and routes will need to get better—but his closing speed helps him make up ground. His arm is average. At the plate, Thompson has quick hand speed and a tick above-average raw power that could be a plus tool as he gets stronger. Thompson's swing and plate discipline leave him with holes, with chase tendencies that led to a 29 percent strikeout rate.

BA GRADE

55 Risk: Extreme

Hit: 45. Power: 55.
Run: 70. Field: 55.
Arm: 50.

THE FUTURE: Thompson's raw tool set is as good as any player's in the organization, giving him a has a ceiling to rival any player in the organization—if he can improve his approach to make more contact. Scouts highest on Thompson believe he has the athleticism to help make those adjustments and turn into an above-average regular in center field.

Year	Club (League)	Class	AVG	G	AB	R	H	2B	3B	HR	RBI	BB	SO	SB	CS	OBP	SLG
2017	Rangers (AZL)	R	.257	30	113	23	29	7	2	3	12	6	28	5	5	.317	.434
2018	Hickory (SAL)	LoA	.289	84	332	52	96	18	5	8	42	23	104	32	7	.344	.446
Minor League Totals			.281	114	445	75	125	25	7	11	54	29	132	37	12	.337	.443

10 MASON ENGLERT, RHP

Born: Nov. 1, 1999. **B-T:** B-R. **HT:** 6-4. **WT:** 205. **Drafted:** HS—Forney, Texas, 2018 (4th round). **Signed by:** Josh Simpson.

TRACK RECORD: The Rangers drafted prep arms with three of their top four picks in the 2018 draft and signed them for seven-figure bonuses, including Englert, who got $1 million as a fourth-rounder. They shut all three of them down from official games after signing, but at instructional league, Englert made a loud impression.

SCOUTING REPORT: Going into the draft, Englert had several positive indicators between his tall, projectable frame, easy mechanics, athleticism and arm speed suggesting more in the tank. At instructs, that projection started to manifest. He went from throwing mostly upper 80s in the summer of 2017 to low 90s in the spring of 2018 and then topped out at 96 mph with good extension after signing. Englert reached that velocity without much effort in his delivery, which is calm and repeatable, helping him locate his fastball to both sides of the plate. He has shown feel to spin both his slider and curveball, both flashing above-average potential but inconsistent. Englert sells his changeup with good arm action, though he didn't throw it often.

THE FUTURE: Englert has the components of a starting pitcher, and he could join fellow 2018 draft pick Cole Winn next season in the short-season Spokane rotation.

BILL MITCHELL

BA GRADE
55 Risk: Extreme
Fastball: 60.
Curve: 60. **Slider:** 55.
Change: 50. **CTL:** 55.

Year	Club (League)	Class	W	L	ERA	G	GS	CG	SV	IP	H	HR	BB	SO	K/9	WHIP	AVG
2018	Did not play																

11 COLE RAGANS, LHP

BA GRADE
55 Risk: Extreme

Born: Dec. 12, 1997. **B-T:** L-L. **HT:** 6-4. **WT:** 195. **Drafted:** HS—Tallahassee, Fla., 2016 (1st round). **Signed by:** Brett Campbell.

TRACK RECORD: Ragans was the No. 30 overall pick in 2016, then impressed scouts the next summer in the short-season Northwest League. Scheduled to make his full-season debut in 2018, Ragans never ended up throwing an inning during the year, as he had Tommy John surgery in March. He should be on a similar timetable the Rangers had fellow lefty Joe Palumbo on for his TJ rehab.

SCOUTING REPORT: When healthy, Ragans was one of the system's top pitching prospects, pitching off a fastball that parked at 89-93 mph and hit 95. Ragans takes advantage of the high spin rate on his fastball by elevating for swing-and-miss up in the zone, then disrupts the timing of hitters with a plus changeup in the low-80s. The pitch has good speed differential off his fastball and the deception in his delivery helps that fastball/changeup combination play up even more. Ragans earned better grades on his curveball than he did in 2017, when it was a fringe-average pitch that needed tightening.

THE FUTURE: Once healthy, he should be ready for low Class A Hickory.

Year	Club (League)	Class	W	L	ERA	G	GS	CG	SV	IP	H	HR	BB	SO	K/9	WHIP	AVG
2016	Rangers (AZL)	R	0	0	4.70	4	2	0	0	8	11	0	6	9	10.6	2.22	.344
2017	Spokane (NWL)	SS	3	2	3.61	13	13	0	0	57	50	5	35	87	13.7	1.48	.234
2018	Did not play—Injured																
Minor League Totals			3	2	3.74	17	15	0	0	65	61	5	41	96	13.3	1.57	.248

12 OSLEIVIS BASABE, SS

BA GRADE
55 Risk: Extreme

Born: Sept. 13, 2000. **B-T:** R-R. **HT:** 6-1. **WT:** 165. **Signed:** Venezuela, 2017. **Signed by:** Carlos Plaza.

TRACK RECORD: After missing out on Shohei Ohtani, the Rangers had extra bonus pool space available in December 2017. Part of their Plan B included signing Basabe, who received a $550,000 bonus. As an amateur, Basabe stood out for his premium speed and athleticism in the middle of the diamond, though several teams saw a lot of risk in his bat. However, Basabe didn't look raw offensively in his pro debut, ranking third in the Dominican Summer League in hitting with nearly as many walks as strikeouts.

SCOUTING REPORT: Basabe has quick hands and he uses them well in his swing to snap the barrel through the zone. He will chase pitches out of the zone with off-balance swings, but when he swings at strikes he doesn't miss much because he has good feel for the barrel. His power is mostly for doubles right now, though in a few years he could grow into 10-15 home run power. Basabe is a plus-plus runner, and while Basabe spent some time in center field as an amateur and a lot of scouts like him better as an outfielder, Basabe prefers to play shortstop and has shown enough to continue playing the position. His arm plays better in the infield and is now plus.

THE FUTURE: A breakout prospect candidate, Basabe should jump to the Rookie-level Arizona League in 2019.

Year	Club (League)	Class	AVG	G	AB	R	H	2B	3B	HR	RBI	BB	SO	SB	CS	OBP	SLG
2018	Rangers1 (DSL)	R	.344	52	192	37	66	16	3	1	34	23	25	12	6	.414	.474
Minor League Totals			.344	52	192	37	66	16	3	1	34	23	25	12	6	.414	.474

13 C.D. PELHAM, LHP

BA GRADE

45 Risk: Medium

Born: Feb. 21, 1995. **B-T:** L-L. **HT:** 6-6. **WT:** 245. **Drafted:** Spartanburg Methodist (S.C.) JC, 2015 (33rd round). **Signed by:** Jay Heafner.

TRACK RECORD: Pelham was a crude, under-the-radar pitcher when the Rangers signed him for $40,000 as a 33rd-round pick in 2015. It took a couple years, but Pelham broke through when he moved to the bullpen for low Class A Hickory in 2017, then in 2018 pitched at two levels, played in the Futures Game and made his major league debut as a September callup.

SCOUTING REPORT: Pelham is a power pitcher who throws in the mid-to-upper 90s, reaching 98 mph with lively cutting action. The extension he's able to generate helps his fastball jump on hitters and he attacks them from a tall, downhill angle. When his slider is right, it's an above-average weapon that he can use to miss bats, though he's still working to master consistency of that pitch. Pelham has significantly improved his control from his early years with the Rangers, but it remains below-average.

THE FUTURE: Pelham should figure into Rangers' big league bullpen mix in 2019, with the upside to become a closer.

Year	Club (League)	Class	W	L	ERA	G	GS	CG	SV	IP	H	HR	BB	SO	K/9	WHIP	AVG
2016	Spokane (NWL)	SS	0	6	6.16	16	7	0	2	38	36	0	43	50	11.8	2.08	.243
2017	Hickory (SAL)	LoA	4	2	3.18	37	0	0	13	62	47	6	26	75	10.8	1.17	.204
2018	Down East (CAR)	HiA	0	0	1.95	23	0	0	11	28	23	0	13	34	11.1	1.30	.215
	Frisco (TL)	AA	2	0	6.16	24	0	0	2	19	20	1	13	19	9.0	1.74	.270
	Texas (AL)	MAJ	0	0	7.04	10	0	0	0	8	12	0	4	7	8.2	2.09	.353
Major League Totals			0	0	7.04	10	0	0	0	8	12	0	4	7	8.2	2.09	.353
Minor League Totals			10	8	4.25	116	7	0	28	165	141	8	108	202	11.0	1.51	.225

14 OWEN WHITE, RHP

BA GRADE

55 Risk: Extreme

Born: Aug. 9, 1999. **B-T:** R-R. **HT:** 6-3. **WT:** 170. **Drafted:** HS—China Grove, N.C., 2018 (2nd round). **Signed by:** Jay Heafner.

TRACK RECORD: The Rangers had a pitching-heavy draft in 2018, and after selecting righthander Cole Winn with their first-round pick, the Rangers drafted White in the second round. He signed for $1.5 million, though he didn't pitch after signing as the Rangers took it slowly with their high school arms.

SCOUTING REPORT: A high school quarterback, White is an excellent athlete for a pitcher. He has clean arm action and fast arm speed that produces a fastball in the low-90s and up to 96. He's still skinny, with enough room on his frame that he might be able to throw harder once he adds more weight. He throws strikes with his fastball to get ahead of hitters and can miss bats with his curveball, which flashes above-average, and while he used a slider as well in high school, he didn't show that pitch after signing at instructional league. White has a changeup but hasn't needed to throw it much yet. White's bouncy athleticism shows in the way he gets off the mound quickly to field his position.

THE FUTURE: White likely will follow the path of Hans Crouse and Cole Ragans by pitching in short-season Spokane in 2019.

Year	Club (League)	Class	W	L	ERA	G	GS	CG	SV	IP	H	HR	BB	SO	K/9	WHIP	AVG
2018	Did not play																

15 JONATHAN ORNELAS, SS/3B

BA GRADE

50 Risk: Extreme

Born: May 26, 2000. **B-T:** R-R. **HT:** 6-1. **WT:** 180. **Drafted:** HS—Glendale, Ariz., 2018 (3rd round). **Signed by:** Levi Lacey.

TRACK RECORD: A third-round pick in the 2018 draft, Ornelas quickly boosted his stock with a strong showing in the Rookie-level Arizona League, where he impressed pro scouts with his hitting ability.

SCOUTING REPORT: Ornelas doesn't have a conventional swing, but it works for him with his ability to consistently barrel the baseball. He can get his body shifted to his front side early, but he's able to keep his hands back and fire with good bat speed and a short path to the ball to connect and do damage, especially against fastballs. Ornelas showed some chase tendencies in the AZL but mostly showed a good plan at the plate and walked at a 12 percent clip. He's wiry strong and projects to have at least average power. A high school shortstop, Ornelas spent more time at third base in pro ball and is likely to shift around between third, shortstop and possibly second base going forward. He has soft hands and a plus arm, but he's a fringe-average runner whose range is light for an everyday shortstop

THE FUTURE: Ornelas has the defensive skill set and offensive profile to fit at either third or second base. He should jump to low Class A Hickory in 2019.

Year	Club (League)	Class	AVG	G	AB	R	H	2B	3B	HR	RBI	BB	SO	SB	CS	OBP	SLG
2018	Rangers (AZL)	R	.302	48	172	34	52	10	4	3	28	25	41	15	5	.389	.459
Minor League Totals			.302	48	172	34	52	10	4	3	28	25	41	15	5	.389	.459

16 DEMARCUS EVANS, RHP

BA GRADE

45 Risk: High

Born: Oct. 22, 1996. **B-T:** R-R. **HT:** 6-5. **WT:** 275. **Drafted:** HS—Petal, Miss., 2015 (25th round). **Signed by:** Brian Morrison.

TRACK RECORD: Years ago, a pitcher like Evans would confound evaluators as to how he was able to get so many empty swings just on a fastball that seemed invisible to hitters. Today, that invisiball is better understood and more accurately measured as a high-spin fastball, which is Evans' strength.

SCOUTING REPORT: Evans' velocity ticked up as the season went along as he better incorporated his lower half into his delivery, and his fastball at 92-96 mph quickly disappears on batters. Pitching primarily off that pitch, Evans struck out a whopping 47 percent of hitters with low Class A Hickory in 2018. He was even better in the second half once he started landing his above-average curveball for strikes.

THE FUTURE: Evans has yet to play above low Class A, but he pitched in the Arizona Fall League and could rise quickly in 2019, with a chance to pitch high-leverage innings in the big leagues.

Year	Club (League)	Class	W	L	ERA	G	GS	CG	SV	IP	H	HR	BB	SO	K/9	WHIP	AVG
2016	Rangers (AZL)	R	1	1	3.10	8	6	0	0	29	19	2	18	44	13.7	1.28	.183
	Spokane (NWL)	SS	0	1	2.77	6	6	0	0	26	20	1	19	31	10.7	1.50	.204
2017	Rangers (AZL)	R	0	1	11.12	3	3	0	0	6	6	0	6	10	15.9	2.12	.273
	Hickory (SAL)	LoA	2	5	4.85	12	6	0	0	30	22	1	25	46	14.0	1.58	.198
	Spokane (NWL)	SS	0	2	2.59	5	5	0	0	24	15	0	9	25	9.2	0.99	.171
2018	Hickory (SAL)	LoA	4	1	1.77	35	0	0	9	56	28	1	27	103	16.6	0.98	.149
Minor League Totals			7	11	3.06	78	26	0	9	182	124	5	110	269	13.3	1.28	.189

17 CHRIS SEISE, SS

BA GRADE

50 Risk: Extreme

Born: Jan. 6, 1999. **B-T:** B-R. **HT:** 6-2. **WT:** 175. **Drafted:** HS—Winter Garden, Fla., 2017 (1st round). **Signed by:** Brett Campbell.

TRACK RECORD: The Rangers had two first-round picks in 2017. They used their first to draft outfielder Bubba Thompson, then used the next to draft Seise at No. 29 overall. After getting an introduction to pro ball that summer in the Rookie-level Arizona League and short-season Northwest League, Seise was scheduled to make his full-season debut in 2018 with low Class A Hickory, but that never happened.

SCOUTING REPORT: Seise suffered a torn labrum in his right shoulder, requiring surgery in May and erasing his entire 2018 season. When healthy, Seise stood out in the field, where he showed a plus arm from shortstop with quick footwork and smooth hands. A slightly above-average runner, Seise ranges well to both sides with good reads off the bat. Seise is a defensive-oriented prospect who showed high strikeout tendencies in his pro debut, struggling at times with his timing and balance. He has a power-over-hit offensive profile, with average raw power that could increase once he gets stronger.

THE FUTURE: Seise is expected to be ready to go again in spring training and take the field with Hickory.

Year	Club (League)	Class	AVG	G	AB	R	H	2B	3B	HR	RBI	BB	SO	SB	CS	OBP	SLG
2017	Rangers (AZL)	R	.336	27	116	23	39	5	3	3	27	9	30	5	0	.395	.509
	Spokane (NWL)	SS	.222	24	99	10	22	3	1	0	9	4	30	1	1	.250	.273
2018	Did not play—Injured																
Minor League Totals			.284	51	215	33	61	8	4	3	36	13	60	6	1	.330	.400

18 TYLER PHILLIPS, RHP

BA GRADE

45 Risk: High

Born: Oct. 27, 1997. **B-T:** R-R. **HT:** 6-5. **WT:** 200. **Drafted:** HS—Pennsauken, N.J., 2015 (16th round). **Signed by:** Takeshi Sakurayama.

TRACK RECORD: The 2018 season marked a major step forward for Phillips. In 2017, Phillips opened the year in low Class A Hickory, but after seven games his ERA swelled to 6.39, so the Rangers demoted him to short-season Spokane. He returned to Hickory in 2018 and flourished, finishing with a late-season

bump to high Class A Down East.

SCOUTING REPORT: Phillips has success by being an elite strike-thrower with a deceptive changeup that plays well off his fastball. He pitches off a four-seam fastball in the low-90s that moves more like a sinker, with the ability to pound strikes down in the zone and get grounders. He backs up his fastball with a plus changeup that looks like a fastball out of his hand but has late fade and tumble to get swing-and-miss or weak contact. He already has plus control, throwing a high percentage of strikes to both sides of the plate. Strike-throwers with a good changeup can often breeze through Class A hitters but run into trouble at higher levels. He throws a slurvy, below-average curveball, so developing a better breaking pitch will be important for Phillips against better hitters.

THE FUTURE: Phillips is ticketed for Down East to start 2019.

Year	Club (League)	Class	W	L	ERA	G	GS	CG	SV	IP	H	HR	BB	SO	K/9	WHIP	AVG
2016	Spokane (NWL)	SS	4	7	6.44	13	13	0	0	59	78	2	20	57	8.7	1.67	.307
2017	Hickory (SAL)	LoA	1	2	6.39	7	4	0	0	25	28	2	9	15	5.3	1.46	.280
	Spokane (NWL)	SS	4	2	3.45	13	13	0	0	73	78	6	11	78	9.6	1.22	.265
2018	Hickory (SAL)	LoA	11	5	2.67	22	22	1	0	128	117	4	14	124	8.7	1.02	.239
	Down East (CAR)	HiA	1	0	1.80	1	1	0	0	5	2	0	2	3	5.4	0.80	.125
Minor League Totals			21	17	3.92	69	53	1	1	305	316	16	57	287	8.5	1.22	.261

19 RANDY FLORENTINO, C

BA GRADE

50 Risk: Extreme

Born: July 5, 2000. **B-T:** L-R. **HT:** 5-11. **WT:** 175. **Signed:** Dominican Republic, 2017. **Signed by:** Danilo Troncoso.

TRACK RECORD: Florentino signed with the Rangers out of the Dominican Republic for just $25,000 on July 2, 2017, but he quickly broke through as one of the team's best lower-level prospects. Florentino debuted in the Dominican Summer League, where he ranked third in OPS (1.004).

SCOUTING REPORT: Florentino has an encouraging mix of patience and power, especially for a player with a chance to stick behind the plate. Florentino has a discerning eye for his age, with his 53 walks tied for third in the DSL. He has plenty of thump in his bat too, with the potential to hit 20-25 home runs and a short swing with the ability to keep his barrel on plane with the pitch for a long time, helping him get to that power in games.

THE FUTURE: Florentino could remain at catcher, but he's an offensive-minded player who will need more work to stay at the position. He has an average arm (he threw out 27 percent of runners) but has to improve his receiving and blocking. The Rookie-level Arizona League should be his next step.

Year	Club (League)	Class	AVG	G	AB	R	H	2B	3B	HR	RBI	BB	SO	SB	CS	OBP	SLG
2018	Rangers2 (DSL)	R	.309	60	191	48	59	18	5	6	35	53	51	8	8	.454	.550
Minor League Totals			.309	60	191	48	59	18	5	6	35	53	51	8	8	.454	.550

20 A.J. ALEXY, RHP

BA GRADE

45 Risk: High

Born: April 21, 1998. **B-T:** R-R. **HT:** 6-4. **WT:** 220. **Drafted:** HS—Elverson, Pa., 2016 (11th round). **Signed by:** Rich Delucia (Dodgers).

TRACK RECORD: Alexy was an over-slot sign in the 11th round of the 2016 draft, with the Dodgers signing him for $597,500. In the midst of Alexy's first full season, the Dodgers traded him along with Willie Calhoun and infielder Brendon Davis to the Rangers for Yu Darvish at the 2017 trade deadline.

SCOUTING REPORT: Switching from the Midwest League to the South Atlantic League, Alexy repeated the low Class A level in 2018, showing swing-and-miss stuff with erratic ability to harness it in the strike zone. Alexy pitches at 91-94 mph and can reach 96, with the movement to get empty swings up in the zone. His best pitch is a curveball that flashes plus, with a slight grip tweak in-season that helped. While the Rangers place a heavy emphasis on fastball command for their lower-level pitchers, the data they had on Alexy's breaking ball prompted them to encourage Alexy to throw it more often. He made progress with his changeup at the end of the season, and the pitch has average potential. Alexy struck out 31 percent of batters, but he also struggles to throw his fastball for strikes, leading to a high walk rate.

THE FUTURE: If Alexy can improve his control, he has the potential to be a back-end starter or better, but his strike-throwing issues create significant risk of him moving to the bullpen. High Class A Down East is up next.

Year	Club (League)	Class	W	L	ERA	G	GS	CG	SV	IP	H	HR	BB	SO	K/9	WHIP	AVG
2016	Dodgers (AZL)	R	1	0	4.61	7	3	0	0	14	17	2	3	12	7.9	1.46	.315
2017	Great Lakes (MWL)	LoA	2	6	3.67	19	19	0	0	74	46	3	37	86	10.5	1.13	.180
	Hickory (SAL)	LoA	1	1	3.05	5	5	0	0	21	13	3	15	27	11.8	1.35	.178
2018	Hickory (SAL)	LoA	6	8	3.58	22	20	0	0	108	89	5	52	138	11.5	1.31	.229
Minor League Totals			10	15	3.63	53	47	0	0	216	165	13	107	263	11.0	1.26	.214

21 TYREQUE REED, 1B

BA GRADE

45 Risk: Very High

Born: June 6, 1997. **B-T:** R-R. **HT:** 6-2. **WT:** 260. **Drafted:** Itawamba (Miss.) JC, 2017 (8th round). **Signed by:** Brian Morrison.

TRACK RECORD: Reed annihilated pitchers while playing junior college ball in Mississippi, leading NJCAA Division II in batting average, slugging and on-base percentage in 2017. He signed with the Rangers for $135,000 as an eighth-round pick after that season, then continued to mash when he got to the Rookie-level Arizona League.

SCOUTING REPORT: The arrows were pointing up for Reed heading into the year, but he arrived at low Class A Hickory in May and hit a wall early, finishing the first half hitting .220/.287/.415 in 35 games. Reed had extraneous movement in his swing that he was able to get away with in the AZL, but he worked to simplify his swing and tightened his strike-zone discipline. He took off in the second half, batting .294/.373/.552 with a lower strikeout rate in 62 games after the all-star break. Reed has a strong, bulky build with plus raw power to take the ball out to any part of the park, though there are scouts who concerns that he generates his power more with strength than bat speed and question how that will play at higher levels. Reed doesn't have much speed or athleticism, though he has shown enough defensively where he might not just be limited to DH duties despite his size.

THE FUTURE: If everything clicks, Reed could develop into a player similar to Brewers first baseman Jesus Aguilar, who also overcame 4-A labels as a prospect. He's ready for high Class A Down East in 2019.

Year	Club (League)	Class	AVG	G	AB	R	H	2B	3B	HR	RBI	BB	SO	SB	CS	OBP	SLG
2017	Rangers (AZL)	R	.350	35	120	35	42	13	2	5	29	22	26	3	1	.455	.617
2018	Hickory (SAL)	LoA	.267	97	344	48	92	27	0	18	53	32	102	1	0	.343	.503
Minor League Totals			.289	132	464	83	134	40	2	23	82	54	128	4	1	.374	.532

22 DAVID GARCIA, C

BA GRADE

45 Risk: Extreme

Born: Feb. 6, 2000. **B-T:** B-R. **HT:** 5-11. **WT:** 170. **Signed:** Venezuela, 2016. **Signed by:** Johnny Gomez.

TRACK RECORD: Garcia was one of the top prospects available for the in the 2016-17 international signing period, with the Rangers signing him for $800,000 out of Venezuela on July 2, 2016. In his U.S. debut, Garcia got off to a rough start offensively in the Rookie-level Arizona League, but he finished with a flourish, batting .426/.491/.617 in August.

SCOUTING REPORT: Garcia projects to stick behind the plate, where he has an above-average arm and gets rid of the ball quickly with swift footwork and accurate throws. He blocks and receives well for his age, and while he's a passionate player, he plays even-keeled and under control, which helped him separate his defensive game during his early-season offensive struggles. Once Garcia made a swing adjustment to be able to better use his hands, his offensive performance spiked. He has a simple, direct swing and makes consistent contact, with doubles power now and enough projection to develop 10-15 home run power.

THE FUTURE: Getting stronger will be crucial for Garcia to be able to drive the ball with more impact against better pitching.

Year	Club (League)	Class	AVG	G	AB	R	H	2B	3B	HR	RBI	BB	SO	SB	CS	OBP	SLG
2017	Rangers2 (DSL)	R	.215	58	186	27	40	7	1	1	26	25	49	1	0	.321	.280
2018	Rangers (AZL)	R	.269	34	119	10	32	8	0	1	20	9	26	0	1	.320	.361
Minor League Totals			.236	92	305	37	72	15	1	2	46	34	75	1	1	.321	.311

23 JOSE RODRIGUEZ, C

BA GRADE

45 Risk: Extreme

Born: Oct. 5, 2001. **B-T:** L-R. **HT:** 6-0. **WT:** 185. **Signed:** Venezuela, 2018. **Signed by:** Jhonny Gomez.

TRACK RECORD: One of the most aggressive teams on the international market, the Rangers were in early on Rodriguez and signed him when he became eligible on July 2, 2018. While a lot of teams didn't see much of Rodriguez leading up to July 2, the Rangers jumped on him because of his offensive potential.

SCOUTING REPORT: Rodriguez puts himself in a good hitting position with his setup and stance in the box, then releases a smooth, calm swing. It's a compact stroke and he drives the ball to the alleys now with a chance to grow into average power in the future. Rodriguez is an offensive-minded catcher who will need a lot of work to be able to stay behind the plate. His arm is strong enough to catch but his receiving, blocking and throwing are all extremely crude, so there's considerable risk he could end up moving to either left field or first base.

THE FUTURE: Rodriguez will in 2019 make his pro debut in the Dominican Summer League.

Year	Club (League)	Class	W	L	ERA	G	GS	CG	SV	IP	H	HR	BB	SO	K/9	WHIP	AVG
2018	Did not play—Signed 2019 contract																

24 KYLE CODY, RHP

Born: Aug. 9, 1994. **B-T:** R-R. **HT:** 6-7. **WT:** 245. **Drafted:** Kentucky, 2016 (6th round). **Signed by:** Mike Medici.

TRACK RECORD: Cody was one of the top breakthrough players in the Rangers' system in 2017, when he rose through two Class A levels and missed plenty of bats with a pair of plus pitches. The 2018 season, however, struck a significant blow to his future. Cody tried to rehab an elbow injury early in the season, but after a setback in that process, he had Tommy John surgery in July.

SCOUTING REPORT: Due to the timing of the surgery, Cody won't pitch in a game against until the 2020 season, so with just five innings pitched in 2018 and none in 2019, the injury essentially wipes out two seasons. When Cody was healthy, he attacked hitters with a lively 93-97 mph fastball coming from a steep angle out of his 6-foot-7, 245-pound frame. His plus slider looks like his fastball coming out of his hand but breaks off with sharp, late tilt as it gets to the plate. His changeup is fringe-average, so the injury sets back much-needed development of his third pitch.

THE FUTURE: Cody has the stuff to be a No. 3 or 4 starter, but his durability is questionable. Cody will be 25 when the 2020 season opens and under an innings limit that season, so a bullpen role may be in his future.

Year	Club (League)	Class	W	L	ERA	G	GS	CG	SV	IP	H	HR	BB	SO	K/9	WHIP	AVG
2016	Spokane (NWL)	SS	2	5	5.13	12	9	0	0	47	56	4	13	53	10.1	1.46	.293
2017	Hickory (SAL)	LoA	6	6	2.83	18	18	0	0	95	77	4	33	101	9.5	1.15	.218
	Down East (CAR)	HiA	3	0	2.05	5	5	0	0	31	25	0	10	35	10.3	1.14	.225
2018	Rangers (AZL)	R	0	0	0.00	2	2	0	0	5	2	0	1	9	16.2	0.60	.118
Minor League Totals			11	11	3.23	37	34	0	0	178	160	8	57	198	10.0	1.22	.238

25 EMMANUEL CLASE, RHP

Born: March 18, 1998. **B-T:** R-R. **HT:** 6-2. **WT:** 205. **Signed:** Dominican Republic, 2015. **Signed by:** Chris Kemp/Emengildo Diaz (Padres).

TRACK RECORD: When the Padres signed Clase out of the Dominican Republic for $125,000 in February 2015, he was an 18-year-old who had quick, clean arm action and an 86-89 mph fastball, which later that year ticked up to 93 mph in the Dominican Summer League. In April 2018, the Rangers traded catcher Brett Nicholas to the Padres for a player to be named, with Clase going to the Rangers a month later.

SCOUTING REPORT: He dominated as the closer for short-season Spokane, posting an ERA of 0.64. Having added 30 pounds since signing, Clase now throws in the mid-to-upper 90s with a peak of 101 mph. His fastball has above-average movement, a blessing and a curse as he can miss barrels with his fastball but is still harnessing his command, though he's generally around the strike zone. Clase is a two-pitch guy but leans heavily on his fastball. His slider flashes as an average pitch with two-plane depth at its best, but it's inconsistent in part because he doesn't always throw it with the same arm speed as his fastball.

THE FUTURE: Low Class A Hickory is the next assignment for Clase, who has the upside to be a high-leverage reliever, with the risk of being another fireballer who flames out in the lower levels.

Year	Club (League)	Class	W	L	ERA	G	GS	CG	SV	IP	H	HR	BB	SO	K/9	WHIP	AVG
2016	Padres (AZL)	R	2	0	4.01	8	2	0	0	25	22	0	12	23	8.4	1.38	.227
2017	Tri-City (NWL)	SS	0	1	13.50	1	0	0	0	3	9	1	0	4	10.8	2.70	.474
	Padres (AZL)	R	2	4	5.30	9	6	0	0	36	40	4	22	42	10.6	1.74	.276
2018	Spokane (NWL)	SS	1	1	0.64	22	0	0	12	28	16	0	6	27	8.6	0.78	.163
Minor League Totals			7	7	3.14	53	18	0	12	146	140	6	61	145	8.9	1.37	.246

26 SCOTT HEINEMAN, OF

Born: Dec. 4, 1992. **B-T:** R-R. **HT:** 6-1. **WT:** 215. **Drafted:** Oregon, 2015 (11th round). **Signed by:** Rick Shroeder.

TRACK RECORD: When Heineman was at Oregon, injuries limited his time on the field, with the Rangers signing him for $100,000 as an 11th-round pick in 2015. In three years of pro ball, Heineman has hit well at every level, including at Triple-A Round Rock in 2018, prompting the Rangers to add him to the 40-man roster in November to protect him from the Rule 5 draft.

SCOUTING REPORT: Heineman turned 26 in December and has never distinguished himself as much of a prospect among pro scouts, but his performance and hard-nosed, high-energy style could help force his way to the major leagues in 2019. There's some length to Heineman's swing, but he makes consistent contact with fringe-average power and manages his at-bats well. Heineman is an average runner with a solid-average arm, splitting time between all three outfield positions. His best defensive fit is on a corner, though his offensive production doesn't profile as an everyday player there.

THE FUTURE: After playing winter ball for Escogido in the Dominican League, Heineman will likely return to Triple-A in 2019, but with a thin Rangers team in Texas, he could be up during the year as a fourth outfielder or up-and-down guy.

Year	Club (League)	Class	AVG	G	AB	R	H	2B	3B	HR	RBI	BB	SO	SB	CS	OBP	SLG
2016	High Desert (CAL)	HiA	.303	134	525	96	159	39	8	17	80	59	120	30	14	.386	.505
2017	Frisco (TL)	AA	.284	117	468	82	133	26	7	9	44	50	121	12	9	.363	.427
2018	Frisco (TL)	AA	.522	7	23	6	12	2	0	1	10	7	5	2	1	.613	.739
	Round Rock (PCL)	AAA	.295	107	424	68	125	20	2	11	57	32	93	16	8	.355	.429
Minor League Totals			.298	365	1440	252	429	87	17	38	191	148	339	60	32	.374	.461

27   DIOSBEL ARIAS, SS/3B

Born: July 21, 1996. **B-T:** R-R. **HT:** 6-2. **WT:** 190. **Signed:** Cuba, 2017.
Signed by: Willy Espinal.

BA GRADE
40 Risk: Very High

TRACK RECORD: In 2014, Arias played on a stacked Cuban 18U national team that also included outfielder Julio Pablo Martinez and first baseman/outfielder Hasuan Viera. He left Cuba, signed with the Rangers for $700,000 on July 2, 2017, then reunited with Martinez and Viera in short-season Spokane, where all three players made their U.S. debuts in 2018.

SCOUTING REPORT: Arias never dominated against his peers in Cuba, but he put himself on the prospect radar by leading the Northwest League in on-base percentage, albeit as a 22-year-old in a college-heavy league. In Spokane, Arias consistently put together quality at-bats with a firm grasp of the strike zone. He has a simple, repeatable swing with good bat control and a line-drive approach, though his power is well-below-average. Arias is a below-average runner whose range and footwork won't play at shortstop. With a solid-average arm, Arias is a better fit defensively at third base, though his lack of power is a concern there, while second base could be another option.

THE FUTURE: Skeptical scouts still see a fringy prospect, but Arias could change that if he continues to hit in full-season ball, with low Class A Hickory his next step.

Year	Club (League)	Class	AVG	G	AB	R	H	2B	3B	HR	RBI	BB	SO	SB	CS	OBP	SLG
2017	Rangers1 (DSL)	R	.419	8	31	4	13	4	0	0	8	1	6	0	0	.438	.548
2018	Spokane (NWL)	SS	.366	61	224	43	82	15	2	3	44	33	39	5	1	.451	.491
Minor League Totals			.373	69	255	47	95	19	2	3	52	34	45	5	1	.449	.498

28   SAM HUFF, C/1B

Born: Jan. 14, 1998. **B-T:** R-R. **HT:** 6-4. **WT:** 230. **Drafted:** HS—Phoenix, 2016 (7th round). **Signed by:** Josh Simpson.

BA GRADE
40 Risk: Very High

TRACK RECORD: Huff helped his draft stock during his senior season of high school by leading the state of Arizona in home runs. Huff signed with the Rangers for $225,000 as a seventh-round pick in 2016, then showed big power with a crude approach the next year when the Rangers held him back in the Rookie-level Arizona League.

SCOUTING REPORT: Promoted to low Class A Hickory in 2018, Huff showed the biggest raw power of any hitters in the organization, though his plate discipline still has a ways to go. Huff has 70 raw power, generating impact with a combination of leverage in his swing and strength in his 6-foot-4, 230-pound frame. When Huff barrels the ball, he can hit it out to any part of the park, but he has holes inside and gets himself into trouble by chasing a lot of pitches outside the strike zone, leading to a 31 percent strikeout rate with a walk in just five percent of his plate appearances last season. Huff's defensive profile has risk as well. He has a plus arm and frames pitches well, but with his size he's going to have to improve his lateral agility, footwork and blocking to be able to stick behind the plate.

THE FUTURE: His overall skill set has similarities to Marlins first baseman Peter O'Brien, a former catcher. High Class A Down East is next for Huff.

Year	Club (League)	Class	AVG	G	AB	R	H	2B	3B	HR	RBI	BB	SO	SB	CS	OBP	SLG
2016	Rangers (AZL)	R	.330	28	97	19	32	10	1	1	17	16	29	0	0	.436	.485
2017	Rangers (AZL)	R	.249	49	197	34	49	9	2	9	31	24	66	3	2	.329	.452
2018	Hickory (SAL)	LoA	.241	118	415	53	100	22	3	18	55	23	140	9	1	.292	.439
Minor League Totals			.255	195	709	106	181	41	6	28	103	63	235	12	3	.324	.449

29 KEYBER RODRIGUEZ, SS/2B

BA GRADE

45 Risk: Extreme

Born: Oct. 24, 2000. **B-T:** B-R. **HT:** 5-9. **WT:** 160. **Signed:** Venezuela, 2017.
Signed by: Carlos Gonzalez.

TRACK RECORD: Rodriguez signed for $1 million out of Venezuela when the 2017-18 international signing period opened on July 2, 2017, making him the organization's top international signing that year. Rodriguez lacks the physicality found among a lot of seven-figure international signings, but the Rangers believed in his all-around, in-game skills and high baseball IQ.

SCOUTING REPORT: Rodriguez showed that in his pro debut in the Dominican Summer League in 2018, though his lack of strength was also evident. Rodriguez built a strong track record of hitting as an amateur and he continued to show good bat control in the DSL. At 5-foot-9, Rodriguez has a small strike zone and he doesn't expand it much, manipulating the barrel well to make frequent contact when he does swing. He's an above-average runner, though he didn't steal much last season. Rodriguez has the bat-to-ball skills and plate discipline to get on base at a high clip, but he has minimal power, which will create issues against better pitching unless he gets significantly stronger. Rodriguez has good athleticism and instincts in the field, but his arm is below-average and will probably push him to second base.

THE FUTURE: Rodriguez is on schedule to make his U.S. debut in the Rookie-level Arizona League in 2019.

Year	Club (League)	Class	AVG	G	AB	R	H	2B	3B	HR	RBI	BB	SO	SB	CS	OBP	SLG
2018	Rangers2 (DSL)	R	.254	51	193	35	49	6	6	1	26	24	36	4	3	.338	.363
Minor League Totals			.254	51	193	35	49	6	6	1	26	24	36	4	3	.338	.363

30 ALEX SPEAS, RHP

BA GRADE

45 Risk: Extreme

Born: March 4, 1998. **B-T:** R-R. **HT:** 6-4. **WT:** 185. **Drafted:** HS—Powder Springs, Ga., 2016 (2nd round). **Signed by:** Derrick Tucker.

TRACK RECORD: The Rangers were excited about Speas' combination of arm speed and outstanding athleticism when they drafted him, though he proved even more raw than expected when he arrived in pro ball. During a difficult year with short-season Spokane in 2017, Speas moved to the bullpen, and he stayed in that role with low Class A Hickory in 2018.

SCOUTING REPORT: While Speas was still wild, he was showing significant signs of progress in a role that seemed to suit him, but he had Tommy John surgery in June, halting his season. Speas has a lively 94-98 mph pitch that explodes late on hitters. That has been Speas' best pitch since he signed, but his slider caught up in 2018. Speas' slider was a fringe-average pitch coming into the season, but he made rapid progress with it in 2018, snapping off plus sliders at times with the confidence to double up with the pitch against hitters. His improved slider helped him miss more bats, with Speas striking out 40 percent of the batters he faced. Speas still is wild, but with his two-pitch mix in a bullpen role, he can be successful with even a little below-average control.

THE FUTURE: Speas won't take the mound again until July or August though, as he continues to rehab.

Year	Club (League)	Class	W	L	ERA	G	GS	CG	SV	IP	H	HR	BB	SO	K/9	WHIP	AVG
2016	Rangers (AZL)	R	0	0	0.00	4	3	0	0	8	4	0	7	11	11.9	1.32	.138
2017	Spokane (NWL)	SS	1	6	6.15	16	7	0	1	34	29	5	25	45	12.0	1.60	.223
2018	Hickory (SAL)	LoA	2	0	2.20	20	0	0	6	29	16	1	21	49	15.4	1.29	.155
Minor League Totals			3	6	3.82	40	10	0	7	71	49	6	53	105	13.4	1.44	.187

Toronto Blue Jays

BY BEN BADLER

After going 76-86 in 2017, the Blue Jays could have hit the reset button and pushed to turn around the major league club for 2019. Instead, the Blue Jays prepared for the 2018 season as though they would be a playoff contender.

It didn't work.

The Blue Jays fell flat, finishing 73-89.

The good news? Vladimir Guerrero Jr. is coming. Guerrero is the best prospect in baseball, not only a favorite to be the American League Rookie of the Year in 2019 but a player who could immediately put himself into MVP conversations.

Guerrero has superstar potential, but more help is on the way. Shortstop Bo Bichette, one of the game's elite prospects, is expected to open in Triple-A. So will second baseman Cavan Biggio, who had a breakout 2018 season. Catcher Danny Jansen and righthander Sean Reid-Foley are two prospects who reached the majors last year, while lefthander Ryan Borucki and infielder Lourdes Gurriel Jr. both showed promising signs in their big league debuts.

Toronto's farm system is strong from top to bottom. Beyond the stacked talent at the upper levels, the Blue Jays have righthander Nate Pearson and shortstop Kevin Smith in the next wave. Their top three 2018 draft picks—shortstop Jordan Groshans, outfielder Griffin Conine and righthander Adam Kloffenstein—were all top-50 talents heading into the draft. Groshans, the No. 12 overall pick, got off to a terrific pro debut and earned glowing praise from evaluators around the Rookie-level Gulf Coast League.

There's more up-and-coming young talent from their Latin American program with righthander Eric Pardinho, infielders Miguel Hiraldo and Leonardo Jimenez, catcher Gabriel Moreno and shortstop Orelvis Martinez, whose $3.5 million bonus was the highest in the 2018 class.

Will the top end of the farm system be enough to push the Blue Jays back into playoff contention in 2019? Guerrero might be a cornerstone talent, but it's likely the next tier of players will experience some hiccups. But if Guerrero and Bichette click right away in 2019, that's a significant upgrade coming to the left side of the infield. If the front office can supplement the roster with the right trades and free agent signings, there's a chance for Toronto to turn things around quickly.

The heart of the lineup that carried the 2016 Blue Jays to their second straight American League Championship Series is gone. The team has already moved on without Jose Bautista and Edwin Encarnacion. Now, the Blue Jays move forward in

Lourdes Gurriel Jr. projects as a middle infield fixture after showing explosive tools in 2018.

PROJECTED 2022 LINEUP

Catcher	Danny Jansen (27)
First Base	Ryan Noda (26)
Second Base	Lourdes Gurriel Jr. (28)
Third Base	Vladimir Guerrero Jr. (23)
Shortstop	Bo Bichette (24)
Left Field	Teoscar Hernandez (29)
Center Field	Kevin Pillar (33)
Right Field	Cavan Biggio (27)
Designated Hitter	Randal Grichuk (30)
No. 1 Starter	Marcus Stroman (31)
No. 2 Starter	Eric Pardinho (21)
No. 3 Starter	Nate Pearson (25)
No. 4 Starter	Aaron Sanchez (29)
No. 5 Starter	Ryan Borucki (28)
Closer	Hector Perez (26)

2019 without Josh Donaldson or Troy Tulowitzki.

Rather than trade Donaldson after the 2017 season, when he hit .270/.385/.559 in 113 games, the Blue Jays kept him and finally traded him in August, selling low for minimal return. The series of deals the Blue Jays made after the All-Star break brought back more spare parts than projected regulars. The Blue Jays received nothing for Tulowitzki, who they released in December rather than go into another spring with the 34-year-old.

The Blue Jays have productively procured talent from the amateur ranks, drafting well and signing good prospects from Latin America. Now, they need to make better strategic decisions at the major league level to capitalize on the those players.

TORONTO BLUE JAYS

TOP 2019 ROOKIE: Vladimir Guerrero Jr., 3B. He is the 2019 AL Rookie of the Year favorite, and while he likely will start in Triple-A, he could be an immediate All-Star.
BREAKOUT PROSPECT: Adam Kloffenstein, RHP. The 6-foot-5 teenager has good body control for a big man and arrows pointing up on his stuff.
SLEEPER: John Aiello, 3B. He followed a dynamite sophomore year with a disappointing junior season at Wake Forest, but he's a potential power-hitting third baseman if he can rebound in 2019.

SOURCE OF TOP 30 TALENT			
Homegrown	23	Acquired	7
College	8	Trade	6
Junior college	1	Rule 5 draft	1
High school	8	Independent league	0
Nondrafted free agent	0	Free agent/waivers	0
International	6		

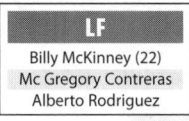

LF
Billy McKinney (22)
Mc Gregory Contreras
Alberto Rodriguez

CF
Anthony Alford (11)
Cal Stevenson (16)
Jonathan Davis
Forrest Wall
Josh Palacios
Dom Abbadessa

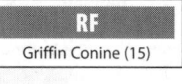

RF
Griffin Conine (15)

3B
Vladimir Guerrero Jr. (1)
Miguel HIraldo (10)
Orelvis Martinez (13)
John Aiello

SS
Bo Bichette (2)
Jordan Groshans (5)
Kevin Smith (7)
Leonardo Jimenez (21)
Logan Warmoth (25)
Kevin Vicuña
Santiago Espinal
Luis de los Santos
Addison Barger

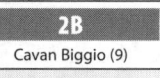

2B
Cavan Biggio (9)

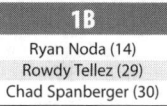

1B
Ryan Noda (14)
Rowdy Tellez (29)
Chad Spanberger (30)

C
Danny Jansen (3)
Gabriel Moreno (20)
Reese McGuire (28)
Alejandro Kirk
Riley Adams
Max Pentecost
Hagen Danner

LHP
LHSP
Thomas Pannone
LHRP
Jose Fernandez
Juan Diaz

RHP
RHSP
Eric Pardinho (4)
Nate Pearson (6)
Sean Reid-Foley (8)
Adam Kloffenstein (12)
Patrick Murphy (17)
Trent Thornton (18)
Hector Perez (19)
T.J. Zeuch (24)
Elvis Luciano (27)
Yennsy Diaz
Elixon Caballero
Maximo Castillo
Joey Murray
Alejandro Melean, rhp
RHRP
David Paulino (23)
Sean Wymer (26)
Jacob Waguespack
Zach Jackson
Brad Wilson

DRAFT ANALYSIS

2018

BEST PURE HITTER: SS Jordan Groshans (1) made a loud impression in his pro debut in the Rookie-level Gulf Coast League, where he showed an advanced approach and a knack for putting the fat part of the bat on the ball. He has the ability to square up premium velocity and drove the ball.
BEST POWER HITTER: OF Griffin Conine (2) has plus raw power and impressive bat speed. He hit nine home runs in 42 games in the Cape Cod League after his sophomore season, though he had a down year as a junior at Duke and will need to better control the strike zone.
FASTEST RUNNER: For OF Adrian Ramos (19), his strengths center around his speed and defense, with 70 speed on the 20-80 scouting scale.
BEST DEFENSIVE PLAYER: OF Hunter Steinmetz (11) is a 5-foot-9 center fielder with plus speed and good defensive instincts. The Blue Jays also drafted C Chris Bec (5), who has strong catch-and-throw skills out of Maine.
BEST ATHLETE: There wasn't one super quick-burst athlete in Toronto's 2018 draft class, but Ramos sticks out for his combination of speed, quickness and athleticism at a premium position.
BEST FASTBALL: The Blue Jays didn't draft a flamethrower like they did in 2017 with Nate Pearson, but RHP Adam Kloffenstein (3) was up to 96 mph this spring at 17 years old. He has the best combination of present fastball and projected future fastball in their class.
BEST SECONDARY PITCH: It depends what day you see him to tell what his best secondary pitch is, but Kloffenstein flashes an assortment of three promising pitches. His curveball is probably his most advanced pitch right now, though he shows feel for a slider and an advanced changeup.
BEST PRO DEBUT: Groshans dominated the GCL as an 18-year-old, batting .331/.390/.500 in 37 games before a late promotion to Rookie-level Bluefield. OF Cal Stevenson (11) had more than

twice as many walks (53) as strikeouts (21), hit .359/.494/.518 and stole 20 base in 21 attempts.
MOST INTRIGUING BACKGROUND: The Blue Jays added to their collection of sons of former '90s and 2000s big league standouts by drafting Conine, whose father Jeff played 17 seasons in the majors. Cobi Johnson (30) is the son of Blue Jays pitching coach Dane Johnson.
CLOSEST TO THE MAJORS: Conine doesn't have a typical fast-track profile after going through some struggles his junior year at Duke and then joining short-season Vancouver, but he is the system's most advanced college hitter. Wymer could move relatively fast as well if he's in a relief role.
BEST LATE-ROUND PICK: Stevenson has tremendous plate discipline and above-average speed that should help him get on base at a high clip. He's not a pure center fielder, but he has above-average speed and good instincts for a player who could rotate around all three outfield spots.
THE ONE WHO GOT AWAY: C Kameron Guangorena (36) ranked as the No. 114 prospect on the BA 500. He had a strong commitment to Cal State Fullerton, where he's going to bring a promising combination of athleticism, strong hands and a plus arm.

— BEN BADLER

TOP DRAFT PICKS OF THE DECADE

Year	Player, Pos.	2018 Org
2009	Chad Jenkins, RHP	Did not play
2010	Deck McGuire, RHP	Angels
2011	*Tyler Beede, RHP	Giants
2012	D.J. Davis, OF	Blue Jays
2013	*Phil Bickford, RHP	Brewers
2014	Jeff Hoffman, RHP	Rockies
2015	Jon Harris, RHP	Blue Jays
2016	T.J. Zeuch, RHP	Blue Jays
2017	Logan Warmoth, SS	Blue Jays
2018	Jordan Groshans, SS	Blue Jays
* Did not sign		

2017

The early results from this class have been mixed, but it still shows solid promise. RHP Nate Pearson (1) lost nearly the whole year to injuries and SS Logan Warmoth (1) struggled. But SS Kevin Smith (5) exceeded expectations and OF Ryan Noda (15) showed off his patience, leading the minor leagues in walks.

GRADE: B

2016

SS Bo Bichette (2) and 2B Cavan Biggio (5) give this class star power. Bichette has become a premier prospect in the game, and Biggio put together a break-out year in Double-A. Both are expected to soon reach the big leagues. RHP T.J. Zeuch (1) is also closing in on Toronto after a solid year in Double-A.

GRADE: B

2015

The Blue Jays failure to sign RHP Brady Singer (2) looms even larger now after his College Player of the Year season for Florida. No player the Blue Jays signed from this draft ranks in the handbook. RHP Jon Harris (1) reached Triple-A and is their best shot at getting something from the class.

GRADE: F

1 VLADIMIR GUERRERO JR., 3B

Born: March 16, 1999. **B-T:** R-R. **Ht.:** 6-2. **Wt.:** 225.
Signed: Dominican Republic, 2015. **Signed by:**
Ismael Cruz/Sandy Rosario/Luciano Del Rosario.

Hall of Famer Vladimir Guerrero Sr. was one of the most dynamic players in baseball history, with a dazzling combination of power, speed, arm strength and ability to hit any pitch. Vlad Jr., who signed with the Blue Jays for $3.9 million at age 16 in 2015, doesn't have his dad's athleticism, but he has the hand-eye coordination, bat speed, power and strike-zone discipline to rival any hitter who has come along in years. Guerrero began 2018 by hitting a walk-off home run against the Cardinals in an exhibition game at Montreal's Olympic Stadium, where his father began his major league career. He proceeded to lead the minors with a 1.073 OPS facing Double-A and Triple-A pitchers, becoming the Baseball America's Minor League Player of the Year.

SCOUTING REPORT: Even as a 19-year-old, Guerrero looked like he belonged in the middle of a major league lineup He is a potential superstar in the mold of Manny Ramirez, and it's not out of the question that Guerrero could develop into an 80 hitter with 80 power. He has a preternatural ability to make hard contact and barrel any type of pitch in any area of the strike zone. He has a simple, powerful swing, unleashing fierce bat speed with a compact, efficient path to the ball. He rarely swings and misses and hammers the ball to all parts of the park. He also has phenomenal strike-zone discipline and rarely chases borderline pitches. As an amateur in the Dominican Republic, Guerrero was a heavyset outfielder with below-average speed and arm strength. After signing, he moved to third base, where his arm strength has improved to plus, giving him a chance to stick there—at least early in his career. Guerrero worked diligently to improve his defense in 2018, but he remains a large, stocky player with a lack of first-step quickness that limits his range. At some point, he might have to move to first base or even DH. Wherever he plays, his offensive production will make him an elite player.

THE FUTURE: Guerrero will be the favorite to win American League Rookie of the Year in 2019, and he might immediately rank among the top overall hitters in baseball. Vladimir Sr. won the AL MVP award in 2004, and Junior has the talent to be in plenty of MVP conversations over the next decade.

BRIAN WESTERHOLT/FOUR SEAM

BA GRADE	SCOUTING GRADES	
80 Risk: Medium	Hit: 80. Power: 70. Run: 40. Field: 40. Arm: 60.	

Projected future grades on 20-80 scouting scale

TOP PROSPECTS OF THE DECADE

Year	Player, Pos.	2018 Org
2009	Travis Snider, OF	Atlantic League
2010	Zach Stewart, RHP	Blue Jays
2011	Kyle Drabek, RHP	Atlantic League
2012	Travis d'Arnaud, C	Mets
2013	Travis d'Arnaud, C	Mets
2014	Aaron Sanchez, RHP	Blue Jays
2015	Daniel Norris, LHP	Tigers
2016	Anthony Alford, OF	Blue Jays
2017	Vladimir Guerrero Jr., 3B	Blue Jays
2018	Vladimir Guerrero Jr., 3B	Blue Jays

BEST TOOLS

Best Hitter For Average	Vladimir Guerrero Jr.
Best Power Hitter	Vladimir Guerrero Jr.
Best Strike-Zone Discipline	Vladimir Guerrero Jr.
Fastest Baserunner	Reggie Pruitt
Best Athlete	D.J. Neal
Best Fastball	Nate Pearson
Best Curveball	Eric Pardinho
Best Slider	Sean Reid-Foley
Best Changeup	Maximo Castillo
Best Control	Eric Pardinho
Best Defensive Catcher	Reese McGuire
Best Defensive Infielder	Kevin Vicuna
Best Infield Arm	Vladimir Guerrero Jr.
Best Defensive Outfielder	Jonthan Davis
Best Outfield Arm	Chavez Young

Year	Club (League)	Class	AVG	G	AB	R	H	2B	3B	HR	RBI	BB	SO	SB	CS	OBP	SLG
2016	Bluefield (APP)	R	.271	62	236	32	64	12	3	8	46	33	35	15	5	.359	.449
2017	Lansing (MWL)	LoA	.312	71	269	53	84	21	1	7	48	40	34	6	2	.406	.476
	Dunedin (FSL)	HiA	.333	48	168	31	56	7	1	6	31	36	28	2	2	.450	.494
2018	Blue Jays (GCL)	R	.333	3	9	3	3	2	0	0	0	1	1	0	0	.400	.556
	Dunedin (FSL)	HiA	.500	1	4	1	2	1	0	0	2	0	0	0	0	.500	.750
	New Hampshire (EL)	AA	.404	60	230	48	93	19	1	14	60	21	27	3	3	.452	.678
	Buffalo (IL)	AAA	.336	30	110	15	37	7	0	6	16	15	10	0	0	.414	.564
Minor League Totals			.330	275	1026	183	339	69	6	41	200	146	135	26	12	.414	.529

2 BO BICHETTE, SS

Born: March 5, 1998. **B-T:** R-R. **Ht.:** 5-11. **Wt.:** 185. **Drafted:** HS—St. Petersburg, Fla., 2016 (2nd round). **Signed by:** Matt Bishoff.

TRACK RECORD: While Dante Bichette hit 274 home runs and made four All-Star games in a 14-year major league career, his son Bo has a chance to be even better. Bichette quickly catapulted from a 2016 second-round pick to one of the best prospects in baseball by the end of 2017. As one of the youngest players in the Double-A Eastern League in 2018, he drew praise for his offense and impressed on defense.

SCOUTING REPORT: Bichette has explosive bat speed and a rhythmic swing that generates a lot of torque. He swings hard—sometimes losing his balance—but he's usually in-sync, on time and on plane. He starts his swing with an aggressive leg kick, though he shortens to a toe tap with two strikes. He drives the ball well to the middle of the field with average raw power, and he has the bat speed and strength projection to hit for above-average power in the future. Bichette has worked diligently on his conditioning and fielding and

BA GRADE

65 **Risk:** Medium

Hit: 70. **Power:** 60.
Run: 50. **Field:** 50.
Arm: 55.

now projects as an average shortstop. He has good body control, quick footwork and ranges well up the middle. He has a tick above-average arm, though he gets tested on balls to his right. With a game built around aggression, Bichette carried that mentality onto the field and often would charge in on groundballs, but in 2018 he did a better job of staying back and making plays under control. He's an average runner whose aggressiveness and reads helped him steal 32 bases.

THE FUTURE: Bichette is scheduled to open 2019 at Triple-A Buffalo, but he could be in the majors by the All-Star break. With a chance to develop into a plus-or-better hitter and stick at shortstop, plenty of All-Star games could be in his future.

Year	Club (League)	Class	AVG	G	AB	R	H	2B	3B	HR	RBI	BB	SO	SB	CS	OBP	SLG
2016	Blue Jays (GCL)	R	.427	22	82	21	35	9	2	4	36	6	17	3	0	.451	.732
2017	Lansing (MWL)	LoA	.384	70	284	60	109	32	3	10	51	28	55	12	3	.448	.623
	Dunedin (FSL)	HiA	.323	40	164	28	53	9	1	4	23	14	26	10	4	.379	.463
2018	New Hampshire (EL)	AA	.286	130	535	95	153	42	7	11	73	48	100	32	11	.344	.452
Minor League Totals			.329	262	1065	204	350	92	13	29	183	96	198	57	18	.386	.521

3 DANNY JANSEN, C

Born: April 15, 1995. **B-T:** R-R. **Ht.:** 6-2. **Wt.:** 225. **Drafted:** HS—Appleton, Wis., 2013 (16th round). **Signed by:** Wes Penick.

TRACK RECORD: After a breakthrough 2017 season, Jansen took another step forward in 2018, posting a .390 on-base percentage for Triple-A Buffalo before getting called up to the majors in August.

SCOUTING REPORT: Jansen is a high on-base threat with a sharp eye for the strike zone. He's a disciplined hitter who recognizes pitches early, stays balanced and doesn't chase much off the plate. He does a good job of putting himself into favorable counts and swinging at pitches he can damage with a compact swing. Jansen set a career-high with 15 home runs between Buffalo and Toronto in 2018, but he's more of a line-drive hitter with just enough pull-side power for average home run totals. Jansen earns high praise for his leadership and ability to manage a pitching staff. He blocks balls well, but his arm is fringe-average. He could improve his footwork and release to get rid of the ball faster after throwing out just 19 percent of basestealers in 2018.

BA GRADE

55 **Risk:** Medium

Hit: 60. **Power:** 40.
Run: 30. **Field:** 45.
Arm: 45.

THE FUTURE: If everything clicks for Jansen, he could have a similar profile to fellow Blue Jays catcher Russell Martin. He's ready for a larger role in Toronto in 2019.

Year	Club (League)	Class	AVG	G	AB	R	H	2B	3B	HR	RBI	BB	SO	SB	CS	OBP	SLG
2016	Blue Jays (GCL)	R	.222	3	9	0	2	0	0	0	2	1	2	0	0	.364	.222
	Dunedin (FSL)	HiA	.218	54	188	18	41	7	0	1	23	22	40	7	1	.313	.271
2017	Dunedin (FSL)	HiA	.369	31	122	19	45	6	0	5	18	8	14	0	0	.422	.541
	New Hampshire (EL)	AA	.291	52	179	23	52	15	1	2	20	22	19	1	0	.378	.419
	Buffalo (IL)	AAA	.328	21	67	8	22	4	1	3	10	11	7	0	0	.423	.552
2018	Buffalo (IL)	AAA	.275	88	298	45	82	21	1	12	58	44	49	5	1	.390	.473
	Toronto (AL)	MAJ	.247	31	81	12	20	6	0	3	8	9	17	0	0	.347	.432
Major League Totals			.247	31	81	12	20	6	0	3	8	9	17	0	0	.347	.432
Minor League Totals			.269	376	1282	177	345	76	3	33	196	166	185	17	3	.367	.410

4 ERIC PARDINHO, RHP

Born: Jan. 5, 2001. **B-T:** R-R. **Ht.:** 5-9. **Wt.:** 200. **Signed:** Brazil, 2017. **Signed by:** Andrew Tinnish/Sandy Rosario.

TRACK RECORD: Pardinho was the top international pitching prospect in the 2017 class when the Blue Jays signed him for $1.4 million out of Brazil. He was so advanced that the Blue Jays skipped him over two levels to debut in the Rookie-level Appalachian League at 17. He picked apart older hitters to rank third in the league in strikeouts.

SCOUTING REPORT: Pardinho has outstanding command, polish and feel to change speeds for his age. With a smooth, fluid arm action and a calm, easy delivery with good extension, he repeats his mechanics consistently to throw a high percentage of strikes and locate his fastball to both sides of the plate. He has an advanced feel to mix his stuff and set up hitters, starting with a fastball that sits at 89-93 mph and tops out at 96 mph. His out-pitch when he signed was a curveball that flashes plus, and he now mixes in a swing-and-miss slider that could give him another plus pitch. Pardinho's changeup was a fairly new pitch for him in 2018, but he has the arm action and enough ability to potentially develop it into an average-or-better offering.

THE FUTURE: As difficult as it is to project a 18-year-old pitcher, Pardinho has the combination of stuff and potentially plus command to develop into a No. 2 or 3 starter. Low Class A Lansing is his next step.

BILL MITCHELL

BA GRADE

60 Risk: Very High

Fastball: 55.
Curve: 60. Slider: 60.
Change: 50. CTL: 60.

Year	Club (League)	Class	W	L	ERA	G	GS	CG	SV	IP	H	HR	BB	SO	K/9	WHIP	AVG
2018	Bluefield (APP)	R	4	3	2.88	11	11	0	0	50	37	5	16	64	11.5	1.06	.199
Minor League Totals			4	3	2.88	11	11	0	0	50	37	5	16	64	11.5	1.06	.199

5 JORDAN GROSHANS, SS/3B

Born: Nov. 10, 1999. **B-T:** R-R. **Ht.:** 6-3. **Wt.:** 180. **Drafted:** HS—Magnolia, Texas, 2018 (1st round). **Signed by:** Brian Johnston.

TRACK RECORD: The Blue Jays drafted Groshans with their first-round pick in the 2018 draft, selecting him No. 12 overall and signing him for $3.4 million. He made his mark immediately in the Rookie-level Gulf Coast League, dominating that level before a mid-August bump to Rookie-level Bluefield.

SCOUTING REPORT: Groshans earned rave reviews from those who saw him in the GCL, where he barreled balls consistently and demonstrated an advanced hitting approach for his age. Long and lanky, he has quick bat speed and a knack for finding the sweet spot, punishing good fastballs with the adjustability in his swing to drive pitches on the outer half to right field. Groshans has plus raw power and can take the ball over the fence anywhere from right-center field to his pull side, though he primarily sticks with a line-drive, all-fields approach. In the GCL, he shared time with others at shortstops and saw time at third base. His above-average arm and defensive actions fit on the left side of the infield, but he's more of an offensive-oriented player whose first-step quickness looks better suited for third base, where he has the attributes to become an above-average defender.

THE FUTURE: If Groshans does slide over to third base, he has the offensive upside to be an everyday regular at the position. An assignment to low Class A Lansing is next.

MIKE JANES/FOUR SEAM

BA GRADE

60 Risk: Very High

Hit: 60. Power: 60.
Run: 50. Field: 50.
Arm: 60.

Year	Club (League)	Class	AVG	G	AB	R	H	2B	3B	HR	RBI	BB	SO	SB	CS	OBP	SLG
2018	Blue Jays (GCL)	R	.331	37	142	17	47	12	0	4	39	13	29	0	0	.390	.500
	Bluefield (APP)	R	.182	11	44	4	8	1	0	1	4	2	8	0	0	.229	.273
Minor League Totals			.296	48	186	21	55	13	0	5	43	15	37	0	0	.353	.446

6 NATE PEARSON, RHP

Born: Aug. 20, 1996. **B-T:** R-R. **Ht.:** 6-6. **Wt.:** 245. **Drafted:** JC of Central Florida, 2017 (1st round). **Signed by:** Matt Bishoff.

TRACK RECORD: The Blue Jays used the second of their two first-round picks in 2017 to select Pearson, who quickly looked like a steal after dominating the short-season Northwest League while touching triple digits. He looked poised for a breakthrough in 2018, but a back injury prevented him from pitching until May 7, when he threw 1.2 innings before a line drive fractured his right forearm and ended his season.

SCOUTING REPORT: As a college starter, Pearson sat 92-94 mph and touched 98 mph regularly. With the Blue Jays, he sits in the mid- to upper 90s. He reaches 101 mph in short stints, though he has yet to have an outing of more than four innings to show he can hold velocity. He throws an explosive fastball with late life to get empty swings up and down the strike zone, with steep downhill angle from his 6-foot-6 frame. Since joining the Blue Jays, Pearson has added more power and sharpness to what was once a slurvy slider, crank-

BA GRADE

60 Risk: Very High

Fastball: 70.
Slider: 55.
Change: 50. **CTL:** 45.

ing it up to the mid- to upper 80s with late tilt. His slider is still inconsistent but flashes above-average. He mixes in an average changeup with late fade.

THE FUTURE: Pearson, who hit 100 mph in the Arizona Fall League, has the stuff to work as a mid-rotation starter if he proves he can handle a starter's workload.

Year	Club (League)	Class	W	L	ERA	G	GS	CG	SV	IP	H	HR	BB	SO	K/9	WHIP	AVG
2017	Blue Jays (GCL)	R	0	0	0.00	1	1	0	0	1	1	0	0	2	18.0	1.00	.250
	Vancouver (NWL)	SS	0	0	0.95	7	7	0	0	19	6	0	5	24	11.4	0.58	.097
2018	Dunedin (FSL)	HiA	0	1	10.80	1	1	0	0	2	5	1	0	1	5.4	3.00	.500
Minor League Totals			0	1	1.66	9	9	0	0	22	12	1	5	27	11.2	0.78	.158

7 KEVIN SMITH, SS/3B

Born: July 4, 1996. **B-T:** R-R. **Ht.:** 6-1. **Wt.:** 190. **Drafted:** Maryland, 2017 (4th round). **Signed by:** Doug Witt.

TRACK RECORD: A three-year starter at Maryland, Smith debuted with the Blue Jays in 2017 after signing that summer as a fourth-round pick. Following the season, Smith called the Blue Jays to ask when was the earliest possible date he could report to their complex in Dunedin, Fla. He worked on his swing and broke through with a strong 2018 season.

SCOUTING REPORT: A student of the game, Smith spent the offseason working to shorten his swing path and increase the amount of time his barrel spends in the hitting zone. His body awareness helped him make that adjustment and be more direct to the ball, and he cut his strikeout rate from 25 percent at Rookie-level Bluefield in 2017 to 21 percent split between two Class A levels in 2018. Smith still projects as a power-over-hit offensive profile, with quick bat speed and plus raw power to drive balls out to all fields. Smith isn't a flashy shortstop, but he is a steady, reliable defender with average defense for

BA GRADE

55 Risk: High

Hit: 45. Power: 60.
Run: 50. Field: 50.
Arm: 60.

the position. He has sure hands and an above-average, accurate arm with a quick release.

THE FUTURE: Smith raised his stock in 2018, albeit as a college player dominating Class A competition. Double-A New Hampshire will give Smith a chance to prove himself against upper-level pitchers.

Year	Club (League)	Class	AVG	G	AB	R	H	2B	3B	HR	RBI	BB	SO	SB	CS	OBP	SLG
2017	Bluefield (APP)	R	.271	61	262	43	71	25	1	8	43	16	70	9	0	.312	.466
2018	Lansing (MWL)	LoA	.355	46	183	36	65	23	4	7	44	17	33	12	1	.407	.639
	Dunedin (FSL)	HiA	.274	83	340	57	93	8	2	18	49	23	88	17	5	.332	.468
Minor League Totals			.292	190	785	136	229	56	7	33	136	56	191	38	6	.343	.507

8 SEAN REID-FOLEY, RHP

Born: Aug. 30, 1995. **B-T:** R-R. **Ht.:** 6-3. **Wt.:** 220. **Drafted:** HS—Jacksonville, 2014 (2nd round). **Signed by:** Matt Bishoff.

TRACK RECORD: Reid-Foley struggled through a rough 2017 season, with inconsistent stuff from start to start and fastball command that would frequently escape him. He opened 2018 repeating Double-A New Hampshire and looked much improved. He reached Triple-A by May and then Toronto in August for his major league debut.

SCOUTING REPORT: The Blue Jays stressed to Reid-Foley the importance of fastball command—especially down and away—and he showed signs of improvement in that area. He has a plus fastball that sits 92-95 mph and reaches 97 mph. The quality of his slider was more consistent in 2018. It's a plus weapon he can bury as a chase pitch away from righthanded hitters or get empty swings when he throws it to the back foot of lefties. He throws an average curveball that sometimes blends with his slider. Reid-Foley switched the way he gripped his changeup in spring training, and at times it showed good action and deception with average potential. Despite unorthodox mechanics, he has been durable.

THE FUTURE: Reid-Foley has the plus stuff to miss bats and potentially develop into a No. 3 or 4 starter, though he will have to continue to improve his fastball command to get there. He should be able to compete for a job in Toronto's starting rotation to open 2019.

BA GRADE
50 Risk: Medium
Fastball: 60.
Curve: 50. Slider: 60.
Change: 45. CTL: 45.

Year	Club (League)	Class	W	L	ERA	G	GS	CG	SV	IP	H	HR	BB	SO	K/9	WHIP	AVG
2016	Lansing (MWL)	LoA	4	3	2.95	11	11	0	0	58	43	2	22	59	9.2	1.12	.208
	Dunedin (FSL)	HiA	6	2	2.67	10	10	0	0	57	35	2	16	71	11.1	0.89	.172
2017	New Hampshire (EL)	AA	10	11	5.09	27	27	0	0	133	145	22	53	122	8.3	1.49	.278
2018	New Hampshire (EL)	AA	5	0	2.03	8	8	0	0	44	27	3	20	52	10.6	1.06	.174
	Buffalo (IL)	AAA	7	5	3.90	16	16	1	0	85	76	5	30	98	10.3	1.24	.235
	Toronto (AL)	MAJ	2	4	5.13	7	7	0	0	33	31	6	21	42	11.3	1.56	.244
Major League Totals			2	4	5.13	7	7	0	0	33	31	6	21	42	11.3	1.56	.244
Minor League Totals			37	33	3.90	106	103	1	0	496	429	38	218	552	10.0	1.30	.232

9 CAVAN BIGGIO, 2B/3B

Born: April 11, 1995. **B-T:** L-R. **Ht.:** 6-1. **Wt.:** 205. **Drafted:** Notre Dame, 2016 (5th round). **Signed by:** Jeff Johnson.

TRACK RECORD: Double-A New Hampshire opened 2018 with Vladimir Guerrero Jr. and Bo Bichette—two top prospects with big league bloodlines. They also had Biggio, the son of Hall of Famer Craig Biggio, who went from long shot minor leaguer to a legitimate prospect with a breakthrough season.

SCOUTING REPORT: After an underwhelming first full season in 2017, Biggio went to work on the load and timing in his swing. He lowered his hands in an attempt to help his bat stay on plane longer through the hitting zone. The mechanical adjustment helped him increase his power and tap into his power more frequently in games. He more than doubled his home run output from 2017, while his isolated power spiked from .130 to .247. Biggio is a three true outcomes player with a high dose of home runs, walks and strikeouts. His swing still has holes—he struck out 26 percent of the time in Double-A—but he's also a patient hitter whose 100 walks ranked third in the minors.

BA GRADE
50 Risk: Medium
Hit: 45. Power: 60.
Run: 50. Field: 45.
Arm: 50.

Strikeouts will limit his batting average, but his patience help keep his OBP up, and he has above-average power. Biggio is a smart, instinctive player and an average runner. He turns the double play quickly at second base with an average arm, but he's still working to soften his hands and improve his footwork and range. He has spent time at third base (where his arm is stretched), first base and the outfield as well.

THE FUTURE: Biggio has a chance to develop into an average regular, whether it be at second base or as an offensive-minded utility man. Triple-A Buffalo is his next stop, and he could finish the year in Toronto.

Year	Club (League)	Class	AVG	G	AB	R	H	2B	3B	HR	RBI	BB	SO	SB	CS	OBP	SLG
2016	Vancouver (NWL)	SS	.282	53	202	24	57	11	3	0	21	29	28	9	3	.382	.366
	Lansing (MWL)	LoA	.222	9	36	3	8	1	0	0	5	4	7	2	0	.310	.250
2017	Dunedin (FSL)	HiA	.233	127	463	75	108	17	5	11	59	74	140	11	7	.342	.363
2018	New Hampshire (EL)	AA	.251	131	447	80	112	22	5	26	99	98	148	20	8	.385	.497
Minor League Totals			.248	320	1148	182	285	51	13	37	184	205	323	42	18	.365	.412

10 MIGUEL HIRALDO, SS

Born: Sept. 5, 2000. **B-T:** R-R. **Ht.:** 5-11. **Wt.:** 175. **Signed:** Dominican Republic, 2017. **Signed by:** Luciano Del Rosario.

TRACK RECORD: As an amateur in the Dominican Republic, Hiraldo earned praise as one of the top hitters in a strong 2017 international class. The Blue Jays signed him for $750,000, and he justified their belief in his bat with a strong offensive showing in the Dominican Summer League.

SCOUTING REPORT: Hiraldo has a knack for driving the ball from a direct, compact swing. He doesn't generate much separation with his hands to load his swing, but he has explosive hand speed that generates plus bat speed. He's an aggressive hitter who mashes fastballs, with strong forearms and legs that he incorporates to generate average power. He's a pull-heavy hitter who's still improving his pitch recognition and selectivity. Blue Jays scouts were more optimistic than others when they signed Hiraldo about his ability to stick at shortstop, citing his hands and arm strength. His range and defensive actions aren't ideal for shortstop, though he has the defensive skill set for third base.

BA GRADE
55 Risk: Extreme
Hit: 55. Power: 60.
Run: 45. Field: 45.
Arm: 55.

THE FUTURE: Hiraldo is still several years away, but he has the offensive upside to profile at third base.

Year	Club (League)	Class	AVG	G	AB	R	H	2B	3B	HR	RBI	BB	SO	SB	CS	OBP	SLG
2018	Blue Jays (DSL)	R	.313	54	214	41	67	18	3	2	33	23	30	15	6	.381	.453
	Blue Jays (GCL)	R	.231	10	39	3	9	4	0	0	3	1	12	3	0	.250	.333
Minor League Totals			.300	64	253	44	76	22	3	2	36	24	42	18	6	.362	.435

11 ANTHONY ALFORD, OF

BA GRADE
45 Risk: Medium

Born: July 20, 1994. **B-T:** R-R. **Ht.:** 6-1. **Wt.:** 215. **Drafted:** HS—Petal, Miss., 2012 (3rd round). **Signed by:** Brian Johnston.

TRACK RECORD: In a year in which several Blue Jays prospects improved their stock, Alford was one of the most disappointing players in the system. He followed a promising 2017 campaign by scuffling at the next level, and his on-base percentage dropped 78 points from Double-A to Triple-A in 2018.

SCOUTING REPORT: At his best, Alford has shown the components to get on base at a high clip, but that didn't come together for him in 2018. He struggled with his timing throughout the year and never seemed to be in sync with his swing. As a result, his strikeout rate jumped from 16 percent in Double-A to 27 percent in Triple-A. Alford doesn't project to hit more than 10-15 home runs in the big leagues, so putting the ball in play more and improving his plan at the plate will be essential for him. Alford is a good athlete and a plus runner, though his arm is below-average. He's a solid-average defender in center field, though the Blue Jays have moved him around all three outfield positions and will likely continue to do so.

THE FUTURE: Alford has the body control and awareness to make adjustments, but his stock tumbled in 2018. The 2019 season will be critical if he's going to rebound and develop into an everyday player.

Year	Club (League)	Class	AVG	G	AB	R	H	2B	3B	HR	RBI	BB	SO	SB	CS	OBP	SLG
2016	Dunedin (FSL)	HiA	.236	92	339	53	80	17	2	9	44	53	117	18	6	.344	.378
2017	Toronto (AL)	MAJ	.125	4	8	0	1	1	0	0	0	0	3	0	0	.125	.250
	Dunedin (FSL)	HiA	.143	6	21	1	3	0	0	0	2	0	8	1	0	.182	.143
	New Hampshire (EL)	AA	.310	68	245	41	76	14	0	5	24	35	45	18	3	.406	.429
	Buffalo (IL)	AAA	.333	3	12	1	4	1	0	0	0	1	2	0	0	.385	.417
2018	Dunedin (FSL)	HiA	.200	7	20	2	4	1	0	0	2	3	8	0	1	.360	.250
	Buffalo (IL)	AAA	.240	105	375	52	90	22	1	5	34	30	112	17	7	.312	.344
	Toronto (AL)	MAJ	.105	13	19	3	2	0	0	0	1	2	9	1	0	.190	.105
Major League Totals			.111	17	27	3	3	1	0	0	1	2	12	1	0	.172	.148
Minor League Totals			.265	413	1519	254	402	83	11	26	149	202	432	92	24	.360	.385

12 ADAM KLOFFENSTEIN, RHP

BA GRADE
55 Risk: Extreme

Born: Aug. 25, 2000. **B-T:** R-R. **Ht.:** 6-5. **Wt.:** 245. **Drafted:** HS—Magnolia, Texas, 2018 (3rd round). **Signed by:** Brian Johnston.

TRACK RECORD: The Blue Jays used their first-round pick in 2018 on shortstop Jordan Groshans, then in the third round they drafted Kloffenstein, his Magnolia (Tex.) HS teammate. The Blue Jays pulled Kloffenstein away from his TCU commitment with an over-slot $2.45 million signing bonus.

SCOUTING REPORT: Kloffenstein has an extra-large frame with good athleticism, body control and balance, helping him throw strikes from a sound delivery. His fastball fluctuated anywhere from 89-95 mph as a senior, but he could add a little extra in time. He shows feel for an array of secondaries, with his slider the most advanced. His slider stays in line well with his fastball before breaking late with hard tilt, projecting as an above-average pitch. Sometimes his curveball is more effective than his slider depending on the day, while his changeup is advanced and could give him another above-average pitch with more experience. He's an intelligent pitcher who earns praise from coaches as a student of the game.

THE FUTURE: Kloffenstein has the potential of a mid-rotation starter, with enough upside for more.

Year	Club (League)	Class	W	L	ERA	G	GS	CG	SV	IP	H	HR	BB	SO	K/9	WHIP	AVG
2018	Blue Jays (GCL)	R	0	0	0.00	2	2	0	0	2	1	0	2	4	18.0	1.50	.143
Minor League Totals			0	0	0.00	2	2	0	0	2	1	0	2	4	18.0	1.50	.143

13 ORELVIS MARTINEZ, SS

BA GRADE

55 Risk: Extreme

Born: Nov. 19, 2001. **B-T:** R-R. **Ht.:** 5-11. **Wt.:** 180. **Signed:** Dominican Republic, 2018. **Signed by:** Alexis de la Cruz/Sandy Rosario.

TRACK RECORD: The Blue Jays have become one of the most aggressive teams in Latin America. They were in early on Martinez and signed him out of the Dominican Republic for $3.5 million

SCOUTING REPORT: With a calm, relaxed swing, Martinez produces loft and easy power, driving the ball well from right-center over to his pull side. He has good bat speed and leverage in his swing with considerable strength projection, so he should be able to develop plus power. Martinez didn't dominate games as an amateur, but he generally performed well, both in terms of hitting ability and power. He starts his swing with his bat wrapped behind his head, creating more length for his barrel to travel. Some scouts have concerns about the adjustability of his swing, although he has quick hands and generally does a good job of keeping them inside the ball. The Blue Jays will keep Martinez at shortstop for now, though most scouts project him as a third baseman given his range and how it will likely decrease as he gets heavier. He's a below-average runner with soft hands and a strong arm, giving him the attributes to fit well at third base.

THE FUTURE: Martinez will likely begin his career in the Rookie-level Gulf Coast League in 2019.

Year	Club (League)	Class	AVG	G	AB	R	H	2B	3B	HR	RBI	BB	SO	SB	CS	OBP	SLG
2018	Did not play—Signed 2019 contract																

14 RYAN NODA, 1B/OF

BA GRADE

50 Risk: Very High

Born: March 30, 1996. **B-T:** L-L. **Ht.:** 6-3. **Wt.:** 220. **Drafted:** Cincinnati, 2017 (15th round). **Signed by:** Coulsin Barbiche.

TRACK RECORD: After piling up strikeouts at Cincinnati, Noda fell to the Blue Jays in the 15th round in 2017. He quickly rebounded in pro ball, winning the Rookie-level Appalachian League MVP award that summer. In 2018, he was bumped to low Class A Lansing, where Noda led the minors with 109 walks.

SCOUTING REPORT: The first two months of the season, Noda drew a lot of walks but did little else, finishing May with a .203/.443/.308 slash line. After that, Noda settled in, batting .281/.409/.570 the rest of the season. Noda combines extreme plate patience (he walked in 21 percent of his plate appearances last year) with strong forearms and plus raw power from the left side. Noda's power comes with a high strikeout rate, so he doesn't project to be better than a .260 hitter. When he's able to square the ball up, however, he has the bat speed, strength and ability to generate lift in his swing, making him a threat to go deep to all fields with the patience to draw plenty of walks and keep his on-base percentage up. A below-average runner, Noda split time between first base and the outfield corners, with adequate defense at each spot.

THE FUTURE: Noda's offensive skill set shouldn't give him any issues at the lower levels. His family of comparable offensive players carries considerable 4-A player-type risk, but he could carve out an Eric Hinske-type career as a patient, power-hitting lefty. High Class A Dunedin is up next in 2019.

Year	Club (League)	Class	AVG	G	AB	R	H	2B	3B	HR	RBI	BB	SO	SB	CS	OBP	SLG
2017	Bluefield (APP)	R	.364	66	214	62	78	18	3	7	39	59	60	7	4	.507	.575
2018	Lansing (MWL)	LoA	.256	124	403	78	103	24	4	20	80	109	135	14	4	.421	.484
Minor League Totals			.293	190	617	140	181	42	7	27	119	168	195	21	8	.451	.515

15 GRIFFIN CONINE, OF

BA GRADE

50 Risk: Very High

Born: July 11, 1997. **B-T:** L-R. **Ht.:** 6-1. **Wt.:** 200. **Drafted:** Duke, 2018 (2nd round). **Signed by:** Jason Beverlin.

TRACK RECORD: With Vladimir Guerrero Jr., Cavan Biggio and Bo Bichette potentially graduating to the majors in 2019, the Blue Jays restocked their stash of prospects whose dads played in the big leagues by drafting Conine in 2018. The son of former Marlins outfielder Jeff Conine, Griffin entered his junior year at Duke as a potential first-round pick, but an underwhelming spring dropped him to the second round.

SCOUTING REPORT: Conine's best tool is his plus power, which he generates with an impressive combination of strength and bat speed. Conine's power has shown up in games, but his elevated swing-and-miss rate raised red flags in college. Conine didn't do anything to quiet those concerns in pro ball after striking out in 27 percent of his plate appearances with short-season Vancouver. Conine isn't a free-swinger, but he will have to make an adjustment to swing at better pitches to keep his whiffs to a reasonable level. Conine is a below-average runner and defender who has a plus arm that fits in right field.
THE FUTURE: If Conine can bounce back in 2019, he has the upside to be an everyday right fielder. Low Class A Lansing is his next step after he serves a 50-game suspension for testing positive for ritalinic acid.

Year	Club (League)	Class	AVG	G	AB	R	H	2B	3B	HR	RBI	BB	SO	SB	CS	OBP	SLG
2018	Blue Jays (GCL)	R	.375	2	8	1	3	1	0	0	3	1	2	0	0	.444	.500
	Vancouver (NWL)	SS	.238	55	206	24	49	14	2	7	30	19	63	5	0	.309	.427
Minor League Totals			.243	57	214	25	52	15	2	7	33	20	65	5	0	.314	.430

16 CAL STEVENSON, OF

BA GRADE
50 Risk: Extreme

Born: Sept. 12, 1996. **B-T:** L-L. **Ht.:** 5-10. **Wt.:** 175. **Drafted:** Arizona, 2018 (10th round). **Signed by:** Darold Brown.
TRACK RECORD: After winning 2015 Mountain West Conference co-freshman of the year at Nevada, Stevenson moved to Chabot (Calif.) JC in 2016 and then Arizona in 2017. He showed strong on-base skills but hit just one home run as a senior, then signed with the Blue Jays for $5,000 as a 10th-rounder.
SCOUTING REPORT: While old for the level, Stevenson had an outstanding pro debut in the Rookie-level Appalachian League, where he led the league in on-base percentage and drew more than twice as many walks (53) as strikeouts (21). He has terrific plate discipline, patiently working the count and rarely expanding the strike zone. He keeps his hands inside the ball with a knack for the barrel, striking out in just eight percent of his Appy League plate appearances. Stevenson is also an above-average runner. While his contact skills and plate discipline are excellent, his power falls on the other end of the scale. He has well below-average power, so he will have to develop more impact for his on-base skills to transfer at higher levels. Stevenson isn't a true burner, but he has the speed and overall baseball savvy to handle center field.
FUTURE: Stevenson should start 2019 at one of the team's Class A affiliates and could move quickly.

Year	Club (League)	Class	AVG	G	AB	R	H	2B	3B	HR	RBI	BB	SO	SB	CS	OBP	SLG
2018	Blue Jays (GCL)	R	.474	6	19	12	9	2	0	0	2	11	3	1	0	.645	.579
	Bluefield (APP)	R	.359	53	195	61	70	13	6	2	29	53	21	20	1	.494	.518
Minor League Totals			.369	59	214	73	79	15	6	2	31	64	24	21	1	.511	.523

17 PATRICK MURPHY, RHP

BA GRADE
45 Risk: High

Born: June 10, 1995. **B-T:** R-R. **Ht.:** 6-4. **Wt.:** 220. **Drafted:** HS—Chandler, Ariz., 2013 (3rd round). **Signed by:** Blake Crosby.
TRACK RECORD: Murphy missed his senior season of high school with an elbow injury that required Tommy John surgery, but the Blue Jays drafted him anyway as a third-round pick in 2013. He returned to the mound in 2014, but had surgery for thoracic outlet syndrome and, when that didn't relieve his symptoms, doctors repositioned nerves in his pitching elbow. Murphy threw just four innings in his first four seasons, but he had a breakthrough 2018, winning the Florida State League pitcher of the year award.
SCOUTING REPORT: Murphy's strikeout rate jumped from 5.8 K/9 with low Class A Lansing in 2017 to 8.3 K/9 in the FSL last year. His velocity has increased over the year, now sitting at 92-95 mph with good movement and reaching 98 mph. He pairs it with a curveball that's still inconsistent but flashes plus. Murphy has tinkered with different grips on his changeup and tried throwing it more often in 2018, but it's still a firm, below-average pitch and a key point for his development. Throwing 152.2 innings was a big development in Murphy's durability and potential to remain a starter given his medical history.
THE FUTURE: Now on the 40-man roster, Murphy should open 2019 in Double-A. If he builds on last year, he could make his MLB debut by the end of the season, with a chance to be a No. 4 starter.

Year	Club (League)	Class	W	L	ERA	G	GS	CG	SV	IP	H	HR	BB	SO	K/9	WHIP	AVG
2016	Lansing (MWL)	LoA	0	1	4.29	8	2	0	2	21	24	3	14	20	8.6	1.81	.286
	Vancouver (NWL)	SS	4	5	2.84	13	13	0	0	70	71	0	23	48	6.2	1.35	.264
2017	Blue Jays (GCL)	R	1	0	0.00	3	2	0	0	9	7	0	1	15	15.0	0.89	.212
	Lansing (MWL)	LoA	4	3	2.94	15	15	0	0	89	87	5	33	57	5.8	1.35	.263
	Dunedin (FSL)	HiA	0	1	7.00	2	2	0	0	9	14	0	3	5	5.0	1.89	.368
2018	New Hampshire (EL)	AA	0	0	3.00	1	1	0	0	6	4	0	3	6	9.0	1.17	.200
	Dunedin (FSL)	HiA	10	5	2.64	26	26	1	0	147	126	5	50	135	8.3	1.20	.233
Minor League Totals			19	16	3.00	71	63	1	2	354	341	13	129	290	7.4	1.33	.255

18 TRENT THORNTON, RHP

BA GRADE

45 Risk: High

Born: Sept. 30, 1993. **B-T:** R-R. **Ht.:** 6-0. **Wt.:** 175. **Drafted:** North Carolina, 2015 (5th round). **Signed by:** Tim Bittner (Astros).

TRACK RECORD: A fifth-round pick of the Astros in 2015, Thornton reached Triple-A two years later, though he struggled in his first exposure to that level. He had better results in 2018, pitched in the Arizona Fall League, then joined the Blue Jays when the Astros traded him for shortstop Aledmys Diaz.
SCOUTING REPORT: Thornton throws a lively, 92-94 mph fastball that can reach 97 mph, though his best pitch is a plus curveball. The spin rate on Thornton's curveball ranks among the highest in baseball, regularly registering above 3,000 rpm. Thornton's innate feel for spinning the baseball carries over to his slider, a solid-average pitch, though his below-average changeup lags behind. Thornton's results often haven't matched his stuff, dating back to his junior year at North Carolina when he posted a 5.08 ERA. That's surprising because he does throw a lot of strikes and has some deception with a herky-jerky delivery.
THE FUTURE: Thornton has the stuff and control to fit as a No. 4 starter with a chance for more, though he could also find success in a bullpen role where his velocity would play up. Thornton will compete for a spot on the big league pitching staff in spring training and should be in Toronto at some point in 2019.

Year	Club (League)	Class	W	L	ERA	G	GS	CG	SV	IP	H	HR	BB	SO	K/9	WHIP	AVG
2016	Lancaster (CAL)	HiA	7	4	4.12	17	14	1	0	90	91	14	16	89	8.9	1.19	.265
	Corpus Christi (TL)	AA	3	1	2.35	7	7	0	0	46	42	5	5	35	6.8	1.02	.243
2017	Corpus Christi (TL)	AA	1	2	6.06	4	3	0	0	16	25	2	0	13	7.2	1.53	.329
	Fresno (PCL)	AAA	8	4	5.09	21	20	0	0	115	137	12	23	88	6.9	1.39	.295
2018	Fresno (PCL)	AAA	9	8	4.42	24	22	0	0	124	118	13	31	122	8.8	1.20	.248
Minor League Totals			32	19	4.23	88	78	1	0	446	475	48	85	395	8.0	1.25	.271

19 HECTOR PEREZ, RHP

BA GRADE

45 Risk: High

Born: June 6, 1996. **B-T:** R-R. **Ht.:** 6-3. **Wt.:** 200. **Signed:** Dominican Republic, 2014. **Signed by:** Oz Ocampo/Roman Ocumarez/Leocadio Guevara (Astros).

TRACK RECORD: The Astros gave Perez $45,000 to sign out of the Dominican Republic in 2014. Within a few years, his velocity exploded and he developed into one of Houston's top pitching prospects. At the 2018 trade deadline, the Astros sent Perez and two others to the Blue Jays for closer Roberto Osuna.
SCOUTING REPORT: Perez's best pitch is his fastball, though his velocity fluctuates from start to start. He can reach 99 mph, though typically he sits around 92-96 mph. Perez has struck out more than a batter per inning at every full-season club he's pitched for, despite not having a true out-pitch. He throws a hard slider that's more notable for its power than its depth, coming in anywhere from 88-91 mph. It flashes as an average pitch, though it's not always at that level. He's also working on a fringe-average splitter that he gained confidence in over the course of the season. Perez has a lot of moving pieces in his delivery that he worked to try to simplify in 2018, but he's still erratic with his control.
THE FUTURE: Added to the 40-man roster, Perez has a chance to make his major league debut in 2019. He will continue to start for the Blue Jays in the minors, but he could ultimately find a fit as a reliever.

Year	Club (League)	Class	W	L	ERA	G	GS	CG	SV	IP	H	HR	BB	SO	K/9	WHIP	AVG
2016	Tri-City (NYP)	SS	2	0	1.57	7	3	0	0	29	19	0	12	36	11.3	1.08	.181
	Quad Cities (MWL)	LoA	2	1	4.60	7	7	0	0	31	28	1	22	44	12.6	1.60	.246
2017	Quad Cities (MWL)	LoA	1	1	2.50	4	3	0	0	18	9	2	11	24	12.0	1.11	.150
	Buies Creek (CAR)	HiA	6	5	3.63	21	14	0	2	89	69	6	67	104	10.5	1.52	.218
2018	Buies Creek (CAR)	HiA	3	3	3.84	17	11	1	2	73	50	5	40	83	10.3	1.24	.196
	Corpus Christi (TL)	AA	0	1	3.24	4	2	0	0	17	12	0	8	18	9.7	1.20	.197
	New Hampshire (EL)	AA	0	1	3.86	6	5	0	0	26	17	1	16	32	11.2	1.29	.193
Minor League Totals			16	12	3.20	83	55	1	5	337	234	15	199	391	10.4	1.28	.197

20 GABRIEL MORENO, C

BA GRADE

45 Risk: Very High

Born: Feb. 14, 2000. **B-T:** R-R. **Ht.:** 5-11. **Wt.:** 170. **Drafted:** Venezuela, 2016. **Signed by:** Francisco Plasencia.

TRACK RECORD: In 2015, the Blue Jays went over their international bonus pool to sign Vladimir Guerrero Jr., rendering them unable to sign anyone for over $300,000 in the 2016 signing period. That left the Blue Jays looking for bargains, and they may have found one in Moreno, who signed for $25,000.
SCOUTING REPORT: Moreno has good rhythm and timing at the plate, with a preternatural ability to make contact. With superb hand-eye coordination and some of the best bat control in the organization, Moreno rarely misses when he swings, striking out in just 12 percent of his plate appearances last season. The next step for Moreno is to learn when not to swing, as he's an extremely aggressive hitter who rarely walks, with his bat-to-ball skills getting him in trouble sometimes because he connects for weak contact

on pitches he should lay off. Moreno showed more power in 2018, and he has enough power potential for 15-20 home runs in the future. He's an athletic catcher whose blocking and receiving need work, but he exchanges the ball quickly to his average arm, erasing 38 percent of basestealers last year.

THE FUTURE: An aggressive, contact-oriented catcher, Moreno is similar to Marlins catcher Tomas Telis.

Year	Club (League)	Class	AVG	G	AB	R	H	2B	3B	HR	RBI	BB	SO	SB	CS	OBP	SLG
2017	Blue Jays (DSL)	R	.248	32	125	9	31	4	1	0	17	6	5	5	4	.274	.296
2018	Blue Jays (GCL)	R	.413	23	92	14	38	12	2	2	22	4	7	1	1	.455	.652
	Bluefield (APP)	R	.279	17	61	10	17	5	0	2	14	3	13	1	0	.303	.459
Minor League Totals			.309	72	278	33	86	21	3	4	53	13	25	7	5	.341	.450

21 LEONARDO JIMENEZ, SS

BA GRADE

45 Risk: Extreme

Born: May 17, 2001. **B-T:** R-R. **Ht.:** 5-11. **Wt.:** 165. **Signed:** Panama, 2017. **Signed by:** Alex Zapata/Sandy Rosario.

TRACK RECORD: Growing up in Panama, Jimenez represented his country in several international tournaments. The Blue Jays spent $825,000 to sign Jimenez in 2017, making him the highest paid Panamanian prospect of the 2017-18 international signing period. The Blue Jays skipped Jimenez over the Dominican Summer League, and he had a steady pro debut in the Rookie-level Gulf Coast League.

SCOUTING REPORT: More than his raw tools, Jimenez sticks out for his baseball acumen that's well beyond his years. Jimenez is a fringe-average runner and doesn't have the quick-twitch explosiveness that a lot of scouts prefer in a shortstop, but he's a savvy, fundamentally sound player with a good internal clock. Some scouts think Jimenez's range would fit better at second base, but he reads the ball well off the bat and has good body control with soft hands and an average arm. Jimenez manages his at-bats well. He doesn't chase much outside the strike zone and uses the whole field, spraying line drives with occasional gap shots, though he might never have more than below-average power.

THE FUTURE: Rookie-level Bluefield or short-season Vancouver is the next stop for Jimenez in 2019.

Year	Club (League)	Class	AVG	G	AB	R	H	2B	3B	HR	RBI	BB	SO	SB	CS	OBP	SLG
2018	Blue Jays (GCL)	R	.250	37	132	13	33	8	2	0	19	16	17	0	0	.333	.341
Minor League Totals			.250	37	132	13	33	8	2	0	19	16	17	0	0	.333	.341

22 BILLY McKINNEY, OF

BA GRADE

40 Risk: Medium

Born: Aug. 23, 1994. **B-T:** L-L. **Ht.:** 6-1. **Wt.:** 205. **Drafted:** HS—Plano, Texas, 2013 (1st round). **Signed by:** Armann Brown (Yankees).

TRACK RECORD: McKinney has been a high-profile prospect since the A's drafted in in the first round of the 2013 draft. He has bounced around since then, getting traded to the Cubs in 2014, the Yankees in 2016, and then last year traded to the Blue Jays alongside third baseman Brandon Drury for J.A. Happ. It was a strange year for McKinney, whose on-base percentage stayed under .300 in Triple-A, but he hit well when the Blue Jays brought him up to Toronto in August.

SCOUTING REPORT: McKinney's projection has dimmed since his early years in Oakland's farm system, but he still has a potential big league role. He has a loose, fluid swing from the left side and is a good fastball hitter, though he can get too aggressive swinging at breaking pitches. McKinney has average raw power and hit a career-best 20 home runs between the minors and majors in 2018, showing power from left-center field over to his pull side. McKinney began his career as a center fielder, but he's now a below-average runner with a fringe-average arm rotating between both outfield corner spots.

THE FUTURE: If McKinney hits like he did in his brief big league stint last year, he has a chance to become a fourth outfielder. He could also become an up-and-down guy bouncing between the big leagues and Triple-A, however.

Year	Club (League)	Class	AVG	G	AB	R	H	2B	3B	HR	RBI	BB	SO	SB	CS	OBP	SLG
2016	Tennessee (SL)	AA	.252	88	298	37	75	12	3	1	31	47	68	2	4	.355	.322
	Trenton (EL)	AA	.234	35	128	15	30	7	1	3	13	12	29	2	2	.310	.375
2017	Trenton (EL)	AA	.250	69	232	34	58	16	4	6	29	30	45	2	1	.339	.431
	Scranton/W-B (IL)	AAA	.306	55	209	32	64	13	3	10	35	9	49	0	0	.336	.541
2018	New York (MAJ)	MAJ	.250	2	4	0	1	0	0	0	0	0	1	0	0	.250	.250
	Tampa (FSL)	HiA	.250	3	8	1	2	1	0	0	3	4	2	0	0	.500	.375
	Trenton (EL)	AA	.222	5	18	2	4	1	0	0	0	3	4	1	1	.333	.278
	Scranton/W-B (IL)	AAA	.226	56	212	27	48	8	5	13	32	21	56	0	0	.299	.495
	Buffalo (IL)	AAA	.203	20	64	10	13	3	2	3	8	8	16	0	0	.292	.453
	Toronto (AL)	MAJ	.252	36	115	14	29	7	0	6	13	11	32	1	0	.320	.470
Major League Totals			.252	38	119	14	30	7	0	6	13	11	33	1	0	.318	.462
Minor League Totals			.269	618	2227	314	600	125	30	57	310	259	462	21	14	.348	.429

23 DAVID PAULINO, RHP

BA GRADE
40 Risk: High

Born: Feb. 6, 1994. **B-T:** R-R. **Ht.:** 6-7. **Wt.:** 235. **Signed:** Dominican Republic, 2010. **Signed by:** Carlos Santana/Ramon Perez/Miguel Garcia (Tigers).

TRACK RECORD: Paulino has had a frustrating career, highlighted by two elbow surgeries and an 80-game suspension after he tested positive for steroids. The Astros dealt him to the Blue Jays for Roberto Osuna.
SCOUTING REPORT: At 6-foot-7, Paulino attacks hitters with downhill plane on his fastball, which sits at 91-94 mph. Paulino can reach back for more, but he doesn't throw as hard as he did a few years ago. Paulino has a knack for manipulating his secondary stuff, throwing his offspeed more than his fastball in many starts. His changeup is an above-average, swing-and-miss pitch with good separation off his fastball. His breaking ball morphs between a curveball and a slider, with the pitch most effective when he's throwing it with more power in the low 80s. Paulino's peripheral numbers were good in 2018, though his upper-level performance hasn't quite matched his stuff yet, with Paulino still needing to improve his command.
THE FUTURE: Paulino's history of medical issues give him a dubious future as a starting pitcher. In September, the Blue Jays used him out of their bullpen, with Paulino having the skill set for middle relief.

Year	Club (League)	Class	W	L	ERA	G	GS	CG	SV	IP	H	HR	BB	SO	K/9	WHIP	AVG
2016	Astros (GCL)	R	0	0	0.75	3	3	0	0	12	9	0	2	14	10.5	0.92	.196
	Corpus Christi (TL)	AA	5	2	1.83	14	9	0	1	64	47	3	11	72	10.1	0.91	.204
	Fresno (PCL)	AAA	0	2	3.86	3	3	0	0	14	16	1	6	20	12.9	1.57	.267
	Houston (AL)	MAJ	0	1	5.14	3	1	0	0	7	6	0	3	2	2.6	1.29	.240
2017	Fresno (PCL)	AAA	0	1	4.50	3	3	0	0	14	11	3	9	13	8.4	1.43	.208
	Houston (AL)	MAJ	2	0	6.52	6	6	0	0	29	36	8	7	34	10.6	1.48	.300
2018	Fresno (PCL)	AAA	0	0	5.50	4	4	0	0	18	16	3	5	23	11.5	1.17	.232
	Astros (GCL)	R	0	0	3.00	3	3	0	0	9	7	0	1	10	10.0	0.89	.226
	Toronto (AL)	MAJ	1	0	1.35	7	0	0	0	7	6	1	2	6	8.1	1.20	.240
Major League Totals			3	1	5.48	16	7	0	0	43	48	9	12	42	8.9	1.41	.282
Minor League Totals			13	10	2.62	58	49	0	2	237	180	12	65	265	10.0	1.03	.208

24 T.J. ZEUCH, RHP

BA GRADE
40 Risk: High

Born: Aug. 1, 1995. **B-T:** R-R. **Ht.:** 6-7. **Wt.:** 225. **Drafted:** Pittsburgh, 2016 (1st round). **Signed by:** Doug Witt.

TRACK RECORD: Zeuch became the highest draft pick ever from Pittsburgh's program when the Blue Jays selected him with the No. 21 overall pick in 2016. Injuries to Zeuch's lower back and hamstring limited him to 65.2 innings in 2017, but he showed excellent durability in 2018 with Double-A New Hampshire.
SCOUTING REPORT: Zeuch's best pitch is is sinker, which he drops on hitters with steep, downhill plane. The pitch has plus velocity in the low to mid-90s and heavy sink, inducing a ton of groundballs and weak contact. He throws a lot of strikes, getting quick, efficient outs by pounding the zone and keeping the ball on the ground. Zeuch's weakness is is lack of a swing-and-miss pitch. His curveball and slider are fringy, with neither looking like it will be a legitimate out-pitch. He also throws a fringe-average changeup.
THE FUTURE: Zeuch's secondaries and add considerable risk to his profile, though scouts highest on him think he has enough offspeed stuff to develop into a back-end starter. He's ready for Triple-A in 2019.

Year	Club (League)	Class	W	L	ERA	G	GS	CG	SV	IP	H	HR	BB	SO	K/9	WHIP	AVG
2016	Blue Jays (GCL)	R	0	0	0.00	1	1	0	0	3	0	0	0	2	6.0	0.00	.000
	Vancouver (NWL)	SS	0	1	3.52	6	6	0	0	23	21	1	5	22	8.6	1.13	.247
	Lansing (MWL)	LoA	0	1	9.00	2	2	0	0	8	10	1	2	14	15.8	1.50	.294
2017	Blue Jays (GCL)	R	0	2	5.14	3	3	0	0	7	9	1	2	5	6.4	1.57	.321
	Dunedin (FSL)	HiA	3	4	3.38	12	11	0	0	59	63	3	17	46	7.1	1.36	.266
2018	Dunedin (FSL)	HiA	3	3	3.47	6	6	1	0	36	34	4	9	24	5.9	1.18	.248
	New Hampshire (EL)	AA	8	5	3.27	20	20	0	0	113	117	7	27	77	6.1	1.27	.251
Minor League Totals			14	16	3.54	50	49	1	0	249	254	17	62	190	6.9	1.27	.258

25 LOGAN WARMOTH, SS

BA GRADE
40 Risk: High

Born: Sept. 6, 1995. **B-T:** R-R. **Ht.:** 6-0. **Wt.:** 190. **Drafted:** North Carolina, 2017 (1st round). **Signed by:** Chris Kline.

TRACK RECORD: The Blue Jays drafted college shortstops with two of their first five picks in 2017. Their fourth-round pick Kevin Smith had a terrific year and is now the team's No. 7 prospect. Warmoth, a first-round pick, fell flat, doing little to distinguish himself in terms of either performance or tools.
SCOUTING REPORT: Pro scouts who saw Warmoth for the first time in 2018 were puzzled at how Warmoth was a first-round pick. Scouts highest on Warmoth in his draft year saw a player who was solid across the board with a high baseball IQ and no weaknesses. But in 2018, he gave scouts more of a vanilla look. Warmoth has some stiffness to his swing, though he does consistently put the ball in play. He doesn't

drive the ball with much impact, and his power is below-average. He's an average runner with an above-average arm and steady hands at shortstop, though a lot of scouts think he's better suited for second base.
THE FUTURE: Warmoth trended in the wrong direction in 2018, so 2019 will be key for him to show that last season was more of an aberration than a sign of things to come.

Year	Club (League)	Class	AVG	G	AB	R	H	2B	3B	HR	RBI	BB	SO	SB	CS	OBP	SLG
2017	Blue Jays (GCL)	R	.273	6	22	3	6	0	0	1	3	1	2	1	0	.304	.409
	Vancouver (NWL)	SS	.306	39	160	18	49	11	2	1	20	7	33	5	2	.356	.419
2018	Blue Jays (GCL)	R	.273	4	11	4	3	0	0	0	2	4	0	0	0	.500	.273
	Dunedin (FSL)	HiA	.248	75	282	31	70	13	2	1	28	30	69	9	0	.322	.319
Minor League Totals			.269	124	475	56	128	24	4	3	51	40	108	15	2	.338	.356

26 SEAN WYMER, RHP

BA GRADE
40 Risk: High

Born: March 19, 1997. **B-T:** R-R. **Ht.:** 6-1. **Wt.:** 190. **Drafted:** Texas Christian, 2018 (4th round). **Signed by:** Gerald Turner/Brandon Bishoff.
TRACK RECORD: Wymer worked out of the bullpen his first two seasons at Texas Christian, then moved to the Horned Frogs' weekend rotation as a junior. He moved back into a multi-inning reliever midway through the season, then signed with the Blue Jays for $478,600 as a fourth-round pick. When he got to short-season Vancouver, Wymer never went more than three innings in an outing
SCOUTING REPORT: Wymer's future is likely as a reliever, a role that suited him best in college. As a starter, he sat in the low 90s, though out of the bullpen he worked at 93-95 mph. His upper-70s curveball is an above-average pitch, and it played up with more sharpness in short stints. Wymer lacks a reliable third pitch, as his changeup is below-average. Wymer fills the strike zone, showing above-average control.
THE FUTURE: Wymer will open 2019 at one of Toronto's Class A affiliates, though he could move quickly if the Blue Jays opt to develop him as a reliever.

Year	Club (League)	Class	W	L	ERA	G	GS	CG	SV	IP	H	HR	BB	SO	K/9	WHIP	AVG
2018	Vancouver (NWL)	SS	4	3	4.84	13	7	0	0	35	35	3	7	34	8.7	1.19	.257
Minor League Totals			4	3	4.84	13	7	0	0	35	35	3	7	34	8.7	1.19	.257

27 ELVIS LUCIANO, RHP

BA GRADE
45 Risk: Extreme

Born: Feb. 15, 2000. **B-T:** R-R. **Ht.:** 6-2. **Wt.:** 185. **Signed:** Dominican Republic, 2016. **Signed by:** Junior Noboa (Diamondbacks).
TRACK RECORD: Luciano was acquired from the D-backs, along with minor league reliever Gabe Speier, in June 2018 in exchange for major league outfielder Jon Jay. He spent most of his first season with the Royals by making 11 starts in the Rookie-level Appalachian League followed by two appearances in the Rookie-level Pioneer League. Since Luciano's original contract with the D-backs was voided before he re-signed with them, he was eligible for the Rule 5 draft, and the Blue Jays selected him with the No. 10 pick.
SCOUTING REPORT: Possessing a good feel for pitching, Luciano works off a low-90s fastball that can touch 95 mph. With an efficient delivery and athletic frame, he could add more velocity as he matures. His 84-86 mph slider flashes plus with late tilt. Rounding out his arsenal is an 82-85 mph changeup with above-average potential, giving him three pitches that he can use to get swings and misses.
THE FUTURE: The Royals weren't even sure Luciano would break camp with a full-season club in 2019, so Luciano is an extreme longshot gamble to be able to stick all year on Toronto's major league roster.

Year	Club (League)	Class	W	L	ERA	G	GS	CG	SV	IP	H	HR	BB	SO	K/9	WHIP	AVG
2017	D-backs (DSL)	R	3	1	2.98	11	6	0	0	48	42	2	15	41	7.6	1.18	.236
	Diamondbacks (AZL)	R	1	0	2.76	4	2	0	1	16	16	0	3	9	5.0	1.16	.242
	Missoula (PIO)	R	0	0	0.00	1	0	0	0	2	0	0	0	2	9.0	0.00	.000
2018	Burlington (APP)	R	3	5	4.66	11	11	0	0	56	55	4	20	56	9.0	1.34	.255
	Idaho Falls (PIO)	R	2	0	0.00	2	1	0	0	11	6	0	3	14	11.5	0.82	.162
Minor League Totals			9	6	3.37	29	20	0	1	134	119	6	41	122	8.2	1.20	.237

28 REESE McGUIRE, C

BA GRADE
40 Risk: High

Born: March 2, 1995. **B-T:** L-R. **Ht.:** 5-11. **Wt.:** 215. **Drafted:** HS—Covington, Wash., 2013 (1st round). **Signed by:** Greg Hopkins (Pirates).
TRACK RECORD: McGuire showed promise when the Pirates drafted him with the 14th pick in 2013, but his stock has steadily slid. He was traded to the Blue Jays in 2016, and at Triple-A Buffalo in 2018, McGuire had a modest year then performed well as a September callup in his first major league action.
SCOUTING REPORT: McGuire's best attributes are on the defensive side. He's a smart, high baseball IQ player who handles a pitching staff well and prepares thoroughly before games. Behind the plate,

McGuire receives pitches well and is solid at blocking. His pure arm strength is average, but it plays up because his quick footwork and technique allow him to get rid of the ball quickly. McGuire has a short, contact-oriented swing with good rhythm and a line-drive approach, though he doesn't do much damage. **THE FUTURE:** With Danny Jansen coming up, McGuire is likely ticketed back to Triple-A in 2019. As a good defender with just enough offense for a catcher, McGuire could carve out a career as a backup.

Year	Club (League)	Class	AVG	G	AB	R	H	2B	3B	HR	RBI	BB	SO	SB	CS	OBP	SLG
2016	Altoona (EL)	AA	.259	77	266	29	69	16	2	1	37	29	26	4	4	.337	.346
	New Hampshire (EL)	AA	.226	15	53	5	12	2	0	0	5	7	8	2	2	.328	.264
2017	Blue Jays (GCL)	R	.409	8	22	4	9	2	0	0	7	3	1	0	1	.462	.500
	Dunedin (FSL)	HiA	.250	3	12	1	3	1	0	0	1	1	2	0	0	.308	.333
	New Hampshire (EL)	AA	.278	34	115	19	32	5	1	6	20	16	19	2	1	.366	.496
2018	Buffalo (IL)	AAA	.233	96	322	31	75	9	2	7	37	33	77	3	2	.312	.339
	Toronto (AL)	MAJ	.290	14	31	5	9	3	0	2	4	2	9	1	0	.333	.581
Major League Totals			.290	14	31	5	9	3	0	2	4	2	9	1	0	.333	.581
Minor League Totals			.263	479	1745	200	459	72	9	17	207	155	235	38	20	.326	.344

29 ROWDY TELLEZ, 1B

BA GRADE
40 Risk: High

Born: March 16, 1995. **B-T:** L-L. **Ht.:** 6-4. **Wt.:** 250. **Drafted:** HS—Elk Grove, Calif., 2013 (30th round). **Signed by:** Darold Brown.
TRACK RECORD: Tellez had a big year as a 21-year-old with Double-A New Hampshire in 2016, when he ranked second in the Eastern League in on-base percentage and third in slugging. He followed it up with a brutal 2017 season in Triple-A Buffalo, then bounced back with a solid year while repeating the level in 2018. He made his major league debut as a September callup, performing well in very limited at-bats.
SCOUTING REPORT: Tellez has flashed the components to be a middle-of-the-order bat, though it's come with roller-coaster performance. He has plus power, generating his thump more from physical strength than pure bat speed. His timing at the plate was better in 2018 than it was the previous year, and he doesn't punch out a ton. Though he got more aggressive when called up to Toronto, Tellez generally sticks with a patient plan at the plate. He's a below-average athlete and runner, and while he did make progress defensively last year, he's still below-average fielder.
THE FUTURE: If everything breaks right for Tellez, he could develop into a player along the lines of Lucas Duda, but there's also risk he could top out as a 4-A slugger.

Year	Club (League)	Class	AVG	G	AB	R	H	2B	3B	HR	RBI	BB	SO	SB	CS	OBP	SLG
2016	New Hampshire (EL)	AA	.297	124	438	71	130	29	2	23	81	63	92	4	3	.387	.530
2017	Buffalo (IL)	AAA	.222	122	445	45	99	29	1	6	56	47	94	6	1	.295	.333
2018	Buffalo (IL)	AAA	.270	112	393	43	106	22	0	13	50	40	74	7	4	.340	.425
	Toronto (AL)	MAJ	.314	23	70	10	22	9	0	4	14	2	21	0	0	.329	.614
Major League Totals			.314	23	70	10	22	9	0	4	14	2	21	0	0	.329	.614
Minor League Totals			.271	560	2034	254	551	120	7	64	327	229	407	26	12	.345	.431

30 CHAD SPANBERGER, 1B

BA GRADE
40 Risk: Very High

Born: Nov. 1, 1995. **B-T:** L-R. **Ht.:** 6-3. **Wt.:** 235. **Drafted:** Arkansas, 2017 (6th round). **Signed by:** Jesse Retzlaf (Rockies).
TRACK RECORD: A sixth-round pick out of Arkansas in 2017, Spangberger was showing promising signs as a hitter when the Rockies traded him to the Blue Jays in the 2018 deal for reliever Seung-Hwan Oh.
SCOUTING REPORT: Power is Spanberger's best tool. He's extremely strong and can turn around quality fastballs, blasting balls out to all fields with 70 raw power. He put the ball in play more frequently in 2018, cutting his strikeout rate from 26 percent in 2017 to 21 percent last season. Spanberger would benefit from a more selective plan at the plate. Spanberger is a below-average runner, but he has some sneaky athleticism for his size. He's a fringe-average defender at first base, and some scouts would like to see him get time in the outfield corners (something he did a little bit at Arkansas) to increase his versatility.
THE FUTURE: Spanberger might be a one-trick pony, but if he can keep making strides with his pure hitting ability and approach, his power will continue to give him opportunities as he moves up. He will likely open 2019 with high Class A Dunedin, with a mid-season move to Double-A New Hampshire possible.

Year	Club (League)	Class	AVG	G	AB	R	H	2B	3B	HR	RBI	BB	SO	SB	CS	OBP	SLG
2017	Grand Junction (PIO)	R	.294	60	235	49	69	15	2	19	51	27	71	2	0	.368	.617
2018	Asheville (SAL)	LoA	.315	92	349	65	110	20	3	22	75	20	82	16	4	.363	.579
	Lansing (MWL)	LoA	.278	9	36	6	10	0	1	2	6	1	6	1	0	.289	.500
	Dunedin (FSL)	HiA	.231	22	78	8	18	2	0	3	9	14	17	0	0	.348	.372
Minor League Totals			.297	183	698	128	207	37	6	46	141	62	176	19	4	.359	.564

Washington Nationals

BY CARLOS COLLAZO

While the Nationals postseason struggles turned into missing out on the playoffs entirely in 2018 during the final year of Bryce Harper's contract, the farm system continues to turn out impact major league players.

While Washington's farm has ranked as a middle of the pack system at best over the last three seasons, the production the team has gotten from players throughout the Top 30 Prospects—both in the form of home grown players taking on major league roles and prospects being traded for major league talent—has allowed the Nationals to remain competitive.

The Nationals will have at least two of their outfield spots solidified for the foreseeable future (regardless of Harper's final landing spot in free agency) with cornerstone international players Juan Soto and Victor Robles. An injury to Robles in 2018 stalled his inevitable rise to Washington regular, but opened the door for Soto—who ranked as the No. 2 prospect behind Robles a year ago—to sprint through the system and pen one of the most impressive rookie seasons of all time. Soto and Robles have more than enough offensive ability to complement an offensive core that includes the homegrown third baseman Anthony Rendon and shortstop Trea Turner, who ranked No. 2 in the Nationals system in 2016; one spot ahead of Robles at the time.

Trades have thinned Washington's system quite a bit over the last few seasons. General manager Mike Rizzo has continued to trade top talents to improve the major league team. Former No. 1 prospect Lucas Giolito was the most notable name traded out of the system in 2016 to acquire outfielder Adam Eaton, but even recently Washington continues to trade prospects to fill major league needs. Outfielder Daniel Johnson would have ranked safely within the top 10 on this year's list and been the club's second-highest ranked outfield prospect, but he was packaged with rookie righthander Jefry Rodriguez—who ranked on the club's top 30 last year—to bring in catcher Yan Gomes from the Indians.

Washington has lost numerous prospects to graduation and trades over the last few years—particularly young pitchers—but the scouting department has made arms a focus of the last two drafts. While the team only has one pitcher who presently has an argument for Top 100 Prospect status, there's is plenty of depth to be found on the mound throughout this system outside of the top 10.

Juan Soto's incredible rookie season included a historic .406 on-base percentage.

PROJECTED 2022 LINEUP

Catcher	Yan Gomes (34)
First Base	Anthony Rendon (32)
Second Base	Luis Garcia (22)
Third Base	Carter Kieboom (24)
Shortstop	Trea Turner (29)
Left Field	Juan Soto (23)
Center Field	Victor Robles (25)
Right Field	Adam Eaton (33)
No. 1 Starter	Max Scherzer (37)
No. 2 Starter	Stephen Strasburg (33)
No. 3 Starter	Patrick Corbin (32)
No. 4 Starter	Mason Denaburg (22)
No. 5 Starter	Wil Crowe (27)
Closer	Erick Fedde (29)

The international scouting and development remains a strength with the Nationals, even outside of Robles and Soto. Shortstop Luis Garcia could be the next breakout star in the system with pristine bat-to-ball skills and offensive aptitude as a teenager, while a full third of the top 30 prospects is made up of international players with plenty of upside on both sides of the ball.

There's a lack of impact bats close to the major leagues outside of Kieboom, and the talent drops off enough outside of the top 10 to prevent Washington from owning a top-15 farm system, but there is still plenty of major league value to be had to keep the Nationals in the playoff hunt on a yearly basis.

WASHINGTON NATIONALS

TOP 2019 ROOKIE: Victor Robles, OF. Injury stalled his ascent to a regular major league role, but he should be locked into the lineup in 2019.
BREAKOUT PROSPECT: Israel Pineda, C. The 18-year-old dealt with a minor injury that limited him to 46 games, but he's shown an impressive hit tool and could start tapping into more game power soon.

SOURCE OF TOP 30 TALENT			
Homegrown	29	Acquired	1
College	14	Trade	1
Junior college	2	Rule 5 draft	0
High school	3	Independent league	0
Nondrafted free agent	0	Free agent/waivers	0
International	10		

SLEEPER: Jake Noll, UT. A righthanded hitter with above-average bat speed and back-to-back double-digit homer seasons, Noll has played second, third, first and will get more looks in the outfield in 2019.

LF
Telmito Agustin (14)
Alec Keller

CF
Victor Robles (1)
Gage Canning (12)
Rafael Bautista
Ricardo Mendez

RF
Justin Connell
Jacob Rhinesmith
Rhett Wiseman

3B
Anderson Franco
Colton Pogue
Jacob Wilson

SS
Carter Kieboom (2)
Luis Garcia (3)
Yasel Antuna (9)
Jose Sanchez (17)

2B
Jake Noll
Cole Freeman

1B
Drew Ward (29)
Jose Marmolejos
Aldrem Corredo
Blake Chisolm

C
Raudy Read (13)
Israel Pineda (15)
Tres Barrera (16)
Taylor Gushue
Jakson Reetz

LHP

LHSP	LHRP
Tim Cate (6)	Ben Braymer (20)
Seth Romero (7)	Taylor Guilbeau
Nick Raquet (19)	Jose Ferrer
	Aaron Fletcher
	Carson Teel

RHP

RHSP	RHRP
Mason Denaburg (4)	Reid Schaller (11)
Wil Crowe (5)	James Bourque (18)
Sterling Sharp (8)	Kyle Johnston (22)
Jake Irvin (10)	Tanner Rainey (24)
Jackson Tetreault (21)	Joan Adon (25)
Brigham Hill (23)	Gabe Klobosits (27)
Tomas Alastre (26)	Ronald Pena (29)
Malvin Pena (28)	Jacob Condra-Bogan
Joan Baez	Jhonatan German
Kyle McGowin	Austen Williams
Austin Voth	Jeremy McKinney
	A.J. Bogucki

DRAFT ANALYSIS

2018

BEST PURE HITTER: OF Gage Canning (5) had no issues at all in the New York-Penn League, hitting .315/.373/.593. He was promoted to low Class A Hagerstown, where he dealt with a minor injury, but when fully healthy Canning brings a solid line-drive swing that should serve him well.

BEST POWER HITTER: OF Pablo O'Connor (27) has above-average raw power and started to tap into it more by getting the ball in the air more consistently. In 52 games at short-season Auburn, O'Connor's isolated slugging improved from .120 to .166 as he tallied three triples and five homers.

FASTEST RUNNER: OF Cody Wilson (13) is a plus runner who stole 19 bases in 21 tries during the spring for Florida Atlantic and has plenty of pro potential on the bases as well.

BEST DEFENSIVE PLAYER: Wilson's speed has allowed him to play a solid outfield. INF Cole Daily (22) was a solid defender at shortstop, third base and second base this summer, with just one error across 453 innings during his debut.

BEST ATHLETE: Denaburg is certainly in the argument here as one of the most athletic pitchers in the 2018 prep class, as a converted catcher who's capable of doing standing backflips. Wilson brings his athleticism to the bases and the outfield, has above-average bat speed and is the more quick-twitch athlete of the two players.

BEST FASTBALL: RHP Mason Denaburg (1), touched as high as 97 mph during the spring of his senior high school season, with impressive arm-side life and control at lower velocities. RHP Reid Schaller (3) sits in the mid-90s and touched 99 mph this spring for Vanderbilt after recovering from Tommy John surgery. Both pitchers could wind up with future 70-grade fastballs.

BEST SECONDARY PITCH: LHP Tim Cate (2) had one of the best breaking balls of the 2018 draft class with a hammer curveball in the upper 70s to lower 80s, which Cate manipulated at will when healthy. The pitch has late-breaking action and is an easy plus offering at its best.

BEST PRO DEBUT: OF Jacob Rhinesmith (18)

TOP DRAFT PICKS OF THE DECADE

Year	Player, Pos	2018 Org
2009	Stephen Strasburg, RHP	Nationals
2010	Bryce Harper, OF	Nationals
2011	Anthony Rendon, 3B	Nationals
2012	Lucas Giolito, RHP	White Sox
2013	Jake Johansen, RHP (2nd round)	White Sox
2014	Erick Fedde, RHP	Nationals
2015	Andrew Stevenson, OF (2nd round)	Nationals
2016	Carter Kieboom, SS	Nationals
2017	Seth Romero, LHP	Nationals
2018	Mason Denaburg, RHP	Nationals

put together an impressive junior campaign with Western Kentucky and hit .283/.358/.380 in 63 games in the New York-Penn League this summer. He impressed Nationals coaches and evaluators with a consistent, professional approach at the plate with solid hands and a repeatable swing.

MOST INTRIGUING BACKGROUND: RHP Ryan Tapani's (21) father Kevin had a 13-year major league career pitching for the Mets, Twins, Dodgers, White Sox and Cubs.

CLOSEST TO THE MAJORS: RHP Jake Irvin (4) has a repeatable delivery and is a solid strike-thrower. He looks more like a big league starter currently than Denaburg, Cate or Schaller. If Cate stays healthy, he's a pitcher who could move through the system quickly as well.

BEST LATE-ROUND PICK: The Nationals are trying to see how much $3,000 can get them in the 27th and 28th rounds with a powerful bat in O'Connor and a solid pro debut from 1B Blake Chisolm (28), who hit .296/.427/.480 in the Gulf Coast League with a physical 6-foot-5 frame.

THE ONE WHO GOT AWAY: RHP Cole Wilcox (37) was the most talented player the Nationals failed to sign, but they took him late enough to know he would wind up at Georgia. RHP Zach Linginfelter (19) is going back to Tennessee for his junior season after posting an 11.62 K/9 rate this spring.

—CARLOS COLLAZO

2017

Between getting sent home from spring training and having Tommy John surgery, LHP Seth Romero (1) has had a tumultuous start to his pro career. RHP Wil Crowe (2) has already reached Double-A.

GRADE: C

2016

LHP Jesus Luzardo (3) has blossomed into one of the best pitching prospects in baseball and was part of the trade for Sean Doolittle. SS Carter Kieboom (1) in 2018 put together his best year as a pro.

GRADE: A

2015

Top pick OF Andrew Stevenson (2) and RHP Koda Glover (8) have graduated to the big leagues. LHP Taylor Hearn (5) has twice been traded for a closer, most recently getting sent to the Rangers.

GRADE: C

1 VICTOR ROBLES, OF

Born: May 19, 1997. **B-T:** R-R. **Ht.:** 6-0. **Wt.:** 190.
Signed: Dominican Republic, 2013.
Signed by: Modesto Ulloa.

The only thing that could have halted Robles' rapid ascent to the major leagues was injury, and of course that's what set the top-ranked talent back in 2018. Robles hyperextended his left elbow during a game with Triple-A Syracuse in early April and didn't return to the International League until July 27. He hit .269/.345/.386 in 36 games with Syracuse before earning a September callup to the big league club, where he looked right at home and hit .288/.348/.525.

SCOUTING REPORT: While Robles overflows with above-average tools, what will make him a perennial all-star candidate is his hitting ability, which grades out as plus thanks to his quick hands and pitch recognition. He opened up his stance a bit in 2018 and can cut himself off at times because of that. Scouts raved about Robles' ability to hit to all fields, and he did that to a larger extent this season compared to 2017. Robles' plus-plus speed will allow him to hit for plenty of extra bases, and while he doesn't have plus raw power he should have enough to hit 15-20 home runs annually. Speed is Robles' loudest tool, and he ranked in the 95th percentile of major leaguers this season with a sprint speed of 29.3 feet per second, according to Statcast. That running ability has allowed him to rack up 129 stolen bases over five minor league seasons and should allow him to become a headache for major league batteries. His natural running ability, as well as the steps he's taken over the past few seasons to improve his jumps, routes and throwing accuracy, should allow him to become an elite defensive center fielder. His plus arm gives him the ability to handle right field without a problem, but there are few outfielders who could force him out of center.

THE FUTURE: Robles should be a regular fixture in the Nationals' outfield in 2019, buttressing a formidable young core alongside Juan Soto. While Soto has a higher offensive ceiling, Robles has the ability to impact the game on both sides of the ball at a high level while hitting at the top of the lineup.

G FIUME/GETTY IMAGES

BA GRADE	SCOUTING GRADES
65 Risk: Medium	**Hit:** 60. **Power:** 55. **Speed:** 70. **Field:** 70. **Arm:** 60.

Projected future grades on 20-80 scouting scale.

TOP PROSPECTS OF THE DECADE

2009	Jordan Zimmermann, RHP	Tigers
2010	Stephen Strasburg, RHP	Nationals
2011	Bryce Harper, OF	Nationals
2012	Bryce Harper, OF	Nationals
2013	Anthony Rendon, 3B	Nationals
2014	Lucas Giolito, RHP	White Sox
2015	Lucas Giolito, RHP	White Sox
2016	Lucas Giolito, RHP	White Sox
2017	Victor Robles, OF	Nationals
2018	Victor Robles, OF	Nationals

BEST TOOLS

Best Hitter for Average	Luis Garcia
Best Power Hitter	Carter Kieboom
Best Strike-Zone Discipline	Carter Kieboom
Fastest Baserunner	Victor Robles
Best Athlete	Sterling Sharp
Best Fastball	Mason Denaburg
Best Curveball	Tim Cate
Best Slider	Seth Romero
Best Changeup	Wil Crowe
Best Control	Kyle McGowin
Best Defensive Catcher	Tres Barrera
Best Defensive Infielder	Jose Sanchez
Best Infield Arm	Juan Pascal
Best Defensive Outfielder	Victor Robles
Best Outfield Arm	Victor Robles

Year	Club (League)	Class	AVG	G	AB	R	H	2B	3B	HR	RBI	BB	SO	SB	CS	OBP	SLG
2017	Potomac (CAR)	HiA	.289	77	291	49	84	25	7	7	33	25	62	16	7	.377	.495
	Harrisburg (EL)	AA	.324	37	139	24	45	12	1	3	14	12	22	11	3	.394	.489
	Washington (NL)	MAJ	.250	13	24	2	6	1	2	0	4	0	6	0	1	.308	.458
2018	Nationals (GCL)	R	.333	8	18	7	6	1	0	0	1	7	4	4	1	.556	.389
	Auburn (NYP)	SS	.188	4	16	0	3	0	0	0	3	1	2	1	0	.235	.188
	Syracuse (IL)	AAA	.278	40	158	25	44	9	1	2	10	18	26	14	6	.356	.386
	Washington (NL)	MAJ	.288	21	59	8	17	3	1	3	10	4	12	3	2	.348	.525
Major League Totals			.277	34	83	10	23	4	3	3	14	4	18	3	3	.337	.506
Minor League Totals			.300	384	1438	274	432	89	26	28	155	129	252	129	45	.392	.457

2 CARTER KIEBOOM, SS

Born: Sept. 3, 1997. **B-T:** R-R. **Ht.:** 6-2. **Wt.:** 190. **Drafted:** HS—Marietta, Ga., 2016 (1st round). **Signed by:** Eric Robinson.

TRACK RECORD: A 2016 first-round selection out of Walton High in Marietta, Ga., Kieboom made the most of his first healthy full season in pro ball in 2018, advancing to Double-A Harrisburg at age 20, more than four years younger than the average Eastern League hitter.

SCOUTING REPORT: The Nationals wanted to see the normally selective Kieboom get more aggressive on fastballs in the strike zone in 2018, and they were happy with the results when he started to figure that out. After hitting .198/.308/.347 during the first month of the season with a 14 percent walk rate, Kieboom went on to hit .301/.370/.469 during his final 99 games, with a 9.5 percent walk rate. Kieboom has excellent balance at the plate and the ability to hit to all fields. He also started to tap into his plus raw power with a career-high 16 home runs. Kieboom improved his consistency at shortstop and showed a strong internal clock, reliably soft hands and a solid first step to go with above-average arm strength.

BA GRADE
55 Risk: High
Hit: 60. Power: 60.
Run: 50. Field: 50
Arm: 55

THE FUTURE: While Kieboom has shown he could handle shortstop, he will get reps at second base to increase his versatility and provide a more clear path to the big leagues—with Trea Turner and Anthony Rendon entrenched on the left side of the infield—where he could provide an impact bat in the middle of the order.

Year	Club (League)	Class	AVG	G	AB	R	H	2B	3B	HR	RBI	BB	SO	SB	CS	OBP	SLG
2016	Nationals (GCL)	R	.244	36	135	22	33	8	4	4	25	12	43	1	2	.323	.452
2017	Nationals (GCL)	R	.417	6	12	1	5	3	0	0	5	3	0	0	0	.563	.667
	Auburn (NYP)	SS	.250	7	28	4	7	1	0	1	4	1	2	1	0	.276	.393
	Hagerstown (SAL)	LoA	.296	48	179	36	53	12	0	8	26	28	40	2	2	.400	.497
2018	Potomac (CAR)	HiA	.298	61	245	48	73	15	0	11	46	36	50	6	1	.386	.494
	Harrisburg (EL)	AA	.262	62	248	36	65	16	1	5	23	22	59	3	1	.326	.395
Minor League Totals			.279	220	847	147	236	55	5	29	129	102	194	13	6	.362	.458

3 LUIS GARCIA, SS/3B

Born: May 16, 2000. **B-T:** L-R. **Ht.:** 6-0. **Wt.:** 190. **Signed:** Dominican Republic, 2016. **Signed by:** Carlos Ulloa.

TRACK RECORD: The No. 3 prospect available in the 2016 international signing class, Garcia signed for $1.3 million and quickly showed that his skills could translate to pro ball with a strong debut season in the Gulf Coast League in 2017. He hit .298 in his full-season debut and even climbed to high Class A Potomac, where he was the only 18-year-old in the Carolina League.

SCOUTING REPORT: Garcia stands out for his excellent feel to hit, with impressive hand-eye coordination, a consistent lefthanded stroke and a strong understanding of what he's trying to do at the plate. Nationals coaches raved about his baseball IQ, and while they didn't directly compare him with Juan Soto, they did point out that he makes adjustments within at-bats in a similar manner. While Garcia doesn't have huge raw power, he homered seven times and scouts noticed increased physicality in 2018, giving him a chance for above-average power in the future. Garcia's run grades seemed to

BA GRADE
55 Risk: High
Hit: 60. Power: 55.
Run: 55. Field: 50.
Arm: 55

be universally lower than a year ago, when he was a plus-plus runner—now he's closer to above-average. Defensively, Garcia has the instincts and arm for shortstop, but he might profile better at second base as he continues to fill out.

THE FUTURE: Garcia should start the 2019 season with Potomac after just 40 games this season but could push his way to Double-A Harrisburg if he continues to hit.

Year	Club (League)	Class	AVG	G	AB	R	H	2B	3B	HR	RBI	BB	SO	SB	CS	OBP	SLG
2017	Nationals (GCL)	R	.302	49	199	25	60	8	3	1	22	9	32	11	2	.330	.387
2018	Hagerstown (SAL)	LoA	.297	78	296	48	88	14	4	3	31	19	49	8	5	.335	.402
	Potomac (CAR)	HiA	.299	49	204	34	61	7	2	4	23	12	33	4	1	.338	.412
Minor League Totals			.299	176	699	107	209	29	9	8	76	40	114	23	8	.335	.401

4 MASON DENABURG, RHP

Born: Aug. 8, 1999. **B-T:** R-R. **Ht.:** 6-4. **Wt.:** 195. **Drafted:** HS—Merritt Island, Fla., 2018 (1st round). **Signed by:** Alan Marr.

TRACK RECORD: A converted catcher, Denaburg established himself as one of the hardest-throwing pitchers in a deep 2018 prep pitching class and did enough over the summer and during his spring season to get selected at No. 27—even though he missed time with biceps tendinitis. He did not pitch after signing for $3 million.

SCOUTING REPORT: An athletic righthander with an ideal starter's frame, Denaburg touched 97 mph at times as an amateur, though he usually settles into the low 90s. At the lower velocities he commands the pitch substantially better. However, as Denaburg continues to refine his understanding of pitching, he has the mechanics, arm action and athleticism that should allow him to develop at least above-average control. In addition to a plus fastball, Denaburg has a curveball in the upper-70s that will need more consistency but has the power and depth to become a second plus offering. Denaburg rarely threw a low-80s changeup as an amateur, but he showed good feel for the pitch at instructional league.

THE FUTURE: Denaburg has middle-of-the-rotation upside and should have more than enough body control to make the small adjustments that will be necessary to handle his first full season in 2019.

MIKE JANES/FOUR SEAM IMAGES

BA GRADE

60 Risk: Extreme

Fastball: 60.
Curveball: 60.
Change: 50. CTL: 55.

Year	Club (League)	Class	AVG	G	AB	R	H	2B	3B	HR	RBI	BB	SO	SB	CS	OBP	SLG
2018	Did not play																

5 WIL CROWE, RHP

Born: Sept. 9, 1994. **B-T:** R-R. **Ht.:** 6-2. **Wt.:** 240. **Drafted:** South Carolina, 2017 (2nd round). **Signed by:** Paul Faulk.

TRACK RECORD: Crowe had a strong 2017 debut for the Nationals after signing for $946,500 in the second round, posting a 2.96 ERA over two leagues. In his first full pro season in 2018, Crowe posted a 2.69 ERA in the Carolina League before earning a promotion to Double-A Harrisburg where he struggled in five starts.

SCOUTING REPORT: Crowe has no plus pitch in his repertoire, and the 6-foot-2 righthander relies on excellent feel for a solid four-pitch mix to succeed. Scouts and Nationals coaches both rave about Crowe's ability to mix his entire repertoire in any count, which includes a willingness and ability to work inside against hitters. His fastball sits in the 91-92 mph range with solid sinking action. He has a curveball and slider that are both average offerings and a changeup that has become his go-to out pitch. Crowe doesn't throw as hard as he did in college, when he had more rest between starts. He also had Tommy John surgery as a sophomore. Still, the emergence of his changeup and his overall strike-throwing ability has allowed him to become of Washington's most consistent pitching prospects.

THE FUTURE: After wearing down a bit at the end of 2018 under the stress of a career high 116 innings, Crowe will likely start 2019 back in Double-A.

BA GRADE

50 Risk: Medium

Fastball: 55.
Change: 55. Curve: 50.
Slider: 50. CTL: 60.

Year	Club (League)	Class	W	L	ERA	G	GS	CG	SV	IP	H	HR	BB	SO	K/9	WHIP	AVG
2017	Nationals (GCL)	R	0	0	4.91	2	2	0	0	4	3	0	1	2	4.9	1.09	.250
	Auburn (NYP)	SS	0	0	2.61	7	7	0	0	21	18	3	3	15	6.5	1.02	.234
2018	Auburn (NYP)	SS	0	0	0.00	1	1	0	0	3	2	0	2	1	3.0	1.33	.222
	Potomac (CAR)	HiA	11	0	2.69	16	15	0	0	87	71	6	30	78	8.1	1.16	.220
	Harrisburg (EL)	AA	0	5	6.15	5	5	0	0	26	31	4	16	15	5.1	1.78	.307
Minor League Totals			11	5	3.33	31	30	0	0	141	125	13	52	111	7.1	1.26	.239

6 TIM CATE, LHP

Born: Sept. 30, 1997. **B-T:** L-L. **Ht.:** 6-0. **Wt.:** 185. **Drafted:** Connecticut, 2018 (2nd round). **Signed by:** John Malzone.

TRACK RECORD: Cate established himself as one of the better lefthanded college pitchers in the 2018 draft class after two strong seasons as a starter with Connecticut. He was in the middle of a third before he was sidelined with an elbow injury. Despite Cate's short stature and injury concerns—he had Tommy John surgery in high school—the Nationals liked him and his curveball enough to sign him for $986,200 in the second round.

SCOUTING REPORT: Scouts don't talk about Cate without raving about his 77-83 mph hammer curveball. One of the best breaking pitches in the 2018 class, it's at least a plus offering and many scouts go as far as throwing a 70 grade on it. Cate lands his curve regularly and uses it as a swing-and-miss offering both inside and outside the strike zone. His fastball is more solid-average, in the 90-92 mph range, but he has touched the mid-90s in the past and the Nationals hope he will be able to get there more regularly in the future with improved body strength. Cate will need to improve the life on his fastball, which gets flat at times, as well as develop his changeup, which is a distant third pitch. He also needs to improve his command, but with a compact delivery and clean, high three-quarter slot, projects to be average in that area.

THE FUTURE: Cate has a middle-of-the-rotation ceiling, but could also be useful as a breaking ball-heavy reliever if his size and injury history limit his workload.

TOMASSO DEROSA

BA GRADE

50 Risk: High

Fastball: 55.
Curveball: 70.
Change: 50. CTL: 50.

Year	Club (League)	Class	W	L	ERA	G	GS	CG	SV	IP	H	HR	BB	SO	K/9	WHIP	AVG
2018	Auburn (NYP)	SS	2	3	4.65	9	8	0	0	31	34	1	10	26	7.5	1.42	.272
	Hagerstown (SAL)	LoA	0	3	5.57	4	4	0	0	21	23	4	6	19	8.1	1.38	.271
Minor League Totals			2	6	5.02	13	12	0	0	52	57	5	16	45	7.8	1.40	.271

7 SETH ROMERO, LHP

Born: April 19, 1996. **B-T:** L-L. **Ht.:** 6-3. **Wt.:** 240. **Drafted:** Houston, 2017 (1st round). **Signed by:** Tyler Wilt.

TRACK RECORD: Romero's pro career has stalled multiple times since the Nationals made him their first-round pick in 2017. He was sent home from spring training in 2018 for violating team rules and later in the year had Tommy John surgery that will sideline him for all of 2019. In college at Houston, he served multiple suspensions and eventually was kicked off the team.

SCOUTING REPORT: Despite a long history of makeup concerns and new question marks about his health, Romero draws raves from scouts for the quality of his stuff on the rare occasions when he has been on the field. He has three plus pitches in his repertoire between a fastball that sits in the mid-90s with good life, a slider with sharp bite and a changeup that has good separation and diving action. The raw stuff has never been the question with Romero. who should have no issues racking up strikeouts, but his delivery will never be described as clean—with plenty of moving parts—and he will continue to face questions about his character until he proves his maturity. Nationals evaluators don't see him as a bad kid, but a player who is still learning how to become a professional.

THE FUTURE: The start to Romero's pro career has been about as bad as anyone could have anticipated, and he will now have to wait until 2020 to prove that he can return healthy and fully take advantage of his obvious talent.

GLEN GASTON

BA GRADE

55 Risk: Extreme

Fastball: 60.
Slider: 60.
Change: 60. CTL: 50.

Year	Club (League)	Class	W	L	ERA	G	GS	CG	SV	IP	H	HR	BB	SO	K/9	WHIP	AVG
2017	Nationals (GCL)	R	0	0	0.00	1	1	0	0	2	0	0	2	3	13.5	1.00	.000
	Auburn (NYP)	SS	0	1	5.40	6	6	0	0	20	19	0	6	32	14.4	1.25	.244
2018	Hagerstown (SAL)	LoA	0	1	3.91	7	7	0	0	25	20	3	8	34	12.1	1.11	.206
Minor League Totals			0	2	4.37	14	14	0	0	47	39	3	16	69	13.1	1.16	.215

8 STERLING SHARP, RHP

Born: May 30, 1995. **B-T:** R-R. **Ht.:** 6-4. **Wt.:** 170. **Drafted:** Drury (Mo.), 2016 (22nd round). **Signed by:** Brandon Larson.

TRACK RECORD: The Nationals signed Sharp out of Drury (Mo.) University despite a 5.90 ERA at the Division II school in 2016, but the lanky, athletic righthander has come into his own in three years in the Nationals system. A gifted athlete, Sharp was recruited to play basketball in college but that athleticism has transferred well to the mound.

SCOUTING REPORT: Sharp doesn't overpower batters with velocity, but uses a sinking fastball in the 90-92 mph range with terrific boring action that he routinely locates in the bottom half of the strike zone. He complements his sinker with a changeup that has diving action as well, with a tick of armside run. The two pitches allowed him to record one of the highest groundball rates in the Nationals' system, with a 61.8 percent groundball rate in high Class A Potomac and a 55.8 percent groundball rate in Double A Harrisburg. Sharp also has a developing slider that could become a third average pitch, but he needs to improve his control of the offering and learn to trust it as much as his fastball and changeup. Sharp's stuff plays up thanks to plus deception, as he hides the ball well behind a lean body, which could be improved with added strength.

THE FUTURE: Sharp reached Double-A Harrisburg in 2018 and will likely return to the Eastern League to begin 2019. He has the overall package to be a back-of-the-rotation starter.

BA GRADE
50 Risk: High
Fastball: 55.
Changeup: 55
Slider: 50. CTL: 55.

Year	Club (League)	Class	W	L	ERA	G	GS	CG	SV	IP	H	HR	BB	SO	K/9	WHIP	AVG
2016	Nationals (GCL)	R	3	0	3.24	11	7	0	2	42	47	2	6	35	7.6	1.27	.287
	Auburn (NYP)	SS	0	0	3.60	1	1	0	0	5	6	0	0	3	5.4	1.20	.316
2017	Hagerstown (SAL)	LoA	4	9	3.69	18	17	1	0	93	100	8	14	69	6.7	1.23	.271
	Potomac (CAR)	HiA	2	2	4.78	6	5	0	0	32	39	4	13	26	7.3	1.63	.307
2018	Potomac (CAR)	HiA	5	3	3.16	14	14	0	0	80	82	4	21	58	6.6	1.29	.262
	Harrisburg (EL)	AA	6	3	4.33	13	13	1	0	69	72	6	26	47	6.2	1.43	.268
Minor League Totals			20	17	3.74	63	57	2	2	320	346	24	80	238	6.7	1.33	.274

9 YASEL ANTUNA, SS/2B

Born: Oct. 26, 1999. **B-T:** B-R. **Ht.:** 6-0. **Wt.:** 170. **Signed:** Dominican Republic, 2016. **Signed by:** Pablo Arias.

TRACK RECORD: The No. 14 international prospect in the 2016 class, Antuna signed for a Nationals international record of $3.85 million and had a strong debut in the Gulf Coast League in 2017 before taking a step back at the plate and having Tommy John surgery in 2018.

SCOUTING REPORT: Antuna signed for nearly $4 million thanks to his offensive potential as a switch-hitter with above-average raw power. In 2018 he struggled mightily with the bat because he lacked a consistent plate approach. He also looked better from the right side than the left. Antuna's power hasn't yet shown up in games, but scouts see raw strength in batting practice. His large frame and terrific work ethic in the gym could produce a more powerful hitter in the future. Defensively, Antuna has smooth actions and strong hands at shortstop, but he had issues with throwing accuracy and sat back on balls too frequently. When healthy, Antuna had plus arm strength, but that will have to be re-evaluated when he returns in mid-2019.

THE FUTURE: Antuna still has upside thanks to his physical tools, but he has plenty of work to do when it comes to refining his game—both offensively and defensively. He must develop a consistent offensive approach and get the reps necessary to improve his confidence.

BA GRADE
50 Risk: Extreme
Hit: 50. Power: 60.
Run: 45. Field: 50.
Arm: 55.

Year	Club (League)	Class	AVG	G	AB	R	H	2B	3B	HR	RBI	BB	SO	SB	CS	OBP	SLG
2017	Nationals (GCL)	R	.301	48	173	25	52	8	3	1	17	23	29	5	5	.382	.399
2018	Hagerstown (SAL)	LoA	.220	87	323	44	71	14	2	6	27	32	79	8	7	.293	.331
Minor League Totals			.248	135	496	69	123	22	5	7	44	55	108	13	12	.324	.355

10 JAKE IRVIN, RHP

TOM DIPACE

Born: Feb. 18, 1997. **B-T:** R-R. **Ht.:** 6-6. **Wt.:** 225. **Drafted:** Oklahoma, 2018 (4th round). **Signed by:** Ed Gustafson.

TRACK RECORD: Irvin improved every year at Oklahoma, culminating in a 6-2 junior campaign in which he posted a 3.41 ERA with 115 strikeouts to just 28 walks in 95 innings. With an impressive Big 12 track record and a large, 6-foot-6, 225-pound frame, the Nationals signed Irvin for $550,000.

SCOUTING REPORT: While his build and college track record are both impressive, Irvin's stuff is more ordinary than overwhelming. He has a solid-average fastball that's routinely in the 90-94 mph range, only occasionally touching 95 or 96. His slider is average, a low 80s breaking ball with solid finish that he's able to throw for strikes in most counts, but the pitch gets slurvy at times and he'll need to sharpen it moving forward. Irvin rarely threw a changeup in college, but scouts thought it had a chance to be a solid pitch in the future and the Nationals like his feel for the offering currently. Irvin will likely never rack up a high number of strikeouts, but he's a solid strike thrower, repeats his delivery and hides the ball well on his backside.

THE FUTURE: A potential quick-mover, Irvin stands out more for his high floor than high upside, and could be a back-of-the-rotation starter or middle reliever.

BA GRADE

45 Risk: High

Fastball: 55.
Slider: 50.
Change: 50. **CTL:** 55.

Year	Club (League)	Class	W	L	ERA	G	GS	CG	SV	IP	H	HR	BB	SO	K/9	WHIP	AVG
2018	Nationals (GCL)	R	1	0	1.42	7	3	0	0	13	10	0	3	9	6.4	1.03	.213
	Auburn (NYP)	SS	0	0	2.25	4	4	0	0	8	6	0	4	6	6.8	1.25	.207
Minor League Totals			1	0	1.74	11	7	0	0	21	16	0	7	15	6.5	1.11	.211

11 REID SCHALLER, RHP

BA GRADE

45 Risk: High

Born: April 2, 1997. **B-T:** R-R. **Ht.:** 6-3. **Wt.:** 210. **Drafted:** Vanderbilt, 2018 (3rd round). **Signed by:** Brian Cleary.

TRACK RECORD: A hard-throwing righthander who missed his first season at Vanderbilt after undergoing Tommy John surgery, Schaller struck out 39 batters in 28.2 relief innings for the Commodores this spring before Washington signed him for $551,100 as a draft-eligible freshman.

SCOUTING REPORT: The Nationals used Schaller in a starting role in Rookie ball and low Class A, but most scouts expect to see Schaller provide major league value in the bullpen thanks to a high-effort delivery. While Washington has not cemented a role for him moving forward, the organization does prefer to give their priority arms more innings as starters and that could be the case here. Schaller has a fastball that sits in the 94-97 mph range in the bullpen and touches as high as 99-100 mph. For secondary offerings, the 6-foot-3 righty has a power slider in the mid-80s with sharp, downward action that could become a put-away pitch, as well as a changeup that needs more work.

THE FUTURE: The Nationals will try and stretch Schaller out more with a full season in 2019 and continue to build his workload as he gets further away from his Tommy John surgery, but without the development of a consistent third pitch, the bullpen will remain his most likely future destination.

Year	Club (League)	Class	W	L	ERA	G	GS	CG	SV	IP	H	HR	BB	SO	K/9	WHIP	AVG
2018	Nationals (GCL)	R	0	1	1.54	5	5	0	0	12	9	1	3	16	12.3	1.03	.209
	Auburn (NYP)	SS	2	2	5.90	7	7	0	0	29	30	0	9	16	5.0	1.34	.268
Minor League Totals			2	3	4.65	12	12	0	0	41	39	1	12	32	7.1	1.25	.252

12 GAGE CANNING, OF

BA GRADE

45 Risk: High

Born: April 23, 1997. **B-T:** L-R. **Ht.:** 5-10. **Wt.:** 175. **Drafted:** Arizona State, 2018 (5th round). **Signed by:** Mitch Sokol.

TRACK RECORD: Canning had a career-year at the plate for Arizona State during his junior season and hit .369/.426/.648 with nine home runs, 11 triples and 17 doubles. At the same time, he moved from right field to center field and had no issues with the position change, prompting the Nationals to sign his solid all-around package for $308,900 in the fifth round.

SCOUTING REPORT: A 5-foot-10, 175-pound lefthanded hitter, Canning will likely never have plus raw power, but he has plenty of strength in his compact frame that leads to 55-grade raw power and could become above-average in-game with some adjustments at the plate. An aggressive hitter, Canning had strikeout concerns throughout college and whiffed almost 29 percent of the time in the South Atlantic and New York-Penn leagues. He'll need to cut down his swing in two-strike counts and learn how to make adjustments within at-bats to project as a solid hitter moving forward. A plus runner, Canning will also need to improve his baserunning to better utilize a strong tool, though it's enough to project him as a solid center fielder moving forward with improved route-running and more reps.

THE FUTURE: Canning has a solid package of tools and a high-energy playing style that is endearing, but refinement will be necessary in all phases of his game.

Year	Club (League)	Class	AVG	G	AB	R	H	2B	3B	HR	RBI	BB	SO	SB	CS	OBP	SLG
2018	Auburn (NYP)	SS	.315	14	54	13	17	3	3	2	7	5	18	0	2	.373	.593
	Hagerstown (SAL)	LoA	.223	31	112	15	25	9	0	4	16	11	36	2	0	.294	.411
Minor League Totals			.253	45	166	28	42	12	3	6	23	16	54	2	2	.319	.470

13 RAUDY READ, C

BA GRADE

45 Risk: High

Born: Oct. 29, 1993. **B-T:** R-R. **Ht.:** 6-0. **Wt.:** 170. **Signed:** Dominican Republic, 2011. **Signed by:** Modesto Ulloa.

TRACK RECORD: After winning the Nationals' Bob Boone Award for professionalism and leadership after a strong 2017 season, Read tested positive for the steroid Boldenone during the offseason and faced an 80-game suspension that limited the 25-year-old catcher to 53 games in 2018.

SCOUTING REPORT: Read's power fell off in 2018 with just one home run every 71 plate appearances, compared to one homer every 26 plate appearances in 2017. Those within the Nationals organization still like his raw power and natural strength, but there is added skepticism of what that tool truly looks like now given his suspension. Read hit well in Double-A but struggled in a 13-game stint in Triple-A, with most evaluators citing his hit tool as fringe-average, though he managed to use the opposite field more this season. Defensively, Read has plus arm strength and has consistently improved behind the plate as he learns how to absorb and use more information related to game-calling as he progresses.

THE FUTURE: Read will need to make up for lost at-bats in 2019, and should be challenged with a full season in Triple-A Syracuse, as he's proven his bat in the Eastern League and is getting old for the level.

Year	Club (League)	Class	AVG	G	AB	R	H	2B	3B	HR	RBI	BB	SO	SB	CS	OBP	SLG
2016	Potomac (CAR)	HiA	.262	101	386	54	101	30	1	9	51	31	53	6	3	.324	.415
2017	Harrisburg (EL)	AA	.265	108	411	44	109	25	1	17	61	27	79	2	0	.312	.455
	Washington (NL)	MAJ	.273	8	11	1	3	0	0	0	0	0	3	0	0	.273	.273
2018	Syracuse (IL)	AAA	.260	13	50	2	13	2	0	0	2	1	8	0	0	.269	.300
	Harrisburg (EL)	AA	.286	40	147	14	42	9	2	3	26	11	30	0	0	.335	.435
Major League Totals			.273	8	11	1	3	0	0	0	0	0	3	0	0	.273	.273
Minor League Totals			.256	550	2031	235	519	134	6	55	300	139	330	18	19	.310	.409

14 TELMITO AGUSTIN, OF

BA GRADE

45 Risk: High

Born: Oct. 9, 1996. **B-T:** L-L. **Ht.:** 5-10. **Wt.:** 160. **Signed:** Dominican Republic, 2013. **Signed by:** Virgilio DeLeon.

TRACK RECORD: After struggling in his first full season in pro ball in 2017, Agustin began having more success in 2018, including a .302/.368/.454 line with high Class A Potomac. However, injuries have continued to limit his at-bats, and he missed time with a broken finger this season.

SCOUTING REPORT: Agustin has made impressive strides forward with his strength, which has translated to the field and allowed the lefthanded hitter to leverage the baseball more effectively and start to hit for more power. Prior to his May injury, Agustin hit .386/.411/.659 including four of the six home runs he hit in total in 2018. Previously, Agustin had the speed to potentially play center field, but he's now a solid-average runner who fits best in the corners and spent all of his time in 2018 in left or right field. While Agustin's run tool has backed up, he's improved both his baserunning and outfield instincts—both of which were previously large question marks in his game.

THE FUTURE: Agustin shows flashes of being a solid fourth outfielder with an intriguing bat, but injuries have prevented him from putting together a full and successful season. He should get his first test in Double-A in 2019.

Year	Club (League)	Class	AVG	G	AB	R	H	2B	3B	HR	RBI	BB	SO	SB	CS	OBP	SLG
2016	Nationals (GCL)	R	.000	1	4	0	0	0	0	0	0	0	2	0	0	.000	.000
	Hagerstown (SAL)	LoA	.265	72	238	35	63	12	1	5	30	16	71	14	9	.309	.387
2017	Potomac (CAR)	HiA	.206	33	102	12	21	4	0	1	14	6	27	3	2	.257	.275
	Hagerstown (SAL)	LoA	.277	80	296	45	82	18	4	9	37	13	74	9	4	.308	.456
2018	Auburn (NYP)	SS	.186	18	70	7	13	2	0	1	5	5	20	1	0	.247	.257
	Potomac (CAR)	HiA	.302	63	205	31	62	10	3	5	30	20	43	7	3	.368	.454
Minor League Totals			.280	372	1295	204	362	69	22	25	179	110	306	69	28	.338	.425

15 ISRAEL PINEDA, C

Born: April 3, 2000. **B-T:** R-R. **Ht.:** 5-11. **Wt.:** 190. **Signed:** Venezuela, 2016.
Signed by: Eduardo Rosario.

BA GRADE
50 Risk: Extreme

TRACK RECORD: The Nationals signed Pineda as part of their big 2016 international class, inking him to a $450,000 deal as an offensive-minded catching prospect whose defense still needed some work. After more than holding his own during his debut pro season in the Gulf Coast League in 2017, Pineda was promoted to the New York-Penn League in 2018 where—at almost three years younger than the average hitter—he hit .273/.341/.388 with four home runs and made the NYPL all-star team.

SCOUTING REPORT: Washington officials were impressed with Pineda's bat-to-ball skills and believe that he'll continue to add strength and physicality to his stocky frame to hit for more power in the future. Praised for his ability to use the entire field, Pineda has pulled more than half of his batted balls in each of the last two seasons, but might use the right-center gap as he's challenged more at the plate in the future. Defensively, Pineda has above-average arm strength and has thrown out an impressive 42 percent of baserunners in his 370 minor league innings behind the plate.

THE FUTURE: A broken bone in his left hand ended Pineda's season in August, but he could shoot up this list in the future given health and further refinement in his game.

Year	Club (League)	Class	AVG	G	AB	R	H	2B	3B	HR	RBI	BB	SO	SB	CS	OBP	SLG
2017	Nationals (GCL)	R	.288	17	59	10	17	5	2	0	12	4	13	0	0	.323	.441
2018	Auburn (NYP)	SS	.273	46	165	25	45	7	0	4	24	12	35	0	0	.341	.388
Minor League Totals			.277	63	224	35	62	12	2	4	36	16	48	0	0	.336	.402

16 TRES BARRERA, C

Born: Sept. 15, 1994. **B-T:** R-R. **Ht.:** 6-0. **Wt.:** 215. **Drafted:** Texas, 2016 (6th round). **Signed by:** Tyler Wilt.

BA GRADE
45 Risk: High

TRACK RECORD: A talented defensive catcher dating back to his college days at Texas—where he also played third and second at times—Barrera signed for $210,000 in the sixth round of the 2016 draft. Since then he's progressed a level each year and continued to impress scouts and teammates with his work behind the plate.

SCOUTING REPORT: A bilingual backstop, Barrera handles the pitching staff well and is athletic behind the plate, with quick actions that allow him to get down and block effectively and soft, quiet hands that allow him to present the ball well to both sides of the plate. His rapid transition and footwork on throws to second base allowed him to throw out 49 percent of baserunners in the Carolina League, and coaches also praised his improved game-calling. Barrera doesn't project to be more than a fringe-average hitter at best, but he does have solid bat speed and raw pull power. He'll need to cut down on his strikeouts and adjust his approach to tap into that potential with any consistency.

THE FUTURE: Barrera could project as a regular if he takes a step forward offensively, but if that doesn't happen he could still become a valuable catch-and-throw backup for a major league team.

Year	Club (League)	Class	AVG	G	AB	R	H	2B	3B	HR	RBI	BB	SO	SB	CS	OBP	SLG
2016	Auburn (NYP)	SS	.244	48	164	19	40	9	1	3	17	15	22	0	0	.337	.366
2017	Hagerstown (SAL)	LoA	.278	67	237	28	66	18	1	8	27	23	58	1	0	.354	.464
2018	Potomac (CAR)	HiA	.263	68	259	36	68	14	0	6	24	22	53	3	0	.334	.386
Minor League Totals			.264	183	660	83	174	41	2	17	68	60	133	4	0	.342	.409

17 JOSE SANCHEZ, SS

Born: July 12, 2000. **B-T:** R-R. **Ht.:** 5-11. **Wt.:** 155. **Signed:** Venezuela, 2016.
Signed by: German Robles.

BA GRADE
50 Risk: Extreme

TRACK RECORD: A $950,000 international signee in Washington's 2016 class that also includes Yasel Antuna and Luis Garcia, Sanchez is the best defender of the group, though he was overmatched at the plate in the Gulf Coast League in 2017 and again in the New York-Penn League this season.

SCOUTING REPORT: Sanchez has plus hands up the middle to go with terrific footwork and mobility from side to side. Nevertheless, he's best described as an average runner overall. With above-average arm strength, Sanchez has all the tools necessary to handle the position and continues to improve his body strength and agility. After splitting time at shortstop, second and third in 2017, Sanchez played all but one game at shortstop this season. One of the youngest players in the New York-Penn League at just 17, Sanchez only managed a .230/.309/.282 line in 64 games, which is a slight improvement from his Rookie ball numbers a year prior.

THE FUTURE: Sanchez should start 2019 back in Auburn to work on figuring out the offensive side of the game and will project as a plus defensive and utility infielder if that doesn't happen.

Year	Club (League)	Class	AVG	G	AB	R	H	2B	3B	HR	RBI	BB	SO	SB	CS	OBP	SLG
2017	Nationals (GCL)	R	.209	48	158	22	33	3	0	1	20	14	26	0	2	.280	.247
2018	Auburn (NYP)	SS	.230	64	209	20	48	9	1	0	23	24	56	1	0	.309	.282
Minor League Totals			.221	112	367	42	81	12	1	1	43	38	82	1	2	.297	.267

18 JAMES BOURQUE, RHP

BA GRADE
50 Risk: Extreme

Born: July 9, 1993. **B-T:** R-R. **Ht.:** 6-4. **Wt.:** 190. **Drafted:** Michigan, 2014 (14th round). **Signed by:** Steve Arnieri.

TRACK RECORD: Bourque split time in the bullpen and rotation during his first two years at Michigan before becoming a primary reliever during his junior year and finding more success in the role. He's followed a similar path during his four years with the Nationals.

SCOUTING REPORT: Washington ran Bourque out as a starter in 2014 and again in 2016 and 2017 after he missed the 2015 season due to Tommy John surgery, but the 6-foot-4 righthander didn't find much success until he moved into the bullpen this summer. Bourque was able to pitch almost exclusively off of a plus fastball and curveball combination, while his control issues were minimized in shorter outings. He posted a career-best 1.70 ERA in 53 innings split between high Class A and Double-A. Bourque's fastball touches as high as 98 and is regularly in the mid-90s, and he complements it with a power curve in the 85-88 mph range. That curve is presently an out-pitch and could wind up being a 70-grade offering. Bourque's lack of a third pitch might not inhibit him as a reliever, but Nationals evaluators liked the progress he made with a changeup during instructional league.

THE FUTURE: Bourque should begin 2019 in Double-A, where he'll try and refine his command, but he could move quickly to the majors as a potential late-inning reliever.

Year	Club (League)	Class	W	L	ERA	G	GS	CG	SV	IP	H	HR	BB	SO	K/9	WHIP	AVG
2016	Hagerstown (SAL)	LoA	5	6	5.03	17	13	0	0	68	81	10	23	55	7.3	1.53	.293
2017	Hagerstown (SAL)	LoA	5	7	5.05	23	20	0	0	114	123	8	35	90	7.1	1.39	.273
2018	Potomac (CAR)	HiA	3	2	2.16	26	0	0	5	33	19	3	12	52	14.0	0.93	.170
	Harrisburg (EL)	AA	1	0	0.92	15	0	0	1	20	11	0	14	24	11.0	1.27	.167
Minor League Totals			17	20	4.24	93	44	0	6	280	287	22	101	254	8.2	1.39	.264

19 NICK RAQUET, LHP

BA GRADE
45 Risk: High

Born: Dec. 12, 1995. **B-T:** R-L. **Ht.:** 6-0. **Wt.:** 215. **Drafted:** William & Mary, 2017 (3rd round). **Signed by:** Bobby Myrick.

TRACK RECORD: The Nationals signed Raquet for $475,000 in the third round after a 2017 season with William & Mary where the southpaw struck out 11 batters per nine innings. After a solid debut last summer, Raquet progressed to the Carolina League in 2018, where he ran into his first professional speed bump, posting a 4.91 ERA over 55 innings of work.

SCOUTING REPORT: Raquet throws with a high-energy, up-tempo delivery and sits in the low to mid-90s with a fastball that features heavy armside running action. He's shown both a slider and a curveball, the former in the mid-80s with some tilt and the latter in the upper 70s that's loopier and more of a change-of-pace offering than an out-pitch. Raquet also works in an average changeup that plays up with his slightly funky delivery. Projected to wind up in the bullpen out of the draft, the Nationals have stuck with Raquet as a starter to this point, and a respectable four-pitch mix plus solid strikethrowing should keep him there until he struggles.

THE FUTURE: Still, Raquet wore down as the season progressed and most scouts think he'd be a better fit in the bullpen, where his stuff could tick up.

Year	Club (League)	Class	W	L	ERA	G	GS	CG	SV	IP	H	HR	BB	SO	K/9	WHIP	AVG
2017	Nationals (GCL)	R	0	0	0.00	1	1	0	0	2	2	0	0	2	9.0	1.00	.250
	Auburn (NYP)	SS	3	2	2.45	11	11	0	0	51	56	2	7	22	3.9	1.23	.283
2018	Hagerstown (SAL)	LoA	4	6	2.79	12	12	2	0	68	68	1	18	56	7.4	1.27	.262
	Potomac (CAR)	HiA	5	3	4.91	12	12	1	0	55	72	3	21	36	5.9	1.69	.319
Minor League Totals			12	11	3.32	36	36	3	0	176	198	6	46	116	5.9	1.39	.286

20 BEN BRAYMER, LHP

BA GRADE
45 Risk: High

Born: April 28, 1994. **B-T:** L-L. **Ht.:** 6-2. **Wt.:** 215. **Drafted:** Auburn, 2016 (18th round). **Signed by:** Eric Robinson.

TRACK RECORD: The Most Valuable Pitcher in the 2015 NJCAA World Series, Braymer led Louisiana State-Eunice JC to a national championship and then went to Auburn for his junior season, where he was a solid bullpen presence in the SEC. The Nationals signed him for $100,000 and he had a few solid seasons before breaking out in 2018.

SCOUTING RPEORT: Washington's co-pitcher of the year, Braymer spent a month in the South Atlantic League as a reliever before moving up to high Class A Potomac where he eventually transitioned into a starting role, with success in both. Braymer works in the 90-93 mph range with his fastball, but gets up to 95 at times and complements the pitch with a plus slider. He's got a solid changeup that he uses to neutralize righthanded hitters, but he is still more effective versus lefthanders, who hit just .174/.273/.231 against him. Braymer was old for both the leagues he pitched in and should be challenged in Double-A in 2019.
THE FUTURE: While the Nationals will continue to start Braymer next season, he could fill a hybrid role or serve as a multi-inning reliever in the future with impressive control, poise and a solid three-pitch mix.

Year	Club (League)	Class	W	L	ERA	G	GS	CG	SV	IP	H	HR	BB	SO	K/9	WHIP	AVG
2016	Nationals (GCL)	R	0	2	4.12	8	2	0	0	20	13	0	13	24	11.0	1.32	.194
2017	Auburn (NYP)	SS	2	0	2.28	6	6	0	0	28	24	1	13	39	12.7	1.34	.226
	Hagerstown (SAL)	LoA	3	2	5.26	7	7	0	0	38	46	3	8	37	8.8	1.43	.295
2018	Hagerstown (SAL)	LoA	3	0	1.75	7	0	0	0	26	18	2	5	25	8.8	0.90	.205
	Potomac (CAR)	HiA	6	3	2.43	21	11	0	2	89	73	4	29	93	9.4	1.15	.223
Minor League Totals			14	7	3.02	49	26	0	2	200	174	10	68	218	9.8	1.21	.234

21 JACKSON TETREAULT, RHP

Born: June 3, 1996. **B-T:** R-R. **Ht.:** 6-5. **Wt.:** 170. **Drafted:** State JC of Florida, 2017 (7th round). **Signed by:** Buddy Hernandez.
TRACK RECORD: A seventh-round draft pick in 2017 who signed for $300,000, Tetreault impressed in his pro debut last season, posting a 2.68 ERA in 40.1 innings—most of which came in the low Class A New York-Penn League. Tetreault made his way to high Class A Potomac in 2018 and improved his strikethrowing ability, lowering his walk rate from 3.8 batters per nine innings to 2.8.
SCOUTING REPORT: Washington officials were impressed with the adjustments that Tetreault made this season, citing improved pitch-usage, though there is still more work to be done on his command and filling out a skinny, projectable frame. Tetreault has a fast, whippy arm, a clean delivery and throws a fastball that's in the low to mid-90s. This season he threw his changeup more frequently, enough to become Tetreault's second-best offering, ahead of a curveball that he throws with solid spin, but doesn't land for strikes as consistently as he needs to.
THE FUTURE: Tetreault started all of his 24 games this season, but previously had collegiate success as a reliever. There's a path to a starting role in the future, but it still involves plenty of projecting on his stuff.

Year	Club (League)	Class	W	L	ERA	G	GS	CG	SV	IP	H	HR	BB	SO	K/9	WHIP	AVG
2017	Nationals (GCL)	R	0	0	4.50	1	0	0	0	2	1	1	1	2	9.0	1.00	.143
	Auburn (NYP)	SS	2	2	2.58	11	6	0	0	38	32	1	16	36	8.5	1.25	.216
2018	Hagerstown (SAL)	LoA	3	8	4.01	20	20	0	0	110	108	10	34	118	9.7	1.29	.255
	Potomac (CAR)	HiA	1	1	4.37	4	4	1	0	23	21	2	7	20	7.9	1.24	.241
Minor League Totals			6	11	3.75	36	30	1	0	173	162	14	58	176	9.2	1.27	.243

22 KYLE JOHNSTON, RHP

Born: July 17, 1996. **B-T:** R-R. **Ht.:** 6-0. **Wt.:** 190. **Drafted:** Texas, 2017 (6th round). **Signed by:** Tyler Wilt.
TRACK RECORD: Part of the Nationals' heavy pitching class in the 2017 draft, Johnston signed for $226,100 after being selected in the 6th round. After a solid three-year career at Texas, Johnston posted a 3.43 ERA in 46.2 innings in the New York-Penn League last summer and progressed to high Class A Potomac in 2018.
SCOUTING REPORT: Johnston has always been lauded for his impressive fastball-slider combination, as both of the offerings grade out as plus pitches. His fastball features plenty of armside movement and sits in the low to mid-90s, with a hard, sharp slider that should be an out-pitch in the future. The knock on Johnston has always been his control, and he didn't take any steps forward in that area in 2018, walking 4.1 batters per nine innings in the South Atlantic League and 5.3 in the Carolina League.
THE FUTURE: The 6-foot righthander has been used as both a starter and reliever in his first two pro seasons, though he's performed much better in the latter role and could make a full transition to the bullpen soon, barring a step forward with a fringy changeup or with his strikethrowing.

Year	Club (League)	Class	W	L	ERA	G	GS	CG	SV	IP	H	HR	BB	SO	K/9	WHIP	AVG
2017	Nationals (GCL)	R	0	0	0.00	1	0	0	0	2	0	0	2	1	4.5	1.00	.000
	Auburn (NYP)	SS	0	2	3.43	14	7	0	0	45	41	2	23	32	6.4	1.43	.241
2018	Hagerstown (SAL)	LoA	2	3	3.42	18	7	0	2	55	50	3	25	59	9.6	1.36	.238
	Potomac (CAR)	HiA	5	2	4.94	10	9	1	0	47	41	4	28	37	7.0	1.46	.237
Minor League Totals			7	7	3.86	43	23	1	2	149	132	9	78	129	7.8	1.41	.237

23 BRIGHAM HILL, RHP

BA GRADE

45 Risk: High

Born: July 8, 1995. **B-T:** R-R. **Ht.:** 6-0. **Wt.:** 185. **Drafted:** Texas A&M, 2017 (5th round). **Signed by:** Tyler Wilt.

TRACK RECORD: Originally drafted in the 20th round in 2016 by the Athletics as a draft-eligible sopho-more, Hill bet on himself and returned to Texas A&M, where he posted another solid campaign and was rewarded with a fifth-round selection and $291,200 signing bonus from the Nationals.

SCOUTING REPORT: Something of a high-floor, low-ceiling arm, Hill stands out more for his pitchability than overwhelming pure stuff, though he does have one of the best changeups in Washington's system—a legitimate plus offering with late tumble. Hill's fastball sits mostly in the 90-92 mph range and occasion-ally touches 94 with a curveball that's fringe-average but impressed Nationals coaches this season. Hill's overall package lends itself more to being a back-of-the-rotation starter than a future bullpen arm as he lacks an impact fastball or breaking ball. His strikeout-to-walk rate backed up this year in the South Atlantic League, though he still managed a 3.08 ERA in almost 50 innings.

THE FUTURE: Hill remains a risky pitching prospect and has a small margin for error given his stuff and smaller frame. The improvement of his breaking ball could end up determining how far Hill goes.

Year	Club (League)	Class	W	L	ERA	G	GS	CG	SV	IP	H	HR	BB	SO	K/9	WHIP	AVG
2017	Auburn (NYP)	SS	0	1	2.63	4	3	0	0	14	12	0	3	9	5.9	1.10	.214
	Hagerstown (SAL)	LoA	0	1	6.07	6	6	0	0	30	41	4	5	30	9.1	1.55	.318
2018	Nationals (GCL)	R	0	2	4.50	2	2	0	0	6	8	0	4	5	7.5	2.00	.348
	Hagerstown (SAL)	LoA	4	3	3.08	10	10	1	0	50	46	0	18	35	6.3	1.29	.250
Minor League Totals			4	7	4.00	22	21	1	0	99	107	4	30	79	7.2	1.38	.273

24 TANNER RAINEY, RHP

BA GRADE

45 Risk: Extreme

Born: Dec. 25, 1992. **B-T:** R-R. **Ht.:** 6-2. **Wt.:** 235. **Drafted:** West Alabama, 2015 (2nd round supplemental). **Signed By:** Ben Jones.

TRACK RECORD: Traded to the Nationals in December in exchange for RHP Tanner Roark, Rainey made a third straight minor league All-Star game with Triple-A Louisivlle with a 2.65 ERA in 51 innings in the International League, but struggled mightily in a brief major league stint with the Reds.

SCOUTING REPORT: The explosive righthander was moved to the bullpen by Cincinnati in 2017 to capi-talize on his two-pitch mix. His fastball is a top of the scale offering, regularly in the 97-99 mph range and touching as high as 101. His slider is also a plus offering, with sharp movement that falls off the table. The biggest issue is his control, which is below-average and currently prevents him from throwing his slider in the strike zone with any sort of consistency.

THE FUTURE: After having success in the upper minors, Rainey should get another crack in a major league bullpen in 2019. Big league hitters were able to lay off his slider, and were able to barrel him up during his brief, eight-game stint with the Reds. Control is the biggest question, but his stuff could play as a back-end bullpen piece if he makes improvements in that area.

Year	Club (League)	Class	W	L	ERA	G	GS	CG	SV	IP	H	HR	BB	SO	K/9	WHIP	AVG
2016	Dayton (MWL)	LoA	5	10	5.57	29	20	0	1	103	109	9	66	113	9.8	1.69	.273
2017	Daytona (FSL)	HiA	2	2	3.80	39	0	0	9	45	21	4	22	77	15.4	0.96	.136
	Pensacola (SL)	AA	1	1	1.59	14	0	0	4	17	8	2	11	27	14.3	1.12	.146
2018	Cincinnati (NL)	MAJ	0	0	24.43	8	0	0	0	7	13	4	12	7	9.0	3.57	.406
	Louisville (IL)	AAA	7	2	2.65	44	0	0	3	51	25	2	35	65	11.5	1.18	.148
Major League Totals			0	0	24.43	8	0	0	0	7	13	4	12	7	9.0	3.57	.406
Minor League Totals			17	17	4.22	141	35	0	17	275	221	19	162	339	11.1	1.39	.221

25 JOAN ADON

BA GRADE

45 Risk: Extreme

Born: Aug. 12, 1998. **B-T:** R-R. **Ht.:** 6-2. **Wt.:** 185. **Signed:** Dominican Republic, 2016. **Signed by:** Pablo Arias.

TRACK RECORD: Part of the Nationals' huge 2016 international class, Adon has quietly impressed the team in his first two professional seasons. After posting a 3.54 ERA in the Dominican Summer League in 2017, Adon came stateside in 2018 and was pushed to the New York-Penn League at just 19-years-old—more than two years younger than the average pitcher.

SCOUTING REPORT: Adon has enough heat on his fastball, which is a plus offering currently in the low to mid-90s, with a solid-average slider and an average changeup that round out his repertoire. The 6-foot-2, 185-pound righty had no issues racking up strikeouts, with 40 in 30.2 innings, but has plenty of work to do limiting walks. He's still learning how to consistently repeat his delivery, stay on line and gather himself over the rubber, but Washington executives are confident those things will come with more time.

THE FUTURE: Adon threw strikes more consistently at instructional league with a few mechanical adjustments. He should start 2019 back in the New York-Penn League.

Year	Club (League)	Class	W	L	ERA	G	GS	CG	SV	IP	H	HR	BB	SO	K/9	WHIP	AVG
2017	Nationals (DSL)	R	2	1	3.54	13	0	0	1	28	24	1	9	31	10.0	1.18	.240
2018	Nationals (GCL)	R	2	0	2.29	13	0	0	2	20	20	0	13	29	13.3	1.68	.250
	Auburn (NYP)	SS	1	1	7.36	7	0	0	0	11	13	2	9	11	9.0	2.00	.310
Minor League Totals			5	2	3.84	33	0	0	3	59	57	3	31	71	10.9	1.50	.257

26 TOMAS ALASTRE, RHP

Born: June 11, 1998. **B-T:** R-R. **Ht.:** 6-4. **Wt.:** 170. **Signed:** Venezuela, 2014. **Signed by:** Eduardo Rosario.

TRACK RECORD: Signed out of Venezuela in 2014, Alastre began his pro career with the Nationals by throwing in the Dominican Summer League during the 2015 season, before coming over to the United States with mixed results.

SCOUTING REPORT: In 2018, Alastre spent the entire season with low Class A Hagerstown, where he threw a career-high 118.1 innings in 23 starts in his age 20 season. Alastre has an average fastball in the low 90s, but leverages the ball well for the most part, occasionally getting flat and leaving the pitch up and over the plate. He's got a downer curveball that's average and a changeup that needs more work to get to average. While Alastre struggled statistically—and in particular needs to cut down his walks—the Nationals love his baseball IQ and decided to challenge him with his Hagerstown assignment.

THE FUTURE: If Washington decides to continue pushing Alastre aggressively he could start the 2019 season in the Carolina League, but given his age he might benefit from another stint with Hagerstown.

Year	Club (League)	Class	W	L	ERA	G	GS	CG	SV	IP	H	HR	BB	SO	K/9	WHIP	AVG
2016	Nationals (GCL)	R	0	3	5.21	7	4	0	0	19	21	1	14	12	5.7	1.84	.292
2017	Auburn (NYP)	SS	0	1	5.63	2	2	0	0	8	11	0	6	6	6.8	2.13	.367
	Nationals (GCL)	R	3	1	2.55	9	6	0	0	42	29	3	14	43	9.1	1.02	.192
2018	Hagerstown (SAL)	LoA	4	8	5.32	23	23	0	0	118	135	21	44	80	6.1	1.51	.290
Minor League Totals			7	18	4.54	55	49	0	0	242	244	27	111	191	7.1	1.47	.265

27 GABE KLOBOSITS, RHP

Born: May 16, 1995. **B-T:** L-R. **Ht.:** 6-7. **Wt.:** 270. **Drafted:** Auburn, 2017 (36th round). **Signed by:** Jimmy Gonzales/Tyler Wilt.

TRACK RECORD: Klobosits was drafted out of high school in 2014 by the Red Sox in the 25th round. Instead of signing, Klobosits went to Galveston (Texas) JC and dominated for two seasons before heading to Auburn, where his results were mediocre at best. After signing with the Nationals in the 36th round, Klobosits wowed by posting a 1.47 ERA in 30.2 innings across three levels, with a 34-8 K/BB ratio.

SCOUTING REPORT: A highly anticipated sophomore season in pro ball was cut short after just 16.1 innings in the Carolina League, as Klobosits underwent Tommy John surgery in May. Massively built at 6-foot-7, 270 pounds, Klobosits has an impressive two-pitch combination between a low to mid-90s fastball with exceptional angle as well as a slider that could wind up being a plus offering. Prior to walking 11 batters in 11 games in 2018, Klobosits had shown remarkable control for a pitcher of his size.

THE FUTURE: It'll be fascinating to see what Klobosits looks like when he returns to the mound at some point in late 2019 or 2020. If he comes back healthy, he could eventually become a weapon in the bullpen.

Year	Club (League)	Class	W	L	ERA	G	GS	CG	SV	IP	H	HR	BB	SO	K/9	WHIP	AVG
2017	Nationals (GCL)	R	0	0	0.00	2	0	0	0	4	3	0	1	5	11.3	1.00	.214
	Auburn (NYP)	SS	0	0	1.66	15	0	0	5	22	19	0	6	18	7.5	1.15	.244
	Hagerstown (SAL)	LoA	0	0	1.80	3	0	0	1	5	1	0	1	11	19.8	0.40	.063
2018	Potomac (CAR)	HiA	1	1	2.20	11	0	0	1	16	14	0	11	18	9.9	1.53	.226
Minor League Totals			2	1	1.72	31	0	0	7	47	37	0	19	52	10.0	1.19	.218

28 MALVIN PENA, RHP

Born: June 24, 1997. **B-T:** R-R0. **Ht.:** 6-2. **Wt.:** 180. **Signed:** Dominican Republic, 2014. **Signed by:** Modesto Ulloa.

TRACK RECORD: Signed as an international free agent out of the Dominican Republic in 2014, Pena struggled early in his pro career, with a 6.50 ERA combined between two stints in the Dominican Summer League in 2014 and 2016, with a Tommy John surgery mixed between. Pena began to get back on track last season in the United States, and had his best year in 2018, reaching Class A Hagerstown.

SCOUTING REPORT: Though Pena dealt with some arm soreness and was eventually shut down due to an oblique injury, when he was on the mound he impressed with a good tempo and an impressive ability to repeat his delivery despite a large frame that is significantly bigger than his listed height and weight.

Pena has a fastball that's typically in the 92-93 mph range and gets up to 95-96 at times, with a curveball and changeup that are both inconsistent but could both become average. He improved the feel for his changeup over the course of the season and coaches were also impressed at times with his breaking ball.
THE FUTURE: Given Pena's impressive strikethrowing ability and three-pitch mix, there's a chance Pena continues to start, but he doesn't project as more than a back-of-the-rotation arm.

Year	Club (League)	Class	W	L	ERA	G	GS	CG	SV	IP	H	HR	BB	SO	K/9	WHIP	AVG
2016	Nationals (DSL)	R	0	2	11.37	2	2	0	0	6	6	0	7	5	7.1	2.05	.240
2017	Auburn (NYP)	SS	0	0	3.86	2	0	0	1	7	10	0	4	5	6.4	2.00	.357
	Nationals (GCL)	R	1	3	5.44	10	7	0	0	41	45	7	18	39	8.5	1.52	.274
2018	Auburn (NYP)	SS	3	0	1.80	4	4	0	0	20	20	0	3	20	9.0	1.15	.253
	Hagerstown (SAL)	LoA	3	1	3.60	6	6	0	0	30	37	1	4	27	8.1	1.37	.289
Minor League Totals			8	7	4.69	37	22	0	1	134	155	10	47	117	7.8	1.50	.284

29 RONALD PENA, RHP

BA GRADE

45 Risk: Extreme

Born: September 19, 1991. **B-T:** R-R. **Ht.:** 6-4. **Wt.:** 210. **Drafted:** Palm Beach State (Fla.) JC, 2012 (16th round). **Signed by:** Alex Morales.
TRACK RECORD: The Nationals signed Pena in the 16th round of the 2012 draft out of Palm Beach (Fla.) JC, where he showed a fastball that touched 94 mph and fringy secondary offerings. Since then, Pena's path has been a long one, as the 6-foot-4, 210-pound righthander spent six seasons in the low minors battling various injury issues.
SCOUTING REPORT: In his seventh season with the organization, Pena rewarded the Nationals' patience with something of a breakout campaign during his age 26 season, reaching Double-A for the first time and posting a 3.27 ERA over two leagues and 52.1 innings, with the best strikeout rate of his career. Pena throws a fastball that's regularly in the mid-90s and has touched 100 mph at times. The pitch has solid life when he keeps it down in the zone, but can flatten out at times when he leaves it up. He also has a power slider that ranges from a fringe-average to above-average offering depending on the day.
THE FUTURE: Pena seems to be figuring himself out at a late age, but there's still work to be done, as he became susceptible to the long ball in Double-A.

Year	Club (League)	Class	W	L	ERA	G	GS	CG	SV	IP	H	HR	BB	SO	K/9	WHIP	AVG
2016	Hagerstown (SAL)	LoA	0	0	3.38	5	0	0	2	8	8	2	3	3	3.4	1.38	.242
	Nationals (GCL)	R	0	0	4.50	4	0	0	0	6	6	0	1	5	7.5	1.17	.240
2017	Potomac (CAR)	HiA	2	3	5.70	31	0	0	1	47	56	3	21	45	8.6	1.63	.292
2018	Potomac (CAR)	HiA	1	1	1.98	17	0	0	1	27	19	0	9	38	12.5	1.02	.196
	Harrisburg (EL)	AA	1	2	4.68	21	0	0	5	25	21	5	15	28	10.1	1.44	.219
Minor League Totals			14	12	4.20	128	24	0	10	274	272	21	104	209	6.9	1.37	.257

30 DREW WARD, 3B

BA GRADE

40 Risk: High

Born: Nov. 25, 1994. **B-T:** L-R. **Ht.:** 6-3. **Wt.:** 215. **Drafted:** HS—Leedey, Okla., 2013 (3rd round) **Signed by:** Ed Gustafson.
TRACK RECORD: The Nationals selected Ward in the third round of the 2013 draft and signed him for $850,000 after he showed impressive power from the left side and graduated from high school in three years. Six minor league seasons later and Ward finally got his first taste of Triple-A, after three years spending time in Double-A.
SCOUTING REPORT: Ward has hit double-digit home runs in each of the last three years, but he's continued to struggle with strikeouts—he has a 25.9 career minor league strikeout percentage—and struggled mightily in an admittedly short, 17-game stint in the International League. While he's continued to swing-and-miss at a high rate, Ward remains a patient hitter and walked 14 percent of the time in Harrisburg and 11 percent in Syracuse. He spent a majority of his time at first base after playing primarily third throughout his previous five seasons, which will hurt his value moving forward. Ward has solid-average arm strength but lacks quickness side-to-side as a below-average runner.
THE FUTURE: While Ward hasn't developed as Washington might have hoped offensively, he still has solid-average power and on-base skills that might allow him to turn the corner. After turning 24 in November, Ward was more than three years younger than the average hitter in the International League.

Year	Club (League)	Class	AVG	G	AB	R	H	2B	3B	HR	RBI	BB	SO	SB	CS	OBP	SLG
2016	Potomac (CAR)	HiA	.278	64	230	36	64	16	0	11	32	34	70	0	1	.377	.491
	Harrisburg (EL)	AA	.219	53	178	19	39	7	0	3	24	22	51	0	1	.310	.309
2017	Harrisburg (EL)	AA	.235	121	413	47	97	20	0	10	53	55	131	0	0	.325	.356
2018	Syracuse (IL)	AAA	.185	17	54	5	10	2	0	0	2	7	20	0	1	.279	.222
	Harrisburg (EL)	AA	.259	98	320	59	83	16	4	13	56	55	95	1	1	.376	.456
Minor League Totals			.254	632	2184	284	554	119	9	55	317	282	650	7	11	.345	.392

Baseball America senior writer Ben Badler and executive editor J.J. Cooper report on international players who were free agents as the Prospect Handbook went to press but are expected to sign with major league organizations for 2019.

YUSEI KIKUCHI, LHP

HAMISH BLAIR/GETTY IMAGES

Born: June 17, 1991. **B-T:** L-L. **Ht.:** 6-0. **Wt.:** 210.

TRACK RECORD: For the second consecutive season, the top Japanese pitcher expected to come to the U.S hails from Hanamaki Higashi High. Kikuchi actually graduated from the school the year before Shohei Ohtani arrived, but Ohtani beat him to the States because Kikuchi waited until he had pitched eight seasons in Japan before being posted. Ohtani came to the U.S. after just five seasons. Kikuchi entertained the idea of coming to the U.S. immediately out of high school but ended up signing as Seibu's first pick in the 2009 draft. Kikuchi's best season in Japan was in 2017 when he went 16-6, 1.97. He missed some time early in 2018 with a stiff shoulder. He was still effective upon his return, but he never showed the same level of dominance.

BA GRADE

55 Risk: Medium

SCOUTING REPORT: Kikuchi's delivery demonstrates his athleticism and balance as he hangs over the rubber on his plant foot through a very extended leg kick that can help disrupt a hitter's timing. He attacks hitters with a 91-93 mph four-seam fastball that can touch 96. It projects as at least an above-average pitch. He'll likely look to add a two-seam fastball when he comes to the U.S. to give him a fastball with some sink. Kikuchi pitches off his fastball more than most Japanese pitchers, using it to set up a plus mid-80s slider. Kikuchi's slider can dive out of the zone away from lefthanded hitters. The pitch is especially effective because he can command it so well. He can bury it or sweep it out of the zone, but he also can tickle the bottom of the zone with it when needed. His 73-78 mph average curveball is more of an early-count surprise pitch. It's a big, slow breaker which is effective because of the change of pace and his ability to throw it for strikes. At its best, his curve can lock up hitters who are looking for a fastball. He has sporadically thrown a straight changeup to righthanders. It's a below-average pitch and he's more effective against righties by working in and out with his fastball. He's shown a comfort and ability to dot the inner corner.

THE FUTURE: Kikuchi is a mid-rotation starter as a lefty with a track record of success, a plus slider and above-average control. He's not as dominant and lacks the ceiling of a Shohei Ohtani, Yu Darvish or Daisuke Matsuzaka, but he should be a useful addition to his signing club's rotation.

FLORENCIO SERRANO, RHP

Born: Feb. 23, 2000. **Height:** 6-2. **Weight:** 210. **B-T:** R-R.

The Cubs went over their international bonus pool in 2015-16, which meant that for the 2017-18 signing period, they were in their second year of the penalty box. Teams in that penalty can't sign any player for more than $300,000, though there's an exception for Mexican League players, where only the amount that goes to the player (often 25 percent, with the Mexican League team keeping the other 75 percent) counts against the major league organization's international bonus pool. That enabled the Cubs to sign Serrano from the Tijuana Toros for $1.2 million in 2017, with just $300,000 counting against the Cubs' pool. However, Major League Baseball voided Serrano's contract when it later determined the Toros had submitted false documentation about the amount going to Serrano, which would have made the Cubs ineligible to sign the righthander. MLB determined the Cubs were not at fault (and even added an extra $300,000 to the team's bonus pool for the 2018-19 period), then put a ban on Mexican League signings until the two leagues worked out a new signing protocol.

That means Serrano is still with Tijuana, though for now unable to sign due to MLB rules. It adds to the unusual path for Serrano, who was born in Corpus Christi, Texas, and pitched at Robstown (Texas) High as a freshman in 2016. After his freshman year, Serrano moved to Mexico, where both of his parents were born, and joined the Toros.

Serrano ranked as the No. 29 international prospect in the 2017 signing class, and his stock has ticked up now that he's throwing harder. As a 17-year-old in 2017, Serrano sat 88-92 mph and touched 94, then touched 95 after signing. Since adding more weight and strength, Serrano reached 97 mph at a showcase at the end of 2018. His slider flashes plus to miss bats and he has shown feel for a changeup as well. Serrano has the repertoire and durable build of a starter, though there's effort in his delivery, which has some scouts questioning whether he might end up in the bullpen.

BA GRADE

50 Risk: Extreme

2018 INTERNATIONAL TOP 50 PROSPECTS

Rk.	Name	Pos.	Country	Team
1	Victor Victor Mesa	OF	Cuba	Marlins
2	Marco Luciano	SS	Dominican Republic	Giants
3	Diego Cartaya	C	Venezuela	Dodgers
4	Noelvi Marte	SS	Dominican Republic	Mariners
5	Osiel Rodriguez	RHP	Cuba	Yankees
6	Richard Gallardo	RHP	Venezuela	Cubs
7	Orelvis Martinez	SS	Dominican Republic	Blue Jays
8	Gabriel Rodriguez	SS	Venezuela	Indians
9	Francisco Alvarez	C	Venezuela	Mets
10	Misael Urbina	OF	Venezuela	Twins
11	Jairo Pomares	OF	Cuba	Giants
12	Alvin Guzman	OF	Dominican Republic	D-backs
13	Alejandro Pie	SS	Dominican Republic	Rays
14	Antonio Gomez	C	Venezuela	Yankees
15	Kevin Alcantara	OF	Dominican Republic	Yankees
16	Starlyn Castillo	RHP	Dominican Republic	Phillies
17	Jose de la Cruz	OF	Dominican Republic	Tigers
18	Omar Florentino	SS	Dominican Republic	Royals
19	Juan Guerrero	SS	Dominican Republic	Rockies
20	Eduardo Lopez	OF	Dominican Republic	Red Sox
21	Junior Sanquintin	SS	Dominican Republic	Indians
22	Abraham Calzadilla	RHP	Venezuela	D-backs
23	Jerming Rosario	RHP	Dominican Republic	Dodgers
24	Sandy Gaston	RHP	Cuba	Rays
25	Alexander Ramirez	OF	Dominican Republic	Angels
26	Malcom Nunez	3B	Cuba	Cardinals
27	Jose Lopez	OF	Dominican Republic	Cubs
28	Eduarqui Fernandez	OF	Dominican Republic	Brewers
29	Freddy Valdez	OF	Dominican Republic	Mets
30	Ryson Polonius	SS	Curacao	Rays
31	Rainer Polonius	SS	Curacao	Rays
32	Fernando Ortega	RHP	Dominican Republic	Phillies
33	Warming Bernabel	SS	Dominican Republic	Rockies
34	Fernando Villalobos	C	Mexico	
35	Sergio Campana	OF	Dominican Republic	Pirates
36	Jose Rodriguez	C	Venezuela	Rangers
37	Luis Matos	OF	Venezuela	Giants
38	Adinso Reyes	SS	Dominican Republic	Tigers
39	Angel Martinez	SS	Dominican Republic	Indians
40	Estanli Castillo	OF	Dominican Republic	Rays
41	Branlyn Jaraba	3B	Colombia	Brewers
42	Joalbert Angulo	LHP	Venezuela	Phillies
43	Denny Larrondo	RHP	Cuba	Yankees
44	Diomedes Sierra	LHP	Dominican Republic	D-backs
45	Jose Bonilla	SS	Dominican Republic	
46	Rafael Morel	SS	Dominican Republic	Cubs
47	Joel Machado	LHP	Venezuela	Cubs
48	Agustin Ramirez	C	Dominican Republic	Yankees
49	Eduardo Garcia	SS	Venezuela	Brewers
50	Daury del Rosario	SS	Dominican Republic	Rays

The athletic Marco Luciano has high offensive upside.

Diego Cartaya's acumen shows on both sides of the ball.

2018 RULE 5 DRAFT

The 2018 Rule 5 draft occurred on Dec. 13, 2018, our transactions deadline for this book. A few of these players rank in their new organizations' Top 30 Prospects, but since all 14 will be in big league spring training camp in 2019, we provide thumbnail scouting reports for all of them in this space.

Pick	2019 Org	Player	Pos	2018 Org	BA Grade/Risk

1. Orioles   **Richie Martin**   **SS**   **Athletics**   **45/Medium**

The Orioles have no true shortstop, so the path is clear for at least a backup role. There are some questions about his bat and he has to watch his weight to keep his quickness, but getting a true shortstop with success at Double-A in the Rule 5 draft is a rare opportunity.

2. Royals   **Sam McWilliams**   **RHP**   **Rays**   **45/High**

Numerous scouts from other organizations described McWilliams as arguably the best combination of stuff and major league readiness available. His fastball/slider combo may be helped by working out of the bullpen. He has battled control issues at times, but a rebuilding Royals team can find ways to keep him around.

3. Rangers   **Jordan Romano**   **RHP**   **Blue Jays**   **40/Medium**

The White Sox could use another quality bullpen arm, and Romano has the stuff and upper-level success to do that. In a best-possible scenario, he could even be a back-end starter with his heavy, mid-90s fastball and hard, nasty slider

4. Marlins   **Riley Farrell**   **RHP**   **Astros**   **45/High**

Ferrell walked too many batters in 2018, but he has the stuff to pitch in the late innings, much like he has throughout his career going back to his days at Texas Christian.

5. Tigers   **Reed Garrett**   **RHP**   **Rangers**   **45/High**

Garrett follows is a reasonably polished pitcher with success in the upper levels. He's more big league-ready than most of the pitchers on this list, and his stuff is good enough that he could work his way into a seventh-inning role

6. Reds   **Connor Joe**   **C**   **Dodgers**   **40/High**

Joe was primarily a first baseman/third baseman last season, but he has toyed with catching in the past. Being able to be even a semi-plausible emergency catcher would help his versatility and chances to stick. Joe has always gotten on base with average power potential. That may be enough to fill a bench role for the Reds.

7. Royals   **Chris Ellis**   **RHP**   **Cardinals**   **40/Medium**

Ellis has shown he can sit 93-95 mph and touch 97 out of the bullpen. His combination of solid fastball velocity and a decent breaking ball would fit for the Royals as a swingman who can handle low-leverage relief and spot starts.

8. Giants   **Travis Bergen**   **LHP**   **Blue Jays**   **40/Medium**

Bergen allowed just two runs in 27 appearances with Double-A New Hampshire, he showed he can get both lefthanders and righthanders out, and he struck out more than 11.7 batters per nine innings.

9. Blue Jays   **Elvis Luciano**   **RHP**   **Royals**   **45/Extreme**

Luciano won't turn 19 until just before spring training, but he was available because he had his contract voided and renegotiated. He has yet to pitch in full-season ball, so the jump to the big leagues is going to be a massive one. If he makes the Blue Jays' roster, it will be expected that he will be buried on the bench to be used in blowouts, much like Brewers lefthander Wei-Chung Wang in 2014.

10. Mets   **Kyle Dowdy**   **RHP**   **Indians**   **45/Extreme**

Dowdy was a high-effort, 92-93 mph starter in college, but now he can touch 97 with a high-spin breaking ball. The results haven't matched the stuff so far. He had a 5.15 ERA in 2018 while posting a 1.48 WHIP.

11. Orioles   **Drew Jackson**   **SS**   **Dodgers**   **40/High**

Jackson actually has louder tools than No. 1 overall pick Richie Martin. He's a plus runner with a plus arm, and his average power is better. Martin has been viewed as a better shortstop and has a better hit tool. Jackson fits the versatile, play-anywhere mold that teams look for in backups. He can play shortstop, second base and center field.

12. D-backs   **Nick Green**   **RHP**   **Yankees**   **40/Medium**

Green coudl become a useful, groundball-oriented reliever. He can go right at hitters with a 92-95 mph fastball that he cuts. He's shown flashes with his changeup, but in a bullpen role, he could rely on cutters to get a lot of weak ground balls.

13. Mariners   **Brandon Brennan**   **RHP**   **Rockies**   **40/High**

After attracting some interest on the minor league free agent market, Brennan now gets a chance to show he can fit in a big league bullpen. The Mariners are playing for 2020 and beyond, so Brennan has a shot to stick around. He throws an average fastball and slider.

14. Giants   **Drew Ferguson**   **OF**   **Astros**   **40/Medium**

Ferguson fits the profile of a fourth outfielder. He can play all three outfield positions plausibly, and he puts the bat on the ball enough to be a useful pinch-hitter or fill-in. He hit .304/.432/.443 last season largely at Triple-A Fresno. A wrist injury cost him time, but he finished the season healthy.

2018 DRAFT   ## TOP 100 PICKS

FIRST ROUND

No. Team: Player, Pos.	Bonus
1. Tigers: Casey Mize, RHP	$7,500,000
2. Giants: Joey Bart, C	$7,025,000
3. Phillies: Alec Bohm, 3B	$5,850,000
4. White Sox: Nick Madrigal, SS	$6,411,400
5. Reds: Jonathan India, 3B	$5,297,500
6. Mets: Jarred Kelenic, OF	$4,500,000
7. Padres: Ryan Weathers, LHP	$5,226,500
8. Braves: Carter Stewart, RHP	Did not sign
9. Athletics: Kyler Murray, OF	$4,660,000
10. Pirates: Travis Swaggerty, OF	$4,400,000
11. Orioles: Grayson Rodriguez, RHP	$4,300,000
12. Blue Jays: Jordan Groshans, SS	$3,400,000
13. Marlins: Connor Scott, OF	$4,038,200
14. Mariners: Logan Gilbert, RHP	$3,883,800
15. Rangers: Cole Winn, RHP	$3,150,000
16. Rays: Matthew Liberatore, LHP	$3,497,500
17. Angels: Jordyn Adams, OF	$4,100,000
18. Royals: Brady Singer, RHP	$4,247,500
19. Cardinals: Nolan Gorman, 3B	$3,231,700
20. Twins: Trevor Larnach, OF	$2,550,000
21. Brewers: Brice Turang, SS	$3,411,100
22. Rockies: Ryan Rolison, LHP	$2,912,300
23. Yankees: Anthony Seigler, C	$2,815,900
24. Cubs: Nico Hoerner, SS	$2,724,000
25. D-backs: Matt McLain, SS	Did not sign
26. Red Sox: Triston Casas, 3B	$2,552,800
27. Nationals: Mason Denaburg, RHP	$3,000,000
28. Astros: Seth Beer, OF	$2,250,000
29. Indians: Bo Naylor, C	$2,578,137
30. Dodgers: J.T. Ginn, RHP	Did not sign
31. Rays: Shane McClanahan, LHP	$2,230,100
32. Rays: Nick Schnell, OF	$2,297,500
33. Royals: Jackson Kowar, RHP	$2,147,500
34. Royals: Daniel Lynch, LHP	$1,697,500
35. Indians: Ethan Hankins, RHP	$2,246,022

SUPPLEMENTAL FIRST ROUND

No. Team: Player, Pos.	Bonus
36. Pirates: Gunnar Hoglund, RHP	Did not sign
37. Orioles: Cadyn Grenier, SS	$1,800,000
38. Padres: Xavier Edwards, SS	$2,600,000
39. D-backs: Jake McCarthy, OF	$1,650,000
40. Royals: Kris Bubic, LHP	$1,597,500
41. Indians: Lenny Torres, RHP	$1,350,000
42. Rockies: Grant Lavigne, 1B	$2,000,000
43. Cardinals: Griffin Roberts, RHP	$1,664,200

SECOND ROUND

No. Team: Player, Pos.	Bonus
44. Tigers: Parker Meadows, OF	$2,500,000
45. Giants: Sean Hjelle, RHP	$1,500,000
46. White Sox: Steele Walker, OF	$2,000,000
47. Reds: Lyon Richardson, RHP	$1,997,500
48. Mets: Simeon Woods-Richardson, RHP	$1,850,000
49. Braves: Greyson Jenista, OF	$1,200,000

No. Team: Player, Pos.	Bonus
50. Athletics: Jameson Hannah, OF	$1,800,000
51. Pirates: Braxton Ashcraft, RHP	$1,825,000
52. Blue Jays: Griffin Conine, OF	$1,350,000
53. Marlins: Osiris Johnson, SS	$1,350,000
54. Mariners: Josh Stowers, OF	$1,100,000
55. Rangers: Owen White, RHP	$1,500,000
56. Rays: Tyler Frank, SS	$997,500
57. Angels: Jeremiah Jackson, SS	$1,194,000
58. Royals: Jonathan Bowlan, RHP	$697,500
59. Twins: Ryan Jeffers, C	$800,000
60. Brewers: Joe Gray, OF	$1,113,500
61. Yankees: Josh Breaux, C	$1,497,500
62. Cubs: Brennen Davis, OF	$1,100,000
63. D-backs: Alek Thomas, OF	$1,200,000
64. Red Sox: Nick Decker, OF	$1,250,000
65. Nationals: Tim Cate, LHP	$986,200
66. Astros: Jayson Schroeder, RHP	$1,200,000
67. Indians: Nick Sandlin, RHP	$750,000
68. Dodgers: Michael Grove, RHP	$1,229,500

SUPPLEMENTAL SECOND ROUND

No. Team: Player, Pos.	Bonus
69. Marlins: Will Banfield, C	$1,800,000
70. Athletics: Jeremy Eierman, SS	$1,232,000
71. Rays: Tanner Dodson, RHP	$772,500
72. Reds: Josiah Gray, RHP	$772,500
73. Brewers: Micah Bello, OF	$550,000
74. Padres: Grant Little, OF	$800,000
75. Cardinals: Luken Baker, 1B	$800,000
76. Rockies: Mitchell Kilkenny, RHP	$550,000
77. Cubs: Cole Roederer, OF	$1,200,000
78. Cubs: Paul Richan, RHP	$450,000

SECOND ROUND

No. Team: Player, Pos.	Bonus
79. Tigers: Kody Clemens, 2B	$600,000
80. Giants: Jake Wong, RHP	$850,000
81. White Sox: Konnor Pilkington, LHP	$650,000
82. Reds: Bren Spillane, OF	$597,500
83. Mets: Carlos Cortes, 2B	$1,000,038
84. Padres: Owen Miller, SS	$500,000
85. Athletics: Hogan Harris, LHP	$660,000
86. Pirates: Connor Kaiser, SS	$625,000
87. Orioles: Blaine Knight, RHP	$1,100,000
88. Blue Jays: Adam Kloffenstein, RHP	$2,450,000
89. Marlins: Tristan Pompey, OF	$645,000
90. Mariners: Cal Raleigh, C	$854,000
91. Rangers: Jonathan Ornelas, SS	$622,800
92. Rays: Ford Proctor, SS	$572,500
93. Angels: Aaron Hernandez, RHP	$547,500
94. Royals: Kyle Isbel, 2B	$592,300
95. Cardinals: Mateo Gil, SS	$900,000
96. Rockies: Terrin Vavra, SS	$550,000
97. Yankees: Ryder Green, OF	$997,500
98. Cubs: Jimmy Herron, OF	$520,000
99. D-backs: Jackson Goddard, RHP	$550,000
100. Red Sox: Durbin Feltman, RHP	$559,600

SIGNING BONUSES

2017 DRAFT

FIRST ROUND

No. Team: Player, Pos.	Bonus
1. Twins: Royce Lewis, SS	$6,725,000
2. Reds: Hunter Greene, RHP	$7,230,000
3. Padres: MacKenzie Gore, LHP	$6,700,000
4. Rays: Brendan McKay, 1B	$7,005,000
5. Braves: Kyle Wright, RHP	$7,000,000
6. Athletics: Austin Beck, OF	$5,303,000
7. D-backs: Pavin Smith, 1B	$5,016,300
8. Phillies: Adam Haseley, OF	$5,100,000
9. Brewers: Keston Hiura, 2B	$4,000,000
10. Angels: Jo Adell, OF	$4,376,800
11. White Sox: Jake Burger, 3B	$3,700,000
12. Pirates: Shane Baz, RHP	$4,100,000
13. Marlins: Trevor Rogers, LHP	$3,400,000
14. Royals: Nick Pratto, 1B	$3,450,000
15. Astros: J.B. Bukauskas, RHP	$3,600,000
16. Yankees: Clarke Schmidt, RHP	$2,184,300
17. Mariners: Evan White, 1B	$3,125,000
18. Tigers: Alex Faedo, RHP	$3,500,000
19. Giants: Heliot Ramos, OF	$3,101,700
20. Mets: David Peterson, LHP	$2,994,500
21. Orioles: D.L. Hall, LHP	$3,000,000
22. Blue Jays: Logan Warmoth, SS	$2,820,200
23. Dodgers: Jeren Kendall, OF	$2,897,500
24. Red Sox: Tanner Houck, RHP	$2,614,500
25. Nationals: Seth Romero, LHP	$2,800,000
26. Rangers: Bubba Thompson, OF	$2,100,000
27. Cubs: Brendon Little, LHP	$2,200,000
28. Blue Jays: Nate Pearson, RHP	$2,452,900
29. Rangers: Chris Seise, SS	$2,000,000
30. Cubs: Alex Lange, RHP	$1,925,000

SUPPLEMENTAL FIRST ROUND

No. Team: Player, Pos.	Bonus
31. Rays: Drew Rasmussen, RHP	Did not sign
32. Reds: Jeter Downs, SS	$1,822,500
33. Athletics: Kevin Merrell, SS	$1,800,000
34. Brewers: Tristen Lutz, OF	$2,352,000
35. Twins: Brent Rooker, OF	$1,935,300
36. Marlins: Brian Miller, OF	$1,888,800

SECOND ROUND

No. Team: Player, Pos.	Bonus
37. Twins: Landon Leach, RHP	$1,400,000
38. Reds: Stuart Fairchild, OF	$1,800,300
39. Padres: Luis Campusano, C	$1,300,000
40. Rays: Michael Mercado, RHP	$2,132,400
41. Braves: Drew Waters, OF	$1,500,000
42. Pirates: Steven Jennings, RHP	$1,900,000
43. Athletics: Greg Deichmann, OF	$1,700,000
44. D-backs: Drew Ellis, 3B	$1,560,100
45. Phillies: Spencer Howard, RHP	$1,150,000
46. Brewers: Caden Lemons, RHP	$1,450,000
47. Angels: Griffin Canning, RHP	$1,459,200
48. Rockies: Ryan Vilade, 3B	$1,425,400
49. White Sox: Gavin Sheets, 1B	$2,000,000
50. Pirates: Calvin Mitchell, OF	$1,357,300

No. Team: Player, Pos.	Bonus
51. Marlins: Joe Dunand, 3B	$1,200,000
52. Royals: M.J. Melendez, C	$2,097,500
53. Astros: Joe Perez, 3B	$1,600,000
54. Yankees: Matt Sauer, RHP	$2,497,500
55. Mariners: Sam Carlson, RHP	$2,000,000
56. Astros: Corbin Martin, RHP	$1,000,000
57. Tigers: Rey Rivera, OF	$850,000
58. Giants: Jacob Gonzalez, 3B	$950,000
59. Mets: Mark Vientos, 3B	$1,500,000
60. Orioles: Adam Hall, SS	$1,300,000
61. Blue Jays: Hagen Danner, C	$1,500,000
62. Dodgers: Morgan Cooper	$867,500
63. Red Sox: Cole Brannen, OF	$1,300,000
64. Indians: Quentin Holmes	$988,970
65. Nationals: Wil Crowe, RHP	$946,500
66. Rangers: Hans Crouse, RHP	$1,450,000
67. Cubs: Cory Abbott, RHP	$901,900

SUPPLEMENTAL SECOND ROUND

No. Team: Player, Pos.	Bonus
68. D-backs: Daulton Varsho, C	$881,100
69. Padres: Blake Hunt, C	$1,600,000
70. Rockies: Tommy Doyle, RHP	$837,300
71. Indians: Tyler Freeman, SS	$816,500
72. Pirates: Conner Uselton, OF	$900,000
73. Royals: Evan Steele, LHP	$826,500
74. Orioles: Zac Lowther, LHP	$779,500
75. Astros: J.J. Matijevic, 2B	$700,000

THIRD ROUND

No. Team: Player, Pos.	Bonus
76. Twins: Blayne Enlow, RHP	$2,000,000
77. Reds: Jacob Heatherly, LHP	$1,047,500
78. Padres: Mason House, OF	$732,200
79. Rays: Taylor Walls, SS	$612,500
80. Braves: Freddy Tarnok, RHP	$1,445,000
81. Athletics: Nick Allen, SS	$2,000,000
82. D-backs: Matt Tabor, RHP	$1,000,000
83. Phillies: Connor Seabold, RHP	$525,000
84. Brewers: K.J. Harrison, C	$667,000
85. Angels: Jacob Pearson, OF	$1,000,000
86. Rockies: Will Gaddis, RHP	$600,000
87. White Sox: Luis Gonzalez, OF	$517,000
88. Pirates: Dylan Busby, 3B	$575,000
89. Marlins: Riley Mahan, 2B	$525,000
90. Royals: Daniel Tillo, LHP	$557,500
91. Astros: Tyler Ivey, RHP	$450,000
92. Yankees: Trevor Stephan, RHP	$797,500
93. Mariners: Wyatt Mills, RHP	$125,000
94. Cardinals: Scott Hurst, OF	$450,000
95. Tigers: Joey Morgan, C	$564,000
96. Giants: Seth Corry, LHP	$1,000,000
97. Mets: Quinn Brodey, OF	$500,000
98. Orioles: Mike Baumann, RHP	$500,000
99. Blue Jays: Riley Adams, C	$542,400
100. Dodgers: Connor Wong, C	$547,500

SIGNING BONUSES

2016 DRAFT

FIRST ROUND

No. Team: Player, Pos.	Bonus
1. Phillies: Mickey Moniak, OF	$6,100,000
2. Reds: Nick Senzel, 3B	$6,200,000
3. Braves: Ian Anderson, RHP	$4,000,000
4. Rockies: Riley Pint, RHP	$4,800,000
5. Brewers: Corey Ray, OF	$4,125,000
6. Athletics: A.J. Puk, LHP	$4,069,200
7. Marlins: Braxton Garrett, LHP	$4,145,000
8. Padres: Cal Quantrill, RHP	$3,963,045
9. Tigers: Matt Manning, RHP	$3,505,800
10. White Sox: Zack Collins, C	$3,380,600
11. Mariners: Kyle Lewis, OF	$3,286,700
12. Red Sox: Jason Groome, LHP	$3,650,000
13. Rays: Josh Lowe, 3B	$2,597,500
14. Indians: Will Benson, OF	$2,500,000
15. Twins: Alex Kirilloff, OF	$2,817,100
16. Angels: Matt Thaiss, C	$2,150,000
17. Astros: Forrest Whitley, RHP	$3,148,000
18. Yankees: Blake Rutherford, OF	$3,282,000
19. Mets: Justin Dunn, RHP	$2,378,800
20. Dodgers: Gavin Lux, SS	$2,314,500
21. Blue Jays: T.J. Zeuch, RHP	$2,175,000
22. Pirates: Will Craig, 3B	$2,253,700
23. Cardinals: Delvin Perez, SS	$2,222,500
24. Padres: Hudson Potts, SS	$1,000,000
25. Padres: Eric Lauer, LHP	$2,000,000
26. White Sox: Zack Burdi, RHP	$2,128,500
27. Orioles: Cody Sedlock, RHP	$2,097,200
28. Nationals: Carter Kieboom, SS	$2,000,000
29. Nationals: Dane Dunning, RHP	$2,000,000
30. Rangers: Cole Ragans, LHP	$2,003,400
31. Mets: Anthony Kay, LHP	$1,100,000
32. Dodgers: Will Smith, C	$1,772,500
33. Cardinals: Dylan Carson, OF	$1,350,000
34. Cardinals: Dakota Hudson, RHP	$2,000,000

SUPPLEMENTAL FIRST ROUND

No. Team: Player, Pos.	Bonus
35. Reds: Taylor Trammell, OF	$3,200,000
36. Dodgers: Jordan Sheffield, RHP	$1,847,500
37. Athletics: Daulton Jefferies, RHP	$1,600,000
38. Rockies: Robert Tyler, RHP	$1,701,600
39. D-backs: Anfernee Grier, OF	$1,500,000
40. Braves: Joey Wentz, LHP	$3,050,000
41. Pirates: Nick Lodolo, LHP	Did not sign

SECOND ROUND

No. Team: Player, Pos.	Bonus
42. Phillies: Kevin Gowdy, RHP	$3,500,000
43. Reds: Chris Okey, C	$2,000,000
44. Braves: Kyle Muller, LHP	$2,500,000
45. Rockies: Ben Bowden, LHP	$1,600,000
46. Brewers: Lucas Erceg, 3B	$1,150,000
47. Athletics: Logan Shore, RHP	$1,500,000
48. Padres: Buddy Reed, OF	$1,075,000
49. White Sox: Alec Hansen, RHP	$1,284,500
50. Mariners: Joe Rizzo, 3B	$1,750,000
51. Red Sox: C.J. Chatham, SS	$1,100,000
52. D-backs: Andy Yerzy, C	$1,214,100
53. Rays: Ryan Boldt, OF	$997,500
54. Orioles: Keegan Akin, LHP	$1,177,200
55. Indians: Nolan Jones, SS	$2,250,000
56. Twins: Ben Rortvedt, C	$900,000
57. Blue Jays: J.B. Woodman, OF	$975,000
58. Nationals: Sheldon Neuse, 3B	$900,000
59. Giants: Bryan Reynolds, OF	$1,350,000
60. Angels: Brandon Marsh, OF	$1,073,300
61. Astros: Ronnie Dawson, OF	$1,056,800
62. Yankees: Nick Solak, 2B	$950,000
63. Rangers: Alex Speas, RHP	$1,024,900
64. Mets: Peter Alonso, 1B	$909,200
65. Dodgers: Mitchell White, RHP	$588,300
66. Blue Jays: Bo Bichette, SS	$1,100,000
67. Royals: A.J. Puckett, RHP	$1,200,000
68. Pirates: Travis MacGregor, RHP	$900,000
69. Orioles: Matthias Dietz, RHP	$1,300,000
70. Cardinals: Connor Jones, RHP	$1,100,000

SUPPLEMENTAL SECOND ROUND

No. Team: Player, Pos.	Bonus
71. Padres: Reggie Lawson, RHP	$1,900,000
72. Indians: Logan Ice, C	$850,000
73. Twins: Jose Miranda, SS	$775,000
74. Twins: Akil Baddoo, OF	$750,000
75. Brewers: Mario Feliciano, C	$800,000
76. Braves: Brett Cumberland, C	$1,500,000
77. Rays: Jake Fraley, OF	$797,500

THIRD ROUND

No. Team: Player, Pos.	Bonus
78. Phillies: Cole Stobbe, SS	$1,100,000
79. Reds: Nick Hanson, RHP	$925,000
80. Braves: Drew Harrington, LHP	$900,000
81. Rockies: Garrett Hampson, SS	$750,000
82. Brewers: Braden Webb, RHP	$700,000
83. Athletics: Sean Murphy, C	$753,100
84. Marlins: Thomas Jones, OF	$1,000,000
85. Padres: Mason Thompson, RHP	$1,750,000
86. White Sox: Alex Call, OF	$719,100
87. Mariners: Bryson Brigman, SS	$700,000
88. Red Sox: Shaun Anderson, RHP	$700,000
89. D-backs: Jon Duplantier, RHP	$686,600
90. Rays: Austin Franklin, RHP	$597,500
91. Orioles: Austin Hays, OF	$665,800
92. Indians: Aaron Civale, RHP	$625,000
93. Twins: Griffin Jax, RHP	$645,600
94. Nationals: Jesus Luzardo, LHP	$1,400,000
95. Giants: Heath Quinn, OF	$625,900
96. Angels: Nonnie Williams, SS	$950,000
97. Astros: Jake Rogers, C	$614,000
98. Yankees: Nolan Martinez, RHP	$1,150,000
99. Rangers: Kole Enright, 3B	$675,000
100. Mets: Blake Tiberi, 3B	$500,000

TOP 20 PROSPECTS

FROM EVERY MINOR LEAGUE

TRIPLE-A

International League

1. Ronald Acuna, OF, Gwinnett (Braves)
1. Eloy Jimenez, OF, Charlotte (White Sox)
2. Michael Kopech, RHP, Charlotte (White Sox)
3. Willy Adames, SS, Durham (Rays)
4. Austin Riley, 3B, Gwinnett (Braves)
5. Austin Meadows, OF, Durham (Rays)
6. Nick Senzel, 3B, Louisville (Reds)
7. Justus Sheffield, LHP, Scranton/W-B (Yankees)
8. Victor Robles, OF, Syracuse (Nationals)
9. Francisco Mejia, C, Columbus (Indians)
10. Touki Toussaint, RHP, Gwinnett (Braves)
11. Mitch Keller, RHP, Indianapolis (Pirates)
12. Lourdes Gurriel Jr., SS, Buffalo (Blue Jays)
13. Shane Bieber, RHP, Columbus (Indians)
14. Kevin Kramer, 2B, Indianapolis (Pirates)
15. Cedric Mullins, OF, Norfolk (Orioles)
16. Jake Bauers, 1B, Durham (Rays)
17. Christin Stewart, OF, Toledo (Tigers)
18. Enyel de los Santos, RHP, Lehigh Valley (Phillies)
19. Brandon Lowe, 2B, Durham (Rays)
20. Kevin Newman, SS, Indianapolis (Pirates)

Pacific Coast League

1. Kyle Tucker, OF, Fresno (Astros)
2. Alex Verdugo, OF, Oklahoma City (Dodgers)
3. Luis Urias, 2B, El Paso (Padres)
4. Griffin Canning, RHP, Salt Lake (Angels)
5. Tyler O'Neill, OF, Memphis (Cardinals)
6. Yordan Alvarez, OF, Fresno (Astros)
7. Freddy Peralta, RHP, Colorado Springs (Brewers)
8. Willie Calhoun, OF, Round Rock (Rangers)
9. Corbin Burnes, RHP, Colorado Springs (Brewers)
10. Ryan McMahon, 1B, Albuquerque (Rockies)
11. Sandy Alcantara, RHP, New Orleans (Marlins)
12. Ramon Laureano, OF, Nashville (Athletics)
13. Dakota Hudson, RHP, Memphis (Cardinals)
14. Peter Alonso, 1B, Las Vegas (Mets)
15. Jose Suarez, LHP, Salt Lake (Angels)
16. Josh James, RHP, Fresno (Astros)
17. Jeff McNeil, 2B, Las Vegas (Mets)
18. Garrett Hampson, SS, Albuquerque (Rockies)
19. Austin Gomber, LHP, Memphis (Cardinals)
20. Franmil Reyes, OF, El Paso (Padres)

DOUBLE-A

Eastern League

1. Vladimir Guerrero Jr., 3B, New Hampshire (Blue Jays)
2. Bo Bichette, SS, New Hampshire (Blue Jays)
3. Brendan Rodgers, SS, Hartford (Rockies)
4. Ke'Bryan Hayes, 3B, Altoona (Pirates)
5. Carter Kieboom, SS, Harrisburg (Nationals)
6. Mitch Keller, RHP, Altoona (Pirates)
7. Daz Cameron, OF, Erie (Tigers)
8. Peter Alonso, 1B, Binghamton (Mets)
9. Peter Lambert, RHP, Hartford (Rockies)
10. Andres Gimenez, SS, Binghamton (Mets)

11. Triston McKenzie, RHP, Akron (Indians)
12. Justin Dunn, RHP, Binghamton (Mets)
13. Cedric Mullins, OF, Bowie (Orioles)
14. Cavan Biggio, 2B, New Hampshire (Blue Jays)
15. Ryan Mountcastle, 3B, Bowie (Orioles)
16. Isaac Paredes, SS, Erie (Tigers)
17. Beau Burrows, RHP, Erie (Tigers)
18. Michael King, RHP, Trenton (Yankees)
19. Taylor Hearn, LHP, Altoona (Pirates)
20. Jeff McNeil, 2B, Binghamton (Mets)

Southern League

1. Eloy Jimenez, OF, Birmingham (White Sox)
2. Keston Hiura, 2B, Biloxi (Brewers)
3. Dylan Cease, RHP, Birmingham (White Sox)
4. Griffin Canning, RHP, Mobile (Angels)
5. Bryse Wilson, RHP, Mississippi (Braves)
6. Tony Santillan, RHP, Pensacola (Reds)
7. Kyle Wright, RHP, Mississippi (Braves)
8. Touki Toussaint, RHP, Mississippi (Braves)
9. Taylor Widener, RHP, Jackson (D-backs)
10. Brandon Lowe, 2B, Montgomery (Rays)
11. Nate Lowe, 1B, Montgomery (Rays)
12. Brent Rooker, OF, Chattanooga (Twins)
13. Corey Ray, OF, Biloxi (Brewers)
14. Genesis Cabrera, LHP, Montgomery (Rays)
15. Dane Dunning, RHP, Birmingham (White Sox)
16. Jon Duplantier, RHP, Jackson (D-backs)
17. Luis Rengifo, SS, Mobile (Angels)
18. Nick Solak, 2B, Montgomery (Rays)
19. Taylor Ward, 3B, Mobile (Angels)
20. Zack Collins, C, Birmingham (White Sox)

Texas League

1. Fernando Tatis Jr., SS, San Antonio (Padres)
2. Jesus Luzardo, LHP, Midland (Athletics)
3. Keibert Ruiz, C, Tulsa (Dodgers)
4. Yordan Alvarez, OF, Corpus Christi (Astros)
5. Yusniel Diaz, OF, Tulsa (Dodgers)
6. Sean Murphy, C, Midland (Athletics)
7. Logan Allen, LHP, San Antonio (Padres)
8. Corbin Martin, RHP, Corpus Christi (Astros)
9. Josh Naylor, 1B, San Antonio (Padres)
10. Will Smith, C, Tulsa (Dodgers)
11. Cionel Perez, LHP, Corpus Christi (Astros)
12. Nicky Lopez, SS, NW Arkansas (Royals)
13. Mitchell White, RHP, Tulsa (Dodgers)
14. DJ Peters, OF, Tulsa (Dodgers)
15. Cal Quantrill, RHP, San Antonio (Padres)
16. Andrew Knizner, C, Springfield (Cardinals)
17. Jonathan Hernandez, RHP, Frisco (Rangers)
18. Richie Martin, SS, Midland (Athletics)
19. Austin Allen, C, San Antonio (Padres)
20. Eli White, 2B, Midland (Athletics)

HIGH CLASS A

California League

1. Jo Adell, OF, Inland Empire (Angels)
2. Adrian Morejon, LHP, Lake Elsinore (Padres)
3. Chris Paddack, RHP, Lake Elsinore (Padres)

4. Gavin Lux, SS, R. Cucamonga (Dodgers)
5. Dustin May, RHP, R. Cucamonga (Dodgers)
6. Jazz Chisholm, SS, Visalia (D-backs)
7. Michel Baez, RHP, Lake Elsinore (Padres)
8. Colton Welker, 3B, Lancaster (Rockies)
9. Hudson Potts, 3B, Lake Elsinore (Padres)
10. Daulton Varsho, C, Visalia (D-backs)
11. Brandon Marsh, OF, Inland Empire (Angels)
12. Tony Gonsolin, RHP, R. Cucamonga (Dodgers)
13. Luis Rengifo, SS, Inland Empire (Angels)
14. Evan White, 1B, Modesto (Mariners)
15. Dean Kremer, RHP, R. Cucamonga (Dodgers)
16. Buddy Reed, OF, Lake Elsinore (Padres)
17. Logan Webb, RHP, San Jose (Giants)
18. Tyler Nevin, 3B, Lancaster (Rockies)
19. Emilio Vargas, RHP, Visalia (D-backs)
20. Bryson Brigman, SS, Modesto (Mariners)

Carolina League

1. Dylan Cease, RHP, Winston-Salem (White Sox)
2. Carter Kieboom, SS, Potomac (Nationals)
3. Luis Garcia, SS, Potomac (Nationals)
4. Keston Hiura, 2B, Carolina (Brewers)
5. Micker Adolfo, OF, Winston-Salem (White Sox)
6. Anderson Tejeda, SS, Down East (Rangers)
7. Khalil Lee, OF, Wilmington (Royals)
8. Bobby Dalbec, 3B, Salem (Red Sox)
9. Jonathan Hernandez, RHP, Down East (Rangers)
10. Luis Robert, OF, Winston-Salem (White Sox)
11. Sam Hentges, LHP, Lynchburg (Indians)
12. Hector Perez, RHP, Buies Creek (Astros)
13. Darwinzon Hernandez, LHP, Salem (Red Sox)
14. Brandon Bielak, RHP, Buies Creek (Astros)
15. C.J. Chatham, SS, Salem (Red Sox)
16. Meibrys Viloria, C, Wilmington (Royals)
17. Blake Rutherford, OF, Winston-Salem (White Sox)
18. Luis Gonzalez, OF, Winston-Salem (White Sox)
19. J.J. Matijevic, OF, Buies Creek (Astros)
20. Ryan McKenna, OF, Frederick (Orioles)

Florida State League

1. Royce Lewis, SS, Fort Myers (Twins)
2. Alex Kirilloff, OF, Fort Myers (Twins)
3. Cristian Pache, OF, Florida (Braves)
4. Sixto Sanchez, RHP, Clearwater (Phillies)
5. Taylor Trammell, OF, Daytona (Reds)
6. Matt Manning, RHP, Lakeland (Tigers)
7. Andres Gimenez, SS, St. Lucie (Mets)
8. Jesus Sanchez, OF, Charlotte (Rays)
9. Ian Anderson, RHP, Florida (Braves)
10. Kyle Muller, LHP, Florida (Braves)
11. Kevin Smith, SS, Dunedin (Blue Jays)
12. Brendan McKay, LHP/1B, Charlotte (Rays)
13. Brusdar Graterol, RHP, Fort Myers (Twins)
14. Tony Santillan, RHP, Daytona (Reds)
15. Nate Lowe, 1B, Charlotte (Rays)
16. Daz Cameron, OF, Lakeland (Tigers)
17. Dylan Carlson, OF, Palm Beach (Cardinals)
18. Tyler Stephenson, C, Daytona (Reds)
19. Adam Haseley, OF, Clearwater (Phillies)
20. Adonis Medina, RHP, Clearwater (Phillies)

LOW CLASS A

Midwest League

1. Royce Lewis, SS, Cedar Rapids (Twins)
2. MacKenzie Gore, LHP, Fort Wayne (Padres)
3. Alex Kirilloff, OF, Cedar Rapids (Twins)
4. Brendan McKay, LHP/1B, Bowling Green (Rays)
5. Hunter Greene, RHP, Dayton (Reds)
6. Matt Manning, RHP, West Michigan (Tigers)
7. Ronaldo Hernandez, C, Bowling Green (Rays)
8. Jeter Downs, SS, Dayton (Reds)
9. Elehuris Montero, 3B, Peoria (Cardinals)
10. Luis Patino, RHP, Fort Wayne (Padres)
11. Vidal Brujan, 2B, Bowling Green (Rays)
12. Miguel Amaya, C, South Bend (Cubs)
13. Moises Gomez, OF, Bowling Green (Rays)
14. Lazaro Armenteros, OF, Beloit (Athletics)
15. Kevin Smith, SS, Lansing (Blue Jays)
16. Esteury Ruiz, 2B, Fort Wayne (Padres)
17. Johan Oviedo, RHP, Peoria (Cardinals)
18. Akil Baddoo, OF, Cedar Rapids (Twins)
19. Nolan Jones, 3B, Lake County (Indians)
20. Patrick Sandoval, LHP, Quad Cities (Astros)

South Atlantic League

1. D.L. Hall, LHP, Delmarva (Orioles)
2. Luis Garcia, SS, Hagerstown (Nationals)
3. Drew Waters, OF, Rome (Braves)
4. Oneil Cruz, SS, West Virginia (Pirates)
5. Bubba Thompson, OF, Hickory (Rangers)
6. M.J. Melendez, C, Lexington (Royals)
7. William Contreras, C, Rome (Braves)
8. Anthony Kay, LHP, Columbia (Mets)
9. Tyler Phillips, RHP, Hickory (Rangers)
10. Heliot Ramos, OF, Augusta (Giants)
11. Calvin Mitchell, OF, West Virginia (Pirates)
12. Spencer Howard, RHP, Lakewood (Phillies)
13. Jose Devers, SS, Greensboro (Marlins)
14. Will Stewart, LHP, Lakewood (Phillies)
15. Edward Cabrera, RHP, Greensboro (Marlins)
16. Huascar Ynoa, RHP, Rome (Braves)
17. Nick Pratto, 1B, Lexington (Royals)
18. Seuly Matias, OF, Lexington (Royals)
19. A.J. Alexy, RHP, Hickory (Rangers)
20. Yefry Del Rosario, RHP, Lexington (Royals)

SHORT-SEASON

Northwest League

1. Joey Bart, C, Salem-Keizer (Giants)
2. Hans Crouse, RHP, Spokane (Rangers)
3. Brailyn Marquez, LHP, Eugene (Cubs)
4. Xavier Edwards, SS, Tri-City (Padres)
5. Geraldo Perdomo, SS, Hillsboro (D-backs)
6. Julio Pablo Martinez, OF, Spokane (Rangers)
7. Tucupita Marcano, SS, Tri-City (Padres)
8. Nelson Velazquez, OF, Eugene (Cubs)
9. Diosbel Arias, SS, Spokane (Rangers)
10. Gregory Santos, RHP, Salem-Keizer (Giants)
11. Jake Wong, RHP, Salem-Keizer (Giants)
12. Josh Stowers, OF, Everett (Mariners)
13. Cal Raleigh, C, Everett (Mariners)

14. Matt Tabor, RHP, Hillsboro (D-backs)
15. Andy Yerzy, C, Hillsboro (D-backs)
16. Owen Miller, SS, Tri-City (Padres)
17. Grant Little, OF, Tri-City (Padres)
18. Henry Henry, RHP, Tri-City (Padres)
19. Terrin Vavra, SS, Boise (Rockies)
20. Jake McCarthy, OF, Hillsboro (D-backs)

New York-Penn League

1. Gilberto Celestino, OF, Tri-City (Astros)
2. Travis Swaggerty, OF, West Virginia (Pirates)
3. Luis Oviedo, RHP, Mahoning Valley (Indians)
4. Juan De Paula, RHP, Staten Island (Yankees)
5. Roansy Contreras, RHP, Staten Island (Yankees)
6. Tanner Dodson, RHP/OF, Hudson Valley (Rays)
7. Alex McKenna, OF, Tri-City (Astros)
8. Alec Bohm, 3B, Williamsport (Phillies)
9. Israel Pineda, C, Auburn (Nationals)
10. Tyler Freeman, SS, Mahoning Valley (Indians)
11. Jeremy Eierman, SS, Vermont (Athletics)
12. Rafael Marchan, C, Williamsport (Phillies)
13. Matt Sauer, RHP, Staten Island (Yankees)
14. Chris Betts, C, Hudson Valley (Rays)
15. Adam Hall, SS, Aberdeen (Orioles)
16. Jameson Hannah, OF, Vermont (Athletics)
17. Eduard Bazardo, RHP, Lowell (Red Sox)
18. Rafael Kelly, RHP, Vermont (Athletics)
19. Marcos Brito, 2B, Vermont (Athletics)
20. Jose Medina, OF, Brooklyn (Mets)

ROOKIE-LEVEL

Appalachian League

1. Wander Franco, SS, Princeton (Rays)
2. Nolan Gorman, 3B, Johnson City (Cardinals)
3. Jarred Kelenic, OF, Kingsport (Mets)
4. Eric Pardinho, RHP, Bluefield (Blue Jays)
5. Trevor Larnach, OF, Elizabethton (Twins)
6. Mike Siani, OF, Greeneville (Reds)
7. Mark Vientos, 3B, Kingsport (Mets)
8. Shane Baz, RHP, Princeton (Rays)
9. Everson Pereira, OF, Pulaski (Yankees)
10. Josiah Gray, RHP, Greeneville (Reds)
11. Shervyen Newton, SS, Kingsport (Mets)
12. Alejandro Kirk, C, Bluefield (Blue Jays)
13. Luis Medina, RHP, Pulaski (Yankees)
14. Luis Rijo, RHP, Elizabethton (Twins)
15. Ryan Jeffers, C, Elizabethton (Twins)
16. Hagen Danner, C, Bluefield (Blue Jays)
17. C.J. Alexander, 3B, Danville (Braves)
18. Austin Cox, LHP, Burlington (Royals)
19. Luis Gil, RHP, Pulaski (Yankees)
20. Lyon Richardson, RHP, Greeneville (Reds)

Pioneer League

1. Grant Lavigne, 1B, Grand Junction (Rockies)
2. Brice Turang, SS, Helena (Brewers)
3. Ryan Rolison, LHP, Grand Junction (Rockies)
4. Kyle Isbel, OF, Idaho Falls (Royals)
5. Kris Bubic, LHP, Idaho Falls (Royals)
6. Ryan Feltner, RHP, Grand Junction (Rockies)
7. Mariel Bautista, OF, Billings (Reds)

8. Miguel Vargas, 3B, Ogden (Dodgers)
9. Alek Thomas, OF, Missoula (D-backs)
10. Jeremiah Jackson, SS, Orem (Angels)
11. James Marinan, RHP, Billings (Reds)
12. Jacob Amaya, SS, Ogden (Dodgers)
13. Blaze Alexander, SS, Missoula (D-backs)
14. D'Shawn Knowles, OF, Orem (Angels)
15. Niko Decolati, OF, Grand Junction (Rockies)
16. Je'Von Ward, OF, Helena (Brewers)
17. Jean Carmona, SS, Helena (Brewers)
18. Jared Solomon, RHP, Billings (Reds)
19. Bryce Bush, OF, Great Falls (White Sox)
20. Kevin Maitan, SS, Orem (Angels)

Arizona League

1. Brayan Rocchio, SS, Indians
2. Jhon Torres, OF, Indians
3. Brice Turang, SS, Brewers
4. Xavier Edwards, SS, Padres
5. Bo Naylor, C, Indians
6. Kristian Robinson, OF, D-backs
7. Cole Roederer, OF, Cubs
8. Jordyn Adams, OF, Angels
9. Alexander Canario, OF, Giants
10. Jonathan Ornelas, SS, Rangers
11. Carlos Vargas, RHP, Indians
12. Frank Lopez, RHP, Padres
13. Tahnaj Thomas, RHP, Indians
14. Geraldo Perdomo, SS, D-backs
15. Alek Thomas, OF, D-backs
16. Jeremiah Jackson, SS, Angels
17. Luis Verdugo, C, Cubs
18. Robinson Ortiz, LHP, Dodgers
19. Tucupita Marcano, SS, Padres
20. Blaze Alexander, SS, D-backs

Gulf Coast League

1. Luis Garcia, SS, Phillies
2. Ronny Mauricio, SS, Mets
3. Matthew Liberatore, LHP, Rays
4. Wenceel Perez, SS, Tigers
5. Jordan Groshans, SS, Blue Jays
6. Jhon Torres, OF, Cardinals
7. Antonio Cabello, OF, Yankees
8. Grayson Rodriguez, RHP, Orioles
9. Freudis Nova, SS, Astros
10. Ivan Herrera, C, Cardinals
11. Parker Meadows, OF, Tigers
12. Anthony Garcia, OF, Yankees
13. Nick Schnell, OF, Rays
14. Yoendrys Gomez, RHP, Yankees
15. Braxton Ashcraft, RHP, Pirates
16. Gabriel Moreno, C, Blue Jays
17. Jack Herman, OF, Pirates
18. Osiris Johnson, SS, Marlins
19. Will Banfield, C, Marlins
20. Leonardo Jimenez, SS, Blue Jays

Devers, Jose (Marlins)	250	Fuentes, Josh (Rockies)	154	Hanhold, Eric (Mets)	302
Diaz, Danny (Red Sox)	75	Funkhouser, Kyle (Tigers)	172	Hanifee, Brenan (Orioles)	58
Diaz, Isan (Marlins)	249			Hankins, Ethan (Indians)	138
Diaz, Jordan (Athletics)	337	**G**		Hannah, Jameson (Athletics)	328
Diaz, Yusniel (Orioles)	53			Hansen, Alec (White Sox)	108
Dibrell, Tony (Mets)	304	Gallardo, Richard (Cubs)	90	Harrison, Monte (Marlins)	246
Didder, Ray-Patrick (Braves)	49	Gallegos, Giovanny (Cardinals)	385	Harvey, Hunter (Orioles)	56
Dietz, Matthias (Orioles)	65	Gallen, Zac (Marlins)	253	Haseley, Adam (Phillies)	343
Diplan, Marcos (Brewers)	270	Gamboa, Arquimedes (Phillies)	352	Hatch, Thomas (Cubs)	94
Dodson, Tanner (Rays)	444	Garabito, Gerson (Royals)	206	Hayes, Ke'Bryan (Pirates)	358
Dohy, Kyle (Phillies)	348	Garcia, Adolis (Cardinals)	380	Hays, Austin (Orioles)	55
Doval, Camilo (Giants)	413	Garcia, Anthony (Yankees)	315	Hearn, Taylor (Rangers)	456
Downs, Jeter (Reds)	121	Garcia, Aramis (Giants)	412	Heatherly, Jacob (Reds)	127
Dubon, Mauricio (Brewers)	264	Garcia, Bryan (Tigers)	174	Heim, Jonah (Athletics)	337
Dugger, Robert (Marlins)	253	Garcia, David (Rangers)	462	Heineman, Scott (Rangers)	463
Dunand, Joe (Marlins)	254	Garcia, Deivi (Yankees)	312	Helman, Michael (Twins)	288
Dunn, Justin (Mariners)	423	Garcia, Edgar (Phillies)	349	Helsley, Ryan (Cardinals)	378
Dunning, Dane (White Sox)	104	Garcia, Eduardo (Brewers)	273	Henry, Payton (Brewers)	266
Dunshee, Parker (Athletics)	332	Garcia, Jose Israel (Reds)	123	Hentges, Sam (Indians)	136
Duplantier, Jon (D-backs)	22	Garcia, Luis (Nationals)	486	Henzman, Lincoln (White Sox)	112
Duran, Jarren (Red Sox)	74	Garcia, Luis (Phillies)	342	Herget, Jimmy (Reds)	126
Duran, Jhoan (Twins)	280	Garcia, Reivaj (Cubs)	95	Hermosillo, Michael (Angels)	221
Duran, Rodolfo (Phillies)	350	Garcia, Rico (Rockies)	158	Hernandez, Aaron (Angels)	223
		Garrett, Braxton (Marlins)	250	Hernandez, Arnaldo (Royals)	208
E		Gatewood, Jake (Brewers)	267	Hernandez, Carlos (Royals)	205
		Gerber, Joey (Mariners)	431	Hernandez, Darwinzon (Red Sox)	70
Eastman, Colton (Phillies)	347	German, Frank (Yankees)	318	Hernandez, Jonathan (Rangers)	456
Edman, Tommy (Cardinals)	378	Gibaut, Ian (Rays)	445	Hernandez, Ronaldo (Rays)	439
Edwards, Xavier (Padres)	398	Gigliotti, Michael (Royals)	208	Hernandez, Wilkel (Tigers)	177
Eierman, Jeremy (Athletics)	330	Gil, Luis (Yankees)	319	Herrera, Carlos (Brewers)	273
Elledge, Seth (Cardinals)	383	Gilbert, Logan (Mariners)	424	Herrera, Ivan (Cardinals)	382
Ellis, Drew (D-backs)	30	Gimenez, Andres (Mets)	293	Herron, Jimmy (Cubs)	96
Encarnacion, Jean Carlos (Orioles)	60	Ginkel, Kevin (D-backs)	33	Hicklen, Brewer (Royals)	205
Englert, Mason (Rangers)	458	Givin, Matt (Marlins)	257	Hill, Adam (Mets)	302
Enlow, Blayne (Twins)	281	Goddard, Jackson (D-backs)	32	Hill, Brigham (Nationals)	495
Erceg, Lucas (Brewers)	265	Gohara, Luiz (Braves)	42	Hilliard, Sam (Rockies)	154
Ernesto, Larry (Brewers)	271	Gomez, Antonio (Yankees)	320	Hinsz, Gage (Pirates)	368
Escobar, Luis (Pirates)	362	Gomez, Moises (Rays)	442	Hiraldo, Miguel (Blue Jays)	474
Espinoza, Anderson (Padres)	394	Gomez, Yoendrys (Yankees)	319	Hiura, Keston (Brewers)	261
Estevez, Omar (Dodgers)	239	Gonsalves, Stephen (Twins)	285	Hjelle, Sean (Giants)	407
Estrada, Thairo (Yankees)	320	Gonsolin, Tony (Dodgers)	233	Hoerner, Nico (Cubs)	85
Eusebio, Breiling (Rockies)	160	Gonzalez, Jacob (Giants)	416	Hoffman, Nolan (Mariners)	431
Evans, DeMarcus (Rangers)	460	Gonzalez, Luis (White Sox)	105	Holloway, Jordan (Marlins)	252
		Gonzalez, Oscar (Indians)	142	Holmes, Clay (Pirates)	364
F		Gordon, Nick (Twins)	283	Holmes, Grant (Athletics)	331
		Gore, MacKenzie (Padres)	390	Holmes, Quentin (Indians)	144
Fabian, Sandro (Giants)	416	Gorman, Nolan (Cardinals)	375	Honeywell, Brent (Rays)	438
Faedo, Alex (Tigers)	170	Graffanino, A.J. (Braves)	48	Houck, Tanner (Red Sox)	72
Fairchild, Stuart (Reds)	122	Graterol, Brusdar (Twins)	278	Houser, Adrian (Brewers)	269
Feigl, Brady (Athletics)	336	Gray, Joe (Brewers)	265	Howard, Brian (Athletics)	332
Feliciano, Mario (Brewers)	270	Gray, Josiah (Reds)	123	Howard, Ryan (Giants)	415
Feltman, Durbin (Red Sox)	74	Greene, Hunter (Reds)	118	Howard, Spencer (Phillies)	345
Feltner, Ryan (Rockies)	157	Grenier, Cadyn (Orioles)	61	Howlett, Brandon (Red Sox)	75
Ferguson, Caleb (Dodgers)	232	Griffin, Foster (Royals)	209	Hudson, Dakota (Cardinals)	374
Fernandez, Eduarqi (Brewers)	270	Grisham, Trent (Brewers)	272	Huff, Sam (Rangers)	464
Fernandez, Vince (Rockies)	159	Groome, Jay (Red Sox)	71	Humphreys, Jordan (Mets)	300
Ferrell, Riley (Marlins)	254	Groshans, Jordan (Blue Jays)	471	Humphreys, Reid (Rockies)	156
Festa, Matt (Mariners)	428	Grove, Michael (Dodgers)	236	Hurst, Scott (Cardinals)	384
Fisher, Braydon (Dodgers)	241	Guduan, Reymin (Astros)	192		
Flores, Antoni (Red Sox)	73	Guerrero Jr., Vladimir (Blue Jays)	469	**I**	
Florez, Santiago (Pirates)	369	Guillorme, Luis (Mets)	299		
Florial, Estevan (Yankees)	309	Gutierrez, Kelvin (Royals)	202	India, Jonathan (Reds)	119
Foley, Jason (Tigers)	177	Gutierrez, Vladimir (Reds)	121	Irvin, Cole (Phillies)	350
Fox, Lucius (Rays)	447	Guzman, Jorge (Marlins)	248	Irvin, Jake (Nationals)	490
Fraley, Jake (Mariners)	427			Isabel, Ibandel (Reds)	128
France, Ty (Padres)	400	**H**		Isbel, Kyle (Royals)	201
Francis, Harrison (D-backs)	32			Ivey, Tyler (Astros)	189
Franco, Wander (Rays)	437	Haake, Zach (Royals)	207		
Frank, Tyler (Rays)	447	Haase, Eric (Indians)	144	**J**	
Franklin, Austin (Rays)	448	Hall, Adam (Orioles)	61		
Freeman, Tyler (Indians)	134	Hall, DL (Orioles)	54	Jackson, Alex (Braves)	47
Frias, Luis (D-backs)	30	Hall, Matt (Tigers)	175	Jackson, Drew (Orioles)	65
Friedl, T.J. (Reds)	124	Hamilton, Ian (White Sox)	107	Jackson, Jeremiah (Angels)	218
		Hampson, Garrett (Rockies)	150	James, Josh (Astros)	183

Jansen, Danny (Blue Jays)	470	Lopez, Eduardo (Red Sox)	79	Mercado, Oscar (Indians)	140
Javier, Wander (Twins)	279	Lopez, Jason (Yankees)	317	Mercer, Matt (D-backs)	32
Jax, Griffin (Twins)	283	Lopez, Nicky (Royals)	199	Merrell, Kevin (Athletics)	334
Jefferies, Daulton (Athletics)	333	Lopez, Yoan (D-backs)	28	Mesa Jr., Victor (Marlins)	257
Jeffers, Ryan (Twins)	281	Lovelady, Richard (Royals)	204	Mesa, Victor Victor (Marlins)	245
Jenista, Greyson (Braves)	44	Lowe, Brandon (Rays)	441	Miller, Brian (Marlins)	251
Jennings, Steven (Pirates)	363	Lowe, Josh (Rays)	444	Miller, Jalen (Giants)	417
Jerez, Williams (Angels)	223	Lowe, Nate (Rays)	441	Miller, Owen (Padres)	399
Jewell, Jake (Angels)	224	Lowther, Zac (Orioles)	60	Mills, Wyatt (Mariners)	429
Jimenez, Eloy (White Sox)	101	Luciano, Elvis (Blue Jays)	480	Miranda, Jose (Twins)	283
Jimenez, Gilberto (Red Sox)	77	Luciano, Marco (Giants)	406	Miroglio, Dominic (D-backs)	31
Jimenez, Leonardo (Blue Jays)	478	Lugo, Dawel (Tigers)	172	Misiewicz, Anthony (Mariners)	431
Joe, Connor (Reds)	129	Lugo, William (Mets)	305	Mitchell, Calvin (Pirates)	361
Johnson, Daniel (Indians)	139	Lund, Brennon (Angels)	225	Mize, Casey (Tigers)	165
Johnson, Osiris (Marlins)	251	Lutz, Tristen (Brewers)	264	Moniak, Mickey (Phillies)	346
Johnson, Tyler (White Sox)	113	Lux, Gavin (Dodgers)	230	Montano, Daniel (Rockies)	158
Johnston, Kyle (Nationals)	494	Luzardo, Jesus (Athletics)	325	Montero, Elehuris (Cardinals)	375
Jones, Jahmai (Angels)	215	Lynch, Daniel (Royals)	198	Morales, Francisco (Phillies)	346
Jones, Nolan (Indians)	134			Morejon, Adrian (Padres)	391
				Morel, Yohanse (Royals)	205
K		**M**		Moreno, Gabriel (Blue Jays)	477
				Moss, Scott (Reds)	129
Kaprielian, James (Athletics)	331	Maciel, Gabriel (Twins)	289	Mountcastle, Ryan (Orioles)	54
Kaufman, Rylan (Royals)	207	MacIver, Willie (Rockies)	161	Muller, Kyle (Braves)	42
Kay, Anthony (Mets)	295	Madero, Luis (Angels)	221	Mundell, Brian (Rockies)	159
Kelenic, Jarred (Mariners)	422	Madrigal, Nick (White Sox)	103	Munoz, Andres (Padres)	396
Keller, Mitch (Pirates)	357	Mahan, Riley (Marlins)	257	Murphy, Patrick (Blue Jays)	476
Kelly, Carson (D-backs)	23	Maitan, Kevin (Angels)	222	Murphy, Sean (Athletics)	326
Kelly, Merrill (D-backs)	28	Manning, Matt (Tigers)	166	Murray, Kyler (Athletics)	327
Kendall, Jeren (Dodgers)	236	Maples, Dillon (Cubs)	93		
Kennedy, Buddy (D-backs)	29	Marcano, Tucupita (Padres)	400	**N**	
Kieboom, Carter (Nationals)	486	Marchan, Rafael (Phillies)	351		
Kikuchi, Yusei (free agent)	498	Marinan, James (Reds)	125	Naylor, Bo (Indians)	135
Kilome, Franklyn (Mets)	297	Marquez, Brailyn (Cubs)	86	Naylor, Josh (Padres)	393
King, Michael (Yankees)	311	Marsh, Brandon (Angels)	214	Neidert, Nick (Marlins)	247
Kirilloff, Alex (Twins)	278	Marte, Jose (Giants)	413	Nelson, James (Marlins)	253
Kline, Branden (Orioles)	62	Marte, Noelvi (Mariners)	425	Nelson, Nick (Yankees)	317
Klobosits, Gabe (Nationals)	496	Martin, Corbin (Astros)	183	Netzer, Brett (Red Sox)	81
Kloffenstein, Adam (Blue Jays)	474	Martin, Jason (Pirates)	362	Neuse, Sheldon (Athletics)	330
Knight, Blaine (Orioles)	58	Martin, Richie (Orioles)	59	Nevin, Tyler (Rockies)	152
Knizner, Andrew (Cardinals)	377	Martinez, Juan (Reds)	126	Newman, Kevin (Pirates)	360
Knowles, D'Shawn (Angels)	219	Martinez, Julio Pablo (Rangers)	454	Newton, Shervyn (Mets)	296
Kopech, Michael (White Sox)	102	Martinez, Orelvis (Blue Jays)	475	Nido, Tomas (Mets)	300
Kowar, Jackson (Royals)	199	Mata, Bryan (Red Sox)	72	Nikorak, Mike (Rockies)	159
Kramer, Kevin (Pirates)	359	Mateo, Jorge (Athletics)	329	Nix, Jacob (Padres)	395
Kremer, Dean (Orioles)	57	Matias, Seuly (Royals)	201	Noda, Ryan (Blue Jays)	475
Krook, Matt (Rays)	449	Matijevic, J.J. (Astros)	191	Northcut, Nick (Red Sox)	77
Kruger, Jack (Angels)	220	Mauricio, Ronny (Mets)	294	Nottingham, Jacob (Brewers)	266
		May, Dustin (Dodgers)	231	Nova, Freudis (Astros)	185
		McArthur, James (Phillies)	353	Nunez, Malcom (Cardinals)	377
L		McCarthy, Jake (D-backs)	25		
		McCarthy, Joe (Rays)	447	**O**	
Lakins, Travis (Red Sox)	76	McCarty, Kirk (Indians)	145		
Lambert, Peter (Rockies)	150	McClanahan, Shane (Rays)	442	O'Hoppe, Logan (Phillies)	347
Lange, Alex (Cubs)	91	McGuire, Reese (Blue Jays)	480	O'Neill, Tyler (Cardinals)	374
Lantigua, Danny (Reds)	128	McKay, Brendan (Rays)	438	Ockimey, Josh (Red Sox)	78
Larnach, Trevor (Twins)	279	McKay, David (Mariners)	432	Oliva, Jared (Pirates)	365
Lavigne, Grant (Rockies)	151	McKenna, Alex (Astros)	192	Ornelas, Jonathan (Rangers)	459
Lawrence, Justin (Rockies)	156	McKenna, Ryan (Orioles)	57	Ornelas, Tirso (Padres)	398
Lawson, Reggie (Padres)	397	McKenzie, Triston (Indians)	133	Ortiz, Jhailyn (Phillies)	351
Leach, Landon (Twins)	287	McKinney, Billy (Blue Jays)	478	Ortiz, Luis (Orioles)	59
Leal, Erick (Cubs)	97	McLanahan, Chad (Brewers)	273	Ortiz, Robinson (Dodgers)	238
Lee, Khalil (Royals)	198	McMillan, Sam (Tigers)	176	Oviedo, Johan (Cardinals)	381
Lemons, Caden (Brewers)	268	McWilliams, Sam (Royals)	203	Oviedo, Luis (Indians)	137
Lewis, Kyle (Mariners)	424	Meadows, Parker (Tigers)	168		
Lewis, Royce (Twins)	277	Medeiros, Kodi (White Sox)	113	**P**	
Leyba, Domingo (D-backs)	31	Medina, Adonis (Phillies)	343		
Liberatore, Matthew (Rays)	439	Medina, Luis (Yankees)	314	Pache, Cristian (Braves)	41
Lindsay, Desmond (Mets)	298	Megill, Tylor (Mets)	305	Paddack, Chris (Padres)	392
Listi, Austin (Phillies)	349	Mejia, Francisco (Padres)	391	Palacios, Richie (Indians)	145
Littell, Zack (Twins)	286	Mejia, Jean Carlos (Indians)	140	Palumbo, Joe (Rangers)	457
Little, Brendon (Cubs)	92	Melendez, MJ (Royals)	200	Pardinho, Eric (Blue Jays)	471
Llovera, Mauricio (Phillies)	347	Mella, Keury (Reds)	125	Paredes, Isaac (Tigers)	166
Loaisiga, Jonathan (Yankees)	310	Menez, Conner (Giants)	415	Parsons, Wes (Braves)	47
Long, Shed (Reds)	120	Mercado, David (Rays)	448		

Patino, Luis (Padres)	392	Robert, Luis (White Sox)	103	Shore, Logan (Tigers)	173
Paulino, David (Blue Jays)	479	Roberts, Griffin (Cardinals)	381	Short, Zack (Cubs)	93
Pearson, Nate (Blue Jays)	472	Robinson, Kristian (D-backs)	24	Shugart, Chase (Red Sox)	79
Pelham, C.D. (Rangers)	459	Robles, Victor (Nationals)	485	Siani, Mike (Reds)	122
Pena, Jeremy (Astros)	191	Robson, Jacob (Tigers)	175	Singer, Brady (Royals)	197
Pena, Malvin (Nationals)	496	Rocchio, Brayan (Indians)	137	Siri, Jose (Reds)	122
Pena, Ronald (Nationals)	496	Rodgers, Brady (Astros)	193	Smith, Drew (Mets)	303
Peraza, Oswald (Yankees)	316	Rodgers, Brendan (Rockies)	149	Smith, Kevin (Blue Jays)	472
Perdomo, Geraldo (D-backs)	23	Rodriguez, Alfredo (Reds)	127	Smith, Pavin (D-backs)	28
Pereda, Jhonny (Cubs)	96	Rodriguez, Carlos (Brewers)	269	Smith, Will (Dodgers)	231
Pereira, Everson (Yankees)	310	Rodriguez, Chris (Angels)	220	Sobotka, Chad (Braves)	46
Perez, Brayan (Mariners)	430	Rodriguez, Gabriel (Indians)	138	Sodders, Austin (Tigers)	173
Perez, Cionel (Astros)	186	Rodriguez, Grayson (Orioles)	55	Solak, Nick (Rays)	443
Perez, Franklin (Tigers)	167	Rodriguez, Johnathan (Indians)	145	Solis, Jairo (Astros)	186
Perez, Hector (Blue Jays)	477	Rodriguez, Jose (Rangers)	462	Solomon, Peter (Astros)	190
Perez, Wenceel (Tigers)	170	Rodriguez, Julio (Mariners)	423	Soriano, Jose (Angels)	218
Perkins, Blake (Royals)	208	Rodriguez, Keyber (Rangers)	465	Soroka, Mike (Braves)	38
Peters, DJ (Dodgers)	234	Rodriguez, Osiel (Yankees)	316	Sosa, Edmundo (Cardinals)	382
Peterson, David (Mets)	296	Roederer, Cole (Cubs)	87	Soto, Gregory (Tigers)	172
Peterson, Kort (Royals)	209	Rogers, Jake (Tigers)	171	Soto, Livan (Angels)	223
Phillips, Tyler (Rangers)	460	Rogers, Josh (Orioles)	64	Spanberger, Chad (Blue Jays)	481
Pilkington, Konnor (White Sox)	110	Rogers, Trevor (Marlins)	250	Speas, Alex (Rangers)	465
Pineda, Israel (Nationals)	492	Rojas, Jose (Angels)	225	Spillane, Bren (Reds)	129
Pint, Riley (Rockies)	153	Rolison, Ryan (Rockies)	152	Stafford, Deon (Pirates)	366
Poche, Colin (Rays)	445	Rom, Drew (Orioles)	63	Staumont, Josh (Royals)	207
Pomares, Jairo (Giants)	411	Romero, JoJo (Phillies)	344	Steele, Justin (Cubs)	89
Pompey, Tristan (Marlins)	252	Romero, Seth (Nationals)	488	Stephan, Trevor (Yankees)	317
Ponce, Cody (Brewers)	272	Rooker, Brent (Twins)	280	Stephens, Jordan (White Sox)	109
Poncedeleon, Daniel (Cardinals)	379	Rooney, John (Dodgers)	239	Stephenson, Tyler (Reds)	120
Pop, Zach (Orioles)	63	Rortvedt, Ben (Twins)	286	Stevenson, Cal (Blue Jays)	476
Potts, Hudson (Padres)	396	Rosario, Jeisson (Padres)	398	Stewart, Christin (Tigers)	169
Povse, Max (Mariners)	432	Ruiz, Esteury (Padres)	400	Stewart, DJ (Orioles)	60
Pratto, Nick (Royals)	200	Ruiz, Keibert (Dodgers)	229	Stewart, Will (Phillies)	346
Puk, A.J. (Athletics)	326	Rutherford, Blake (White Sox)	105	Stokes Jr., Troy (Brewers)	268
		Ryan, Ryder (Mets)	303	Stowers, Josh (Mariners)	425
				Straw, Myles (Astros)	188
Q				Strotman, Drew (Rays)	448
		S		Stubbs, Garrett (Astros)	187
Quantrill, Cal (Padres)	394			Suarez, Jose (Angels)	215
Querecuto, Juan (Mariners)	429	Salinas, Raimfer (Yankees)	320	Suarez, Ranger (Phillies)	345
Quinn, Heath (Giants)	411	Sanchez, Jesus (Rays)	440	Supak, Trey (Brewers)	266
		Sanchez, Jose (Nationals)	492	Swaggerty, Travis (Pirates)	359
		Sanchez, LoLo (Pirates)	362	Swanda, John (Angels)	225
R		Sanchez, Sixto (Phillies)	341	Swanson, Erik (Mariners)	426
		Sandlin, Nick (Indians)	143	Szapucki, Thomas (Mets)	298
Ragans, Cole (Rangers)	458	Sandoval, Patrick (Angels)	218		
Rainey, Tanner (Nationals)	495	Sanquintin, Junior (Indians)	144		
Raleigh, Cal (Mariners)	426	Santana, Cristian (Dodgers)	235	**T**	
Raley, Luke (Twins)	287	Santana, Dennis (Dodgers)	232		
Ramirez, Manny (Astros)	192	Santana, Luis (Mets)	299	Tabor, Matt (D-backs)	27
Ramirez, Tyler (Athletics)	335	Santillan, Tony (Reds)	119	Tarnok, Freddy (Braves)	44
Ramos, Heliot (Giants)	406	Santos, Gregory (Giants)	408	Tate, Dillon (Orioles)	58
Ramos, Jeffrey (Braves)	48	Santos, Junior (Mets)	305	Tatis Jr., Fernando (Padres)	389
Ramos, Roberto (Rockies)	160	Sauer, Matt (Yankees)	314	Taveras, Leody (Rangers)	454
Raquet, Nick (Nationals)	493	Sborz, Josh (Dodgers)	238	Tejeda, Anderson (Rangers)	455
Ray, Corey (Brewers)	262	Schaller, Reid (Nationals)	490	Tellez, Rowdy (Blue Jays)	481
Read, Raudy (Nationals)	491	Schellenger, Zach (Red Sox)	78	Tetreault, Jackson (Nationals)	494
Reed, Buddy (Padres)	399	Scherff, Alex (Red Sox)	79	Thaiss, Matt (Angels)	217
Reed, Tyreque (Rangers)	462	Schmidt, Clarke (Yankees)	314	Then, Juan (Yankees)	318
Reid-Foley, Sean (Blue Jays)	473	Schnell, Nick (Rays)	443	Thomas, Alek (D-backs)	25
Rengifo, Luis (Angels)	216	Schrock, Max (Cardinals)	383	Thomas, Cody (Dodgers)	241
Reyes, Alex (Cardinals)	373	Schroeder, Jayson (Astros)	189	Thomas, Lane (Cardinals)	376
Reyes, Denyi (Red Sox)	77	Scott, Connor (Marlins)	247	Thomas, Tahnaj (Pirates)	363
Reyes, Pablo (Pirates)	366	Seabold, Connor (Phillies)	352	Thompson-Williams, Dom (M's)	428
Reynolds, Bryan (Pirates)	361	Seigler, Anthony (Yankees)	311	Thompson, Bubba (Rangers)	457
Richan, Paul (Cubs)	88	Seise, Chris (Rangers)	460	Thompson, Keegan (Cubs)	97
Richardson, Lyon (Reds)	124	Senzel, Nick (Reds)	117	Thompson, Riley (Cubs)	93
Riley, Austin (Braves)	37	Serrano, Florencio (free agent)	499	Thompson, Zach (White Sox)	112
Riley, Trey (Braves)	48	Severino, Yunior (Twins)	282	Thornton, Trent (Blue Jays)	477
Rincon, Carlos (Dodgers)	240	Sharp, Sterling (Nationals)	489	Thorpe, Lewis (Twins)	284
Rios, Edwin (Dodgers)	234	Shaw, Chris (Giants)	410	Tinoco, Jesus (Rockies)	155
Rivas, Alfonso (Athletics)	333	Shawaryn, Mike (Red Sox)	73	Toffey, Will (Mets)	301
Rivera, Blake (Giants)	417	Sheets, Gavin (White Sox)	107	Toribio, Luis (Giants)	409
Rivera, Emmanuel (Royals)	206	Sheffield, Justus (Mariners)	421	Toro, Abraham (Astros)	188
Rivera, Laz (White Sox)	108	Sherfy, Jimmie (D-backs)	33	Torres, Christopher (Marlins)	256
Rizzo, Joe (Mariners)	430				

Torres, Jhon (Cardinals)	381	Vilade, Ryan (Rockies)	153	Widener, Taylor (D-backs)	24
Torres, Lenny (Indians)	142	Viloria, Meibrys (Royals)	203	Willeman, Zach (Dodgers)	238
Torres, Nicolas (Phillies)	352	Vogelbach, Dan (Mariners)	428	Williams, Garrett (Giants)	414
Toussaint, Touki (Braves)	39			Williams, Justin (Cardinals)	379
Trammell, Taylor (Reds)	118	**W**		Wilson, Bryse (Braves)	40
Travis, Sam (Red Sox)	80			Wilson, DJ (Cubs)	95
Tucker, Cole (Pirates)	360	Wade, LaMonte (Twins)	286	Wilson, Israel (Braves)	48
Tucker, Kyle (Astros)	182	Walker, Steele (White Sox)	106	Wilson, Marcus (D-backs)	29
Turang, Brice (Brewers)	263	Walls, Taylor (Rays)	446	Wingenter, Trey (Padres)	399
Turnbull, Spencer (Tigers)	174	Walsh, Jared (Angels)	219	Winn, Cole (Rangers)	455
Tyler, Robert (Rockies)	157	Walton, Donnie (Mariners)	432	Wong, Connor (Dodgers)	236
		Ward, Drew (Nationals)	496	Wong, Jake (Giants)	410
U		Ward, Je'Von (Brewers)	271	Woodford, Jake (Cardinals)	380
		Warmoth, Logan (Blue Jays)	479	Woodrow, Daniel (Tigers)	175
Uceta, Edwin (Dodgers)	240	Warner, Austin (Cardinals)	385	Woods-Richardson, Simeon (Mets)	297
Urbina, Misael (Twins)	282	Warren, Art (Mariners)	432	Wright, Kyle (Braves)	39
Urias, Luis (Padres)	390	Warren, Zach (Phillies)	349	Wymer, Sean (Blue Jays)	480
Uselton, Connor (Pirates)	367	Waters, Drew (Braves)	40		
		Weathers, Ryan (Padres)	395	**Y**	
V		Weaver, Caberea (White Sox)	111		
		Webb, Braden (Brewers)	267	Yamamoto, Jordan (Marlins)	252
Valdez, Framber (Astros)	184	Webb, Jacob (Braves)	46	Yerzy, Andy (D-backs)	27
Valera, George (Indians)	135	Webb, Logan (Giants)	408	Ynoa, Huascar (Braves)	45
Vargas, Carlos (Indians)	139	Weigel, Patrick (Braves)	43	Young, Andy (D-backs)	26
Vargas, Emilio (D-backs)	31	Weiss, Ryan (D-backs)	29	Young, Jared (Cubs)	95
Vargas, Miguel (Dodgers)	237	Welker, Colton (Rockies)	151		
Varland, Gus (Athletics)	336	Wells, Alex (Orioles)	61	**Z**	
Varsho, Daulton (D-backs)	22	Wendelken, J.B. (Athletics)	336		
Vavra, Terrin (Rockies)	155	Wentz, Joey (Braves)	43	Zamora, Daniel (Mets)	303
Velazquez, Andrew (Rays)	445	White, Eli (Athletics)	329	Zavala, Seby (White Sox)	108
Velazquez, Nelson (Cubs)	91	White, Evan (Mariners)	422	Zeuch, T.J. (Blue Jays)	479
Verdugo, Alex (Dodgers)	230	White, Mitchell (Dodgers)	233		
Verdugo, Luis (Cubs)	90	White, Owen (Rangers)	459		
Viall, Chris (Mets)	304	Whitefield, Aaron (Twins)	288		
Vientos, Mark (Mets)	295	Whitley, Forrest (Astros)	181		
Vierling, Matt (Phillies)	353	Whitlock, Garrett (Yankees)	316		